AutoCAD® 2010 for Interior Design and Space Planning

AutoCAD® 2010 for Interior Design and Space Planning

James M. Kirkpatrick

Eastfield College

Beverly L. Kirkpatrick

Adjunct Faculty, Eastfield College

with cover art and chapter opening art from
Pei Cobb Freed & Partners, Architects, LLP

Prentice Hall
Boston Columbus Indianapolis New York San Francisco Upper Saddle River
Amsterdam Cape Town Dubai London Madrid Milan Munich Paris Montreal Toronto
Delhi Mexico City Sao Paulo Sydney Hong Kong Seoul Singapore Taipei Tokyo

Vice President and Executive Editor: Vernon R. Anthony
Acquisitions Editor: Jill Jones-Renger
Editorial Assistant: Doug Greive
Director of Marketing: David Gesell
Marketing Manager: Kara Clark
Senior Marketing Coordinator: Alicia Wozniak
Senior Managing Editor: JoEllen Gohr
Associate Managing Editor: Alexandrina Wolf
Project Manager: Maren L. Miller
Senior Operations Supervisor: Pat Tonneman
Operations Specialist: Deidra Schwartz
Senior Art Director: Diane Y. Ernsberger
Cover Designer: Ali Mohrman
AV Project Manager: Janet Portisch
Full-Service Project Management: Karen Fortgang, bookworks publishing services
Composition: Aptara®, Inc.
Printer/Binder: Edwards Brothers, Inc.
Cover Printer: Coral Graphic Services, Inc.
Text Font: Berkeley Book

Certain images and materials contained in this publication were reproduced with the permission of Autodesk, Inc. © 2009. All rights reserved. Autodesk, AutoCAD, DWG, and the DWG logo are registered trademarks of Autodesk, Inc., in the U.S.A. and certain other countries.

Cover art and chapter opening art used with the permission of and under the copyright of Pei Cobb Freed & Partners, Architects, LLP.

Disclaimer:
This publication is designed to provide tutorial information about AutoCAD® and/or other Autodesk computer programs. Every effort has been made to make this publication complete and as accurate as possible. The reader is expressly cautioned to use any and all precautions necessary, and to take appropriate steps to avoid hazards, when engaging in the activities described herein.

Neither the author nor the publisher makes any representations or warranties of any kind, with respect to the materials set forth in this publication, express or implied, including without limitation any warranties of fitness for a particular purpose or merchantability. Nor shall the author or the publisher be liable for any special, consequential, or exemplary damages resulting, in whole or in part, directly or indirectly, from the reader's use of, or reliance upon, this material or subsequent revisions of this material.

Copyright © 2010 by Pearson Education, Inc., publishing as Prentice Hall, One Lake Street, Upper Saddle River, New Jersey 07458. All rights reserved. Manufactured in the United States of America. This publication is protected by Copyright, and permission should be obtained from the publisher prior to any prohibited reproduction, storage in a retrieval system, or transmission in any form or by any means, electronic, mechanical, photocopying, recording, or likewise. To obtain permission(s) to use material from this work, please submit a written request to Pearson Education, Inc., Permissions Department, One Lake Street, Upper Saddle River, New Jersey, 07458.

Many of the designations by manufacturers and seller to distinguish their products are claimed as trademarks. Where those designations appear in this book, and the publisher was aware of a trademark claim, the designations have been printed in initial caps or all caps.

Library of Congress Control Number: 2009921696

10 9 8 7 6 5 4 3 2

Prentice Hall
is an imprint of

www.pearsonhighered.com

ISBN-10: 0-13-506992-0
ISBN-13: 978-0-13-506992-9

Preface

AutoCAD has become the industry standard graphics program for interior design and space planning. This program is used to complete the many drawings that make up a design project. Many design firms have adopted AutoCAD as their standard because:

- ☐ It saves time.
- ☐ Affiliated professions have chosen it so that they can exchange files and work on the same drawing.
- ☐ Their competitors use it.
- ☐ Their clients expect it.

To be successful in design today, students must be proficient in the use of AutoCAD as it relates to interior design and space planning. The need for an AutoCAD textbook geared specifically to this field is what led us to write *AutoCAD for Interior Design and Space Planning*.

This text, newly updated for AutoCAD 2010, is divided into three parts:

- ☐ Part I: Preparing to Draw with AutoCAD (Chapter 1)
- ☐ Part II: Two-Dimensional AutoCAD (Chapters 2-13)
- ☐ Part III: Three-Dimensional AutoCAD (Chapters 14-16)

This new edition includes many features designed to help you master AutoCAD 2010:

- ☐ The prompt-response format is now clearly defined with numbered steps. This step-by-step approach is used in the beginning tutorials of all chapters and then moves to an outline form in exercises at the end of most chapters. This allows students to learn commands in a drawing situation and then practice applying them on their own.
- ☐ Lineweights have been carefully assigned to provide line contrast in all drawing exercises.
- ☐ Plotting has been added to Chapter 2 to allow students to plot their first drawings sooner.
- ☐ Chapter 4 has been extensively reworked. Students can now plot drawings containing different scales with plot styles and a student-created drawing format.
- ☐ Tutorials are geared to architects, interior designers, and space planners, allowing students to work with real-world situations.
- ☐ More than 500 illustrations (many printed to scale) support the text and reinforce the material.
- ☐ Screen shots help the user locate AutoCAD commands within the AutoCAD menus and ribbons.
- ☐ Boxed "Tips" and "Notes" give students additional support and information.
- ☐ Practice exercises in every chapter review the commands learned.
- ☐ Learning objectives and review questions in every chapter reinforce the learning process.
- ☐ An on-line Instructor's Manual (which is updated with new exercises between editions) is available to support the text.

Organized around architectural projects, *AutoCAD for Interior Design and Space Planning* gives students an understanding of the commands and features of AutoCAD 2010 and demonstrates how to use the program to complete interior design and space planning projects. Building on 14 years of updates, the book is appropriate for self-paced and lecture classes and covers both two-dimensional and three-dimensional drawings.

Throughout the tutorials in this book, numbered steps in bold type provide instructions. Prompt and Response columns in the numbered steps provide step-by-step instructions for starting and completing a command. The Prompt column text repeats the AutoCAD prompt that appears in the Command area of the AutoCAD screen. The Response column text shows how you should respond to the AutoCAD prompt. Blue ruled lines separate the numbered steps from further discussion and explanation. Screen shots of menus show you how to locate the command you are using.

Using numerous illustrations, the text captures the essence of this powerful program and the importance it plays in the interior design, architecture, and space planning professions.

Most importantly, this text was written to help you, the reader, master the AutoCAD program, which will be a valuable tool in your professional career.

Hallmark Features

Progresses from basic commands to complex drawing exercises

- ☐ Builds confidence and basic skills before moving on to more complex assignments.
- ☐ Ensures students have mastered the fundamental features and commands of the AutoCAD program before they apply it to more complex problems.
- ☐ Guides readers step-by-step through each new AutoCAD command.
- ☐ Encourages students to learn commands and features on their own.

Provides over 100 tutorials and exercises

- ☐ Gives students the opportunity to work with a variety of real-world situations, including both commercial and residential projects.

Highlights seven projects appropriate for interior design, space planning and architecture students

- ☐ Highlights seven projects—a tenant space, hotel room, wheelchair accessible residential bathroom, wheelchair accessible commercial restroom, log cabin, house, and bank.
- ☐ Includes project floor plans, dimension plans, elevations, furniture plans, reflected ceiling plans and voice/data/power plans, as well as isometric drawings, a presentation sheet, and the sheet set command that combines multiple plans.
- ☐ Includes a 15-unit condominum building as an exercise in Appendix C.

Includes over 500 figures

- ☐ Helps students by allowing them to compare their work and progress with the many figures available.
- ☐ Shows many drawings to scale so students can assess and check their understanding of chapter material.

Introduces the AutoCAD DesignCenter

- ☐ The DesignCenter is used in Chapter 6 to import blocks, and again in Chapters 9 and 10 to import blocks, layers, and dimension styles from other drawings into existing drawings. 3D objects from the DesignCenter are used in Chapters 14, 15, and 16.

Covers solid modeling in three separate chapters

- ☐ Splits solid modeling material into three chapters: Chapter 14, Solid Modeling; Chapter 15, Complex Solid Models with Materials, Lighting, Rendering, and Animation; and Chapter 16, Advanced Modeling.
- ☐ Uses the 3DWALK and Animation Motion commands to create walk-through presentations.

Online Instructor Materials

To access supplementary materials online, instructors need to request an instructor access code. Go to **www.pearsonhighered.com/irc**, where you can register for an instructor access code. Within 48 hours after registering, you will receive a confirming e-mail, including an instructor access code. Once you have received your code, go to the site and log on for full instructions on downloading the materials you wish to use.

Autodesk Learning License

Learning licenses may only be purchased by ordering a special textbook package ISBN. Instructors should contact their local Pearson Professional and Career sales representative. For the name and number of your sales representative, please contact Pearson Faculty Services at 1-800-526-0485.

Acknowledgments

We would like to thank the reviewers Scott Anthony Boudreau, Joliet Junior College; Zane D. Curry, Texas Tech University; David R. Epperson, University of Tennessee at Chattanooga; Stephen Huff, High Point University; and Elizabeth Pober, University of Oklahoma.

We would also like to acknowledge the following people, who contributed ideas and drawings: Mary Peyton, IALD, IES (Lighting Consultant), Roy Peyton, John Sample, Katherine Broadwell, Curran C. Redman, S. Vic Jones, W. M. Stevens, John Brooks, Dr. David R. Epperson, Valerie Campbell, the CAD students at Eastfield College and Kelly McCarthy, McCarthy Architecture. Thank you also to Pei Cobb Freed & Partners for cover art and chapter opening art. Finally, we would like to thank Autodesk, Inc.

B.L.K.
J.M.K.

Contents

Preface v

Part 1 **Preparing to Draw with AutoCAD** 1

1 **Introducing the AutoCAD Screen** 1

Introduction 1
- Interior Designers and Space Planners 2

Tutorial 1–1: Examine the AutoCAD Screen and Save a Workspace 2
- Examine the AutoCAD Screen 2
- Application Menu Button 3
- Ribbon 4
  - Expanded Panels 4
  - Dialog Boxes and Palettes 4
  - Tooltips 5
  - Flyouts 5
- Quick Access Toolbar 5
- Customization Button 5
- InfoCenter 7
- Subscription Center 7
- Communication Center 7
- Favorites 7
- Help 7
- Drawing Window and Graphics Cursor 7
- Command Line Window (Ctrl+9) 7
- User Coordinate System Icon 8

Status Bar 9
Cursor Coordinate Values (Ctrl+I) 9
Drawing Tools 9
Quick Properties (Ctrl+SHIFT+P) 10
Model/Layout1 10
Quick View Tools 10
Navigation Tools 10
Annotation Scaling Tools 11
Workspace Switching 11
Lock/Unlock Toolbar and Window Positions 11
Plot/Publish Detail Report 11
Application Status Bar Menu 11
Clean Screen (Ctrl+0 (Zero)) 11
Modify and Save a Workspace 11
Close AutoCAD 13
Review Questions 14

Part II **Two-Dimensional AutoCAD 17**

2 Drawing with AutoCAD: Basic Settings and Commands 17

Introduction 17
Following the Tutorials in This Book 17
Tutorial 2–1: Part 1, Beginning an AutoCAD Drawing: Saving Your Work; Setting Units, Limits, Grid, and Snap; Creating Layers 18
Beginning an AutoCAD Drawing 18
Saving the Drawing 19
Save 19
SaveAs 19
Drawing Name and File Name Extension 21
Units 22
Controlling Your Drawing 23
Drawing Scale 23
Drawing Limits and the Cartesian Coordinate System 24
GRIDDISPLAY 25
GRID 25
SNAP 25
ZOOM 26
Drafting Settings Dialog Box 26
Layers 27
Linetypes 30
Lineweights 30
Lineweight Settings Dialog Box 30
LWT 32
Annotation Scale 34
Saving the Drawing 34
Using the Mouse and Right-Click Customization 35

Tutorial 2–1: Part 2, Drawing Lines, Circles, Arcs, Ellipses, and Donuts 36
ORTHO 36
Drawing Lines Using the Grid Marks and Snap Increments 36
ERASE and UNDO 38
Drawing Lines Using Absolute Coordinates 39
Drawing Lines Using Relative Coordinates 40
Drawing Lines Using Polar Coordinates 40
Drawing Lines Using Direct Distance Entry 41
DYN 42
CIRCLE 42
Center, Radius 43
Center, Diameter 44
2 Points 44
3 Points 44
TTR 45
Ltscale 45
ZOOM 45
Zoom-Window 45
Zoom-All 46
Zoom-Previous 47
Zoom-Extents 47
Zoom-Object 47
Zoom Realtime 47
Wheel Mouse 48
Pan Realtime 48
Wheel Mouse 48
Transparent Commands 48
BLIPMODE 48
REDRAW 48
REGEN 49
HIGHLIGHT 49
Move and Editing Commands Selection Set 49
Window (W) and Crossing Window (C) 52
All (All) 52
Fence (F) 52
Remove (R) and Add (A) 52
Last (L) and Previous (P) 52
Undo (U) 53
Grips 53
UNDO and REDO 54
ARC 55
3-Point 55
Start, Center, End 56
Start, Center, Angle 57
Start, Center, Length 57
Start, End, Angle 57
Start, End, Direction 57

Start, End, Radius 57
Continue 57
ELLIPSE 57
Axis, End 58
Center 58
DONUT 59
SCALE 60
<Scale factor> 60
Reference 60
Tutorial 2–2: Plot Responses for CH2-TUTORIAL1, Using the Model Tab 62
Plot - Name 63
Page Setup 63
Printer/Plotter 63
Plot to File 64
Browse for Plot File... 64
Plot Style Table (Pen Assignments) 64
Paper Size 65
Plot Area 66
Plot Scale 66
Annotative Property and Annotation Scale 67
Plot Offset (Origin Set to Printable Area) 67
Shaded Viewport Options 67
Plot Options 67
Drawing Orientation 68
Preview... 68
Review Questions 69
Exercises 72
Exercise 2–1: Drawing Shapes I 72
Exercise 2–2: Drawing a Pattern 73
Exercise 2–3: Drawing Shapes II 75
Exercise 2–4: Drawing a Door 76
Exercise 2–5: Drawing Shapes III 77

3 Drawing with AutoCAD: Conference and Lecture Rooms 79

Tutorial 3–1: Drawing a Rectangular Conference Room, Including Furniture 79
Drawing Template 81
Polyline 82
Undo 84
Offset 84
Through 85
Erase 85
Layer 85
Explode 85
ID Point 86
Trim 88

Chamfer 89
Polyline 91
Undo 91
Angle 91
Trim 91
mEthod 91
Multiple 91
Fillet 92
Copy and Osnap-Midpoint 94
Rotate 95
Reference 96
Point 96
Divide 97
Measure 98
Copy, Osnap-Midpoint, Osnap-Node 98
Pickbox Size 100
Osnap 101
Activating Osnap 101
Osnap Modes That Snap to Specific Drawing Features 101
Running Osnap Modes 103
Osnap Settings: Marker, Aperture, Magnet, Tooltip 103
Tutorial 3–2: Drawing a Rectangular Lecture Room, Including Furniture 104
Solid Walls Using Polyline and Solid Hatch 105
From 106
Break 106
First 107
@ 107
Polyline Edit 107
Hatch 108
Array 111
Rectangular 112
Distance 113
Position the Chair Array 113
Tutorial 3–3: Drawing a Curved Conference Room, Including Furniture 115
Polyline 116
Width 116
Half Width 116
Length 116
Close 116
Arc 116
FILL ON, FILL OFF 118
Polygon 118
Edge 119
Array 120
Polar 120
Tutorial 3–4: Drawing a Conference Room Using Polar Tracking 121
Polar Tracking 122
From and Osnap 124

Zero Radius Fillet 125
Polyline Edit 125
Draw the Double Door 126
Rectangle 127
Tracking 127
Complete the Conference Room 128
Review Questions 129
Exercises 131
Exercise 3–1: Drawing a Rectangular Conference Room, Including Furniture 131
Exercise 3–2: Drawing a Rectangular Lecture Room, Including Furniture 133

4 Adding Text, Tables, and Raster Images to the Drawing 135

Tutorial 4–1: Placing Text on Drawings 135
Making Settings for Text Style... 136
Using the Single Line Text Command to Draw Text 140
Align 142
Fit 142
Center 142
Middle 142
Right 143
TL/TC/TR/ML/MC/MR/BL/BC/BR 143
Using Standard Codes to Draw Special Characters 144
Using the Multiline Text Command to Draw Text Paragraphs in Columns 147
Changing Text Properties 148
Checking the Spelling 152
Tutorial 4–2: Using the Table... Command to Create a Door Schedule 153
Tutorial 4–3: Using the Table... Command to Create a Window Schedule 162
Tutorial 4–4: Using Text and Raster Images to Make a Title Block and a Drawing Format 163
Review Questions 169

5 Advanced Plotting: Using Plot Styles, Paper Space, Multiple Viewports, and PDF Files 173

Layer Names, Colors, and Linewights 173
Plot Styles 174
Named Plot Style (STB) 174
Color-Dependent Plot Style (CTB) 177
Tutorial 5–1: Making a Color-Dependent Plot Style to Change Colors to Plot Black 178
Tutorial 5–2: Plotting CH3-TUTORIAL1, Using a Color-Dependent Plot Style and Page Setup Manager 179

Model, Layout1, and Layout2 Tabs 179
Plotting Multiple Viewports 183
Tutorial 5–3: Plotting Using Create Layout Wizard and Multiple Viewports at Two Different Scales on an 8-1/2″ × 11″ Sheet 183
Tutorial 5–4: Plotting Using Page Setup Manager, Multiple Viewports with Different Floor Plans, and the D-Size Format 187
Tutorial 5–5: Making PDF Files That Can Be Attached to Emails and Opened Without the AutoCAD Program 193
Review Questions 196

6 Drawing the Floor Plan: Walls, Doors, and Windows 199

The Tenant Space Project 199
Tutorial 6–1: Tenant Space Floor Plan 200
Rectangle 201
Hatch 202
Array 202
Multiline Style... 204
Multiline 206
Edit Multiline 211
Extend 213
Properties... 214
List 215
Color 216
Example 1 217
Example 2 217
Linetype 217
Lineweight 217
Make Object's Layer Current 218
Match Properties 218
Block-Make... 219
Wblock 222
Insert-Block... 225
Insertion Point 227
X Scale Factor, Y Scale Factor 227
Annotative Text 228
Inserting Entire Drawings as Blocks 230
Advantages of Using Blocks 230
Tutorial 6–2: Hotel Room Floor Plan 231
Hatch 233
Review Questions 239
Exercises 241
Exercise 6–1: Wheelchair Accessible Commercial Restroom Floor Plan 241
Exercise 6–2: Wheelchair Accessible Residential Bathroom Floor Plan 242
Exercise 6–3: Log Cabin Floor Plan 243
Exercise 6–4: House Floor Plan 245
Exercise 6–5: Bank Floor Plan 245

7 **Dimensioning and Area Calculations** **251**

Six Basic Types of Dimensions 251
Dimensioning Variables 252
Tutorial 7–1: Dimensioning the Tenant Space Floor Plan Using Linear Dimensions 254
Set the Dimensioning Variables Using the Dim: Prompt 255
Set the Dimensioning Variables Using the Dimension Style Manager Dialog Box 256
Fit Tab—Scale for Dimension Features 262
Use Overall Scale Of: (DIMSCALE) 262
Annotative 263
Summary of DIMSCALE and ANNOTATION SCALE 264
Linear and Continue Dimensioning 265
Aligned Dimensioning 269
Baseline Dimensioning 270
Break 272
Adjust Space 273
Tutorial 7–2: Revisions and Modifying Dimensions 274
DIMASSOC System Variable 274
Associative Dimension Commands 274
Oblique 276
Align Text-Home-Angle-Left-Center-Right 276
Override 277
Update 277
Defpoints Layer 278
Properties 278
Match Properties 278
Grips 278
Revision Cloud 279
Tutorial 7–3: Tenant Space Total Square Feet 281
Area 281
CAL 284
QUICKCALC 285
Tutorial 7–4: Tenant Space Square Foot Summary Table 285
Tutorial 7–5: Use QDIM to Dimension the Conference Room from Tutorial 3–1 286
Review Questions 288
Exercises 290
Exercise 7–1: Hotel Room Dimensioned Floor Plan 290
Exercise 7–2: Wheelchair Accessible Commercial Restroom Dimensioned Floor Plan 292
Exercise 7–3: Wheelchair Accessible Residential Bathroom Dimensioned Floor Plan 292
Exercise 7–4: Log Cabin Dimensioned Floor Plan 293
Exercise 7–5: House Dimensioned Floor Plan 293
Exercise 7–6: Bank Dimensioned Floor Plan 297

8 **Drawing Elevations, Wall Sections, and Details 299**

Introduction 299
Tutorial 8–1: Tenant Space: Elevation of Conference Room Cabinets 299
UCS 301
UCS Icon 302
Mirror 304
Stretch 306
Tutorial 8–2: Using the Multileader Command 319
Tutorial 8–3: Tenant Space: Section of Conference Room Cabinets with Hatching 329
Preparing to Use the Hatch Command with the Select Objects Boundary Option 331
Hatch... Hatch and Gradient Dialog Box; Hatch Tab 335
Type and Pattern 335
Angle and Scale 335
Hatch Origin 336
Boundaries 337
Options 337
More Options 337
Islands 337
Boundary Retention 337
Boundary Set 338
Gap Tolerance 338
Inherit Options 338
Hatch... Hatch and Gradient Dialog Box; Gradient Tab 338
Editing Hatch Patterns 343
Tutorial 8–4: Detail of Door Jamb with Hatching 347
Tutorial 8–5: Using POINT FILTERS and OTRACK to Draw an Orthographic Drawing of a Conference Table 348
Review Questions 354
Exercises 355
Exercise 8–1: Different Hatch Styles 355
Exercise 8–2: Elevation of the Wheelchair Accessible Commercial Restrooms 356
Exercise 8–3: Drawing a Mirror from a Sketch 359
Exercise 8–4: Elevation 1 of the Log Cabin Kitchen 360
Exercise 8–5: Elevation 2 of the Log Cabin Kitchen 363
Exercise 8–6: Detail Drawing of a Bar Rail 365

9 **Drawing the Furniture Installation Plan, Adding Specifications, and Extracting Data 367**

Introduction 367
Tutorial 9–1: Tenant Space Furniture Installation Plan with Furniture Specifications 368
Draw the Furniture Symbols 368
Define Attributes... (ATTDEF) 371
Edit Text (DDEDIT) 379

Wblock the Furniture with Attributes Symbol 379
Insert the Wblock with Attributes into the Drawing 380
Complete the Tenant Space Furniture Installation Plan 382
Attribute, Single... 382
Attribute, Global 383
Attribute Display (ATTDISP) 385
Redefining an Inserted Block with Attributes Using the Block Command 385
Block Attribute Manager (BATTMAN) 386
Synchronize Attributes (ATTSYNC) 386
Tutorial 9–2: Extracting Attributes from the Tenant Space Furniture Installation Plan 387
Data Extraction... 388
Review Questions 393
Exercises 394
Exercise 9–1: Hotel Room Furniture Installation Plan 394
Exercise 9–2: Log Cabin Furniture Installation Plan 395
Exercise 9–3: House Furniture Installation Plan 396
Exercise 9–4: Bank Furniture Installation Plan 396

10 DesignCenter, Dynamic Blocks, and External References 401

Introduction 401
Tutorial 10–1: Reception Area Furniture Installation Plan Using the AutoCAD DesignCenter 401
The AutoCAD DesignCenter 402
DesignCenter Tabs 403
DesignCenter Buttons 403
Tutorial 10–2: Training Room Furniture Installation Plan Using the AutoCAD DesignCenter and Dynamic Blocks 406
Dynamic Blocks 410
Tutorial 10–3: Attach an External Reference to an Office Plan 421
XATTACH 421
External Reference (XREF) 422
XBIND 422
Features of External References 422
Review Questions 427

11 Drawing the Reflected Ceiling Plan and Voice/Data/Power Plan 429

Introduction 429
Tutorial 11–1: Part 1, Tenant Space Lighting Legend and Reflected Ceiling Plan 429
Tenant Space Lighting Legend Symbols 431
Tenant Space Reflected Ceiling Plan 431
Tutorial 11–1: Part 2, Tenant Space Voice/Data/Power Legend and Plan 432
Tenant Space Voice/Data/Power Legend Symbols 432
Tenant Space Voice/Data/Power Plan 432

Review Questions 435
Exercises 435
Exercise 11–1: Hotel Room Power/Communication/Lighting Legend and Plan 435
Exercise 11–2: Wheelchair Accessible Commercial Restroom Lighting Legend and Plan 438
Exercise 11–3: Wheelchair Accessible Residential Bathroom Power/Communication/Lighting Legend and Plan 439
Exercise 11–4: Log Cabin Lighting Legend and Plan 441
Exercise 11–5: Log Cabin Power/Communication Legend and Plan 443
Exercise 11–6: House Power/Communication/Lighting Legend and Plan 445
Exercise 11–7: Bank Lighting Legend and Reflected Ceiling Plan 448
Exercise 11–8: Bank Voice/Data/Power Legend and Plan 450

12 Creating Presentations with Layouts and Sheet Sets 453

Model Space and Paper Space 453
Tutorial 12–1: Creating a Printed Presentation of the Tenant Space Project by Combining Multiple Plans on One Sheet of Paper 454
Viewports (VPORTS) 455
REDRAW, REDRAWALL, REGEN, and REGENALL 457
Tilemode 457
MVIEW 458
Create Layout Wizard 459
Working in Model Space with Paper Space Viewports Visible 461
Paper Space 464
MVSETUP 465
Tilemode Set to 1 (ON) 467
Tilemode Set to 0 (OFF) 467
Label the Views While in Paper Space 467
Tutorial 12–2: Creating a Four-Sheet Drawing with Different Layers Frozen on Each Sheet 468
Quick View 472
Tutorial 12–3: Making a Sheet Set Containing Four Drawing Layouts and a Title Page 473
Make a Title Page 474
Sheet Set... 475
eTransmit... 481
Review Questions 483

13 Isometric Drawing and Gradient Hatch Rendering 485

Axonometric Drawing 485
Isometric Drawing 485
Tutorial 13–1: Fundamentals of Isometric Drawing 486
Drafting Settings Dialog Box 487
Shape 1: Drawing the Isometric Rectangle 488
Shape 2: Drawing Isometric Ellipses 489

Shape 3: Drawing a Chair with Ellipses That Show the Thickness of a Material 491
Shape 4: Drawing a Shape That Has a Series of Isometric Ellipses Located on the Same Centerline 495
Shape 5: Isometric Detail with Rounded Corners 496
Shape 6: A TV Shape with an Angled Back 498
Shape 7: Isometric Detail—A Hexagonal-Shaped Vase 500
Tutorial 13–2: Tenant Space Reception Desk in Isometric 502
Dimensioning in Isometric 509
Gradient Hatch 509
Tutorial 13–3: Using Gradient Patterns to Render the Shapes of Tutorial 13–1 510
Review Questions 517
Exercises 518
Exercise 13–1: Using Gradient Patterns to Render the Reception Desk of Tutorial 13–2 518
Exercise 13–2: Tenant Space Reception Seating Area in Isometric 519
Exercise 13–3: Tenant Space Conference Chair in Isometric 519
Exercise 13–4: Conference Room Walls and Table in Isometric 519
Exercise 13–5: Log Cabin Kitchen Isometric Cutaway Drawing 524

Part III **Three-Dimensional AutoCAD 529**

14 Solid Modeling 529

Introduction 529
Solids Commands Used to Create Basic Shapes 529
Solids Commands Used to Create Composite Solids 530
Solids Commands Used to Edit Solids 530
Mesh Modeling 530
SOLIDEDIT 531
Controlling UCS in Three Dimensions 531
Dynamic UCS 531
Commands to View Solids 531
3D Views Menu Options 531
SteeringWheels 533
ViewCube 533
Other Commands That Can Be Used to Edit Solids 533
Settings That Control How the Solid Is Displayed 533
Tutorial 14–1: Part 1, Drawing Primitive Solids 534
Box 536
Sphere 536
Wedge 537
Cone 537
Cylinder 538
Torus 538

Tutorial 14–1: Part 2, Using Extrude to Draw Extruded Solids 539
Draw an Extruded Circle 539
Draw an Extruded Polygon 539
Draw an Extruded Rectangle 540
Draw an Extruded Structural Angle 541
Draw an Extruded Shape 543
Tutorial 14–1: Part 3, Using Revolve to Draw Revolved Solids; Using 3D Rotate to Rotate Solids About the X, Y, and Z Axes 543
Draw Revolved Shape 1 543
Draw a Revolved Rectangle 545
Draw a Revolved Paper Clip Holder 546
Rotate 3D 547
Tutorial 14–1: Part 4, Using Chamfer and Fillet to Form Chamfers and Fillets on Solid Edges 548
Chamfer and Fillet the Top Four Edges of Two Separate Boxes 548
Chamfer and Fillet on the Top Edge of Two Separate Cylinders 549
Tutorial 14–1: Part 5, Using Union to Join Two Solids; Using Subtract to Subtract Solids from Other Solids 550
Draw Solid Shape 1 550
Draw Solid Shape 2 550
Union 552
Subtract 552
Hide 552
Tutorial 14–1: Part 6, Using Sweep, Helix, Subtract, Loft, Planar Surface, Thicken, and Polysolid to Draw Solid Shapes 553
Sweep 553
Loft 556
Create a Bowl-Shaped Object 557
Planar Surface 557
Polysolid 558
Tutorial 14–1: Part 7, Using Intersection to Form a Solid Model from the Common Volume of Two Intersecting Solids 560
Draw Two Extruded Shapes at Right Angles to Each Other 560
Intersect 561
Wblock the Intersected Model 562
Complete Tutorial 14–1 563
Tutorial 14–2: Using Grips to Modify Solid Shapes 564
Tutorial 14–3: Creating a Solid Model of Chair 1 568
Draw One Side of the Chair Legs and Arms 569
Draw the Cushion of the Chair 570
Draw the Back of the Chair 572
Complete the Leg and Arm Assembly 572
Draw the Chair Platform 574
Orbit 575
Tutorial 14–4: Creating Mesh Models 577
Mesh Box and MESHSMOOTHMORE 578
Mesh Cone 579
Mesh Cylinder 580

Mesh Wedge 580
Mesh Torus 581
Make Solid Models 582
Review Questions 587
Exercises 589
Exercise 14–1: Drawing Solid Models of Eight Objects 589
Exercise 14–2: Drawing a Solid Model of a Lamp Table 590
Exercise 14–3: Drawing a Solid Model of a Sofa 591
Exercise 14–4: Drawing a Solid Model of a Lamp and Inserting It and the Lamp Table into the Sofa Drawing 592
Exercise 14–5: Drawing a Solid Model of the Tenant Space Reception Seating 593
Exercise 14–6: Drawing a Solid Model of a Conference Chair 594
Exercise 14–7: Drawing a Solid Model of a Conference Table and Inserting Chairs Around It 595

15 Complex Solid Models with Materials, Lighting, Rendering, and Animation 597

Introduction 597
Tutorial 15–1: Creating a Solid Model of Chair 2 598
Tutorial 15–2: Creating a Solid Model of a Patio 601
Render 611
Render Quality 611
Destinations 611
Lights 611
Materials 612
Other Commands Available to Render, Animate, and Shade 3D Models 612
Tutorial 15–3: Use Render Commands to Make a Photo-Realistic Rendering of the Solid Model in Tutorial 15–2 613
Tutorial 15–4: Create a Walk-Through AVI File for the Rendered 3D Patio 625
Review Questions 630

16 Advanced Modeling 633

Introduction 633
Tutorial 16–1: Make a New Material Using the Advanced Material Type, Attach It to a Model, and Render the Model 633
Tutorial 16–2: Save a Carpet Sample Image from a Manufacturer's Website and Use the Image to Make a New Material 636
Advanced Render Settings 639
General 639
Tutorial 16–3: Build a Solid Model of a Living Room with Furniture, Attach Materials, Add Lights, and Render It 640
Review Questions 649
Exercises 651

Exercise 16–1: Make a Solid Model of the Chair Shown in the Sketch. Use Render Commands to Make a Photo-Realistic Rendering of the Solid Model 651
Exercise 16–2: Make a Solid Model of the Picnic Table Shown in the Sketch. Use Render Commands to Make a Photo-Realistic Rendering of the Solid Model 651
Exercise 16–3: Make a Solid Model of the Table Shown in the Sketch. Use Render Commands to Make a Photo-Realistic Rendering of the Solid Model 652
Exercise 16–4: Make a Solid Model of the Lounge Shown in the Sketch. Use Render Commands to Make a Photo-Realistic Rendering of the Solid Model 653

Appendix A Keyboard Shortcuts 655

Appendix B Shortcut and Temporary Override Keys 659

Appendix C Floor Plans and Interior Elevations of a 15-Unit Condominium Building 661

Index 663

AutoCAD® 2010 for Interior Design and Space Planning

Part I Preparing to Draw with AutoCAD

chapter

1

Introducing the AutoCAD Screen

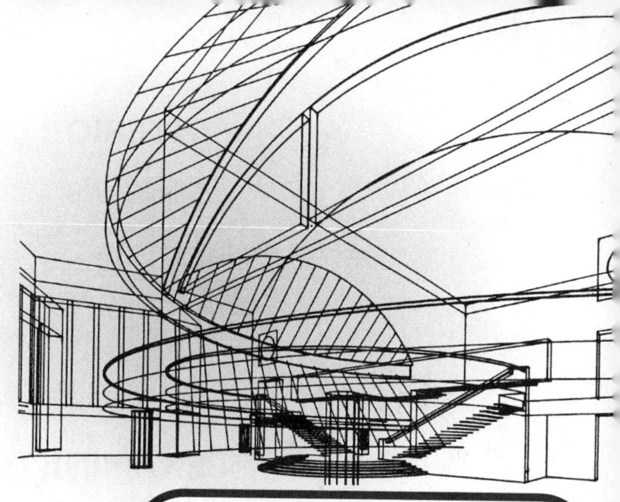

objectives

When you have completed this chapter, you will be able to:

Describe the AutoCAD screen and begin using parts of the screen.

Modify and save a workspace.

INTRODUCTION

Before you start using the tutorials in this book, you need to understand their structure and purpose.

Throughout the tutorials in this book, *numbered steps in bold type provide instructions.* **Prompt** and **Response** columns in the numbered steps provide step-by-step instructions for starting and completing a command. The ***Prompt*** *column text* repeats the AutoCAD prompt that appears in the Command: area of the AutoCAD screen. The ***Response*** *column text* shows your response to the AutoCAD prompt. *Blue ruled lines* separate the numbered steps from further discussion and explanation. *Menus* show you how to locate the command you are using.

INTERIOR DESIGNERS AND SPACE PLANNERS

This book is written for interior designers and space planners who want to learn the AutoCAD program in the most effective and efficient manner—by drawing with it. The tutorials specifically cover interior design and space planning drawings. Tutorial 1–1 introduces you to the AutoCAD 2D Drafting and Annotation workspace and the AutoCAD screen.

Tutorial 1–1: Examine the AutoCAD Screen and Save a Workspace

EXAMINE THE AutoCAD SCREEN

The AutoCAD screen provides the drawing window and easy access to drawing menus and drawing tools. A brief introduction to each part of the screen, Figure 1–1, follows:

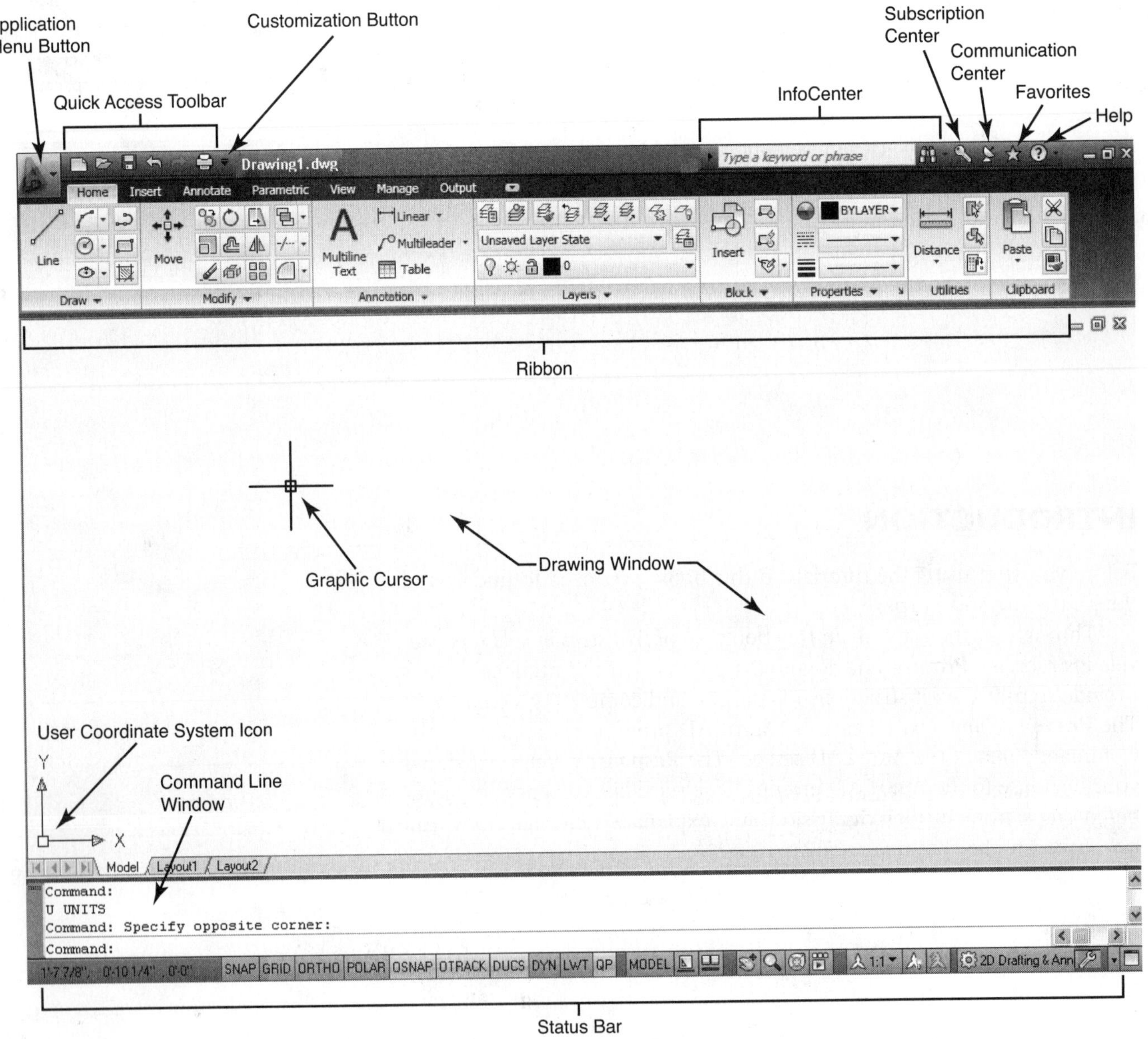

FIGURE 1–1
The AutoCAD Screen

Step 1. Start AutoCAD

APPLICATION MENU BUTTON

When you click (quickly press and release the left mouse button) on the Application menu button, the Application menu opens. The Application commands (Figure 1–2) can be used to:

- Create a drawing
- Open an existing drawing
- Save a drawing
- Export your drawing to a different format
- Print a drawing
- Publish a drawing
- E-mail your drawing
- Access tools to maintain your drawing
- Close a drawing

At the top of the Application menu, you can enter key words to search for additional menu items.

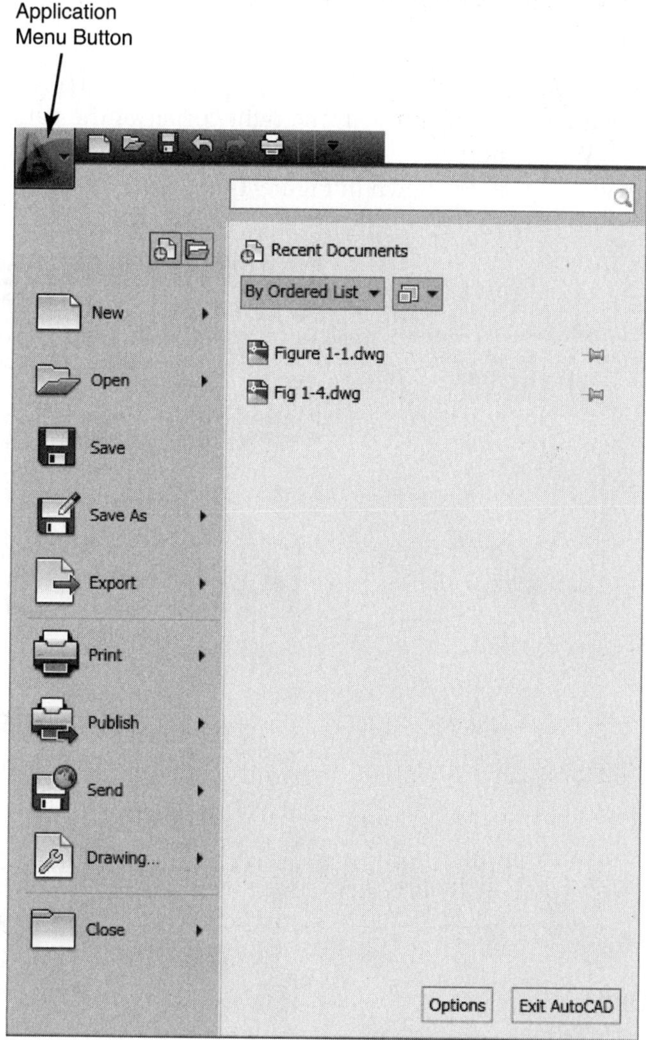

FIGURE 1–2
Application Menu

Step 2. **Click the application button with your left mouse button to open it. Hold your mouse over each command to see the brief descriptions of the command options. Press the Esc key to exit the Application menu.**

RIBBON

The Ribbon displays the commands used to create a drawing. It can be displayed as horizontal, vertical, or floating, or you can turn the Ribbon off. You can create your own Ribbon panels or modify the commands on an existing panel. You can also drag individual panels of the Ribbon into your drawing window and float them.

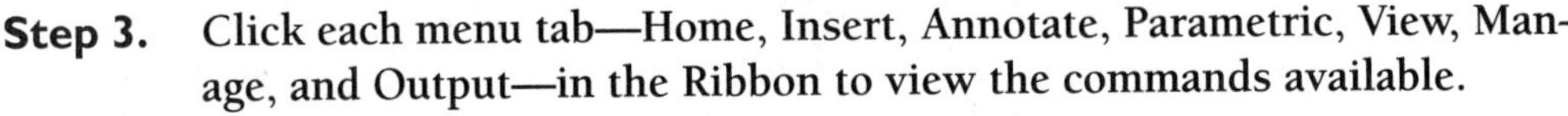

Step 3. **Click each menu tab—Home, Insert, Annotate, Parametric, View, Manage, and Output—in the Ribbon to view the commands available.**

FIGURE 1–3
Expanded Panel

Expanded Panels

Panels with an arrow to the right of the panel title can be expanded to display additional commands. When you click the left mouse button on the arrow, the panel will expand. When expanded, you can use the push pin icon to the left of the panel title to keep the panel expanded (Figure 1–3).

Dialog Boxes and Palettes

Panels with a diagonal arrow in the right corner of the panel title have dialog boxes or palettes. When you click the left mouse button on the diagonal arrow, a dialog box or palette will appear, as shown in Figure 1–4.

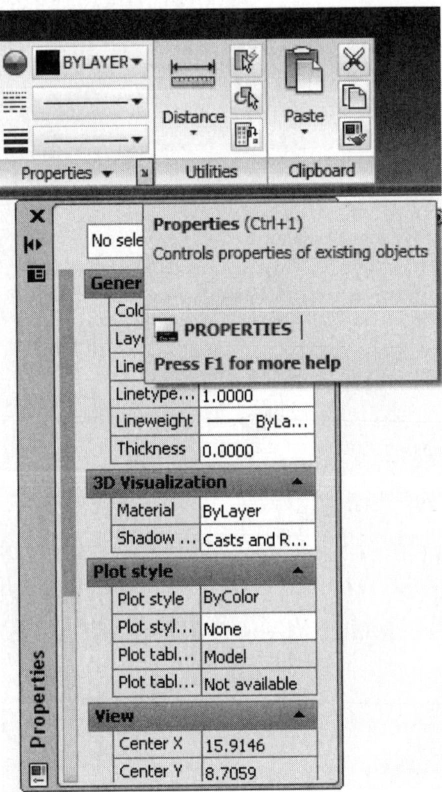

FIGURE 1–4
Properties Palette

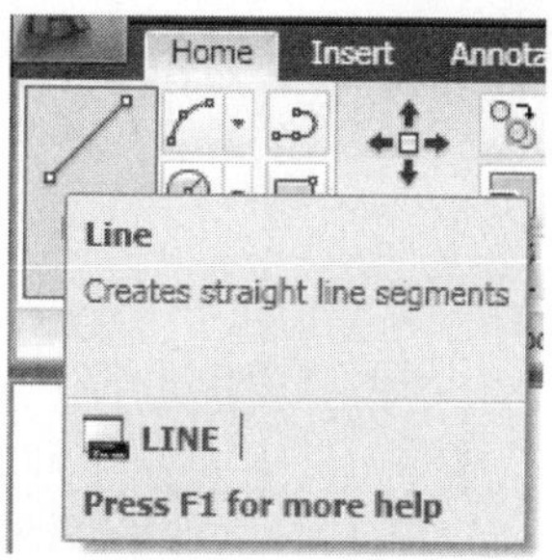

FIGURE 1–5
Tooltips

Tooltips

When you hold the mouse pointer steady (do not click) on any command in the browser or Ribbon, a tooltip will display the name of the command, and a text string gives a brief description of the command (Figure 1–5).

Flyouts

Commands with a small arrow have flyouts. When you click the left mouse button on the command, the flyout will appear, as shown in Figure 1–6. When you click on a command in the flyout, a command is activated.

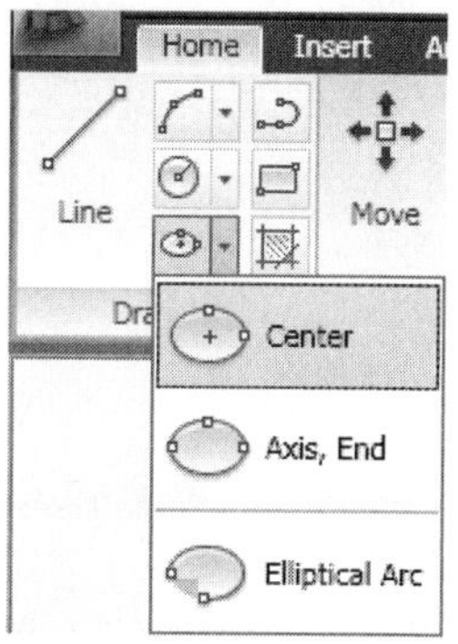

FIGURE 1–6
Flyouts

QUICK ACCESS TOOLBAR

This toolbar contains the New, Open, Save, Undo, Redo, and Plot commands.

When you right-click on the Quick Access Toolbar, the right-click menu shown in Figure 1–7 appears:

The first option in the right-click menu allows you to remove commands from the Quick Access Toolbar.
The second option allows you to add a separator line between command icons in the Quick Access Toolbar.
The third option allows you to add frequently used commands to the Quick Access Toolbar.
The fourth option allows you to move the Quick Access Toolbar to below the Ribbon.

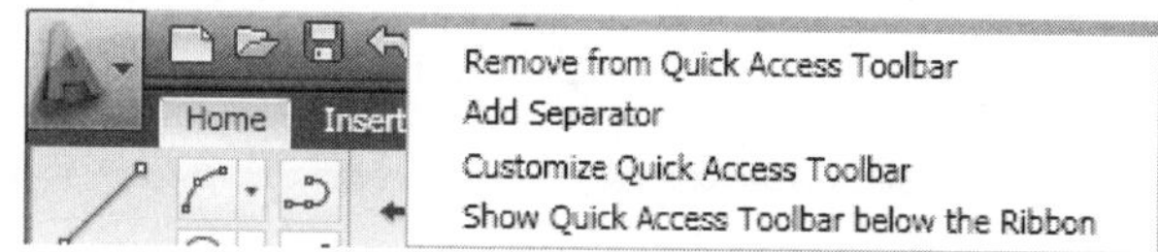

FIGURE 1–7
Right-Click on the Quick Access Toolbar

CUSTOMIZATION BUTTON

When you click the down arrow to the right of the Quick Access Toolbar, the menu shown in Figure 1–8 appears:

Commands Clicking a command to display the check mark adds the command icon to the Quick Access Menu.
More Commands... Takes you to the Customize User Interface Editor and allows you to add frequently used commands to the Quick Access Toolbar.
Show Menu Bar Allows you to display the Menu Bar shown in Figure 1–9.
Show Below the Ribbon Allows you to move the Quick Access Toolbar below the Ribbon.

Step 4. **Hold your mouse steady over each icon in the Quick Access Toolbar to see the text string that gives a brief description of each command.**

Step 5. **Right-click on the Quick Access Toolbar (Figure 1–7) to view the right-click menu. Press the Esc key to exit the right-click menu.**

Step 6. **Click on the customization button to view the menu shown in Figure 1–8. Press the Esc key to exit the menu.**

FIGURE 1–8
Customize Quick Access Toolbar

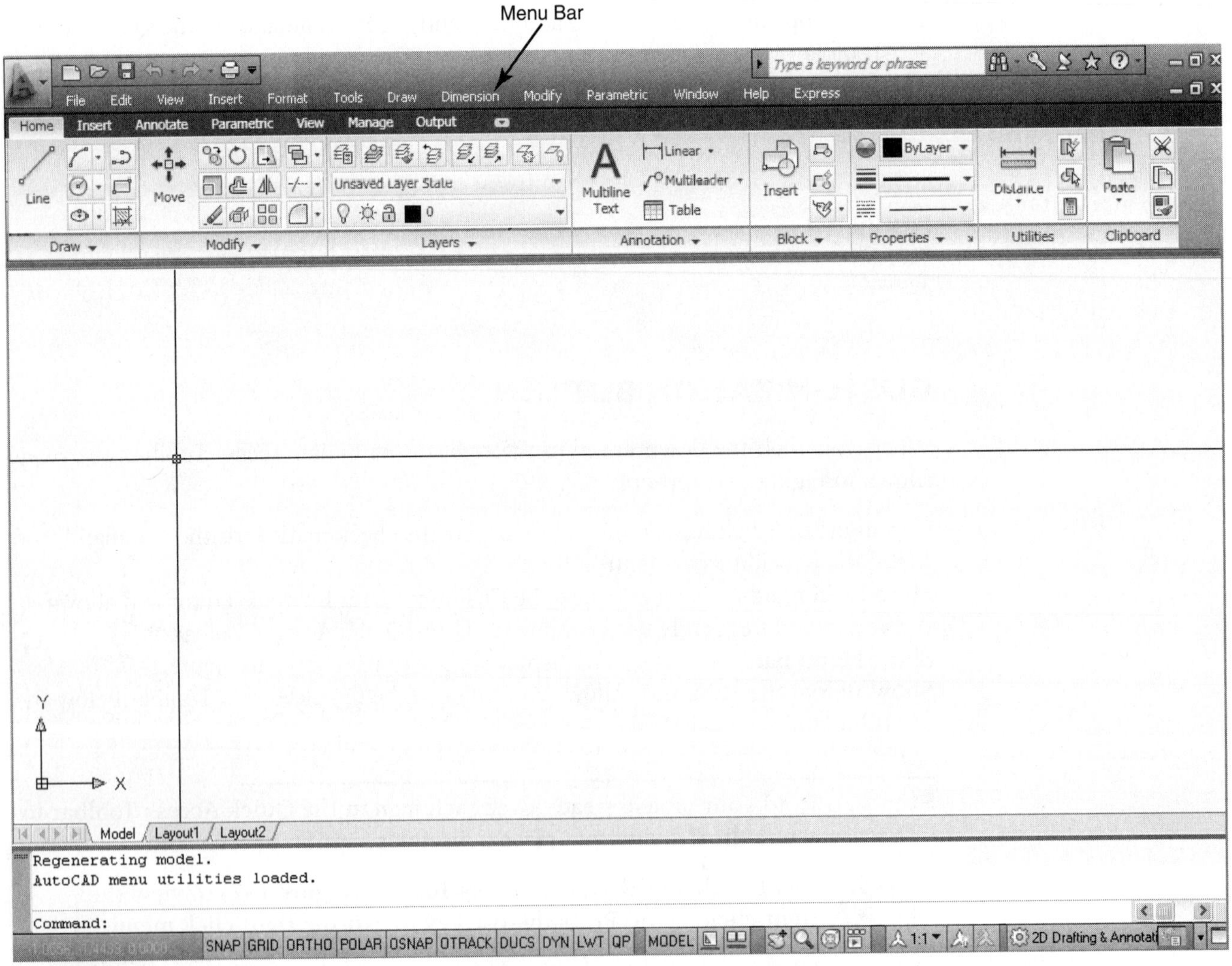

Menu Bar

FIGURE 1–9
Display the Menu Bar

InfoCENTER

You can enter a word or phrase in the InfoCenter to search for information. Click on the Search button to the right of the InfoCenter box to access search results. You can collapse the InfoCenter by clicking the arrow to the left of the InfoCenter box.

SUBSCRIPTION CENTER

You can access subscription services here.

COMMUNICATION CENTER

You can find information regarding product updates and announcements here.

FAVORITES

You can save and access favorite topics here.

HELP

You can access the help menu here.

DRAWING WINDOW AND GRAPHICS CURSOR

The drawing window is where your drawing is displayed. The graphics cursor (or crosshair) follows the movement of a mouse when points of a drawing are entered or a command is selected. The box at the center of the crosshairs is called a pickbox. The size of the cursor and pickbox can be changed to accommodate any individual preference.

Step 7. Locate the Options dialog box where the size of the graphics cursor and pickbox can be changed, as described next:

Prompt	Response
Command:	TYPE: **OP<enter>** (in this book, **<enter>** means to press the Enter key or press the right mouse button for enter)
The Options dialog box appears (Figure 1–10)	CLICK: **the Display tab**
The Display tab appears:	Click the Crosshair size slider in the lower right to decrease or increase the size of the crosshair CLICK: **the Selection tab**
The Selection tab appears:	Click the Pickbox size slider in the upper left to decrease or increase the size of the pickbox Exit the Options dialog box

COMMAND LINE WINDOW (Ctrl+9)

The command line window shown at the bottom of the screen may be moved and resized or turned off. The command line window is where you can see AutoCAD respond to a command you have started. After a command is started, AutoCAD prompts you to enter specific information. Always watch the command line to make sure you and AutoCAD are communicating.

FIGURE 1–10
Options Dialog Box

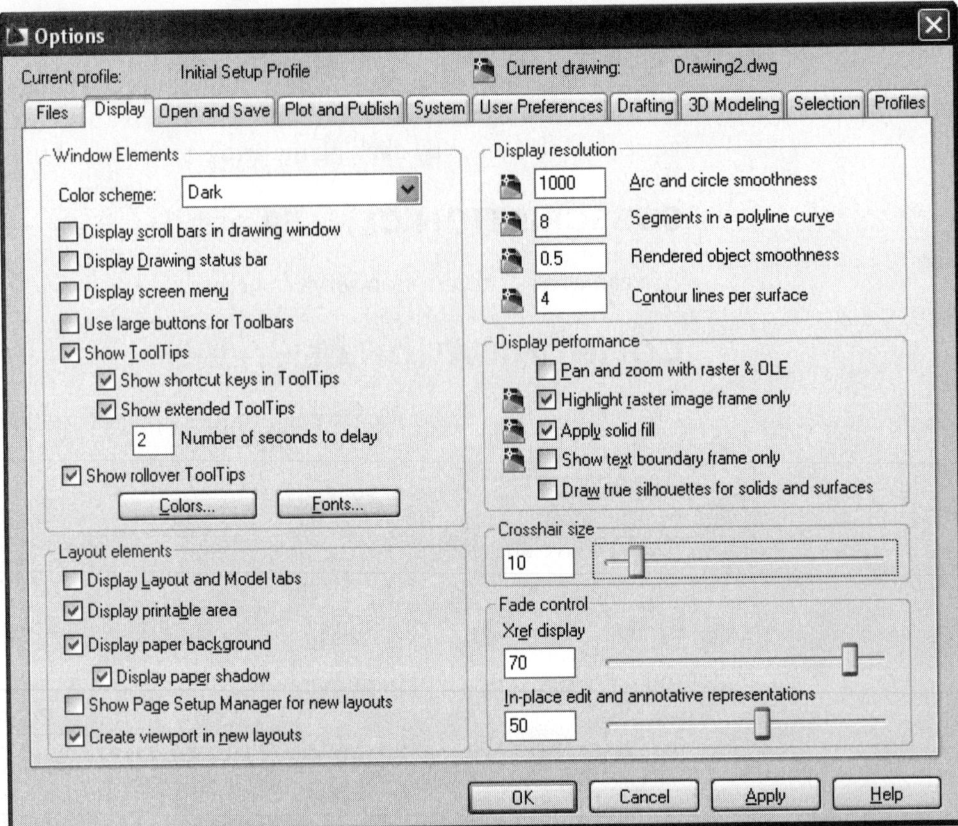

USER COORDINATE SYSTEM ICON

All AutoCAD drawings are made on a coordinate system (Figure 1–11). The user coordinate system (UCS) icon in the lower left corner of the drawing window shows the orientation of the X, Y, and Z axes of the current coordinate system. In 2D drawings, only the X and Y axes are used. The UCS icon is located at the origin of the UCS (0,0). In this figure, the dots (grid marks) are spaced ½″ apart. The crosshairs of the cursor are located 3″ to the right (the X direction) and 2″ up (the Y direction) from 0,0. The numbers in the gray area show the cursor coordinate values (the location of the crosshairs).

FIGURE 1–11
The AutoCAD User Coordinate System—Cartesian Coordinates

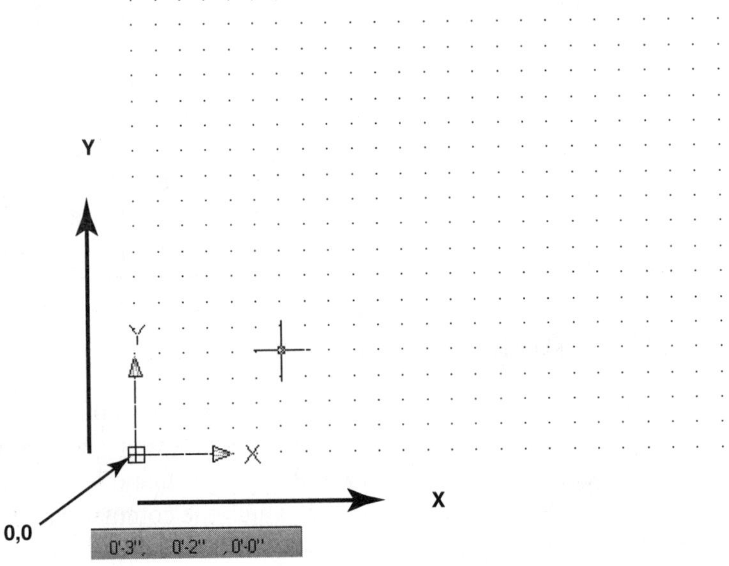

STATUS BAR

The Status Bar (Figure 1–12) at the bottom of the screen contains the following options.

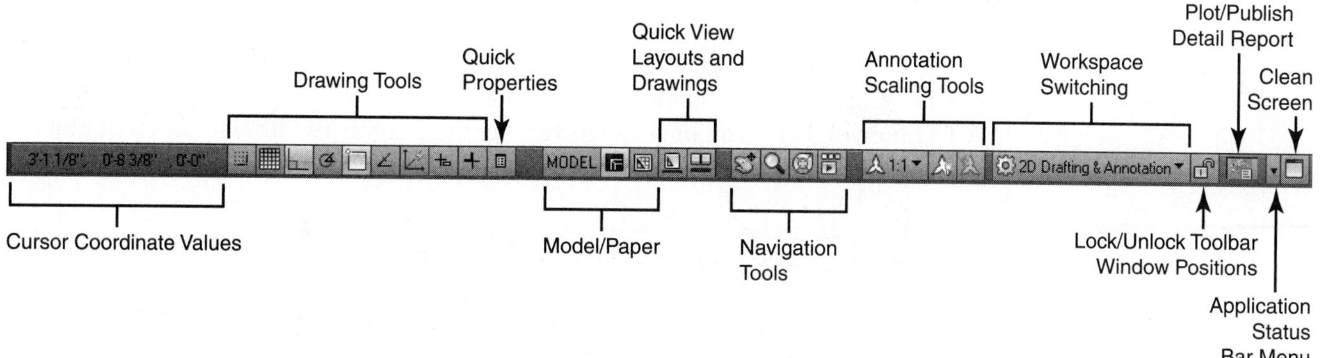

FIGURE 1–12
Status Bar

Cursor Coordinate Values (Ctrl+I)

Using an X- and Y-axis system, the cursor coordinate display number in the lower left corner tells you where the cursor on the screen is located in relation to 0,0 (the lower left corner). Clicking on the coordinates turns them on and off.

Drawing Tools

The Drawing Tools buttons at the bottom of the screen allow you to turn on or off nine drawing tools that affect your drawing. You can also turn the tools off and on using the function keys. The tools and the function keys are:

SNAP (F9) Your graphics cursor (crosshair) snaps to invisible snap points as you move the cursor across the screen when SNAP is on. You set the size between snap points.

GRID (F7) A visible pattern of dots you see on the screen when GRID is on. You set the size between grid dots.

ORTHO (F8) Allows you to draw only horizontally and vertically when on.

POLAR (F10) Shows temporary alignment paths along polar angles when on (Figure 1–13).

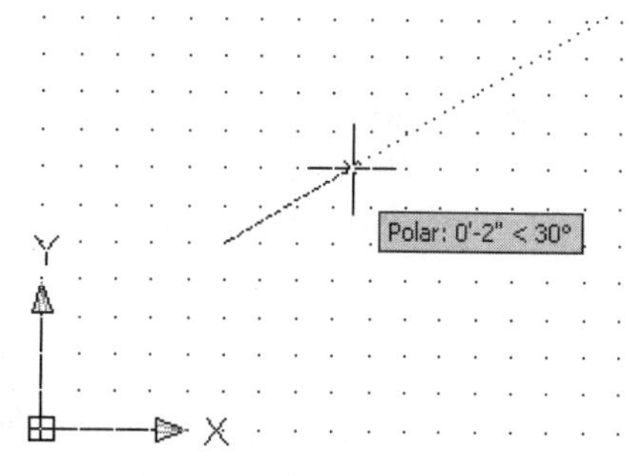

FIGURE 1–13
Polar Angles with Polar On

OSNAP (F3) This is object snap. Osnap contains command modifiers that help you draw very accurately.

OTRACK (F11) Shows temporary alignment paths along object snap points when on.

DUCS (Dynamic UCS) (F6) This is used in 3D to move the user coordinate system.

DYN (Dynamic Input) (F12) Gives you information attached to the cursor regarding commands, coordinates, and tooltips. This is the same information that AutoCAD gives you in the command line window.

LWT (Lineweight) You may assign varying lineweights (widths) to different objects in your drawing. When this toggle is on, the lineweights are displayed on the screen.

The drawing tools buttons can be represented by icons or words (Figure 1–14). The right-click menu of each drawing tool displays settings specific for that tool. Each drawing tool has a "use icons" setting on the right-click menu (Figure 1–15). When a check mark is beside that option, icons are used.

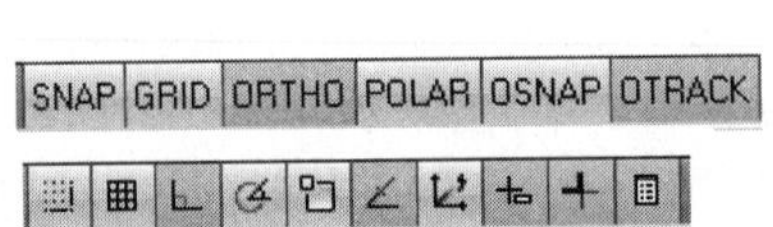

FIGURE 1–14
Drawing Tool Buttons Shown as Words or Icons

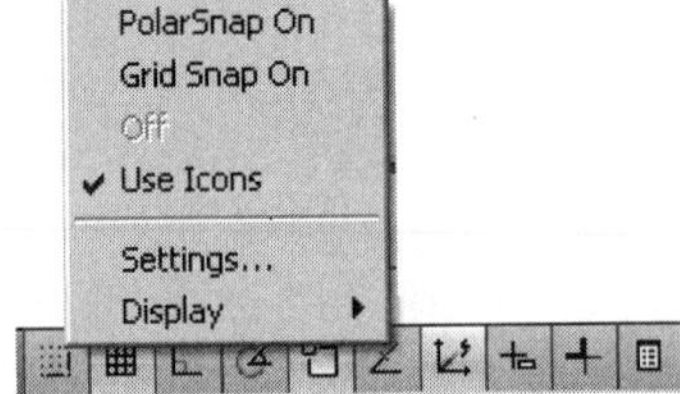

FIGURE 1–15
Right-Click Menu for Drawing Tools

Step 8. RIGHT-CLICK: on one of the drawing tools to see the right-click menu shown in Figure 1–15. SELECT: Use icons (to see either the words or the icons). Set the option (words or icons) that you prefer.

Quick Properties (Ctrl+SHIFT+P)

Every drawing object that you draw has properties such as color, layer, and linetype. When this button is on, the Quick Properties panel appears when you select an object and allows you to view and change the settings for the properties of the object.

Model/Layout1

These buttons control the visibility of the Model and Layout working environments.

Quick View Tools

Quick View Layouts Allows you to preview and switch between open layouts.

Quick View Drawings Allows you to preview and switch between open drawings.

Navigation Tools

Pan Like panning with a camera, pan does not change the magnification of the screen view but allows you to move to parts of the drawing that may be off the screen and not visible in the display.

Zoom Uses the Zoom command and all of its options to zoom a window, zoom all, and move about your drawing.

Steering Wheels Can be used in 2D or 3D to pan and zoom or to rotate a 3D view.

Show Motion Used in 3D to record animation.

Annotation Scaling Tools

These buttons affect annotative objects such as text and dimensions that are added to drawings and need to be scaled when plotted.

Annotation Scale This button allows you to control how annotative text and dimensions appear on the drawing.

Annotation Visibility When you have annotative objects on your drawing that support different scales, this button controls their visibility. When it is off, only the annotative objects with the current annotation scale are visible.

Automatically add scales to annotative objects when the annotation scale changes When this button is on and the annotation scale is changed, the annotative objects change on the screen to reflect the new scale size. The object then supports two scales.

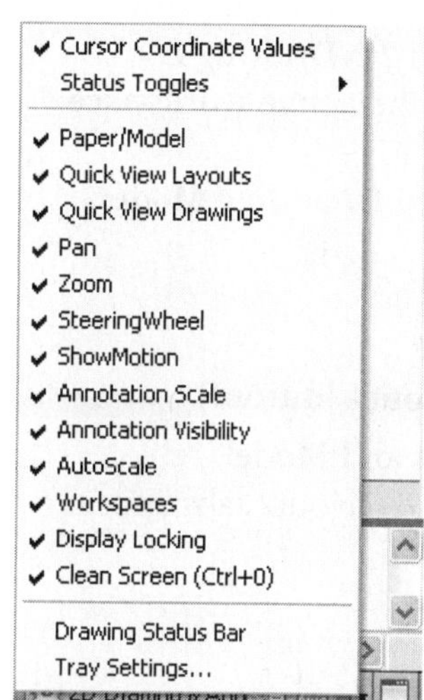

FIGURE 1–16
Application Status Bar Menu

Workspace Switching

A workspace is the environment in which you work. It is defined by which menus, toolbars, or palettes appear on the workspace. This button allows you to switch between defined workspaces.

Lock/Unlock Toolbar and Window Positions

Toolbars and windows can be added to your workspace. This button allows you to lock and unlock the location of these toolbars and windows.

Plot/Publish Detail Report

If a drawing has recently been plotted or published, a report is available.

Application Status Bar Menu

When this arrow is clicked, a menu appears (Figure 1–16) that allows you to turn off and on the visibility of the buttons in the Status Bar.

Clean Screen (Ctrl+0 (Zero))

When on, this button clears the screen of the Ribbon, toolbars, and dockable windows, excluding the command line.

MODIFY AND SAVE A WORKSPACE

AutoCAD provides you with three different workspaces to choose from when making your own workspace: 2D Drafting & Annotation, 3D Modeling, and AutoCAD Classic. Each workspace is defined by a set of menus, toolbars, and palettes. The 3D Modeling workspace is used when you make 3D models. The Classic workspace looks similar to how the AutoCAD screen has looked in past years. In AutoCAD 2010, the 2D Drafting & Annotation workspace has a Ribbon and Application menu.

Step 9. Make sure the 2D Drafting & Annotation workspace is current, as described next:

Prompt	Response
Command:	CLICK: **Workspace Switching button on the status bar**
The Workspace Switching menu appears (Figure 1–17)	If there is a check mark beside 2D Drafting & Annotation, it is active

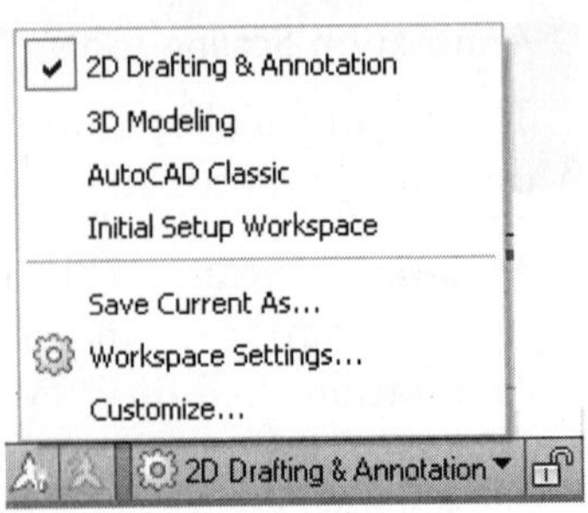

FIGURE 1–17
Workspace Switching Menu

If it is active, PRESS: **Esc to exit the menu**
If it is not active, CLICK: **2D Drafting & Annotation to make it the active workspace**

Step 10. **Modify the 2D Drafting & Annotation workspace by adding Model, Layout1, and Layout2 tabs as described next:**

Prompt	Response
Command:	RIGHT-CLICK: **the Layout1 button**
The right-click menu appears.	CLICK: **Display Layout and Model Tabs** (the Model, Layout1, and Layout2 tabs appear, as shown in Figure 1–18)

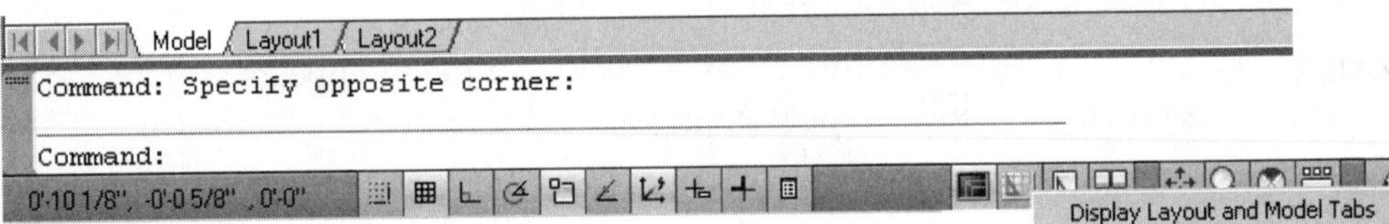

FIGURE 1–18
Right-Click Layout1 Icon and Click: Display Layout and Model Tabs

Step 11. **Add the Menu Bar to the AutoCAD screen as described next:**

Prompt	Response
Command:	CLICK: **the Customization button** (to the right of the Quick Access Toolbar) CLICK: **Show Menu Bar** (Figure 1–19) (the Menu Bar appears as shown in Figure 1–9)

Step 12. **Save your workspace, as described next:**

Prompt	Response
Command:	CLICK: **Workspace Switching button**
The Workspace Switching menu appears:	CLICK: **Save Current As...**
The Save Workspace textbox appears:	TYPE: **your name in the Name: textbox<enter>**

FIGURE 1–19
Show Menu Bar

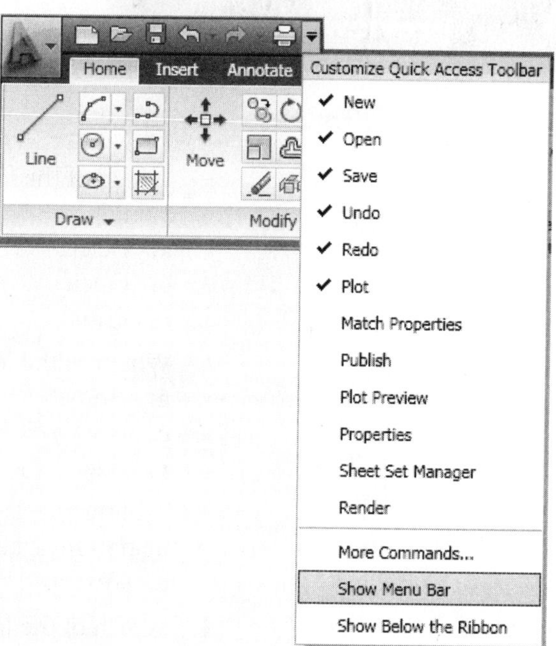

As you become familiar with AutoCAD, you may want to add menus, toolbars, or palettes to your drawing display and keep that display. CLICK: **Save Current As...**, locate your name in the Name: textbox, and save the modified drawing display as your named workspace again.

CLOSE AutoCAD

For now, you will not name or save this exercise. The new workspace is already saved.

Step 13. Click the Close button (the X) in the upper right corner of the AutoCAD screen to exit AutoCAD.

---

review questions

1. Which of the following is *not* one of the commands in the Application menu?
   a. Delete
   b. Open
   c. Print
   d. Close
   e. Publish
2. Which of the following is a Ribbon panel?
   a. Home
   b. File
   c. Edit
   d. Draw
   e. View
3. Tooltips display the name of the command but do not give any other information regarding the command.
   a. True
   b. False
4. Which of the following icons on the Draw panel of the Ribbon have flyouts?
   a. Line
   b. Polygon
   c. Rectangle
   d. Arc
   e. Hatch
5. Ribbon panels with a diagonal arrow in the right corner display which of the following when the diagonal arrow is clicked?
   a. Flyouts
   b. A dialog box or palette
   c. Additional commands
   d. The Help menu
   e. Options
6. List the six commands on the Quick Access Toolbar (before it has been customized).

   ________ ________ ________ ________ ________ ________
7. Describe the purpose of the InfoCenter.

   ____
8. List the tab on the Options dialog box that allows you to change the size of the crosshairs.

   ____
9. List the tab on the Options dialog that allows you to change the size of the pickbox.

   ____
10. List the nine drawing tool buttons on the Status Bar and the function keys that can be used to turn the tools on and off.

    ____

    ____
11. Describe how to add the Menu Bar to the AutoCAD screen.

    ____

    ____
12. List the two navigation tools on the Status Bar that are used for 2D drawings only.

    ____

13. List the three different workspaces that are provided by AutoCAD.

____

____

____

14. Which button can be right-clicked to display Layout and Model tabs?

____

15. If you have modified a workspace and want to save it, which Workspace Switching command option must be clicked?

____

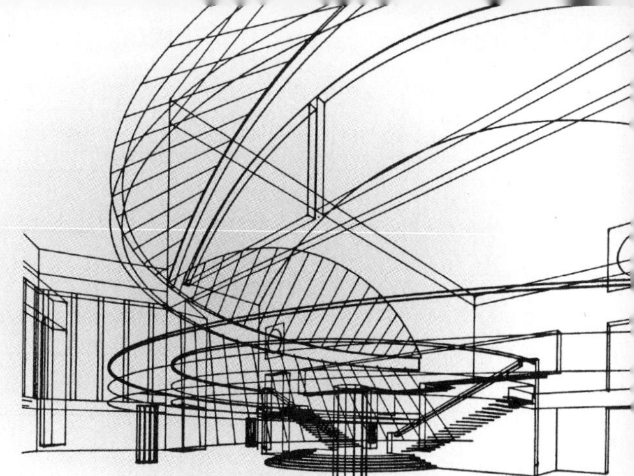

chapter 2

Drawing with AutoCAD: Basic Settings and Commands

objectives

When you have completed this chapter, you will be able to:

Begin a new AutoCAD drawing.

Make settings for an AutoCAD drawing to include Units, Limits, Grid, and Snap.

Make layers and assign color, linetype, and lineweight to each layer.

Use function keys F7 (grid) and F9 (snap) to control grid and snap.

Use the commands Save and SaveAs... to save work.

Use grips to modify objects.

Turn ORTHO mode (F8) on and off to control drawing horizontal and vertical lines.

Use annotation scale to control how text and other annotative objects appear on the drawing.

Correctly use the following commands and settings:

Arc	Erase	Redo
BLIPMODE	Highlight	Redraw
Circle	Line	Regen
Donut	Ltscale	Scale
DYN	Move	Undo
Ellipse	Pan	Zoom

Correctly use the following selection set options:

All	Remove
Window	Add
Last	Undo
Previous	Fence
Crossing window	

Draw using:

Absolute, relative, and polar coordinates, and direct distance entry.

Print/Plot drawings from a Model tab.

INTRODUCTION

Tutorial 2–1, Part 1 of this chapter describes the settings that must be made when preparing to draw with AutoCAD. Tutorial 2–1, Part 2 describes how to draw using basic AutoCAD commands. When you have completed Tutorial 2–1, your drawing will look similar to Figure 2–1. Tutorial 2–2 describes how to print your drawing.

The following is a hands-on step-by-step procedure to complete your first drawing using AutoCAD.

FOLLOWING THE TUTORIALS IN THIS BOOK

You are probably using a mouse with a small wheel between the buttons. The left button is the pick button used to select commands and click points on the drawing. The **Response** column item used in the tutorials describes the location of points on the drawing that are clicked by the left button on your mouse. Figures are provided throughout the chapters to show the location of the points. The points are indicated in bold type in the **Response** column by a **D** followed by a number; for example, **D1**, **D2**. Look at the figure referenced in the step to locate the point on the drawing, and click a point in the same place on your drawing.

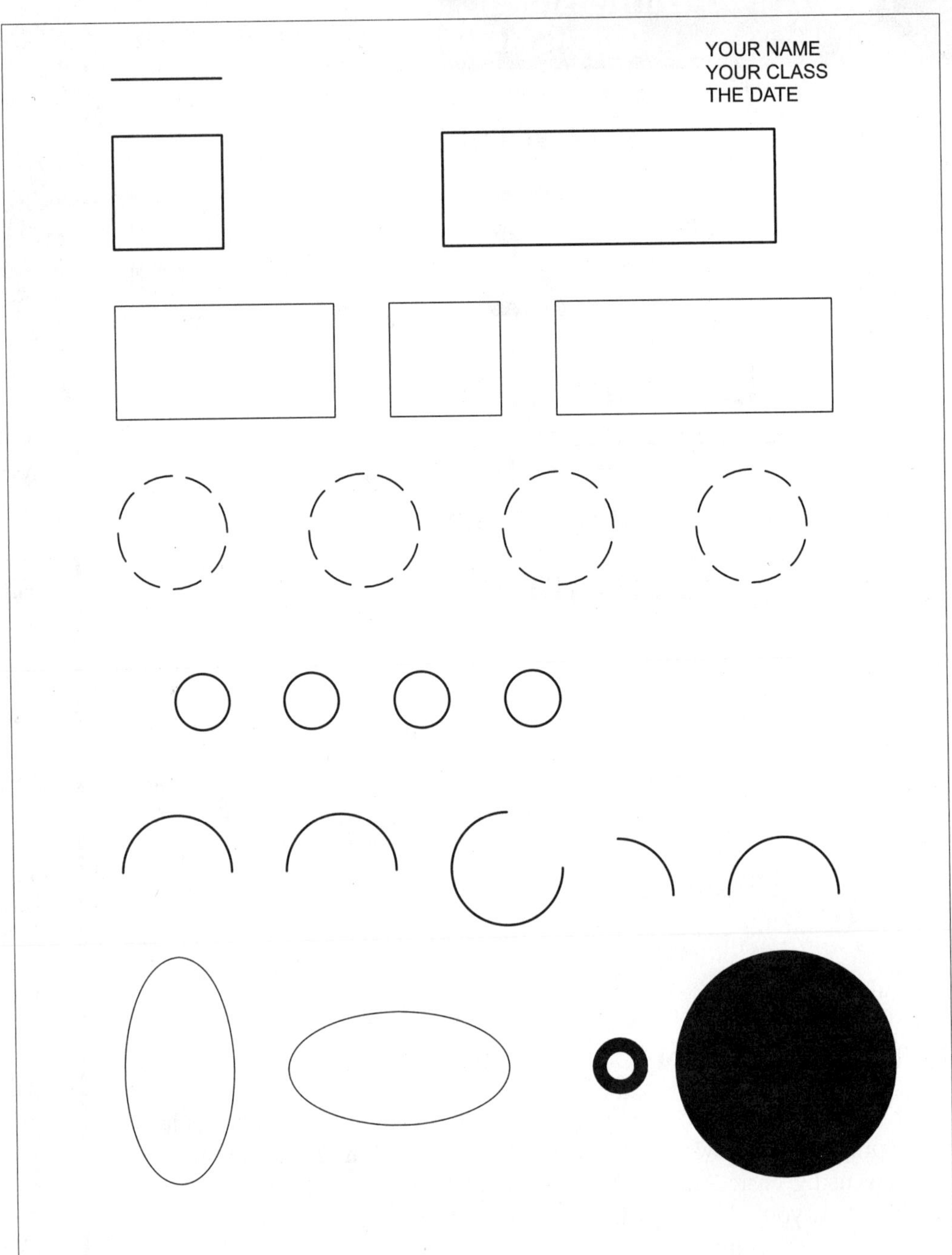

FIGURE 2–1
Tutorial 2–1—Complete

Tutorial 2–1: Part 1, Beginning an AutoCAD Drawing: Saving Your Work; Setting Units, Limits, Grid, and Snap; Creating Layers

BEGINNING AN AutoCAD DRAWING

When you CLICK: **New...** from the Quick Access Toolbar or **New** from the Application menu button, AutoCAD allows you to select a template file from the Template folder. A template file has settings already established. These settings can include units, limits, grid, snap, and a border and title block. Templates save time because the settings are already made.

If you CLICK: **New...** and select the acad.dwt template, you are in the same drawing environment as when you simply open the AutoCAD program and begin drawing. AutoCAD uses the acad.dwt template for the drawing settings if no other template is selected.

You do not need to CLICK: **New...** from the File menu. You can stay in the drawing environment that appeared when you started AutoCAD.

Step 1. If your named workspace is not active, select it by using the Workspaces command on the Tools menu. If it is not available, repeat the steps under the heading "Modify and Save a Workspace" in Tutorial 1–1.

SAVING THE DRAWING

You must understand two commands, Save and SaveAs, and their uses to name and save your work in the desired drive and folder.

Save

When the Save command is clicked for a drawing that *has not been named,* the Save Drawing As dialog box is activated. You may name the drawing by typing a name in the File name: input box. You also select a drive and folder where you want the drawing saved.

When the Save command is clicked and the drawing *has been named* and already saved, no dialog box appears, and the drawing is saved automatically to the drive and folder in which you are working. At this time, the existing drawing file (.dwg) becomes the backup file (.bak) file, and a new drawing file is created.

SaveAs

SaveAs activates the Save Drawing As dialog box *whether or not the drawing has been named* and allows you to save your drawing to any drive or folder you choose.

Some additional features of the SaveAs command are as follows:

1. A drawing file can be saved, and you may continue to work because with the SaveAs command the drawing editor is not exited.
2. If the default drive is used (the drive on which you are working), and the drawing has been opened from that drive, .dwg and .bak files are created when "Create backup copy with each save" is checked on the Open and Save tab on the Options dialog box as shown in Figure 2–2. To access the Options dialog box, TYPE: **OP <enter>**.
3. If a drive other than the default is specified, only a .dwg file is created.
4. To change the name of the drawing, you may save it under a new name by typing a new name in the File name: input box. The drawing is still saved under the original name as well as the new name. You can save the drawing under as many names as you need.
5. If the drawing was previously saved, or if a drawing file already exists with the drawing file name you typed, AutoCAD gives you the message "drawing name.dwg already exists. Do you want to replace it?" When you are updating a drawing file, the old .dwg file is replaced with the new drawing, so the answer to click is Yes. If an error has been made and you do not want to replace the file, click No.
6. A drawing may be saved to as many disks or to as many folders on the hard disk as you wish. You should save your drawing in two different places as insurance against catastrophe.
7. Any drawing can be saved as a template by selecting AutoCAD Drawing Template (*.dwt) in the Files of type: input box in the Save Drawing As dialog box. AutoCAD automatically adds the file extension .dwt to the template name.

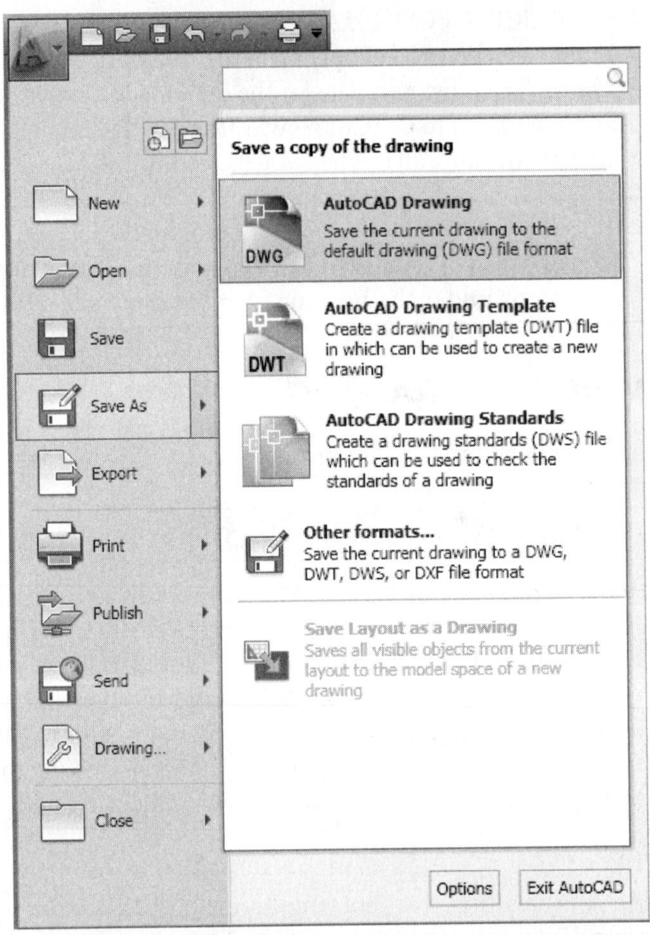

FIGURE 2–2
Options Dialog Box, Open and Save Tab

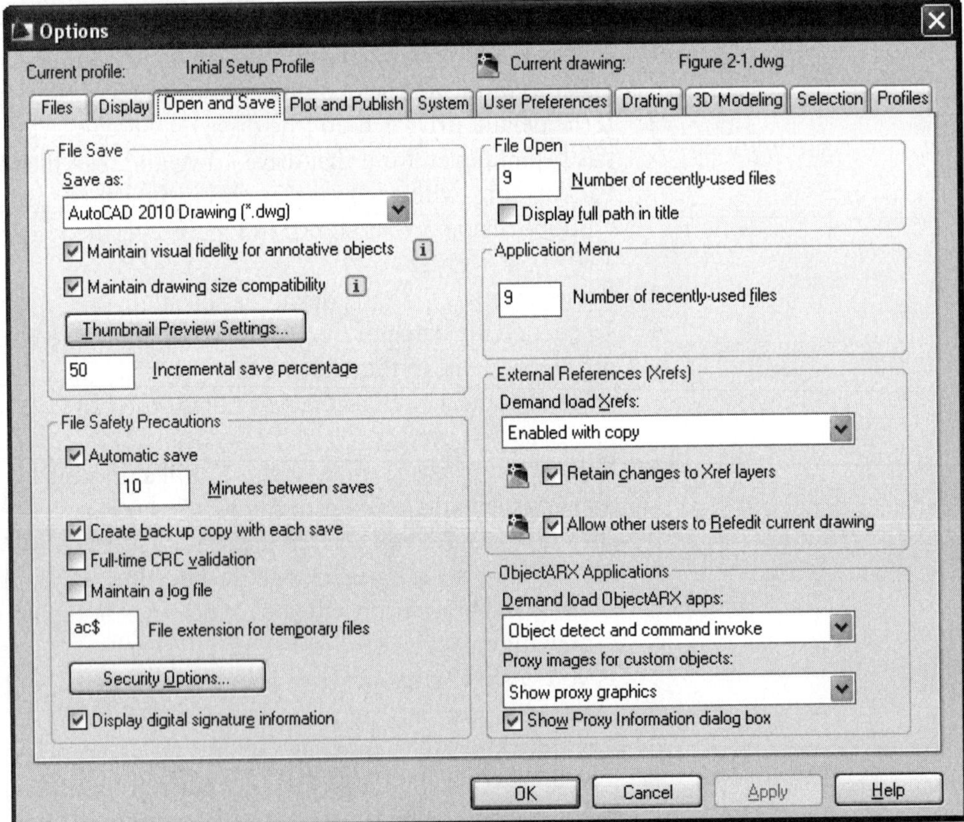

Step 2. **Name and save Tutorial 2–1 on the drive and/or folder you want (Figure 2–3), as described next:**

Prompt	Response
Command:	**Save**
The Save Drawing As dialog box appears with the file name highlighted:	TYPE: **CH2-TUTORIAL1**
The Save Drawing As dialog box appears, as shown in Figure 2–3:	**Select the drive and/or folder in which you want to save CH2-TUTORIAL1.** CLICK: **Save**

FIGURE 2–3
Save Drawing As Dialog Box; Save CH2-TUTORIALI

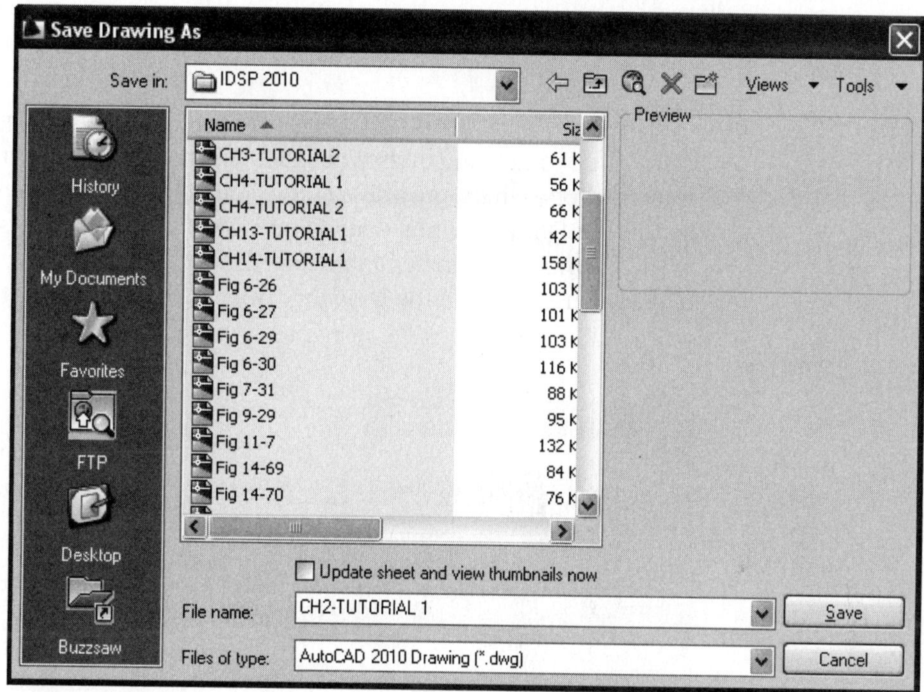

Drawing Name and File Name Extension

The drawing name can be up to 255 characters long and can have spaces. The drawing name cannot have special characters that the AutoCAD or Microsoft® Windows programs use for other purposes. The special characters that cannot be used include the less-than and greater-than symbols (<>), forward slashes and backslashes (/ \), backquotes (`), equal signs (=), vertical bars (|), asterisks (*), commas (,), question marks (?), semicolons (;), colons (:), and quotation marks ("). As you continue to learn AutoCAD, other objects will be also named, such as layers. These naming conventions apply to all named objects.

AutoCAD automatically adds the file extension .dwg to the drawing name and .bak to a backup file. The icon to the left of the file name in the Save Drawing As dialog box describes the file type. If you would also like to see the .dwg and .bak extensions, activate Windows Explorer and complete the following steps:

1. CLICK: **Folder Options...** on the Tools menu in Windows.
2. Select the View tab. Remove the check in the check box before the setting "Hide extensions for known file types."

If you lose a drawing file, the drawing's .bak file can be renamed as a .dwg file and used as the drawing file. Using Windows Explorer, RIGHT-CLICK: on the file name and select Rename from the menu. Simply keep the name, but change the file extension. If the .dwg file is corrupted, you may give the .bak file a new name and change the extension to .dwg. Don't forget to add the .dwg extension in either case, because the file will not open without a .dwg extension.

NOTE: To cancel a command, PRESS: Esc (from the keyboard).

UNITS

Units refers to drawing units. For example, an inch is a drawing unit. In this book, architectural units, which provide feet and fractional inches, are used. The Precision: input box in the Drawing Units dialog box allows you to set the smallest fraction to display when showing coordinates and defaults on the screen. There is no reason to change any of the other settings in the Drawing Units dialog box at this time.

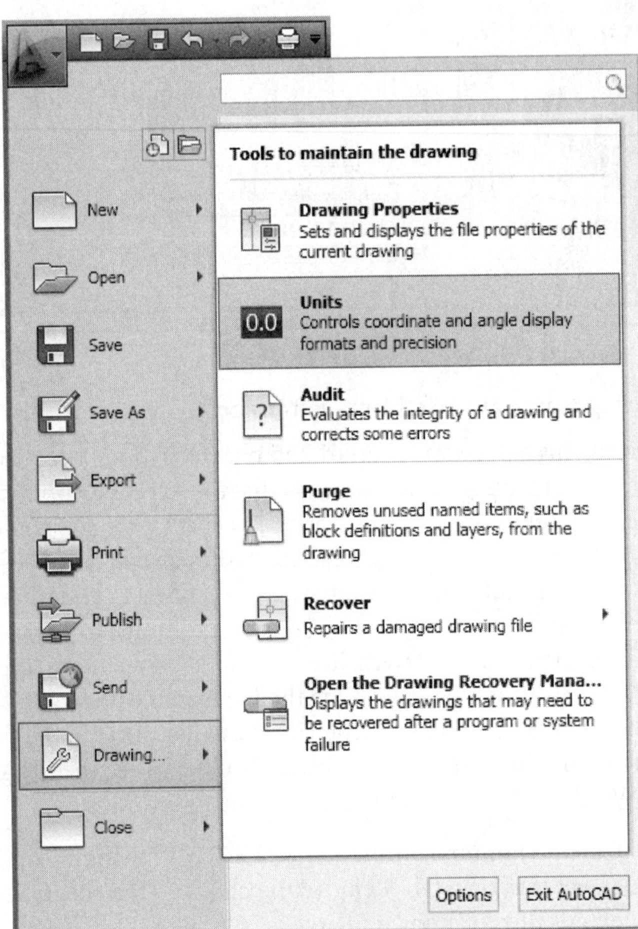

Step 3. Set Drawing Units... (Figure 2–4), as described next:

Prompt	Response
Command:	**Units...** (or TYPE: **UN<enter>**)
The Drawing Units dialog box appears (Figure 2–4):	CLICK: **Architectural** (for Type: under Length) CLICK: **0′-0 1/16″** (for Precision: under Length) CLICK: **OK**

FIGURE 2–4
Drawing Units Dialog Box

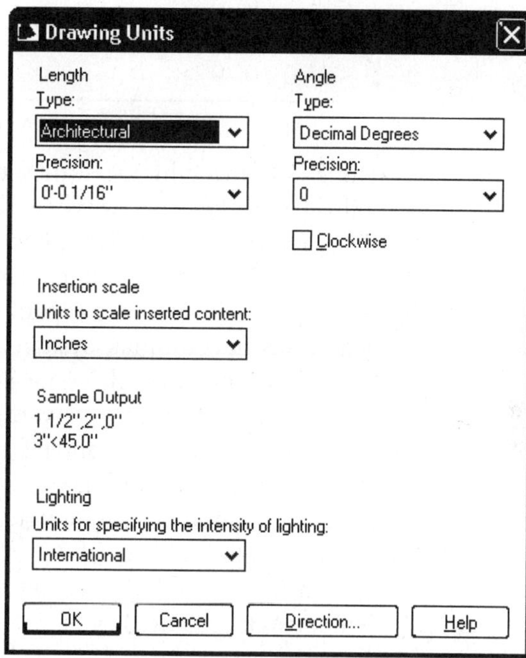

NOTE: The Precision: input box has no bearing on how accurately AutoCAD draws. It allows you to set the smallest fraction to display values shown on the screen such as coordinates and defaults. No matter what the Precision: setting, AutoCAD draws with extreme accuracy.

CONTROLLING YOUR DRAWING

When you begin drawing with AutoCAD, you may click a tab or drawing tool that you do not need. If you select the Layout1 or Layout2 tabs at the bottom of your drawing window and are not sure where you are in the drawing, simply select the Model tab to return to your drawing. The Layout tabs are used for printing or plotting and will be described later.

Step 4. **Make sure SNAP and GRID are on in the status bar and that ORTHO, POLAR, OSNAP, OTRACK, DUCS, DYN, LWT and QP are off.**

DRAWING SCALE

A drawing scale factor does not need to be set. When using AutoCAD to make drawings, always draw full scale, using real-world feet and inches. Full-scale drawings can be printed or plotted at any scale.

DRAWING LIMITS AND THE CARTESIAN COORDINATE SYSTEM

Step 5. Set drawing limits, as described next:

Prompt	Response
Command:	TYPE: **LIMITS<enter>**
Specify lower left corner or [ON/OFF] <0′-0″, 0′-0″>:	**<enter>**
Specify upper right corner <1′-0″, 0′-9″>:	TYPE: **8-1/2,11<enter>**

Think of drawing limits as the sheet size or sheet boundaries. This sheet of paper is also called the *workplane*. The workplane is based on a Cartesian coordinate system. A Cartesian coordinate system has three axes, X, Y, and Z. Here, 8-1/2,11 was set as the drawing limits. In the Cartesian coordinate system, that value is entered as 8-1/2,11 using a comma with no spaces to separate the X- and Y-axis coordinates. The X-axis coordinate of a Cartesian coordinate system is stated first (8-1/2) and measures drawing limits from left to right (horizontally). The Y-axis coordinate is second (11) and measures drawing limits from bottom to top (vertical). You will be drawing on a vertical 8-1/2″ × 11″ workplane similar to a standard sheet of typing paper. The Z axis is used in 3D.

The lower left corner, the origin point of the drawing boundaries, is 0,0 and is where the X and Y axes intersect. The upper right corner is 8-1/2,11 (Figure 2–5). These are the limits for Tutorial 2–1. To turn the 8-1/2″ × 11″ area horizontally, enter the limits as 11,8-1/2. With units set to Architectural, AutoCAD defaults to inches, so the inch symbol is not required.

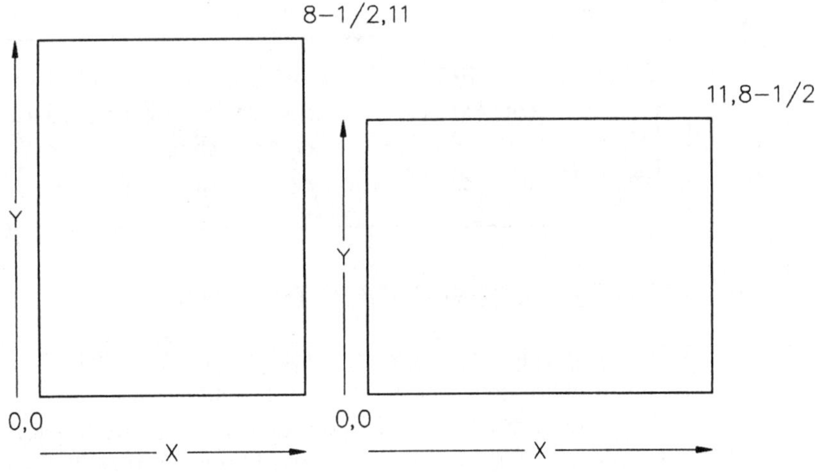

FIGURE 2–5
Drawing Limits

The coordinate display numbers in the extreme lower left corner of the AutoCAD screen tell you where the crosshair on the screen is located in relation to the 0,0 origin. The display updates as you move the cursor.

If you need to change the drawing limits, you may do so at any time by entering new limits to the "Specify upper right corner:" prompt. Changing the drawing limits will automatically show the grid pattern for the new limits.

GRIDDISPLAY

GRIDDISPLAY is a system variable that controls the display of the grid.

Step 6. **Set GRIDDISPLAY to zero so the grid will show the area specified by the limits, as described next:**

Prompt	Response
Command:	TYPE: **GRIDDISPLAY<enter>**
Enter new value for GRIDDISPLAY <2>:	TYPE: **0<enter>**

GRID

Step 7. **Set the Grid Spacing, as described next:**

Prompt	Response
Command:	TYPE: **GRID<enter>**
Specify grid spacing(X) or [ON/OFF/Snap/Major/aDaptive/Limits/Follow/Aspect] <0′-0 1/2″>:	TYPE: **1/4<enter>**

You have just set 1/4″ as the grid spacing. The grid is the visible pattern of dots on the display screen. With a setting of 1/4″, each grid dot is spaced 1/4″ vertically and horizontally. The grid is not part of the drawing, but it helps in getting a sense of the size and relationship of the drawing elements. It is never plotted.

Pressing function key F7 or Ctrl+G turns the grid on or off. The grid can also be turned on or off by selecting either option in response to the prompt "Specify grid spacing(X) or [ON/OFF/Major/aDaptive/Follow/Aspect]" or by clicking the GRID button at the bottom of the screen.

SNAP

Step 8. **Set the Snap Spacing, as described next:**

Prompt	Response
Command:	TYPE: **SN<enter>**
Specify snap spacing or [ON/OFF/Aspect/Style/Type] <0′-0 1/2″>:	TYPE: **1/8<enter>**

You have set 1/8″ as the snap spacing. Snap is an invisible grid on the display screen. As you move the mouse across the screen, the crosshair will snap, or lock, to an invisible snap grid when SNAP is on. With a setting of 1/8″, each snap point is spaced 1/8″ horizontally and vertically.

Pressing function key F9 or Ctrl+B turns the snap on or off. The snap can also be turned on or off by selecting either option in response to the prompt "Specify snap spacing or [ON/OFF/Aspect/Style/Type]" or by clicking the SNAP button at the bottom of the screen.

It is helpful to set the snap spacing the same as the grid spacing or as a fraction of the grid spacing so the crosshair snaps to every grid point or to every grid point and in between. The snap can be set to snap several times in between the grid points.

Some drawings or parts of drawings should never be drawn with snap off. Snap is a very important tool for quickly locating or aligning elements of your drawing. You may need to turn snap off and on while drawing, but remember that a drawing entity drawn on snap is easily moved, copied, or otherwise edited.

ZOOM

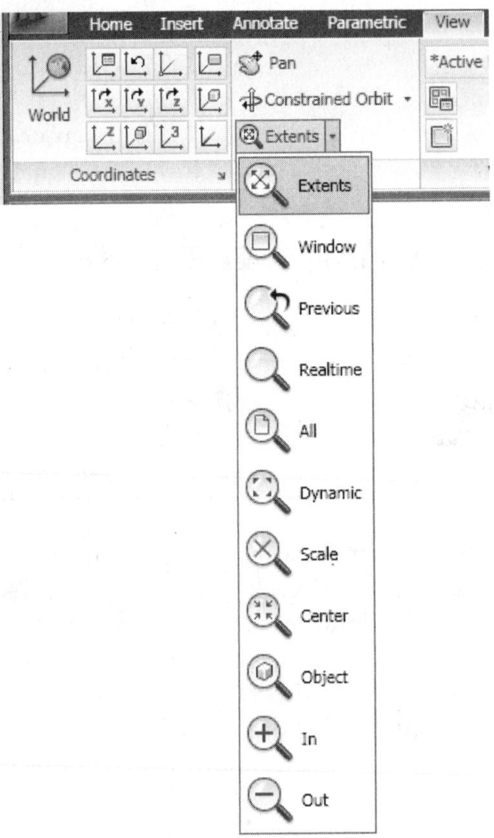

Step 9. View the entire drawing area, as described next:

Prompt	Response
Command:	Zoom-All (or TYPE: **Z<enter>**)
Specify corner of window, enter a scale factor (nX or nXP), or [All/ Center/Dynamic/Extents/Previous/ Scale/Window/object]<real time>:	TYPE: **A<enter>**

Always use the Zoom-All command after setting up or entering an existing drawing so that you are familiar with the size and shape of your limits and grid. Otherwise, you may be viewing only a small part of the drawing limits and not realize it.

DRAFTING SETTINGS DIALOG BOX

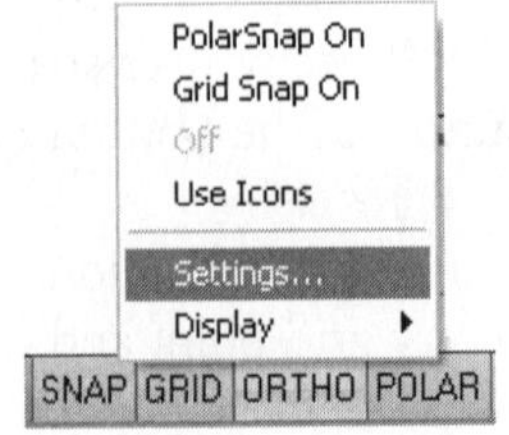

You can also set snap and grid by using the Drafting Settings dialog box (Figure 2–6).

To locate the Drafting Settings dialog box, RIGHT-CLICK: on SNAP or GRID in the status bar and CLICK: **Settings....** The dialog box is a handy tool to use in setting the snap and grid spacing, but if you are a fair typist, typing these commands from the keyboard is faster.

FIGURE 2–6
Drafting Settings Dialog Box

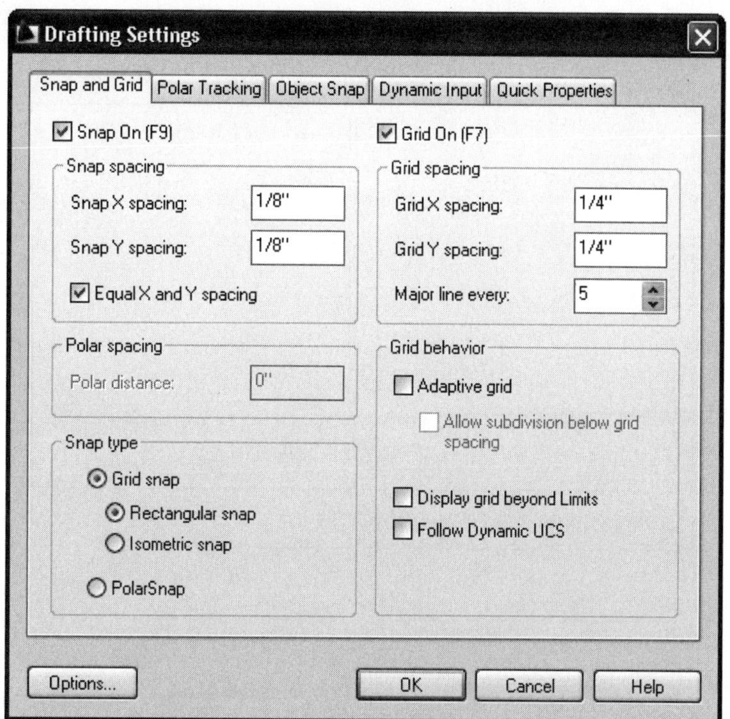

LAYERS

Different parts of a project can be placed on separate layers. The building shell may be on one layer, the interior walls on another, the electrical on a third layer, the furniture on a fourth layer, and so on. There is no limit to the number of layers you may use in a drawing. Each is perfectly aligned with all the others. Each layer may be viewed on the display screen separately, one layer may be viewed in combination with one or more of the other layers, or all layers may be viewed together. Each layer may also be plotted separately or in combination with other layers, or all layers may be plotted at the same time. The layer name can be from 1 to 255 characters in length.

Step 10. Create layers using the Layer Properties Manager dialog box (Figures 2–7 and 2–8), as described next:

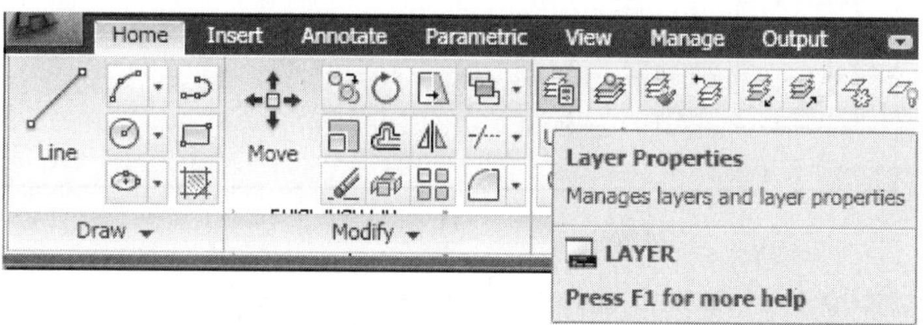

Prompt	Response
Command:	**Layer Properties** (or TYPE: **LA<enter>**)
The Layer Properties Manager dialog box appears:	CLICK: **the New Layer icon three times** (see Figure 2–7)
Layer1, Layer2, Layer3 appear in the Layer Name list (Figure 2–8):	CLICK: **the box under Color, beside Layer1**

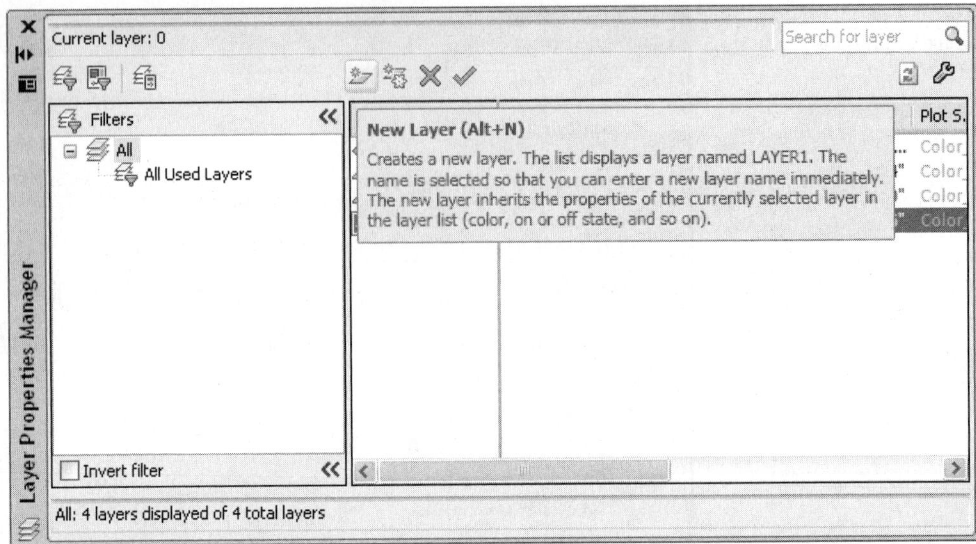

FIGURE 2–7
Layer Properties Manager Dialog Box

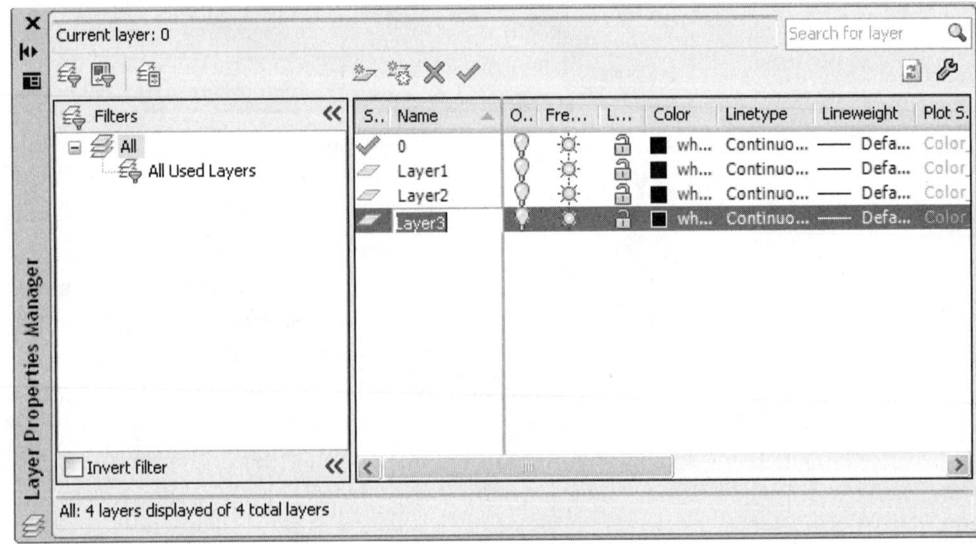

FIGURE 2–8
Layer1, Layer2, and Layer3 Appear in the Layer Name List

NOTE: The Standard Colors are: 1 (red), 2 (yellow), 3 (green), 4 (cyan), 5 (blue), 6 (magenta), and 7 (white or black).

Step 11. **Assign colors to layers (Figure 2–9), as described next:**

Prompt	Response
The Select Color dialog box appears:	CLICK: **the color white** (Index color: 7) (Figure 2–9) CLICK: **OK**
The Layer Properties Manager dialog box appears:	CLICK: **the box under Color, beside Layer2**
The Select Color dialog box appears:	CLICK: **the color blue** (Index color: 5) CLICK: **OK**

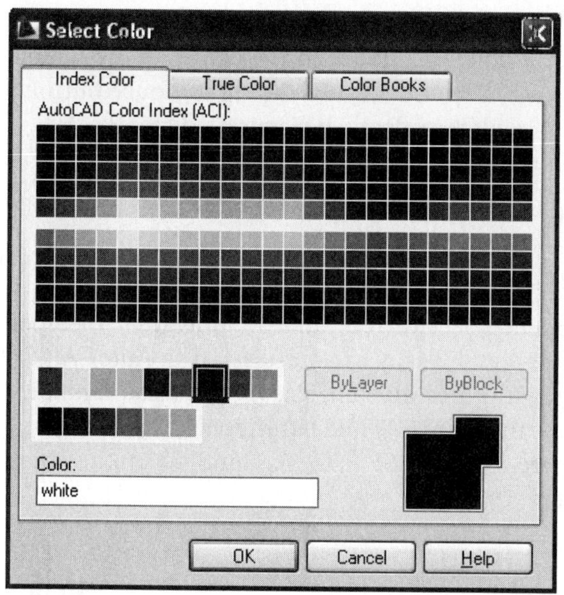

FIGURE 2–9
Select Color Dialog Box

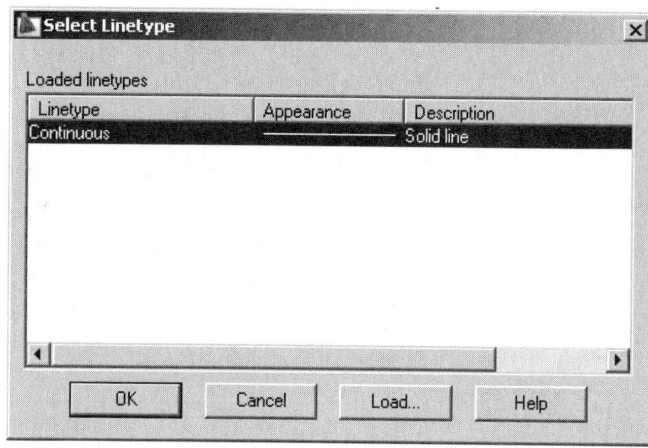

FIGURE 2–10
Select Linetype Dialog Box

The Layer Properties Manager dialog box appears:	CLICK: **the box under Color, beside Layer3**
The Select Color dialog box appears:	CLICK: **the color green** (Index color: 3) CLICK: **OK**

Step 12. **Assign linetypes to layers (Figures 2–10, 2–11, and 2–12), as described next:**

Prompt	Response
The Layer Properties Manager dialog box appears:	CLICK: **the word "continuous" under Linetype, beside Layer2**
The Select Linetype dialog box appears (Figure 2–10):	CLICK: **Load...** (to load linetypes so they can be selected)

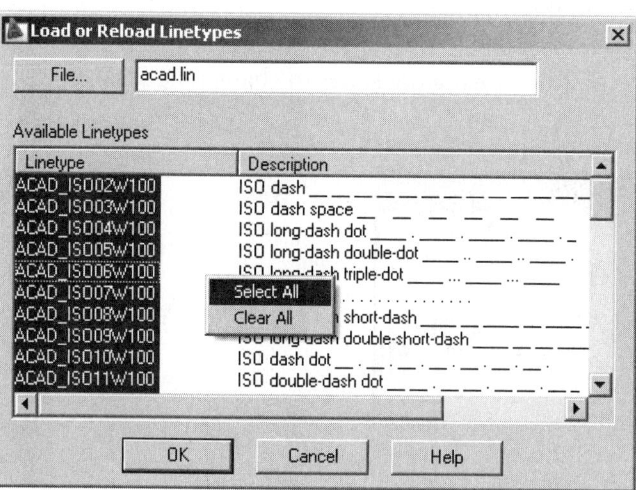

FIGURE 2–11
Load or Reload Linetypes Dialog Box

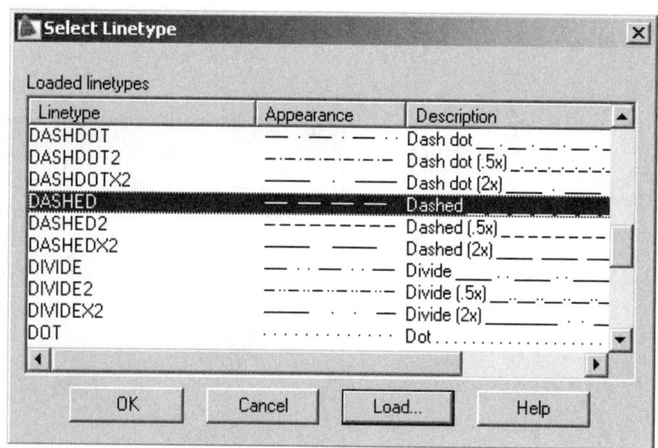

FIGURE 2–12
Select the DASHED Linetype

Prompt	Response
The Load or Reload Linetypes dialog box appears:	**Move the mouse to the center of the dialog box and** CLICK: **the right mouse button** CLICK: **Select All** (Figure 2–11) CLICK: **OK**

LINETYPES

Linetypes must be loaded before they can be selected. You can load individual linetypes or you can load several by holding down the Shift key as you select. The AutoCAD library of standard linetypes provides you with three different sizes of each standard linetype other than continuous. For example, the DASHED line has the standard size called DASHED, a linetype half the standard size called DASHED2(.5x), and a linetype twice the standard size called DASHEDX2(2x).

Prompt	Response
The Select Linetype dialog box appears (Figure 2–12):	CLICK: **Dashed** CLICK: **OK** CLICK: **the close button (X) in the upper left corner of the dialog box**

LINEWEIGHTS

Lineweights are expressed in millimeters or inches. The default lineweight initially set for all layers is .25 mm or .010 inches. Lineweights need to be varied, for example, to show thick lines for walls and thin lines for dimensions, to emphasize something on the drawing, to show existing and new construction, or to show existing and new furniture. Lineweight is an important component for drawing legibility. Lineweights are displayed in pixels on the screen; they plot with the exact width of the assigned lineweight.

Lineweight Settings Dialog Box

To locate the Lineweight Settings dialog box (Figure 2–13), RIGHT-CLICK: **LWT** in the status bar and CLICK: **Settings....** In this dialog box, you can change the Units for Listing from millimeters to inches or reset the default lineweight. You can also adjust the Model tab display scale of lineweights by moving the slider to change the scale.

FIGURE 2–13
Change Lineweight Settings to Inches

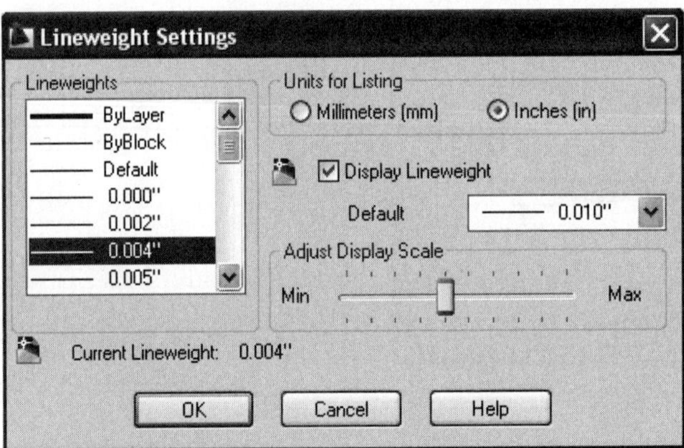

Step 13. Change the Units for Listing in the Lineweight Settings dialog box to inches. The lineweights will now read in inches in the Layer Properties Manager dialog box instead of millimeters. If you prefer millimeters, leave it set to millimeters.

Step 14. Assign lineweights to layers (Figure 2–14), as described next:

Prompt	Response
Command:	**Layer Properties** (or TYPE: **LA<enter>**)
The Layer Properties Manager dialog box appears:	CLICK: **The word Default under Lineweight, beside Layer1**
The Lineweight dialog box appears (Figure 2–14):	CLICK: **0.014″ (.35mm)** CLICK: **OK**
The Layer Properties Manager dialog box appears:	CLICK: **The word Default under Lineweight, beside Layer2**
The Lineweight dialog box appears:	CLICK: **0.010″ (.25mm)** CLICK: **OK**
The Layer Properties Manager dialog box appears:	CLICK: **The word Default under Lineweight, beside Layer3**
The Lineweight dialog box appears:	CLICK: **0.006″ (.15mm)** CLICK: **OK**

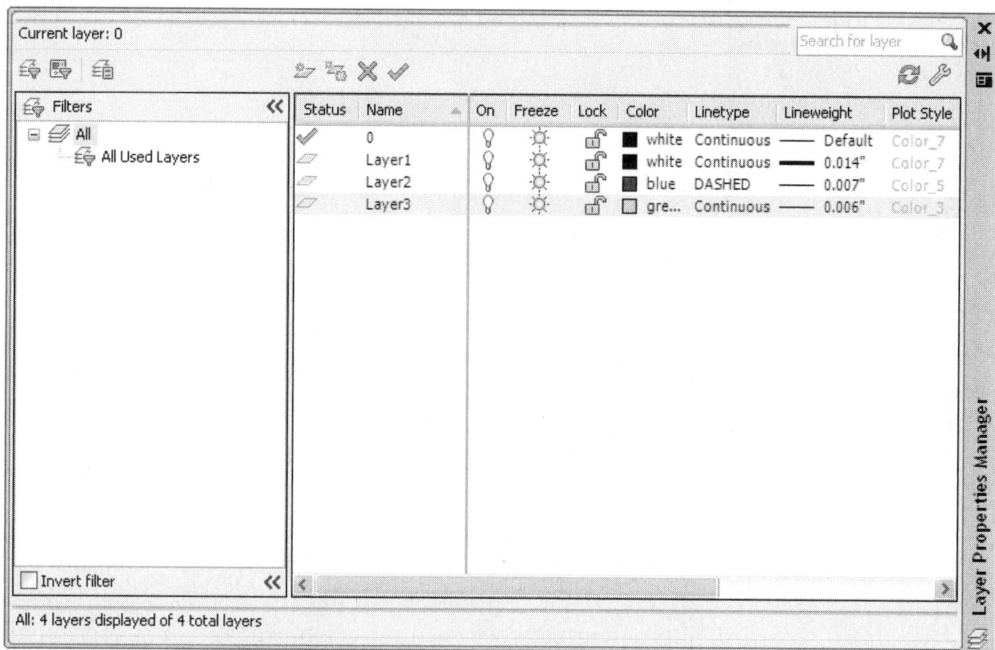

FIGURE 2–14
Assign Lineweight to Layers

LWT

The display of the lineweights in your drawing is controlled by CLICKING: LWT on the status bar. Lineweights are not displayed unless LWT is ON.

Step 15. Turn LWT ON (in the Status Bar).

Step 16. Make a layer current (Figure 2–15), as described next:

Prompt	Response
The Layer Properties Manager dialog box appears with layer names, colors, and linetypes assigned:	CLICK: **Layer1** (to select it) (Figure 2–15). Be sure to CLICK: on a layer name, not on one of the other properties such as lock or color. CLICK: **Set Current** (the green check icon) CLICK: the close button (X) in the upper left corner of the dialog box

You can also double-click the layer name to set it current. Anything drawn from this point until another layer is set current will be on Layer1.

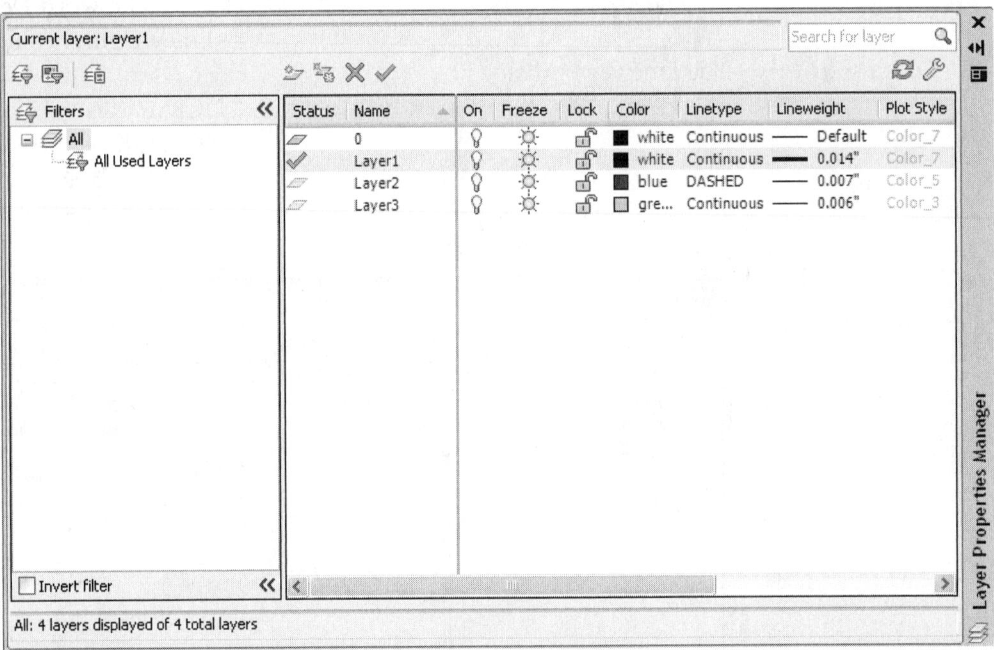

FIGURE 2–15
Layers with Colors, Linetypes, Lineweights Assigned, and Layer1 Current

To change a layer name after using New Layer to create layers, CLICK: the layer name to highlight it, then slowly left-click the name again in the Name: input area, and type over the existing name. You can also click the layer name and then use Rename from the right-click menu to rename a layer. You can initially name the layers by clicking New and then typing the layer names separated by a comma. When you type the comma, you move to the next layer.

FIGURE 2–16
Layer Status on the Layers Panel of the Home Ribbon

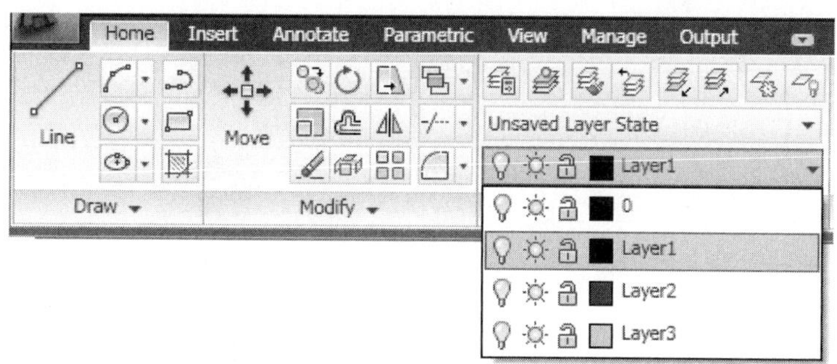

The Layer Combo Control option icons on the Layers panel of the Home Ribbon (Figure 2–16) that can be changed, reading from left to right, are:

1. *Turn a Layer On or Off for entire drawing:* These pertain to the visibility of layers. When a layer is turned OFF, it is still part of the drawing, but any entity drawn on that layer is not visible on the screen and cannot be plotted. For instance, the building exterior walls layer, interior walls layer, and electrical layer are turned ON and all other layers turned OFF to view, edit, or plot an electrical plan. One or more layers can be turned OFF and ON as required.
2. *Freezes or Thaws Layer for entire drawing:* These also pertain to the visibility of layers. The difference between ON/OFF and FREEZE/THAW is a matter of how quickly the drawing regenerates on the display screen. If a layer is frozen, it is not visible and cannot be plotted, and AutoCAD spends no time regenerating it. A layer that is turned OFF is not visible and cannot be plotted, but AutoCAD does regenerate it.

NOTE: When a layer is off or frozen and it aligns with other layers, it is important not to move objects that align with a frozen or off layer. Objects on the off or frozen layer do not move and will not be aligned with the moved items when you turn the off layer on or thaw the frozen layer. However, when ALL objects are selected (when you TYPE: **ALL<enter>** to select objects), objects on a layer that is OFF and thawed will move.

3. *Lock or Unlock a Layer globally for entire drawing:* When a layer is locked, it is visible, and you can draw on it. You cannot use any of the Edit commands to edit any of the drawing entities on the layer. You cannot accidentally change any entity that is already drawn.

To change the state of any layer, pick the icon to select the alternate state. For example, Figure 2–17 shows that Layer1 was turned off by picking the lightbulb to turn it off. Three additional layer properties that are shown in the Layer Properties Manager dialog box are:

1. *Plot Style:* Plot styles are created using a plot style table to define various properties such as color, grayscale, and lineweight. A layer's plot style overrides the layer's color, linetype, and lineweight. Plot styles are used when you want to plot the same drawing with different settings or different drawings with the same settings.

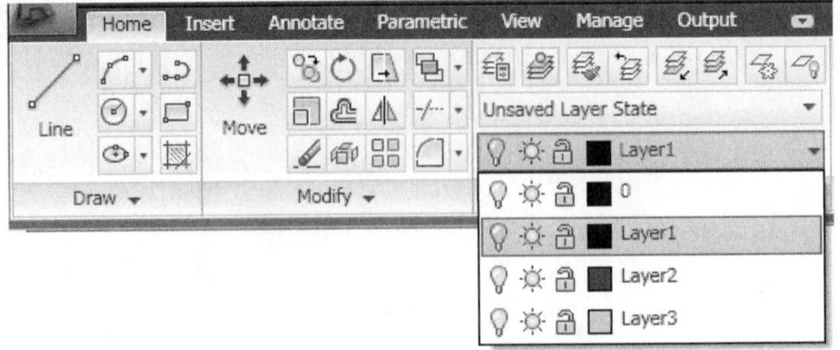

FIGURE 2–17
Turn Off Layer1

2. *Plot:* This allows you to make visible layers nonplottable. For example, you may not want to plot a layer that shows construction lines. When a layer is nonplottable, it is displayed but not plotted.
3. *New VP Freeze:* Allows you to freeze layers in a newly created viewport.

If you create some layers that you do not need, delete them by highlighting them and picking the Delete icon.

ANNOTATION SCALE

Annotation scale controls how the text and other annotative objects appear on the drawing. This setting affects annotative objects, such as text and dimensions, that are added to drawings that need to be scaled when plotted (e.g., Scale: 1/4″ = 1′-0″). Each object, such as text or dimensions, has an annotative property that must be set to ON for this setting to apply.

Step 17. Make sure your Annotation Scale located in the lower right corner of the AutoCAD screen is set to the default 1:1 (Figure 2–18).

SAVING THE DRAWING

Step 18. Save the drawing, as described next:

Prompt	Response
Command:	**Save**
The drawing is saved in the drive and folder selected at the beginning of this exercise.	

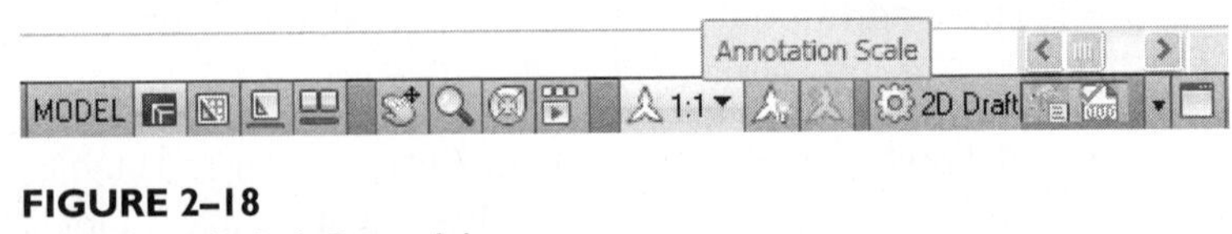

FIGURE 2–18
Annotation Scale Is Set to 1:1

NOTE: Make sure you save your drawing often, so you do not lose any of your work.

USING THE MOUSE AND RIGHT-CLICK CUSTOMIZATION

The Right-Click Customization dialog box settings control what happens when the right mouse button (shown as **<enter>** in this book) is clicked. To access the Right-Click Customization dialog box, TYPE: **OP<enter>**. Select the User Preferences tab of the Options dialog box (Figure 2–19). CLICK: the **Right-click Customization...** button in the Windows Standard Behavior area, and the Right-Click Customization dialog box (Figure 2–20) appears.

In the Response columns of the tutorials, **<enter>** indicates that the right mouse button should be clicked. Notes in parentheses are used to clarify how **<enter>** is used; for example, **<enter>** (to return the Line command prompt). Leave the Right-Click Customization dialog box set to the default as shown in Figure 2–20. As you become more familiar with AutoCAD, you may decide to change this setting.

FIGURE 2–19
Options Dialog Box with User Preferences Tab Clicked

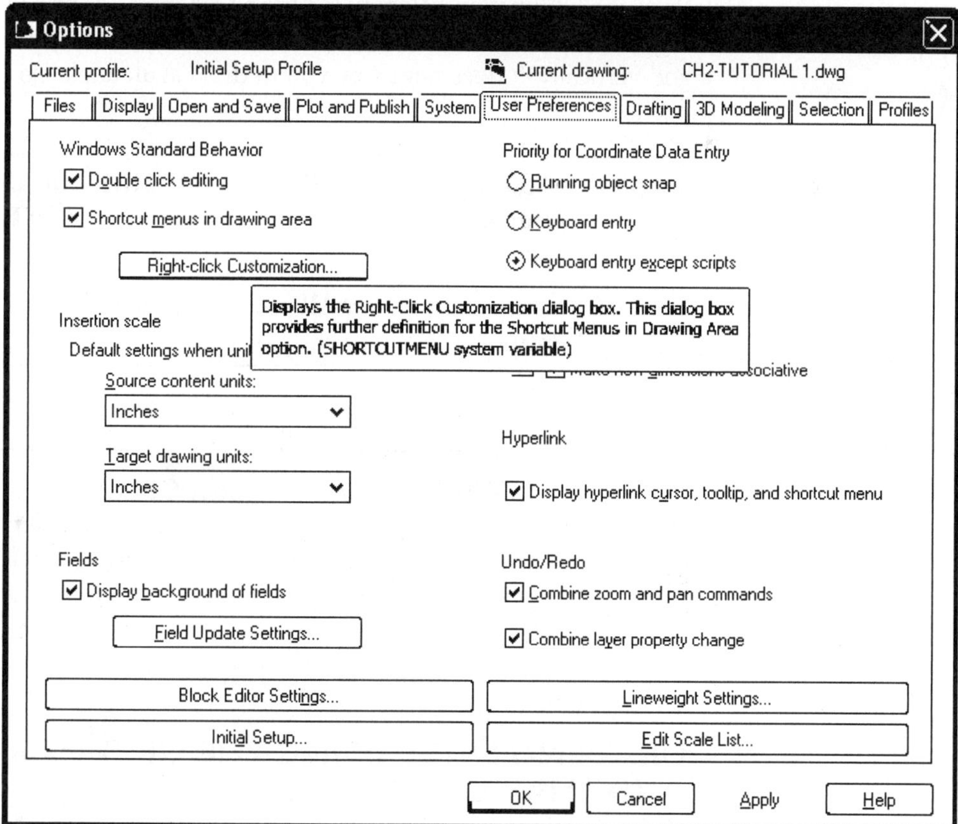

FIGURE 2–20
Right-Click Customization Dialog Box

Right-Click Customization

☐ Turn on time-sensitive right-click:
Quick click for ENTER
Longer click to display Shortcut Menu
Longer click duration: ____ milliseconds

Default Mode
If no objects are selected, right-click means
○ Repeat Last Command
◉ Shortcut Menu

Edit Mode
If one or more objects are selected, right-click means
○ Repeat Last Command
◉ Shortcut Menu

Command Mode
If a command is in progress, right-click means
○ ENTER
○ Shortcut Menu: always enabled
◉ Shortcut Menu: enabled when command options are present

Apply & Close | Cancel | Help

Tutorial 2–1: Part 2, Drawing Lines, Circles, Arcs, Ellipses, and Donuts

ORTHO

Press the F8 function key to turn Ortho ON and OFF, or CLICK: **ORTHO** at the bottom of your screen. Ortho mode, when ON, helps you to draw lines perfectly, horizontally and vertically. It does not allow you to draw at an angle, so turn Ortho OFF and ON as needed.

Step 19. Make sure that GRID, SNAP, ORTHO, and LWT are ON and the remaining buttons in the Status Bar are OFF. Make sure Layer1 is current.

Step 20. Complete a Zoom-All command to make sure you are looking at the entire 8-1/2 × 11 limits of your drawing.

NOTE: When Ortho mode is ON, drawing or editing a drawing part is restricted to horizontal and vertical movements only. Hold down the Shift key as a temporary override key to turn ORTHO off and on. See Appendix A for additional temporary override keys.

DRAWING LINES USING THE GRID MARKS AND SNAP INCREMENTS

Use Figure 2–21 as a guide when locating the line, squares, and rectangles drawn using the Line command.

FIGURE 2–21
Draw a Line, Squares, and Rectangles

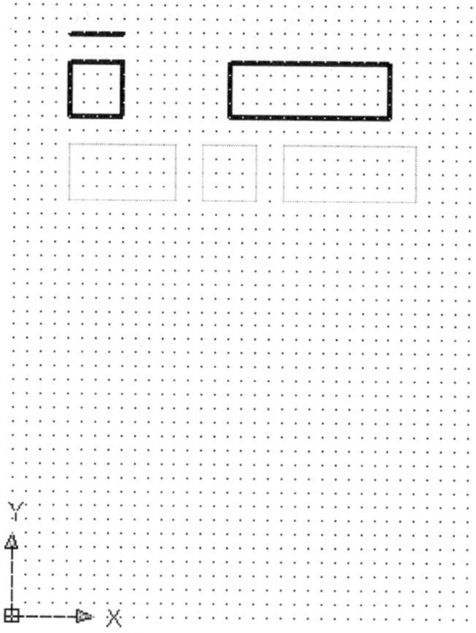

Lines can be drawn by snapping to the grid marks visible on the screen. The snap is set at 1/8″, and the grid is set at 1/4″. The grid provides a visual cue for the snap points that snap on every grid mark and in between every grid mark.

Step 21. Draw a horizontal line 1″ long, using the snap increments and grid marks (Figure 2–21), as described next:

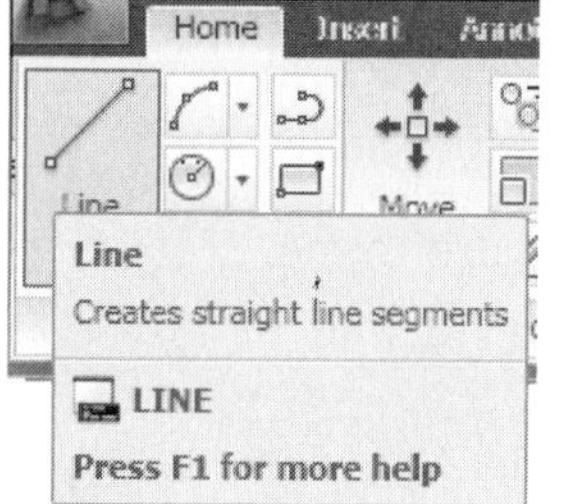

Prompt	Response
Command:	**Line** (or TYPE: **L<enter>**)
Specify first point:	**D1** (Do not type "D1." Look at Figure 2–21 and click the point D1, approximately two grid spaces down (1/2″) and four grid spaces to the right (1″) of the upper left corner of the page.)
Specify next point or [Undo]:	**D2** (move your mouse four grid marks to the right and click the point D2)
Specify next point or [Undo]:	**<enter> When the right mouse button is used for Enter, a shortcut menu appears, and Enter must be clicked on the shortcut menu to complete the command. When the keyboard Enter key is used, the command is completed, and the shortcut menu does not appear.**

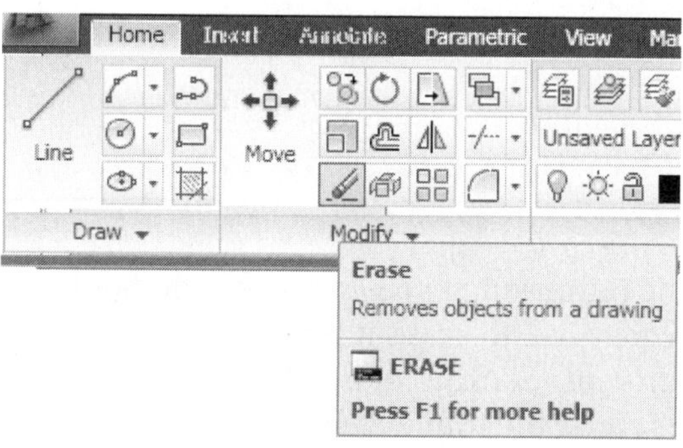

ERASE AND UNDO

Step 22. Erase the line and bring it back again, as described next:

Prompt	Response
Command:	**Erase** (or TYPE: **E<enter>**)
Select objects:	**Position the small box that replaces the crosshair any place on the line and click the line.**
Select objects: 1 found	
Select objects:	**<enter>** (the line disappears)
Command:	TYPE: **U<enter>** (the line reappears)

Do not be afraid to draw with AutoCAD. If you make a mistake, you can easily erase it using the Erase command. The Undo feature will restore everything erased by the Erase command. When you are using the Erase command, a small box replaces the screen crosshair. The small box is called the *pickbox*.

Step 23. Draw a 1″ square using the snap increments and grid marks and undo the last two lines (Figure 2–22), as described next:

Prompt	Response
Command:	**Line**
Specify first point:	**D1** (CLICK: **a point 1/2″ directly below the left end of the line just drawn**)
Specify next point or [Undo]:	**D2** (Figure 2–22)
Specify next point or [Undo]:	**D3**
Specify next point or [Close/Undo]:	**D4**
Specify next point or [Close/Undo]:	**D5**
Specify next point or [Close/Undo]:	TYPE: **U<enter>** (move your mouse to see that the line is undone)
Specify next point or [Close/Undo]:	TYPE: **U<enter>**
Specify next point or [Close/Undo]:	**<enter>** (to stop and return to the Command: prompt)

FIGURE 2–22
Draw a 1″ Square Using Grid Marks

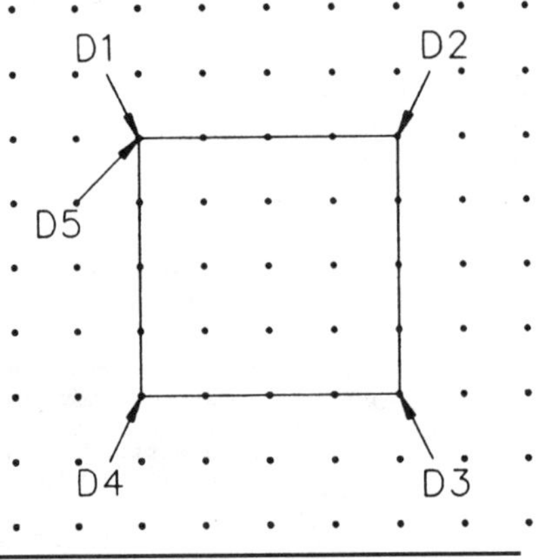

While in the Line command, if you decide you do not like the last line segment drawn, use the Undo command to erase it and continue on with the Specify next point of [Close/Undo]: prompt. Clicking more than one undo will backtrack through the line segments in the reverse order in which they were drawn.

Step 24. Complete the square (Figure 2–22), as described next:

Prompt	Response
Command:	**<enter>** (to return the Line command prompt)
Specify first point:	**<enter>** (the line is attached)
Specify next point or [Undo]:	**D4**
Specify next point or [Undo]:	**D5**
Specify next point or [Close/Undo]:	**<enter>** (to stop)

The Line command has a very handy feature: If you respond to the Specify first point: prompt by pressing the Enter key or the space bar, the line will start at the end of the most recently drawn line.

NOTE: Pressing the Esc key cancels the command selection process and returns AutoCAD to the Command: prompt. Use Esc if you get stuck in a command.

DRAWING LINES USING ABSOLUTE COORDINATES

Remember, 0,0 is the lower left corner of the page, the origin point of the Cartesian coordinate system. When you use absolute coordinates to draw, the X-axis coordinate is entered first and identifies a location on the horizontal axis. The Y-axis coordinate is entered second and identifies a location on the vertical axis. The page size is 8-1/2,11. A little adding and subtracting to determine the absolute coordinates will locate the rectangle on the page as follows.

Step 25. Draw a rectangle using absolute coordinates (Figure 2–23), as described next:

Prompt	Response
Command:	**Line** (move the crosshair to the center of the screen)
Specify first point:	TYPE: **4,10<enter>** (the line begins)
Specify next point or [Undo]:	TYPE: **7,10<enter>**
Specify next point or [Undo]:	TYPE: **7,9<enter>**
Specify next point or [Close/Undo]:	TYPE: **4,9<enter>**
Specify next point or [Close/Undo]:	TYPE: **C<enter>**

Step 26. CLICK: on the coordinate display to turn the screen coordinate display on (if needed) and move your pointer to each corner of the square. Watch how the screen coordinate display shows the X,Y coordinate position of each corner. Compare those coordinates with the coordinates you just typed and entered. They are the same.

Step 27. Complete a Zoom-All command. Hold the crosshair of the cursor (with snap on) on the lower left corner of the grid; the coordinate display reads 0′-0″, 0′-0″. Move the cursor to the upper right corner of the grid; the coordinate display reads 0′-8′ 1/2″, 0′-11″.

FIGURE 2–23
Draw a Rectangle Using Absolute Coordinates

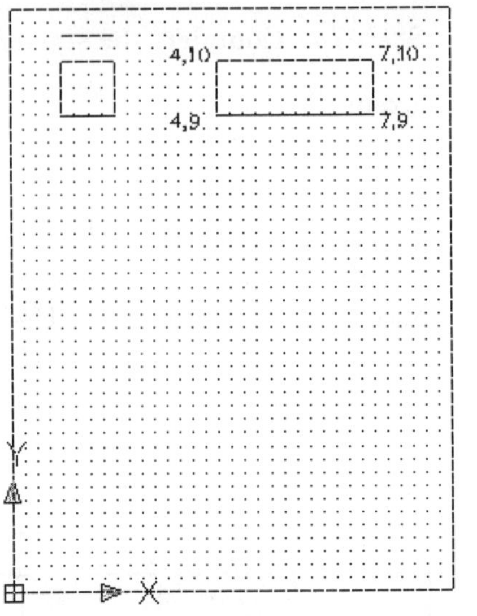

NOTE: If you turn DYN on by clicking it on the Status Bar, you will see the dynamic input display attached to the cursor. The appearance of dynamic input display is controlled by the settings made in the Drafting Settings dialog box. RIGHT-CLICK: on DYN in the Status Bar to access these settings.

DRAWING LINES USING RELATIVE COORDINATES

Relative coordinates are used after a point is entered. (Relative to what? Relative to the point just entered.) After a point has been clicked on the drawing, relative coordinates are entered by typing @, followed by the X,Y coordinates. For example, after a point is entered to start a line, typing and entering @1,0 will draw the line 1″ in the X direction, 0″ in the Y direction.

Step 27. **Set Layer3 current. Layer3 has a 0.50 lineweight.**

Step 28. **Draw a rectangle using relative coordinates, as described next:**

Prompt	Response
Command:	**Line**
Specify first point:	CLICK: **a point on the grid 1/2″ below the lower left corner of the first square drawn**
Specify next point or [Undo]:	TYPE: **@2,0<enter>**
Specify next point or [Undo]:	TYPE: **@0,−1<enter>**
Specify next point or [Close/Undo]:	TYPE: **@−2,0<enter>**
Specify next point or [Close/Undo]:	TYPE: **C<enter>**

A minus sign (−) is used for negative line location with relative coordinates. Negative is to the left for the X axis and down for the Y axis.

DRAWING LINES USING POLAR COORDINATES

Absolute and relative coordinates are extremely useful in some situations; however, for many design applications (for example, drawing walls) polar coordinates or direct distance entry is used. Be sure you understand how to use all types of coordinates.

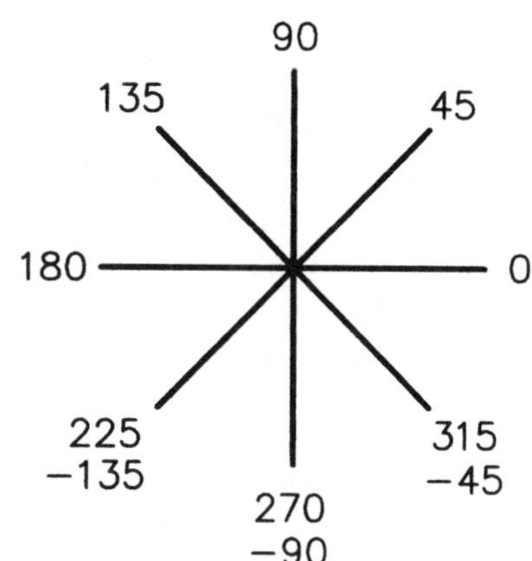

FIGURE 2–24
Polar Coordinate Angles

Polar coordinates are also relative to the last point entered. They are typed starting with an @, followed by a distance and angle of direction. Figure 2–24 shows the polar coordinate angle directions. The angle of direction is always preceded by a < sign when polar coordinates are entered.

Step 29. Draw a 1″ square using polar coordinates, as described next:

Prompt	Response
Command:	**<enter>** (to return the Line command prompt)
Specify first point:	CLICK: **a point on the grid 1/2″ to the right of the upper right corner of the last rectangle drawn**
Specify next point or [Undo]:	TYPE: **@1<0<enter>**
Specify next point or [Undo]:	TYPE: **@1<270<enter>**
Specify next point or [Close/Undo]:	TYPE: **@1<180<enter>**
Specify next point or [Close/Undo]:	TYPE: **C<enter>**

DRAWING LINES USING DIRECT DISTANCE ENTRY

Direct distance entry is a quick, accurate, and easy way to draw lines. It can also be used with any other command that asks you to specify a point. Move your mouse in the direction you want to draw, TYPE: **the distance**, and PRESS: **<enter>**.

Step 30. Draw a rectangle using direct distance entry, as described next:

Prompt	Response
Command:	**Line (with ORTHO ON)**
Specify first point:	CLICK: **a point on the grid 1/2″ to the right of the upper right corner of the square just drawn**
Specify next point or [Undo]:	**Move your mouse to the right;** TYPE: **2-1/2<enter>**
Specify next point or [Undo]:	**Move your mouse down;** TYPE: **1<enter>**
Specify next point or [Close/Undo]:	**Move your mouse to the left;** TYPE: **2-1/2<enter>**
Specify next point or [Close/Undo]:	TYPE: **C<enter>**

DYN

As you gain more experience, you may want to use Dynamic Input to draw lines. CLICK: **DYN** at the bottom of your screen to turn Dynamic Input ON and OFF. When ON, DYN mode displays three tooltips of command information near your cursor. These are Pointer Input, Dimension Input, and Dynamic Prompts (see Figure 2–26).

When DYN is on, you can enter coordinate values into the input fields instead of using the command line. They are entered as follows:

To enter *absolute coordinates* type the pound sign (#) prefix, the absolute coordinates, and PRESS **<enter>** (example: **#4,4<enter>**).
Entering *relative coordinates* is the default. To enter relative coordinates type the relative coordinates without the at sign (@) (example: **5,3<enter>**).
To enter *polar coordinates:* TYPE: **the distance from the first point<enter>**, PRESS: **TAB** (to lock the value), TYPE: **the angle value<enter>**.

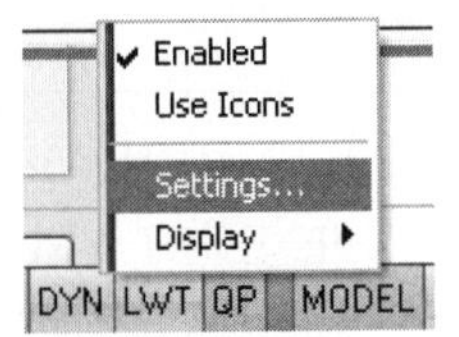

FIGURE 2–25
Right-Click: DYN;
Click: Settings...

Right-click DYN on the Status Bar, then click **Settings...** (Figure 2–25) to access the Dynamic Input tab of the Drafting Settings dialog box (Figure 2–26). On this tab, you can control the display of the three tooltips near your cursor when DYN is on. Hold F12 down to turn DYN off temporarily.

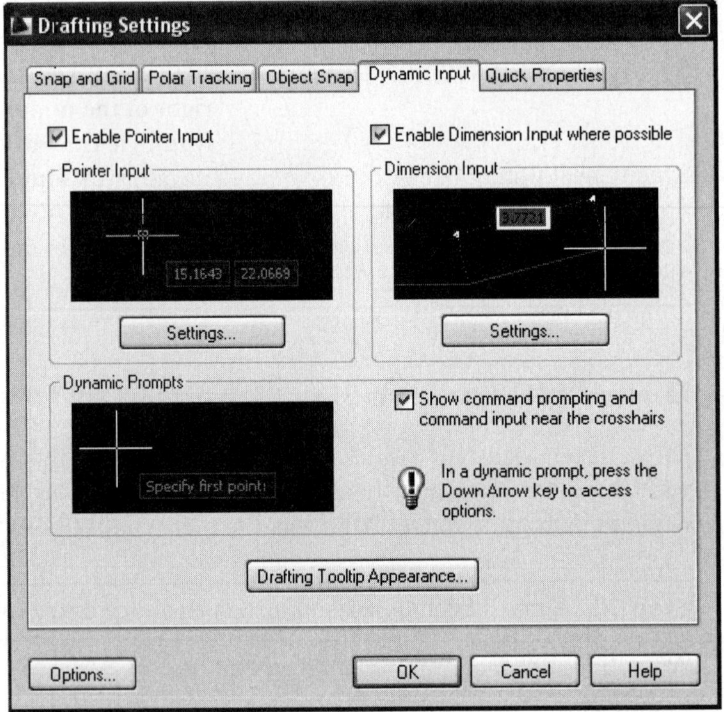

FIGURE 2–26
Drafting Settings Dialog Box, Dynamic Input Tab

CIRCLE

Step 31. Look at Figure 2–27 to determine the approximate location of the four dashed-line circles you will draw.

Step 32. Set Layer2 current. Layer2 has a dashed linetype.

Step 33. Turn ORTHO OFF.

FIGURE 2–27
The Location of Four Circles

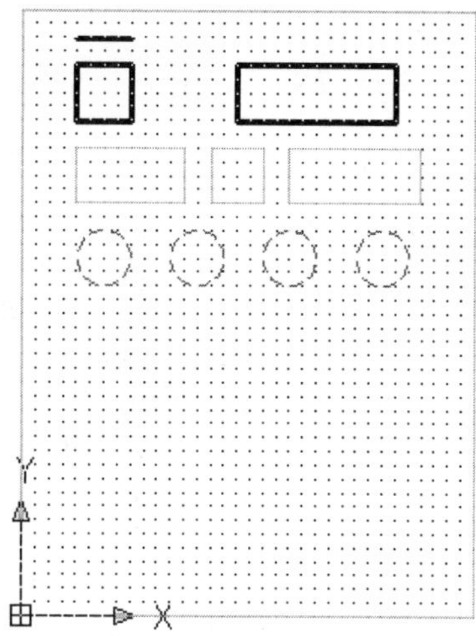

Center, Radius

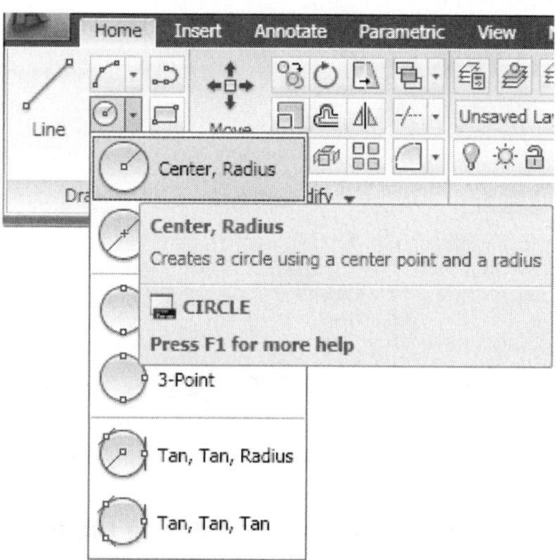

Step 34. **Draw a circle with a 1/2″ radius (Figure 2–28), as described next:**

Prompt	Response
Command:	**Center, Radius**
Specify center point for circle or [3P/2P/Ttr(tan tan radius)]:	**D1** (Figure 2–28)
Specify radius of circle or [Diameter]:	TYPE: **1/2<enter>** (the circle appears)

FIGURE 2–28
Draw the Same-Size Circle Using Four Different Methods

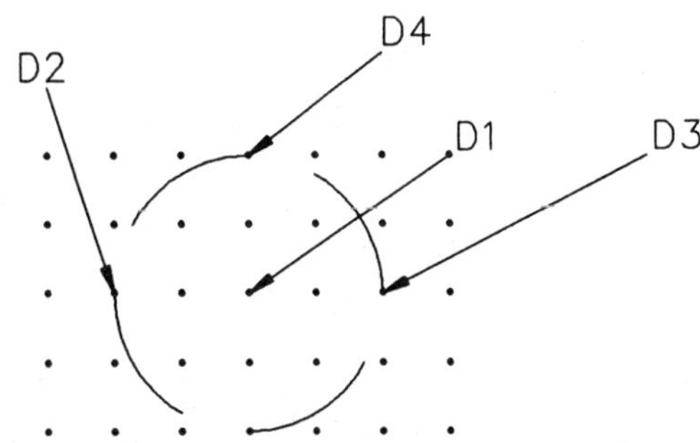

Center, Diameter

Step 35. **Draw a circle with a 1″ diameter (Figure 2–28), as described next:**

Prompt	Response
Command:	**<enter>** (to return Circle command prompt)
Specify center point for circle or [3P/2P/Ttr(tan tan radius)]:	**D1** (Figure 2–28)
Specify radius of circle or [Diameter]<0′-0 1/2″>:	TYPE: **D<enter>** (to specify diameter)
Specify diameter of circle <0′-1″>:	**<enter>** (the circle appears)

2 Points

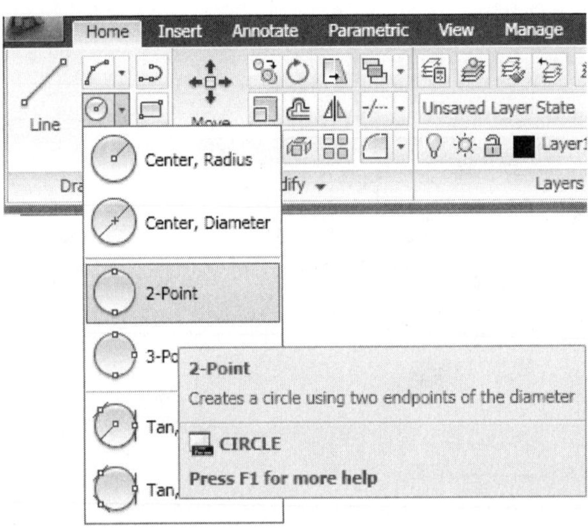

Step 36. **Draw a 1″ diameter circle by locating the two endpoints of its diameter (Figure 2–28), as described next:**

Prompt	Response
Command:	**2 Point**
Specify center point for circle or [3P/2P/Ttr(tan tan radius)]: _2p	
Specify first endpoint of circle's diameter:	**D2** (on a grid mark, Figure 2–28)
Specify second endpoint of circle's diameter:	**D3** (move four grid spaces to the right)

3 Points

Step 37. **Draw a 1″ diameter circle by clicking three points on its circumference (Figure 2–28), as described next:**

Prompt	Response
Command:	**3 Point**
Specify center point for circle or [3P/2P/Ttr(tan tan radius)]: _3p	

Prompt	Response
Specify first point on circle:	**D2** (Figure 2–28)
Specify second point on circle:	**D3** (move four grid spaces to the right)
Specify third point on circle:	**D4** (the center of the top of the circle)

You have just learned four different methods of drawing the same size circle. You can watch the size of the circle change on the screen by moving the pointer, and you can select the desired size by clicking the point that indicates the size.

TTR

The next option of the Circle command is Tan, Tan, Radius. This stands for tangent, tangent, and radius. A tangent touches a circle at a single point.

Ltscale

AutoCAD provides a variety of linetypes that you may use. For example, the dashed linetype provided by AutoCAD consists of 1/2″ line segments with 1/4″ spaces in between. The given line segment length (1/2″) and spacing (1/4″) for the dashed linetype are drawn when the global linetype scale factor is set to 1 (the default).

To make the line segment length or spacing smaller, enter a linetype scale factor smaller than 1 but larger than 0 to the Ltscale prompt. To make the line segment length and spacing larger, enter a linetype scale factor larger than 1. Look closely to see the circle's DASHED linetype scale change when the following is entered.

Step 38. Use Ltscale to change the size of the DASHED linetype, as described next:

Prompt	Response
Command:	TYPE: **LTSCALE<enter>**
Enter new linetype scale factor <1.0000>:	TYPE: **1/2<enter>**
Regenerating model.	

ZOOM

The most commonly used Zoom commands (Extents, Window, Previous, Realtime, and All) help you control how you view the drawing area on the display screen. While drawing the lines and circles for this chapter, you have been able to view the entire 8-1/2″ × 11″ drawing limits on the screen. The Zoom-All command was used earlier to assure that view. The Zoom commands are located on the Menu Bar and the Ribbon.

Zoom-Window

The Zoom-Window command allows you to pick two opposite corners of a rectangular window on the screen. The cursor changes to form a rubber band that shows the size of the window on the screen. The size of the window is controlled by the movement of the mouse. The part of the drawing inside the windowed area is magnified to fill the screen when the second corner of the window is clicked.

The following will use the Zoom-Window command to look more closely at the three tangent circles previously drawn.

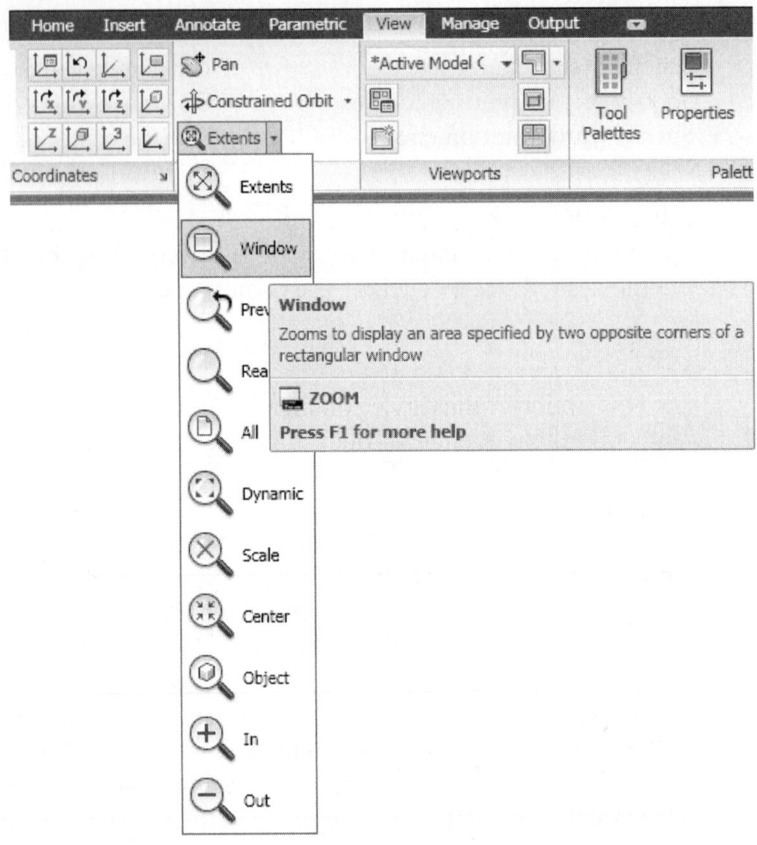

Step 39. Use Zoom-Window to look more closely at the four circles (Figure 2–29), as described next:

Prompt	Response
Command:	TYPE: **Z<enter>**
Specify corner of window, enter a scale factor (nX or nXP), or [All/Center/Dynamic/Extents/Previous/Scale/Window/Object] <real time>:	**D1** (lower left corner of the window, Figure 2–29)
Specify opposite corner:	**D2** (upper right corner of the window)

FIGURE 2–29
Use Zoom-Window

D2

D1

Zoom-All

Now that you have a windowed area of the drawing, how do you return to the entire drawing view? The drawing extents include whatever graphics are actually drawn on the page. If only half of the page is full of graphics, the extents will take up half of the page. Sometimes, graphics are drawn outside the limits; this, too, is considered the drawing extents. The limits of the drawing are set with the Limits command. The Zoom-All command displays the entire drawing limits or extents, whichever is larger. In this instance, Zoom-All will provide a view of the drawing limits.

Step 40. Use Zoom-All to view the entire drawing, as described next:

Prompt	Response
Command:	**Zoom-All** (or TYPE: **Z<enter>**)
Specify corner of window, enter a scale factor (nX or nXP), or [All/Center/Dynamic/Extents/Previous/Scale/Window/Object] <real time>:	TYPE: **A<enter>**

Zoom-Previous

Zoom-Previous is a very convenient feature. AutoCAD remembers up to 10 previous views. This is especially helpful and saves time if you are working on a complicated drawing.

Step 41. Use Zoom-Previous to see the last view of the tangent circles again, as described next:

Prompt	Response
Command:	**<enter>** (to repeat the Zoom command)
Specify corner of window, enter a scale factor (nX or nXP), or [All/Center/Dynamic/Extents/Previous/Scale/Window/Object] <real time>:	TYPE: **P<enter>**

Zoom-Extents

The extents of a drawing include whatever graphics are actually drawn on the page. The Zoom-Extents command provides a view of all drawing entities on the page as large as possible to fill the screen.

Step 42. Use Zoom-Extents to view the extents of drawing CH2-TUTORIAL1.

Zoom-Object

Zoom-Object allows you to select an object or objects to describe the area that will be displayed.

Zoom Realtime

PRESS: **<enter>** to the Zoom prompt to activate Zoom Realtime. The Zoom Realtime command is located on the Navigate panel of the View ribbon and the View menu under Zoom on the Menu bar. After activating the command, to zoom in or out, hold down the left mouse button and move the mouse up or down to change the magnification of the drawing. PRESS: **the right mouse button** to get a shortened Zoom and Pan menu. CLICK: **Exit** or PRESS: **Esc** to exit from the command.

Wheel Mouse You can also zoom in and out by turning the wheel of a two-button mouse.

PAN REALTIME

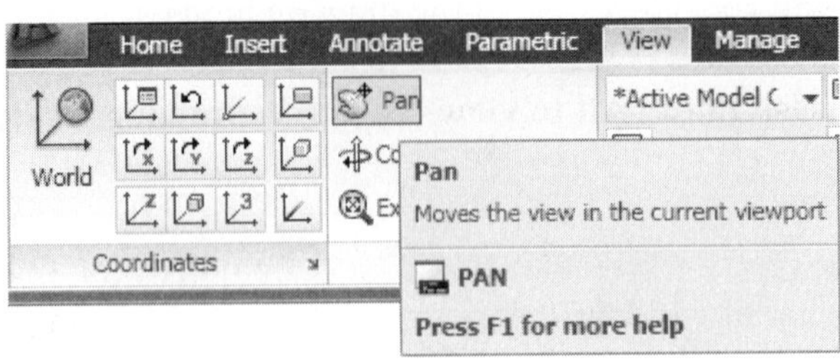

The Pan Realtime command allows you to maintain the current display magnification and see parts of the drawing that may be off the screen and not visible in the display. Like panning with a camera, pan does not change the magnification of the view.

You may also TYPE: **P<enter>** to activate this command. To move the view of your drawing at the same magnification, hold down the left button on your mouse and move the mouse in any direction to change the view of your drawing.

Wheel Mouse If you have a wheel mouse, you can pan by pressing down on the wheel and moving the mouse.

TRANSPARENT COMMANDS

A *transparent command* is one that can be used while another command is in progress. It is convenient to be able to change the display while a command such as Line is in progress. All the Zoom commands and the Pan command from the Menu Bar and the Ribbon may be used transparently; you can simply click them.

Commands that do *not* select objects, create new objects, or end the drawing session also usually can be used transparently. The grid and snap settings can be used transparently. After you have entered a command such as Line, you can TYPE: **'CAL<enter>** to start the calculator command transparently, TYPE: **'P<enter>** to start the Pan command, or TYPE: **'grid** to change the grid setting. An apostrophe (') must precede the command name. The >> preceding the command prompt in the command line window indicates the command is being used transparently.

BLIPMODE

When a point is entered on a drawing, AutoCAD generates small marker blips on the screen. Commands such as Redraw or Regen that redraw or regenerate the drawing erase the marker blips. When you TYPE: **BLIPMODE<enter>**, the Blipmode command has two responses: ON and OFF. When the Blipmode command is OFF, no marker blips are displayed. When the Blipmode command is ON, the marker blips appear.

REDRAW

When you pick Redraw from the View menu or TYPE: **R<enter>**, AutoCAD redraws and cleans up your drawing. Any marker blips on the screen disappear, and drawing entities affected by editing of other objects are redrawn. Pressing function key F7 twice turns the Grid OFF and ON and also redraws the screen.

REGEN

When you click Regen from the View menu, AutoCAD regenerates the entire drawing.

HIGHLIGHT

When you select any object such as a circle or line to erase or move or otherwise modify, the circle or line is highlighted. This highlighting is controlled by the HIGHLIGHT system variable. When you TYPE: **HIGHLIGHT<enter>**, the Highlight command has two responses: enter 1 to turn highlighting ON, or 0 to turn highlighting OFF. You will need to have this variable on so the items selected are confirmed by the highlighting.

MOVE AND EDITING COMMANDS SELECTION SET

You may want to move some of the items on your page to improve the layout of the page. The Move command allows you to do that.

Step 43. **Set Layer1 current.**

Step 44. **Use Zoom-All to view the entire drawing. Use Zoom-Realtime as needed to draw the circles in the next step.**

Step 45. **Draw a row of four 1/2″-diameter circles, 1″ on center (1″ from the center of one circle to the center of the next circle), as shown in Figure 2–30.**

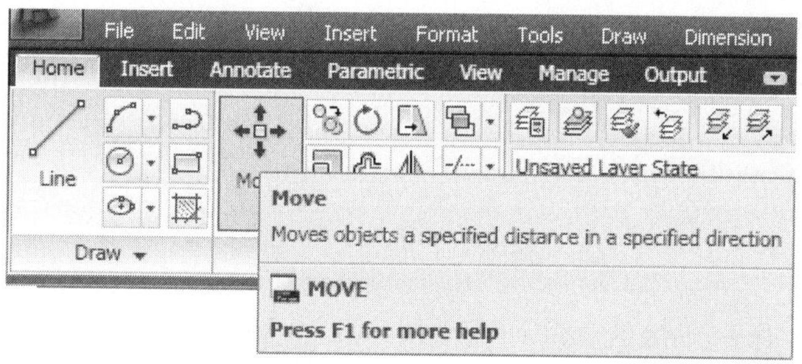

FIGURE 2–30
Draw a Row of Four 1/2″-Diameter Circles, 1″ on Center

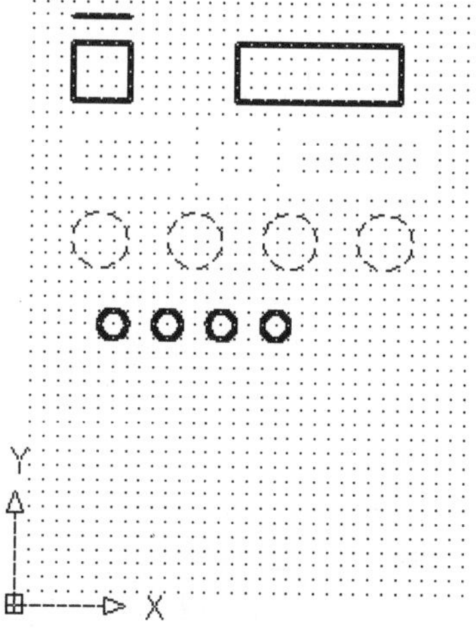

Step 46. **Pick Move from the Ribbon (or TYPE: M<enter>).**

After you pick Move, the prompt in the prompt line asks you to "Select objects:". Also, a pickbox replaces the screen crosshair. The pickbox helps you select the item or group of items to be moved by positioning the pickbox on the item. The item or group of items selected is called the *selection set*. Many of the AutoCAD Modify commands provide the same prompt, the pickbox, and also the same options used to select the object or objects to be edited. To view all the options used to select an object or objects, type and enter a **?** at the Select objects: prompt. The options are Window/Last/Crossing/BOX/ALL/Fence/WPolygon/CPolygon/Group/Add/Remove/Multiple/Previous/Undo/AUto/SIngle/SUbobject/Object. We will cover some of the more commonly used options used to select objects.

The Move command is used in the following part of this tutorial to demonstrate various options that many of the Modify commands use to select objects. Notice that when the item is selected, AutoCAD confirms your selection by highlighting it.

TIP: PRESS: function key F9 or CTRL+B to turn Snap OFF if it interferes with clicking on an object; turn it back ON as soon as the object is selected.

Step 47. Select a circle by clicking a point on the circle, and move it (Figure 2–31), as described next:

Prompt	Response
Select objects:	**D1** (any point on the circumference of the circle, as shown in Figure 2–31)
Select objects: 1 found	
Select objects:	**<enter>** (you have completed selecting objects)
Specify base point or [Displacement] <Displacement>:	**D2** (the center of the circle—be sure SNAP is ON)
Specify second point or <use first point as displacement>:	CLICK: **a point three grid marks (3/4″) to the right** **-or-** **with ORTHO ON, move your mouse to the right.** TYPE: **3/4<enter>**

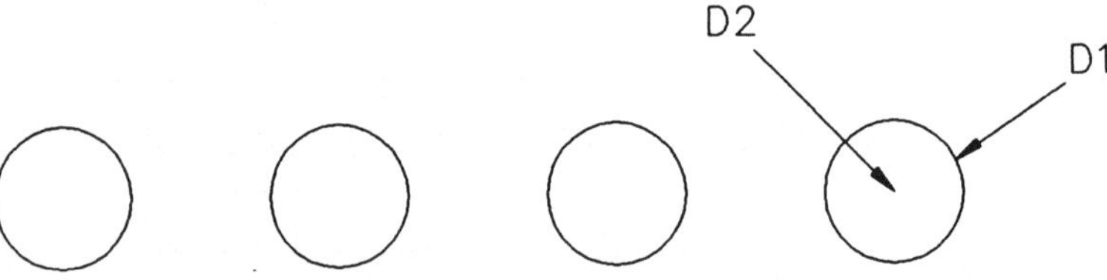

FIGURE 2–31
Select a Circle by Clicking a Point on the Circle, and Move It

NOTE: Keep Snap ON while moving a drawing entity. Snap from one grid point (base point or displacement) to another (second point).

FIGURE 2–32
Select a Circle by Clicking a Point on the Circle, and Move It by Entering Relative Coordinates

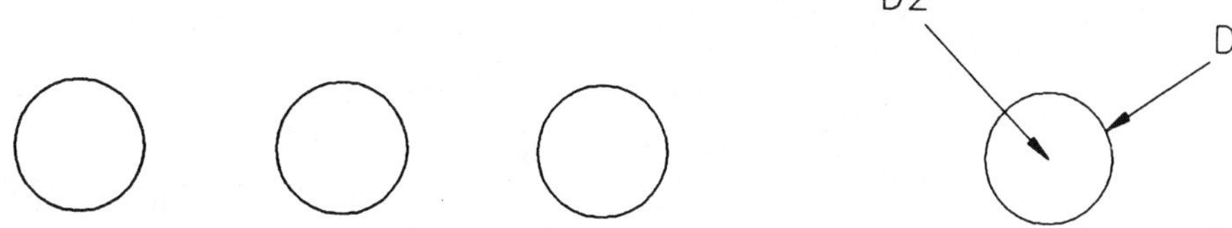

Step 48. **Select a circle by clicking a point on the circle, and move it by entering relative coordinates (Figure 2–32), as described next:**

Prompt	Response
Command:	**<enter>** (to repeat Move command prompt)
Select objects:	**D1** (Figure 2–32)
Select objects: 1 found	
Select objects:	**<enter>**
Specify base point or [Displacement] <Displacement>:	**D2** (the center of the circle)
Specify second point or <use first point as displacement>:	TYPE: **@-3/4,0<enter>**

You can give the second point of displacement by clicking a point on the screen or by using absolute, relative, or polar coordinates, or direct distance entry.

TIP: When using the Move command, the base point can be any place on the drawing, if you give a specific direction and distance for the second point.

Step 49. **Select items to be edited by using a window, and then remove an item from the selection set (Figure 2–33), as described next:**

Prompt	Response
Command:	**<enter>**
Select objects:	**D1** (Figure 2–33)
Specify opposite corner:	**D2**
4 found	
Select objects:	TYPE: **R<enter> (or hold down the Shift key)**

FIGURE 2–33
Select Items to Be Edited by Using a Window, and Then Remove an Item from the Selection Set

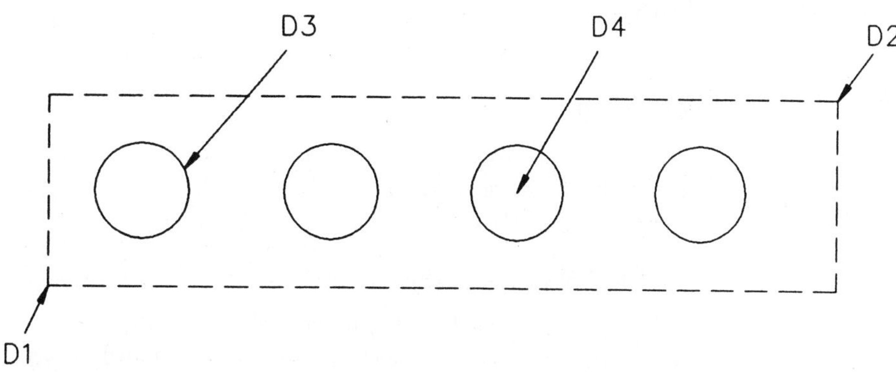

Prompt	Response
Remove objects:	**D3**
Remove objects:	**<enter>**
Specify base point or [Displacement] <Displacement>:	**D4** (the center of the circle or any place on the drawing)
Specify second point or <use first point as displacement>:	**With ORTHO ON, move your mouse down.** TYPE: **1/2<enter>**

Window (W) and Crossing Window (C)

The Window (picking left to right) and Crossing Window (picking right to left) responses allow you to pick two opposite corners of a rectangular window on the screen. The crosshair of the pointer changes to form a rubber band that shows the size of the window on the screen. The size of the window is controlled by the movement of the pointer.

With the Window response, only the parts of the drawing that are *entirely contained within the window* are selected to be edited. If the window covers only a part of a drawing entity, that entity is not selected. You may also TYPE: **W<enter>** at the Select objects: prompt to activate the Window response.

When you use the Crossing Window command, any part of the drawing that is contained within or *crossed by the crossing window* is included in the selection set. With a crossing window, a drawing entity such as a line or circle does not have to be entirely contained within the window to be selected—it only has to be touched by the crossing window. The colors of both the crossing window and the window are controlled by the Visual Effect Settings on the Selection tab of the Options dialog box.

Picking an empty area on the drawing and moving your mouse to the right creates a window. Picking and moving to the left creates a crossing window.

TIP: **Typing W<enter> or C<enter> to activate a window or a crossing window is helpful when the drawing area is dense and clicking an empty area is difficult or impossible.**

Step 50. Return the circles to the approximate location as shown in Figure 2–30.

All (All)

Selects all objects on thawed layers.

Fence (F)

Fence allows you to click points that draw a line that selects any objects it crosses.

Remove (R) and Add (A)

The Remove response allows you to remove a drawing part from the selection set. If you are in the Remove mode and decide to add another drawing part to the selection set, TYPE: **A<enter>** to return to the Add mode.

Last (L) and Previous (P)

The Last response selects the most recent drawing entity created. The Previous response selects the most recent selection set. Both are handy if you want to use several editing commands on the same drawing entity or the same selection set. You may also type and enter **L** or **P** from the keyboard while you are in a command and selecting objects.

Undo (U)

While in an editing command, if you decide you do not want something in a selection set, you may use the Undo command to remove it and continue on with the Select objects: prompt. Typing **U<enter>** backtracks through the selection sets in the reverse of the order in which they were selected.

GRIPS

Grips are small squares that appear on an object if it is selected with no command active. Grips are very useful and can speed up your use of many of the Modify commands.

TIP: If grips appear when you do not want them, PRESS: **the Esc key.**

Step 51. Use grips to change the size of a circle; then move, scale, and rotate several circles at the same time, as described next:

Prompt	Response
Command:	With no command active, CLICK: **on one of the circles you have drawn**
Small blue squares (grips) appear at each quadrant and at the center of the circle:	CLICK: **one of the grips at one of the quadrants of the circle**
The grip changes color (becomes HOT). Specify stretch point or [Base point/Copy/Undo/eXit]:	**Move your mouse to see that the size of the circle changes, then** TYPE: **3/4<enter>**
The radius of the circle is now 3/4″	CLICK: **Undo** (or TYPE: **U<enter>**) to return the circle to its previous size
Command:	Using a window, SELECT: **all four 1/2″-diameter circles**
Grips appear at each quadrant and at the centers of all circles:	CLICK: **the grip at the far left quadrant**
The grip changes color (becomes HOT). **STRETCH** Specify stretch point or [Base point/Copy/Undo/eXit]:	PRESS: **the space bar to advance to the MOVE grip mode in the command area**
MOVE Specify move point or [Base point/Copy/Undo/eXit]:	**Move your mouse to the right to see that the circles move with your cursor.** You can

Prompt	Response
	now TYPE: **the distance to move the circles** or you can CLICK: **the destination point.** For now, TYPE: **5<enter>** to move the circles 5″ to the right.
With all circles still displaying grips:	CLICK: **the grip at the far left quadrant**
The grip changes color (becomes HOT). **STRETCH** Specify stretch point or [Base point/ Copy/Undo/eXit]:	PRESS: **the space bar twice to advance to the ROTATE grip mode**
ROTATE Specify rotation angle or [Base point/ Copy/Undo/Reference/eXit]:	**Move your mouse so you can see that the circles are rotated.** You can now TYPE: **an angle** or you can CLICK: **a point to select the angle.** For now, TYPE: **45<enter>** to rotate the circles 45°.
Command:	CLICK: **Undo twice** (or TYPE: **U<enter> twice**) to return the circles to their original position.

UNDO AND REDO

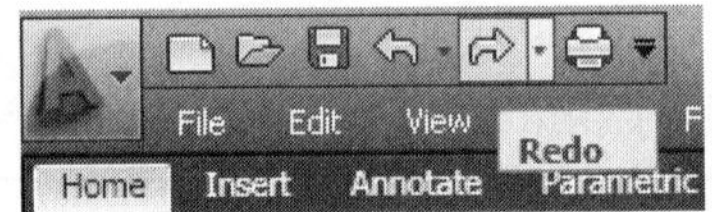

Understanding how to use the Undo command can be very helpful when drawing with AutoCAD.

When the Undo icon on the Quick Access Toolbar is clicked, the most recent command is undone. To undo more than one command, click the Undo icon more than once. Use the Redo icon to redo as many undos as you need.

When **U** is typed from the keyboard to the Command: prompt, and the Enter key is pressed, the most recent command operation is undone. Most of the time the operation that is undone is obvious, such as when a line that you have just drawn is undone. The most recent mode settings that are not obvious, such as Snap, will be undone also. Typing **REDO** and pressing **<enter>** will redo only one undo, and must immediately follow the **U** or **UNDO** command.

When **U** is typed and entered from the keyboard, no prompt line appears. If you TYPE: **UNDO <enter>**, the prompt "Enter the number of operations to undo or [Auto/Control/BEgin/End/Mark/Back] <1>:" appears. The default is <1>. You may enter a number for the number of operations to be undone. For instance, if 5 is entered at the prompt, five operations will be undone. If you decide you went too far, you can TYPE: **REDO<enter>** or select Redo from the Standard toolbar, and all five operations will be restored.

Typing **U** from the keyboard and pressing the Enter key is the same as entering the number 1 to the Undo prompt. In that instance, **Redo** will redo only one undo, no matter how many times you typed and entered **U**. Right-click menus also have the Undo and Redo commands.

FIGURE 2–34
Draw Arcs

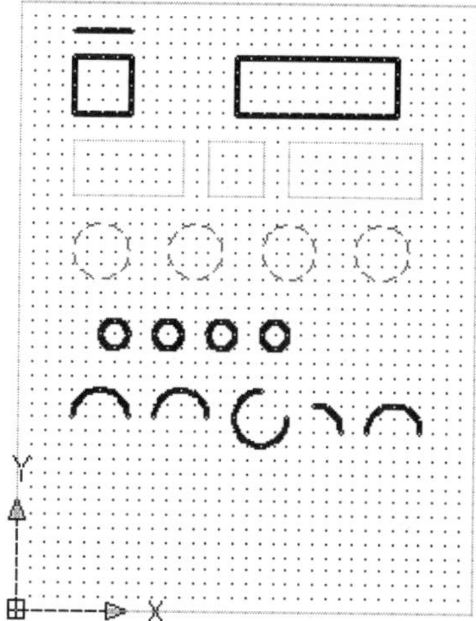

ARC

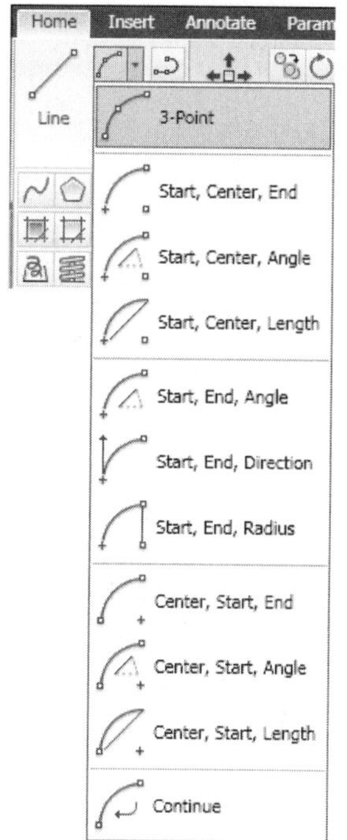

There are many methods from which to choose when you are drawing arcs. Whatever the situation, you can select a method to suit your needs. Experiment with the different methods described next and decide which ones you prefer to use. Use Figure 2–34 as a guide when locating the approximate location of the arcs on your drawing.

3-Point

Using the 3-point method, you can draw an arc clockwise or counterclockwise by specifying the start point, second point, and endpoint of the arc.

Step 52. Draw three arcs using the 3-point method (Figure 2–35), as described next:

Prompt	Response
Command:	**3 Point** (or TYPE: **A<enter>**)
Specify start point of arc or [Center]:	**D1**
Specify second point of arc or [Center/End]:	**D2** (Figure 2–35)
Specify endpoint of arc:	**D3**
Command:	**<enter>** (repeat ARC)
Specify start point of arc or [Center]:	**D4**

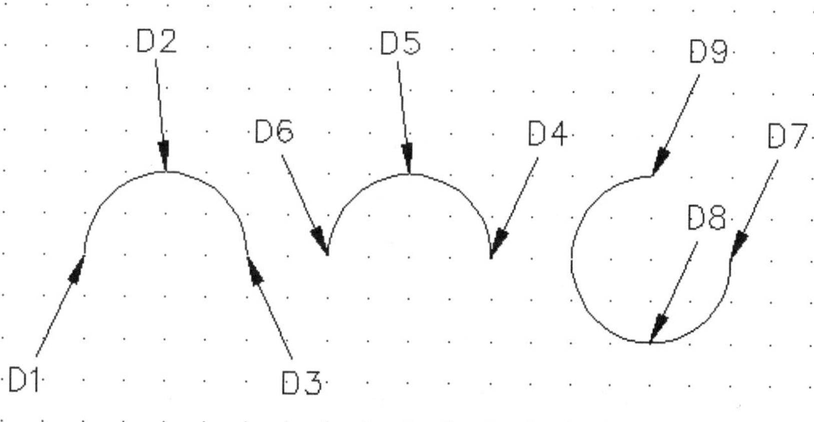

FIGURE 2–35
Draw Arcs Using the 3-Point Method

Prompt	Response
Specify second point of arc or [Center/End]:	**D5**
Specify endpoint of arc:	**D6**
Command:	**<enter>** (repeat ARC)
Specify start point of arc or [Center]:	**D7**
Specify second point of arc or [Center/End]:	**D8**
Specify endpoint of arc:	**D9**

Start, Center, End

The Start, Center, End method allows you to draw an arc only counterclockwise, by specifying the start, center, and end.

Step 53. Draw two arcs using the Start, Center, End method (Figure 2–36), as described next:

Prompt	Response
Command:	**Arc-Start, Center, End**
Specify start point of arc or [Center]:	**D1**
Specify second point of arc or [Center/End]:_c Specify center point of arc:	**D2** (Figure 2–36)
Specify endpoint of arc or [Angle/chord Length]:	**D3**
Command:	**Arc-Start, Center, End**
Specify start point of arc or [Center]:	**D4** (Figure 2–36)
Specify second point of arc or [Center/End]:_c Specify center point of arc:	**D5**
Specify endpoint of arc or [Angle/chord Length]:	**D6**

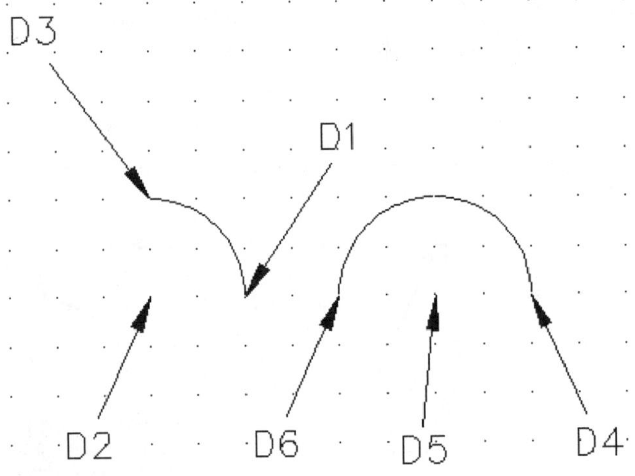

FIGURE 2–36
Draw Arcs Using the Start, Center, End Method

Start, Center, Angle

In the Start, Center, Angle method, A is the included angle (the angle the arc will span). A positive angle will draw the arc counterclockwise; a negative angle will draw the arc clockwise.

Start, Center, Length

In the Start, Center, Length method, L is the chord length. A *chord* is a straight line that connects an arc's start point and endpoint. A positive chord length can be entered to draw a minor arc (less than 180°), and a negative chord length can be entered to draw a major arc (more than 180°). Both are drawn counterclockwise.

Start, End, Angle

With the Start, End, Angle method, after the start point and endpoint of the arc have been picked, a positive angle draws the arc counterclockwise; a negative angle keeps the same start and endpoints but draws the reverse arc or draws clockwise.

Start, End, Direction

In this method, Direction is the specified direction that the arc takes from the start point. The direction is specified in degrees. You can also specify the direction by pointing to a single point. Major, minor, counterclockwise, and clockwise arcs can be drawn with the Start, End, Direction method.

Start, End, Radius

In the Start, End, Radius method, Radius is the arc radius. When you use this method, enter a positive radius to draw a minor arc (less than 180°), and enter a negative radius to draw a major arc (more than 180°). Both are drawn counterclockwise.

Continue

If Continue is picked at the first prompt of any of the arc methods that start with S, the new arc starts at the endpoint of the last arc or line drawn. Pressing the Enter key has the same effect. The new arc's direction follows the direction of the last arc or line drawn.

ELLIPSE

Look at Figure 2–37 to determine the approximate location of the ellipses drawn with the Ellipse command.

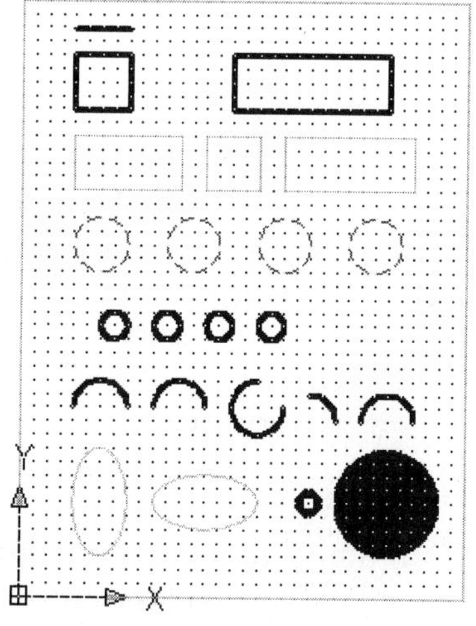

FIGURE 2–37
Draw Ellipses and Donuts

Axis, End

The minor axis of an ellipse is its smaller axis, and the major axis is the larger axis.

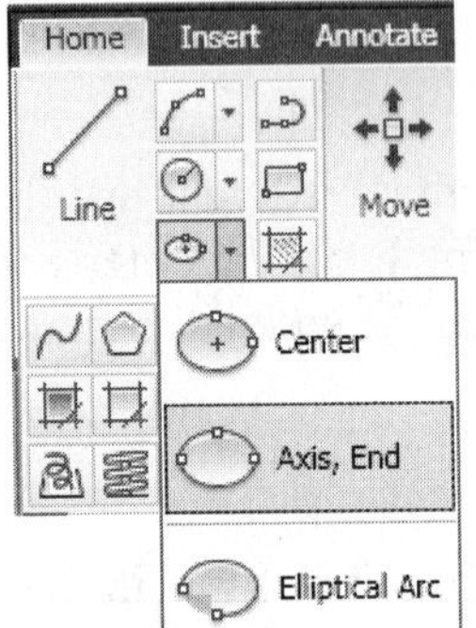

Step 54. **Set Layer3 current.**

Step 55. **Draw an ellipse by entering points for the minor axis of the ellipse (Figure 2–38), as described next:**

Prompt	Response
Command:	**Ellipse-Axis, End** (or TYPE: **EL<enter>**)
Specify axis endpoint of ellipse or [Arc/Center]:	**D1** (Figure 2–38)
Specify other endpoint of axis:	**D2—With ORTHO ON, move your mouse to the right;** TYPE: **1<enter>**
Specify distance to other axis or [Rotation]:	**D3—With ORTHO ON, move your mouse up;** TYPE: **1<enter>**

Step 56. **Draw an ellipse by entering points for the major axis of the ellipse (Figure 2–38), as described next:**

Prompt	Response
Command:	**Ellipse-Axis, End**
Specify axis endpoint of ellipse or [Arc/Center]:	**D4** (Figure 2–38)
Specify other endpoint of axis:	**D5—With ORTHO ON, move your mouse to the right;** TYPE: **2<enter>**
Specify distance to other axis or [Rotation]:	**D6—With ORTHO ON, move your mouse up;** TYPE: **1/2<enter>**

FIGURE 2–38
Draw an Ellipse by Entering Points for the Minor and Major Axes of the Ellipse

D3
D6
D1
D2
D4
D5

Center

You may also draw an ellipse by specifying the center point, the endpoint of one axis, and the length of the other axis. Type **C** and press **<enter>** to the prompt "Specify axis endpoint of ellipse or [Arc/Center]:" to start with the center of the ellipse. Entering the center point first is similar to the first two methods described above, and either the minor or major axis may be constructed first. As with all methods of drawing an ellipse, you can specify the points by clicking a point on the drawing, by typing and entering coordinates, or by direct distance entry.

DONUT

Look at Figure 2–37 to determine the approximate location of the solid ring and solid circle drawn using the Donut command.

Step 57. Set Layer1 current.

Step 58. Use the Donut command to draw a solid ring (Figure 2–39), as described next:

Prompt	Response
Command:	**Donut** (or TYPE: **DO<enter>**)
Specify inside diameter of donut <default>:	TYPE: **1/2<enter>**
Specify outside diameter of donut <default>:	TYPE: **1<enter>**
Specify center of donut or <exit>:	CLICK: **a point on the drawing**
Specify center of donut or <exit>:	**<enter>**

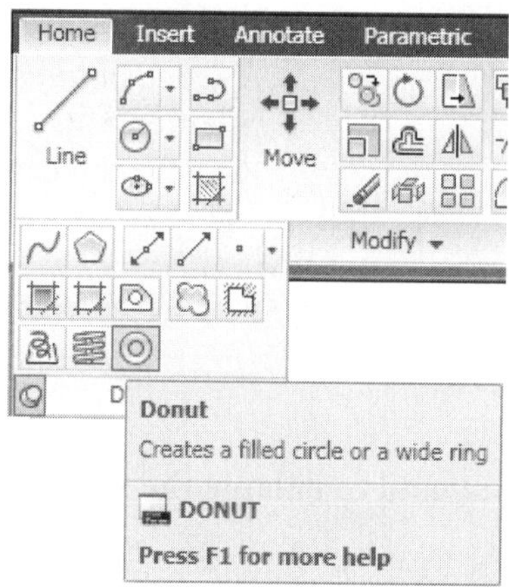

FIGURE 2–39
Use the Donut Command to Draw a Solid Ring and a Solid Circle

Step 59. Use the Donut command to draw a solid circle (Figure 2–39), as described next:

Prompt	Response
Command:	**<enter>** (Repeat DONUT)
Specify inside diameter of donut <0′-0 1/2″>:	TYPE: **0<enter>** (so there is no center hole)
Specify outside diameter of donut <0′-1″>:	**<enter>**
Specify center of donut or <exit>:	CLICK: **a point on the drawing**
Specify center of donut or <exit>:	**<enter>**

The Donut command can be used to draw solid dots of any size as well as solid rings with different inside and outside diameters.

SCALE

The Scale command lets you reduce or enlarge either drawing entities or an entire drawing. The Copy option of the Scale command allows you to copy and enlarge or reduce the object at the same time.

<Scale factor>

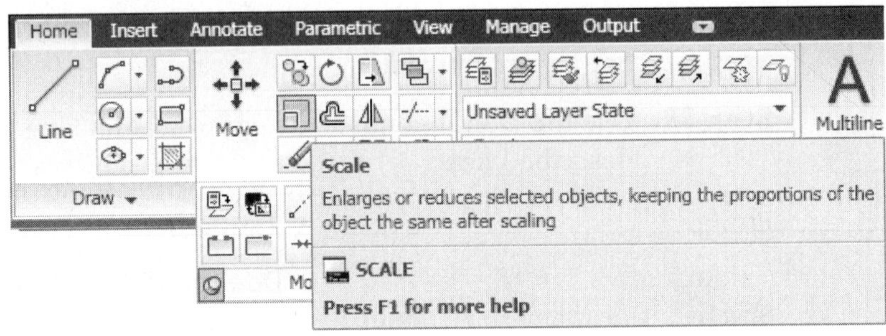

Step 60. Use the Scale command to reduce the solid ring (Figure 2–40), as described next:

Prompt	Response
Command:	**Scale** (or TYPE: **SC<enter>**)
Select objects:	**Window the ring** (or click the outside edge of the ring)
Select objects:	**<enter>**
Specify base point:	CLICK: **the center of the ring**
Specify scale factor or [Copy/Reference]:	TYPE: **.5<enter>**

The relative scale factor of .5 was used to reduce the rectangle. A relative scale factor of 2 would have enlarged the rectangle.

Reference

Step 61. Use the Scale command to enlarge the solid circle (Figure 2–40), as described next:

Prompt	Response
Command:	**<enter>** (Repeat SCALE)
Select objects:	**Window the circle**
Select objects:	**<enter>**
Specify base point:	CLICK: **the center of the circle**
Specify scale factor or [Copy/Reference] <default>:	TYPE: **R<enter>**
Specify reference length <0′-1″>:	**<enter>** (to accept 1 as the default)
Specify new length or [Points] <0′-1″>:	TYPE: **2<enter>**

The Reference option allows you to type and enter a number for the Reference (current) length of a drawing entity. You can also enter the Reference (current) length by picking two points on the drawing to show AutoCAD the Reference (current) length. You can

FIGURE 2–40
Tutorial 2–1, Part 2—Complete

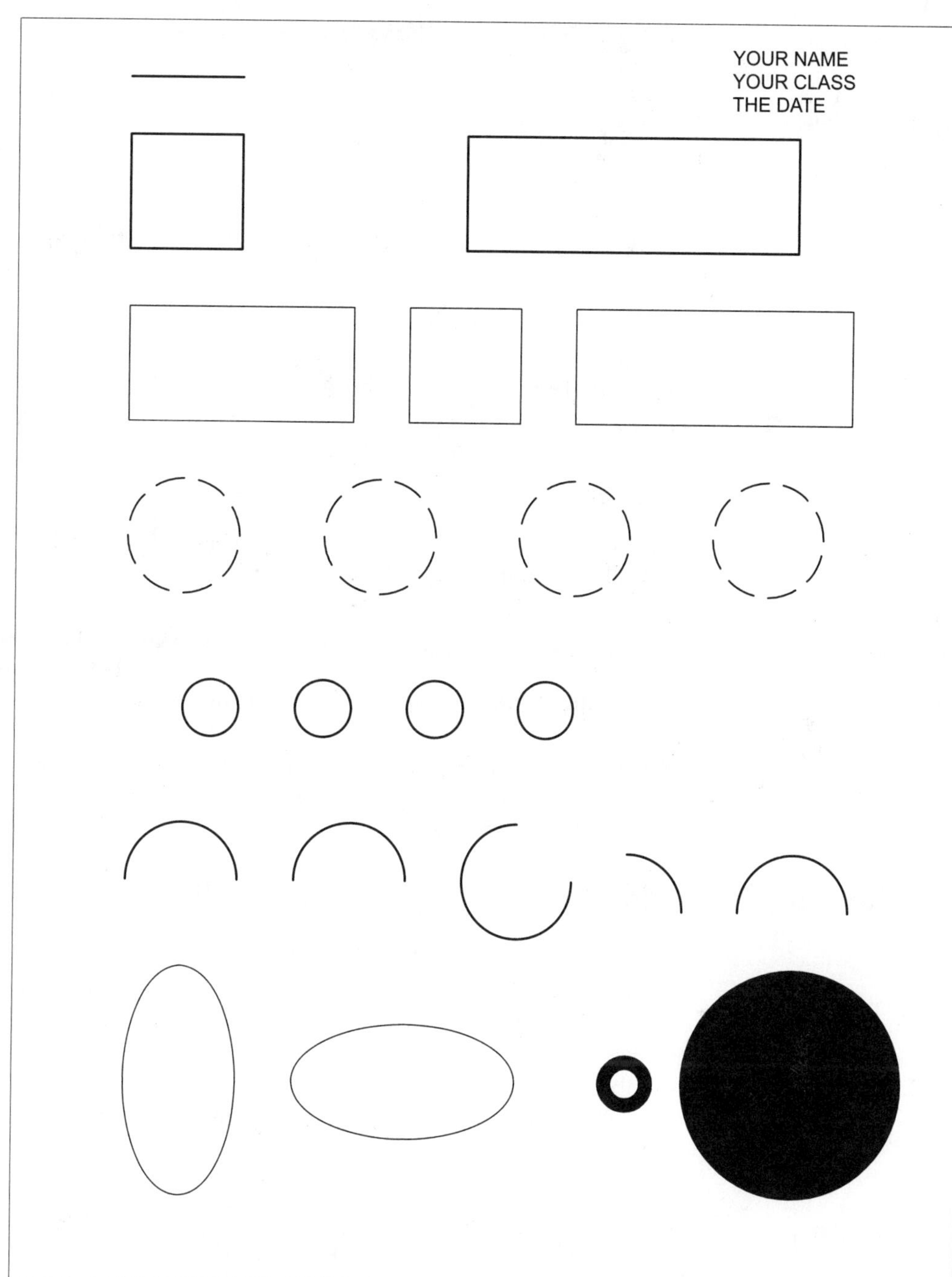

type and enter the new length by using a number, or you can enter it by picking two points on the drawing to show the new length.

Step 62. **Set Layer3 current.**

Step 63. **Add your name, class, and date to the upper right corner of your drawing as described next:**

Prompt	Response
Command:	**Single Line Text** (or TYPE: **DT<enter>**)
Specify start point of text or [Justify/Style]:	CLICK: **a point in the upper right corner to start typing your name as shown in Figure 2–40**

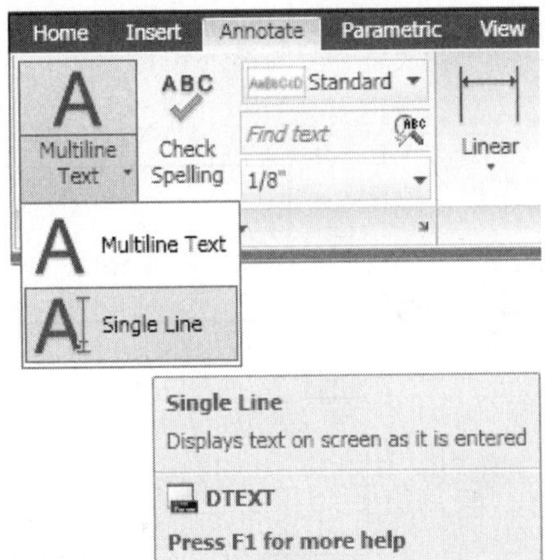

Prompt	Response
Specify height <default>:	TYPE: **1/8<enter>**
Specify rotation angle of text <0>:	**<enter>** (to accept the 0 default rotation)
The In-Place Text Editor appears:	TYPE: **YOUR NAME<enter>** **YOUR CLASS<enter>** **THE DATE<enter>**
The In-Place Text Editor:	**<enter>** (to close the In-Place Text Editor)

Step 63. When you have completed Tutorial 2–1, Part 2 (Figure 2–40), save your drawing in at least two places.

Tutorial 2–2: Plot Responses for CH2-TUTORIAL1, Using the Model Tab

When you start a new drawing, AutoCAD provides a single Model tab and two Layout tabs at the bottom of the drawing window. Thus far you have been working on the Model tab in model space. Model space is the 2D (and also 3D) environment where you create your drawings. You can also plot (or print) from the Model tab. Tutorial 2–2 describes how to print from the Model tab.

The following is a hands-on, step-by-step tutorial to make a hard copy of CH2-TUTORIAL1.

Step 1. **Open drawing CH2-TUTORIAL1 so it is displayed on the screen. Remember, if your drawing has been saved on a disk, open it from the disk and save it on the hard drive or network drive.**

Step 2. **Make sure the Model tab is current.**

Step 3. **Click the Plot command from the Quick Access toolbar, or** CLICK: **Plot... from the File menu, or** TYPE: **PLOT, <enter> to access the Plot dialog box. Pressing Ctrl+P will also access the Plot dialog box.**

Step 4. **Click the More Options arrow in the lower right corner of the Plot dialog box to display the entire Plot dialog box (Figure 2–41).**

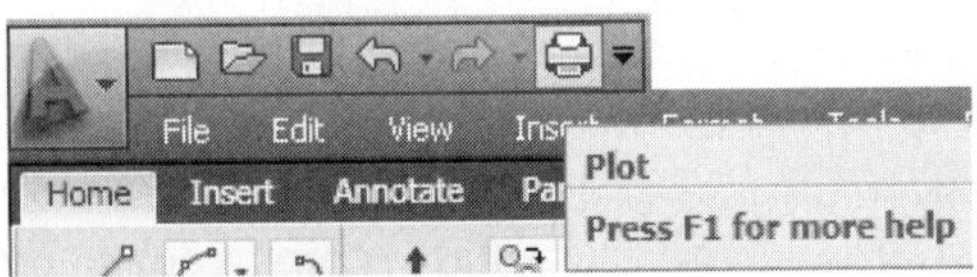

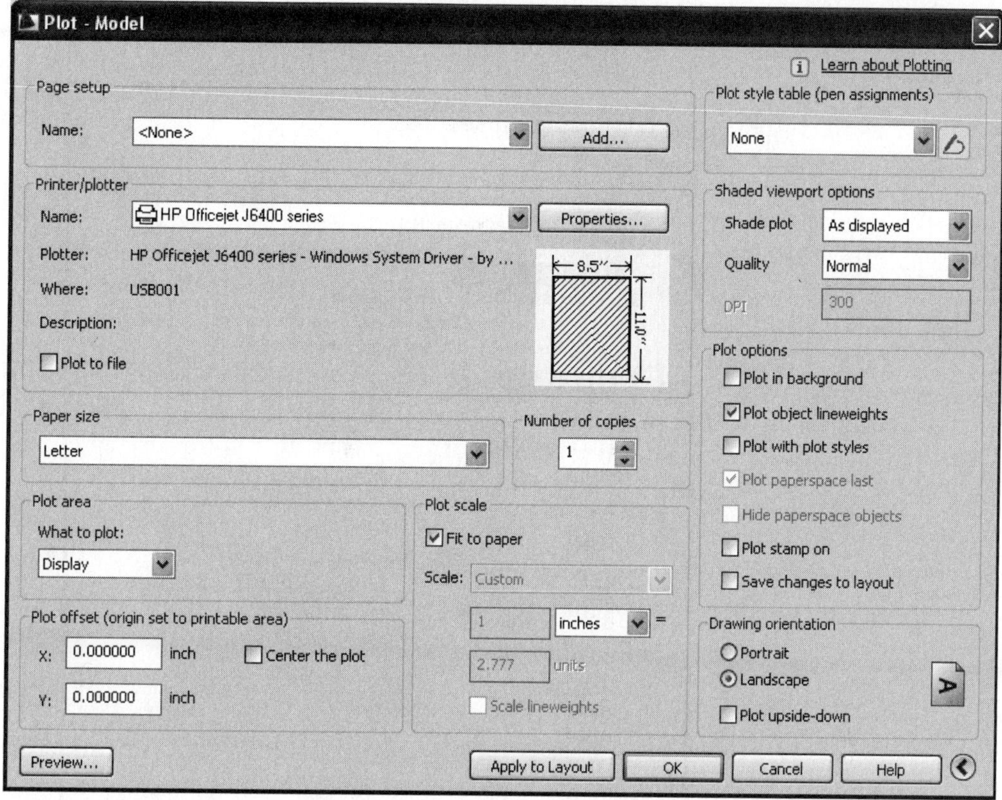

FIGURE 2–41
Plot Dialog Box

PLOT - NAME

The strip at the top of the dialog box displays the current layout tab name or shows whether the Model tab is current. It shows "Model" now, because the Model tab is current.

PAGE SETUP

Name: Layout settings (the settings that control the final plot output) are referred to as *page setups.* This list box displays any named or saved page setups that you can select to apply to the current page setup.

Add... When this button is clicked, the Add Page Setup dialog box is displayed. You can specify a name for the new page setup.

Step 5. Set the Page setup to None.

PRINTER/PLOTTER

The Name: line displays the current plot device (plotter or printer). When the down arrow is clicked, a list of the available plotting devices is displayed in the Name: list. You can select the plot device that you want to use.

Properties... When this button is clicked, the Plotter Configuration Editor (Figure 2–42) is displayed. The Plotter Configuration Editor allows you to view or to modify current plot device information.

Custom Properties... When this button of the Plotter Configuration Editor is clicked, a Properties dialog box for the configured plotter (or printer) appears. Each plotter (or printer) has a unique Properties dialog box; you can customize settings for the vector colors, print quality, and raster corrections for your plotter (or printer) using the Properties dialog box.

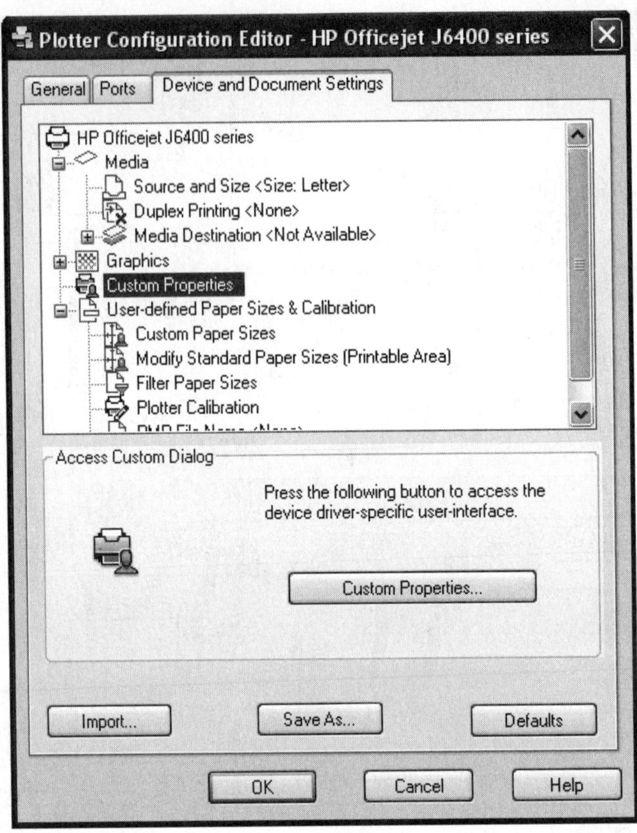

FIGURE 2–42
Plot Configuration Editor Dialog Box

Step 6. Select the printer that you will use. If the Name: line does not show the correct plot device, click the down arrow and select the printer that you will use.

If you need to add a plot device, the Plotter Manager (under File in the Menu Bar) is used to add or modify plotter and printer configuration files.

PLOT TO FILE

If you do not check the Plot to file button, AutoCAD plots directly from your computer. If there is a cable leading from your computer to the printer or plotter, or if you are plotting from a network, do not check the Plot to file button.

If you do check the Plot to file button, a file is created with the extension .plt.

BROWSE FOR PLOT FILE...

When Plot to file is selected, and OK is clicked, the Browse for Plot File dialog box is displayed. This box allows you to determine where the plot file is to be stored.

Step 7. Select the correct setting for the Plot to file check box, for your situation.

PLOT STYLE TABLE (PEN ASSIGNMENTS)

Plot styles allow you to plot the same drawing in different ways. The Plot style table (Figure 2–43) can be used to create, edit, or store plot style files. Plot styles are explained in Chapter 5.

FIGURE 2–43
Plot Style Table

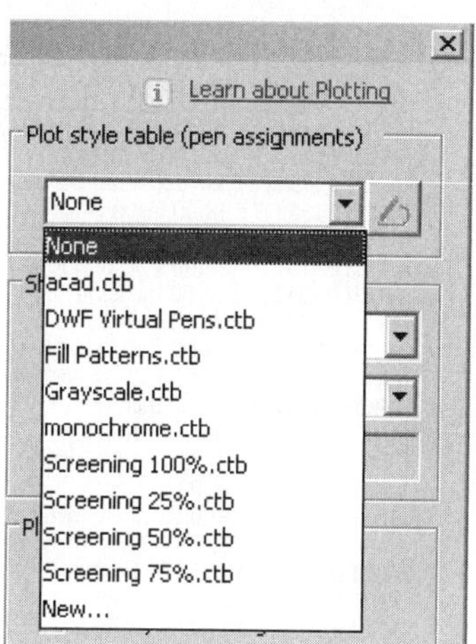

Step 8. **Set the Plot style table to None.**

PAPER SIZE

The Paper size: line displays the current paper size. When the down arrow is clicked, it lists the paper sizes the printer (Figure 2–44) or plotter (Figure 2–45) can accommodate; the current size is highlighted. An A, B, D, or E displayed beside the size indicates a standard American National Standards Institute (ANSI) paper size. ARCH displayed beside the size indicates a standard architectural paper size.

Step 9. **Select the Letter (8.5 × 11 in.) paper size, and 1 for the Number of copies.**

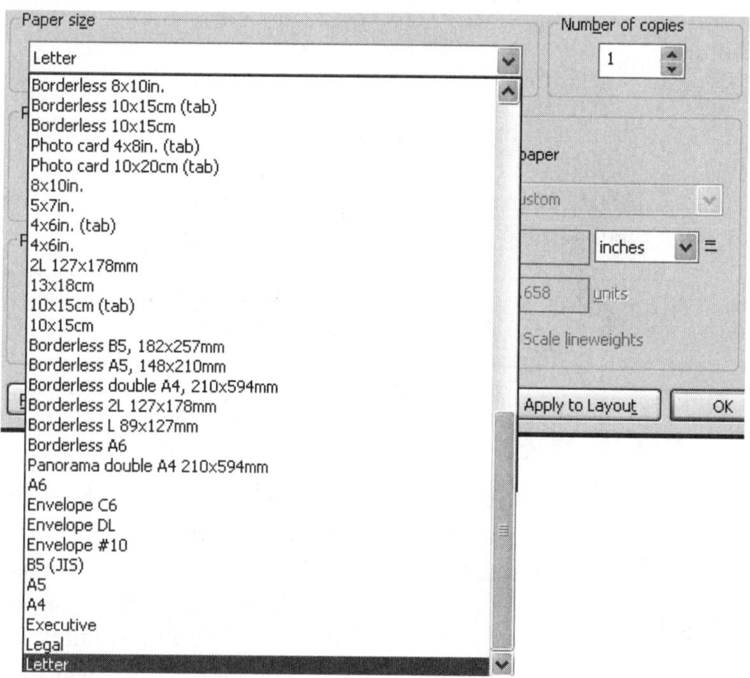

FIGURE 2–44
Paper Sizes for a Printer

FIGURE 2–45
Paper Sizes for a Plotter

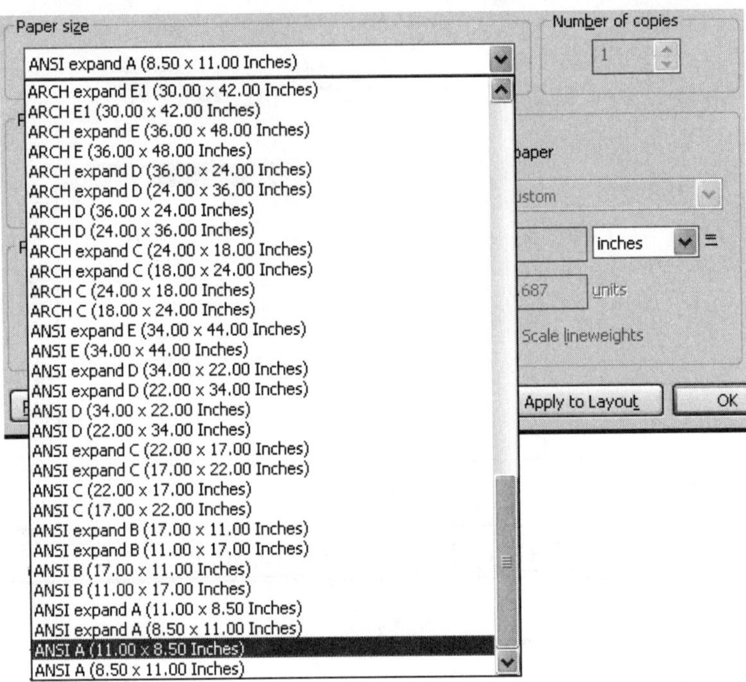

PLOT AREA

When you click the down arrow, the following options are displayed (view will not be displayed because you have not named and saved a view in your drawing):

Limits This option plots the part of the drawing that lies within the drawing limits. The limits for drawing CH2-TUTORIAL1 are 8-1/2,11.

Extents This option plots the drawing extents. The drawing extents are whatever graphics are actually drawn, including any graphics that lie outside the limits of the drawing area.

Display This option plots the part of the drawing that is displayed on the screen at the time the plot is made.

Window This selection allows you to pick two corners of a window and plot only the part of the drawing that is within the window. When the Window < button is clicked, it clears the Plot dialog box so you can view your drawing and use your mouse to click the two corners of a window. AutoCAD then returns to the Plot dialog box.

Step 10. CLICK: **Extents to select the drawing extents as part of the drawing that is to be printed.**

PLOT SCALE

Scale: The Scale: line displays the scale at which the drawing will be plotted. If the scale list is gray, CLICK: the check mark in the Fit to paper check box so a scale may be selected. When the down arrow is clicked, a list of available scales is displayed. You can select the scale that you want to use. To be able to measure a plotted drawing accurately using a scale, you must enter a specific plotting scale.

You may respond by selecting Fit to paper instead of entering a specific scale. When you select this option, AutoCAD scales the selected plot area as large as possible to fit the specified paper size.

ANNOTATIVE PROPERTY AND ANNOTATION SCALE

Objects such as text, dimensions, hatches, and leaders can be annotative. For text to be annotative, you can turn the annotative property on in the Text Style dialog box. Also, before you add the text to your drawing, you must set the Annotation Scale, located in the lower right corner of the status bar.

When a drawing such as a large house or building is drawn full scale, the text that is added to the drawing must also be large. For instance, if you want the text of a drawing to be 1/8″ high when plotted at a scale of 1/4″ = 1′-0″, the text that you add while drawing full scale will need to be 6″ high.

Annotation scale controls how the text and other annotative objects appear on the drawing. When you make the text annotative and set the annotation scale of the drawing, AutoCAD automatically does the arithmetic for you and controls how the text looks on your screen. When adding the text, you have to enter only the size of the text you want in the plotted drawing, and AutoCAD automatically calculates the size of the text on the drawing using the annotation scale setting.

If you have annotative objects on your drawing and have set the annotation scale, it is usually best to plot your drawing at the same scale as the annotation scale that you have set. If there are no annotative objects on your drawing, the annotation scale does not affect anything. If the plot scale and the annotation scale differ, when the plot is initiated, AutoCAD prompts you with "The annotation scale is not equal to the plot scale. Do you wish to Continue?" You can answer with "OK" or "Cancel."

Step 11. Select a scale of 1:1, which is 1 plotted inch = 1 drawing unit.

PLOT OFFSET (ORIGIN SET TO PRINTABLE AREA)

Center the plot To center the drawing on the paper, place a check in the Center the plot check box, and the plot will be automatically centered on the paper.

X and Y offset The plot offset specifies the location of the plot, on the paper, from the lower left corner of the paper. The X: input line moves the plotted drawing in the X direction on the paper, and the Y: input moves the drawing in the Y direction. You can enter either positive or negative values.

Step 12. Place a check in the Center the plot check box.

Notice that the X and Y inputs are automatically calculated to center the selected plotting area (extents) in the paper size (8½″ × 11″).

SHADED VIEWPORT OPTIONS

These options relate to 3D drawings and control how shaded and rendered viewports are plotted. This is described in Chapters 14, 15, and 16.

PLOT OPTIONS

Plot in background A check mark in this box allows you to continue working while your drawing is being plotted.

Plot object lineweights A check mark in this box tells AutoCAD to plot the drawing using the lineweights you have assigned to any object in the drawing.

Plot with plot styles This option allows you to use a plot style. Since you are not using a plot style, this box will not be checked.

Plot paperspace last When this option is checked, model space will be plotted first. Usually, paper space drawings are plotted before model space drawings.

Hide paperspace objects The Hide paperspace objects check box refers to 3D objects only. When you use the Hide command, AutoCAD hides any surface on the screen that is behind another surface in 3D space. If you want to do the same on your paper space plot, you must click the Hide paperspace objects check box so a check appears in the box. This shows only in the full plot preview window.

Another way to hide in paper space is to select the viewport in which you want to have hidden lines, click Properties under Modify in the Menu Bar, and turn Shade plot to Hidden.

Plot stamp on A check mark here allows you to place signatures and other stamps on the drawing.

Save changes to layout Checking this box allows you to save any changes you have made in the Plot dialog box.

Step 13. Put a check in the Plot object lineweights box. (Plot paperspace last and Hide paperspace objects are grayed out because no Layout tabs were used.)

DRAWING ORIENTATION

The paper icon represents the orientation of the selected paper size. The letter A icon represents the orientation of the drawing on the paper.

Portrait This button allows you to specify a vertical orientation of the drawing on the page.

Landscape This button allows you to specify a horizontal orientation of the drawing on the page. If a plot shows only half of what should have been plotted, the orientation may need to be changed.

Plot upside-down This check box allows you to plot the drawing, in a portrait or landscape orientation, upside-down.

Step 14. Select the Portrait orientation.

PREVIEW...

The Preview... button shows you exactly how the final plot will appear on the sheet.

Step 15. CLICK: **the Preview... button.**

Preview your plot for CH2-TUTORIAL1, Part 2, Figure 2–46. If there is something wrong with the plot, press the space bar and make the necessary adjustments. If the preview looks OK, press the space bar to end the preview. You may also click the right mouse button to access the menu shown in Figure 2–47.

Step 16. CLICK: **OK from the Plot dialog box (or** CLICK: **Plot from the right-click menu).**

The plot proceeds from this point. If you have not created a plot file, remove the completed plot from the printer or plotter. If you have created a .plt file, take your disk to the plot station or send your plot via a network.

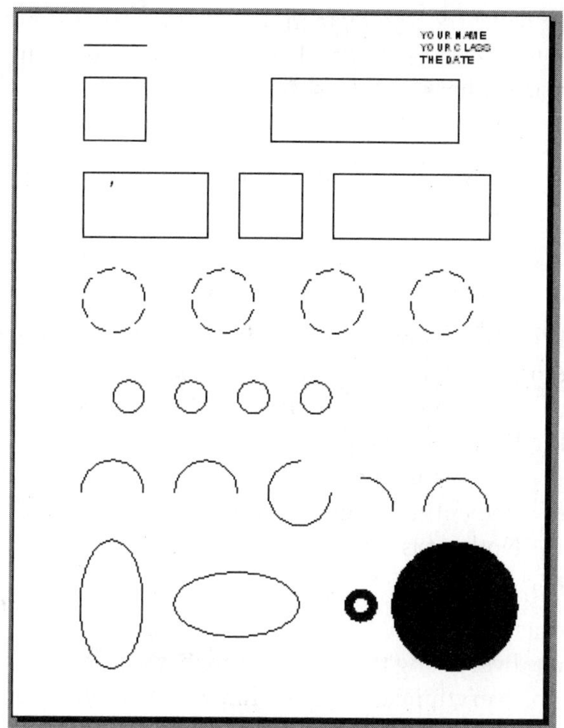

FIGURE 2–46
Plot Preview

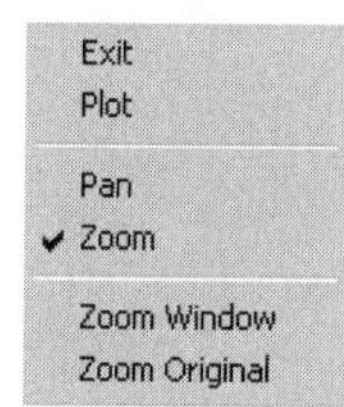

FIGURE 2–47
Preview Right-Click Menu

review questions

1. The default lower left corner of the drawing limits is 8-1/2,11.
   a. True
   b. False
2. The function key F7 described in this chapter does which of the following?
   a. Provides a checklist of the layers created
   b. Turns Snap ON or OFF
   c. Flips the screen from the text display to the graphics display
   d. Turns Grid ON or OFF
   e. Turns Ortho ON or OFF
3. Which of the following function keys is used to turn Snap ON or OFF?
   a. F1
   b. F2
   c. F7
   d. F8
   e. F9
4. How many layers may be used in a drawing?
   a. 1
   b. 2
   c. 3
   d. 16
   e. An unlimited number
5. AutoCAD provides how many sizes of each standard linetype (except continuous)?
   a. 1
   b. 2
   c. 3
   d. 4
   e. As many as you want

6. To make the line segment length and spacing larger for a dashed linetype, enter a number larger than 1 to the Ltscale prompt "Enter new linetype scale factor <1.0000>:".
   a. True b. False
7. Always use the Zoom-All command after setting up a new drawing.
   a. True b. False
8. Snap may be turned OFF and ON while you are drawing.
   a. True b. False
9. When the Move command is used with a selection window (CLICK: left, drag right), not a crossing window,
   a. Everything the window touches is selected.
   b. Everything entirely within the window is selected.
   c. The last item clicked is selected.
   d. The entire screen is selected.
   e. Nothing is selected.
10. When the Move command is used with a crossing window (CLICK: right, drag left),
   a. Everything the window touches is selected.
   b. Everything entirely within the window is selected.
   c. The last item clicked is selected.
   d. The entire screen is selected.
   e. Nothing is selected.
11. The 3-point method of drawing arcs allows you to draw arcs clockwise or counterclockwise.
   a. True b. False
12. The Reference option of the Scale command allows you to pick two points on the drawing to show AutoCAD the current length of the drawing entity to be reduced or enlarged.
   a. True b. False
13. Pressing the Esc key cancels a command.
   a. True b. False

Complete.

14. Explain what .dwg and .dwt files are.
   .dwg: ____
   .dwt: ____
15. Name the three axes of a Cartesian coordinate system and describe them.
   ____
   ____
   ____
   ____
16. Describe how Save differs from SaveAs when the drawing has been named.
   ____
   ____
17. Using relative coordinates to draw a 3″ square, write the information you type and enter in response to the Command: line prompt "Specify next

point or [Undo]:" after the first point of the square has been clicked. Draw the square to the right and up.

a. ______

b. ______

c. ______

d. ______

18. Using absolute coordinates to draw a 3″ square, write the information that you type and enter in response to the Command: line prompt "Specify next point or [Undo]:" after the first point of the square has been clicked. The first point of the square is at coordinates 4,4. Draw the square to the right and up.

a. ______

b. ______

c. ______

d. ______

19. Using polar coordinates to draw a 3″ square, write the information that you type and enter in response to the Command: line prompt "Specify next point or [Undo]:" after the first point of the square has been clicked. Draw the square to the right and up.

a. ______

b. ______

c. ______

d. ______

20. Write the name of the function key that when pressed helps to draw lines perfectly, horizontally and vertically.

______

21. Write the name of the small squares that appear on an object when it is selected with no command active.

______

22. Name the Zoom command option that displays only the graphics actually drawn on the page.

______

23. Describe what is meant by a transparent command.

______

______

24. What is the inside diameter size of the donut when the Donut command is used to draw a solid circle?

______

25. When plotting from the Model tab, which of the following will produce a plot of the part of the drawing that is displayed on the screen?

a. Display
b. Extents
c. Limits
d. View
e. Window

26. When plotting from the Model tab, which of the following will produce a plot of the entire drawing, even if part of it is outside the limits?

a. All
b. Extents
c. Limits
d. View
e. Window

27. The Shaded viewport options part of the Plot dialog box relates to which of the following?
    a. 3D drawings
    b. Isometric drawings
    c. Hidden linetypes
    d. 2D drawings
    e. Slide files
28. A drawing that is to be plotted using the Model tab so that it fits on a particular size sheet without regard to the scale requires which scale response?
    a. 1:1
    b. Full
    c. 1:2
    d. Fit to Paper
    e. MAX
29. If you want your text to be 1/8″ high when plotted on a drawing that is to be scaled at 1/4″ = 1′-0″, how high is the text while you are drawing full scale?

    ____
30. List the 12 properties listed in the Plot Style Table Editor that can be set.

    __________ __________ __________
    __________ __________ __________
    __________ __________ __________
    __________ __________ __________

exercises

Exercise 2–1: Drawing Shapes I

Draw, full size, the shapes shown in Figure 2–48. Use the dimensions shown. Locate the shapes approximately as shown. Use your workspace to make the following settings:

1. **Use SaveAs... to save the drawing with the name CH2-EX1.**
2. Set drawing Units: **Architectural**
3. Set Drawing Limits: **8-1/2,11**
4. Set GRIDDISPLAY: **0**
5. Set Grid: **1/4″**
6. Set Snap: **1/8″**
7. Create the following layers:

LAYER NAME	COLOR	LINETYPE	LINEWEIGHT
Layer1	blue	continuous	.010″ (.25 mm)

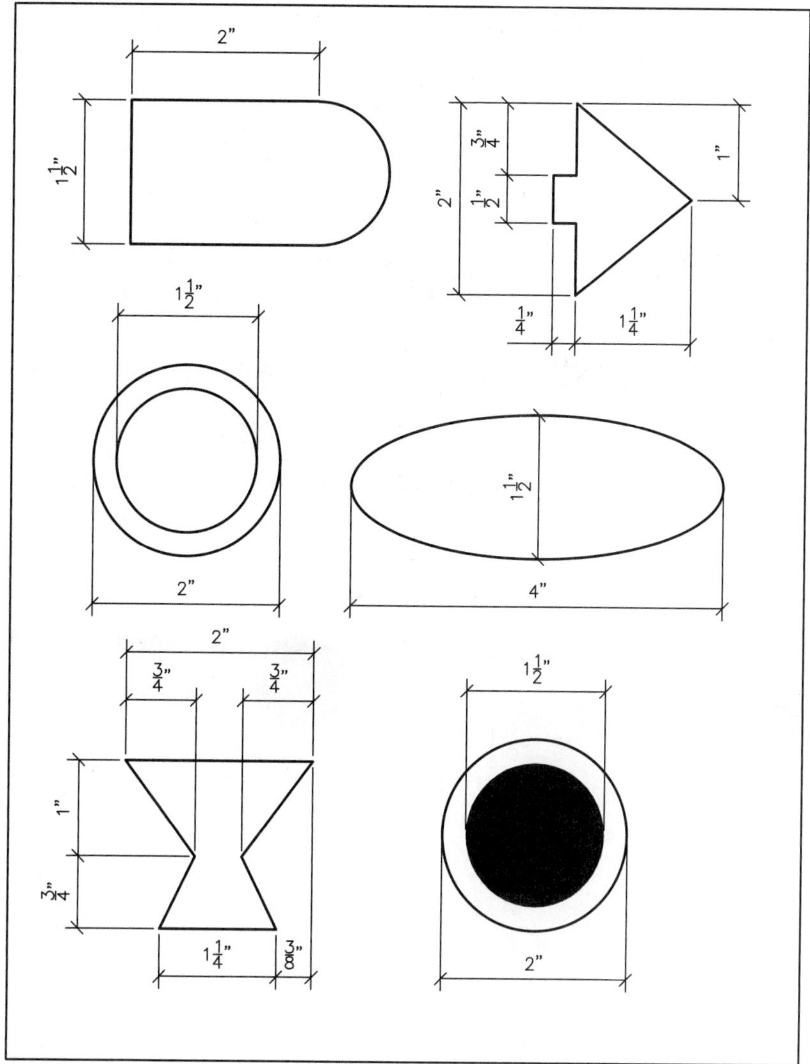

FIGURE 2–48
Exercise 2–1: Drawing Shapes I

Exercise 2–2: Drawing a Pattern

Draw the pattern shown in Figure 2–49. Use an architectural scale to measure the pattern and draw it full scale. Use your workspace to make the following settings:

1. **Use SaveAs... to save the drawing with the name CH2-EX2.**
2. Set drawing Units: **Architectural**
3. Set Drawing Limits: **8-1/2,11**
4. Set GRIDDISPLAY: **0**
5. Set Grid: **1/4″**
6. Set Snap: **1/8″**
7. **Create the layers on your own.**

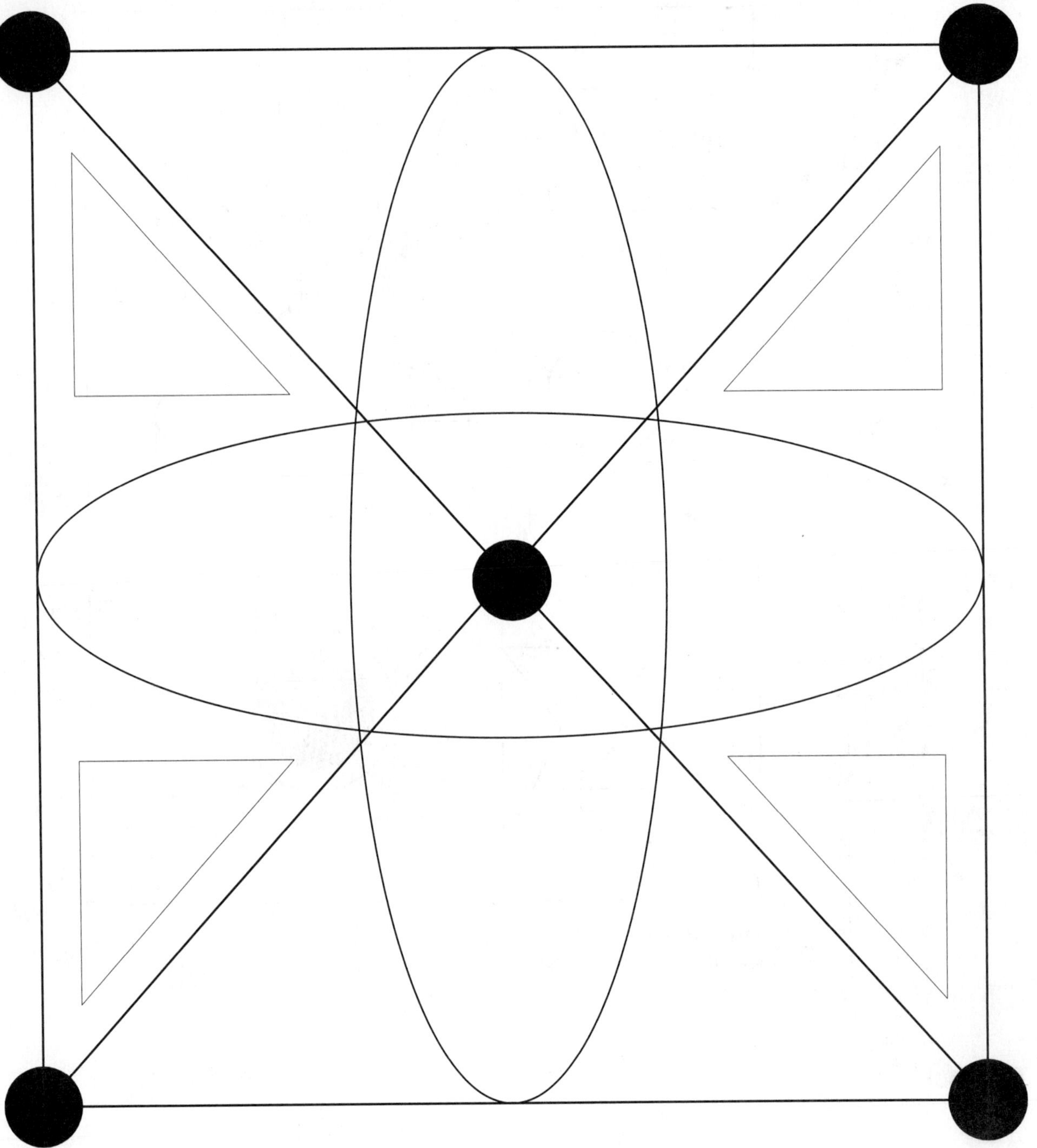

FIGURE 2–49
Exercise 2–2: Drawing a Pattern (Scale: 1″ = 1″)

Exercise 2–3: Drawing Shapes II

Draw the shapes shown in Figure 2–50. Use an architectural scale to measure the shapes and draw them full scale. Your drawing will be the size shown in the figure. Use your workspace to make the following settings:

1. **Use SaveAs... to save the drawing with the name CH2-EX3.**
2. Set drawing Units: **Architectural**
3. Set Drawing Limits: **8-1/2,11**
4. Set GRIDDISPLAY: **0**
5. Set Grid: **1/4″**
6. Set Snap: **1/8″**
7. **Create the layers on your own.**

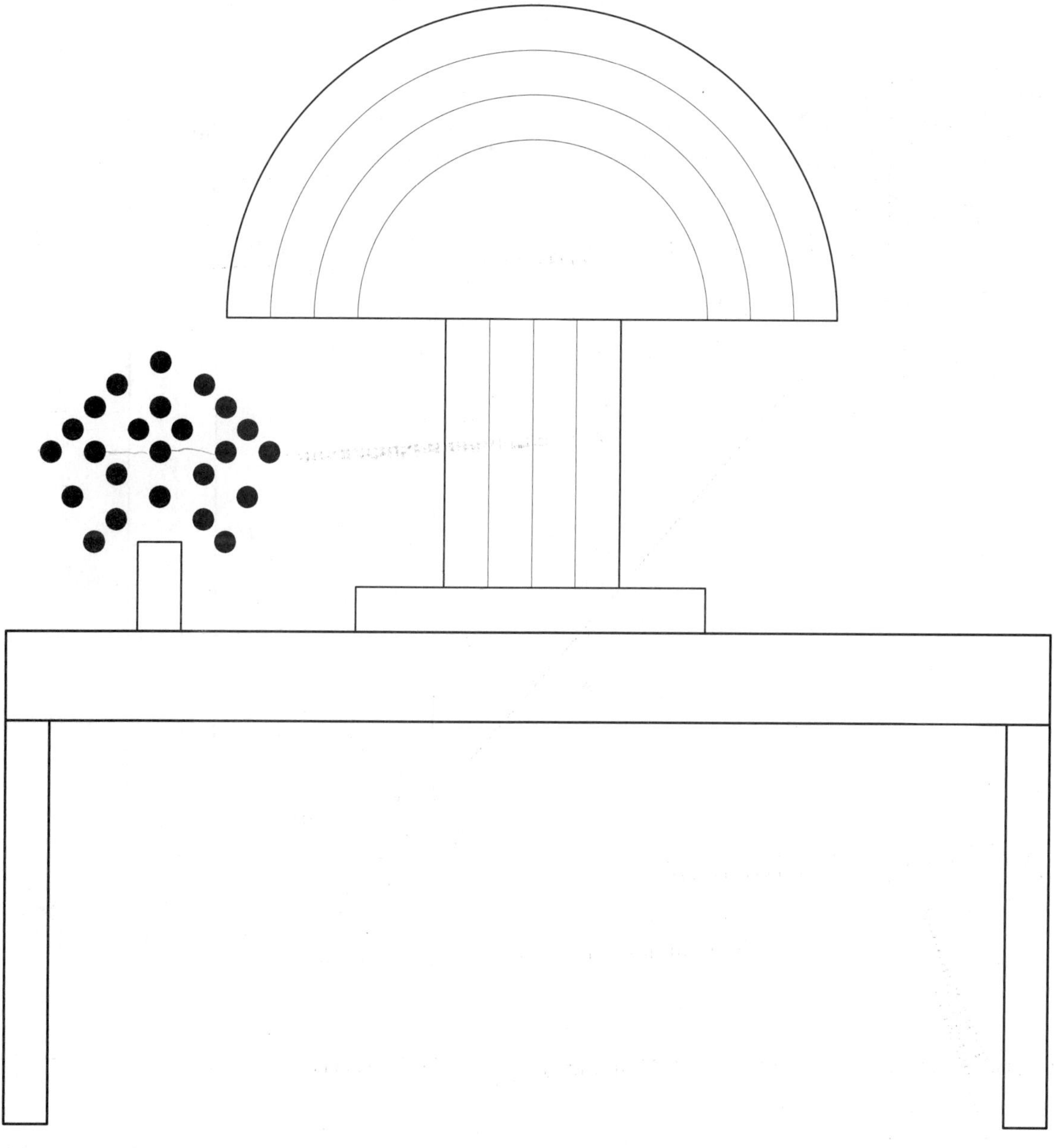

FIGURE 2–50
Exercise 2–3: Drawing Shapes II (Scale: 1″ = 1″)

Exercise 2–4: Drawing a Door

Draw the door shape shown in Figure 2–51. Use an architectural scale to measure the figure and draw it full scale. Use your workspace to make the following settings:

1. **Use SaveAs... to save the drawing with the name CH2-EX4.**
2. Set drawing Units: **Architectural**
3. Set Drawing Limits: **8-1/2,11**
4. Set GRIDDISPLAY: **0**
5. Set Grid: **1/4″**
6. Set Snap: **1/8″**
7. **Create the layers on your own.**

FIGURE 2–51
Exercise 2–4: Drawing a Door
(Scale: 1″ = 1″)

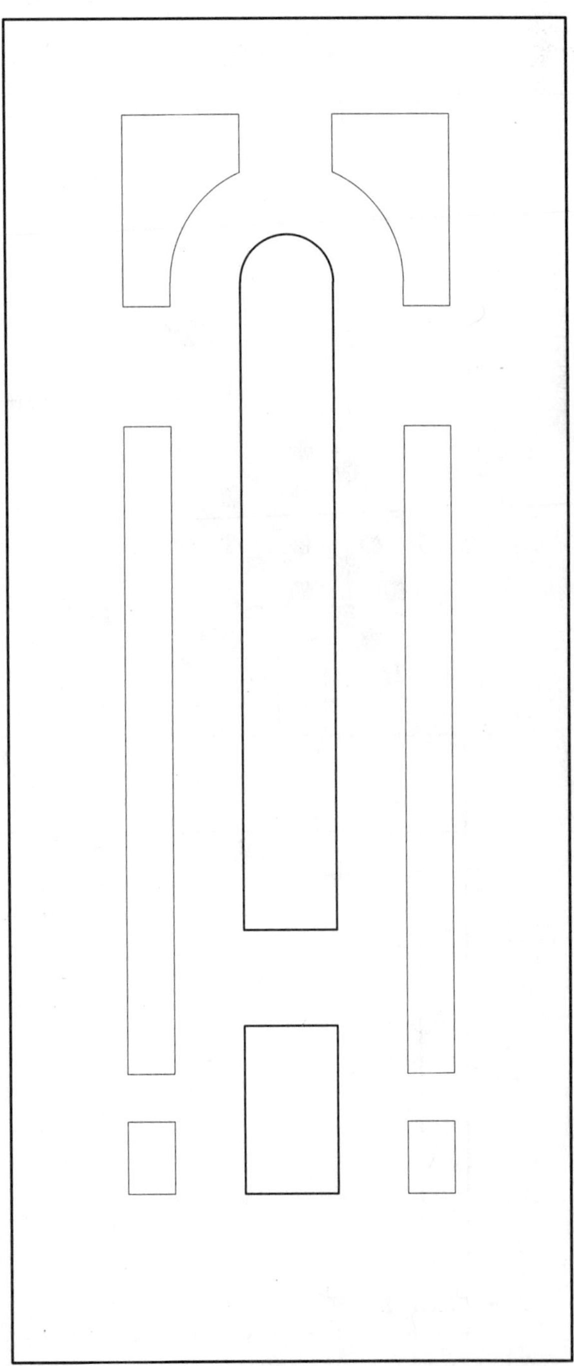

Exercise 2–5: Drawing Shapes III

Draw the shape shown in Figure 2–52. Use an architectural scale to measure the figure and draw it full scale. Use your workspace to make the following settings:

1. **Use SaveAs... to save the drawing with the name CH2-EX5.**
2. Set drawing Units: **Architectural**
3. Set Drawing Limits: **8-1/2,11**
4. Set GRIDDISPLAY: **0**
5. Set Grid: **1/4″**
6. Set Snap: **1/8″**
7. **Create the layers on your own.**

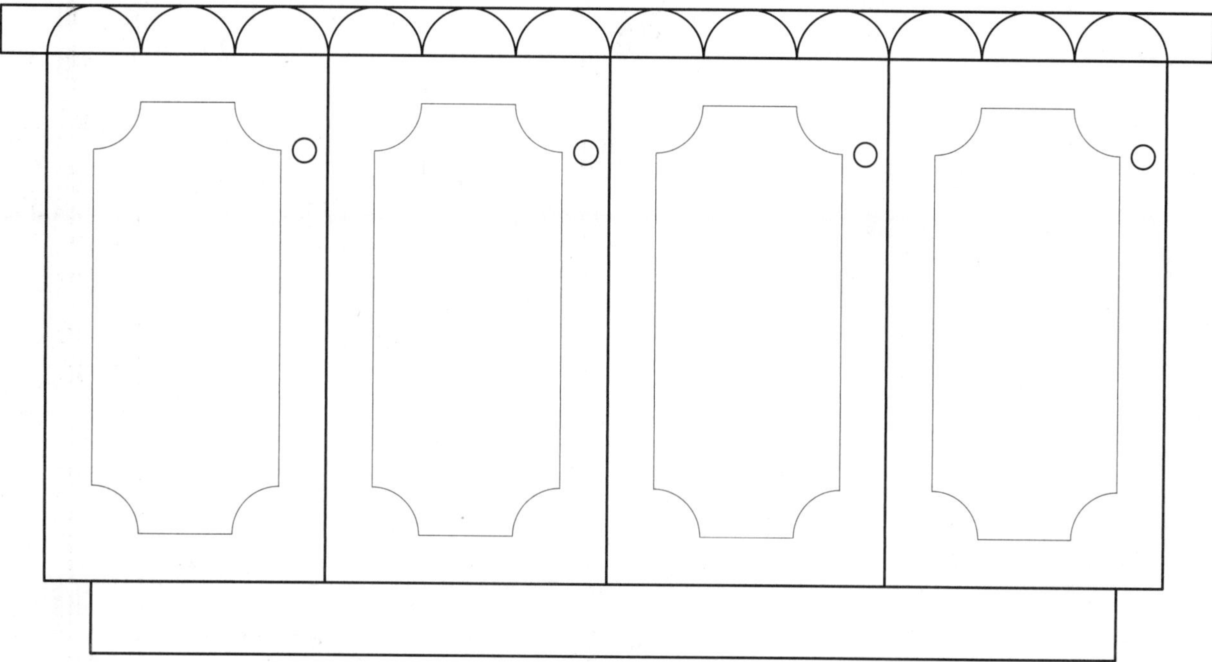

FIGURE 2–52
Exercise 2–5: Drawing Shapes III (Scale: 1″ = 1″)

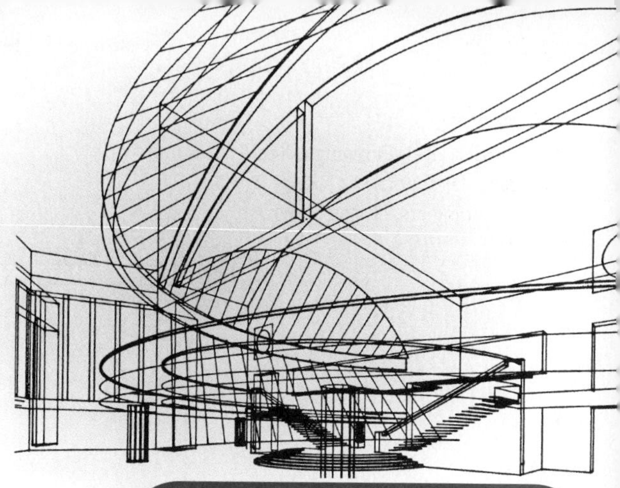

chapter 3

Drawing with AutoCAD: Conference and Lecture Rooms

objectives

When you have completed this chapter, you will be able to:

Correctly use the following commands and settings:

- Arc
- Array
- Break
- Chamfer
- Copy
- Distance
- Divide
- Drawing Template
- Explode
- Fill
- Fillet
- From
- Hatch
- ID Point
- Line
- Measure
- Mirror
- Offset
- Osnap
- Pickbox
- Point
- Polygon
- Polyline
- Polyline Edit
- Rectangle
- Rotate
- Tracking
- Trim

Draw using polar tracking.

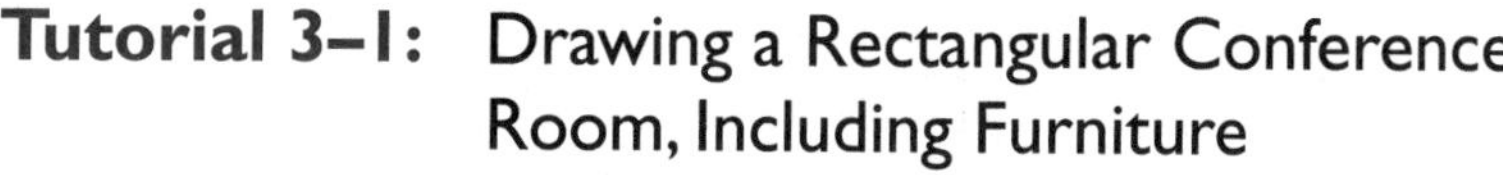

Tutorial 3–1: Drawing a Rectangular Conference Room, Including Furniture

A conference room, including walls and furnishings, is drawn in Tutorial 3–1. When you have completed Tutorial 3–1, your drawing will look similar to Figure 3–1.

FIGURE 3–1
Tutorial 3–1: Drawing a Rectangular Conference Room Including Furniture (Scale: 1/4″ = 1′-0″)

NAME
CLASS
DATE

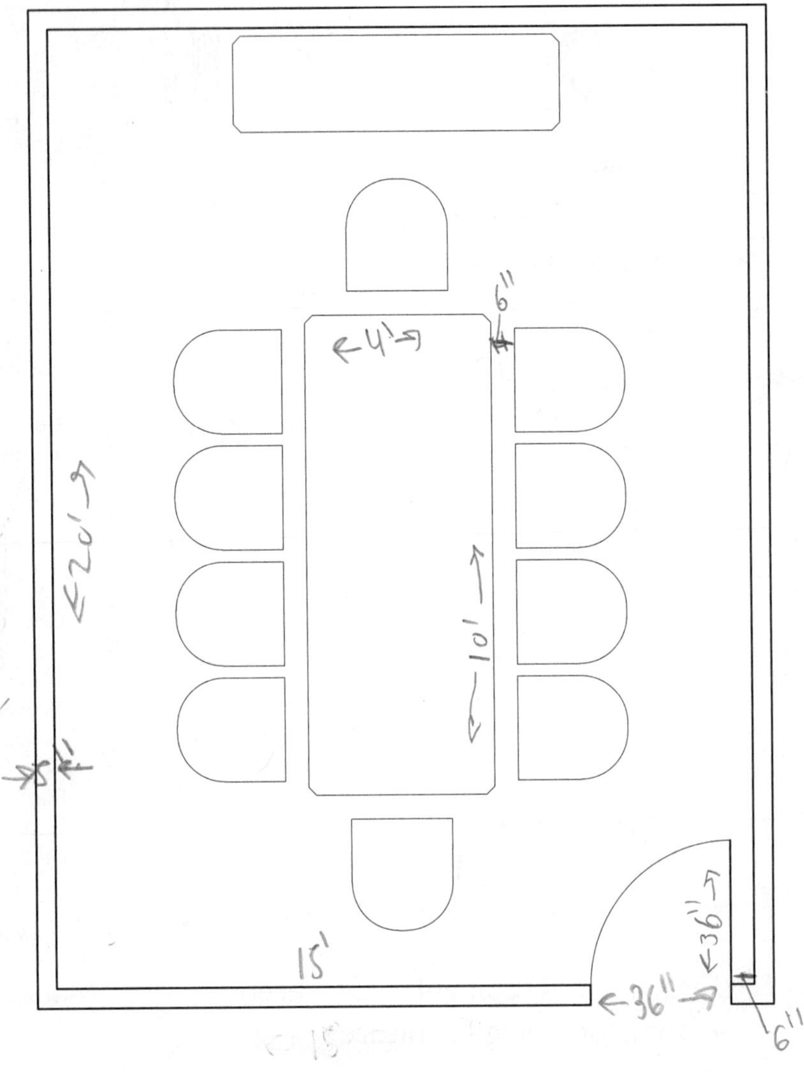

Step 1. **Use your workspace to make the following settings:**

1. **Use SaveAs... to save the drawing with the name CH3-TUTORIAL1.**
2. Set drawing Units: **Architectural**
3. Set Drawing Limits: **25′,35′** (Don't forget the foot mark.)
4. Set GRIDDISPLAY: **0**
5. Set Grid: **12″**
6. Set Snap: **6″**
7. Create the following layers:

LAYER NAME	COLOR	LINETYPE	LINEWEIGHT
a-anno-text	green	continuous	.006″ (.15mm)
a-door-sgl	blue	continuous	.007″ (.18mm)
a-door-swng	red	continuous	.004″ (.09mm)
a-wall-intr	blue	continuous	.007″ (.18mm)
i-furn	cyan	continuous	.004″ (.09mm)

8. Set **Layer a-wall-intr** current.
9. Use **Zoom-All** to view the limits of the drawing.
10. **Turn SNAP, GRID, and LWT ON**. The remaining buttons in the Status Bar are OFF.

DRAWING TEMPLATE

You will be able to use these settings for the remaining tutorials in Chapter 3. Making a template of the settings will save you the time of setting up Tutorials 3–2, 3–3, and 3–4.

Step 2. Save the drawing as a template on the drive and/or folder in which you want to save (Figures 3–2 and 3–3), as described next:

Prompt	Response
Command:	**SaveAs...**
The Save Drawing As dialog box appears:	CLICK: **the down arrow in the Files of type: input box and move the cursor to** CLICK: **AutoCAD Drawing Template [*.dwt]** TYPE: **Ch3-conference-rm-setup** (in the File name: input box so the Save Drawing As dialog box appears as shown in Figure 3–2). Notice the Save in: input box has changed to Template.

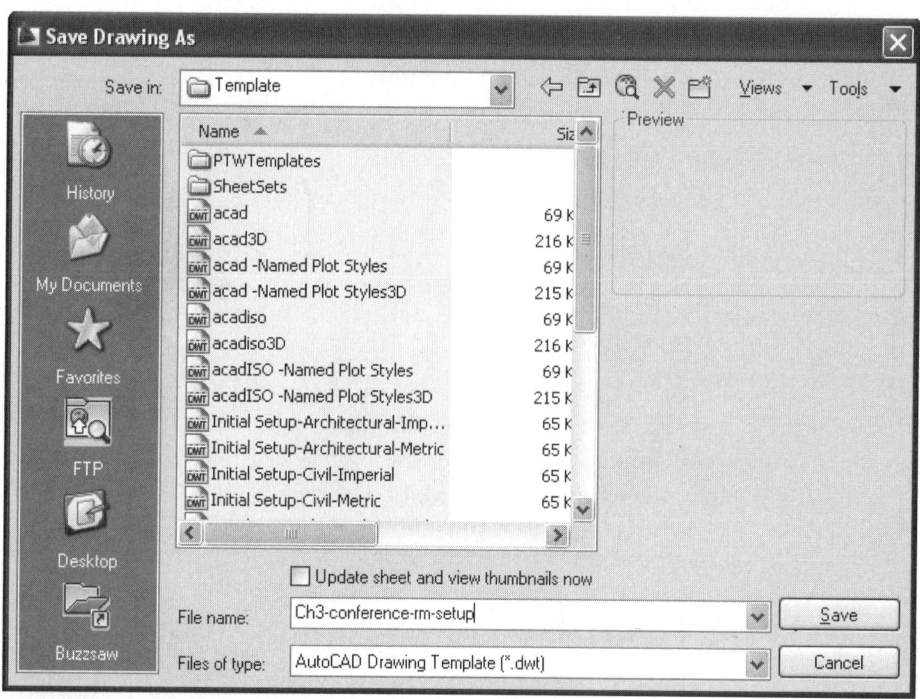

FIGURE 3–2
Save the Drawing as a Template

FIGURE 3–3
Template Options Dialog Box

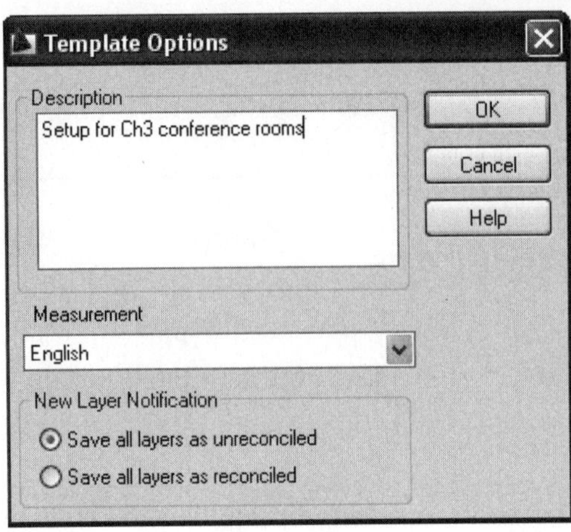

Prompt	Response
	CLICK: **the down arrow in the Save in: input box, highlight the drive and folder in which you want to save.**
	CLICK: **Save**
The Template Options dialog box appears (Figure 3–3):	TYPE: **Setup for Ch3 conference rooms** (as shown in Figure 3–3)
	CLICK: **OK**

Step 3. **The drawing remains as a template in the Template folder, so you must save it again as a drawing file. Save the drawing as a drawing file on the drive and/or folder in which you want to save, as described next:**

Prompt	Response
Command:	**SaveAs...**
The Save Drawing As dialog box appears:	CLICK: **the down arrow in the Files of type: input box and move the cursor to**
	CLICK: **AutoCAD 2010 Drawing [*.dwg]**
	CLICK: **the down arrow in the Save in: input box, highlight the drive and folder in which you want to save.**
	CLICK: **CH3-TUTORIAL1** (to appear in the File name: input box)
	CLICK: **Save**
The Save Drawing As dialog box appears saying the drawing already exists. Do you want to replace it?	CLICK: **Yes**

POLYLINE

Begin by drawing the conference room walls using the Polyline command. Polylines are different from regular lines in that regardless of the number of segments that make up a polyline, AutoCAD treats a polyline drawn with one operation of the Polyline command as a single entity. This is especially helpful when you are drawing walls, because after you draw the outline of a single room or entire building, you can offset the entire polyline to show the thickness of the walls.

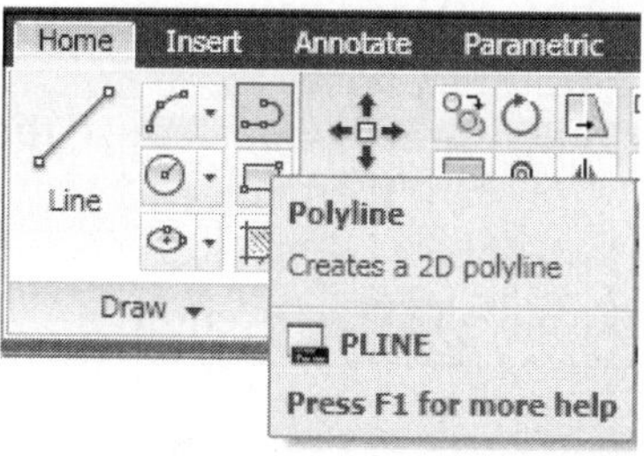

Step 4. Use Polyline to draw the inside lines of the conference room walls (Figure 3–4), as described next:

Prompt	Response
Command:	**Polyline** (or TYPE: **PL<enter>**)
Specify start point:	TYPE: **5′,5′<enter>**
	(You have just entered absolute coordinates; the polyline starts 5′ to the right on the X axis and 5′ up on the Y axis.)
	Set ORTHO ON (PRESS: **F8** or CLICK: **ORTHO**)
Current line-width is 0′-0″.	
Specify next point or [Arc/Halfwidth/Length/Undo/Width]:	**Move your mouse to the right and** TYPE: **15′<enter>** (direct distance entry)

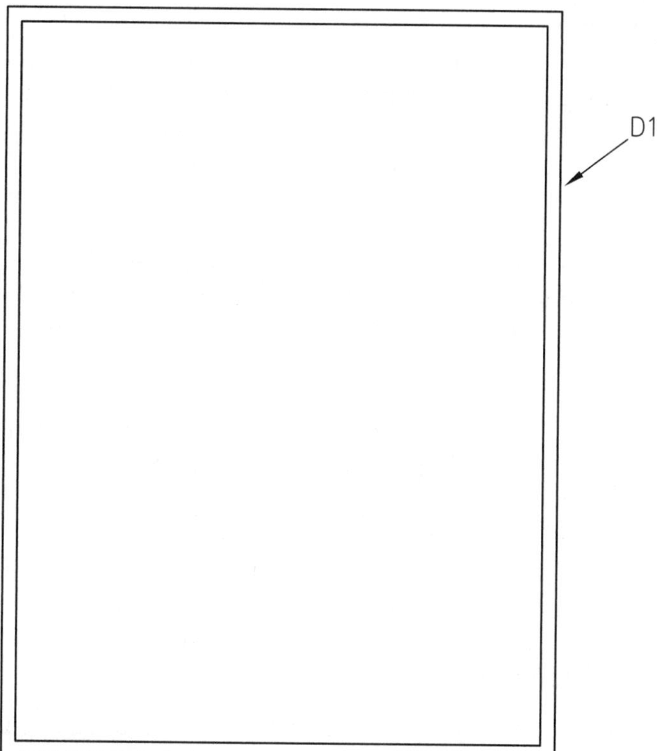

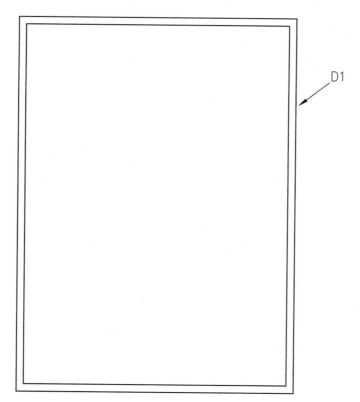

FIGURE 3–4
Draw the Conference Room Walls

Prompt	Response
Specify next point or [Arc/Close/ Halfwidth/Length/Undo/Width]:	**Move your mouse up and** TYPE: **20′<enter>**
Specify next point or [Arc/Close/ Halfwidth/Length/Undo/Width]:	**Move your mouse to the left and** TYPE: **15′<enter>**
Specify next point or [Arc/Close/ Halfwidth/Length/Undo/Width]:	TYPE: **C<enter>**

Undo

The Polyline Undo option is similar to the Line command. If you do not like the last polyline segment drawn, use the Undo option to erase it and continue with the "Specify next point or [Arc/Close/Halfwidth/Length/Undo/Width]:" prompt.

You can enter any of the capitalized options in the Polyline prompt by typing the letters in either upper- or lowercase. The remaining options in the Polyline prompt will be described later in this chapter.

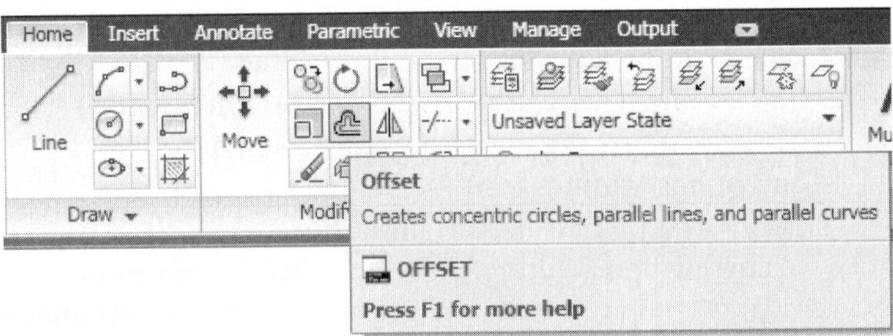

OFFSET

Because the polyline is treated as a single entity, when you click one point on the polyline, you are able to offset the entire outline of the conference room at once. If the outline of the room had been drawn with the Line command, using Offset would offset each line segment individually, and the corners would not meet.

Step 5. **Use Offset to draw the outside line (showing depth) of the conference room walls (Figure 3–4), as described next:**

Prompt	Response
Command:	**Offset** (or TYPE: **O<enter>**)
Specify offset distance or [Through/ Erase/Layer] <Through>:	TYPE: **5<enter>**
Select object to offset or [Exit/Undo] <Exit>:	CLICK: **anyplace on the polyline**
Specify point on side to offset or [Exit/Multiple/Undo] <Exit>:	**D1** (outside of the rectangle, Figure 3–4)
Select object to offset or [Exit/Undo] <Exit>:	**<enter>**

There are four options in the Offset prompt: offset distance, Through, Erase, and Layer. To complete the conference room wall, 5″ was set as the offset distance. To use any of the other options, type and enter the capital letter shown for the option in the command line or press Enter to start the <Through> default option.

Through

When the Through option is started and the object to be offset has been selected, AutoCAD prompts: "Specify through point or [Exit/Multiple/Undo] <Exit>:". You respond by clicking a point on the drawing through which you want the object to be offset.

Erase

When the Erase option is started, AutoCAD prompts: "Erase source object after offsetting? [Yes/No] <No>:". You can then respond with Yes or No, and AutoCAD continues by asking you to specify the offset distance, object to offset, and point on side to offset.

Layer

When the Layer option is started, AutoCAD prompts: "Enter layer option for offset objects [Current/Source] <Source>:" You can then respond with the selection of current or source layer, and AutoCAD continues by asking you to specify the offset distance, object to offset, and point on side to offset.

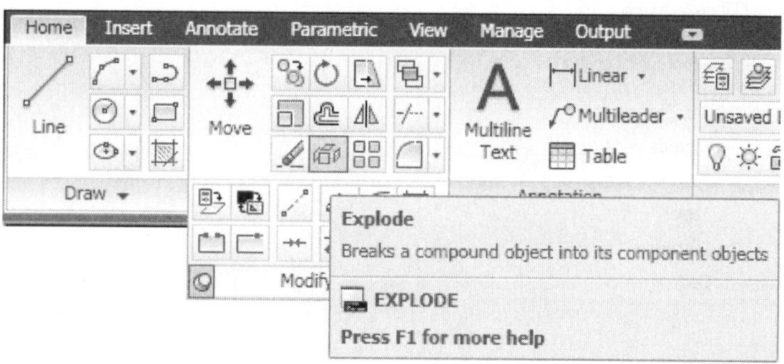

EXPLODE

Because the polyline is treated as a single entity, it must be "exploded" before individual line segments can be edited. The Explode command splits the solid polyline into separate line segments. After the polyline is exploded into separate line segments, you will be able to add the conference room door.

Step 6. **Use Explode to split the two polylines that make the conference room walls, as described next:**

Prompt	Response
Command:	**Explode** (or TYPE: **X<enter>**)
Select objects:	CLICK: **anyplace on the outside polyline**
Select objects:	CLICK: **anyplace on the inside polyline**
Select objects:	**<enter>**

After you use the Explode command, the walls do not look different, but each line segment is now a separate entity.

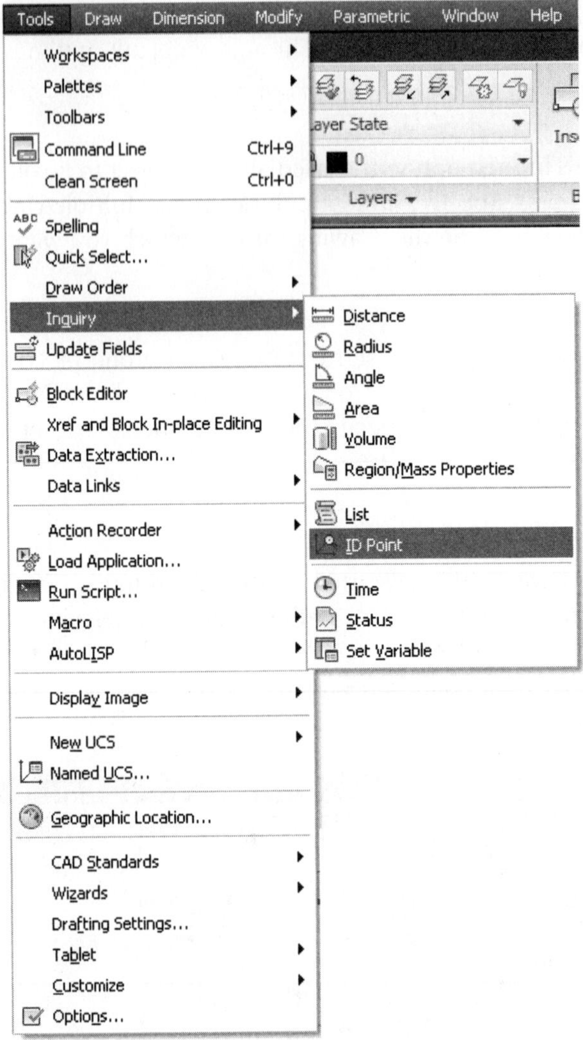

ID POINT

A very useful command, ID Point allows you to locate a point on a drawing and have the position of the point displayed in coordinates. AutoCAD remembers the coordinate location of the point. A command, such as Line, can be initiated *immediately* after the ID Point command has located a point on the drawing. You can enter the start point of the Line command by using relative or polar coordinates, or you may also use direct distance entry, to specify a distance from the established ID Point location.

Step 7. **Use Zoom-Window to magnify the lower right corner of the conference room where the door will be located.**

Step 8. **Use ID Point to locate a point on the drawing. Use Line to draw the right side of the door opening (Figure 3–5), as described next:**

Prompt	Response
Command:	**ID Point** (or TYPE: **ID<enter>**)
Specify point:	**D1** (with SNAP ON, snap to the inside lower right corner of the conference room, Figure 3–5)
Point: X = 20′-0″ Y = 5′-0″ Z = 0′-0″	

FIGURE 3–5
Draw the Door Opening and Door; Draw a Credenza and Conference Table

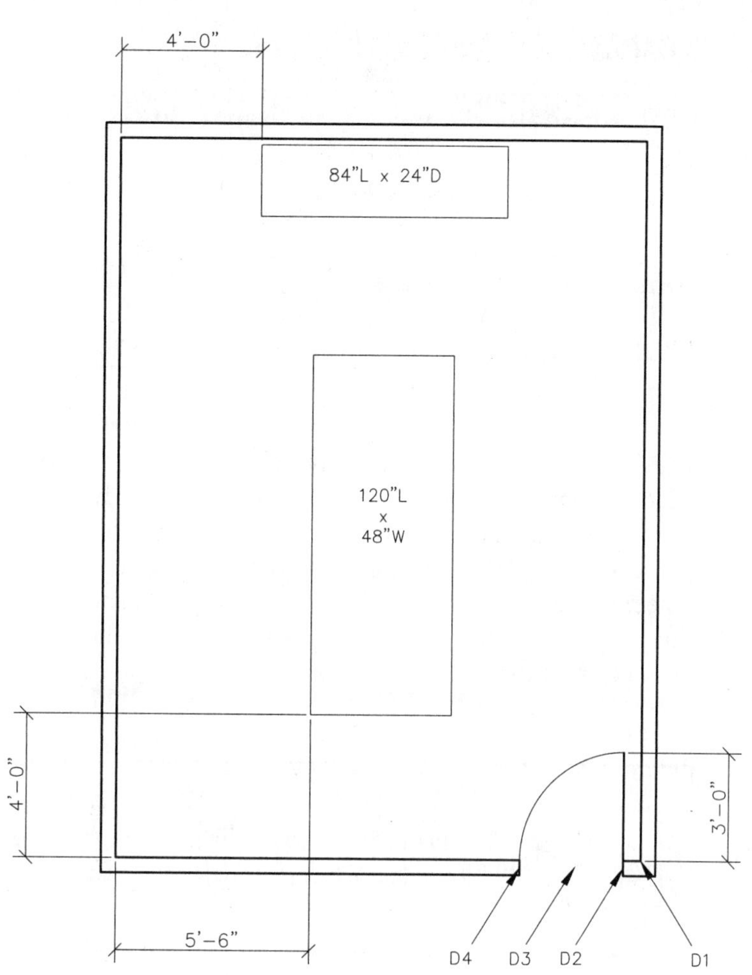

Prompt	Response
Command:	TYPE: **L<enter>**
Specify first point:	TYPE: **@6<180<enter>** (you have just entered polar coordinates; move your mouse so you can see where the line is attached)
Specify next point or [Undo]:	TYPE: **@5<−90<enter>** (using polar coordinates; the line goes down 5″)
Specify next point or [Undo]:	**<enter>**

Step 9. Offset the line 3′ to the left to form the door opening, as described next:

Prompt	Response
Command:	**Offset** (or TYPE: **O<enter>**)
Specify offset distance or [Through/Erase/Layer] <0′-5″>:	TYPE: **3′<enter>**
Select object to offset or [Exit/Undo]<Exit>:	**D2** (the 5″ line you just drew; turn SNAP OFF if necessary; Figure 3–5)
Specify point on side to offset or [Exit/Multiple/Undo]<Exit>:	**D3** (pick to the left)
Select object to offset or [Exit/Undo]<Exit>:	**<enter>**

TRIM

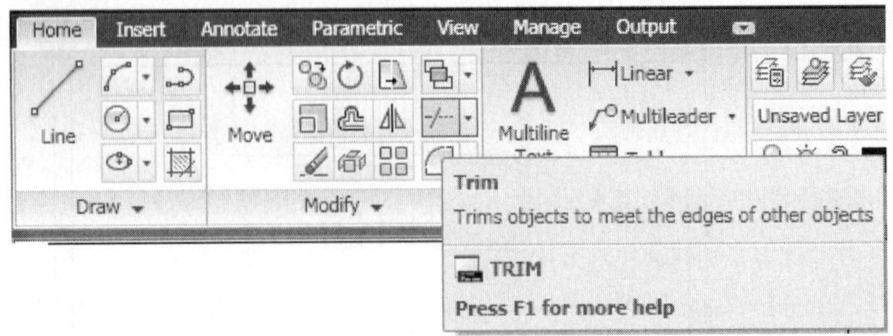

Watch the Trim prompts carefully. You cannot pick the objects to trim until all cutting edges (the edge to which the object is trimmed) have been selected and the Enter key is pressed, so that the prompt "Select object to trim or shift-select to extend or [Fence/Crossing/Project/Edge/eRase/Undo]:" appears. If you are unable to trim an object because it does not intersect a cutting edge, and you have selected **all** as the cutting edges, hold the Shift key down and click on the entity to extend while still in the Trim command.

NOTE: Press Enter to the Trim prompt "Select objects or <select all>:" to select all objects as cutting edges.

Step 10. Use Trim to trim the horizontal wall lines between the two 5′ vertical lines that represent the door opening (Figure 3–5), as described next:

Prompt	Response
Command:	**Trim** (or TYPE: **TR<enter>**)
Current settings: Projection = UCS Edge = None	
Select cutting edges	
Select objects or <select all>:	**D2** (the 5″ vertical line, Figure 3–5)
Select objects: 1 found	
Select objects:	**D4** (the second 5″ vertical line)
Select objects: 1 found, 2 total	
Select objects:	**<enter>**
Select object to trim or shift-select to extend or [Fence/Crossing/Project/Edge/eRase/Undo]:	**Click the two horizontal wall lines between D2 and D4** (Figure 3–5). **<enter>** (to complete the command; if you turned SNAP OFF to pick the lines, be sure to turn it back ON)

Step 11. Set Layer a-door-sgl current.

Step 12. Use the Line command to draw a 3′ vertical door line. Snap (be sure SNAP is ON) to the upper right corner of the door opening to begin the door line. Draw the line using polar coordinates or direct distance entry (Figure 3–5).

Step 13. Set Layer a-door-swng current.

Step 14. Use the Arc-Start, Center, End method to draw the door swing arc, counterclockwise. Note that the start of the arc is the top of the door line, the center is the bottom of the door line, and the end is the upper left corner of the door opening (Figure 3–5).

Step 15. Set Layer i-furn current. Use Zoom-Extents.

Step 16. Use the Polyline command to draw a credenza (84″ long by 24″ deep) centered on the 15′ rear wall of the conference room, 2″ away from the wall. Locate an ID point by snapping to the inside upper left corner of the conference room. Start the Polyline @48,−2 (relative coordinates) away from the point. Finish drawing the credenza by using direct distance entry. You can use feet or inches. Remember, AutoCAD defaults to inches in Architectural Units, so use the foot (′) symbol if you are using feet. Be sure to draw the credenza using one operation of Polyline so it is one continuous polyline. *Use the Close option for the last segment of the polyline* (Figure 3–5).

Step 17. Draw a conference table 120″ long by 48″ wide using the Line command. You can determine the location of the first point by using ID Point or by using grid and snap increments. Use direct distance entry to complete the table. Refer to Figure 3–5 for the location of the table in the room.

Step 18. Use Zoom-Window to zoom in on the table.

CHAMFER

A chamfer is an angle (usually 45°) formed at a corner. The following will use the Chamfer command to make the beveled corners of the conference table and credenza.

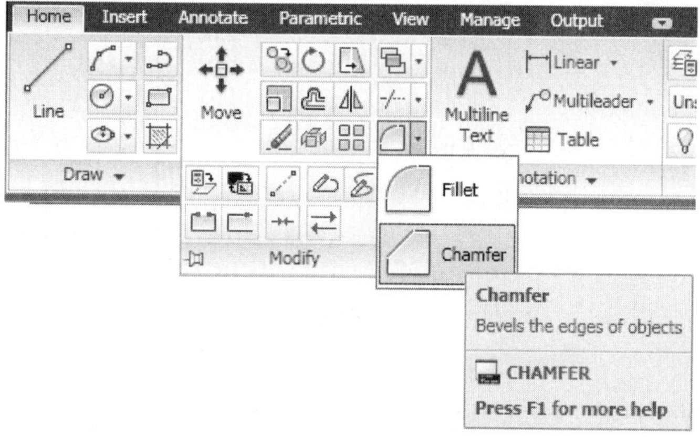

Step 19. **Use Chamfer to bevel the corners of the table (Figure 3–6), as described next:**

Prompt	Response
Command:	**Chamfer** (or TYPE: **CHA<enter>**)
(TRIM mode) Current chamfer Dist1 = 0′-0″ Dist2 = 0′-0″	
Select first line or [Undo/Polyline/ Distance/Angle/Trim/mEthod/ Multiple]:	TYPE: **D<enter>**
Specify first chamfer distance <0′-0″>:	TYPE: **2<enter>**
Specify second chamfer distance <0′-2″>:	**<enter>**
Select first line or [Undo/Polyline/ Distance/Angle/Trim/mEthod/ Multiple]:	**D1** (Figure 3–6)
Select second line:	**D2**
Command:	**<enter>** (repeat CHAMFER)
(TRIM mode) Current chamfer Dist1 = 0′-2″, Dist2 = 0′-2″	
Select first line or [Undo/Polyline/ Distance/Angle/Trim/mEthod/ Multiple]:	**D2**
Select second line:	**D3**

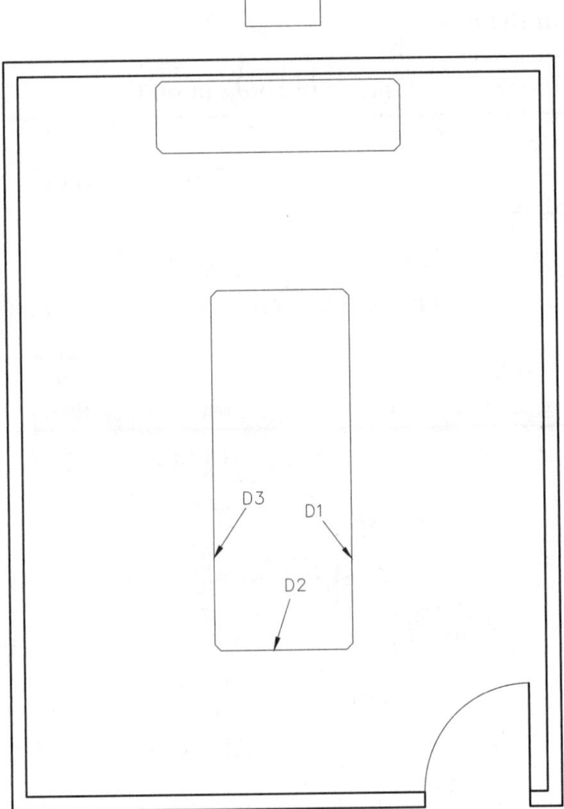

FIGURE 3–6
Chamfer the Corners of the Table and Credenza; Draw a Rectangular Shape

TIP: TYPE: **M<enter>** (for Multiple) at the Chamfer prompt so you do not have to repeat the Chamfer command.

Step 20. **Chamfer the other corners of the table (Figure 3–6).**

Step 21. **Use Zoom-Window to zoom in on the credenza.**

Polyline

Because the credenza was drawn using one operation of the Polyline command, and the Close option was used to complete the credenza rectangle, it is treated as a single entity. The Chamfer command Polyline option chamfers all corners of a continuous polyline with one click.

Undo

Allows you to undo the previous chamfer.

Angle

This option of the Chamfer command allows you to specify an angle and a distance to create a chamfer.

Trim

This option of both the Chamfer and Fillet commands allows you to specify that the part of the original line removed by the chamfer or fillet remains as it was. To do this, TYPE: **T<enter>** at the Chamfer prompt and **N<enter>** at the Trim/No trim <Trim>: prompt. Test this option on a corner of the drawing so you know how it works. Be sure to return it to the Trim option.

mEthod

The mEthod option of the Chamfer command allows you to specify whether you want to use the Distance or the Angle method to specify how the chamfer is to be drawn. The default is the Distance method.

Multiple

Allows you to chamfer multiple corners without repeating the Chamfer command.

Step 22. **Use Chamfer distance 2″ to bevel the corners of the credenza (Figure 3–6), as described next:**

Prompt	Response
Command:	**Chamfer**
(TRIM mode) Current chamfer Dist1 = 0′-2″, Dist2 = 0′-2″	
Select first line or [Undo/Polyline/ Distance/Angle/Trim/mEthod/ Multiple]:	TYPE: **P<enter>** (accept 2″ distances as previously set)
Select 2D polyline:	CLICK: **anyplace on the credenza**
4 lines were chamfered	

NOTE: **If the last corner of the credenza does not chamfer, this is because the Close option of the Polyline command was not used to complete the polyline rectangle. Explode the credenza and use the Chamfer command to complete the chamfered corner.**

When setting the chamfer distance, you can set a different distance for the first and second chamfers. The first distance applies to the first line clicked, and the second distance applies to the second line clicked. You can also set the distance by clicking two points on the drawing.

You can set a chamfer distance of zero and use it to remove the chamfered corners from the table. Using a distance of zero will make 90° corners on the table. Then you can erase the old chamfer lines. This will change the table but not the credenza because it does not work with a polyline. If you have two lines that do not meet to form an exact corner or that overlap, use the Chamfer command with 0 distance to form an exact corner. The Chamfer command will chamfer two lines that do not intersect. It automatically extends the two lines until they intersect, trims the two lines according to the distance entered, and connects the two trimmed ends with the chamfer line.

NOTE: Save your drawing often so you do not lose your work.

Step 23. **Zoom in on a portion of the grid outside the conference room walls.**

Step 24. **Draw a rectangle 26″ wide by 28″ deep using the Line command (Figure 3–6). Be sure to have SNAP ON when you draw the rectangle. Next, you will edit this rectangle using the Fillet command to create the shape of a chair.**

NOTE: Remember to turn Snap OFF and ON as needed. Turn Snap OFF when it interferes with selecting an entity. Turn it back ON as needed.

FILLET

The Fillet command is similar to Chamfer, except the Fillet command creates a round instead of an angle.

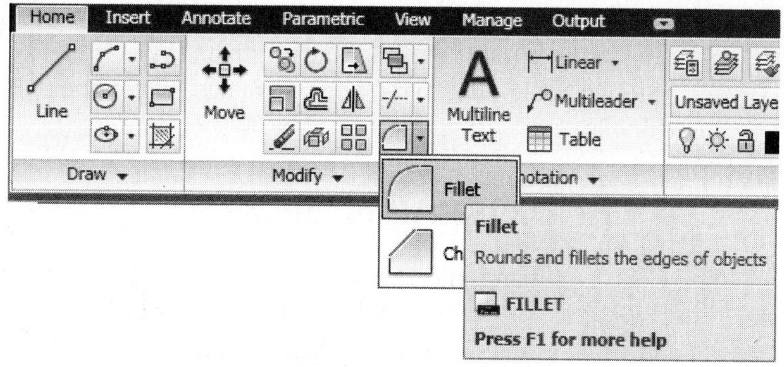

Step 25. Use Fillet to edit the back of the rectangle to create the symbol of a chair (Figure 3–7), as described next:

Prompt	Response
Command:	**Fillet** (or TYPE: **F<enter>**)
Current settings: Mode = TRIM, Radius = 0′-0″	
Select first object or [Undo/ Polyline/Radius/Trim/Multiple]:	TYPE: **R<enter>**
Specify fillet radius <0′-0″>:	TYPE: **12<enter>**
Select first object or [Undo/ Polyline/Radius/Trim/Multiple]:	TYPE: **T<enter>**
Enter Trim mode option [Trim/No trim]<Trim>:	TYPE: **T<enter>** (verify Trim option)
Select first object or [Undo/ Polyline/Radius/Trim/Multiple]:	**D1** (Figure 3–7)
Select second object:	**D2**
Command:	**<enter>** (repeat Fillet)
Current settings: Mode = TRIM, Radius = 1′-0″	
Select first object or [Undo/ Polyline/Radius/Trim/Multiple]:	**D3**
Select second object:	**D4**

FIGURE 3–7
Use Fillet to Create the Chair Symbol

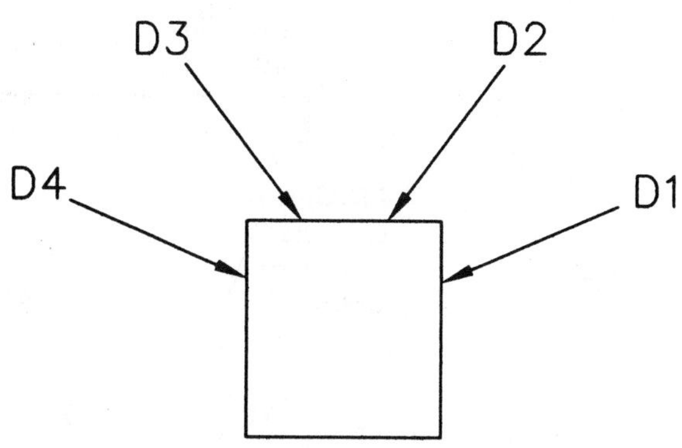

The Polyline option of Fillet automatically fillets an entire continuous polyline with one click. Remember to set the fillet radius first.

Fillet will also fillet two circles, two arcs, a line and a circle, a line and an arc, or a circle and an arc.

COPY AND OSNAP-MIDPOINT

The Copy command allows you to copy any part of a drawing either once or multiple times. Object Snap modes, when combined with other commands help you to draw very accurately. As you become more familiar with the Object Snap modes, you will use them constantly to draw with extreme accuracy. The following introduces the Osnap-Midpoint mode, which helps you to snap to the midpoint of a line or arc.

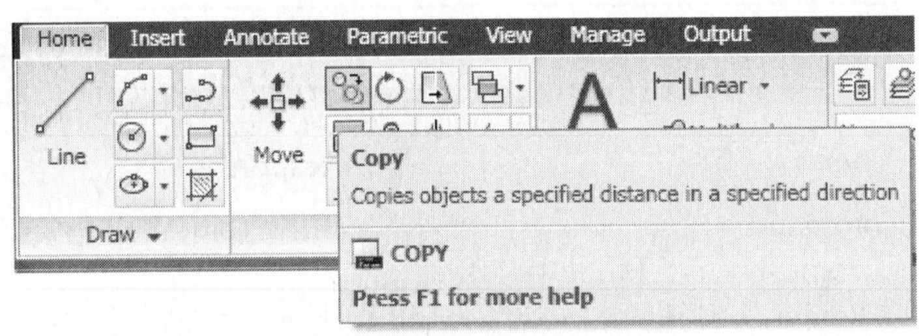

Step 26. Use the Copy command, combined with Osnap-Midpoint, to copy the chair you have just drawn three times (Figure 3–8), as described next:

Prompt	Response
Command:	**Copy** (or TYPE: **CP<enter>**)
Select objects:	CLICK: **the first corner of a window that will include the chair**
Specify opposite corner:	CLICK: **the other corner of the window to include the chair**
Select objects:	**<enter>**
Specify base point or [Displacement/ mOde]<Displacement>:	TYPE: **MID<enter>**
Mid of	**D1** (Figure 3–8)
Specify second point or <use first point as displacement>:	**D2,D3,D4** (be sure SNAP is ON, and leave enough room to rotate the chairs, Figure 3–9)
Specify second point of displacement or [Exit/Undo] <Exit>:	**<enter>**

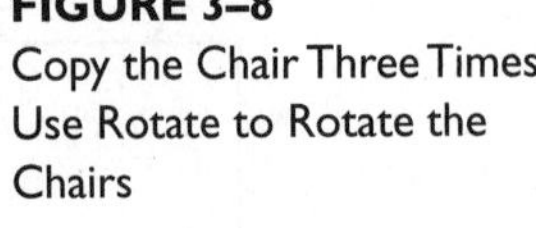

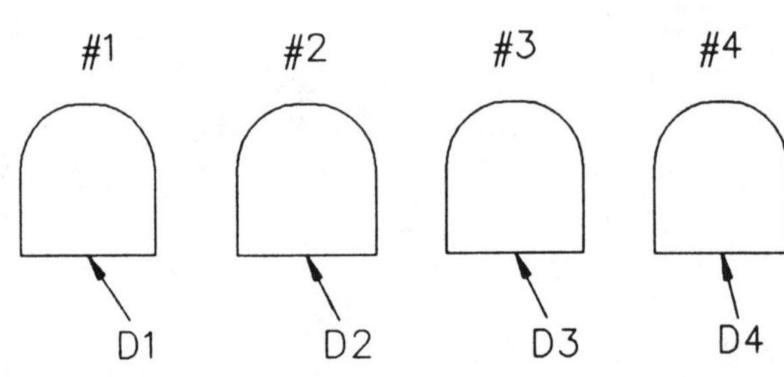

FIGURE 3–8
Copy the Chair Three Times; Use Rotate to Rotate the Chairs

The Osnap-Midpoint mode helped you snap very accurately to the midpoint of the line; you used the midpoint of the line that defines the front of the chair as the base point. When using the Copy command, carefully choose the base point so that it helps you easily locate the copies.

ROTATE

The Rotate command rotates a selected drawing entity in the counterclockwise direction; 90° is to the left, and 270° (or −90°) is to the right. You select a base point of the entity to be rotated, and the entity rotates about that base point.

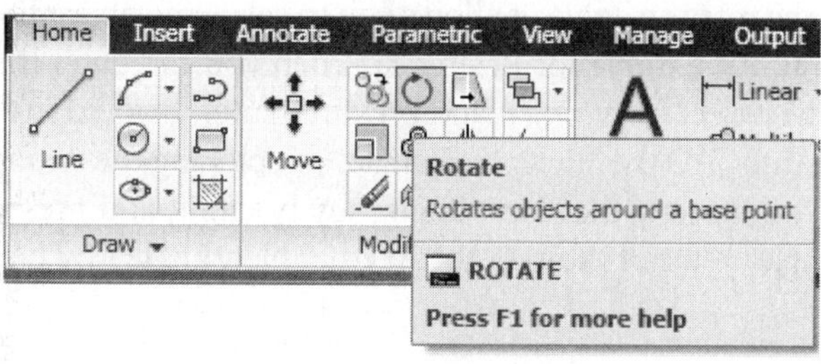

Step 27. Use the Rotate command to rotate chairs 2 and 3 (Figure 3–9), as described next:

Prompt	Response
Command:	**Rotate** (or TYPE: **RO<enter>**)
Select objects:	**Start the window to include chair 2**
Specify opposite corner:	**Complete the window to include chair 2**
Select objects:	**<enter>**
Specify base point:	TYPE: **MID<enter>**
Mid of	**D2** (Figure 3–8)
Specify rotation angle or [Copy/Reference]:	TYPE: **90<enter>**
Command:	**<enter>** (Repeat ROTATE)
Select objects:	**Window chair 3**
Select objects:	**<enter>**
Specify base point:	TYPE: **MID<enter>**
mid of	**D3** (Figure 3–8)
Specify rotation angle or [Copy/Reference]:	TYPE: **180<enter>**

#1 #2 #3 #4

90 DEGREES 180 DEGREES −90 DEGREES

FIGURE 3–9
Rotated Chairs

NOTE: If part of the entity that is to be rotated lies on the specified base point, that part of the entity remains on the base point while the entity's orientation is changed.

Step 28. Rotate chair 4 using a 270° (or −90°) rotation angle (Figure 3–9).

Reference

The Reference option of the Rotate prompt is sometimes easier to use, especially if you do not know the rotation angle. It allows you to select the object to be rotated and click the base point. TYPE: **R<enter>** for Reference. Then you can enter the "Reference angle:" (current angle) of the object by typing it and pressing Enter. If you don't know the current angle, you can show AutoCAD the "Reference angle:" by picking the two endpoints of the line to be rotated. You can specify the "New angle:" by typing it and pressing Enter. If you don't know the new angle, you can show AutoCAD the "New angle:" by picking a point on the drawing.

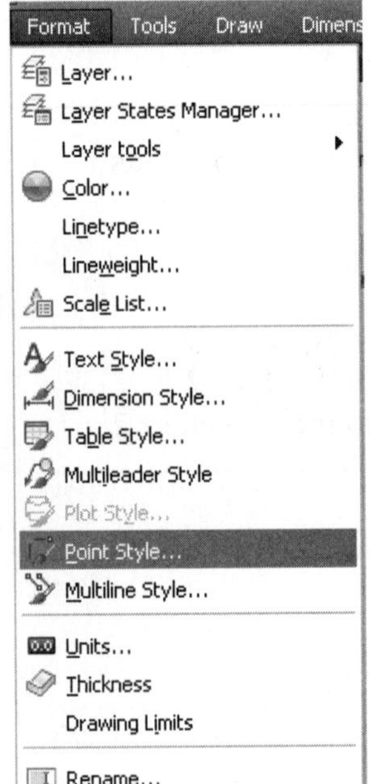

POINT

The Point command allows you to draw points on your drawing. Object Snap recognizes these points as nodes. The Osnap mode Node is used to snap to points.

There are many different types of points to choose from. The appearance of these points is determined by the Pdmode (point definition mode) and Pdsize (point definition size) options within the Point command.

Step 29. Use the Point Style... command to set the appearance of points, as described next:

Prompt	Response
Command:	**Point Style...** (or TYPE: **DDPTYPE<enter>**)
The Point Style dialog box appears (Figure 3–10):	CLICK: **the X box** CLICK: **Set Size in Absolute Units** TYPE: **6″ in the Point Size: input box** CLICK: **OK**

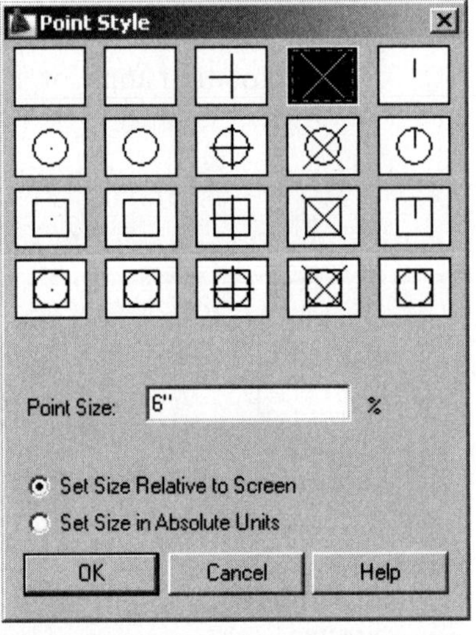

FIGURE 3–10
Point Style Dialog Box

You have just set the points to appear as an X, and they will be 6″ high. The Point Style dialog box shows the different types of points available. The size of the point may be set in a size relative to the screen or in absolute units.

Step 30. Use the Offset command to offset the two lines that define the long sides of the conference table. The chairs will be placed 6″ from the edge of the table, so set 6″ as the offset distance. Offset the lines on each side, outside the table, as shown in Figure 3–11. These lines will be used as construction lines to help locate the chairs.

FIGURE 3–11
Offset the Two Lines Defining the Long Sides of the Conference Table; Divide the Lines into Eight Equal Segments; Copy Chair 4

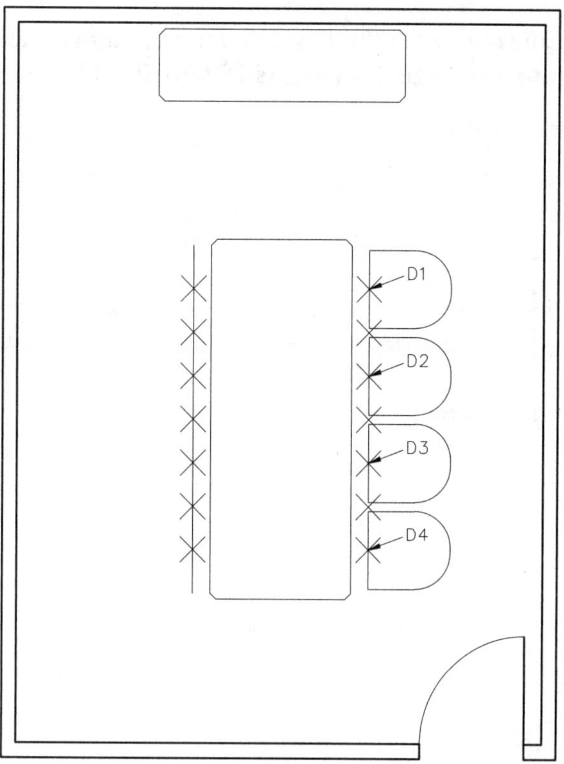

DIVIDE

The Divide command divides an entity into equal parts and places point markers along the entity at the dividing points. The Pdmode has been set to 3 (an X point), so an X will appear as the point marker when you use Divide.

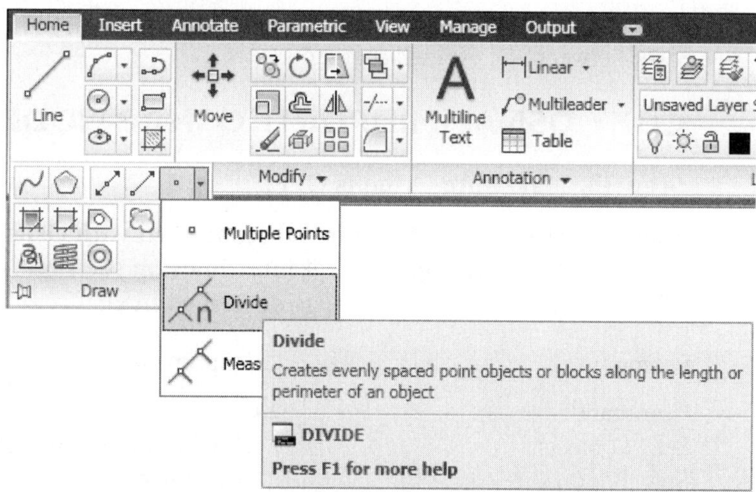

Step 31. Use Divide to divide the offset lines into eight equal segments (Figure 3–11), as described next:

Prompt	Response
Command:	**Divide** (or TYPE: **DIV<enter>**)
Select object to divide:	CLICK: **anyplace on one of the offset lines**
Enter the number of segments or [Block]:	TYPE: **8<enter>** (the X points divide the line into eight equal segments)

Step 32. Continue with the Divide command and divide the other offset line into eight equal segments (Figure 3–11).

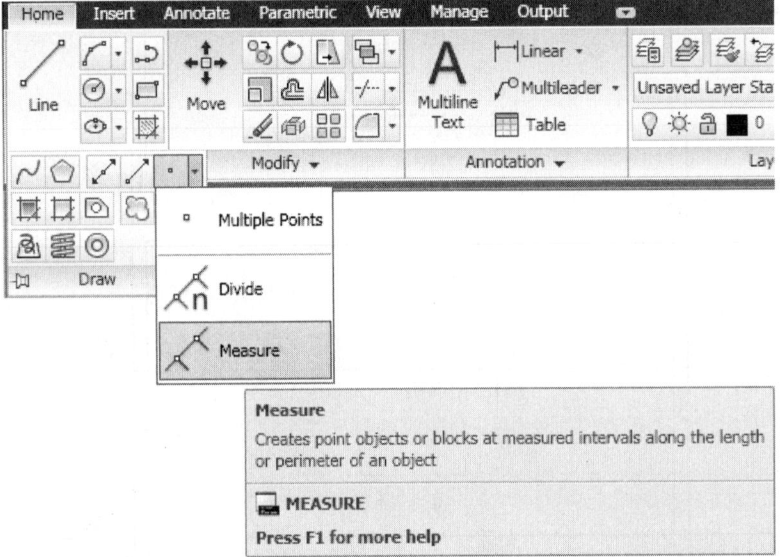

MEASURE

The Measure command is similar to the Divide command, except that with Measure you specify the distance. Divide calculates the interval to divide an entity into a specified number of equal segments. The Measure command places point markers at a specified distance along an entity.

The measurement and division of a circle start at the angle from the center that follows the current Snap rotation. The measurement and division of a closed polyline start at the first vertex drawn. The Measure command also draws a specified block at each mark between the divided segments.

COPY, OSNAP-MIDPOINT, OSNAP-NODE

Step 33. Make sure Ortho is OFF.

Step 34. Use the Copy command (combined with Osnap-Midpoint and Osnap-Node) to copy chair 4 four times on the right side of the conference table (Figure 3–11), as described next:

Prompt	Response
Command:	**Copy** (or TYPE: **CP<enter>**)
Select objects:	CLICK: **below and to the left of chair 4**
Specify opposite corner:	**Window chair 4**

Prompt	Response
Select objects:	**<enter>**
Specify base point or [Displacement/ mOde] <Displacement>:	TYPE: **MID<enter>**
_mid of	CLICK: **anyplace on the straight line that forms the front of the chair symbol**
Specify second point or <use first point as displacement>:	TYPE: **NOD<enter>**
of	**D1** (Figure 3–11)
Specify second point or [Exit/Undo] <Exit>:	TYPE: **NOD<enter>**
of	**D2**
Specify second point or [Exit/Undo] <Exit>:	TYPE: **NOD<enter>**
of	**D3**
Specify second point or [Exit/Undo] <Exit>:	TYPE: **NOD<enter>**
of	**D4**
Specify second point or [Exit/Undo] <Exit>:	**<enter>**

The points act as nodes (snapping exactly on the center of the X) for Object Snap purposes.

Step 35. Continue with the Copy, Osnap-Midpoint, and Osnap-Node commands, and place four chairs on the left side of the table (Figure 3–12).

FIGURE 3–12
Complete Tutorial 3–1

NAME
CLASS
DATE

Step 36. Use the Copy command to place a chair at each end of the conference table. Because you will be copying each chair only once, go immediately to Osnap-Midpoint to specify the base point. Use the grid and snap to determine the "Second point of displacement:" for each chair (Figure 3–12).

Step 37. TYPE: **PDMODE<enter>** at the Command: prompt. Set the Pdmode to 1, and the drawing is regenerated. The Xs will disappear. You have set the Pdmode to be invisible.

Step 38. Erase the offset lines used to locate the chairs on each long side of the table. Use F7 to redraw when it looks like part of the chairs have been erased.

Step 39. Erase the chairs you have drawn outside the conference room walls; Tutorial 3–1 is complete.

Step 40. Set Layer a-anno-text current.

Step 41. Use the Single Line Text command (TYPE: **DT<enter>**) to type your name, class number, and date, 6″ H. in the upper right corner. When plotted to a scale of 1/4″ = 1′-0″, the 6″ H. text will be 1/8″ H.

Step 42. When you have completed Tutorial 3–1, save your work in at least two places.

Step 43. Print your drawing from the Model tab at a scale of 1/4″ = 1′-0″.

In Chapter 5 you will learn about using a color dependent plot style to change layer colors 1 through 7 to the color black when printing and plotting.

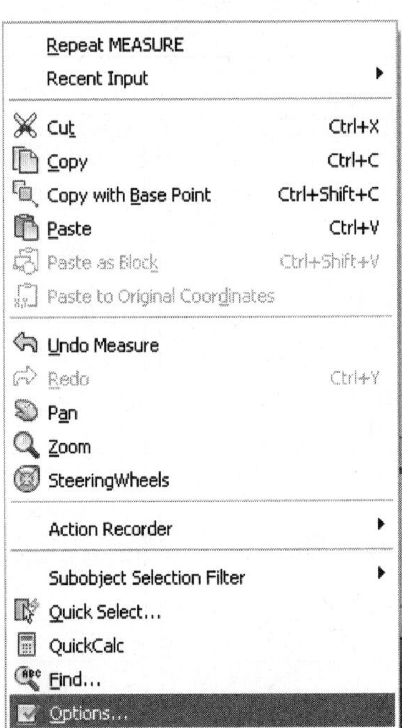

PICKBOX SIZE

The Pickbox Size slider bar on the Selection tab under Options... on the right-click menu (Figure 3–13) can be used to change the size of the target box, the small box that rides on the screen crosshair and appears when the Modify commands are used.

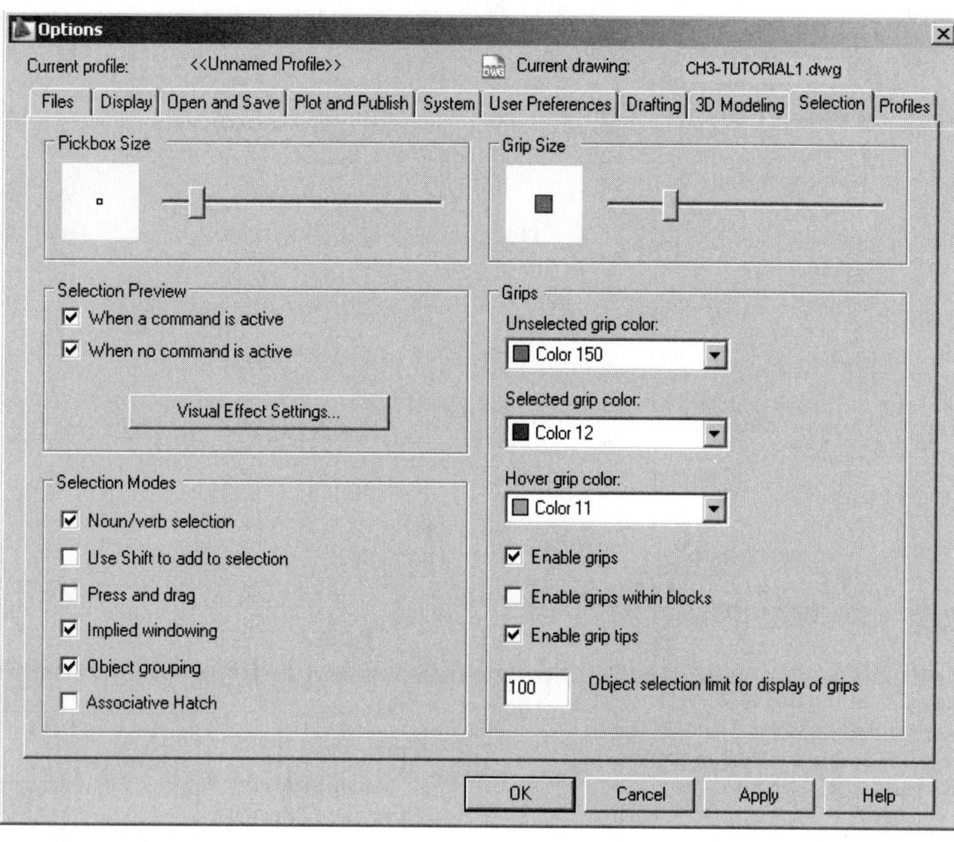

FIGURE 3–13
Options Dialog Box, Selection Tab, Pickbox Size Slider Bar

OSNAP

It is important that you become familiar with and use Object Snap modes in combination with Draw, Modify, and other AutoCAD commands. When an existing drawing object is not located on a snap point, it is impossible to connect a line or other drawing entity exactly to it. You may try, and you may think that the two points are connected, but a close examination (Zoom-Window) will reveal that they are not. Object Snap modes are used in combination with other commands to connect exactly to points of existing objects in a drawing. You need to use Object Snap modes constantly for complete accuracy.

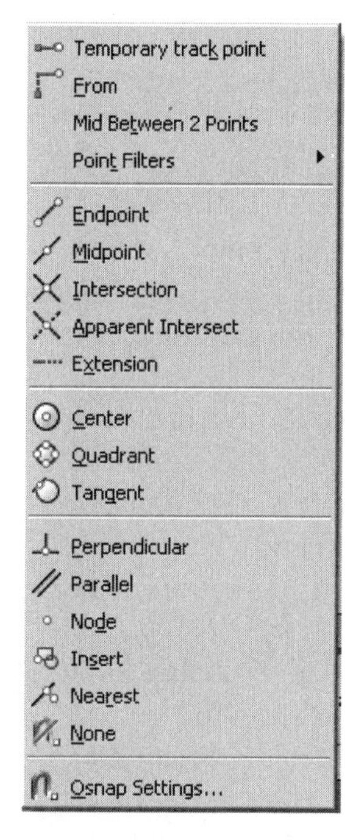

FIGURE 3–14
Activate the Osnap Menu by Pressing Shift and Right-Clicking in the Drawing Area

Activating Osnap

An Osnap mode can be activated in the following ways:

1. Typing the Osnap abbreviation (first three letters of the Object Snap mode).
2. Pressing Shift and right-clicking in the drawing area, then choosing an Object Snap mode from the Object Snap menu that appears (Figure 3–14).
3. Right-clicking OSNAP on the Status Bar, then clicking Settings... (Figure 3–15) to access the Drafting Settings dialog box (Figure 3–16).

Osnap Modes That Snap to Specific Drawing Features

You have already used Osnap-Midpoint and Node. They are examples of Osnap modes that snap to drawing features. Midpoint snaps to the midpoint of a line or arc, and Node snaps to a point entity.

The following list describes other Osnap modes that snap to specific drawing features. AutoCAD Osnap modes treat each edge of a solid and each polyline segment as a line. You will use many of these Osnap modes while completing the exercises in this book.

Mid Between 2 Points Snaps to a point midway between two points that you pick on the drawing.

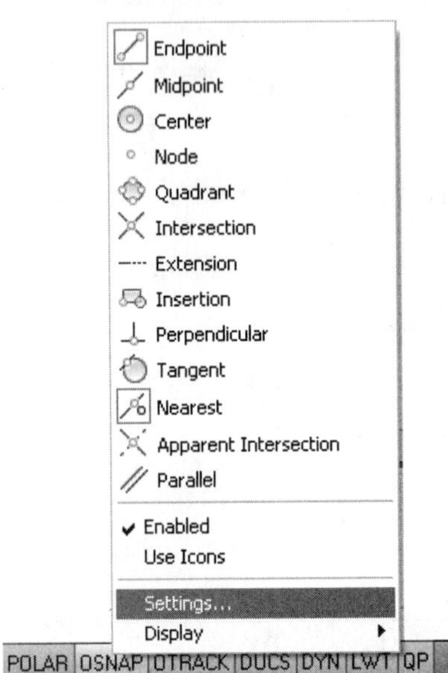

FIGURE 3–15
Activate OSNAP by Right-Clicking OSNAP on the Status Bar, Then Clicking Settings... to Access the Drafting Settings Dialog Box

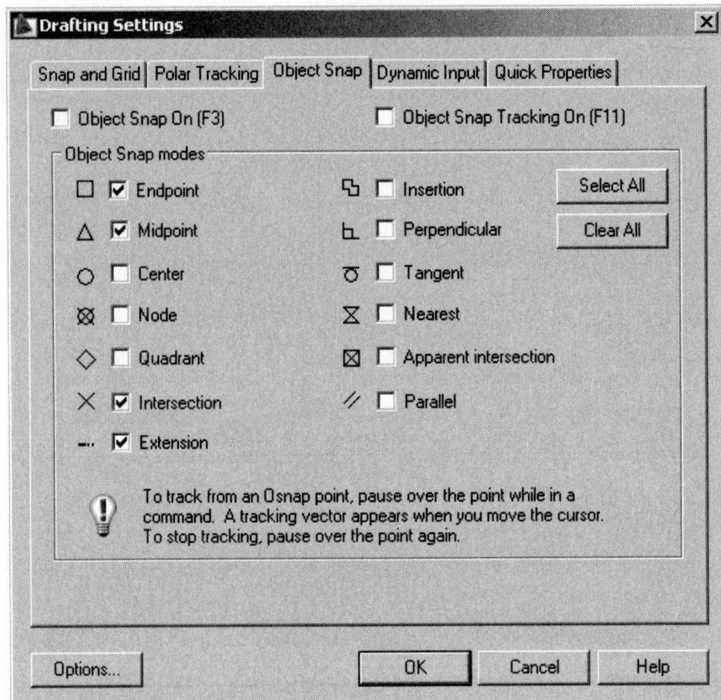

FIGURE 3–16
Drafting Settings Dialog Box with Endpoint, Midpoint, Intersection, and Extension Selected

Endpoint Snaps to the endpoint of a line or arc. The end of the line or arc nearest the point picked is snapped to.

Midpoint Snaps to the midpoint of a line or arc.

Center Snaps to the center of an arc or circle.

Node Snaps to a point (POINT: command).

Quadrant Snaps to the closest quadrant point of an arc or circle. These are the 0°, 90°, 180°, and 270° points on a circle, arc, or ellipse.

Intersection Snaps to the intersection of two lines, a line with an arc or circle, or two circles and/or arcs.

Extension Extends a line or arc. With a command and the extension mode active, pause over a line or arc, and after a small plus sign is displayed, slowly move along a temporary path that follows the extension of the line or arc. You can draw objects to and from points on the extension path line.

Insertion Snaps to the insertion point of text, attribute, or block. (These objects are described in later chapters.)

Perpendicular Snaps to the point on a line, circle, or arc that forms a 90° angle from that object to the last point. For example, if you are drawing a line, click the first point of the line, then use Perpendicular to connect the line to another line. The new line will be perpendicular to the first pick.

Tangent Snaps to the point on a circle or arc that when connected to the last point entered forms a line tangent to (touching at one point) the circle or arc.

Nearest Snaps to the point on a line, arc, or circle that is closest to the position of the crosshair; also snaps to any point (POINT: command) node that is closest to the crosshair. You will use this mode when you want to be sure to connect to a line, circle, or point, and cannot use another Osnap mode.

Apparent intersect Snaps to what appears to be an intersection even though one object is above the other in 3D space.

Parallel Draws a line parallel to another line. With the Line command active, click the first point of the new line you want to draw. With the Parallel mode active, pause over the line you want to draw parallel to, until a small parallel line symbol is displayed. Move the cursor away from but parallel to the original line, and an alignment path is displayed for you to complete the new line.

For the Line command, you can also use the Tangent and Perpendicular modes when picking the first point of the line. This allows you to draw a line tangent to, or perpendicular to, an existing object.

Running Osnap Modes

You can use individual Osnap modes while in another command, as you did with Midpoint and Node. You can also set a running Osnap mode. A running Osnap mode is constantly in effect while you are drawing, until it is disabled. For example, if you have many intersections to which you are connecting lines, set the Intersection mode as a running mode. This saves time by eliminating your constant return to the Osnap command for each intersection pick.

You can set a running Osnap mode using Drafting Settings... from the Status Bar. When the Drafting Settings dialog box appears, Figure 3–16, make sure the Object Snap tab is active. Click a check mark beside the desired Osnap mode or modes. Be sure to disable the running Osnap mode when you are through using it, as it can interfere with your drawing. Clicking OSNAP on in the Status Bar (or pressing function key F3) will activate any running Osnap modes you have set, and clicking it off will disable any running Osnap modes you have set.

Osnap Settings: Marker, Aperture, Magnet, Tooltip

Note the markers (small symbols) beside each Object Snap mode in the Drafting Settings dialog box, Object Snap tab (Figure 3–16). The display of the markers is controlled under the Drafting tab of the Options dialog box (Figure 3–17). A check mark

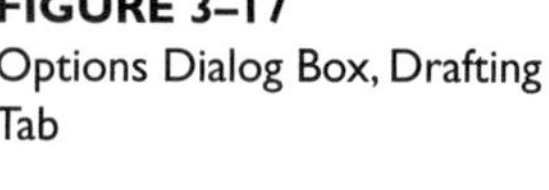

FIGURE 3–17
Options Dialog Box, Drafting Tab

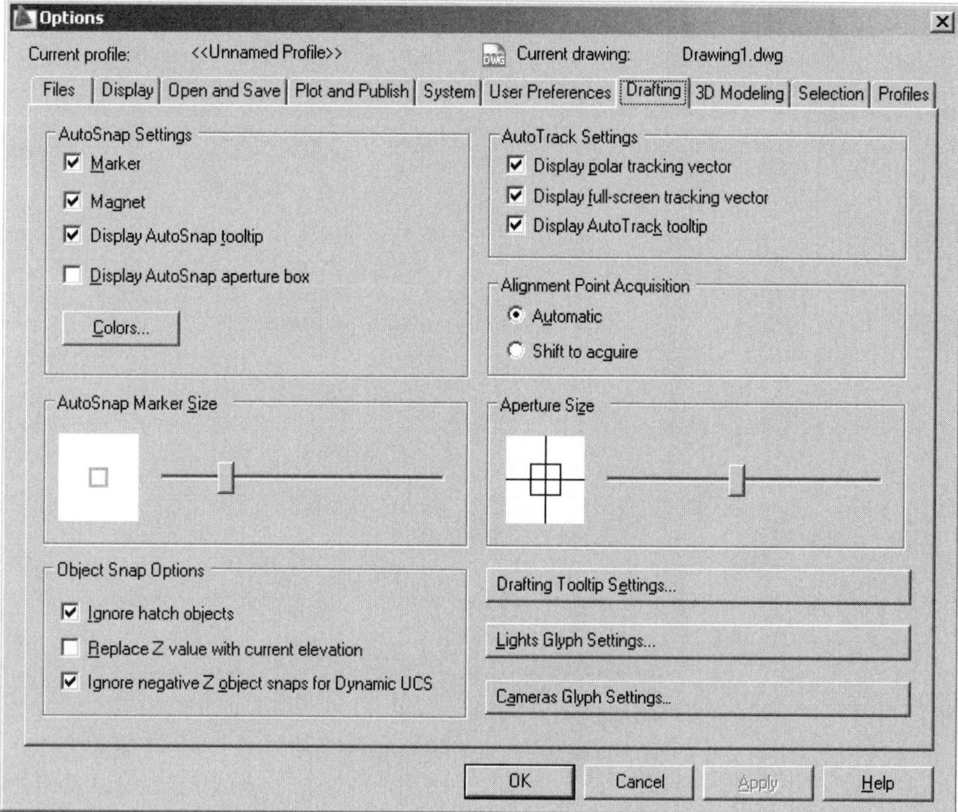

beside Marker will add the marker symbol to the crosshair. The AutoSnap Marker Size slider bar near the bottom of the dialog box specifies the size of the marker.

When Osnap is activated, a small target box called an *aperture* can also be added to the screen crosshair. This small box shows the area within which AutoCAD will search for Object Snap candidates. The Aperture Size slider bar on the right side of the dialog box specifies the size of the box.

Tutorial 3–2: Drawing a Rectangular Lecture Room, Including Furniture

A lecture room, including walls and furnishings, is drawn in Tutorial 3–2. When you have completed Tutorial 3–2, your drawing will look similar to Figure 3–18.

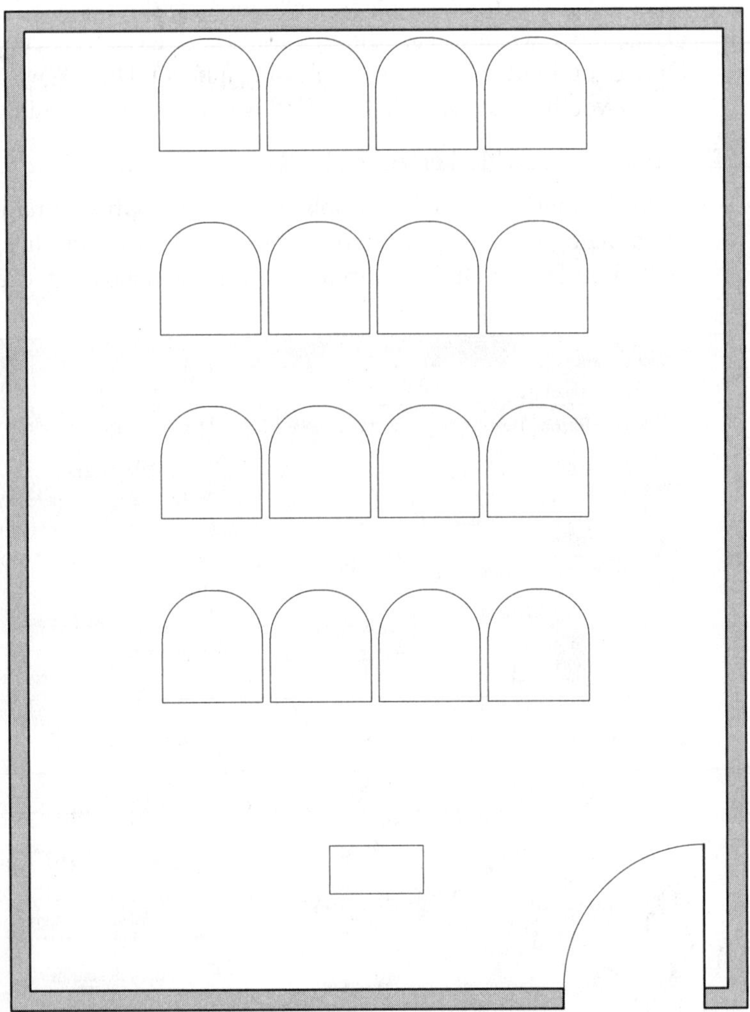

FIGURE 3–18
Tutorial 3–2: Drawing a Rectangular Lecture Room, Including Furniture
(Scale: 1/4″ = 1′-0″)

Step 1. CLICK: **Open..., change the Files of type: input box to Drawing Template (*.dwt) and open template** *Ch3-conference-rm-setup*, **previously made at the beginning of Tutorial 3–1.**

Step 2. CLICK: **SaveAs..., change the Files of type: input box to AutoCAD 2010 Drawing (.dwg) and save the template as a drawing file named CH3-TUTORIAL2.**

-or-

Step 3. **Use your workspace to make the following settings:**

1. **Use SaveAs... to save the drawing with the name CH3-TUTORIAL2.**
2. Set drawing Units: **Architectural**
3. Set Drawing Limits: **25′,35′**
4. Set GRIDDISPLAY: **0**
5. Set Grid: **12″**
6. Set Snap: **6″**
7. Create the following layers:

LAYER NAME	COLOR	LINETYPE	LINEWEIGHT
a-wall-intr	blue	continuous	.007″ (.18mm)
a-anno-text	green	continuous	.006″ (.15mm)
a-door-sgl	blue	continuous	.007″ (.18mm)
a-door-swng	red	continuous	.004″ (.09 mm)
i-furn	cyan	continuous	.004″ (.09mm)

Step 4. **Set Layer a-wall-intr current.**

Step 5. **Use Zoom-All to view the limits of the drawing.**

Step 6. **Turn SNAP, GRID and LWT ON. The remaining buttons in the Status Bar should be OFF.**

SOLID WALLS USING POLYLINE AND SOLID HATCH

In Tutorial 3–2 you will use the Line command to draw the lecture room walls; then you will use the Polyline Edit command to change the lines to a polyline before you offset the walls. After you have completed drawing the walls, you will use the Hatch command to make the walls solid.

Step 7. **Use Line to draw the walls of the lecture room (Figure 3–19), as described next:**

Prompt	Response
Command:	**Line** (or TYPE: **L<enter>**)
Specify first point:	TYPE: **5′,7′<enter>**
Specify next point or [Undo]:	**Turn ORTHO ON** **Move your mouse to the right** and TYPE: **15′<enter>**
Specify next point or [Undo]:	**Move your mouse straight up** and TYPE: **20′<enter>**
Specify next point or [Close/Undo]:	**Move your mouse to the left** and TYPE: **15′<enter>**
Specify next point or [Close/Undo]:	TYPE: **C<enter>**

FIGURE 3–19
Use Line to Draw the Lecture Room Walls

Step 8. **Use Zoom-Window to magnify the lower right corner of the lecture room where the door will be drawn.**

FROM

FROM is a command modifier that locates a base point and then allows you to locate an offset point from that base point. It is similar to ID Point, but differs in that FROM is used within a command; ID Point must be used before the command is activated. FROM is used at a prompt that wants you to locate a point, and it does not work unless a command is active to issue that prompt. Both FROM and ID Point are usually used in combination with Object Snap modifiers when locating the initial base point.

BREAK

The Break command can be used to erase a part of a drawing object.

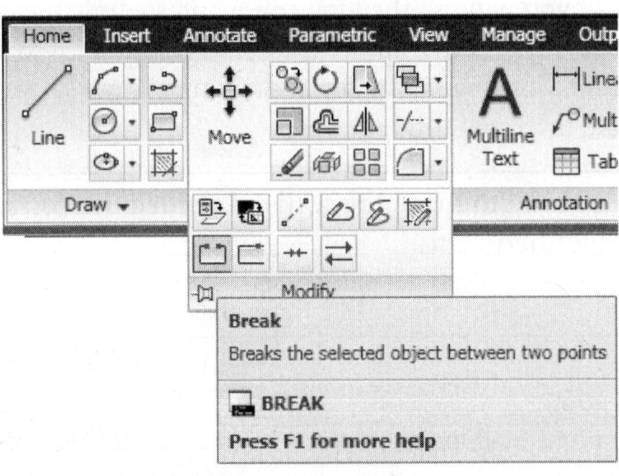

Step 9. **Use Break to create an opening for the lecture room door (Figure 3–20), as described next:**

Prompt	Response
Command:	**Break** (or TYPE: **BR<enter>**)
Select object:	CLICK: **anyplace on the bottom horizontal line**

FIGURE 3–20
Use Break to Create an Opening for the Conference Room Door

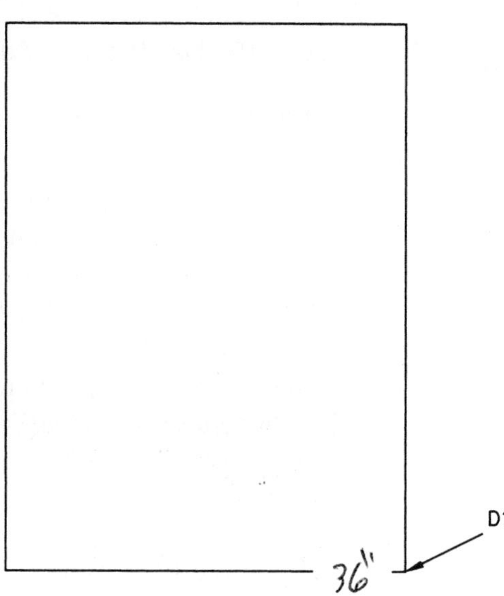

Prompt	Response
Specify second break point or [First point]:	TYPE: **F<enter>** (for first point)
Specify first break point:	TYPE: **FRO<enter>** (abbreviation for FROM)
Base point:	**OSNAP-Intersection**
int of	**D1** (Figure 3–20)
<Offset>:	TYPE: **@6<180<enter>** (polar coordinate)
Specify second break point:	TYPE: **@36<180<enter>** (polar coordinate)

First

When selecting an entity to break, you may use the point entered in the selection process as the first break point, or you may TYPE: **F<enter>** to be able to select the first break point.

@

Sometimes you need only to break an entity and not erase a section of it. In that case, use @ as the second break point. The line will be broken twice on the same point; no segments will be erased from the line.

POLYLINE EDIT

Polyline Edit is a modify command used to edit polylines or to change lines into polylines. It can join lines or arcs together and make them a single polyline. It can also be used to change the width of a polyline.

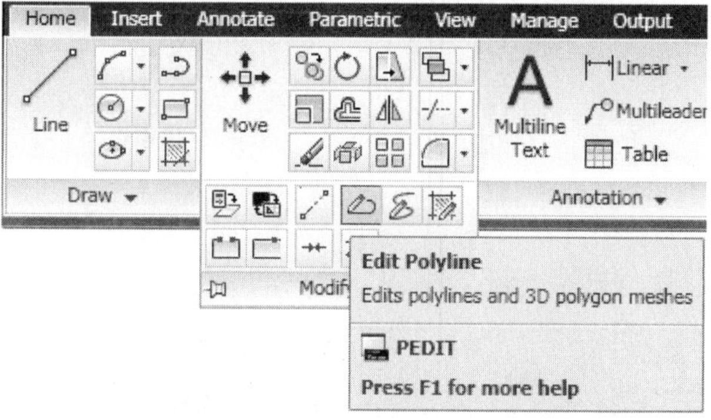

Step 10. Use Polyline Edit to change the lines into a polyline, as described next:

Prompt	Response
Command:	**Polyline Edit** (or TYPE: **PE<enter>**)
Select polyline or [Multiple]:	CLICK: **any of the lines drawn**
Object selected is not a polyline	
Do you want to turn it into one? <Y>	**<enter>** (to tell AutoCAD yes, you want to turn it into a polyline)
Enter an option [Close/Join/Width/Edit vertex/Fit/Spline/Decurve/Ltype gen/Reverse/Undo]:	TYPE: **J<enter>** (for Join)
Select objects:	TYPE: **ALL<enter>** (to select all the lines)
5 found	
Select objects:	**<enter>**
4 segments added to polyline	
Enter an option [Open/Join/Width/Edit vertex/Fit/Spline/Decurve/Ltype gen/Reverse/Undo]:	**<enter>**

Step 11. Use the Offset command to offset the polyline 5″ to the outside of the current polyline.

Step 12. Use the Line command with a running OSNAP endpoint to close the polyline. TYPE: **L<enter>** CLICK: **D1,D2<enter><enter>** CLICK: **D3,D4<enter> as shown in Figure 3–21.**

Step 13. Use Zoom-Extents so you can see the entire drawing graphics.

HATCH

The Hatch and Gradient dialog box is discussed in detail in Chapters 8 and 12. For now you will use a single hatch pattern to create solid walls as shown in Figure 3–18.

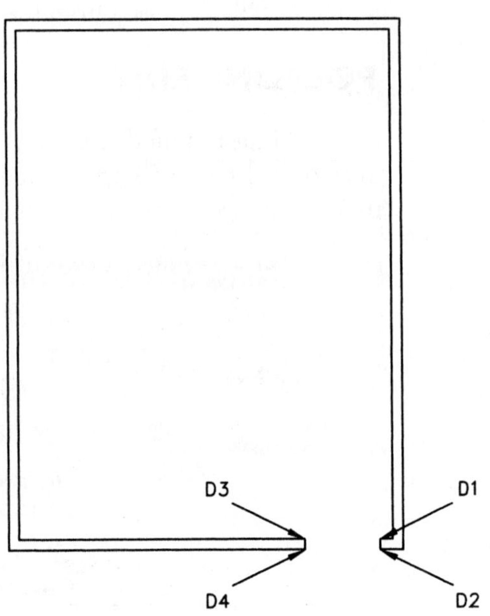

FIGURE 3–21
Use the Line Command to Close the Ends of the Polyline

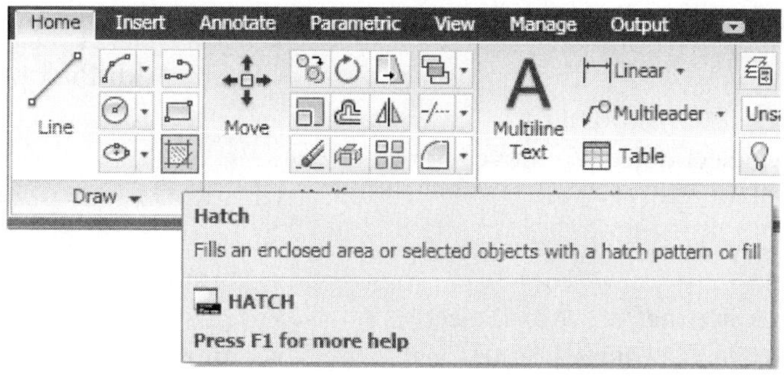

Step 14. Create the following new layer and set it as the current layer:

LAYER NAME	COLOR	LINETYPE	LINEWEIGHT
a-wall-pat1	gray (253)	continuous	.010″ (.25mm)

Step 15. Use the Hatch command to make the walls solid, as described next:

Prompt	Response
Command:	**Hatch...** (or TYPE: **H<enter>**)
The Hatch and Gradient dialog box appears:	**With the Hatch Tab selected:** CLICK: **the Pattern: list and scroll up to the SOLID pattern** CLICK: **on it, as shown in Figure 3–22**

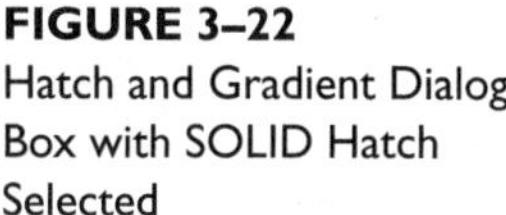

FIGURE 3–22
Hatch and Gradient Dialog Box with SOLID Hatch Selected

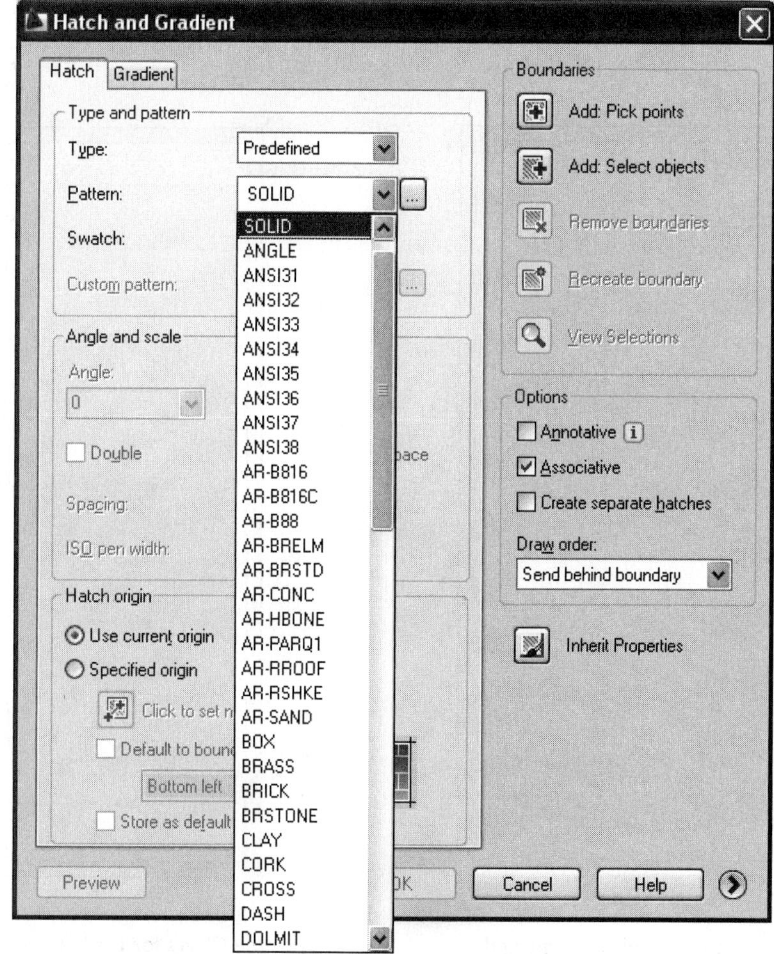

Prompt	Response
	CLICK: **Add: Pick points**
Pick internal point or [Select objects/remove Boundaries]:	CLICK: **D1** (any point between polylines forming the wall, Figure 3–23—you will have to turn SNAP OFF)
Pick internal point or [Select objects/remove Boundaries]:	**<enter>**
The Hatch and Gradient dialog box or right-click menu appears:	CLICK: **Preview**
Pick or press Esc to return to the dialog box or <Right-click to accept hatch>:	**Right-click** (if the pattern looks correct) **or** PRESS: **Esc** (and fix the dialog box)

Step 16. **Set Layer a-door-sgl current.**

Step 17. **Use the Line command to draw a 3′ vertical door line. Snap (be sure SNAP is ON) to the upper right corner of the door opening to begin the door line. Draw the line using polar coordinates or direct distance entry (Figure 3–24).**

Step 18. **Set Layer a-door-swng current.**

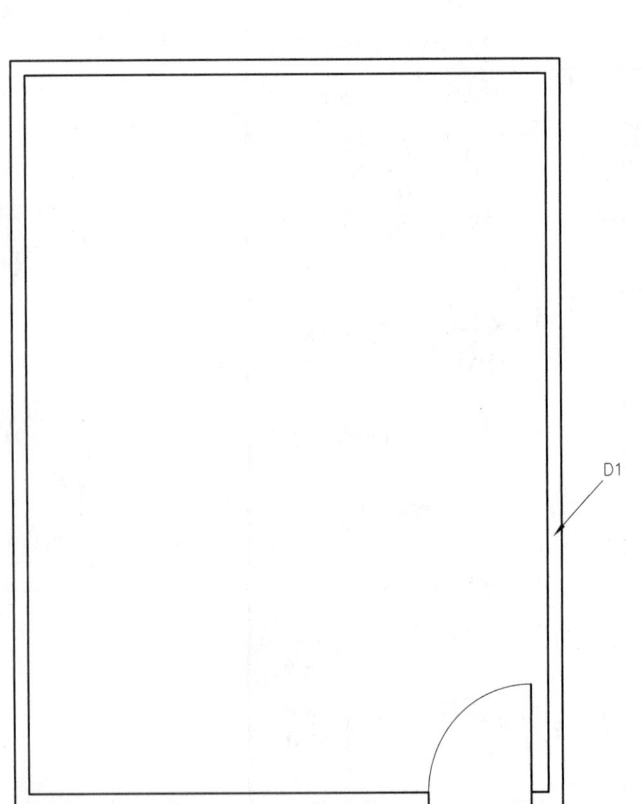

FIGURE 3–23
CLICK: Any Point Between the Two Polylines Forming the Wall

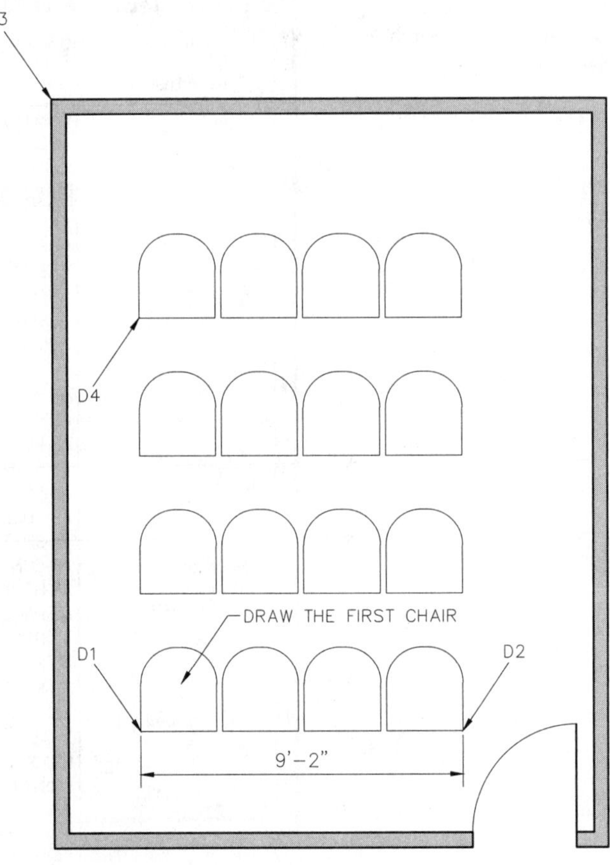

FIGURE 3–24
Draw the Chairs for the Lecture Room

Step 19. Use the Arc-Start, Center, End method to draw the counterclockwise door swing arc. Use Osnap-Endpoint for the start, center, and end connections.

Step 20. Set Layer i-furn current.

Step 21. To draw the first chair in the group of chairs, zoom in on a portion of the grid inside the lecture room walls in the lower left area (Figure 3–24).

Step 22. Use the Line command to draw a rectangle 26″ wide by 28″ deep. This chair shape will be used to draw the entire group of 16 chairs and will be moved to the correct position later. For now, just be sure it is located in the general area of the lower left corner of the room, shown in Figure 3–24.

Step 23. Edit the rectangle, using the Fillet command, 12″ Radius to form the shape of the chair.

Step 24. Zoom-Extents after you finish drawing the chair.

ARRAY

Array allows you to make multiple copies of an object in a rectangular or polar (circular) array. The Rectangular option is used to draw all the chairs in the lecture room; the Polar option is described in Tutorial 3–3.

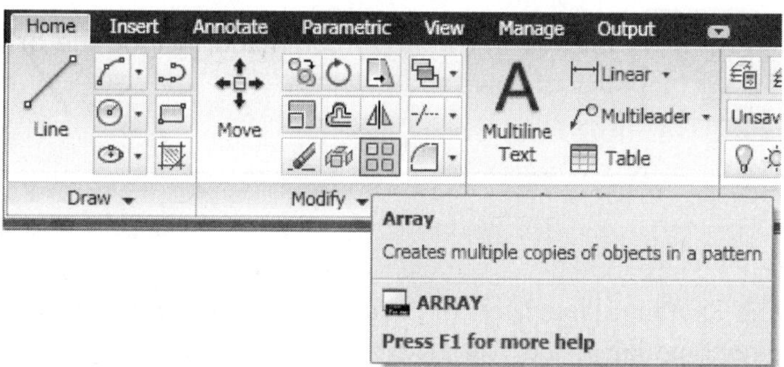

Step 25. Use the Array command to make a rectangular pattern of 16 chairs (Figures 3–24 and 3–25), as described next:

Prompt	Response
Command:	**Array** (or TYPE: **AR<enter>**)
The Array dialog box appears:	CLICK: **the Select objects button**
Select objects:	PICK: **any point to locate the first corner of a window to include the entire chair**
Specify opposite corner:	**Window the chair just drawn**
Select objects:	**<enter>**
The Array dialog box appears:	CLICK: **the Rectangular Array button**
	TYPE: **4 in the Rows: text box**
	TYPE: **4 in the Columns: text box**

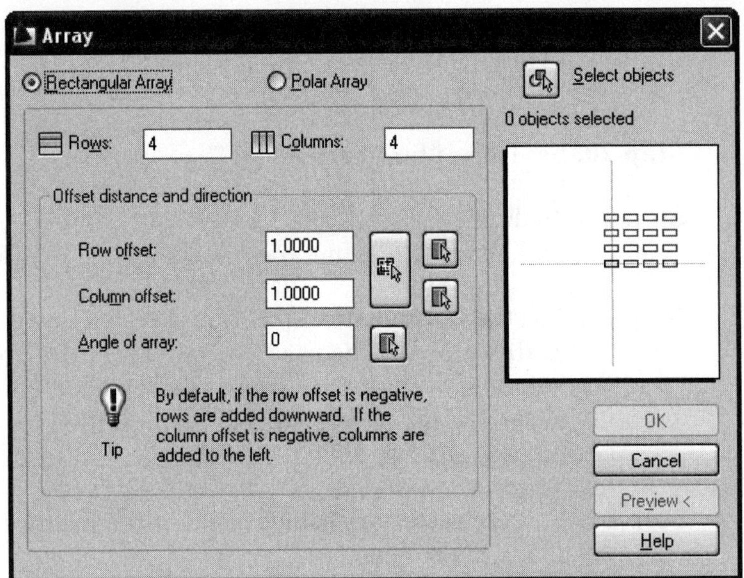

FIGURE 3–25
Array Dialog Box

Prompt	Response
	TYPE: **46 in the Row offset: text box** TYPE: **28 in the Column offset: text box** TYPE: **0 in the Angle of array: text box** CLICK: **OK**

NOTE: In the Array command, include the original item in the number of rows and columns.

Rectangular

The Rectangular option of Array allows you to make multiple copies of an object in a rectangular array. The array is made up of horizontal rows and vertical columns. The direction and spacing of the rows and columns are determined by the distance you specify between each. In the previous example we used the chair as the cornerstone element in the lower left corner of the array. Positive numbers were used for the distance between the rows and columns, and the array went up and to the right. When a positive number is entered for the rows, they proceed up; when a negative number is entered, they proceed down. When a positive number is entered for the columns, they proceed to the right; when a negative number is entered, they proceed to the left.

NOTE: To rotate a rectangular array, set the Angle of array to the desired angle and then create the array.

DISTANCE

The Distance command can be used to determine measurements. We know the interior width of the room is 15′. To center the array of chairs accurately in the lecture room, we need to measure the width of the array. The depth appears to be fine for the room size.

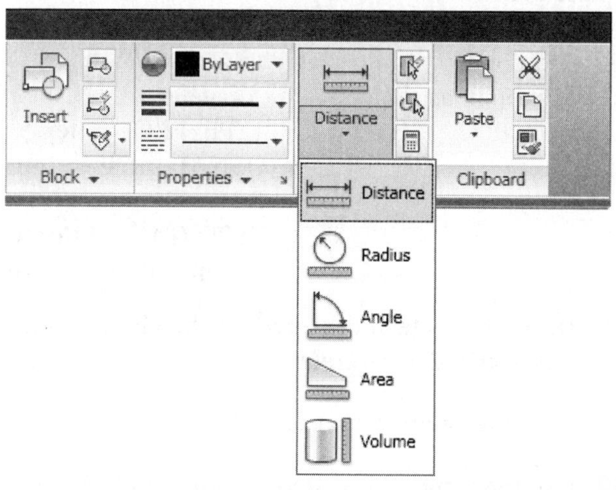

Step 26. Use Distance to measure a specified distance (Figure 3–24), as described next:

Prompt	Response
Command:	**Distance** (or TYPE: **DI<enter>**)
Specify first point:	**OSNAP-Intersection**
int of	**D1** (Figure 3–24)
Specify second point or [multiple points]:	**OSNAP-Intersection**
int of	**D2**
Distance = 9′-2″, Angle in XY Plane = 0,Angle from XY Plane = 0, Delta X = 9′-2″,Delta Y = 0′-0″, Delta Z = 0′-0″	

The room width, 180″ (15′), minus the array width, 110″ (9′-2″), is 70″. You can leave 35″-wide aisles on each side of the array.

Position the Chair Array

To locate the chair array precisely, use Move, FROM, and OSNAP-Intersection. The array will be located 2″ away from the back wall of the lecture room and will have 35″-wide aisles on each side.

Using the outside upper left corner of the room as the base point, the aisle width of 35″, plus the 5″ wall, is 40″ on the X axis. The chair depth, 28″, plus the distance of the wall, 5″, and away from the wall, 2″, is 35″ on the Y axis. Make sure ORTHO is OFF.

Step 27. Locate the chair array (Figure 3–24), as described next:

Prompt	Response
Command:	**Move** (or TYPE: **M<enter>**)
Select objects:	CLICK: **any point to locate the first corner of a window to include the entire array**

Prompt	Response
Specify opposite corner:	**Window the entire array**
Select objects:	**<enter>**
Specify base point or [Displacement] <Displacement>:	**OSNAP-Intersection**
int of	**D4**
Specify second point or <use first point as displacement>:	TYPE: **FRO<enter>**
Base point:	**OSNAP-Intersection**
int of	**D3**
<Offset>:	TYPE: **@40,-35<enter>** (do not forget the minus in front of the 35)

Step 28. **Draw the lectern centered on the chair array, as shown in Figure 3–26; Tutorial 3–2 is complete.**

Step 29. **Set Layer a-anno-text current.**

Step 30. **Use the Single Line Text command** (TYPE: **DT<enter>**) **to type your name, class number, and date, 6″ H. in the upper right corner.**

Step 31. **When you have completed Tutorial 3–2, save your work in at least two places.**

Step 32. **Print your drawing from the Model tab at a scale of 1/4″ = 1′-0″.**

FIGURE 3–26
Complete Tutorial 3–2

FIGURE 3–27
Tutorial 3-3: Drawing a Curved Conference Room, Including Furniture
(Scale: 1/4″ = 1′-0″)

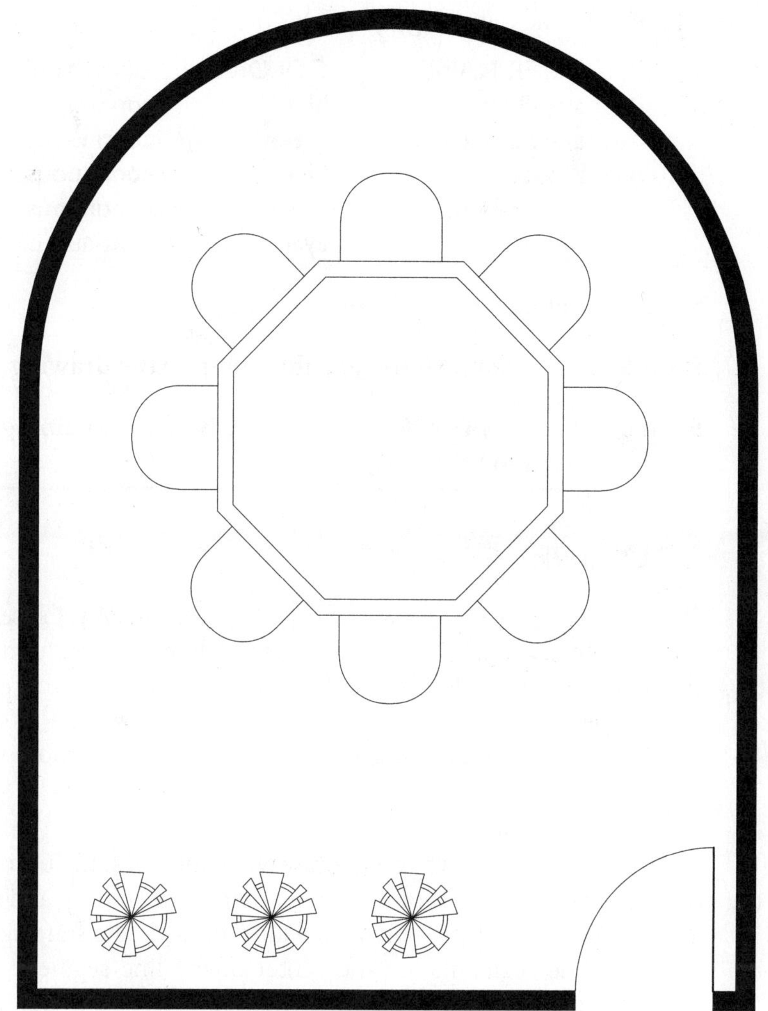

Tutorial 3–3: Drawing a Curved Conference Room, Including Furniture

A conference room, including walls and furnishings, is drawn in Tutorial 3–3. When you have completed Tutorial 3–3, your drawing will look similar to Figure 3–27.

Step 1. **CLICK: Open..., change the Files of type: input box to Drawing Template (*.dwt) and open the Ch3-conference-rm-setup template, previously made at the beginning of Tutorial 3–1.**

Step 2. **CLICK: Save As..., change the Files of type: input box to AutoCAD 2010 Drawing (.dwg), and save the template as a drawing file named CH3-TUTORIAL3.**

-or-

Step 3. **Use your workspace to make the following settings:**

1. **Use SaveAs... to save the drawing with the name CH3-TUTORIAL3.**
2. Set drawing Units: **Architectural**

3. Set Drawing Limits: **25′,35′**
4. Set GRIDDISPLAY: **0**
5. Set Grid: **12″**
6. Set Snap: **6″**
7. Create the following layers:

LAYER NAME	COLOR	LINETYPE	LINEWEIGHT
a-wall-intr	blue	continuous	.007″ (.18mm)
a-anno-text	green	continuous	.006″ (.15mm)
a-door-sgl	blue	continuous	.007″ (.18mm)
a-door-swng	red	continuous	.004″ (.09mm)
i-furn	cyan	continuous	.004″ (.09mm)

Step 4. Set Layer a-wall-intr current.

Step 5. Use Zoom-All to view the limits of the drawing.

Step 6. Turn SNAP, GRID and LWT ON. The remaining buttons in the Status Bar should be OFF.

POLYLINE

The Polyline prompt is "Specify next point or [Arc/Close/Halfwidth/Length/Undo/Width]:". In Tutorial 3–1, a continuous polyline was used to draw the inside lines of the conference room walls; then Offset was used to draw the outside line showing wall depth. The Width option of the Pline prompt allows you to specify a thickness for the polyline. The Width option is used to draw the lecture room walls in Tutorial 3–3.

Width

The Width option allows you to draw wide polylines. In Tutorial 3–3, a 5″-wide polyline is used to draw the walls of the lecture room. The starting and ending points of the polyline are the *center* of the polyline's width. Because the starting and ending points of the wide polyline segments are the center of the line segment, 5″ is added to each line length to compensate for the 2-1/2″ wall thickness on each side of the center line.

When a wide polyline is exploded, the width information is lost, and the polyline changes to a line segment.

Half Width

This specifies the width of the polyline from the center of the polyline to either edge.

Length

The Length option in the Polyline prompt allows you to draw a polyline segment at the same angle as the previously drawn polyline segment, by specifying the length of the new segment.

Close

It is always best to use the Close option when you are completing a wide polyline. The effect of using Close is different from clicking or entering a point to complete the polyline. With the Close option, the last corner is completely closed.

Arc

The Polyline Arc command is similar to the Arc command in the Draw menu.

Step 7. **Draw the walls of the conference room, using a wide polyline and wide polyarc (Figure 3–28), as described next:**

Prompt	Response
Command:	**Polyline** (or TYPE: **PL<enter>**)
Specify start point:	TYPE: **4′9-1/2,4′9-1/2<enter>**
Current line-width is 0′-0″	
Specify next point or [Arc/ Halfwidth/Length/Undo/Width]:	TYPE: **W**
Specify starting width <0′-0″>:	TYPE: **5<enter>**
Specify ending width <0′-5″>:	**<enter>**
Specify next point or [Arc/ Halfwidth/Length/Undo/Width]:	TYPE: **@15′5<0<enter>**
Specify next point or [Arc/Close Halfwidth/Length/Undo/Width]:	TYPE: **@12′9<90<enter>**
Specify next point or [Arc/Close/ Halfwidth/Length/Undo/Width]:	TYPE: **A<enter>**
Specify endpoint of arc or [Angle/ CEnter/CLose/Direction/ Halfwidth/Line/Radius/ Second pt/Undo/Width]:	TYPE: **@15′5<180<enter>**
Specify endpoint of arc or [Angle/ CEnter/CLose/Direction/	

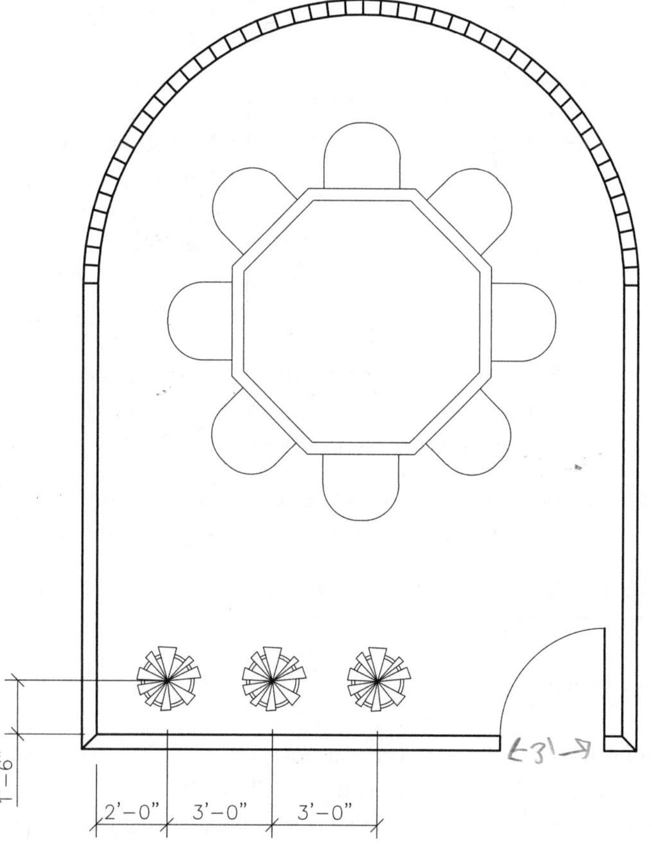

FIGURE 3–28
Draw Tutorial 3–3

Prompt	Response
Halfwidth/Line/Radius/Second pt/ Undo/Width]:	TYPE: **L<enter>**
Specify next point or [Arc/Close/ Halfwidth/Length/Undo/Width]:	TYPE: **C<enter>**

When you subtract 2-1/2″ (half the polyline width) from coordinates 5′,5′ to get your starting point of coordinates 4′9-1/2,4′9-1/2, the lower left inside corner of the lecture room is located on the grid mark at coordinates 5′,5′. Turn coordinates on and snap to the lower left inside corner of the lecture room to verify this.

Notice that you do not have to insert the inch symbol in the polar coordinates, because architectural units default to inches.

FILL ON, FILL OFF

The settings FILL ON and FILL OFF affect the appearance of the polyline and solid hatch. To have an outline of the polyline, TYPE: **FILL<enter>**, then **OFF<enter>** and regenerate the drawing. To have it appear solid again, TYPE: **FILL<enter>**, then TYPE: **ON<enter>** and regenerate the drawing (TYPE: **RE<enter>**).

Step 8. TYPE: FILL<enter>, then TYPE: OFF<enter> and regenerate the drawing to create an open polyline (Figure 3–28).

Step 9. Use the Break command and From to create a 3′ door opening (Figure 3–28):

Prompt	Response
Command:	**Break** (or TYPE: **BR<enter>**)
Select Object:	CLICK: **anyplace on the polyline**
Specify second break point or [First point]:	TYPE: **F<enter>**
Specify first break point:	TYPE: **FRO<enter>** (abbreviation for FROM)
Base point:	**OSNAP-Intersection**
int of	CLICK: **the lower right intersection of the polylines**
<Offset>:	TYPE: **@8-1/2<180<enter>**
Specify second break point:	TYPE: **@36<180<enter>**

Step 10. Set Layer a-door-sgl current. Use the Line command to draw a 3′ vertical door line. Start the door line at the inside corner of the door opening, with snap ON (Figure 3–28).

Step 11. Set Layer a-door-swng current. Use the Arc-Start, Center, End method to draw the door swing arc (Figure 3–28).

Step 12. Set Layer i-furn current.

POLYGON

The Polygon command draws a polygon with 3 to 1024 sides. After the number of sides is specified, the Polygon prompt is "Specify center of polygon or [Edge]:". When the center of the polygon (default option) is specified, the polygon can then be inscribed in a circle or circumscribed about a circle. When the polygon is inscribed in a circle, all the vertices lie on the circle, and the edges of the polygon are inside the circle. When the polygon is circumscribed about a circle, the midpoint of each edge of the polygon lies on the circle, and the vertices are outside the circle. A polygon is a closed polyline.

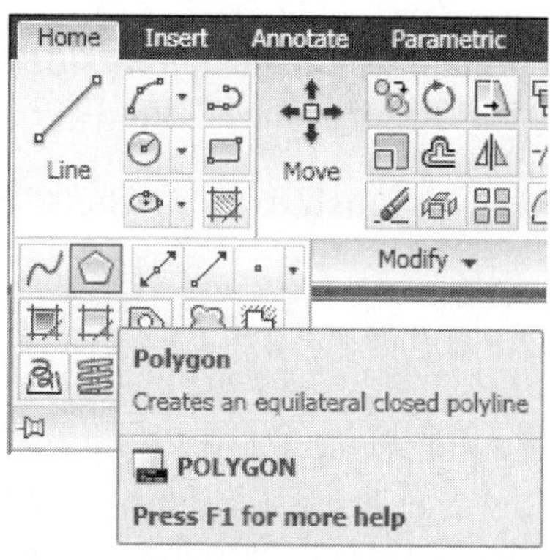

Step 13. Use the Polygon command to draw the conference table (Figure 3–28), as described next:

Prompt	Response
Command:	**Polygon** (or TYPE: **POL<enter>**)
Enter number of sides <4>:	TYPE: **8<enter>**
Specify center of polygon or [Edge]:	TYPE: **12′6,16′6<enter>**
Enter an option [Inscribed in circle/ Circumscribed about circle]<I>:	TYPE: **I<enter>** (or just **<enter>** if I is the default
Specify radius of circle:	TYPE: **48<enter>**

The method of specifying the radius controls the orientation of the polygon. When the radius is specified with a number, as above, the bottom edge of the polygon is drawn at the current snap angle—horizontal in the polygon just drawn. When the radius of an inscribed polygon is specified with a point, a vertex of the polygon is placed at the point location. When the radius of a circumscribed polygon is specified with a point, an edge midpoint is placed at the point's location.

Edge

When the Edge option of the prompt is selected, AutoCAD prompts "Specify first endpoint of edge:" and "Specify second endpoint of edge:". The two points entered to the prompts specify one edge of a polygon that is drawn counterclockwise.

Step 14. To draw the first chair of the eight chairs that are placed around the conference table, zoom in on a portion of the grid inside the conference room walls (Figure 3–28).

Step 15. Use the Line command to draw a rectangle 26″ wide by 28″ deep using polar coordinates or direct distance entry.

Step 16. Edit one of the 26″-wide sides of the rectangle, using the Fillet command, 12″ Radius to form the back of the chair.

Step 17. The chairs are located 6″ in from the outside edge of the table. Use the Move command, Osnap-Midpoint (to the front of the chair), and FROM

to locate the front of the chair 6″ inside the midpoint of an edge of the conference table polygon (Figure 3–28).

Step 18. **Use the Trim and Erase commands to erase the part of the chair that is under the conference table.**

Step 19. **Use the Offset command to offset the outside edge of the conference table 4″ to the inside, to form the 4″ band (Figure 3–28).**

Step 20. **Zoom-Extents after you finish drawing the 4″ band.**

ARRAY

Polar

The Polar option of Array allows you to make multiple copies of an object in a circular array. The 360° "Angle to fill" can be specified to form a full circular array. An angle less than 360° can be specified to form a partial circular array. When a positive angle is specified, the array is rotated counterclockwise (+=ccw). When a negative angle is specified, the array is rotated clockwise (−=cw).

AutoCAD constructs the array by determining the distance from the array's center point to a point on the object selected. If more than one object is selected, the reference point is on the last item in the selection set. When multiple items are arrayed and are not rotated as they are copied, the resulting array depends on the reference point used.

If one of the two array parameters used above—the number of items in the array or the angle to fill—is not specified, AutoCAD will prompt for a third parameter—"Angle between items:". Any two of the three array parameters must be specified to complete an array.

Step 21. **Use the Array command to make a polar (circular) pattern of eight chairs (Figure 3–28), as described next:**

Prompt	Response
Command:	**Array** (or TYPE: **AR<enter>**)
The Array dialog box appears:	CLICK: **the Select objects button**
Select objects:	CLICK: **the first corner for a window to select the chair just drawn**
Specify opposite corner:	**Window the chair just drawn.**
Select objects:	**<enter>**
	CLICK: **the Polar Array button**
	CLICK: **the button that allows you to pick a center point**
Specify center point of array:	CLICK: **the center point of the polygon** (or TYPE: **12′6,16′6<enter>**)
	TYPE: **8 in the Total number of items: input area**
	TYPE: **360 in the Angle to fill: input box** **Make sure there is a check in the Rotate items as copied: check box.**
	CLICK: **OK**

Step 22. **Use Zoom-Window to zoom in on the area of the conference room where the plants and planters are located (Figure 3–28).**

Step 23. Use the Circle command, 9″ Radius, to draw the outside shape of one planter.

Step 24. Use the Offset command, offset distance 1″, offset to the inside of the planter, to give a thickness to the planter.

Step 25. Use the Line command to draw multisegmented shapes (to show a plant) in the planter (Figure 3–28).

Step 26. Use Trim to trim the lines of the pot beneath the plant leaves. Window the entire planter to select the cutting edges, and then select the lines to trim.

Step 27. Use the Copy command to draw the next two planters, as shown in Figure 3–28.

Step 28. Set FILL ON and regenerate the drawing to have the walls appear solid again; Tutorial 3–3 is complete.

Step 29. Set Layer a-anno-text current.

Step 30. Use the Single Line Text command (TYPE: DT<enter>) to type your name, class number, and date, 6″ H. in the upper right corner.

Step 31. When you have completed Tutorial 3–3, save your work in at least two places.

Step 32. Print your drawing from the Model tab at a scale of 1/4″ = 1′-0″.

Tutorial 3–4: Drawing a Conference Room Using Polar Tracking

In Tutorial 3–4, Polar Tracking is used to draw lines at angles in 15° increments. The Polyline Edit command is used to join lines together and to change the width of the existing polyline. Zero Radius Fillet is used to join lines to form a square corner, and furniture is added.

When you have completed Tutorial 3–4, your drawing will look similar to Figure 3–29.

Step 1. CLICK: Open..., change the Files of type: input box to Drawing Template (*.dwt) and open the Ch3-conference-rm-setup template, previously created at the beginning of Tutorial 3–1.

Step 2. CLICK: SaveAs..., change the Files of type: input box to AutoCAD 2010 Drawing (.dwg) and save the template as a drawing file named CH3-TUTORIAL4.

-or-

Step 3. Use your workspace to make the following settings:

1. Use SaveAs... to save the drawing with the name CH3-TUTORIAL4.
2. Set drawing Units: **Architectural**
3. Set Drawing Limits: **25′,35′**
4. Set GRIDDISPLAY: **0**
5. Set Grid: **12″**
6. Set Snap: **6″**

FIGURE 3–29
Tutorial 3–4: Drawing a Conference Room Using Polar Tracking (Scale 1/4″ = 1′-0″)

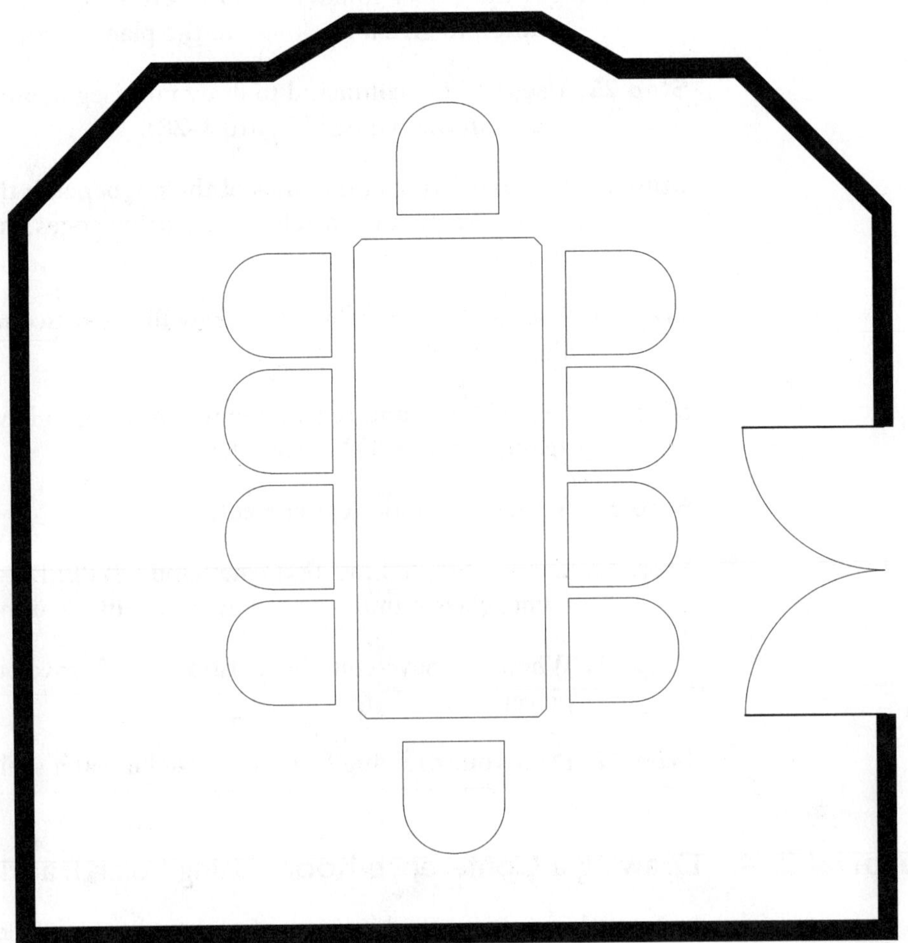

7. Create the following layers:

LAYER NAME	COLOR	LINETYPE	LINEWEIGHT
a-wall-intr	blue	continuous	.007″ (.18mm)
a-anno-text	green	continuous	.006″ (.15mm)
a-door-sgl	blue	continuous	.007″ (.18mm)
a-door-swng	red	continuous	.004″ (.09mm)
i-furn	cyan	continuous	.004″ (.09mm)

Step 4. Set Layer a-wall-intr current.

Step 5. Use Zoom-All to view the limits of the drawing.

Step 6. Turn SNAP, GRID, and LWT ON. The remaining buttons in the Status Bar should be OFF.

POLAR TRACKING

Step 7. Set Polar Tracking angles at 15°, as described next:

Prompt	Response
Command:	**Place your mouse over POLAR on the status bar and** RIGHT-CLICK

FIGURE 3–30
Set Polar Tracking Angles

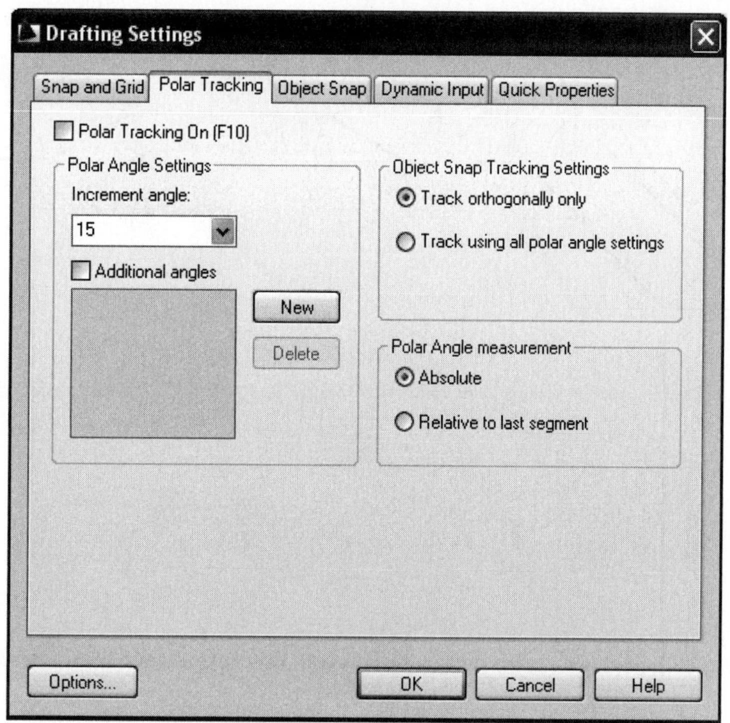

Prompt	Response
A shortcut menu appears:	CLICK: **Settings...**
The Drafting Settings dialog box appears with the Polar Tracking tab selected:	CLICK: **the list under Increment angle: and** CLICK: **15** (as shown in Figure 3–30) CLICK: **OK**

Step 8. Use the Line command with direct distance entry and Polar Tracking to draw most of the wall symbols (Figure 3–31), as described next:

Prompt	Response
Command:	**Line** (or TYPE: **L<enter>**)
Specify first point:	TYPE: **11′,7′<enter>**
Specify next point or [Undo]:	**Turn ORTHO ON**
	Move your mouse to the left and TYPE: **7′6<enter>**
Specify next point or [Undo]:	**Move your mouse straight up and** TYPE: **15′<enter>**
Specify next point or [Close/Undo]:	CLICK: **POLAR** (ORTHO turns OFF automatically)
	Move your mouse so that 45° shows and TYPE: **4′3<enter>**
Specify next point or [Close/Undo]:	**Move your mouse so that <0° shows and** TYPE: **2′6<enter>**
Specify next point or [Close/Undo]:	**Move your mouse so that <30° shows** and TYPE: **2′<enter>**
Specify next point or [Close/Undo]:	**Move your mouse so that <0° shows and** TYPE: **4′<enter>**

FIGURE 3–31
Measurements for the Walls

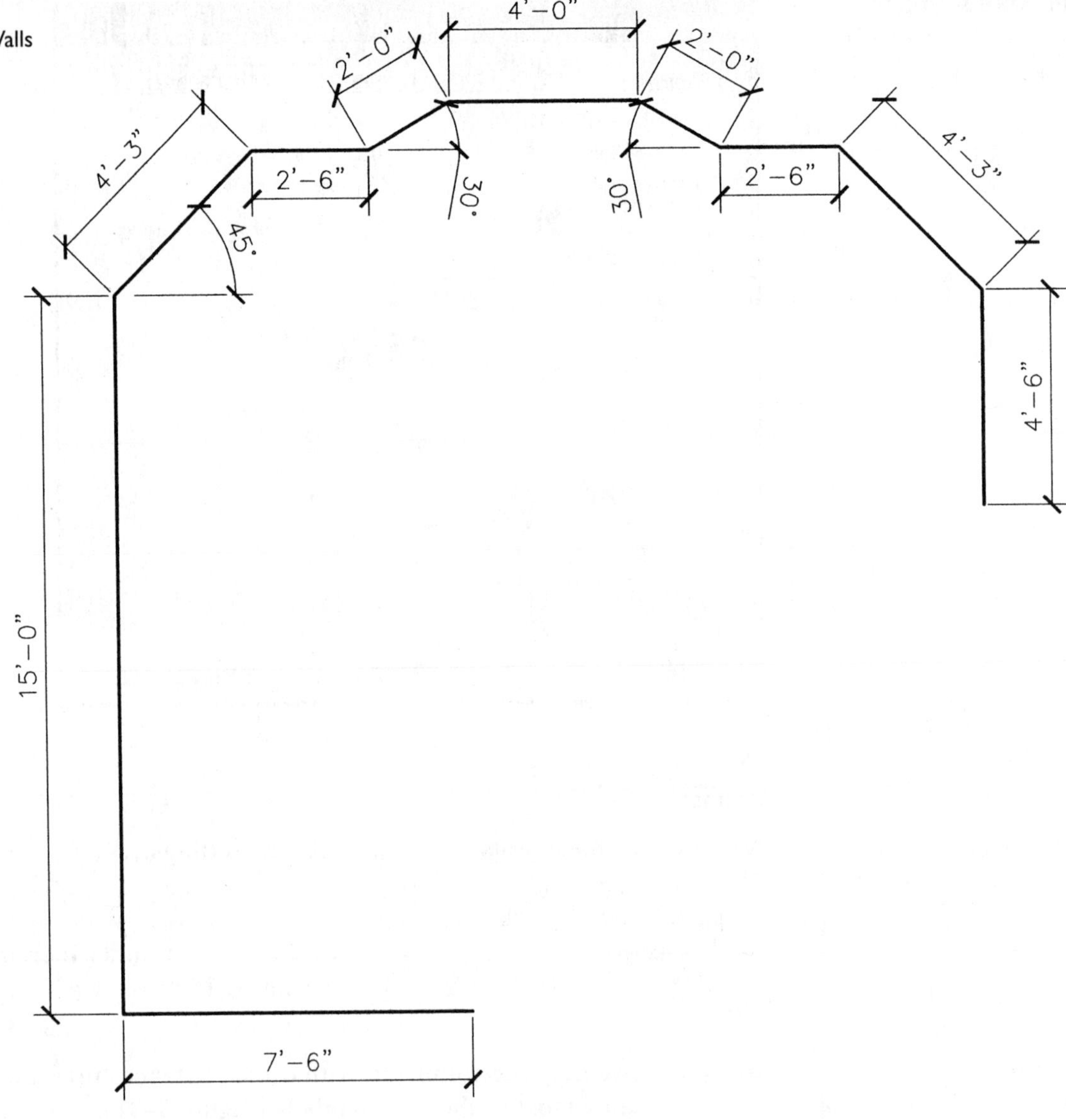

Prompt	Response
Specify next point or [Close/Undo]:	**Move your mouse so that <330° shows and** TYPE: **2'<enter>**
Specify next point or [Close/Undo]:	**Move your mouse so that <0° shows and** TYPE: **2'6<enter>**
Specify next point or [Close/Undo]:	**Move your mouse so that <315° shows and** TYPE: **4'3<enter>**
Specify next point or [Close/Undo]:	**Move your mouse straight down so that <270° shows and** TYPE: **4'6<enter>**
Specify next point or [Close/Undo]:	**<enter>** (to complete the Line command)

FROM AND OSNAP

Step 9. Draw an opening for the double door (Figure 3–32), as described next:

Prompt	Response
Command:	**<enter>** (to repeat the Line command)
Specify first point:	TYPE: **FRO<enter>**
Base point:	**OSNAP-Endpoint**

FIGURE 3–32
Draw the Door Opening and Use Zero Radius Fillet to Draw a Square Corner

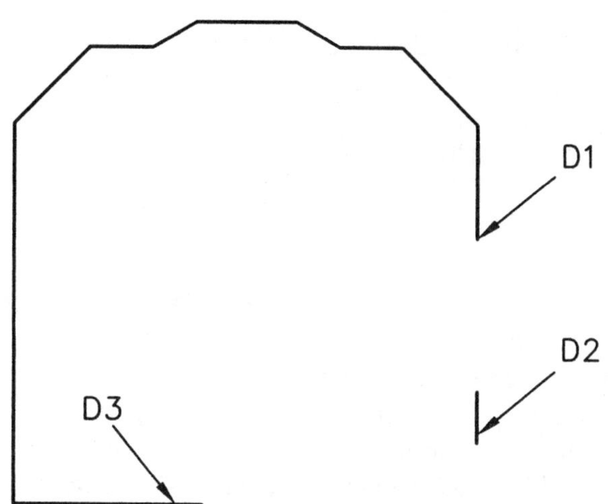

Prompt	Response
end of:	CLICK: **D1** (Figure 3–32)
<Offset>:	TYPE: **@6′<270<enter>**
Specify next point or [Undo]:	**Turn ORTHO ON**
	Move your mouse straight down and TYPE: **2′<enter>**
Specify next point or [Undo]:	**<enter>**

ZERO RADIUS FILLET

Step 10. Use Zero Radius Fillet to make a square corner on the lower left, as described next:

Prompt	Response
Command:	**FILLET** (or TYPE: **F<enter>**)
Current settings: Mode = TRIM, Radius = 0′-0″	TYPE: **R<enter>** (this is not necessary if the radius is already set at 0)
Specify fillet radius <default>:	TYPE: **0<enter>**
Select first object or [Undo/Polyline/Radius/Trim/Multiple]:	CLICK: **D2** (Figure 3–32)
Select second object or shift-select to apply corner:	CLICK: **D3**

POLYLINE EDIT

Step 11. Use Polyline Edit to join all lines into a single polyline and make it 5″ wide, as described next:

Prompt	Response
Command:	**Polyline Edit** (or TYPE: **PE<enter>**)
Select polyline or [Multiple]:	CLICK: **any of the lines**
Object selected is not a polyline	
Do you want to turn it into one? <Y>	**<enter>**

Prompt	Response
Enter an option [Close/Join/Width/ Edit vertex/Fit/Spline/Decurve/ Ltype gen/Reverse/Undo]:	TYPE: **J<enter>**
Select objects:	TYPE: **ALL<enter>** (or use a crossing window to select all)
11 found	
Select objects:	**<enter>**
10 segments added to polyline	
Enter an option [Close/Join/Width/ Edit vertex/Fit/Spline/Decurve/ Ltype gen/Reverse/Undo]:	TYPE: **W<enter>**
Specify new width for all segments:	TYPE: **5<enter>**
Enter an option [Close/Join/Width/ Edit vertex/Fit/Spline/Decurve/ Ltype gen/Reverse/Undo]:	**<enter>**

DRAW THE DOUBLE DOOR

Step 12. Set Layer a-door-sgl current. Draw one line of the double door using the Line command, as described next:

Prompt	Response
Command:	**Line** (or TYPE: **L<enter>**)
Specify first point:	**OSNAP-Endpoint**
end of:	CLICK: **D1** (Figure 3–33)
Specify next point or [Undo]:	**Turn ORTHO ON**
	Move your mouse to the left and TYPE: **3′<enter>**
Specify next point or [Undo]:	**<enter>**

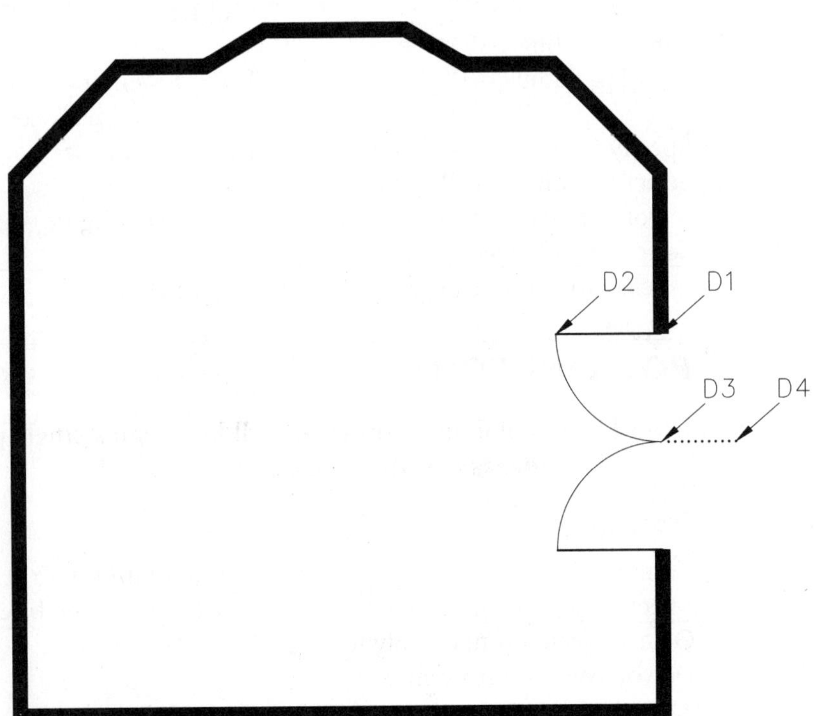

FIGURE 3–33
Use Line, Arc, and Mirror to Draw the Double Door

Step 13. **Set Layer a-door-swng current. Complete drawing the double door using the Arc and Mirror commands, as described next:**

Prompt	Response
Command:	**Arc-Center, Start, End**
Specify center point of arc: (Figure 3–33)	CLICK: **with a running Osnap-Endpoint, D1**
Specify start point of arc:	CLICK: **D2**
Specify end point of arc or [Angle/chord Length]:	**Move your mouse down and** CLICK: **D3**
Command:	**Mirror** (or TYPE: **MI<enter>**)
Select objects:	CLICK: **the line and the arc of the single door**
Select objects:	**<enter>**
Specify first point of mirror line:	CLICK: **D3** (Figure 3–33) (**running OSNAP-Endpoint**)
Specify second point of mirror line:	**With ORTHO ON**, CLICK: **D4** (or any point directly to the left or right of D3)
Erase source objects? [Yes/No] <N>:	**<enter>** (to answer No, do not erase the first door)

RECTANGLE

The Rectangle command allows you to draw a rectangle, chamfer or fillet the corners, and give width to the polyline that is created.

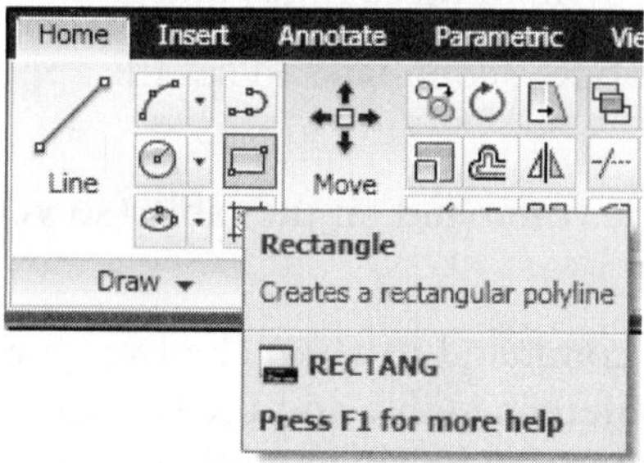

TRACKING

Tracking, which is similar to the ID Point command, allows you to specify points, except that you can activate Tracking whenever AutoCAD asks for a point. You can also specify as many points as you need until you arrive at the desired location, then you press Enter to end the tracking mode.

Step 14. **Set Layer i-furn current. Draw the table using Rectangle and Osnap-Tracking (Figure 3–29), as described next:**

Prompt	Response
Command:	**Rectangle** (or TYPE: **REC<enter>**)
Specify first corner point or [Chamfer/Elevation/Fillet/Thickness/Width]:	TYPE: **C<enter>**
Specify first chamfer distance for rectangles <0′-0″>:	TYPE: **2<enter>**
Specify second chamfer distance for rectangles <0′-2″>:	**<enter>**

Prompt	Response
Specify first corner point or [Chamfer/Elevation/Fillet/ Thickness/Width]:	TYPE: **TRACK<enter>**
First tracking point: int of	TYPE: **INT<enter> the lower left inside corner of the room**
Next point (Press ENTER to end tracking):	**Move your mouse to the right and** TYPE: **7′3 <enter>**
Next point (Press ENTER to end tracking):	**Move your mouse up and** TYPE: **4′6<enter>**
Next point (Press ENTER to end tracking):	**<enter>** (to end tracking)
Specify other corner point or [Area/Dimensions/Rotation]:	TYPE: **@48,120<enter>** (relative coordinates)

COMPLETE THE CONFERENCE ROOM

Step 15. Draw a rectangle 26″ wide and 28″ deep using the Line command (Figure 3–34).

Step 16. Use Fillet (12″ Radius) to edit the back of the rectangle to create the symbol of a chair.

Step 17. Copy the chair symbol three times and rotate it 90°, 180°, and −90°.

Step 18. Use the Point Style... command to set the appearance of points to X and size to 6″.

Step 19. Use the Explode command on the table (so you can use the Offset command).

Step 20. Use the Offset command to offset the two lines that define the long sides of the conference table and the two lines that define the ends of the conference table. The chairs will be placed 6″ from the edge of the table, so set 6″ as the offset distance. Offset the lines outside the table. These lines will be used as construction lines to help locate the chairs.

Step 21. Use Divide to divide the long offset lines into eight equal segments.

Step 22. Use the Copy command (combined with Osnap-Midpoint and Osnap-Node) to copy the chairs on all four sides of the conference table.

Step 23. Set Pdmode to 1 (invisible).

Step 24. Erase the offset lines used to locate the chairs; Tutorial 3–4 is complete.

Step 25. Set Layer a-anno-text current.

Step 26. Use the Single Line Text command (TYPE: DT<enter>) to type your name, class number, and date, 6″ H. in the upper right corner, Figure 3–34.

Step 27. When you have completed Tutorial 3–4, save your work in at least two places.

Step 28. Print your drawing from the Model tab at a scale of 1/4″ = 1′-0″.

FIGURE 3–34
Tutorial 3-4 Complete (Scale: 1/4″ = 1′-0″)

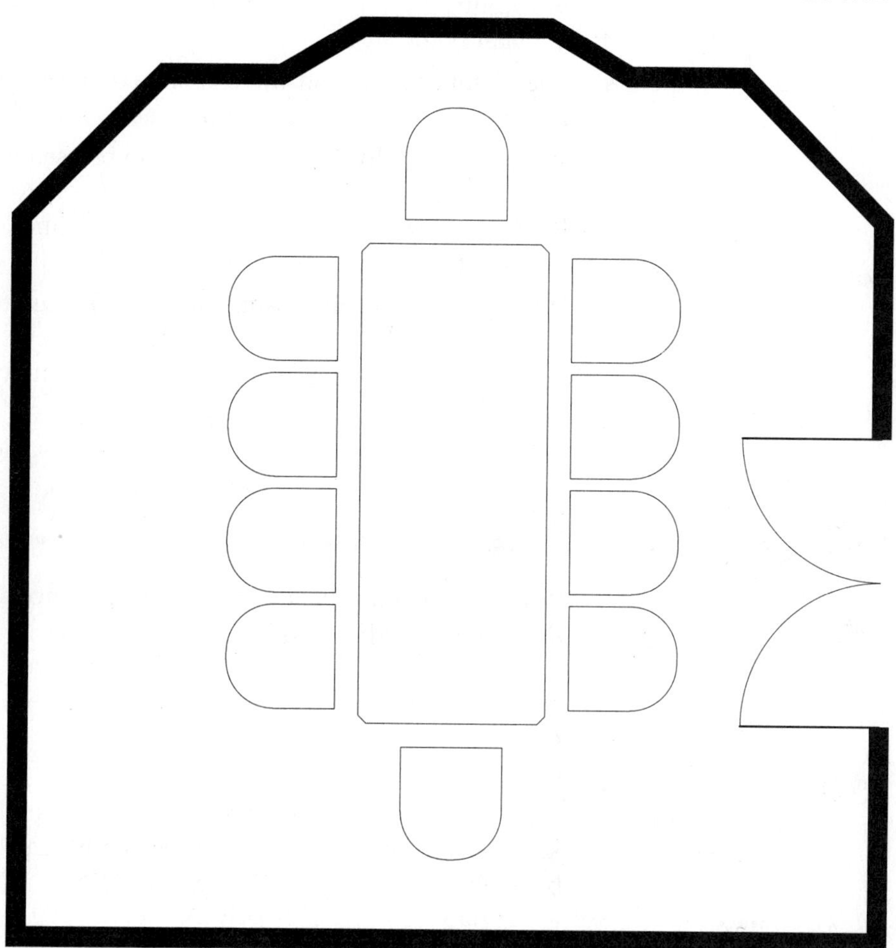

review questions

1. When the outline of the walls of a room is drawn with a zero-width polyline, which of the following commands can be used to draw most quickly the second line that shows the depth of the walls?
   a. Line
   b. Polyline
   c. Offset
   d. Copy
   e. Array
2. Which of the following commands is used to split a solid polyline into separate line segments?
   a. ID Point
   b. Offset
   c. Array
   d. Trim
   e. Explode

3. Which of the following commands is used to locate a point on a drawing and have the position of that point displayed in coordinates?
   a. ID Point
   b. Inquiry
   c. First point
   d. Aperture
   e. Distance
4. The Chamfer command will chamfer two lines that do not intersect.
   a. True
   b. False
5. Which of the following commands can be used to draw a rounded corner?
   a. Chamfer
   b. Fillet
   c. Offset
   d. Trim
   e. Edit Polyline
6. Which of the following Osnap modifiers is used to snap to a point entity?
   a. Perpendicular
   b. Endpoint
   c. Node
   d. Midpoint
   e. Intersection
7. Which of the following rotation angles is the same as −90°?
   a. 90
   b. 180
   c. 270
   d. 300
   e. 330
8. Which of the following controls the appearance of the markers used in the Divide command?
   a. Aperture Size
   b. Point Style
   c. Osnap
   d. Pickbox Size
   e. ID Point
9. Which of the following is used to change the size of the target box that appears when Modify commands are used?
   a. Aperture Size
   b. Point Style
   c. Osnap
   d. Pickbox Size
   e. ID Point
10. Which of the following commands can be used to join lines or arcs together and make them a single polyline?
   a. Explode
   b. Polyline Edit
   c. Polyline
   d. Close
   e. Edit vertex

Complete.

11. Describe the difference between a square drawn with the Line command and a square drawn with the Polyline command when Offset is used to offset the lines or polyline.

____

____

____

12. Describe what the Trim prompt "Select cutting edges... Select objects:" means.

____

____

13. Describe how to chamfer the corners of a rectangle using only the Rectangle command.

____

14. Describe how to change the width of an existing polyline.

____

15. Which command is used to determine the exact distance from one point to another?

____

16. Describe four different ways an Osnap mode can be activated.

____

____

____

____

17. When creating a counterclockwise polar array of six chairs arranged in a half circle, which "Angle to fill" would you use to form the array?

____

18. Describe the use of the option FROM.

____

19. Which Polyline Arc option allows you to draw a straight-line polyline after a polyline arc has been drawn?

____

20. Describe the use of Tracking.

____

exercises

Exercise 3–1: Drawing a Rectangular Conference Room, Including Furniture

A rectangular conference room including furniture (Figure 3–35) is drawn in Exercise 3–1. Use your workspace to make the following settings:

Step 1. CLICK: **Open..., change the Files of type: input box to Drawing Template (*.dwt) and open the Ch3-conference-rm-setup template, previously created at the beginning of Tutorial 3–1.**

Step 2. CLICK: **Save As…, change the Files of type: input box to AutoCAD 2010 Drawing (.dwg) and save the template as a drawing file named CH3-EX1.**

-or-

Step 3. Use your workspace to make the following settings:

1. **Use SaveAs… to save the drawing with the name CH3-EX1.**
2. Set drawing Units: **Architectural**
3. Set Drawing Limits: **25′,35′**
4. Set GRIDDISPLAY: **0**
5. Set Grid: **12″**
6. Set Snap: **6″**

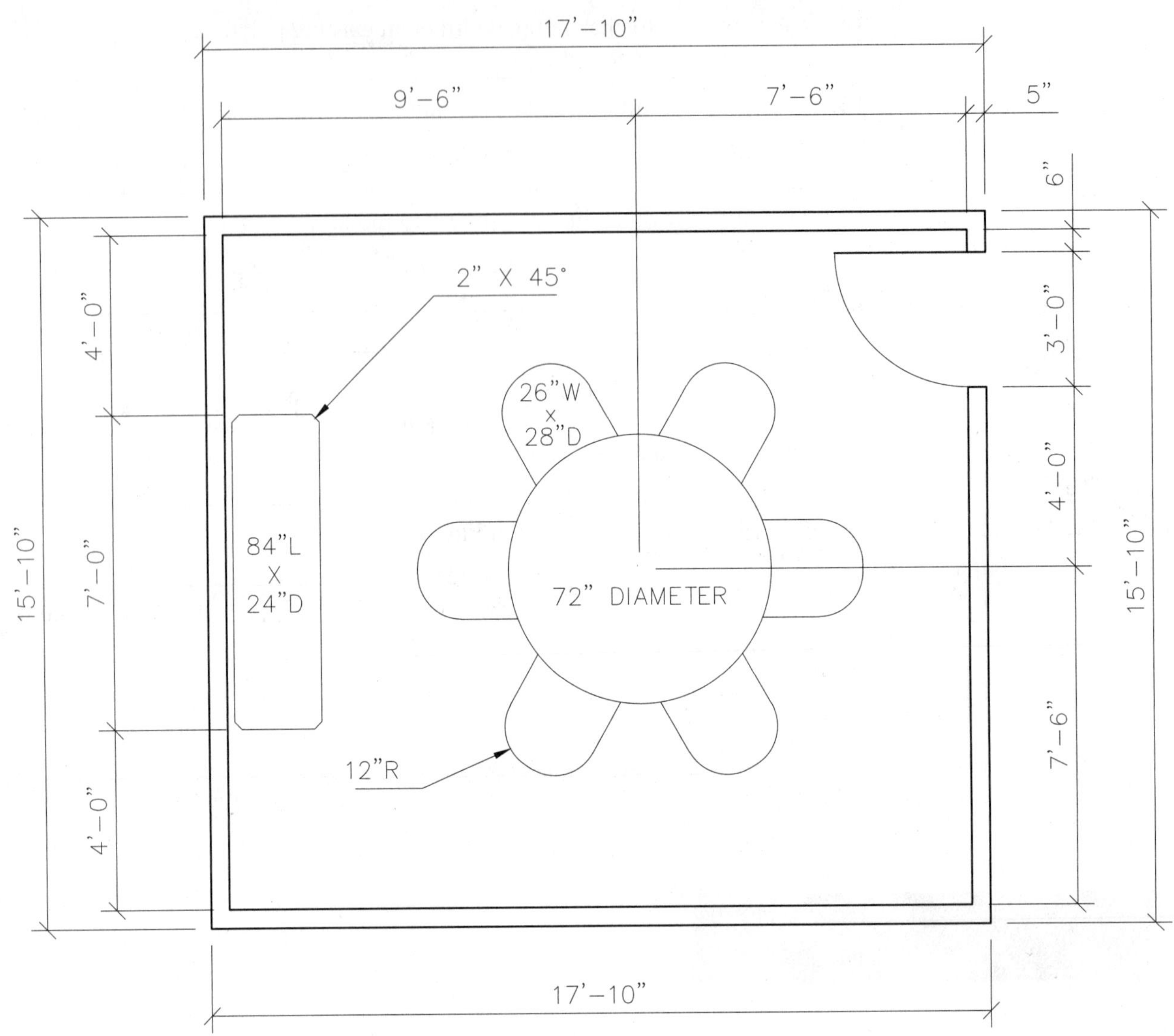

FIGURE 3–35
Exercise 3–1: Drawing a Rectangular Conference Room, Including Furniture (Scale: 1/4" = 1'-0")

7. Create the following layers:

LAYER NAME	COLOR	LINETYPE	LINEWEIGHT
a-wall-intr	blue	continuous	.007" (.18mm)
a-anno-text	green	continuous	.006" (.15mm)
a-door	blue	continuous	.007" (.18mm)
a-door-swng	red	continuous	.004" (.09mm)
i-furn	cyan	continuous	.004" (.09mm)

Step 4. Set Layer a-wall-intr current.

Step 5. Use Zoom-All to view the limits of the drawing.

Step 6. Turn SNAP, GRID, and LWT ON. The remaining buttons in the Status Bar should be OFF.

Step 7. Use the measurements shown in Figure 3–35 to draw the conference room full scale. Do not add the dimensions.

Step 8. Set Layer a-anno-text current.

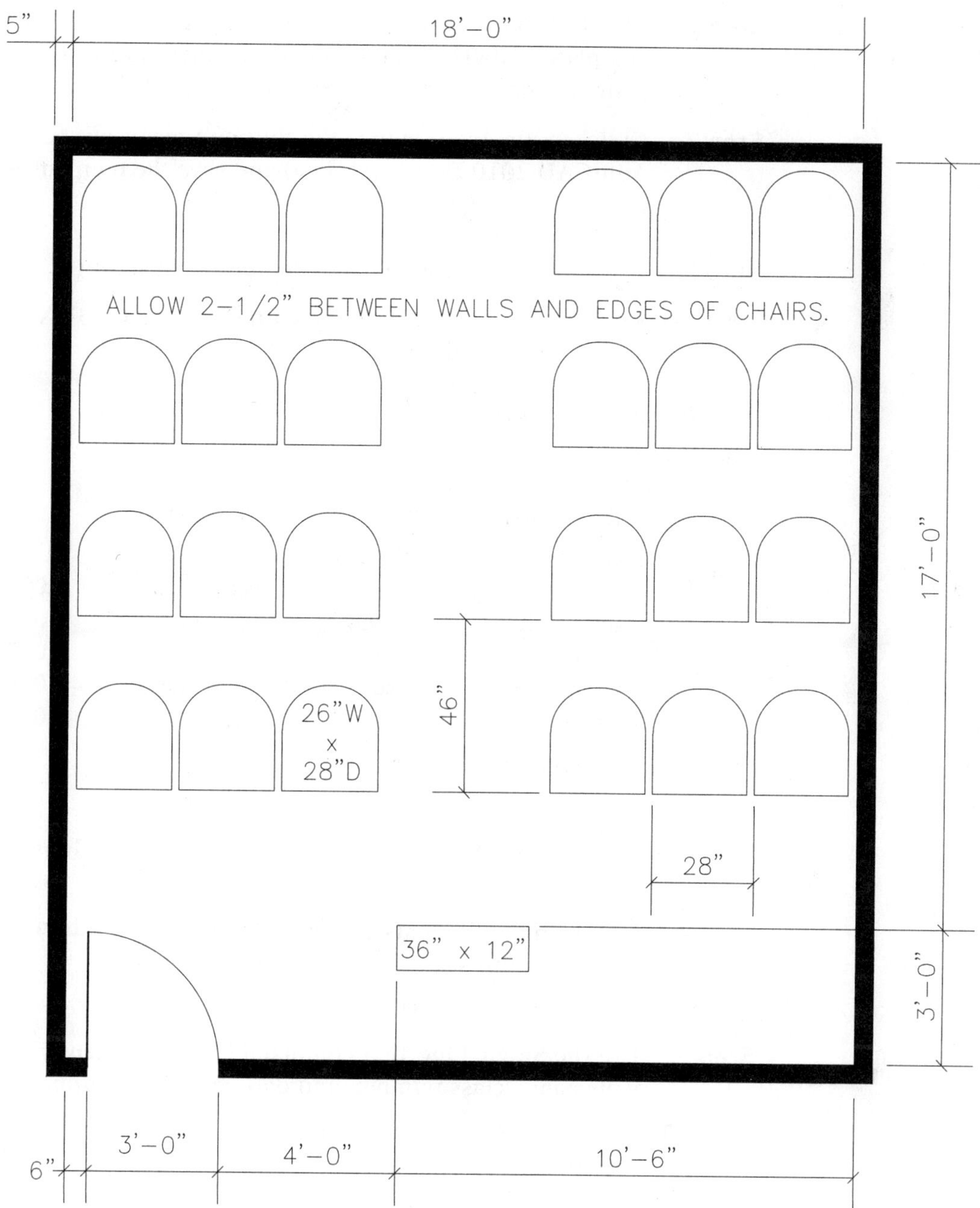

FIGURE 3–36
Exercise 3–2: Drawing a Rectangular Lecture Room, Including Furniture (Scale: 1/4" = 1'-0")

Step 9. Use the Single Line Text command (Type: DT<enter>) to type your name, class number, and date, 6"H. in the upper right corner.

Step 10. When you have completed Exercise 3–1, save your work in at least two places.

Step 11. Print your drawing from the Model tab at a scale of 1/4" = 1'-0".

Exercise 3–2: Drawing a Rectangular Lecture Room, Including Furniture

A lecture room including furniture (Figure 3–36) is drawn in Exercise 3–2. Use your workspace to make the following settings:

Step 1. CLICK: Open..., change the Files of type: input box to Drawing Template (*.dwt) and open the Ch3-conference-rm-setup template, previously created at the beginning of Tutorial 3–1.

Step 2. CLICK: Save As..., change the Files of type: input box to AutoCAD 2010 Drawing (.dwg) and save the template as a drawing file named CH3-EX2.

-or-

Step 3. Use your workspace to make the following settings:

1. Use SaveAs... to save the drawing with the name CH3-EX2.
2. Set drawing Units: **Architectural**
3. Set Drawing Limits: 25′,35′
4. Set GRIDDISPLAY: 0
5. Set Grid: 12″
6. Set Snap: 6″
7. Create the following layers:

LAYER NAME	COLOR	LINETYPE	LINEWEIGHT
a-wall-intr	blue	continuous	.007″ (.18mm)
a-anno-text	green	continuous	.006″ (.15mm)
a-door	blue	continuous	.007″ (.18mm)
a-door-swng	red	continuous	.004″ (.09mm)
i-furn	cyan	continuous	.004″ (.09mm)

Step 4. Set Layer a-wall-intr current.

Step 5. Use Zoom-All to view the limits of the drawing.

Step 6. Turn SNAP, GRID, and LWT ON. The remaining buttons in the Status Bar should be OFF.

Step 7. Use the measurements shown in Figure 3–36 to draw the conference room full scale. Do not add the dimensions.

Step 8. Set Layer a-anno-text current.

Step 9. Use the Single Line Text command (Type: DT<enter>) to type your name, class number, and date, 6″H. in the upper right corner.

Step 10. When you have completed Exercise 3-2, save your work in at least two places.

Step 11. Print your drawing from the Model tab at a scale of 1/4″ = 1′-0″.

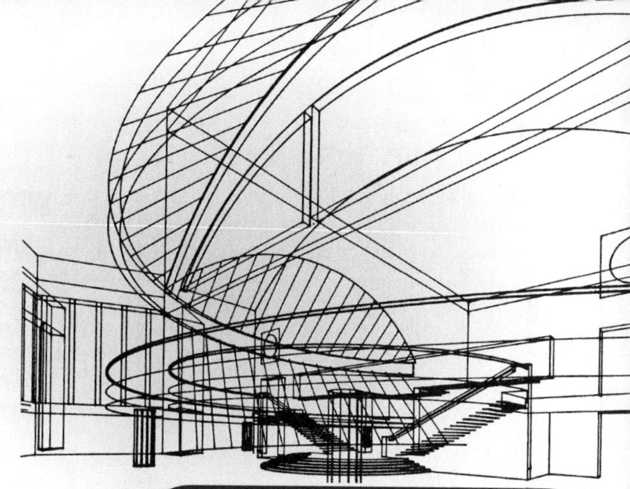

chapter

4

Adding Text, Tables, and Raster Images to the Drawing

objectives

When you have completed this chapter, you will be able to:

- Define the terms *style* and *font* and describe the function of each.
- Use different fonts on the same drawing.
- Place text on several different parts of the drawing with a single command.
- Use the modifiers Align, Fit, Center, Middle, Right, Top, and Style.
- Use the Text Style... setting to create condensed, expanded, rotated, backward, inclined, and upside-down text.
- Use the Text Style... setting to change any style on the drawing to a different font.
- Use standard codes to draw special characters such as the degree symbol, the diameter symbol, the plus and minus symbol, and underscored and overscored text.
- Use Mtext (multiline text) to create paragraph text.
- Spell check your drawing.
- Use the Table... command to create door and window schedules.
- Use Raster Image commands to insert pictures into AutoCAD drawings.

Tutorial 4–1: Placing Text on Drawings

To make complete drawings with AutoCAD, you need to know how text is added to the drawings. The following AutoCAD commands, used to place lettering on drawings, are examined in Tutorial 4–1.

Text Style... Used to control the appearance of text.
Single Line Text (Dtext) Used to draw text that is not in paragraph form.
Multiline Text (Mtext) Used to draw text that is in paragraph form.

When you have completed Tutorial 4–1, your drawing will look similar to the drawing in Figure 4–1.

FIGURE 4–1
Tutorial 4–1: Placing Text on Drawings

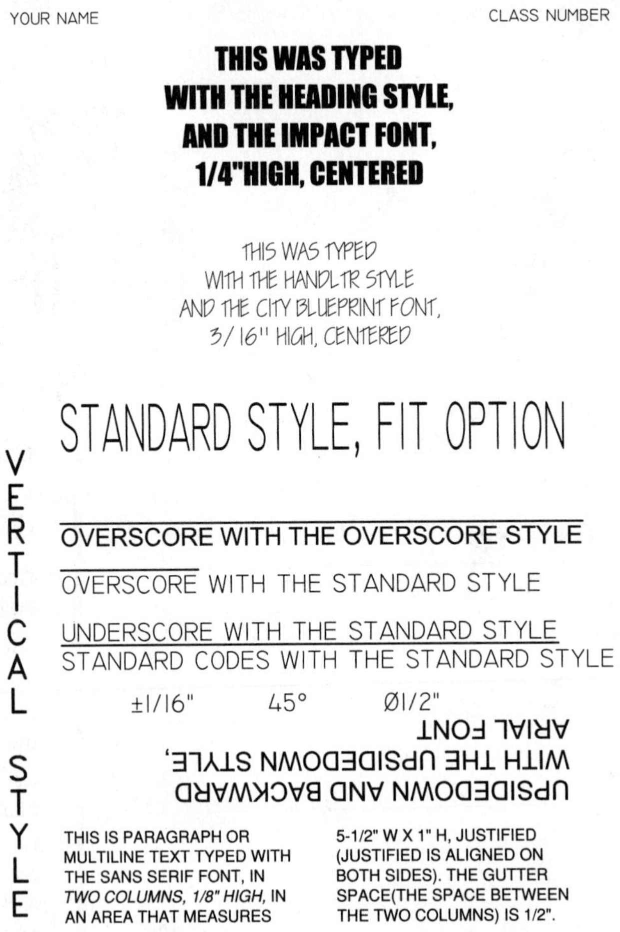

YOUR NAME CLASS NUMBER

THIS WAS TYPED
WITH THE HEADING STYLE,
AND THE IMPACT FONT,
1/4"HIGH, CENTERED

THIS WAS TYPED
WITH THE HANDLTR STYLE
AND THE CITY BLUEPRINT FONT,
3/16" HIGH, CENTERED

STANDARD STYLE, FIT OPTION

VERTICAL STYLE

OVERSCORE WITH THE OVERSCORE STYLE

OVERSCORE WITH THE STANDARD STYLE

UNDERSCORE WITH THE STANDARD STYLE

STANDARD CODES WITH THE STANDARD STYLE

±1/16" 45° Ø1/2"

UPSIDEDOWN AND BACKWARD
WITH THE UPSIDEDOWN STYLE,
ARIAL FONT

THIS IS PARAGRAPH OR MULTILINE TEXT TYPED WITH THE SANS SERIF FONT, IN *TWO COLUMNS, 1/8" HIGH,* IN AN AREA THAT MEASURES 5-1/2" W X 1" H, JUSTIFIED (JUSTIFIED IS ALIGNED ON BOTH SIDES). THE GUTTER SPACE(THE SPACE BETWEEN THE TWO COLUMNS) IS 1/2".

Step 1. Use your workspace to make the following settings:

1. **Use SaveAs... to save the drawing with the name, CH4-TUTORIAL1.**
2. Set drawing Units: **Architectural**
3. Set Drawing Limits: **8-1/2,11** (the inch mark is not needed)
4. Set GRIDDISPLAY: **0**
5. Set GRID: **1/4**
6. Set SNAP: **1/8**
7. Create the following layers:

LAYER NAME	COLOR	LINETYPE	LINEWEIGHT
a-anno-text	green	continuous	.006″ (.15mm)
a-area-iden	magenta	continuous	.006″ (.15mm)

8. Set **a-anno-text current**.
9. Use **Zoom-All** to view the limits of the drawing.

MAKING SETTINGS FOR TEXT STYLE...

It is important to understand the difference between the terms *style name* and *font name* with regard to text:

Style name This is a category that can be assigned any name you choose. The style name is used to separate fonts. You may use the same name for the style as is used for the font, or you may use a different name, single number, or letter for the style name. AutoCAD provides by default a style named Standard.

Font name: This is the name of any alphabet that you select to assign to a style name. A font has to be in the AutoCAD program before it can be selected and assigned to a style name. AutoCAD assigns the Arial font to the Standard style by default.

You may have only one font per style, but you can have many styles with the same font. For example,

Style Name	Font Name
SIMPLEX	SIMPLEX
CLIENT NAME	ITALIC
NOTES	SIMPLEX
ITALIC	ITALIC
BANNER	MONOTEXT
COMPANY NAME	ROMAND
ROMAND	ROMAND

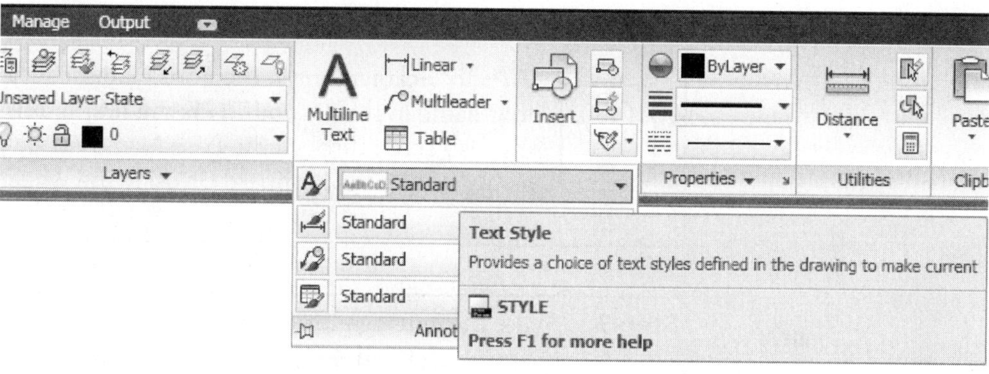

Step 2. Make the setting for the STANDARD style (Figure 4–2), as described next:

Prompt	Response
Command:	**Text Style...** (or TYPE: **ST<enter>**)
The Text Style dialog box appears:	CLICK: **TechnicLite** (in the Font Name: list)
	CLICK: **Apply**

FIGURE 4–2
Select the TechnicLite Font for the Standard Style

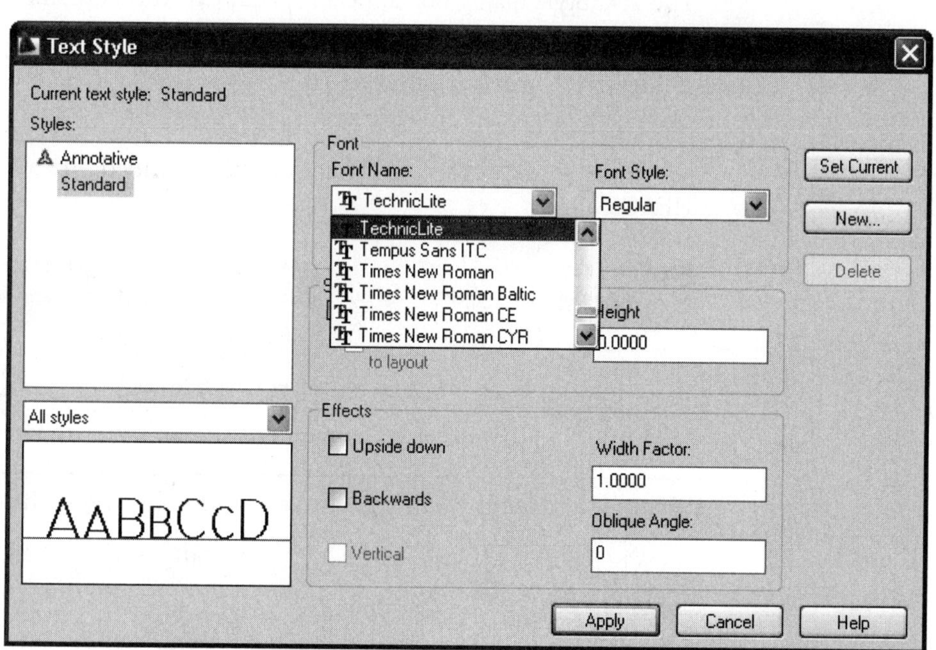

Any text typed while the STANDARD style is active will now contain the TechnicLite font. Notice the preview area in the lower left corner that shows you what the font looks like. Notice also that the vertical setting is grayed out, indicating that this font cannot be drawn running up and down.

The other settings should be left as they are. If you leave the text height set at 0, you will be able to draw different heights of the same style and you will be able to change the height of text if you need to. Leave the text height set to 0 in all cases. The Width Factor allows you to stretch letters so they are wider by making the Width Factor greater than 1, narrower by making the Width Factor less than 1. The Oblique Angle slants the letters to the right if the angle is positive and to the left if the angle is negative.

AutoCAD also provides a style named Annotative. This style is used when text is added to a drawing that will be plotted to scale (e.g., 1/4″ = 1′-0″). Any style can be made annotative in the Text Style dialog box by clicking the box under Size and beside Annotative to put a check in the box. Annotative will be described and used in Chapter 6.

TIP: To locate a font in the Font Name: list, hold your cursor over any font name in the list and TYPE: the first letter of the desired font. You can also scroll through the Font Name: list by pressing the up or down arrow key on the keyboard or using the wheel on your wheel mouse.

Step 3. Make the settings for a new style that will be used on the drawing (Figures 4–3 and 4–4), as described next:

Prompt	Response
The Text Style dialog box:	CLICK: **New...** (button on the right)
The New Text Style dialog box appears with a Style Name that AutoCAD assigns, style1:	TYPE: **HEADING** (to name the style, Figure 4–3) CLICK: **OK** (or PRESS: **<enter>**)
The Text Style dialog box appears:	CLICK: **romand.shx** (in the Font Name: list, Figure 4–4) Remove the check in the Annotative box CLICK: **Apply**

You now have two styles that have been defined on your drawing, STANDARD and HEADING.

FIGURE 4–3
Name the Style, HEADING

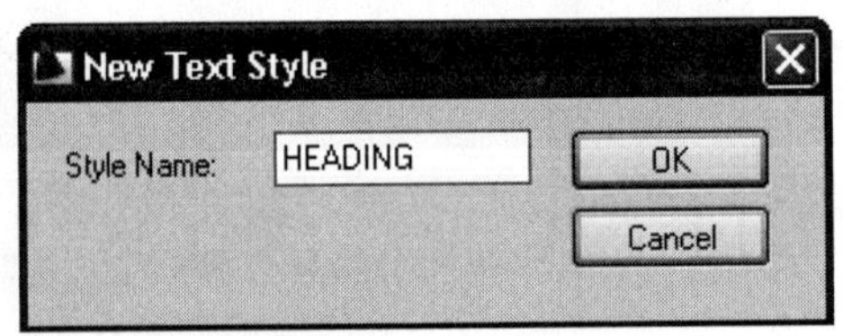

Step 4. Make the settings for the following new styles (Figure 4–5):

Style Name	Font Name	Other Settings
HANDLTR	CityBlueprint	None
OVERSCORE	Arial	None

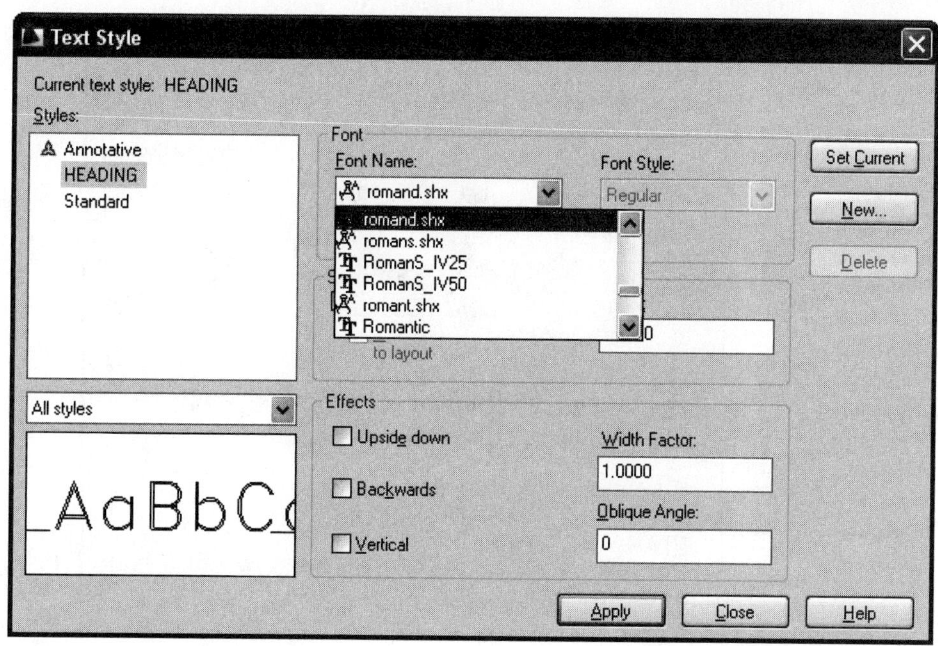

FIGURE 4–4
Select the romand.shx Font for the HEADING Style

UPSIDEDOWN	Arial	Place checks in the Effects box labeled Upside down and the box labeled Backwards.
VERTICAL	romand.shx	Place a check in the Effects box labeled Vertical, Figure 4–5. Remove checks in Upside down and Backwards.

Step 5. **Click the down arrow in the Styles list to determine whether your list matches the one shown in Figure 4–6.**

Step 6. **Click the HEADING style name and the Set Current button to make it current; close the dialog box.**

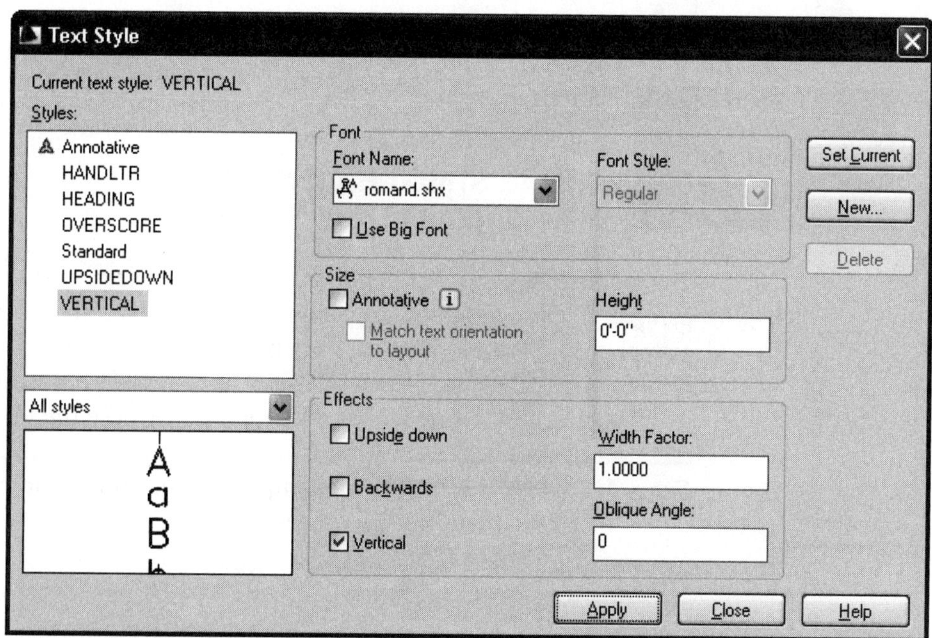

FIGURE 4–5
Make Settings for the VERTICAL Style

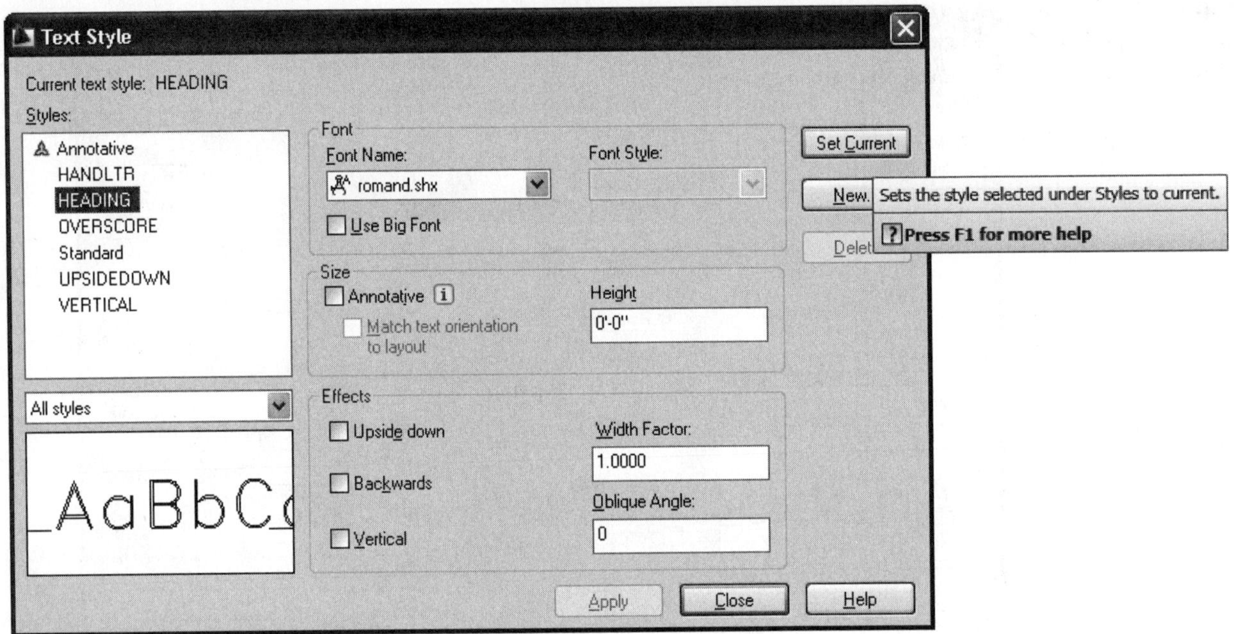

FIGURE 4–6
Check the Styles List and Set the HEADING Style Current

NOTE: If you make a mistake while making the settings for a new style, go back to the Text Style dialog box, highlight the style name, change or fix the settings, and CLICK: **Apply**.

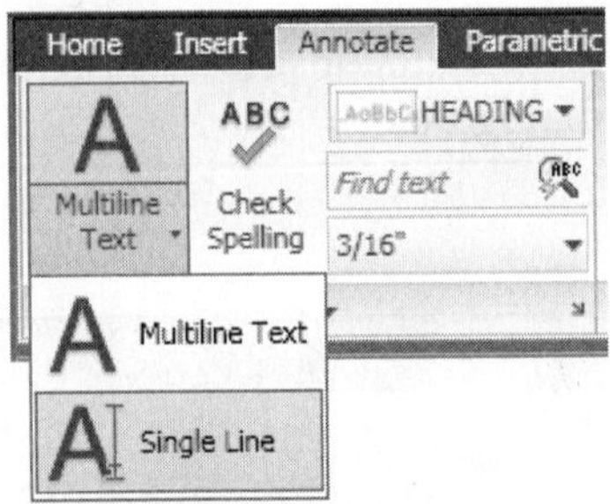

USING THE SINGLE LINE TEXT COMMAND TO DRAW TEXT

The Single Line Text command (also known as Dtext) is used to draw text that is not in paragraph form. Although the name of the command might lead you to believe that only a single line can be drawn, such is not the case. To draw one line under another, just PRESS: **<enter>**, and the next line can be drawn with the same settings as the first line.

If you are not happy with the location of text, use the Move command to relocate it.

Step 7. Draw the first two examples at the top of the page using single line text (Figure 4–7), as described next:

Prompt	Response
Command:	**Single Line Text** (or TYPE: **DT<enter>**)

FIGURE 4–7
First Two Examples of Single Line Text

THIS WAS TYPED
WITH THE HEADING STYLE,
AND THE ROMAND FONT,
1/4" HIGH

THIS WAS TYPED
WITH THE HANDLTR STYLE,
AND THE CITY BLUEPRINT FONT,
3/16" HIGH, CENTERED

Prompt	Response
Specify start point of text or [Justify/Style]:	TYPE: **C<enter>**
Specify center point of text:	TYPE: **4-1/4,10<enter>** (You are locating the center of the line of text using absolute coordinates, 4-1/4″ to the right and 10″ up)
Specify height <0′-0 3/16″>:	TYPE: **1/4<enter>**
Specify rotation angle of text <0>:	**<enter>**
The In-Place Text Editor appears ON the screen:	TYPE: **THIS WAS TYPED<enter>**
	TYPE: **WITH THE HEADING STYLE, <enter>**
Command:	TYPE: **AND THE ROMAND FONT,<enter>**
	TYPE: **1/4″ HIGH<enter>**
	<enter> (to exit the Text Editor)
	<enter> (repeat DTEXT)
Specify start point of text or [Justify/Style]:	TYPE: **S<enter>** (to change styles)
Enter style name or [?] <HEADING>:	TYPE: **HANDLTR<enter>**
Specify start point of text or [Justify/Style]:	TYPE: **C<enter>**
Specify center point of text:	TYPE: **4-1/4,8<enter>**
Specify height <0′-0 1/4″>:	TYPE: **3/16<enter>**
Specify rotation angle of text <0>:	**<enter>**
The In-Place Text Editor appears:	TYPE: **THIS WAS TYPED<enter>**
	TYPE: **WITH THE HANDLTR STYLE,<enter>**
	TYPE: **AND THE CITY BLUEPRINT FONT, <enter>**
	TYPE: **3/16″ HIGH, CENTERED <enter>**
	<enter>

Step 8. **Draw the next block of text using the Fit option of single line text with the STANDARD style (Figure 4–8), as described next:**

Prompt	Response
Command:	**Single Line Text** (or TYPE: **DT<enter>**)
Specify start point of text or [Justify/Style]:	TYPE: **S<enter>** (to change styles)
Enter style name or [?] <HANDLTR>:	TYPE: **STANDARD<enter>**

FIGURE 4–8
Using the Fit Option of Single Line Text

THIS WAS TYPED
WITH THE HEADING STYLE,
AND THE ROMAND FONT,
1/4" HIGH

THIS WAS TYPED
WITH THE HANDLTR STYLE,
AND THE CITY BLUEPRINT FONT,
3/16" HIGH, CENTERED

STANDARD STYLE, FIT OPTION

Prompt	Response
Specify start point of text or [Justify/Style]:	TYPE: **F<enter>** (for Fit)
Specify first endpoint of text baseline:	TYPE: **1-1/2,6<enter>**
Specify second endpoint of text baseline:	TYPE: **7,6<enter>**
Specify height <0′-0 3/16″>:	TYPE: **1/2<enter>**
The In-Place Text Editor appears:	TYPE: **STANDARD STYLE, FIT OPTION <enter> <enter>**

When you activate the Single Line Text command, the prompt is "Specify start point of text or [Justify/Style]:". The Style option allows you to select a different style (that has already been defined) for the text you are about to draw. If you TYPE: **J<enter>**, the prompt then becomes "Enter an option [Align/Fit/Center/Middle/Right/TL/TC/TR/ML/MC/MR/BL/BC/BR]:".

Align

Align draws the text between two points that you click. It does not condense or expand the font but instead adjusts the letter height so that the text fits between the two points.

Fit

Fit draws the text between two clicked points like the Align option, but instead of changing the letter height, Fit condenses or expands the font to fit between the points.

Center

Center draws the text so that the bottom of the line of lettering is centered on the clicked point. You may also choose the top or the middle of the line of lettering by typing TC or MC at the justify prompt.

Middle

Middle draws the text so that the middle of the line of lettering is centered around a clicked point. This is useful when a single line of text must be centered in an area such as a box.

Right

Right draws the text so that each line of text is right justified (ends at the same right margin). The top or center of the line may also be selected by typing TR or MR at the justify prompt.

TL/TC/TR/ML/MC/MR/BL/BC/BR

These are alignment options: Top Left, Top Center, Top Right, Middle Left, Middle Center, Middle Right, Bottom Left, Bottom Center, Bottom Right. They are used with horizontal text.

Step 9. Draw a line of text using the VERTICAL style (Figure 4–9), as described next:

(Remember that you checked Vertical in the Text Style dialog box for this text style.)

Prompt	Response
Command:	**<enter>** (repeat DTEXT)
Specify start point of text or [Justify/Style]:	TYPE: **S<enter>**
Enter style name or [?] <Standard>:	TYPE: **VERTICAL<enter>**
Specify start point of text or [Justify/Style]:	TYPE: **1,6<enter>**
Specify height <0′-0″ 3/16″>:	TYPE: **1/4<enter>**
Specify rotation angle of text <270>:	**<enter>**
The In-Place Text Editor appears:	TYPE: **VERTICAL STYLE<enter> <enter>**

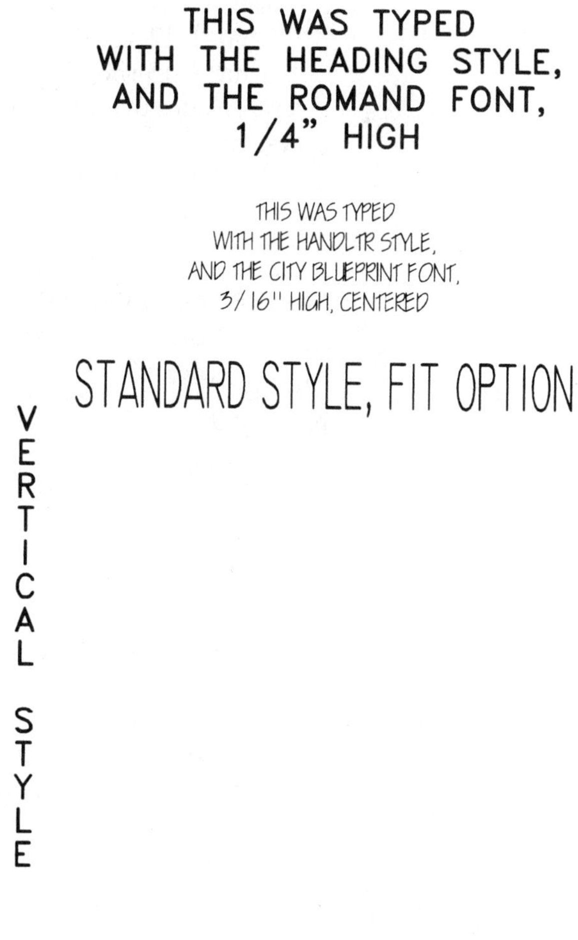

FIGURE 4–9
Using the Vertical Option of Single Line Text

THIS WAS TYPED
WITH THE HEADING STYLE,
AND THE ROMAND FONT,
1/4" HIGH

THIS WAS TYPED
WITH THE HANDLTR STYLE,
AND THE CITY BLUEPRINT FONT,
3/16" HIGH, CENTERED

STANDARD STYLE, FIT OPTION

VERTICAL STYLE

45%%D

45°

FIGURE 4–10
Degree Symbol Code

%%C.500

⌀.500

FIGURE 4–11
Diameter Symbol Code

%%P.005

±.005

FIGURE 4–12
Plus–Minus Symbol Code

%%UUNDERSCORE

UNDERSCORE

%%UUNDERSCORE%%U LETTERS

UNDERSCORE LETTERS

FIGURE 4–13
Underscore Code

%%OOVERSCORE

OVERSCORE

%%OOVERSCORE%%O LETTERS

OVERSCORE LETTERS

FIGURE 4–14
Overscore Code

USING STANDARD CODES TO DRAW SPECIAL CHARACTERS

Figures 4–10 through 4–14 show the use of codes to obtain several commonly used symbols, such as the degree symbol, the diameter symbol, the plus–minus symbol, and underscored and overscored text. The top line of Figure 4–10 shows the code that must be typed to obtain the degree symbol following the number 45. Two percent symbols followed by the letter D produce the degree symbol.

Figure 4–11 illustrates that two percent symbols followed by the letter C produce the diameter symbol.

Figure 4–12 shows the code for the plus–minus symbol.

Figure 4–13 shows the code for underscore: two percent symbols followed by the letter U. Notice that the first line contains only one code. The second line contains two codes: one to start the underline and one to stop it.

Figure 4–14 shows the code for overscored text. The same code sequence for starting and stopping the overscore applies.

Step 10. Draw five lines containing special codes for the overscore, underscore, plus–minus, degree, and diameter symbols (Figure 4–15), as described next:

Prompt	Response
Command:	**<enter>** (repeat DTEXT)
Specify start point of text or [Justify/Style]:	TYPE: **S<enter>**
Enter style name or [?] <VERTICAL>:	TYPE: **OVERSCORE<enter>**
Specify start point of text or [Justify/Style]:	TYPE: **1-1/2,5<enter>**
Specify height <0′-0 3/16″>:	TYPE: **3/16<enter>**
Specify rotation angle of text <0>:	**<enter>**
The In-Place Text Editor appears:	TYPE: **%%OOVERSCORE WITH THE OVERSCORE STYLE<enter><enter>**
Command:	**<enter>** (repeat DTEXT)

FIGURE 4–15
Using Single Line Text to Draw Symbols with Standard Codes

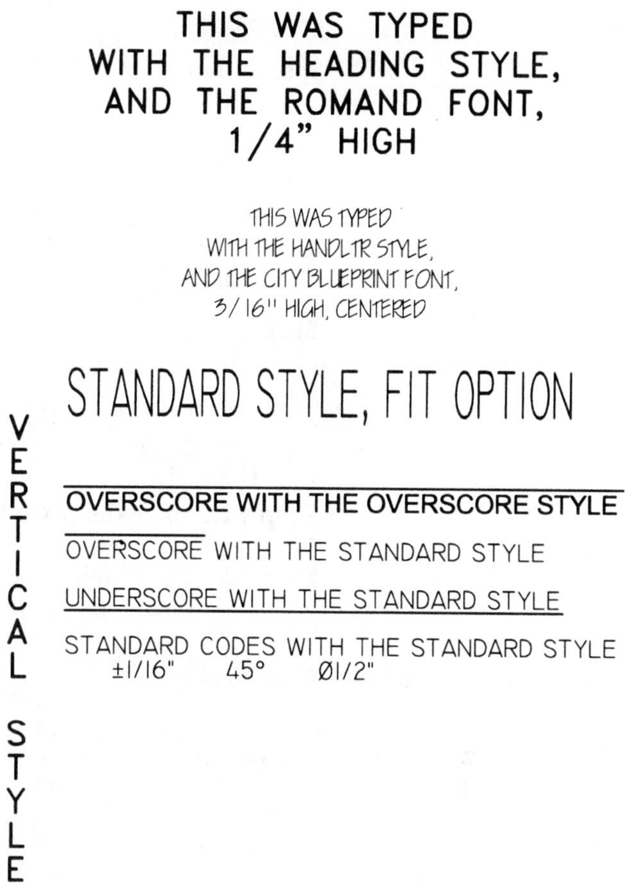

THIS WAS TYPED
WITH THE HEADING STYLE,
AND THE ROMAND FONT,
1/4" HIGH

THIS WAS TYPED
WITH THE HANDLTR STYLE,
AND THE CITY BLUEPRINT FONT,
3/16" HIGH, CENTERED

STANDARD STYLE, FIT OPTION

VERTICAL STYLE

OVERSCORE WITH THE OVERSCORE STYLE

OVERSCORE WITH THE STANDARD STYLE

UNDERSCORE WITH THE STANDARD STYLE

STANDARD CODES WITH THE STANDARD STYLE
±1/16" 45° Ø1/2"

Prompt	Response
Specify start point of text or [Justify/Style]:	TYPE: **S<enter>**
Enter style name or [?] <OVERSCORE>:	TYPE: **STANDARD<enter>**
Specify start point of text or [Justify/Style]:	TYPE: **1-1/2,4-1/2<enter>**
Specify height <0′-0 1/2″>:	TYPE: **3/16<enter>**
Specify rotation angle of text <0>:	**<enter>**
The In-Place Text Editor appears:	TYPE: **%%OOVERSCORE%%O WITH THE STANDARD STYLE<enter> <enter>**
Command:	**<enter>** (Repeat DTEXT)
Specify start point of text or [Justify/Style]:	TYPE: 1-1/2,4**<enter>**
Specify height <0′-0 1/2″>:	TYPE: **3/16<enter>**
Specify rotation angle of text <0>	**<enter>**
The In-Place Text Editor appears:	TYPE: **%%UUNDERSCORE WITH THE STANDARD STYLE<enter> <enter>**
Command:	**<enter>** (Repeat DTEXT)
Specify start point of text or [Justify/Style]:	**<enter>**
The In-Place Text Editor appears:	TYPE: **STANDARD CODES WITH THE STANDARD STYLE<enter> <enter>**
Command:	**<enter>** (Repeat DTEXT)

Prompt	Response
Specify start point of text or [Justify/Style]:	CLICK: **a point in the approximate location ±1/16″, as shown in Figure 4–15**
Specify height <0′-0 3/16″>:	**<enter>** (to accept the 3/16″ default height)
Specify rotation angle of text <0>:	**<enter>**
The In-Place Text Editor appears:	TYPE: **%%P1/16″<enter> <enter>**
Command:	

Step 11. **Use Single Line Text (DTEXT) to add the following text (3/16 height) to your drawing, as shown in Figure 4–15:**

45° (45 %%D)
Ø1/2″ (%%C1/2″)

Step 12. **Make the Style Name UPSIDEDOWN current.**

Step 13. **Use Single Line Text to draw the following phrase (3/16 height) upside down and backward with its start point at 7,2-1/2 (Figure 4–16):**

UPSIDEDOWN AND BACKWARD <enter>
WITH THE UPSIDEDOWN STYLE, <enter>
ARIAL FONT <enter> <enter>

THIS WAS TYPED
WITH THE HEADING STYLE,
AND THE ROMAND FONT,
1/4" HIGH, CENTERED

THIS WAS TYPED
WITH THE HANDLTR STYLE,
AND THE CITY BLUEPRINT FONT,
3/16" HIGH, CENTERED

STANDARD STYLE, FIT OPTION

VERTICAL STYLE

OVERSCORE WITH THE OVERSCORE STYLE

OVERSCORE WITH THE STANDARD STYLE

UNDERSCORE WITH THE STANDARD STYLE

STANDARD CODES WITH THE STANDARD STYLE
±1/16" 45° Ø1/2"

UPSIDE DOWN AND BACKWARD
WITH THE UPSIDEDOWN STYLE,
ARIAL FONT

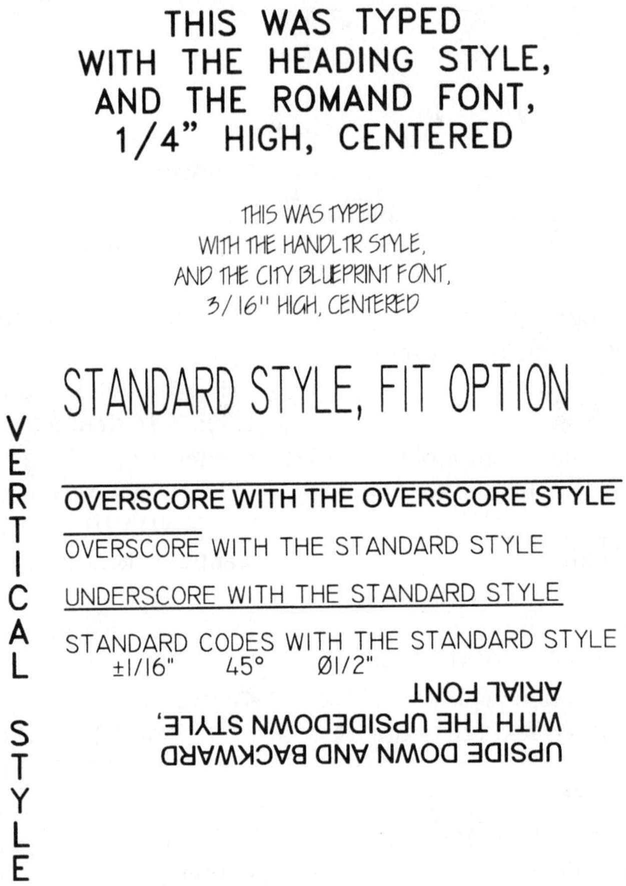

FIGURE 4–16
Draw a Phrase Upside Down and Backward with the UPSIDE-DOWN Style

USING THE MULTILINE TEXT COMMAND TO DRAW TEXT PARAGRAPHS IN COLUMNS

The Multiline Text command (also known as Mtext) is used to draw text in paragraph form. The command activates the Text Formatting Editor, which has many of the same features that other Windows Text Editors have. You can select a defined style, change the text height and case, boldface and italicize some fonts, select a justification style, specify the width of the paragraph (or columns and the space between columns within the paragraph), rotate a paragraph, search for a word and replace it with another, undo, import text, number lines, insert bullets, and select symbols for use on your drawing. In this exercise, you will create a paragraph in two columns using the SansSerif font.

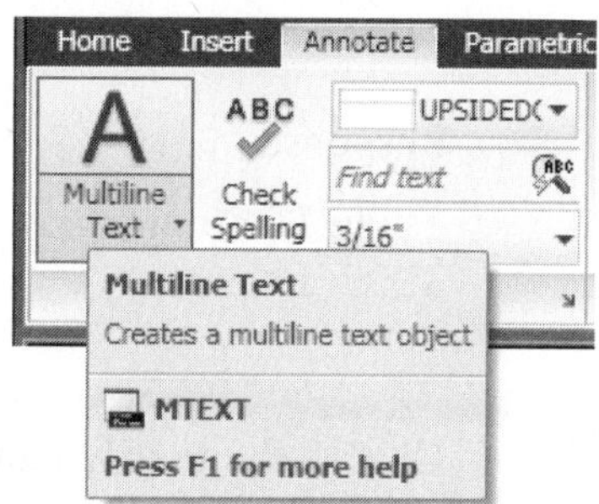

Step 14. Create a new text style and use Multiline Text to draw a paragraph in two columns, as described next:

Prompt	Response
Command:	TYPE: **ST<enter>**
The Text Style dialog box appears:	CLICK: **New**
The New Text Style dialog box appears:	TYPE: **PARAGRAPH** (as the new style name) CLICK: **OK**
The Text Style dialog box appears:	Change the Font Name: to **SansSerif** **Remove checks from Annotative, Upside-down, and Backward** (if these are checked) CLICK: **Set Current**
The current style has been modified. Do you want to save your changes?	CLICK: **Yes** CLICK: **Close**
Command:	**Multiline Text...** (or TYPE: **MT<enter>**)
Specify first corner:	TYPE: **1-1/2, 2<enter>**
Specify opposite corner or [Height/Justify/Line spacing/Rotation/Style/Width/Columns]:	TYPE: **H<enter>**
Specify height <3/16″>:	TYPE: **1/8<enter>**
Specify opposite corner or [Height/Justify/Line spacing/Rotation/Style/Width/Columns]:	TYPE: **C<enter>**
Enter column type [Dynamic/Static/No columns] <Dynamic>:	TYPE: **S<enter>**
Specify total width: <1′-3″>:	TYPE: **5-1/2<enter>**
Specify number of columns: <2>:	TYPE: **2<enter>**

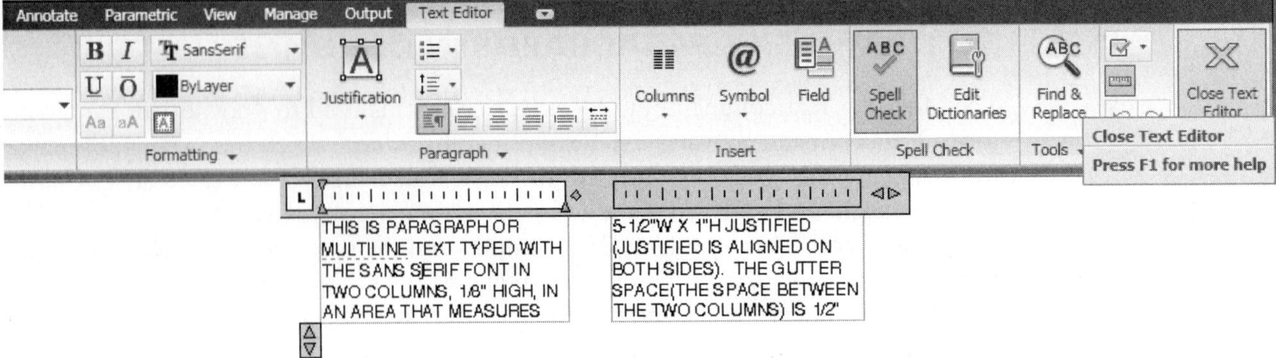

FIGURE 4–17
Multiline Text in Two Columns

Prompt	Response
Specify gutter width: <1″>:	TYPE: **1/2<enter>**
Specify column height: <2″>:	TYPE: **1<enter>**
The Text Formatting Editor appears, and the Ribbon changes:	CLICK: **the Justify icon** (so the text is flush right and flush left) TYPE: **The paragraph shown in Figures 4–17 and 4–19.** When you type 1/8 in the paragraph, the dialog box shown in Figure 4–18 appears. Remove the check from Enable Autostacking After the paragraph is typed correctly, CLICK: **Close Text Editor** (on the Ribbon)

CHANGING TEXT PROPERTIES

Sometimes you will need to change the text font, height, or content. AutoCAD has several commands that can be used to do this:

Text Style... Use this command to change the font of a text style that already exists on your drawing.

FIGURE 4–18
Do Not Stack Fractions and Tolerances

FIGURE 4–19
Type Multiline Text in Two Columns

THIS WAS TYPED
WITH THE HEADING STYLE,
AND THE ROMAND FONT,
1/4"HIGH

THIS WAS TYPED
WITH THE HANDLTR STYLE
AND THE CITY BLUEPRINT FONT,
3/16" HIGH, CENTERED

STANDARD STYLE, FIT OPTION

VERTICAL STYLE

OVERSCORE WITH THE OVERSCORE STYLE

OVERSCORE WITH THE STANDARD STYLE

UNDERSCORE WITH THE STANDARD STYLE

STANDARD CODES WITH THE STANDARD STYLE

±1/16"   45°   Ø1/2"

ARIAL FONT
WITH THE UPSIDEDOWN STYLE,
UPSIDEDOWN AND BACKWARD

THIS IS PARAGRAPH OR MULTILINE TEXT TYPED WITH THE SANS SERIF FONT . IN TWO COLUMNS, 1/8" HIGH, IN AN AREA THAT MEASURES 5-1/2" W X 1" H. JUSTIFIED (JUSTIFIED IS ALIGNED ON BOTH SIDES). THE GUTTER SPACE(THE SPACE BETWEEN THE TWO COLUMNS) IS 1/2".

DDEDIT (same as DOUBLE-CLICK) Use this command if you want to change the text contents only for Single Line Text. This command allows you to select multi-line text to change its contents and several of its properties.

Properties Use this command to change any of the text's characteristics: properties, origin, style, height, rotation angle, the text content, or any of several other properties.

Step 15. Use the Text Style... command to change the font of text typed with the HEADING name from Romand to Impact (Figure 4–20), as described next:

Prompt	Response
Command:	**Text Style...** (or TYPE: **ST<enter>**)
The Text Style dialog box appears:	CLICK: **HEADING** (in the Styles: list)
	CLICK: **Set Current**
	CLICK: **Impact** (from the Font Name: list, Figure 4–20)
	CLICK: **Apply**
	CLICK: **Close**

Notice that everything you typed with the HEADING style name is now still the HEADING style but changed to the Impact font.

FIGURE 4–20
Select the Impact Font for the HEADING Style

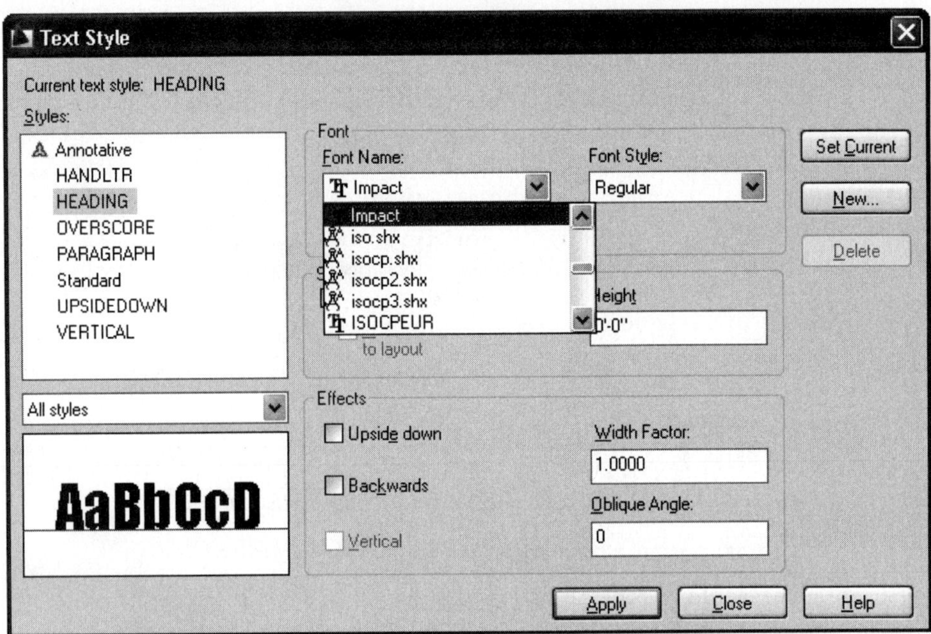

FIGURE 4–21
Change Text Using DDEDIT (Edit Text)

THIS WAS TYPED
WITH THE HEADING STYLE,
AND THE IMPACT FONT,
1/4" HIGH

Step 16. **Use the DDEDIT command to change "AND THE ROMAND FONT" at the top of the page to "AND THE IMPACT FONT" (Figure 4–21), as described next:**

Prompt	Response
Command:	DOUBLE-CLICK: **AND THE ROMAND FONT**
The In-Place Text Editor appears:	CLICK: **to the right of ROMAND, backspace over ROMAND** and TYPE: **IMPACT** (Figure 4–21)
Select an annotation object or [Undo]:	**<enter><enter>**

NOTE: Double-click on any text to edit it.

FIGURE 4–22
Change Multiline Text to Italic

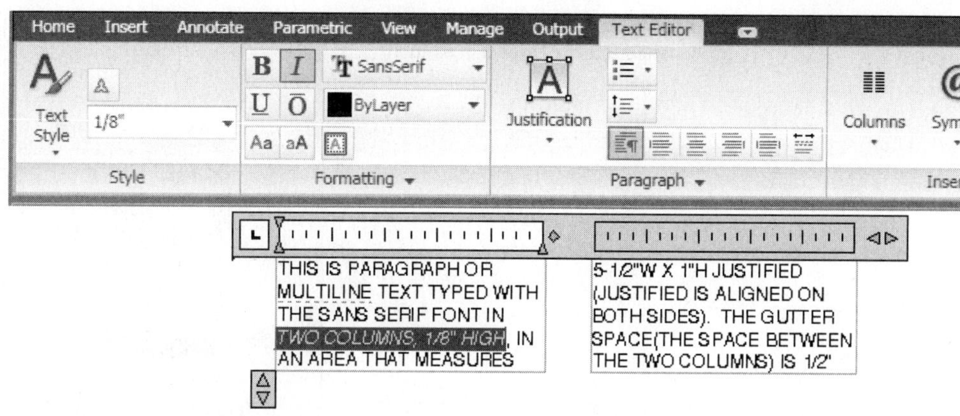

Step 17. DOUBLE-CLICK on the line of text that reads "1/4″ HIGH" and change it to "1/4″ HIGH, CENTERED."

Step 18. Use DDEDIT to change the words TWO COLUMNS, 1/8″ HIGH to the italic font (Figure 4–22), as described next:

Prompt	Response
Command:	DOUBLE-CLICK: **any point on the multiline text**
The Text Formatting Editor (Figure 4–22) appears:	CLICK: **the left mouse button to the left of the word TWO, hold it down, and drag to the end to the word HIGH so that TWO COLUMNS, 1/8″ HIGH is highlighted**, then CLICK: **I** (for italic)
	CLICK: **OK**

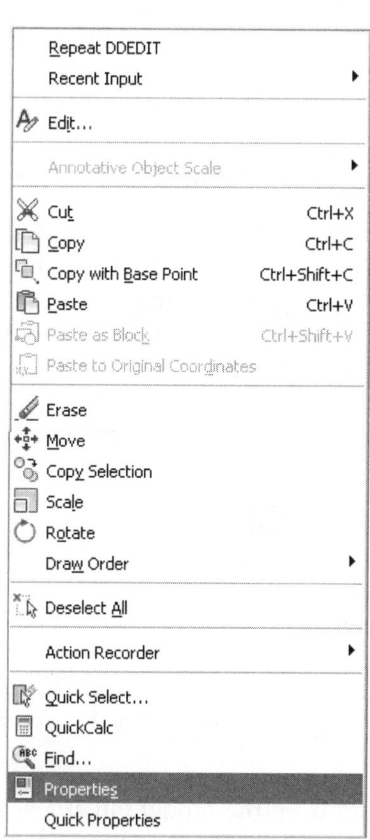

FIGURE 4–23
Change Text to Layer a-area-iden

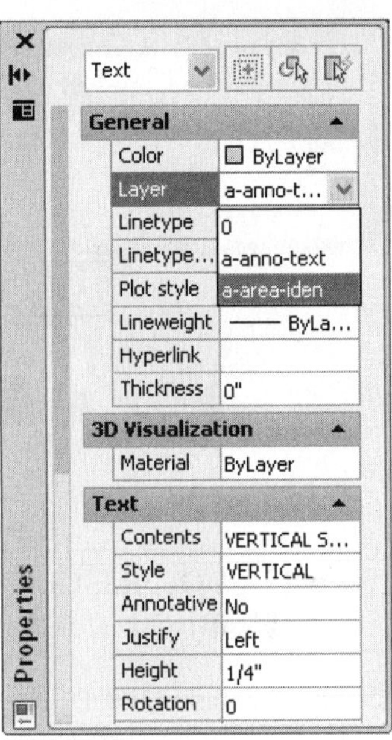

Step 19. **Use Properties to change the vertical line of text from Layer a-anno-text to Layer a-area-iden (Figure 4–23), as described next:**

Prompt	Response
Command:	CLICK: **the vertical line of text (VERTICAL STYLE)** and RIGHT-CLICK
The right-click menu appears:	CLICK: **Properties**
The Properties palette appears:	CLICK: **Layer**
	CLICK: **the down arrow** (Figure 4–23)
	CLICK: **a-area-iden**
	CLICK: **the X in the upper left corner to close**
	VERTICAL STYLE is now changed to a-area-iden

Step 20. **Use Single Line Text, STANDARD style, 1/8″ high to place your name and class number in the upper left and upper right corners, respectively. The start point for your name is 1,10-1/2. Use right-justified text for class number (at the Dtext prompt "Specify start point of text or [Justify/Style]:"** TYPE: **R<enter>. The right endpoint of text baseline is 7-1/2,10-1/2.**

CHECKING THE SPELLING

AutoCAD has a spell checker that allows you to check the spelling on your drawing. The Spelling command is located on the Annotate panel, or TYPE: **SP<enter>** at the Command: prompt to access it.

Step 21. **When you have completed Tutorial 4–1, save your work in at least two places.**

Step 22. **Print your drawing from the Model tab at a scale of 1:1.**

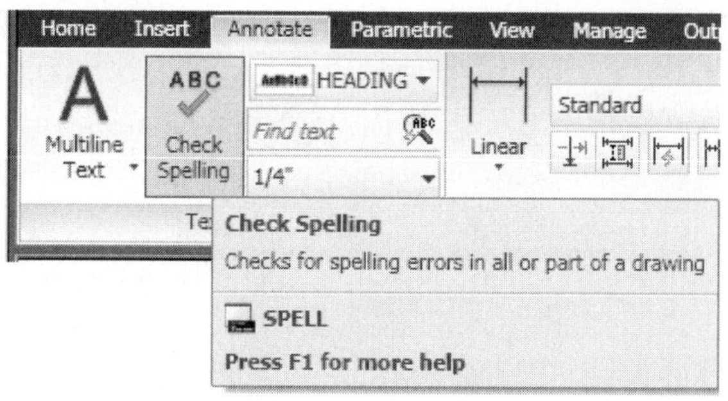

DOOR SCHEDULE			
MARK	SIZE	QUANTITY	REMARKS
1	2'0"X 6'8"	8	FLUSH DOOR
2	2'6"X 6'8"	2	FLUSH DOOR
3	2'6"X 6'8"	1	EXT FLUSH DOOR
4	3'0"X 7'0"	1	EXT FLUSH DOOR
5	4'0"X 6'8"	3	DOUBLE DOOR
6	3'0"X 6'8"	1	DOUBLE DOOR
7	9'4"X 6'8"	1	SLIDING DOOR

FIGURE 4–24
Door Schedule

Tutorial 4–2: Using the Table... Command to Create a Door Schedule

The Table... command in AutoCAD 2009 is a tool to create professional appearing tables such as door schedules, tables for drawing sets, tabular drawings, window schedules, and similar items.

When you have completed Tutorial 4–2, your drawing will look similar to Figure 4–24. This is a commonly used means of specifying the number and types of doors used in a commercial or residential building.

Step 1. Use your workspace to make the following settings:

1. **Use SaveAs... to save the drawing with the name CH4-TUTORIAL2.**
2. Set drawing Units: **Architectural**
3. Set drawing Limits: **11,8-1/2**
4. Set GRIDDISPLAY: **0**
5. Set Grid: **1/4″**
6. Set Snap: **1/8″**
7. **Make a new text style, name it Table, change the font from Arial to simplex and set the Table style current.**
8. **Create the following layer:**

LAYER NAME	COLOR	LINETYPE	LINEWEIGHT
a-anno-legn	blue	continuous	.007″ (.18mm)

9. **Set Layer a-anno-legn current.**
10. **Use Zoom-All to view the limits of the drawing.**

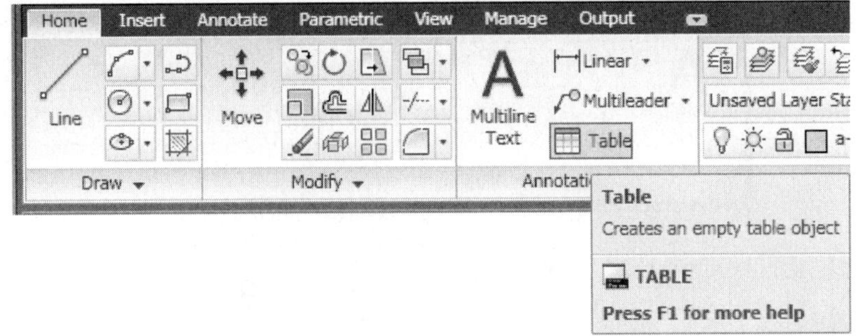

Step 2. Use the Table… command to draw the table, as described next:

Prompt	Response
Command:	CLICK: **Table** (or TYPE: **TABLE<enter>**)
The Insert Table dialog box, Figure 4–25, appears:	**Make the settings shown in Figure 4–25:** **6 columns (you will need only 4, but specify 6 anyway—you will delete 2 of them). Set column width at 2″ (you will change the column widths as you create the table).** **5 rows (you will need 7, but specify 5 for now—adding rows is very easy)** **Set Row height: at 1 if it is not the default** CLICK: **the Launch the Table Style dialog icon (the icon next to the Standard Table style name)**
The Table Style dialog box, Figure 4–26, appears:	**At this point you could specify a New Table name, but for now just modify the Standard table.** CLICK: **Modify...**

FIGURE 4–25
Insert Table Dialog Box

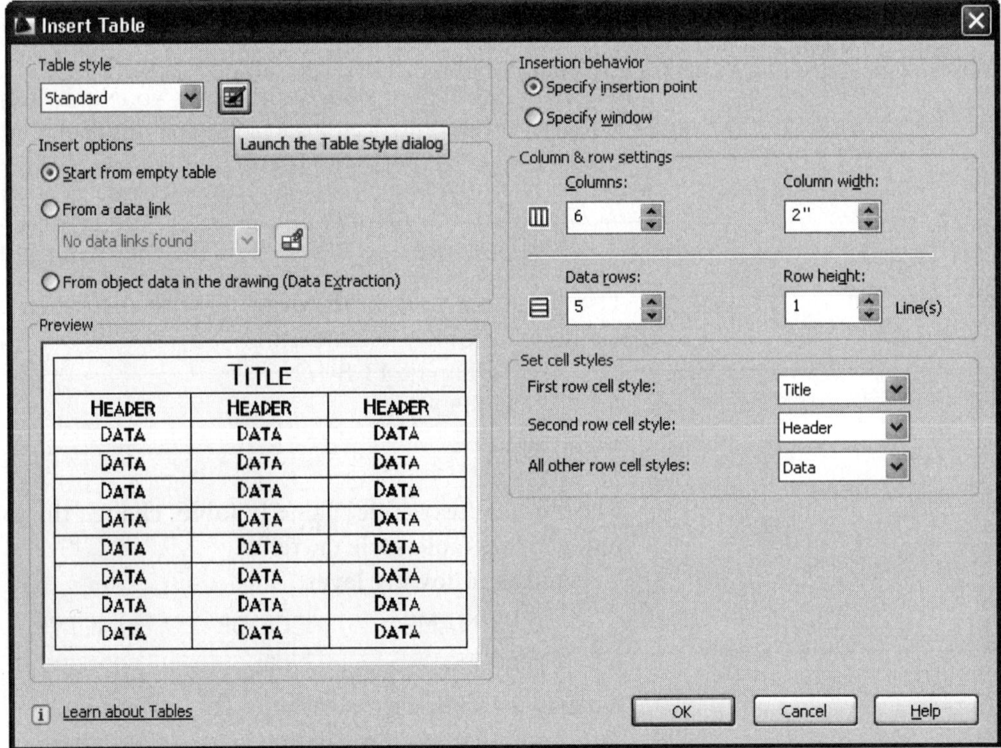

FIGURE 4–26
Table Style Dialog Box

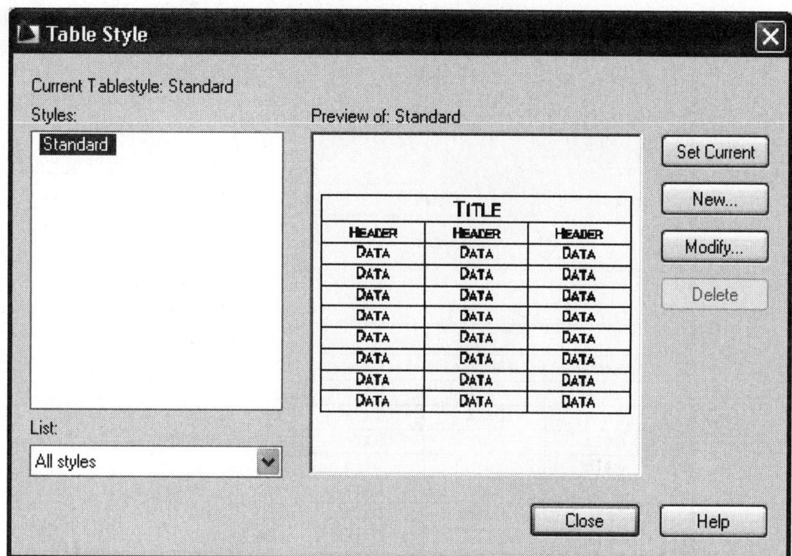

Prompt	Response
The Modify Table Style Standard dialog box, Figure 4–27, appears:	**There are three tabs: General, Text, and Borders**. CLICK: **the Text tab (Figure 4–28)**
	CLICK: **Title (under Cell styles, Figure 4–29)**
	CLICK: **the General tab (Figure 4–30)**
	CLICK: **the Fill Color: list and select Color 9 (a light gray) as the background color for the Title cell** (You have to CLICK: **Select Color...** at the bottom of the list to access the Index Color tab, Figure 4–30.)
	CLICK: **OK**

FIGURE 4–27
Modify Table Style: Standard Dialog Box

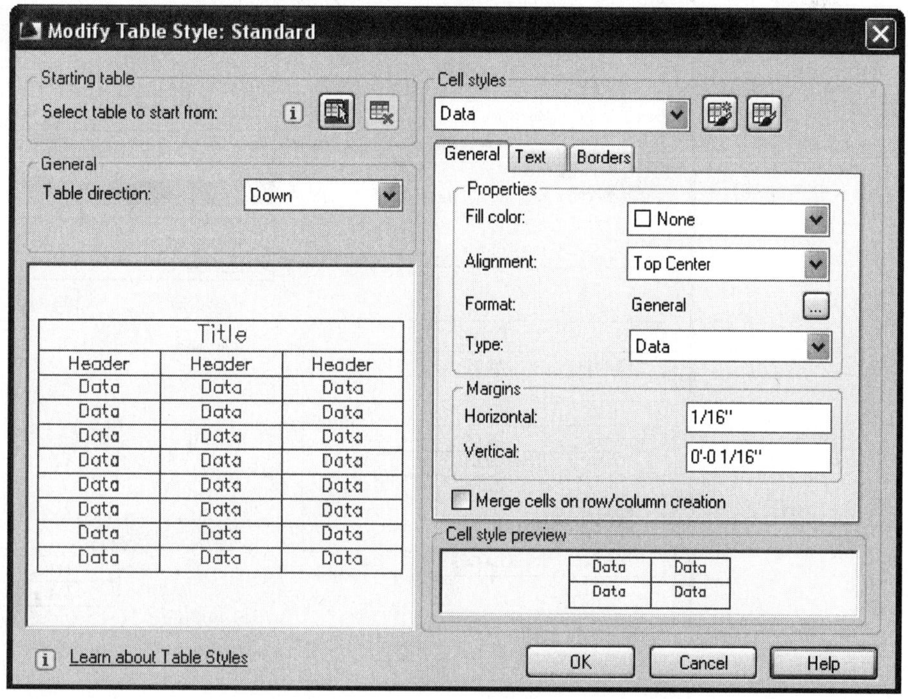

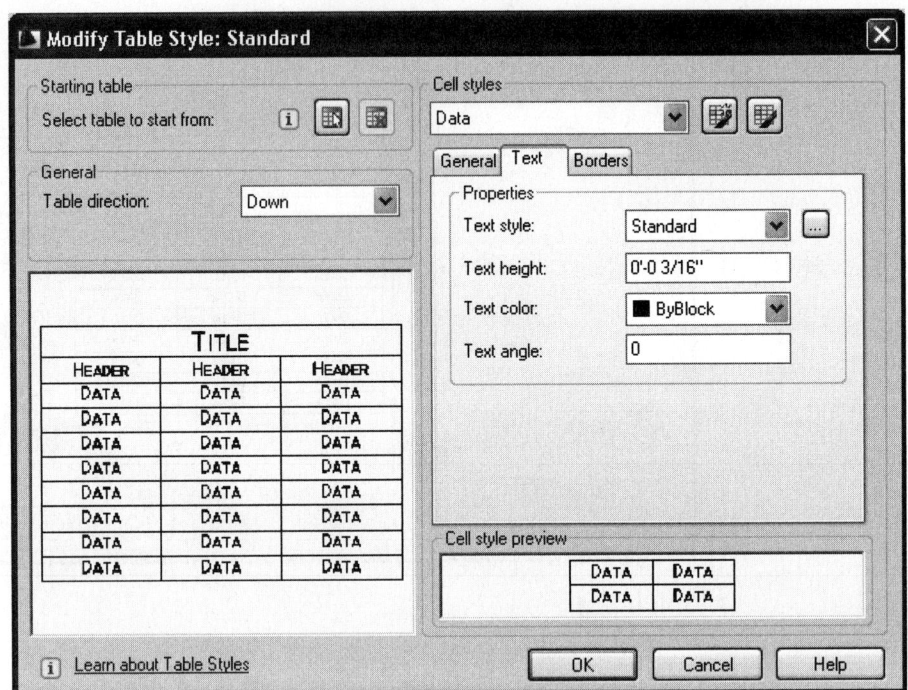

FIGURE 4–28
Select the Text Tab

Prompt	Response
The Table Style dialog box appears:	CLICK: **Close**
The Insert Table dialog box appears:	**Check to make sure you still have 6 Columns and 5 Data rows**, then CLICK: **OK**

Step 3. Insert the table and type the title, as described next:

Prompt	Response
Specify insertion point:	CLICK: **a point to place the table in the approximate center of the page (It will hang outside the drawing limits for now.)**

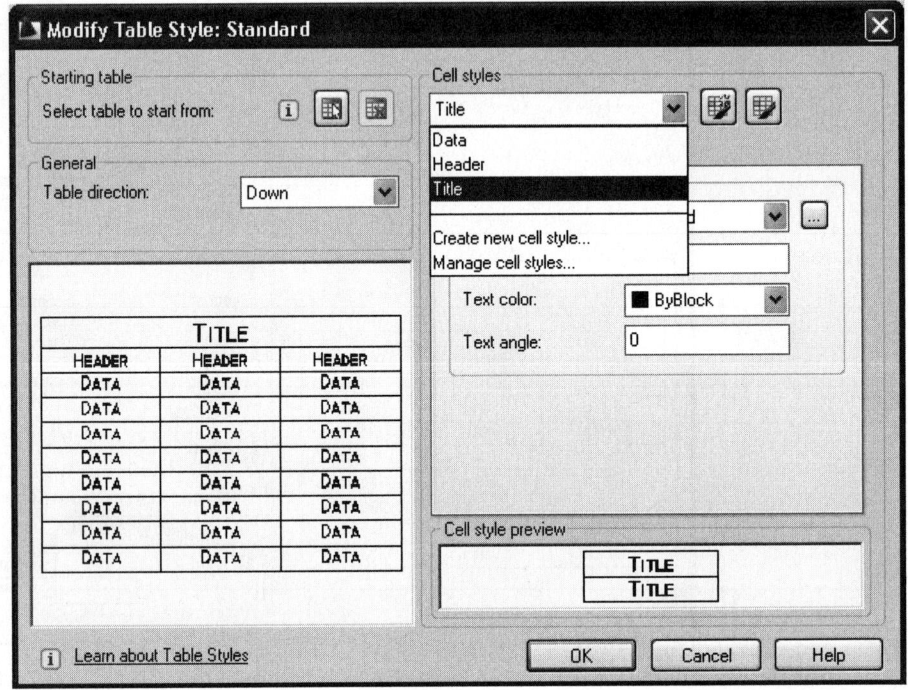

FIGURE 4–29
Select Title Cell

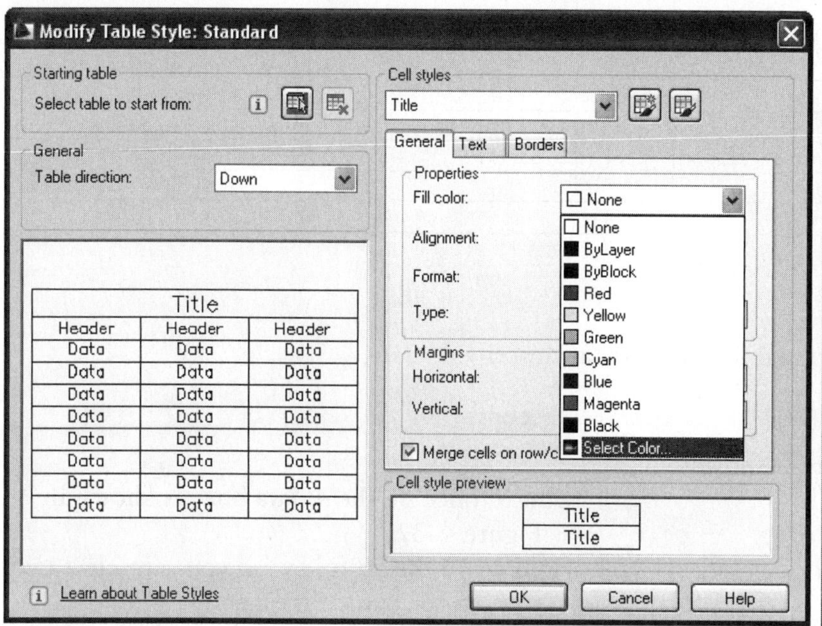

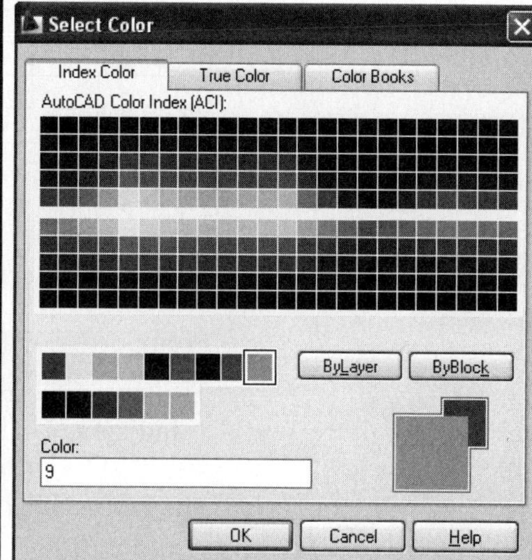

FIGURE 4–30
Select Fill Color for the Title Cell

Prompt	Response
The Text Formatting dialog box appears with the cursor flashing in the center of the Title area:	TYPE: **DOOR SCHEDULE<enter>**

Step 4. Create column 1 head and all data in column 1, as described next:

Prompt	Response
The Text Formatting dialog box appears with the cursor flashing in the center of the column 1 Header area:	TYPE: **MARK<enter>**
The Text Formatting dialog box appears with the cursor flashing in the center of the first data area:	TYPE: **1<enter>**
The Text Formatting dialog box appears with the cursor flashing in the center of the second data area:	TYPE: **2<enter>** **3<enter>** **Through 5** **(So the table appears as shown in Figure 4–31. If numbers in the data cells are not in the center**, CLICK: **once on each number**, then RIGHT-CLICK: and CLICK: **Alignment—Middle Center. You can also select all of the data cells at once using a crossing window and align them all at once.)**

FIGURE 4–31
Door Schedule Title and First Column

DOOR SCHEDULE					
MARK					
1					
2					
3					
4					
5					

Step 5. **Insert and delete rows, as described next:**

Prompt	Response
The table appears as shown in Figure 4–31:	CLICK: **once on the 4 data box, as shown in Figure 4–32**
The Ribbon changes (Figure 4–32):	**Hold down the Shift key (so you can select two rows at the same time), and** CLICK: **the next row Below, release the Shift key, then** CLICK: **Insert Below on the Row panel**
	CLICK: **the blank box under item 5** and TYPE: **6<enter>**, and **7<enter>**

Step 6. **Add the remaining column headers (Figure 4–33), as described next:**

Prompt	Response
	DOUBLE-CLICK: **the second column head area**
The Ribbon changes and the cursor flashes in the center of the column 2 header:	TYPE: **SIZE** (do not press **<enter>**) PRESS: **the Tab key**
The cursor is flashing in the center of the third column header:	TYPE: **QUANTITY** PRESS: **the Tab key**
The cursor is flashing in the center of the fourth column header:	TYPE: **REMARKS** CLICK: **any point in the screen area**

FIGURE 4–32
Insert Two Rows Below

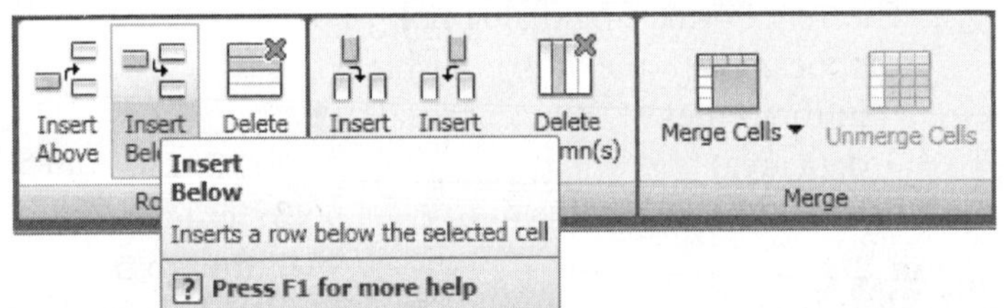

	A	B	C	D	E	F
1	DOOR SCHEDULE					
2	MARK					
3	1					
4	2					
5	3					
6	4					
7	5					
8						
9						

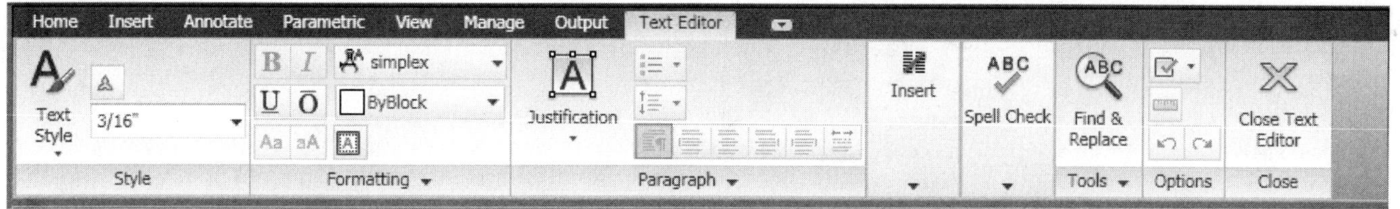

	A	B	C	D	E	F
1	DOOR SCHEDULE					
2	MARK	SIZE	QUANTITY	REMARKS		
3	1					
4	2					
5	3					
6	4					
7	5					
8	6					
9	7					

FIGURE 4–33
Text Editor and the Door Schedule

Step 7. Delete unneeded columns (Figure 4–34), as described next:

Prompt	Response
	CLICK: **the two columns to the right of the REMARKS column** (Hold down the Shift key to select the second column.)
	With the two blank columns highlighted, CLICK: **Delete Column(s)** (Figure 4–34)

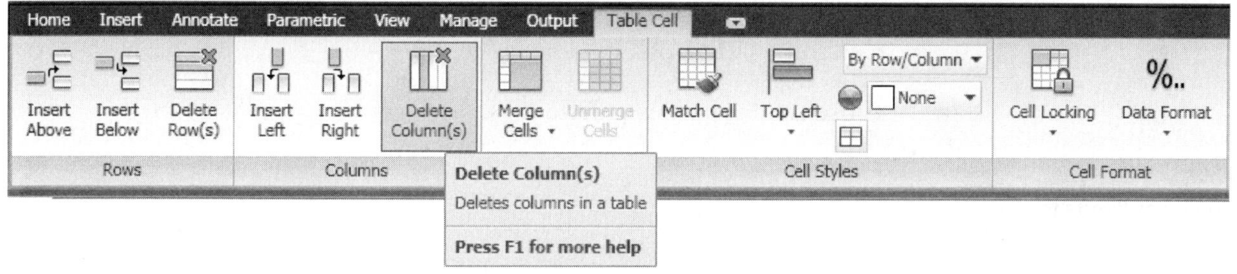

	A	B	C	D	E	F
1	DOOR SCHEDULE					
2	MARK	SIZE	QUANTITY	REMARKS		
3	1					
4	2					
5	3					
6	4					
7	5					
8	6					
9	7					

FIGURE 4–34
Delete Columns

FIGURE 4–35
Change Cell Width and Height

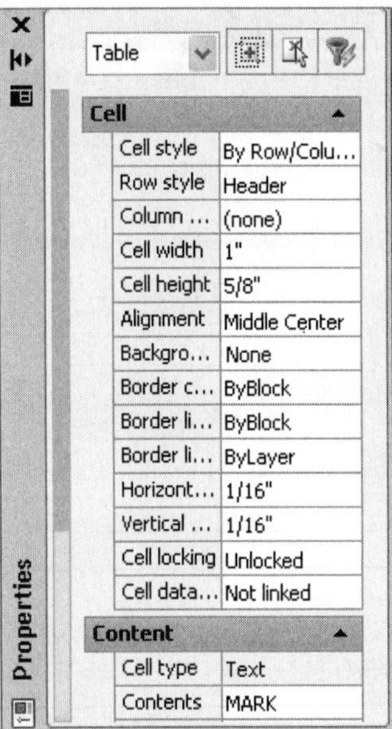

	A	B	C	D
1	DOOR SCHEDULE			
2	MARK	SIZE	QUANTITY	REMARKS
3	1			
4	2			
5	3			
6	4			
7	5			
8	6			
9	7			

Step 8. **Change the width of the columns to fit the data text (Figure 4–35), as described next:**

Prompt	Response
	CLICK: **once on the first column header (MARK) and RIGHT-CLICK:**
The right-click menu appears:	CLICK: **Properties**
The Properties palette appears:	**Change Cell width to 1″ and Cell height to 5/8″** (Figure 4–35)

Step 9. **Change the width of the remaining columns (Figure 4–36):**

Column 2 (SIZE)—leave at 2″.
Column 3 (QUANTITY)—change to 1-1/2″
Column 4 (REMARKS)—change to 2-3/4″

Close the Properties palette

FIGURE 4–36
Use the Properties Palette to Change Cell Width

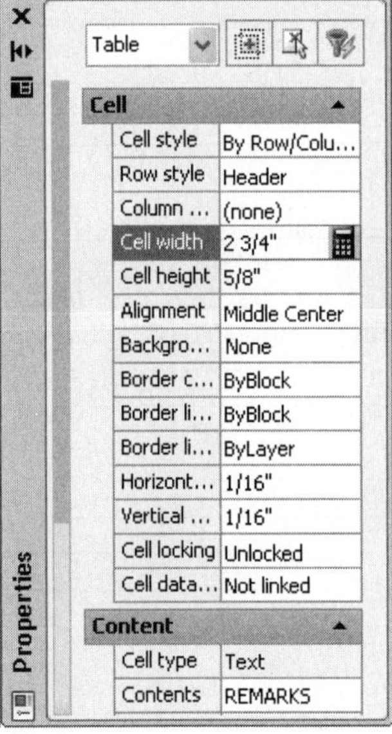

	A	B	C	D
1	DOOR SCHEDULE			
2	MARK	SIZE	QUANTITY	REMARKS
3	1			
4	2			
5	3			
6	4			
7	5			
8	6			
9	7			

FIGURE 4–37
Door Schedule QUANTITY and REMARKS Columns Not Aligned Correctly

DOOR SCHEDULE			
MARK	SIZE	QUANTITY	REMARKS
1	2'0" X 6'8"	8	FLUSH DOOR
2	2'6" X 6'8"	2	FLUSH DOOR
3	2'6" X 6'8"	1	EXT FLUSH DOOR
4	3'0" X 7'0"	1	EXT FLUSH DOOR
5	4'0" X 6'8"	3	DOUBLE DOOR
6	3'0" X 6'8"	1	DOUBLE DOOR
7	9'4" X 6'8"	1	SLIDING DOOR

Step 10. CLICK: **the first cell under the SIZE column header and** TYPE: **2′0″ × 6′8″<enter>.** TYPE: **each remaining door size (Figure 4–37)** and PRESS: **<enter>.**

Step 11. DOUBLE-CLICK: **the first cell under the QUANTITY column header and** TYPE: **each door quantity (Figure 4–37)** and PRESS: **<enter>.**

Step 12. DOUBLE-CLICK: **the first cell under the REMARKS column header and** TYPE: **each door description (Figure 4–37)** and PRESS: **<enter>.**

Step 13. Align data in the REMARKS column flush left (Figures 4–38, 4–39, and 4–40), as described next:

Prompt	Response
With no command active:	CLICK: **D1** (Figure 4–38)
Specify opposite corner:	CLICK: **D2** (to window the data in the REMARKS column)
The right-click menu appears:	CLICK: **Alignment—Middle Left** (from the Cell Styles panel, Figure 4–39)

FIGURE 4–38
Select All Cells in the REMARKS Column

DOOR SCHEDULE			
MARK	SIZE	QUANTITY	REMARKS
1	2'0"X 6'8"	8	FLUSH DOOR
2	2'6"X 6'8"	2	FLUSH DOOR
3	2'6"X 6'8"	1	EXT FLUSH DOOR
4	3'0"X 7'0"	1	EXT FLUSH DOOR
5	4'0"X 6'8"	3	DOUBLE DOOR
6	3'0"X 6'8"	1	DOUBLE DOOR
7	9'4"X 6'8"	1	SLIDING DOOR

D1
D2

Step 14. Align SIZE column data—middle left (Figure 4–40).

Step 15. Align QUANTITY column data—middle center.

Step 16. TYPE: **your name 1/8″ high in the upper right corner.**

Step 17. When you have completed Tutorial 4–2, save your work in at least two places.

Step 18. Print your drawing from the Model tab at a scale of 1:2.

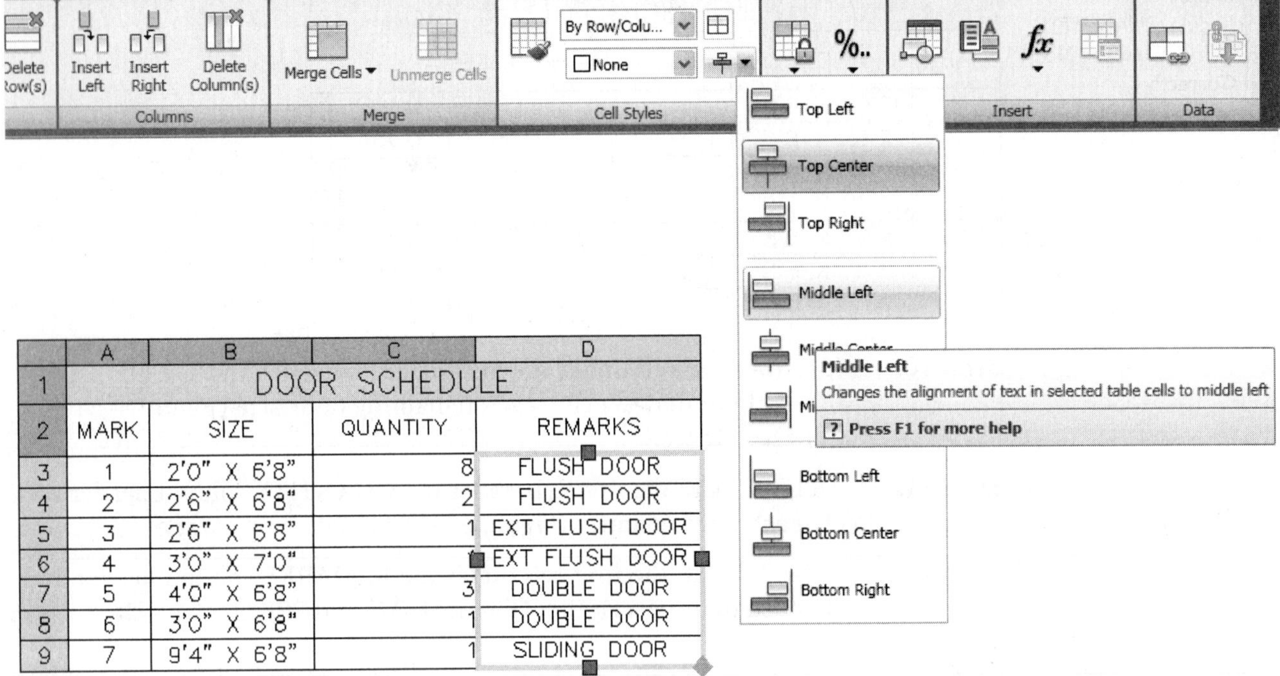

FIGURE 4–39
Align REMARKS Column Middle Left

FIGURE 4–40
Completed Door Schedule Table

DOOR SCHEDULE			
MARK	SIZE	QUANTITY	REMARKS
1	2'0"X 6'8"	8	FLUSH DOOR
2	2'6"X 6'8"	2	FLUSH DOOR
3	2'6"X 6'8"	1	EXT FLUSH DOOR
4	3'0"X 7'0"	1	EXT FLUSH DOOR
5	4'0"X 6'8"	3	DOUBLE DOOR
6	3'0"X 6'8"	1	DOUBLE DOOR
7	9'4"X 6'8"	1	SLIDING DOOR

Tutorial 4–3: Using the Table... Command to Create a Window Schedule

When you have completed Tutorial 4–3, your drawing will look similar to Figure 4–41. This is a commonly used means of specifying the number and types of windows used in a commercial or residential building.

FIGURE 4–41
Completed Window Schedule Table

WINDOW SCHEDULE				
MARK	WIDTH	HEIGHT	QUANTITY	REMARKS
A	4' 5-1/8""	4' 2-5/8"	1	METAL FRAME
B	3' 1-1/8"	4' 2-5/8"	9	METAL FRAME
C	6'-0"	4' 2-5/8"	1	METAL FRAME
D	5'-0"	4' 2-5/8"	1	METAL FRAME
E	9-0"	4' 2-5/8"	1	METAL FRAME

Step 1. **Use the steps described in Tutorial 4–2 to complete the window schedule shown in Figure 4–41.**

Step 2. You may copy CH4-TUTORIAL2, save it as CH4-TUTORIAL3, and make changes as needed to make the new table.

Tutorial 4–4: Using Text and Raster Images to Make a Title Block and a Drawing Format

In this tutorial you will use the text command and insert pictures (raster images) into an AutoCAD drawing format to create your own border and title block that you will use in the plotting chapter. The format shown in Figure 4–42 is for reference. You may select your own picture for the logo or you may choose to select a logo from the Internet.

FIGURE 4–42
Tutorial 4–4 Complete

Step 1. Locate a school or company logo such as the one shown in Figure 4–43.

Step 2. Make a folder that will contain this image if you do not already have a folder of your drawings.

Step 3. Save this image in .jpg format to the folder. You may need to do a print screen to save your image and paste it into Paint or another such program before you save it.

Step 4. Use your workspace to make the following settings:

1. Use SaveAs... to save the drawing with the name, CH4-TUTORIAL4.
2. Set drawing Units: **Architectural**

FIGURE 4–43
Logo Example

3. Set Drawing Limits: **8-1/2,11**
4. Set GRIDDISPLAY: **0**
5. Set GRID: **1/4**
6. Set SNAP: **1/8**
7. Create the following layer:

LAYER NAME	COLOR	LINETYPE	LINEWEIGHT
a-anno-ttlb	magenta	continuous	.008″ (.20mm)

8. Set **a-anno-ttlb current**.
9. Use **Zoom-All** to view the limits of the drawing.

Step 5. Use Create Layout Wizard to make a new layout with an architectural format, as described next:

Prompt	Response
Command:	CLICK: **Create Layout Wizard** (from the Insert-Layout Menu on the Menu Bar)
The Create Layout Wizard appears with the name Layout3:	CLICK: **Next**
The Printer option appears:	CLICK: **DWF6 ePlot.pc3** (or a plotter that plots ARCH D-size [24.00 × 36.00 inches]) CLICK: **Next**
The Paper Size option appears:	**Locate: ARCH D (24.00 × 36.00 inches) in the paper list and** CLICK: **on it** CLICK: **Next**

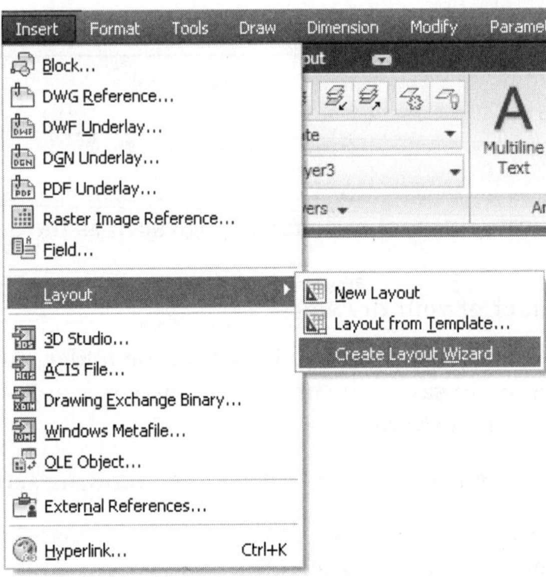

Prompt	Response
The Orientation option appears:	CLICK: **Landscape** CLICK: **Next**
The Title Block option appears:	CLICK: **Architectural Title Block** CLICK: **Next**
The Define Viewports option appears:	**With Single in the Viewport setup box selected,** CLICK: **Next**
The Pick Location option appears:	CLICK: **Next**
The Finish option appears:	CLICK: **Finish**

You are now in Paper Space with an Architectural D-Size title block.

Step 6. Erase the paper space viewport, as described next:

Prompt	Response
Command:	TYPE: **E<enter>**
Select objects:	CLICK: **D1 (Figure 4–44), the rectangle that is not part of the border** (that is the paper space viewport, which will be discussed in detail later)
Select objects:	**<enter>**

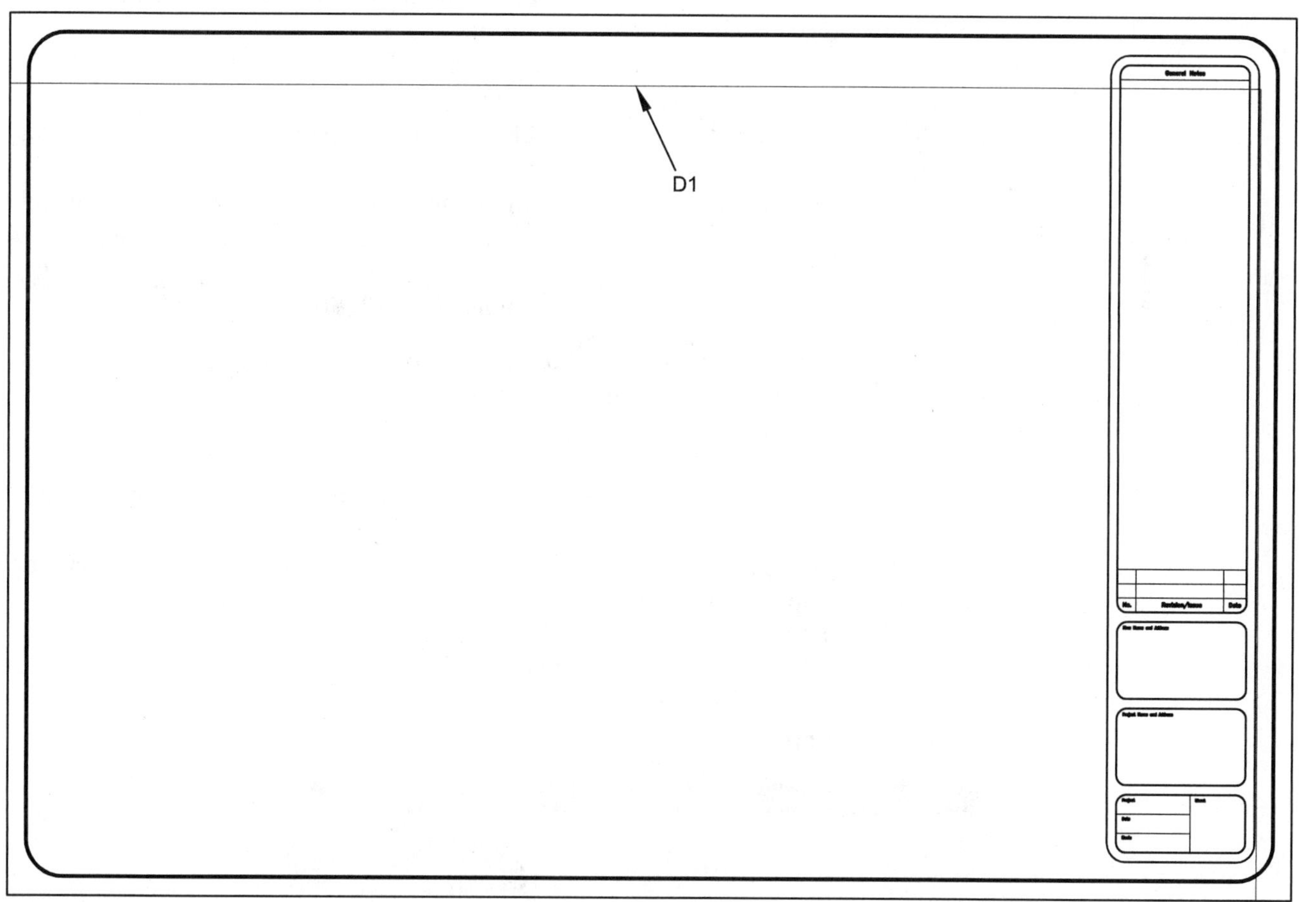

FIGURE 4–44
Erase the Paper Space Viewport

Step 7. **Explode the Architectural title block, as described next:**

Prompt	Response
Command:	TYPE: **X<enter>**
Select objects:	CLICK: **Any point on the Architectural title block**

Step 8. **Erase three words on the left side of the border and the words "Firm Name and Address" in the title block.**

Step 9. **Insert the Raster Image from your folder, as described next:**

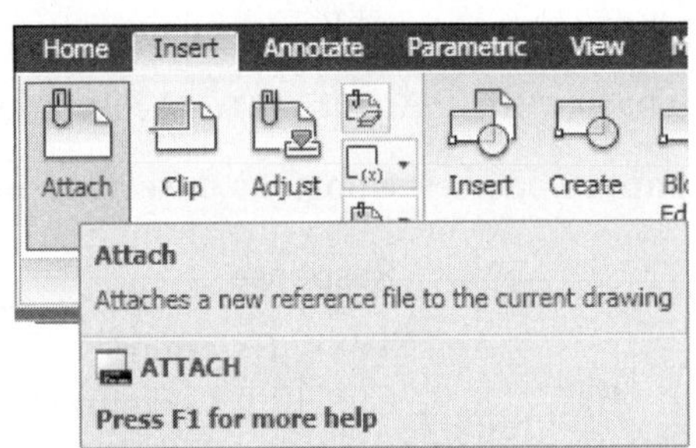

Prompt	Response
Command:	**attach** (or TYPE: **IMAGEATTACH<enter>**)
The Select Reference File dialog box appears:	**Find your LOGO in your folder** and CLICK: **on it**
	CLICK: **Open**
	CLICK: **OK**
Specify insertion point <0,0>:	CLICK: **An open space in your Architectural Format**
Specify scale factor or [Unit] <1>:	**Slowly move your mouse upward to the right to enlarge the image until you are satisfied it is about the correct size**, then CLICK: **that point (Figure 4–45)**

Step 10. **Clip the image to get rid of any part of it that you do not need (Figure 4–46), as described next:**

Prompt	Response
Command:	CLICK: **any point on the outside edge of the inserted image**
The Ribbon changes:	**Create Clipping** (or TYPE: **IMAGECLIP<enter>**)
Enter image clipping option [ON/OFF/Delete/New boundary] <New>:	**<enter>**
Specify clipping boundary or select invert option:	

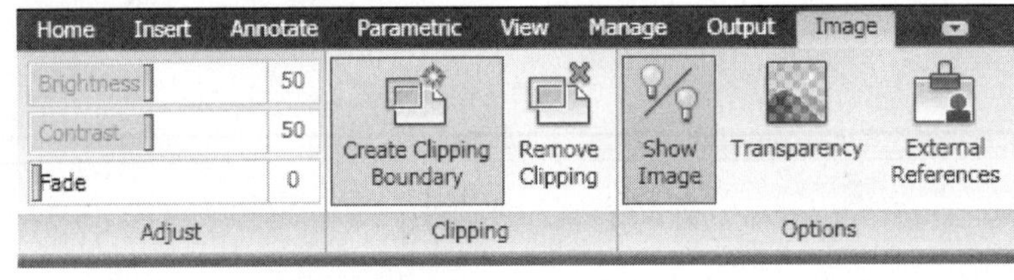

FIGURE 4–45
Insert the LOGO

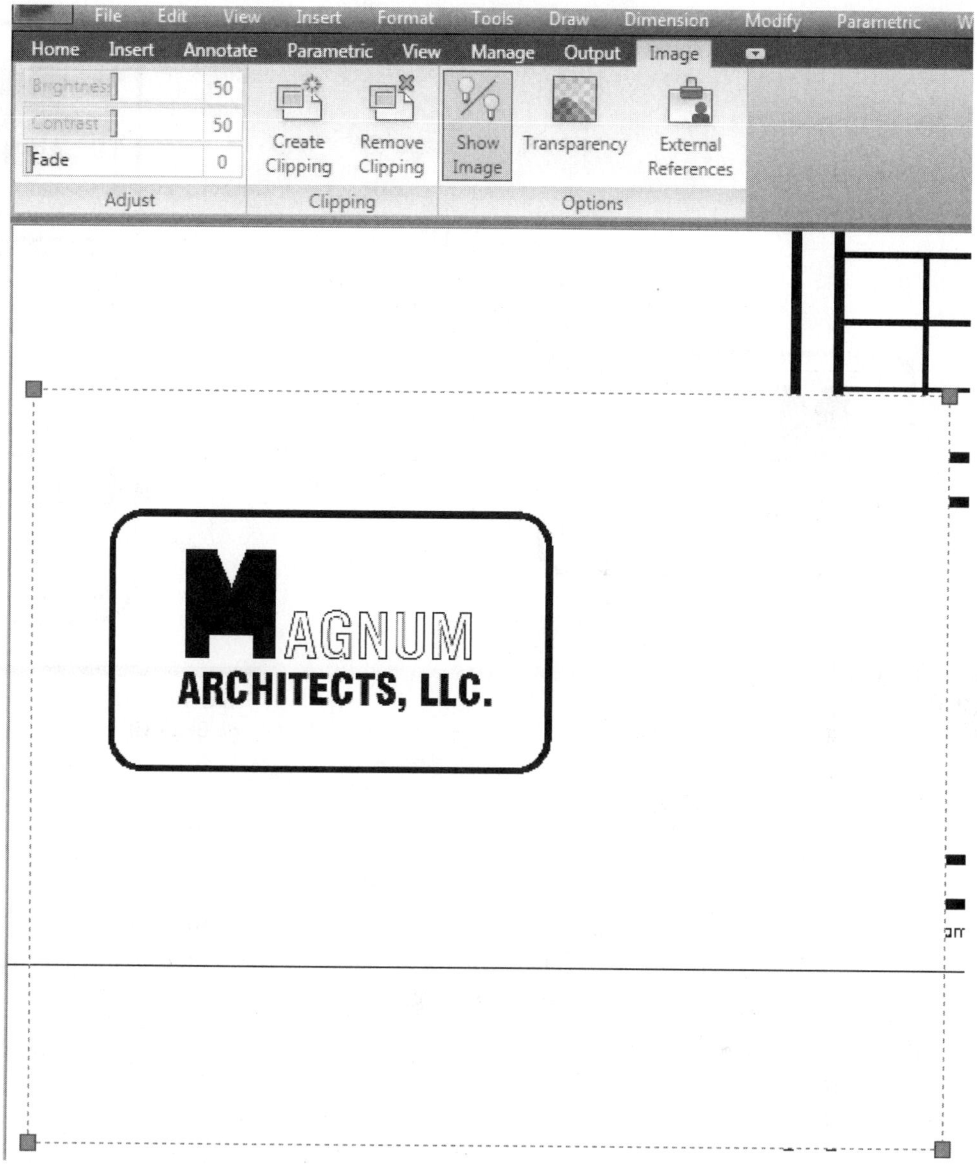

TIP: If your logo cannot be clipped as a rectangle, TYPE: **P<enter>** to select the polygonal option for clipping. This option allows you to CLICK: several points to form a shape that conforms to the outline of your logo.

Prompt	Response
[Select polyline/Polygonal/ Rectangular/Invert clip] <Rectangular>:	**<enter>**
Specify first corner point:	**D1** (Figure 4–46)
Specify opposite corner point:	**D2**

Step 11. On your own, move the clipped logo to the title block as shown in Figure 4–47.

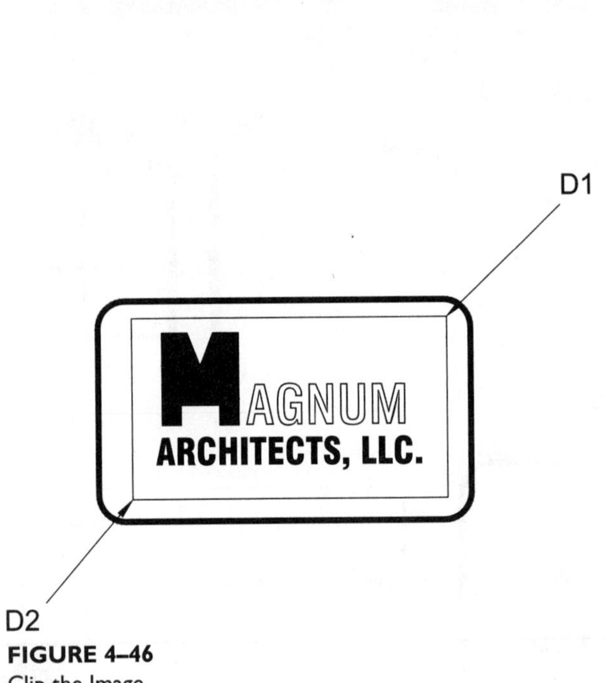

FIGURE 4–46
Clip the Image

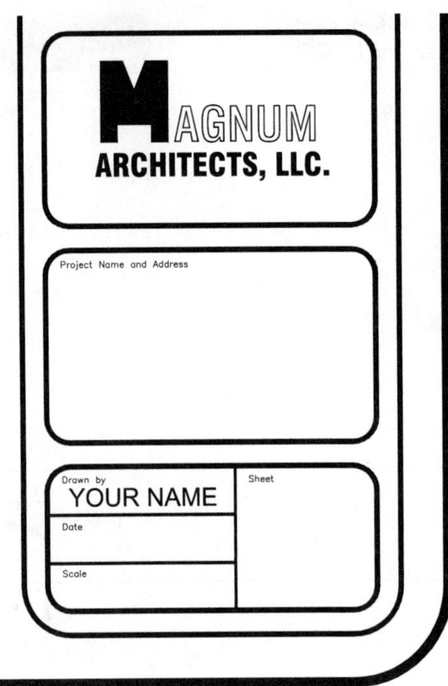

FIGURE 4–47
Title Block Changes

Step 12. DOUBLE-CLICK: **the word Project and change it to read Drawn By. Then add your name to the title block 3/16″ high in the Arial font as shown in Figure 4–47.**

Step 13. Turn off the frame around the clipped image as described next:

Prompt	Response
Command:	TYPE: **IMAGEFRAME<enter>**
Enter new value for IMAGEFRAME<1>:	TYPE: **0<enter>**

Step 14. Because items in paper space cannot be inserted into another drawing and items in model space can, you will have to move your format from paper space into model space as described next. (You will use your format on several drawings in later assignments.)

Prompt	Response
Command:	TYPE: **B<enter>**
The Block Definition dialog box appears:	TYPE: **D-size** (in the Name: box) CLICK: **Select objects**
Select objects:	TYPE: **ALL<enter>**
Select objects:	**<enter>**
The Block Definition dialog box appears:	CLICK: **Pick point**

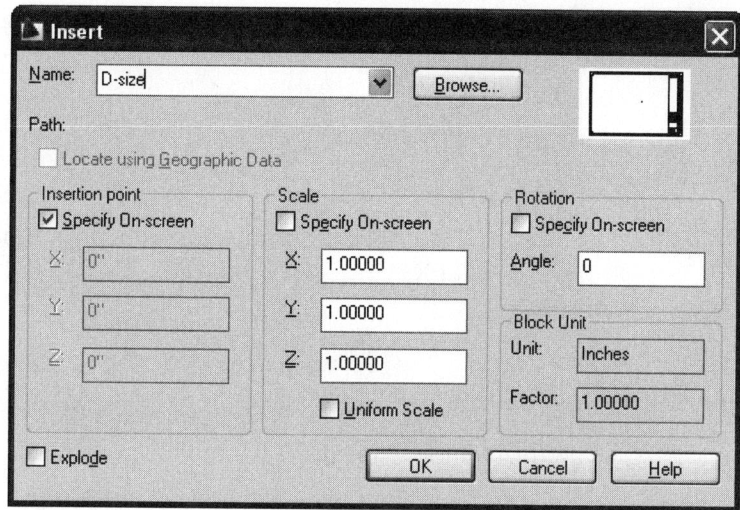

FIGURE 4–48
Insert Dialog Box

Prompt	Response
Specify insertion base point:	TYPE: **0,0<enter>**
The Block Definition dialog box appears:	CLICK: **OK**
Command:	CLICK: **PAPER on the Status Bar or** TYPE: **MS<enter>**
You are now in MODEL space.	
Command:	TYPE: **I<enter>**
The Insert dialog box appears:	**Locate: D-size in the list of blocks and** CLICK: **on it as shown in Figure 4–48**
	CLICK: **OK**
Specify insertion point or [Basepoint/Scale/X/Y/Z/Rotate]:	TYPE: **0,0<enter>**

The architectural format is now in model space and can be used with any drawing. You may want to Zoom-All to see the entire format.

Step 15. **Save the drawing with the name D-size format in at least two places.**

Step 16. **Print the format to fit on an 8-1/2″ × 11″ sheet, using the landscape option.**

review questions

1. The command used in this chapter to place line text (text not in paragraph form) on drawings is
   - **a.** Single Line Text (Dtext)
   - **b.** TXT
   - **c.** Multiline Text (Mtext)
   - **d.** DDedit
   - **e.** MS-DOS Text Editor

2. The command used in this chapter to place paragraph text on drawings is
   a. Single Line Text (Dtext)
   b. TXT
   c. Multiline Text (Mtext)
   d. DDedit
   e. MS-DOS Text Editor
3. Which of the following could be used as a style name?
   a. SIMPLEX
   b. TITLE
   c. NAMES
   d. A
   e. All the above could be used as a style name.
4. Which of the following is a font name?
   a. SIMPLEX
   b. TITLE
   c. NAMES
   d. A
   e. All the above could be used as a font name.
5. You can change from one text style to another from within the Single Line Text command.
   a. True
   b. False
6. When you set the text style, which of the following text height settings will allow you to draw different heights of the same text style?
   a. 1/4
   b. 0′-0″
   c. 1
   d. 1000
   e. —
7. Which of the following Single Line Text options draws text between two clicked points and adjusts the text height so that it fits between the two points?
   a. Fit
   b. Align
   c. Justify
   d. Middle
   e. Style
8. Which of the following Single Line Text options draws text between two clicked points and condenses or expands the text to fit between the two points but does not change the text height?
   a. Fit
   b. Align
   c. Justify
   d. Middle
   e. Style
9. The justification letters MR stand for
   a. Middle, Right-justified
   b. Margin, Right-justified
   c. Midpoint, Left-justified
   d. Bottom, Right-justified
   e. Margin Release
10. Which of the following modifiers should be selected if you want the bottom of the line of text to end 1/2″ above and 1/2″ to the left of the lower right corner of the drawing limits?
   a. TL
   b. BR
   c. BL
   d. TR
   e. MR

Complete.

11. List three commands that can be used to change text.

____

____

____

12. List the command that allows you to change only the text contents for Single Line Text.

____

13. List the command that allows you to change text height, contents, properties, justification, style, and geometry.

____

14. List the command used to create a paragraph of text.

____

15. List the command that will spell check any line or paragraph of text you select.

____

16. List the command used to insert image files (.jpg, .tiff) into your drawing.

____

17. Describe how to delete columns in a table created with the Table… command.

____

18. List the command used to trim off unneeded parts of an inserted image file.

____

____

19. List the default text style name and font that AutoCAD provides for you by default.

____

____

20. List the standard codes for the following.

a. Degree symbol: ______________________________

b. Plus–minus symbol: ______________________________

c. Diameter symbol: ______________________________

d. Underscore: ______________________________

e. Overscore: ______________________________

chapter

5

Advanced Plotting: Using Plot Styles, Paper Space, Multiple Viewports, and PDF Files

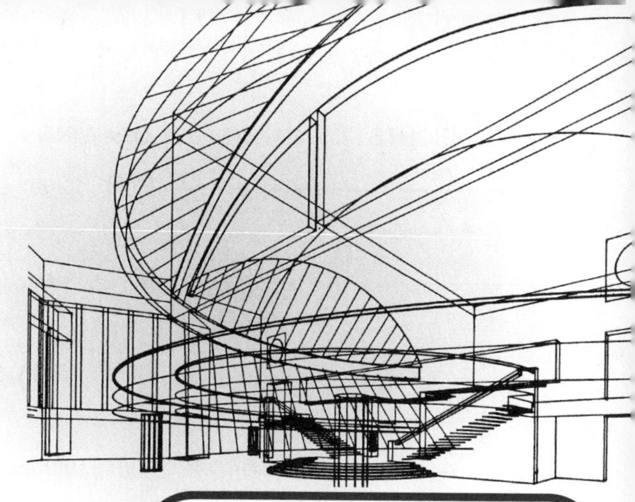

objectives

When you have completed this chapter, you will be able to:

- Create a color-dependent plot style.
- Create different layout tabs for your drawing.
- Print/Plot drawings with multiple viewports from layout tabs.
- Print/Plot drawings using a layout wizard.
- Print/Plot drawings at various scales on the same sheet.
- Print/Plot Drawings to a PDF file.

Layer Names, Colors, and Lineweights

Layers, their colors, and lineweights are very significant in plotting and printing. Varying the thickness of different types of lines such as those that are used to draw walls, doors, text, and furniture can make a drawing much more useful and esthetically pleasing.

The AIA CAD Layer Guidelines have been used as a guide for naming the layers used in this book. Five lineweights have been used to provide drawing legibility in the plans: very heavy, heavy, medium, light, and very light. Colors have been selected to be applied consistently to these layers.

Figure 5–1 shows the lineweights. There are two sets of lineweights, one for A- and B-size sheets and one for C- and D-size sheets. Larger lineweights are used on the C- and D-size sheets to accommodate the larger scale of the drawings.

Figure 5–2 shows the layer names, colors, and lineweights used in this book. This provides a basic outline of layers, colors, and lineweights for architectural plans, which can be adjusted or changed as required for individual needs or preferences.

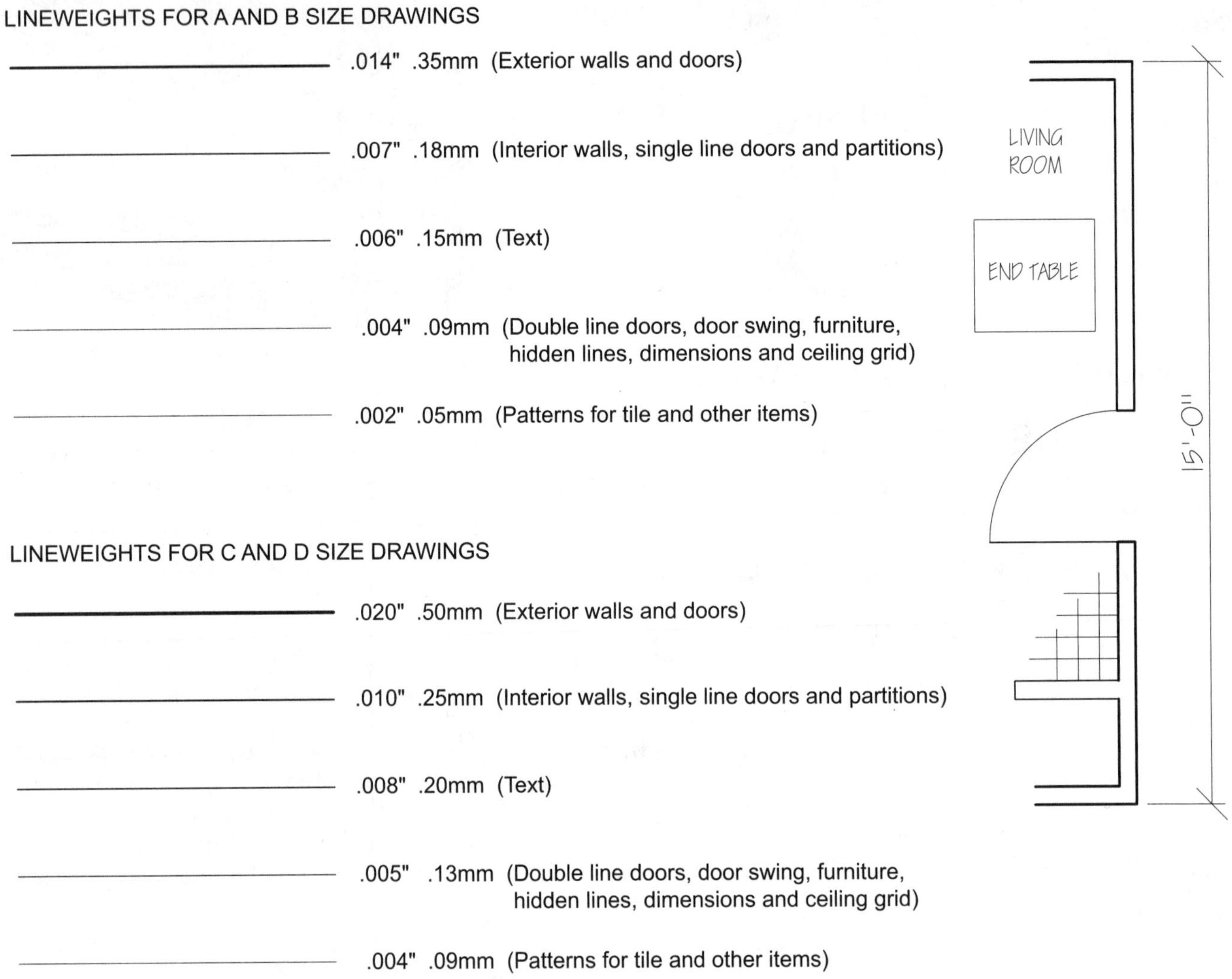

LINEWEIGHTS FOR A AND B SIZE DRAWINGS

.014" .35mm (Exterior walls and doors)

.007" .18mm (Interior walls, single line doors and partitions)

.006" .15mm (Text)

.004" .09mm (Double line doors, door swing, furniture, hidden lines, dimensions and ceiling grid)

.002" .05mm (Patterns for tile and other items)

LINEWEIGHTS FOR C AND D SIZE DRAWINGS

.020" .50mm (Exterior walls and doors)

.010" .25mm (Interior walls, single line doors and partitions)

.008" .20mm (Text)

.005" .13mm (Double line doors, door swing, furniture, hidden lines, dimensions and ceiling grid)

.004" .09mm (Patterns for tile and other items)

FIGURE 5–1
Lineweights for A-, B-, C-, and D-Size Drawings

Plot Styles

Plot styles allow you to plot the same drawing in different ways. AutoCAD provides some plot styles, or you can create your own. A plot style contains settings that can override an object's color, linetype, and lineweight.

The Plot Styles table list (Figure 5–3) can be used to create, edit, or store plot files. The Add Plot Style Table Wizard (Figure 5–4), located under Wizards in the Tools menu, leads you through creating a plot style. There are two types of plot styles: Named and Color-Dependent.

NAMED PLOT STYLE (STB)

Named plot styles assign colors and lineweights to objects. For example, furniture can be assigned the color red with a lineweight of .004″ with a named plot style, no matter what layer it is on. To change the way an object plots, you should change its plot style instead of its color or layer.

LAYER NAME	DESCRIPTION	COLOR	LINEWEIGHT			
			A & B SIZE		C & D SIZE	
Architectural						
a-anno-area	area calculations	green	.006"	.15mm	.008"	.20mm
a-anno-dims	dimensions	red	.004"	.09mm	.005"	.013mm
a-anno-text	text	green	.006"	.15mm	.008"	.20mm
a-anno-ttbl	border and title block	magenta	.006"	.15mm	.008"	.20mm
a-clng-grid	ceiling grid	red	.004"	.09mm	.005"	.13mm
a-door-dbl	doors (double line)	red	.004"	.09mm	.005"	.13mm
a-door-sgl	doors (single line)	blue	.007"	.18mm	.010"	.25mm
a-door-swng	door swing arc	red	.004"	.09mm	.005"	.13mm
a-elev	elevations	blue	.007"	.18mm	.010"	.25mm
a-elev-dims	dimensions	red	.004"	.09mm	.005"	.13mm
*a-elev-hid	dashed line	red	.004"	.09mm	.005"	.13mm
a-elev-pat	textures and hatch patterns	cyan	.002"	.05mm	.004"	.09mm
a-elev-text	text	green	.006"	.15mm	.008"	.20mm
a-flor-iden	room numbers, names, targets	green	.006"	.15mm	.008"	.20mm
a-flor-wdwk	architectural woodwork	blue	.007"	.18mm	.010"	.25mm
a-glaz	windows, curtain walls, glazed partitions	green	.006"	.15mm	.008"	.20mm
a-sect	sections	blue	.007"	.18mm	.010"	.25mm
a-sect-dims	dimensions	red	.004"	.09mm	.005"	.13mm
a-sect-pat1	textures and hatch patterns	gray (255)	.010"	.25mm	.010"	.25mm
a-sect-text	text	green	.006"	.15mm	.008"	.20mm
a-wall-extr	exterior building wall	white	.014"	.35mm	.020"	.50mm
a-wall-head	door/window headers (on reflected ceiling plans	blue	.007"	.18mm	.010"	.25mm
a-wall-intr	interior building wall	blue	.007"	.18mm	.010"	.25mm
a-wall-pat1	textures and hatch patterns	gray (253)	.010"	.25mm	.010"	.25mm
a-wall-pat2	textures and hatch patterns	white	.014"	.35mm	.020"	.50mm
Electrical						
e-lite	lighting	white	.014"	.35mm	.020"	.50mm
*e-lite-circ	lighting circuits	white	.014"	.35mm	.020"	.50mm
e-lite-text	text	green	.006"	.15mm	.008"	.20mm
e-powr	power	white	.014"	.35mm	.020"	.50mm
e-powr-text	text	green	.006"	.15mm	.008"	.20mm
Interiors						
i-furn	furniture	cyan	.004"	.09mm	.005"	.13mm

*All layers have a continuous linetype, except those with an * beside them.
The * denotes a layer with a dashed linetype.

FIGURE 5–2
Outline of Layer Names, Colors, and Linetypes

Plot Styles

File Edit View Favorites Tools Help

Back Search Folders

Address C:\Documents and Settings\Kirkpatrck\Application Data\Autodesk\AutoCAD Gator Beta 2\R18.0\enu\Plot Styles Go

File and Folder Tasks

Make a new folder

Publish this folder to the Web

Share this folder

Other Places

enu

My Documents

Shared Documents

My Computer

My Network Places

Details

acad AutoCAD Color-dependent Plo... 5 KB

acad AutoCAD Plot Style Table File 1 KB

Add-A-Plot Style Table Wizard Shortcut 1 KB

Autodesk-Color AutoCAD Plot Style Table File 1 KB

Autodesk-MONO AutoCAD Plot Style Table File 1 KB

COLOR1-7TOBLACK AutoCAD Color-dependent Plo... 5 KB

DWF Virtual Pens AutoCAD Color-dependent Plo... 6 KB

Fill Patterns AutoCAD Color-dependent Plo... 5 KB

Grayscale AutoCAD Color-dependent Plo... 5 KB

monochrome AutoCAD Color-dependent Plo... 5 KB

monochrome AutoCAD Plot Style Table File 1 KB

plot Text Document 1 KB

Screening 25% AutoCAD Color-dependent Plo... 5 KB

Screening 50% AutoCAD Color-dependent Plo... 5 KB

Screening 75% AutoCAD Color-dependent Plo... 5 KB

Screening 100% AutoCAD Color-dependent Plo... 5 KB

Westwind AutoCAD Color-dependent Plo...

Your Name Color to Black1 AutoCAD Color-dependent Plo...

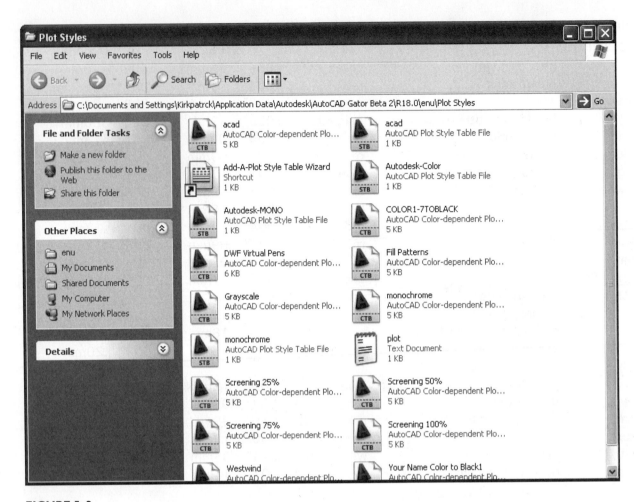

FIGURE 5–3
Plot Styles Table List

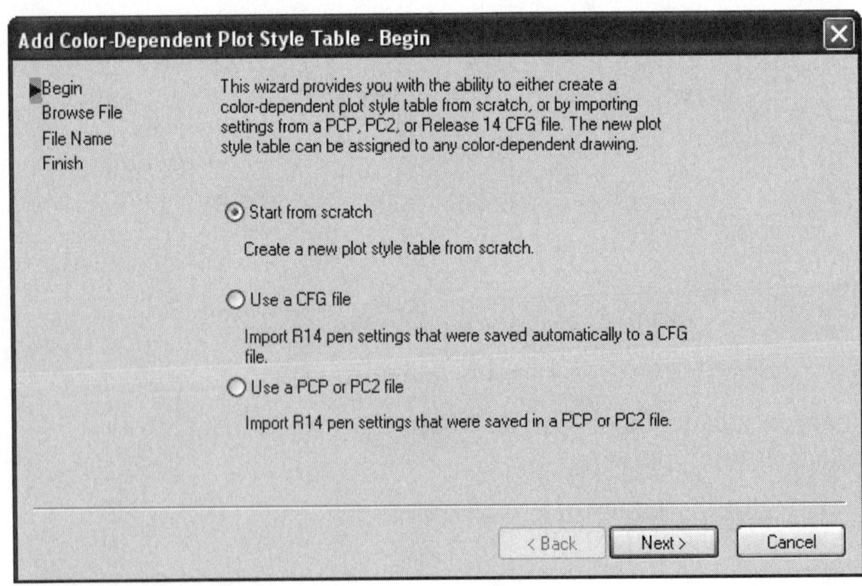

FIGURE 5–4
Add Color-Dependent Plot Style Table Wizard

All colors in this book are assigned by layer so using a named plot style becomes more complex than using a color-dependent plot style. Color-dependent plot styles are used by a vast majority of architects and are used in this book.

COLOR-DEPENDENT PLOT STYLE (CTB)

With a color-dependent plot style, any object that has the same color will be plotted using the same characteristics described in the plot style. For example, the color-dependent plot style can be set for the colors green and blue to be printed black with a lineweight of .006″. The color-dependent plot style can also be set for green and blue to be printed black but with the lineweight assigned by the layer on which the object was drawn. The plot style allows you to plot with either of the following:

Lineweight assigned to the layer
Lineweight assigned to the plot style

This same method applies to linetype; for example, all blue lines will print as hidden lines.

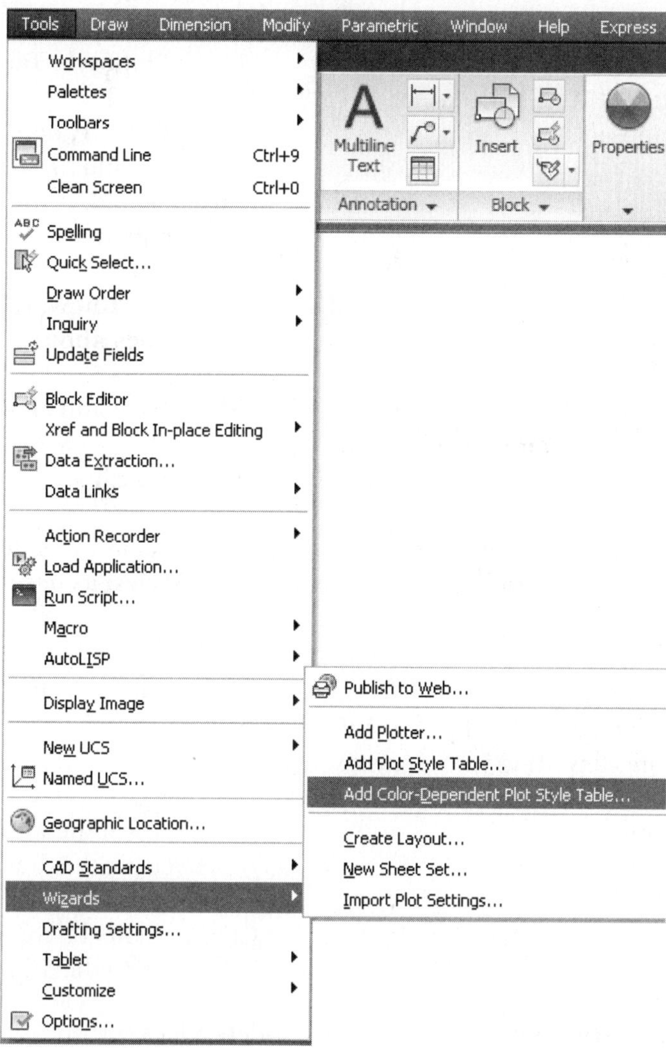

In Tutorial 5–1 you will make your own color-dependent plot style, then plot a drawing using that plot style in Tutorial 5–2. This plot style will print or plot colors 1 (red) through 7 (black) as black with the lineweight assigned by the layer on which the item was drawn.

Tutorial 5–1: Making a Color-Dependent Plot Style to Change Colors to Plot Black

Step 1. Open drawing CH3-TUTORIAL1

Step 2. Add color-dependent plot style tables, as described next:

Prompt	Response
Command:	CLICK: **Add Color-Dependent Plot Style Table Wizard**
The Add Color-Dependent Plot Style Table dialog box (Figure 5–4) appears:	CLICK: **Start from scratch** CLICK: **Next** TYPE: **Your name Color to Black (in the File name box)** CLICK: **Next** CLICK: **Plot Style Table Editor (Figure 5–5)**
The Plot Style Table Editor appears:	CLICK: **Color 1, hold down the shift key and** CLICK: **Color 7 so that Colors 1 through 7 are selected:** In the Properties: area CLICK: **Black** **Use object lineweights and Use object linetypes should be active as shown in Figure 5–5.** CLICK: **Save and close**
The Add Color-Dependent Plot Style Table dialog box appears:	CLICK: **Finish**

Step 3. Use the Convert Plot Styles command to make sure your drawings are set to use color-dependent plot styles, as described next:

Prompt	Response
Command:	TYPE: **CONVERTPSTYLES<enter>**
A warning indicating that you are converting your drawing to a different type of plot style appears:	CLICK: **OK** if the warning shows you are converting the drawing to a color-dependent plot style CLICK: **Cancel** if the warning shows you are converting the drawing to a named plot style

Your drawing is now set to use color-dependent plot styles.

FIGURE 5–5
Plot Style Table Editor Changing Colors 1 Through 7 to Plot Black

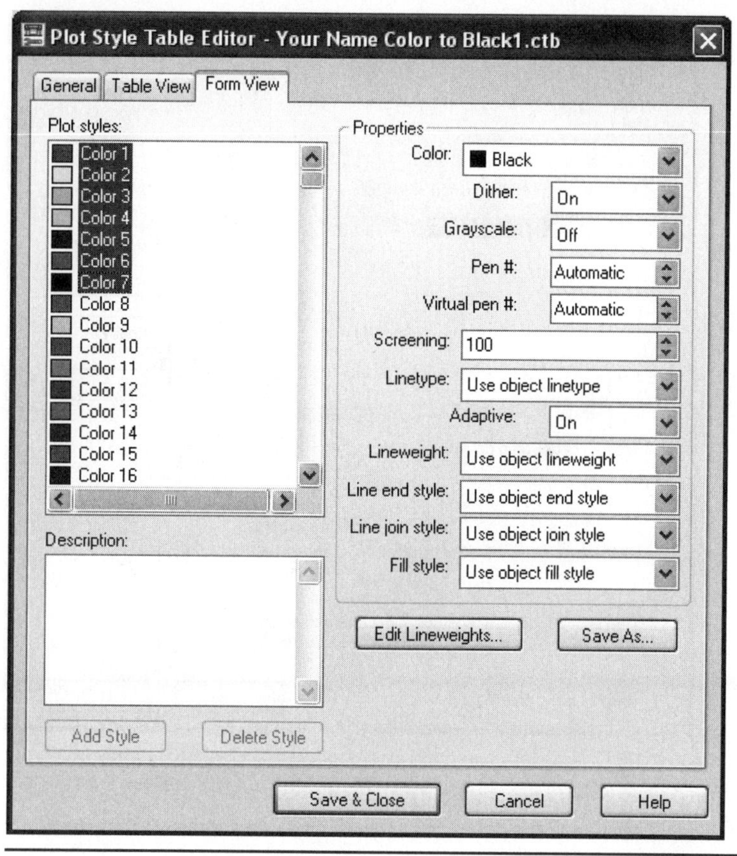

Tutorial 5–2: Plotting CH3-TUTORIAL1, Using a Color-Dependent Plot Style and Page Setup Manager

The following is a hands-on, step-by-step exercise to make a hard copy of CH3-TUTORIAL1 using a color-dependent plot style.

Step 1. **Open drawing CH3-TUTORIAL1 so it is displayed on the screen.**

Step 2. **Make a new layer named Viewport. Make its color green and set it current.**

MODEL, LAYOUT1, AND LAYOUT2 TABS

At the bottom of the drawing window are Model, Layout1, and Layout2 tabs. Model space is the 2D (and also 3D) environment in which you have been working to this point. Model space is where your 2D and 3D models (drawings) are created and modified. You can also print from the Model tab. A Layout tab is used to view paper space. Paper space shows the actual printed or plotted drawing on a real size piece of paper.

Step 3. CLICK: **the Layout1 tab at the bottom of drawing CH3-TUTORIAL1. You are now in paper space. Notice that the tab near the center on the Status Bar shows the paper space icon or reads PAPER. Clicking it will change it to MODEL. Make sure you are in paper space.**

FIGURE 5–6
Page Setup Manager

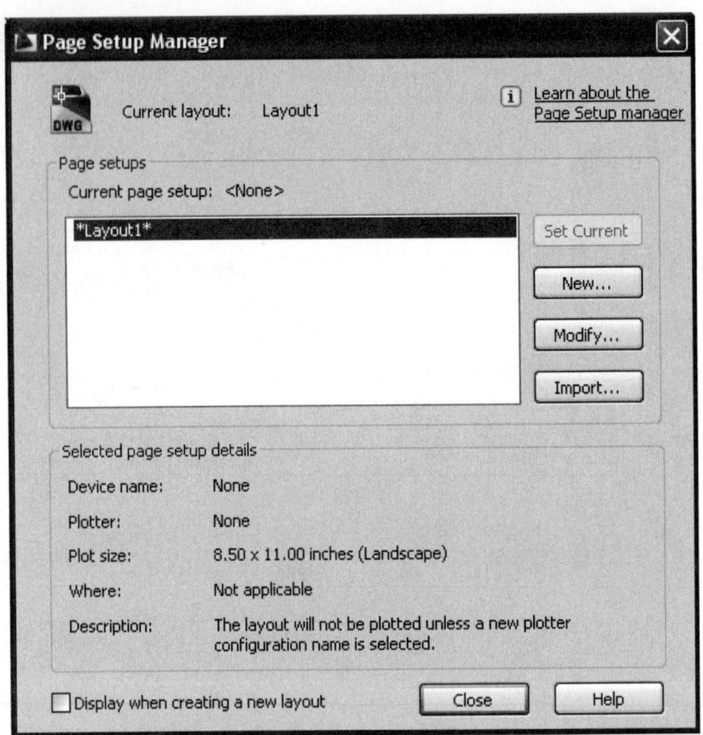

NOTE: It may be helpful to turn the grid off while in MODEL space. Be sure to return to PAPER space.

Step 4. RIGHT-CLICK: **the Layout1 tab and** CLICK: **Page Setup Manager.... The Page Setup Manager, Figure 5–6, appears.**

Step 5. **With Layout1 in Page setups selected,** CLICK: **Modify.... The Page Setup dialog box for Layout1 appears.**

Step 6. **Select the printer you will use.**

Step 7. **Set the Plot Style table to Your Name Color to Black.**

Step 8. **Make the settings shown in Figure 5–7 in the Page Setup dialog box.**

Step 9. **Make sure the Portrait drawing orientation is selected and the Plot scale is 1:1 (Figure 5–7).**

Because you are plotting the Layout tab that will be scaled using the viewport boundary line, use the Plot scale of 1:1 in the Page Setup dialog box.

Step 10. CLICK: **OK. The Page Setup Manager appears.**

Step 11. CLICK: **Close**

If you completed Steps 1 and 2 and created a new layer with the color green, the viewport boundary line is green.

FIGURE 5–7
Page Setup Dialog Box for Layout1

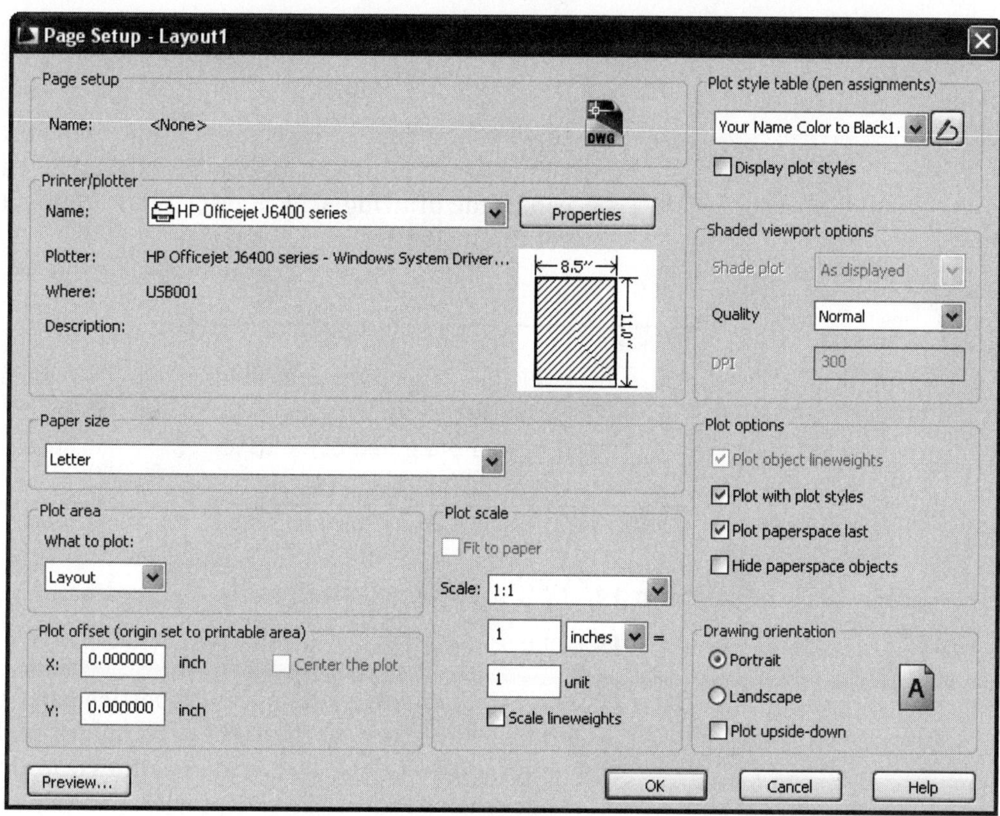

Step 12. CLICK: the green viewport boundary line to select it. If your viewport boundary line is not shaped as shown in Figure 5–8, CLICK: one of the small squares on each corner (called grips). It becomes red. Reshape the viewport by moving the grip. Be sure ORTHO is off.

FIGURE 5–8
Select the Viewport Boundary

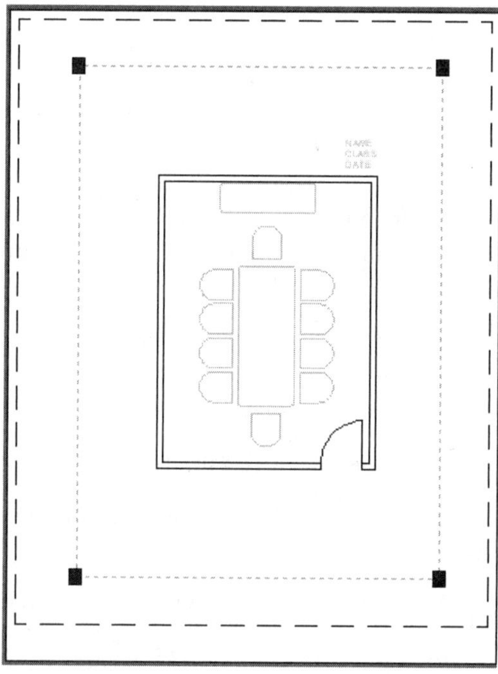

You can reshape, resize, move, erase, and copy the viewport. Additional information regarding the plotting of multiple viewports in 2D and 3D is covered in later chapters.

Step 13. **If your drawing is not centered in the viewport,** CLICK: **PAPER in the status bar to return to model space. Use the Pan or Zoom commands to center the drawing.** CLICK: **MODEL to return to paper space before continuing with the plot setup.**

NOTE: The viewport boundary line (green line) comes in on the layer that is current. That's why you created a layer named Viewport and assigned the green color to it.

Step 14. CLICK: **the green viewport boundary line to select it (Figure 5–8).**

Step 15. CLICK: **Properties from the Properties Panel.**

Step 16. CLICK: **Standard scale in the Properties palette (Figure 5–9).** CLICK: **the arrow to the right of Standard scale and scroll down to select 1/4″ = 1′-0″. This scale is applied to the drawing in the paper space viewport.** CLICK: **Display locked (above the scale) and** CLICK: **Yes to lock the display scale for this viewport. Close the Properties palette.**

Step 17. **Turn the Viewport layer off so the viewport boundary line will not print.**

When the display is locked, you cannot accidentally zoom in or out while in model space and lose the 1/4″ = 1′-0″ scale. If you zoom in or out while in paper space, you do not change the scale because you are zooming in or out on the paper only. When the display is locked, you cannot reposition the drawing. If you need to reposition or change the drawing in any way, you must turn the Viewport layer back on, select the viewport boundary line, select Properties, and unlock the display to make any changes.

Step 18. CLICK: **PAPER to return to MODEL space and erase the existing name, class, and date on the upper right of your drawing. Then** CLICK: **MODEL to return to PAPER space.**

Step 19. **Make a text style using the CityBlueprint font, set Layer a-anno-text current, and add your name, your class, and the date in all capitals, 3/16″ high, to the paper (Figure 5–10).**

Step 20. RIGHT-CLICK: **the Layout1 tab. The right-click menu appears.**

Step 21. CLICK: **Rename.** TYPE: **Furniture Plan for the new layout name.** PRESS: **<enter>.**

Step 22. RIGHT-CLICK: **the Furniture Plan tab.** The right-click menu appears.

Step 23. CLICK: **Plot...** The Plot dialog box appears.

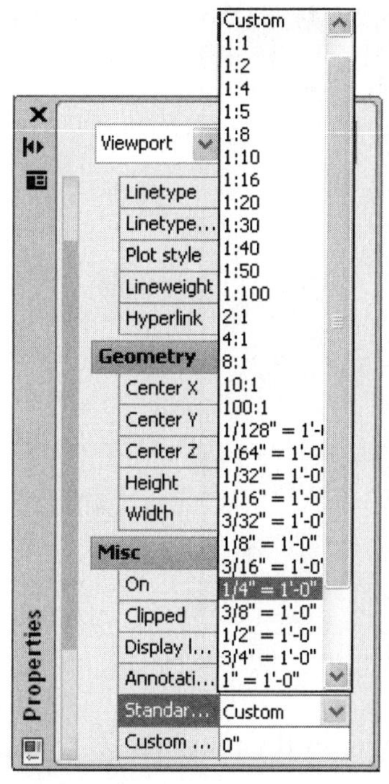

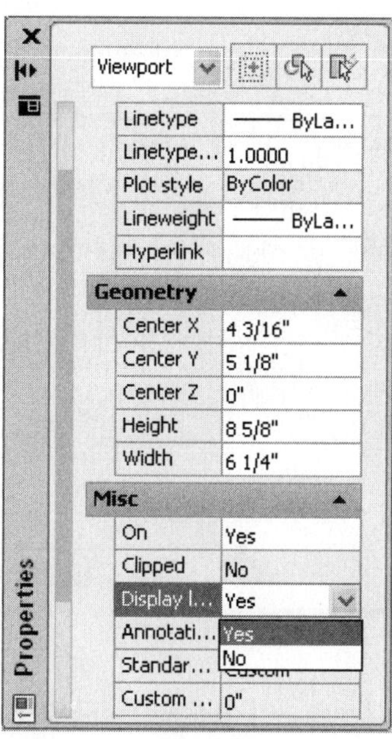

FIGURE 5–9
Set Viewport Scale to 1/4″ = 1′-0″ and Lock the Display

FIGURE 5–10
Add Your Name, Class, and the Current Date 3/16″ High in the City Blueprint Font

Step 24. CLICK: **Preview... If the preview is OK,** RIGHT-CLICK **and** CLICK: **Plot. If not, Exit and correct the problem.** The plot proceeds from this point.

PLOTTING MULTIPLE VIEWPORTS

While in the Model tab, you can use the command Viewports (VPORTS) to divide the display screen into multiple viewports. Model space is limited in that, although multiple viewports may be visible on the display screen, only one viewport can be plotted. In a Layout tab and in paper space, you can have multiple viewports. Each viewport can be treated as a single sheet of paper with a different part of the drawing showing and can be copied, stretched, erased, moved, or scaled. Paper space is not limited, in that you can plot all the viewports at the same time.

Tutorial 5–3: Plotting Using Create Layout Wizard and Multiple Viewports at Two Different Scales on an 8-1/2″ × 11″ sheet

Step 1. **Open drawing CH3-TUTORIAL2 so it is displayed on the screen and save it as CH5-TUTORIAL3.**

Step 2. **Make sure the Model tab is current. Turn the grid OFF.**

Step 3. **Make a new layer named Viewport. Make its color green and set it current.**

Step 4. CLICK: **Wizards (in the Tools menu on the menu bar).** CLICK: **Create Layout... (in the Wizards menu) to access the Create Layout dialog box (Figure 5–11).**

FIGURE 5–11
Create Layout Dialog Box; Enter a Name for the Layout

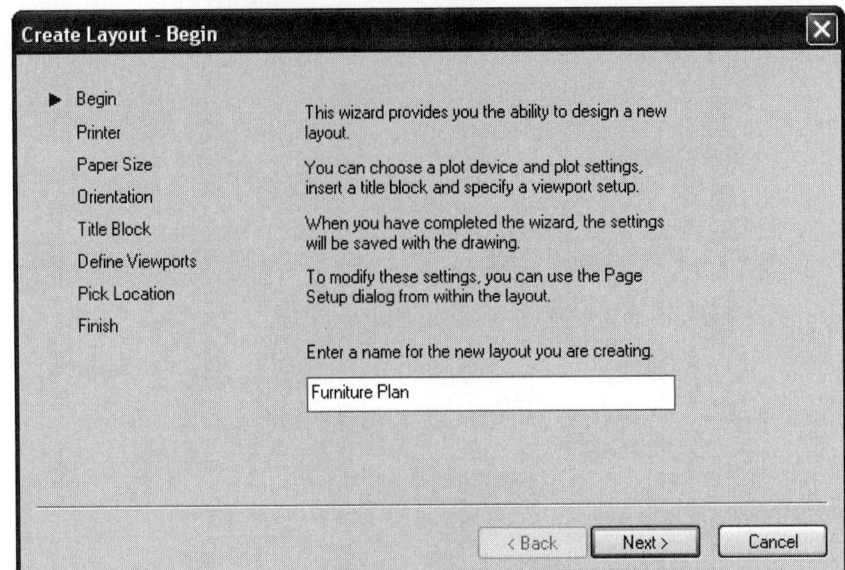

Step 5. TYPE: "**Furniture Plan**" **for the new layout name in the text box (Figure 5–11).** CLICK: **Next>.**

Step 6. **Select a configured printer for the new layout.** CLICK: **Next>.**

Step 7. **Select a paper size of Letter (8.5 × 11 in.).** CLICK: **Next>.**

Step 8. **Select the Portrait orientation of the drawing on the paper.** CLICK: **Next>.**

Step 9. **Select None for your title block (Figure 5–12).** CLICK: **Next>.**

Step 10. **Select the Array option button so you will have two viewports. Select 1/8″ = 1′-0″ as the Viewport scale: (Figure 5–13).** CLICK: **Next>.**

Step 11. CLICK: **Next>. AutoCAD will locate the viewport.**

Step 12. CLICK: **Finish. The Layout tab named Furniture Plan is created with the CH3-TUTORIAL1 conference room shown twice at 1/8″ = 1′-0″ scale. Check to make sure the scales are correct.**

FIGURE 5–12
Select None for No Title Block

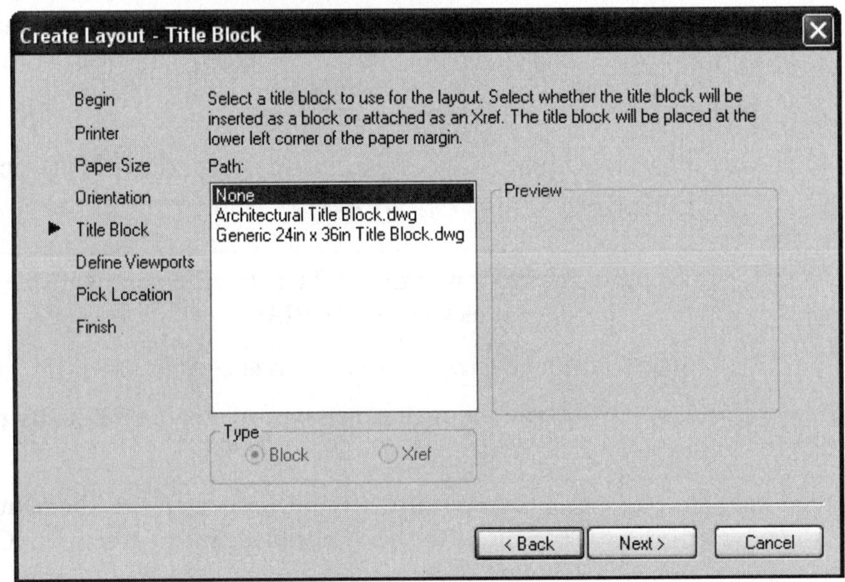

FIGURE 5–13
Select the Array Viewport Setup with Two Rows and One Column at a Scale of 1/8″ = 1′-0″

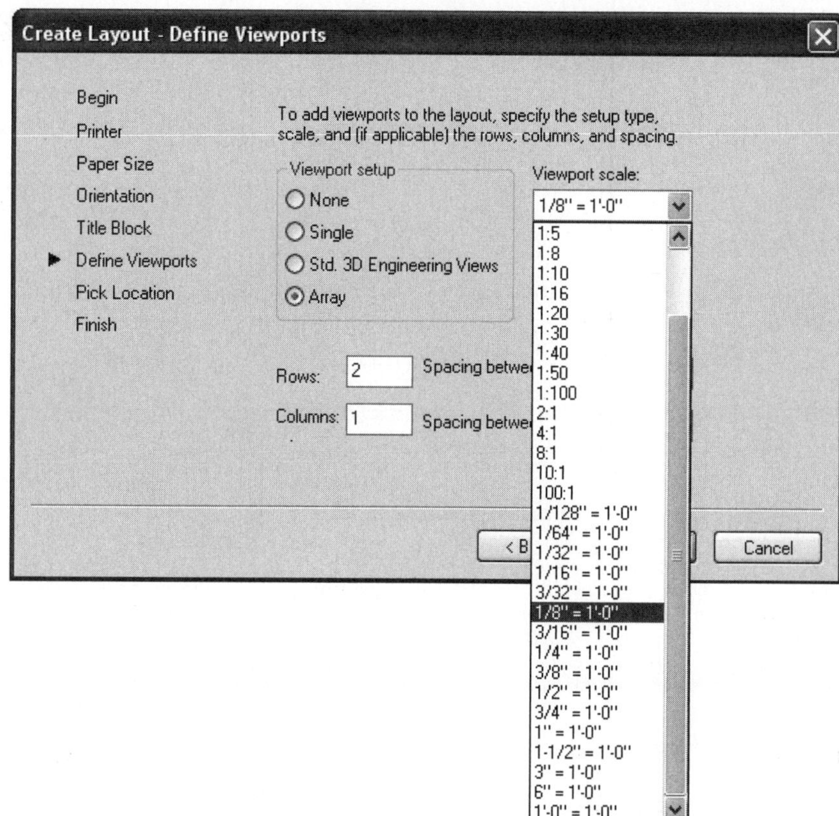

CLICK: the viewport boundary, RIGHT-CLICK and select Properties, then click: Standard scale under Misc. Set the top viewport at 1/8″ = 1′-0″. PRESS: Esc, then use propterties to set the bottom viewport at 3/16″ = 1′-0″.

Step 13. The outline of the viewport (shown in green on your screen) needs to be turned off. Turn the Viewport layer off so it will not print.

Step 14. If your conference rooms are not centered within the dashed lines, change to model space (TYPE: MS <enter> or CLICK: PAPER on the status bar to switch to model space). Use Pan to center the conference rooms and move the bottom view up so it is closer to the top viewport. CLICK: MODEL on the status bar to return to paper space.

NOTE: If you accidentally use a Zoom command while in model space and change the scale of the drawing, turn the viewport layer on. Click on the viewport boundary line and then click on Properties. Locate the scale you want the drawing to be under Misc and the Standard scale input area. Zooming while you are in paper space will not change the scale of the drawing.

Step 15. Use Figure 5–14 as a guide. While in paper space, set the Layer a-anno-text current and use CityBlueprint font, 1/8″ high, to type your name, class, and the date. Complete as shown in Figure 5–14.

FIGURE 5–14
Type Your Name, Class, and Date in the Upper Part of the Drawing

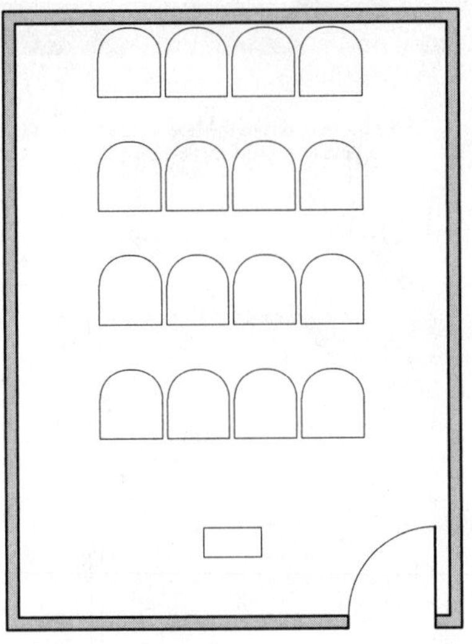

NOTE: When you type your name or anything else 1/8″ high in paper space, it will be printed 1/8″ high when the page is printed at a scale of 1:1.

Step 16. RIGHT-CLICK: **the Furniture Plan tab.** CLICK: **Plot.... Make sure the scale is set 1:1. (The Viewport scales are already set to 1/8″ = 1″-0′ and 3/16″ = 1′-0″; you are plotting the 8-1/2 × 11 paper at 1:1.)**

Step 17. CLICK: **Preview... if the preview is OK,** RIGHT-CLICK **and** CLICK: **Plot. If not, Exit and correct the problem.**

Step 18. **Save the drawing in at least two places.**

Tutorial 5–4: Plotting Using Page Setup Manager, Multiple Viewports with Different Floor Plans, and the D-Size Format

Step 1. **Open drawing CH3-TUTORIAL1 so it is displayed on the screen and save it as CH5-TUTORIAL4.**

Step 2. **Insert CH3-TUTORIAL2, 3, 4 into the current drawing as described next:**

Prompt	Response
Command:	TYPE: **I<enter>**
The Insert dialog box appears:	**Use Browse to locate CH3-TUTORIAL2 in your folder and** CLICK: **on it as shown in Figure 5–15**
The Select Drawing File dialog box appears:	CLICK: **Open**
The Insert Dialog box appears:	CLICK: **OK**

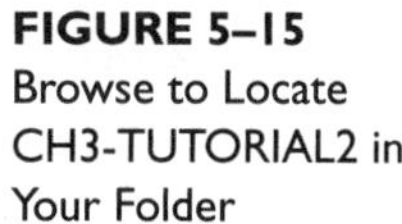

FIGURE 5–15
Browse to Locate CH3-TUTORIAL2 in Your Folder

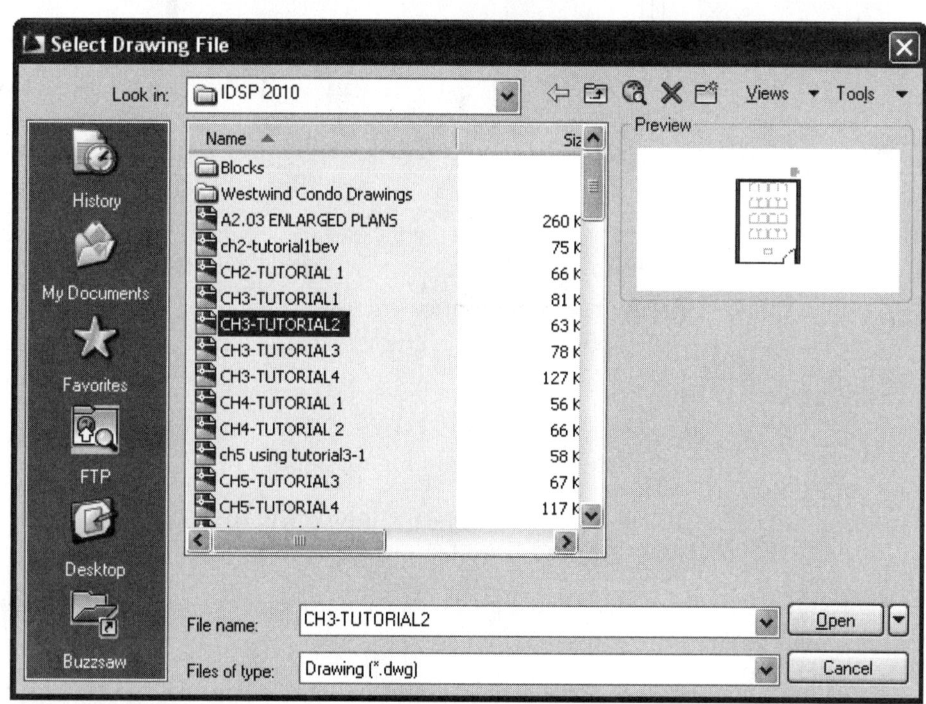

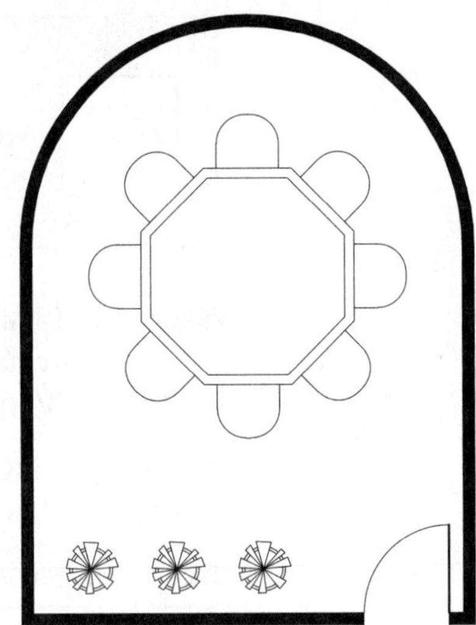
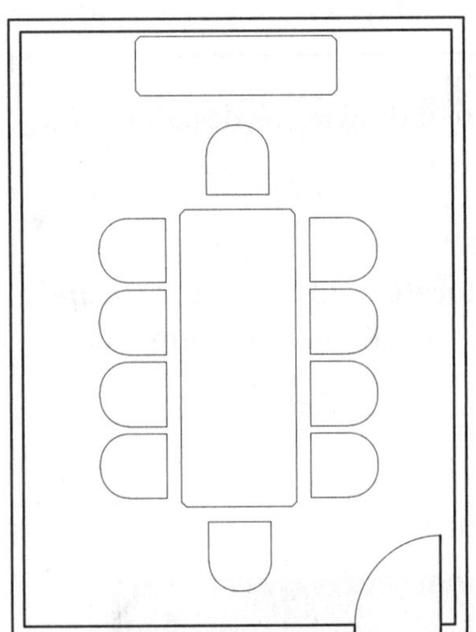
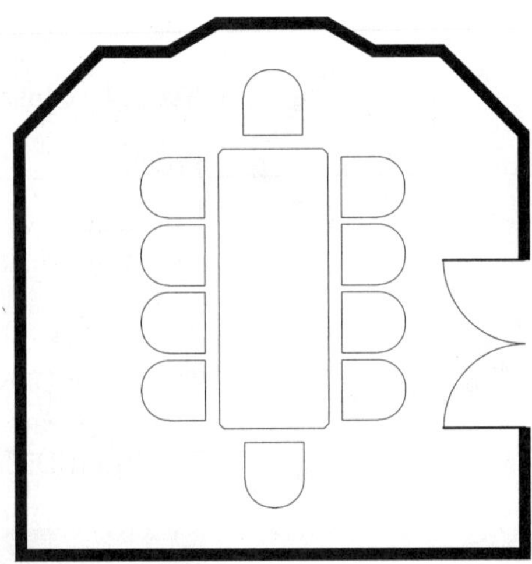

FIGURE 5–16
Insert Tutorials 3–2, 3–3, and 3–4

Prompt	Response
Specify insertion point or [Basepoint/Scale/X/Y/Z/Rotate]:	CLICK: **A point to locate the drawing directly above CH3-TUTORIAL1, Figure 5–16**

Repeat the above for CH3-TUTORIAL3 and CH3-TUTORIAL4. Position the blocks approximately as shown in Figure 5–16.

Step 3. **On your own, explode the inserted blocks and erase the Name, Class, and Date from all four drawings.**

Step 4. **Make a new layer named Viewport. Make its color green and set it current.**

Step 5. **Modify Layout1 using the Page Setup Manager as described next.**

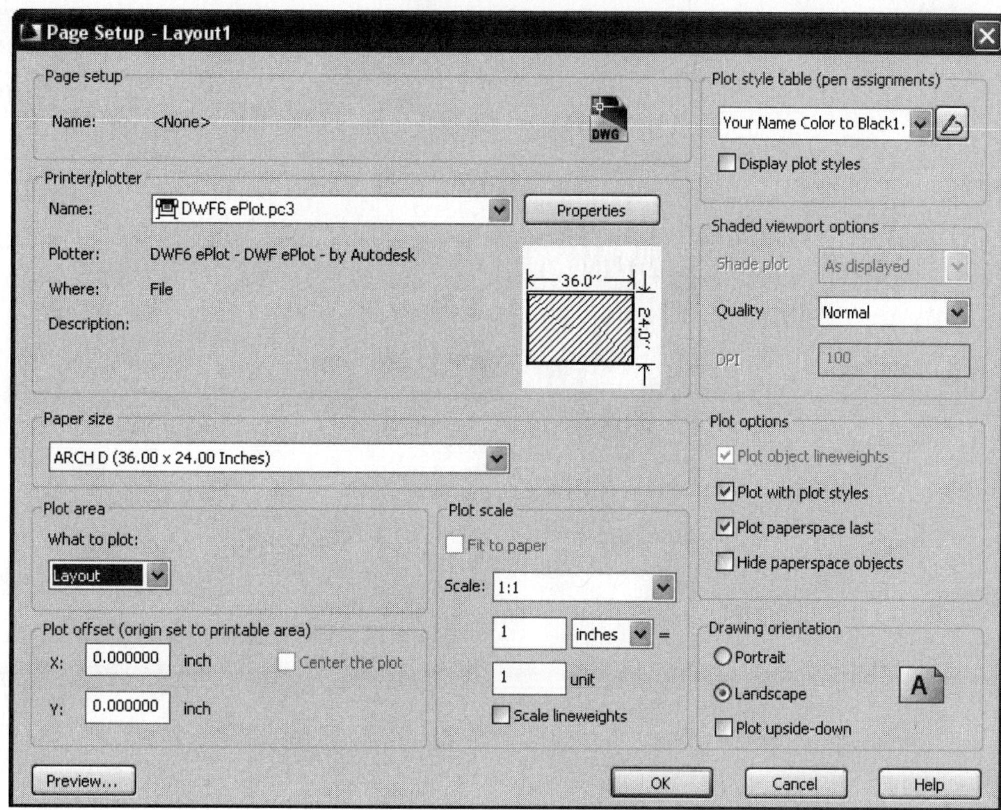

FIGURE 5–17
Page Setup-Layout1 Dialog Box

Prompt	Response
Command:	CLICK: **Layout1**
The picture of the first tutorial appears in paper space.	RIGHT-CLICK: Layout1
	CLICK: **Page Setup Manager...**
The Page Setup Manager appears:	CLICK: **Modify...**
Page Setup - Layout1 appears:	**In the Paper size list** CLICK: **ARCH D (36.00 × 24.00 inches).** Check to see that all other settings are as shown in Figure 5–17
	CLICK: **OK**
The Page Setup Manager appears:	CLICK: **Close**

A 36″ × 24″ area appears on the screen with the first tutorial in the lower left corner.

Step 6. On your own, make a new layer named a-anno-ttbl, color magenta, lineweight .012″, and set it current.

Step 7. Insert the D-Size Title Block you made in an earlier chapter.

Prompt	Response
Command:	TYPE: **I<enter>**
The Insert dialog box appears:	**Use Browse to locate your D-size drawing in your folder and** CLICK: **on it as shown in Figure 5–18**
The Select Drawing File dialog box appears:	CLICK: **Open**
The Insert Dialog box appears:	CLICK: **OK**

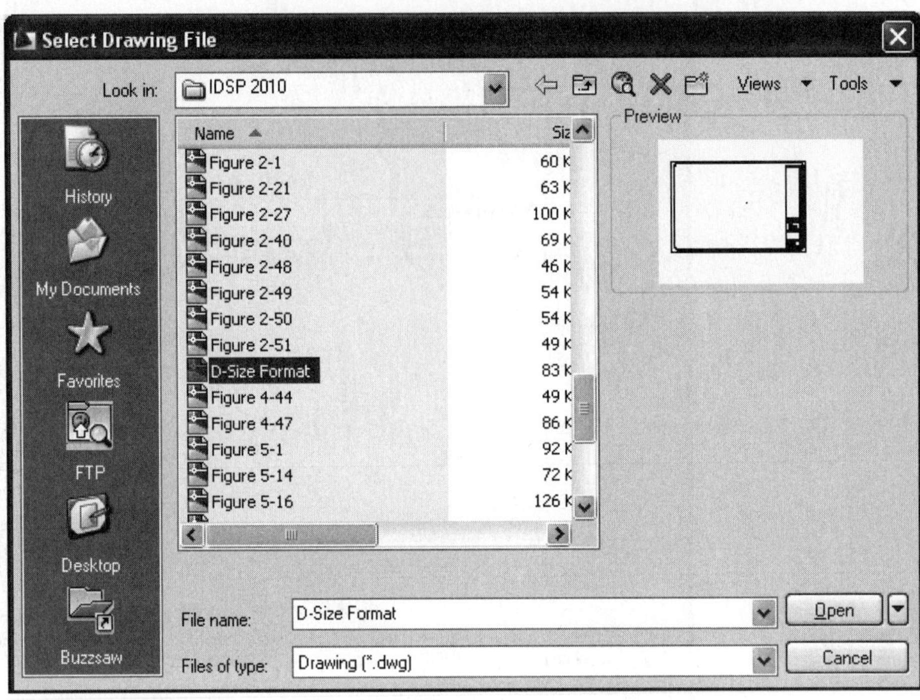

FIGURE 5–18
Locate Your D-Size Format and CLICK: on It

Prompt	Response
Specify insertion point or [Basepoint/Scale/X/Y/Z/Rotate]:	TYPE: **0,0 <enter>**

Step 8. On your own, copy the viewport three times (CLICK: any point on the rectangle that is the viewport to select it) and move them to the approximate locations shown in Figure 5–19.

Step 9. Go to MODEL space and center each conference room floor plan in the viewports (Figure 5–20) as described next

Prompt	Response
Command:	CLICK: **PAPER** (or TYPE: **MS<enter>**) to go to MODEL space CLICK: **The center viewport on the bottom** **Zoom out or Zoom-All** **Pan so the second conference room is centered in the viewport. Then Zoom a window around the conference room so it appears as shown** **Repeat for the third and fourth viewports**

Step 10. Return to PAPER space and set the scales for the individual viewports as described next:

Prompt	Response
Command:	CLICK: **MODEL** (or TYPE: **PS<enter>**) to go to PAPER space

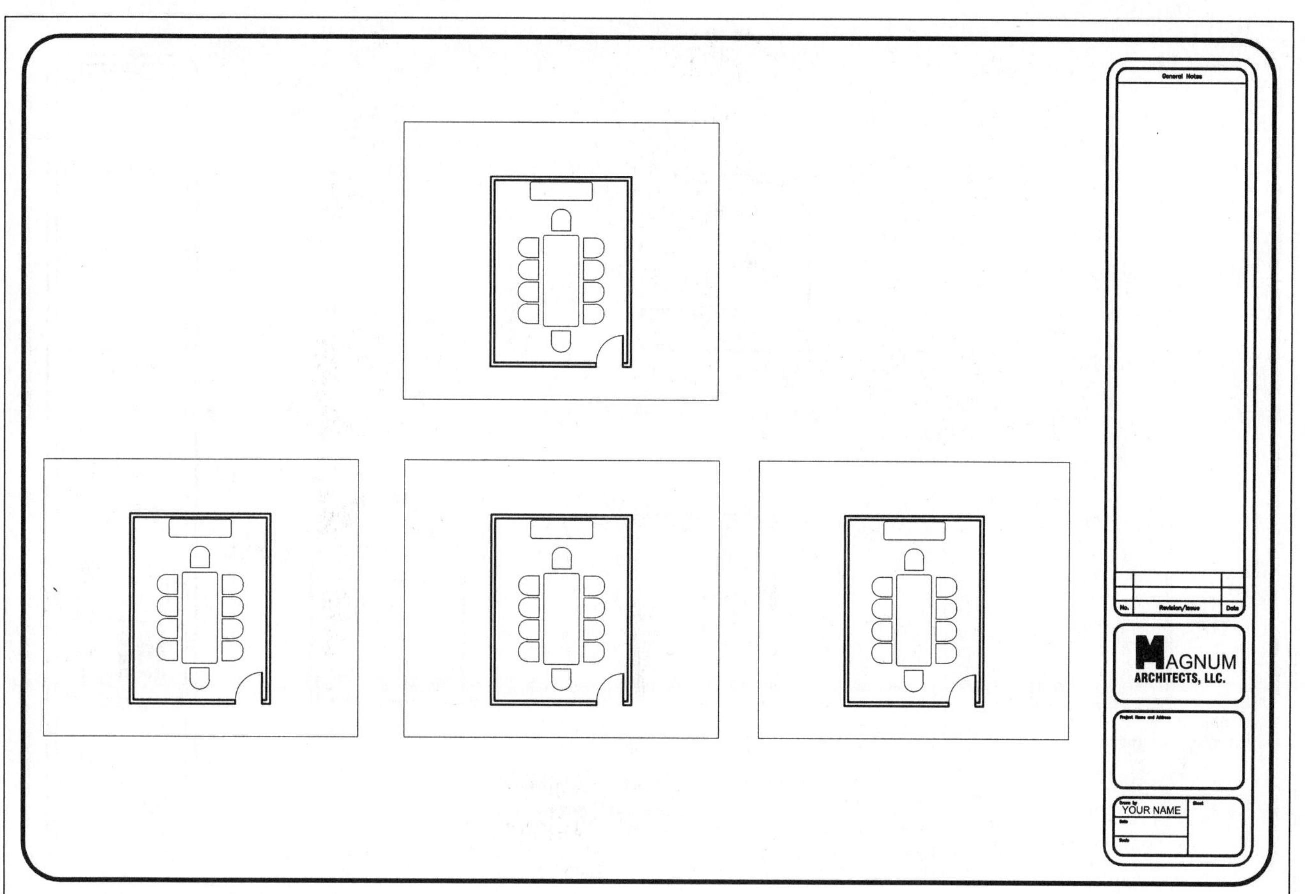

FIGURE 5–19
Copy the First Viewport Three Times

Prompt	Response
	CLICK: **Any point on the lower left viewport**
	CLICK: **Any point on the lower right viewport**
	RIGHT-CLICK: and CLICK: **Properties**
The Properties palette appears:	CLICK: **Standard scale under Misc**
	CLICK: **the arrow to the right of Standard scale and scroll to select 1/4″ = 1′-0″.** This scale is applied to the drawings in the lower left and lower right viewports.
	PRESS: **the Esc key** (to deselect the lower left and lower right viewports)
	CLICK: **Any point on the lower center viewport**
The Properties palette appears:	CLICK: **Standard scale under Misc**
	CLICK: **the arrow to the right of Standard scale and scroll to select 3/16″ = 1′-0″.** This scale is applied to the drawing in the lower center viewport
	PRESS: **the Esc key**
	CLICK: **Any point on the upper viewport**
	RIGHT-CLICK: and CLICK: **Properties**

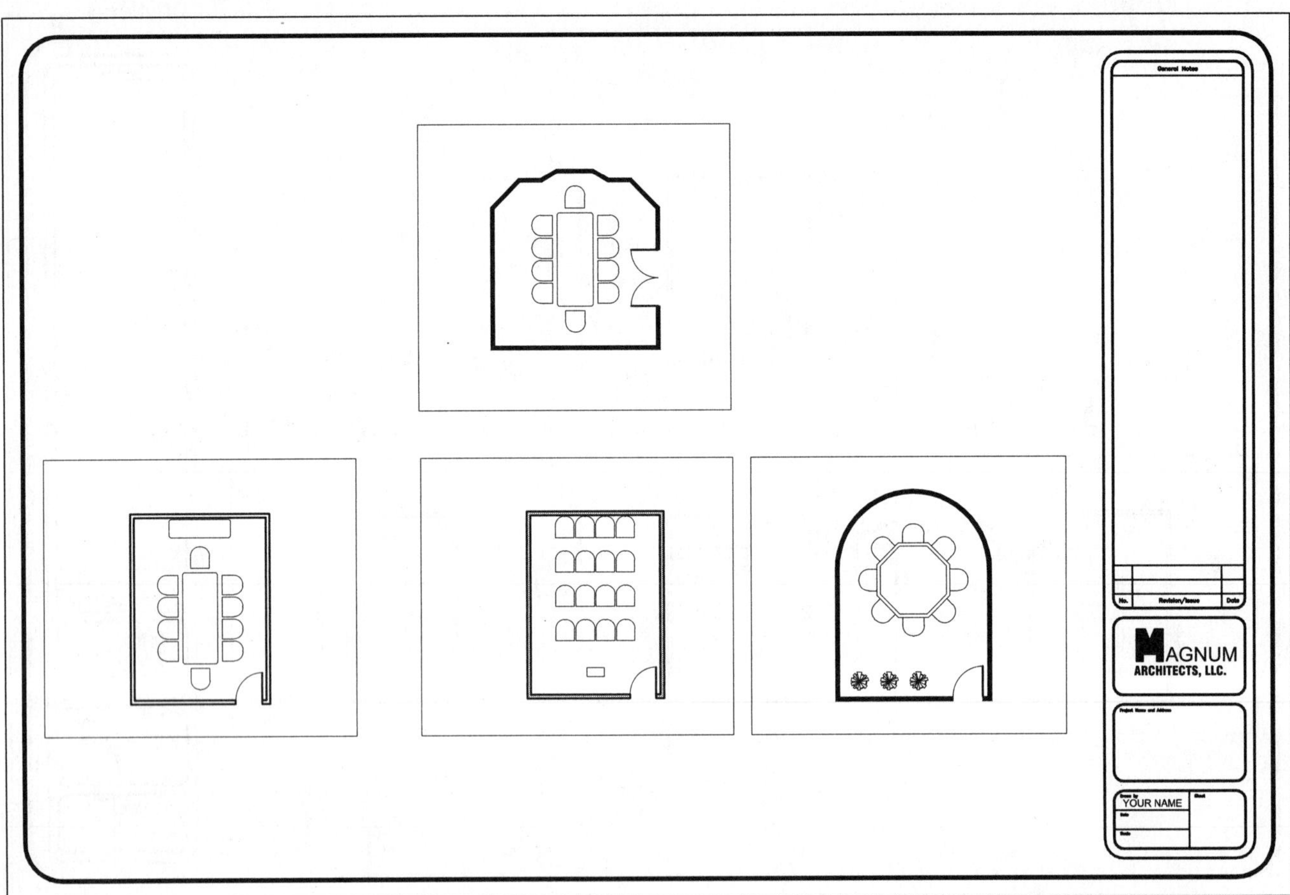

FIGURE 5–20
Conference Rooms Centered in Individual Viewports

Prompt	Response
The Properties palette appears:	CLICK: **Standard scale under Misc** CLICK: **the arrow to the right of Standard scale and scroll to select 3/8″ = 1′-0″.** This scale is applied to the drawing in the upper viewport PRESS: **the Esc key**

The drawing appears approximately as shown in Figure 5–21.

Step 11. Change the shapes of the upper and lower center viewports so the complete drawing for each conference room is shown in viewport as described next:

Prompt	Response
Command:	CLICK: **Any point on the upper viewport**
Grips (small blue squares) appear at all four corners:	CLICK: **the upper right grip to make it hot** (it turns red) **Move your mouse to make the viewport larger or smaller as needed** **Repeat for the lower center viewport**

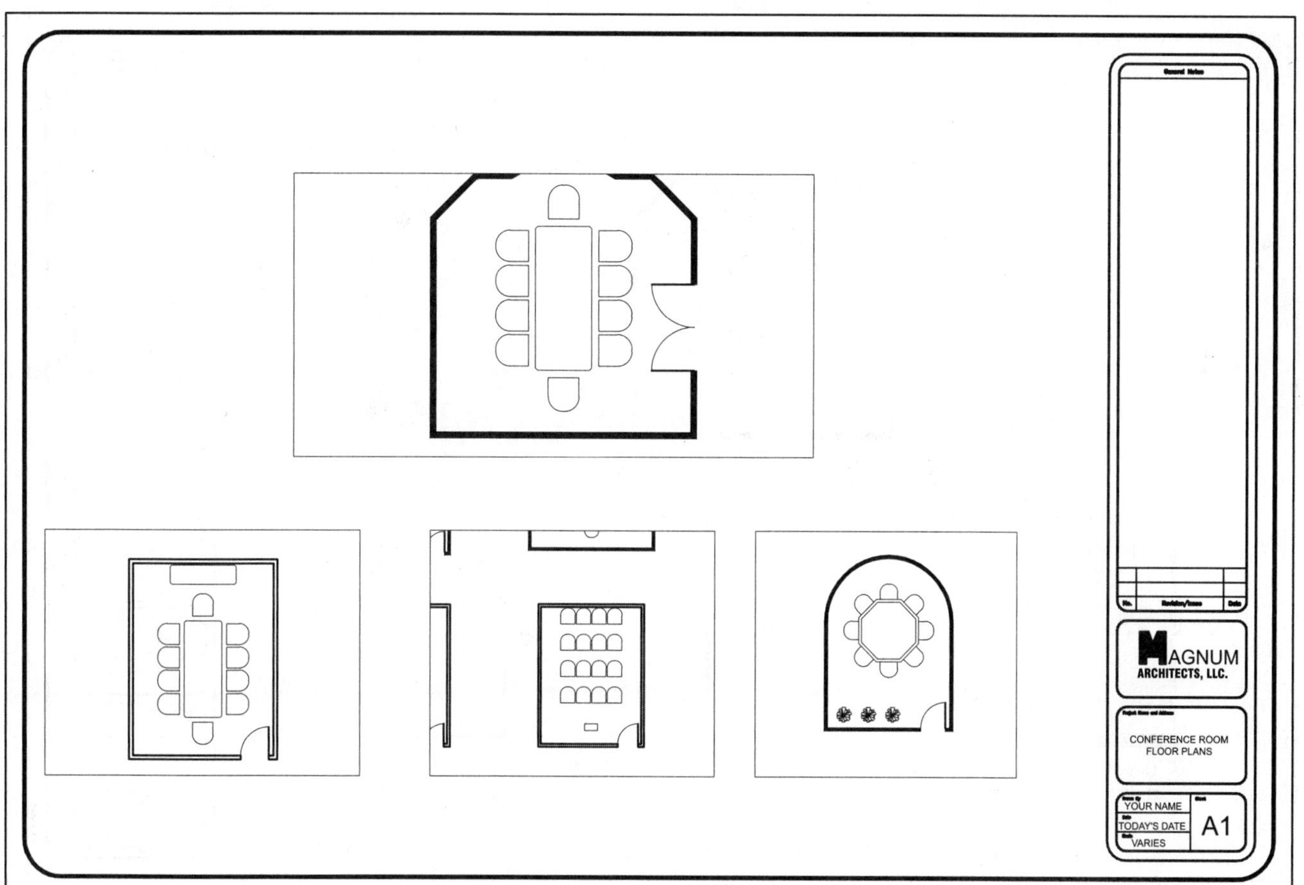

FIGURE 5–21
Set the Scales for Individual Viewports

Step 12. On your own, turn off the Viewport Layer.

Step 13. In the City Blueprint font, 1/4″ high, TYPE: the scale under each conference room floor plan as shown in Figure 5–22.

Step 14. In the Arial font, 3/16″ high, TYPE: the title block information shown in Figure 5–23.

Step 15. Save the drawing in at least two places.

Step 16. Plot the drawing at a scale of 1:1 on a D-size sheet (24″ × 36″) using your Color to Black plot style.

Tutorial 5–5: Making PDF Files That Can Be Attached to Emails and Opened Without the AutoCAD Program

Often it is necessary to send files to clients who do not have the AutoCAD program. PDF files can be used to show drawings without sending .dwg files. The following tutorial shows you how to do that.

Step 1. Open drawing CH5-TUTORIAL4 so it is displayed on the screen.

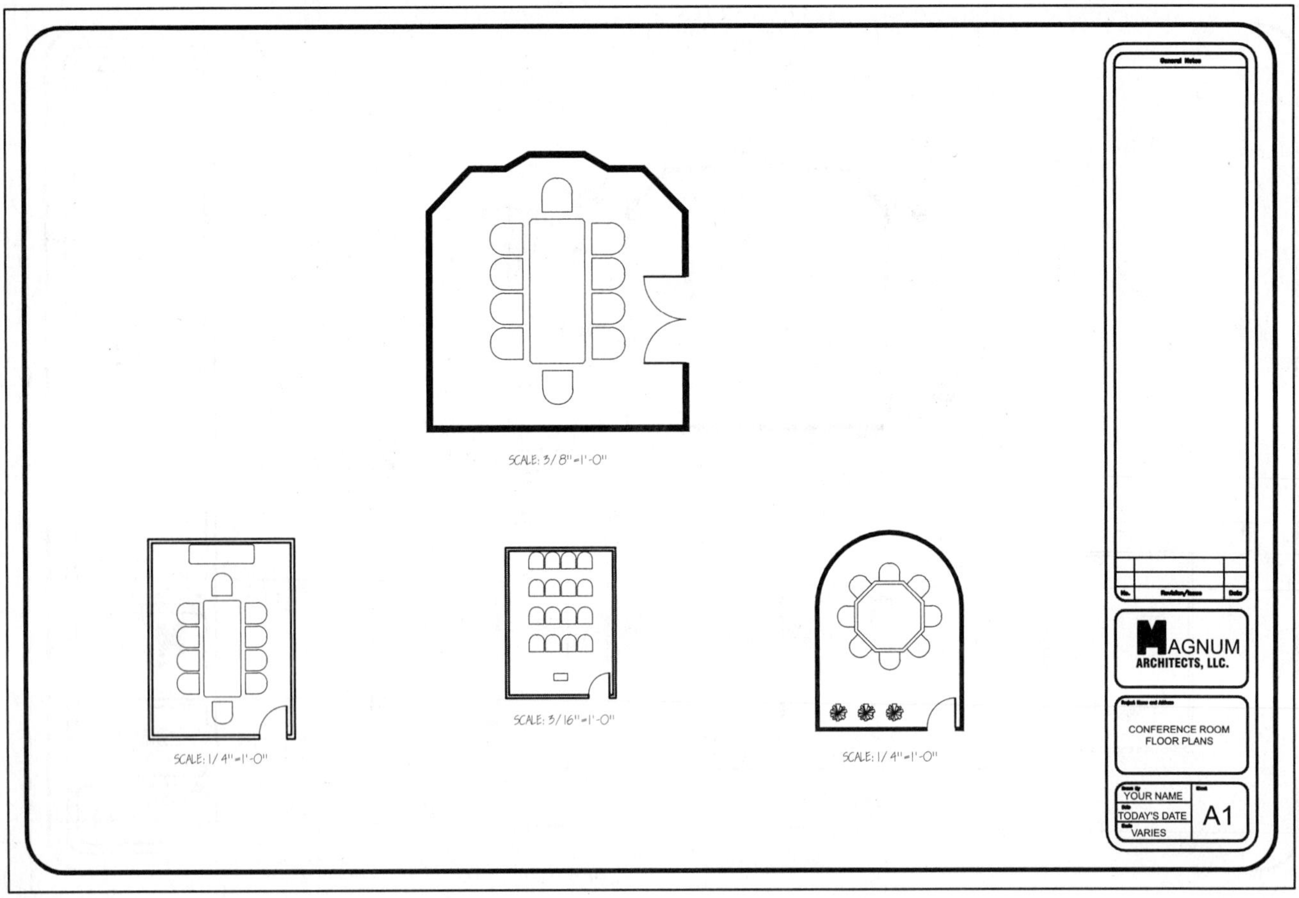

FIGURE 5–22
Type the Scale for Individual Viewports

FIGURE 5–23
Title Block Information

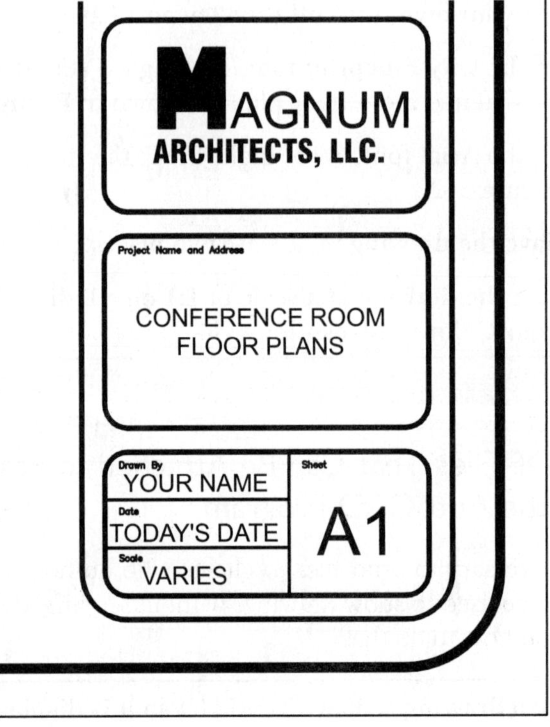

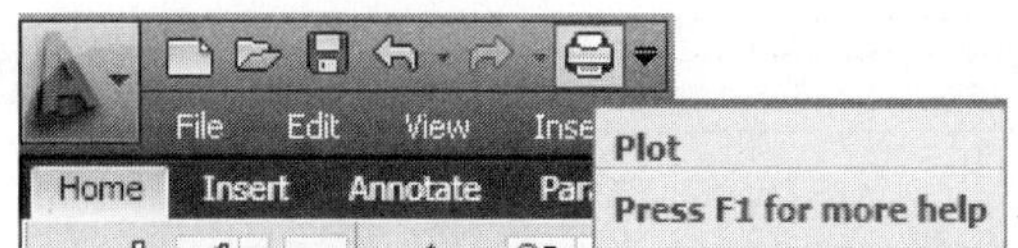

Step 2. Make a PDF file from the CH5-TUTORIAL4 drawing, as described next:

Prompt	Response
Command:	CLICK: **PLOT**
The Plot dialog box appears.	**In the Printer/Plotter Name: box,** CLICK: **DWG to PDF.pc3** as shown in Figure 5–24 **Check other parts of the Plot dialog box to be sure all settings are as shown in Figure 5–24** CLICK: **OK**
The Browse for Plot File box appears:	**Locate the folder and drive where you want to save the file and change the name to CH5-TUTORIAL5 as shown in Figure 5–25** CLICK: **Save**
The PDF image appears:	**If the image is complete, close the program. If not, redo the plot making any necessary changes such as plotting Extents on a larger sheet of paper**

That's it. You now have a PDF file of your drawing that can be sent to anyone and they can view it whether they have AutoCAD or not.

FIGURE 5–24
Plot-Layout1 to PDF Dialog Box

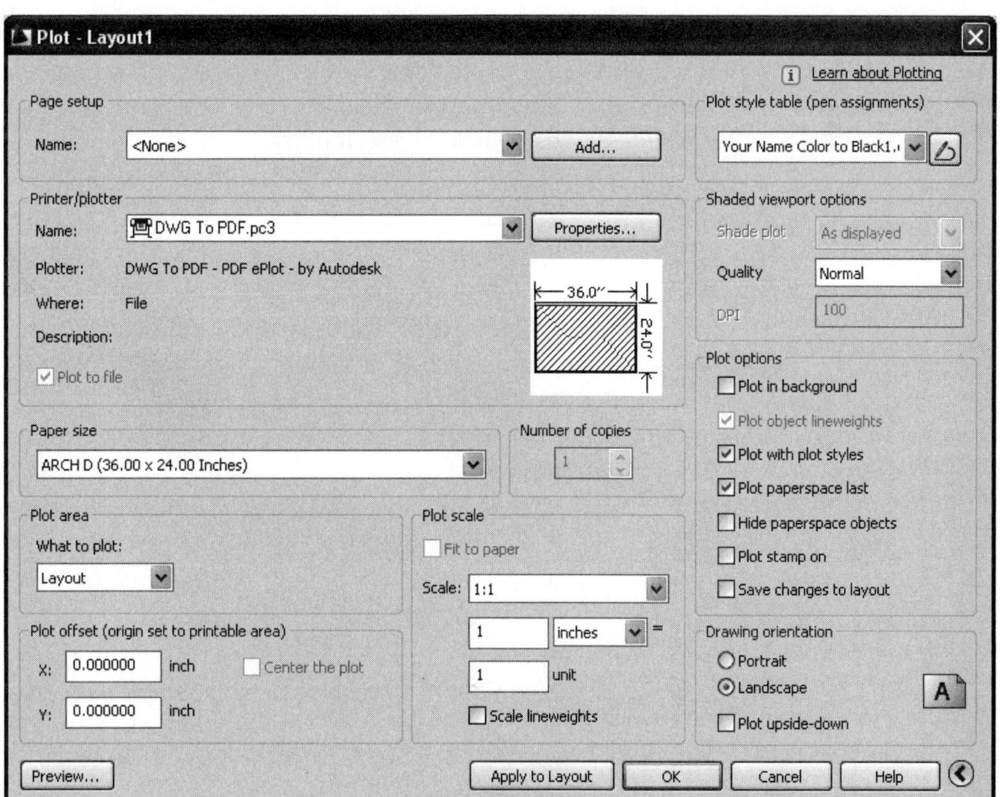

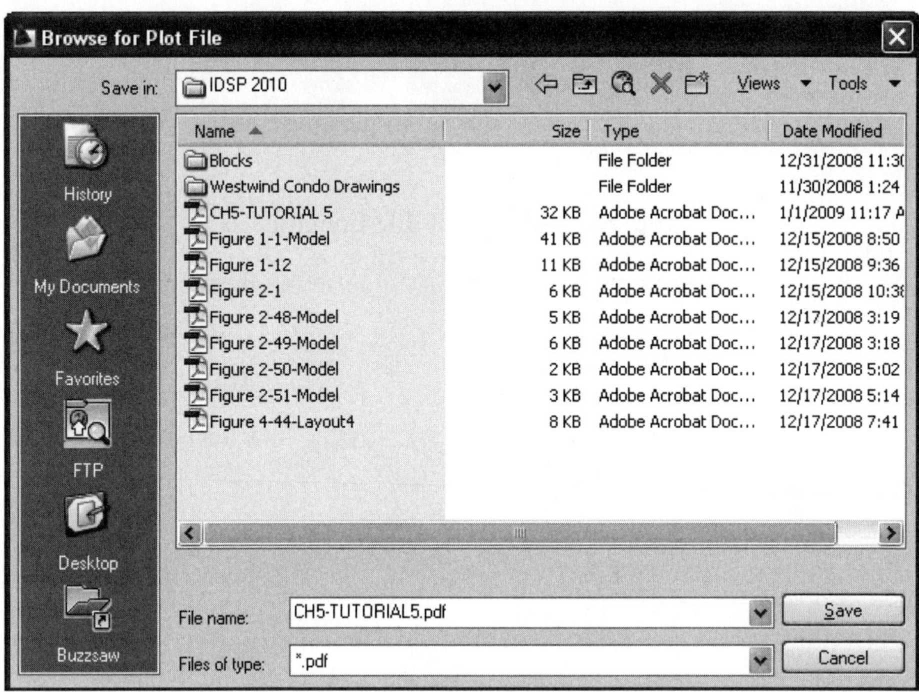

FIGURE 5–25
Locate the Folder to Save the PDF File and Change the Name to CH5-TUTORIAL5

review questions

1. Which of the following contains the Plot... command?
   a. Home panel
   b. Annotate panel
   c. Quick Access Toolbar
   d. View panel
   e. Manage panel
2. Properties that can be set in a plot style table are
   a. Pen #
   b. Dithering
   c. Grayscale
   d. Screening
   e. All the above
3. When plotting from the Model tab, which of the following will produce a plot of the part of the drawing that is displayed on the screen?
   a. Display
   b. Extents
   c. Limits
   d. View
   e. Window
4. When plotting from the Model tab, which of the following will produce a plot of the entire drawing, even if part of it is outside the limits?
   a. All
   b. Extents
   c. Limits
   d. View
   e. Window
5. A plot file has which of the following extensions?
   a. .bak
   b. .dwg
   c. .plt
   d. .cfk
   e. .dwf

6. When plotting from the Model tab, a plot that shows only half of what should have been plotted could probably be corrected by doing which of the following?
   a. Moving the origin .5
   b. Selecting View instead of Extents
   c. Writing the plot to a file
   d. Selecting Landscape instead of Portrait
   e. Selecting a smaller page

7. A color-dependent plot style can be made to allow you to plot with the lineweights that are assigned to the layers in the drawing.
   a. True
   b. False

8. A drawing that is to be plotted using the Model tab so that it fits on a particular size sheet without regard to the scale requires which scale response?
   a. 1:1
   b. Full
   c. 1:2
   d. Fit to Paper
   e. MAX

9. Which of the following menus on the Menu Bar used in this chapter contains the command to create a Layout Wizard?
   a. File
   b. View
   c. Insert
   d. Tools
   e. Window

10. When you are using the Plot command to plot a Layout tab that has a single viewport that is already scaled to 1/2″ = 1′-0″, in the Plot dialog box use a Plot scale of:
    a. 1/2″ = 1′-0″
    b. 1:1
    c. 1:2
    d. 1:48
    e. Scaled to Fit

Complete.

11. Name the three tabs that are at the bottom of the drawing window (when Model and Layout tabs are displayed).

    ____________________ ____________________ ____________________

12. Name the two different types of plot styles.

    ____________________ ____________________

13. Describe why you would use different plot styles to plot the same drawing.

    ____

14. While in the Plot dialog box, name the three different drawing orientations you can select when plotting.

    ____

    ____

    ____

15. If you want your text to be 1/8″ high when plotted on a drawing that is to be scaled at 1/4″ = 1′-0″, how high is the text while you are drawing full scale?

    ____

16. List 12 commands that are on the right-click menu of a Layout tab when you are in paper space.

______________	______________	______________
______________	______________	______________
______________	______________	______________

17. Name the type of drawing file that can be viewed without using AutoCAD.

____

18. When using a Layout Wizard, describe how to center your drawing within a viewport boundary.

____

19. When plotting from a Layout tab, why do you turn off the boundary line of the paper space viewport?

____

20. List the 12 properties listed in the Plot Style Table Editor that can be set.

______________	______________	______________
______________	______________	______________
______________	______________	______________
______________	______________	______________

chapter

6

Drawing the Floor Plan: Walls, Doors, and Windows

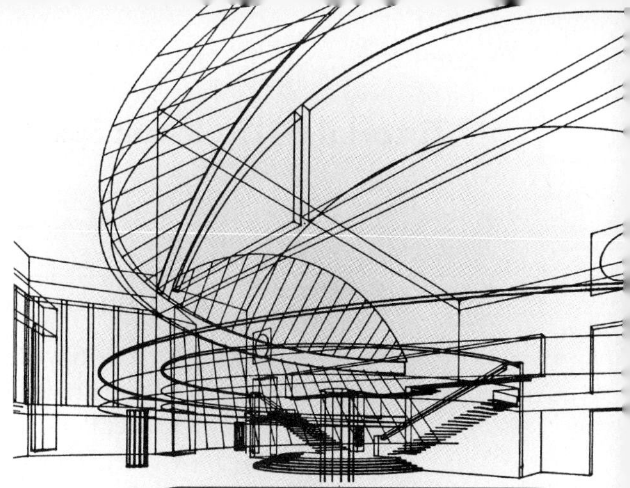

objectives

When you have completed this chapter, you will be able to:

Correctly use the following commands and settings:

- Annotative Text
- Block-Make...
- Color
- Edit Multiline
- Extend
- Hatch
- Insert-Block...
- Linetype
- Lineweight
- List
- Make Objects Layer Current
- Match Properties
- Multiline
- Multiline Style...
- Properties...
- Wblock

THE TENANT SPACE PROJECT

The Polyline or Multiline commands can be used to draw walls quickly. Polyline was described and used in Chapter 3. With Multiline, walls with up to 16 lines are drawn. Tutorial 6–1 contains step-by-step instructions for using Multiline to draw the exterior and interior walls of a tenant space that is located in the northwest corner of a building. The tutorial also contains step-by-step instructions for inserting windows and doors into the plan.

Chapters 7, 8, 9, and 11 provide step-by-step instructions to complete the tenant space project started in this chapter. Each chapter will use the building plan drawn in this chapter to complete a part of the project as described next.

Chapter 7: The tenant space is dimensioned and the square feet calculated.

Chapter 8: Elevations, sections, and details are drawn.

Chapter 9: Furniture is drawn, attributes are assigned (furniture specifications), and the furniture is added to the plan.

Chapter 11: The reflected ceiling plan and voice/data/power plan are drawn.

Tutorial 6–1: Tenant Space Floor Plan

When you have completed Tutorial 6–1, the tenant space floor plan, your drawing will look similar to Figure 6–1.

Step 1. Use your workspace to make the following settings:

1. **Use SaveAs... to save the drawing with the name CH6-TUTORIAL1.**
2. Set drawing Units: **Architectural**
3. Set Precision: **1/32″**
4. Set Drawing Limits: **75′,65′**
5. Set GRIDDISPLAY: **0**
6. Set Grid: **12″**
7. Set Snap: **6″**

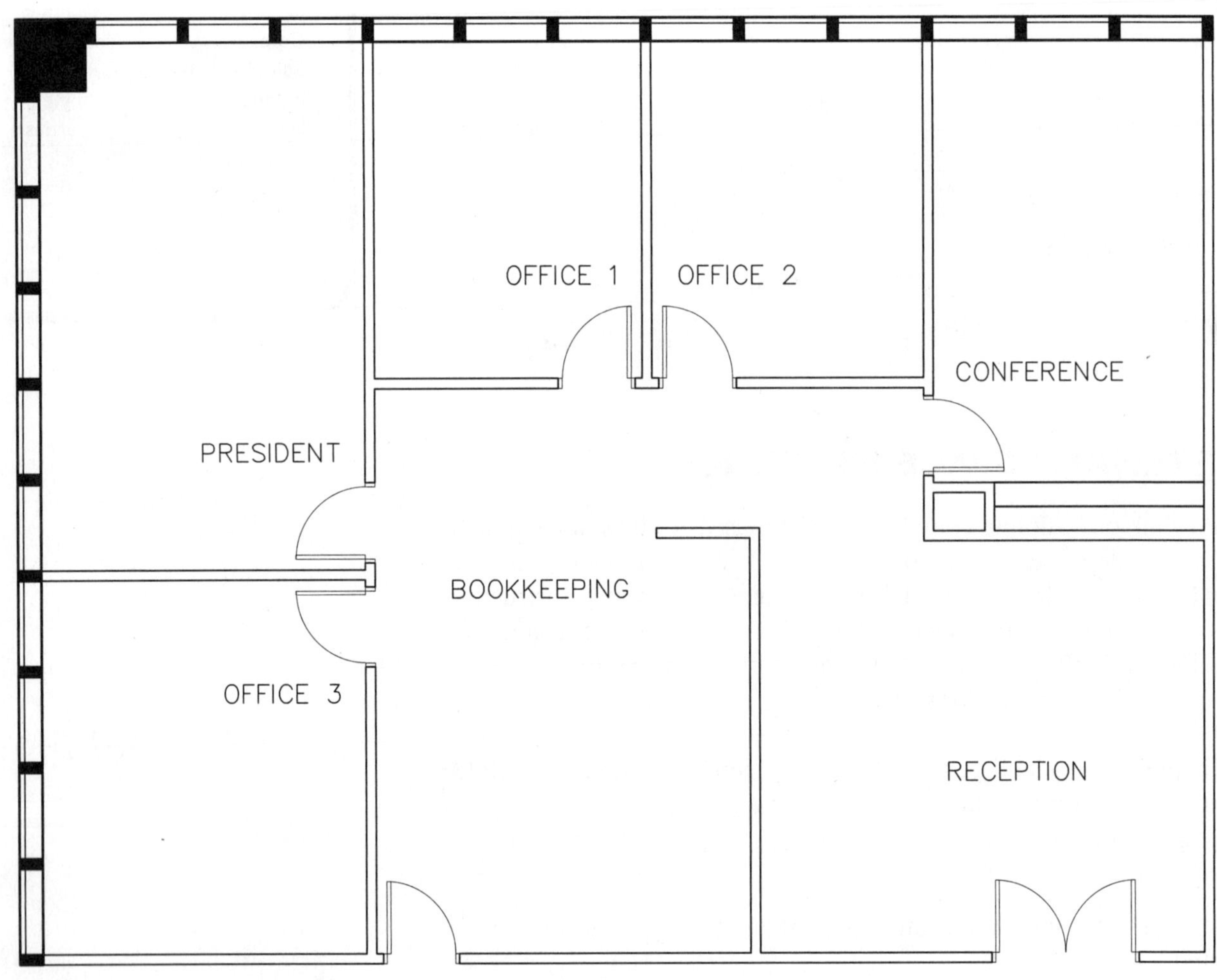

FIGURE 6–1
Tutorial 6–1: Tenant Space Floor Plan (Scale: 1/8″ = 1′-0″)

8. **Create the following layers.** Be sure to type and enter a comma after each layer name. The cursor will move to the next line so you can type the next layer name:

LAYER NAME	COLOR	LINETYPE	LINEWEIGHT
Architectural			
a-anno-area	green	continuous	.006″ (.15mm)
a-anno-dims	red	continuous	.004″ (.09mm)
a-anno-text	green	continuous	.006″ (.15mm)
a-clng-grid	red	continuous	.004″ (.09mm)
a-door-dbl	red	continuous	.004″ (.09mm)
a-door-swng	red	continuous	.004″ (.09mm)
a-flor-iden	green	continuous	.006″ (.15mm)
a-flor-wdwk	blue	continuous	.007″ (.18mm)
a-glaz	green	continuous	.006″ (.15mm)
a-wall-extr	white	continuous	.014″ (.35mm)
a-wall-head	blue	continuous	.007″ (.18mm)
a-wall-intr	blue	continuous	.007″ (.18mm)
a-wall-pat2	white	continuous	.014″ (.35mm)
Electrical			
e-lite	white	continuous	.014″ (.35mm)
e-lite-circ	white	dashedx2	.014″ (.35mm)
e-lite-text	green	continuous	.006″ (.15mm)
e-powr	white	continuous	.014″ (.35mm)
e-powr-text	green	continuous	.006″ (.15mm)
Interiors			
i-furn	cyan	continuous	.004″ (.09mm)

9. Set **Layer a-wall-extr** current.
10. Use **Zoom-All** to view the limits of the drawing.

NOTE: If you cannot see the entire name of the layer, right-click on one of the titles such as Name, Color, or LInetype, and a right-click menu will appear. CLICK: **Maximize all columns** in the right-click menu to be able to see the entire layer name you have typed.

RECTANGLE

The following part of Tutorial 6–1 uses the Rectangle and Hatch commands to draw the window mullions and the 3′-square corner column located in the northwest corner of the tenant space.

Step 2. Use Rectangle to draw the 3′-square corner column (Figure 6–2), as described next:

Prompt	Response
Command:	**RECTANGLE** (or TYPE: **REC<enter>**)
Specify first corner point or [Chamfer/Elevation/Fillet/Thickness/Width]:	TYPE: **17′,51′<enter>**

FIGURE 6–2
Use the Rectangle and Solid Hatch Command to Draw the Corner Column and Two Mullions

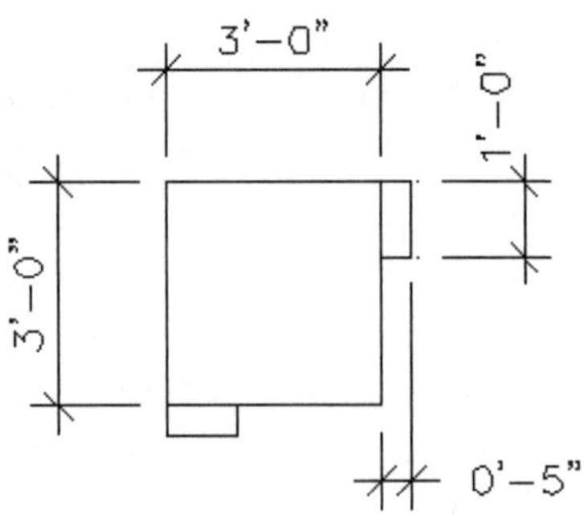

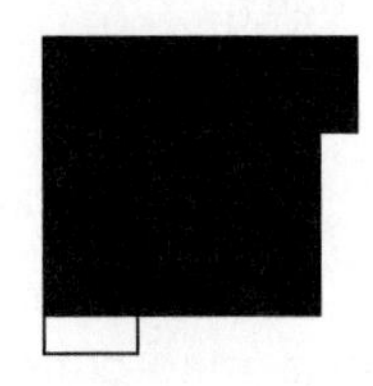

Prompt	Response
Specify other corner point or [Area/ Dimensions/Rotation]:	TYPE: **@3′,-3′<enter>**(be sure to include the minus)

Step 3. **Zoom in close around the column, and use the rectangle command to draw the two separate mullions (5″ × 12″) that are on the east and south sides of the column just drawn, as shown in Figure 6-2. Use snap and relative coordinates (CLICK: the top right corner for first point, then @5,-12 for the other corner points) to draw the mullion much like you just drew the corner column. Remember, with relative coordinates, enter the X axis first, then a comma, then the Y axis.**

Step 4. **Set Layer a-wall-pat2 current.**

HATCH

Step 5. **Use the Hatch command to make the corner column solid (Figure 6-2), as described next:**

Prompt	Response
Command:	**HATCH** (or TYPE: **H<enter>**)
The Hatch and Gradient dialog box appears:	**Select SOLID** in the Pattern list and CLICK: **Add: Pick points**
Pick internal point or [Select objects/ remove Boundaries]:	CLICK: **Any point inside the rectangle**
Pick internal point or [Select objects/ remove Boundaries]:	**<enter>**
The Hatch and Gradient dialog box reappears:	CLICK: **OK**

Step 6. **Use the Hatch command to make the mullions solid. Hatch one mullion, then exit the Hatch command before hatching the second mullion so you can array them separately.**

ARRAY

The Rectangular option of Array allows you to make copies of an object in a rectangular pattern. The array is made up of horizontal rows and vertical columns.

You specify the direction and spacing of rows and columns:

When a positive number is specified for the distance between rows, the array is drawn up. When a negative number is specified, the array is drawn down.

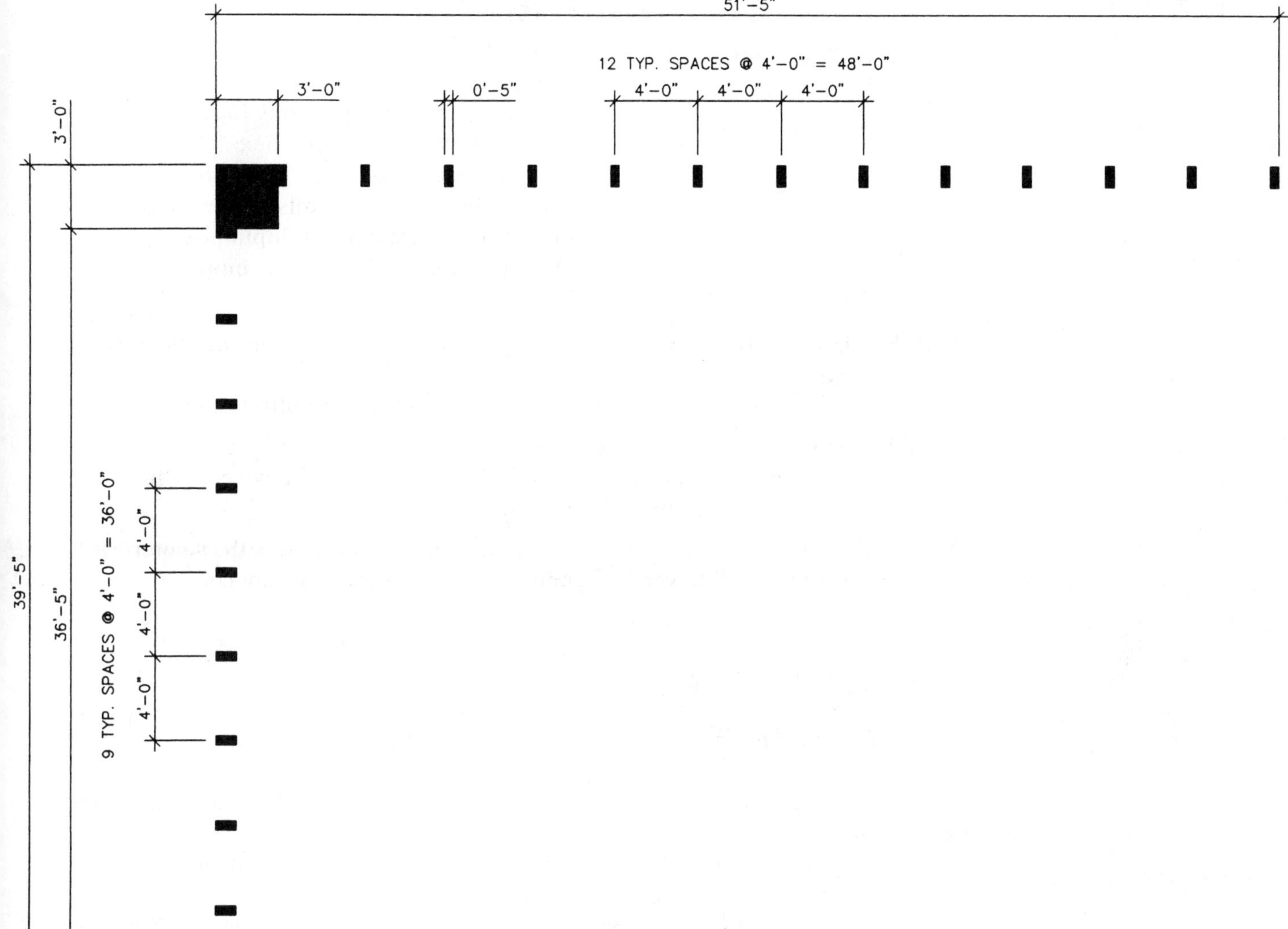

FIGURE 6–3
Use the Array Command to Finish Drawing the Mullions (Scale: 1/8″ = 1′-0″)

When a positive number is specified for the distance between columns, the array is drawn to the right. When a negative number is specified, the array is drawn to the left.

Step 7. Use Array to finish drawing the mullions on the north exterior wall (Figure 6–3), as described next:

Prompt	Response
Command:	**Array** (or TYPE: **AR<enter>**)
The Array dialog box appears:	CLICK: **the Select objects button**
Select objects:	CLICK: **the mullion located on the east side of the column. Select the rectangle and the hatch pattern.**

Prompt	Response
Select objects: 2 found	
Select objects:	**<enter>**
	CLICK: **the Rectangular Array button**
	TYPE: **1 in the Rows: input box**
	TYPE: **13 in the Columns: input box**
	TYPE: **4′ in the Column offset: input box**
	TYPE: **0 in the Row offset: input box**
	TYPE: **0 in the Angle of array: input box**
	CLICK: **OK**

Step 8. **Use the Array command to draw the remaining mullions on the west exterior wall, as shown in Figure 6–3. Specify 10 rows, 1 column, −4′ in the Row offset: input box, and 0 in the Column offset: input box.**

Step 9. **Next, you will draw the walls using Multiline. It is helpful if the column and mullions are not solid. Set FILL OFF and regenerate the drawing so that the columns and mullions are not solid.**

Step 10. **Zoom-Extents and use the Distance command** (TYPE: **DIST<enter>**) **with OSNAP to verify that all of your measurements are correct.**

Step 11. **Set Layer a-wall-extr current.**

MULTILINE STYLE...

With the column and mullions now completed, you are ready to use Multiline to draw the walls. The Multiline Style dialog box allows you to make the settings necessary to draw up to 16 lines at the same time with the Multiline command. You can specify color and linetype for any of the 16 lines and endcaps for each multiline. You can specify the walls as solid (background fill) or not. You must add the name of the multiline style to the list of current styles before you can draw with it.

Next, you will use Multiline Style . . . to create a multiline style named THREE for the north exterior wall of the tenant space. You will make settings to have one line at 0, one at 9″, and one at 12″ (the 3″ glass line is offset 3″ from the outside line of the 12″ wall).

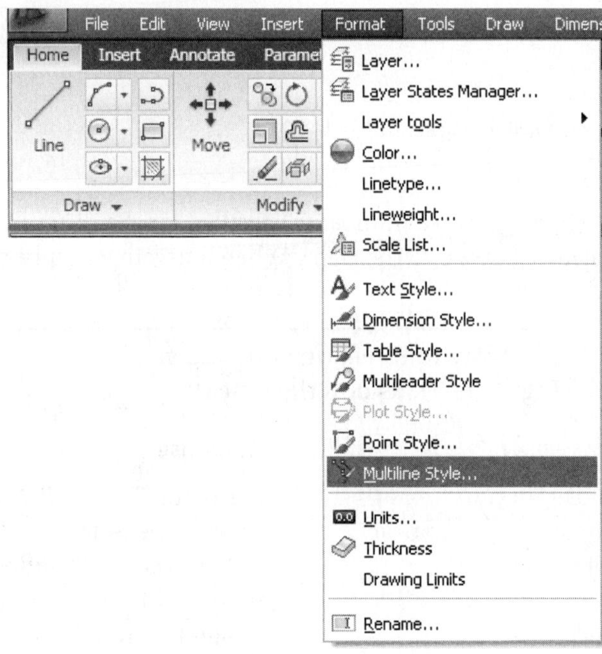

Step 12. Use Multiline Style... to make the settings for a new style named THREE (Figures 6–4 and 6–5), as described next:

Prompt	Response
Command:	**Multiline Style...** (or TYPE: **MLSTYLE<enter>**)
The Multiline Style dialog box appears with Standard highlighted:	CLICK: **New...**
The Create New Multiline Style dialog box appears:	TYPE: **THREE** in the New Style Name box CLICK: **Continue**
The New Multiline Style: THREE dialog box appears:	TYPE: **WALLS in the Description: box** HIGHLIGHT: **0.500** in the Offset: input box (below the Add and Delete buttons) and TYPE: **9** CLICK: **Add** HIGHLIGHT: **0.000** in the Offset: input box and TYPE: **12** CLICK: **Add** Do you have a scroll bar in the Elements list box that indicates more lines? If so, scroll down to look. If you have a −0.5 offset, CLICK: **−0.5** in the list and CLICK: **Delete** to delete an unnecessary offset.

You should now have a 12, a 9, and 0 in the Elements list, as shown in Figure 6–4 and nothing else—no scroll bar to the right indicating more lines. You could now assign

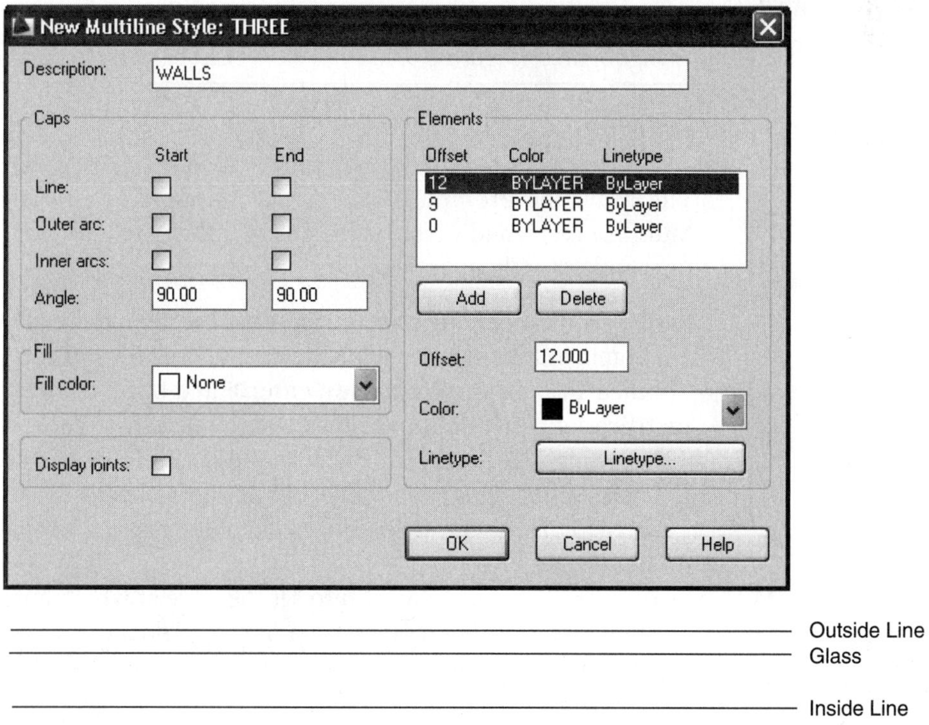

FIGURE 6–4
Wall Style THREE and Element Properties with Offsets of 0″, 9″, and 12″

Outside Line
Glass
Inside Line

FIGURE 6–5
Multiline Style Named THREE

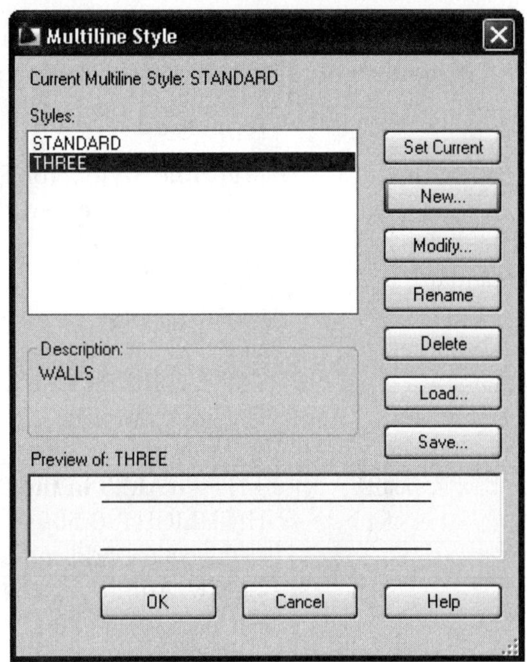

colors and linetypes to the lines. If you do not assign colors or linetypes, the lines will assume the color and linetype of the layer on which the multilines are drawn. Leave colors and linetypes assigned BYLAYER.

Prompt	Response
	CLICK: **OK**
The Multiline Style dialog box appears with THREE highlighted (Figure 6–5)	CLICK: **Set Current** CLICK: **OK**

MULTILINE

The Multiline prompt is "Specify start point or [Justification/Scale/STyle]:". The Multiline command uses the current Multiline Style to draw up to 16 lines at the same time with or without end caps.

Style You can set any style current that has been defined with the Multiline Style... command if it is not already current (TYPE: **ST<enter>** to the Multiline prompt, then TYPE: **the style name<enter>** and begin drawing).

Justification This option allows you to select Top, Zero, or Bottom lines to begin drawing multilines. The default is Top. In this case Zero and Bottom are the same because there are no negative offsets. If you have a positive 3 offset, a 0, and a negative 3 offset, your three lines will be drawn from the middle line with justification set to zero.

Scale This option allows you to set the scale at which lines will be drawn. If your multiline style has a 10 offset, a 6 offset, and a 0, and you set the scale at .5, the lines will be drawn 5″ and 3″ apart. The same style with a scale of 2 draws lines 20″ and 12″ apart.

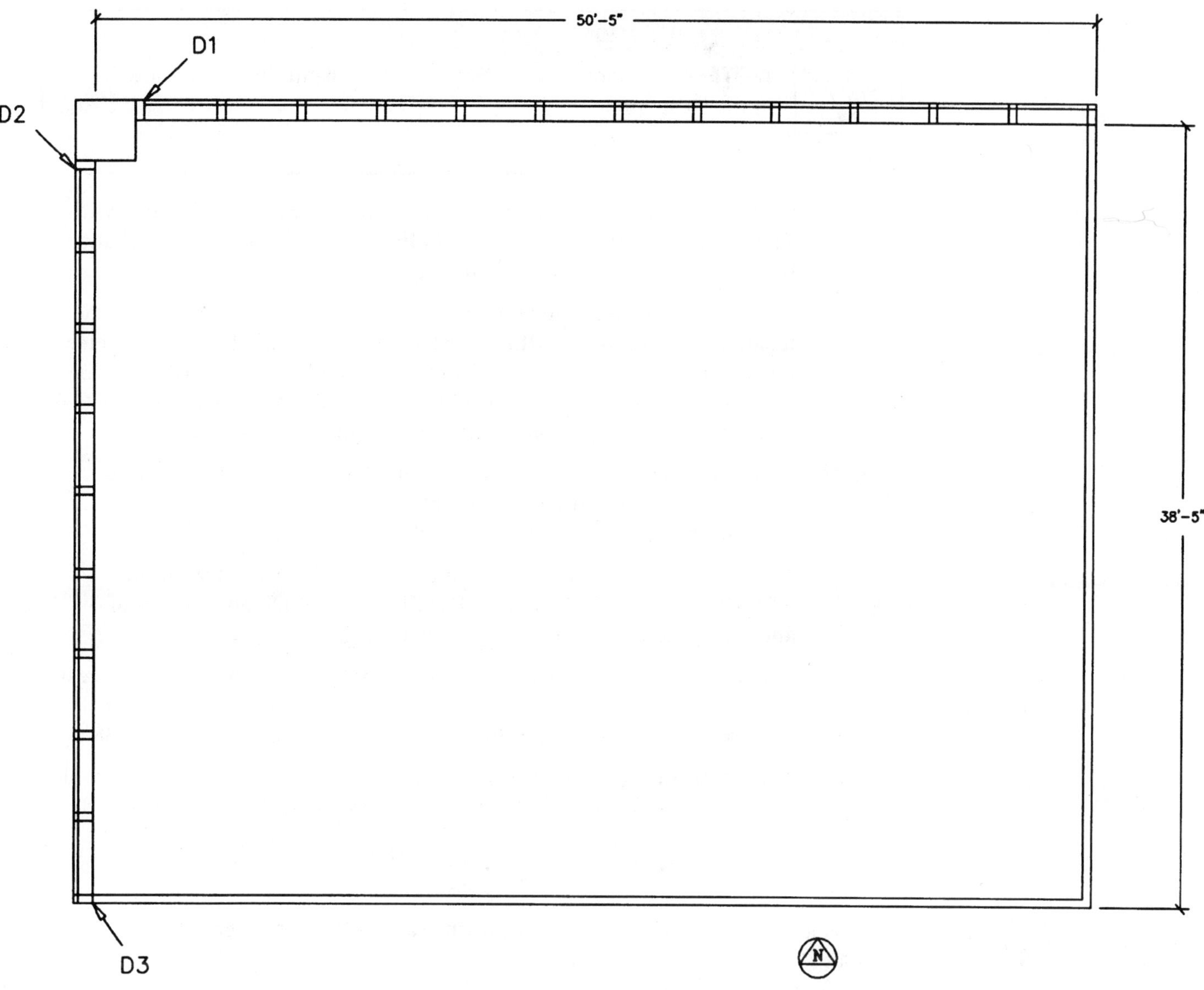

FIGURE 6–6
Use Multiline to Draw Exterior Walls with the Multiline Styles THREE, THREE-WEST, and TWO (Scale: 1/8″ = 1′-0″)

Step 13. Use Multiline to draw the north exterior wall of the tenant space (Figure 6–6), as described next:

Prompt	Response
Command:	**Multiline** (or TYPE: **ML<enter>**)
Current settings: Justification = Top, Scale =1.00, Style = THREE	
Specify start point or [Justification/ Scale/STyle]:	**OSNAP-Intersection**
of	**D1** (Figure 6–6)
Specify next point:	**Turn ORTHO ON. Move your mouse to the right and** TYPE: **48′<enter>**
Specify next point or [Undo]:	**<enter>**

NOTE: You cannot have spaces in the style name, but spaces are OK in the Description.

Step 14. Create a new multiline style with the name THREE-WEST; start with THREE. Description: WALLS; and offsets of 0, 3, and 12. Just change the 9 to 3. Set this style current (Figure 6–7).

Step 15. Use Multiline with a justification of Bottom to draw the west wall of the tenant space with the THREE-WEST multiline style. Use OSNAP-Intersection and CLICK: D2 (Figure 6–6) to start the multiline and make the line 36′ long (subtract 2′5″ from the dimension on the right side of Figure 6–6 to account for the 3′-square corner column and the 5″ mullion).

Step 16. Next the interior walls are drawn. Keep Layer a-wall-extr current. The layer on which the interior walls are drawn will be changed to a-wall-intr in this tutorial with the Properties... command.

Step 17. Create a new multiline style with the name TWO; start with the STANDARD style Description: INTERIOR WALLS; and offsets of 0 and 5 (Figure 6–8). Set this style current.

Step 18. Use Multiline with a justification of Bottom to draw the south and east walls of the tenant space. Use OSNAP-Intersection and CLICK: D3 (Figure 6–6) and make the line to the right 50′5″ and the line up 38′5″.

Step 19. Use Multiline with the Multiline Style TWO to draw 5″-wide horizontal and vertical interior walls inside the tenant space (Figure 6–9), as described next:

Prompt	Response
Command:	**Multiline** (or TYPE: **ML<enter>**)
Current settings: Justification = Bottom, Scale = 1.00, Style = TWO	

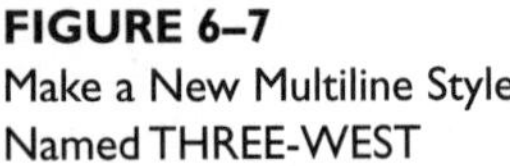

FIGURE 6–7
Make a New Multiline Style Named THREE-WEST

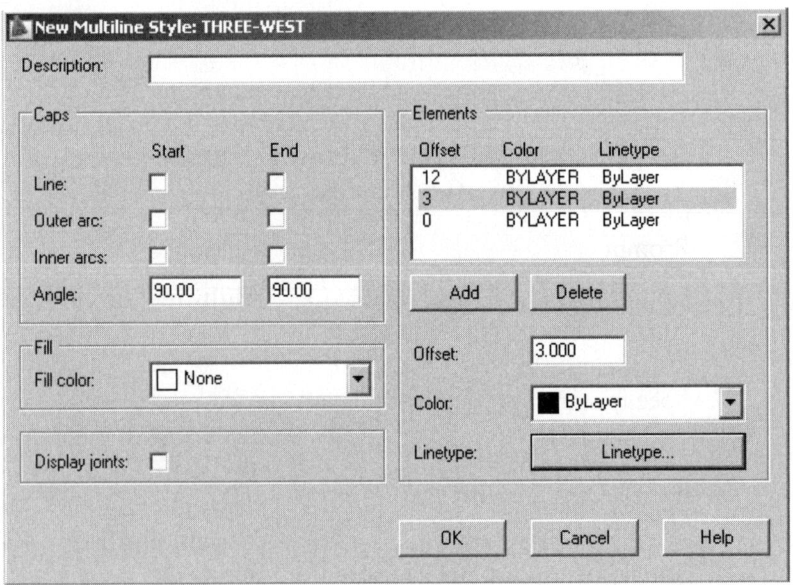

FIGURE 6–8
Make a New Multiline Style Named TWO

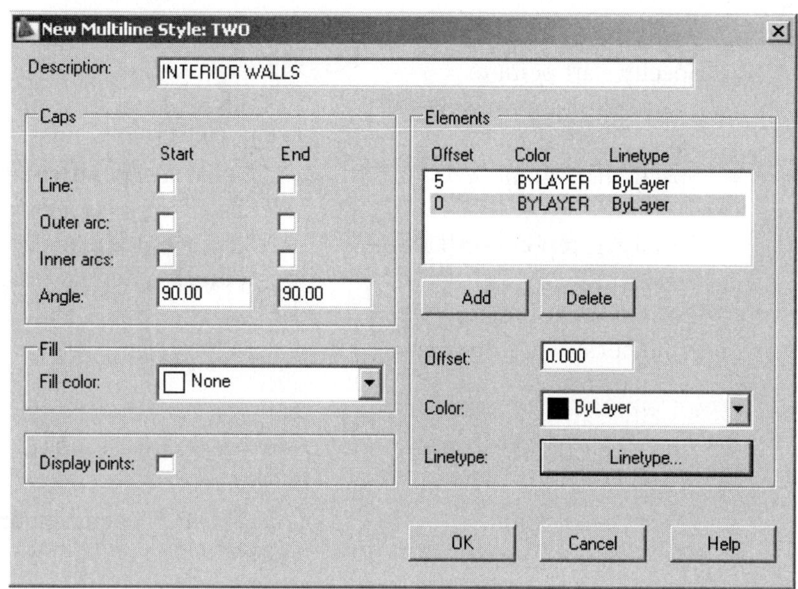

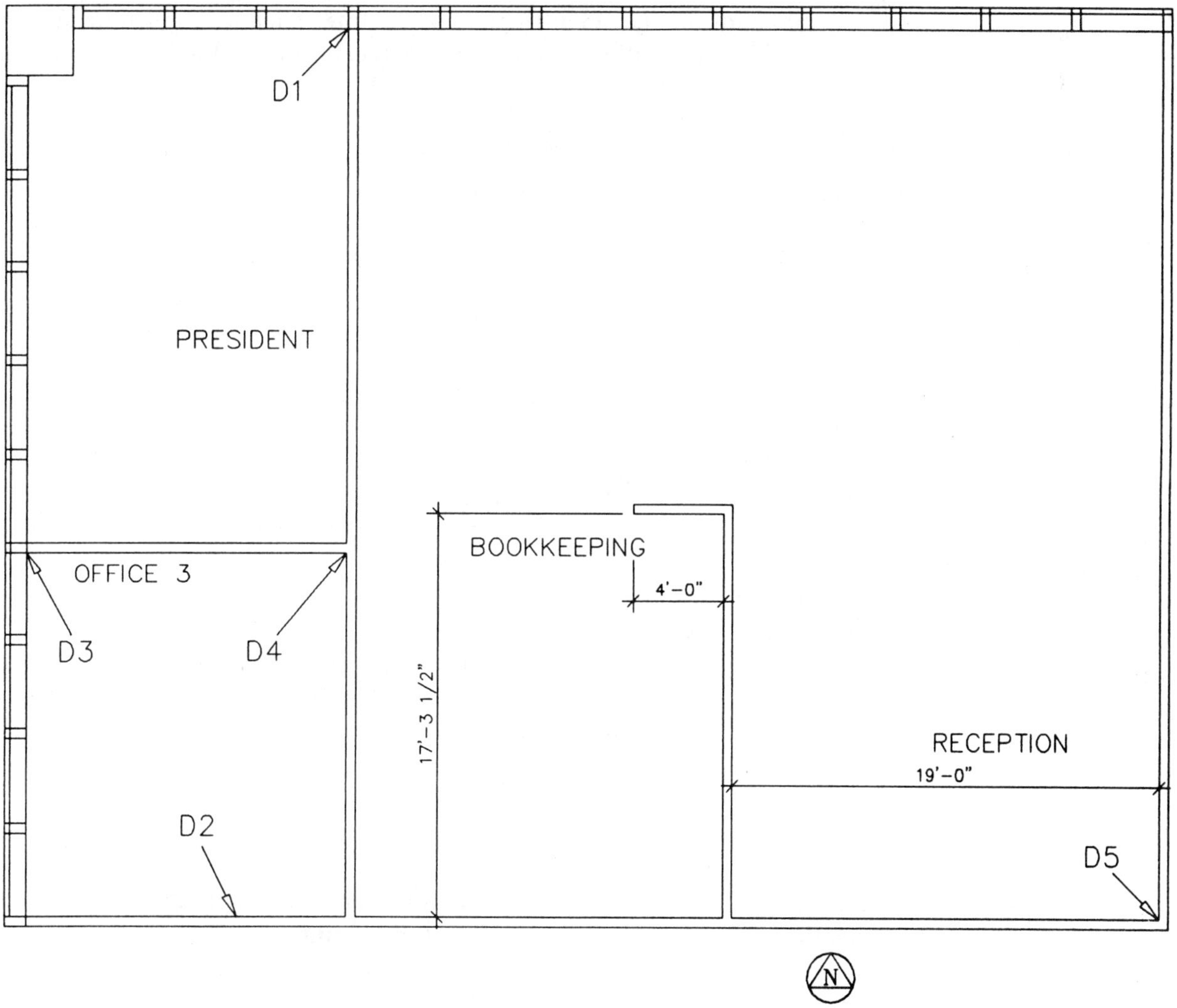

D1
PRESIDENT
OFFICE 3
D3
D4
D2
BOOKKEEPING
4'–0"
17'–3 1/2"
RECEPTION
19'–0"
D5
N

FIGURE 6–9
Use Multiline to Draw Interior Walls (Scale: 1/8″ = 1′-0″)

Prompt	Response
Specify start point or [Justification/Scale/STyle]:	**OSNAP-Intersection**
of	CLICK: **D1** (Figure 6–9)
Specify next point:	**OSNAP-Perpendicular** (turn Snap off as needed)
to	**D2**
Specify next point or [Undo]:	**<enter>** (the intersection will be edited later)
Command:	**<enter> (Repeat MLINE)**
Current settings: Justification = Bottom, Scale = 1.00, Style = TWO:	
Specify start point or [Justification/Scale/STyle]:	**OSNAP-Intersection**
of	**D3**
Specify next point:	**OSNAP-Perpendicular**
to	**D4**
Specify next point or [Undo]:	**<enter>** (the intersection will be edited later)

Step 20. Create a new multiline style that uses the settings of the TWO style but adds an endcap at the end of the line. Then use Multiline and From to draw the wall that separates the reception and bookkeeping areas (Figures 6–9 and 6–10), as described next:

Prompt	Response
Command:	**Multiline Style...**
The Multiline Style dialog box appears:	CLICK: **TWO** and CLICK: **New...**
The Create New Multiline Style dialog box appears:	TYPE: **TWO-CAP-END** in the New Style Name box CLICK: **Continue**
The New Multiline Style: TWO-CAP-END dialog box appears:	In the Caps area CLICK: **End** in the Line: row so a check appears in it, as shown in Figure 6–10. CLICK: **OK**
The Multiline Styles dialog box appears with TWO-CAP-END highlighted:	CLICK: **Set Current;** CLICK: **OK**
Command:	TYPE: **ML<enter>**
Current settings: Justification = Bottom, Scale = 1.00, Style = TWO-CAP-END	
Specify start point or [Justification/Scale/STyle]:	**From** (or TYPE: **FRO<enter>**)
Base point:	**OSNAP-Endpoint**
of	**D5** (Figure 6–9)
<Offset>:	TYPE: **@19′<180<enter>**
Specify next point:	**Turn ORTHO ON. Move your mouse up and** TYPE: **17′3-1/2<enter>**

FIGURE 6–10
Add an Endcap to the Interior Walls

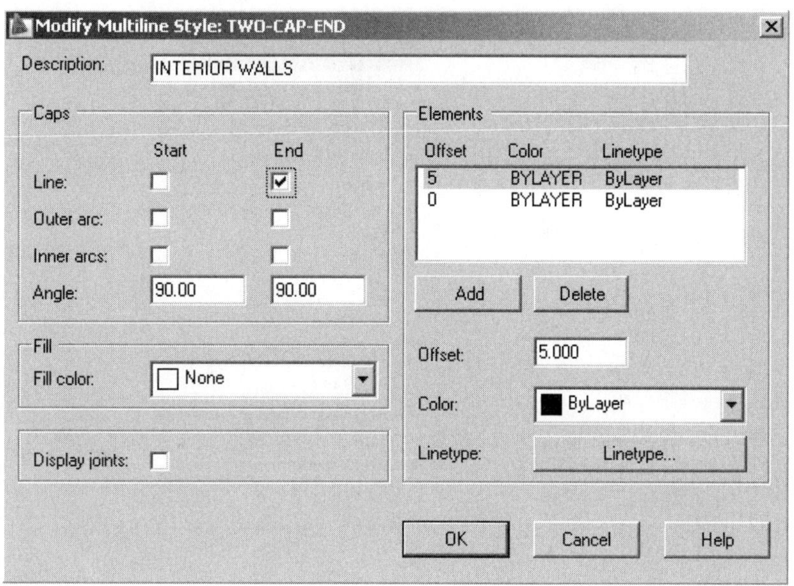

Prompt	Response
Specify next point or [Undo]:	**Move your mouse to the left and** TYPE: **4′<enter>**
Specify next point or [Close/Undo]:	**<enter>** (the intersection will be edited next)

Look at the Fill color: area, Figure 6–10. When a color is selected from the list, the walls are drawn with a solid fill and can be filled with any color.

EDIT MULTILINE

The Edit Multiline command allows you to change the intersections of multilines in a variety of ways, as shown in Figure 6–11. Just CLICK: the change you want, and then CLICK: the two multilines whose intersection you want to change.

FIGURE 6–11
Edit Multiline Tools

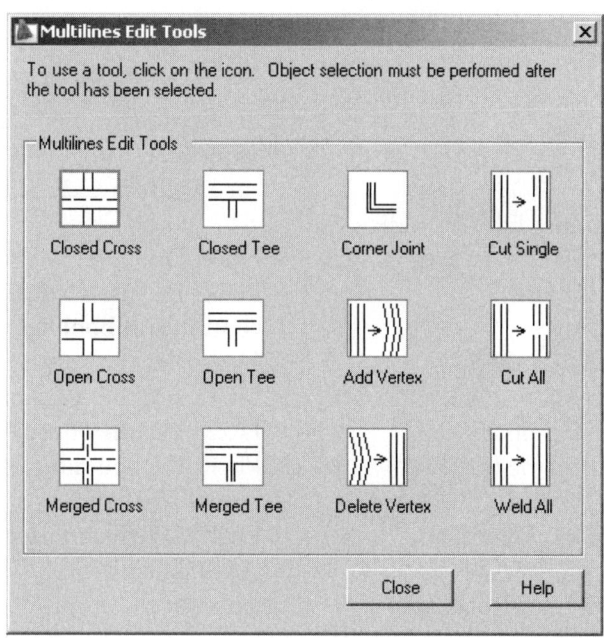

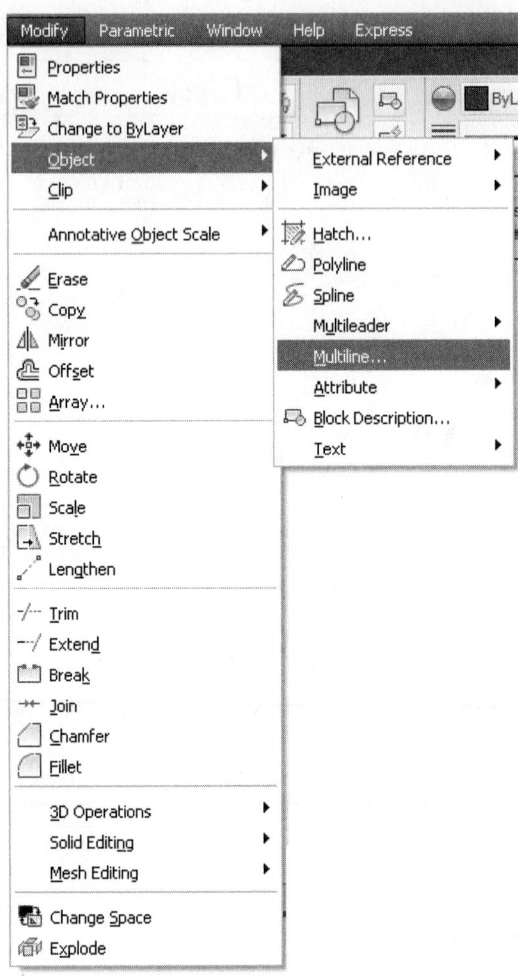

Step 21. Use Edit Multiline to trim the intersections of the multilines forming the interior walls to an Open Tee (Figures 6–11 and 6–12), as described next:

Prompt	Response
Command:	CLICK: **Modify**, then **Object**, then **Multiline...** (or TYPE: **MLEDIT<enter>** or DOUBLE-CLICK: **any multiline**)
The Multilines Edit Tools dialog box appears (Figure 6–11):	CLICK: **Open Tee**
Select first mline:	CLICK: **D1, the vertical wall separating the reception and bookkeeping areas (Figure 6–12)**
Select second mline:	CLICK: **D2, the south horizontal wall**
Select first mline (or Undo):	CLICK: **D3, the interior vertical wall of office 3**
Select second mline:	CLICK: **D2, the south horizontal wall**
Select first mline (or Undo):	CLICK: **D4, the interior horizontal wall of the president's office**
Select second mline:	CLICK: **D3, the interior vertical wall of the president's office**
Select first mline (or Undo):	**<enter>**

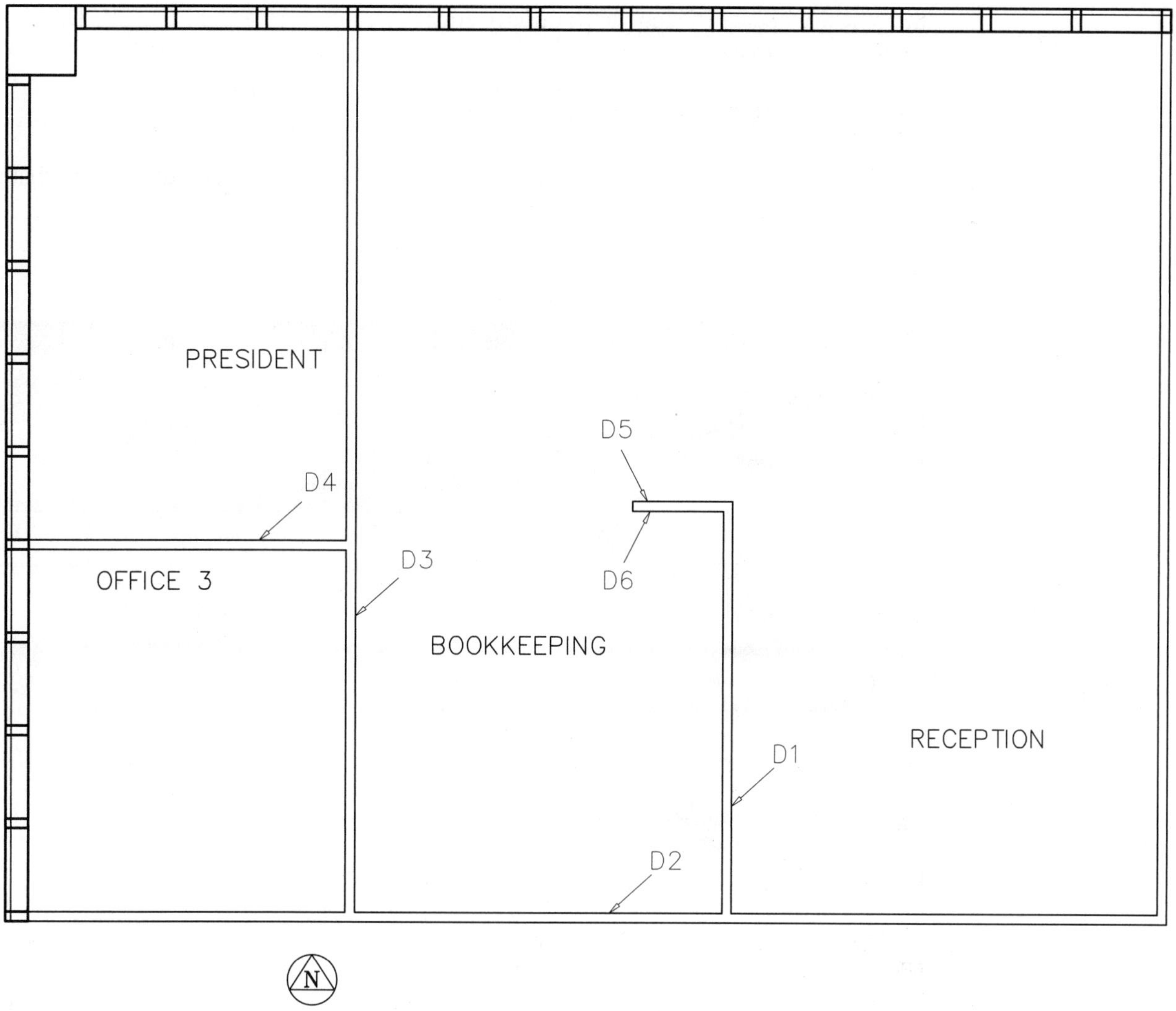

PRESIDENT

D5

D4

OFFICE 3

D3

D6

BOOKKEEPING

RECEPTION

D1

D2

N

FIGURE 6–12
Using the Extend Command (Scale: 1/8″ = 1′-0″)

If you made a mistake while drawing the walls, you must first explode the multiline. Then use a Modify command to edit the multiline, which becomes a series of lines after it is exploded.

EXTEND

The Extend command allows you to lengthen an existing line or arc segment to meet a specified boundary edge. You will find it useful when drawing walls. Figure 6–12 shows

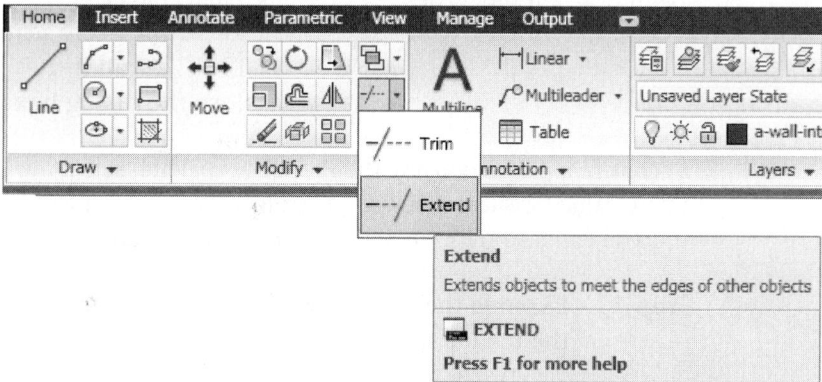

the line selected as **D3** for the boundary edge; press <enter> then CLICK: **D5** and **D6** as the objects to extend.

PROPERTIES...

The Properties palette (Figure 6–13) allows you to change any property that can be changed.

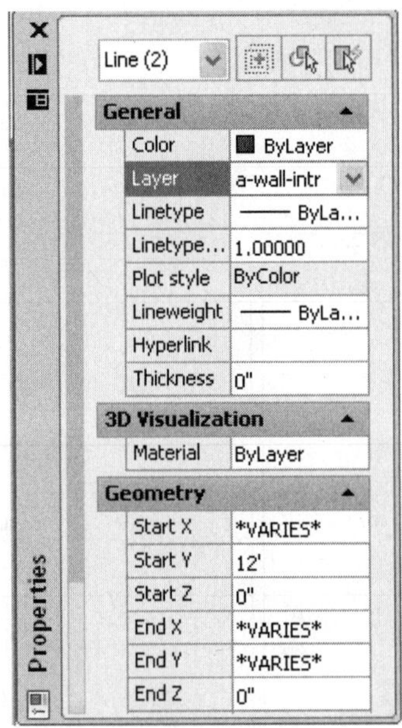

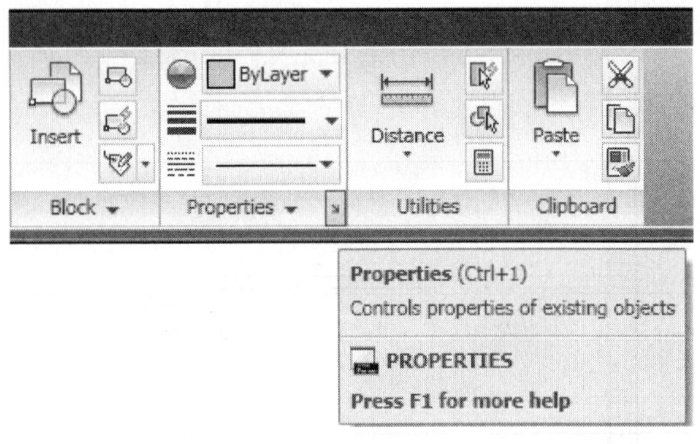

FIGURE 6–13
Properties Palette

Step 22. Use the Properties... command to change the layer of the interior walls from the a-wall-extr Layer to the a-wall-intr Layer, as described next:

Prompt	Response
Command:	**Properties...**
The Properties palette appears:	**Use a crossing window to select all the interior walls.**
The Properties palette lists all the interior wall properties:	CLICK: **Layer...**
	CLICK: **the down arrow**
	CLICK: **a-wall-intr**
	Close the dialog box and PRESS: **Esc**

To change a property using the Properties palette, select the object and then either enter a new value or select a new value from a list. You can leave the Properties palette open, and you can also right-click in the Properties palette to dock it.

Step 23. Explode the outside wall line of the exterior north and west walls of the tenant space.

Step 24. Use the Properties command to change the layer property of the glass line (the middle line on the north and west walls) from the a-wall-extr Layer to the a-glaz Layer.

TIP: You can also move an object to another layer by clicking on it and then clicking the new layer in the layer list.

LIST

After you have changed the property of an entity and would like to confirm the change, or if you need additional information about an entity, using the List command is very helpful. Depending on the type of entity selected, the List command provides a screen display of the data stored for the entity.

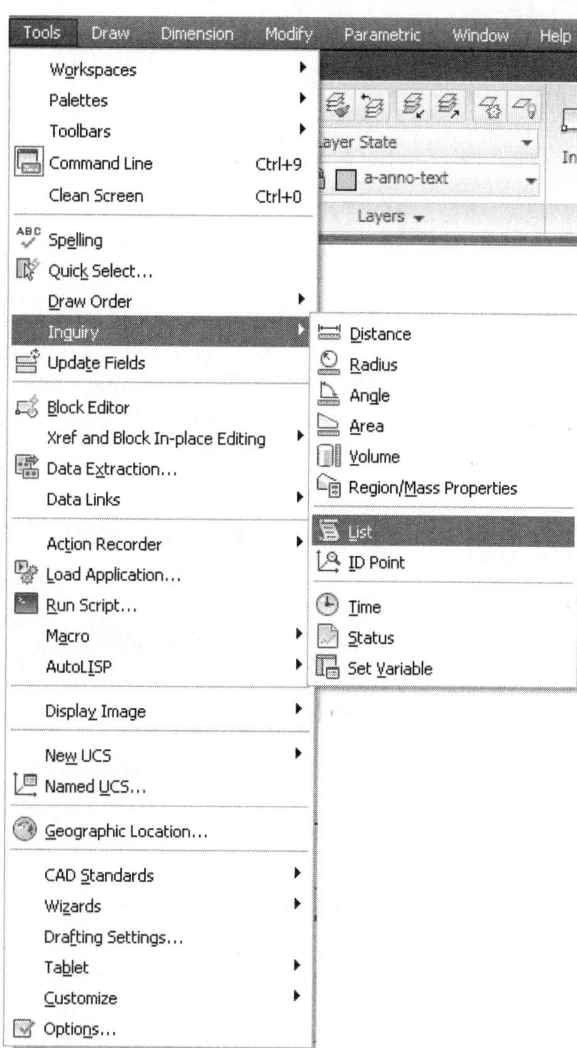

Step 25. **Use the List command to examine the data stored for one line of an interior wall, as described next:**

Prompt	Response
Command:	**List** (or TYPE: **LI<enter>**)
Select objects:	CLICK: **only one line of an interior wall <enter>**
	PRESS: **F2**

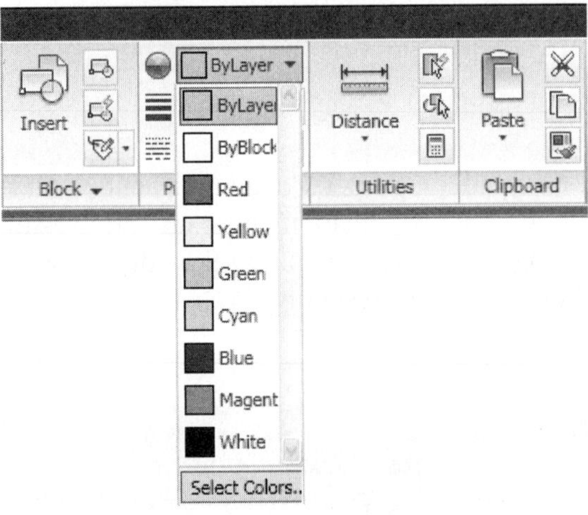

COLOR

To access the Select Color dialog box (Figure 6–14), CLICK: **Select Colors...** on the properties panel (or TYPE: **COL<enter>**).

Set Color ByLayer We have discussed and used Color by assigning color to a layer, thus controlling the color "ByLayer." The object is drawn with a layer current and inherits the color assigned to the layer. The Select Color dialog box sets the color for drawing. When ByLayer is selected, the objects are drawn with the color of the layer on which they are drawn.

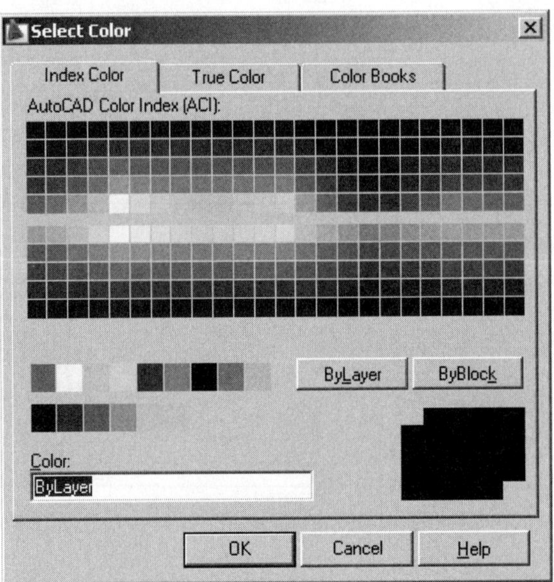

FIGURE 6–14
Select Color Dialog Box

Set Color Individually The color property of objects can also be set individually. When a color, such as red, is selected in the Select Color dialog box, the objects subsequently drawn are red. The objects will be red regardless of the layer that is current when they are drawn.

To keep your drawing simple, when a new color is needed, create a layer and assign the new color to that layer.

Set Color ByBlock Library parts that are blocks can be drawn on the 0 Layer, which is the same as setting the color, lineweight, and linetype properties to ByBlock. The reason for this is explained in the following examples.

Example 1

A door (library part) is drawn on a layer named DOOR that is assigned the color red, and a Wblock is made of the door. The door block is inserted into a new project. Because the block was originally drawn on a layer named DOOR (color red), the layer name is dragged into the new drawing layer listing, and the door will be red, regardless of the layer current in the new drawing.

Example 2

A door (library part) is drawn on the 0 Layer, Wblock is made of the door, and the door Wblock is inserted into a new project. Because the block was originally drawn on the 0 Layer, the door is generated on the drawing's current layer and inherits all properties of that layer.

Before any drawing entity that will be used as a block is drawn, you need to decide how it will be used in future drawings; that will determine how color, lineweight, and linetype are assigned.

TIP: If everything you draw is one color regardless of the layer it is drawn on, check the color setting, and set it to ByLayer.

LINETYPE

When the Linetype command is selected from the Format menu, the Linetype Manager dialog box appears. Like the Color command, the linetype property can be set to ByLayer, individually, or ByBlock.

LINEWEIGHT

When Lineweight... is selected from the Format menu, the Lineweight Settings dialog box (Figure 6–15) is displayed. Like the Color and Linetype commands, the lineweight property can be set to ByLayer, individually, or ByBlock. CLICK: **LWT** on the status bar to display lineweight properties.

NOTE: You can set the color, linetype, and lineweight of an object individually. Make sure you do not do that. Create a new layer and assign the new color, linetype, or lineweight to the layer.

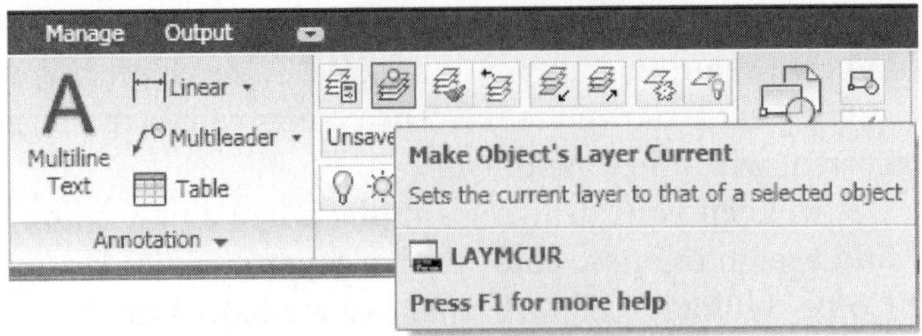

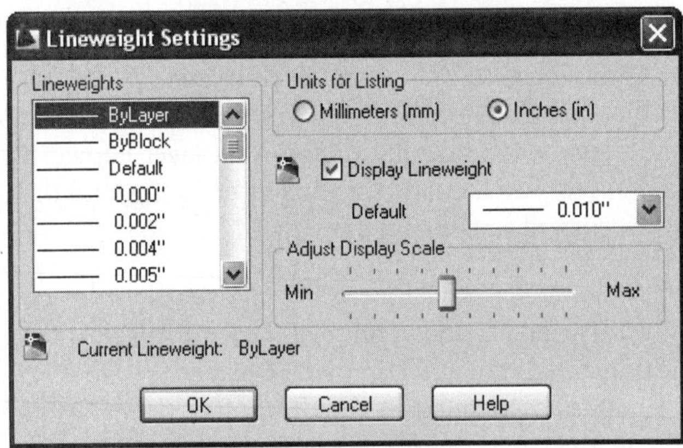

FIGURE 6–15
Lineweight Settings Dialog Box

MAKE OBJECT'S LAYER CURRENT

This is another useful command on the Layers panel. When you activate this command and pick any object, the layer that object is on becomes current.

MATCH PROPERTIES

When the Match Properties command is selected from the Modify menu, or **MATCHPROP** is typed and entered at the Command: prompt, the prompt is "Select source object:". At that prompt you can select the object whose properties you want to copy, and a paintbrush is attached to the cursor. The prompt changes to "Select destination object(s) or [Settings]:" and you can then select the object to which you want to copy the properties.

When you type and enter the Settings option to the Match Properties prompt, the Property Settings dialog box is displayed (Figure 6–16). Properties that can be copied are shown in Figure 6–16. By default, all properties are selected and show a check in the box beside the property name. Remove the check if you do not want a property copied.

Step 26. **Set Layer a-wall-intr current. Use Multiline with the correct Multiline Style current to finish drawing the interior walls of the tenant space. Use the dimensions shown in Figure 6–17. Remember that you can use the Modify commands (Extend, Trim, Edit Multiline, and so on) to fix the Multiline. To use Extend and Trim, you must first explode the multiline.**

Step 27. **Set FILL ON and regenerate the drawing.**

Step 28. **Use the dimensions shown in Figure 6–18 to draw the two door types—single door and double door—that will be defined as blocks and inserted into the tenant space. Draw the lines representing the doors and door frames on the a-door-dbl Layer. Draw the arcs showing**

FIGURE 6–16
Property Settings Dialog Box

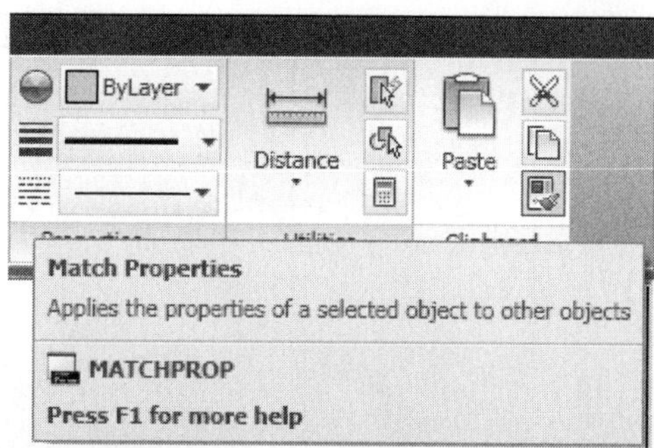

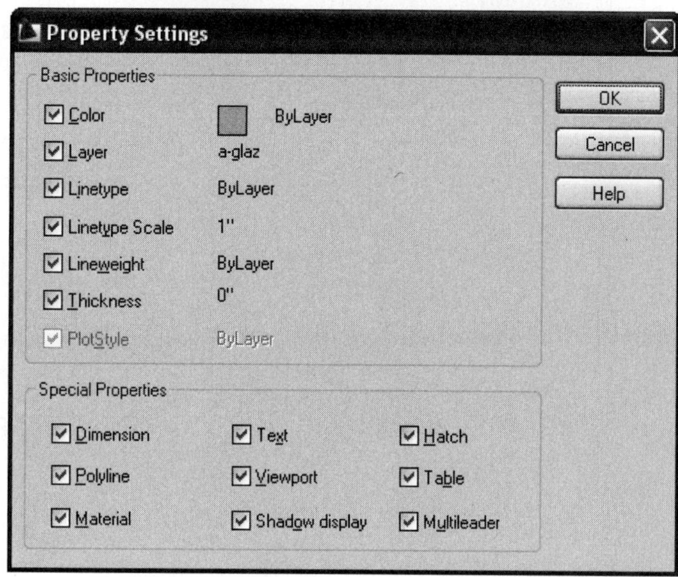

the door swings on the a-door-swng Layer. Pick any open space on your drawing and draw each door full size. In the following part of this tutorial, the Block and Wblock commands are used to define the doors as blocks.

BLOCK-MAKE...

The Block-Make... command allows you to define any part of a current drawing as a block. Copies of the block can be inserted only into that drawing. Copies of a block defined with the Block-Make... command cannot be used in any other drawing without using the AutoCAD DesignCenter (described in Chapter 10).

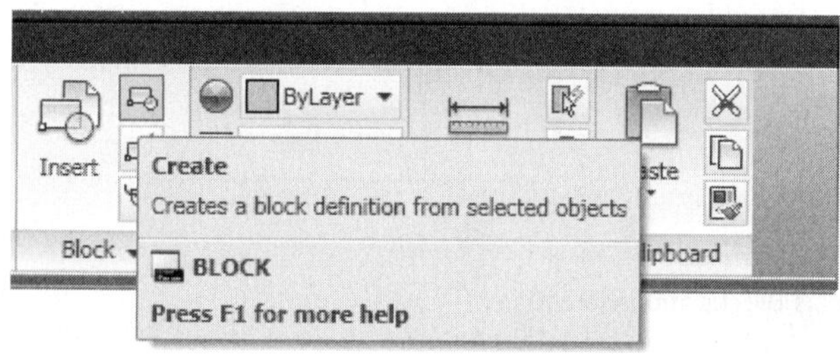

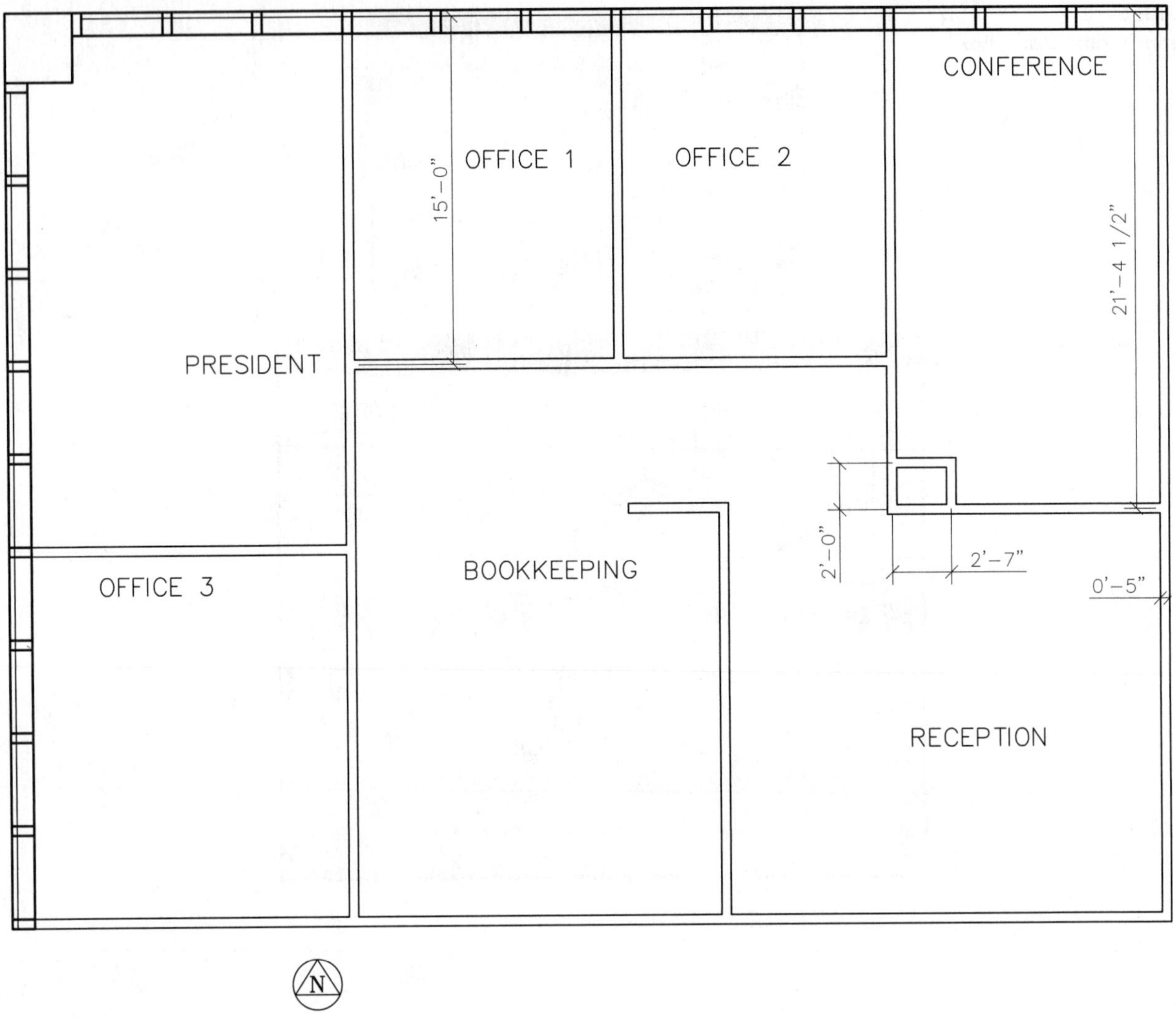

CONFERENCE
OFFICE 1
OFFICE 2
15'–0"
21'–4 1/2"
PRESIDENT
BOOKKEEPING
OFFICE 3
2'–0"
2'–7"
0'–5"
RECEPTION
N

FIGURE 6–17
Use Multiline to Finish Drawing the Interior Walls (Scale: 1/8" = 1'-0")

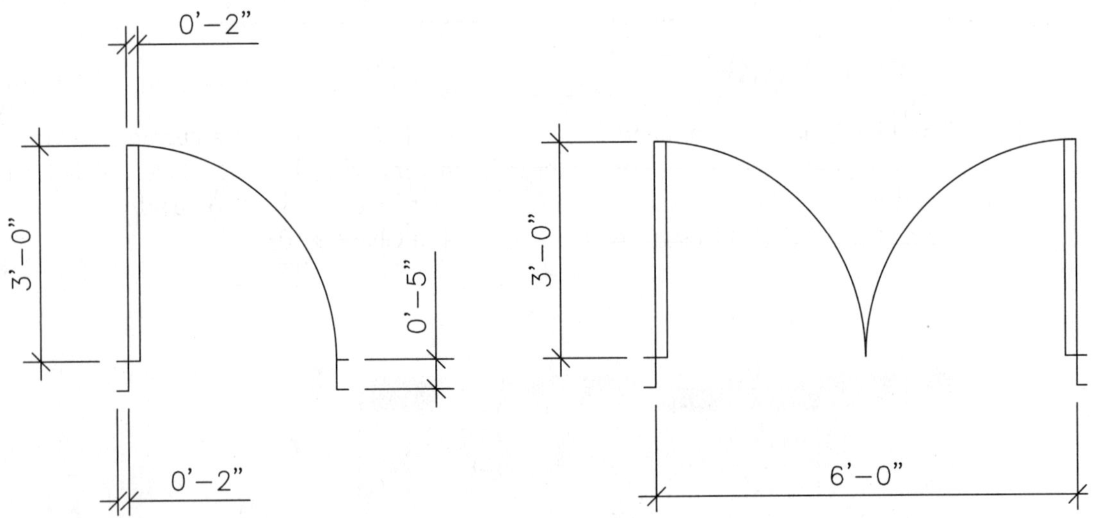

FIGURE 6–18
Two Door Types That Will Be Defined as Blocks and Inserted into the Tenant Space

Step 29. **Use the Block-Make... command to define the single-door drawing as a block named DOOR stored in the current drawing (Figure 6–19), as described next:**

Prompt	Response
Command:	**Block-Make...** (or TYPE: **B<enter>**)
The Block Definition dialog box appears:	TYPE: **DOOR** in the Name: input box CLICK: **the Delete option button under Objects** CLICK: **the Pick point button**
Specify insertion base point:	**OSNAP-Endpoint**
of:	**D1** (Figure 6–19)
The Block Definition dialog box appears:	CLICK: **the Select objects button**
Select objects:	CLICK: **a point to locate the first corner of a selection window**
Specify opposite corner:	**Window only the single-door drawing**
Select objects:	**<enter>**
The Block Definition dialog box appears:	CLICK: **OK**
The single-door symbol is gone and is now defined as a block within your drawing.	

The three option buttons in the Objects area of the Block Definition dialog box specify what happens to the selected object (in this instance, the door) after you create the block:

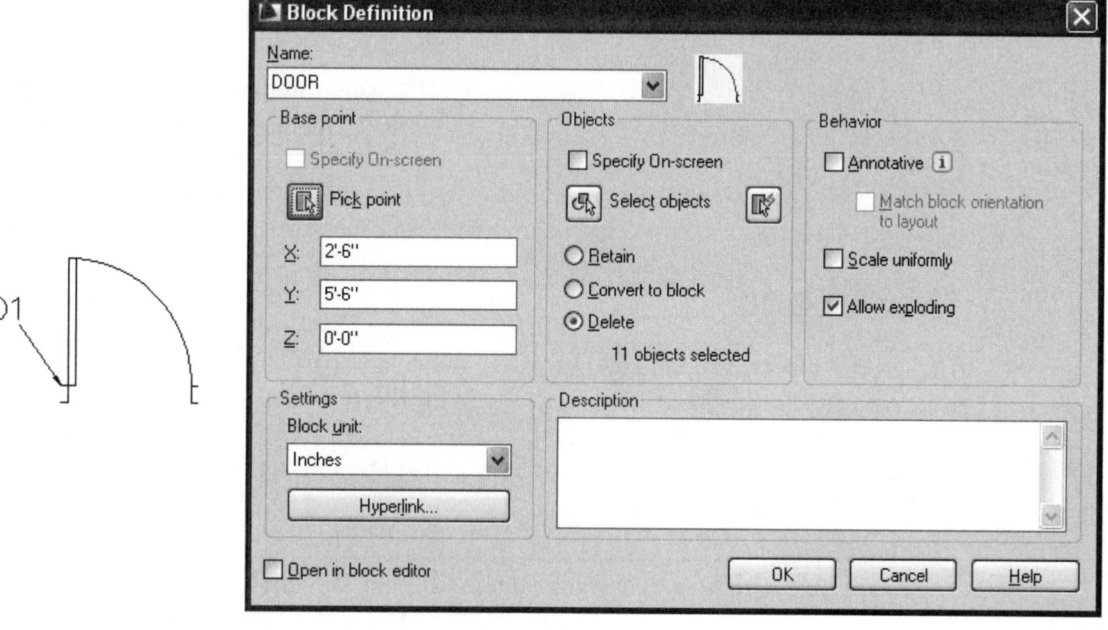

FIGURE 6–19
Make a Block of the Door; Name It DOOR

Retain After the block is created, the door symbol will remain in the drawing but will not be a block.

Convert to block After the block is created, the door symbol will remain in the drawing and will be a block.

Delete After the block is created, the door symbol will be deleted.

The three check boxes in the Behavior area of the Block Definition dialog box, Figure 6–19, specify the following:

Annotative Annotative blocks can be used for inserting objects such as elevation reference symbols that contain a circle (balloon) and numbers. When the annotative balloon and number block is inserted into a drawing, the sizes change according to the annotation scale. They are always the same size when plotted, regardless of the scale of the plotted drawing, if the annotation scale is the same as the plot scale. In this chapter we do not annotate the blocks because the Tenant Space is drawn full scale and we want the door plotted sizes to change depending on the plotted scale.

Match block orientation to layout When Annotative is checked, this specifies that the orientation of the block in paper space matches the orientation of the layout.

Scale uniformly When checked, the block is uniformly scaled in X, Y, and Z planes—DO NOT CHECK THIS BOX.

Allow exploding When checked, the block can be exploded.

A block name can be 1 to 255 characters long. It may include only letters, numbers, and three special characters—$ (dollar sign), - (hyphen), and _ (underscore).

The Insert command is used later in this tutorial to insert copies of the DOOR block into your drawing. The "Specify insertion base point:" is the point on the inserted block to which the crosshair attaches. It allows you to position copies of the block exactly into the drawing. It is also the point around which the block can be rotated when it is inserted.

Step 30. Use the Block-Make... command to view a listing of the block just created, as described next:

Prompt	Response
Command:	**Block-Make...** (or TYPE: **B<enter>**)
The Block Definition dialog box appears:	CLICK: **the down arrow below Name:**
The block name appears:	CLICK: **<cancel>**

When you want to build a library of parts defined as blocks that can be inserted into any drawing, use the Wblock command, described next.

WBLOCK

The Wblock command allows you to define any part of a drawing or an entire drawing as a block. Blocks created with the Wblock command can be stored on a disk, CD, DVD, or on the hard drive or network. Copies of the blocks can then be inserted into any drawing. These Wblocks become drawing files with a .dwg extension, just like any other AutoCAD drawing.

Step 31. Create a new folder named Blocks in which to store your Wblocks.

Step 32. Use Wblock to save the double-door drawing as a block on your hard drive or on a network (Figure 6–20), as described next:

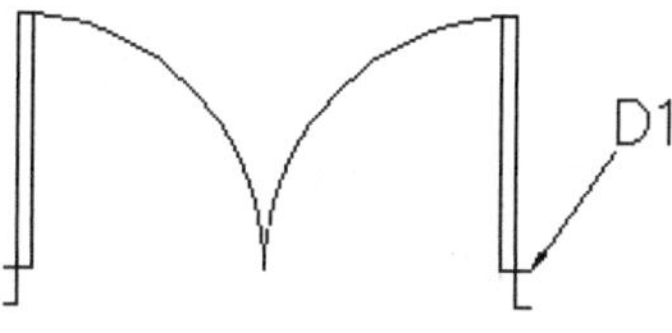

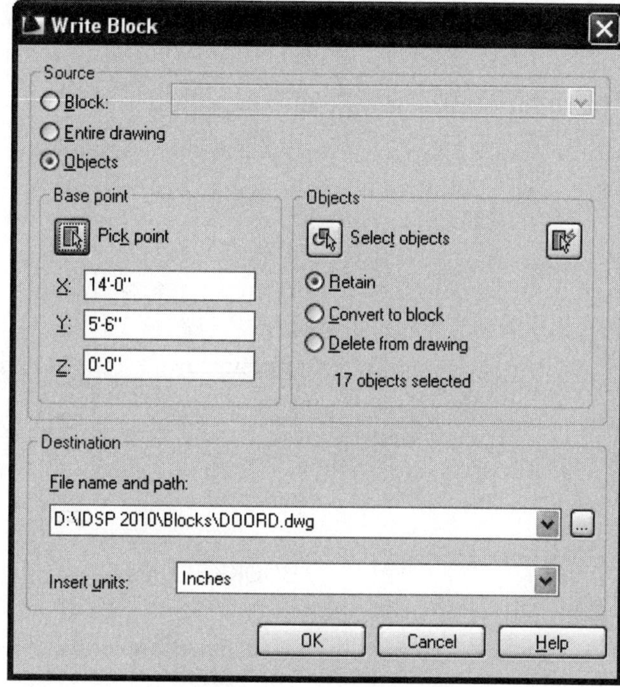

FIGURE 6–20
Write Block Dialog Box for DOORD Drawing

Prompt	Response
Command:	TYPE: **W<enter>**
The Write Block dialog box appears:	TYPE: **DOORD** (to replace the "new block" name in the File name and path: input box) CLICK: **the ... button** (to the right of File name and path:). This will allow you to Browse: for files or folders and select the path to where you want to save.
The Browse for Drawing File dialog box appears:	CLICK: **the down arrow in the Save in: input box to select the drive and folder where you want to save the double-door-drawing** CLICK: **Save**
The Write Block dialog box appears:	CLICK: **Delete from drawing button** CLICK: **Pick point button**
Specify insertion base point:	**OSNAP-Endpoint**
of	**D1** (Figure 6–20)
The Write Block dialog box appears:	CLICK: **the Select objects button**
Select objects:	**Window the entire double-door drawing**
Select objects:	**<enter>**
The Write Block dialog box appears:	CLICK: **OK**

The double-door drawing disappears and is saved as a block.

The double-door drawing is now saved as a drawing file with a .DWG file extension. Copies of the DOORD drawing can be recalled and inserted into any other drawing. It is obvious that building a library of parts that can be inserted into any drawing saves time.

The three option buttons in the Source area of the Write Block dialog box specify what you are defining as a Wblock:

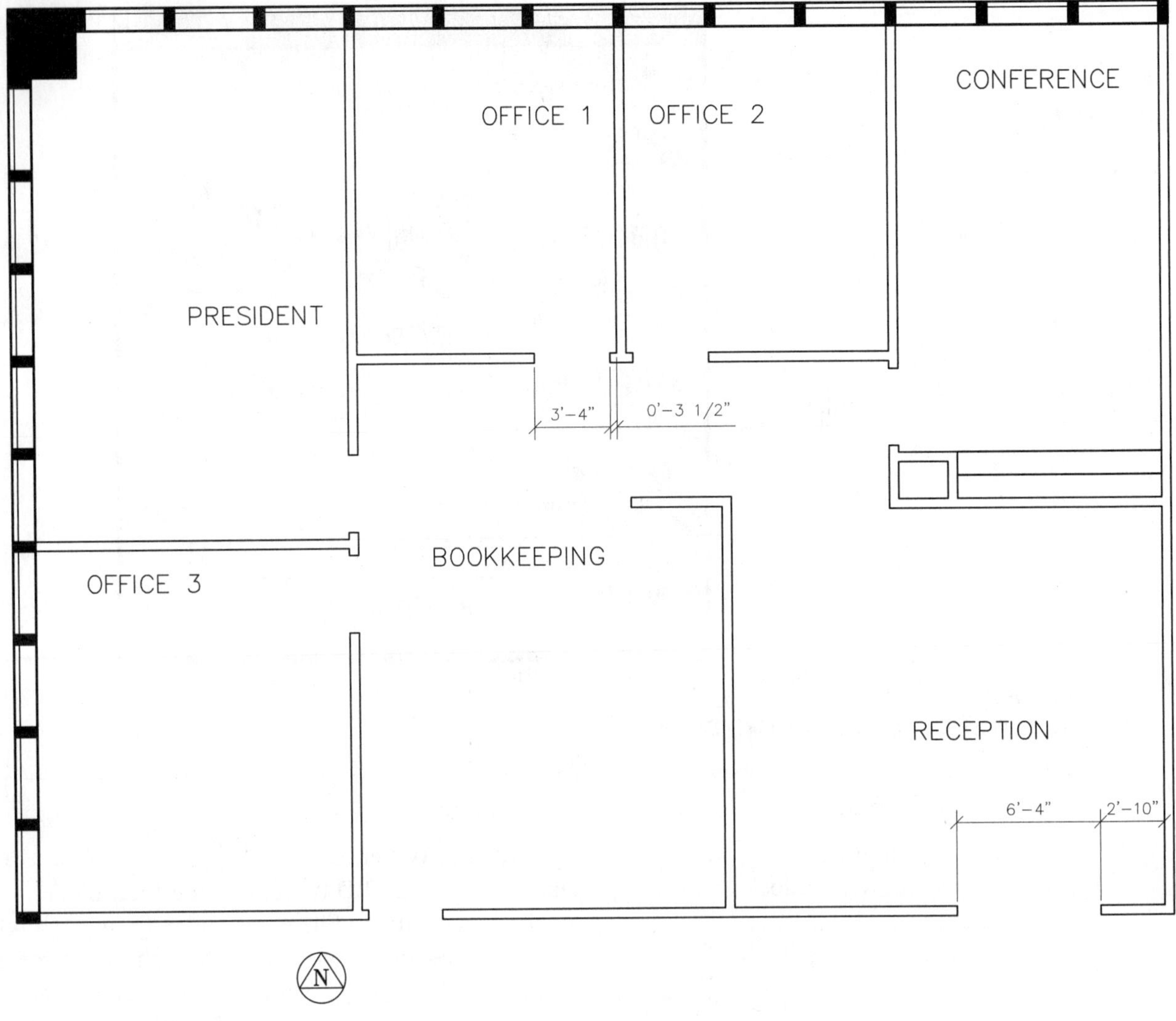

FIGURE 6–21
Use the Dimensions Shown to Draw the Openings for All Doors (Scale: 1/8″ = 1′-0″)

Block This helps define a block that is stored in a current drawing as a Wblock.

Entire drawing Not only parts of a drawing but also an entire drawing can be defined as a block. Use 0,0,0 as the base point when defining an entire drawing as a block.

Objects Allows you to select an object to define as a block.

Step 33. **Use the Wblock command to write the DOOR block stored in your current drawing to a disk and folder of your choice.**

Step 34. **In the following part of this tutorial, the doors will be inserted into the tenant space. Before the doors are inserted, openings for all doors must be added to the drawing. Each single door is 3′4″ wide, including the 2″ frame, so each opening for a single door is 3′4″ wide. As shown in Figure 6–21, the dimension from the corner of each room to the outside edge of the single door frame is 3-1/2″. The dimensions shown in Figure 6–21 for the door to OFFICE 1 apply to all single-door openings.**

Use the dimensions shown in Figure 6–21 to draw the openings for the five single doors (Layer a-wall-intr) and for the double-entry door (Layer a-wall-extr). A helpful hint: Use From or ID with the Line command

to draw the first door opening line, and Offset for the second door opening line. Then use Trim to complete the opening. If Trim does not work, explode the multiline first, then trim.

INSERT-BLOCK...

The Insert-Block... command allows you to insert the defined blocks into your drawing. It may be used to insert a block defined with either the Block-Make command or the Wblock command.

The Insert mode found in the Osnap menu allows you to snap to the insertion point of Text or a Block entity.

The following part of the tutorial uses the Insert command to insert the DOOR block into the tenant space. Don't forget to zoom in on the area of the drawing on which you are working. Remember also that the insertion point of the DOOR block is the upper left corner of the door frame.

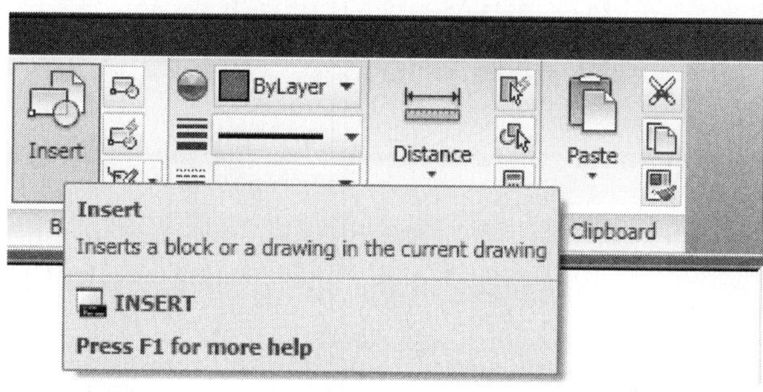

Step 35. **Use the Insert command to insert the block named DOOR into OFFICE 2 (Figures 6–22 and 6–23), as described next:**

Prompt	Response
Command:	**Insert-Block...** (or TYPE: **I<enter>**)
The Insert dialog box appears (Figure 6–22):	CLICK: **DOOR** (in the Name: input box) (Be sure there is a check in the Specify On-screen box under Insertion point and in the Uniform Scale check box.) CLICK: **OK**

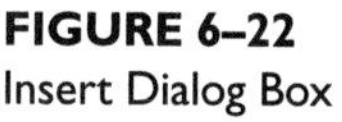
FIGURE 6–22
Insert Dialog Box

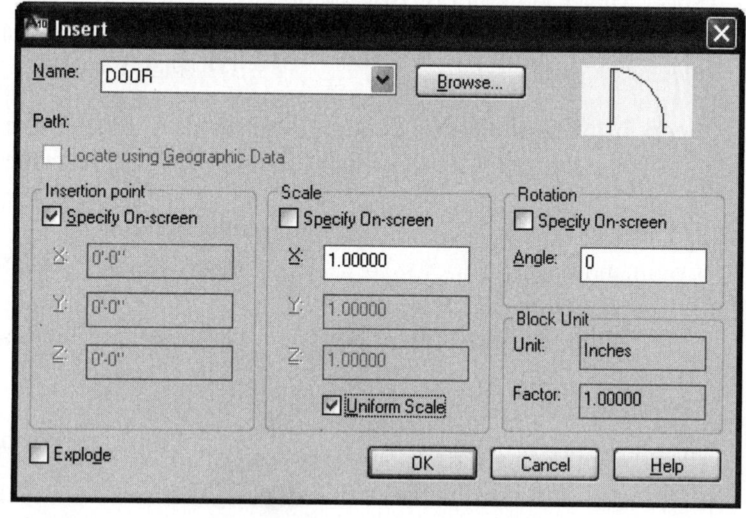

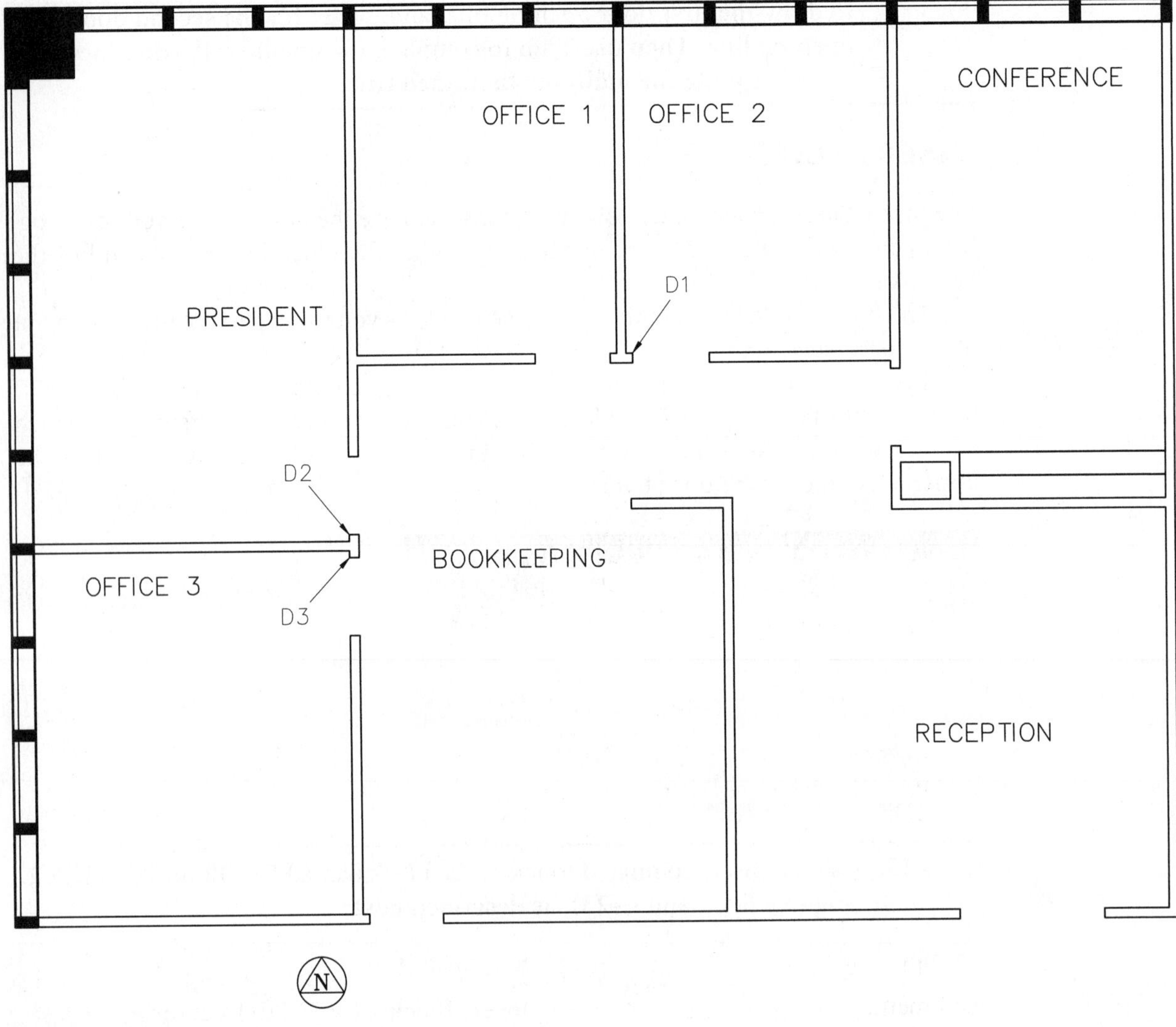

FIGURE 6–23
Use the Insert-Block... Command to Insert the Block Named DOOR (Scale: 1/8″ = 1′-0″)

Prompt	Response
Specify insertion point or [Basepoint/ Scale/Rotate]:	**OSNAP-Intersection**
of	**D1** (Figure 6–23)

Step 36. Use the Insert-Block... command to insert the block named DOOR into the president's office (Figure 6–23), as described next:

Prompt	Response
Command:	**Insert-Block...** (or TYPE: **I<enter>**)
The Insert dialog box appears with DOOR in the Name: input box:	TYPE: **90** (in the Rotation Angle: input box) CLICK: **OK**
Specify insertion point or [Basepoint/ Scale/Rotate]:	**OSNAP-Intersection**
of	**D2**

NOTE: Door blocks originally drawn on the a-door-dbl and a-door-swng Layers will be on those layers in the drawing, regardless of what layer is current when they are inserted into the drawing.

When a copy of a block is inserted into the drawing, it is inserted as a single object. Before the Trim command can be used or a copy of a block can be edited, the block must be exploded. When a block is exploded, it returns to separate objects.

If you want a block to be inserted already exploded, check the Explode box in the lower left corner of the Insert dialog box.

Insertion Point

The "Insertion point:" of the incoming block is the point where the "insertion base point" specified when the door was defined as a block will be placed. In the preceding tutorials, the Osnap mode Intersection was used to position copies of the block exactly into the drawing. You can also use the ID command or From (on the Osnap menu) when inserting a block. Use the ID command to identify a point on the drawing, and then initiate the Insert-Block... command after the point has been located. You can then enter the "Insertion point:" of the block by using relative or polar coordinates to specify a distance from the established point location.

X Scale Factor, Y Scale Factor

The X and Y scale factors provide flexibility in how the copy of the block will appear when it is inserted. The default X and Y scale factor is 1. A scale factor of 1 inserts the block as it was originally drawn.

New scale factors can be typed and entered in response to the prompts. AutoCAD multiplies all X and Y dimensions of the block by the X and Y scale factors entered. By default, the Y scale factor equals the X scale, but a different Y scale factor can be entered separately. This is helpful when you are inserting a window block into a wall with windows of varying lengths. The block can be inserted, the X scale factor can be increased or decreased by the desired amount, and the Y scale factor can remain stable by being entered as 1.

Negative X or Y scale factors can be entered to insert mirror images of the block. When the X scale factor is negative, the Y scale factor remains positive. When the Y scale factor is negative, the X scale factor remains positive. Either a negative X or Y scale factor will work in the following example, but negative X will be used.

Step 37. Use the Insert-Block... command and a negative X scale factor, and rotate the angle of the block to insert the block named DOOR into office 3 (Figure 6–23), as described next:

Prompt	Response
Command:	**Insert-Block...**
The Insert dialog box appears with DOOR in the Name: input box:	UNCHECK: the Uniform Scale box TYPE: **–1** (in the X scale input box); TYPE: **90** (in the Rotation Angle: input box) CLICK: **OK**
Specify insertion point or [Basepoint/Scale/X/Y/Z/Rotate]:	**OSNAP-Intersection**
of	**D3**

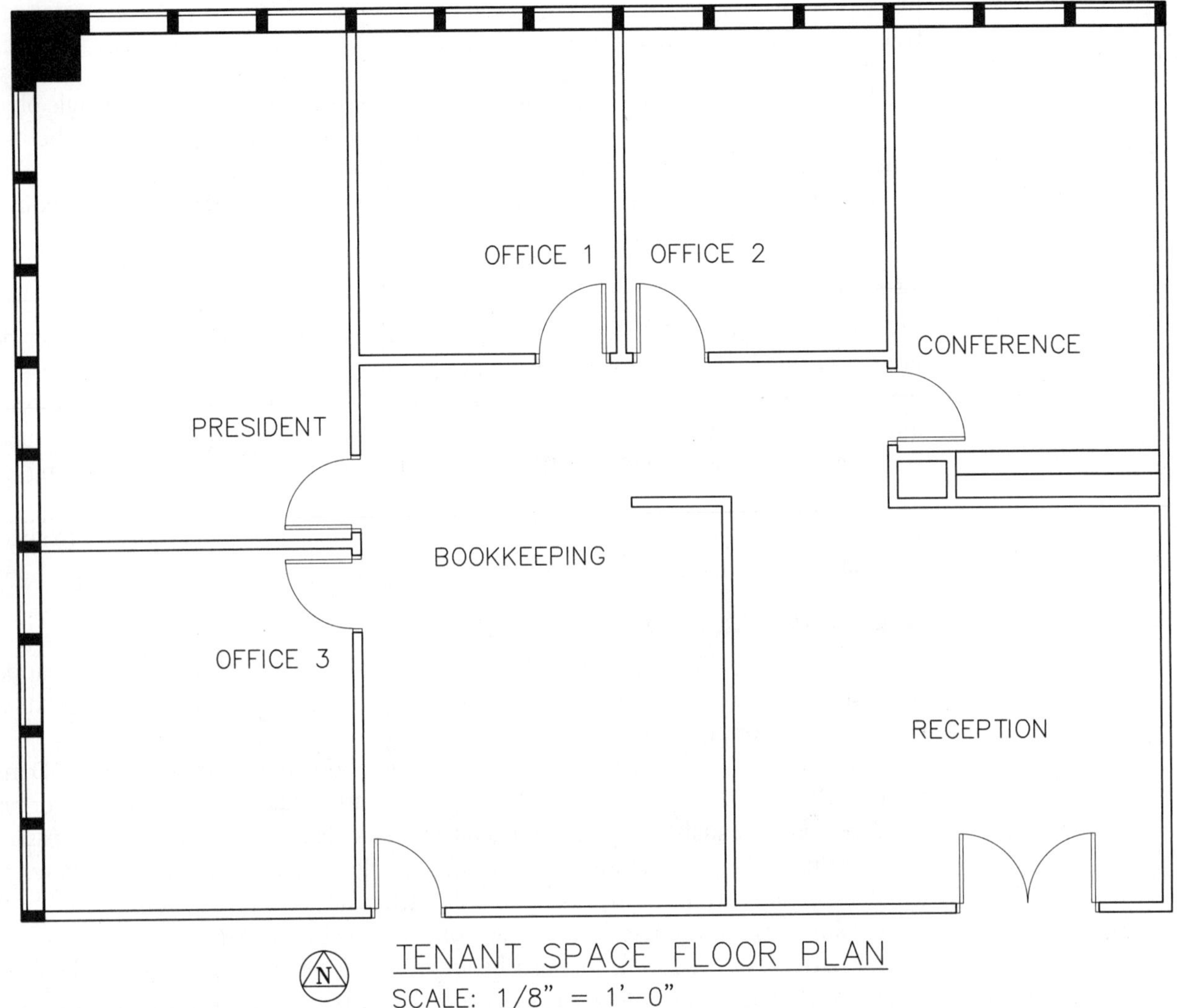

FIGURE 6–24
Tutorial 6–1: Tenant Space Floor Plan (Scale: 1/8″ = 1′-0″)

Step 38. **Use the Insert-Block... command to complete the insertion of all doors in the tenant space. Use Browse... to locate the Wblock DOORD (double door) for the Reception area (Figure 6–24).**

Step 39. **Set Layer a-flor-wdwk current. Draw two lines to show the cabinets in the conference room. The upper cabinets are 12″ deep (Figure 6–24).**

Step 40. **Set Layer a-flor-iden current.**

Step 41. **In the Text Style dialog box, change the text style Standard so that it has the simplex font.**

ANNOTATIVE TEXT

When a drawing such as the tenant space floor plan is drawn full scale, the text that is added to the drawing must also be large. For instance, if you want the text to be 1/8″

high when plotted at a scale of 1/8″ = 1′-0″, the text will need to be 12″ high on the drawing. When you set the annotation scale of the drawing and make the text annotative, AutoCAD automatically does the arithmetic for you and controls how the text looks on your screen. When adding the text, you have to enter only the size of the text you want in the printed drawing, and AutoCAD automatically calculates the size of the text on the drawing using the annotative scale setting.

You have two places where you can make the text annotative. You can select the Annotative style, or you can select the box beside Annotative under Size. When the text is annotative, the annotation scale controls how the text and other annotative objects appear on the drawing. You must set the Annotation Scale, located in the lower right corner of the Status Bar.

If you have annotative objects on your drawing and have set the annotation scale, it is usually best to plot your drawing at the same scale as the annotation scale that you have set. If there are no annotative objects on your drawing, the annotation scale does not affect anything. If the plot scale and the annotation scale differ, when the plot is initiated, AutoCAD prompts you with "The annotation scale is not equal to the plot scale. Do you wish to Continue?" You can answer with "OK" or "Cancel."

You can change the annotation scale of an annotative object. In the Status Bar, if you hold your mouse over the icon that is near the Annotation Scale input area, the tooltip will display "Automatically add scales to annotative objects when the annotation scale changes." When this icon is on and the annotation scale is changed, the annotative objects change on the screen to reflect the new scale size, and the object; then supports two scales. You can see the new scales by clicking on the object; the current scale is highlighted, and the scale size that is not current will show as dimmed. You can also use the Annotation Object Scale command in the Modify window to add or delete a current scale or any of the scales you have added to the annotative object.

You can select the object and use the Properties command to change the annotative scale of an object or use the Properties command to change an object that is not annotative, to annotative.

If you hold your mouse over a second icon that is near the Annotation Scale input area, the tooltip will display, "Annotation Visibility: Show annotative objects for all scales." When you have annotative objects on your drawing that support different scales, this icon controls their visibility. When it is off, only the annotative objects with the current annotation scale are visible.

Step 42. **In the Text Style dialog box, select the box beside Annotative under Size to make sure the annotative property is set to ON (Figure 6–25).**

Step 43. **Set the drawing Annotation Scale to 1/8″ = 1′-0″ (located in the lower right area on the AutoCAD screen, Figure 6–26).**

Step 44. **Use Dtext, height 3/32″ to type the identifying name in each room. Use the approximate locations, as shown in Figure 6–24; the names can be moved as needed when furniture is inserted into the drawing.**

Step 45. **Set Layer a-anno-text current. Use Dtext, height 1/8″ to type your name, class, and date in the upper right area, as shown in Figure 6–24.**

Step 46. **Use Dtext, height 1/8″ to type the underlined text, TENANT SPACE FLOOR PLAN.**

Step 47. **Use Dtext, height 3/32″ to type the drawing scale.**

Step 48. **Draw the North arrow similar to the North arrow on Figure 6–24. Use a 2′-2″ diameter circle. Make a new text style, named North Arrow, Romant font, not annotative, and set it current. Use Dtext to make an 8″-high letter N in the circle.**

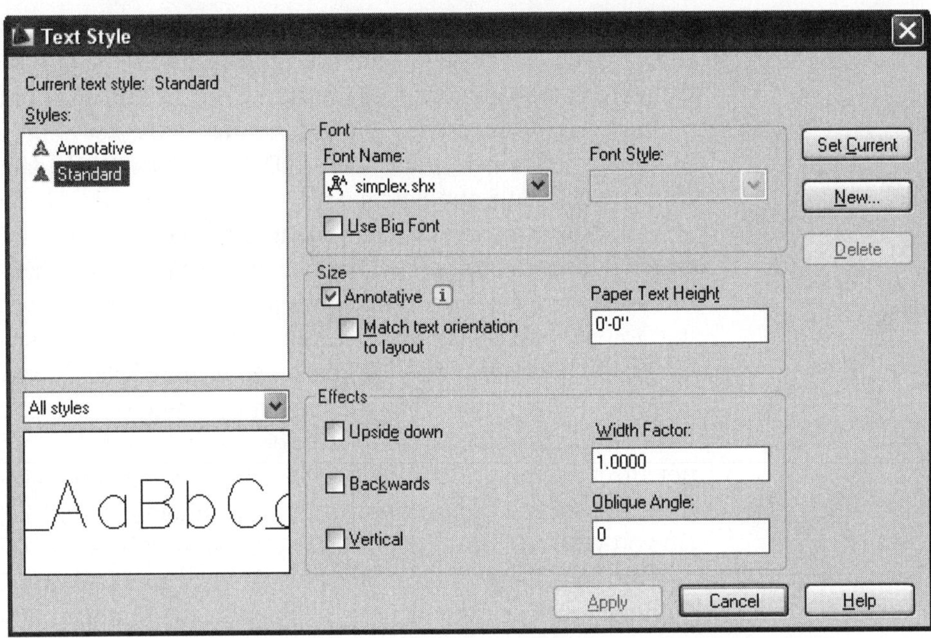

FIGURE 6–25
Text Style Dialog Box with Simplex Font and Annotative Selected

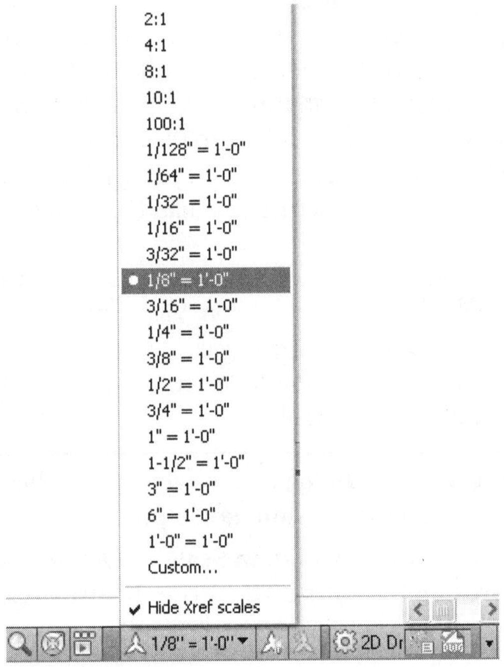

FIGURE 6–26
Set Annotation Scale to 1/8″ = 1′-0″

INSERTING ENTIRE DRAWINGS AS BLOCKS

The Insert-Block... command can be used to insert into the current drawing any drawing that has not been defined as a block and to define it as a block within that drawing. Simply use the Insert-Block... command to insert the drawing. Use the Browse... button in the Insert dialog box to locate the drawing.

ADVANTAGES OF USING BLOCKS

The use of blocks in drawings has many advantages that can save you time.

1. A library of drawing parts allows you to draw an often-used part once instead of many times.
2. Blocks can be combined with customized menus to create a complete applications environment around AutoCAD that provides the building and furnishings parts that are used daily.
3. Once a block is defined and inserted into the drawing, you can update all references to that block by redefining the block.
4. Because AutoCAD treats a block as a single object, less disk space is used for each insertion of a block.

Step 49. When you have completed Tutorial 6–1, save your work in at least two places.

Step 50. Print the Tenant Space Floor Plan at a scale of 1/8″ = 1′-0″.

Tutorial 6–2: Hotel Room Floor Plan

In Tutorial 6–2, the AutoCAD Design Center is used to insert existing fixtures such as a tub, toilet, sink, and faucet into the floor plan. Lineweights are used to make the drawing more attractive, and a solid hatch pattern with a gray color is used to make the walls solid. When you have completed Tutorial 6–2, your drawing will look similar to Figure 6–27 without dimensions.

Step 1. Use your workspace to make the following settings:

1. **Use SaveAs... to save the drawing with the name CH6-TUTORIAL2.**
2. Set drawing Units: **Architectural**
3. Set Drawing Limits: **40′,40′**
4. Set GRIDDISPLAY: **0**
5. Set Grid: **12″**
6. Set Snap: **6″**
7. Create the following layers:

LAYER NAME	COLOR	LINETYPE	LINEWEIGHT
a-anno-center	red	center	.004″ (.09mm)
a-anno-dims	red	continuous	.004″ (.09mm)
a-anno-text	green	continuous	.006″ (.15mm)
a-bldg-hidn	green	hidden	.006″ (.15mm)
a-bldg-misc	blue	continuous	.007″ (.18mm)
a-door-dbl	red	continuous	.004″ (.09mm)
a-door-swng	red	continuous	.004″ (.09mm)
a-fixt-bath	green	continuous	.006″ (.15mm)
a-fixt-pfix	yellow	continuous	.002″ (.05mm)
a-glaz	green	continuous	.006″ (.15mm)
a-wall-intr	blue	continuous	.007″ (.18mm)
a-wall-patl	gray (253)	continuous	.002″ (.05mm)
i-furn	cyan	continuous	.004″ (.09mm)

8. Set **Layer a-wall-intr** current.

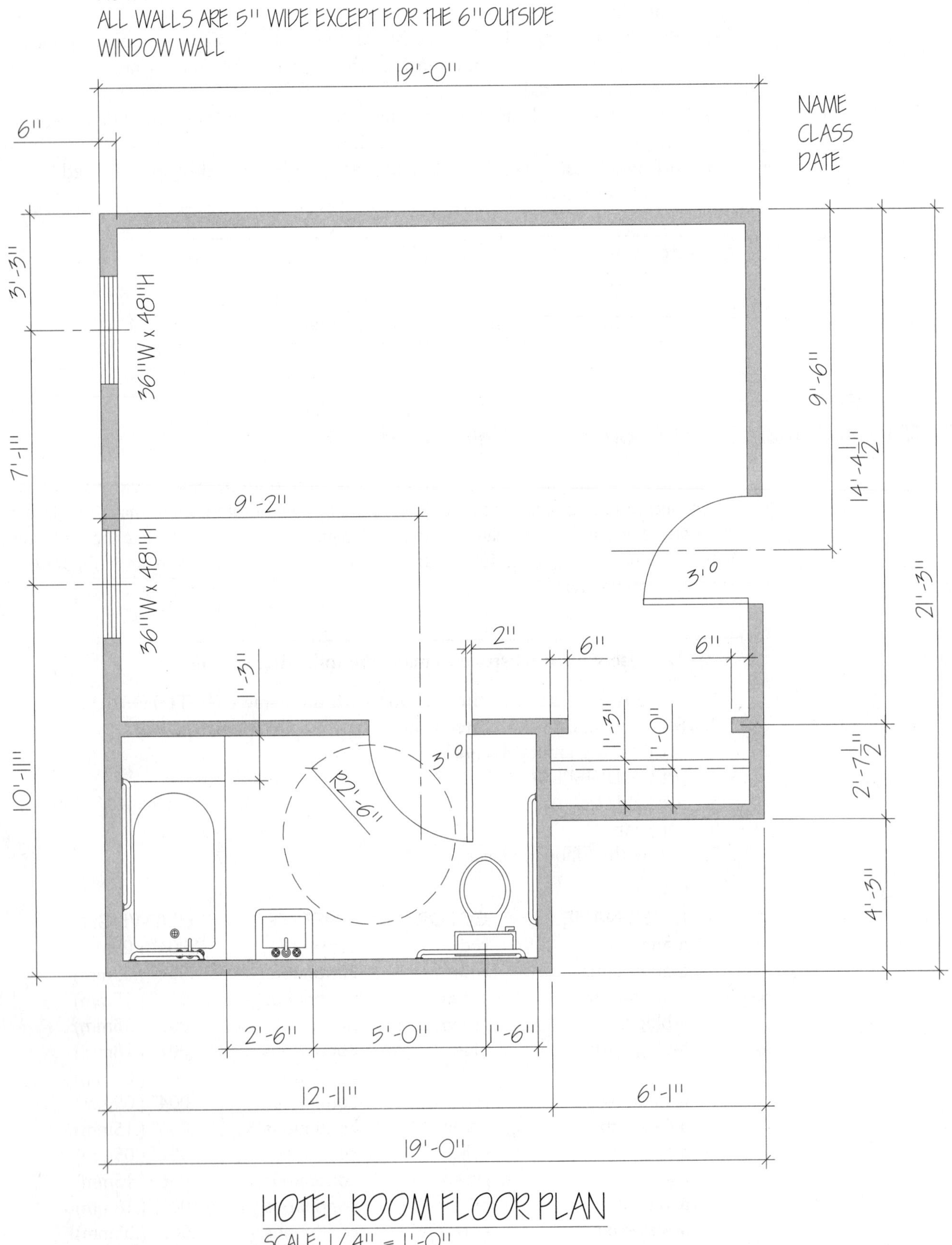

FIGURE 6–27
Tutorial 6–2: Hotel Room Floor Plan (Scale: 1/4″ = 1′-0″)

Step 2. **Use Polyline to draw the outside walls, as described next:**

Prompt	Response
Command:	**Polyline** (or TYPE: **PL<enter>**)
Specify start point:	TYPE: **29′,32′<enter>**
Specify next point or [Arc/Halfwidth/Length/Undo/Width]:	**Turn ORTHO ON, move your mouse straight up**, and TYPE: **8′<enter>**
Specify next point or [Arc/Close/Halfwidth/Length/Undo/Width]:	**Move your mouse to the left**, and TYPE: **19′<enter>**
Specify next point or [Arc/Close/Halfwidth/Length/Undo/Width]:	**Move your mouse straight down**, and TYPE: **21′3<enter>**
Specify next point or [Arc/Close/Halfwidth/Length/Undo/Width]:	**Move your mouse to the right**, and TYPE: **12′11<enter>**
Specify next point or [Arc/Close/Halfwidth/Length/Undo/Width]:	**Move your mouse straight up**, and TYPE: **4′3<enter>**
Specify next point or [Arc/Close/Halfwidth/Length/Undo/Width]:	**Move your mouse to the right**, and TYPE: **6′1<enter>**
Specify next point or [Arc/Close/Halfwidth/Length/Undo/Width]:	**Move your mouse straight up**, and TYPE: **6′<enter>**
Specify next point or [Arc/Close/Halfwidth/Length/Undo/Width]:	**<enter>**

Step 3. **Offset the polyline just drawn 5″ to the inside (Figure 6–27).**

Step 4. **Explode the offset polyline and move the inside line on the left 1″ to the right to make a 6″ wall on the window side. Trim where necessary, or use 0 distance chamfer to make square corners (Figure 6–27).**

Step 5. **Draw the following (Figures 6–27 and 6–28):**

Layer	**Object**
a-bldg-misc	closet shelf
a-bldg-hidn	closet rod
a-door-dbl	double line door
a-door-swng	door swing
a-wall-intr	remaining walls and door and window openings

Do not draw the window. It will be inserted as a block later.

Step 6. **Change LTSCALE as needed to show the Hidden linetype of the rod.**

HATCH

Next you will add a solid hatch pattern to shade the walls of the hotel room. The most important aspect of using the Hatch command is to create a clear boundary for the hatch pattern. If the boundary of the hatching area is not clearly defined, the Hatch command will not work, or will not appear, as you want it to. Any small gap at intersections will cause an error message with the Hatch command.

FIGURE 6–28
Complete Outside and Inside Walls and Closet Details

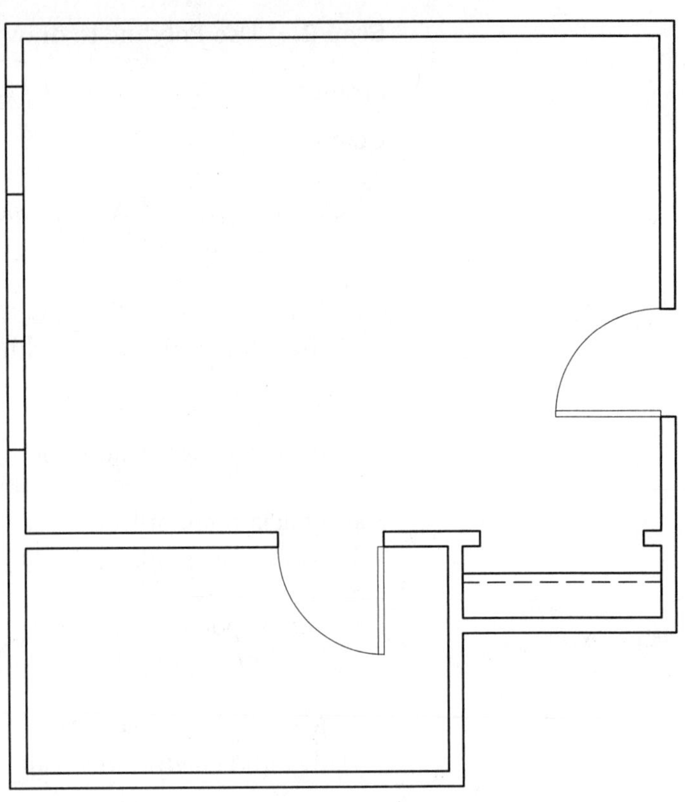

Step 7. **Set Layer a-wall-patl current.**

Step 8. **Use the Hatch command to add shading to the walls of the hotel room, as described next:**

Prompt	Response
Command:	**Hatch** (or TYPE: **H<enter>**)
The Hatch and Gradient dialog box appears:	CLICK: **Predefined** in the pattern Type area CLICK: **...** (to the right of the Pattern: list box) CLICK: **the Other Predefined tab** CLICK: **SOLID** CLICK: **OK** CLICK: **Add: Pick points**
Pick internal point or [Select objects/remove Boundaries]:	CLICK: **the points inside the lines defining the walls**
Pick internal point or [Select objects/remove Boundaries]:	**<enter>**
The Hatch and Gradient dialog box appears:	CLICK: **Preview** or **OK**

The walls are now hatched. If you get an error message, check that there are no gaps in the lines that form the boundaries for the walls.

Step 9. **Set Layer a-fixt-bath current.**

FIGURE 6–29
Select the Bathtub 26″ × 60″ from the DesignCenter

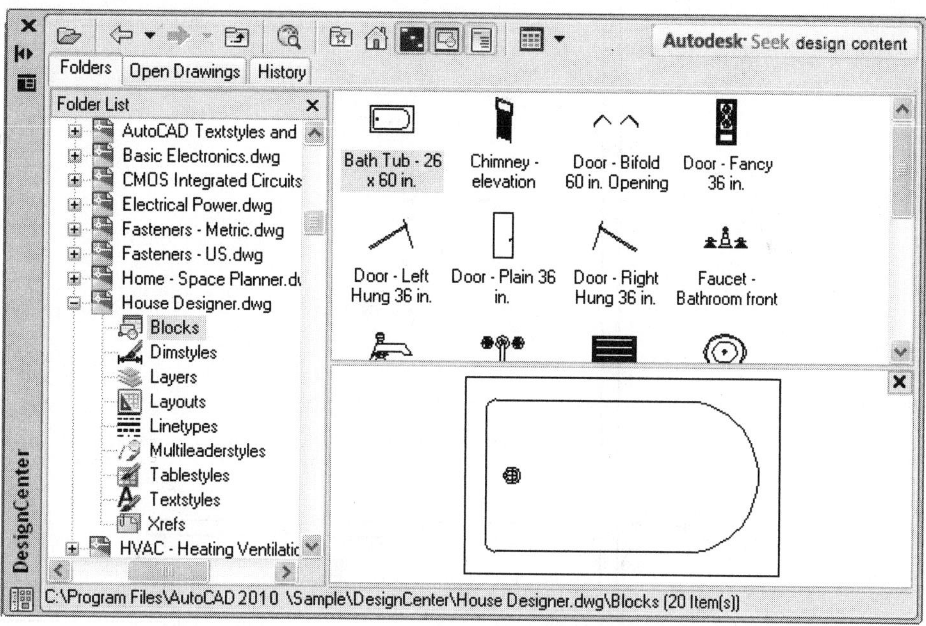

Step 10. **Open the AutoCAD DesignCenter and locate the 2D Architectural House Designer blocks drawing (Figure 6–29), as described next:**

Prompt	Response
Command:	TYPE: **DC<enter>**
The DesignCenter appears:	CLICK: **AutoCAD 2010, Sample, DesignCenter, House Designer.dwg.Blocks (Follow the path shown in Figure 6–29.)**
The available blocks appear in the area to the right:	CLICK: **26″ × 60″ Bathtub Plan View** (Hold down the CLICK: button and drag and drop the bathtub into the drawing) (Note: The bathtube size is 36″ × 60″)

Step 11. **Rotate the tub and use OSNAP-intersection to locate the tub (Figure 6–30). Add a line to show the tub seat (Figure 6–31).**

Step 12. **Insert the toilet in the location shown (Figure 6–31). Locate the toilet symbol in the DesignCenter, House Designer.dwg, Blocks, Toilet-top.**

Step 13. **Draw the sink using the dimensions shown in Figure 6–32.**

Step 14. **Set Layer a-fixt-pfix current and insert the top view of the faucet in the locations shown (Figure 6–31) in the bathtub and sink. You will have to insert it on the a-fixt-pfix layer because the faucet is so detailed the lines will flow together unless they are very thin. Locate the faucet symbol in the DesignCenter, House Designer.dwg, Blocks, Faucet-Bathroom top.**

Step 15. **Draw the grab bars on the a-fixt-bath Layer, using the dimensions shown in Figures 6-31 and 6-32, or set Layer a-fixt-bath current and use the Autodesk Seek design content to locate the grab bars, as described next, Figure 6-33:**

FIGURE 6–30
Insert the Bathtub

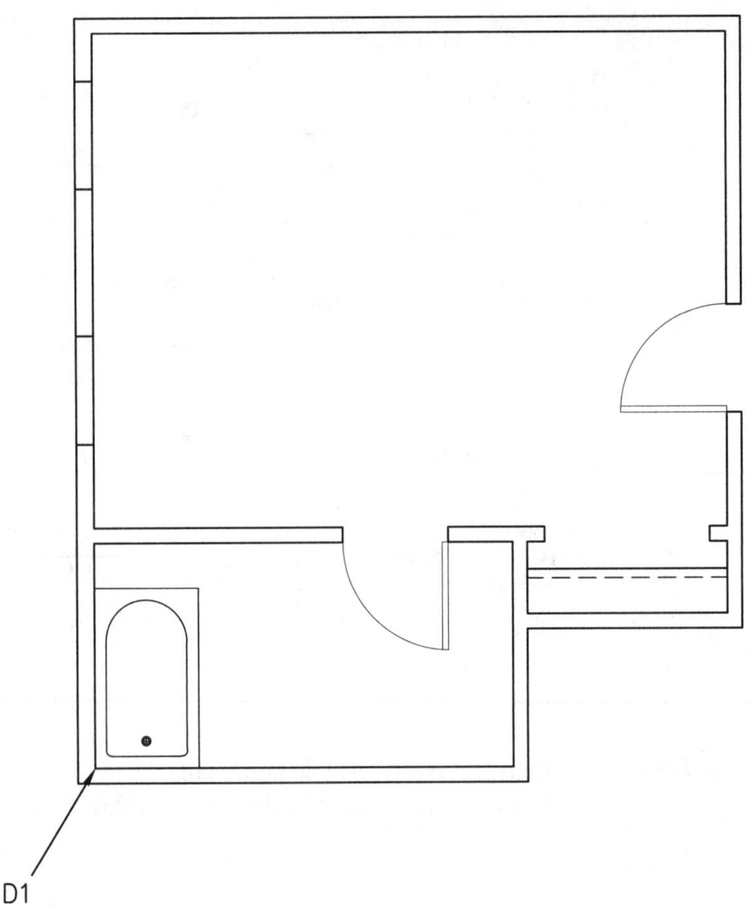

Prompt	Response
Command:	TYPE: **DC<enter>**
The DesignCenter appears:	CLICK: **Autodesk Seek design content button** (in the upper right corner)
The Autodesk Seek online source for product specifications and design files appears:	CLICK: **DWG** (for file type in the search input area, Figure 6-33) TYPE: **grab bar** (in the search input area, Figure 6-33) CLICK: **Search button**
The product specification files appear:	**Scroll down to the Autodesk Library image area and drag-and-drop the grab bars into the drawing**

NOTE: Before Autodesk Seek can be used to drag and drop drawings, a free plug-in must be installed. CLICK: the note "About idrop" and follow the directions to install the plug-in.

Step 16. **Trim the toilet, sink , faucet, and tub seat lines that show through the grab bars. You will have to explode the blocks before you can trim. When the blocks are exploded they will return to the 0 Layer. Window the exploded**

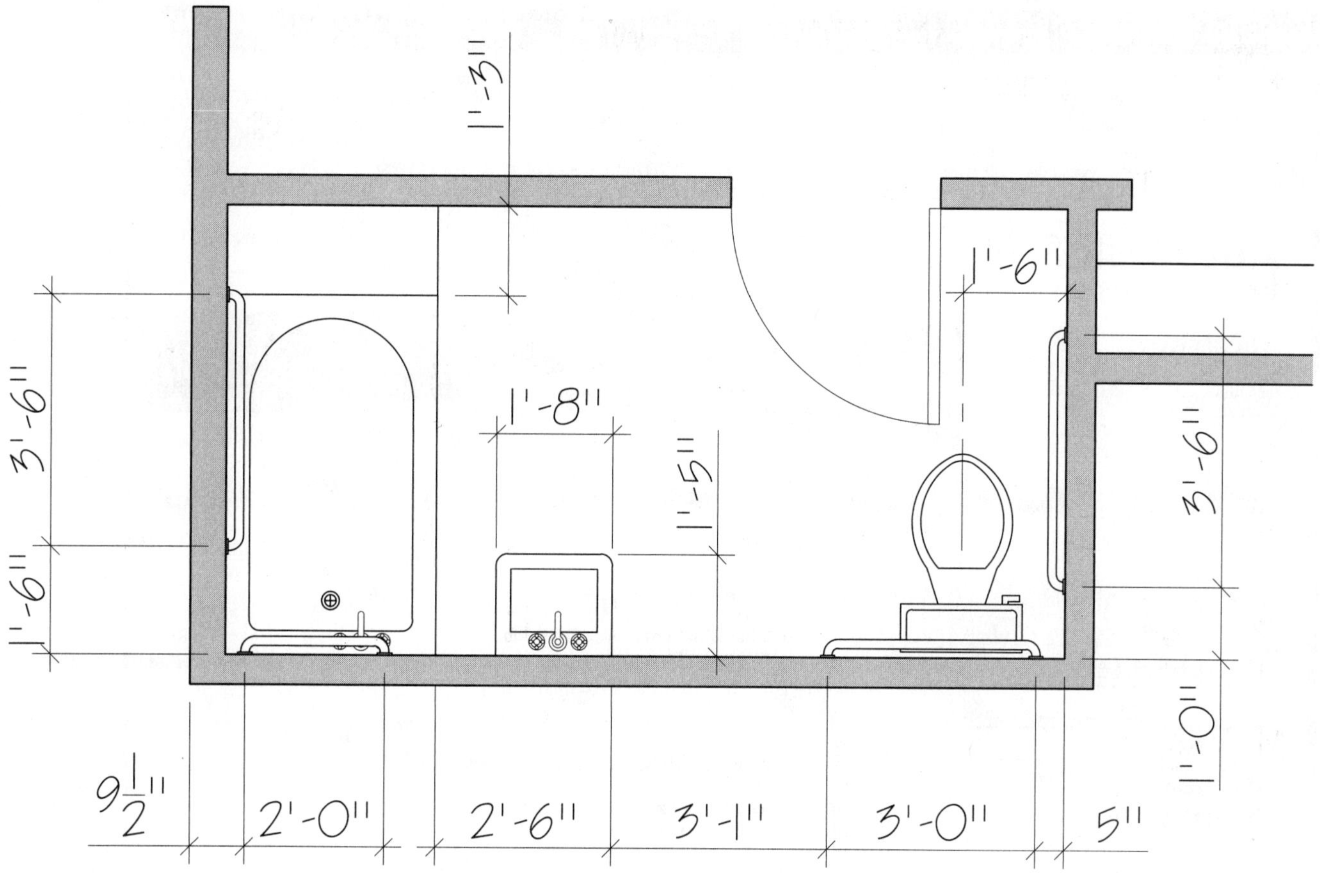

FIGURE 6–31
Bathroom Dimensions for Tutorial 6–2: Hotel Room Floor Plan (Scale: 3/8″ = 1′-0″)

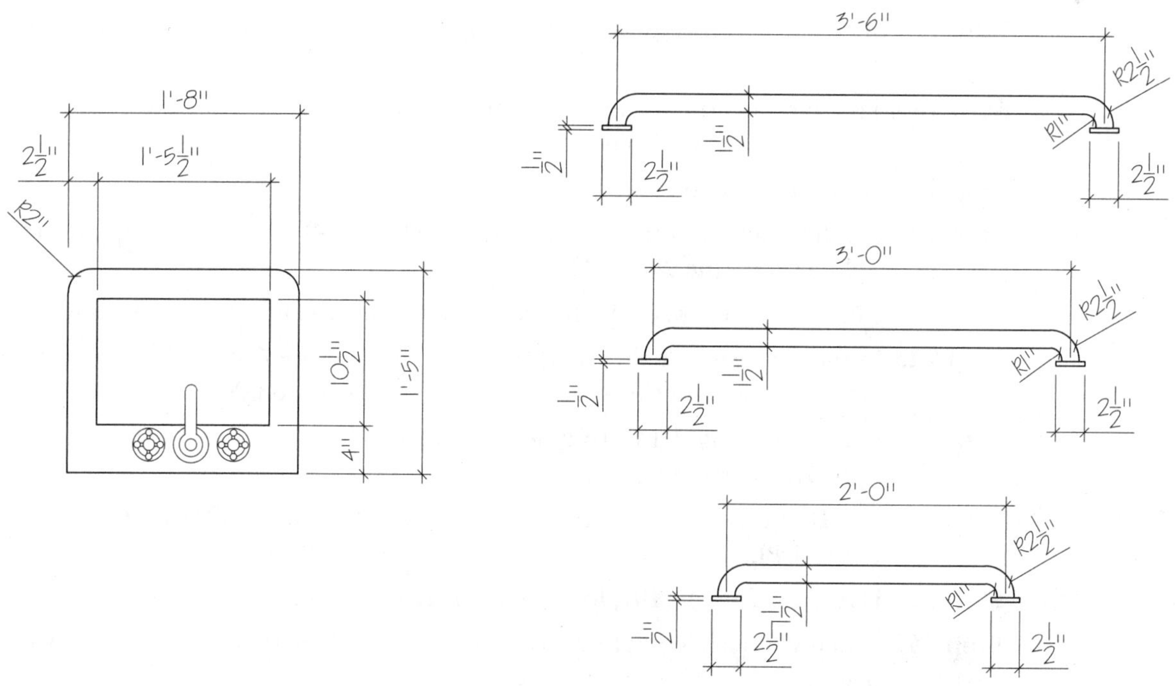

FIGURE 6–32
Sink and Grab Bar Dimensions

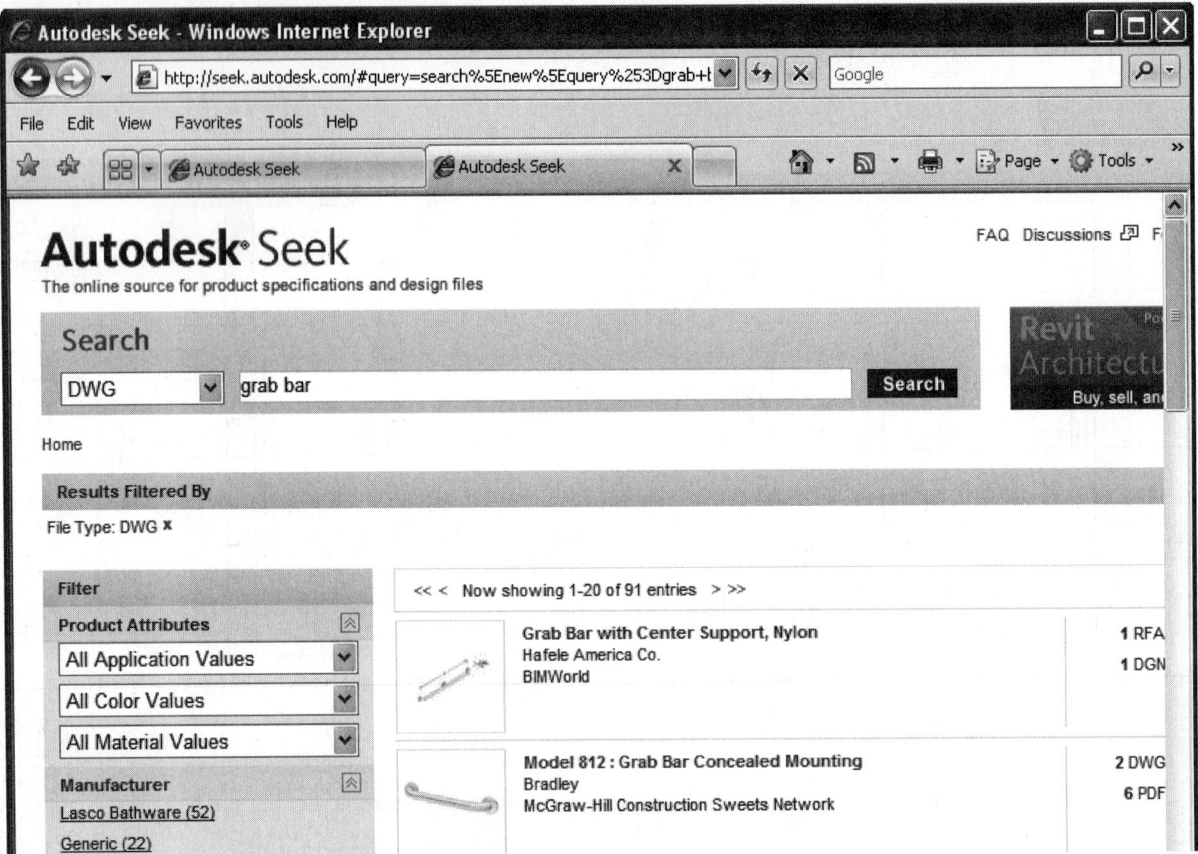

FIGURE 6–33
Autodesk Seek Online

blocks and put them back on the green a-fixt-bath Layer so they will plot with the correct lineweight.

Step 17. Set Layer a-bldg-hidn current and draw the 60″-diameter wheelchair turning space.

Step 18. Set Layer a-glaz current and insert the 36″ wood frame windows from the DesignCenter, House Designer.dwg, Blocks.

Step 19. Set Layer a-anno-text current.

Step 20. Set the drawing Annotation Scale to 1/4″ = 1′-0″ (located in the lower right area on the AutoCAD screen).

Step 21. Change the text style Standard so that it has the CityBlueprint font.

Step 22. In the Text Style dialog box, select the box beside Annotative under Size to make sure the annotative property is set to ON.

Step 23. Use Dtext, height 1/8″ to type your name, class, and date in the upper right area (Figure 6–27).

Step 24. Use Dtext, height 3/16″ to type the underlined text, HOTEL ROOM FLOOR PLAN.

Step 25. Use Dtext, height 1/8″ to type the drawing scale.

Step 26. When you have completed Tutorial 6–2, save your work in at least two places.

Step 27. Print the Hotel Room Floor Plan at a scale of 1/4″ = 1′-0″.

review questions

1. What is the maximum number of lines you can draw at the same time with Multiline?
   a. 2
   b. 4
   c. 8
   d. 12
   e. 16
2. Which of the following Multiline justification options can be used to draw a three-line multiline that has a 3 offset, a 0, and a negative 3 offset, using the middle line?
   a. Top
   b. Right
   c. Bottom
   d. Left
   e. Zero
3. When you have created a new Multiline Style, what must you pick in the Multiline Style dialog box to set the new style current?
   a. Add
   b. Save...
   c. New
   d. Set Current
   e. Load...
4. Which of the following must be selected first when using the Extend command?
   a. The correct color
   b. The correct layer
   c. Object to be trimmed
   d. Object to extend
   e. Boundary edge
5. Which of the following may *not* be changed with the Properties... command?
   a. Color
   b. Layer
   c. Linetype
   d. Lineweight
   e. Drawing name
6. Which of the following commands tells you which layer a line is on and its length?
   a. Status
   b. Dist
   c. Area
   d. List
   e. Utility
7. If a block is inserted with a check in the Explode block, which of the following is true?
   a. The block must be exploded before it can be edited.
   b. Each element of the block is a separate object.
   c. The block assumes the color of the current layer.

d. A Wblock is created with the same name.
e. AutoCAD will not accept the block name.

8. The Wblock command does which of the following?
   a. Creates a block that can be used on the current drawing only
   b. Creates a drawing file on any disk
   c. Creates a drawing file on the hard disk only
   d. Creates blocks of parts of the current drawing only
   e. Uses only named blocks on the current drawing

9. Which scale factor can be used to create a mirror image of a block with the use of the Insert-Block… command?
   a. Negative X, Positive Y
   b. Positive X, Positive Y
   c. Negative X, Negative Y
   d. Mirrored images cannot be created with the Insert-Block… command.

Complete.

10. List the command that attaches a paint brush to the cursor so you can copy properties from one object to another.

    ____

11. List the command that allows you to pick an object on the drawing and the layer that object is on becomes current.

    ____

12. Describe what happens when a block is created using the Block-Make… command, and the Retain objects option button is selected.

    ____

    ____

13. Describe how several entities drawn on a single layer may each be a different color.

    ____

    ____

14. List four advantages of using blocks.
    a. ______________________________

    ____

    b. ______________________________

    ____

    c. ______________________________

    ____

    d. ______________________________

    ____

15. If you want your annotative text to be 1/8″ high on your drawing when plotted at a scale of 1/8″ = 1′0″, how high is the text while you are drawing full scale?

    ____

Exercise 6–1: Wheelchair Accessible Commercial Restroom Floor Plan

1. Draw the floor plan of the commercial restroom shown in Figure 6–34. Use the dimensions shown in Figure 6–34 (Sheets 1 and 2), or use an architectural scale to measure the floor plan and draw it full scale. Your drawing should look similar to Figure 6–34 without dimensions.
2. Plot or print the drawing to scale.

FIGURE 6–34
Sheet 1 of 2, Exercise 6–1: Wheelchair Accessible Commercial Restroom Floor Plan (Scale: 3/16″ = 1′-0″)

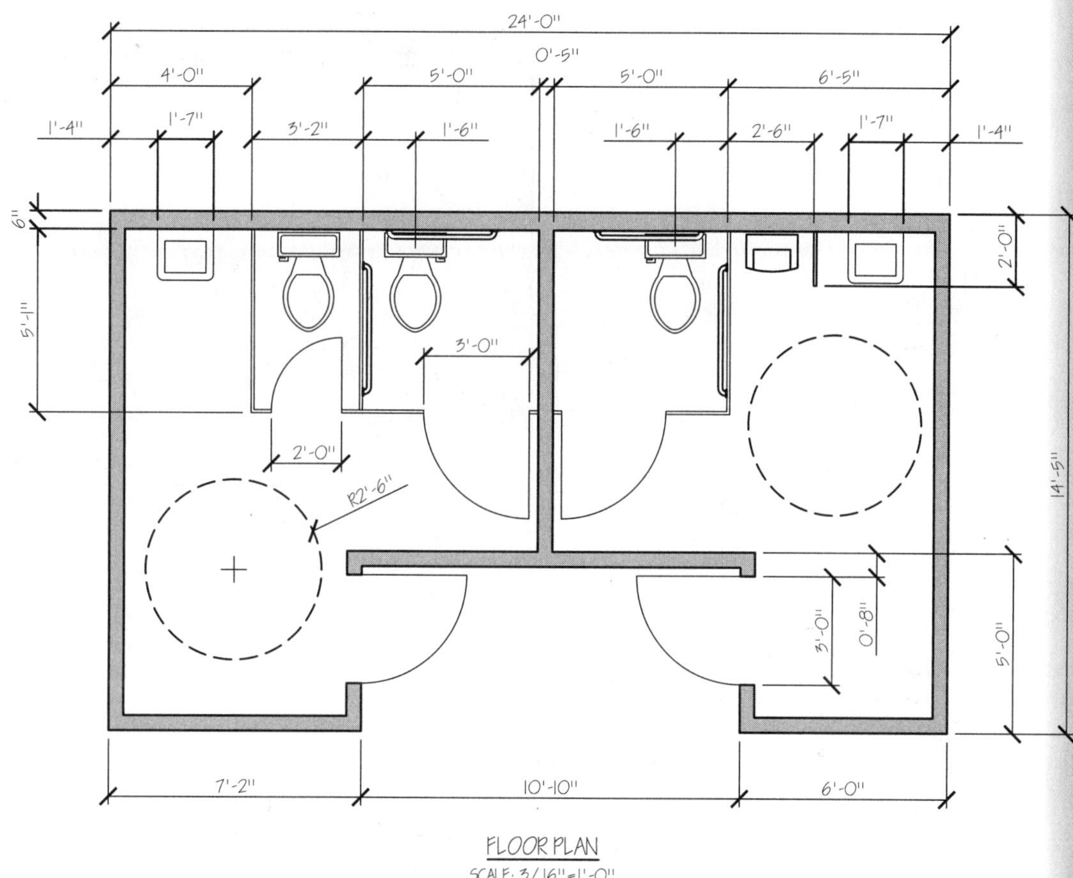

FIGURE 6–34
Sheet 2 of 2, Exercise 6–1: Wheelchair Accessible Commercial Restroom Floor Plan, Grab Bar Detail (Scale: 3/16″ = 1′-0″)

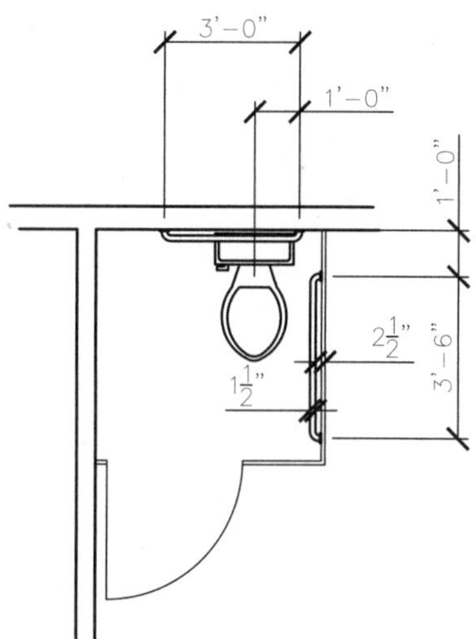

Exercise 6–2: Wheelchair Accessible Residential Bathroom Floor Plan

1. Draw the floor plan of the residential bathroom shown in Figure 6–35. Use the dimensions shown in Figure 6–35, or use an architectural scale to measure the floor plan and draw it full scale. Your drawing should look similar to Figure 6–35 without dimensions.
2. Plot or print the drawing to scale.

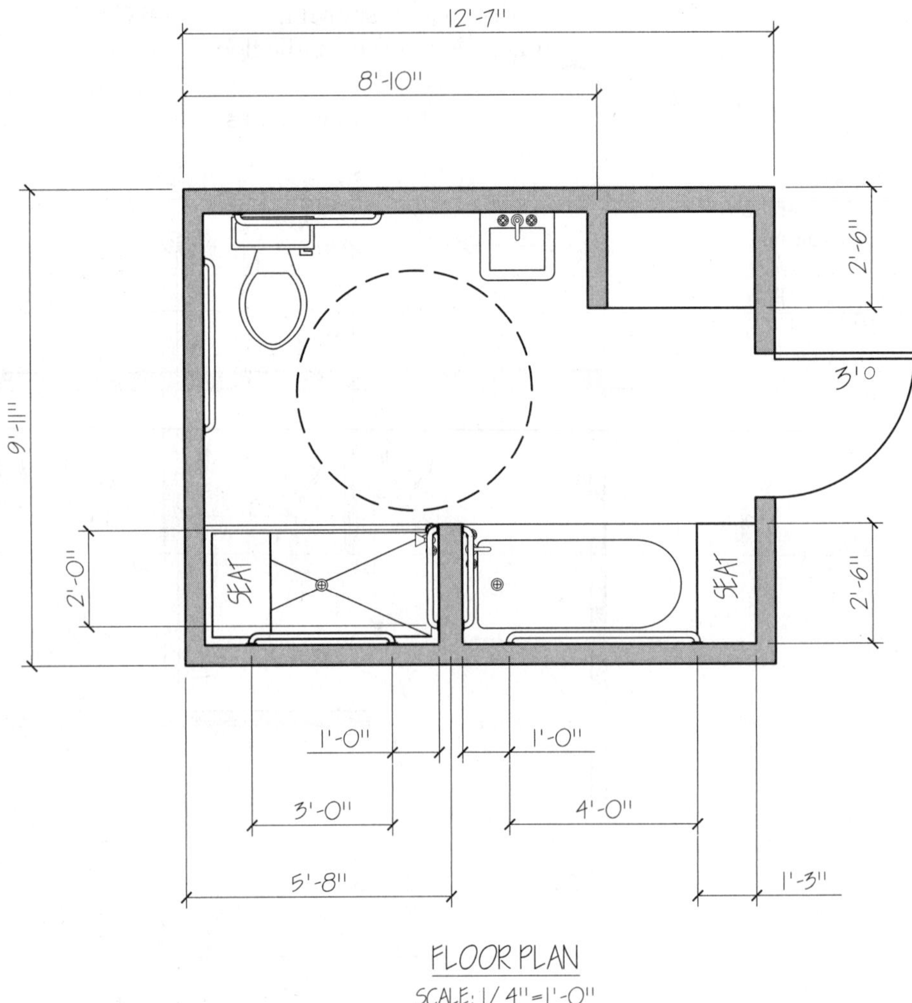

FIGURE 6–35
Exercise 6–2: Wheelchair Accessible Residential Bathroom Floor Plan (Scale: 1/4" = 1'-0")

Exercise 6–3: Log Cabin Floor Plan

1. Draw the floor plan of the log cabin shown in Figure 6–36. Use the dimensions shown in Figure 6–37 (Sheets 1 and 2), or use an architectural scale to measure the floor plan or fireplace detail and draw it full scale. Your drawing should look similar to Figure 6–37 (Sheet 2) without dimensions.
2. Plot or print the drawing to scale.

FIGURE 6–36
Log Cabin-Huntsman (Courtesy of Tech Art)

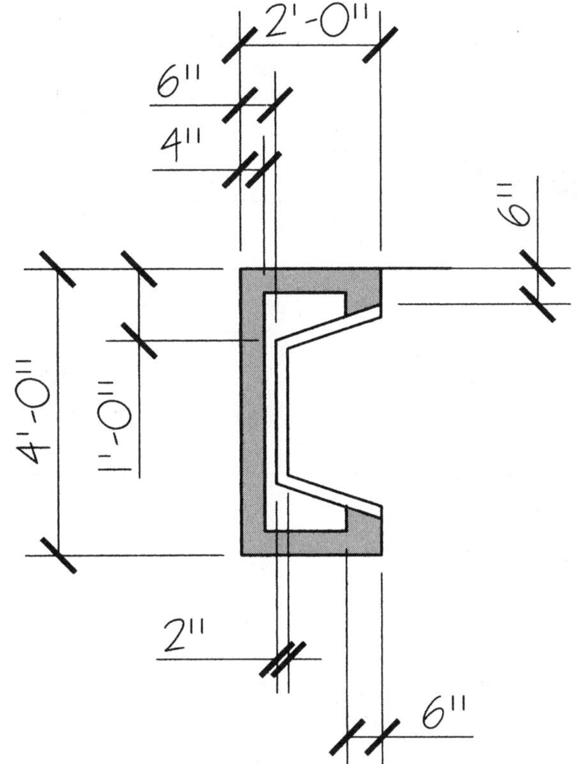

FIGURE 6–37
Sheet 1 of 2, Exercise 6–3: Log Cabin Floor Plan, Fireplace Dimensions (Scale: 3/16" = 1'-0") (Courtesy of Tech Art)

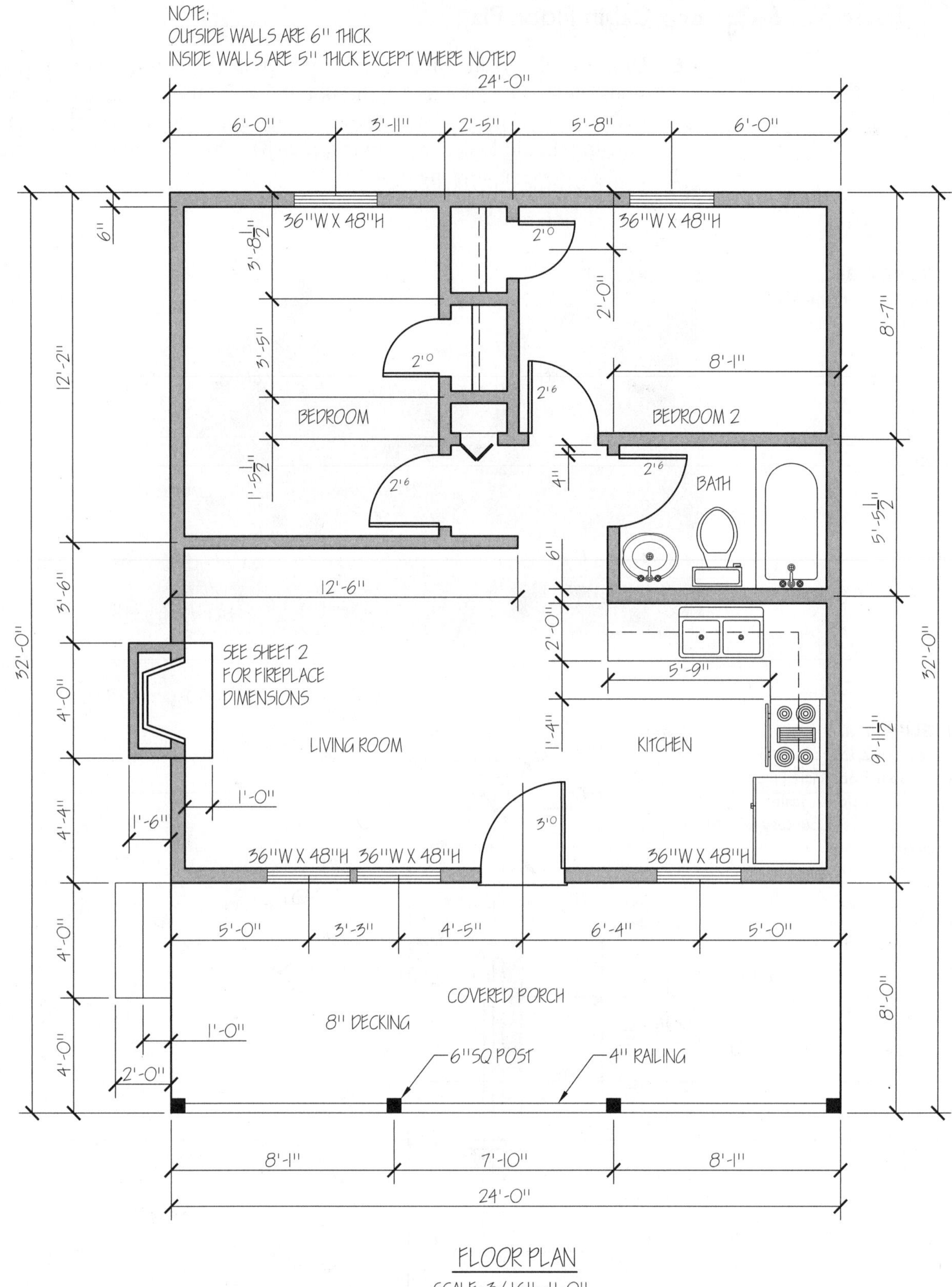

FIGURE 6–37
Sheet 2 of 2, Exercise 6–3: Log Cabin Floor Plan (Scale: 3/16″ = 1′-0″)

Exercise 6–4: House Floor Plan

1. Draw the lower and upper levels of the house floor plan as shown in Figure 6–38 (Sheets 1 and 2). Use the dimensions shown, or use an architectural scale to measure the floor plan and draw it full scale. Your drawing should look similar to Figure 6–38 without dimensions.
2. Use a Layout Wizard or Page Setup Manager to create a layout. Plot or print the drawing to scale.

Exercise 6–5: Bank Floor Plan

1. Draw the bank floor plan as shown in Figure 6–39 (Sheets 1 and 2). Use the dimensions shown, or use an architectural scale to measure the floor plan and draw it full scale. Your drawing should look similar to Figure 6–39 without dimensions.
2. Use a Layout Wizard or Page Setup Manager to create a layout. Plot or print the drawing to scale.

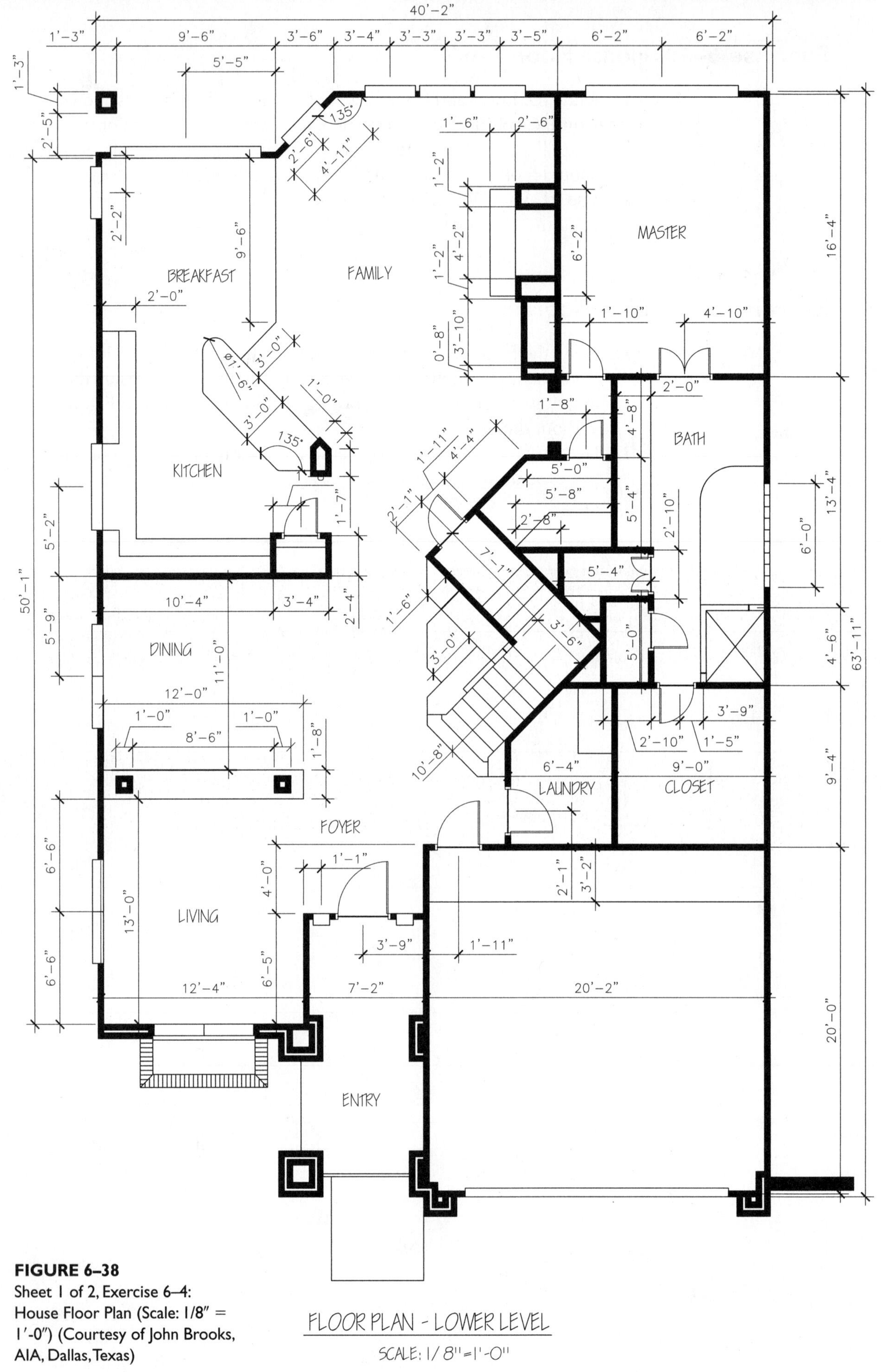

FIGURE 6–38
Sheet 1 of 2, Exercise 6–4: House Floor Plan (Scale: 1/8" = 1'-0") (Courtesy of John Brooks, AIA, Dallas, Texas)

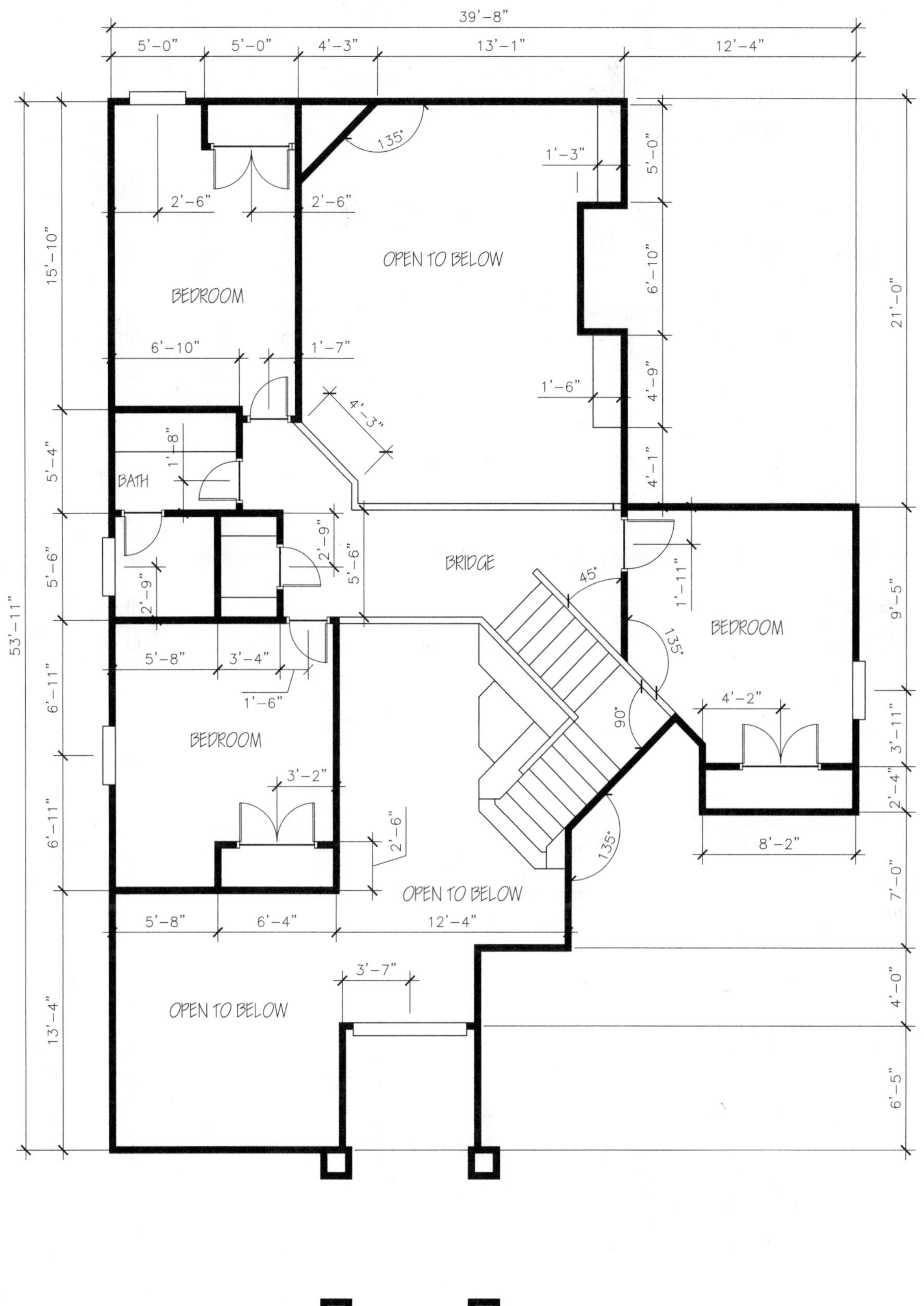

FIGURE 6–38
Sheet 2 of 2, Exercise 6–4: House Floor Plan (Scale: 1/8" = 1'-0") (Courtesy of John Brooks, AIA, Dallas, Texas)

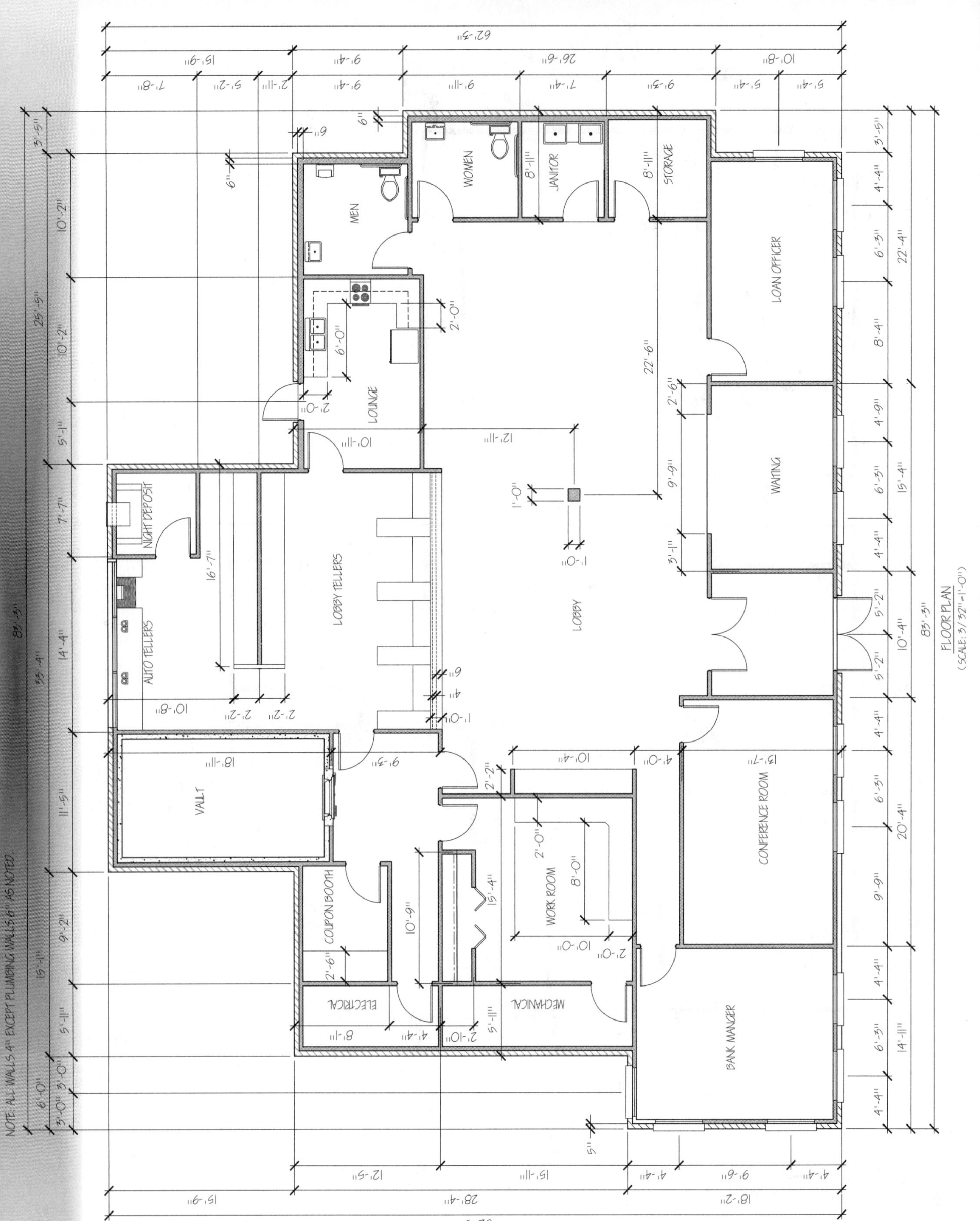

FIGURE 6–39
Sheet 1 of 2, Exercise 6–5: Bank Floor Plan (Scale: 3/32″ = 1′-0″)
(Courtesy of Benjamin Puente, Jr.)

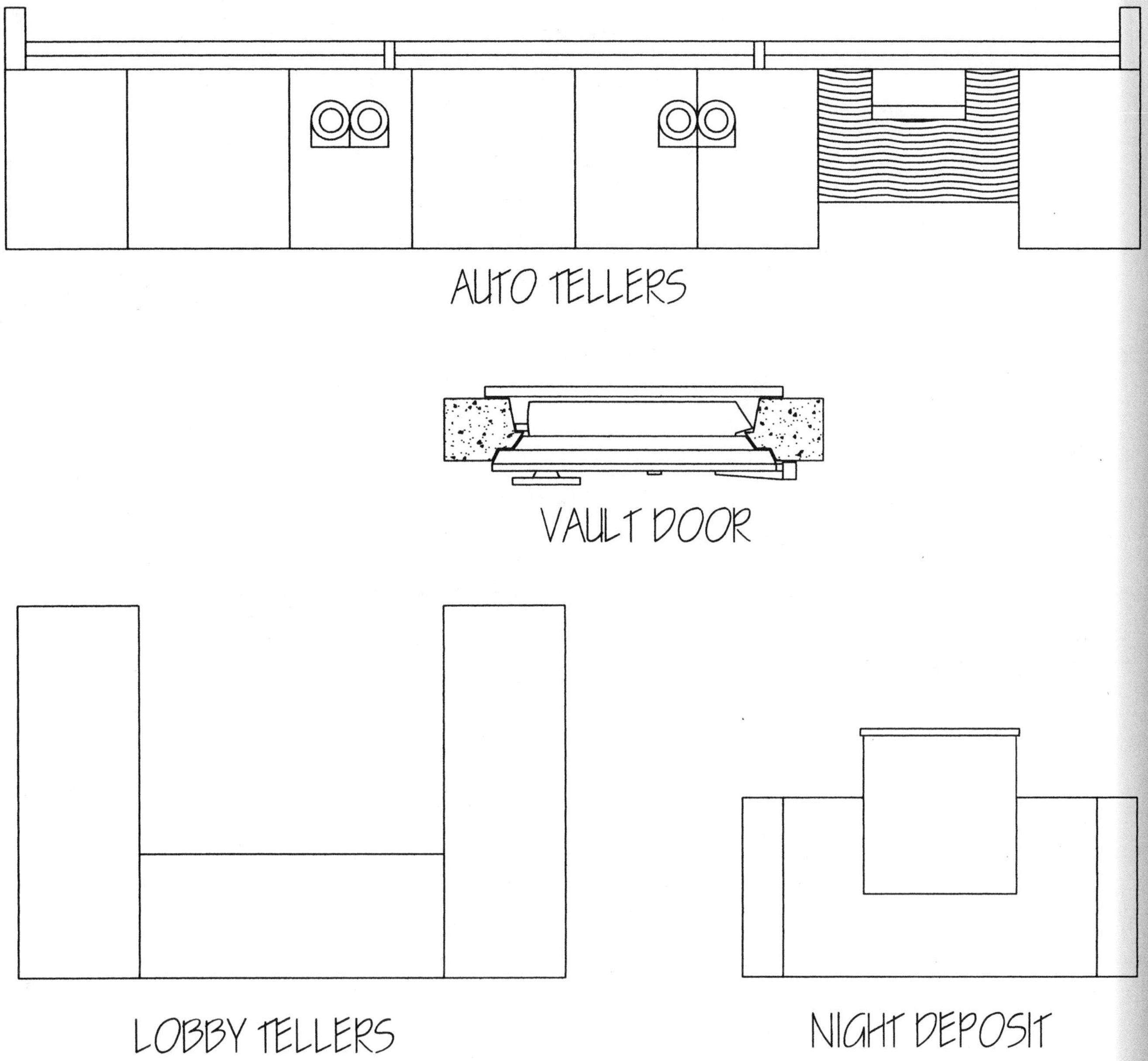

AUTO TELLERS

VAULT DOOR

LOBBY TELLERS

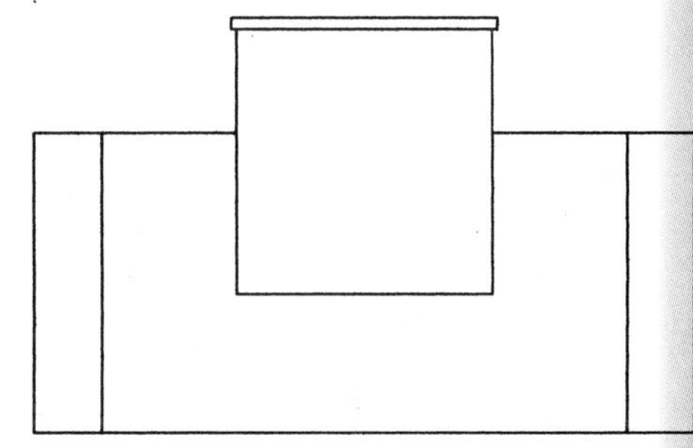

NIGHT DEPOSIT

FIGURE 6–39
Sheet 2 of 2, Exercise 6–5: Bank Floor Plan Details (Scale: 1/2″ = 1′-0″)
(Courtesy of Benjamin Puente, Jr.)

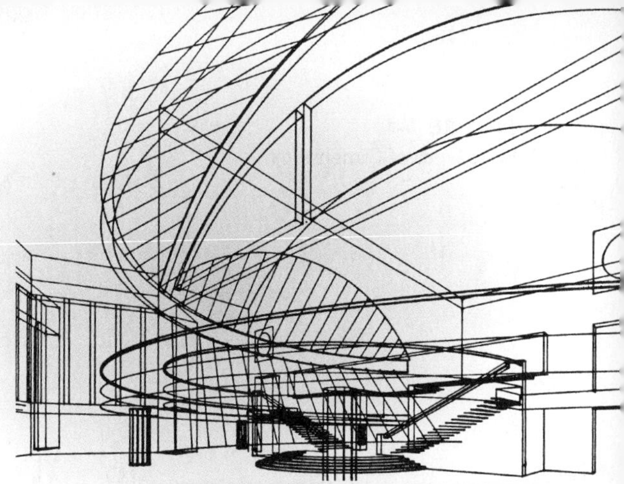

chapter

7

Dimensioning and Area Calculations

objectives

When you have completed this chapter, you will be able to:

Understand the function of dimensioning variables.

Set dimensioning variables.

Save and restore dimensioning styles.

Correctly use the following commands and settings:

Aligned Dimensioning
Align Text
Area
Baseline Dimensioning
Cal
Continue Dimensioning
DIMASSOC
DIMBREAK
DIMDLE
DIMEDIT
Dimension Edit
Dimension Style...
DIMSCALE
DIMSPACE
DIMTXT
Grips
Linear Dimensioning
MATCHPROP
Oblique
Override
QDIM
REVCLOUD
Status
Update

SIX BASIC TYPES OF DIMENSIONS

Six basic types of dimensions can be automatically created using AutoCAD. They are linear (and arc length), aligned, ordinate, radius, diameter, and angular. They are listed in the Dimension menu of the Menu Bar and are shown on the Annotate tab of the ribbon. Each dimension type shown in Figure 7–1 can be activated by selecting one of the following:

Linear For dimensioning the length of horizontal, vertical, and angled lines.
Arc Length For dimensioning the length of an arc.
Aligned For showing the length of features that are drawn at an angle.
Ordinate To display the X or Y coordinate of a feature.
Radius To create radius dimensioning for arcs and circles.
Diameter To create diameter dimensioning for arcs and circles.
Angular For dimensioning angles.

Additionally, leaders and center marks can be drawn by selecting Multileader or Center Mark.

FIGURE 7–1
Basic Types of Dimensions

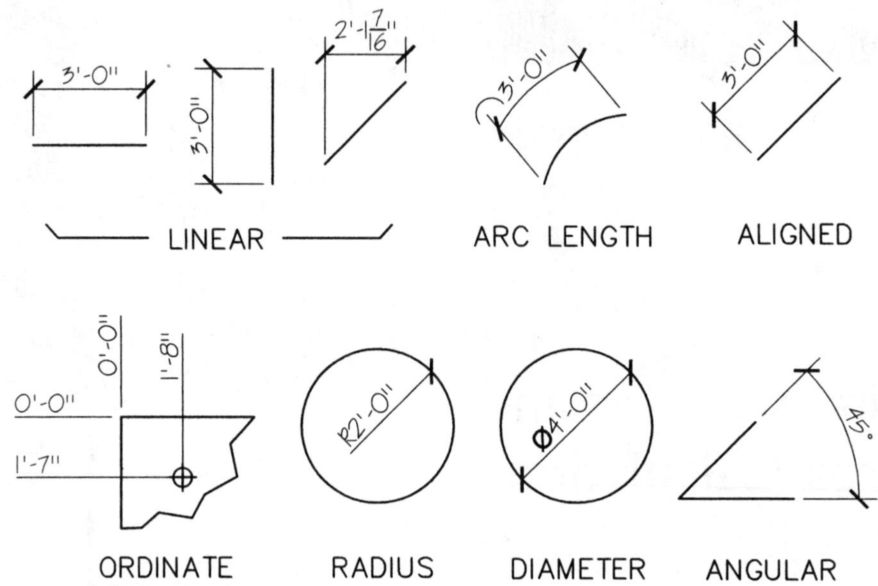

The appearance of these six basic types of dimensions, leaders, and center marks when they are drawn and plotted is controlled by settings called dimensioning variables.

DIMENSIONING VARIABLES

Dimensioning variables are settings that determine what your dimensions look like on your drawing. For instance, as shown in Figure 7–2, setting the dimension variables will determine the size of a tick mark, how far the dimension line extends beyond the tick, how far the extension line extends beyond the dimension line, and so on.

A list of dimensioning variables and a brief description of each variable appears when STATUS is typed from the Dim: prompt. (TYPE: **DIM<enter>**, TYPE: **STATUS <enter>**, PRESS: **F2** to return to the graphics screen). Figure 7–3 shows the list of dimensioning variables and the default setting for each as they appear when STATUS is typed from the Dim: prompt and Architectural units have been set. Some users of AutoCAD prefer to use the STATUS list to set dimensioning variables. Others like to use the Dimension Style Manager dialog box.

The Dimension Style Manager dialog box (Figure 7–4) allows you to set the dimensioning variables using a dialog box. It allows you to name the dimension style and change dimension variables using tabs on the dialog box. While dimensioning the same drawing, you may want some of the dimensions to have different variable settings from

FIGURE 7–2
Dimension Terms and Variables

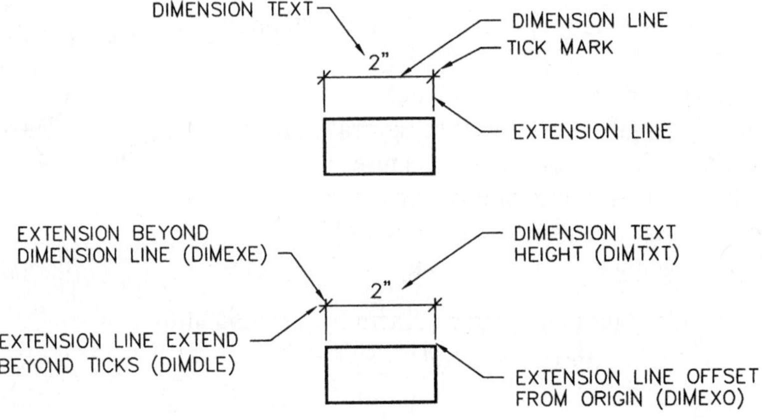

DIMASO	Off	Create dimension objects	DIMLIM	Off	Generate dimension limits
DIMSTYLE	Standard	Current dimension style (read-only)	DIMLTEX1	BYBLOCK	Linetype extension line 1
DIMADEC	0	Angular decimal places	DIMLTEX2	BYBLOCK	Linetype extension line 2
DIMALT	Off	Alternate units selected	DIMLTYPE	BYBLOCK	Dimension linetype
DIMALTD	2	Alternate unit decimal places	DIMLUNIT	2	Linear unit format
DIMALTF	25.40000	Alternate unit scale factor	DIMLWD	-2	Dimension line-leader lineweight
DIMALTMZF	8'-4"	Alternate sub-zero factor for metric dimensions	DIMLWE	-2	Extension line lineweight
DIMALTMZS		Alternate sub-zero suffix for metric dimensions	DIMMZF	8'-4"	Sub zero factor for metric dimensions
DIMALTRND	0"	Alternate units rounding value	DIMMZS		Sub zero suffix for metric dimensions
DIMALTTD	2	Alternate tolerance decimal places	DIMPOST		Prefix and suffix for dimension text
DIMALTTZ	0	Alternate tolerance zero suppression	DIMRND	0"	Rounding value
DIMALTU	2	Alternate units	DIMSAH	Off	Separate arrow blocks
DIMALTZ	0	Alternate unit zero suppression	DIMSCALE	1.00000	Overall scale factor
DIMAPOST		Prefix and suffix for alternate text	DIMSD1	Off	Suppress the first dimension line
DIMARCSYM	0	Arc length symbol	DIMSD2	Off	Suppress the second dimension line
DIMASZ	3/16"	Arrow size	DIMSE1	Off	Suppress the first extension line
DIMATFIT	3	Arrow and text fit	DIMSE2	Off	Suppress the second extension line
DIMAUNIT	0	Angular unit format	DIMSOXD	Off	Suppress outside dimension lines
DIMAZIN	0	Angular zero suppression	DIMTAD	0	Place text above the dimension line
DIMBLK	ClosedFilled	Arrow block name	DIMTDEC	4	Tolerance decimal places
DIMBLK1	ClosedFilled	First arrow block name	DIMTFAC	1.00000	Tolerance text height scaling factor
DIMBLK2	ClosedFilled	Second arrow block name	DIMTFILL	0	Text background enabled
DIMCEN	3/32"	Center mark size	DIMTFILLCLR	BYBLOCK	Text background color
DIMCLRD	BYBLOCK	Dimension line and leader color	DIMTIH	On	Text inside extensions is horizontal
DIMCLRE	BYBLOCK	Extension line color	DIMTIX	Off	Place text inside extensions
DIMCLRT	BYBLOCK	Dimension text color	DIMTM	0"	Minus tolerance
DIMDEC	4	Decimal places	DIMTMOVE	0	Text movement
DIMDLE	0"	Dimension line extension	DIMTOFL	Off	Force line inside extension lines
DIMDLI	3/8"	Dimension line spacing	DIMTOH	On	Text outside horizontal
DIMDSEP	.	Decimal separator	DIMTOL	Off	Tolerance dimensioning
DIMEXE	3/16"	Extension above dimension line	DIMTOLJ	1	Tolerance vertical justification
DIMEXO	1/16	Extension line origin offset	DIMTP	0"	Plus tolerance
DIMFRAC	0	Fraction format	DIMTSZ	0"	Tick size
DIMFXL	1"	Fixed Extension Line	DIMTVP	0.00000	Text vertical position
DIMFXLON	Off	Enable Fixed Extension Line	DIMTXSTY	Standard	Text style
DIMGAP	3/32"	Gap from dimension line to text	DIMTXT	3/16"	Text height
DIMJOGANG	45	Radius dimension jog angle	DIMTXTDIRECTION	Off	Dimension text direction
DIMJUST	0	Justification of text on dim line	DIMTZIN	0	Tolerance zero suppression
DIMLDRBLK		Leader block name	DIMUPT	Off	User positioned text
DIMLFAC	1.00000	Linear unit scale factor	DIMZIN	0	Zero suppression

FIGURE 7–3
Dimensioning Variables

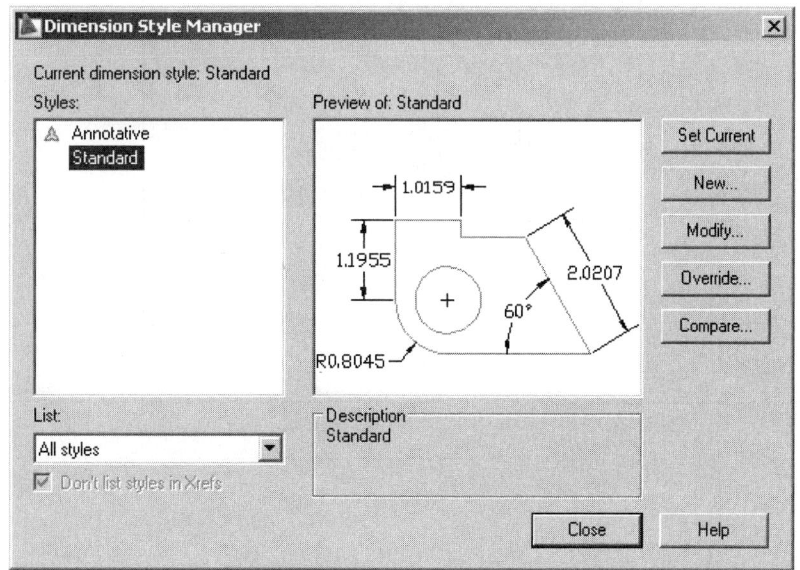

FIGURE 7–4
Dimension Style Manager Dialog Box

the rest of the dimensions. Two or more distinct styles of dimensioning can be used in the same drawing. Each style (and the variable settings for that style) may be saved separately and recalled when needed.

Tutorial 7–1: Dimensioning the Tenant Space Floor Plan Using Linear Dimensions

Tutorial 7–1 provides instructions for setting the dimensioning variables for the tenant space floor plan drawn in Tutorial 6–1, saving the dimensioning variables, and dimensioning the exterior and interior of the tenant space floor plan using linear dimensions. When you have completed Tutorial 7–1, your drawing will look similar to Figure 7–5.

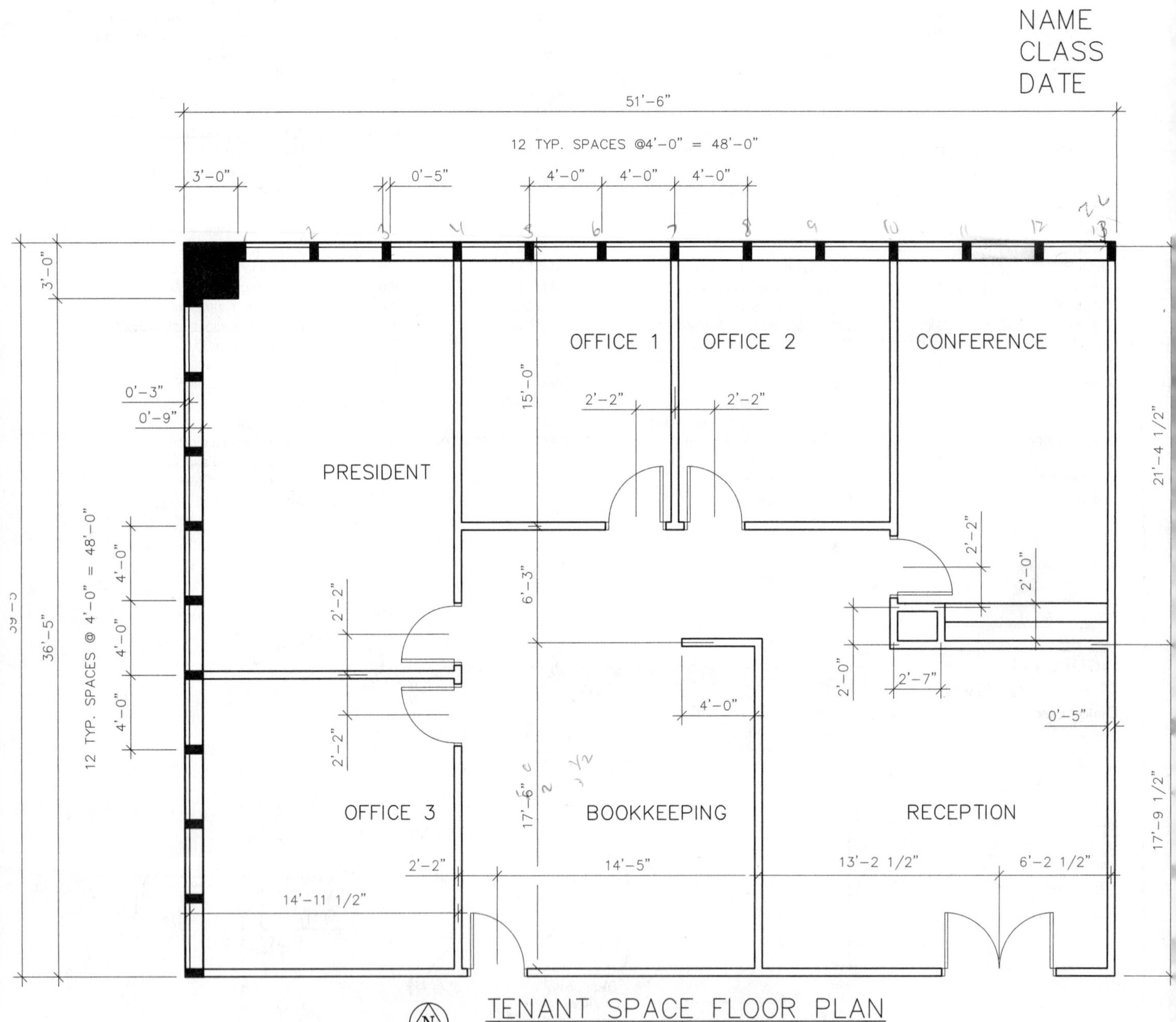

FIGURE 7–5
Tutorial 7–1: Dimensioning the Tenant Space Floor Plan Using Linear Dimensions (Scale: 1/8" = 1'-0")

Step 1. Begin drawing CH7-TUTORIAL1 by opening existing drawing CH6-TUTORIAL1 and saving it as CH7-TUTORIAL1 on the hard drive or network drive, as described next:

Prompt	Response
Command:	CLICK: **Open...**
The Select File dialog box appears:	LOCATE: **CH6-TUTORIAL1** DOUBLE-CLICK: **CH6-TUTORIAL1**
CH6-TUTORIAL1 is opened.	
Command:	**SaveAs...**
The Save Drawing As... dialog box is displayed:	TYPE: **CH7-TUTORIAL1** (replace CH6–TUTORIAL1 in the File Name: input box) CLICK: the correct drive and folder CLICK: **Save**

You are now working on the hard drive or network with a drawing named CH7-TUTORIAL1.

Step 2. Verify that UNITS is set to Architectural, as described next:

Prompt	Response
Command:	TYPE: **UNITS<enter>**
The Drawing Units dialog box appears:	SELECT: **Architectural** in the Type: input box SELECT: 0′-0 1/32″ in the Precision: input box CLICK: **OK**

NOTE: Be sure to select 32 as the denominator of the smallest fraction to display when setting drawing Units so that the dimensioning variable settings will display the same fraction if they are set in 32nds.

There are two different ways the dimensioning variables can be set. They can be set using the Dim: prompt, or by using the Dimension Style Manager dialog box. The following describes the two ways to set dimensioning variables.

SET THE DIMENSIONING VARIABLES USING THE DIM: PROMPT

Step 3. Use STATUS to view the current status of all the dimensioning variables and change the setting for DIMDLE, as described next:

Prompt	Response
Command:	TYPE: **DIM<enter>**
Dim:	TYPE: **STATUS<enter>**
(The dimension variables appear on the screen.)	CLICK: **the maximize button** (Scroll to see how the variables are currently set.)

Prompt	Response
Dim:	TYPE: **DLE<enter>** (dimension line extension)
Dim: dle	
Enter new value for dimension variable <default>:	TYPE: **1/16<enter> <enter>** (The second **<enter>** is so the variables will scroll and you can see the new setting.)
Dim:	PRESS: **F2**
	PRESS: **Esc**

NOTE: When the Dim: prompt is current, you can type the dimensioning variable name without the "DIM" prefix (example: DLE). When the Command: prompt is current, you must type the "DIM" Prefix (example: DIMDLE).

SET THE DIMENSIONING VARIABLES USING THE DIMENSION STYLE MANAGER DIALOG BOX

The Dimension Style Manager dialog box (Figure 7–6) allows you to change dimension variables using tabs on the dialog box. The default dimension style is Standard. Notice that there is a *style override* to the Standard dimension style. The override was created when you just typed a new setting for DIMDLE, using the command line. You can also create an override using the dialog box (see the Override... button). A dimension style override changes a dimensioning system variable without changing the current dimension style. All dimensions created in the style include the override until you delete the override, save the override to a new style, or set another style current.

You can use the Modify... button to modify the existing Standard style, or you can name a new style and make that style current when you begin dimensioning. In this exercise you will create a new style that has several dimensioning variables that are different from the Standard style.

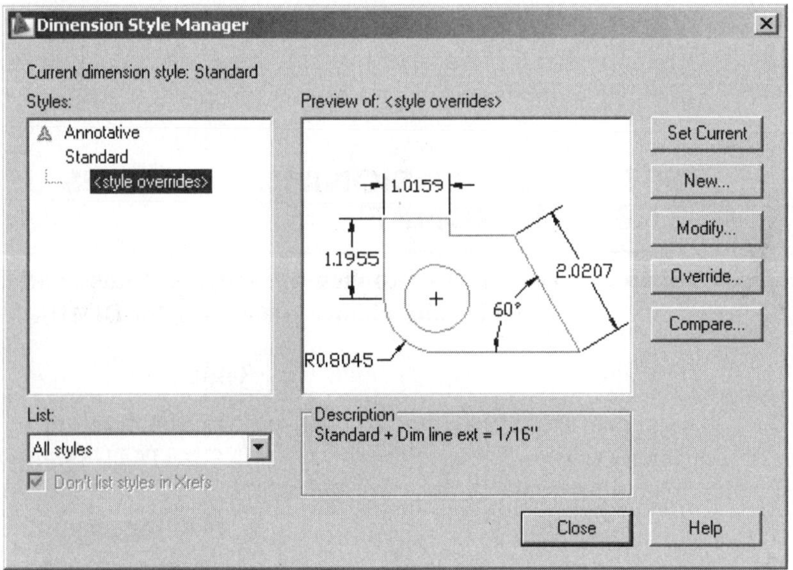

FIGURE 7–6
Dimension Style Manager Dialog Box Showing a Style Override

Dim style

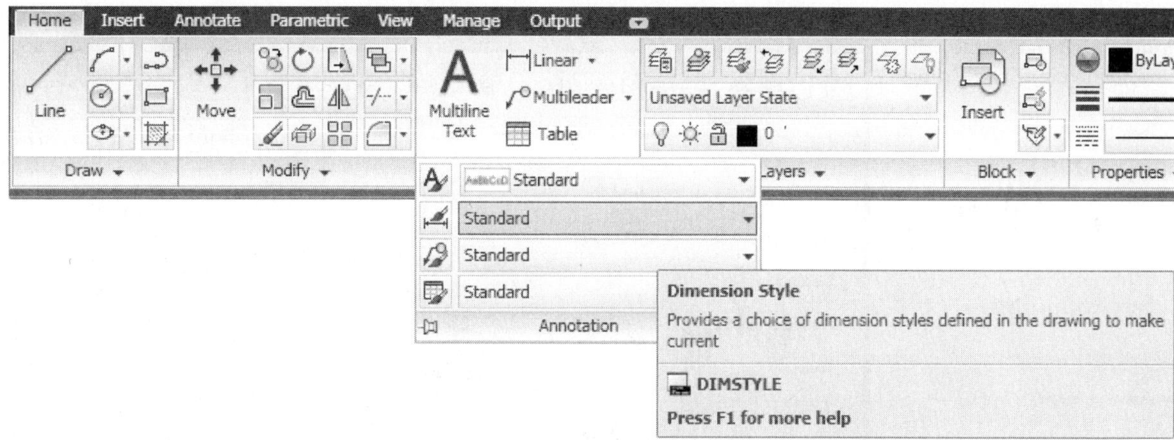

Step 4. **Use the Dimension Style Manager to create a new style (Figures 7–6 through 7–13), as described next:**

Prompt	Response
Command:	**Dimension Style...** (or TYPE: **DDIM<enter>**)
The Dimension Style Manager dialog box (Figure 7–6) appears:	CLICK: **New...**
The Create New Dimension Style dialog box (Figure 7–7) appears:	TYPE: **STYLE1** in the New Style Name: input box CLICK: **Start with: Standard** CLICK: **Continue** (or PRESS:**<enter>**)
The New Dimension Style dialog box appears:	CLICK: **the Primary Units tab** (Figure 7–8) (Setting the Primary Units first will allow you to view how dimensions will appear as you set other variables.)
The Primary Units tab is shown:	SELECT: **Architectural** in the Unit format: input box SELECT: **0′-0 1/2″** in the Precision: input box **Set all other variables for this tab as shown in Figure 7–8.** CLICK: **the Symbols and Arrows tab** (Figure 7–9)

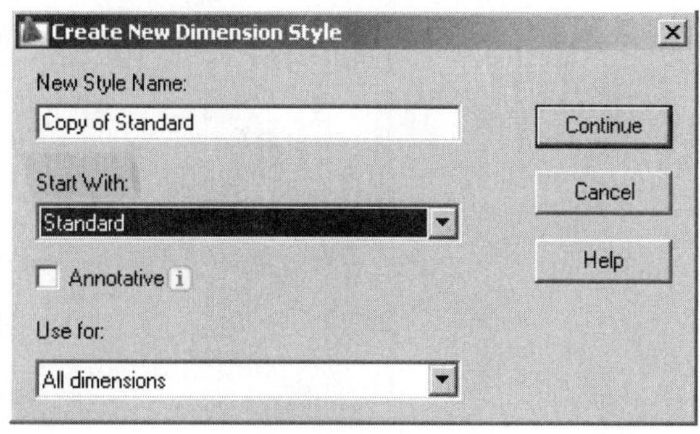

FIGURE 7–7
Create New Dimension Style Dialog Box

FIGURE 7–8
Primary Units Tab of the New Dimension Style Dialog Box

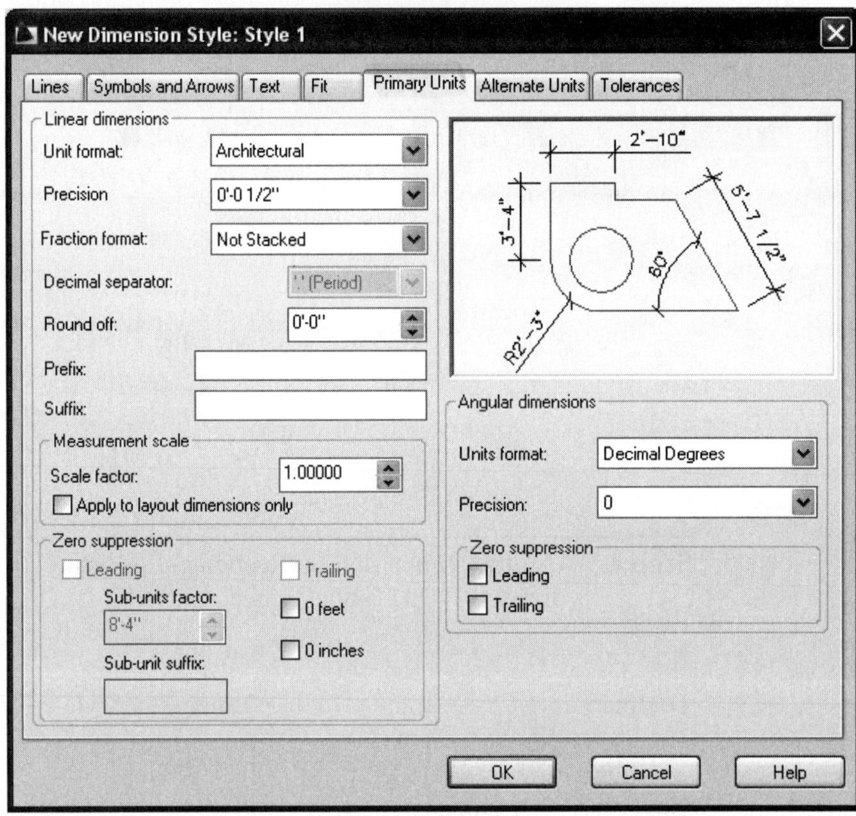

FIGURE 7–9
Symbols and Arrows Tab

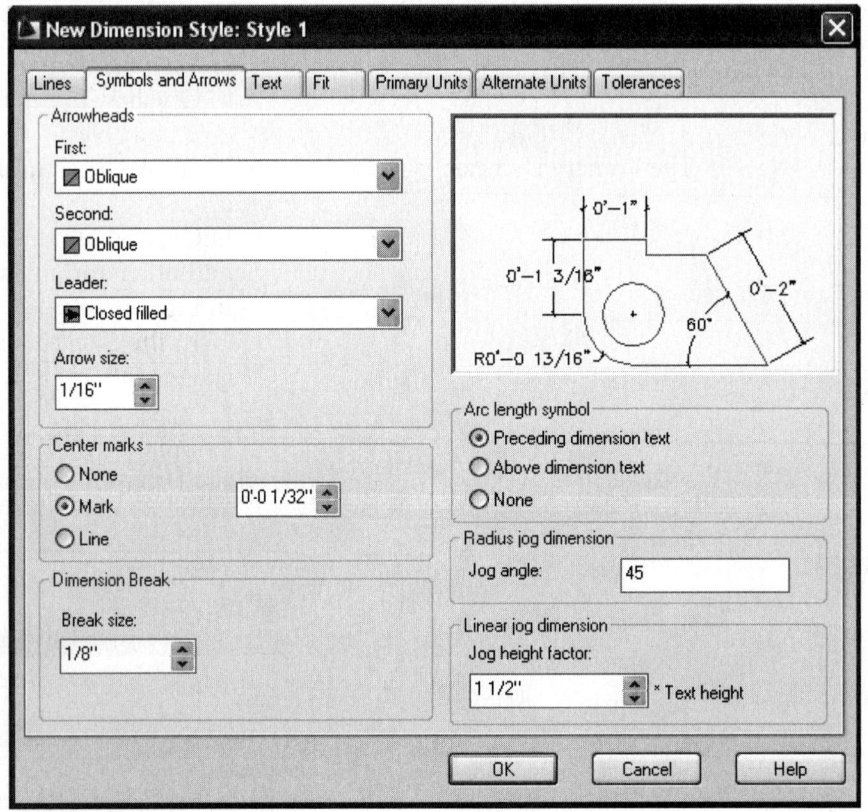

Prompt	Response
The Symbols and Arrows tab is shown:	CLICK: **Oblique** in the Arrowheads First: list SELECT: **1/16″** in the Arrow size: list SELECT: **1/32″** in the Center marks Size: list **Set all other variables for this tab, as shown in Figure 7–9.** CLICK: **the Lines tab** (Figure 7–10)
The Lines tab is shown:	CLICK: **the down arrow so that 1/16″ appears in the Extend beyond dim lines: box in the Extension lines area** CLICK: **the down arrow so that 1/16″ appears in the Extend beyond ticks: box in the Dimension lines area** **Set all other variables for this tab as shown in Figure 7–10** CLICK: **the Text tab**

NOTE: If you want a thicker tick, select Architectural tick in the Arrowheads First: list on the symbols and arrows tab.

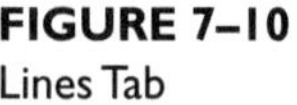

FIGURE 7–10
Lines Tab

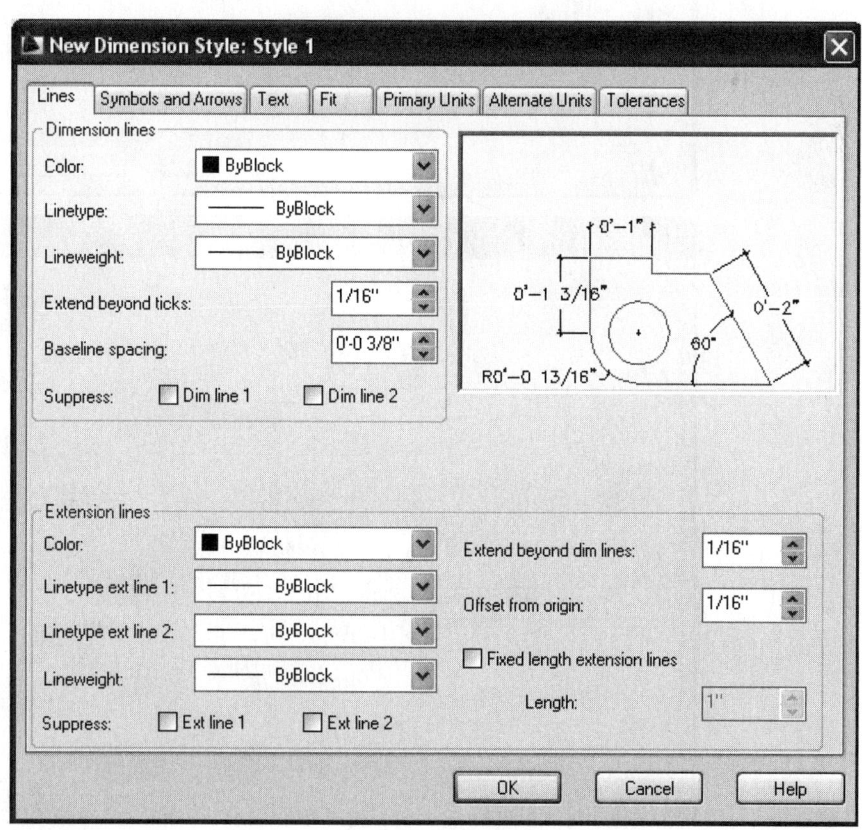

Prompt	Response
The Text tab is shown:	CLICK: **1/16″** in the Text height: box (Figure 7–11) CLICK: **Above** in the Vertical: box of the Text placement area (This places dimension text above the dimension line.) CLICK: **0′-0 1/32″** in the Offset from dim line: box in the Text placement area CLICK: the **Aligned with dimension line** option button in the Text alignment area

FIGURE 7–11
Text Tab and Text Style Dialog Box

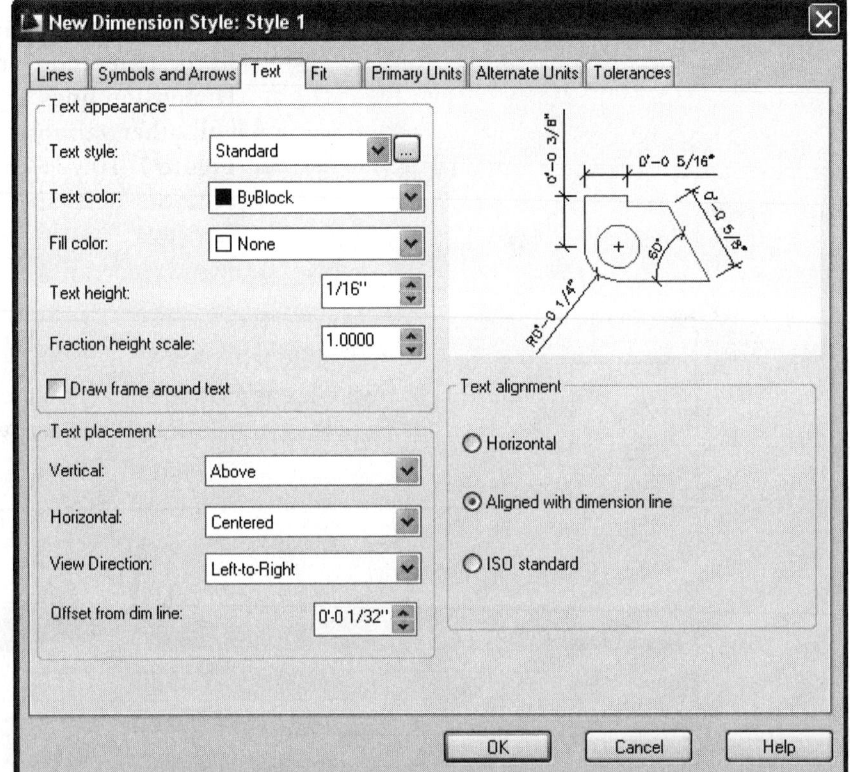

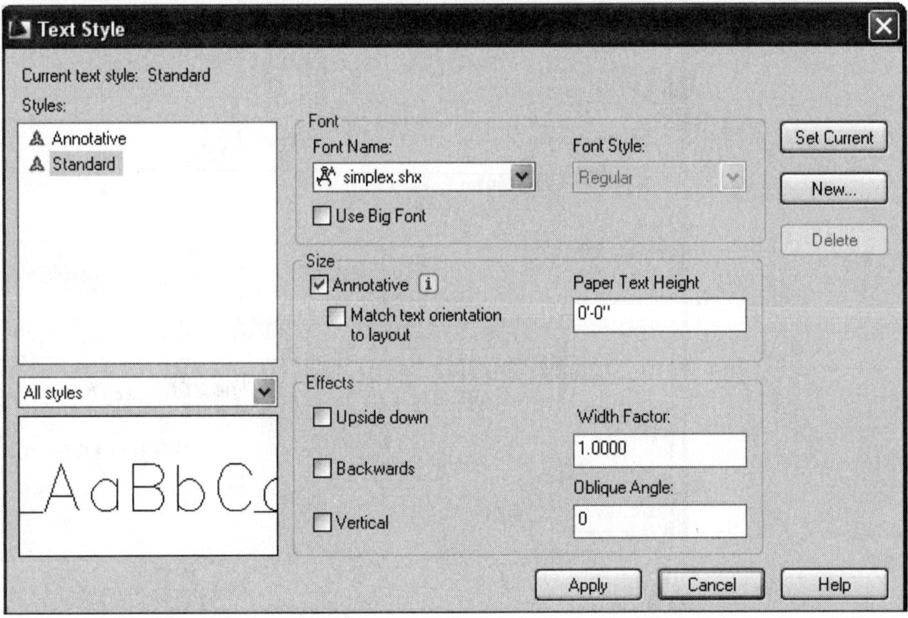

Prompt	Response
	CLICK: **the three dots (ellipsis) to the right of the Standard Text style: input box**
The Text Style dialog box appears:	CLICK: **simplex.shx** in the Font Name: input box
	CLICK: **Apply** and **Close** (or **Cancel** if simplex is already the font)
	Set all other variables for this tab as shown in Figure 7–11.
	CLICK: **the Fit tab**
The Fit tab is shown:	CLICK: the **Either text or arrows (best fit)** option button in the Fit options area (Figure 7–12)
	CLICK: the **Use overall scale of:** option button
	HIGHLIGHT: **the text** in the Use overall scale of: text box and TYPE: **96** (This sets a DIMSCALE of 1/8″ = 1′ [8 × 12] so that all dimensioning variables are multiplied by 96. For example, as you are dimensioning the drawing, the text height, originally set at 1/16″, will actually measure 1/16″ × 96, or 6″. When the layout is created using 1/8″ = 1′ scale, all variables will be the size set originally. For example, text height will be 1/16″ [or 6″ ÷ 96].)
	Set all other variables for this tab as shown in Figure 7–12.
	CLICK: **OK**

FIGURE 7–12
Fit Tab

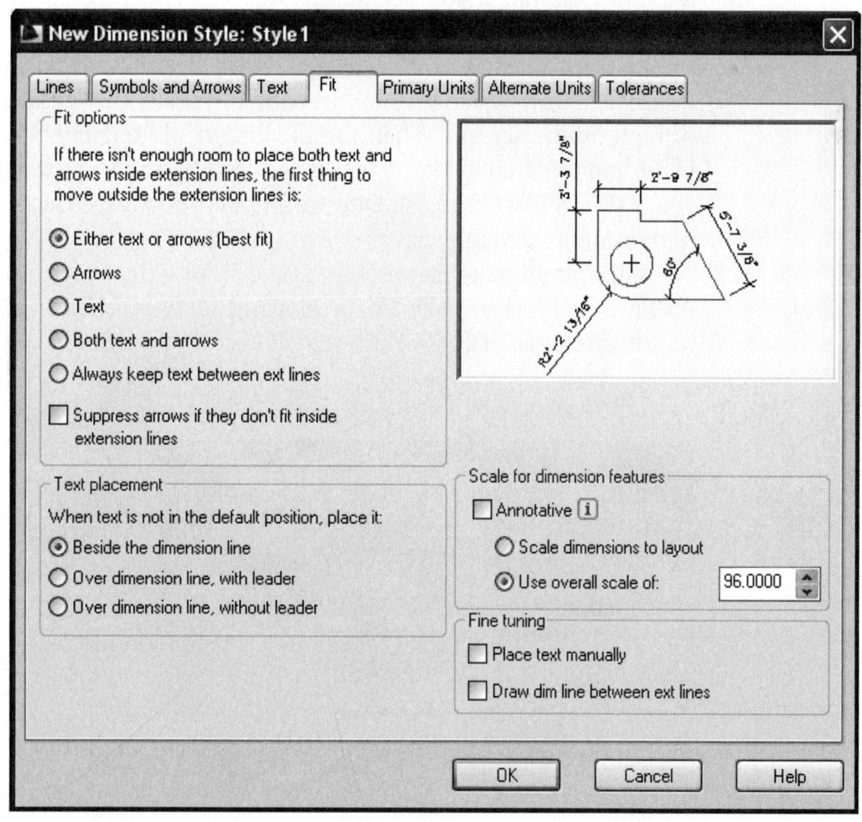

Prompt	Response
The AutoCAD Alert dialog box appears:	CLICK: **OK**
The Dimension Style Manager appears with STYLE1 highlighted:	CLICK: **Set Current** (to set STYLE1 current)
	CLICK: **Close**

FIT TAB—SCALE FOR DIMENSION FEATURES

The preceding section set dimensioning variables that govern the sizes, distances, and spacing of dimensioning elements. It is important to understand how the value that is entered for a variable that governs a size, distance, or spacing of a dimensioning element relates to your drawing as it appears on the screen and when the drawing is plotted. This is controlled by the following settings as shown on the Fit tab in Figure 7–12.

USE OVERALL SCALE OF: (DIMSCALE)

This setting is also referred to as overall scale factor and the variable DIMSCALE. When a drawing such as the tenant space or a large house is drawn full scale, the dimensions that are added to the drawing must also be large. For example, if you want the text of the dimensions to be 1/16″ high when plotted at a scale of 1/8″ = 1′-0″, the text of the dimensions that you add while dimensioning full scale will be 6″ high. DIMSCALE is the variable that controls the overall scale factor, or how the dimensioning parts appear on the screen display while you are drawing full scale and how they appear when plotted. For example, if you decide that the dimensioning text (DIMTXT) will be 1/16″ high when a drawing is plotted, enter 1/16″ for the text height value (DIMTXT). If you plan to plot the drawing at 1/8″ = 1′-0″, set the overall scale factor (DIMSCALE) to 96 (1/8″ = 12, 1 = 96). While you are drawing full scale, the text height will be 1/16″ × 96, or 6″ high on the screen. When the drawing is plotted at 1/8″ = 1′-0″, the entire drawing including the dimensioning text is reduced by a scale factor of 96 (6″ ÷ 96 = 1/16″). If you TYPE: **STATUS** to the Dim: prompt, you will see this setting as DIMSCALE in the dimensioning variable list, as shown in Figure 7–13.

The overall scale factor (DIMSCALE) for a drawing that is plotted at 1/4″ = 12″ is 48 (1/4 = 12, 1 = 48). For a plotting ratio of 1/2″ = 12″, the overall scale factor (DIMSCALE) is 24 (1/2 = 12, 1 = 24).

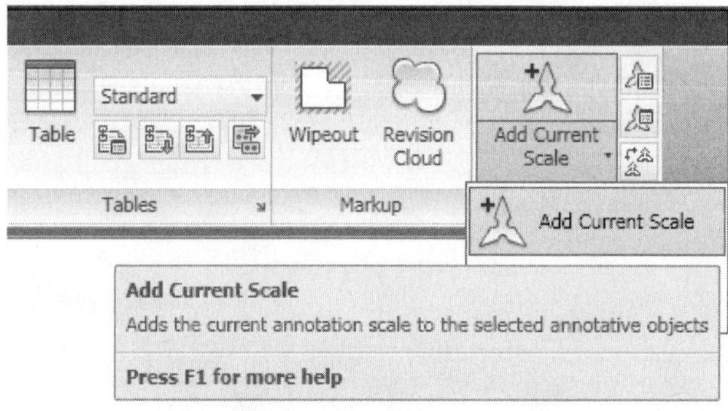

DIMASO	Off	Create dimension objects
DIMSTYLE	Style1	Current dimension style (read-only)
DIMADEC	0	Angular decimal places
DIMALT	Off	Alternate units selected
DIMALTD	2	Alternate unit decimal places
DIMALTF	25.40000	Alternate unit scale factor
DIMALTMZF	8'-4"	Alternate sub-zero factor for metric dimensions
DIMALTMZS		Alternate sub-zero suffix for metric dimensions
DIMALTRND	0"	Alternate units rounding value
DIMALTTD	2	Alternate tolerance decimal places
DIMALTTZ	0	Alternate tolerance zero suppression
DIMALTU	2	Alternate units
DIMALTZ	0	Alternate unit zero suppression
DIMAPOST		Prefix and suffix for alternate text
DIMARCSYM	0	Arc length symbol
DIMASZ	1/16"	Arrow size
DIMATFIT	3	Arrow and text fit
DIMAUNIT	0	Angular unit format
DIMAZIN	0	Angular zero suppression
DIMBLK	Oblique	Arrow block name
DIMBLK1	ClosedFilled	First arrow block name
DIMBLK2	ClosedFilled	Second arrow block name
DIMCEN	0"	Center mark size
DIMCLRD	BYBLOCK	Dimension line and leader color
DIMCLRE	BYBLOCK	Extension line color
DIMCLRT	BYBLOCK	Dimension text color
DIMDEC	1	Decimal places
DIMDLE	1/16"	Dimension line extension
DIMDLI	3/8"	Dimension line spacing
DIMDSEP	.	Decimal separator
DIMEXE	1/16"	Extension above dimension line
DIMEXO	1/16	Extension line origin offset
DIMFRAC	2	Fraction format
DIMFXL	1"	Fixed Extension Line
DIMFXLON	Off	Enable Fixed Extension Line
DIMGAP	1/32"	Gap from dimension line to text
DIMJOGANG	45	Radius dimension jog angle
DIMJUST	0	Justification of text on dim line
DIMLDRBLK	ClosedFilled	Leader block name
DIMLFAC	1.00000	Linear unit scale factor
DIMLIM	Off	Generate dimension limits
DIMLTEX1	BYBLOCK	Linetype extension line 1
DIMLTEX2	BYBLOCK	Linetype extension line 2
DIMLTYPE	BYBLOCK	Dimension linetype
DIMLUNIT	4	Linear unit format
DIMLWD	-2	Dimension line-leader lineweight
DIMLWE	-2	Extension line lineweight
DIMMZF	8'-4"	Sub zero factor for metric dimensions
DIMMZS		Sub zero suffix for metric dimensions
DIMPOST		Prefix and suffix for dimension text
DIMRND	0"	Rounding value
DIMSAH	Off	Separate arrow blocks
DIMSCALE	96.00000	Overall scale factor
DIMSD1	Off	Suppress the first dimension line
DIMSD2	Off	Suppress the second dimension line
DIMSE1	Off	Suppress the first extension line
DIMSE2	Off	Suppress the second extension line
DIMSOXD	Off	Suppress outside dimension lines
DIMTAD	1	Place text above the dimension line
DIMTDEC	1	Tolerance decimal places
DIMTFAC	1.00000	Tolerance text height scaling factor
DIMTFILL	0	Text background enabled
DIMTFILLCLR	BYBLOCK	Text background color
DIMTIH	Off	Text inside extensions is horizontal
DIMTIX	Off	Place text inside extensions
DIMTM	0"	Minus tolerance
DIMTMOVE	0	Text movement
DIMTOFL	Off	Force line inside extension lines
DIMTOH	Off	Text outside horizontal
DIMTOL	Off	Tolerance dimensioning
DIMTOLJ	1	Tolerance vertical justification
DIMTP	0"	Plus tolerance
DIMTSZ	0"	Tick size
DIMTVP	0.00000	Text vertical position
DIMTXSTY	Standard	Text style
DIMTXT	1/16"	Text height
DIMTXTDIRECTION	Off	Dimension text direction
DIMTZIN	0	Tolerance zero suppression
DIMUPT	Off	User positioned text
DIMZIN	1	Zero suppression

FIGURE 7–13
Dimensioning Variables with DIMSCALE Set to 96

ANNOTATIVE

When you make the dimensioning annotative and set the annotation scale of the drawing, AutoCAD automatically does the overall scale factor arithmetic for you and controls how the dimensioning looks on your screen. When adding the dimensioning, you have to enter only the size of the text and other variables you want in the plotted drawing, and AutoCAD automatically calculates the size of the text on the drawing using the annotative scale setting.

You have two places where you can make the dimensions annotative. If the Annotative box is checked on the Fit tab, the dimensions are annotative, and the "Scale dimensions to layout" and "Use overall scale of:" options are grayed out. If you select the Annotative style when the Dimension Style Manager dialog box is first opened, these two selections are grayed out also. When the dimensioning is annotative, DIMSCALE is set to 0.

When the dimensioning is annotative, the annotation scale controls how the text and other annotative objects appear on the drawing. You must set the Annotation Scale, located in the lower right corner of the Status Bar.

If you have annotative objects on your drawing and have set the annotation scale, it is usually best to plot your drawing at the same scale as the annotation scale that you have set. If there are no annotative objects on your drawing, the annotation scale does not affect anything. If the plot scale and the annotation scale differ, when the plot is initiated, AutoCAD prompts you with "The annotation scale is not equal to the plot scale. Do you wish to Continue?" You can answer with "OK" or "Cancel."

You can change the annotation scale of an annotative object. In the Status Bar, if you hold your mouse over the icon that is near the Annotation Scale input area, the tooltip will display, "Automatically add scales to annotative objects when the annotation scale changes." When this icon is on and the annotation scale is changed, the annotative objects change on the screen to reflect the new scale size, and the object then supports two scales. You can see the new scales by clicking on the object, the current scale is highlighted, and the scale size that is not current will show as dimmed. You can also use the Annotative Object Scale command in the Modify window to add or delete a current scale or any of the scales you have added to the annotative object.

You can select the object and use the Properties command to change the annotative scale of an object or use the Properties command to change an object that is not annotative, to annotative.

If you hold your mouse over a second icon that is near the Annotation Scale input area, the tooltip will display, "Annotation Visibility: Show annotative objects for all scales." When you have annotative objects on your drawing that support different scales, this icon controls their visibility. When it is off, only the annotative objects with the current annotation scale are visible.

SUMMARY OF DIMSCALE AND ANNOTATION SCALE

1. **Set dimensioning variables to the size you want on the printed page.** For example: Text height: 1/16″ (DIMTXT) and all other variables proportional to 1/16″.
2. If the dimension style **IS NOT** annotative: **Set DIMSCALE to the ratio of the full-size drawing compared to the printed page.** If you plan to plot at:

   1/8″ = 1′-0″ set DIMSCALE to 96.
   Dimension text (and all other dimensioning variables) on the drawing is multiplied by 96, so that the text height on the full-size drawing becomes 1/16″ × 96 or 6″.

   1/4″ = 1′-0″ set DIMSCALE to 48.
   Dimension text (and all other dimensioning variables) on the drawing is multiplied by 48, so that the text height on the full-size drawing becomes 1/16″ × 48 or 3″.

   1/2″ = 1′-0″ set DIMSCALE to 24.
   Dimension text (and all other dimensioning variables) on the drawing is multiplied by 24, so that the text height on the full-size drawing becomes 1/16″ × 24 or 1-1/2″.

3. If the dimension style **IS** annotative: DIMSCALE is automatically set to 0, and the annotative scale acts the same as DIMSCALE. If you plan to plot at:

   1/8″ = 1′-0″ set ANNOTATION SCALE to 1/8″ = 1′-0″.
   Dimension text (and all other dimensioning variables, all other annotative text and other annotative objects) on the drawing is multiplied by 96, so that the text height on the full-size drawing becomes 1/16″ × 96 or 6″.

1/4″ = 1′-0″ set ANNOTATION SCALE to 1/4″ = 1′-0″.
Text height on the full-size drawing becomes 3″.
1/2″ = 1′-0″ set ANNOTATION SCALE to 1/2″ = 1′-0″.
Text height on the full-size drawing becomes 1-1/2″.

NOTE: Start a drawing, set the dimensioning variables, and save the drawing as a template for future dimensioning projects.

Step 5. **Set Layer a-anno-dims current.**

Step 6. **Use Zoom-All to view the entire drawing.**

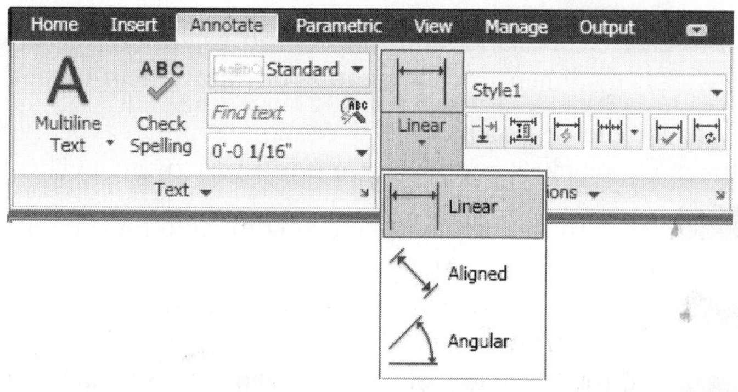

LINEAR AND CONTINUE DIMENSIONING

Step 7. **Using Linear, dimension the column and one mullion on the north exterior wall of the tenant space floor plan (Figure 7–14), as described next:**

Prompt	Response
Command:	**Linear** (or Type: **HOR<enter>** from the Dim: prompt)
Specify first extension line origin or <select object>:	**D1** (with Snap ON)
Specify second extension line origin:	**D2**
Specify dimension line location or [Mtext/Text/Angle/Horizontal/Vertical/Rotated]:	**D3** (on snap, three grid marks up, with 12″ grid)
Command:	**<enter>** (repeat **Linear**)
Specify first extension line origin or <select object>:	**OSNAP-Intersection**
of	**D4**
Specify second extension line origin:	**OSNAP-Intersection**
of	**D5**

FIGURE 7–14
Linear Dimensioning

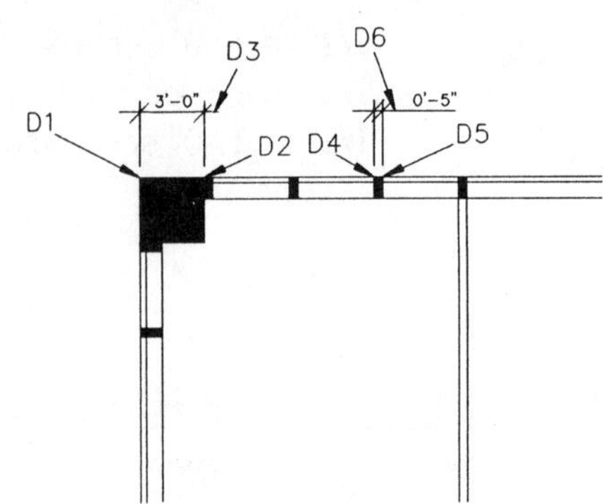

Prompt	Response
Specify dimension line location or [Mtext/Text/Angle/Horizontal/ Vertical/Rotated]:	**D6** (on snap, three grid marks up)

In the Linear command, after the second extension line origin is selected, the prompt reads: Specify dimension line location or [Mtext/Text/Angle/Horizontal/Vertical/Rotated]:

Before you pick a dimension line location, you may type the first letter of any of the options in the brackets and press **<enter>** to activate it. These options are as follows:

Mtext To activate the multiline text command for dimensions requiring more than one line of text.
Text To replace the default text with a single line of text. To suppress the text entirely, press the space bar.
Angle To rotate the text of the dimension to a specific angle.
Horizontal To specify that you want a horizontal dimension; this is normally not necessary.
Vertical To specify that you want a vertical dimension; this is normally not necessary.
Rotated To specify that you want to rotate the entire dimension.

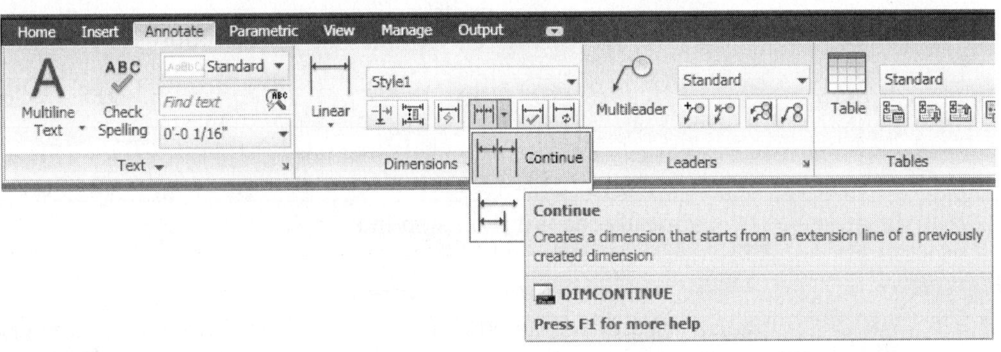

Step 8. **Using Linear and Continue, dimension horizontally (center to center) the distance between four mullions on the north exterior wall of the tenant space (Figure 7–15), as described next. (Before continuing, Zoom in or Pan over to the four mullions to be dimensioned.)**

FIGURE 7–15
Linear Dimensioning with the Continue Command to Draw Horizontal Dimensions

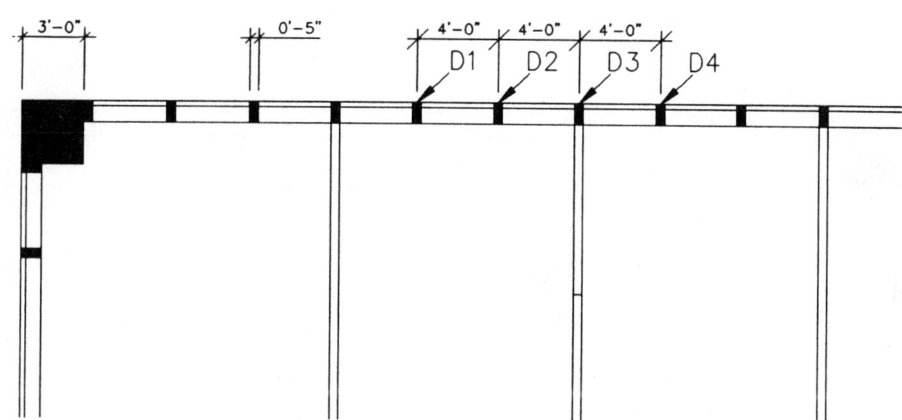

Prompt	Response
Command:	**Linear** (from the Dimensions panel)
Specify first extension line origin or <select object>:	**OSNAP-Midpoint**
of	**D1**
Specify second extension line origin:	**OSNAP-Midpoint**
of	**D2**
Specify dimension line location or [Mtext/Text/Angle/Horizontal/Vertical/Rotated]:	CLICK: **a point on snap, three grid marks up, to align with previous dimensions.**
Command:	**Continue** (from the Dimension menu)
Specify a second extension line origin or [Undo/Select]<Select>:	**OSNAP-Midpoint**
of	**D3**
Specify a second extension line origin or [Undo/Select]<Select>:	**OSNAP-Midpoint**
of	**D4**
Specify a second extension origin or [Undo/Select]<Select>:	**<enter>**
Select continued dimension:	**<enter>** (to complete the command)

NOTE: You may change the dimension string at the prompt "Specify dimension line location," by typing **T<enter>**, then typing new dimensions from the keyboard and pressing **<enter>**.

Step 9. **Using Linear and Continue, dimension vertically (center to center) the distance between four mullions on the west exterior wall of the tenant space (Figure 7–16), as described next. (Before continuing, Zoom in on the four mullions to be dimensioned.)**

Prompt	Response
Command:	**Linear** (or TYPE: **VER<enter>** from the Dim: prompt)

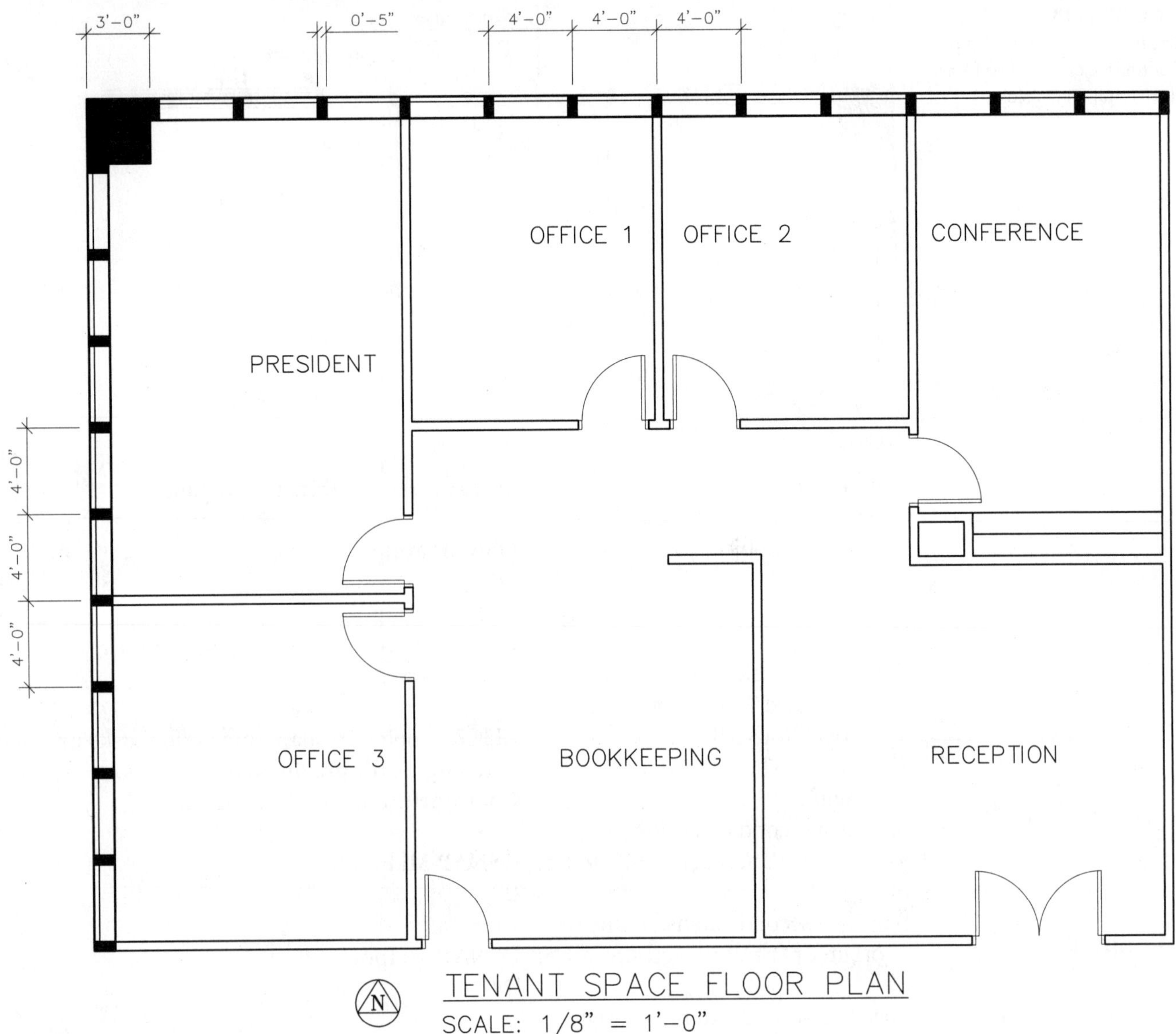

FIGURE 7–16
Linear Dimensioning with the Continue Command to Draw Vertical Dimensions (Scale: 1/8" = 1'-0")

Prompt	Response
Specify first extension line origin or <select object>:	**OSNAP-Midpoint**
of	CLICK: **the first mullion** (Dimension south to north)
Specify second extension line origin:	**OSNAP-Midpoint**
of	PICK: **the second mullion**
Specify dimension line location or [Mtext/Text/Angle/Horizontal/Vertical/Rotated]:	PICK: **a point on snap, three grid marks to the left, similar to previous dimension line locations**
Command:	**Continue** (on the Dimensions panel)
Specify a second extension line origin or [Undo/Select]<Select>:	**OSNAP-Midpoint**

Prompt	Response
of	PICK: **the third mullion**
Specify a second extension line origin or [Undo/Select]<Select>:	**OSNAP-Midpoint**
of	PICK: **the fourth mullion**
Specify a second extension line origin or [Undo/Select]<Select>:	**<enter>**
Select continued dimension:	**<enter>**

TIP: Use Osnap commands to select extension line origins. Set a running Osnap mode.

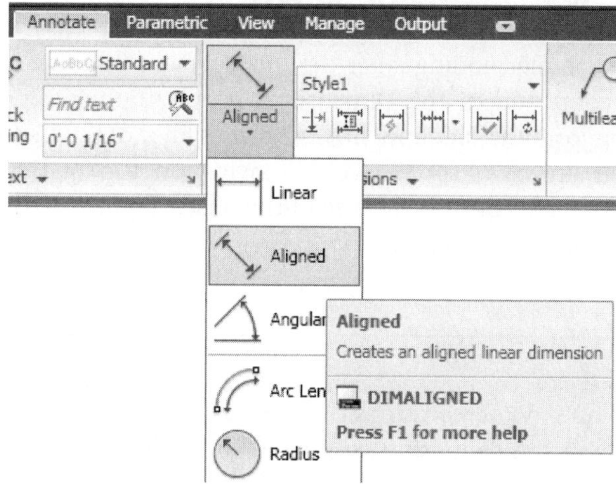

ALIGNED DIMENSIONING

When Aligned is used, you can select the first and second extension line origin points of a line that is at an angle, and the dimension line will run parallel to the origin points. Figure 7–17 shows an example of aligned dimensioning.

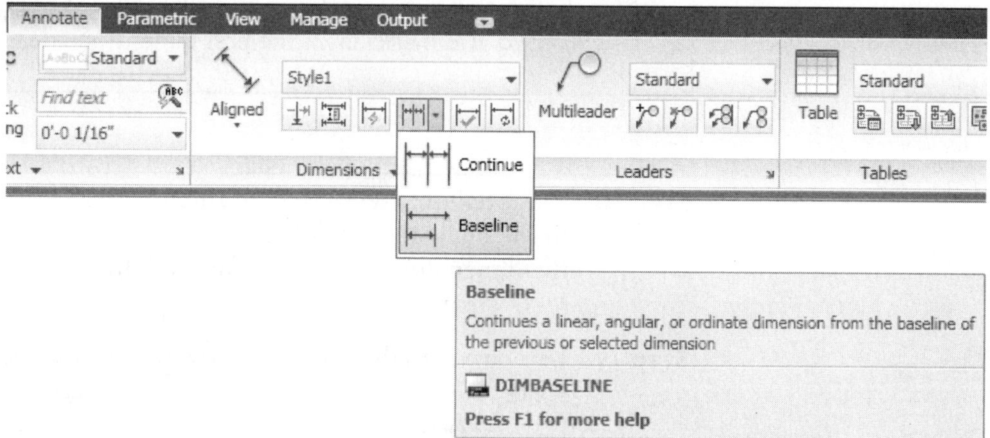

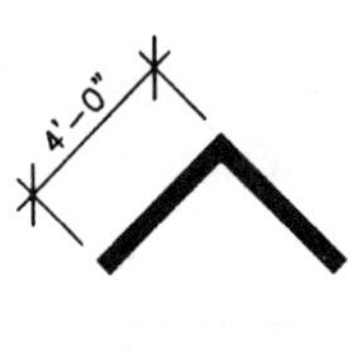

FIGURE 7–17
Dimensioning with the Aligned Command

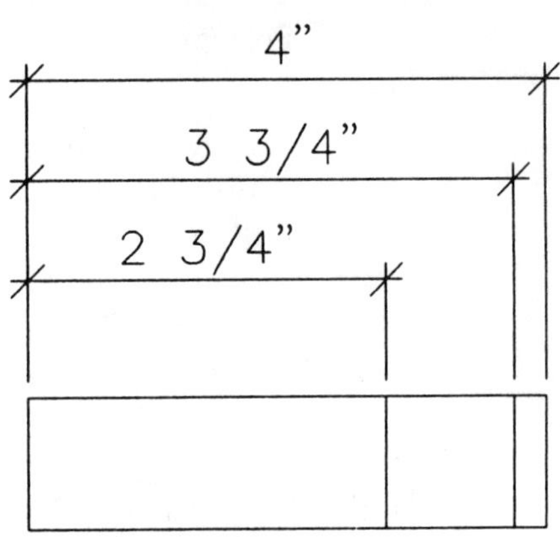

FIGURE 7–18
Linear Dimensioning with the Baseline Command

BASELINE DIMENSIONING

With linear dimensioning, after the first segment of a line is dimensioned, picking the Baseline command in the Dimensions panel automatically continues the next linear dimension from the baseline (first extension line) of the first linear dimension. The new dimension line is offset to avoid drawing on top of the previous dimension. The DIMDLI variable controls the size of the offset. Figure 7–18 shows linear dimensioning with the Baseline command.

CAUTION: When erasing construction lines, avoid selecting definition points; otherwise, the dimension associated with that point will be erased.

NOTE: When stacking dimension lines, locate the first dimension line farther from the object being dimensioned than subsequent dimension lines are from each other. For example, locate the first dimension line three grid marks from the object and the second dimension line two grid marks from the first dimension line.

Step 10. **Use Dtext, centered, to add the text "12 TYP. SPACES @ 4′-0″ = 48′-0″ to the plan (Figure 7–19). Place it two grid marks (on a 12″ grid) above the dimension line of the mullions dimension. Set the text height to 1/16″ (text is annotative).**

Step 11. **Use Linear to dimension the overall north exterior wall of the tenant space. You may snap to the tick (intersection) of a previous dimension (Figure 7–19).**

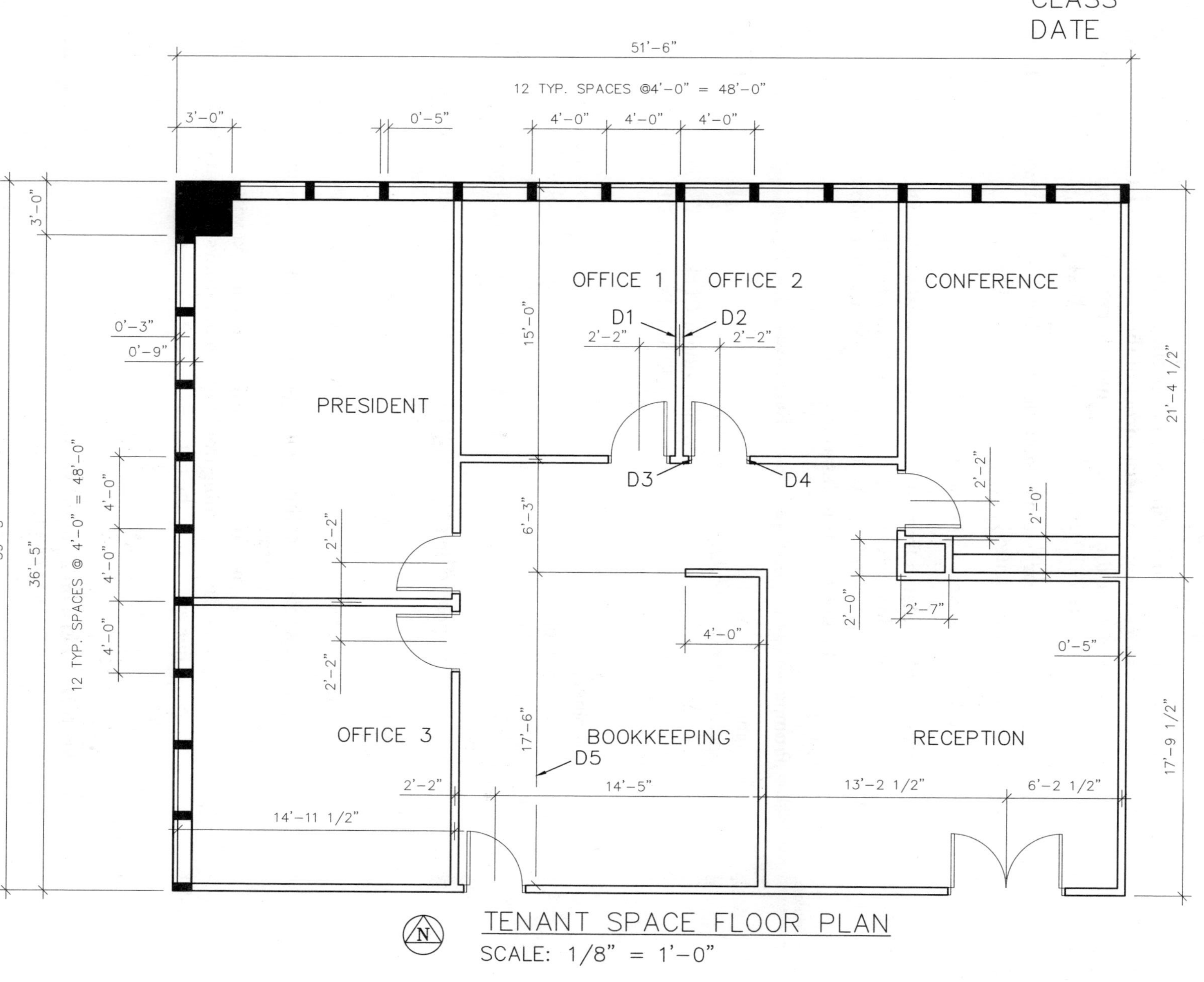

FIGURE 7–19
Tutorial 7–1 Complete (Scale: 1/8" = 1'-0")

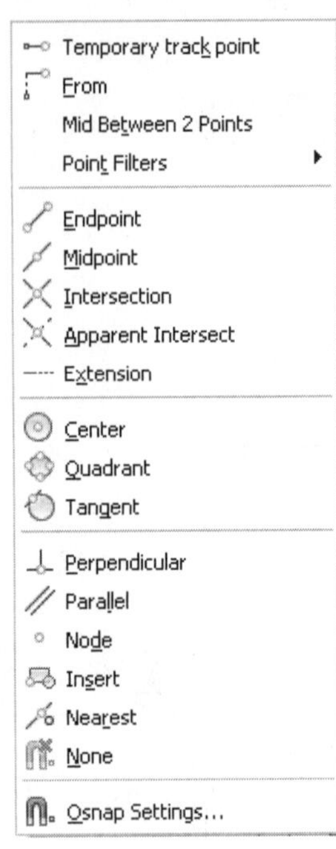

Step 12. Use Dtext, centered, to add the text "9 TYP. SPACES @ 4′-0″ = 36′-0″ to the plan (Figure 7–19). Place it two grid marks (on a 12″ grid) above the dimension line of the mullions dimension. Set the text height to 1/16″.

Step 13. Use Linear to dimension from the southwest corner of the tenant space to the southern corner of the column. Use Continue to continue the dimension to the outside northwest corner of the building (Figure 7–19).

Step 14. Use Linear to dimension the overall west exterior wall of the tenant space (Figure 7–19).

Step 15. Set a running Osnap mode of Nearest.

Step 16. Dimension from the middle of the west wall of Office 2 to the center of the door in Office 2. Use the Shift key and right-click to get the Osnap menu and PICK: "Mid Between 2 Points" to complete the dimension (Figure 7–19), as described next:

Prompt	Response
Command:	**Linear**
Specify first extension line origin or <select object>:	**Shift-Right Click** CLICK: **Mid Between 2 Points**
Specify first extension line origin or <select object>: _m2p First point of mid:	CLICK: **D1 (left side of wall symbol)**
Second point of mid:	CLICK: **D2 (right side of wall symbol)**
Specify second extension line origin:	**Shift-Right Click** CLICK: **Mid Between 2 Points**
Specify second extension line origin: _m2p First point of mid:	CLICK: **D3** (left side of door opening)
Second point of mid:	CLICK: **D4** (right side of second wall)
Specify dimension line location or [Mtext/Text/Angle/Horizontal/Vertical/Rotated]:	PICK: **a point to locate the dimension**

Step 17. Complete the dimensioning using the Linear dimension commands and the appropriate Osnap modifiers. When you are dimensioning from left to right, any outside dimension line and text will be placed to the right. Dimensioning from right to left draws any outside dimension line and text to the left.

BREAK

Step 18. Add a break in the vertical dimension line in the Bookkeeping Area that crosses over another dimension line, as described next, Figure 7–19:

Prompt	Response
Command:	**Break** (or TYPE: **DIMBREAK<enter>**)
Select dimension to add/remove break or [Multiple]:	**D5** (Figure 7–19)

Prompt	Response
Select object to break dimension or [Auto/Manual/Remove]<Auto>:	**<enter>**
1 object modified	
The break is added	

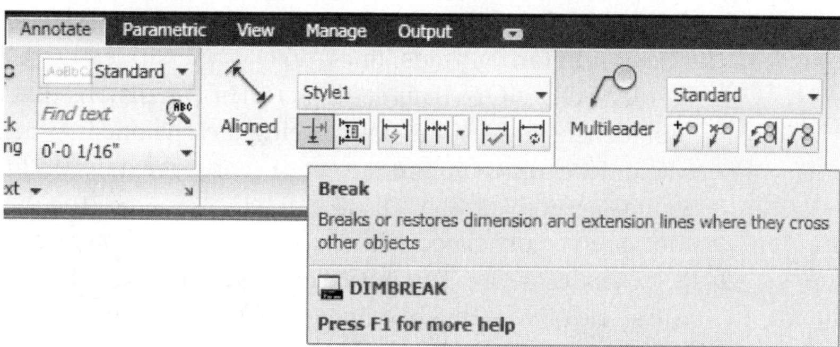

A break can be added to a dimension line, extension line, or to a multileader (described in Chapter 8).

Multiple Allows you to select more than one dimension line that you want to break.
Manual Allows you to pick the first and second break point for the break.
Remove Allows you to select the dimension and remove the break from that dimension.

ADJUST SPACE

Adjust Space (DIMSPACE) is used to make the spacing between parallel dimension lines equal. This command asks you to select a base dimension—the dimension you do not want to move. The command then asks you to select dimensions that are parallel to the base dimension and that you want to space equally. You can then enter a distance (for example, 24″), or you can press **<enter>** and the dimensions will be automatically spaced—the automatic space is twice the height of the dimension text.

If you have a series of dimensions that you want to align, enter a 0 for the spacing value, and they will align.

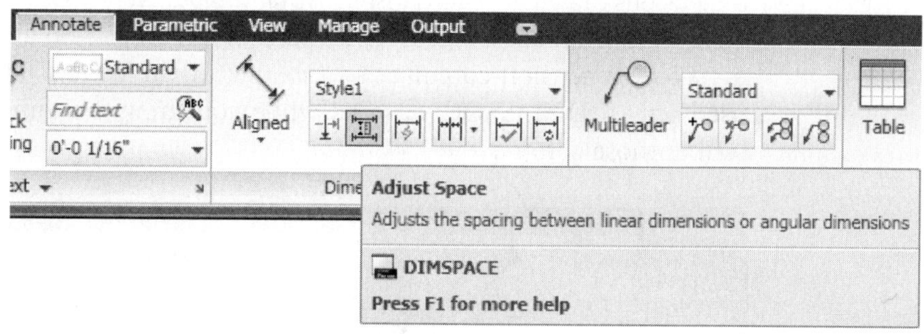

Step 19. **Move your name, class, and date outside any dimension lines, if needed.**

Step 20. **When you have completed Tutorial 7–1, save your work in at least two places.**

Step 21. **Print Tutorial 7–1 from the Model tab at a scale of 1/8″ = 1′-0″.**

Tutorial 7–2: Revisions and Modifying Dimensions

DIMASSOC SYSTEM VARIABLE

This setting is not one of the dimensioning variables and is not stored in a dimension style, but it does affect how dimensions behave in relation to the object being dimensioned. It has three states:

0 DIMASSOC is OFF. This setting creates exploded dimensions. Each part of the dimension (arrowheads, lines, text) is a separate object.

1 DIMASSOC is ON. This setting creates dimensions that are single objects but are not associated with the object being dimensioned. When the dimension is created, definition points are formed (at the ends of extension lines, for example). If these points are moved, as with the Stretch command, the dimension changes, but it is not directly associated with the object being dimensioned.

2 DIMASSOC is ON. This setting creates associative dimension objects. The dimensions are single objects, and one or more of the definition points on the dimension are linked to association points on the object. When the association point on the object moves, the dimension location, orientation, and text value of the dimension change. For example: Check DIMASSOC to make sure the setting is 2 (TYPE: DIMASSOC<enter>. If the value is not 2, TYPE: 2<enter>). Draw a 2″ circle and dimension it using the diameter dimensioning command. With no command active, CLICK: any point on the circle so that grips appear at the quadrants of the circle. CLICK: any grip to make it hot and move the grip. The dimension changes as the size of the circle changes.

Tutorial 7–2 describes commands that can be used to modify dimensions and how to make a revision cloud. When you have completed Tutorial 7–2, your drawing will look similar to Figure 7–20.

Step 1. Open drawing CH7-TUTORIAL1 and save it as CH7-TUTORIAL2 to the hard drive or network drive.

ASSOCIATIVE DIMENSION COMMANDS

When the DIMASSOC variable is on, each dimension that is drawn is created as a block. That means that the extension lines, dimension lines, ticks or arrows, text, and all other parts of the dimensions are entered as a single object. When DIMASSOC is ON and set to 2, the dimensions drawn are called *associative dimensions.* When DIMASSOC is OFF, the extension lines, dimension lines, and all other parts of the dimension are drawn as separate entities.

Four dimension commands—Oblique, Align Text, Override, and Update—can be used only if DIMASSOC was ON while you drew the dimensions. The following describes those commands.

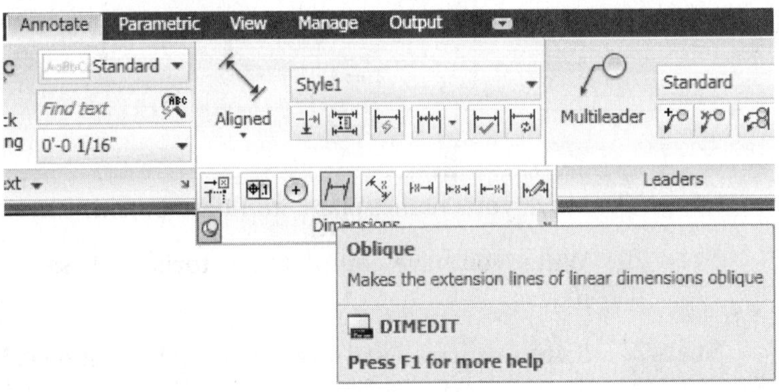

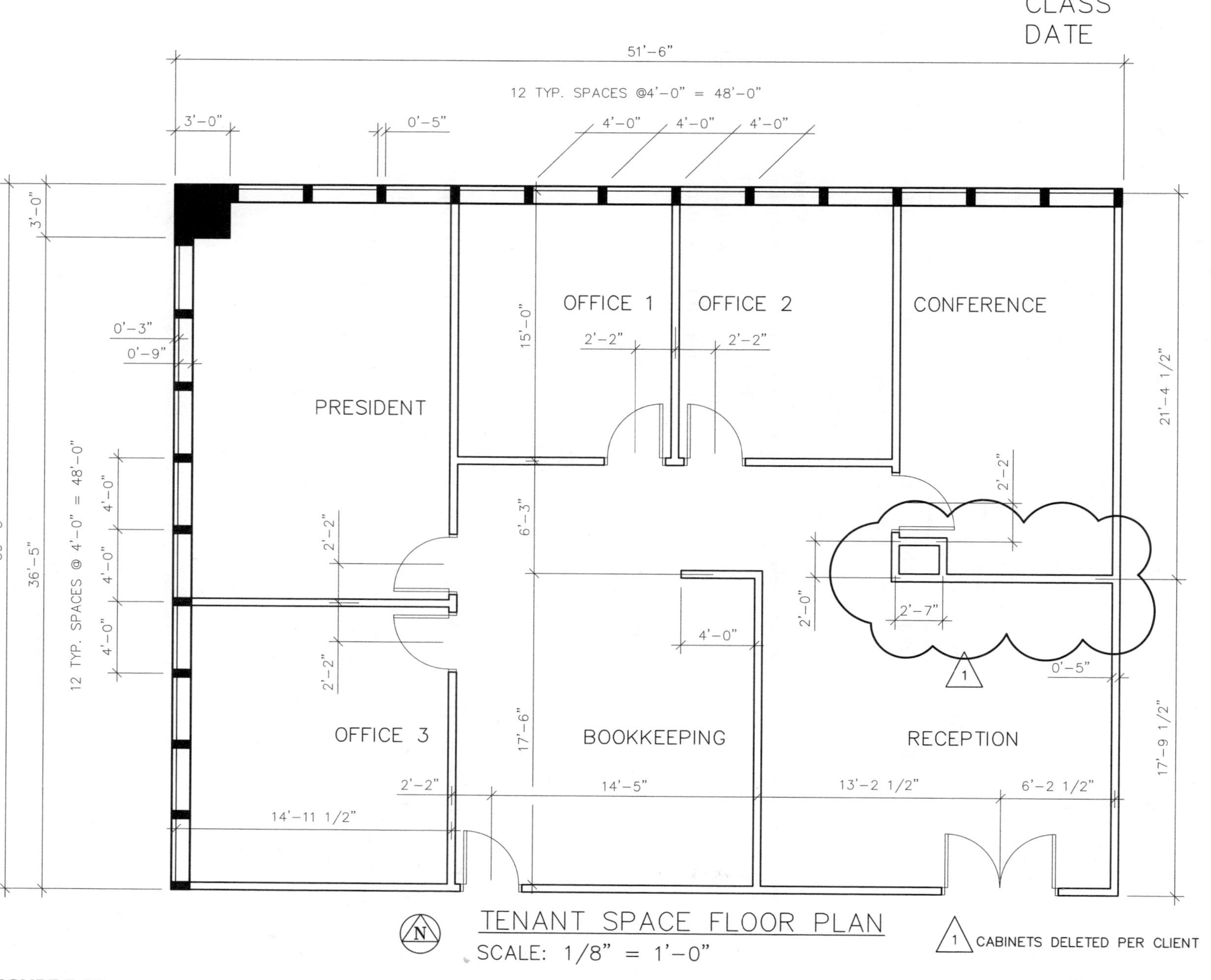

FIGURE 7–20
Tutorial 7–2 Complete (Scale: 1/8" = 1'-0")

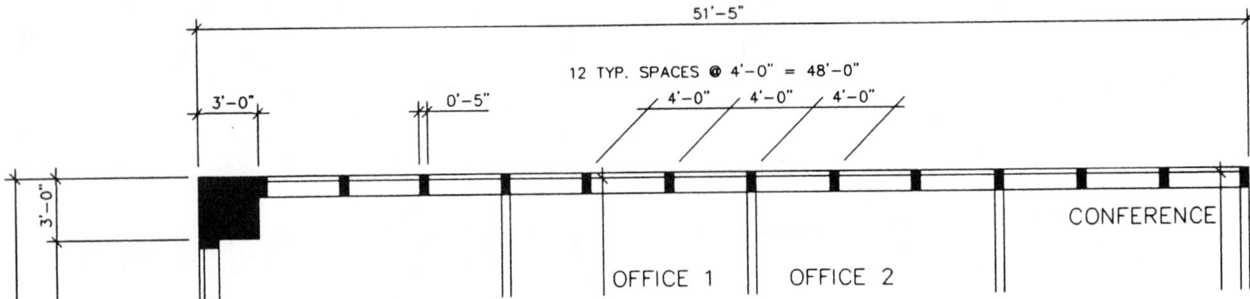

FIGURE 7–21
Using the Oblique Command

OBLIQUE

Step 2. **Create an oblique angle for the extension lines of the four mullions on the north exterior wall of the tenant space (Figure 7–21), as described next:**

Prompt	Response
Command:	**Oblique** (or TYPE: **OB<enter>** from the Dim: prompt)
Select objects:	PICK: **the extension lines of the mullion dimensions on the north exterior wall until they are all highlighted.**
Select objects:	**<enter>**
Enter obliquing angle (press <enter> for none):	TYPE: **45<enter>**
The extension lines of the mullion dimensions appear as shown in Figure 7–21.	

ALIGN TEXT-HOME-ANGLE-LEFT-CENTER-RIGHT

Step 3. **Change the placement of the text for the overall dimension on the west exterior wall of the tenant space to flush right, and return it to the center position, as described next:**

Prompt	Response
Command:	**Right Justify**
Select dimension:	PICK: **the dimension text, 39′-5″**

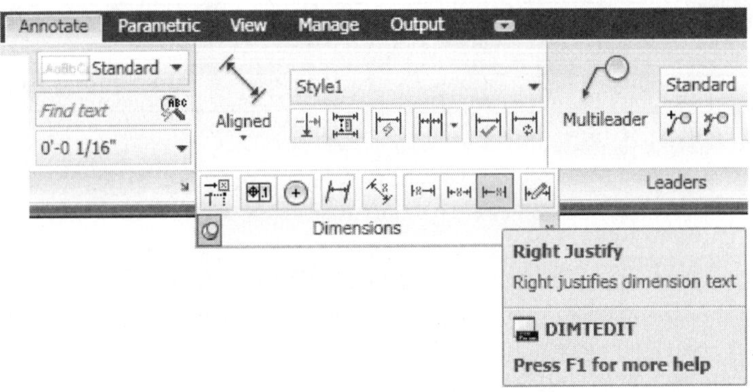

Prompt	Response
The text moves to the right side of the dimension line (if the dimension line was drawn bottom to top, the dimension moves to the bottom).	
Command:	**Center Justify**
Select objects:	PICK: **the same dimension<enter>**
The text moves back to the center of the dimension line.	

The Left option left justifies the text along the dimension line. The Angle option allows you either to type a new text angle (and PRESS: **<enter>**) or to pick two points to show AutoCAD the new text angle. The Home option returns the dimension text to its home position.

OVERRIDE

The Override command is helpful when you are in the middle of dimensioning a project or have completed dimensioning a project and decide that one or more of the dimension variables in a named style need to be changed. The Override command can be used to change one or more dimension variables for selected dimensions but does not affect the current dimension style.

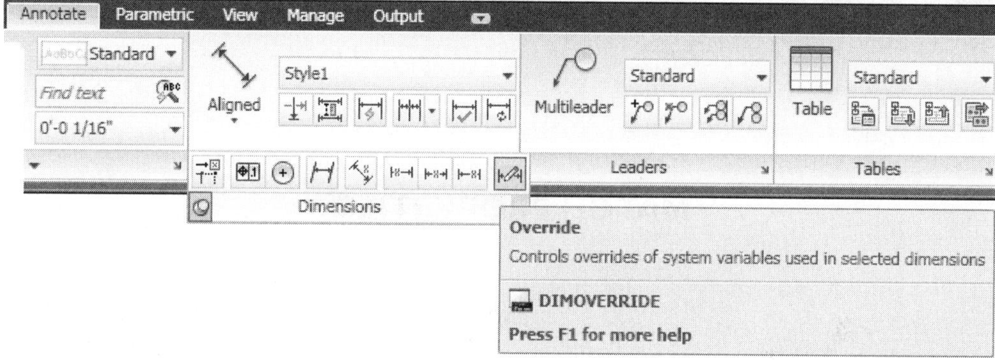

UPDATE

Update differs from Override in that it updates dimensions using the current settings of the dimension style. For example, if you decide a dimension variable needs to be changed in a dimension style, change the variable. You may click the Save button in the Dimension Styles dialog box to save the changed variable to the dimension style. If you do not save the changed variable, AutoCAD prompts you with an ALERT dialog box, "Save changes to current style?" when you change dimension styles. Use Update to include the new variable settings in all or part of the dimensions within the drawing.

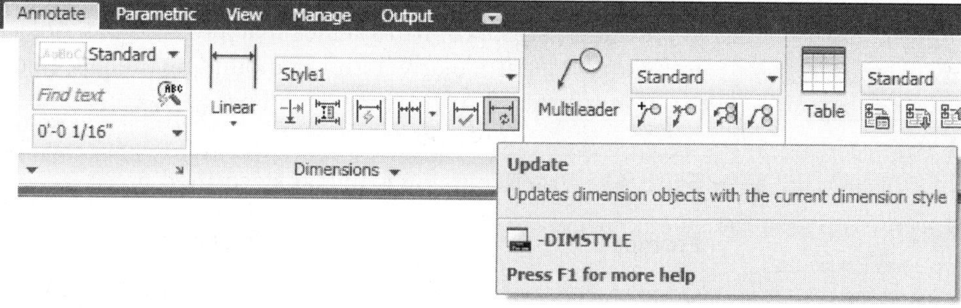

DEFPOINTS LAYER

When DIMASSOC is on, a special layer named Defpoints is also created. Definition points for dimensions are drawn on the Defpoints Layer. They are small points on the drawing that are not plotted but are used to create the dimension. When the dimension is updated or edited, the definition points are redefined.

PROPERTIES

The Properties command can be used to change the properties of any dimension, as shown in Figure 7–22. Begin by selecting the dimension to be modified, then CLICK: **Properties** from the Modify menu on the Ribbon, or RIGHT-CLICK and CLICK: **Properties**. The Properties palette appears. Clicking the arrows to the right of the Property group displays a list of those items that can be changed. To change dimension text, CLICK: **Text override** (below **Measure...**) and TYPE: **the new text** in the box to the right.

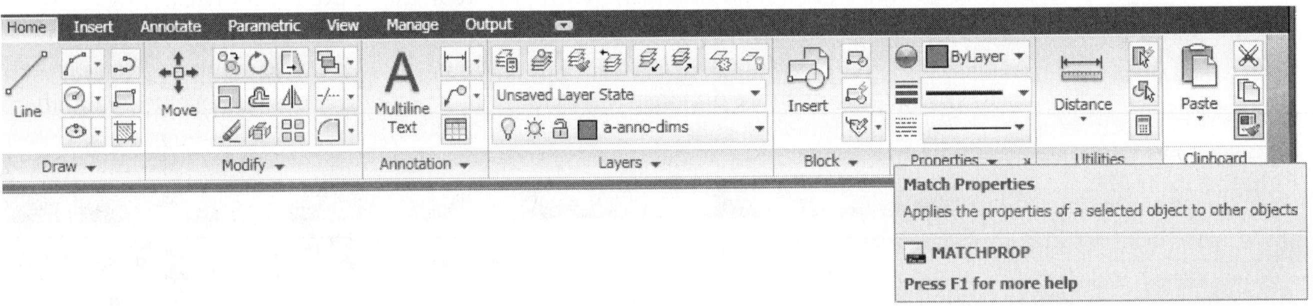

Text	
Fill color	None
Fraction...	Not stacked
Text color	■ ByBlock
Text hei...	0'-0 1/16"
Text offset	0'-0 1/32"
Text out...	On
Text pos...	Centered
Text pos...	Above
Text style	Standard
Text insi...	On
Text pos...	30'-7 27/32"
Text pos...	54'-6 9/16"
Text rot...	0
Text vie...	Left-to-Right
Measure...	0'-5"
Text ov...	
Fit	

FIGURE 7–22
Use the Properties Palette to Change Dimension Text

MATCH PROPERTIES

When the Match Properties command is selected, or **MATCHPROP** is typed and entered at the Command: prompt, the prompt is "Select source object:". At that prompt you can select the dimension whose properties you want to copy, and a paintbrush is attached to the cursor. The prompt changes to "Select destination object(s) or [Settings]:", and you can then select the dimension to which you want to copy the properties.

When you type and enter the Settings option to the Match Properties: prompt, the Property Settings dialog box is displayed. Properties that can be copied are shown in the Property Settings dialog box. By default, all properties are selected and show a check in the box beside the property name. You can copy some or all of the properties of a dimension. If you do not want a property copied, suppress that property in the Property Settings dialog box.

GRIPS

Grips are small, solid-filled squares that appear on an object when you click on the object. Grips are particularly useful in modifying the placement of dimension text and the location of extension and dimension lines.

Step 4. Practice using grips, as described next:

Prompt	Response
Command:	CLICK: **the 14′-11 1/2″ dimension in OFFICE 3**

Prompt	Response
Five squares appear on the dimension; one at the end of each extension line, one at the center of each tick, and one in the center of the dimension text:	CLICK: **the grip in the center of the dimension text**

NOTE: To use multiple grips and to keep the shape of the dimension or any object with which you are using grips, hold down the Shift key before selecting the grips to make them hot.

The grip changes color (becomes HOT): Specify stretch point or [Base point/Copy/Undo/eXit]:	**With SNAP and ORTHO ON, move your mouse up and** CLICK: **a point two grid marks up**
The dimension is stretched up two grid marks:	CLICK: **the same grip to make it hot, move your mouse to the right, and** CLICK: **a point two grid marks to the right**
The dimension text moves two grid marks to the right:	CLICK: **the grip at the origin of the first extension line to make it hot, and move your mouse up two grid marks**
The origin of the first extension line moves up two grid marks:	CLICK: **the grip in the center of the dimension text to make it hot, and** PRESS: **the space bar one time**
The prompt changes to Specify move point or [Base point/Copy/Undo/eXit]:	**Move your cursor two grid marks down and** CLICK: **a point**
The entire dimension moves down two grid marks:	PRESS: **Esc**
The grips disappear:	TYPE: **U<enter>, and continue pressing <enter> until the dimension is returned to its original state**

To use grips, select a grip to act as the base point. Then select one of the grip modes—stretch, move, rotate, scale, or mirror. You can cycle through these modes by pressing **<enter>** or the space bar, or right-click to see all the modes and options.

REVISION CLOUD

Any change on a plan is submitted with a change-order. A revision cloud is used to identify any area of a plan that has been changed. The cloud is coordinated with a note in the title block that gives a brief description of the change.

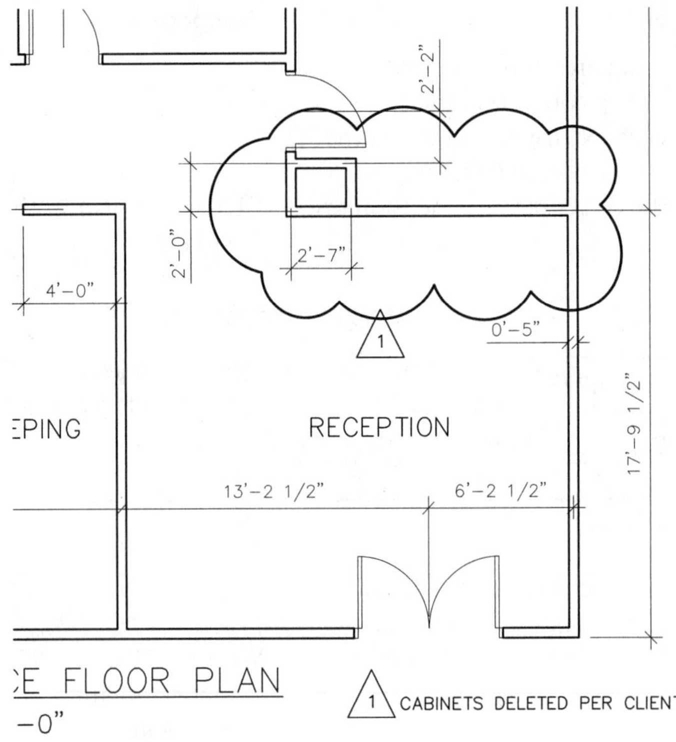

FIGURE 7–23
Draw a Revision Cloud to Identify an Area That Has Been Changed

---

Step 5. Create the following new layer and set it as the current layer:

LAYER NAME	COLOR	LINETYPE	LINEWEIGHT
a-anno-revs	white	continuous	.014″ (.35mm)

Step 6. Erase the two lines that represent the cabinets in the Conference Room.

Step 7. Draw a revision cloud to identify the area on the plan that has been changed (Figure 7–23), as described next:

Prompt	Response
Command:	**Revision Cloud** or TYPE: **REVCLOUD<enter>**
Minimum arc length: 4′-0″ Maximum arc length: 4′-0″ Style: Normal Specify start	

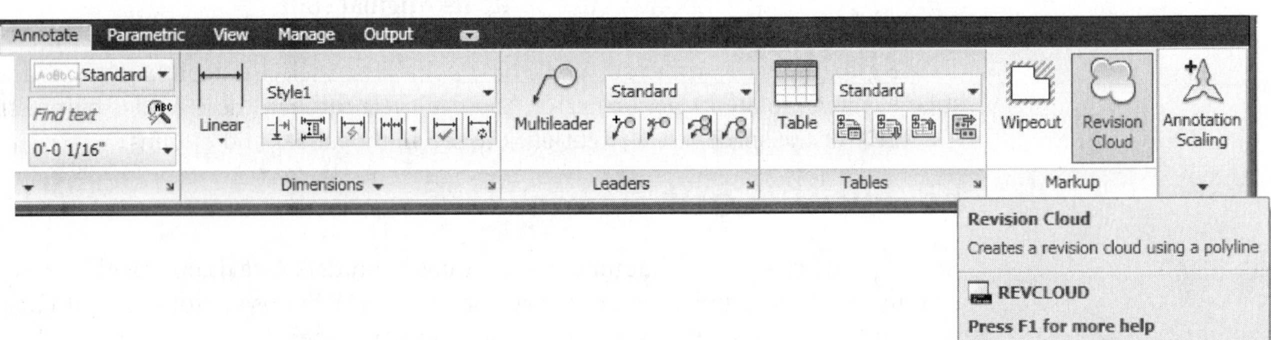

Prompt	Response
point or [Arc length/Object/ Style] <Object>:	**Pick any place to start the cloud (Figure 7–20)**
Guide crosshairs along cloud path...	**Guide your cursor along the cloud path**
Revision cloud finished.	

Arc Length Allows you to specify the minimum and maximum arc length in the revision cloud.

Object Allows you to select an object to convert to a revision cloud. You can convert a circle, ellipse, polyline, or spline to a revision cloud.

Style Allows you to select a style named Calligraphy, which gives the appearance of a revision cloud drawn with a pen.

Step 8. **Use grips to move any dimensions that are hidden by the cloud or to edit individual arcs in the revision cloud.**

Step 9. **Set Layer a-anno-text current and add the triangle that is 2′ × 2′, revision number, and revision note to the plan (Figure 7–23).**

Step 10. **When you have completed Tutorial 7–2, save your work in at least two places.**

Step 11. **Print Tutorial 7–2 at a scale of 1/8″ = 1′-0″.**

Tutorial 7–3: Tenant Space Total Square Feet

Tutorial 7–3 provides step-by-step instructions for using the Area command to compute the total square feet of the tenant space floor plan. It also provides instructions for using the Cal (calculator) command. When you have completed Tutorial 7–3, your drawing will look similar to Figure 7–24.

Step 1. **Open drawing CH7-TUTORIAL1 and save it as CH7-TUTORIAL3 to the hard drive.**

AREA

In order for the total square feet of any space to be computed, the exact area that is to be included must be identified. In the tenant space, the face of the exterior building glass on the north and west walls is used as the building's exterior measuring points, and the center of the south and east walls will be used as the interior measuring points.

Step 2. **Freeze Layers a-anno-dims and Defpoints, and set Layer a-anno-area current.**

Step 3. TYPE: **FILL<enter> then OFF<enter> so that the column and mullions are not solid. Regenerate the drawing (**TYPE: **RE<enter>).**

Step 4. **To be able to select the defining points of the exact area, as described above, use the Line command to draw separate lines in each corner of the tenant space to which you can snap using OSNAP-Intersection and OSNAP-Midpoint. Each corner with the added lines is shown in Figure 7–25.**

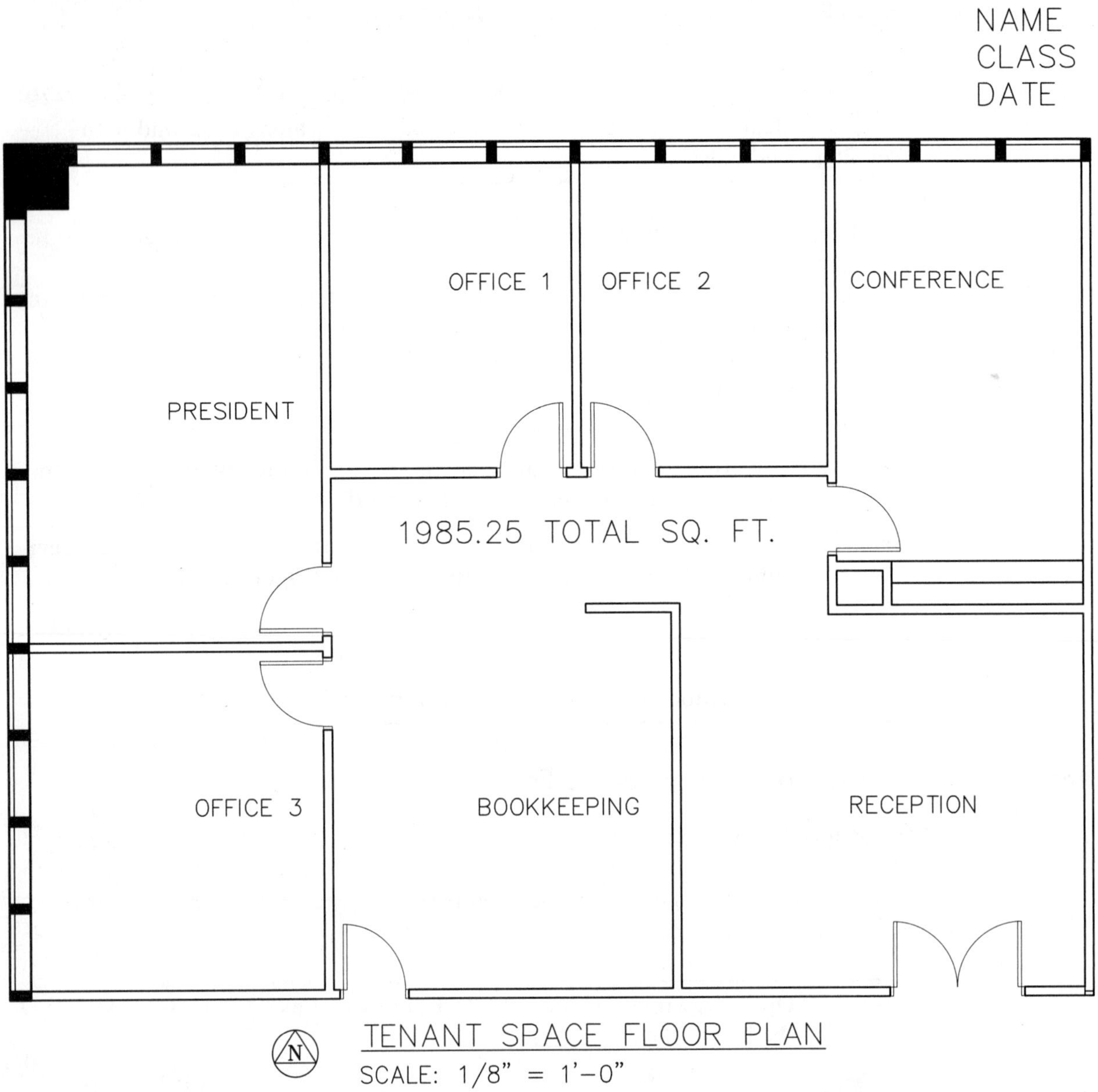

NAME
CLASS
DATE

OFFICE 1
OFFICE 2
CONFERENCE
PRESIDENT
1985.25 TOTAL SQ. FT.
OFFICE 3
BOOKKEEPING
RECEPTION

N

TENANT SPACE FLOOR PLAN
SCALE: 1/8" = 1'-0"

FIGURE 7–24
Tutorial 7–3: Tenant Space Total Square Feet (Scale: 1/8″ = 1′-0″)

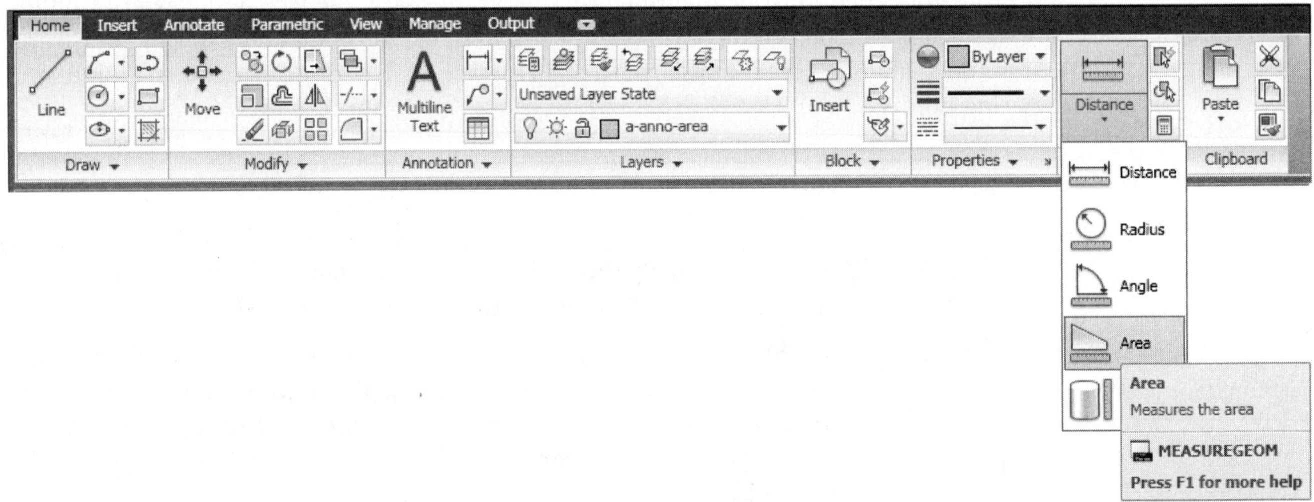

FIGURE 7–25
Defining Points of the Exact Area Included in the Total Square Feet of the Tenant Space

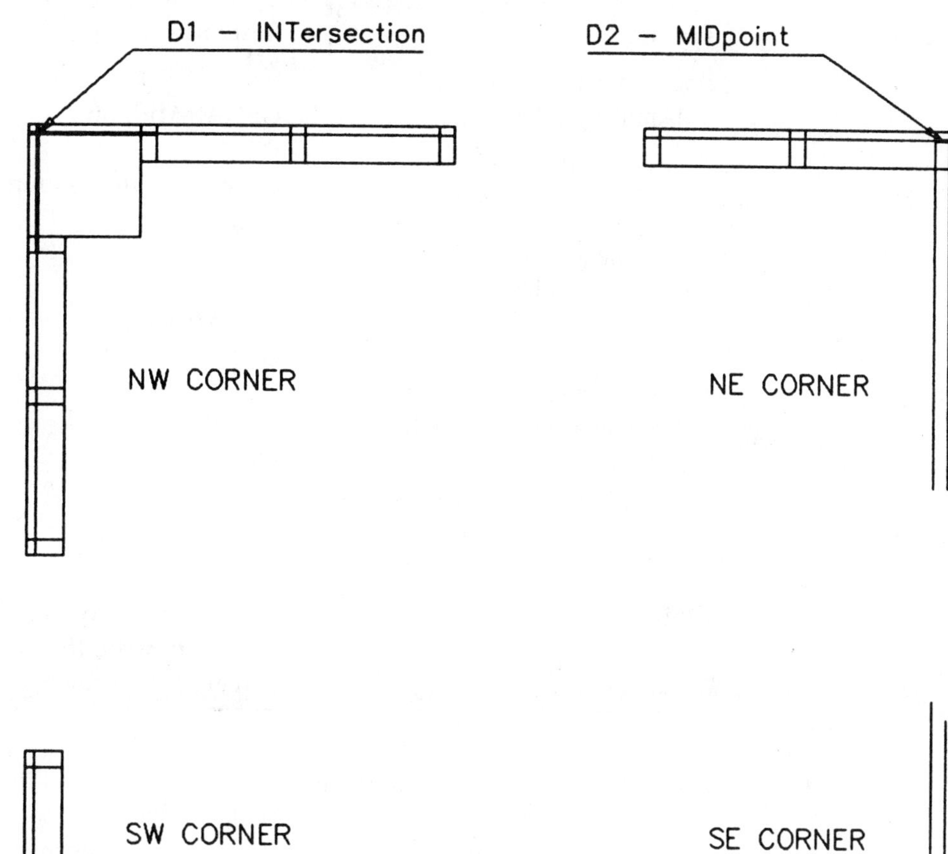

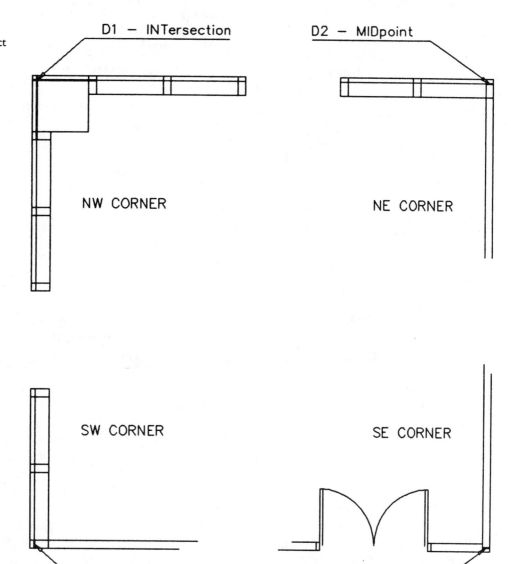

Step 5. Compute the total square feet of the tenant space (Figure 7–25), as described next:

Prompt	Response
Command:	**Area** (or TYPE: **AREA<enter>**)
Specify first corner point or [Object/ Add area/Subtract area]: <object>:	**OSNAP-Intersection** **Zoom a window around the northwest corner**
of	**D1** (Figure 7–25) **Zoom a window around the northeast corner**
Specify next point or [Arc/Length/Undo]:	**OSNAP-Midpoint**
of	**D2** **Zoom a window around the southeast corner**

Prompt	Response
Specify next point or [Arc/Length/Undo]:	**OSNAP-Midpoint**
of	**D3**
	Zoom a window around the southwest corner.
Specify next point or [Arc/Length/Undo/Total] <Total>:	**OSNAP-Midpoint**
of	**D4**
Specify next corner point or [Arc/Length/Undo/Total] <Total>:	**<enter>**
Area = 285876.25 square in. (1985.2517 square ft), Perimeter = 179′-10″	
Command:	**Use the Dtext command 1/8″ high (annotative text) to write the number of total square feet of the drawing (Figure 7–24).**

Add When Add is picked, the Area command is placed in an add mode. Add must be picked before the first space (of all the spaces to be added together) is specified. When the first space is specified, the area information is displayed. When the second space is specified, its individual area information is displayed along with the total area information of the two spaces together. Each subsequent space specified is displayed as an individual area total and is added to the running total.

Subtract When Subtract is picked, each subsequent space specified is displayed as an individual area total and is subtracted from the running total.

Object Object allows you to compute the area of a selected circle ellipse, polygon, solid, or closed polyline. For a circle, the area and circumference are displayed. When a wide, closed polyline is picked, the area defined by the center line of the polyline is displayed (the polyline width is ignored). Object is the fastest way to find the area of a closed polyline.

Step 6. Turn FILL ON.

Step 7. Regenerate the drawing (TYPE: **RE<enter>**).

CAL

AutoCAD provides a handy calculator that functions much like many handheld calculators. The following uses the add and divide features of the calculator. You may want to try other features on your own.

Use CAL to add three figures:

+ = add
− = subtract
× = multiply
/ = divide

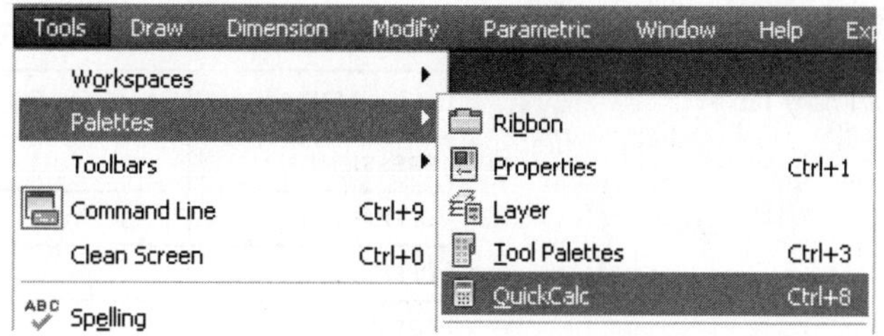

TIP: CAL can be used within any command, such as Line or Move, to specify a point. This avoids having to add and subtract dimensions beforehand. You must add an apostrophe before the CAL ('CAL) to use it within a command.

Prompt	Response
Command:	TYPE: **CAL<enter>**
>>Expression:	TYPE: **2′6 + 6′2 + 4′1<enter>**
12′-9″	

QUICKCALC

AutoCAD also has a calculator that can be used for scientific calculations, unit conversion, and basic calculations.

Step 8. **When you have completed Tutorial 7–3, save your work in at least two places.**

Step 9. **Print Tutorial 7–3 at a scale of 1/8″ = 1′-0″.**

Tutorial 7–4: Tenant Space Square Foot Summary Table

Step 1. **Use your workspace to make the following settings:**

1. **Use SaveAs. . . to save the drawing on the hard drive or network drive with the name CH7-TUTORIAL4.**
2. Set drawing Units: **Architectural**
3. Set Drawing Limits: **8-1/2,11″**
4. Set GRIDDISPLAY: **0**
5. Set Grid: **1/4″**
6. Set Snap: **1/8″**
7. Create the following layer:

LAYER NAME	COLOR	LINETYPE	LINEWEIGHT
a-anno-area	green	continuous	.006″ (.15mm)

8. Set **Layer a-anno-area** current.
9. Use **Zoom-All** to view the limits of the drawing.

Step 2. **Use the Area command to find the total square footage of each area (Figure 7–26) in the tenant space. Use the face of the exterior building glass on the north and west walls as the boundaries and measure to the**

FIGURE 7–26
Tutorial 7–4: Tenant Space Square Foot Summary Table

SQUARE FOOT SUMMARY	
AREA	SQ. FT.
PRESIDENT	
OFFICE 1	
OFFICE 2	
OFFICE 3	
CONFERENCE	
BOOKKEEPING	
RECEPTION	
HALL	
TOTAL SQ. FT.	

center of the remaining walls in each area. Include the square footage of the walled-in area next to the cabinets in the conference room.

President
Office 1
Office 2
Office 3
Conference
Bookkeeping
Reception
Hall

Step 3. Create a new text style named Summary with the Arial font.

Step 4. Create a Table style named Summary. Use the Table command to list the name and square footage of each area, and the total square footage, as shown in Figure 7–26.

Step 5. The table will include the following:

Text: Arial font
Title text—3/32″ High
Header text—3/32″ High
Data text—1/16″ High
Data text alignment—Middle Left
Column width—1″

Step 6. Make the text for the TOTAL SQ. FT. bold.

Step 7. When you have completed Tutorial 7–4 save your work in at least two places.

Step 8. Plot or print the drawing at scale of 1:1.

Tutorial 7–5: Use QDIM to Dimension the Conference Room from Tutorial 3–1

Tutorial 7–5 gives you practice in using the QDIM command from the Dimension menu or toolbar. QDIM allows you to select the objects you want to dimension and to specify which type of dimensioning you want to use and then automatically dimensions the geometry for you. Although you can select any areas to be automatically dimensioned,

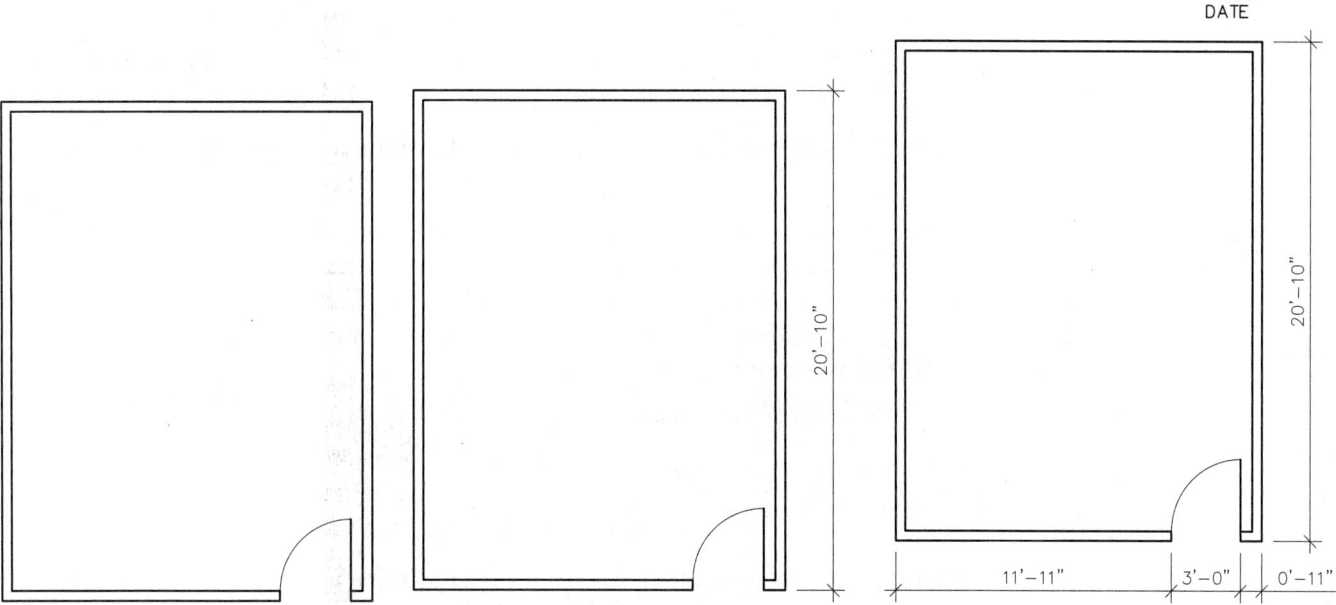

FIGURE 7–27
CH3-TUTORIAL1 with Furniture Erased

FIGURE 7–28
Use Quick Dimension to Dimension the Right Side

FIGURE 7–29
Use Quick Dimension to Dimension the Bottom

the more complex the geometry (for example, a complex floor plan), the more careful you have to be in selecting objects because QDIM dimensions everything.

Step 1. Begin this exercise by opening CH3-TUTORIAL1 and saving it as CH7-TUTORIAL5 to the hard drive.

Step 2. Erase the furniture from the drawing so the drawing appears as shown in Figure 7–27.

Step 3. Set the standard text style font to simplex and set it current.

Step 4. Use the DesignCenter to insert the Dimension Style, STYLE1 from CH7-TUTORIAL1. Open the DesignCenter, locate the drawing, and drag STYLE1 into CH7-TUTORIAL5.

Step 5. Create the following new layer and set it as the current layer:

LAYER NAME	COLOR	LINETYPE	LINEWEIGHT
a-anno-dims	red	continuous	.004" (.09mm)

Step 6. Use Quick Dimension to dimension the drawing (Figures 7–28 and 7–29), as described next:

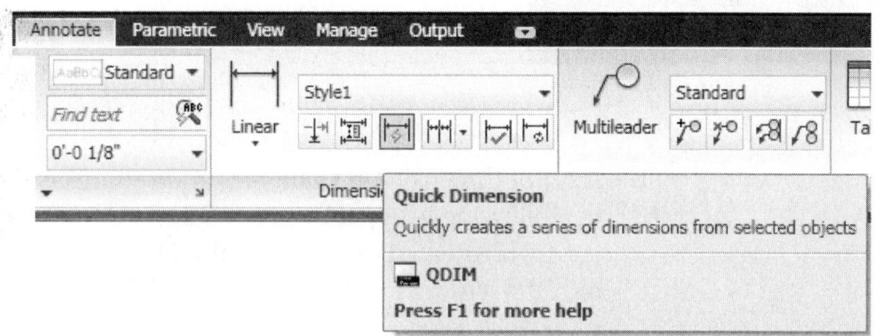

Prompt	Response
Command:	**Quick Dimension** (from the Dimension menu or toolbar) (or TYPE: **QDIM** from the Command: prompt)
Select geometry to dimension:	CLICK: **on the outside right side wall line of the floor plan**
Select geometry to dimension:	**<enter>**
Specify dimension line position, or [Continuous/Staggered/Baseline/Ordinate/Radius/Diameter/datumPoint/Edit/seTtings] <Continuous>:	CLICK: **a point two grid marks to the right of the right side**
The drawing is dimensioned as shown in Figure 7–28.	
Command:	**<enter>** (repeat **QDIM**)
Select geometry to dimension:	CLICK: **the bottom wall line of the floor plan including the wall to the right of the door opening**
Select geometry to dimension:	**<enter>**
Specify dimension line position, or [Continuous/Staggered/Baseline/Ordinate/Radius/Diameter/datumPoint/Edit/seTtings] <Continuous>:	CLICK: **a point two grid marks below the bottom of the floor plan**

The plan is dimensioned as shown in Figure 7–29.

Step 7. **Add your name, class, and the current date in the upper right, Figure 7–29.**

Step 8. **When you have completed Tutorial 7–5, save your work in at least two places.**

Step 9. **Print Tutorial 7–5 to scale.**

review questions

1. A list of dimensioning variables and settings is displayed when which of the following is typed from the Dim: prompt?
   a. LINEAR
   b. DIM VARS
   c. STATUS
   d. DIMSTYLE
   e. UPDATE

2. Which of the following dimensioning variables controls the height of text used in the dimension?
   a. DIMSTYLE
   b. DIMTSZ
   c. DIMASZ
   d. DIMTXT
   e. DIMTIX

3. Which tab on the New Dimension Style dialog box would you use to change a tick to a closed, filled arrowhead?
   a. Lines
   b. Symbols and Arrows
   c. Text
   d. Fit
   e. Primary Units
   f. Alternate Units

4. Which tab on the New Dimension Style dialog box would you use to change the appearance of the dimension text from one text style to another?
   a. Lines
   b. Symbols and Arrows
   c. Text
   d. Fit
   e. Primary Units
   f. Alternate Units

5. Which tab on the New Dimension Style dialog box would you use to change the overall scale factor from 96 to 48?
   a. Lines
   b. Symbols and Arrows
   c. Text
   d. Fit
   e. Primary Units
   f. Alternate Units

6. Which tab on the New Dimension Style dialog box would you use to set the distance that the dimension line extends beyond the tick?
   a. Lines
   b. Symbols and Arrows
   c. Text
   d. Fit
   e. Primary Units
   f. Alternate Units

7. Which tab on the New Dimension Style dialog box would you use to make a setting that will have the dimension text always appear horizontal on the page?
   a. Lines
   b. Symbols and Arrows
   c. Text
   d. Fit
   e. Primary Units
   f. Alternate Units

8. If a full-size drawing is to be plotted at a plotting ratio of 1/8″ = 12″, the DIMSCALE value should be set to
   a. 1
   b. 12
   c. 24
   d. 48
   e. 96

9. A Defpoints layer is created when a dimension is drawn with which of the following variables set to ON?
   a. DIMSTYLE
   b. DIMTOH
   c. DIMTAD
   d. DIMASSOC
   e. DIMTIH

10. To find the area of a closed polyline most quickly, which of the Area command options should be used?
   a. Object
   b. Poly
   c. Add
   d. Subtract
   e. First point

Complete.

11. List the seven tabs in the New Dimension Style dialog box:
    a. ______
    b. ______
    c. ______
    d. ______
    e. ______
    f. ______
    g. ______
12. Which setting must be made for dimensioning variable values to be displayed in 32nds of an inch?

    ______

    ______
13. What is the DIMSCALE setting when the dimensioning is annotative?

    ______
14. Describe what happens to the dimension of a 2″-diameter circle when the circle is enlarged to 40″ if DIMASSOC is set to 2.

    ______
15. List the five grip modes you can cycle through.
    a. ______
    b. ______
    c. ______
    d. ______
    e. ______
16. List the two styles available in the Revision Cloud command.
    a. ______
    b. ______

exercises

Exercise 7–1: Hotel Room Dimensioned Floor Plan

1. Set dimensioning variables for the hotel room floor plan.
2. Dimension the hotel room floor plan (Figure 7–30) on the Dim Layer.
3. Locate the first row of dimensions farther from the drawing (e.g., 2′) than the first row of dimensions is from the second row of dimensions (e.g., 1′6″). Consistently space each row of dimensions on all four sides of the drawing.
4. Plot or print the drawing to scale.

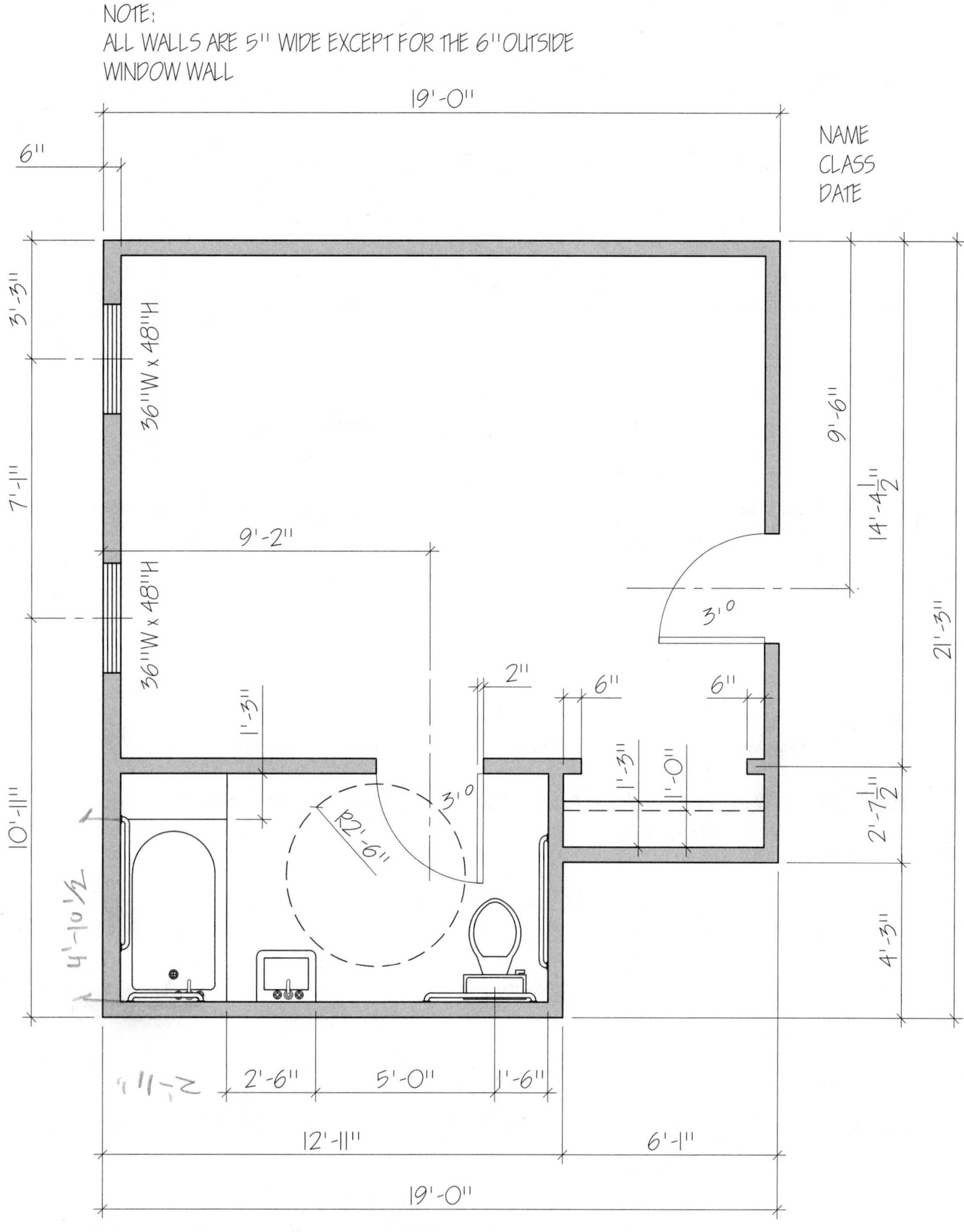

FIGURE 7–30
Exercise 7–1: Hotel Room Dimensioned Floor Plan (Scale: 1/4″ = 1′-0″)

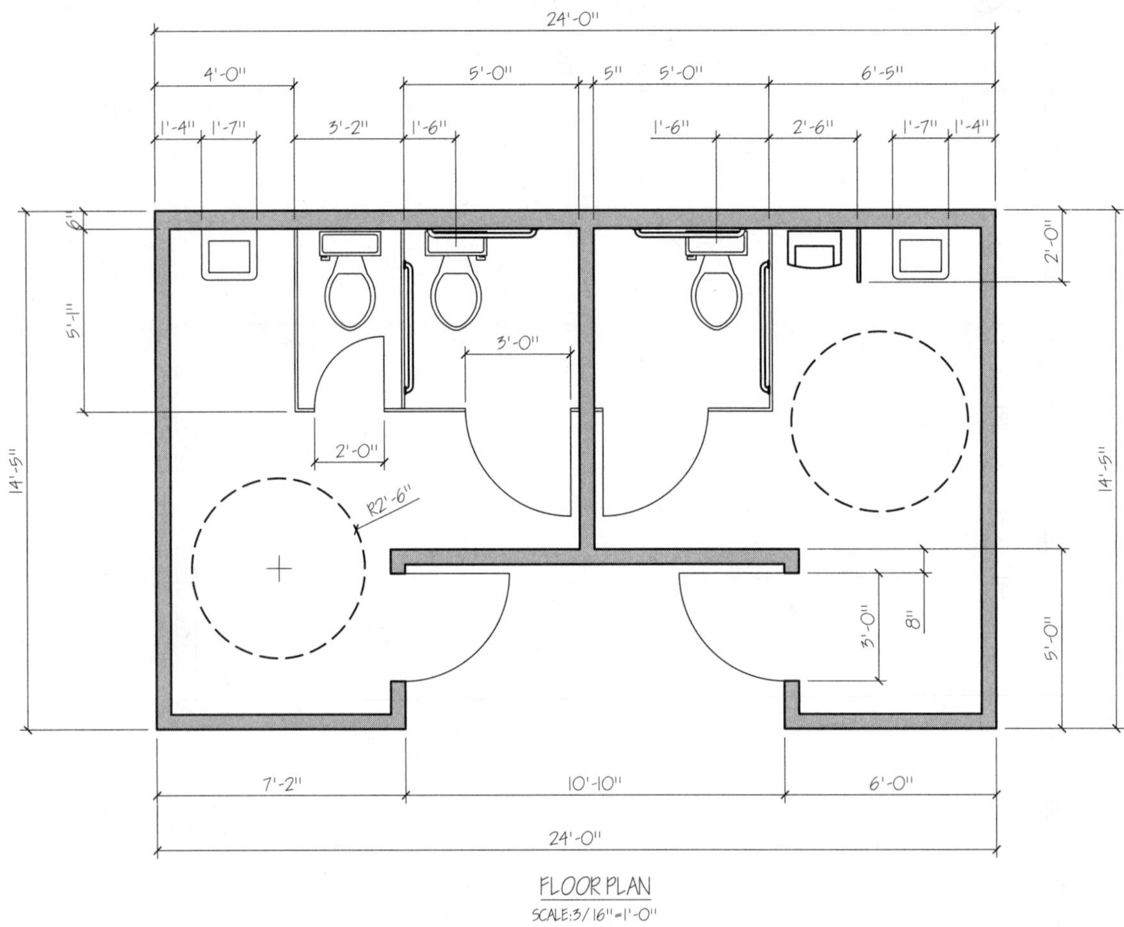

FIGURE 7–31
Exercise 7–2: Wheelchair Accessible Commercial Restroom Dimensioned Floor Plan (Scale: 3/16″ = 1′-0″)

Exercise 7–2: Wheelchair Accessible Commercial Restroom Dimensioned Floor Plan

1. Set dimensioning variables for the commercial restroom floor plan.
2. Create a new layer for dimensions, and dimension the commercial restroom floor plan (Figure 7–31).
3. Locate the first row of dimensions farther from the drawing (e.g., 2′) than the first row of dimensions is from the second row of dimensions (e.g., 1′6″). Consistently space each row of dimensions on all four sides of the drawing.
4. Plot or print the drawing to scale.

Exercise 7–3: Wheelchair Accessible Residential Bathroom Dimensioned Floor Plan

1. Set dimensioning variables for the residential bathroom floor plan.
2. Create a new layer for dimensions, and dimension the residential bathroom floor plan (Figure 7–32).
3. Locate the first row of dimensions farther from the drawing (e.g., 2′) than the first row of dimensions is from the second row of dimensions (e.g., 1′6″). Consistently space each row of dimensions on all four sides of the drawing.
4. Plot or print the drawing to scale.

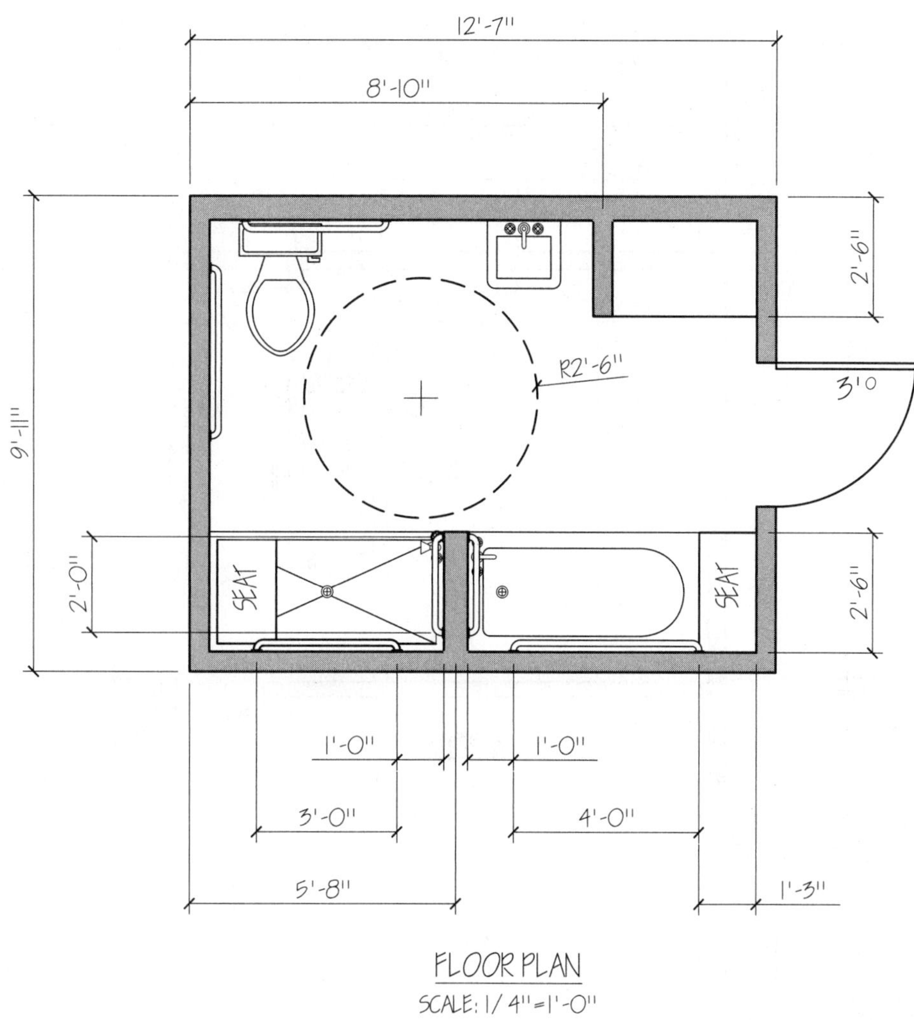

FIGURE 7–32
Exercise 7–3: Wheelchair Accessible Residential Bathroom Dimensioned Floor Plan (Scale: 1/4″ = 1′-0″)

Exercise 7–4: Log Cabin Dimensioned Floor Plan

1. Set dimensioning variables for the log cabin floor plan.
2. Create a new layer for dimensions, and dimension the log cabin floor plan (Figure 7–33).
3. Locate the first row of dimensions farther from the drawing (e.g., 2′) than the first row of dimensions is from the second row of dimensions (e.g., 1′6″). Consistently space each row of dimensions on all four sides of the drawing.
4. Plot or print the drawing to scale.

Exercise 7–5: House Dimensioned Floor Plan

1. Set dimensioning variables for the house floor plan.
2. Create a new layer for dimensions, and dimension the house floor plan (Figure 7–34, Sheets 1 and 2).
3. Locate the first row of dimensions farther from the drawing (e.g., 2′) than the first row of dimensions is from the second row of dimensions (e.g., 1′6″). Consistently space each row of dimensions on all four sides of the drawing.
4. Plot or print the drawing to scale.

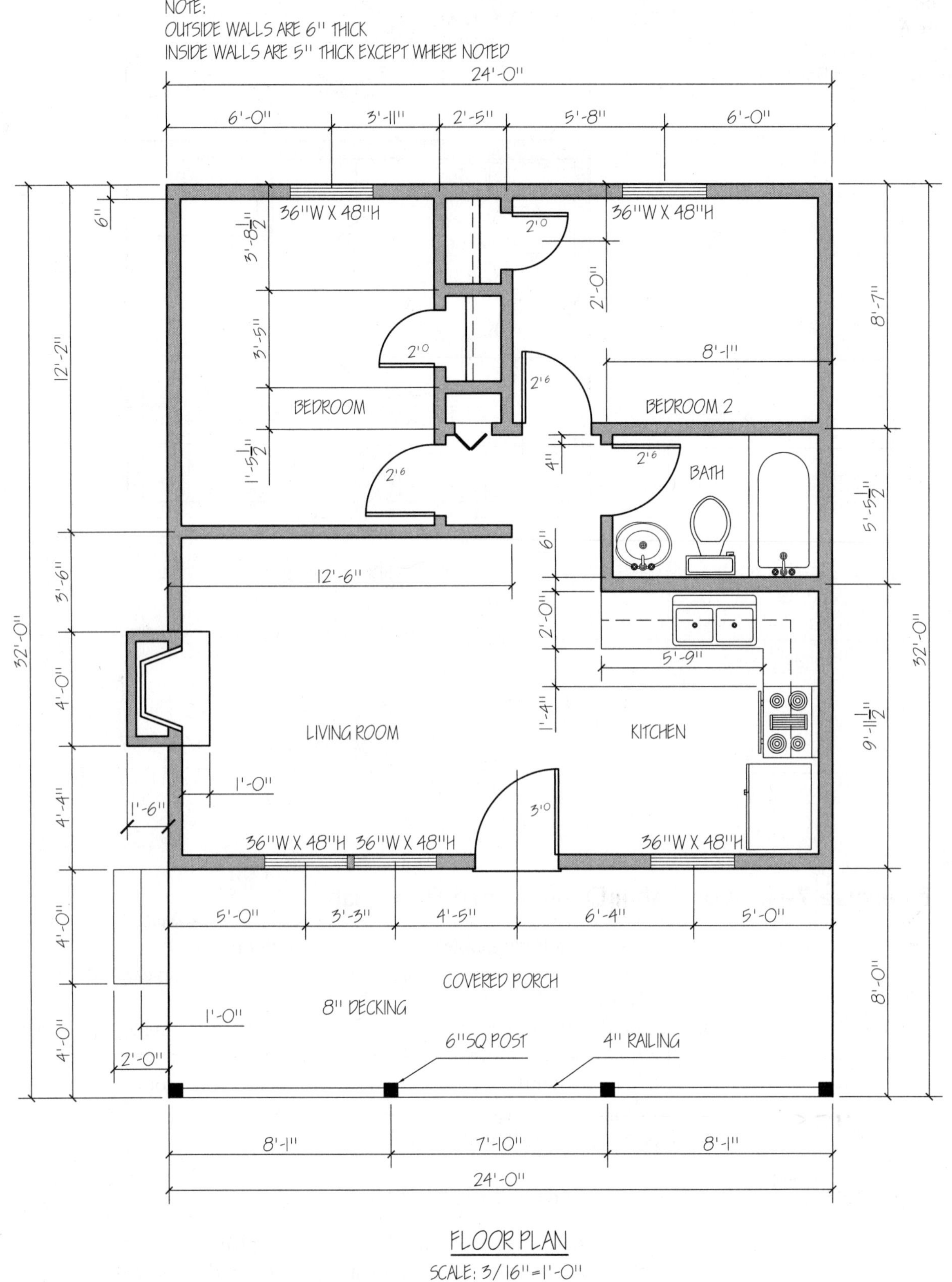

FIGURE 7–33
Exercise 7–4: Log Cabin Dimensioned Floor Plan (Scale: 3/16″ = 1′-0″)

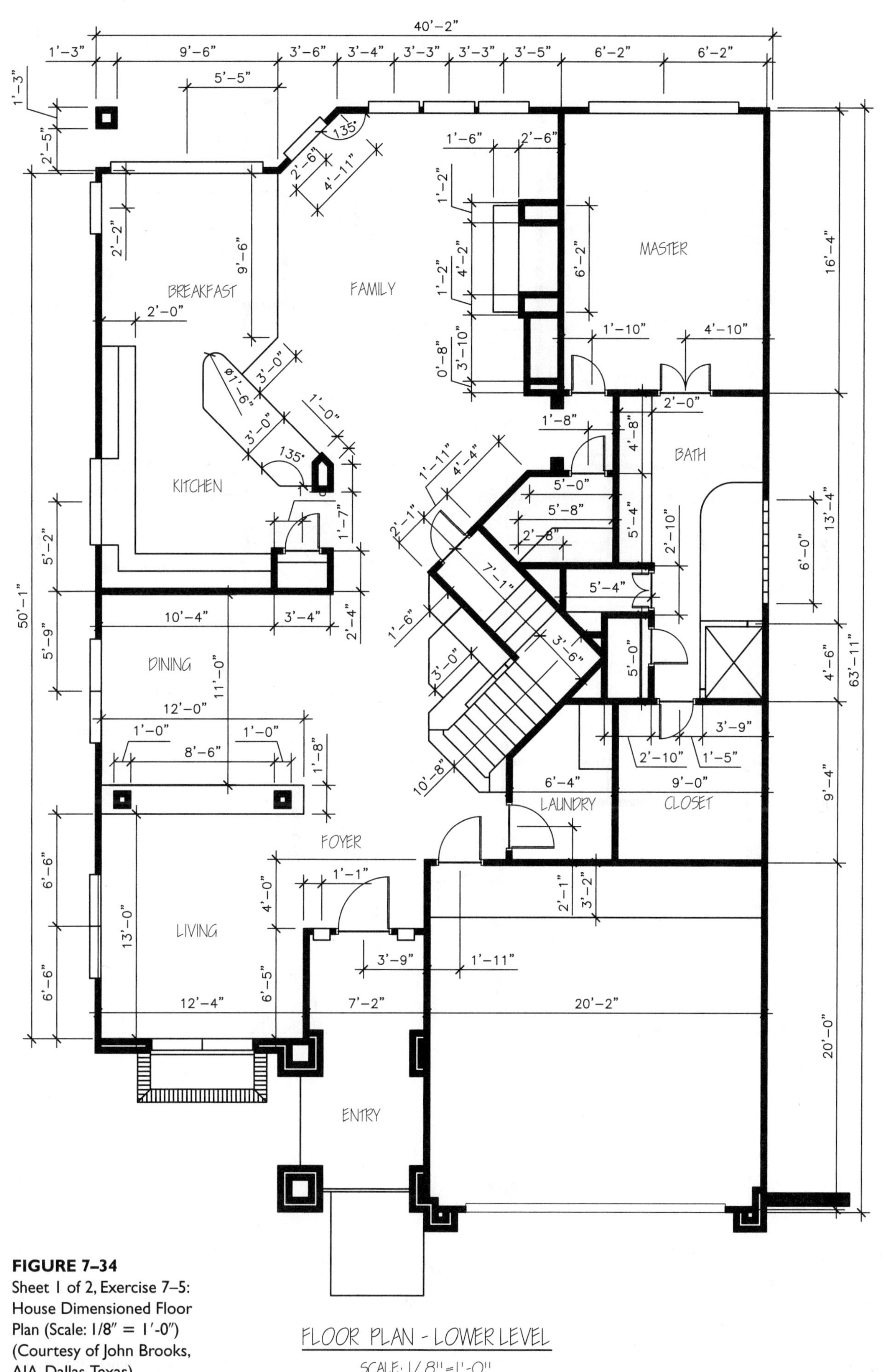

FIGURE 7–34
Sheet 1 of 2, Exercise 7–5: House Dimensioned Floor Plan (Scale: 1/8″ = 1′-0″) (Courtesy of John Brooks, AIA, Dallas, Texas)

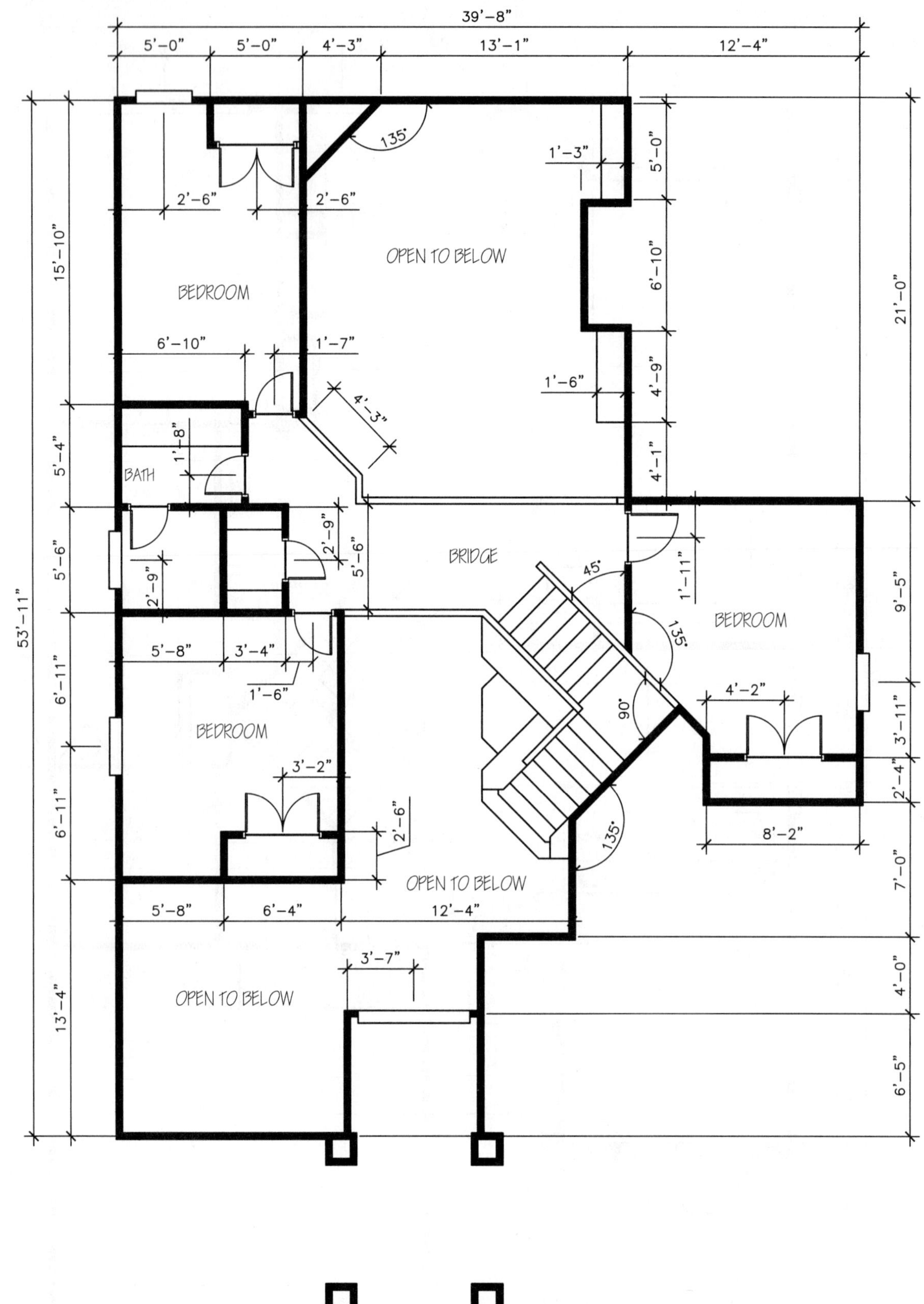

FIGURE 7–34
Sheet 2 of 2, Exercise 7–5: House Dimensioned Floor Plan (Scale: 1/8" = 1'-0") (Courtesy of John Brooks, AIA, Dallas, Texas)

Exercise 7–6: Bank Dimensioned Floor Plan

1. Set dimensioning variables for the bank plan.
2. Create a new layer for dimensions, and dimension the bank floor plan (Figure 7–35).
3. Locate the first row of dimensions farther from the drawing (e.g., 2′) than the first row of dimensions is from the second row of dimensions (e.g., 1′6″). Consistently space each row of dimensions on all four sides of the drawing.
4. Plot or print the drawing to scale.

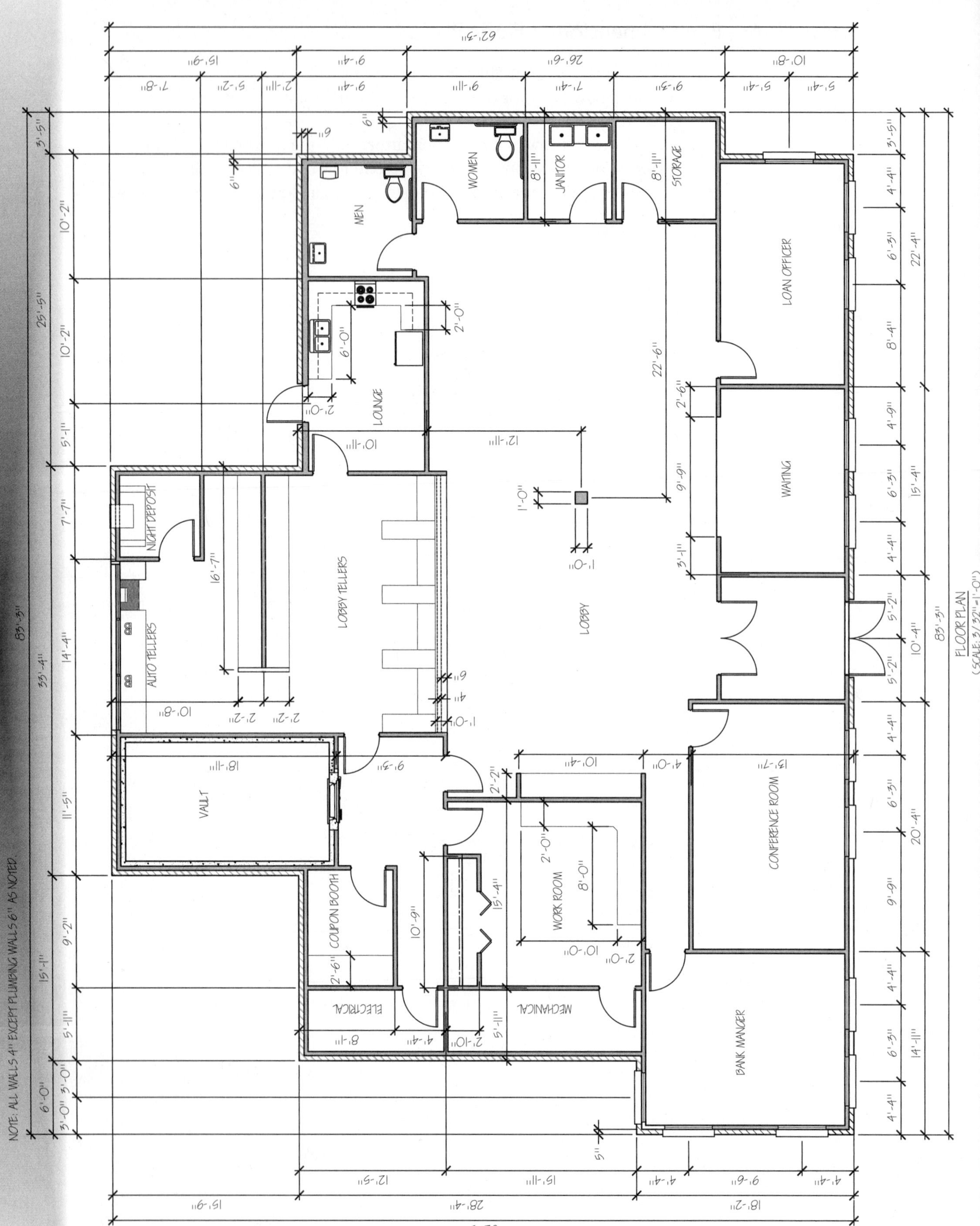

FIGURE 7–35
Exercise 7–6: Bank Dimensioned Floor Plan (Scale: 3/32″ = 1′-0″)

chapter 8

Drawing Elevations, Wall Sections, and Details

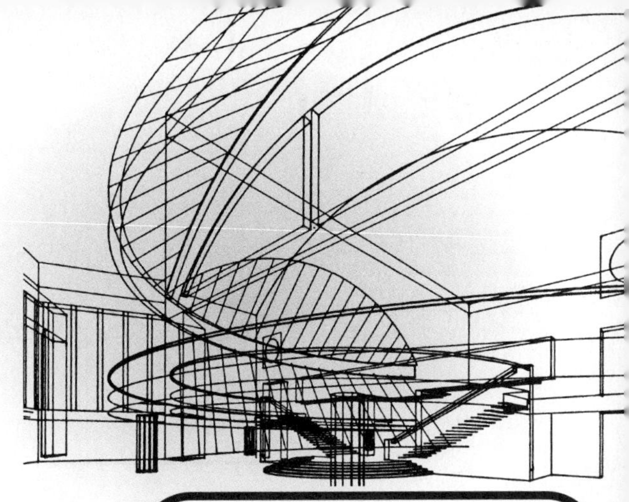

objectives

When you have completed this chapter, you will be able to:

Correctly use the following commands and settings:

Edit Hatch	OTRACK
Editing Hatch Patterns	Point Filters
Hatch...	Stretch
Mirror	UCS
Multileader	UCS Icon

INTRODUCTION

The AutoCAD program makes it possible to produce clear, accurate, and impressive drawings of elevations, sections, and details. Many of the commands you have already learned are used in this chapter, along with some new commands.

Tutorial 8–1: Tenant Space: Elevation of Conference Room Cabinets

In Tutorial 8–1, an elevation of the south wall of the tenant space conference room is drawn. The south wall of the tenant space conference room has built-in cabinets that include a refrigerator and a sink. When you have completed Tutorial 8–1, your drawing will look similar to Figure 8–1.

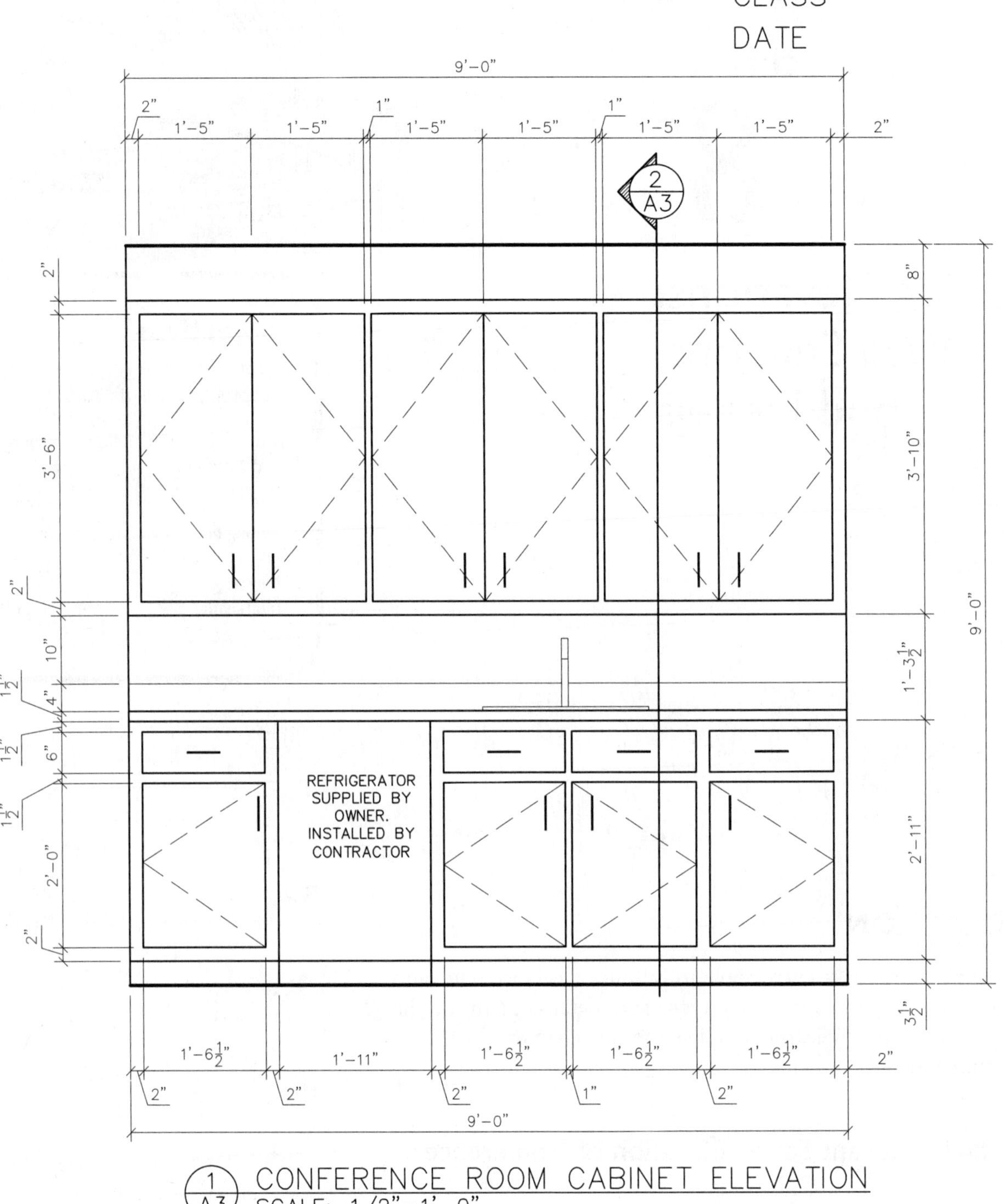

FIGURE 8–1
Tutorial 8–1: Tenant Space, Elevation of Conference Room Cabinets (Scale: 1/2″ = 1′-0″)

Step 1. Use your workspace to make the following settings:

1. **Use SaveAs… to save the drawing on the hard drive with the name CH8-TUTORIAL1.**
2. Set drawing Units: **Architectural**
3. Set Drawing Limits: **25′,24′**

4. Set GRIDDISPLAY: **0**
5. Set Grid: **12″**
6. Set Snap: **6″**
7. Create the following layers:

LAYER NAME	COLOR	LINETYPE	LINEWEIGHT
a-elev-pat	cyan	continuous	.002″(.05mm)
a-elev	blue	continuous	.010″(.25mm)
a-elev-hid	red	hidden	.004″(.09mm)
a-elev-text	green	continuous	.006″(.15mm)
a-elev-dim	red	continuous	.004″(.09mm)
a-wall-extr	white	continuous	.014″(.35mm)

8. Set **Layer a-elev** current.
9. **Zoom-All**

UCS

While you were drawing with AutoCAD in previous chapters, the UCS (user coordinate system) icon was located in the lower left corner of your drawings. A coordinate system is simply the X, Y, and Z coordinates used in your drawings. For two-dimensional drawings, only the X and Y coordinates are meaningful. The Z coordinate is used for a three-dimensional model.

Notice that the 2D UCS icon (Figure 8–2) has a W on it. The W stands for *world coordinate system*. This is the AutoCAD fixed coordinate system, which is common to all AutoCAD drawings. Your version of AutoCAD uses the 3D icon by default showing only X and Y axes.

The UCS command is used to set up a new user coordinate system. When UCS is typed from the Command: prompt, the prompt is "Specify origin of UCS or [Face/NAmed/OBject/Previous/View/World/X/Y/Z/ZAxis] <World>". The Z coordinate is described and used extensively in the chapters that cover three-dimensional modeling. The UCS command options that apply to two dimensions are listed next.

Specify origin of UCS Allows you to create a new UCS by selecting a new origin and a new X axis. If you select a single point, the origin of the current UCS moves without changing the orientation of the X and Y axes.

NAmed When this option is entered, the prompt "Enter an option [Restore/Save/Delete/?]" appears. It allows you to restore, save, delete, and list named user coordinate systems.

OBject Allows you to define a new UCS by pointing to a drawing object such as an arc, point, circle, or line.

Previous Makes the previous UCS current.

World This is the AutoCAD fixed coordinate system, which is common to all AutoCAD drawings. In most cases you will want to return to the world coordinate system before plotting any drawing.

FIGURE 8–2
2D Model Space, 3D Model Space, and Paper Space UCS Icons

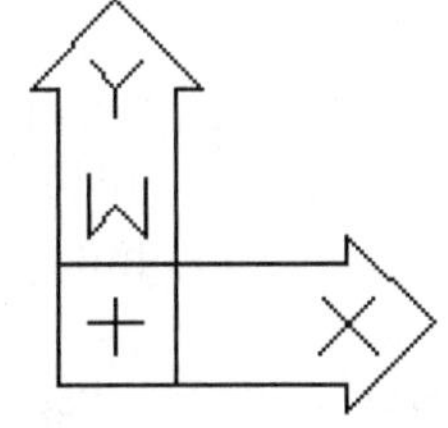

2D MODEL SPACE ICON

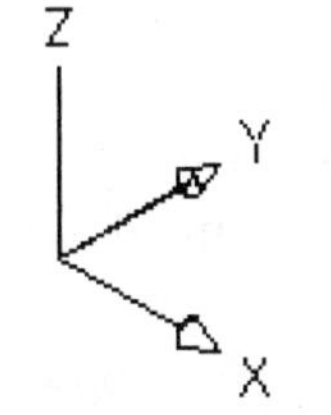

3D MODEL SPACE ICON

PAPER SPACE ICON

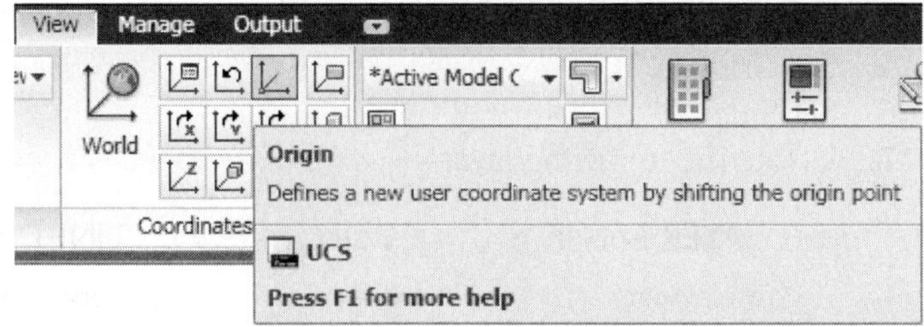

Step 2. Use the UCS command to change the origin of the current UCS, as described next:

Prompt	Response
Command:	TYPE: **UCS<enter>** (or CLICK: **UCS-origin**
Specify origin of UCS or [Face/NAmed/OBject/Previous/	and just TYPE: **8′,12′<enter>**
View/World/X/Y/Z/ZAxis] <World>	TYPE: **8′,12′<enter>**
Specify point on X-axis or <Accept>:	**<enter>**

The origin for the current user coordinate system is now 8′ in the X direction and 12′ in the Y direction. The UCS icon may not have moved from where 0,0 was originally located. The UCS Icon command, described next, is used to control the orientation and visibility of the UCS icon.

NOTE: You can change the UCS so you can move 0,0 to any point on your drawing to make it more convenient to locate points.

UCS ICON

There are two model space UCS icons that you can choose to use: one for 2D drawings and one for 3D drawings. The default is the 3D icon, which you will probably use for both 2D and 3D. The UCS Icon command is used to control the visibility and orientation of the UCS icon (Figure 8–2). The UCS icon appears as arrows (most often located in the lower left corner of an AutoCAD drawing) that show the orientation of the X, Y, and Z axes of the current UCS. It appears as a triangle in paper space. The UCS Icon command options are "ON/OFF/All/Noorigin/ORigin/Properties:". The UCS Icon command options are listed next.

ON Allows you to turn on the UCS icon if it is not visible.

OFF Allows you to turn off the UCS icon when it gets in the way. This has nothing to do with the UCS location—only the visibility of the UCS icon.

All Allows you to apply changes to the UCS icon in all active viewports. (The Viewports command, which allows you to create multiple viewports, is described in Chapter 12.)

Noorigin When Noorigin is current, the UCS icon is displayed at the lower left corner of the screen.

FIGURE 8–3
UCS Icon Dialog Box

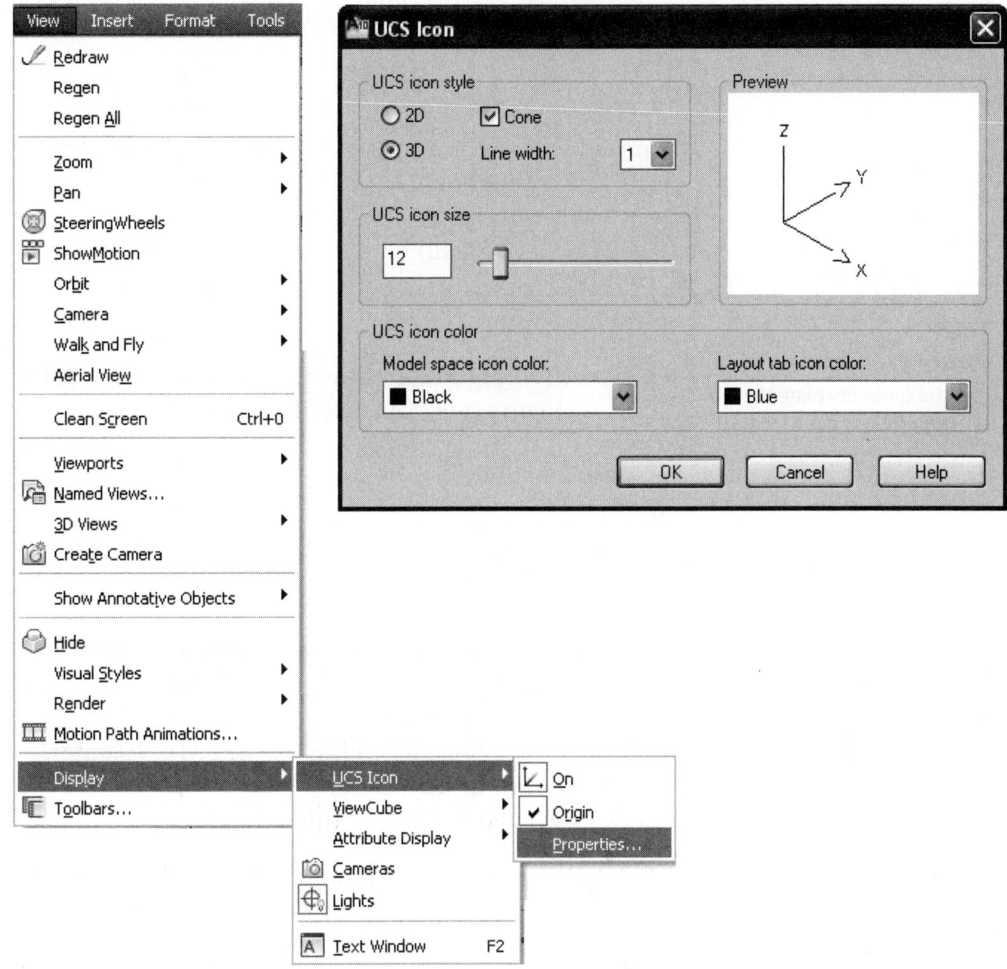

ORigin Forces the UCS icon to be displayed at the origin of the current UCS. For example, when USC Icon - Origin is clicked, the new UCS that you just created will appear in its correct position. If the origin of the UCS is off the screen, the icon is still displayed in the lower left corner of the screen.

Properties When Properties is selected, the UCS Icon dialog box apppears (Figure 8–3). This box allows you to select the 2D or 3D model space icon and to change the size and color of model space and paper space (Layout tab) icons.

Step 3. If the UCS icon did not move, use the UCS Icon command to force the UCS icon to be displayed at the origin of the new, current UCS, as described next:

Prompt	Response
Command:	TYPE: **UCSICON<enter>**
Enter an option [ON/OFF/All/ Noorigin/ORigin/Properties] <ON>:	TYPE: **OR<enter>** (The UCS icon moves to the 8′,12′ coordinate location.)

Step 4. Using absolute coordinates, draw a rectangle forming the first upper cabinet door. Start the drawing at 2,2 (two inches above and

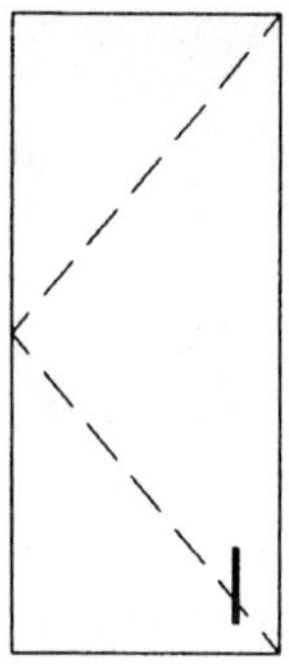

FIGURE 8–4
Draw the Lines Forming the First Upper Cabinet Door

two inches to the right of the new UCS), Figure 8–4, as described next:

Prompt	Response
Command:	**Rectangle (or** TYPE: **REC<enter>)**
Specify first corner point or [Chamfer/Elevation/ Fillet/Thickness/Width]:	TYPE: **2,2<enter>**
Specify other corner point or [Area/Dimensions/Rotation]:	TYPE: **19,44<enter>**

Step 5. **Use Polyline to draw the door hardware using absolute coordinates (Figure 8–4), as described next:**

Prompt	Response
Command:	**Polyline** (or TYPE: **PL<enter>**)
Specify start point:	TYPE: **16,4<enter>**
Specify next point or [Arc/ Halfwidth/Length/Undo/Width]:	TYPE: **W<enter>**
Specify starting width <0′-0″>:	TYPE: **1/4<enter>**
Specify ending width <0′-0 1/4″>:	**<enter>**
Specify next point or [Arc/ Halfwidth/Length/Undo/Width]:	TYPE: **16,9<enter>**
Specify next point or [Arc/Close/ Halfwidth/Length/Undo/Width]:	**<enter>**

Step 6. **Set Layer a-elev-hid current and draw the dashed lines of the door using absolute coordinates (Figure 8–4), as described next:**

Prompt	Response
Command:	**Line** (or TYPE: **L<enter>**)
Specify first point:	TYPE: **19,3′8<enter>**
Specify next point or [Undo]:	TYPE: **2,23<enter>**
Specify next point or [Undo]:	TYPE: **19,2<enter>**
Specify next point or [Close/Undo]:	**<enter>**

Step 7. **Change the linetype scale of the Hidden linetype to make it appear as dashes, change the linetype to Hidden2, or both. A large linetype scale such as 12 is needed. (**TYPE: **LTSCALE <enter>, then** TYPE: **12 <enter>.)**

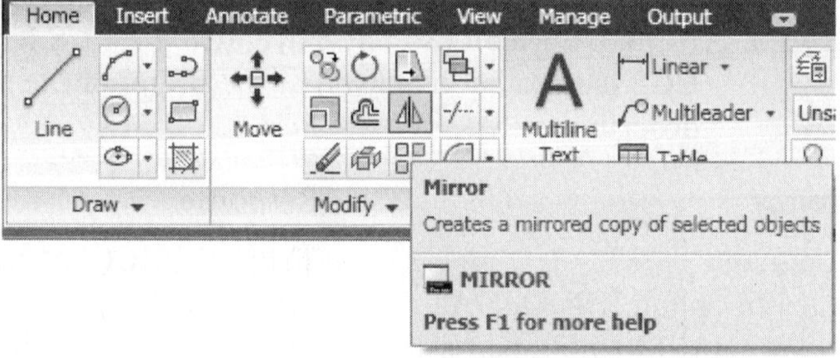

MIRROR

The Mirror command allows you to mirror about an axis any entity or group of entities. The axis can be at any angle.

FIGURE 8–5
Use the Mirror Command to Copy the Cabinet Door

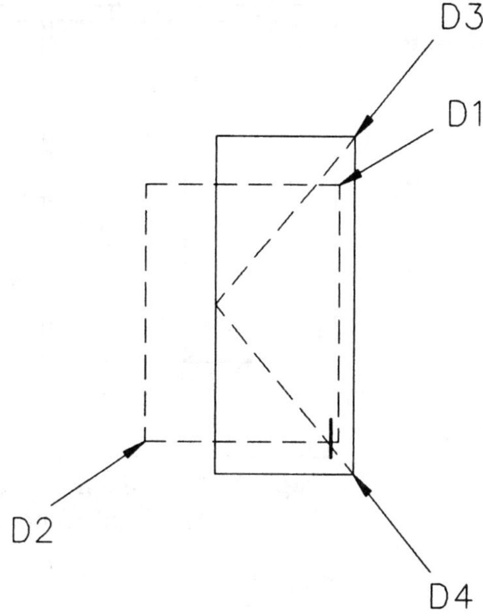

Step 8. **Draw the second cabinet door, using the Mirror command to copy the cabinet door just drawn (Figure 8–5), as described next:**

Prompt	Response
Command:	**Mirror** (or TYPE: **MI<enter>**)
Select objects:	**D1**
Specify opposite corner:	**D2**
Select objects:	**<enter>**
Specify first point of mirror line:	**D3** (with ORTHO and SNAP ON)
Specify second point of mirror line:	**D4**
Erase source objects? [Yes/No] <N>:	**<enter>** (to complete command)

NOTE: If you want to mirror a part of a drawing containing text but do not want the text to be a mirror image, change the MIRRTEXT system variable setting to 0. This allows you to mirror the part and leave the text "right reading." When MIRRTEXT is set to 1, the text is given a mirror image. To change this setting, TYPE: **MIRRTEXT <enter>**, then TYPE: **0<enter>**.

Step 9. **Set Layer a-elev current. Using relative coordinates, draw a rectangle forming the upper cabinet. Start the rectangle at the 0,0 location of the new UCS (Figure 8–6), as described next:**

Prompt	Response
Command:	**Rectangle (or** TYPE: **REC<enter>)**
Specify first corner point or [Chamfer/Elevation/Fillet/Thickness/Width]:	TYPE: **0,0<enter>**
Specify other corner point or [Area/Dimensions/Rotation]:	TYPE: **@9',3'10<enter>**

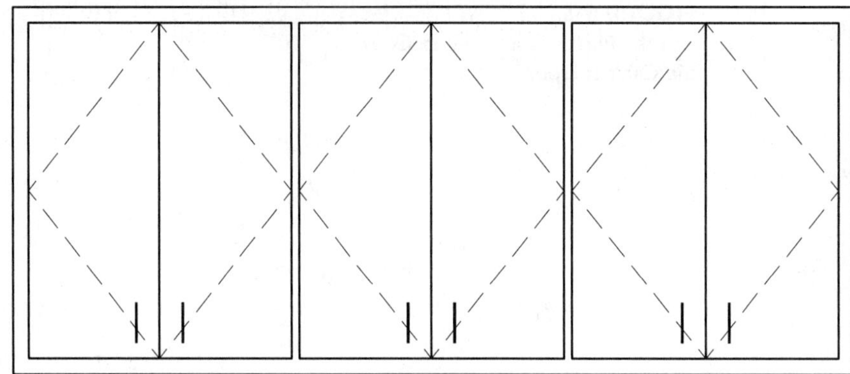

FIGURE 8–6
Draw the Upper Cabinets

Step 10. **Copy the first two cabinet doors 2′11″ and 5′10″ to the right (Figure 8–6) as described next:**

Prompt	Response
Command:	**Copy (or** TYPE: **CP<enter>)**
Select objects:	**Use a window to select the first two cabinet doors.**
Select objects:	**<enter>**
Specify base point or [Displacement/ mOde] <Displacement>:	CLICK: Any point
Specify second point or <use first point as displacement>:	**With ORTHO ON, move your mouse to the right** and TYPE: **2′11<enter>**
Specify second point or [Exit/Undo] <Exit>:	**Move the mouse to the right and** TYPE: **5′10<enter>**
Specify second point or [Exit/Undo] <Exit>:	**<enter>**

Step 11. **Use the Mirror command to draw the first lower cabinet door (Figure 8–7), as described next:**

Prompt	Response
Command:	**Mirror** (or TYPE: **MI<enter>**)
Select objects:	**D2** (left to right)
Specify opposite corner:	**D1**
Select objects:	**<enter>**
Specify first point of mirror line:	**D3** (with ORTHO and SNAP ON; the lower cabinets will be moved to the accurate location later)
Specify second point of mirror line:	**D4**
Erase source objects? [Yes/No] <N>:	**<enter>** (The lower cabinet is now too high and too narrow.)

STRETCH

The Stretch command can be used to stretch entities to make them longer or shorter. It can also be used to move entities that have other lines attached to them without removing the

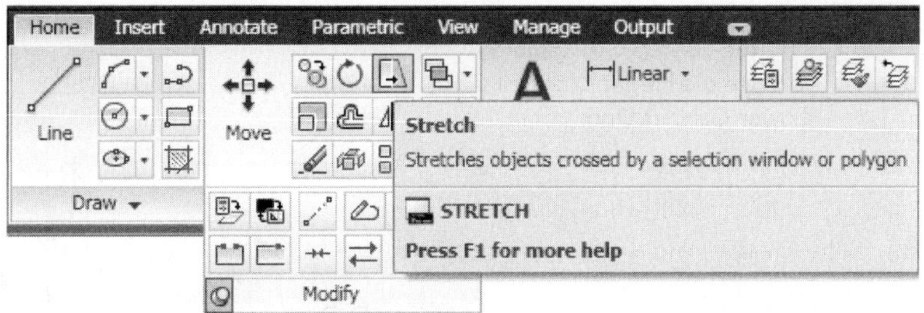

attached lines (described later in this exercise). Stretch requires you to use a crossing window to select objects. As with many other Modify commands, you may select objects initially, then remove or add objects to the selection set before you perform the stretch function.

Step 12. Use the Stretch command to change the height of the first lower cabinet door just drawn (Figure 8–8), as described next:

Prompt	Response
Command:	**Stretch** (or TYPE: **S<enter>**)
Select objects to stretch by crossing-window or crossing-polygon...	
Select objects:	**D1**
Specify opposite corner:	**D2**

FIGURE 8–7
Use the Mirror Command to Draw the First Lower Cabinet Door

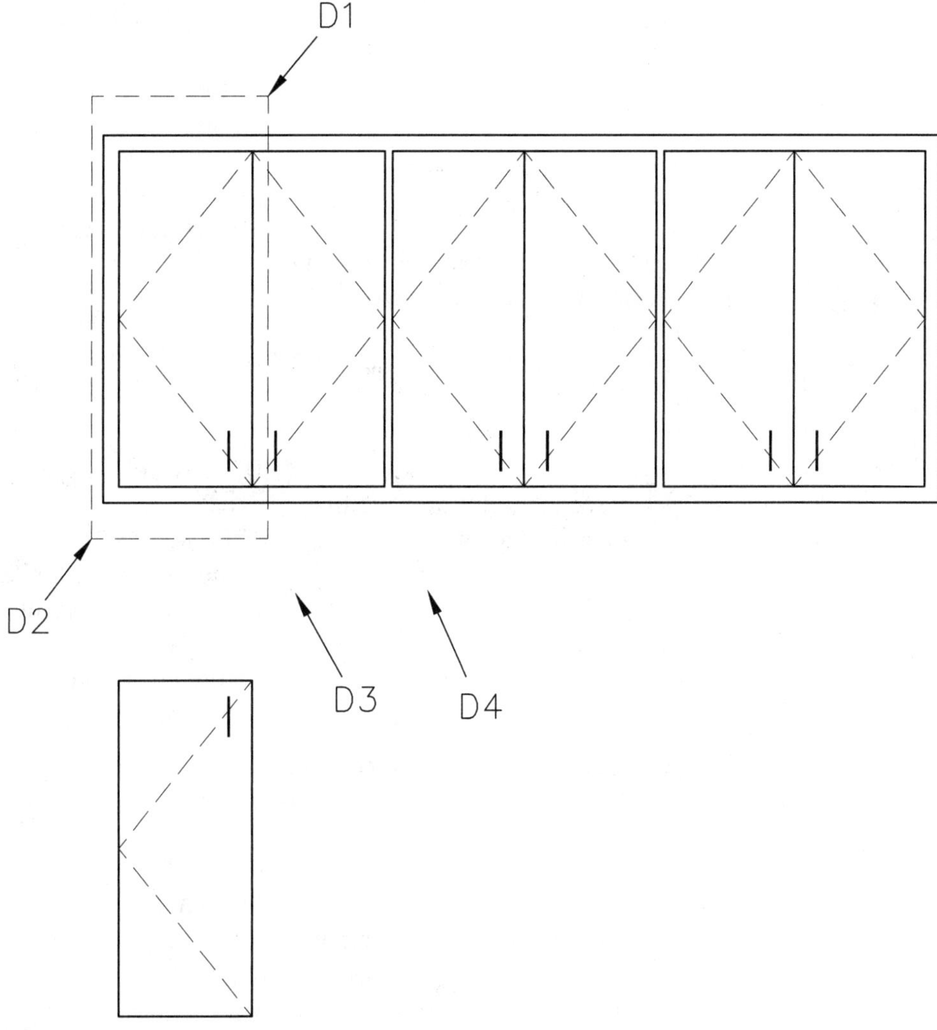

FIGURE 8–8
Use the Stretch Command to Change the Height of the First Lower Cabinet Door

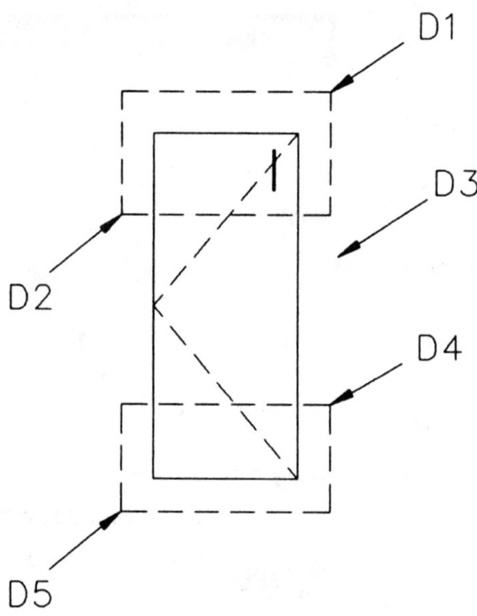

Prompt	Response
Select objects:	**<enter>**
Specify base point or [Displacement] <Displacement>:	**D3** (any point)
Specify second point or <use first point as displacement>:	TYPE: **@9<270<enter>** (or with ORTHO ON move your mouse down and TYPE: **9 <enter>**) (the upper door height, 3′6″, minus the lower door height, 2′, divided by 2; take half off the top of the door and half off the bottom)
Command:	**Stretch** (or PRESS: **<enter>**)
Select objects to stretch by crossing-window or crossing-polygon...	
Select objects:	**D4**
Specify opposite corner:	**D5**
Select objects:	**<enter>**
Specify base point or [Displacement] <Displacement>:	**D3** (any point)
Specify second point or <use first point as displacement>:	TYPE: **@9<90<enter>** (or move your mouse up and TYPE: **9 <enter>**) The lower cabinet door should now be 18″ shorter than the upper cabinet door from which it was mirrored (3′6″ minus 18″ equals 2′, the cabinet door height).

Step 13. Use the Stretch command to change the width of the cabinet door (Figure 8–9), as described next:

Prompt	Response
Command:	**Stretch**
Select objects to stretch by crossing-window or crossing-polygon...	
Select objects:	**D1**

FIGURE 8–9
Use the Stretch Command to Change the Width of the Cabinet Door

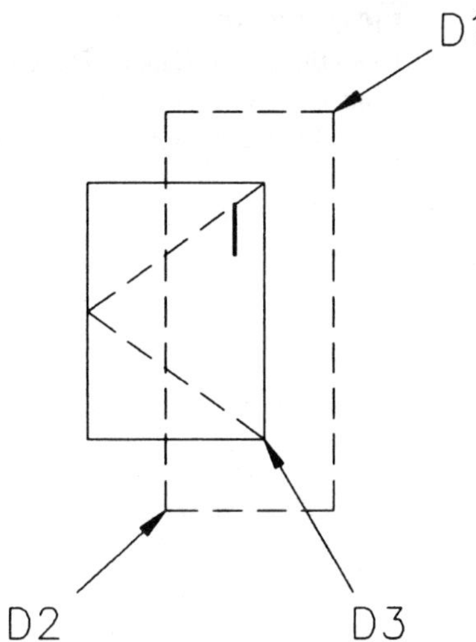

Prompt	Response
Specify opposite corner:	**D2**
Select objects:	**<enter>**
Specify base point or [Displacement] <Displacement>:	**D3** (any point)
Specify second point or <use first point as displacement>:	TYPE: **@1-1/2<0<enter>** (or move the mouse to the right and TYPE: **1-1/2 <enter>**) (the upper door width, 1′5″, plus 1-1/2″, equals the lower door width, 1′6-1/2″)

Step 14. **Save the current UCS used to draw the upper cabinets, as described next:**

Prompt	Response
Command:	TYPE: **UCS<enter>**
Specify origin of UCS or [Face/ NAmed/OBject/Previous/View/ World/X/Y/Z/ZAxis] <World>:	TYPE: **S<enter>**
Enter name to save current UCS or [?]:	TYPE: **UPPER<enter>**

Step 15. **Create a new UCS origin for drawing the lower cabinets by moving the existing UCS origin –4′2-1/2″ in the Y direction, as described next:**

Prompt	Response
Command:	**<enter>** (repeat UCS)
Specify origin of UCS or [Face/ NAmed/OBject/Previous/View/ World/X/Y/Z/ZAxis] <World>:	TYPE: **O<enter>**
Specify new origin point <0,0,0>:	TYPE: **0,-4′2-1/2<enter>** (be sure to include the minus)

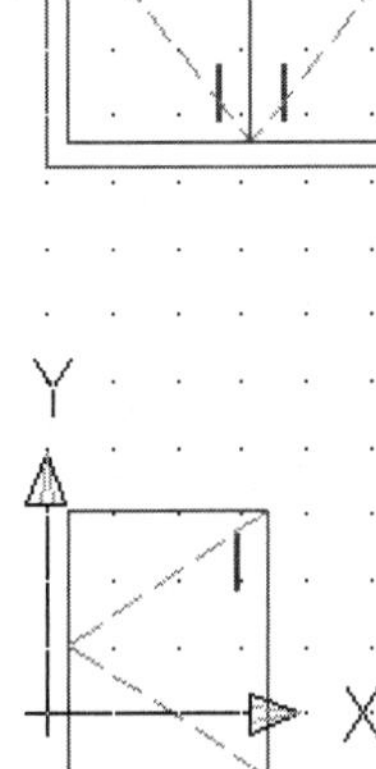

Step 16. **Move the lower cabinet door to a point 2″ above and 2″ to the right of the origin of the current UCS (Figure 8–10), as described next:**

Prompt	Response
Command:	**Move** (or TYPE: **M<enter>**)
Select objects:	**D1** (Figure 8–10)
Specify opposite corner:	**D2**
Select objects:	**<enter>**

FIGURE 8–10
Move the Lower Cabinet Door to a Point 2″ Above and 2″ to the Right of the Origin of the Current UCS

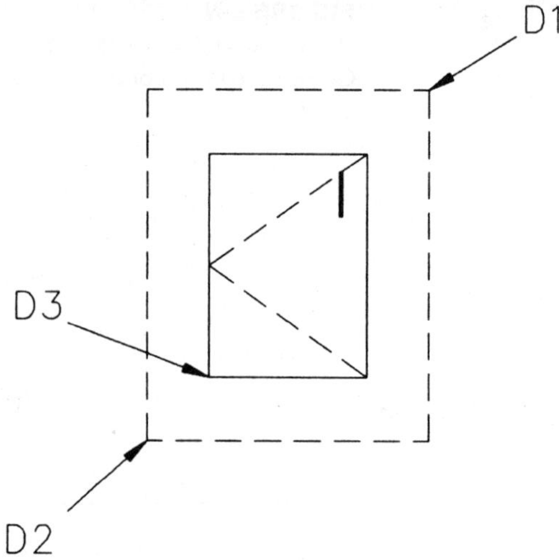

Prompt	Response
Specify base point or [Displacement] <Displacement>:	**OSNAP-Intersection**
of	**D3**
Specify second point or <use first point as displacement>:	TYPE: **2, 2<enter>**

Step 17. Using relative coordinates, draw a rectangle forming the drawer above the lower cabinet door (Figure 8–11), as described next:

Prompt	Response
Command:	**Rectangle** (or TYPE: **REC<enter>**)
Specify first corner point or [Chamfer/Elevation/Fillet/Thickness/Width]:	TYPE: **FRO<enter>**

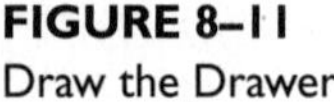
FIGURE 8–11
Draw the Drawer

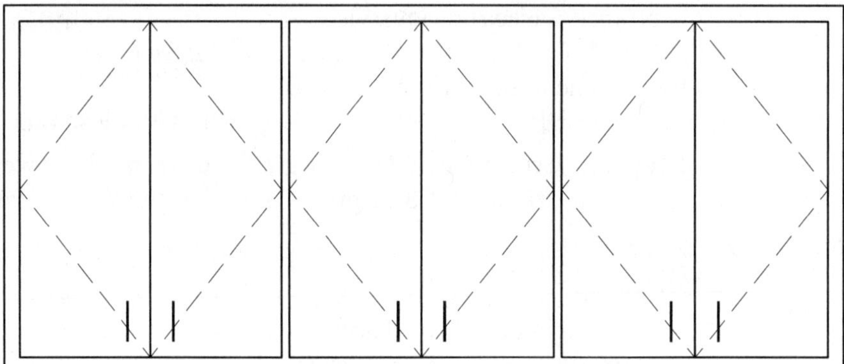

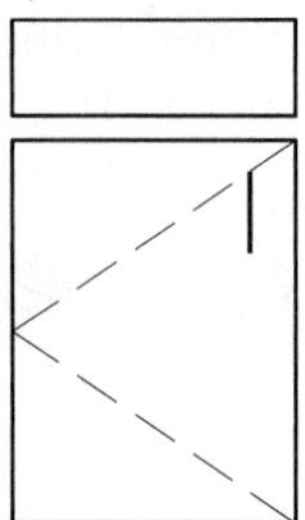

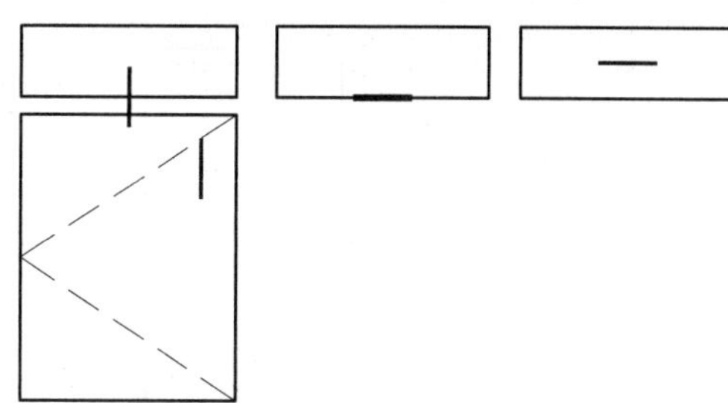

FIGURE 8–12
Copy the Door Handle, Rotate It, and Move It

Prompt	Response
Base point:	CLICK: **The upper left corner of the lower cabinet door.**
<Offset>:	TYPE: **@1-1/2<90<enter>**
Specify other corner point or [Area/Dimensions/Rotation]:	TYPE: **@1′6-1/2,6<enter>**

Step 18. **Copy the door handle to the midpoint of the bottom line of the drawer, rotate it 90 degrees, and move it up 3″ as shown in Figure 8–12.**

Step 19. **Explode the upper cabinet rectangle. Offset the bottom line of the rectangle several times and change two lines to other layers (Figure 8–13) as described below:**

Offset the bottom line of the rectangle 10″ and change it to the a-elev-pat Layer.
Offset the bottom line of the rectangle 14″.
Offset that line 1-1/2″.
Offset that line 2′11″.
Offset that line 3-1/2″ and change the offset line to the a-wall-extr Layer.

FIGURE 8–13
Explode the Cabinet Rectangle and Offset the Bottom Line

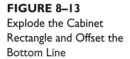

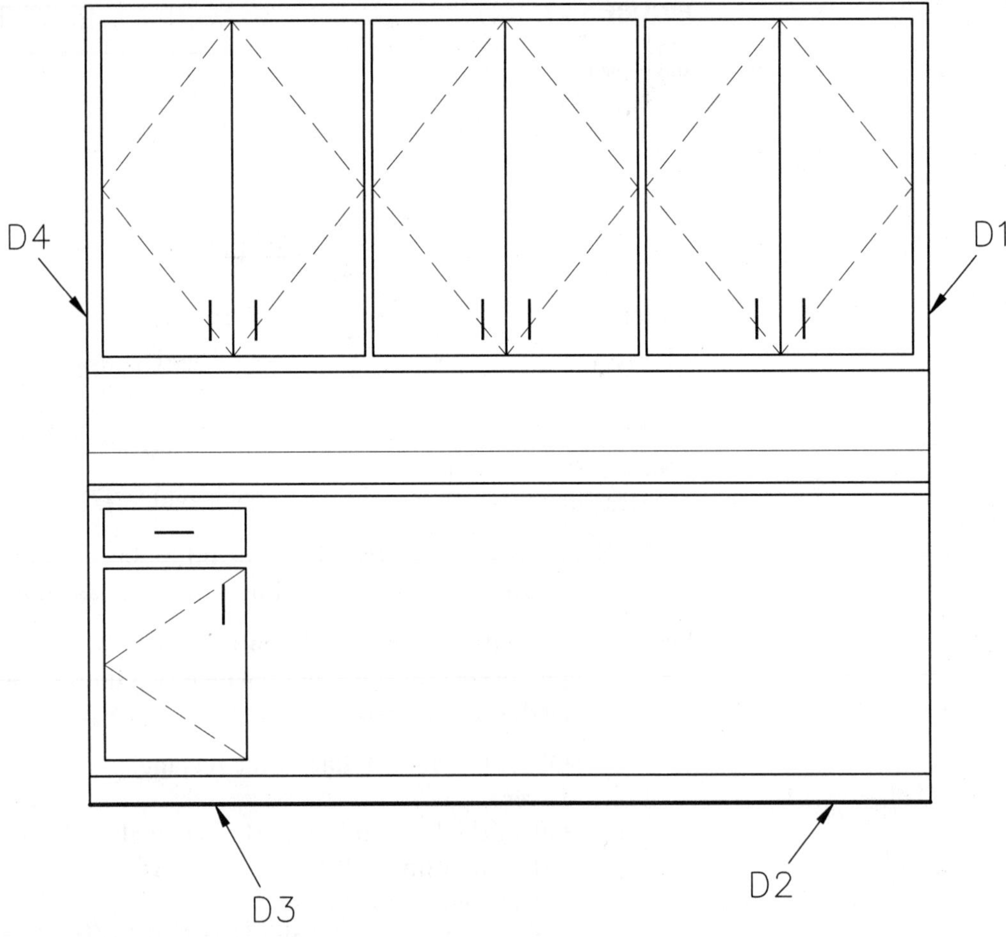

FIGURE 8–14
Use Fillet to Extend Lines on Both Sides

Step 20. **Use zero radius fillet to extend lines on both sides of the cabinets as described next:**

Prompt	Response
Command:	**Fillet (or** TYPE: **F<enter>)**
Select first object or [Undo/ Polyline/Radius/Trim/Multiple]:	TYPE: **M<enter>**
Select first object or [Undo/ Polyline/Radius/Trim/Multiple]:	CLICK: **D1** (Figure 8–14)
Select second object or shift-select to apply corner:	CLICK: **D2**
Select first object or [Undo/ Polyline/Radius/Trim/Multiple]:	CLICK: **D3**
Select second object or shift-select to apply corner:	CLICK: **D4**
Select first object or [Undo/ Polyline/Radius/Trim/Multiple]:	<enter>

Step 21. **Use the Mirror command to draw the door and drawer on the right side of the lower cabinet, as shown in Figure 8–15.**

Step 22. **Use the Copy command to copy the door and drawer on the left 3′9-1/2″ to the right, Figure 8–16.**

FIGURE 8–15
Use Mirror to Draw the Door and Drawer on the Far Right

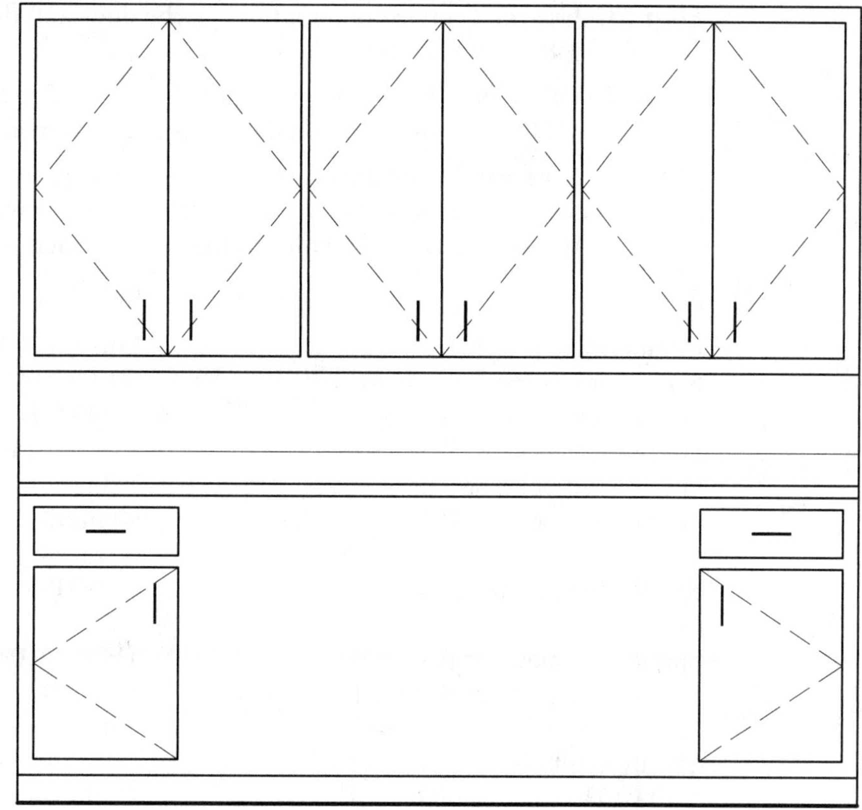

FIGURE 8–16
Copy Drawers and Doors Offset and Trim Lines to Form the Refrigerator

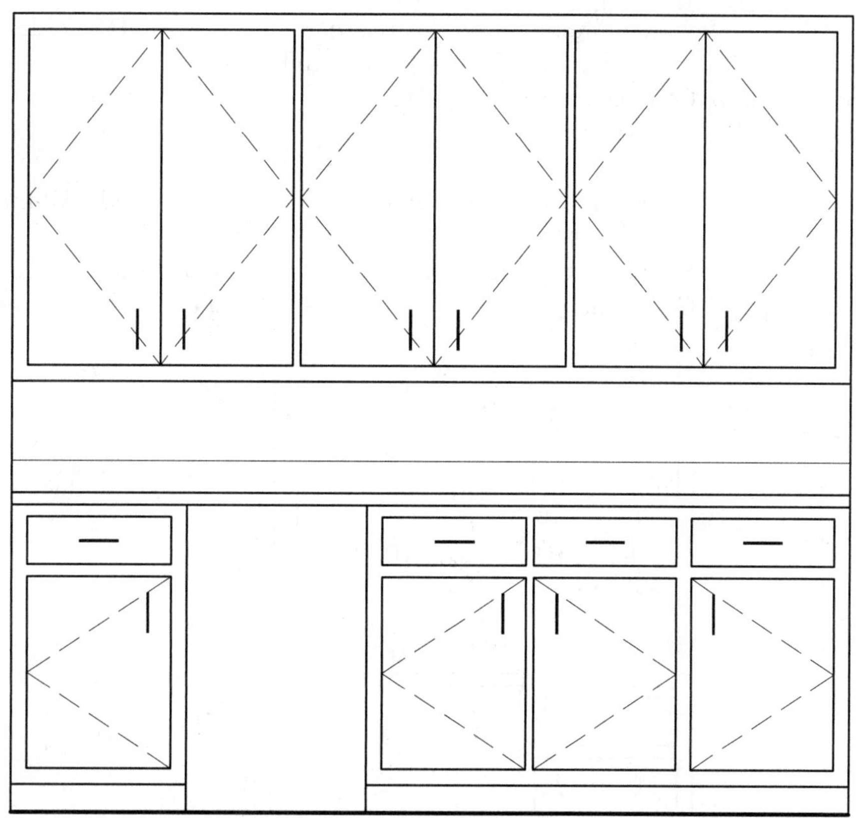

Step 23. Use the Copy command to copy the door and drawer on the right 1′8-1/2″ to the left.

Step 24. Offset the cabinet line on the far left, 1′10-1/2″ to the right. Offset that line 1′11″ to the right to form the refrigerator. Trim lines as needed, Figure 8-16.

Step 25. Set Layer a-elev-dim current. Draw the sink in the approximate location shown in Figure 8–17 (the Stretch command will be used later to move the sink to the correct location), as described next:

Prompt	Response
Command:	**Line** (or TYPE: **L<enter>**)
Specify first point:	**D1** (OSNAP-Nearest)
Specify next point or [Undo]:	TYPE: **@1/2<90<enter>**
Specify next point or [Undo]:	TYPE: **@25<0<enter>**
Specify next point or [Close/Undo]:	TYPE: **@1/2<270<enter>**
Specify next point or [Close/Undo]:	**<enter>**
Command:	**<enter>** (Repeat LINE)
Specify first point:	**OSNAP-Midpoint**
of	**D2**
Specify next point or [Undo]:	TYPE: **@10<90<enter>**
Specify next point or [Undo]:	**<enter>**
Command:	**Offset** (or TYPE: **O<enter>**)
Specify offset distance or [Through/ Erase/Layer]<default>:	TYPE: **1/2<enter>**
Select object to offset or [Exit/Undo] <Exit>:	**D3** (the line just drawn)
Specify point on side to offset or [Exit/Multiple/Undo] <Exit>:	**D4** (to the right)
Select object to offset or [Exit/Undo] <Exit>:	**D3**
Specify point on side to offset or [Exit/Multiple/Undo] <Exit>:	**D5** (to the left)
Select object to offset or [Exit/Undo] <Exit>:	**<enter>**
Command:	**Line**
Specify first point:	**OSNAP-Endpoint**
of	**D6**
Specify next point or [Undo]:	**OSNAP-Endpoint**
of	**D7**
Specify next point or [Undo]:	**<enter>** (to complete the command)
Command:	**Offset**

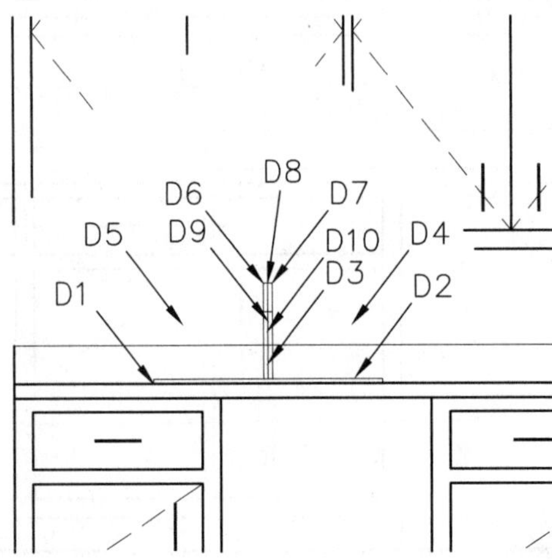

FIGURE 8–17
Draw the Sink in the Approximate Location Shown

Prompt	Response
Specify offset distance or [Through/ Erase/Layer] <0′-1/2″>:	TYPE: **3<enter>**
Select object to offset or [Exit/Undo] <Exit>:	**D8**
Specify point on side to offset or [Exit/Multiple/Undo] <Exit>:	**D10**
Select object to offset or [Exit/Undo] <Exit>:	**<enter>**
Command:	**Erase** (or TYPE: **E<enter>**)
Select objects:	**D9** (the center vertical line)
Select objects:	**<enter>**

Step 26. **Trim out the line of the backsplash where it crosses the faucet.**

Step 27. **You can use the Stretch command to move entities that have other lines attached to them without removing the attached lines. Use Stretch to move the sink to its correct location (Figure 8–18), as described next:**

Prompt	Response
Command:	**Stretch** (or TYPE: **S<enter>**)
Select objects to stretch by crossing-window or crossing-polygon...	
Select objects:	**D2**
Specify opposite corner:	**D1**
Select objects:	**<enter>**
Specify base point or [Displacement], Displacement.:	**OSNAp-Midpoin**t

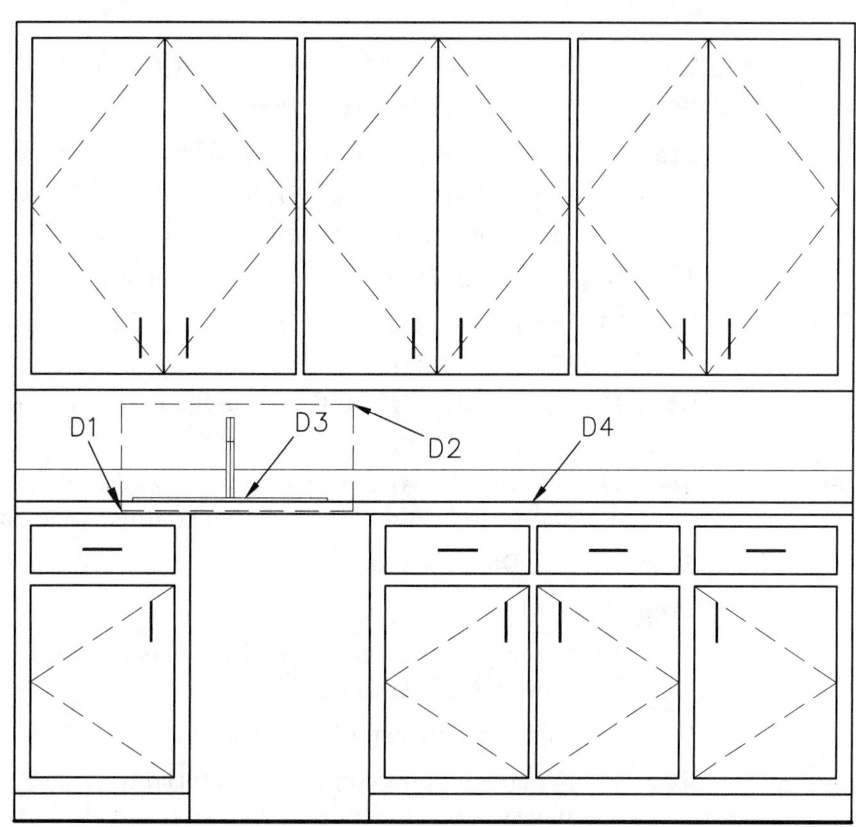

FIGURE 8–18
Use Stretch to Move the Sink to Its Correct Location

Prompt	Response
of	**D3**
Specify second point or <use first point as displacement>:	**D4** (with ORTHO ON, PICK: **a point directly above the space between the two center doors**)

Step 28. **Use Offset and Extend to draw the ceiling line above the cabinets (Figure 8–19). Change the ceiling line to the a-wall-extr Layer.**

Step 29. **Use the UCS command to save the current UCS, and name it LOWER. Set the UCS to World.**

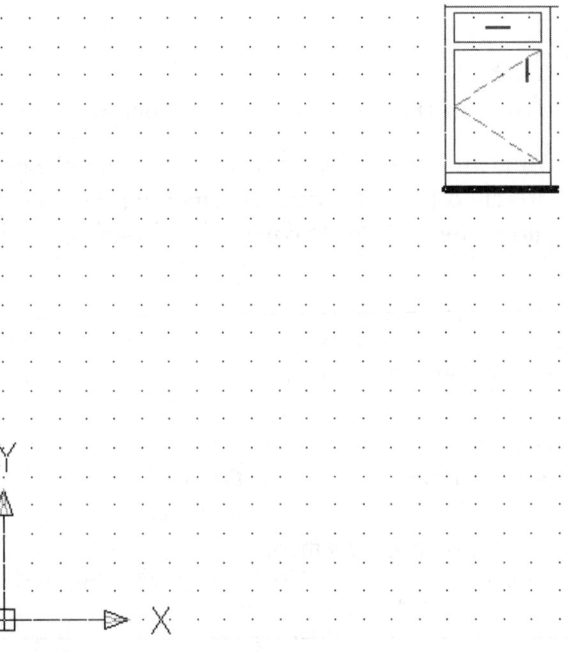

Step 30. **Set the drawing Annotation Scale to 1/2″ = 1′-0″.**

Step 31. **Set Layer a-elev-text current.**

Step 32. **Change the text style to Standard with the simplex font.**

Step 33. **In the Text Style dialog box, select the box beside Annotative under Size to make sure the annotative property is set to ON.**

Step 34. **Use Dtext, height 1/16″ to place the note on the refrigerator.**

Step 35. **Use Dtext, height 1/8″ to type your name, class, and the current date in the upper right area.**

Step 36. **Use Dtext, height l/8″ to type the underlined text, CONFERENCE ROOM CABINET ELEVATION.**

Step 37. **Add the elevation and section symbols to the elevation drawing, as shown in Figure 8–19. Use a 4″ radius circle and 3/32″ high text.**

Step 38. **Use Dtext, height 3/32″ to type the drawing scale.**

Step 39. **Set Layer a-elev-dim current.**

Step 40. **Set the dimensioning variables as described in Tutorial 7–1, with DIMSCALE set to 24.**

Step 41. **Add the dimensions as shown in Figure 8–19.**

Step 42. **When you have completed Tutorial 8–1, save your work in at least two places.**

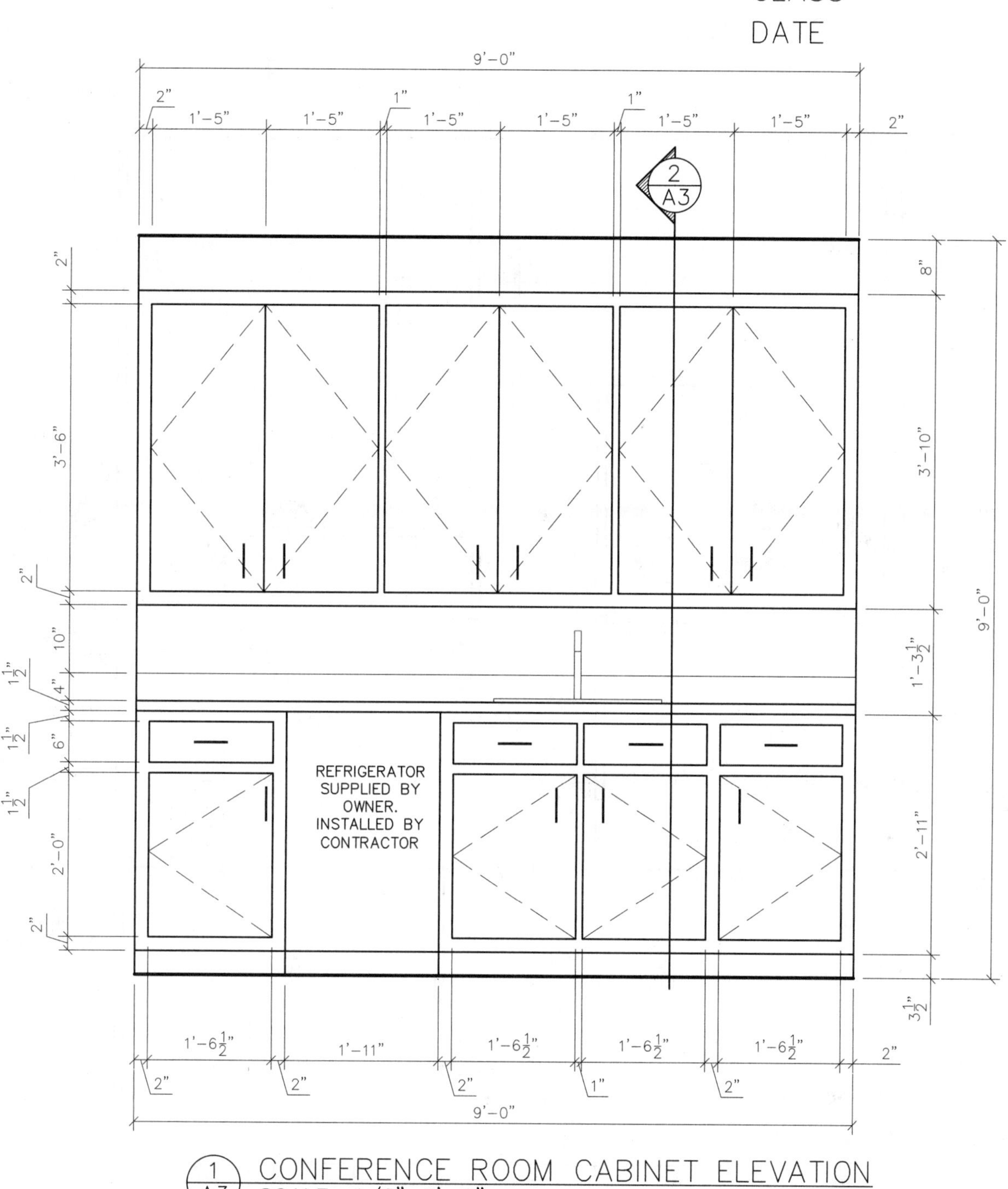

FIGURE 8–19
Complete the Elevation Drawing (Scale: 1/2″ = 1′-0″)

Step 43. Print Tutorial 8–1 to a scale of 1/2″ = 1′-0″.

Step 44. Add the elevation symbol, as shown in Figure 8–20, to your Tutorial 7–1: TENANT SPACE FLOOR PLAN drawing. Use a 1′ radius circle and 1/16″ high text (annotative).

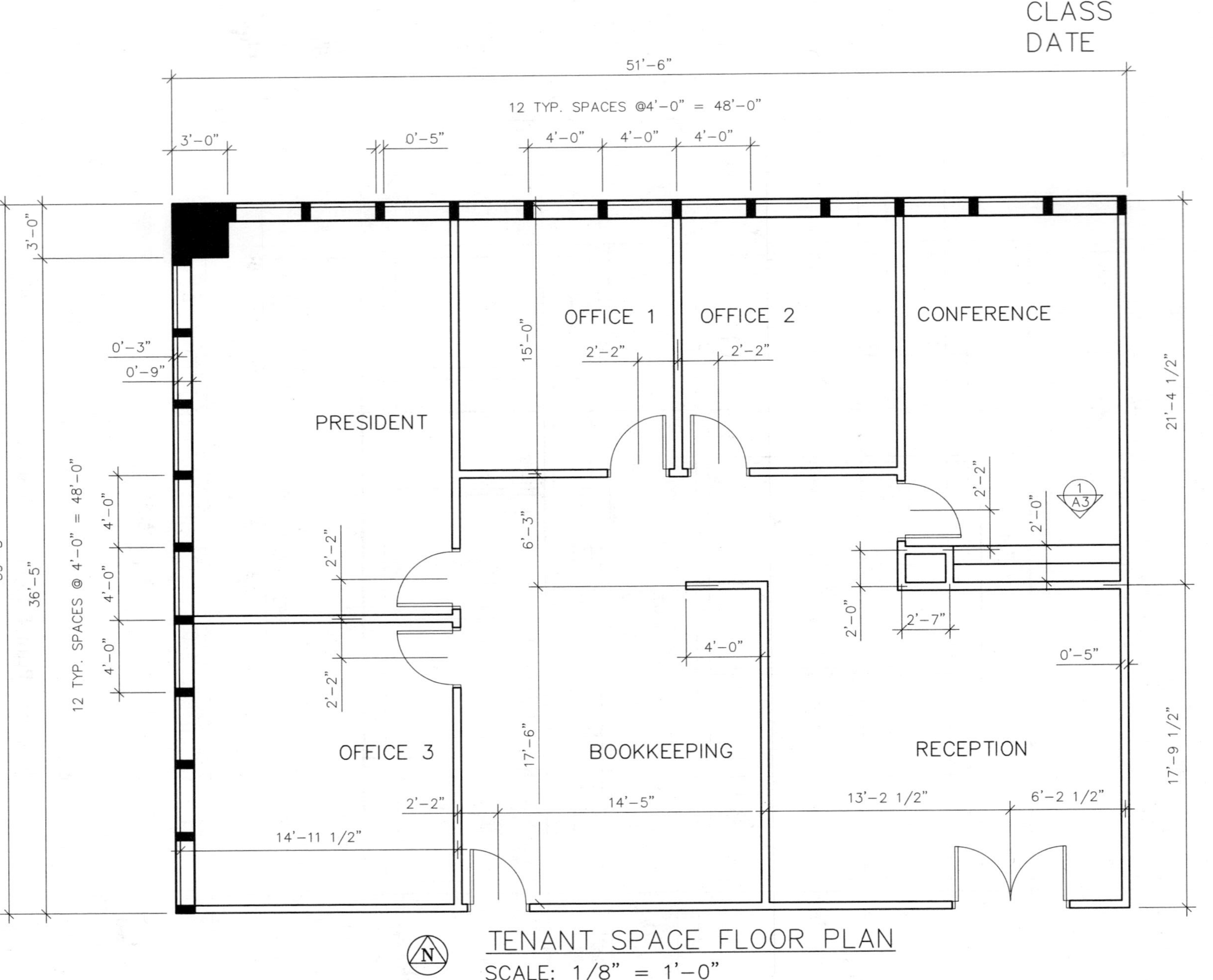

FIGURE 8–20
Tenant Space Floor Plan with Elevation Symbol (Scale: 1/8″ = 1′-0″)

Tutorial 8–2: Using the Multileader Command

The Multileader command can be used in a variety of ways. With Multileader you can draw a leader arrowhead first, tail first, or content first. You can align the text or balloons after you have drawn them. You can gather balloons so you have several balloons on the same leader, and you can add or delete leaders. In Tutorial 8–2, all of these options are used.

Step 1. Use your workspace to make the following settings:

1. Set drawing Units: **Architectural**
2. Set Drawing Limits: **8-1/2,11**
3. Set GRIDDISPLAY: **0**
4. Set Grid: **1/2″**
5. Set Snap: **1/8″**
6. Create the following layers:

LAYER NAME	COLOR	LINETYPE	LINEWEIGHT
Layer1	magenta	continuous	Default
Layer2	red	continuous	.004″(.09mm)

7. Set **Layer2** current.
8. Change the Standard text style from Arial font to simplex.
9. Set ATTDIA: to 0
10. Save the drawing as **CH8-TUTORIAL2**.

Step 2. Draw all of the 1/4″ radius circles shown in Figure 8–21 in the approximate locations shown. Space the circles 1″ apart so you have space for the leaders. Draw the concentric circles as shown in the lower left. Radii for the concentric circles are 1/4, 3/8, 1/2, and 5/8.

FIGURE 8–21
Draw 1/4″ Radius Circles and 1/4″, 3/8″, 1/2″, and 5/8″ Radius Concentric Circles

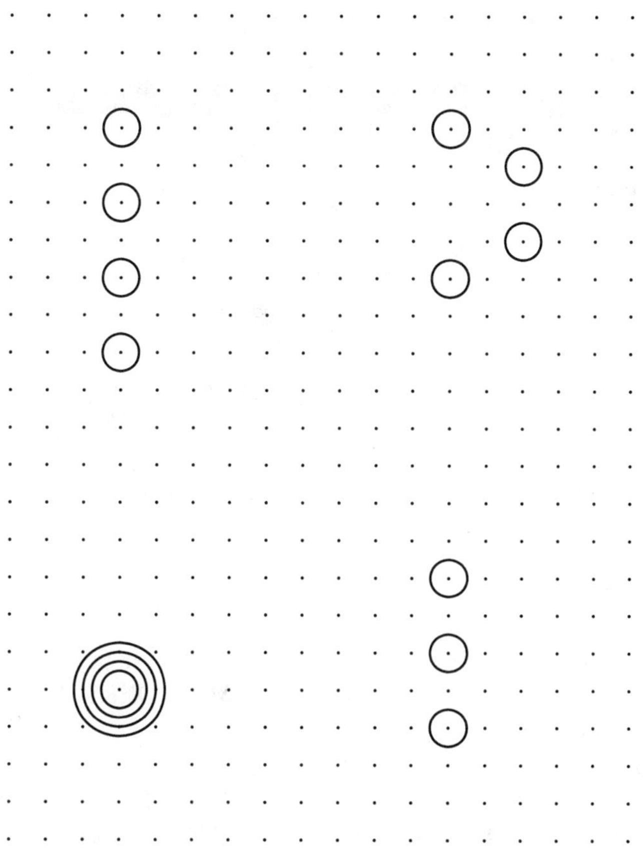

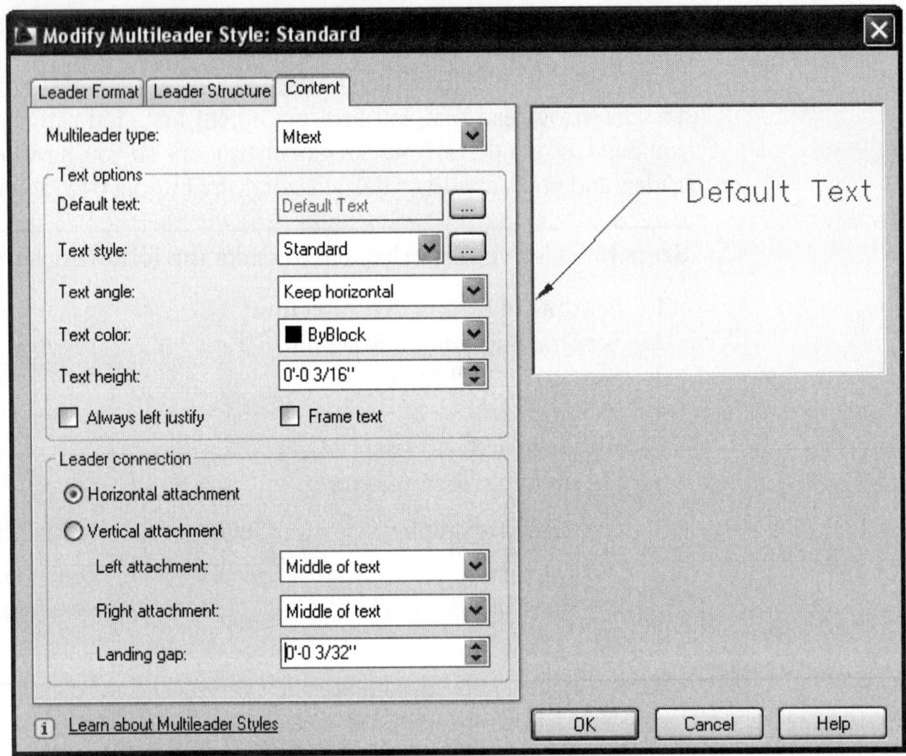

FIGURE 8–22
Modify Multileader Style: Standard Dialog Box, Content Tab

Step 3. **Set Layer1 current.**

Step 4. **Open the Multileader Style dialog box and make the settings (Figure 8–22), as described next:**

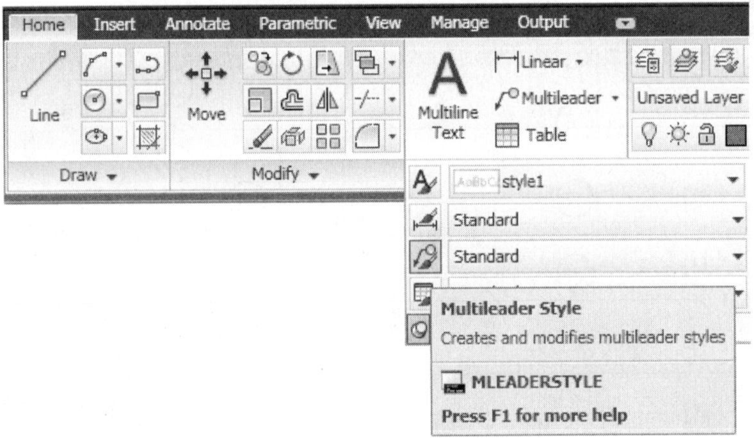

Prompt	Response
Command:	**Multileader Style** (or TYPE: **MLEADERSTYLE<enter>**)
The Multileader Style Manager appears:	CLICK: **Modify...**
The Modify Multileader Style: Standard dialog box appears:	CLICK: **the Content tab**

FIGURE 8–23
Modify Multileader Style: Standard Dialog Box, Leader Structure Tab

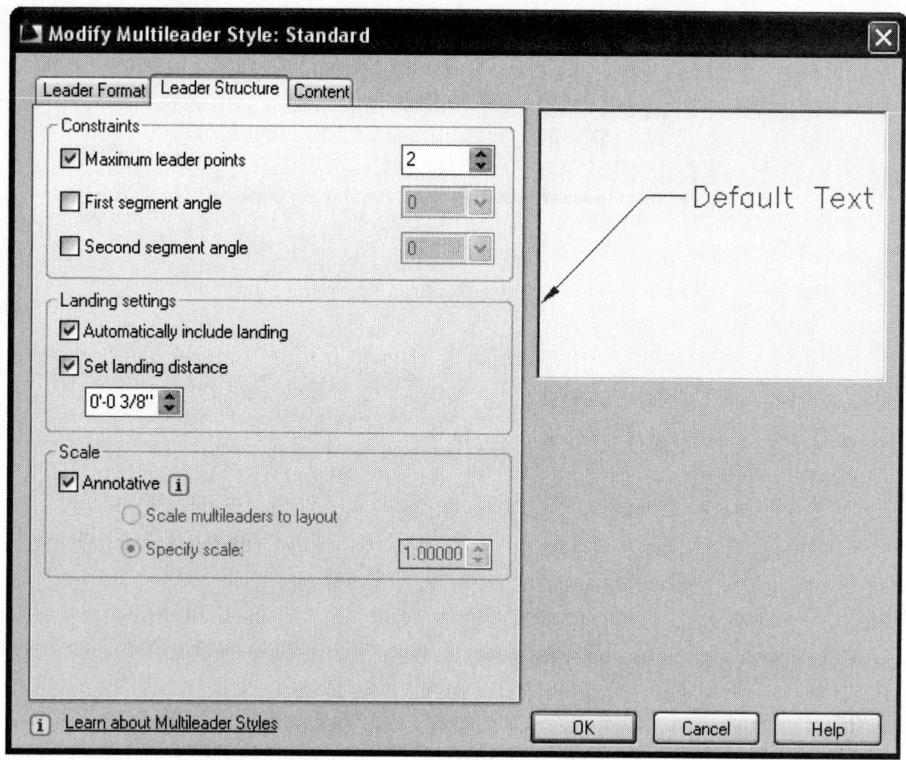

Prompt	Response
	Make the settings shown in Figure 8–22 if they are not there already: Multileader type: **Mtext** Text height: **3/16** Left attachment: **Middle of text** Right attachment: **Middle of text** Landing gap: **3/32** (The landing is the horizontal line of the leader, and the landing gap is the distance between the landing and the text.) CLICK: **the Leader Structure tab, Figure 8–23, and make these settings:** Landing distance: **3/8″** Scale – CHECK: **Annotative** (so leaders are annotative) CLICK: **the Leader Format tab, Figure 8–24, and make these settings:** Type: **Straight** Arrowhead Symbol: **Closed filled** Arrowhead Size: **3/16″** CLICK: **OK**
The Multileader Style Manager appears:	CLICK: **Set Current** CLICK: **Close**

Step 5. **Draw four multileaders using the Standard Multileader style. Draw two leaders arrowhead first, one leader landing first, and one leader content first, as described next:**

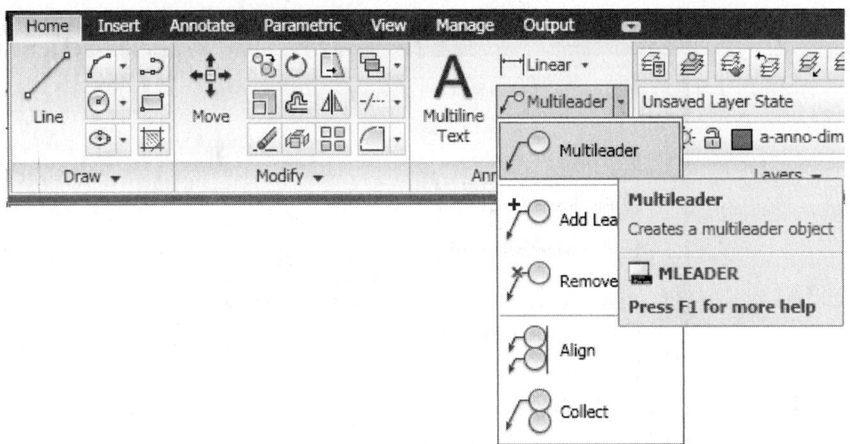

Prompt	Response
Command:	**Multileader** (or TYPE: **MLEADER<enter>**)
The Select Annotation Scale dialog box appears:	**Set the annotation scale to 1:1** CLICK: **OK**
Specify leader arrowhead location or [leader Landing first/Content first/ Options] <Options>:	**OSNAP-Nearest** (The arrow should touch the outside of the circle, but point toward the center of the circle.)
to	**Dl** (Figure 8–25)
Specify leader landing location:	**D2**
The Multiline Text Editor appears:	TYPE: **CIRCLE1** CLICK: **Close Text Editor** (on the Ribbon)

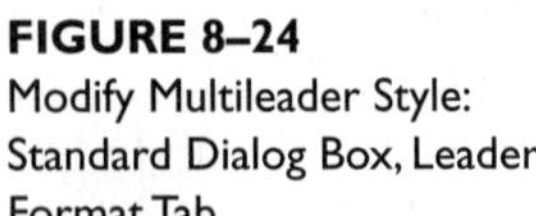

FIGURE 8–24
Modify Multileader Style: Standard Dialog Box, Leader Format Tab

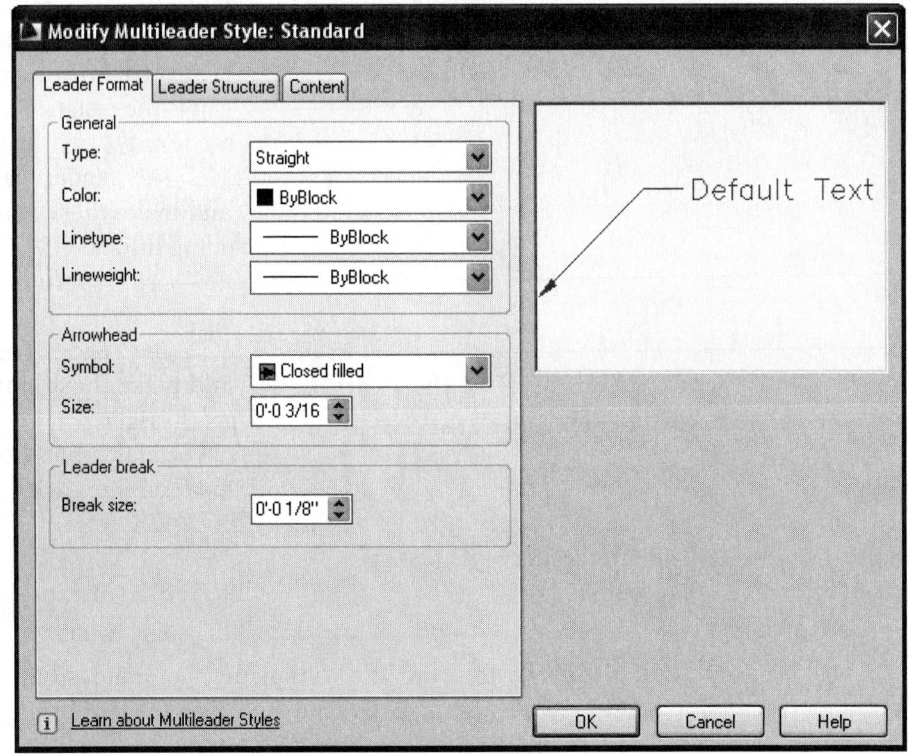

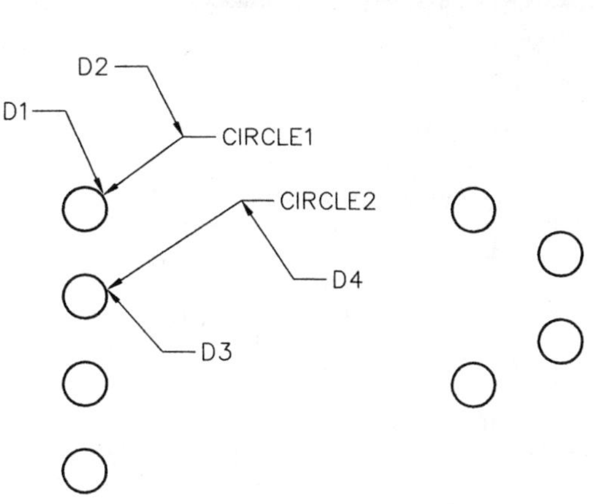

FIGURE 8–25
Draw Two Leaders Arrowhead First with the Standard Multileader Style

FIGURE 8–26
Draw One Leader Landing First (Dl, D2), Draw Another Leader Content First (D3, D4, D5)

Prompt	Response
Command:	**<enter>**
Specify leader arrowhead location or [leader Landing first/Content first/Options] <Options>:	**OSNAP-Nearest**
to	**D3** (Figure 8–25)
Specify leader landing location:	**D4**
The Multiline Text Editor appears:	TYPE: **CIRCLE2** CLICK: **Close Text Editor**
Command:	**<enter>**
Specify leader arrowhead location or [leader Landing first/Content first/ Options] <Options>:	TYPE: **L<enter>** (to select Landing first)
Specify leader landing location or [leader arrowHead first/Content first/Options] <Content first>:	**Dl** (Figure 8–26)
Specify leader arrowhead location:	**D2 (OSNAP-Nearest)**
The Multiline Text Editor appears:	TYPE: **CIRCLE3** CLICK: **Close Text Editor**
Command:	**<enter>**
Specify leader arrowhead location or [leader Landing first/Content first/Options] <Options>:	TYPE: **C<enter>**
Specify first corner of text or [leader arrowHead first/leader Landing first/Options] <Options>:	**D3**
Specify opposite corner:	**D4**
The Multiline Text Editor appears:	TYPE: **CIRCLE4** CLICK: **Close Text Editor**
Specify leader arrowhead location:	**D5 (OSNAP-Nearest)**

Step 6. **Align the leaders so all of the text starts at the same distance from the left, as described next:**

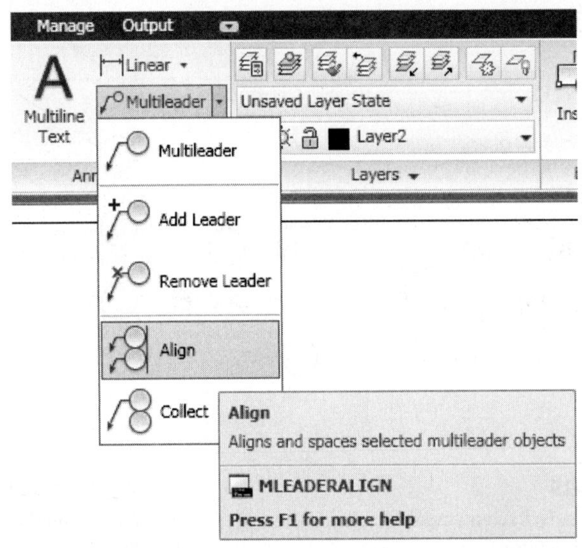

Prompt	Response
Command:	**Align Multileaders** (or TYPE: **MLEADERALIGN <enter>**)
Select multileaders:	**Use a window to select all four leaders** (The window can include the circles also.)
Specify opposite corner: 4 found	
Select multileaders:	**<enter>**
Current mode: Use current spacing	
Select multileader to align to or [Options]:	CLICK: **the top leader (CIRCLE1)**
Specify direction:	**With ORTHO ON**, CLICK: **a point below the bottom leader (CIRCLE4)**

The leaders are aligned, Figure 8–27.

Step 7. Set a Multileader Style so the text appears inside a circle, as described next:

Prompt	Response
Command:	**Multileader Style** (or TYPE: **MLEADERSTYLE<enter>**).
The Multileader Style Manager appears:	CLICK: **New...**
The Create New Multileader Style dialog box appears:	TYPE: **BALLOON** in the New style name: text box (Figure 8–28) CLICK: **Continue**
The Modify Multileader Style: BALLOON dialog box appears with the Content tab active:	CLICK: **the Content tab** CLICK: **Block** in the Multileader type: list CLICK: **Circle** (Figure 8–29) CLICK: **the Leader Structure tab** CLICK: **the Check in Annotative** so it disappears. CLICK: **the Specify scale:** option button

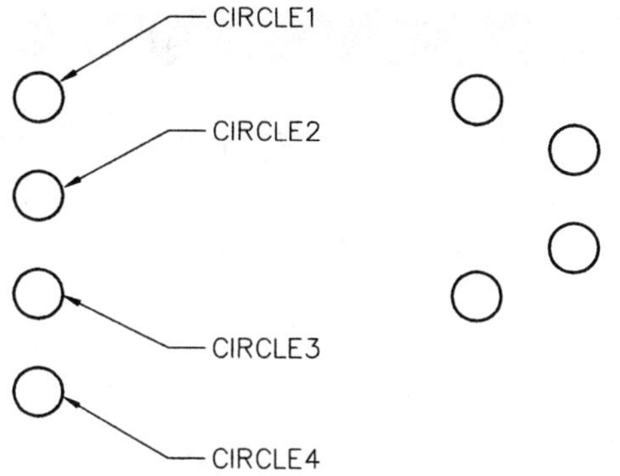

FIGURE 8–27
Leaders Are Aligned

Create New Multileader Style
New style name:
BALLOON
Continue
Cancel
Help
Start with:
Standard
Annotative

FIGURE 8–28
Name a New Multileader Style, BALLOON

Prompt	Response
	TYPE: **2** in the Specify scale: text box (Figure 8–30)
	CLICK: **the Leader Format tab and change the arrowhead Size: to 3/32.**
	CLICK: **OK**
The Multileader Style Manager appears:	CLICK: **Set Current**
	CLICK: **Close**

Step 8. **Draw four multileaders using the BALLOON Multileader Style. Draw all four with the content first, as described next:**

Prompt	Response
Command:	**Multileader** (or TYPE: **MLEADER<enter>**)

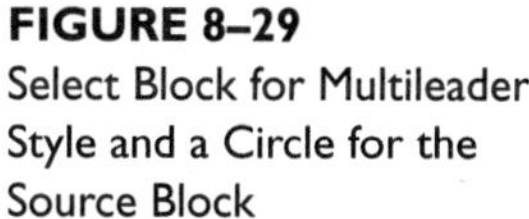

FIGURE 8–29
Select Block for Multileader Style and a Circle for the Source Block

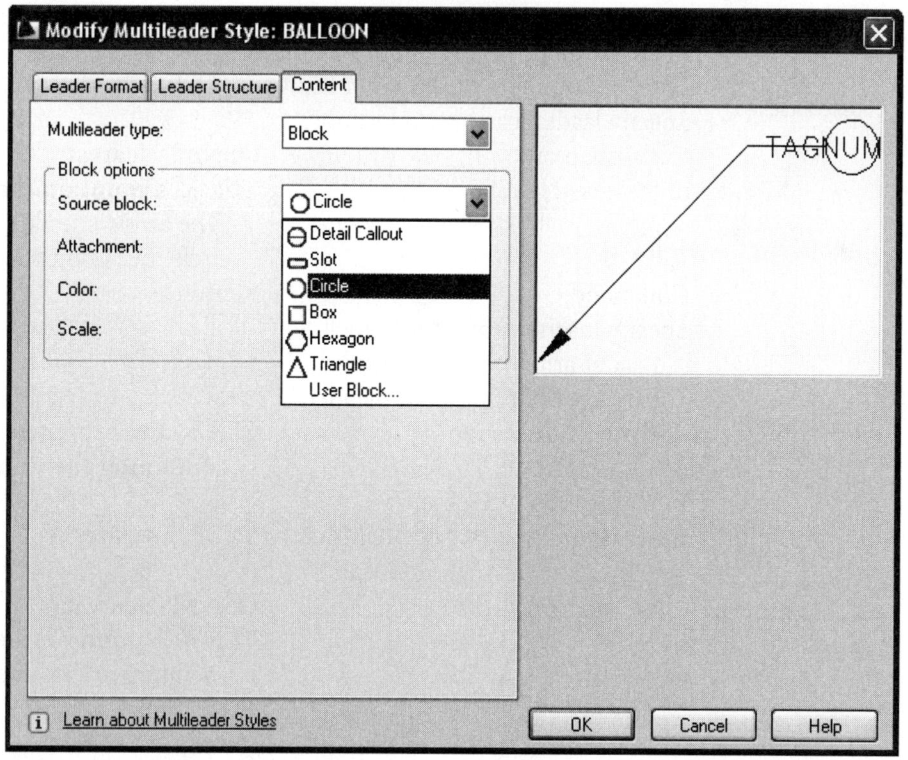

FIGURE 8–30
Deactivate Annotative and Specify a Scale of 2

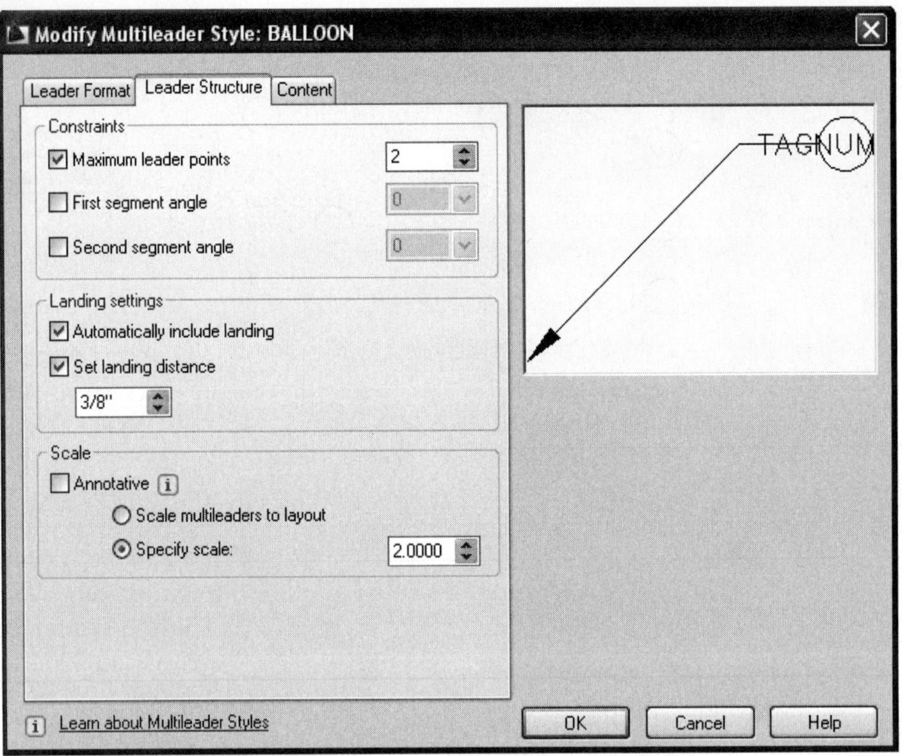

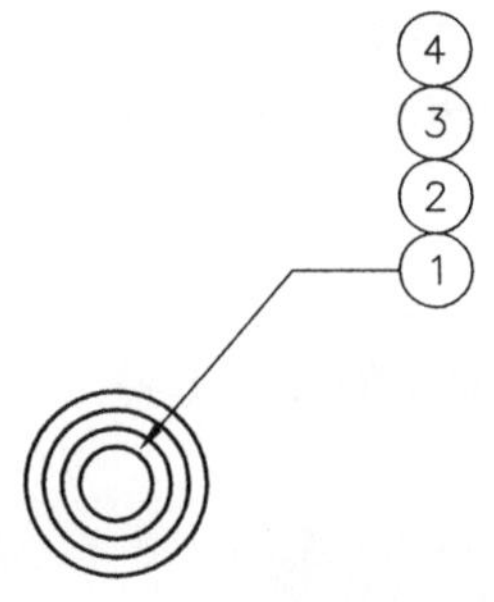

FIGURE 8–31
Collected Content Attached to One Leader

Prompt	Response
Specify insertion point for block or [leader arrowHead first/leader Landing first/Options] <leader arrowHead first>:	A circle appears on your cursor. CLICK: **a snap point on the drawing, to locate the center point of the circle, containing the number 1** (Figure 8–31)
Enter attribute values	
Enter tag number <TAGNUMBER>:	TYPE: **1<enter>**
Specify leader arrowhead location: <Osnap on>	**OSNAP-Nearest**
to	CLICK: **a point on the 1/4″ radius circle** (The arrow should touch the outside of the circle, but point toward the center of thecircle.)
Command:	**<enter>**
Specify insertion point for block or [leader arrowHead first/leader Landing first/Options] <leader arrowHead first>:	CLICK: **the center point of the circle containing the number 2** (Figure 8–31)
Enter attribute values	
Enter tag number <TAGNUMBER>:	**TYPE: 2<enter>**
Specify leader arrowhead location: <Osnap on>	**OSNAP-Nearest**
to	CLICK: **a point on the 3/8″ radius circle** (pointing toward the center is not important on the circles containing the numbers 2, 3, and 4)
Command:	**<enter>**

Prompt	Response
Specify insertion point for block or [leader arrowHead first/leader Landing first/Options] <leader arrowHead first>:	CLICK: **the center point of the circle containing the number 3** (Figure 8–31)
Enter attribute values	
Enter tag number <TAGNUMBER>:	TYPE: **3<enter>**
Specify leader arrowhead location: <Osnap on>	**OSNAP-Nearest**
to	CLICK: **a point on the 1/2″ radius circle**
Command:	**<enter>**
Specify insertion point for block or [leader arrowHead first/leader Landing first/Options] <leader arrowHead first>:	CLICK: **the center point of the circle containing the number 4** (Figure 8–31)
Enter attribute values	
Enter tag number <TAGNUMBER>:	TYPE: **4<enter>**
Specify leader arrowhead location: <Osnap on>	**OSNAP-Nearest**
to	CLICK: **a point on the 5/8″ radius circle**
Command:	**<enter>**

Step 9. **Collect the four leaders so all of the balloons are attached to one leader, as described next:**

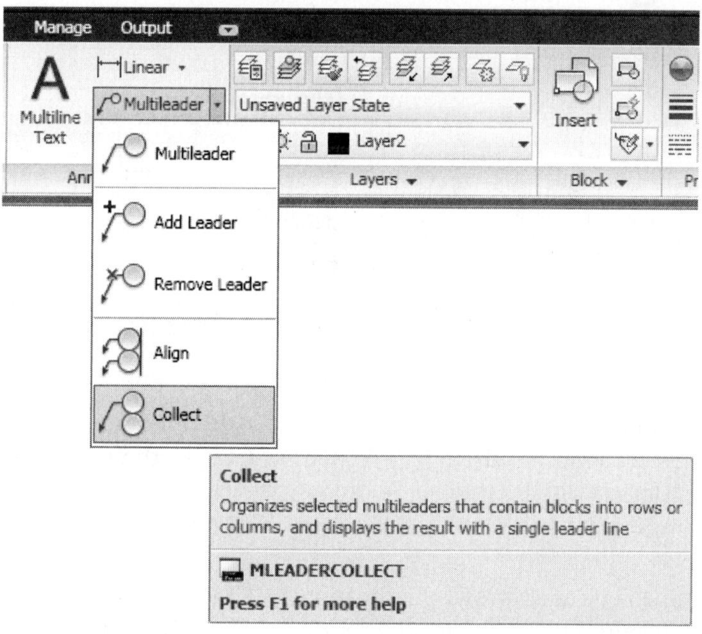

Prompt	Response
Command:	**Collect Multileaders** (or TYPE: **MLEADERCOLLECT<enter>**)
Select multileaders:	**select all four leaders**
Select multileaders:	**<enter>**

Prompt	Response
Specify collected multileader location or [Vertical/Horizontal/ Wrap] <Horizontal>:	TYPE: **V<enter>**
Specify collected multileader location or [Vertical/Horizontal/ Wrap] <Vertical>:	CLICK: **a point in the approximate location shown in Figure 8–31**

Step 10. Draw a multileader and add three leaders to it, as described next:

Prompt	Response
Command:	**Multileader** (or TYPE: **MLEADER<enter>**)
Specify insertion point for block or [leader arrowHead first/ leader Landing first/Options] <Options>:	A circle appears on your cursor. CLICK: **a snap point on the drawing, to locate the center point of the circle, containing the number 5** (Figure 8–32)
Enter attribute values	
Enter tag number <TAGNUMBER>:	TYPE: **5<enter>**
Specify leader arrowhead location:	CLICK: **a point on the top circle** (Figure 8–32)

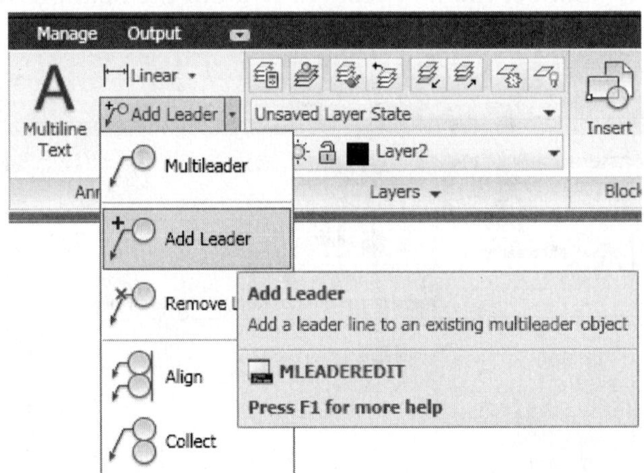

Prompt	Response
Command:	**Add Leader**
Select a multileader:	CLICK: **the multileader you just drew**
1 found	
Specify leader arrowhead location:	CLICK: **a point on the next circle** (Figure 8–33)
Specify leader arrowhead location:	CLICK: **a point on the next circle**
Specify leader arrowhead location:	CLICK: **a point on the last circle<enter>**

Step 11. Make a new Multileader Style with the following settings and draw three leaders from a hexagon labeled 6 (Figure 8–34), as described next:

1. **Name it HEX (start with a copy of BALLOON).**
2. **Not Annotative. Scale of 2.**
3. **Change Landing distance to 1/8″.**

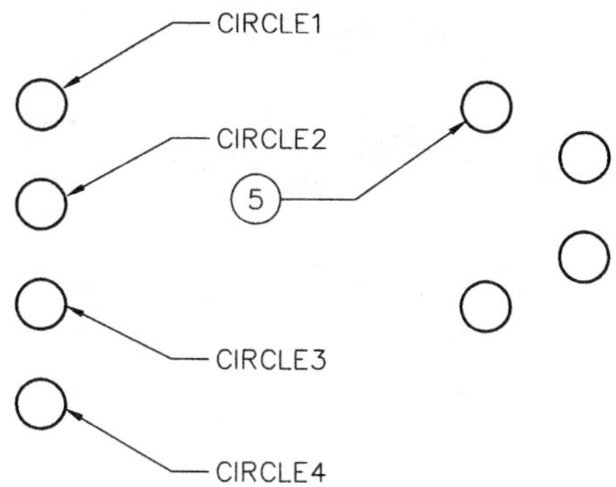

FIGURE 8–32
Draw the Multileader for the Number 5

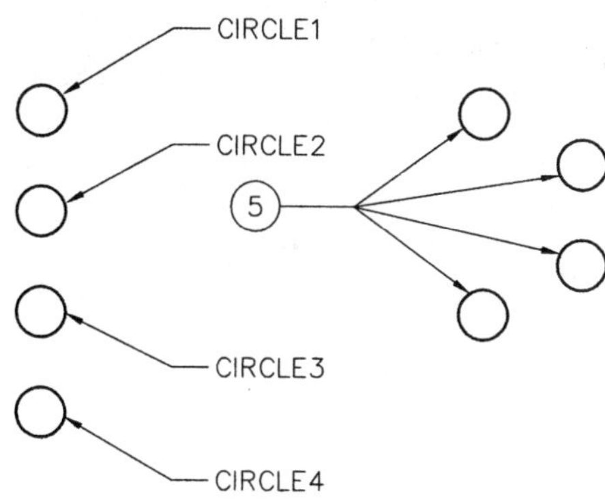

FIGURE 8–33
Draw One Leader and Add Three More

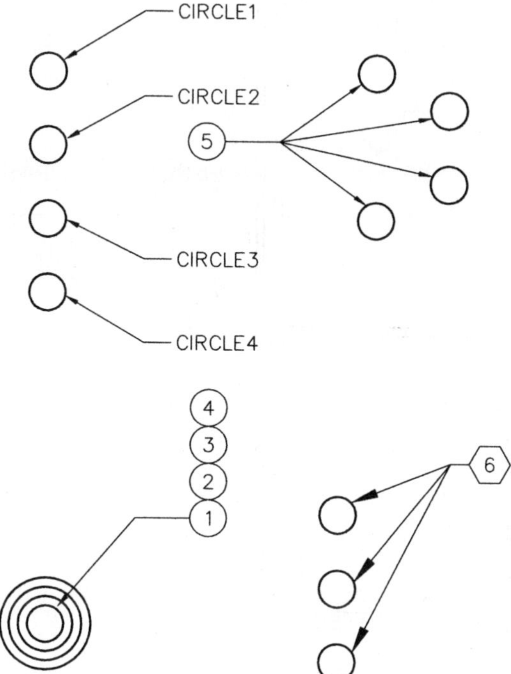

FIGURE 8–34
Tutorial 8–2: Complete

4. **Use a content Block—Hexagon.**
5. **Draw one leader with a 6 in the hexagon and add two leaders to it. Tutorial 8–2 is now complete.**

Step 12. **Save your drawing in two places.**

Step 13. **Print the drawing at a scale of 1:1.**

Tutorial 8–3: Tenant Space: Section of Conference Room Cabinets with Hatching

In Tutorial 8–3, a sectional view of the built-in cabinets on the south wall of the tenant space conference room is drawn. The sectional view of the south wall of the cabinets (Figure 8–35) shows many construction details that elevation and plan views cannot. Sectional views are imaginary cuts through an area. Hatched lines are used to show where the imaginary saw used to make these imaginary cuts touches the cut objects.

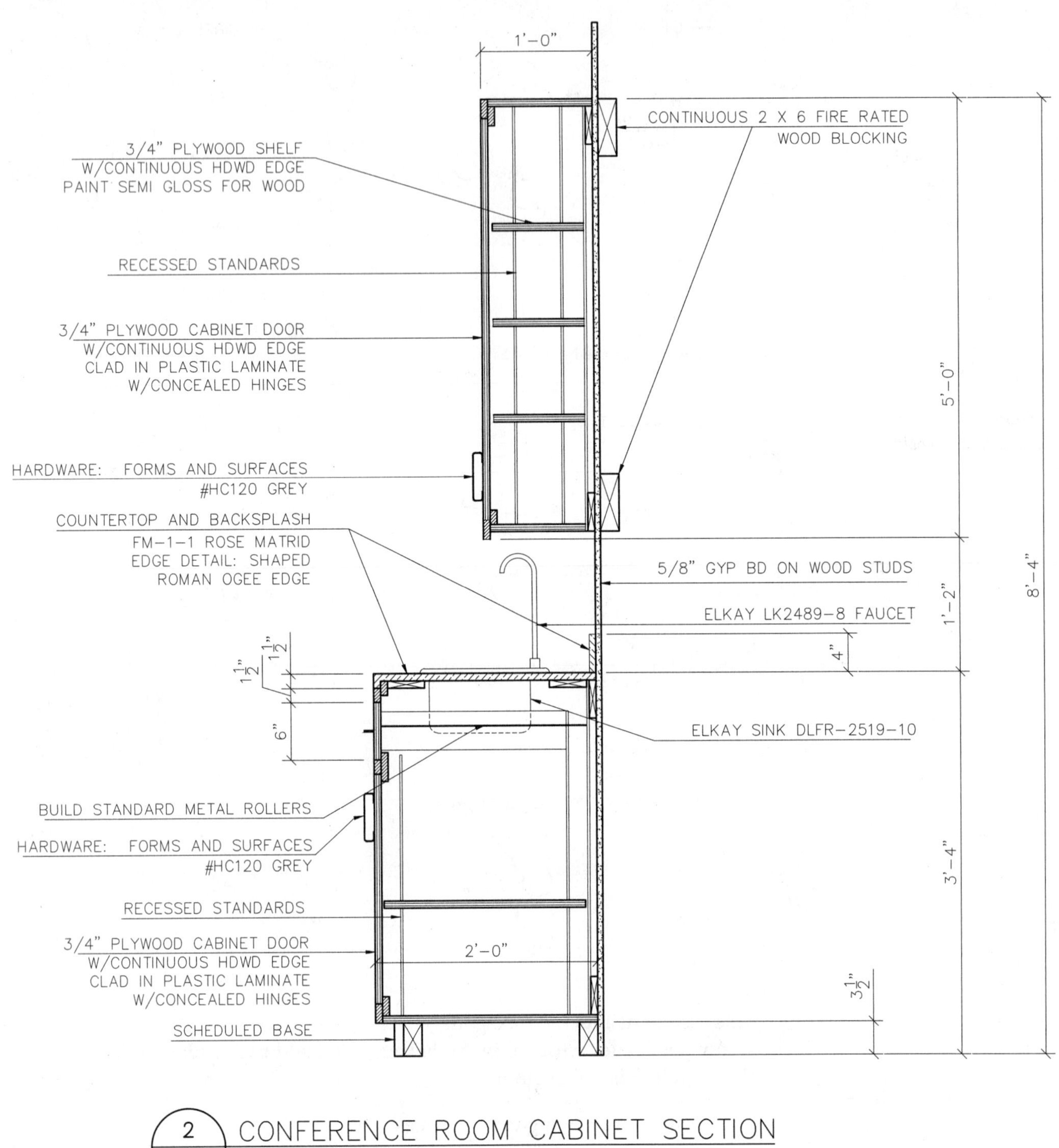

FIGURE 8–35
Tutorial 8–3: Tenant Space, Section of Conference Room Cabinets with Hatching (Scale: 3/4″ = 1′-0″)

This crosshatching is done in AutoCAD by drawing hatch patterns. Tutorial 8–3 will describe the Hatch command, used to draw hatch patterns.

When you have completed Tutorial 8–3, your drawing will look similar to Figure 8–35.

Step 1. Begin drawing CH8-TUTORIAL3 on the hard drive or network drive by opening existing drawing CH8-TUTORIAL1 and saving it to the hard

drive or network drive with the name CH8-TUTORIAL3. You can use all the settings and text created for Tutorial 8–1.

Step 2. Reset Drawing Limits, Grid, and Snap as needed.

Step 3. Create the following layers by renaming the existing layers and changing the Hidden linetype to Continuous:

LAYER NAME	COLOR	LINETYPE	LINEWEIGHT
a-sect	blue	continuous	.010″ (.25mm)
a-sect-pat1	cyan	continuous	.002″ (.05mm)
a-sect-text	green	continuous	.006″ (.15mm)
a-sect-dims	red	continuous	.004″ (.09mm)

Step 4. Set Layer a-sect current.

Step 5. After looking closely at Figure 8–35, you may want to keep some of the conference room elevation drawing parts. Use Erase to eliminate the remainder of the drawing.

Step 6. Change the underlined text to read <u>CONFERENCE ROOM CABINET SECTION</u>, change the top number in the balloon, and change the drawing scale to read as shown in Figure 8–35.

Step 7. Set the drawing Annotation Scale to 3/4″ = 1′-0″.

Step 8. The cabinet section must be drawn before you use the Hatch command to draw the hatching. Draw the sectional view of the south wall of the tenant space conference room full size (measure features with an architectural scale of 3/4″ = 1′ to find the correct size), as shown in Figure 8–36. Include the text and the dimensions. Use Layer a-sect to draw the view, Layer a-sect-text for the 1/16″ high (annotative) text and leaders, and Layer a-sect-dims, for the dimensions. Hatch patterns as shown in Figure 8–35 will be drawn on Layer a-sect-pat1.

Step 9. When the cabinet section is complete with text and dimensions, freeze Layers a-sect-text and a-sect-dims so that they do not interfere with drawing the hatch patterns.

PREPARING TO USE THE HATCH COMMAND WITH THE SELECT OBJECTS BOUNDARY OPTION

The most important aspect of using the Hatch command when you use "Select Objects" to create the boundary is to have the boundary of the area to be hatched defined clearly on the drawing. If the boundary of the hatching area is not clearly defined, the hatch pattern will not appear as you want it to. For example, some of the hatch pattern may go outside the boundary area, or the boundary area may not be completely filled with the hatch pattern.

Before you use the Hatch command in this manner, all areas to which hatching will be added must be prepared so that none of their boundary lines extend beyond the area to be hatched. When the views on which you will draw hatching have already been drawn, it is often necessary to use the Break command to break the boundary lines into line segments that clearly define the hatch boundaries. The Break command is used to break any of the lines that define the area to be hatched so that those lines do not extend beyond the boundary of the hatching area.

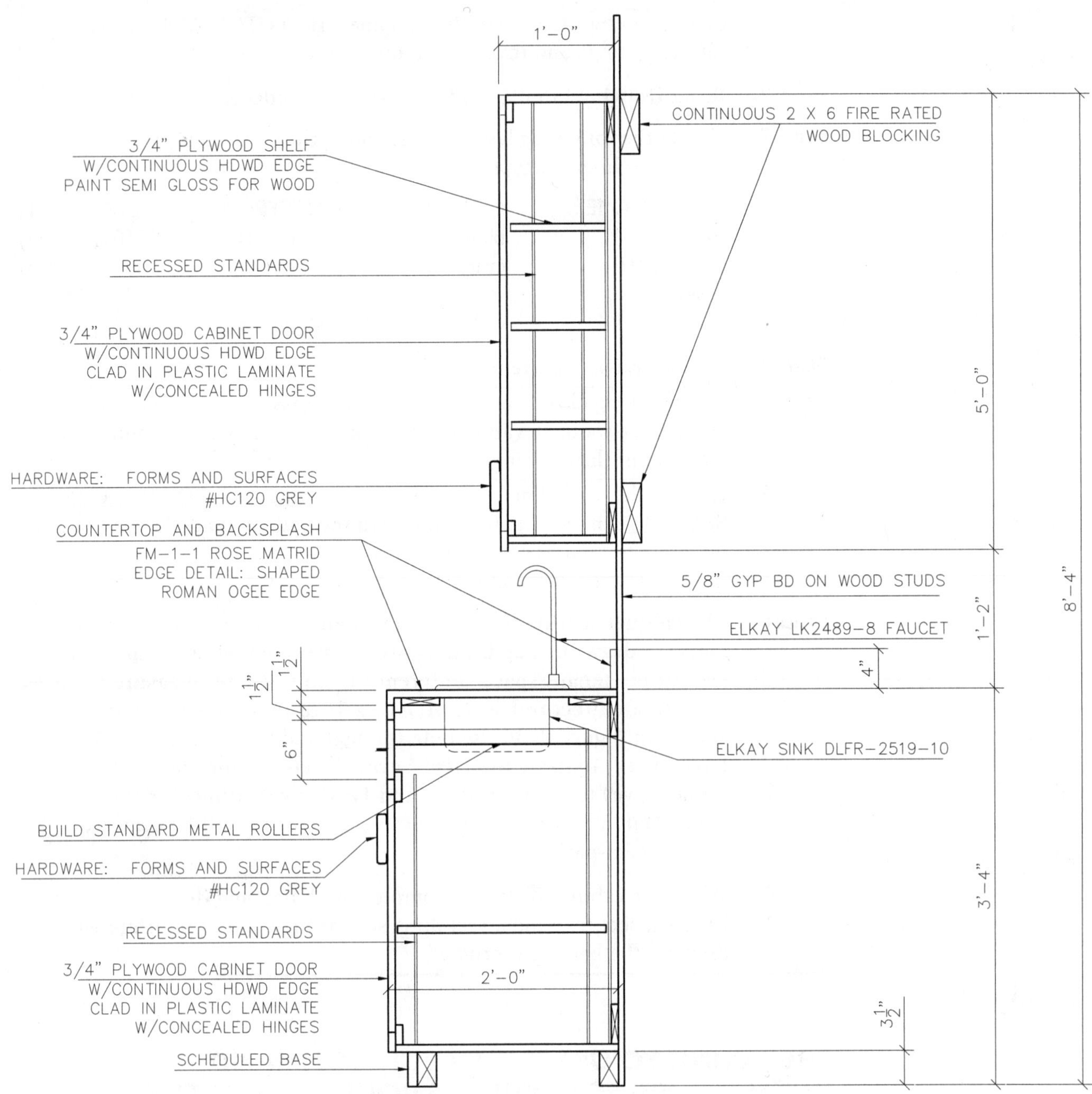

FIGURE 8–36
Tutorial 8–3: Tenant Space, Section of Conference Room Cabinets Before Hatching (Scale: 3/4" = 1'-0")

Step 10. **Use the Break command to help clearly define the right edge of the horizontal plywood top of the upper cabinets (Figure 8–37), as described next:**

Prompt	Response
Command:	**Break** (or TYPE: **BR<enter>**)
Select object:	**D1** (to select the vertical line)
Specify second break point or [First point]:	TYPE: **F<enter>**
Specify first break point:	**D2** (use **OSNAP-Intersection**)

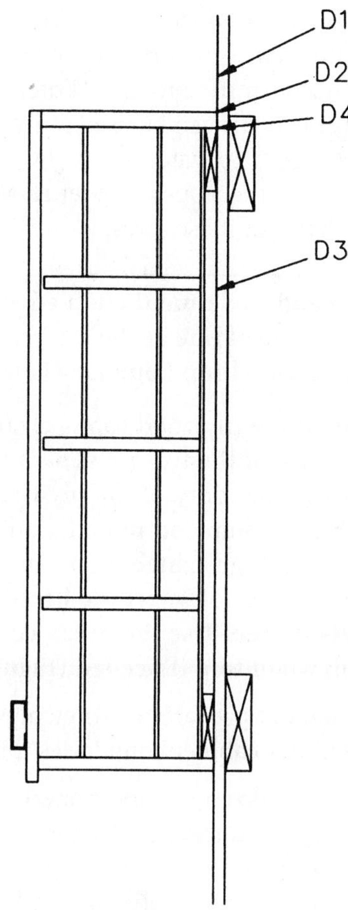

FIGURE 8–37
Use the Break Command to Clearly Define the Right Edge of the Horizontal Top Area of the Upper Cabinets

Prompt	Response
Specify second break point:	TYPE: @**<enter>** (places the second point exactly at the same place as the first point, and no gap is broken out of the line)
Command:	**<enter>** (repeat BREAK)
Select object:	**D3** (to select the vertical line)
Specify second break point or [First point]:	TYPE: **F<enter>**
Specify first break point:	**D4** (use **OSNAP-Intersection**)
Specify second break point:	TYPE: @**<enter>**

You have just used the Break command with the @ option to break the vertical line so that it is a separate line segment that clearly defines the right edge of the plywood top area.

TIP: You can also use the Break at Point command from the Modify panel on the Ribbon and eliminate typing F for first point.

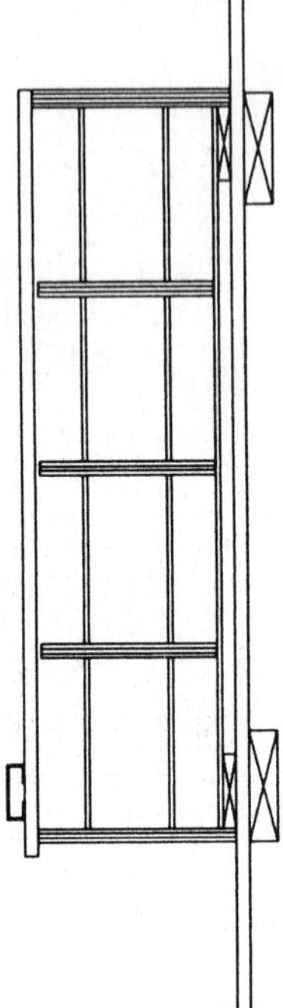

FIGURE 8–38 Upper Cabinets with Hatch Patterns Drawn

The Break command can also be used to erase or break a gap out of an entity. To break a gap out of an entity, simply click the first and second points of the desired gap at the command prompts. As shown in the prompt, "Enter second point (or F for first point):", the point used to "Select object:" can be used as the first point of the break.

Before using the Hatch command to hatch the plywood top, the three plywood shelves, and the plywood bottom of the upper cabinet as shown in Figure 8–38, you need to define clearly the boundaries of those areas.

Step 11. **Use the Break command to define the left edge of the plywood top boundary. Break the vertical line at the intersection of the bottom of the left edge of the plywood top boundary (Figure 8–38).**

Step 12. **When the boundary of the plywood top is clearly defined, the top, bottom, right, and left lines of the top are separate line segments that do not extend beyond the boundary of the plywood top. To check the boundary, use the Erase command to pick and highlight each line segment. When each line is highlighted, you can see clearly if it needs to be broken. Use the Esc key to cancel the Erase command so that the lines are not actually erased. Use the Break command on the top horizontal line of the plywood top, if needed (Figure 8–38).**

Step 13. Use the Break command to prepare the three plywood shelves and the plywood bottom of the upper cabinet boundaries for hatching (Figure 8–38).

Step 14. The Hatch command will also not work properly if the two lines of an intersection do not meet, that is, if there is any small gap. If you need to check the intersections of the left side of the plywood shelves to make sure they intersect properly, do this before continuing with the Hatch command.

TIP: You may prefer to draw lines on a new layer over the existing ones to form the enclosed boundary area instead of breaking, as described in this procedure. These additional lines may be erased easily with a window after you turn off all layers except the one to be erased. This is sometimes faster and allows the line that was to be broken to remain intact.

TIP: If there is a small gap at the intersection of two lines, change the gap tolerance (HPGAPTOL) system variable. TYPE: **HPGAPTOL <enter>** at the Command: prompt. Any gaps equal to or smaller than the value you specify in the hatch pattern gap tolerance are ignored, and the boundary is treated as closed. You can also use the Chamfer command (0 distance) or the Fillet command (0 radius) to connect two lines to form a perfect 90° angle.

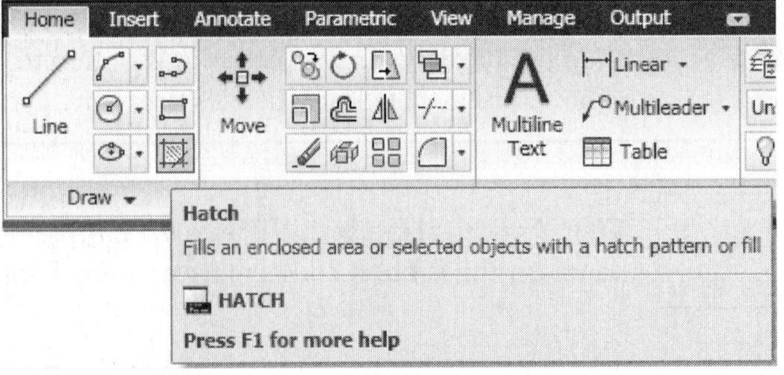

HATCH... HATCH AND GRADIENT DIALOG BOX; HATCH TAB

Type and Pattern

When the Hatch command is activated (TYPE: **H<enter>**), the Hatch and Gradient dialog box with the Hatch tab selected appears (Figure 8–39). As listed in the Type and pattern: list box, the pattern types can be as follows:

Predefined Makes the Pattern... button available.
User-defined Defines a pattern of lines using the current linetype.
Custom Specifies a pattern from the ACAD.pat file or any other PAT file.

To view the predefined hatch pattern options, CLICK: **the ellipsis (...)** to the right of the Pattern: list box. The Hatch Pattern Palette appears (Figure 8–40). Other parts of the Hatch and Gradient dialog box are as follows:

Pattern: Specifies a predefined pattern name.
Custom pattern This list box shows a custom pattern name. This option is available when Custom is selected in the Type: area.

Angle and Scale

Angle: Allows you to specify an angle for the hatch pattern relative to the X axis of the current UCS.
Scale: This allows you to enlarge or shrink the hatch pattern to fit the drawing. It is not available if you have selected User-defined in the Type: list box.

FIGURE 8–39
Hatch and Gradient Dialog Box, Hatch Tab

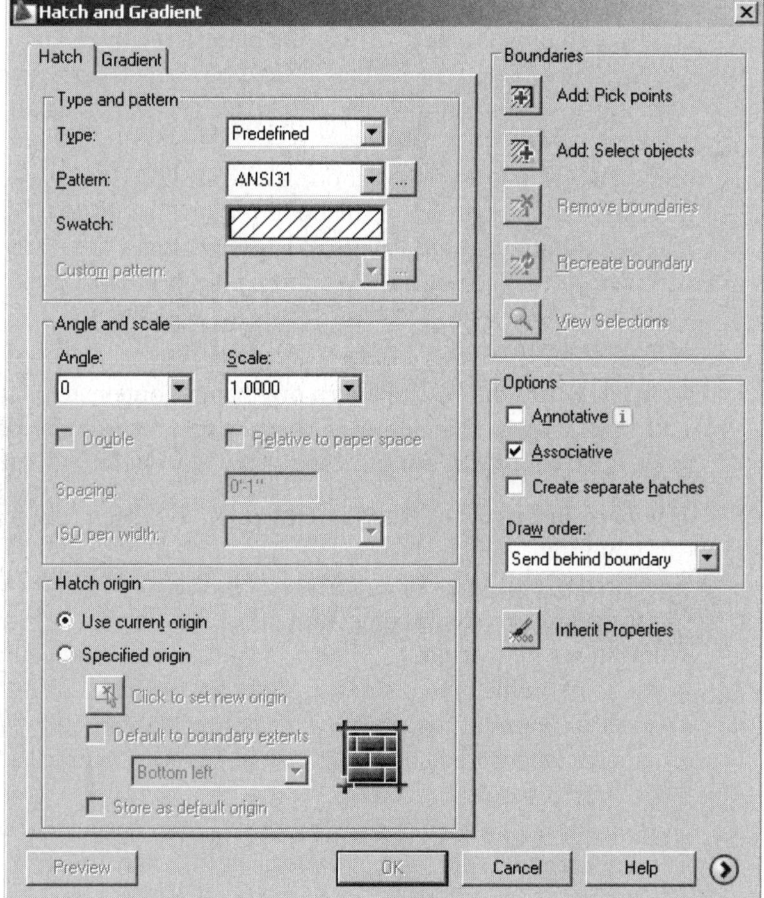

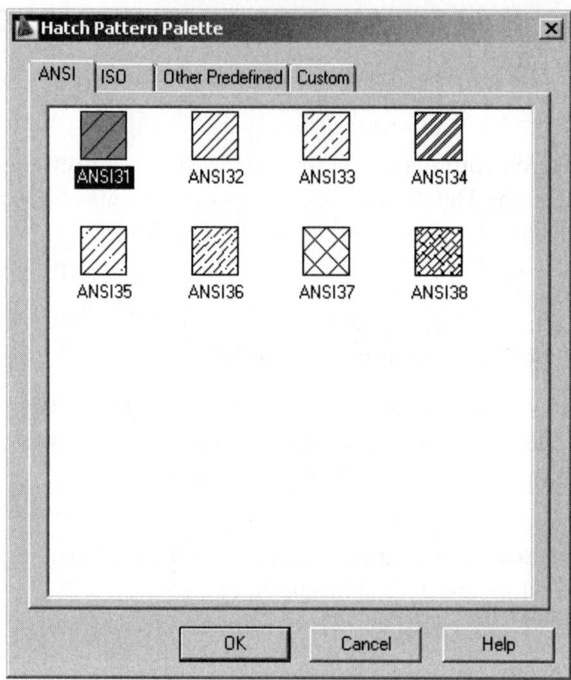

FIGURE 8–40
Hatch Pattern Palette

Double When you check this box, the area is hatched with a second set of lines at 90° to the first hatch pattern (available when User-defined pattern type is selected).

Relative to paper space Scales the pattern relative to paper space so you can scale the hatch pattern to fit the scale of your paper space layout.

Spacing Allows you to specify the space between lines on a user-defined hatch pattern.

ISO pen width If you select one of the 14 ISO (International Organization of Standardization) patterns at the bottom of the list of hatch patterns and on the ISO tab of the Hatch Pattern Palette, this option scales the pattern based on the selected pen width. Each of these pattern names begins with ISO.

Hatch Origin

Controls where the hatch pattern originates. Some hatch patterns, such as brick, stone, and those used as shingles, need to start from a particular point on the drawing. By default, all hatch origins are the same as the current UCS origin.

Use current origin Uses 0,0 as the origin by default. In most cases this will be what you want.

Specified origin Specifies a new hatch origin. When you CLICK: this option, the following options become available.

Click to set new origin When you CLICK: this box, you are then prompted to pick a point on the drawing as the origin for the hatch pattern.

Default to boundary extents This option allows you to select a new origin based on the rectangular extents of the hatch. Choices include each of the four corners of the extents and its center.

Store as default origin This option sets your specified origin as the default.

Preview button Allows you to preview the hatch pattern before you apply it to a drawing.

Boundaries

Add: Pick points Allows you to pick points inside a boundary to specify the area to be hatched.

Add: Select objects Allows you to select the outside edges of the boundary to specify the area to be hatched.

Remove boundaries Allows you to remove from the boundary set objects defined as islands by the Pick Points< option. You cannot remove the outer boundary.

Recreate boundary Allows you to create a polyline or a region around the hatch pattern.

View Selections Displays the currently defined boundary set. This option is not available when no selection or boundary has been made.

Options

Annotative You can make the hatch annotative by selecting the box beside Annotative under Options in the dialog box. To add the annotative hatch to your drawing, first, set the desired Annotation Scale for your drawing. Second, hatch the object (using type, pattern, angle, and scale) so you can see that the hatch is the correct size and appearance. If you change the plotting scale of your drawing, you can change the size of the hatch pattern by changing the Annotation Scale, located in the lower right corner of the status bar.

Associative When a check appears in this button, the hatch pattern is a single object and stretches when the area that has been hatched is stretched.

Create separate hatches When this button is clicked so that a check appears in it, you can create two or more separate hatch areas by using the Hatch command only once. You can erase those areas individually.

Draw order: The Draw order: list allows you to place hatch patterns on top of or beneath existing lines to make the drawing more legible.

Inherit Properties Allows you to pick an existing hatch pattern to use on another area. The pattern picked must be associative (attached to and defined by its boundary).

MORE OPTIONS

When the More Options arrow in the lower right corner is clicked, the following options, Figure 8–41, appear.

Islands

The following Island display style options are shown in Figure 8–41:

Normal When Normal is clicked (and a selection set is composed of areas inside other areas), alternating areas are hatched, as shown in the Island display style: area.

Outer When Outer is clicked (and a selection set is composed of areas inside other areas), only the outer area is hatched, as shown in the Island display style: area.

Ignore When Ignore is clicked (and a selection set is composed of areas inside other areas), all areas are hatched, as shown in the Island display style: area.

Boundary Retention

Retain boundaries Specifies whether the boundary objects will remain in your drawing after hatching is completed.

Object type: Allows you to select either a polyline or a region if you choose to retain the boundary.

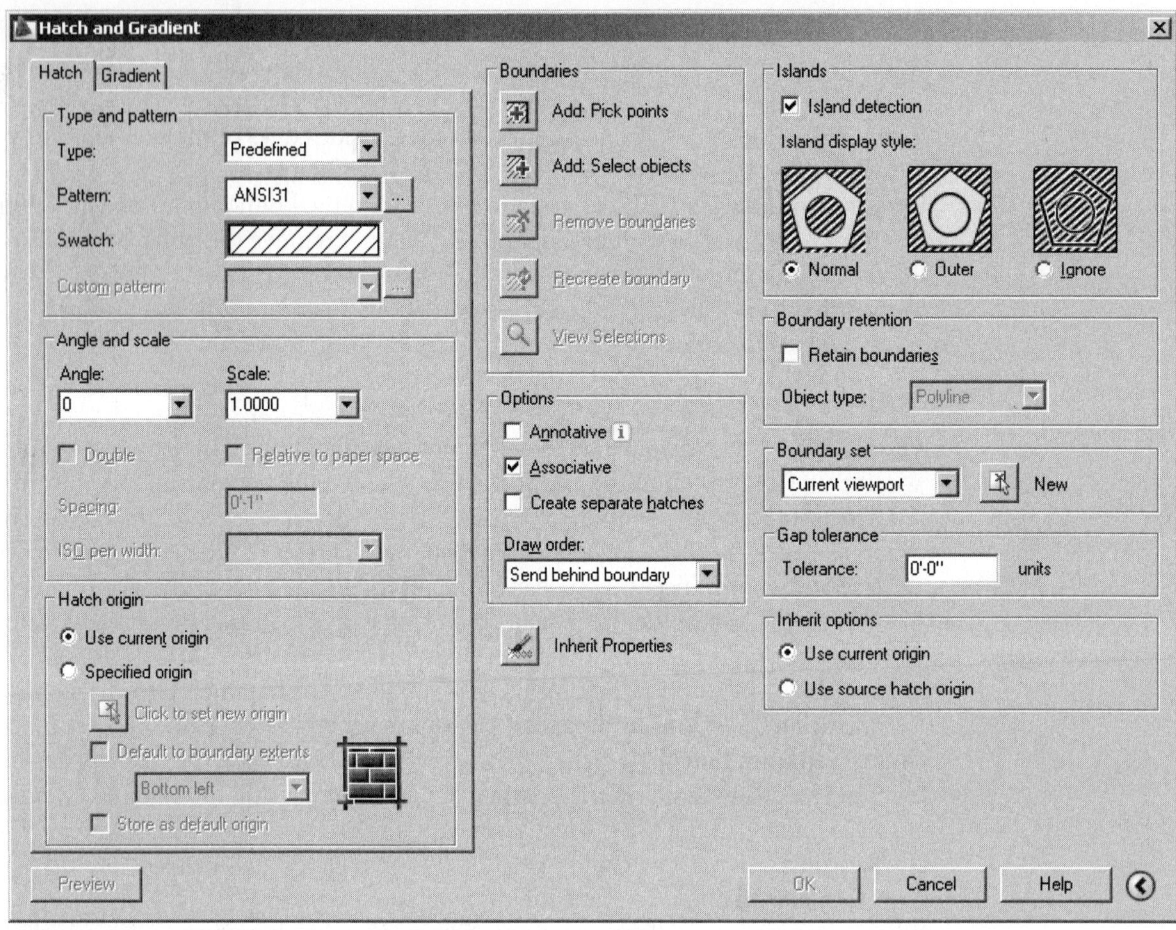

FIGURE 8–41
Hatch and Gradient Dialog Box, More Options

Boundary Set

List box This box allows you to select a boundary set from the current viewport or an existing boundary set.

New When New is clicked, the dialog box temporarily closes and you are prompted to select objects to create the boundary set. AutoCAD includes only objects that can be hatched when it constructs the new boundary set. AutoCAD discards any existing boundary set and replaces it with the new boundary set. If you don't select any objects that can be hatched, AutoCAD retains any current set.

Gap Tolerance

Allows a gap tolerance between 0 and 5000 units to hatch areas that are not completely enclosed.

Inherit Options

Allows you to choose either the current hatch origin or the origin of the inherited hatch for the new hatch pattern.

HATCH... HATCH AND GRADIENT DIALOG BOX; GRADIENT TAB

The Gradient tab (Figure 8–42) is discussed fully in Chapter 13.

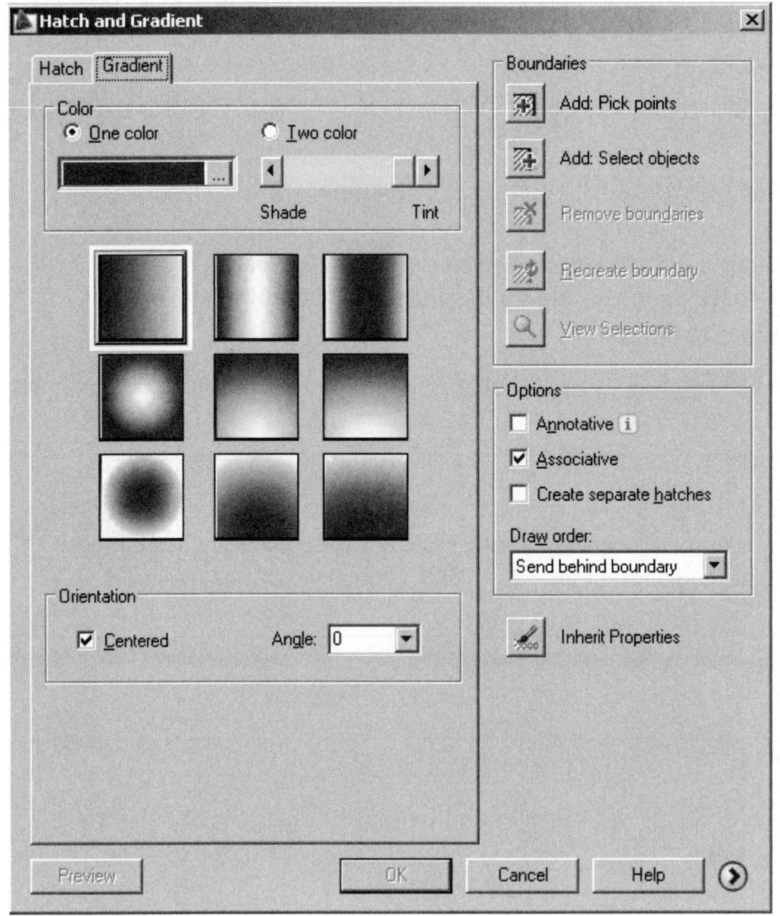

FIGURE 8–42
Gradient Tab

FIGURE 8–43
Use the Hatch Command with the Select Objects< Boundary Option to Draw a Uniform Horizontal-Line Hatch Pattern on the Plywood Top of the Upper Cabinets

---

Step 15. **Set Layer a-sect-patl current.**

Step 16. **Use the Hatch command with the Select Objects boundary option to draw a uniform horizontal-line hatch pattern on the plywood top of the upper cabinets (Figure 8–43), as described next:**

Prompt	Response
Command:	**Hatch** (or TYPE: **H<enter>**)
The Hatch and Gradient dialog box appears:	CLICK: **User-defined** in the pattern Type: area Angle: **0** Spacing: **1/4″** CLICK: **Add: Select objects**
Select objects or [picK internal point/remove Boundaries]:	CLICK: **D1**
Specify opposite corner:	CLICK: **D2**
Select objects or [picK internal point/remove Boundaries]:	**<enter>**
The Hatch and Gradient dialog box appears:	CLICK: **Preview**
Pick or press Esc to return to dialog or <Right-click to accept hatch>:	

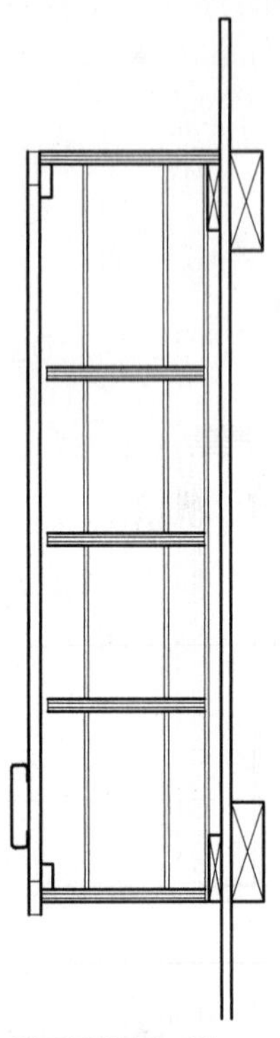

FIGURE 8–44
Draw a Hatch Pattern on the Three Plywood Shelves and the Plywood Bottom of the Upper Cabinet

Prompt	Response
(A preview of your hatching appears):	**RIGHT-CLICK** (if the correct hatch pattern was previewed; if not, CLICK: **Esc** and fix the problem)

The plywood top of the upper cabinet is now hatched.

Step 17. Use the same hatching procedure to draw a hatch pattern on the three plywood shelves and the plywood bottom of the upper cabinet, as shown in Figure 8–44.

NOTE: Although the "Pick Points" method of creating hatch boundaries is often much easier, you must know how to use "Select Objects" as well. There are instances when "Pick Points" just does not work.

TIP: Turn off or freeze the text and dimension layers if they interfere with hatching.

When you use the Pick Points boundary option to create a boundary for the hatch pattern, AutoCAD allows you to pick any point inside the area, and the boundary is automatically created. You do not have to prepare the boundary of the area as you did with the Select Objects boundary option, but you have to make sure there are no gaps in the boundary.

Step 18. Use the Hatch command with the Pick Points boundary option to draw a uniform vertical-line hatch pattern on the upper cabinet door (Figure 8–45), as described next:

Prompt	Response
Command:	**Hatch** (or TYPE: **H<enter>**)
The Hatch and Gradient dialog box appears:	CLICK: **User-defined** in the pattern Type: area Angle: **90** Spacing: **1/4″** CLICK: **Add: Pick points**
Pick internal point or [Select objects/remove Boundaries]:	CLICK: **D1** (inside the door symbol)
Pick internal point or [Select objects/remove Boundaries]:	**<enter>**

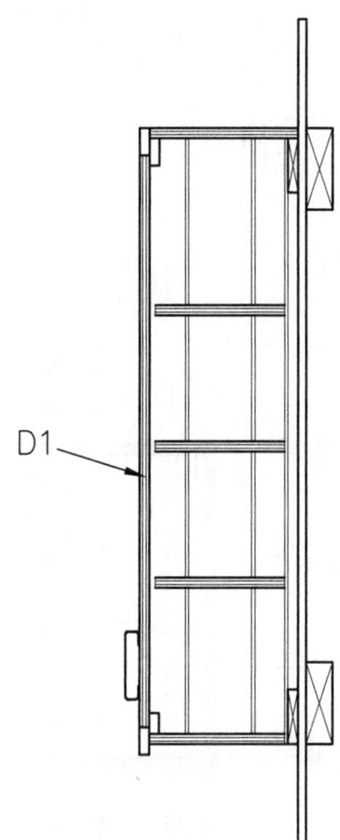

FIGURE 8–45
Use the Hatch Command with the Pick Points Boundary Option to Draw a Uniform Vertical-Line Hatch Pattern on the Upper Cabinet Door

Prompt	Response
The Hatch and Gradient dialog box appears:	CLICK: **Preview**
Pick or press Esc to return to dialog or <Right-click to accept hatch>:	
(A preview of your hatching appears):	**RIGHT-CLICK** (if the correct hatch pattern was previewed; if not, CLICK: **Esc** and fix the problem)

TIP: You may have to draw a line across the top of the 5/8″ gypsum board to create the hatch pattern on the gypsum board.

Step 19. Use the Hatch command with the Pick Points boundary option to draw the AR-SAND hatch pattern on the 5/8″ gypsum board (Figures 8–46, 8–47, and 8–48), as described next:

Prompt	Response
Command:	**Hatch**
The Hatch and Gradient dialog box appears:	CLICK: **Predefined** CLICK: ... (to the right of the Pattern: list box)
The Hatch Pattern Palette appears:	CLICK: **the Other Predefined tab** CLICK: **AR-SAND** (Figure 8–46) CLICK: **OK**
The Hatch and Gradient dialog box appears (Figure 8–47):	CLICK: **0** (in the Angle box) TYPE: **3/8″** (in the Scale: box) CLICK: **Add: Pick points**

NOTE: Remember when you use the Pick Points button, often the complete boundary of the area to be hatched must be visible on the screen.

Prompt	Response
Pick internal point or [Select objects/remove Boundaries]:	CLICK: **any point inside the lines defining the 5/8″ gypsum board boundary** (Figure 8–48)
Pick internal point or [Select objects/remove Boundaries]:	**<enter>**
The Hatch and Gradient dialog box appears:	CLICK: **OK**

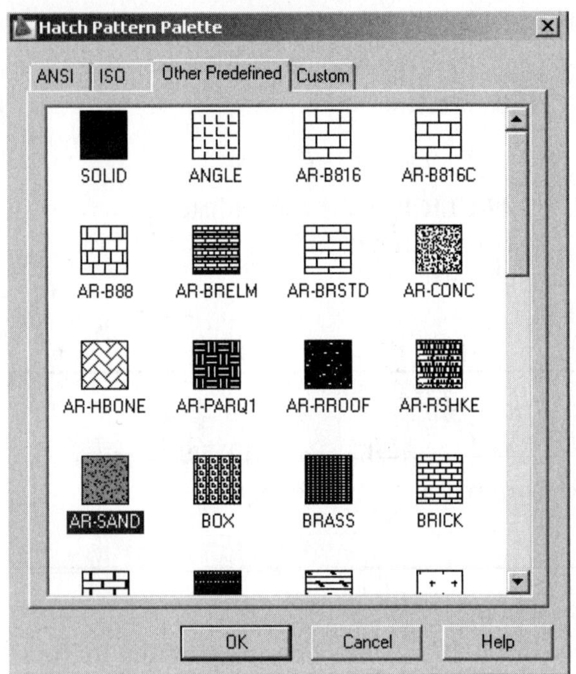

FIGURE 8–46
Select AR-SAND

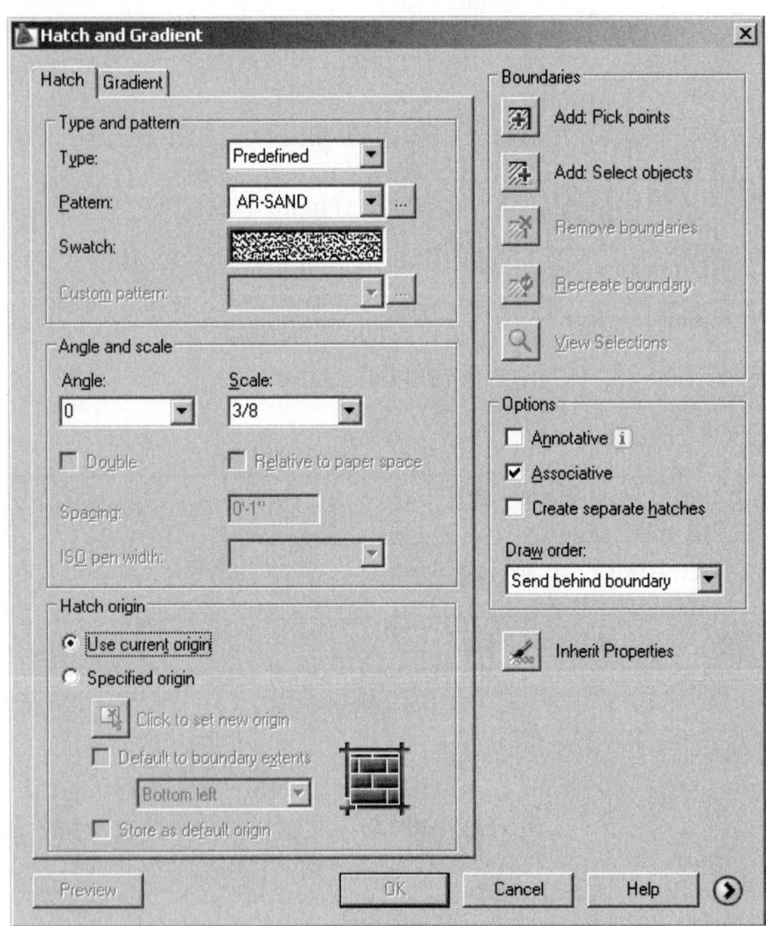

FIGURE 8–47
Specify Scale for AR-SAND

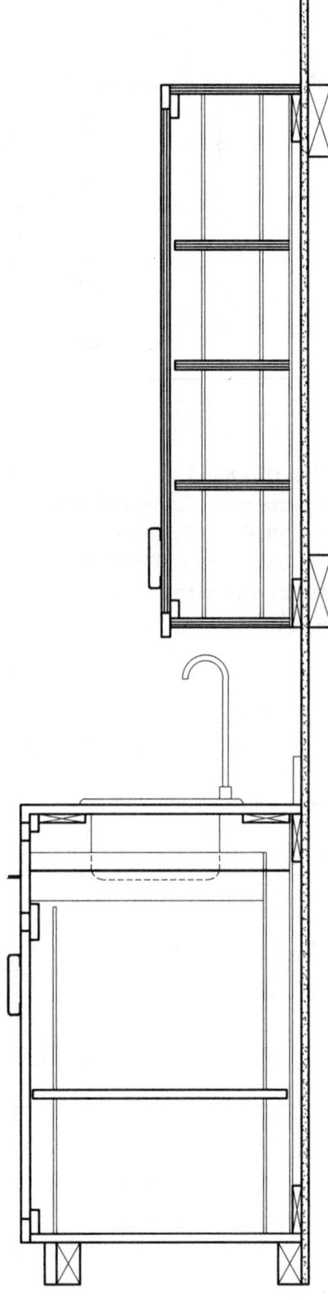

FIGURE 8–48
Use the Hatch Command to Draw the AR-SAND Hatch Pattern on the 5/8″ Gypsum Board

The 5/8″ gypsum board is now hatched. (If you get an error message, try 1/2″ for scale in the Scale: box or draw a line across the top of the gypsum board.)

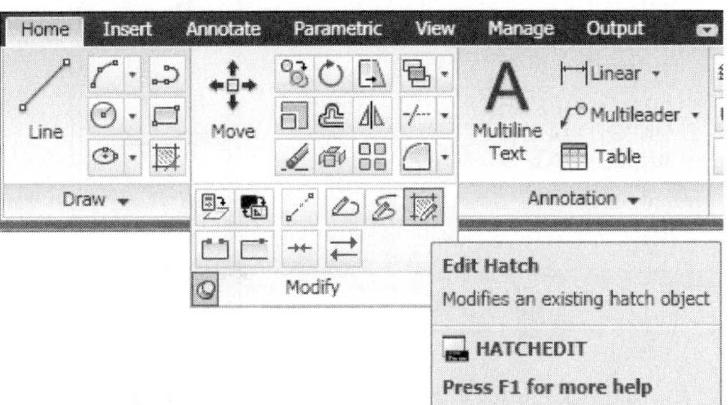

EDITING HATCH PATTERNS

Select **Edit Hatch...** or TYPE: **HE<enter>** or DOUBLE-CLICK: **on a hatch pattern** to access the Hatch Edit dialog box (Figure 8–49). You can edit the pattern, angle, scale, origin, and draw order of the hatch pattern.

If you already have an associative hatch pattern on a drawing that has one or two lines extending outside the hatch area, if necessary, explode the hatch pattern. The lines may then be trimmed, because they are individual lines.

FIGURE 8–49
Hatch Edit Dialog Box

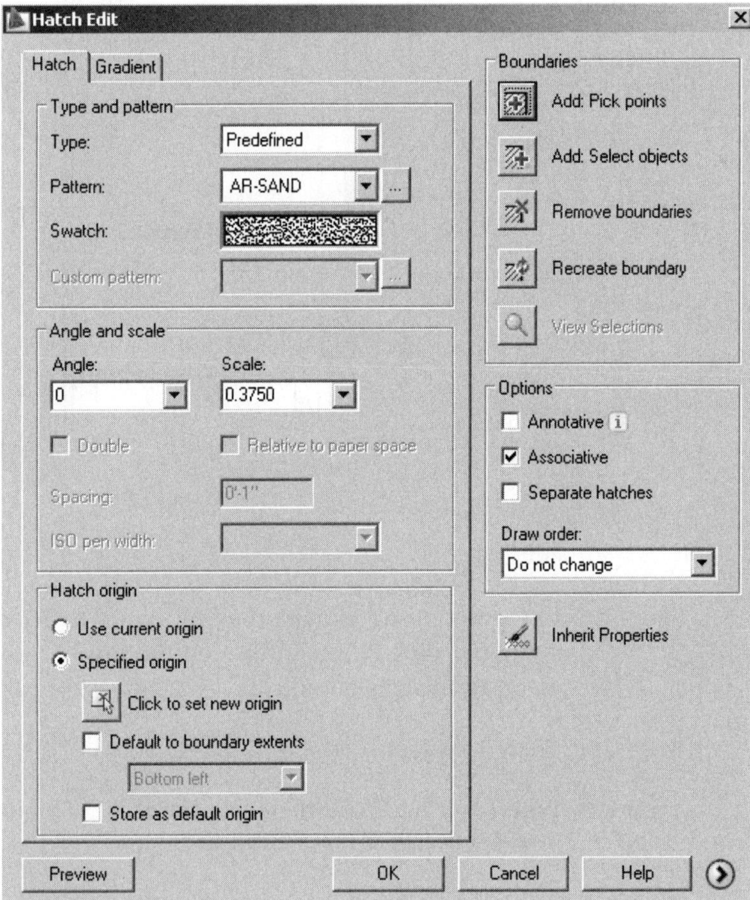

FIGURE 8–50
Draw the Hatch Patterns on the Upper and Lower Cabinets as Shown

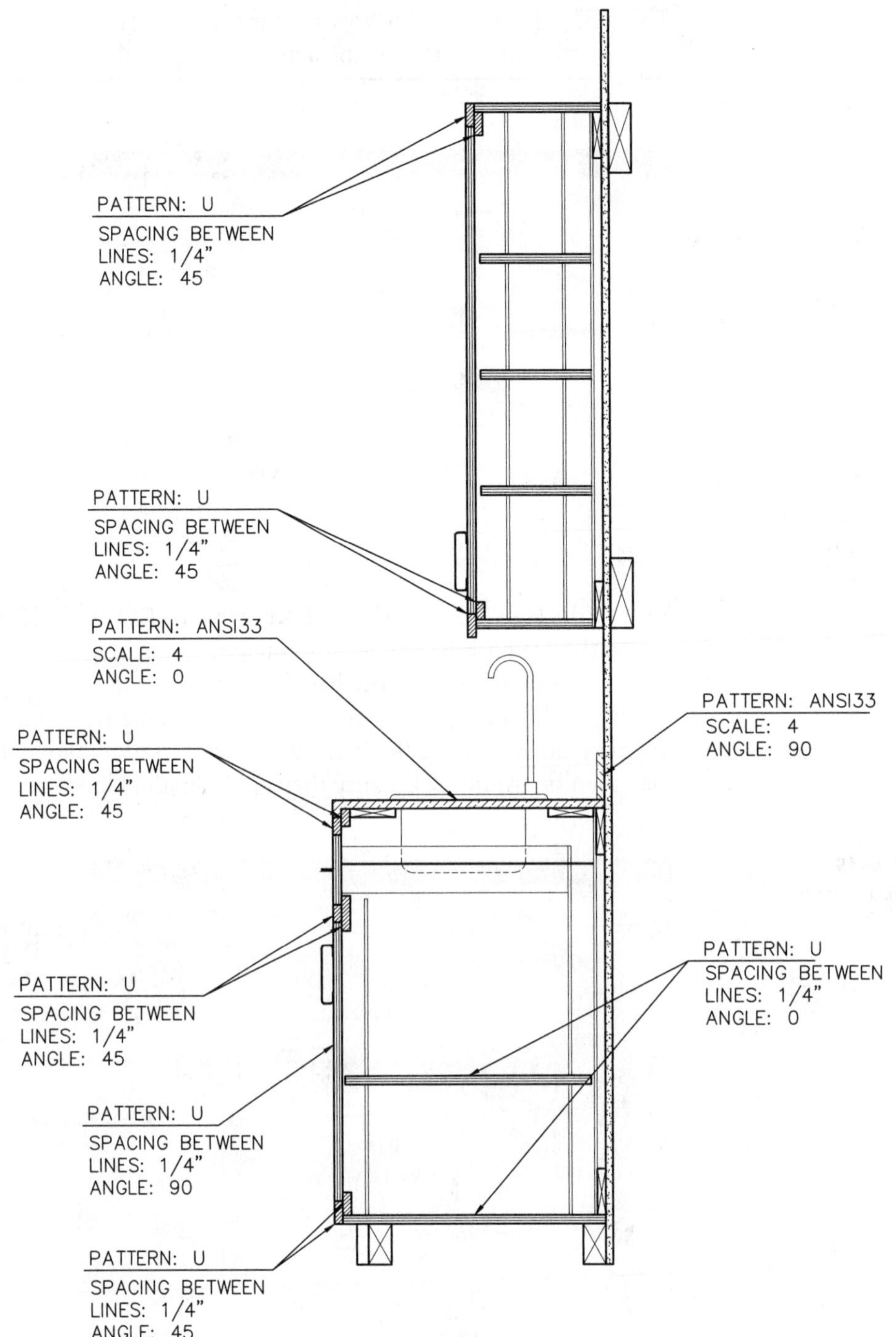

Step 20. Using the patterns described in Figure 8–50, draw hatch patterns by using the Pick Points option on the lower cabinets and the end views of wood in the upper cabinets.

Step 21. Thaw Layers a-sect-text and a-sect-dims.

Step 22. When you have completed Tutorial 8–3 (Figure 8–51), save your work in at least two places.

Step 23. Print Tutorial 8–3 at a scale of 3/4″ = 1′-0″.

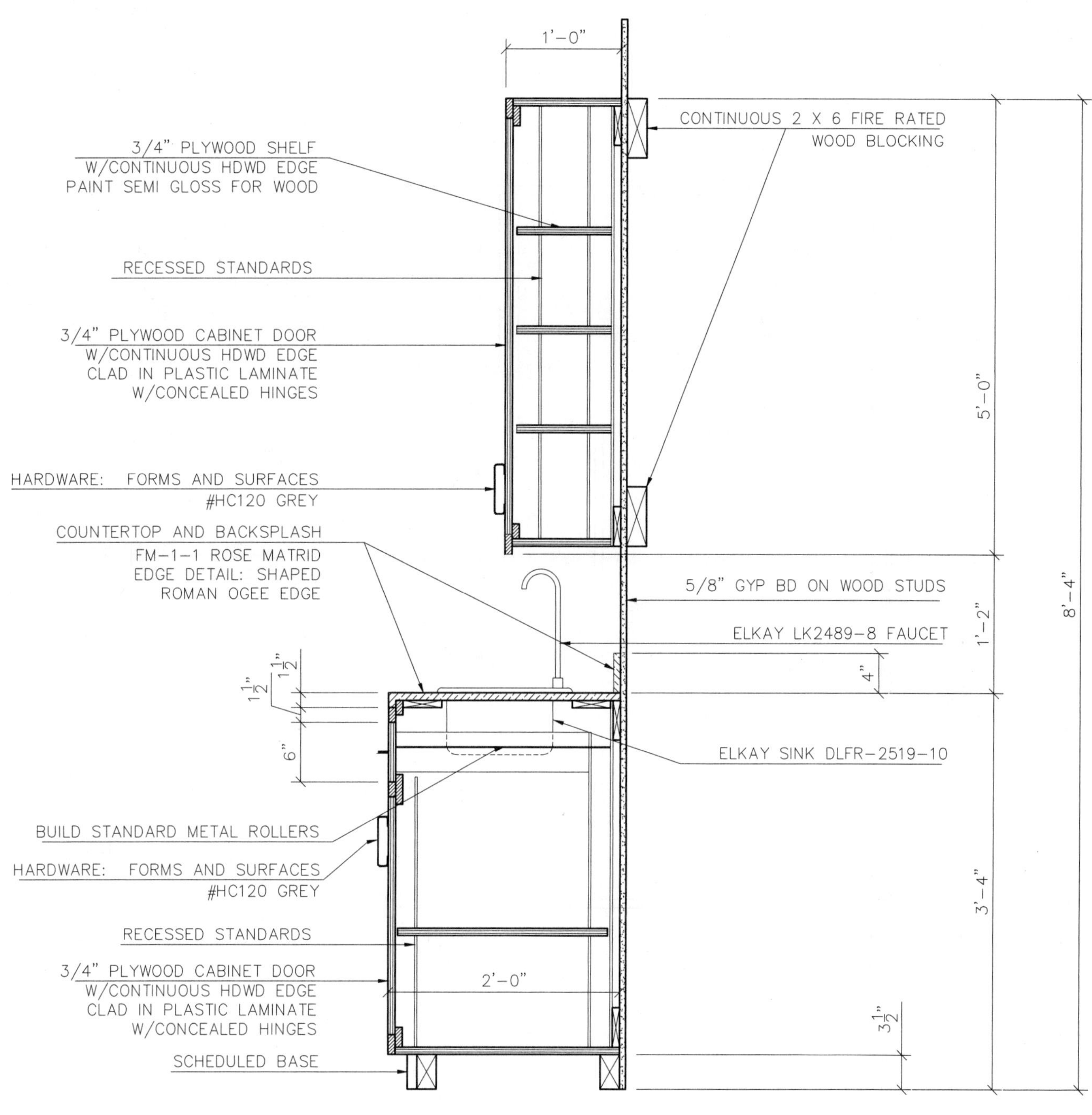

FIGURE 8–51
Tutorial 8–3: Completed Section Drawing (Scale: 3/4″ = 1′-0″)

Step 24. Add the section symbol as shown in Figure 8–52 to your TENANT SPACE FLOOR PLAN drawing. Use a 1′ radius circle and 1/16″ high text (annotative). You may need to move two dimensions as shown and add a layer for the cutting plane line below the symbol. Use PHANTOM 2 linetype and .004″ lineweight, color red.

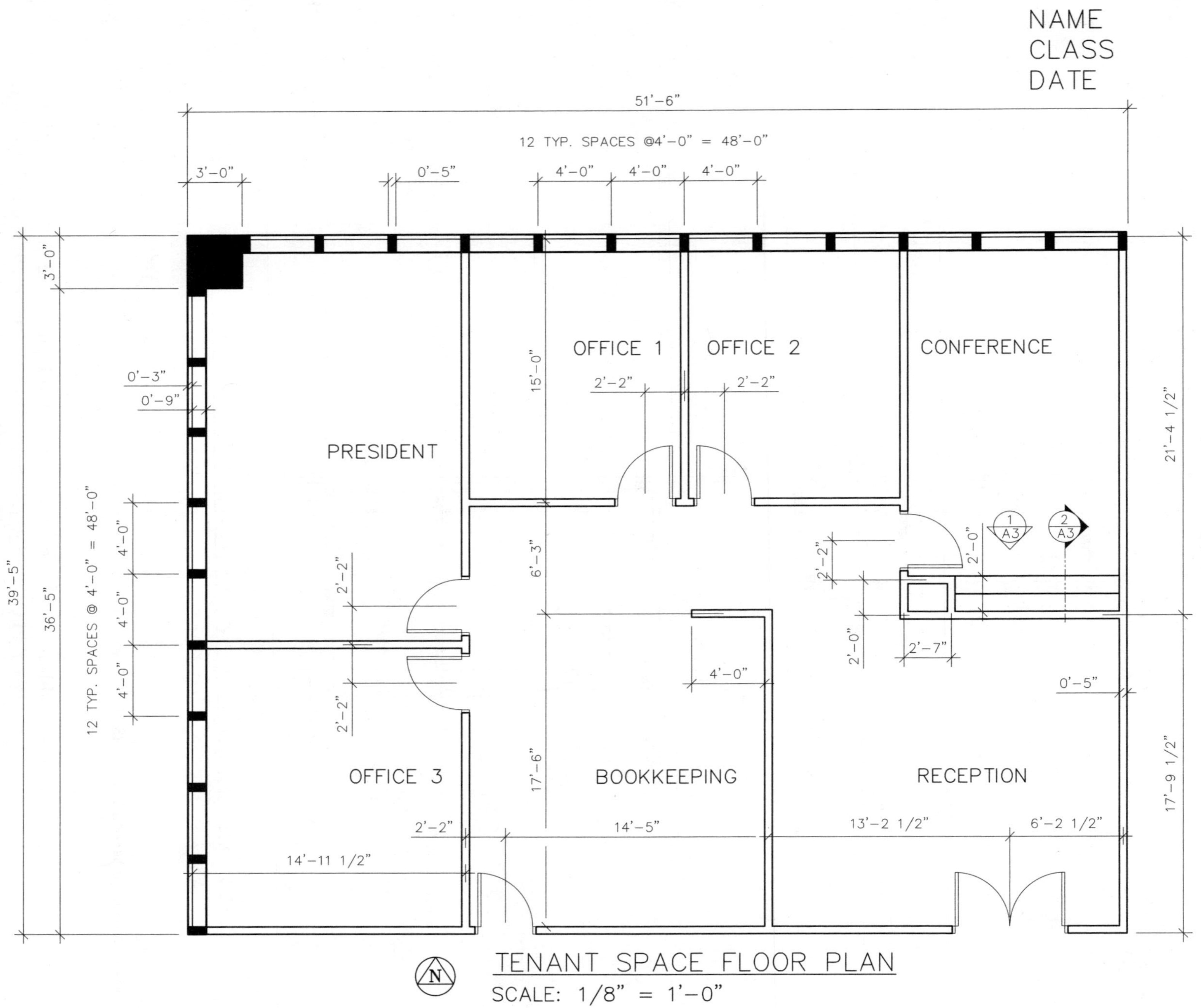

NAME
CLASS
DATE

51'–6"
12 TYP. SPACES @4'–0" = 48'–0"
3'–0"
0'–5"
4'–0"
4'–0"
4'–0"
39'–5"
36'–5"
12 TYP. SPACES @ 4'–0" = 48'–0"
0'–3"
0'–9"
PRESIDENT
OFFICE 1
OFFICE 2
CONFERENCE
15'–0"
2'–2"
2'–2"
21'–4 1/2"
6'–3"
2'–2"
2'–0"
1 A3
2 A3
2'–7"
2'–0"
4'–0"
0'–5"
OFFICE 3
BOOKKEEPING
RECEPTION
17'–6"
17'–9 1/2"
2'–2"
14'–5"
13'–2 1/2"
6'–2 1/2"
14'–11 1/2"

TENANT SPACE FLOOR PLAN
SCALE: 1/8" = 1'–0"

FIGURE 8–52
Tenant Space Floor Plan with Elevation and Section Symbols (scale: 1/8" = 1'-0")

FIGURE 8–53
Tutorial 8–4: Detail of a Door Jamb with Crosshatching (Scale: 3″ = 1′-0″)

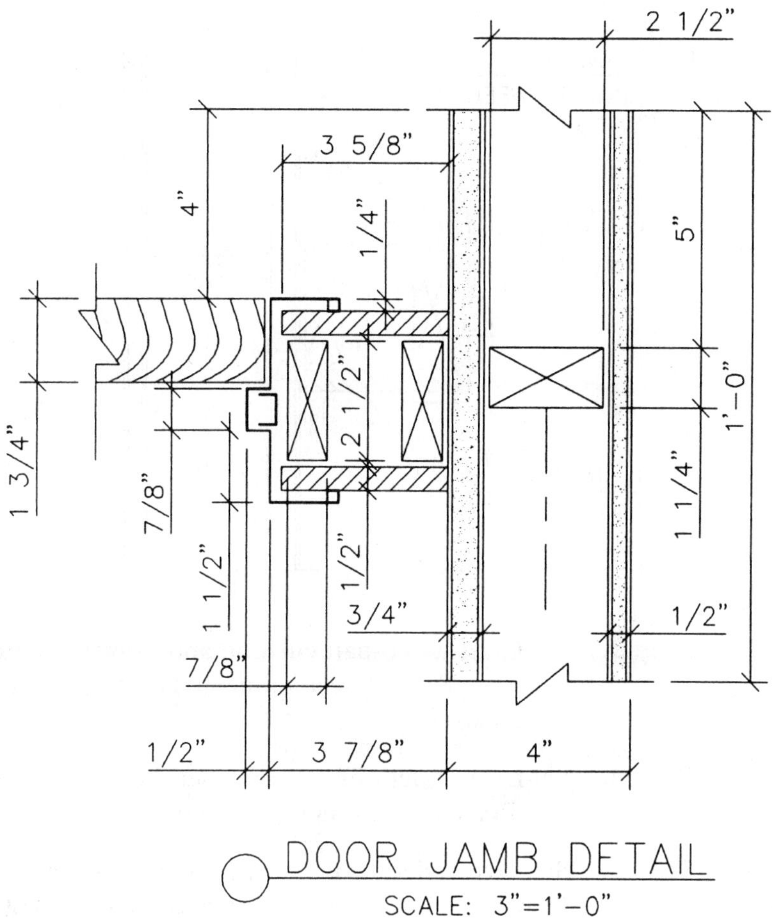

Tutorial 8–4: Detail of Door Jamb with Hatching

In Tutorial 8–4, a detail of a door jamb is drawn. When you have completed Tutorial 8–4, your drawing will look similar to Figure 8–53.

Step 1. **Use your workspace to make the following settings:**

1. **Use SaveAs... to save the drawing on the hard drive with the name CH8-TUTORIAL4.**
2. **Set Drawing Units, Limits, Grid, and Snap.**
3. **Create the following layers:**

LAYER NAME	COLOR	LINETYPE	LINEWEIGHT
a-detl	blue	continuous	.010″(.25mm)
a-detl-patt	cyan	continuous	.002″(.05mm)
a-detl-text	green	continuous	.006″(.15mm)
a-detl-dim	red	continuous	.004″(.09mm)

4. **Set Layer a-detl current.**

Step 2. **Using the dimensions shown in Figure 8–53, draw all the door jamb components. Drawing some of the components separately and copying or moving them into place will be helpful. Measure any dimensions not shown with a scale of 3″ = 1′-0″.**

FIGURE 8–54
Tutorial 8–4: Hatch Patterns

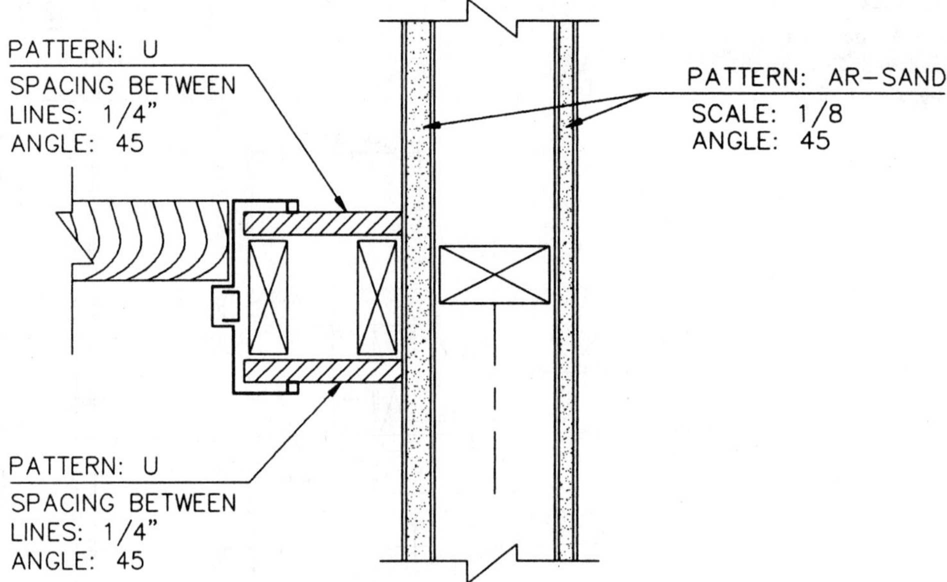

Step 3. Set Layer a-detl-patt current, and draw the hatch patterns as described in Figure 8–54. Use a Spline and array it to draw the curved wood grain pattern.

Step 4. Set Layer a-detl-dim current, set the dimensioning variables, and draw the dimensions as shown in Figure 8–53.

Step 5. Set Layer a-detl-text current, and add the name of the detail as shown in Figure 8–53. Add your name, class, and current date in the upper right.

Step 6. Save the drawing in two places.

Step 7. Print the drawing at a scale of 3″ = 1′-0″.

Tutorial 8–5: Using POINT FILTERS and OTRACK to Draw an Orthographic Drawing of a Conference Table

In Tutorial 8–5, the AutoCAD features called Point Filters and Otrack are used. These features are helpful when you are making two-dimensional drawings showing the top, front, and side views of an object. All of the features in these views must line up with the same features in the adjacent view. When you have completed Tutorial 8–5 your drawing will look similar to Figure 8–55.

Step 1. **Use your workspace to make the following settings:**

1. Set drawing Units: **Architectural**
2. Set Drawing Limits: **16′, 14′**
3. Set GRIDDISPLAY: **0**
4. Set Grid: **2″**
5. Set Snap: **1″**
6. Create the following layers:

LAYER NAME	COLOR	LINETYPE	LINEWEIGHT
a-furn	cyan	continuous	.004″(.09mm)
a-furn-hid	red	HIDDEN	.004″(.09mm)
a-furn-text	green	continuous	.006″(.15mm)

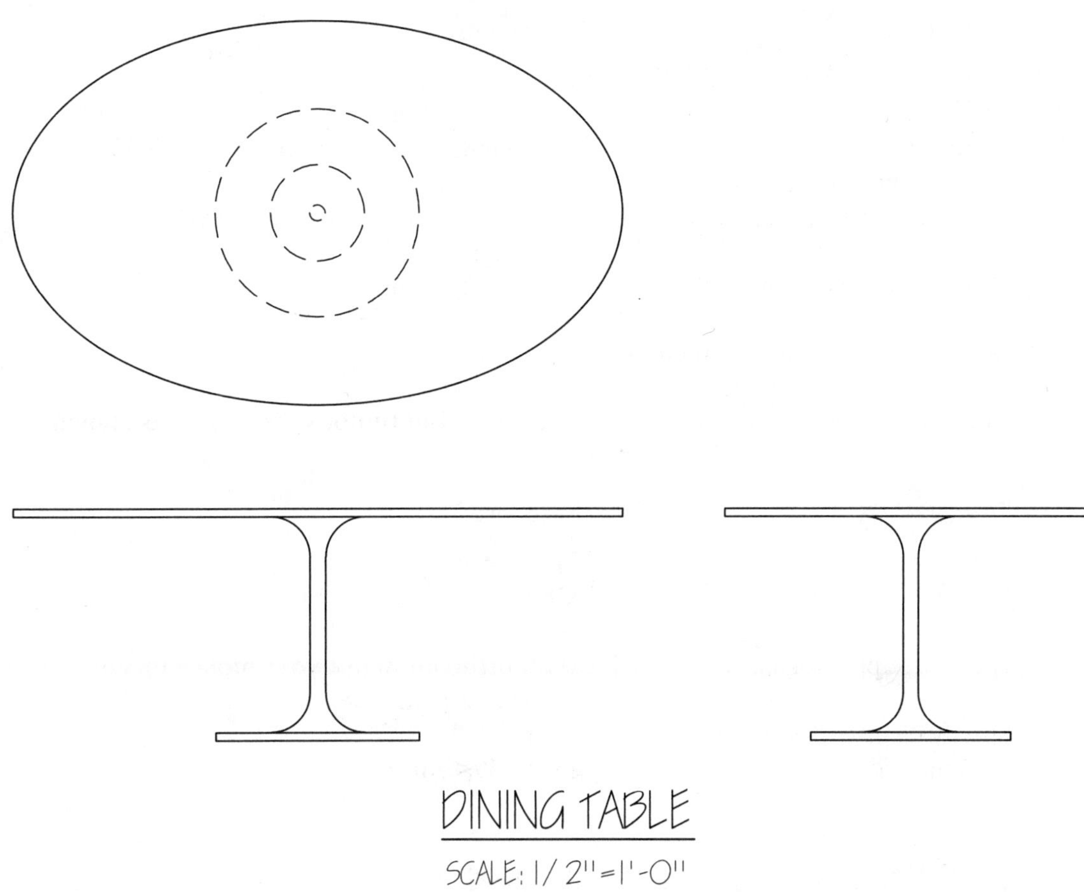

FIGURE 8–55
Tutorial 8–5: Using Point Filters and OTRACK to Draw Three Views of a Dining Table (Scale: 1/2″ = 1′-0″)

7. Set **Layer a-furn-hid** current.
8. Set LTSCALE: **16**

Step 2. Draw the base and column of the table (HIDDEN Line), as shown in the top view (Figure 8–56), as described next:

Prompt	Response
Command:	**Circle-Center, Diameter** (not Radius)
Specify center point for circle or [3P/2P/Ttr (tan tan radius)]:	TYPE: **4′,9′<enter>**

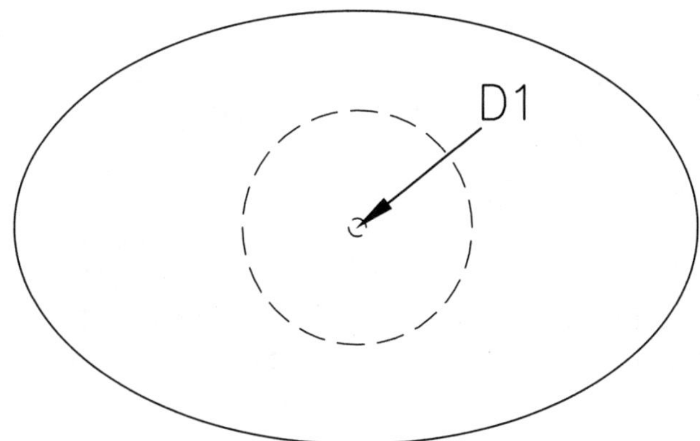

FIGURE 8–56
Draw the Top View of the Base, Column, and Top of the Table

Prompt	Response
Specify diameter of circle <default>:	TYPE: **2′2<enter>**
Command:	**Circle-Center, Diameter** (not Radius)
Specify center point for circle or [3P/2P/Ttr (tan tan radius)]:	TYPE: **4′,9′**(the same center as the first circle)
Specify diameter of circle <default>:	TYPE: **2<enter>**

Step 3. **Set Layer a-furn current.**

Step 4. **Draw the elliptical top of the table (Continuous Linetype), as shown in the top view (Figure 8–56), as described next:**

Prompt	Response
Command:	**Ellipse-Center**
Specify center of ellipse:	**OSNAP-Center**
of	**D1**
Specify endpoint of axis:	**With ortho on, move your mouse up and** TYPE: **2′<enter>**
Specify distance to other axis or [Rotation]:	TYPE: **39<enter>**

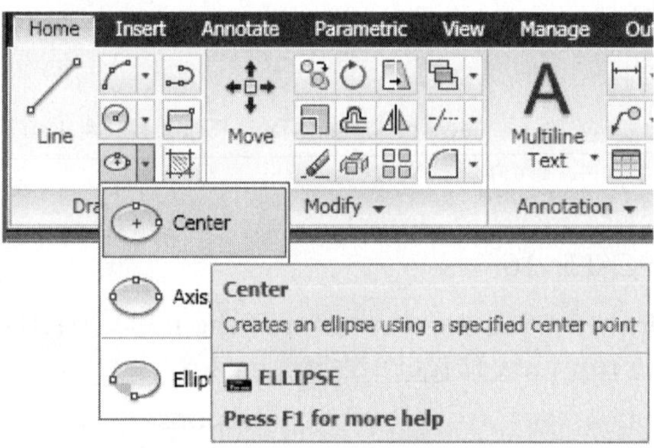

Step 5. **Use Point Filters to draw the front view of the top of this elliptical table (Figure 8–57), as described next:**

Prompt	Response
Command:	**Line**
Specify first point:	TYPE: **.X<enter>**
of	**OSNAP-Quadrant**
of	**D1** (Figure 8–57)
(need YZ):	**D2** (with SNAP ON, **pick a point in the approximate location shown in Figure 8–57**)
Specify next point or [Undo]:	TYPE: **.X<enter>**
of	**OSNAP-Quadrant**
of	**D3**

FIGURE 8–57
Draw the Front View of the Top of the Table Using Point Filters

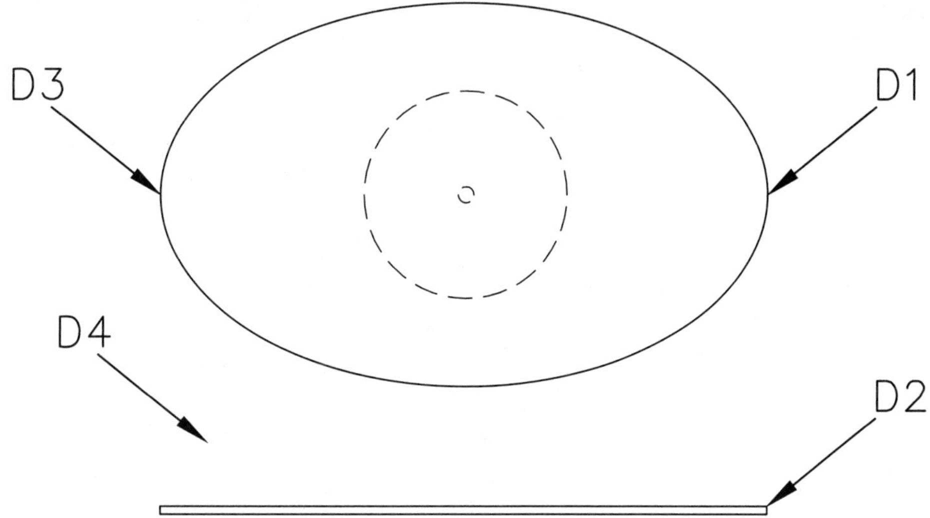

Prompt	Response
(need YZ):	**D4** (with ORTHO ON, **pick any point to identify the Y component of the point;** ORTHO makes the Y component of the new point the same as the Y component of the previous point)
Specify next point or [Close/Undo]:	With ORTHO ON, **move your mouse straight down,** and TYPE: **1<enter>**
Specify next point or [Close/Undo]:	TYPE: **.X<enter>**
of	**OSNAP-Endpoint**
of	**D2**
(need YZ):	With ORTHO ON, **move your mouse to the right, and pick any point**
Specify next point or [Close/Undo]:	TYPE: **C<enter>**

Step 6. **Set running Osnap modes of Endpoint, Quadrant, and Intersection and turn OSNAP and OTRACK ON.**

Step 7. **Use OTRACK and Offset to draw the front view of the column (Figure 8–58), as described next:**

Prompt	Response
Command:	**Line**
Specify first point:	**Move your mouse to the quadrant shown as D1** (Figure 8–58) but do not CLICK: **Hold it until the Quadrant symbol shows, then move your mouse straight down until the dotted line shows the intersection symbol on the bottom line of the tabletop as shown, then** CLICK: **the intersection point.**
Specify next point or [Undo]:	With ORTHO ON, **move your mouse straight down** and TYPE: **27<enter>**
Specify next point or [Undo]:	**<enter>**

FIGURE 8–58
Use OTRACK to Draw the Front View of the Column

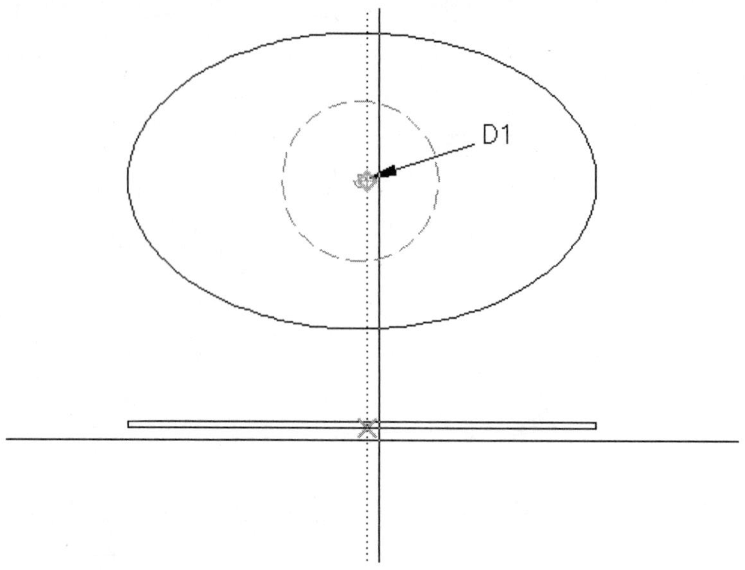

Prompt	Response
Command:	**Offset** (or TYPE: **O<enter>**)
Specify offset distance or [Through/Erase/Layer] <Through>:	TYPE: **2<enter>**
Select object to offset or [Exit/Undo] <Exit>:	CLICK: **D1** (Figure 8–59)
Specify point on side to offset or [Exit/Multiple/Undo] <Exit>:	CLICK: **D2 (any point to the left of the 27″ line)**
Select object to offset or [Exit/Undo] <Exit>:	**<enter>**

Step 8. Use OTRACK to draw the front view of the base (Figure 8–59), as described next:

Prompt	Response
Command:	**Line**
Specify first point:	**Move your mouse to the quadrant shown as** D3 **(Figure 8–59) but do not** CLICK. **Hold it**

FIGURE 8–59
Use OTRACK to Draw the Front View of the Base

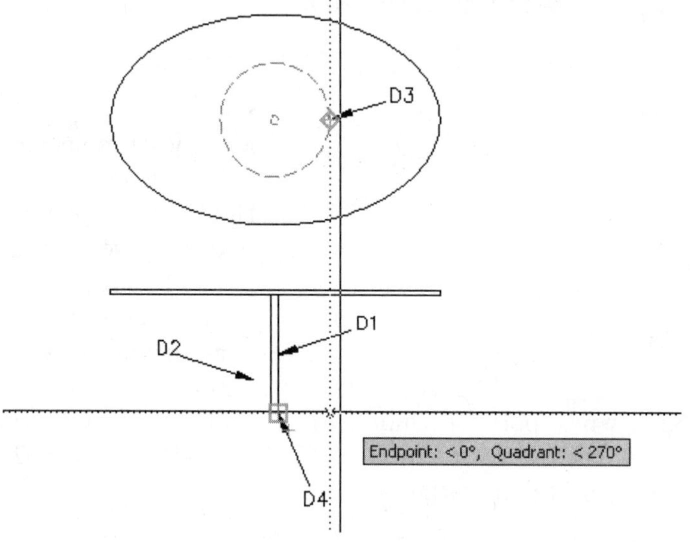

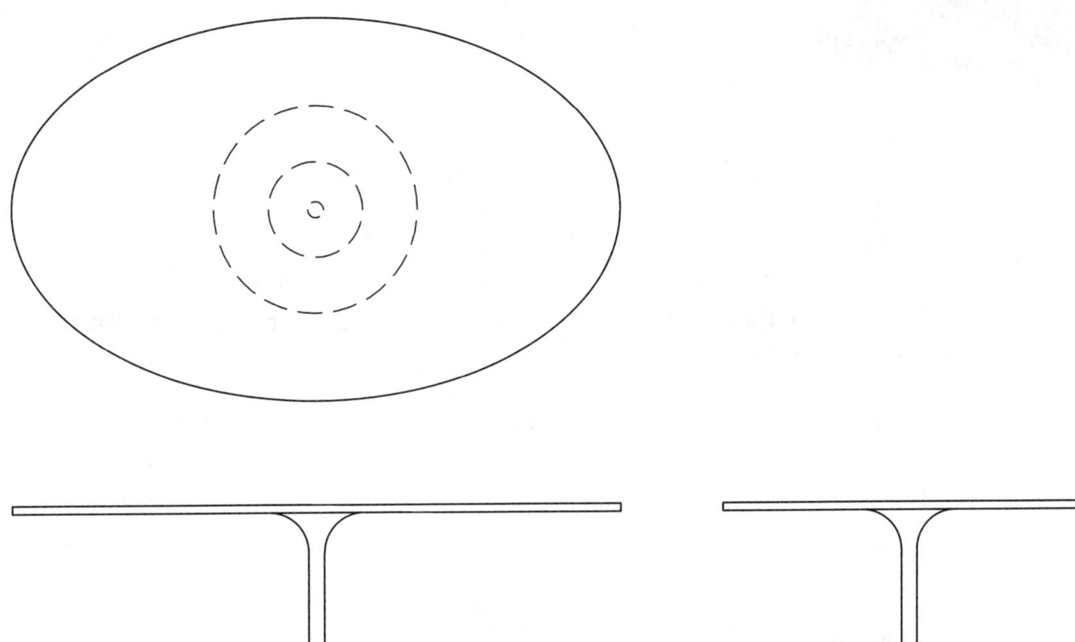

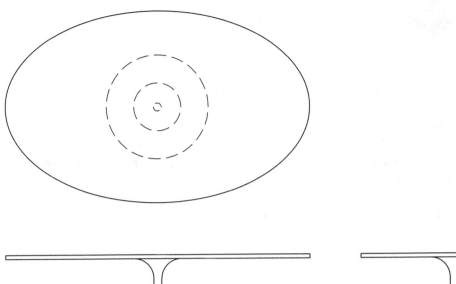

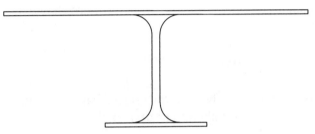

FIGURE 8–60
Draw the Right Side View Using Copy, Line, and OTRACK. Complete Front and Right Side Views with a 5″ No Trim Radius and the Trim Command.

Prompt	Response
	until the Quadrant symbol shows, then move your mouse to D4 (do not CLICK) **(the dotted line shows the endpoint symbol), then move your mouse back to the vertical dotted line and** CLICK:
Specify next point or [Undo]:	With ORTHO ON, **move your mouse straight down** and TYPE: **1<enter>**
Specify next point or [Undo]:	With ORTHO ON, **move your mouse to the left** and TYPE: **26<enter>**
Specify next point or [Close/Undo]:	With ORTHO ON, **move your mouse straight up**, and TYPE: **1<enter>**
Specify next point or [Close/Undo]:	TYPE: **C<enter>**

Step 9. **Use OTRACK to draw the right side view of the table with the Line and Copy commands (Figure 8–60). Be sure to get depth dimensions from the top view.**

Step 10. **Use a 5″ Radius fillet (no trim) and trim to complete front and right side views.**

Step 11. **Label the drawing as shown in Figure 8–55. Add your name, class, and current date in the upper right.**

Step 12. **Save your drawing in two places.**

Step 13. **Print the drawing at a scale of 1/2″ = 1′-0″.**

review questions

1. Which of the following patterns produces evenly spaced dots?
   a. U
   b. DOTS
   c. ANSI34
   d. DOLMIT
   e. LINE

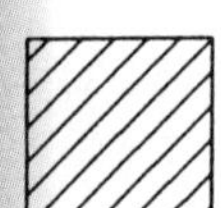

FIGURE 8–61

2. Which of the following angles produces the User-defined pattern shown in Figure 8–61?
   a. 45
   b. 90
   c. 0
   d. 135
   e. 105

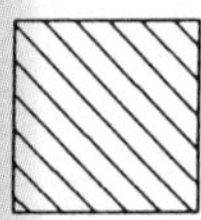

FIGURE 8–62

3. Which of the following angles produces the User-defined pattern shown in Figure 8–62?
   a. 45
   b. 90
   c. 0
   d. 135
   e. 105
4. Which of the following commands can be used to correct a hatch pattern that extends outside a hatch boundary, after it has been exploded?
   a. Array
   b. Copy
   c. Move
   d. Trim
   e. Break

FIGURE 8–63

5. Which of the following describes the User-defined pattern shown in Figure 8–63?
   a. X pat
   b. 45,145
   c. Double
   d. Double section
   e. Line-two
6. Which of the following in the Spacing: input box in the Hatch and Gradient dialog box produces hatch lines 1/4″ apart (User-defined pattern)?
   a. 1/4″
   b. 1
   c. 1-4
   d. 4
   e. Depends on the size of the drawing.
7. After a Hatch command that spaced lines 1/8″ apart has been performed, what is the default setting in the Spacing: input box for the next hatch pattern?
   a. 0″
   b. 1/4″
   c. 1/8″
   d. 1″
   e. Depends on the size of the drawing.
8. Which setting allows an image to be Mirrored without mirroring the text?
   a. MIRRTEXT = 1
   b. MIRRTEXT = 0
   c. MIRRTXT = 1
   d. MIRRTXT = 0
   e. DTEXT-STYLE = 0
9. The Stretch command is best used for
   a. Stretching an object in one direction
   b. Shrinking an object in one direction
   c. Moving an object along attached lines
   d. All the above
   e. None of the above

10. Which Hatch option allows you to hatch only the outermost boundary of multiple areas within a selection window?

a. Pattern
b. Scale
c. Outer
d. Normal
e. Ignore

Complete.

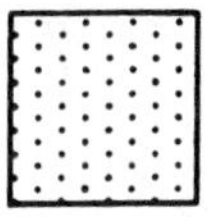

11. What is the correct name of the pattern in Figure 8–64?

____

FIGURE 8–64

12. How can the predefined Hatch pattern options (Hatch Pattern Palette) be called up on the screen?

____

____

FIGURE 8–65

13. Correctly label the User-defined pattern shown in Figure 8–65. Show angle and spacing at full scale.

Angle _______________ Spacing _______________

FIGURE 8–66

14. Correctly label the Predefined pattern shown in Figure 8–66. Show pattern and angle.

Pattern _______________ Angle _______________

15. What is the name of the UCS Icon command option that forces the UCS icon to be displayed at the 0,0 point of the current UCS?

____

16. How can all the lines of an associative 35-line hatch pattern be erased?

____

17. List the command that allows you to change a hatch pattern from Associative to individual lines.

____

18. Describe what the landing of a leader is.

____

19. What is the name of the system variable that can be changed to allow a small gap in the intersection of two lines in a hatch boundary?

____

exercises

Exercise 8–1: Different Hatch Styles

1. Draw the figure (without hatching) shown in Figure 8–67. Use an Architectural scale of 1/2″ = 1″ to measure the figure, and draw it full scale. Copy it two times, leaving 1″ between figures.
2. Shade each figure with a different Hatch Style (CLICK: the More Options arrow in the lower right corner of the Hatch and Gradient dialog box) as shown: Normal, Outer, and Ignore. Use the same hatch pattern: User-defined, 1/8″ spacing, 45° angle.
3. Save the drawing in two places, and plot or print the drawing to scale.

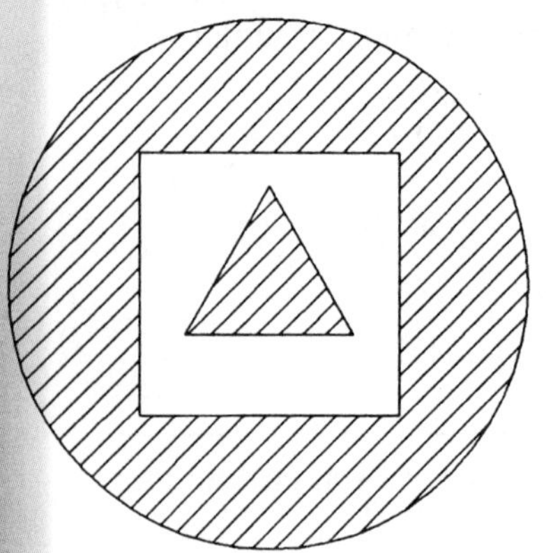
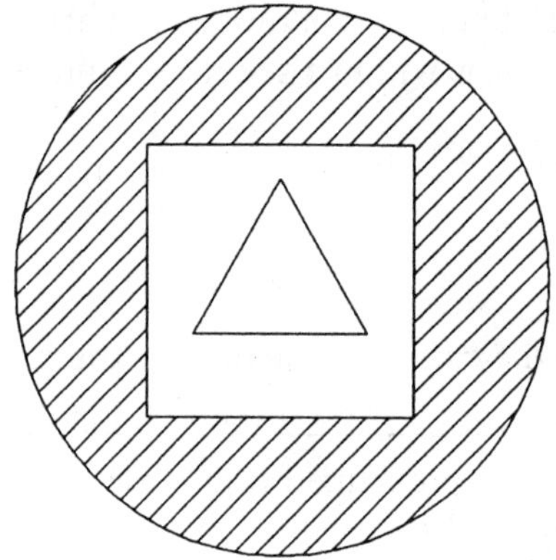
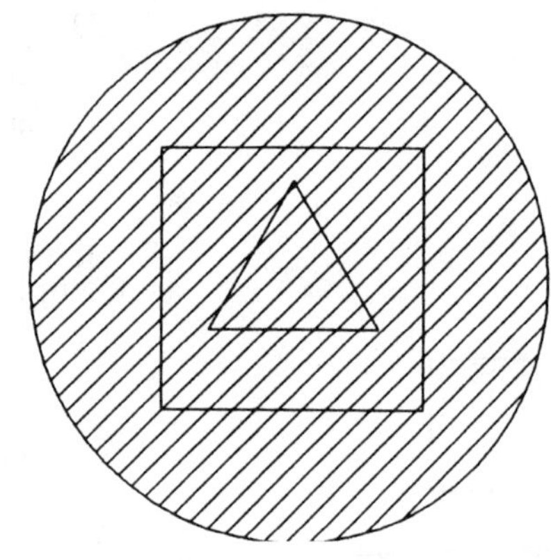

FIGURE 8–67
Practice Exercise 8–1: Different Hatch Styles (Scale: 1/2″ = 1″)

Exercise 8–2: Elevation of the Wheelchair Accessible Commercial Restrooms

Figure 8–68 shows the floor plan of the commercial restrooms with the elevations indicated. The line of text at the bottom of Figure 8–69 shows where the House Designer drawing is located in the AutoCAD DesignCenter. The front view of the toilets, urinals, sinks, grab bars, faucets, and toilet paper holders are blocks contained within this drawing and in the DesignCenter Online. Just DOUBLE-CLICK: on any of these blocks to activate the Insert command, and insert these blocks into your elevation drawing as needed. You may need to modify the sink, and you will have to draw the mirror and paper towel holder.

Draw elevation 1 of the commercial wheelchair accessible restrooms as shown in Figure 8–70. Use the dimensions shown or use an Architectural scale of 1/4″ = 1′0″ to measure elevation 1, and draw it full scale without dimensions. Use lineweights to make the drawing more attractive and a solid hatch pattern with a gray color to make the walls solid. Use the same gray color for the layer on which you draw the ceramic tile. When you have completed Exercise 8–2, your drawing will look similar to Figure 8–70 without dimensions.

1. **Use your workspace to make the following settings:**
    1. Set drawing Units: **Architectural**
    2. Set Drawing Limits: **25′,20′**
    3. Set GRIDDISPLAY: **0**
    4. Set Grid: **12″**
    5. Set Snap: **3″**
    6. Create the following layers:

LAYER NAME	COLOR	LINETYPE	LINEWEIGHT
a-elev-pfix	blue	continuous	.008″(.30mm)
a-elev-text	green	continuous	.006″(.15mm)
a-elev-pat2	253	continuous	.010″(.25mm)
a-elev-pat1	cyan	continuous	.002″(.05mm)
a-elev	blue	continuous	.010″(.25mm)
a-wall-extr	white	continuous	.014″(.35mm)

2. **Use the Rectangle command to draw the mirror above the sinks (25″,37″) on the a-elev-pfix layer and offset the rectangle 3/4″ to the inside.**

3. Use the Rectangle command to draw the partitions between toilets (1″,60″ and 1″,36″) on the a-elev-pfix Layer.
4. Draw lines on the a-elev-pat1 Layer and array them in 4″ spaces between rows and layers and trim them as needed to create the 4″ tiles.
5. Insert all blocks on the a-elev-pfix Layer. Put wall outlines on the a-elev layer and the solid hatch pattern inside the walls on the a-elev-pat2 Layer.
6. Draw upper and lower lines of the elevation on the a-wall-extr Layer.
7. Label the drawing on the a-elev-text layer, add the scale, and place your name, class, and the current date in the upper right corner with the CityBlueprint font 5″ high.
8. Save the drawing in two places and print the drawing to scale.

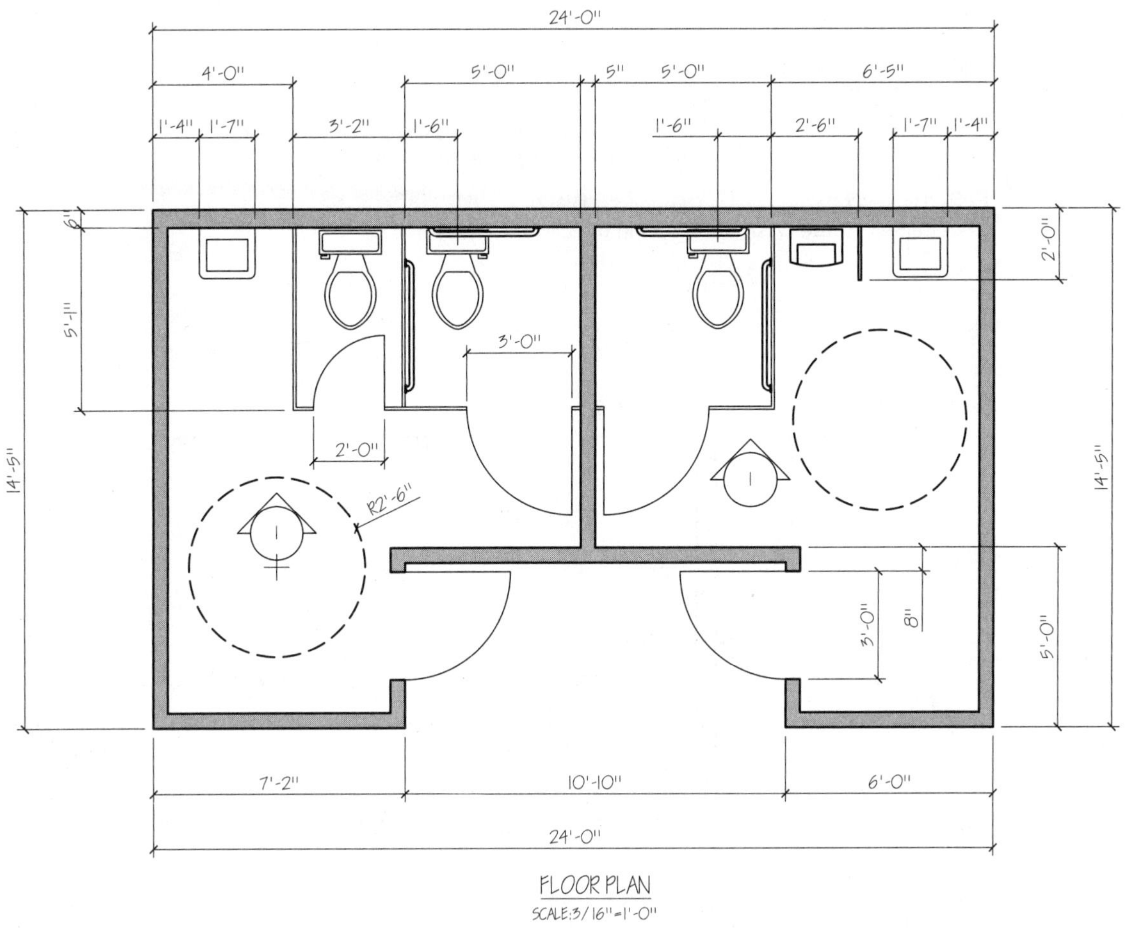

FIGURE 8–68
Exercise 8–2: Floor Plan of the Wheelchair Accessible Commercial Restrooms (Scale: 3/16″ = 1′-0″)

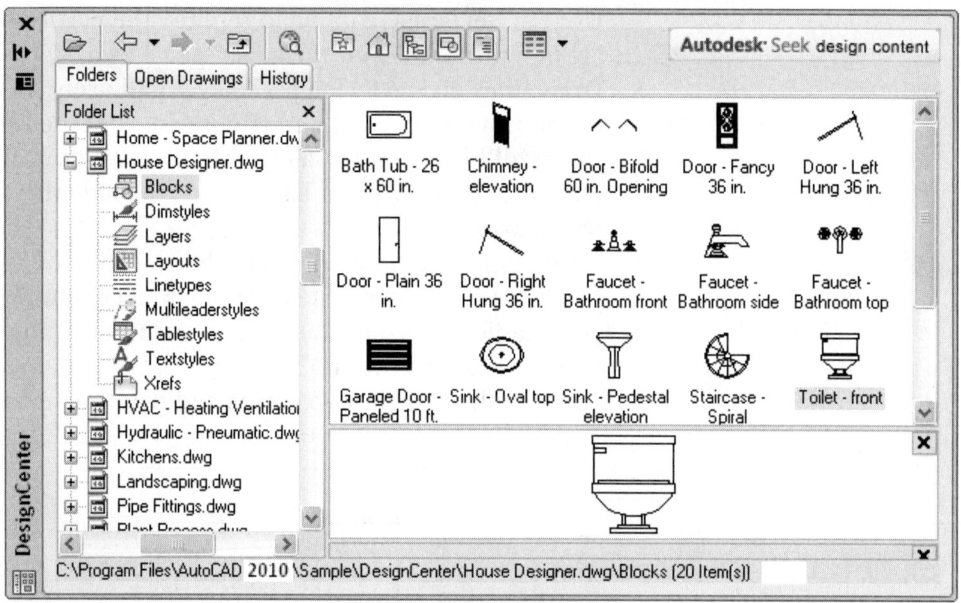

FIGURE 8–69
Exercise 8–2: House Designer Blocks in the DesignCenter

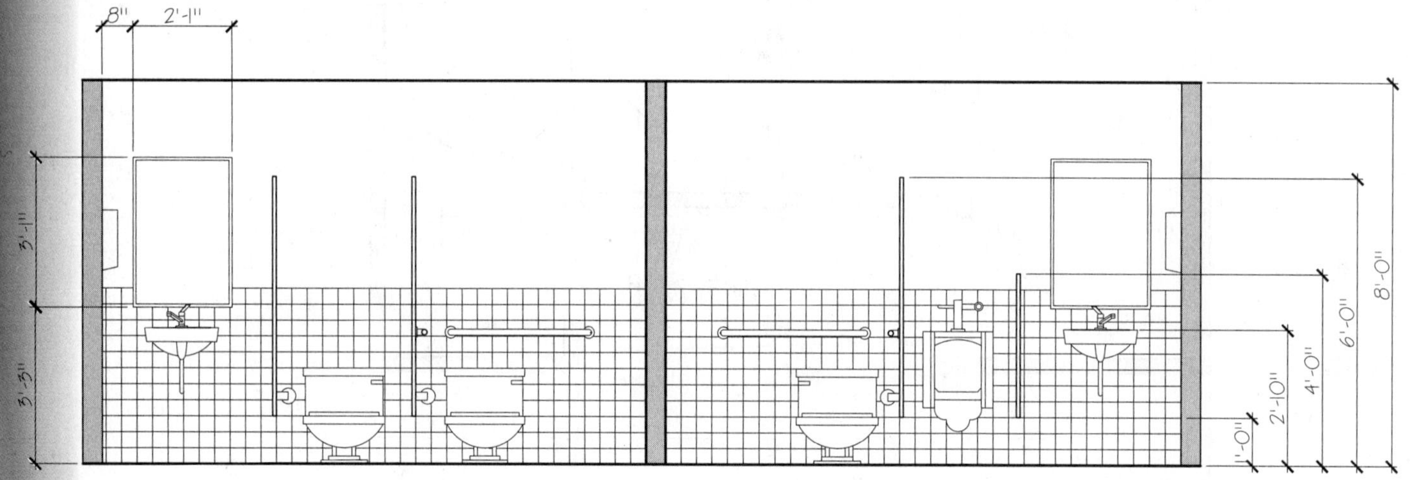

FIGURE 8–70
Exercise 8–2: Elevation of the Wheelchair Accessible Commercial Restrooms (Scale: 1/4″ = 1′-0″)

Exercise 8–3: Drawing a Mirror from a Sketch

1. Use the dimensions shown to draw the mirror in Figure 8–71 using AutoCAD.
2. Set your own drawing limits, grid, and snap. Create your own layers as needed.
3. Do not place dimensions on this drawing, but do show the cutting plane lines and label them as shown.
4. Do not draw Detail A. This information is shown so you can draw that part.
5. Draw and label sections A-A, B-B, and C-C in the approximate locations shown on the sketch. Use the ANSI31 hatch pattern for the sectional views, or draw splines and array them to show wood. Do not show dimensions.
6. Save the drawing in two places and print the drawing to scale.

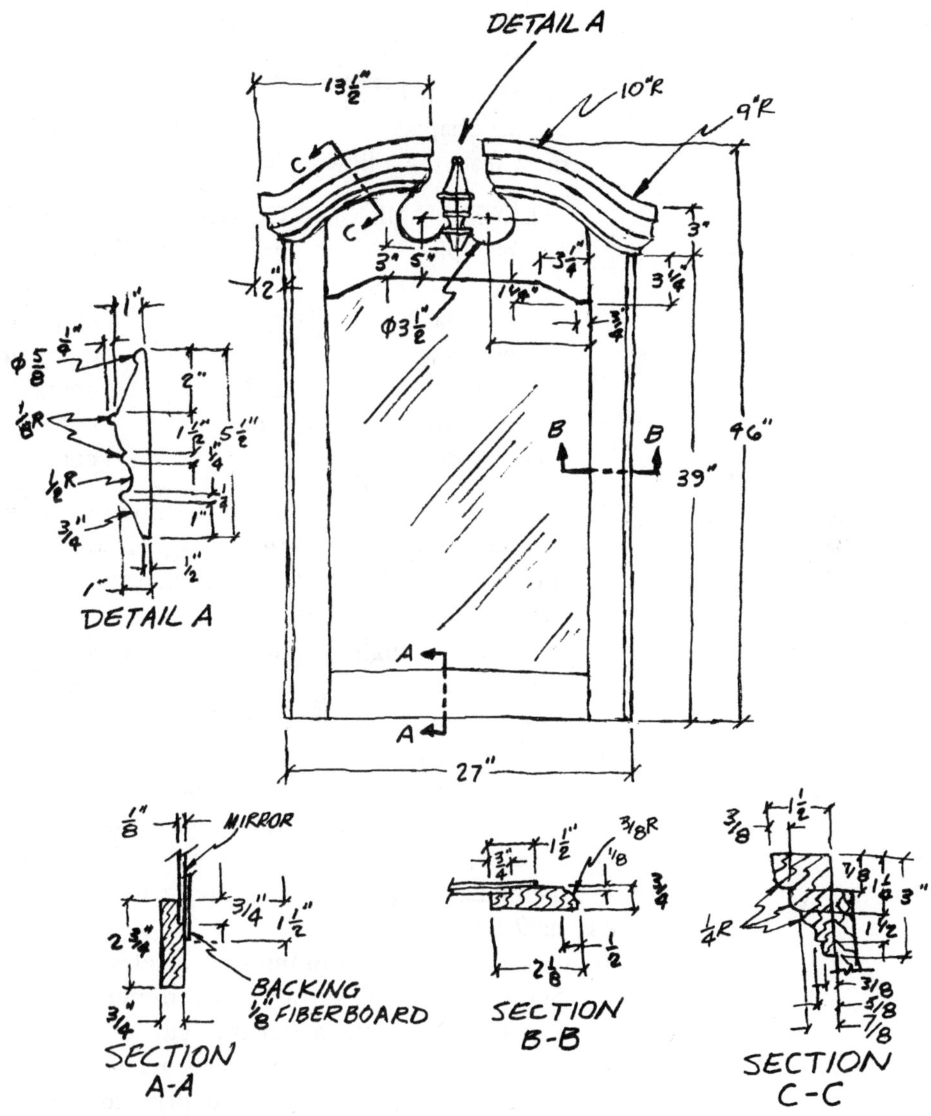

FIGURE 8–71
Exercise 8–3: Mirror

Exercise 8–4: Elevation 1 of the Log Cabin Kitchen

Figure 8–72 shows the floor plan of the log cabin kitchen with two elevations indicated. The line of text at the bottom of Figure 8–73 shows where the Kitchen drawing is located in the AutoCAD DesignCenter. The front view of the dishwasher, faucet, range-oven, and refrigerator are blocks contained within this drawing. Just DOUBLE-CLICK: on any of these blocks to activate the Insert command, and insert these blocks into your elevation drawing as needed.

Draw elevation 1 of the log cabin kitchen as shown in Figure 8–74. Use the dimensions shown or use an Architectural scale of 1/2″ = 1′0″ to measure elevation 1, and draw it full scale with dimensions. Use lineweights to make the drawing more attractive and a solid hatch pattern with a gray color to make the walls solid.

When you have completed Exercise 8–4, your drawing will look similar to Figure 8–74 with dimensions.

1. **Use your workspace to make the following settings:**
    1. Set drawing Units: **Architectural**
    2. Set Drawing Limits: **15′,19′**
    3. Set GRIDDISPLAY: **0**
    4. Set Grid: **12″**
    5. Set Snap: **3″**
    6. Create the following layers:

LAYER NAME	COLOR	LINETYPE	LINEWEIGHT
a-elev-pfix	green	continuous	.006″(.15mm)
a-elev	blue	continuous	.010″(.25mm)
a-elev-pat1	cyan	continuous	.002″(.05mm)
a-elev-text	green	continuous	.006″(.15mm)
a-elev-pat2	253	continuous	.010″(.25mm)
a-wall-extr	white	continuous	.014″(.35mm)
a-elev-dim	red	continuous	.004″(.09mm)

2. **Use the Rectangle command to draw the cabinet doors on the a-elev-pfix Layer, and offset the rectangle 2″ to the inside, then 1/2″ twice more to get the three lines showing the door pattern. Place the three offset lines on the a-elev-pat1 Layer.**
3. **Use the Rectangle command to draw the drawers (next to the range-oven) on the a-elev-pat1 Layer, and offset that rectangle 1/2″ to the inside. Leave 1/2″ between each drawer.**
4. **Use a user-defined hatch pattern with a 45° angle, double hatch, 4″ spacing, and create the hatch pattern on the a-elev-pat2 Layer to create the backsplash behind the range-oven.**
5. **Insert all blocks on the a-elev-pfix Layer. Put wall outlines on the a-elev Layer and the solid hatch pattern inside the walls on the a-elev-pat2 Layer.**
6. **Place top and bottom lines of the elevation on the a-wall-extr Layer.**
7. **Set dimensioning variables and dimension the drawing as shown in Figure 8–74 on the a-elev-dim Layer.**
8. **Label the drawing and add your name, class, and current date in the upper right using the CityBlueprint font on the a-elev-text Layer.**
9. **Save the drawing in two places and print the drawing to scale.**

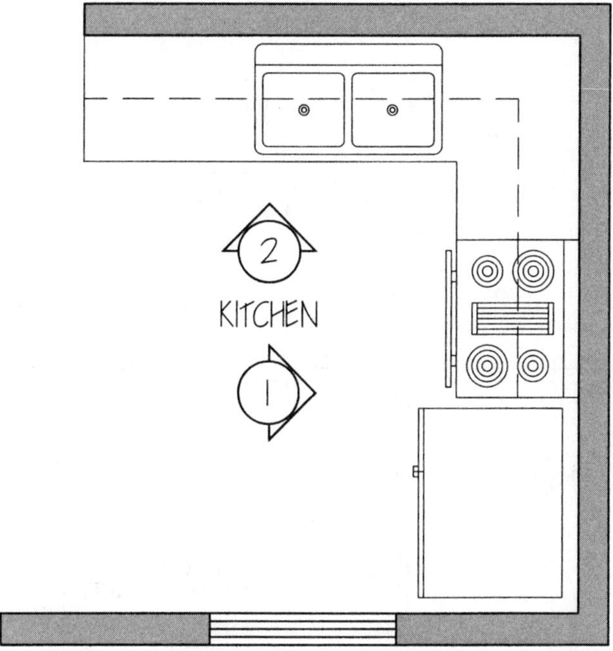

FIGURE 8–72
Exercise 8–4: Plan View of the Log Cabin Kitchen

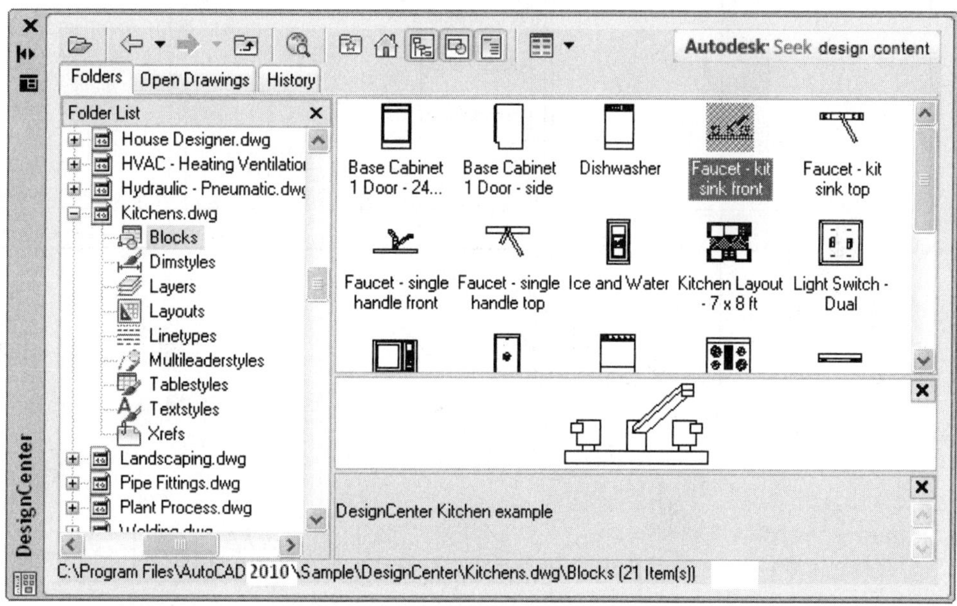

FIGURE 8–73
Exercise 8–4: DesignCenter with the Kitchen Drawing Blocks Displayed

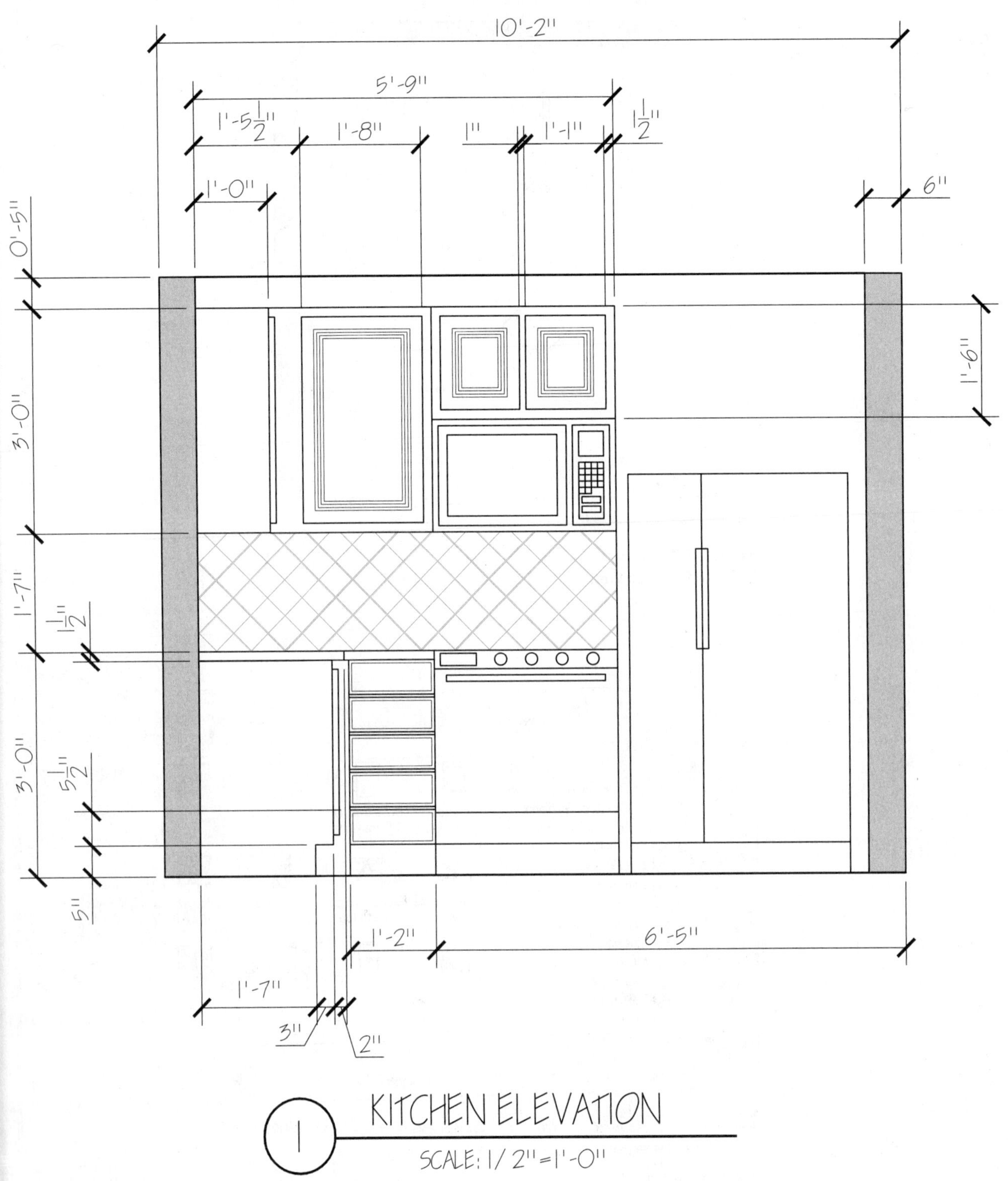

FIGURE 8–74
Exercise 8–4: Elevation 1 of the Log Cabin Kitchen (Scale: 1/2″ = 1′–0″)

Exercise 8–5: Elevation 2 of the Log Cabin Kitchen

Figure 8–72 shows the floor plan of the log cabin kitchen with arrows indicating the line of sight for two elevations of this room. The line of text at the bottom of Figure 8–73 shows where the Kitchen drawing is located in the AutoCAD Design Center. The front view of the dishwasher, faucet, range-oven, and refrigerator are blocks contained within this drawing. Just DOUBLE-CLICK: on any of these blocks to activate the Insert command, and insert these blocks into your elevation drawing as needed.

Draw elevation 2 of the log cabin kitchen as shown in Figure 8–75. Use the dimensions shown or use an Architectural scale of 1/2″ = 1′0″ to measure elevation 2, and draw it full scale with dimensions. Use lineweights to make the drawing more attractive and a solid hatch pattern with a gray color to make the walls solid.

When you have completed Exercise 8–5, your drawing will look similar to Figure 8–75 with dimensions.

1. **Use your workspace to make the following settings:**
    1. Set drawing Units: **Architectural**
    2. Set Drawing Limits: **15′,19′**
    3. Set GRIDDISPLAY: **0**
    4. Set Grid: **12″**
    5. Set Snap: **3″**
    6. Create the following layers (if you do not have them already):

LAYER NAME	COLOR	LINETYPE	LINEWEIGHT
a-elev-pfix	green	continuous	.006″(.15mm)
a-elev	blue	continuous	.010″(.25mm)
a-elev-pat1	cyan	continuous	.002″(.05mm)
a-elev-text	green	continuous	.006″(.15mm)
a-elev-pat2	253	continuous	.010″(.25mm)
a-wall-extr	white	continuous	.014″(.35mm)
a-elev-dim	red	continuous	.004″(.09mm)

2. **Use the Rectangle command to draw the cabinet doors on the e-elev-pfix Layer, and offset the rectangle 2″ to the inside, then 1/2″ twice more to get the three lines showing the door pattern. Place the three offset lines on the a-elev-pat1 Layer.**
3. **Use a user-defined hatch pattern with a 45° angle, double hatch, 4″ spacing, and create the hatch pattern on the a-elev-pat2 Layer to create the backsplash behind the sink.**
4. **Insert all blocks except the faucet on the a-elev-pfix layer. Put the faucet on the a-elev-pat1 Layer, wall outlines on the a-elev Layer, and the solid hatch pattern inside the walls on the a-elev-pat2 Layer.**
5. **Place top and bottom lines of the elevation on the a-wall-extr Layer.**
6. **Set dimensioning variables and dimension the drawing on the a-elev-dim Layer as shown in Figure 8–75.**
7. **Label the drawing and add your name, class, and current date in the upper right using the CityBlueprint font on the a-elev-text Layer.**
8. **Save the drawing in two places and print the drawing to scale.**

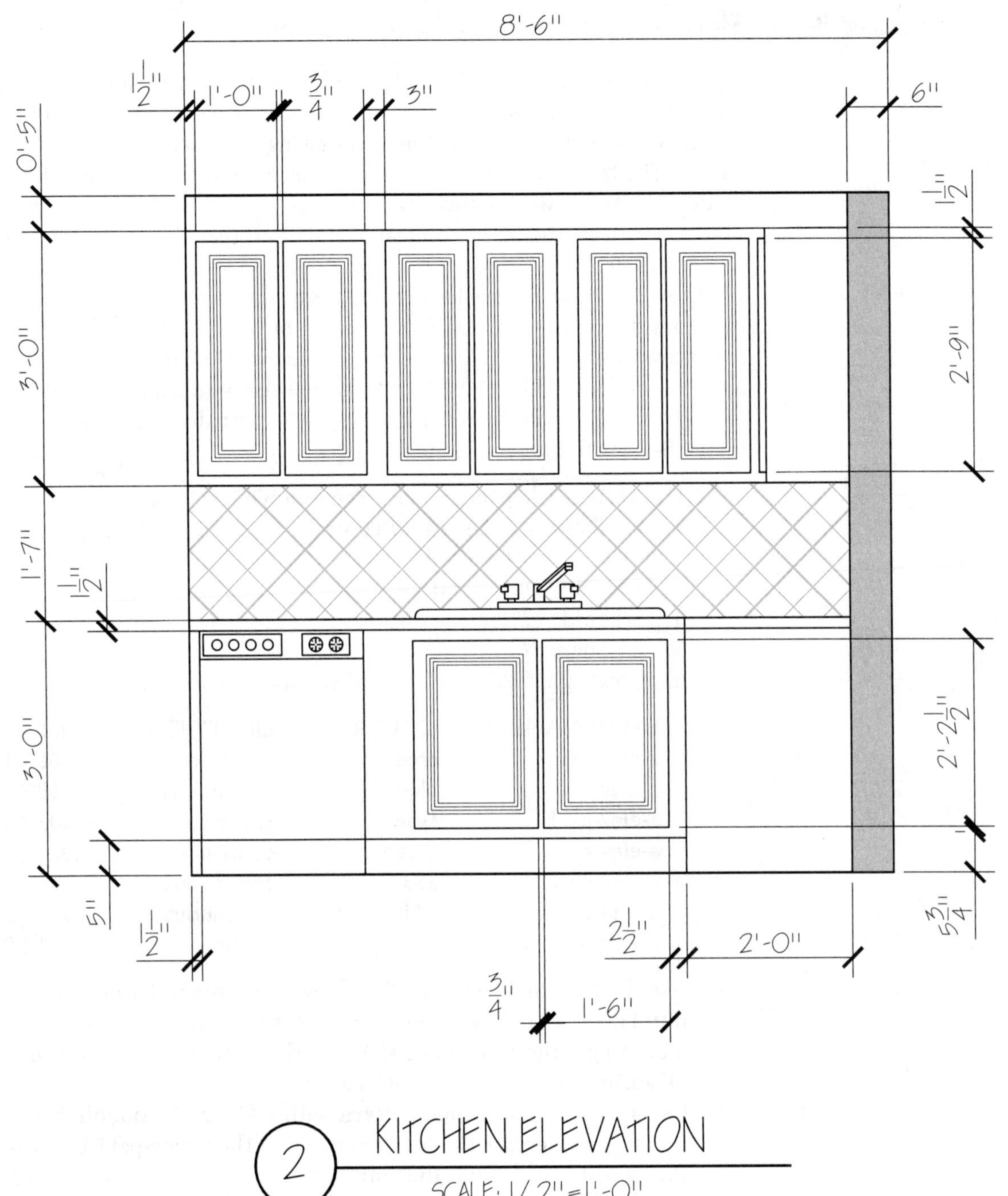

FIGURE 8–75
Exercise 8–5: Elevation 2 of the Log Cabin Kitchen (Scale: 1/2″ = 1′–0″)

Exercise 8–6: Detail Drawing of a Bar Rail

1. Draw the bar rail detail shown in Figure 8–76. Measure the drawing with an architectural 1/2 scale and draw it full size (1:1) using AutoCAD.
2. Set your own drawing limits, grid, and snap. Create your own layers with varying lineweights as needed.
3. Label the drawing as shown in Figure 8–76 in the City Blueprint font. Add your name, class, and the current date in the upper right.
4. Save the drawing in two places and print the drawing at a scale of 1:2.

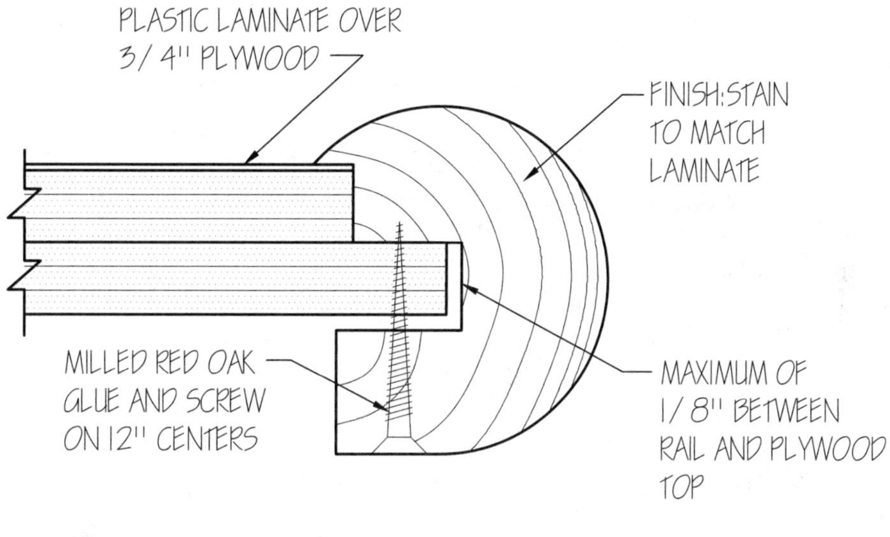

FIGURE 8–76
Exercise 8–6: Bar Rail Detail

chapter

9

Drawing the Furniture Installation Plan, Adding Specifications, and Extracting Data

objectives

When you have completed this chapter, you will be able to:

Correctly use the following commands and settings:

ATTDIA system variable
Attribute Display (ATTDISP)
Block Attribute Manager (BATTMAN)
Data Extraction...
Define Attributes... (ATTDEF)
Edit Text (DDEDIT)
Modify Attribute Global (-ATTEDIT)
Modify Attribute Single (EATTEDIT)
Synchronize Attributes (ATTSYNC)
Write Block (WBLOCK)

INTRODUCTION

This chapter describes the AutoCAD commands that allow specifications to be added to furnishings and how the specifications are extracted from the drawing. These commands are especially important because they reduce the amount of time it takes to count large amounts of like furniture pieces (with specifications) from the plan. There are many software programs available that can be used with AutoCAD to save even more time. These programs provide furniture symbols already drawn and programs that extract specification information in a form that suits your individual needs. Although you may ultimately combine one of these programs with the AutoCAD program, learning the commands included in this chapter will help you to understand how they interact with AutoCAD.

Tutorial 9–1: Tenant Space Furniture Installation Plan with Furniture Specifications

When you have completed Tutorial 9–1, your drawing will look similar to Figure 9–1.

Step 1. Use your workspace to make the following settings:

1. Begin drawing CH9-TUTORIAL1 on the hard drive or network drive by opening existing drawing CH7-TUTORIAL1 and saving it as CH9-TUTORIAL1.
2. Set Layer0 current.
3. Freeze Layers a-anno-dims, Defpoints, and a-anno-area.

DRAW THE FURNITURE SYMBOLS

Step 2. The furniture symbols must be drawn in plan view before you add specifications. Draw the tenant space reception furniture symbols as shown in Figures 9–2, 9–3, 9–4, and 9–5. Draw each piece full scale on

NAME
CLASS
DATE

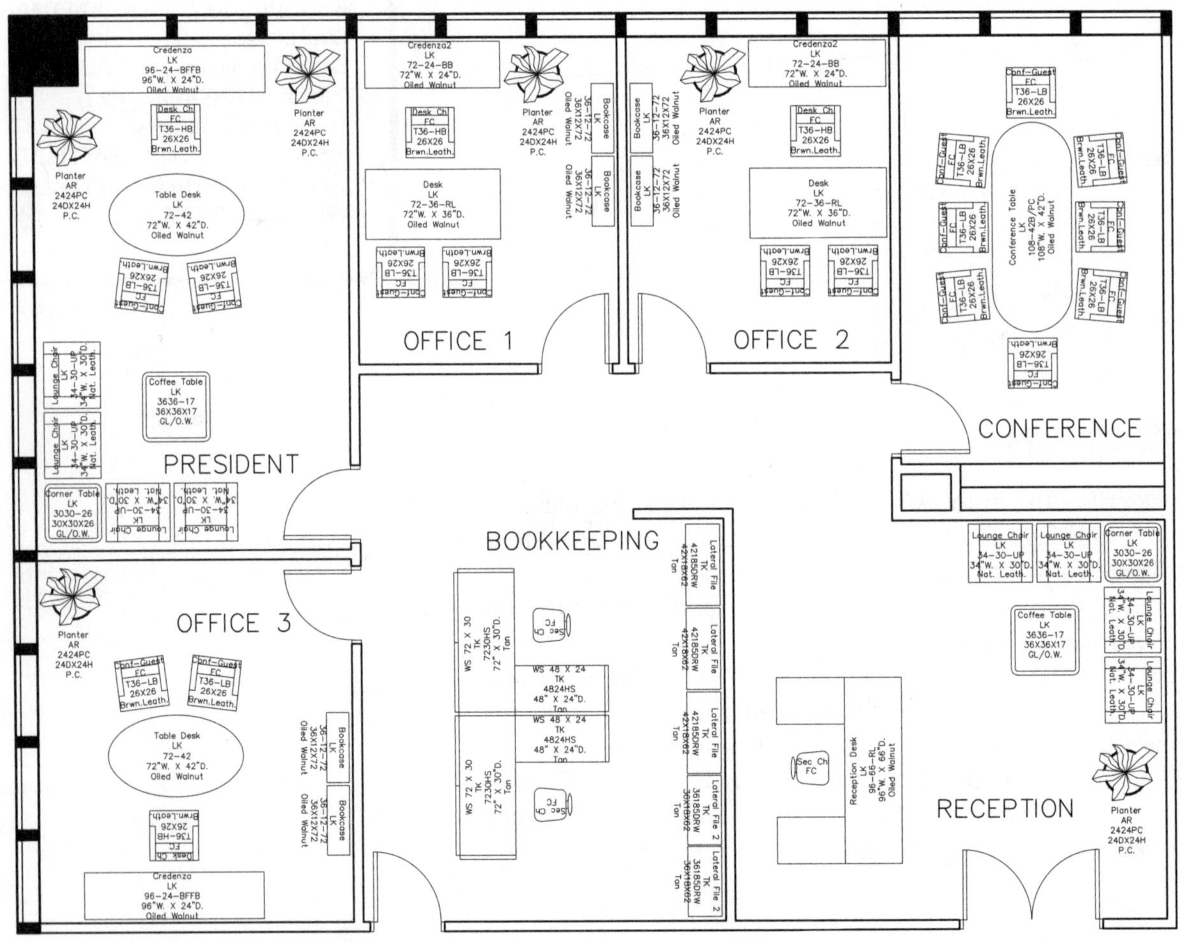

FURNITURE INSTALLATION PLAN
SCALE: 1/8" = 1'–0"

FIGURE 9–1
Tutorial 9–1: Tenant Space Furniture Installation Plan with Furniture Specifications (Scale: 1/8" = 1'-0")

FIGURE 9–2
Tenant Space Furniture Symbols with Specifications (Scale: 1/4″ = 1′-0″)

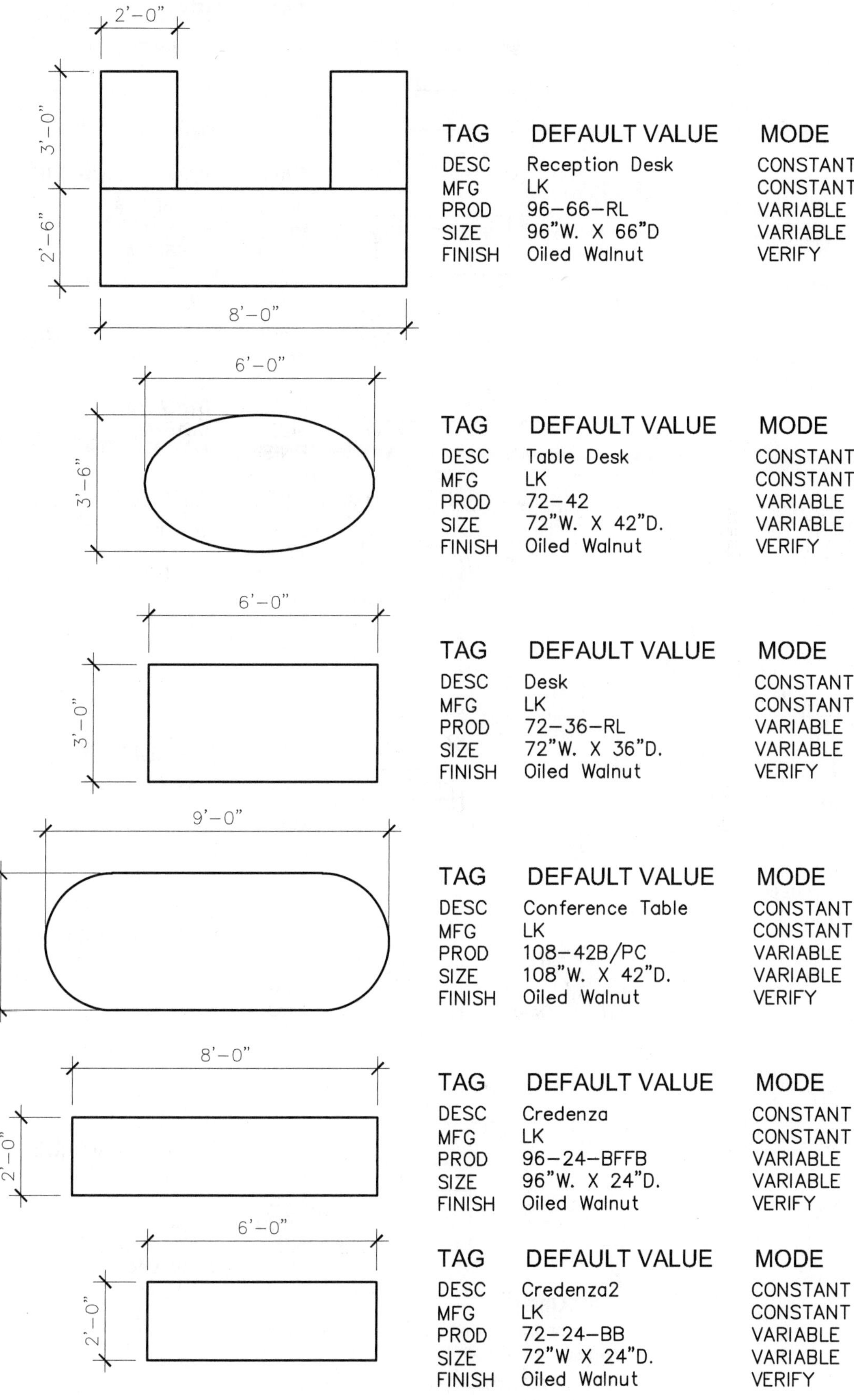

TAG	DEFAULT VALUE	MODE
DESC	Reception Desk	CONSTANT
MFG	LK	CONSTANT
PROD	96–66–RL	VARIABLE
SIZE	96"W. X 66"D	VARIABLE
FINISH	Oiled Walnut	VERIFY

TAG	DEFAULT VALUE	MODE
DESC	Table Desk	CONSTANT
MFG	LK	CONSTANT
PROD	72–42	VARIABLE
SIZE	72"W. X 42"D.	VARIABLE
FINISH	Oiled Walnut	VERIFY

TAG	DEFAULT VALUE	MODE
DESC	Desk	CONSTANT
MFG	LK	CONSTANT
PROD	72–36–RL	VARIABLE
SIZE	72"W. X 36"D.	VARIABLE
FINISH	Oiled Walnut	VERIFY

TAG	DEFAULT VALUE	MODE
DESC	Conference Table	CONSTANT
MFG	LK	CONSTANT
PROD	108–42B/PC	VARIABLE
SIZE	108"W. X 42"D.	VARIABLE
FINISH	Oiled Walnut	VERIFY

TAG	DEFAULT VALUE	MODE
DESC	Credenza	CONSTANT
MFG	LK	CONSTANT
PROD	96–24–BFFB	VARIABLE
SIZE	96"W. X 24"D.	VARIABLE
FINISH	Oiled Walnut	VERIFY

TAG	DEFAULT VALUE	MODE
DESC	Credenza2	CONSTANT
MFG	LK	CONSTANT
PROD	72–24–BB	VARIABLE
SIZE	72"W X 24"D.	VARIABLE
FINISH	Oiled Walnut	VERIFY

MAKE SURE YOU DRAW THE FURNITURE AND THE ATTRIBUTES ON THE 0 LAYER

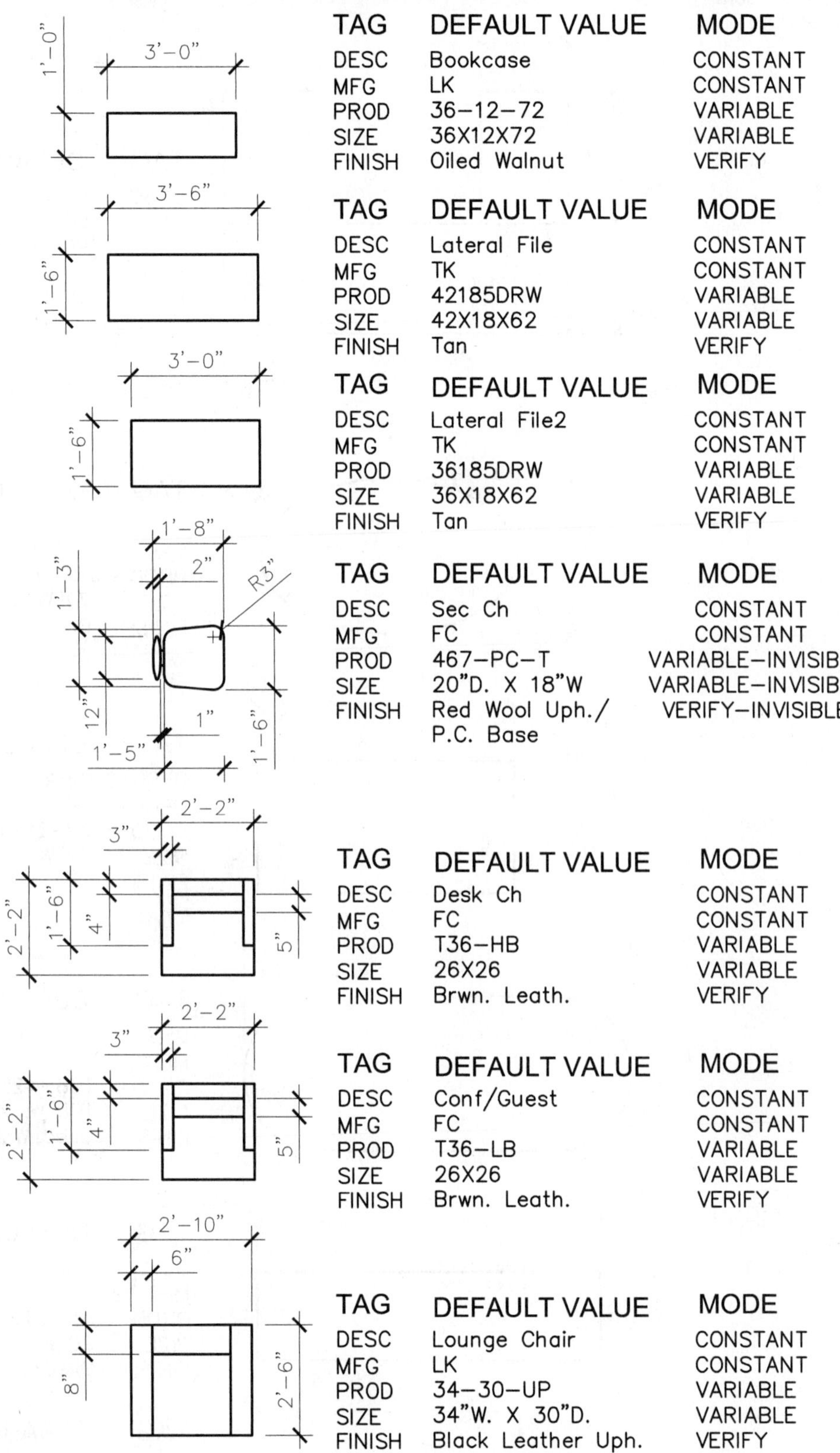

TAG DEFAULT VALUE MODE
DESC Bookcase CONSTANT
MFG LK CONSTANT
PROD 36–12–72 VARIABLE
SIZE 36X12X72 VARIABLE
FINISH Oiled Walnut VERIFY
TAG DEFAULT VALUE MODE
DESC Lateral File CONSTANT
MFG TK CONSTANT
PROD 42185DRW VARIABLE
SIZE 42X18X62 VARIABLE
FINISH Tan VERIFY
TAG DEFAULT VALUE MODE
DESC Lateral File2 CONSTANT
MFG TK CONSTANT
PROD 36185DRW VARIABLE
SIZE 36X18X62 VARIABLE
FINISH Tan VERIFY
TAG DEFAULT VALUE MODE
DESC Sec Ch CONSTANT
MFG FC CONSTANT
PROD 467–PC–T VARIABLE–INVISIBLE
SIZE 20"D. X 18"W VARIABLE–INVISIBLE
FINISH Red Wool Uph./ P.C. Base VERIFY–INVISIBLE
TAG DEFAULT VALUE MODE
DESC Desk Ch CONSTANT
MFG FC CONSTANT
PROD T36–HB VARIABLE
SIZE 26X26 VARIABLE
FINISH Brwn. Leath. VERIFY
TAG DEFAULT VALUE MODE
DESC Conf/Guest CONSTANT
MFG FC CONSTANT
PROD T36–LB VARIABLE
SIZE 26X26 VARIABLE
FINISH Brwn. Leath. VERIFY
TAG DEFAULT VALUE MODE
DESC Lounge Chair CONSTANT
MFG LK CONSTANT
PROD 34–30–UP VARIABLE
SIZE 34"W. X 30"D. VARIABLE
FINISH Black Leather Uph. VERIFY

FIGURE 9–3
Tenant Space Furniture Symbols with Specifications
(Scale: 1/4″ = 1′-0″)

MAKE SURE YOU DRAW THE FURNITURE AND THE ATTRIBUTES ON THE 0 LAYER

TAG	DEFAULT VALUE	MODE
DESC	Panel 48	CONSTANT–INVISIBLE
MFG	TK	CONSTANT–INVISIBLE
PROD	T4812TS	VARIABLE–INVISIBLE
SIZE	48" X 2" 62"H	VARIABLE–INVISIBLE
FINISH	Rose Fabric	VERIFY–INVISIBLE

TAG	DEFAULT VALUE	MODE
DESC	Panel 36	CONSTANT–INVISIBLE
MFG	TK	CONSTANT–INVISIBLE
PROD	T3612TS	VARIABLE–INVISIBLE
SIZE	48" X 2" 62"H	VARIABLE–INVISIBLE
FINISH	Rose Fabric	VERIFY–INVISIBLE

TAG	DEFAULT VALUE	MODE
DESC	Panel 30	CONSTANT–INVISIBLE
MFG	TK	CONSTANT–INVISIBLE
PROD	T3012TS	VARIABLE–INVISIBLE
SIZE	48" X 2" 62"H	VARIABLE–INVISIBLE
FINISH	Rose Fabric	VERIFY–INVISIBLE

TAG	DEFAULT VALUE	MODE
DESC	Panel 24	CONSTANT–INVISIBLE
MFG	TK	CONSTANT–INVISIBLE
PROD	T2412TS	VARIABLE–INVISIBLE
SIZE	24" X 2" 62"H	VARIABLE–INVISIBLE
FINISH	Rose Fabric	VERIFY–INVISIBLE

TAG	DEFAULT VALUE	MODE
DESC	WS 72 X 30	CONSTANT
MFG	TK	CONSTANT
PROD	7230HS	VARIABLE
SIZE	72" X 30"D.	VARIABLE
FINISH	Tan.	VERIFY

TAG	DEFAULT VALUE	MODE
DESC	WS 48 X 24	CONSTANT
MFG	TK	CONSTANT
PROD	4824HS	VARIABLE
SIZE	48" X 24"D.	VARIABLE
FINISH	Tan.	VERIFY

FIGURE 9–4
Tenant Space Furniture Symbols with Specifications (Scale: 1/4" = 1'-0")

your drawing. Pick any open space on your drawing to draw the furniture, similar to Figure 9–5. Draw each symbol on the 0 Layer. Blocks will be made of each symbol so it does not matter where the furniture is drawn on the plan.

DEFINE ATTRIBUTES... (ATTDEF)

The Define Attributes . . . command allows you to add attributes (furniture specifications) to the furniture symbols drawn in plan view. After the attributes are added, a block is made of the symbol. When the block is inserted into a drawing, the specifications

MAKE SURE YOU DRAW THE FURNITURE AND THE ATTRIBUTES ON THE 0 LAYER

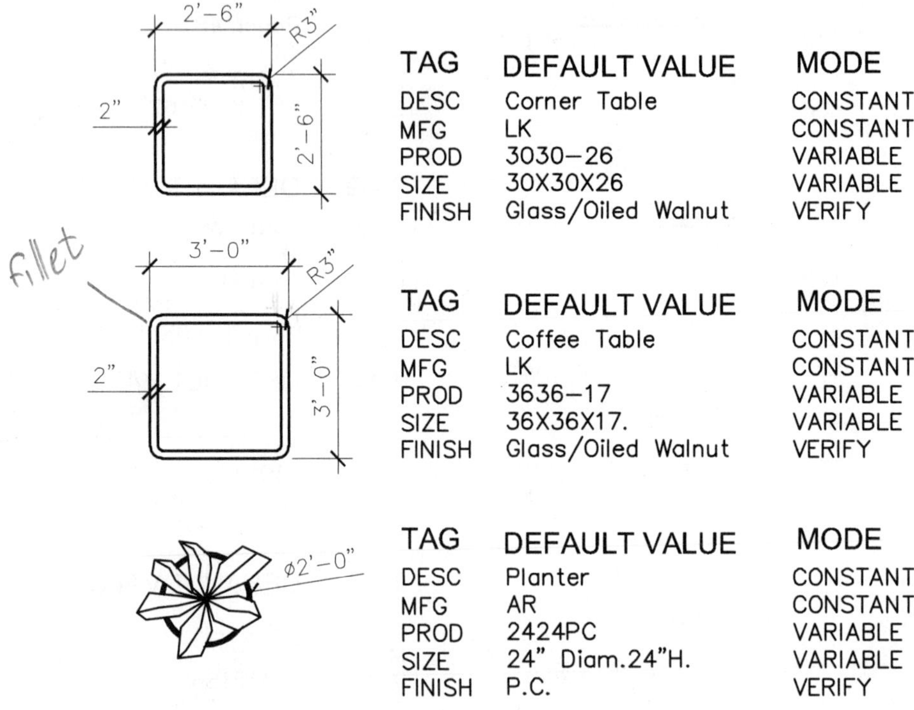

2'–6"
R3"
2"
2'–6"
TAG DEFAULT VALUE MODE
DESC Corner Table CONSTANT
MFG LK CONSTANT
PROD 3030–26 VARIABLE
SIZE 30X30X26 VARIABLE
FINISH Glass/Oiled Walnut VERIFY
fillet
3'–0"
R3"
2"
3'–0"
TAG DEFAULT VALUE MODE
DESC Coffee Table CONSTANT
MFG LK CONSTANT
PROD 3636–17 VARIABLE
SIZE 36X36X17. VARIABLE
FINISH Glass/Oiled Walnut VERIFY
⌀2'–0"
TAG DEFAULT VALUE MODE
DESC Planter CONSTANT
MFG AR CONSTANT
PROD 2424PC VARIABLE
SIZE 24" Diam.24"H. VARIABLE
FINISH P.C. VERIFY

FIGURE 9–5 Tenant Space Furniture Symbols with Specifications (Scale: 1/4" = 1'-0")

appear on the drawing if they have been defined as visible (attributes can be visible or invisible). You can then extract the attribute information from the drawing using the Data Extraction… dialog box.

As shown in Figures 9–2, 9–3, 9–4, and 9–5, each piece of furniture in the tenant space has five attributes. An attribute is made up of two parts: the tag and the value. The tag is used to name the attribute but does not appear on the inserted drawing. It does appear on the drawing while attributes are being defined and before it is made into a block. The tag is used when the attribute information is extracted from the drawing. The attribute tag may contain any characters, but no spaces, and it is automatically converted to uppercase.

The value is the actual specification, such as Reception Desk, LK, 96-66-RL, 96″W × 66″D, and Oiled Walnut. The attribute value may contain any characters, and it may also have spaces. The value appears on the drawing after it is inserted as a block. It appears exactly as it was entered.

There are eight optional modes for the value of ATTDEF; these are set at the beginning of the attribute definition:

Invisible This value is not displayed on the screen when the block is inserted. You may want to use the Invisible mode for pricing, or you may want to make some attributes invisible so that the drawing does not become cluttered.

Constant This value is fixed and cannot be changed. For example, if the same chair is used throughout a project but the fabric varies, then the furniture manufacturer value of the chair will be constant, but the finish value will vary. A Constant value cannot be edited.

Verify This mode allows the value to be variable and allows you to check (verify) the value you have entered. Changes in the value may be entered as needed when the block is inserted.

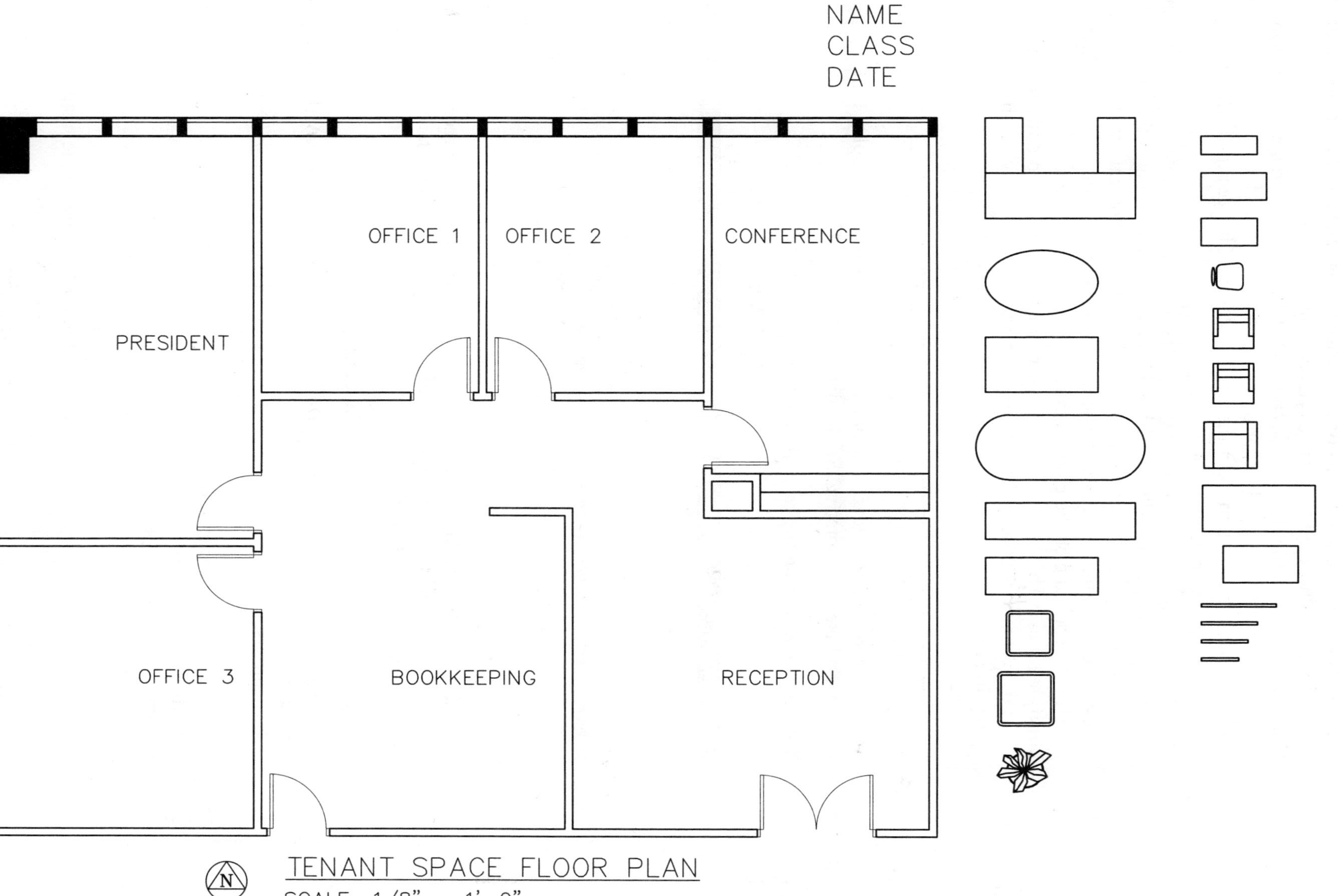

FIGURE 9–6
Draw Furniture Symbols Outside (or Inside) the Tenant Space Floor Plan

Preset This mode allows the value to be variable. It is similar to Constant, but unlike a Constant value, the Preset value can be changed.

Variable If none of the above modes is selected, the value is Variable. The Variable mode allows the value to be changed.

Lock Position This option locks the attribute location inside the block. This is useful when dynamic blocks are used.

Annotative An attribute can be annotative. The annotative attribute is always the same size when plotted, regardless of the scale of the plotted drawing, if the annotation scale is the same as the plot scale. In this chapter we do not annotate the attributes because the furniture is drawn full scale, and we want the plotted attribute size to change depending on the plotted scale.

Multiple Lines This option allows the attribute value to contain multiple lines of text. When this option is selected, you can specify a boundary width for the attribute.

Step 3. Keep the 0 Layer current.

Step 4. Create a new text style named Attribute with the simplex font. Do not make it Annotative. Set it current.

Step 5. Zoom in on the reception desk.

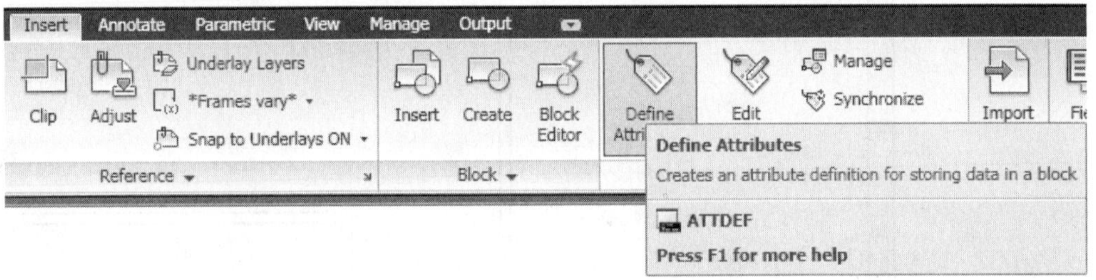

Step 6. Use Define Attributes... to define the attributes of the reception desk. Make the first two attributes of the reception desk Constant (Figure 9–7), as described next:

Prompt	Response
Command:	**Define Attributes...** (or TYPE: **ATT<enter>**)
The Attribute Definition dialog box appears:	CLICK: **Constant** (so a check appears in that Mode check box)
The Prompt: text box is grayed (if the attribute is Constant, there can be no prompt).	TYPE: **DESC** in the Tag: box TYPE: **Reception Desk** in the Default: (value) box. CLICK: **the down arrow** in the Justification box and CLICK: **Center** Text style: **Attribute** TYPE: **3** in the Text height: box

All other parts of the dialog box should be as shown in Figure 9–7.

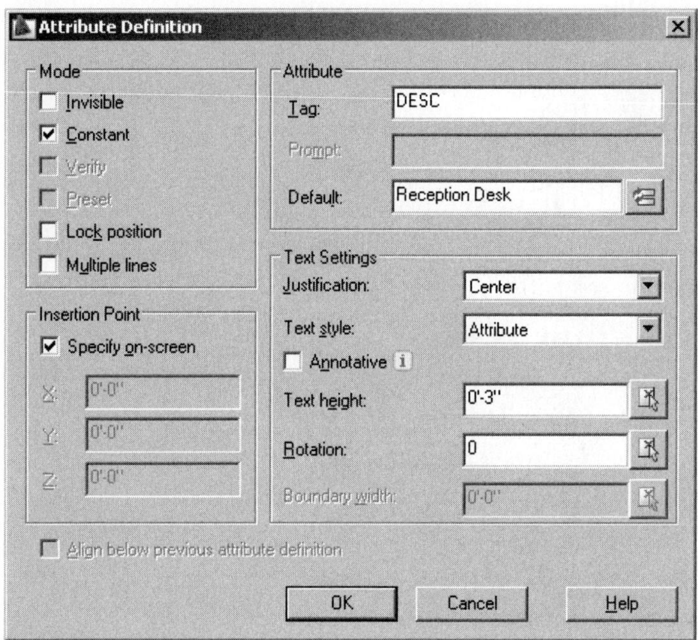

FIGURE 9–7
Use Define Attributes... to Define the First Constant Attribute

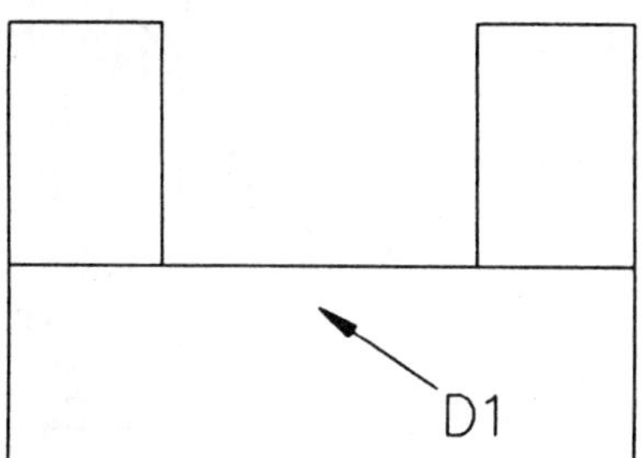

FIGURE 9–8
Specify the Start Point of the First Attribute

Prompt	Response
	CLICK: **OK**
Specify start point:	**D1** (Figure 9–8)
The first attribute is complete; the Attribute Tag appears on the drawing.	
Command:	**<enter>** (repeat ATTDEF)
The Attribute Definition dialog box appears:	**Constant** is checked already, if not, CLICK: **Constant** (so a check appears in that Mode check box)
The Prompt: text box is grayed (if the attribute is Constant there can be no prompt).	TYPE: **MFG** in the Tag: box TYPE: **LK** in the Default: (value) box CLICK: **Align below previous attribute definition** (so a check appears in that Mode check box)

All other parts of the dialog box should be as shown in Figure 9–9. Notice that the Insertion Point and Text Settings areas are grayed when Align below previous attribute definition is checked.

Prompt	Response
	CLICK: **OK**
The second attribute is complete; the Attribute Tag appears on the drawing.	

FIGURE 9–9
Define the Second Constant Attribute

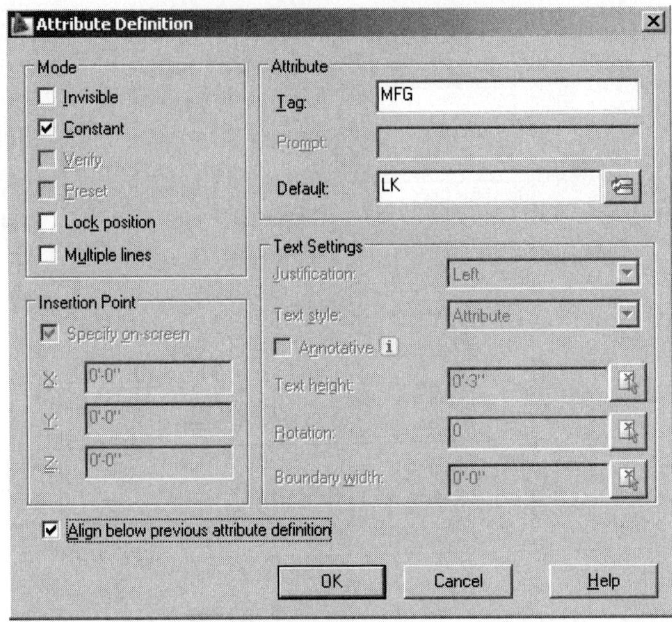

Step 7. Make the third and fourth attributes variable and the fifth one verify as described next:

Prompt	Response
Command:	**<enter>** (repeat ATTDEF)
The Attribute Definition dialog box appears:	**Clear all the checks in the Mode area** (the third attribute is variable)
The Prompt: text box is no longer grayed (this attribute is Variable so a prompt is needed).	TYPE: **PROD** in the Tag: box TYPE: **Enter product number** in the Prompt: box TYPE: **96-66-RL** in the Default: (value) box CLICK: **Align below previous attribute definition** (so a check appears in that Mode check box)

The dialog box should be as shown in Figure 9–10.

Prompt	Response
	CLICK: **OK**
The third attribute is complete; the Attribute Tag appears on the drawing.	
Command:	**<enter>** (repeat ATTDEF)
The Attribute Definition dialog box appears:	
This attribute is also variable so there should be no checks in the Mode boxes.	TYPE: **SIZE** in the Tag: box TYPE: **Enter size** in the Prompt: box TYPE: **96″ W. × 66″ D.** in the Default: (value) box CLICK: **Align below previous attribute definition** (so a check appears in that Mode check box)

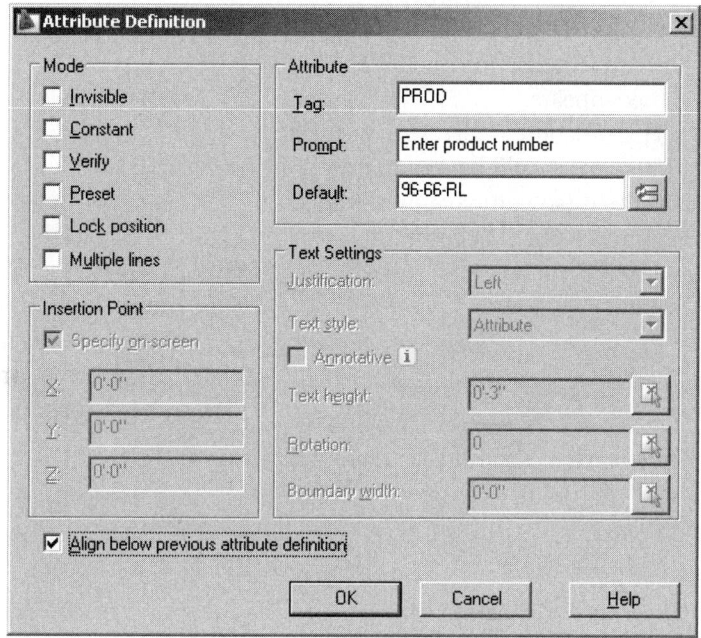

FIGURE 9–10
Define the Third Attribute and Make It Variable

The dialog box should be as shown in Figure 9–11.

Prompt	Response
	CLICK: **OK**
The fourth attribute is complete; the Attribute Tag appears on the drawing.	
Command:	**<enter>** (repeat ATTDEF)

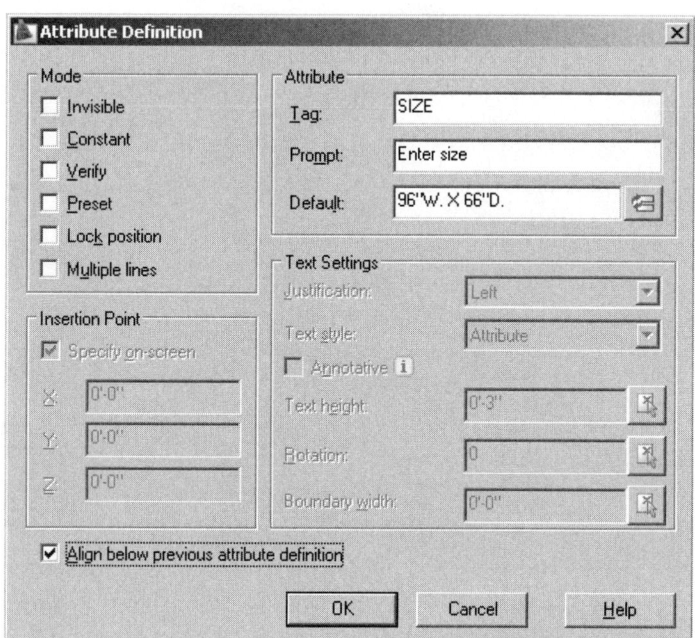

FIGURE 9–11
Define the Fourth Attribute and Make It Variable

Prompt	Response
The Attribute Definition dialog box appears: This attribute is also variable and this one should be one that is verified (so you have two chances to make sure it is correct).	CLICK: **Verify** in the Mode check box. TYPE: **FINISH** in the Tag: box TYPE: **Enter finish** in the Prompt: box TYPE: **Oiled Walnut** in the Default: (value) box CLICK: **Align below previous attribute definition** (so a check appears in that Mode check box)

The dialog box should be as shown in Figure 9–12.

Prompt	Response
	CLICK: **OK**
The fifth attribute is complete; that Attribute Tag appears on the drawing.	

When you have completed defining the five attributes, your drawing of the reception desk will look similar to the desk in Figure 9–13.

NOTE: **If you are not happy with the location of the Attribute Tags, use the Move command to relocate them before using the Block command.**

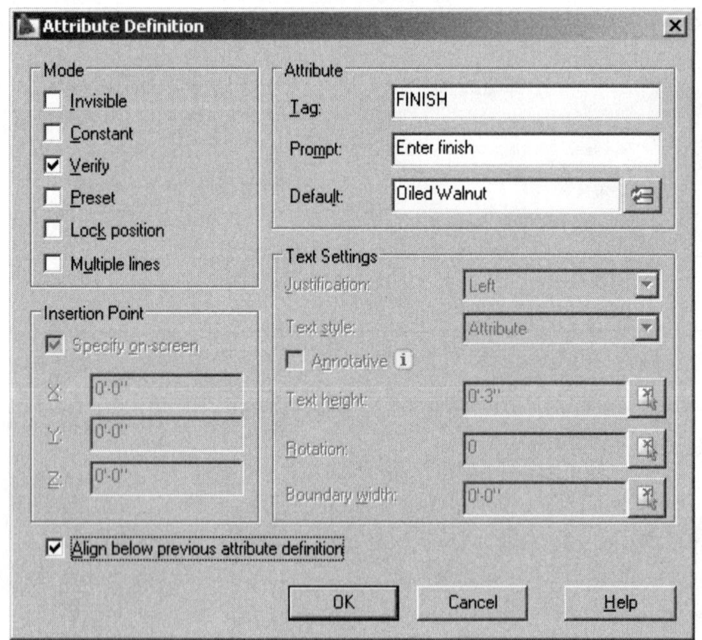

FIGURE 9–12
Define the Fifth Attribute and Make It a Verify One

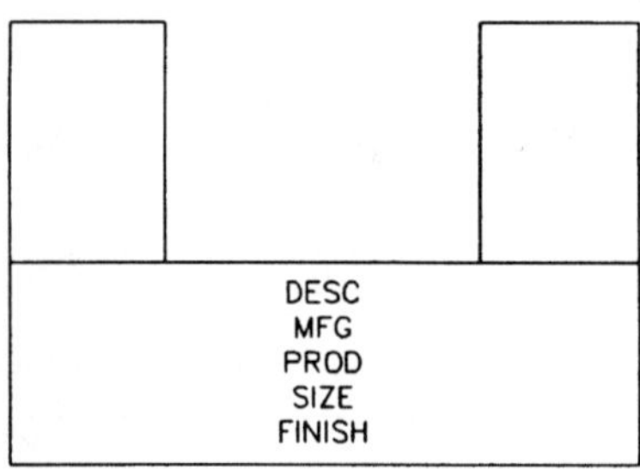

FIGURE 9–13
Reception Desk with Attribute Tags

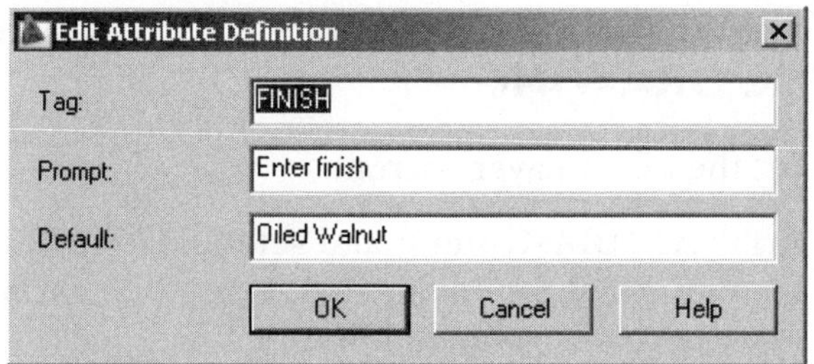

FIGURE 9–14
Edit Attribute Definition Dialog Box

EDIT TEXT (DDEDIT)

Did you make a mistake while typing the attribute tag, attribute prompt, or default attribute value? The Edit Text command allows you to use the Edit Attribute Definition dialog box (Figure 9–14) to correct any typing mistakes you may have made while defining the attributes. You can DOUBLE-CLICK any attribute tag (or TYPE: **ED<enter>**, then CLICK: **the tag**) to activate the Edit Attribute Definition dialog box. The Edit Text prompt is "Select an annotation object or [Undo]:". When you pick a tag, the Edit Attribute Definition dialog box appears and allows you to change the attribute tag, prompt, or default value for a Variable, Verify, or Preset attribute. The tag and the default (actually the value) can be changed for a Constant attribute; adding a prompt for an attribute defined as Constant does not change the attribute mode, and the prompt does not appear.

WBLOCK THE FURNITURE WITH ATTRIBUTES SYMBOL

Step 8. **Use the Write Block command (Figure 9–15) to save the reception desk as a Wblock (a drawing). Save the reception desk to the folder named Blocks that you created in Chapter 6. Name the Wblock Reception Desk. Use the insertion base point as shown in Figure 9–16. Have the desk oriented as shown in Figure 9–16.**

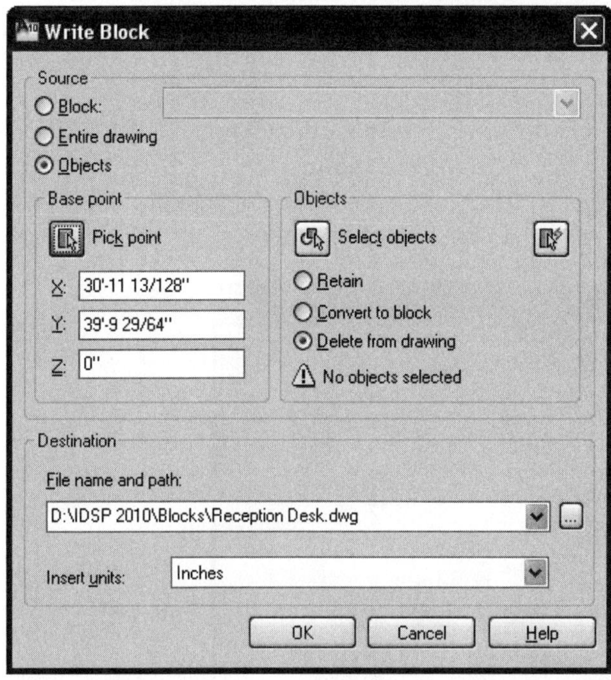

FIGURE 9–15
Write Block Dialog Box

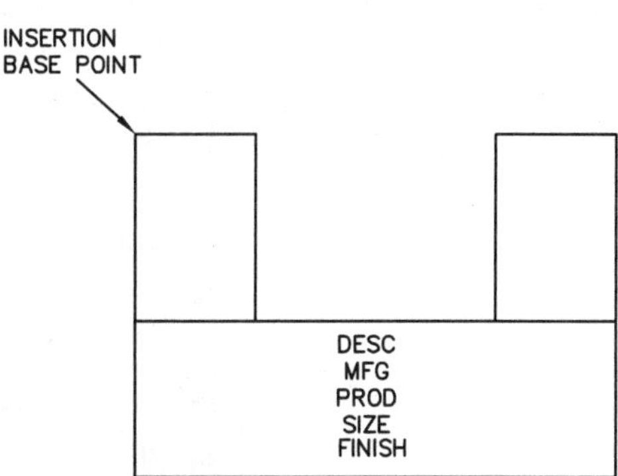

FIGURE 9–16
Save the Reception Desk as a Wblock (a Drawing) to the Folder Named Blocks

INSERT THE WBLOCK WITH ATTRIBUTES INTO THE DRAWING

Step 9. Set the i-furn Layer current.

Step 10. TYPE: **ATTDIA<enter> and set ATTDIA to 1. With ATTDIA set to 1, the Edit Attributes dialog box is used for the attributes. When ATTDIA is set to 0, the command prompts are used.**

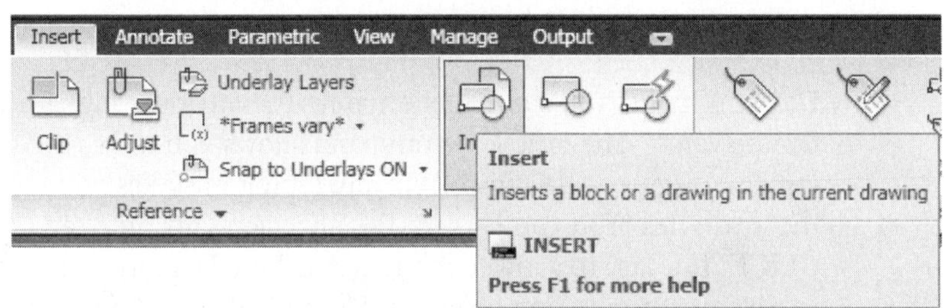

Step 11. **Use the INSERT command to insert the Reception Desk Wblock into the Tenant Space Floor Plan. Use From (on the OSNAP menu) to help position the block, as described next.**

Prompt	Response
Command:	**INSERT** (or TYPE: **I<enter>**)
The Insert dialog box appears:	CLICK: **Browse...**
The Select Drawing File dialog box appears:	LOCATE and CLICK: **the Reception Desk file** CLICK: **Open**
The Insert dialog box appears with Reception Desk in the Name: box:	**Place a check mark in the two Specify On-screen boxes for Insertion point and Rotation** (Figure 9–17). CLICK: **OK**
Specify insertion point or [Basepoint/Scale/X/Y/Z/Rotate]:	TYPE: **FRO<enter>**
Base point:	**OSNAP-Endpoint**
Of	**D1**, Figure 9–18
<Offset>:	TYPE: **@24,30<enter>**

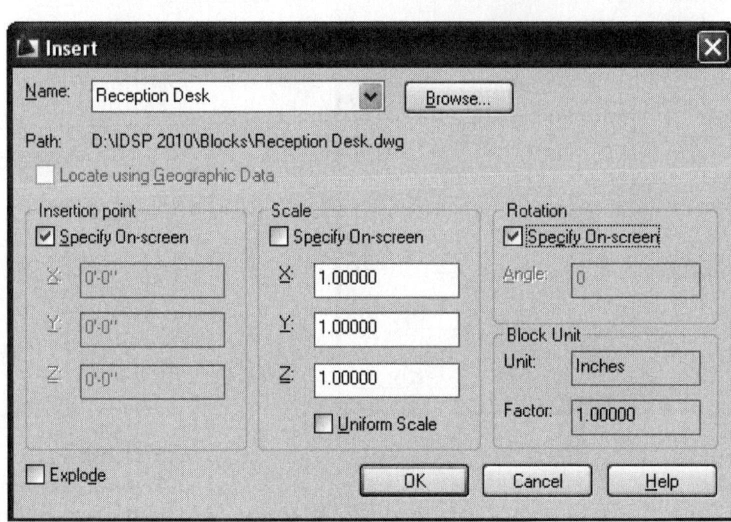

FIGURE 9–17
Insert Dialog Box

FIGURE 9–18
Use the Insert Command to Insert the Reception Desk Block into the Tenant Space Floor

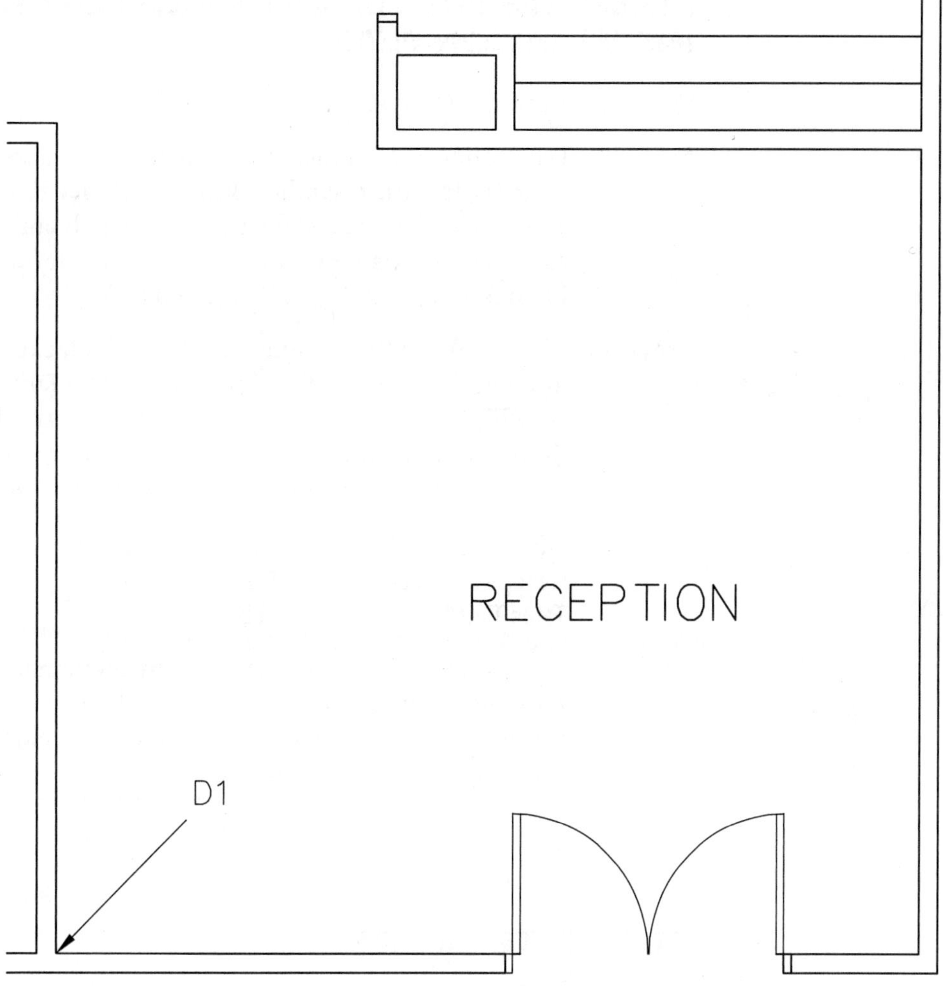

Prompt	Response
Specify rotation angle <0>:	TYPE: **90<enter>**
The Edit Attributes dialog box appears (Figure 9–19):	**Change anything that needs to be changed**—then CLICK: **OK**

FIGURE 9–19
Edit Attributes Dialog Box

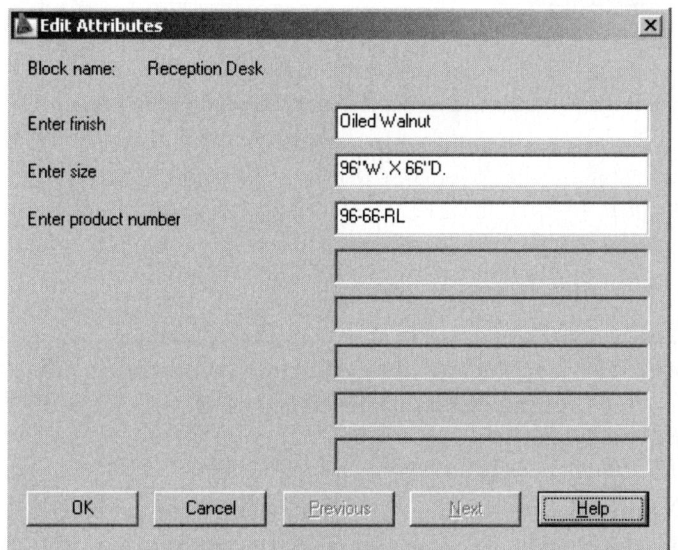

COMPLETE THE TENANT SPACE FURNITURE INSTALLATION PLAN

Step 12. Keep the 0 Layer current.

Step 13. Use Define Attributes... to define the five attributes for each of the remaining furniture symbol drawings. Refer to Figures 9–2, 9–3, 9–4, and 9–5 to determine the attribute tag, default value, and mode for each symbol. Use the same Text Settings for all attributes as shown in Figures 9–7, 9–9, 9–10, 9–11, and 9–12.

Step 14. Use the Write Block command to Wblock each of the furniture symbol drawings into the Blocks folder using the DESC value as the Wblock drawing name. Select an insertion base point that is helpful in positioning the block when you insert it into the drawing. Refer to Figures 9–2, 9–3, 9–4, and 9–5, for example:

DESC	WBLOCK NAME
Reception Desk	Reception Desk
Table Desk	Table Desk

Step 15. Use the INSERT command to insert the remaining furniture symbols into the tenant space furniture installation plan (Figure 9–1). Locate the furniture approximately as shown. Once a block is inserted, it can be copied or moved to a different location.

Some of the values that appeared on the corner table are too long; they go outside the table symbol. This will be fixed next.

ATTRIBUTE, SINGLE...

The Attribute, Single... command uses the Enhanced Attribute Editor dialog box (Figure 9–20) to edit Variable, Verify, and Preset Attributes values of each inserted block at a time. Attributes defined with the Constant mode cannot be edited.

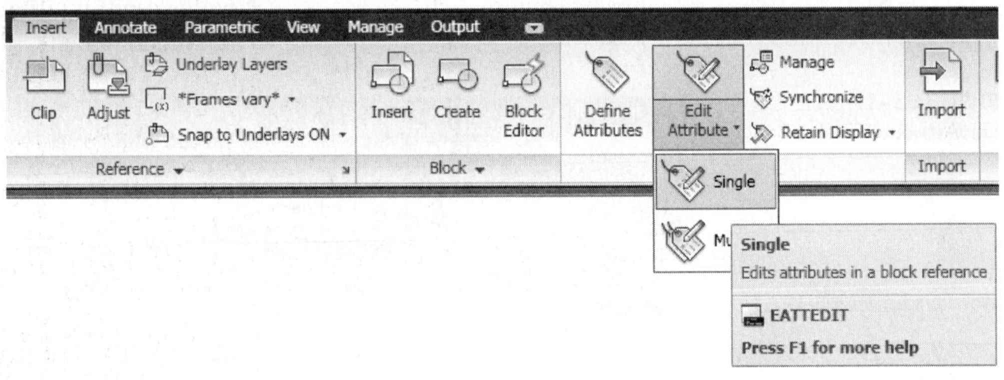

Step 16. Use the Attribute, Single... command to edit the values on the inserted corner table, as described next:

Prompt	Response
Command:	**Edit Attribute...** (or TYPE: **EATTEDIT<enter>**)
Select a block:	PICK: **any place on the corner table.**

FIGURE 9–20
Enhanced Attribute Editor Dialog Box

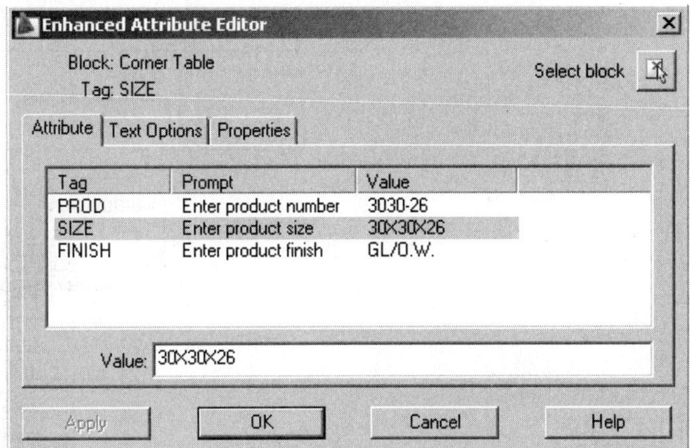

Prompt	Response
The Enhanced Attribute Editor dialog box appears (Figure 9–20):	**Use the dialog box to change the FINISH value to GL/O.W. Highlight the attribute, then change the value in the Value: text box.** CLICK: **Apply** CLICK: **OK**

The values that appear on the corner table now fit within the table symbol (Figure 9–21).

ATTRIBUTE, GLOBAL

The Attribute, Global command uses prompts to edit inserted attribute values. Constant values cannot be edited.

The Attribute, Global prompts allow you to narrow the value selection by entering a specific block name, tag specification, and value specification.

Only visible attributes can be edited when you respond with "Yes" to the prompt "Edit attributes one at a time?". If you respond with "No" to the prompt, visible and invisible attribute value text strings can be edited.

Let's use the Attribute, Global command to edit a value on the eight lounge chairs all at once.

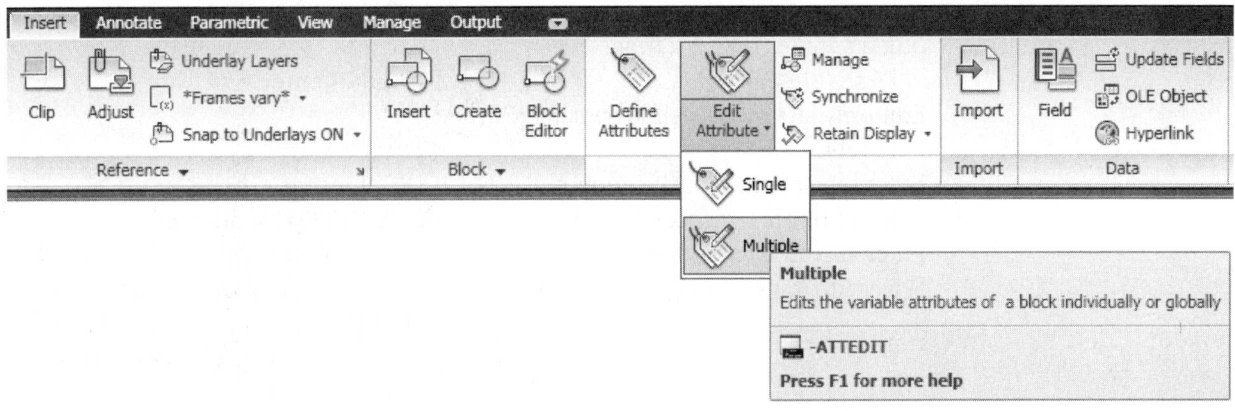

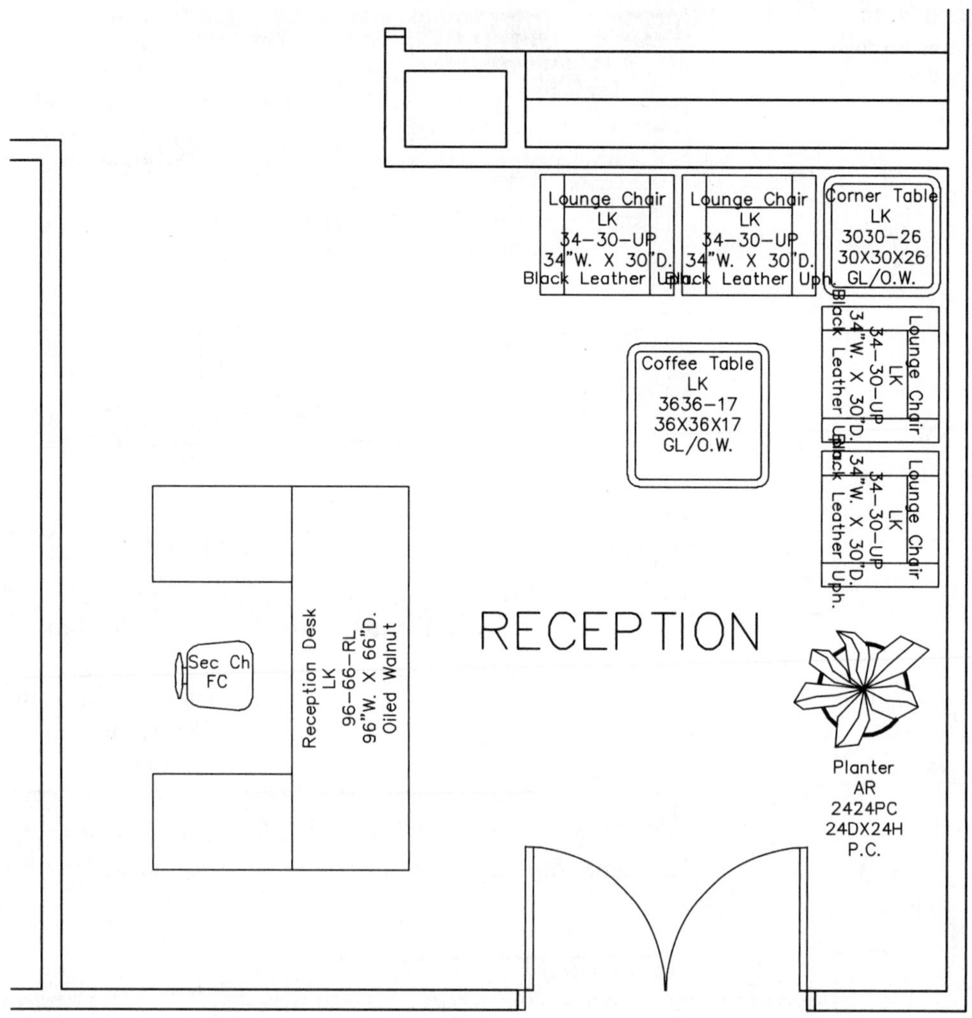

FIGURE 9–21
Tenant Space Reception Area (Scale: 1/4" = 1'-0")

Step 17. Use the Edit Attributes command to edit the text string of the FINISH value on all the lounge chairs at once, as described next:

Prompt	Response
Command:	**Edit Attributes** (or TYPE: **-ATTEDIT <enter>**) (Be sure to include the dash)
Edit attributes one at a time? [Yes/No] <Y>	TYPE: **N<enter>**
Edit only attributes visible on screen? [Yes/No] <Y>	**<enter>**
Enter block name specification <*>:	TYPE: **Lounge Chair<enter>**
Enter attribute tag specification <*>:	TYPE: **FINISH<enter>**
Enter attribute value specification <*>:	TYPE: **Black Leather Uph.<enter>**
Select Attributes:	CLICK: **the Black Leather Uph. attribute on all four chairs in the reception area and the four lounge chairs in the president's office<enter>**

Prompt	Response
4 attributes selected.	
Enter string to change:	TYPE: **Black Leather Uph.<enter>**
Enter new string:	TYPE: **Nat. Leath.<enter>**

Type and enter the block name, tag, and value exactly. You may also enter "No" in response to the prompt "Edit only attributes visible on screen?" and invisible attribute values may also be changed.

ATTRIBUTE DISPLAY (ATTDISP)

The Attribute Display (ATTDISP) command allows you to turn on the Invisible attributes of the secretarial chair. The prompt is "Enter attribute visibility setting [Normal/ ON/ OFF] <Normal>:".

ON Pick ON to make the Invisible attributes appear. Try this, and you will be able to see the Invisible attributes of the secretarial chair.

OFF Pick OFF to make all the attributes on the drawing Invisible. Try this, and you will see that all the attributes are not visible.

Normal Pick Normal to make visible attributes defined as Visible and to make invisible attributes defined as Invisible. Set Normal as the default.

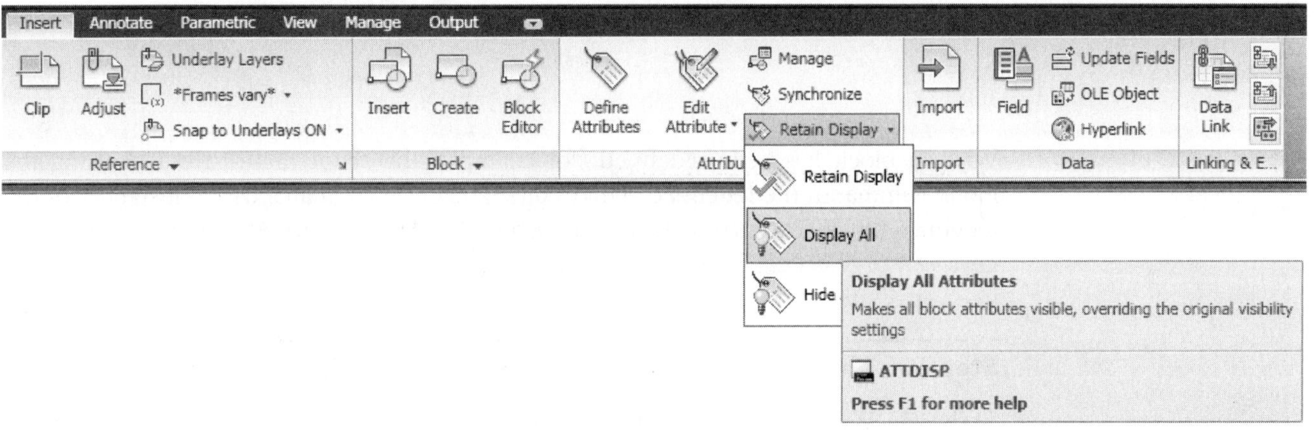

REDEFINING AN INSERTED BLOCK WITH ATTRIBUTES USING THE BLOCK COMMAND

As described in Chapter 6, you can redefine a block using the Block command. When a block that has attributes assigned is redefined using the Block command, previous insertions of the block are affected as follows:

1. Old constant attributes are lost, replaced by new constant attributes, if any.
2. Variable attributes remain unchanged, even if the new block definition does not include those attributes.
3. New variable attributes are not added.

Future insertions of the block will use the new attributes. The previous insertions of the block must be erased and inserted again to use the new attributes.

BLOCK ATTRIBUTE MANAGER (BATTMAN)

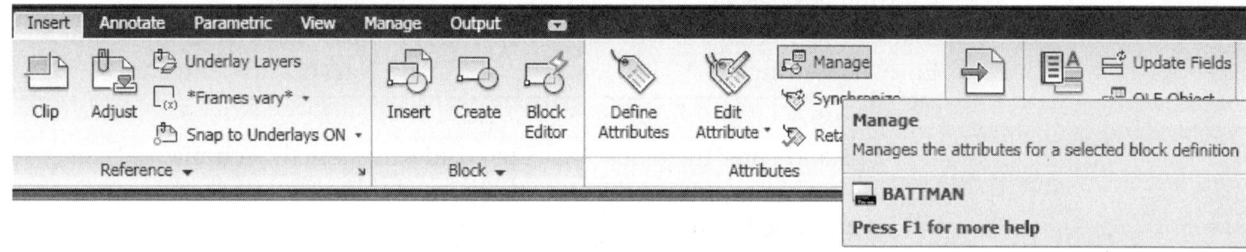

The Block Attribute Manager allows you to locate blocks in the drawing and edit attributes within those blocks in the current drawing. You can also remove attributes from blocks and change the order in which you are prompted for attribute values when inserting a block (Figure 9–22).

SYNCHRONIZE ATTRIBUTES (ATTSYNC)

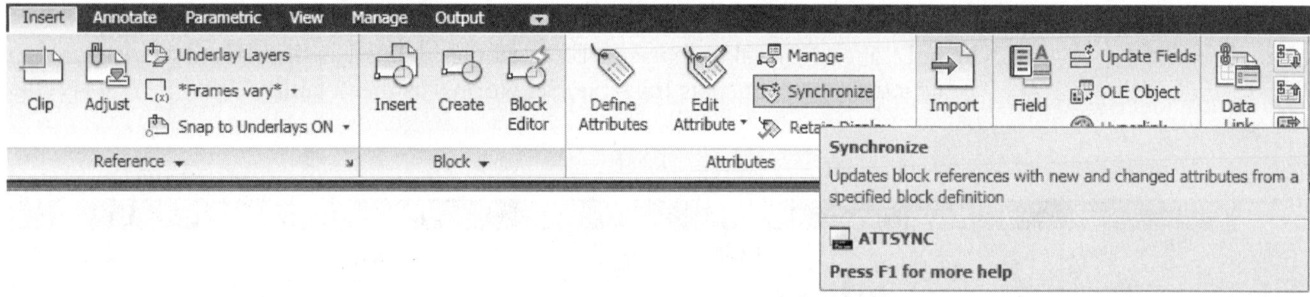

When a block has been redefined (for example, the shape and attributes) using the Block command, the redefined symbol or shape changes in all existing instances of the redefined block. The attributes do not change. The Synchronize Attributes command allows you to select each block whose attributes you want to update to the current redefined attributes.

Step 18. **Change the underlined title text to read as shown in Figure 9–23.**

Step 19. **When you have completed Tutorial 9–1, save your work in at least two places.**

Step 20. **Print Tutorial 9–1 to scale.**

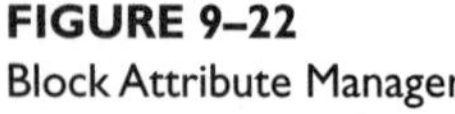

FIGURE 9–22
Block Attribute Manager

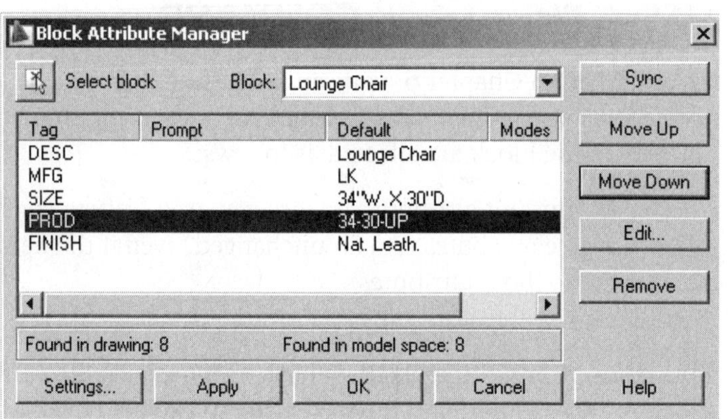

NAME
CLASS
DATE

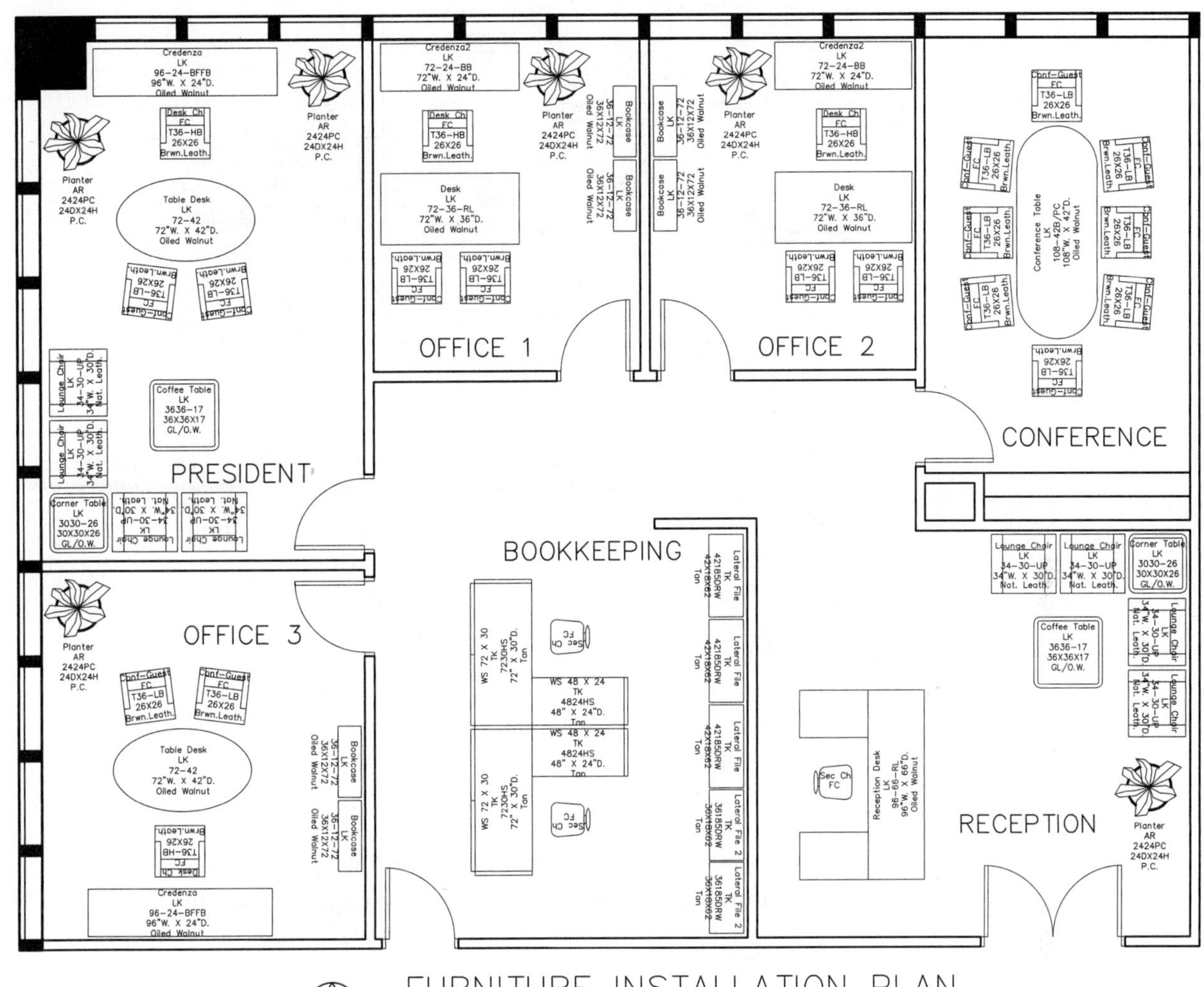

FIGURE 9–23
Tenant Space Furniture Installation Plan with Furniture Specifications (Scale: 1/8" = 1'-0")

Tutorial 9–2: Extracting Attributes from the Tenant Space Furniture Installation Plan

When you have completed Tutorial 9–2, your drawing will look similar to Figure 9–24.

Step 1. Begin drawing CH9-TUTORIAL2 on the hard drive or network drive by opening the existing drawing CH9-TUTORIAL1 and saving it as CH9-TUTORIAL2.

Step 2. Set Layer a-anno-text current.

Step 3. Prepare the drawing to accept the extracted attributes in a tabular form as follows:

FIGURE 9–24
Tutorial 9–2: Complete

NAME
CLASS
DATE

FURNITURE TOTALS						
Count	Name	DESC	FINISH	MFG	PROD	SIZE
1	Panel 48	Panel 48	Rose Fabric	TK	T4812TS	48" X 2" X 62" H.
1	Reception Desk	Reception Desk	Oiled Walnut	LK	96-66-RL	96"W. X 66"D.
1	Conference Table	Conference Table	Oiled Walnut	LK	108-428/PC	108"W. X 42"D.
2	Corner Table	Corner Table	GL/O.W.	LK	3030-26	30X30X26
2	Coffee Table	Coffee Table	GL/O.W.	LK	3636-17	36X36X17
2	WS 72 X 30	WS 72 X 30	Tan	TK	7230HS	72" X 30"D.
2	Panel 24	Panel 24	Rose Fabric	TK	T2412TS	24" X 2" X 62" H.
2	WS 48 X 24	WS 48 X 24	Tan	TK	4824HS	48" X 24"D.
2	Desk	Desk	Oiled Walnut	LK	72-36-RL	72"W. X 36"D.
2	Table Desk	Table Desk	Oiled Walnut	LK	72-42	72"W. X 42"D.
2	Credenza	Credenza	Oiled Walnut	LK	96-24-BFFB	96"W. X 24"D.
2	Lateral File 2	Lateral File 2	Tan	TK	3618SDRW	36X18X62
2	Credenza2	Credenza2	Oiled Walnut	LK	72-24-BS	72"W. X 24"D.
3	Panel 30	Panel 30	Rose Fabric	TK	T3012TS	30" X 2" X 62" H.
3	Lateral File	Lateral File	Tan	TK	4218SDRW	42X18X62
3	Sec Ch	Sec Ch	Red Wool Uph./P.C. Base	FC	467-PC-T	20"D X 18"W
4	Panel 36	Panel 36	Rose Fabric	TK	T3612TS	36" X 2" X 62" H.
4	Desk Ch	Desk Ch	Brwn.Leath.	FC	T36-HB	26X26
6	Planter	Planter	P.C.	AR	2424PC	24DX24H
6	Bookcase	Bookcase	Oiled Walnut	LK	36-12-72	36X12X72
8	Lounge Chair	Lounge Chair	Nat. Leath.	LK	34-30-UP	34"W. X 30"D.
16	Conf-Guest	Conf-Guest	Brwn.Leath.	FC	T36-LB	26X26

1. **Make a new Layout using the Create Layout Wizard (on the Insert menu):**

Begin:	**Name it Furniture Totals**
Printer:	**Select a printer**
Paper Size:	**Letter (8.5″ × 11″)**
Orientation:	**Landscape**
Title Block:	**None**
Define Viewports:	**Single**
Viewport Scale:	**1:1**
Pick Location:	**CLICK: Next>**
Finish:	**CLICK: Finish**

2. **Erase the viewport border created on the new layout so this layout will contain nothing but the table with the extracted attributes (Figure 9–24).**
3. **Make sure the Furniture Totals Layout tab is selected, to continue.**

DATA EXTRACTION...

The Data Extraction Wizard can be used to produce a parts list or bill of materials directly from a drawing that contains blocks with attributes. The drawing you made in this chapter is an excellent example of this type of drawing. With the Data Extraction Wizard, you can extract existing attributes and create a table as described in this tutorial.

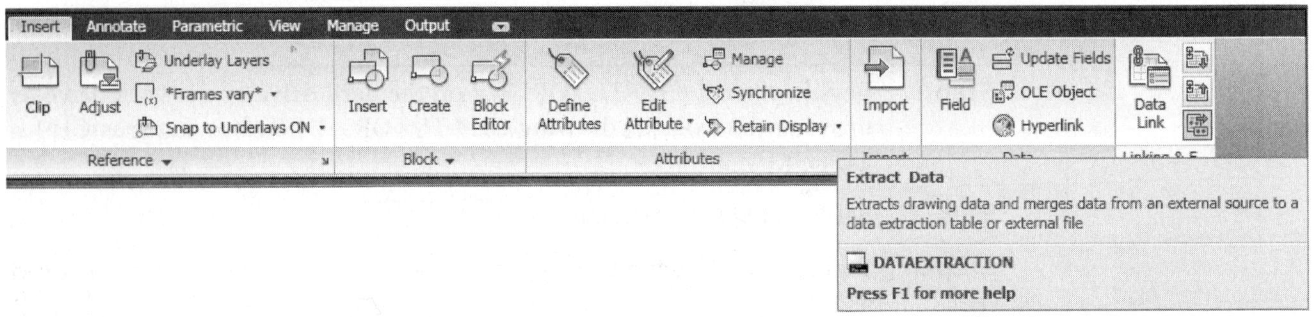

Step 4. **Extract attributes from this drawing using the Data Extraction... command and create a table on the blank Furniture Totals layout, as described next:**

Prompt	Response
Command:	**Data Extraction...**
The Data Extraction Wizard, Figure 9–25, appears:	With the **Create a new data extraction** button selected, CLICK: **Next**
The Save Data Extraction As dialog box appears:	**Select the folder where your drawings are stored,** and name the File: **FURNITURE TOTALS** CLICK: **Save**
The Data Extraction—Define Data Source (Page 2 of 8) appears:	CLICK: **Next**
Select Objects (Page 3 of 8) appears:	**Make sure checks are in Display blocks with attributes only** and **Display objects currently in-use only. Have the Display blocks only radio button on (Figure 9–26).** CLICK: **Next>**
Select Properties (Page 4 of 8) appears:	**Place a check mark in Attribute** only (Figure 9–27) CLICK: **Next**
Refine Data (Page 5 of 8) appears:	**RIGHT-CLICK:** on the column name for any blank columns if there are any and CLICK: **Hide Column** (Figure 9–28) CLICK: **Next**

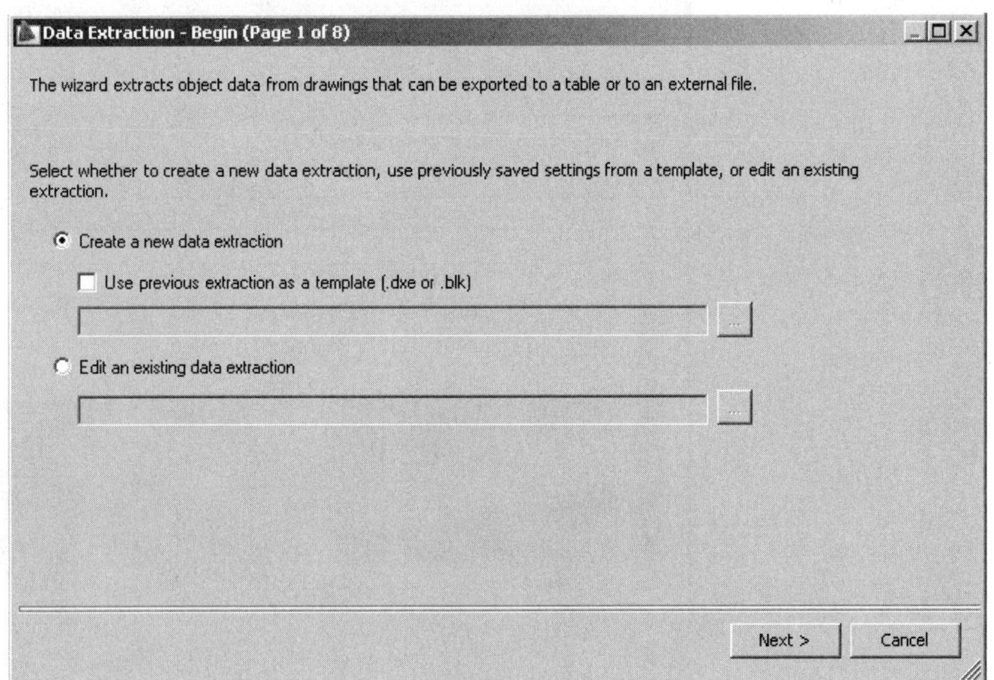

FIGURE 9–25
Data Extraction Wizard - Begin (Page 1 of 8)

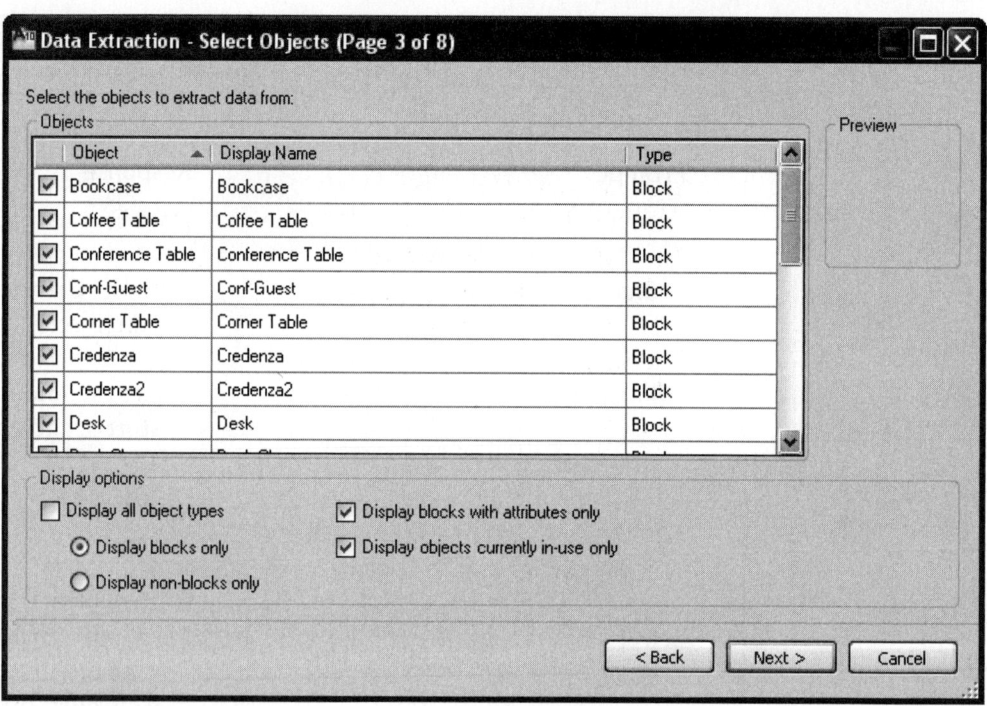

FIGURE 9–26
Data Extraction - Select Objects (Page 3 of 8)

Prompt	Response
Choose Output (Page 6 of 8) appears:	**Place a check mark in Insert data extraction table into drawing.** CLICK: **Next**
Table Style (Page 7 of 8) appears:	TYPE: **FURNITURE TOTALS** in the Enter a title for your table: box (Figure 9–29) CLICK: **Next**
Finish (Page 8 of 8) appears:	CLICK: **Finish**
Specify insertion point:	TYPE: **1/2,8<enter>**

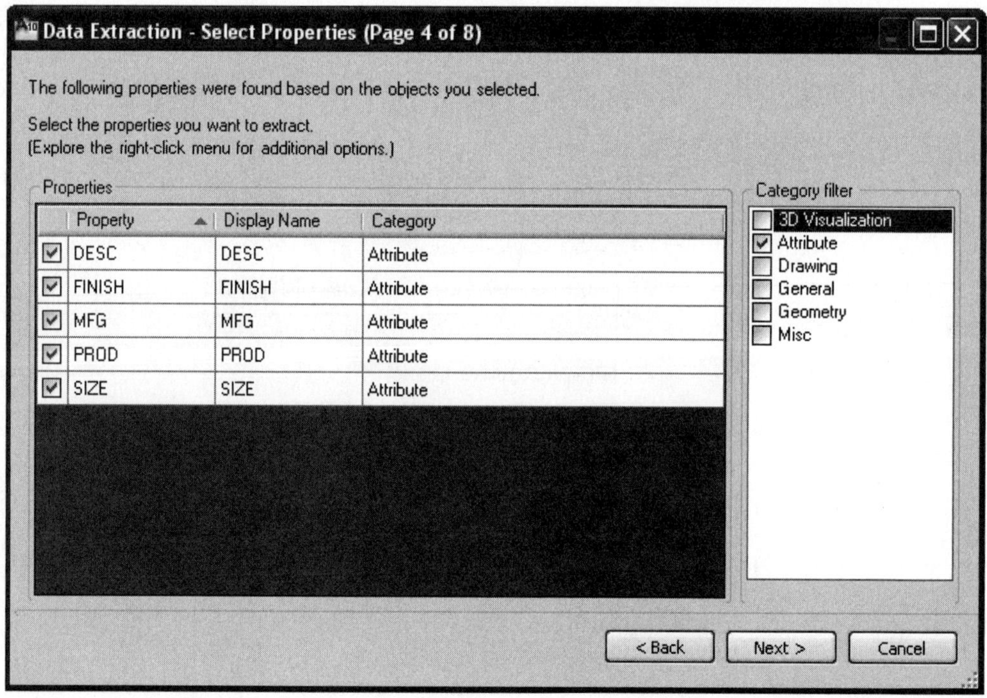

FIGURE 9–27
Data Extraction - Select Properties (Page 4 of 8)

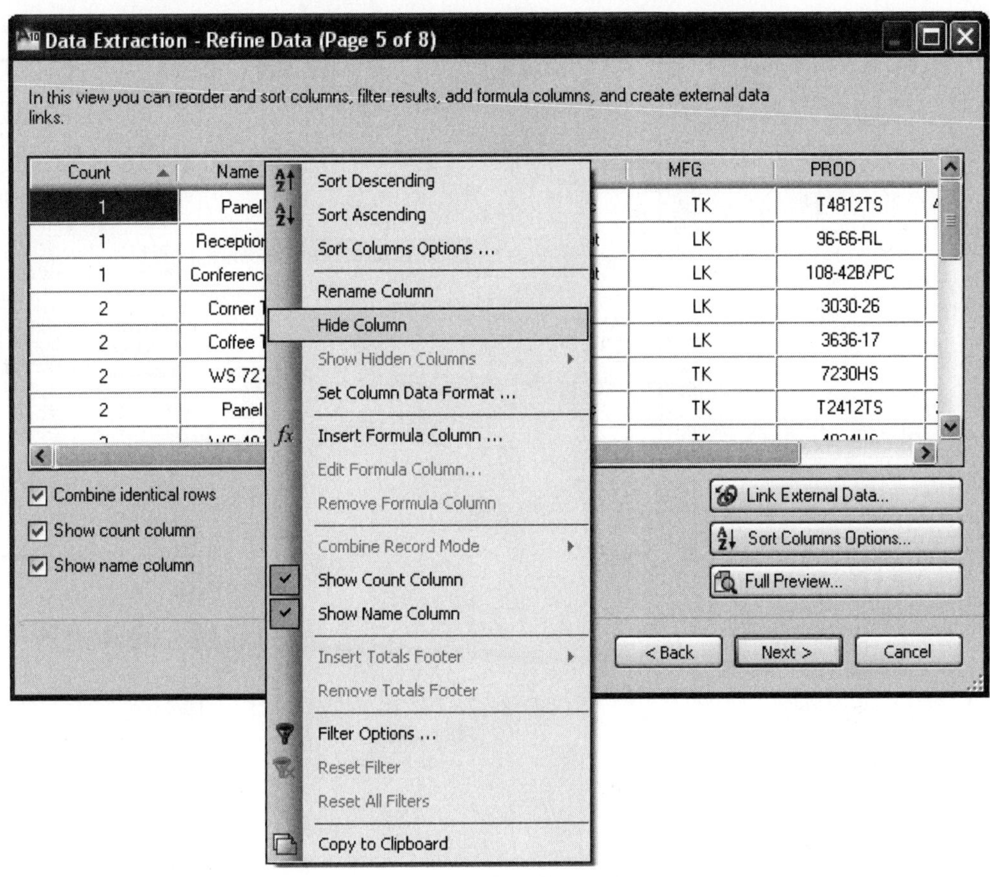

FIGURE 9–28
Data Extraction - Refine Data (Page 5 of 8) Hide Any Blank Columns

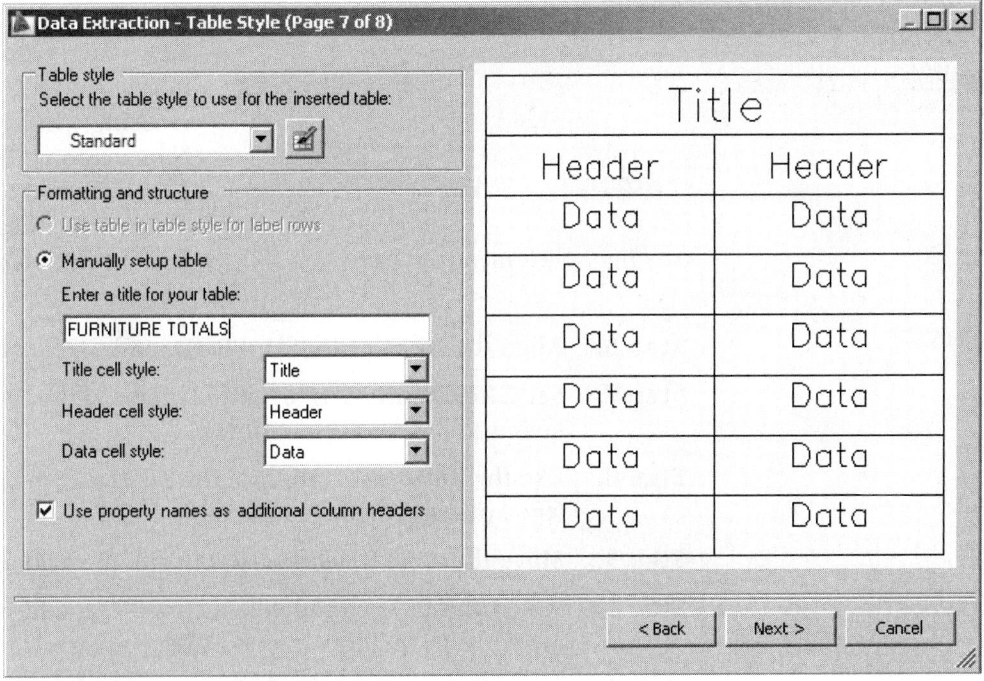

FIGURE 9–29
Data Extraction - Table Style (Page 7 of 8) Name the Table FURNITURE TOTALS

FIGURE 9–30
Align Columns Middle Left

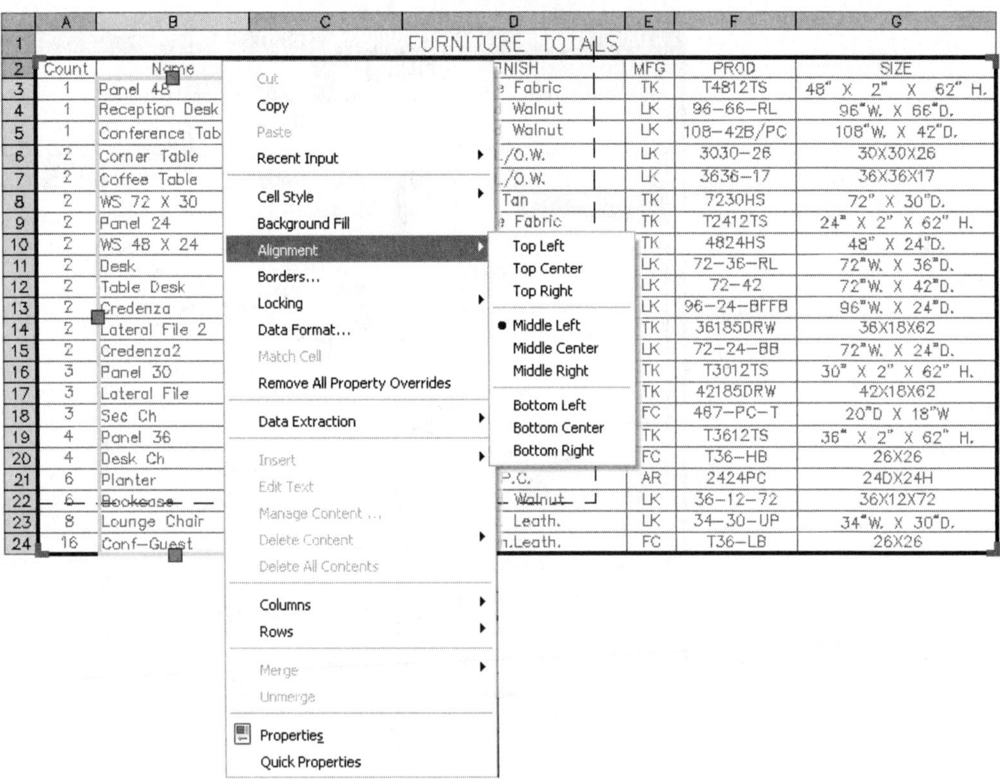

Step 5. Align DESC, FINISH, Name, PROD, and SIZE columns Middle Left (Figure 9–30), as described next:

Prompt	Response
Command:	CLICK: **the open area to the right in the first cell under the Name column to start a crossing window and move your mouse to the left and down so your crossing window selects all cells in the Name column but DOES NOT CROSS THE BOTTOM LINE OF THE TABLE** **Then,** RIGHT-CLICK:
The right-click menu appears:	SELECT: **Alignment - Middle Left** (Figure 9–30)

Step 6. Align the DESC, FINISH, PROD, and SIZE columns middle left.

Step 7. Set GRIDDISPLAY to 0, and set the grid for the FURNITURE TOTALS layout to 1/4″ (so it is visible).

Step 8. Use the Reference option of the SCALE command to scale the long side (the horizontal side) of the table to 10″.

Step 9. Move the table if necessary so it fits the grid as shown in Figure 9–24.

Step 10. When you have completed Tutorial 9–2, add your name, class, and current date to the drawing and save your work in at least two places.

Step 11. Print the Furniture Totals layout at a scale of 1:1 on an 11″ × 8-1/2″ sheet.

review questions

1. In which of the following parts of an attribute definition may spaces *not* be used?
   a. Value
   b. Default Value
   c. Prompt
   d. Tag
   e. Spaces may be used in all the above.
2. AutoCAD can automatically align an attribute definition below one that was defined with the previous Define Attributes... ATTDEF command.
   a. True
   b. False
3. Which of the following part of an attribute appears on the inserted furniture symbol when the attribute mode is *not* Invisible?
   a. Tag
   b. Prompt
   c. Value
   d. Mode
   e. Block name
4. To use the Edit Attributes dialog box to change or accept default values of attributes when inserting blocks or wblocks, which of the following system variables must be set to 1?
   a. ATTREQ
   b. ATTDIA
   c. ATTMODE
   d. ANGDIR
   e. AUPREC
5. Which of the following commands can be used to make invisible all the visible attributes on the drawing?
   a. EATTEDIT
   b. ATTEXT
   c. ATTDEF
   d. -ATTEDIT
   e. ATTDISP
6. Which of the following commands can be used to edit Variable, Verify, Preset, and Constant attribute values of an inserted block using a dialog box?
   a. ATTEXT
   b. ATTDEF
   c. -ATTEDIT
   d. ATTDISP
   e. Constant attributes cannot be edited.

Complete.

7. List the command that uses the Enhanced Attribute Editor dialog box to edit Variable, Verify, and Preset Attribute values of one inserted block at a time.

   ____

   ____
8. When a block that has attributes assigned is redefined with the Block command, what happens to existing Variable attributes on the drawing?

   ____
9. List the command that allows you to select each redefined block whose attributes you want to update to the current redefined attributes.

   ____
10. The command used to extract attributes from a drawing is:

    ____

Exercise 9–1: Hotel Room Furniture Installation Plan

1. Begin CH9-EX1 on the hard drive or network drive by opening the existing hotel room floor plan and saving it as CH9-EX1. Your final drawing will look similar to Figure 9–31.
2. Set the i-furn Layer current and turn off any layers that are not needed.

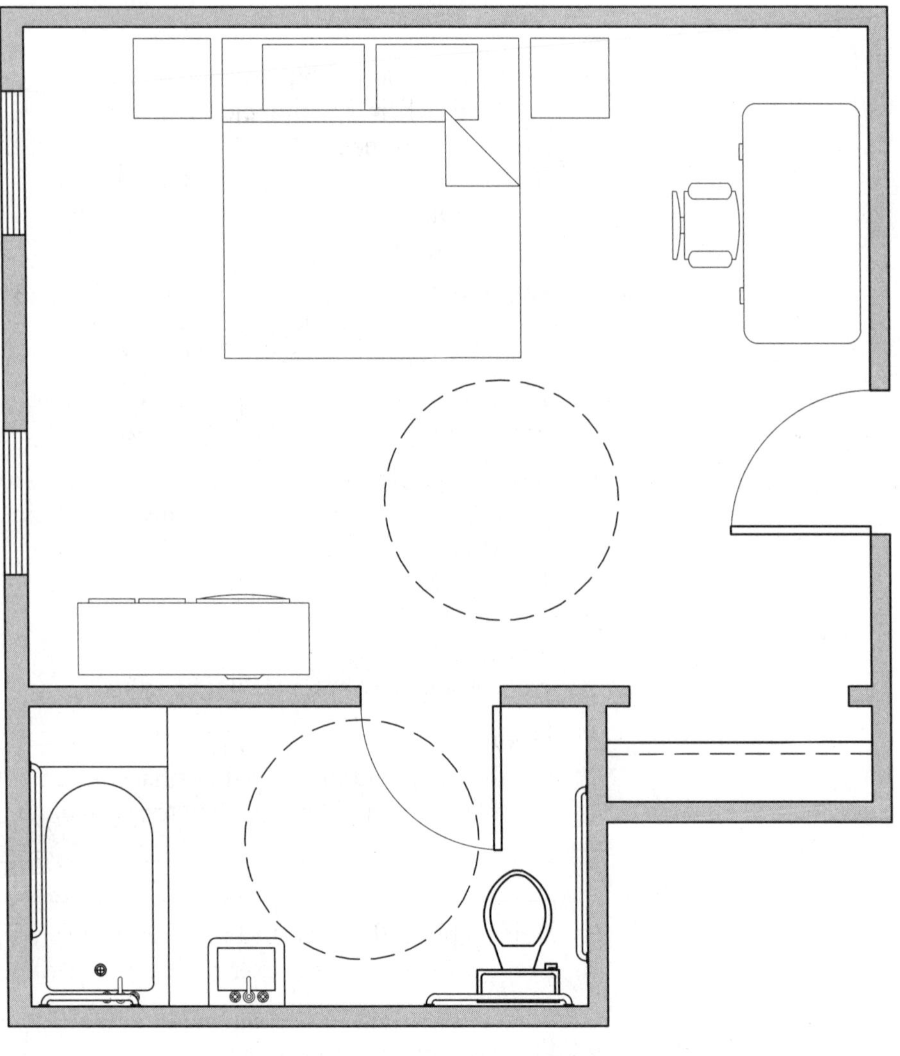

FIGURE 9–31
Exercise 9–1: Hotel Room Furniture Installation Plan (Scale: 1/4″ = 1′-0″)

3. Select furniture from the DesignCenter, and insert it by double-clicking on the furniture symbol. Place the furniture in the approximate locations shown in Figure 9–31. You will find all this furniture in the Home - Space Planner drawing.
4. Save the drawing in two places, and plot or print the drawing to scale.

Exercise 9–2: Log Cabin Furniture Installation Plan

1. Begin CH9-EX2 by opening the existing log cabin floor plan and saving it as CH9-EX2. Your final drawing will look similar to Figure 9–32.
2. Set the i-furn Layer current and turn off any layers that are not needed.

FIGURE 9–32
Exercise 9–2: Log Cabin Furniture Installation Plan (Scale: 3/16″ = 1′-0″)

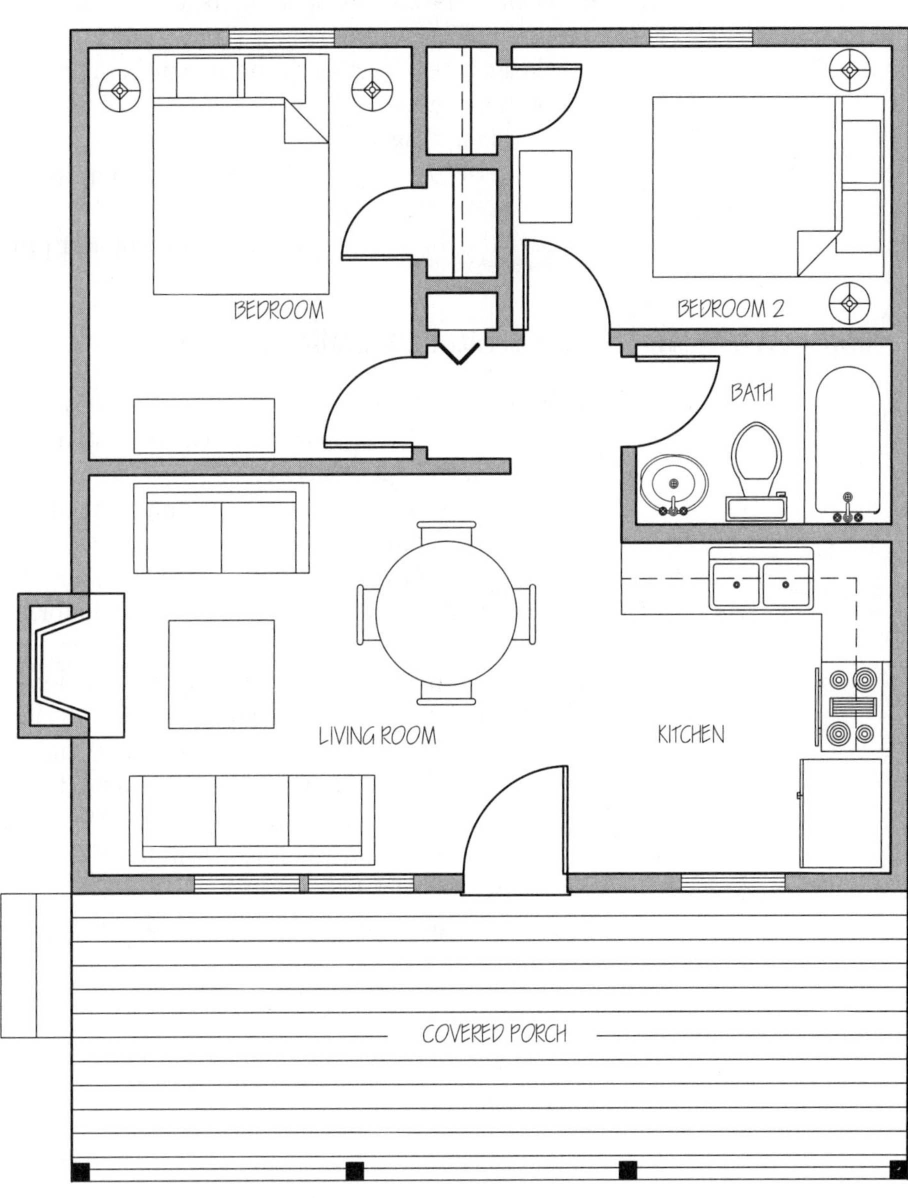

3. Select furniture from the DesignCenter, and insert it by double-clicking on the furniture symbol. Place the furniture in the approximate locations shown in Figure 9–32. You will find this furniture in the Home - Space Planner drawing and 2D Architectural Online. Use a 3/16″ = 1′-0″ architectural scale to measure any furniture you do not find, and draw it full scale.
4. Save the drawing in two places, and plot or print the drawing to scale.

Exercise 9–3: House Furniture Installation Plan

1. Begin CH9-EX3 by opening the existing house floor plan and saving it as CH9-EX3.
2. Create a new layer for furniture and set it current. Turn off any layers that are not needed.
3. Your final drawing will look similar to Figure 9–33, Lower and Upper Levels. Use a 1/8″ = 1′-0″ architectural scale to measure the furniture, and draw it full scale.
4. Save the drawing in two places, and plot or print the drawing to scale.

Exercise 9–4: Bank Furniture Installation Plan

1. Begin CH9-EX4 by opening the existing bank floor plan and saving it as CH9-EX4. Get detail dimensions for customer service representative areas from Figure 9-34, Sheet 2.
2. Create a new layer for furniture and set it current. Turn off any layers that are not needed.
3. Your final drawing will look similar to Figure 9–34, Sheet 1. Select furniture from the DesignCenter, and insert it by double-clicking on the furniture symbol.

   Place the furniture in the approximate locations shown in Figure 9–34. You will find this furniture in the Home - Space Planner drawing and 2D Architectural Online. Use a 3/32″ = 1′-0″ architectural scale to measure any furniture you do not find, and draw it full scale.
4. Measure the two areas shown on Figure 9–34, Sheet 2, with a 1/4″ = 1′-0″ architectural scale, and draw them full size in the approximate location shown on Sheet 1.
5. Save the drawing in two places, and plot or print the drawing to scale.

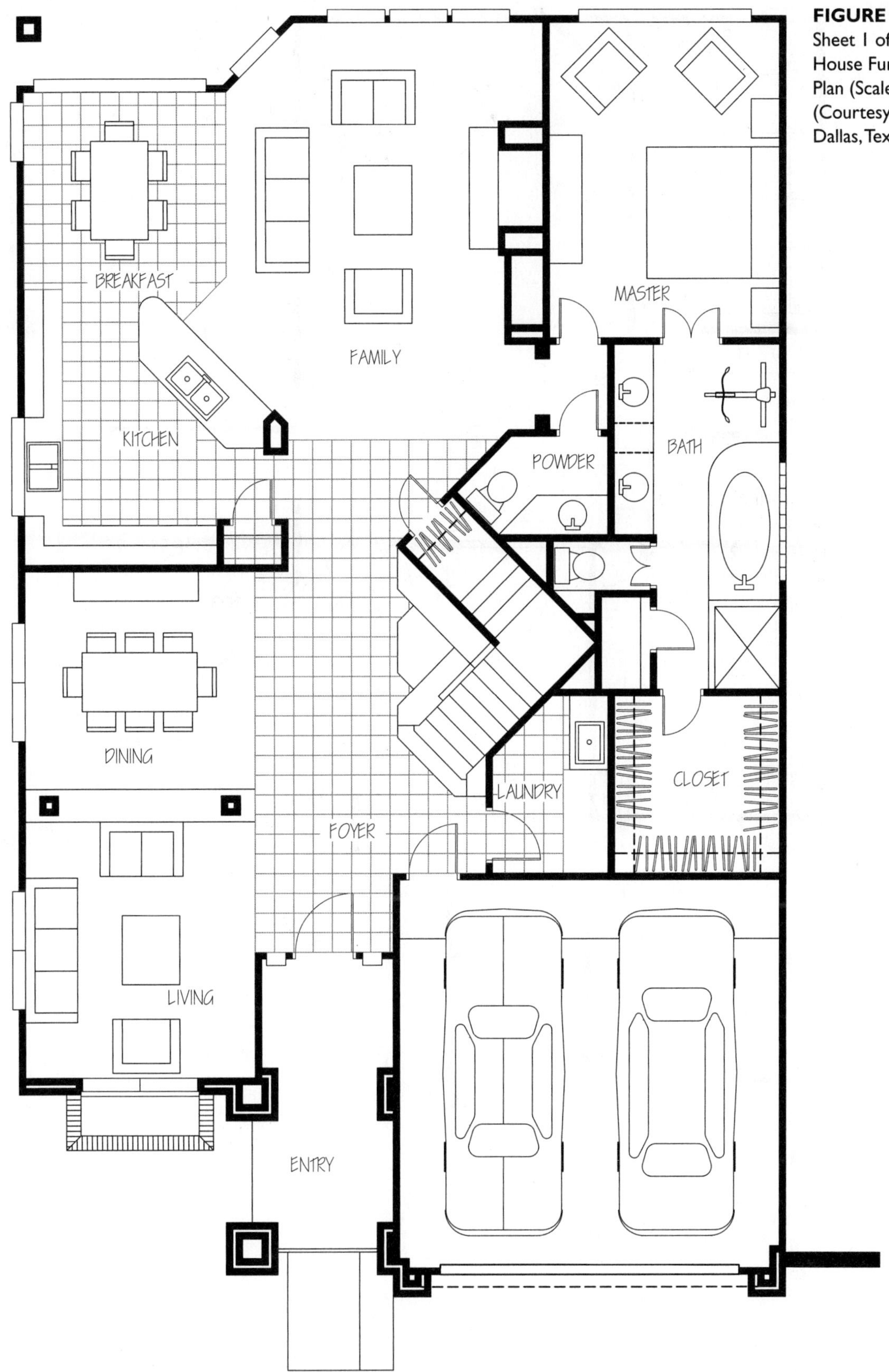

FIGURE 9–33
Sheet 1 of 2, Exercise 9–3: House Furniture Installation Plan (Scale: 1/8″ = 1′-0″) (Courtesy of John Brooks, AIA, Dallas, Texas)

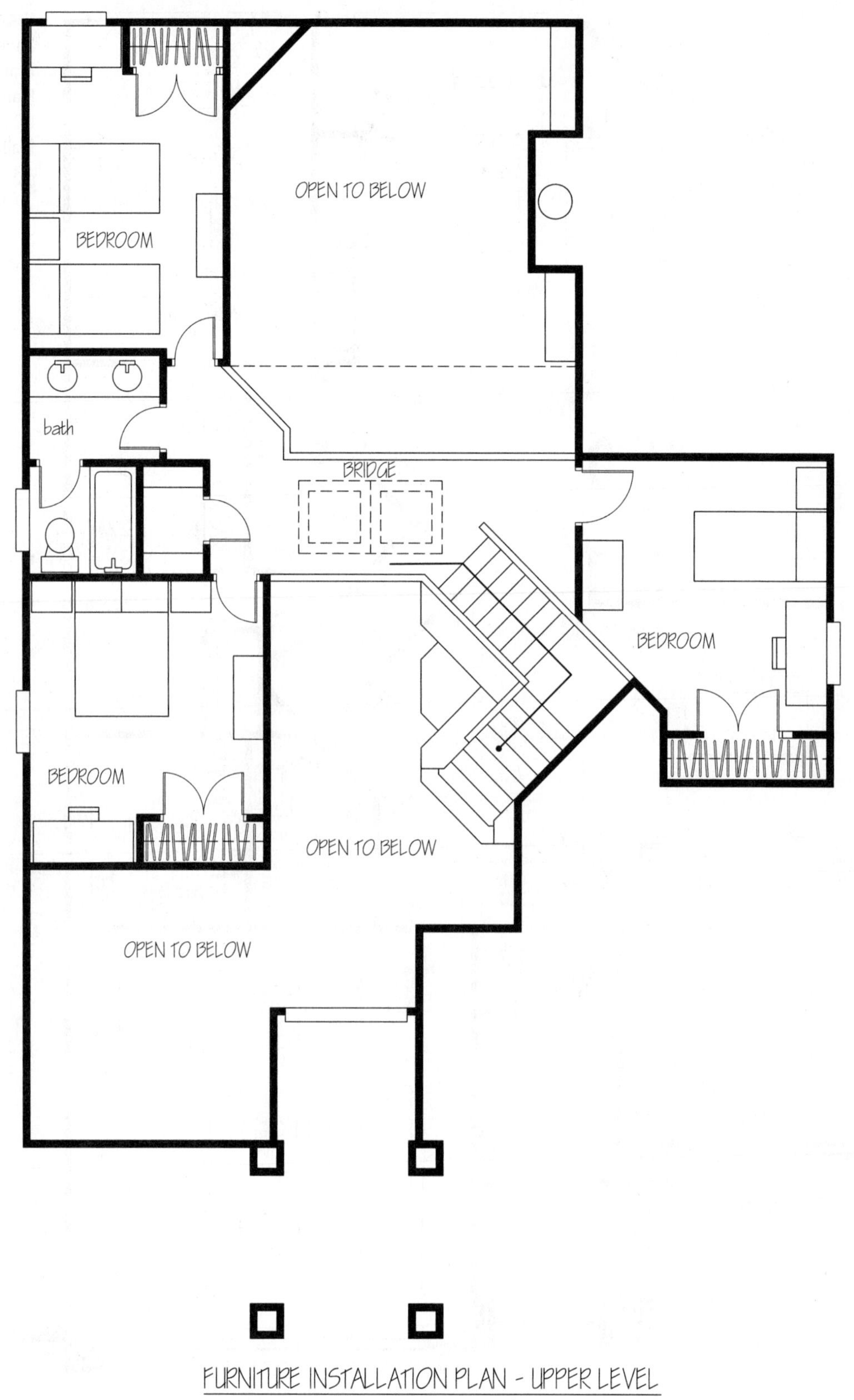

FIGURE 9–33
Sheet 2 of 2, Exercise 9–3: House Furniture Installation Plan (Scale: 1/8″ = 1′-0″) (Courtesy of John Brooks, AIA, Dallas, Texas)

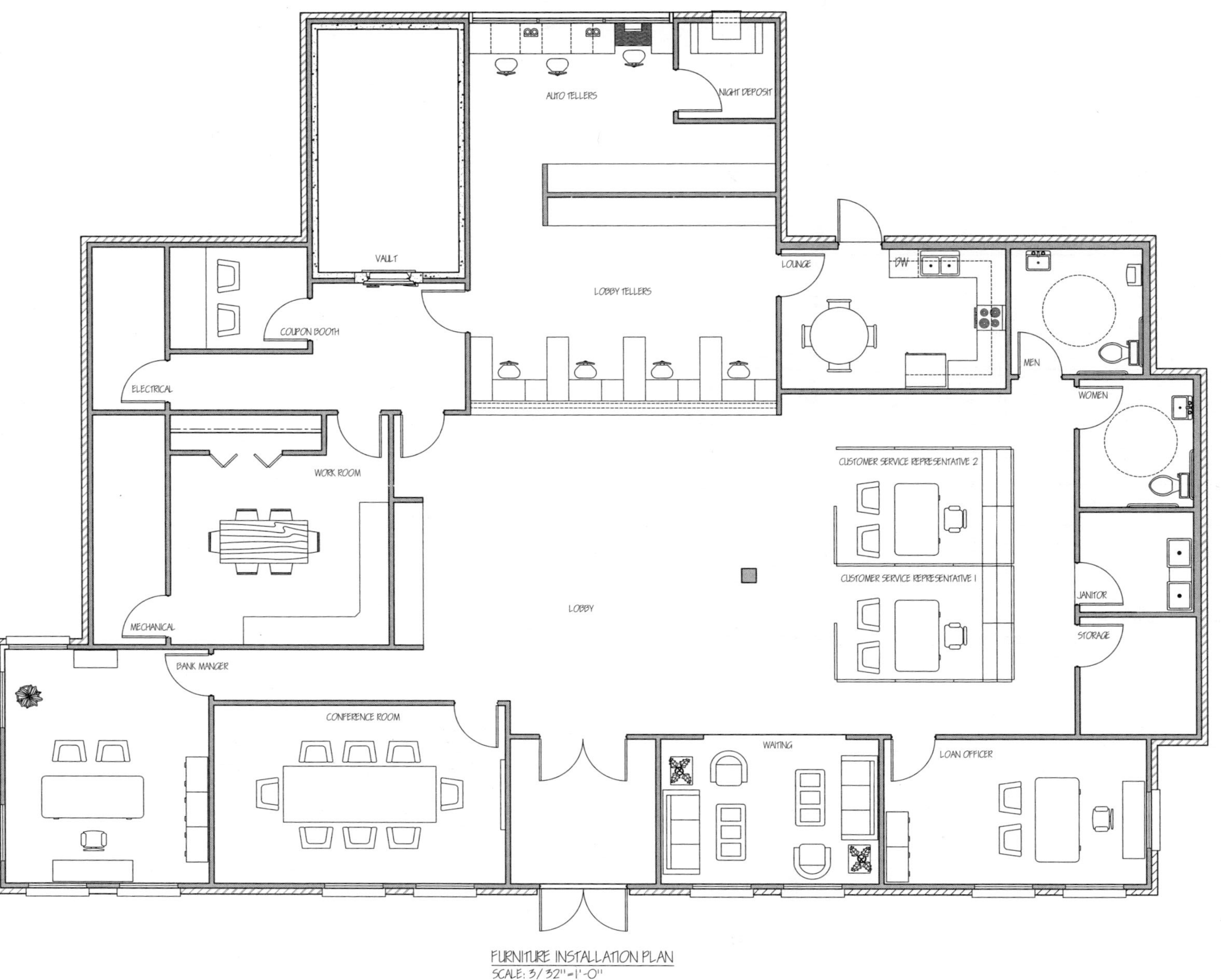

FIGURE 9–34
Sheet 1 of 2, Exercise 9–4: Bank Furniture Installation Plan (Scale: 3/32″ = 1′-0″)

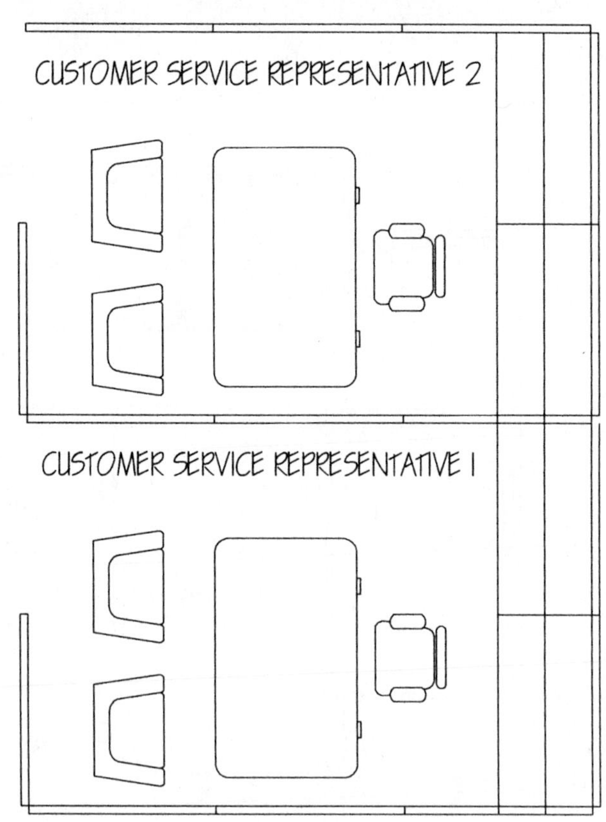

FIGURE 9–34
Sheet 2 of 2, Exercise 9–4: Bank Furniture Plan (Scale: 1/4″ = 1′-0″)

chapter

10

DesignCenter, Dynamic Blocks, and External References

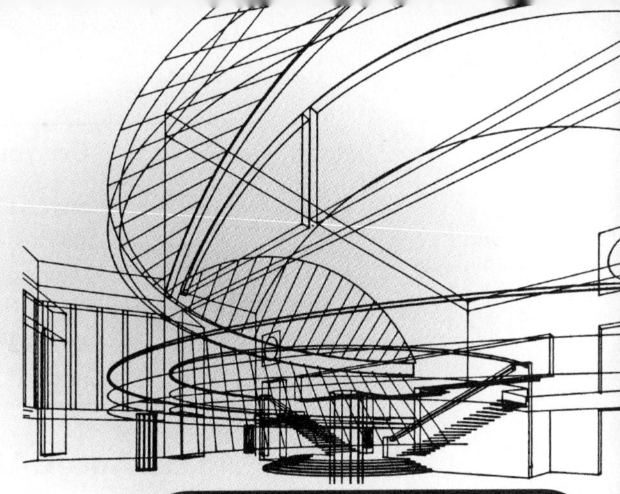

objectives

When you have completed this chapter, you will be able to:

Correctly use the following commands and settings:

AutoCAD DesignCenter (DC)
Dynamic Block Editor (BE)
External Reference (XREF)
XATTACH
XBIND (External Bind)

INTRODUCTION

In this chapter, you will use the AutoCAD DesignCenter to copy layers and blocks (furniture) from one drawing to another. You will also make blocks that perform actions dynamically. Finally you will use external reference commands that allow you to attach drawings to other drawings so that they appear in the primary drawing without inserting them.

Tutorial 10–1: Reception Area Furniture Installation Plan Using the AutoCAD DesignCenter

When you have completed Tutorial 10–1, your drawing will look similar to Figure 10–3 without dimensions.

Step 1. Use your workspace to make the following settings:

1. **Use SaveAs... to save the drawing with the name CH10–TUTORIAL1.**
2. Set drawing Units: **Architectural**
3. Set Drawing Limits: **44′,34′**
4. Set GRIDDISPLAY: **0**
5. Set Grid: **12″**
6. Set Snap: **6″**

THE AutoCAD DESIGNCENTER

The AutoCAD DesignCenter allows you to do the following:

Use existing blocks arranged in categories that AutoCAD has provided.
Use blocks, layers, linetypes, text and dimension styles, and external references from any existing drawing using drag-and-drop.
Examine drawings and blocks as either drawing names or pictures.
Search for drawings and other files.

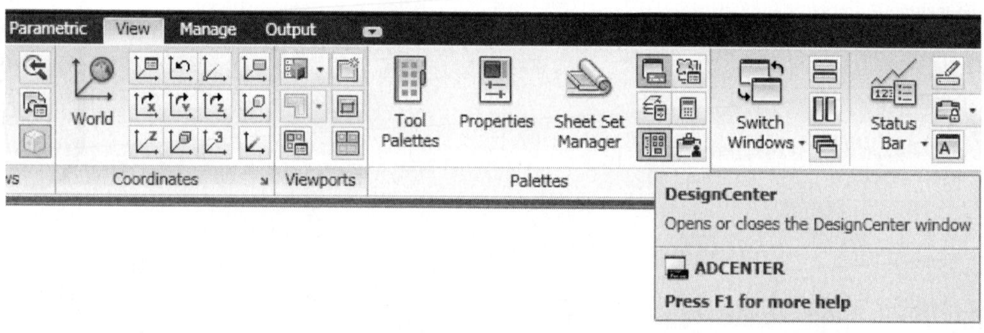

Step 2. Open the DesignCenter and examine it, as described next:

Prompt	Response
Command:	**DesignCenter** (or TYPE: **DC<enter>**)
The DesignCenter appears:	CLICK: **Load** (the icon on the left—above the Folders tab)
The Load dialog box appears:	**Look at the bottom of Figure 10–1. Use the same or similar path to locate the Design Center folder** DOUBLE-CLICK: **DesignCenter** CLICK: **Home - Space Planner.dwg**
The DesignCenter shows the Blocks and other items in the Home - Space Planner.dwg (Figure 10–1). Your Design-Center may appear different, depending on what is selected in the Views icon or Tree View toggle at the top of the DesignCenter.	DOUBLE-CLICK: **Blocks**
All the predefined blocks for this drawing appear.	

FIGURE 10–1
The DesignCenter—Home - Space Planner Drawing

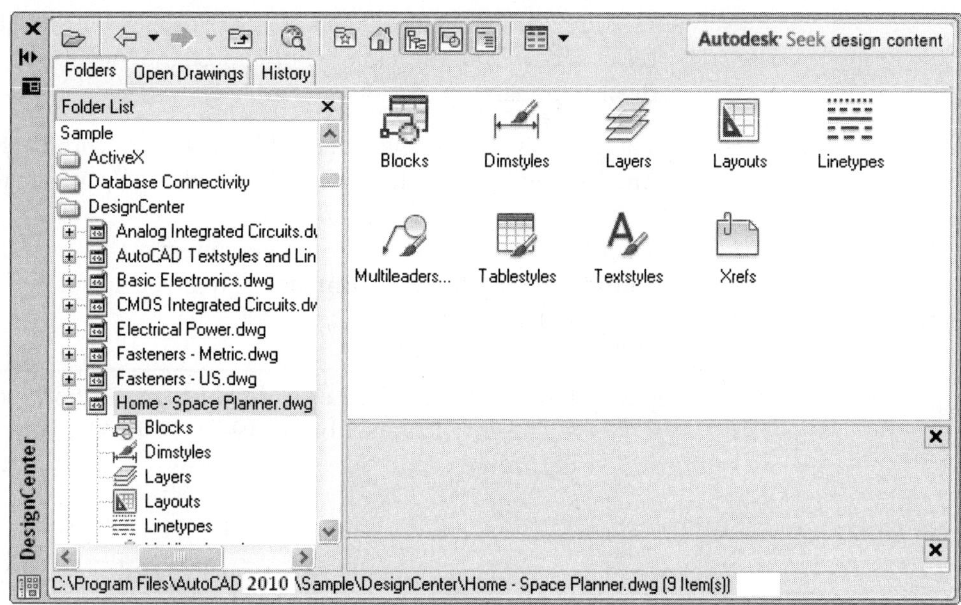

You can now click on any of these drawings, hold down the left mouse button, drag the drawing into the current drawing, and drop it. However, do not do that for this tutorial. You will use layers and blocks from CH9-TUTORIAL1 to complete CH10-TUTORIAL1. Let's look at the parts of the DesignCenter.

DesignCenter Tabs

The tabs at the top of the DesignCenter allow you to access all the following options of the DesignCenter:

Folders Tab Clicking this tab shows you the folders existing on the hard drive of your computer.
Open Drawings Tab Shows you the drawing that is currently open.
History Tab Shows you a list of the most recently opened drawings.

DesignCenter Buttons

Now examine the buttons above the tabs. They are listed below, starting from the first one on the left. Click the Folders tab to display all the icons.

Load Allows you to load drawings and other items that you want to use in your current drawing.
Back Returns you to the previous screen.
Forward Sends you forward from a screen obtained from clicking back.
Up Sends you to the next higher folder structure.
Search Allows you to search for and locate data you need.
Favorites Shows what you have in the Favorites folder. You can save your most-often-used items here.
Home Returns you to the default starting folder.
Tree View Toggle Displays and hides the tree view. The tree view shows the structure of the files and folders in the form of a chart, the area on the left.
Preview Allows you to look at a preview of any selected item. If there is no preview image saved with the selected item, the Preview area will be empty.
Description Shows a text description of any selected item.

Views Provide you with different display formats for the selected items. You can select a view from the View list or choose the View button again to cycle through display formats.

Large Icons Show the names of loaded items with large icons.
Small Icons Show the names of loaded items with small icons.
List Shows a list of loaded items.
Details Places a name for each item in an alphabetical list.
Autodesk Seek Design Content Gives you access to thousands of blocks from manufacturers.

Step 3. Use the DesignCenter to load i-furn, a-door, a-door-swng, and a-wall-intr Layers from CH9-TUTORIAL1 into the new drawing, as described next:

Prompt	Response
Command:	CLICK: **Load** CLICK: **Locate drawing CH9-TUTORIAL1 and** DOUBLE-CLICK: **CH9-TUTORIAL1** DOUBLE-CLICK: **Layers**
The display (Figure 10–2) appears:	CLICK: **Layer a-door, hold down the pick button, drag it into the current drawing (to the right of the DesignCenter), and release the pick button** **Repeat the previous for Layers i-furn, a-door-swng, a-wall-intr** **Close the DesignCenter**

Step 4. Set Layer a-wall-intr current.

Step 5. Use Polyline to draw the outside walls of the reception area using the dimensions from Figure 10–3. Set an offset of 5″ for the wall thickness.

Step 6. Set Layer a-door current.

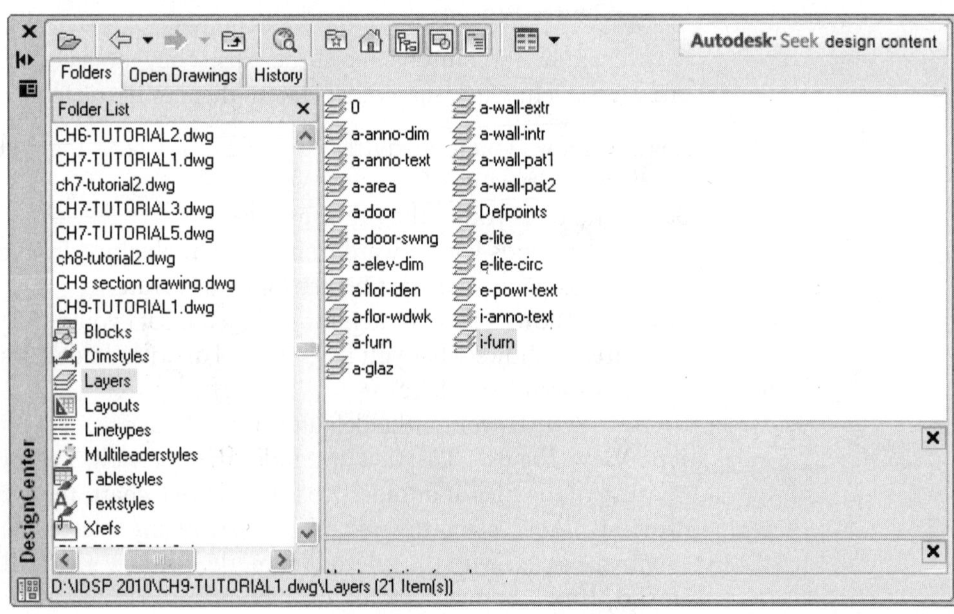

FIGURE 10–2
Layers in CH9-TUTORIAL1

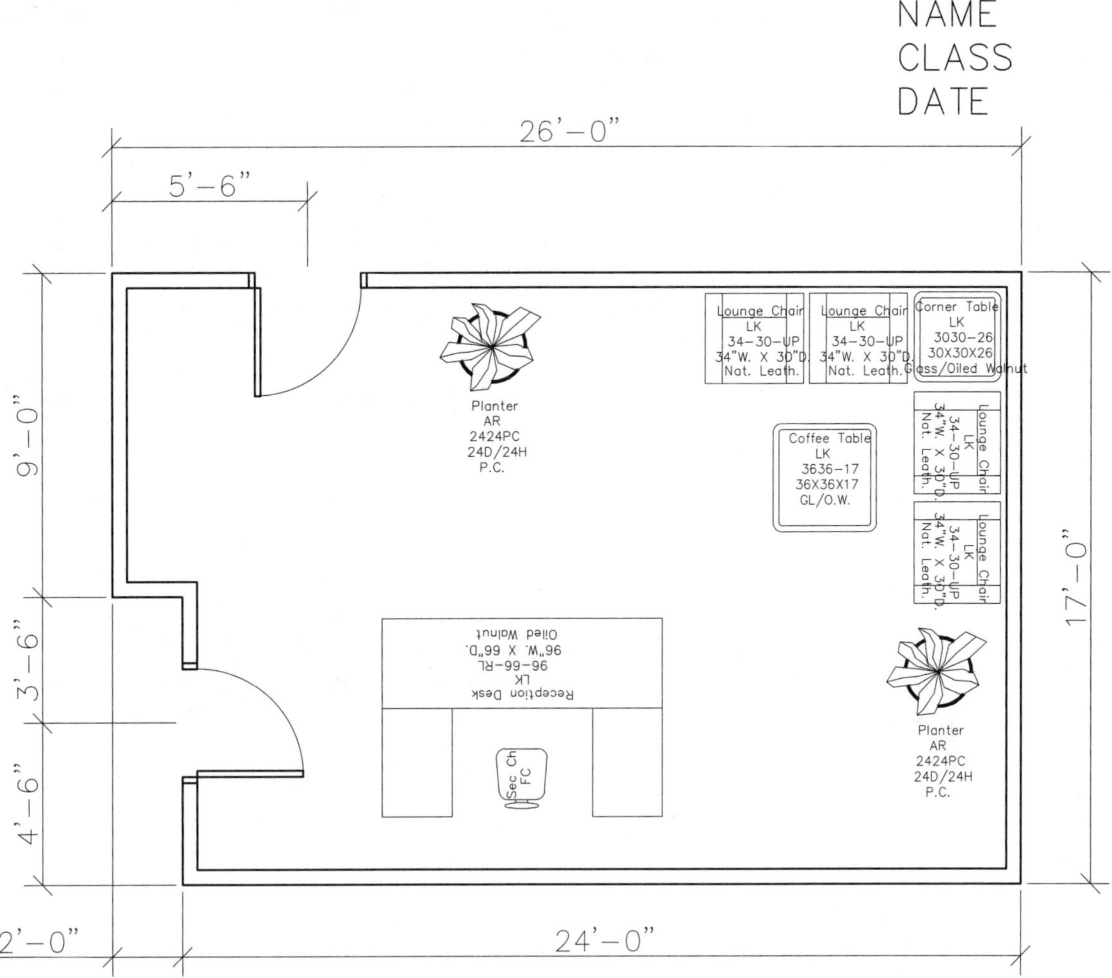

FIGURE 10–3 Dimensions for Tutorial 10–1 (Scale: 3/16″=1′-0″)

Step 7. Open the DesignCenter and CLICK: **Blocks under CH9-TUTORIAL1, find the block named DOOR, and drag and drop it into the current drawing.**

Step 8. **Use the Mirror and Rotate commands if necessary to correctly position the door.**

Step 9. **Place doors in the correct locations using the dimensions from Figure 10–3.**

Step 10. **Use the Trim command to trim the walls from the door openings.**

Step 11. **Set Layer i-furn current.**

Step 12. CLICK: **Blocks under CH9-TUTORIAL1, find the blocks named Planter, Corner Table, Coffee Table, Reception Desk, Sec Ch, and Lounge Chair, and drag and drop them into the current drawing.**

Step 13. **Place furniture in the approximate locations shown in Figure 10–3.**

Step 14. **When you have completed Tutorial 10–1, add your name, class, and the current date to the drawing in the upper right and save your work in at least two places.**

Step 15. **Print Tutorial 10–1 to scale.**

Tutorial 10–2: Training Room Furniture Installation Plan Using the AutoCAD DesignCenter and Dynamic Blocks

When you have completed Tutorial 10–2 your drawing will look similar to Figure 10–4.

Step 1. Use your workspace to make the following settings:

1. **Open Drawing CH3-TUTORIAL2 and save it to the hard drive with the name CH10-TUTORIAL2.**
2. **Erase all furniture and the door so that only the walls remain.**
3. **Set Layer a-door current.**

Step 2. Use a block from the DesignCenter - House Designer drawing to draw a new door, as described next:

Prompt	Response
Command:	**DesignCenter** (or TYPE: **DC<enter>**)
The DesignCenter appears:	CLICK: **the Folders tab**
	CLICK: **Load** (the icon on the left—above the Folders tab)
The Load dialog box appears:	**Locate the C: drive, then** DOUBLE-CLICK: **Program Files/AutoCAD 2010/Sample/ DesignCenter** folder, as shown in **Figure 10–5**
	In the DesignCenter folder, DOUBLE-CLICK: **House Designer.dwg**

FIGURE 10–4
Tutorial 10–2: Training Room

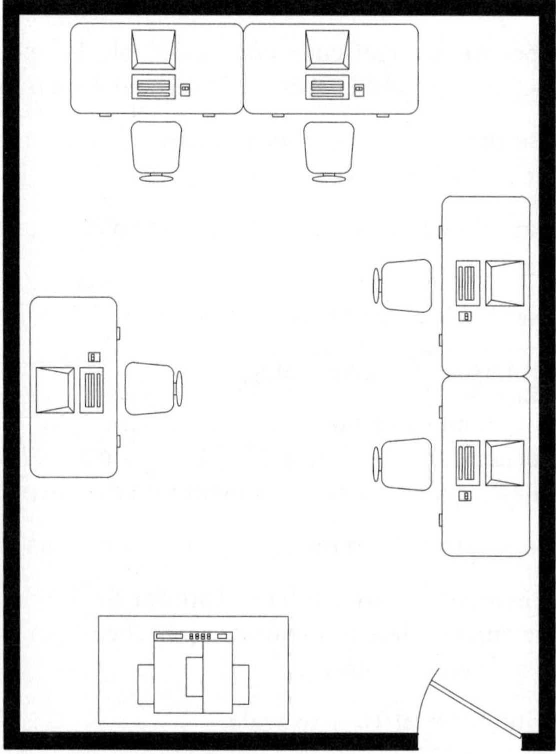

FIGURE 10–5
Locate House Designer Blocks

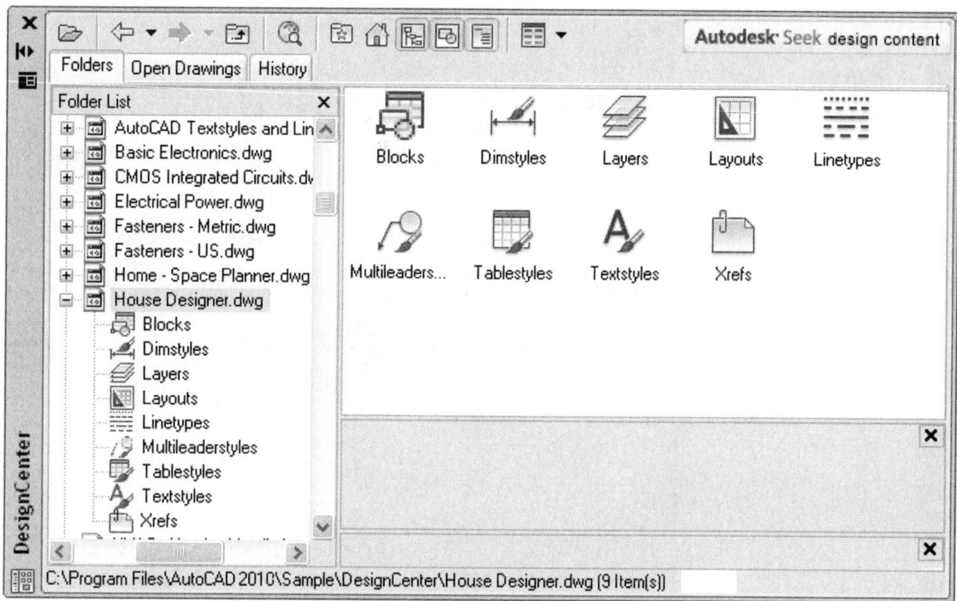

Prompt	Response
The available items in the House Designer drawing appear:	DOUBLE-CLICK: **Blocks** and CLICK: **Large Icons in the Views list, as shown in Figure 10–6.** CLICK:**Tree View Toggle to remove the Tree View.**
	CLICK: **on the Door - Right Hung 36 in. icon and continue to hold down the left mouse button, Figure 10–7. Drag the Door off the Design-Center and use Osnap-Endpoint to place it as shown in Figure 10–8.**

Step 3. **Set the i-furn layer current.**

FIGURE 10–6
CLICK: Blocks and Large Icons in the Views List. CLICK: Tree View Toggle.

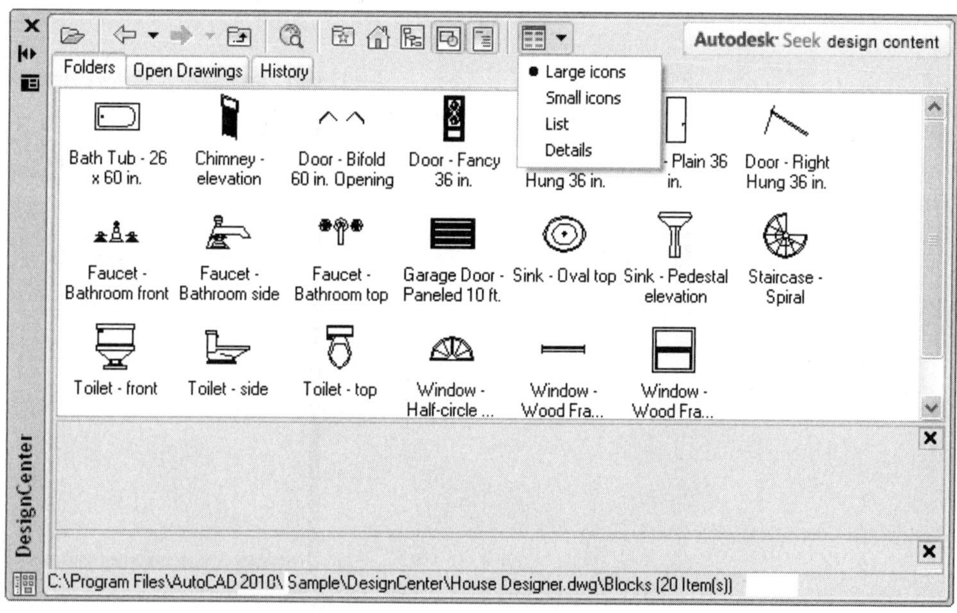

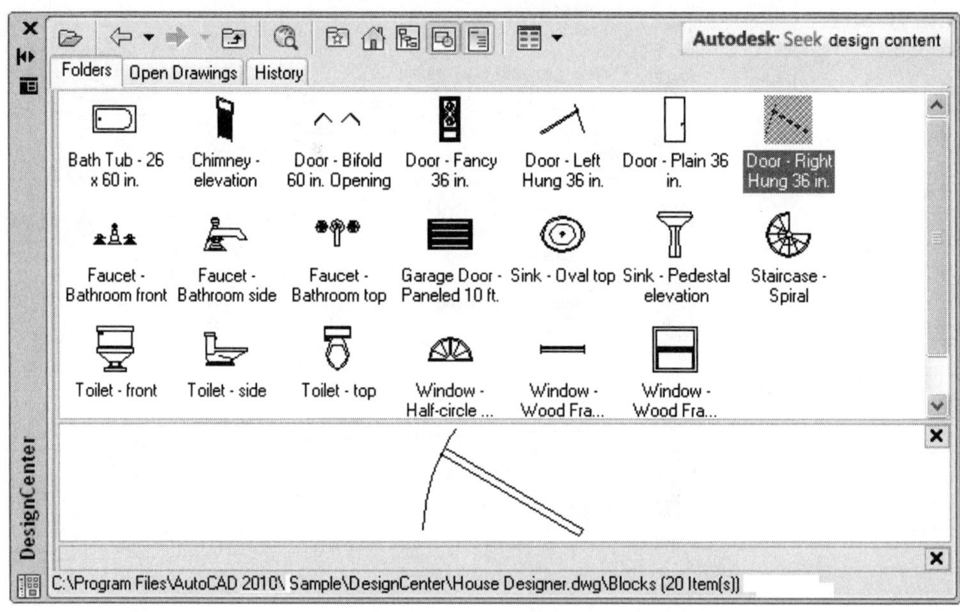

FIGURE 10–7
CLICK: The Door - Right Hung 36 in. Hold Down the Pick Button and Drag the Door Off the DesignCenter

Step 4. Drag and drop blocks from the Home-Space Planner drawing to create furniture in the Training Room, as described next:

Prompt	Response
Command:	**Move your mouse back to the DesignCenter palette**
The DesignCenter opens up again:	DOUBLE-CLICK: **Home-Space Planner.dwg, Figure 10–9**
The available items in the Home-Space Planner.dwg appear:	DOUBLE-CLICK: **Blocks** CLICK: **on the Desk - 30 × 60 in. icon and continue to hold down the left mouse button as you drag the Desk off the DesignCenter and place it on the drawing**

FIGURE 10–8
Use Osnap-Endpoint to Place the Door in the Opening

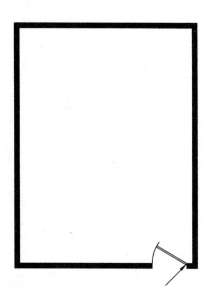

FIGURE 10–9
Open Home - Space Planner Drawing

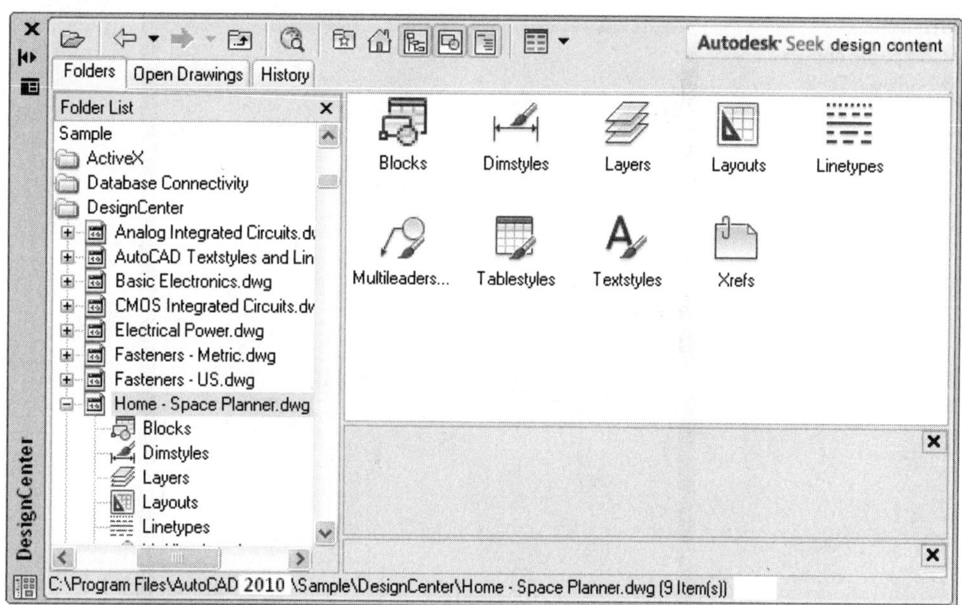

TIP: To minimize the DesignCenter, CLICK: on the Auto-hide button (the two triangles below the X) in the upper left corner.

Step 5. Drag and drop the following blocks from the Home - Space Planner drawing (Figure 10–10):

1. Computer Terminal
2. Table Rectangular Woodgrain 60 × 30 in.

FIGURE 10–10
Home - Space Planner Drawing Blocks

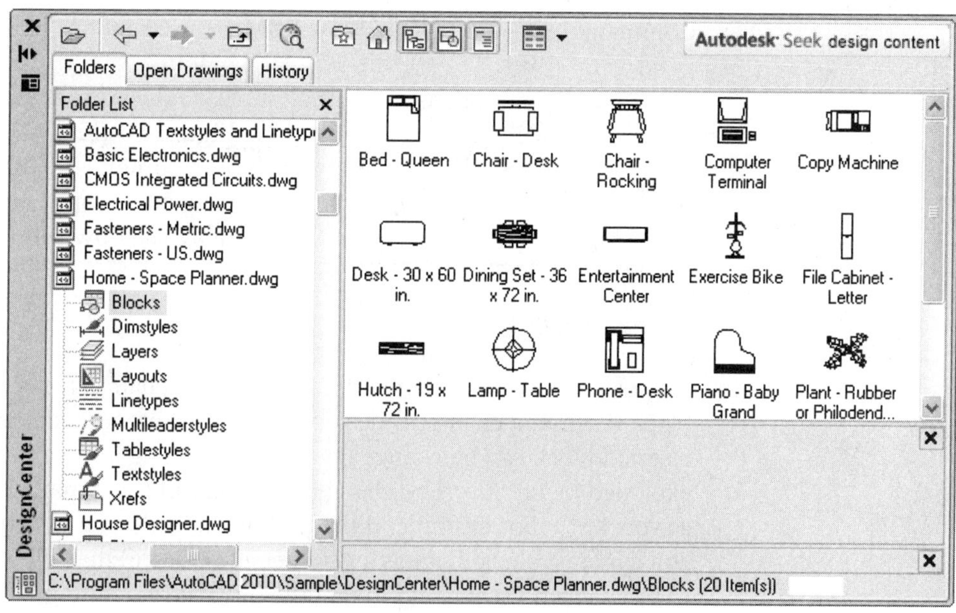

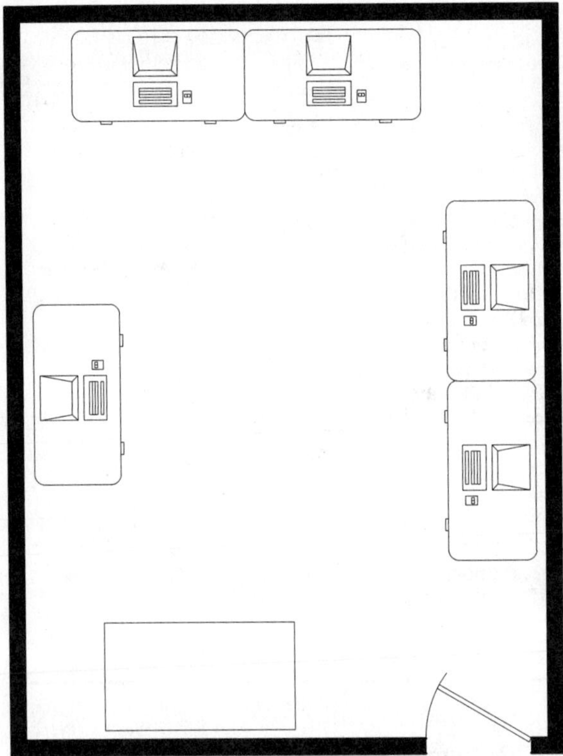

FIGURE 10–11
Desk, Computer, and Rectangular Woodgrain Table with Woodgrain Erased

Step 6. **Move the Computer Terminal on top of the Desk - 30 × 60 in., Figure 10–11.**

Step 7. **Explode the Table - Rectangular Woodgrain 60 × 30 in. and erase the woodgrains so you can see the items you are going to place on top of it.**

Step 8. **Place the woodgrain table in the drawing. Copy and rotate the desk and computer terminal, so your drawing looks like Figure 10–11.**

Step 9. **Locate a copier in DesignCenter Autodesk Seek, and drag-and-drop it on top of the woodgrain table to complete the drawing, as described next:**

Prompt	Response
Command:	**Move your mouse back to the DESIGNCENTER palette**
The DesignCenter opens up again:	CLICK: **the Autodesk Seek button, Figure 10–12.**
	Find a copier, CLICK: **the copier and drag-and-drop it on top of the woodgrain table as shown in Figure 10–4**

DYNAMIC BLOCKS

Part of an inserted dynamic block such as a chair can be moved within the dynamic block (such as a chair-and-desk combination) without exploding the block. A dynamic inserted block can be changed without exploding it. A standard inserted block must be exploded before it can be changed. The size of the dynamic block can also be changed as you work. For example, if the desk is available in a variety of sizes, you can define it as a dynamic block that has a parameter (a feature) that allows the width, depth, or both to be changed without exploding the block or redefining it.

FIGURE 10–12
Autodesk Seek - 2D/3D Copier

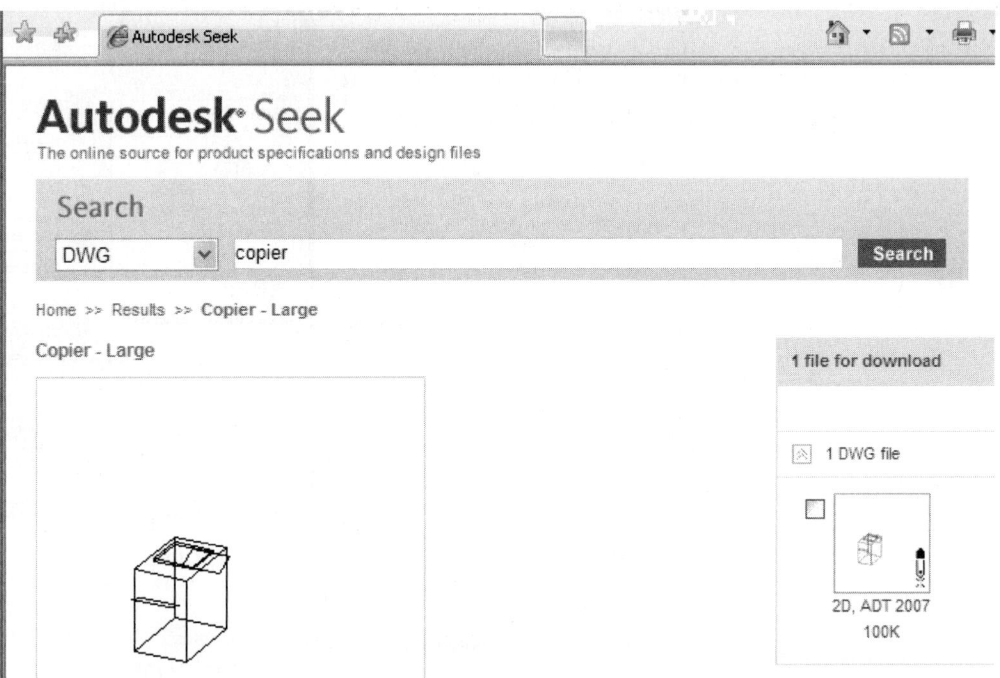

You use the Block Editor to create dynamic blocks. The Block Editor allows you to add the elements that make a block dynamic. You can create a block from scratch, or you can add dynamic features to an existing block.

In the following part of this tutorial, you will redefine the existing woodgrain table as a dynamic block that can change size. You will add dynamic blocks of desk chairs that can be visible or invisible. You will also redefine the existing Door - Right Hung 36 in. as a dynamic block that can flip from one side of the wall to the other. Start with the woodgrain table.

Step 10. Use the Block Editor to add a linear parameter to the woodgrain table (so the length can be easily changed) as described next:

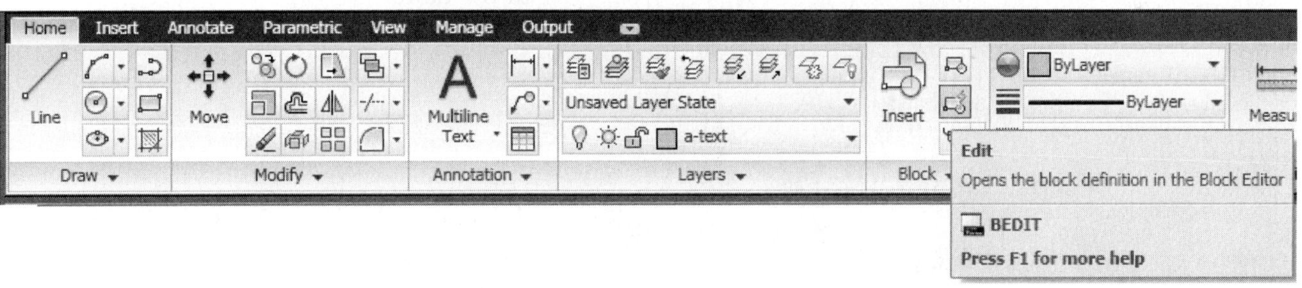

Prompt	Response
Command:	**Block Editor** (or TYPE: **BE<enter>**)
The Edit Block Definition dialog box appears:	CLICK: **Table - Rectangular Woodgrain,** Figure 10–13 CLICK: **OK**
The table appears with woodgrain (you are still in the Block Editor)	**Erase the woodgrain** CLICK: **The Parameters tab of the Block Authoring Palette** CLICK: **Linear**

FIGURE 10–13
CLICK: Table - Rectangular Woodgrain 60 × 30 in. in the List of Blocks

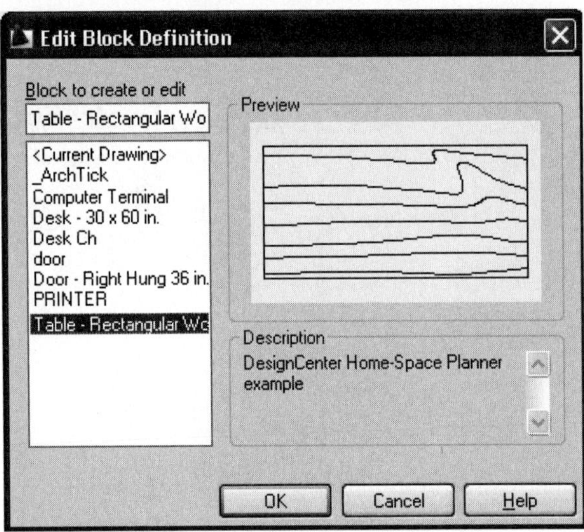

Prompt	Response
Specify start point or [Name/Label/Chain/Description/Base/Palette/Value set]:	CLICK: **OSNAP - Endpoint, the upper left corner of the table.**
Specify endpoint:	CLICK: **OSNAP-Endpoint, the upper right corner of the table.**
Specify label location:	CLICK: **to place the label as shown in Figure 10–14**
	CLICK: **The Actions tab of the Block Authoring Palette**
	CLICK: **Stretch**
Select parameter:	CLICK: **Distance** (on the top of the table).
Specify parameter point to associate with action or enter [sTart point/Second point] <Second>:	CLICK: **The arrow on the upper right corner of the table.**

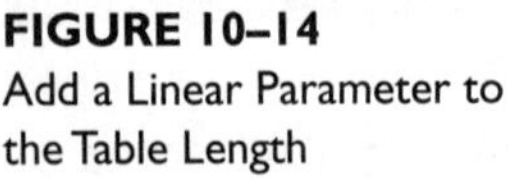
FIGURE 10–14
Add a Linear Parameter to the Table Length

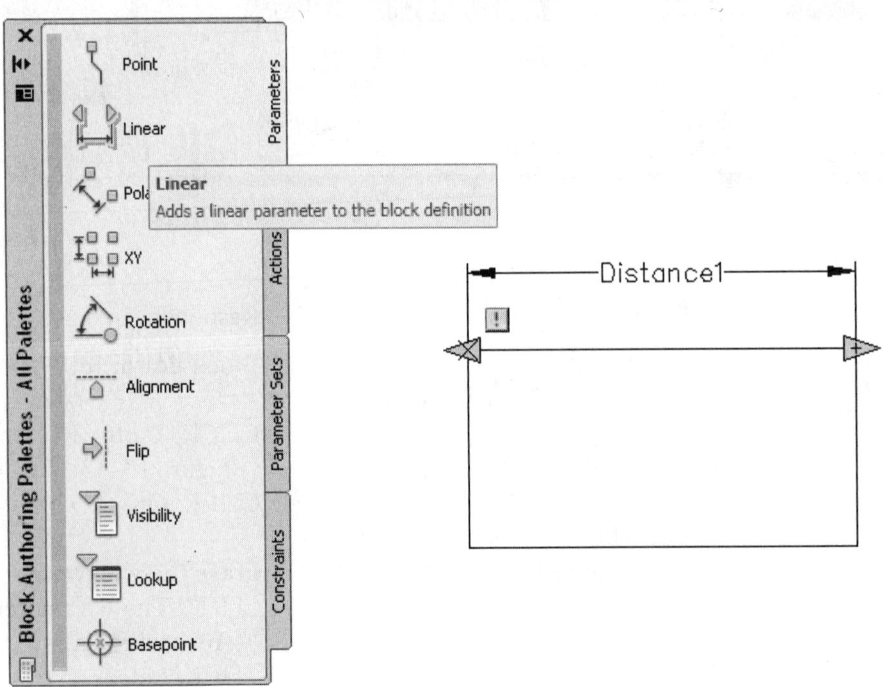

FIGURE 10–15
Add the Stretch Action to the Linear Parameter

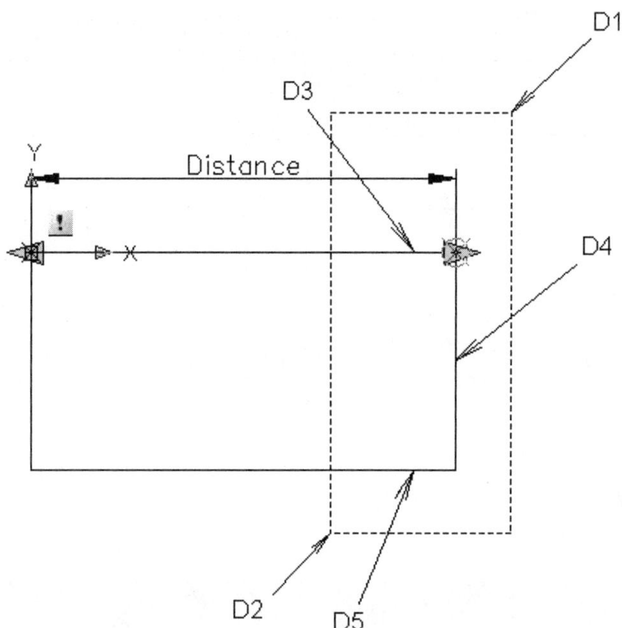

Prompt	Response
Specify first corner of stretch frame or [CPolygon]:	CLICK: **D1, Figure 10–15**
Specify opposite corner:	CLICK: **D2, Figure 10–15**
Specify objects to stretch:	CLICK: **D3**
Select objects:	CLICK: **D4**
Select objects:	CLICK: **D5**
Select objects:	**<enter>**

Step 11. Add a Lookup parameter and a Lookup action that will appear when the block is inserted (so you can just CLICK: a number and the block becomes longer or shorter) **as described next:**

Prompt	Response
	CLICK: **The parameters tab of the Block Authoring Palette**
	CLICK: **Lookup**
Specify parameter location or [Name/Label/Description/Palette/]:	CLICK: **A point close to the table above it**
	CLICK: **The Actions tab of the Block Authoring Palette**
	CLICK: **Lookup**
Select parameter:	CLICK: **The Lookup parameter you just made**
Specify action location:	CLICK: **A point close to the table above it, Figure 10–16**
The Property Lookup Table appears:	CLICK: **Add properties...**
The Add Parameter Properties dialog box appears with Linear selected and Add input properties checked	CLICK: **OK**
The Property Lookup Table appears:	TYPE: **The properties shown in Figure 10–17. Be sure both columns are identical.**

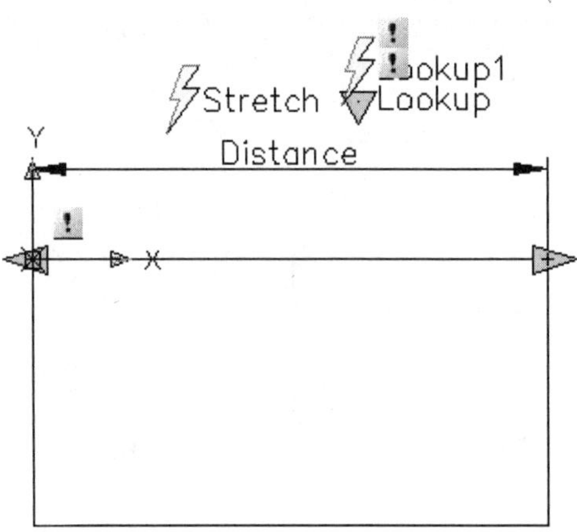

FIGURE 10–16
Locating Parameters and Actions

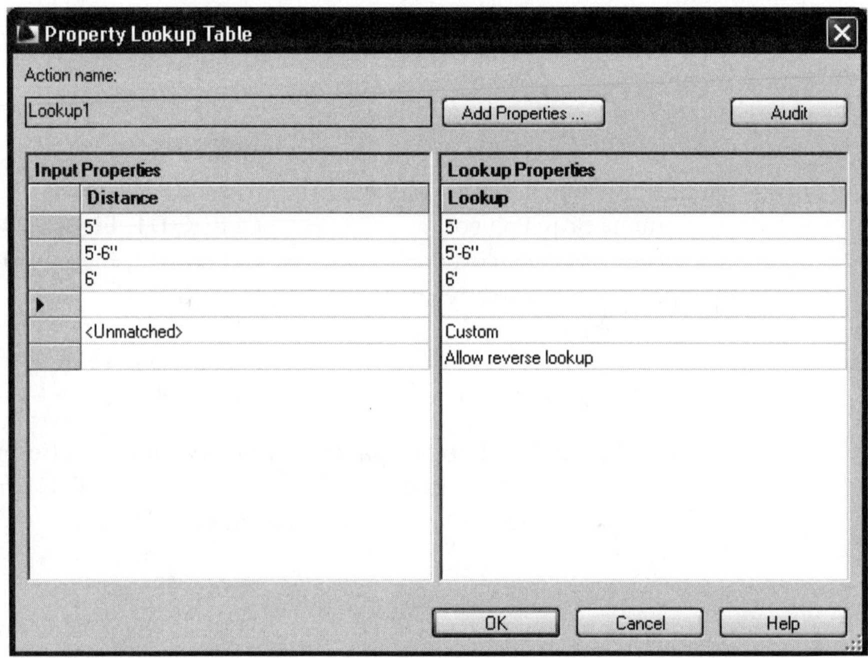

FIGURE 10–17
Look up Properties for Lookup1 Action

Prompt	Response
	CLICK: **Audit** (if both columns are identical, you will get the message that no errors were found)
	CLICK: **Close**
	CLICK: **OK** (to exit the Property Lookup Table)
	CLICK: **Save Block As** (or TYPE: **BSAVEAS<enter>**)
The Save Block As dialog box appears:	In the Block Name Box, TYPE: **Table 5′-5′6-6′**
	CLICK: **OK**

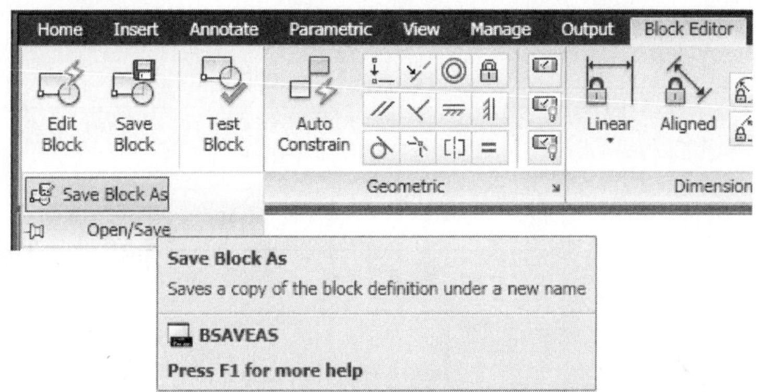

Step 12. **Close the Block Editor and insert your dynamic block as described next:**

Prompt	Response
The Block Editor is open.	TYPE: **BC<enter>** (to close the Block Editor)
The current drawing appears:	
Command:	**Erase the existing Woodgrain Table** (do not erase the Copier)
Command:	TYPE: **I<enter>**
The Insert dialog box appears:	Select: **Table 5′-5′6-6′**
	CLICK: **OK**
Specify insertion point or [Basepoint/Scale/X/Y/Z/Rotate]:	CLICK: **a point to replace the Woodgrain Table you just erased**
	CLICK: **any point on the inserted table**
	CLICK: **the Lookup symbol, Figure 10–18** (to see the three sizes)

Step 13. **You can now** CLICK: **on any of the three numbers, and the block changes length. Change the length to 5′6″.**

Step 14. PRESS: **the Esc key, to get rid of the block parameters.**

Step 15. **Add a linear parameter to make the depth of the table dynamic so you have 2′-6″ and 3′ table depths as described next:**

Prompt	Response
Command:	**Block Editor** (or TYPE: **BE<enter>**)
The Edit Block Definition dialog box appears:	CLICK: **Table 5′-5′6-6′**
	CLICK: **OK**

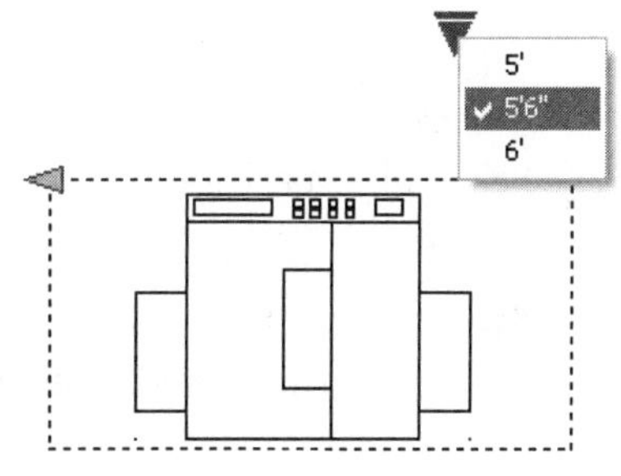

FIGURE 10–18
Insert the Dynamic Block and CLICK: the Lookup Symbol

FIGURE 10–19
Add the Stretch Action to the Linear Parameter, Distance1

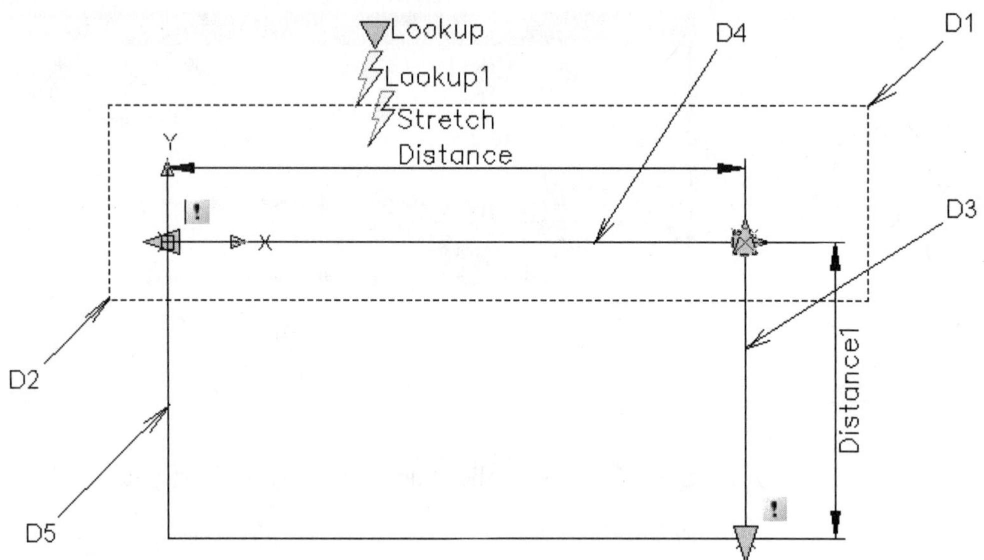

Prompt	Response
	CLICK: **The Parameters tab of the Block Authoring Palette**
	CLICK: **Linear**
Specify start point or [Name/ Label/Chain/Description/Base/ Palette/Value set]:	CLICK: **OSNAP - Endpoint, the lower right corner of the table**
Specify endpoint:	CLICK: **OSNAP - Endpoint, the upper right corner of the table**
Specify label location:	CLICK: **to place the label (Distance1) on the right side of the table, Figure 10–19**
	CLICK: **The Actions tab of the Block Authoring Palette**
	CLICK: **Stretch**
Select parameter:	CLICK: **Distance1** (on the right side of the table)
Specify parameter point to associate with action or enter [sTart point/Second point] <Second>:	CLICK: **The arrow on the upper right corner of the table**
Specify first corner of stretch frame or [CPolygon]:	CLICK: **D1, Figure 10–19**
Specify opposite corner:	CLICK: **D2, Figure 10–19**
Specify objects to stretch:	CLICK: **D3**
Select objects: 1 found	CLICK: **D4**
Select objects: 1 found, 2 total	CLICK: **D5**
Select objects: 1 found, 3 total	**<enter>**

Step 16. Add a Lookup parameter and a Lookup action that will appear when the block is inserted (so you can just CLICK: a number and the block becomes more or less deep) **as described next:**

Prompt	Response
	CLICK: **The parameters tab of the Block Authoring Palette**
	CLICK: **Lookup**
Specify parameter location or [Name/Label/Description/Palette/]:	CLICK: **A point above and to the left of the table**
	CLICK: **The Actions tab of the Block Authoring Palette**
	CLICK: **Lookup**
Select parameter:	CLICK: **The Lookup parameter you just made**
Specify action location:	CLICK: **A point above the word Lookup1**
The Property Lookup Table appears:	CLICK: **Add properties...**
The Add Parameter Properties dialog box appears with Linear selected and Add input properties checked	CLICK: **Linear1**
	CLICK: **OK**
The Property Lookup Table appears:	TYPE: **The properties shown in Figure 10–20. Be sure both columns are identical.**
	CLICK: **Audit** (if both columns are identical, you will get the message that no errors were found)
	CLICK: **OK**
	CLICK: **OK** (to exit the Property Lookup Table)
	CLICK: **Save Block As** (or TYPE: **BSAVEAS<enter>)**
The Save Block As dialog box appears:	CLICK: **Table 5′-5′6-6′** (so it appears in the Block Name area)
	CLICK: **OK**
The AutoCAD warning appears: Block name: is already defined as a block. What do you want to do?	CLICK: **Redefine block**

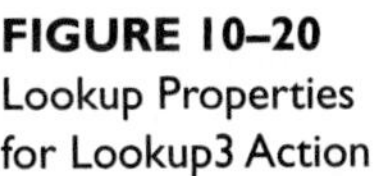
FIGURE 10–20
Lookup Properties for Lookup3 Action

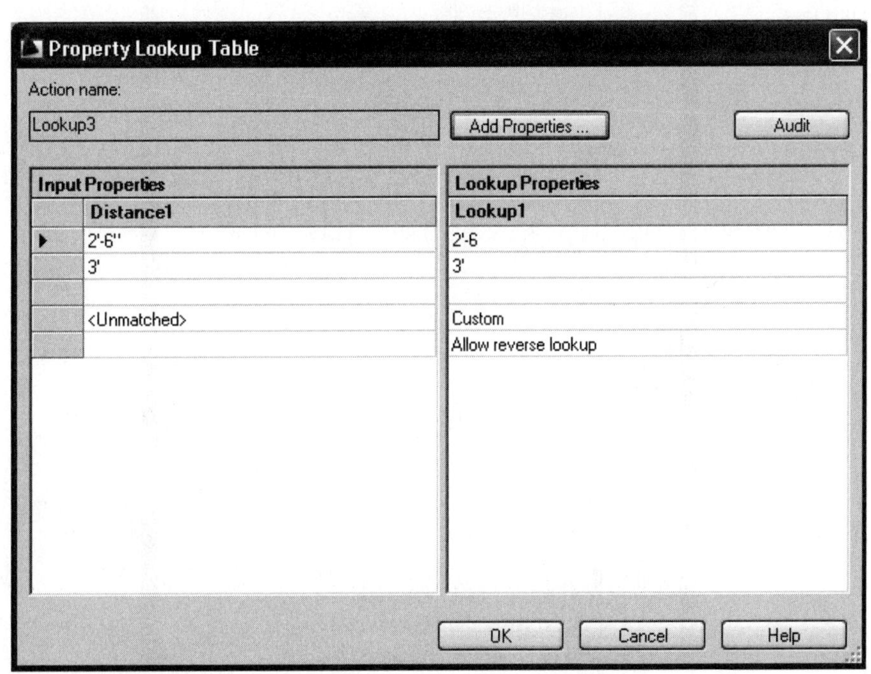

FIGURE 10–21
Lookup Symbols for Depth and Length

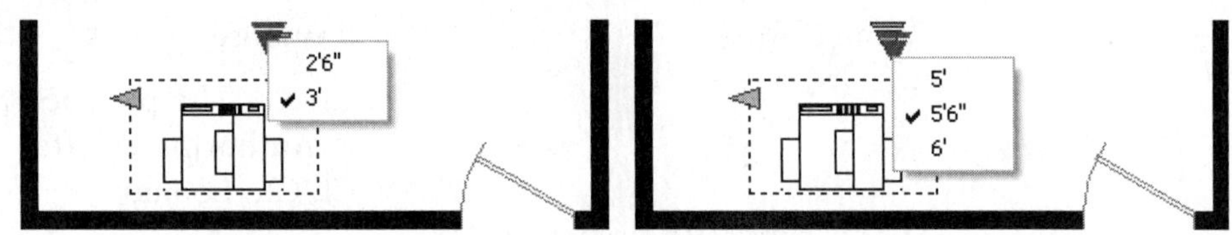

Step 17. On your own, close the Block Editor, erase the previous Table 5′-5′6-6′ block, and insert the new dynamic block.

Step 18. CLICK: any point on the inserted table and CLICK: the Lookup symbol showing depth.

Step 19. You can now CLICK: on any of the two numbers, and the block changes depth. Change the depth to 3′. The table is now 5′6″ × 3′.

Step 20. PRESS: the Esc key to get rid of the block parameters (Figure 10–21).

Step 21. Make the Sec Ch and Desk Ch blocks dynamic so you can make one or the other invisible by clicking on it as described next:

1. Open the DesignCenter (TYPE: DC<enter>). Use the Folders tab to open your drawing CH9-TUTORIAL1.
2. Locate the two blocks, Sec Ch and Desk Ch, and insert both of them into the current drawing, CH10-TUTORIAL2.
3. Explode both drawings and erase the attribute tags.
4. Rotate the chairs so they both face the same direction (Figure 10–22).
5. Block the Desk Ch drawing with the name chair1.
6. Block the Sec Ch drawing with the name chair2.
7. Open the Block Editor, Select chair1 (Figure 10–23) and CLICK: OK.

FIGURE 10–22
Insert Desk Ch and Sec Ch Blocks, Explode Them, and Erase the Attribute Tags

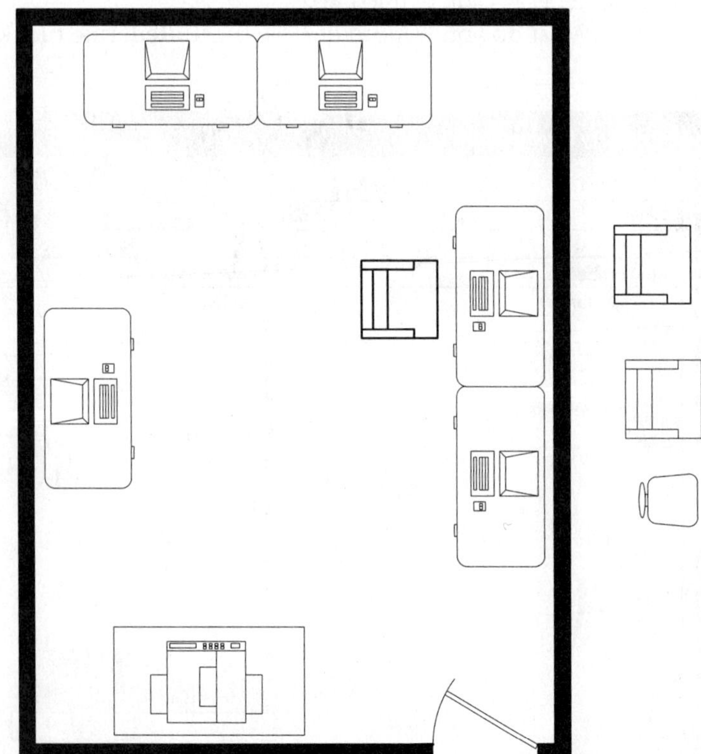

FIGURE 10–23
Select Chair1 to Edit

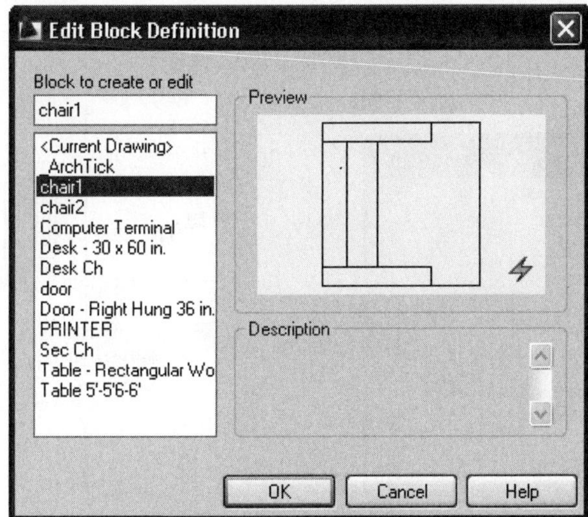

8. CLICK: **The parameters tab of the Block Authoring Palette,** CLICK: **the Visibility parameter, and place the parameter below the chair** (Figure 10–24). (Below the chair will make it easy to find after the block is inserted again.)
9. CLICK: **Visibility States on the Visibility Ribbon.**
10. CLICK: **New** (Figure 10–25) **and** CLICK: **Hide all existing objects in new state.** CLICK: **OK** (to exit New Visibility State dialog box).
11. CLICK: **OK** (to exit Visibility States dialog box—you are still in the Block Editor).
12. **Save the dynamic block as chair1** (TYPE: **BSAVEAS) and close the Block Editor** (TYPE: **BC<enter>).**
13. **Insert chair1 in the approximate location shown in front of a desk** (Figure 10–26). CLICK: **on chair1 and test your visibility parameter, VisibilityState0 and VisibilityState1.** Chair1 should be visible for State0 and invisible for State1.

FIGURE 10–24
Select the Visibility Parameter and Locate It as Shown

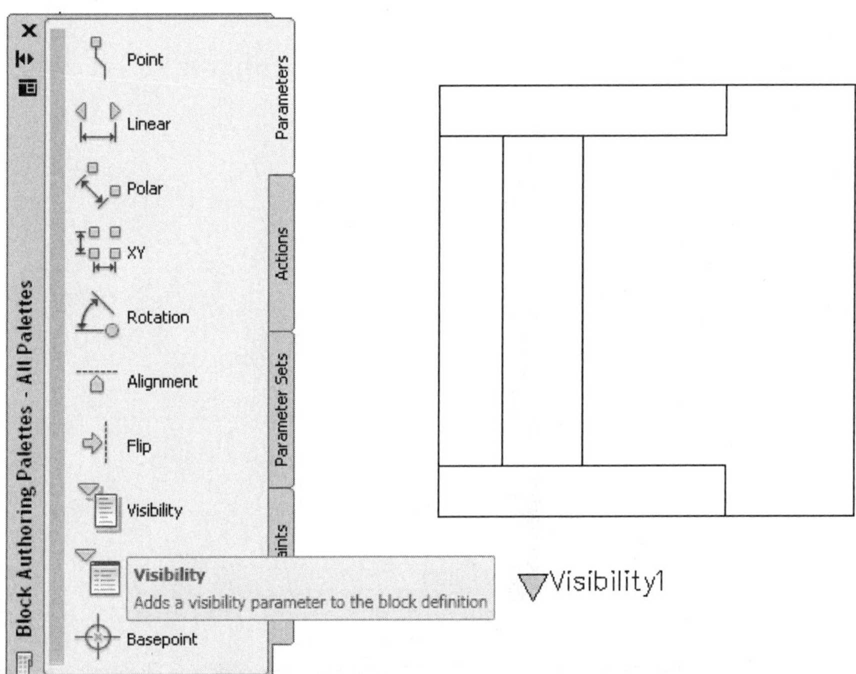

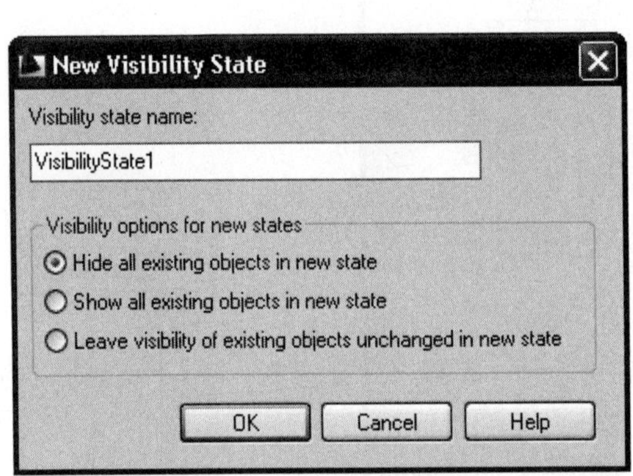

FIGURE 10–25
Make a Visibility State That Hides Chair1

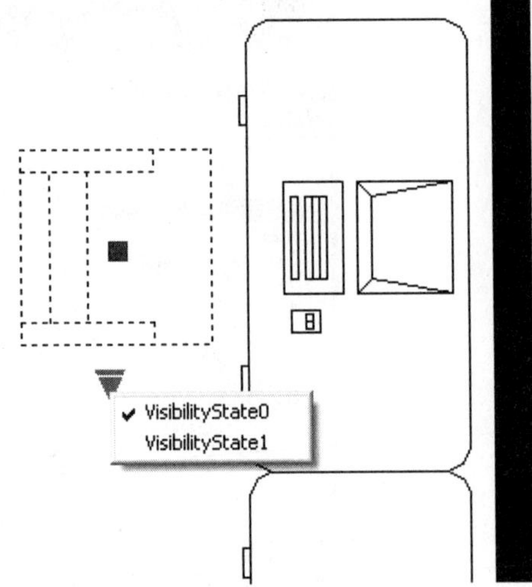

FIGURE 10–26
Chair1 Inserted with Two Visibility States—Visible and Invisible

14. **Repeat items 6 through 11 for chair2.**
15. **Move chair2 so it is positioned as shown in Figure 10–27.**
16. **Copy chair1 and chair2 so each desk has the two chairs.**
17. **Make all chair2s visible and all chair1s invisible as shown in Figure 10–4.**

Step 22. Make the door a dynamic block so it will open in or out as described next:

1. **Open the Block Editor, Select Door - Right Hung 36 in. and** CLICK: **OK.**
2. **Draw a line from D1** (Figure 10–28) **2-1/2″ straight down.** (This line goes to the middle of the wall, so the flip action will flip the door to either side of the room.)
3. CLICK: **the parameters tab of the Block Authoring Palette,** CLICK: **the Flip parameter.**

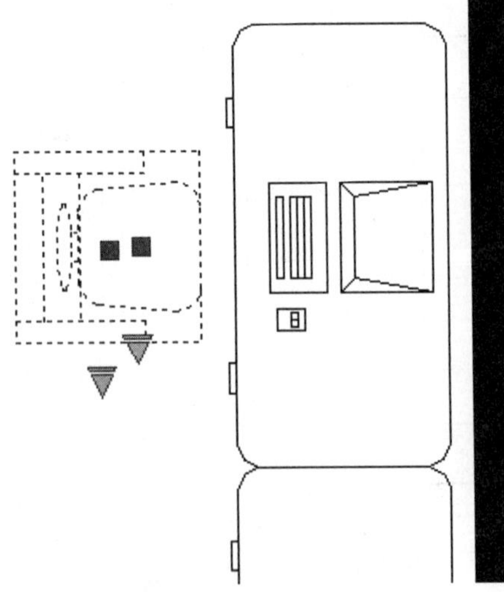

FIGURE 10–27
Both Chairs with Visibility Parameters

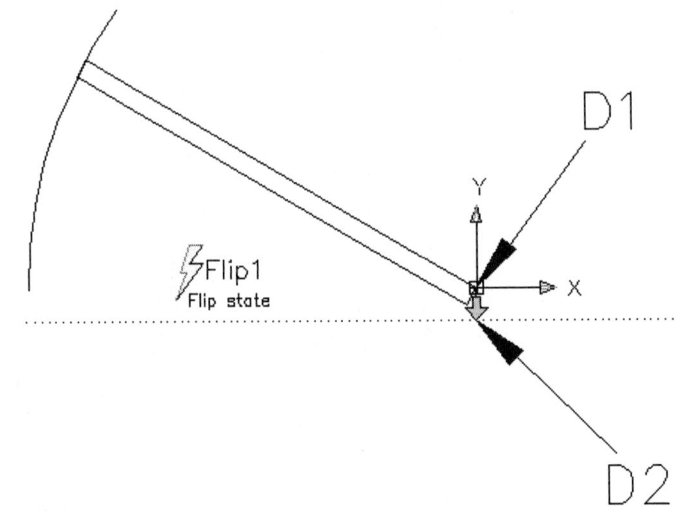

FIGURE 10–28
Add the Flip Parameter and Flip Action to the Door

4. CLICK: **D2** (Figure 10–28) **as the base point of the reflection line. With ORTHO on,** CLICK: **any point to the left of the base point as the endpoint of the reflection line.**
5. **Locate the label (Figure 10–28).**
6. CLICK: **The Actions tab of the Block Authoring Palette,** CLICK: **Flip action,** CLICK: **the Flip state parameter, and then** SELECT: **the entire door.**
7. **Locate the Action location, Flip 1** (Figure 10–28).
8. **Save the dynamic block as Door - Right Hung 36 in. to redefine the block and close the Block Editor.**
9. CLICK: **any point on the door so the flip action is available, flip the door so you see that it works, then leave it as shown in Figure 10–4.**

Step 23. **When you have completed Tutorial 10–2, add your name, class, and current date to the drawing in the upper right and save your work in at least two places.**

Step 24. **Print Tutorial 10–2 to scale.**

Tutorial 10–3: Attach an External Reference to an Office Plan

XATTACH

Before starting the XATTACH command, your primary drawing must be open. When you activate the XATTACH command, the Select Reference File dialog box opens and allows you to select the drawing that you want to attach. When you select and open a drawing to be attached as an external reference to your primary drawing, the External Reference dialog box opens. The External Reference dialog box allows you to specify whether the xref will be an attachment or an overlay.

Attachment An attached xref that is then attached to another drawing becomes a nested xref with all its features fully recognized.

Overlay An overlay is ignored when the drawing on which it is overlaid is then attached as an xref to another drawing.

The XATTACH command allows you to attach an external reference (xref) (drawing) to a primary drawing. For each drawing, the data are stored in their own separate file. Any changes made to the external reference drawing are reflected in the primary drawing each time the primary drawing is loaded into the Drawing Editor.

There are three distinct advantages to using external references:

1. The primary drawing always contains the most recent version of the external reference.
2. There are no conflicts in layer names and other similar features (called *named objects*), such as linetypes, text styles, and block definitions. AutoCAD automatically precedes the external reference layer name or other object name with the drawing name of the xref and a slash (/). For example, if the primary drawing and the external reference (named CHAIR) have a layer named Symbol, then the current drawing layer retains the name Symbol, and the external reference layer in the current drawing becomes Chair/symbol.
3. Drawing files are often much smaller.

External references are used, for example, for drawing a large furniture plan containing several different levels of office types, such as assistant, associate, manager, vice president, and president. Each office typical (furniture configuration used in the office) is attached to the current drawing as an external reference. When changes are made to the external reference drawing of the manager's office (as a result of furniture substitution, for example), the change is reflected in each instance of a manager's office in the primary large furniture plan when it is loaded into the Drawing Editor.

EXTERNAL REFERENCE (XREF)

When you activate the XREF command, the External Reference palette appears. After an external reference has been attached to your drawing, you can right-click on the external reference drawing name to select from the following options:

Attach... The Attach option allows you to attach any drawing as an external reference to the current drawing. There is no limit to the number of external references that you can attach to your drawing. This is the same command as XATTACH.

Detach The Detach option lets you remove unneeded external references from your drawing.

Reload The Reload option allows you to update the current drawing with an external reference that has been changed since you began the current drawing. You do not have to exit from the current drawing to update it with an external reference that you or someone else changed while in the current drawing.

Unload Temporarily clears the external reference from the current drawing until the drawing is reloaded.

Bind... The Insert option in the Bind dialog box creates a block of the external reference in the current drawing and erases any reference to it as an external reference. The Bind option binds the selected xref to the drawing and renames layers in a manner similar to that of the attached xref. This is the same command as XBIND.

XBIND

The XBIND (External Bind) command allows you to bind a selected subset of an external reference's dependent symbols to the current drawing. For example, if you did not want to create a block of the entire external reference but wanted permanently to add only a dimension style of the external reference to the drawing, you could use XBIND.

FEATURES OF EXTERNAL REFERENCES

Following is a list of external reference features:

1. An external reference cannot be exploded.
2. An external reference can be changed into a block with the Bind... option and then exploded. The advantage of using the external reference is then lost. The Bind option would be used if you wanted to send a client a disk or file containing only the current drawing without including external references.
3. External references can be nested. That means that a current drawing containing external references can itself be used as an external reference on another current drawing. There is no limit to the number of drawings you can nest like this.
4. An xref icon appears in the lower right corner of the screen when xrefs are attached to a drawing.

Step 1. Draw the floor plan shown in Figure 10–29 and save it as CH10-TUTORIAL3.

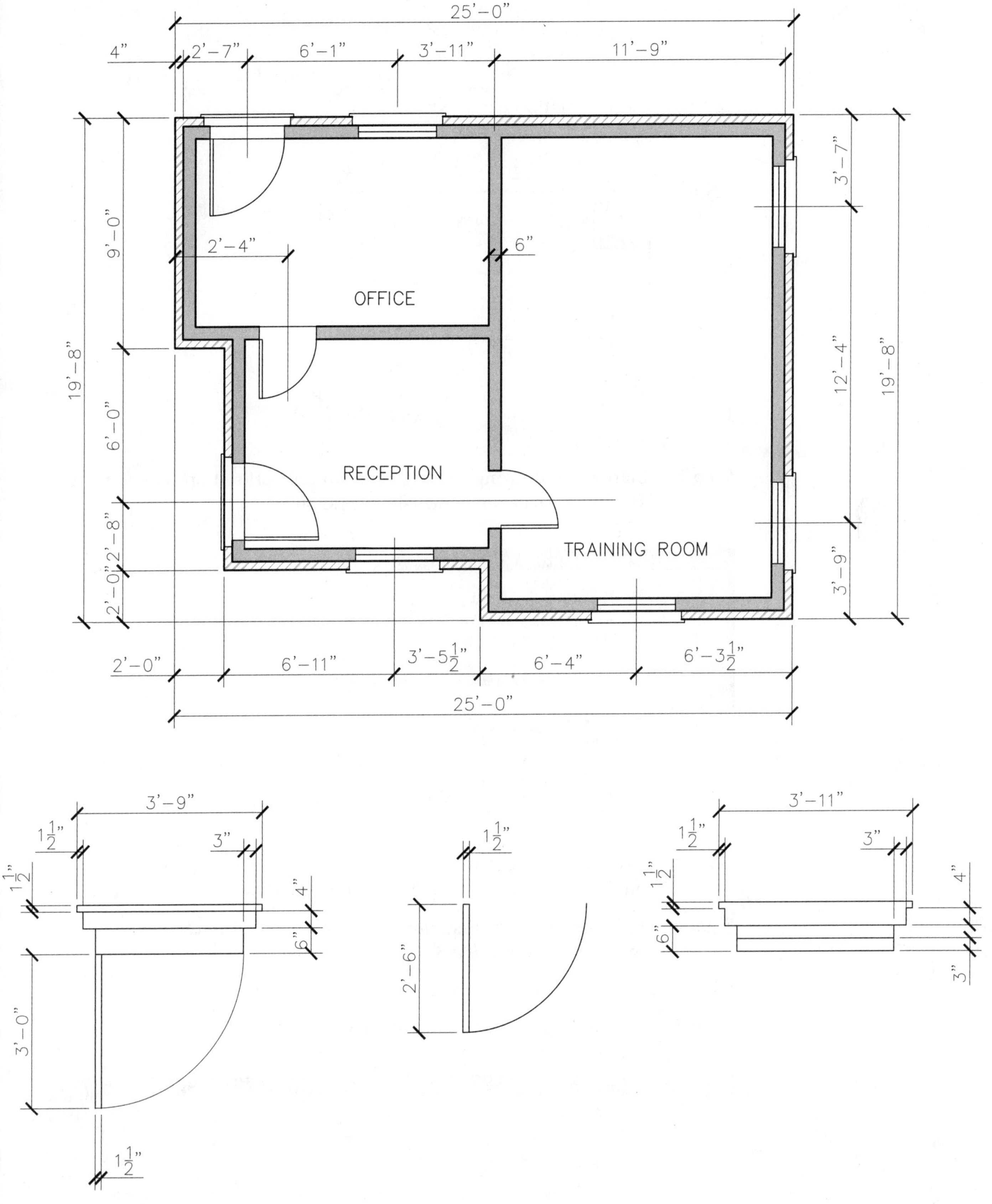

25'–0"
4"
2'–7"
6'–1"
3'–11"
11'–9"
OFFICE
RECEPTION
TRAINING ROOM
2'–4"
6"
9'–0"
19'–8"
6'–0"
2'–8"
2'–0"
3'–7"
12'–4"
19'–8"
3'–9"
2'–0"
6'–11"
3'–5½"
6'–4"
6'–3½"
25'–0"
3'–9"
1½"
3"
4"
6"
3'–0"
1½"
1½"
2'–6"
3'–11"
1½"
3"
1½"
4"
6"
3"

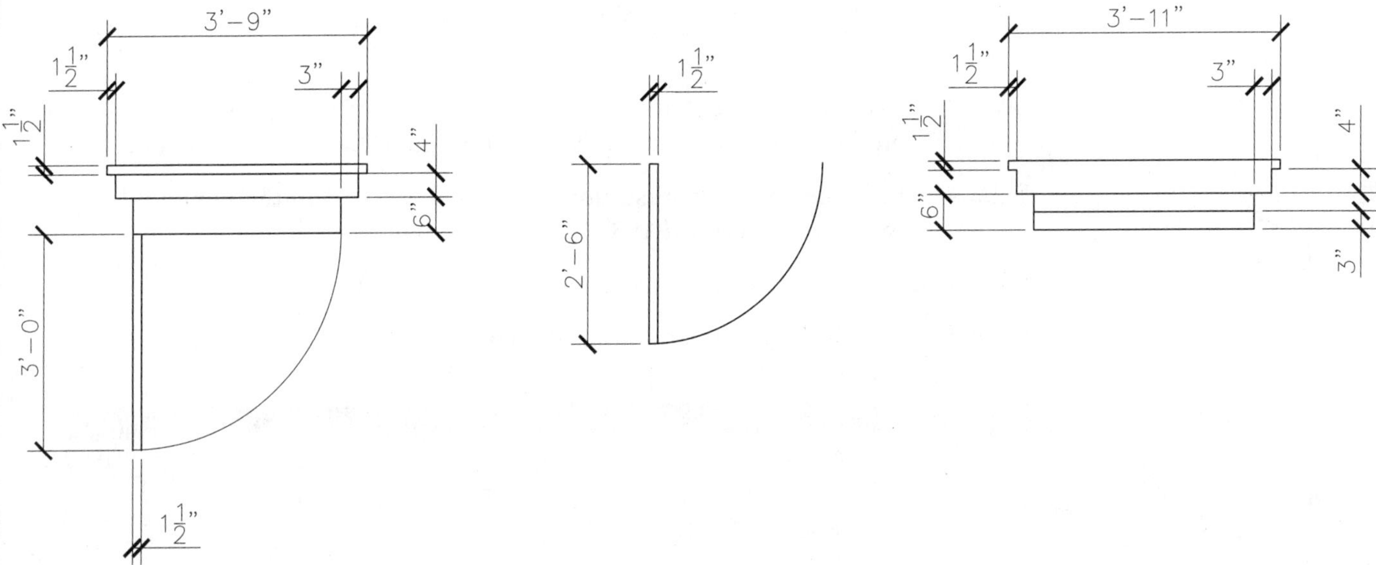

FIGURE 10–29
Tutorial 10–3: Floor Plan Dimensions (Scale: 3/16″ = 1′-0″)

FIGURE 10–30
Tutorial 10–3: Typical Workstation Dimensions

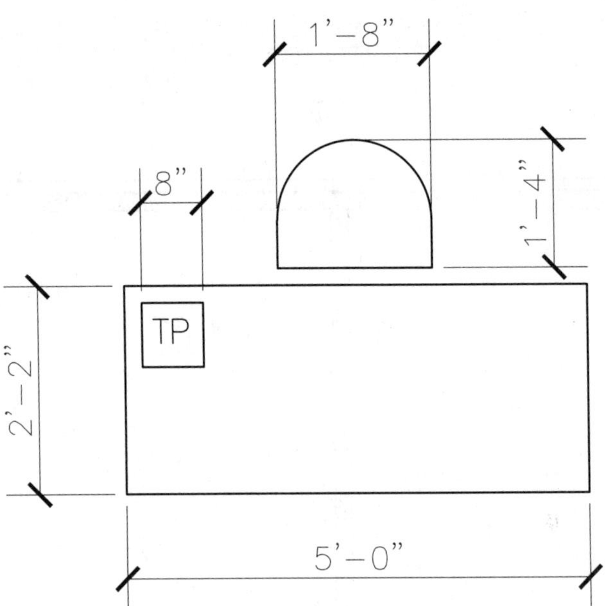

Step 2. Start a new drawing and draw the typical workstation shown in Figure 10–30. Estimate any dimension not shown.

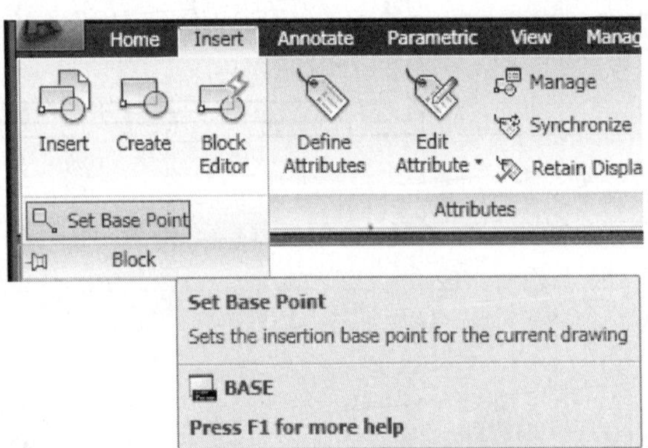

Step 3. Use the Set Base Point command (or TYPE: BASE) to select the midpoint on the arc of the chair as the insertion point for the workstation.

Step 4. Save the typical workstation drawing as WS10-1 in the same folder with CH10-TUTORIAL3. Exit the drawing.

Step 5. Open the floor plan drawing CH10-TUTORIAL3.

Step 6. Attach the workstation to the floor plan drawing as described next:

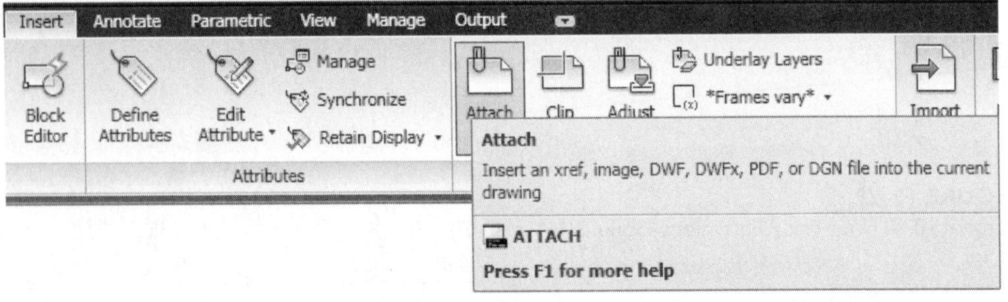

FIGURE 10–31
Locate Drawing WS10-1, and Select It

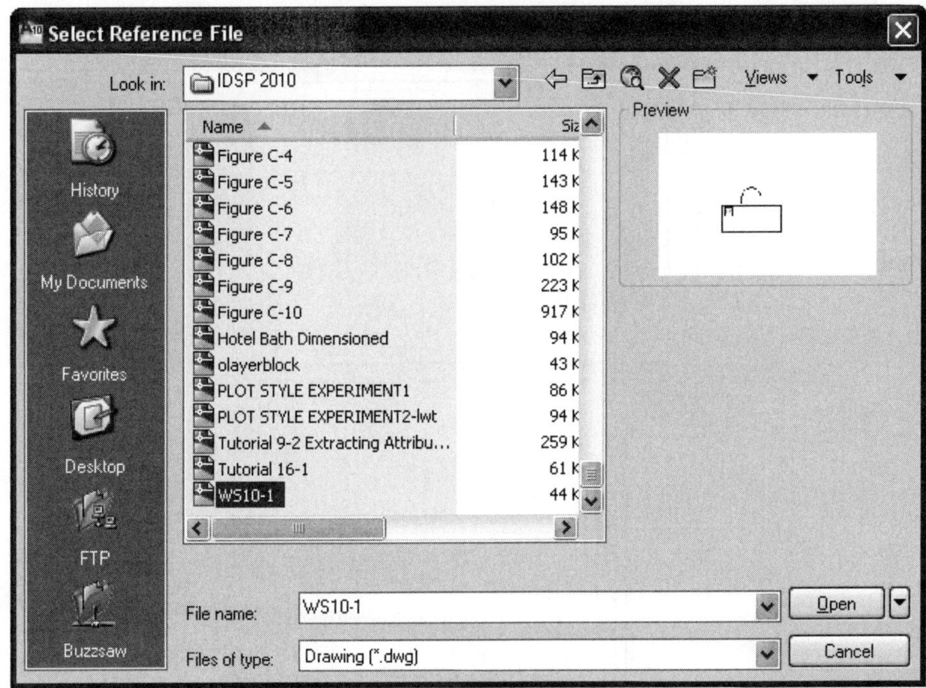

Prompt	Response
Command:	**XATTACH**
The Select Reference File dialog box (Figure 10–31) appears:	**Locate drawing WS10-1 and** CLICK: **on it**
	CLICK: **Open**
The External Reference dialog box (Figure 10–32) appears:	CLICK: **OK**

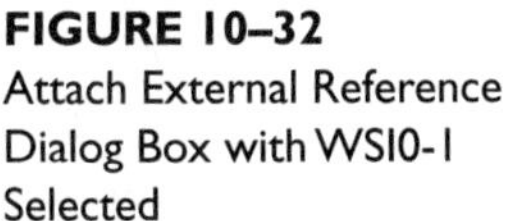
FIGURE 10–32
Attach External Reference Dialog Box with WS10-1 Selected

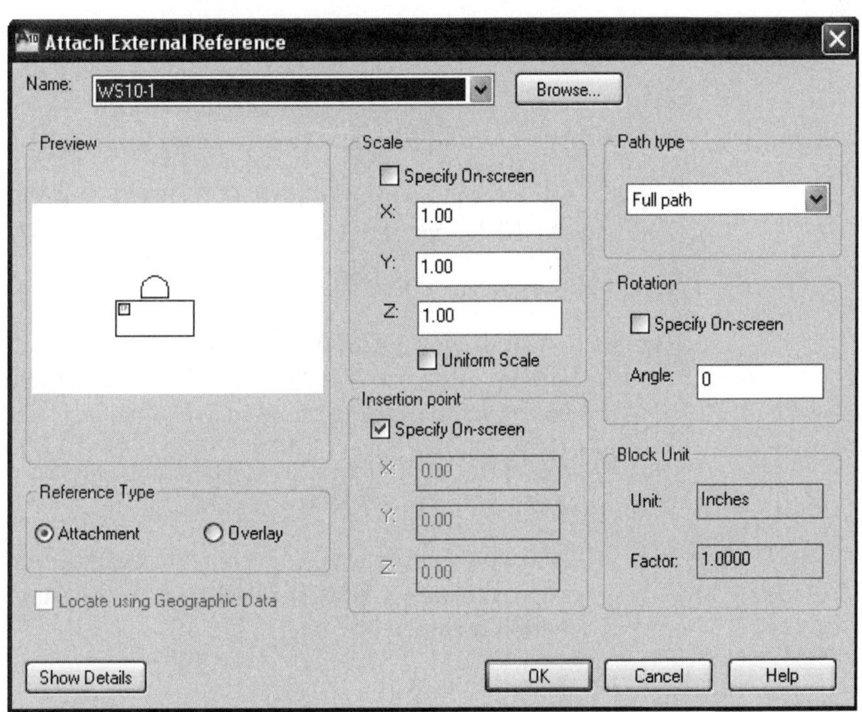

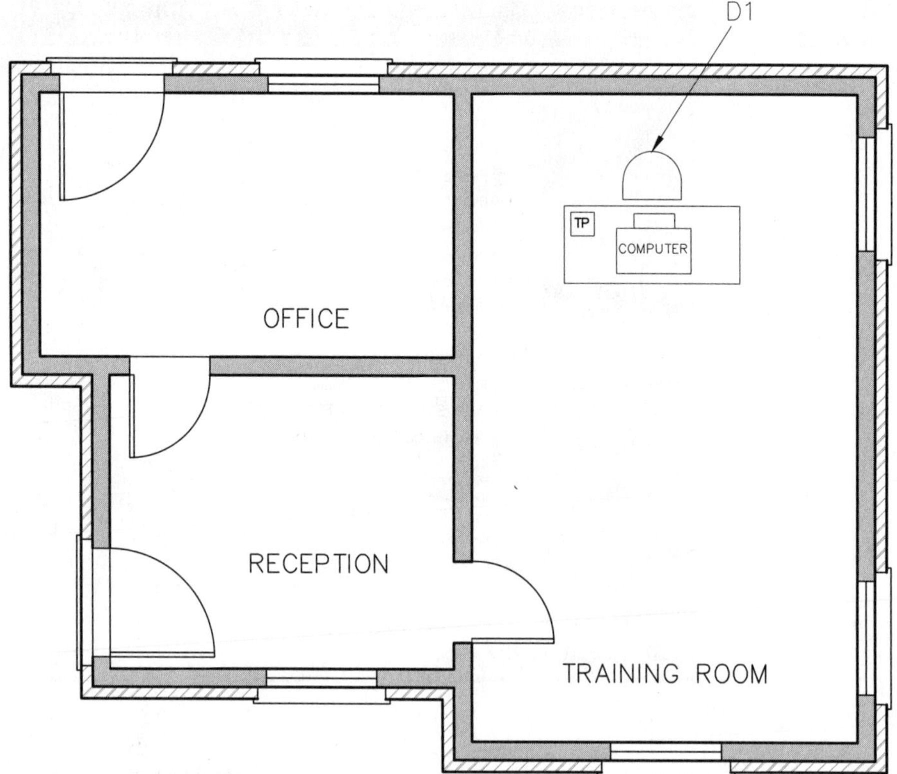

FIGURE 10–33
Insert the External Reference

Prompt	Response
Specify insertion point or [Scale/X/Y/Z/Rotate/PScale/PX/PY/PZ/PRotate]:	CLICK: **D1** (Figure 10–33)

That's all there is to attaching an external reference to another drawing.

Step 7. **Copy the external reference to four other locations on the floor plan as shown in Figure 10–34 (the exact location is not important).**

Step 8. **Save your drawing (CH10-TUTORIAL3) to the same folder or disk as WS10-1. Exit the drawing.**

You have been informed that all of the workstations must now have a computer.

Step 9. **Open drawing WS10-1 and draw a computer approximately the size shown in Figure 10–35 and label it. Save the new workstation drawing in the same place from which it came.**

Step 10. **Open drawing CH10-TUTORIAL3. It should appear as shown in Figure 10–36.**

Step 11. **Add your name, class, and current date to the drawing in the upper right and save CH10-TUTORIAL3 in the same folder or disk from which it came.**

Step 12. **Print the drawing to scale.**

FIGURE 10–34
Copy the External Reference to Four Other Locations

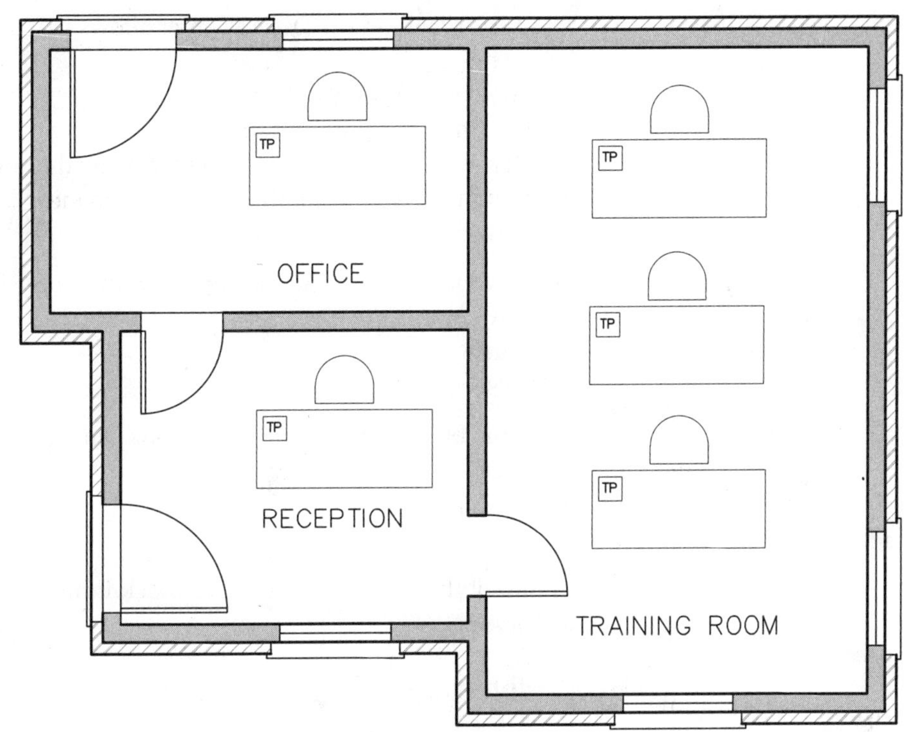

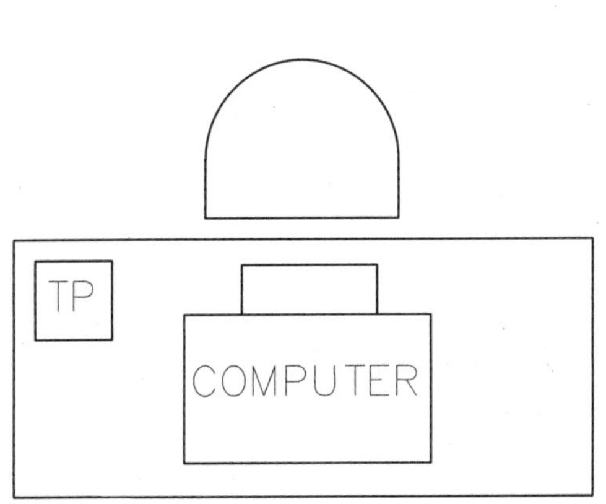

FIGURE 10–35
The New Workstation

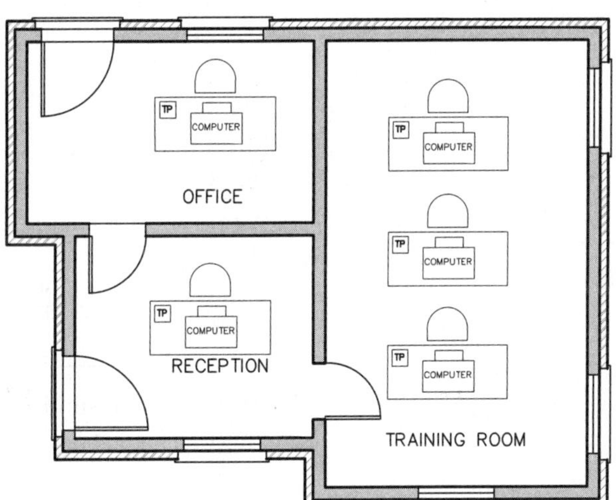

FIGURE 10–36
The Office Floor Plan with New Workstations

review questions

1. The AutoCAD DesignCenter allow you to drag-and-drop blocks, layers, linetypes, text styles, dimension styles, and external references from an existing drawing into the current drawing.
   a. True
   b. False

2. The History tab on the DesignCenter allows you to do which of the following?
   a. Look at a preview of a selected item
   b. Return to the previous screen
   c. Display a list of the most recently opened drawings
   d. Search for data using the search command
   e. Return to the default starting folder
3. Blocks (not Wblocks) can be copied from one drawing to another using the DesignCenter.
   a. True
   b. False
4. Dynamic block parameters and actions can only be added to a block in the Block Editor.
   a. True
   b. False
5. Which of the following opens the Block Editor?
   a. BOPEN
   b. BE
   c. EDITORB
   d. BLOCKE
   e. BED
6. Which of the following closes the Block Editor?
   a. BCL
   b. CLOSE
   c. BC
   d. EDCL
   e. CLOSEB

Complete.

7. What action must be added to a linear parameter to make it change the length of an existing rectangle?

   ____

8. What three visibility options are available in the New Visibility State dialog box?

   ____

   ____

   ____

9. Which External Reference option allows you to make a block of an external reference on the present drawing?

   ____

10. How many external references can be attached to a primary drawing?

   ____

11. List three advantages of using external references.

   ____

   ____

   ____

chapter

11

Drawing the Reflected Ceiling Plan and Voice/Data/Power Plan

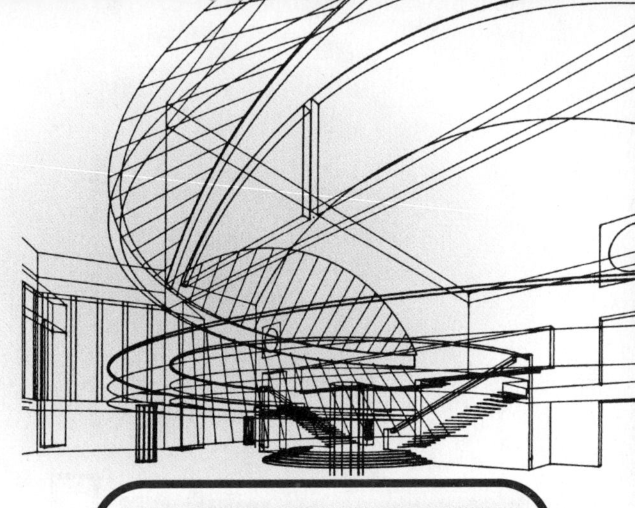

objectives

When you have completed this chapter, you will be able to:

Draw a reflected ceiling plan.

Draw a voice/data/power plan.

INTRODUCTION

Previously learned commands are used to draw the tenant space reflected ceiling plan in Tutorial 11–1, Part 1, and the tenant space voice/data/power plan in Tutorial 11–1, Part 2. Helpful guidelines for drawing Tutorial 11–1, Parts 1 and 2, are provided.

The reflected ceiling plan shows all the lighting symbols and other items such as exit signs that attach to the ceiling in their correct locations in the space. The plan also shows all the switching symbols needed to turn the lights on and off.

The voice/data/power plan shows symbols for telephones (voice), computers (data), and electrical outlets (power).

Tutorial 11–1: Part 1, Tenant Space Lighting Legend and Reflected Ceiling Plan

In Tutorial 11–1, Part 1, you will make a Wblock of each lighting symbol and then insert each symbol into the tenant space reflected ceiling plan. When you have completed Tutorial 11–1, Part 1, your reflected ceiling plan drawing will look similar to Figure 11–1.

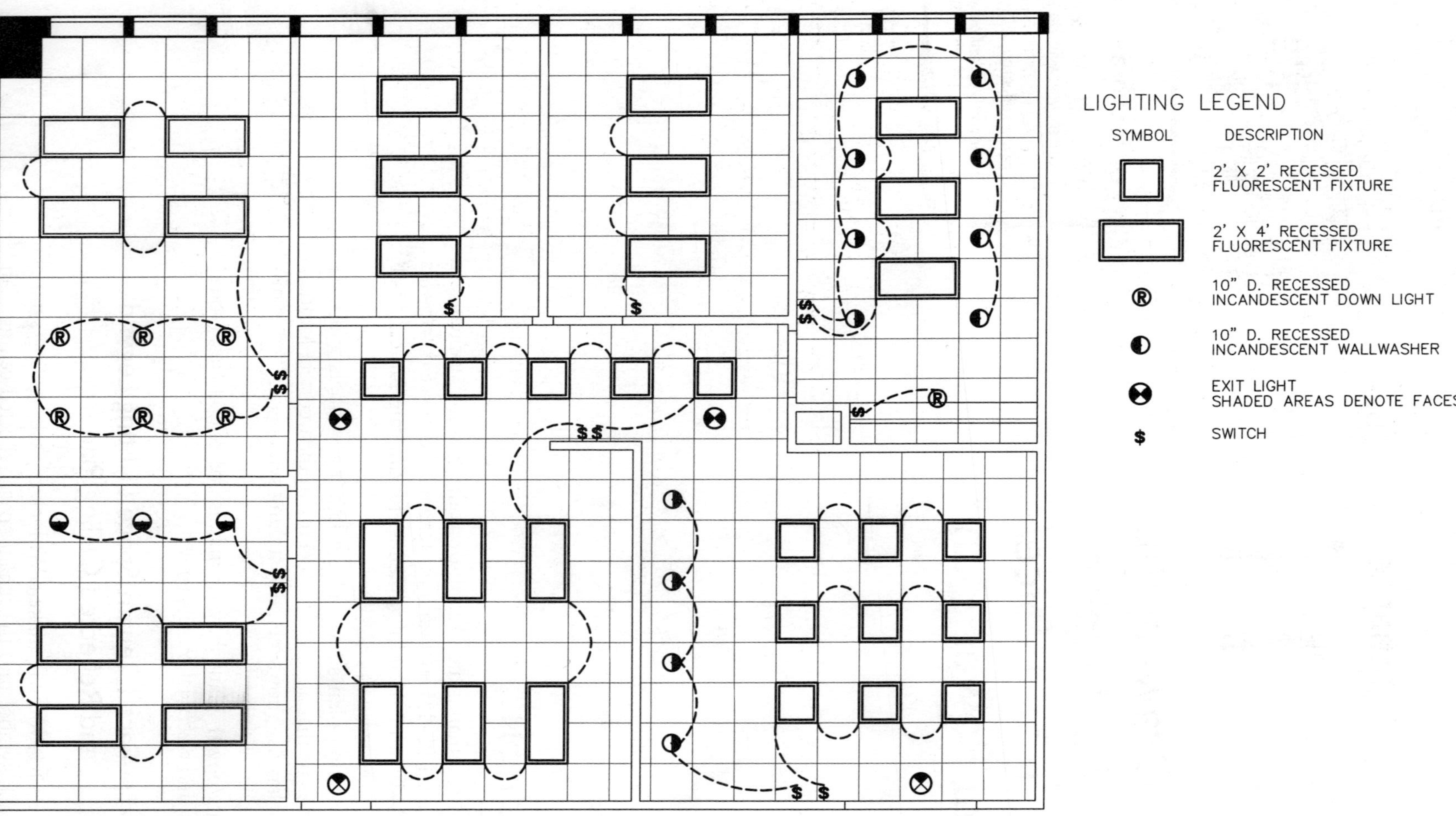

FIGURE 11–1
Tutorial 11–1: Part 1, Tenant Space Reflected Ceiling Plan (Scale: 1/8" = 1'-0")

FIGURE 11–2
Tutorial 11–1: Part 1, Tenant Space Lighting Legend (Scale: 1/4" = 1'-0")

LIGHTING LEGEND

SYMBOL	DESCRIPTION
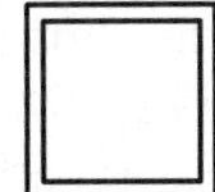	2' X 2' RECESSED FLUORESCENT FIXTURE
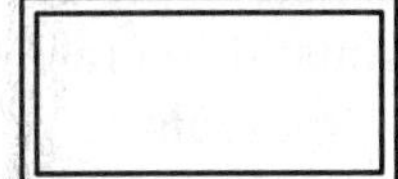	2' X 4' RECESSED FLUORESCENT FIXTURE
Ⓡ	10" D. RECESSED INCANDESCENT DOWN LIGHT
◐	10" D. RECESSED INCANDESCENT WALLWASHER
⊗	EXIT LIGHT SHADED AREAS DENOTE FACES
$	SWITCH

TENANT SPACE LIGHTING LEGEND SYMBOLS

Step 1. Draw each lighting symbol, as shown in Figure 11–2, on the e-lite Layer, full size. Wblock each symbol to a new folder named Lighting Symbols. Identify a logical insertion point, such as a corner of a rectangle or center of a circle.

TENANT SPACE REFLECTED CEILING PLAN

Step 2. Begin drawing CH11-TUTORIAL1-REFLECTED CEILING on the hard drive or network drive by opening existing drawing CH9-TUTORIAL1 and saving it as CH11-TUTORIAL1-REFLECTED CEILING.

Step 3. Freeze the following layers that are not needed to draw the reflected ceiling plan:

a-anno-area
a-anno-dims
a-door-dbl
a-door-swng
a-flor-iden
i-furn

Step 4. Set Layer a-wall-head current. Draw lines across the door openings, as shown in Figure 11–1.

Step 5. Set Layer a-clng-grid current and draw the 2′ × 2′ ceiling grid, as shown in Figure 11–1. Draw a separate balanced grid in each area as shown in Figure 11–1.

Step 6. Insert the lighting legend symbols, full scale, into the location shown on the tenant space reflected ceiling plan in Figure 11–1.

Step 7. Set Layer e-lite-text current.

Step 8. Add the text to the lighting legend as shown in Figure 11–1, and make it annotative. The words LIGHTING LEGEND are 3/32″ high text; the remaining text is all 1/16″ high.

Step 9. Prepare the ceiling grid for insertion of the 2′ × 4′ recessed fixture symbols by using the Erase command to erase the ceiling grid lines that will cross the centers of the symbols.

Use the Copy command and an Osnap modifier to copy the lighting symbols from the legend and place them on the plan, as shown in Figure 11–1.

The wallwasher, 2′ × 4′ fixture, and switch symbols appear on the reflected ceiling plan in several different orientations. Copy each symbol and Rotate the individual symbols into the various positions, then use Copy to draw the additional like symbols in the correct locations on the plan.

Step 10. Set Layer e-lite-circ current. Use the Arc command to draw the symbol for the circuitry. Adjust LTSCALE as needed so lines appear as dashed.

Step 11. Change the title text to read as shown in Figure 11–1.

Step 12. When you have completed Tutorial 11–1, Part 1, save your work in at least two places.

Step 13. Plot or print Tutorial 11–1, Part 1, to scale.

Tutorial 11–1: Part 2, Tenant Space Voice/Data/Power Legend and Plan

In Tutorial 11–1, Part 2, you will make a Wblock of each voice, data, and power symbol and then insert each symbol into the tenant space voice/data/power plan. When you have completed Tutorial 11–1, Part 2, your voice/data/power plan drawing will look similar to Figure 11–3.

TENANT SPACE VOICE/DATA/POWER LEGEND SYMBOLS

Step 1. Draw each voice, data, and power symbol, as shown in Figure 11–4, on the e-power Layer, full size. Wblock each symbol to a new folder named Voice Data Power Symbols. Identify a logical insertion point, such as the tip of a triangle or center of a circle.

TENANT SPACE VOICE/DATA/POWER PLAN

Step 2. Begin drawing CH11-TUTORIAL1-VOICE-DATA-POWER on the hard drive or network drive by opening existing drawing CH11-TUTORIAL1-REFLECTED CEILING and saving it as CH11-TUTORIAL1-VOICE-DATA-POWER.

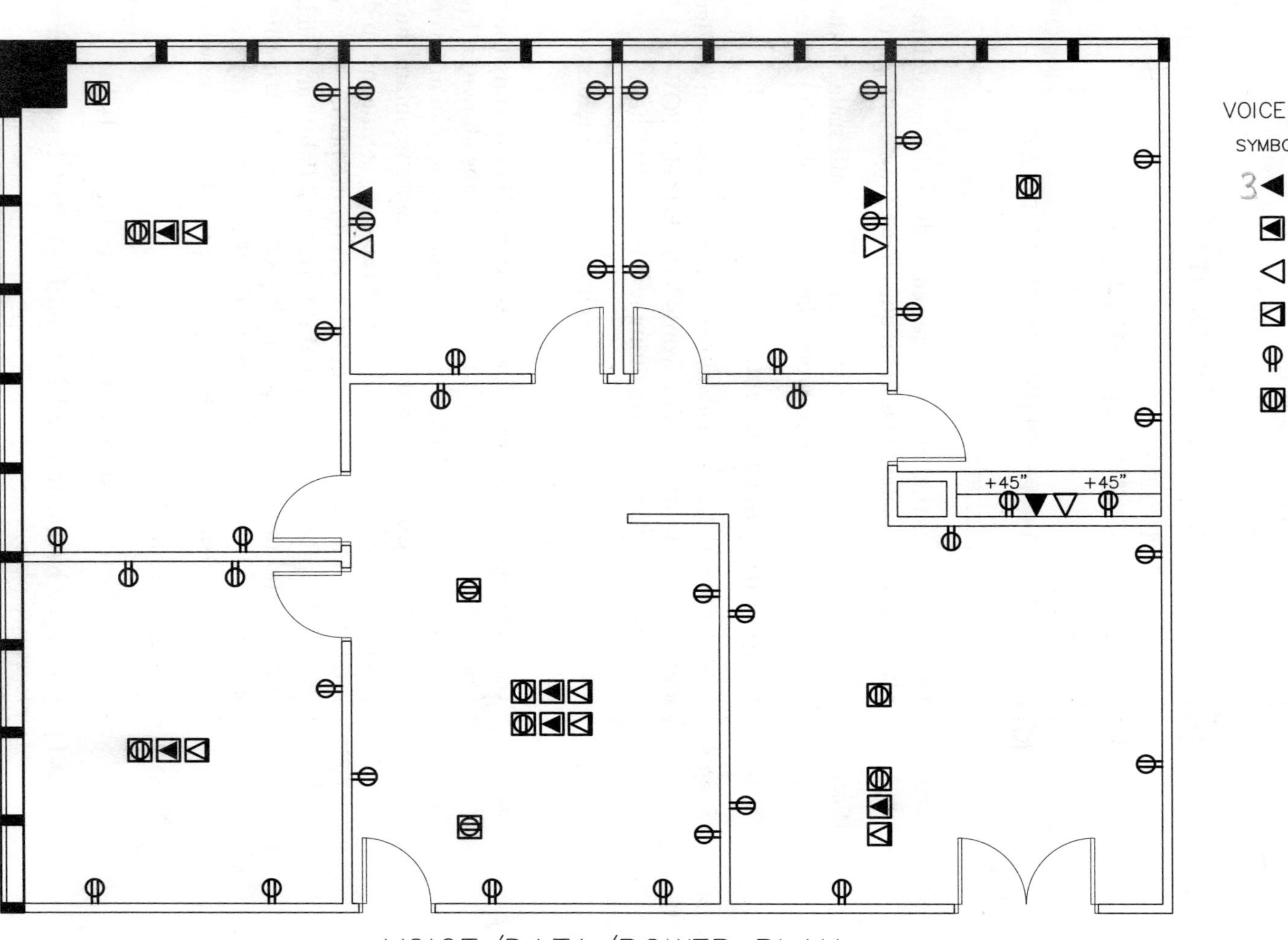

FIGURE 11–3
Tutorial 11–1: Part 2, Tenant Space Voice/Data/Power Plan (Scale: 1/8" = 1'-0")

FIGURE 11–4
Tutorial 11–1: Part 2, Tenant Space Voice/Data/Power Legend (Scale: 1/4″ = 1′-0″)

VOICE/DATA/POWER LEGEND

SYMBOL	DESCRIPTION
◀	TELEPHONE OUTLET
⧈	FLOOR TELEPHONE OUTLET
◁	DATA OUTLET
⧈	FLOOR DATA OUTLET
⏀	DUPLEX RECEPTACLE
⧈	FLOOR DUPLEX RECEPTACLE

Step 3. Freeze all layers that are not required to draw the voice/data/power plan. Thaw any layers that are required, as shown in Figure 11–3.

Step 4. Insert the voice/data/power legend symbols, full scale, in the location shown on the tenant space voice/data/ power plan in Figure 11–3.

Step 5. Set Layer e-powr-text current.

Step 6. Add the text to the voice/data/power legend as shown in Figure 11–4, and make it annotative. The words VOICE/DATA/POWER LEGEND are 3/32″ high text; the remaining text is all 1/16″ high.

Step 7. Thaw the i-furn Layer. Use the furniture to help you locate the voice/data/power symbols.

Step 8. Use the Copy command and an Osnap modifier to copy the symbols from the legend and place them on the plan as shown in Figure 11–3.

The duplex receptacle symbol appears on the plan in several different orientations. Copy the symbol, and use Rotate to obtain the rotated positions as shown on the plan. Use the Copy command to draw like rotated symbols in the correct locations on the plan.

It is helpful to use Osnap-Mid Between 2 Points and pick the two endpoints of the two lines in the duplex receptacle. Use this point to locate the duplex receptacle along the walls when using the Copy command. Use Osnap-Center to help locate the floor receptacle symbol.

Step 9. Freeze the i-furn Layer.

Step 10. Change the title text to read as shown in Figure 11–3.

Step 11. When you have completed Tutorial 11–1, Part 2, save your work in at least two places.

Step 12. Plot or print Tutorial 11–1, Part 2, to scale.

review questions

Complete.

1. When the annotative scale is set to 1/8″ = 1′-0″ and you place annotative text on the drawing at 1/8″ paper height, how high is the text on the drawing (model height)?

   ____

2. List the setting that controls the sizes of linetypes as they appear on the screen (so dashed lines appear dashed).

   ____

3. If a drawing entity is created on a layer that has the color property green, what color does it assume when it is inserted on a layer with the color property red?

   ____

   ____

4. Which of the following plans would most likely contain a symbol for a duplex receptacle?
   a. Lighting
   b. Power
   c. Voice
   d. Data
   e. None of the above
5. Which of the following plans would most likely contain a symbol for a fluorescent fixture?
   a. Lighting
   b. Power
   c. Voice
   d. Data
   e. None of the above

exercises

Exercise 11–1: Hotel Room Power/Communication/Lighting Legend and Plan

1. Draw the hotel room power/communication/lighting symbols as shown in Figure 11–5. Do not redraw any symbols you have already drawn and Wblocked to a folder. Use an architectural scale to measure the symbols and draw them full scale.
2. Wblock each symbol to the appropriate folder.
3. Begin CH11-EX1 by opening the existing Hotel Room Furniture Installation plan, CH9-EX1, and saving it as CH11-EX1.
4. Complete the hotel room power/communication/lighting plan as shown in Figure 11–6. The 45″ notation on the receptacles in the bathroom shows the distance from the floor to the receptacles.
5. Plot or print the drawing to scale.

POWER/COMMUNICATION/LIGHTING LEGEND

SYMBOL	DESCRIPTION
	DUPLEX RECEPTACLE
GFIC	DUPLEX RECEPTACLE WITH GROUND FAULT INTERRUPTER CIRCUIT
	TELEPHONE OUTLET
	DATA OUTLET
TV	CABLE TV OUTLET
S/A	SMOKE ALARM – WIRE DIRECT W/BATTERY BACK-UP
	CEILING MOUNTED LIGHT FIXTURE
	WALL MOUNTED LIGHT FIXTURE
EX	EXHAUST FAN/LIGHT COMBINATION
$	SWITCH

FIGURE 11–5
Exercise 11–1: Hotel Room Power/Communication/Lighting Legend (Scale: 1/4″ = 1′-0″)

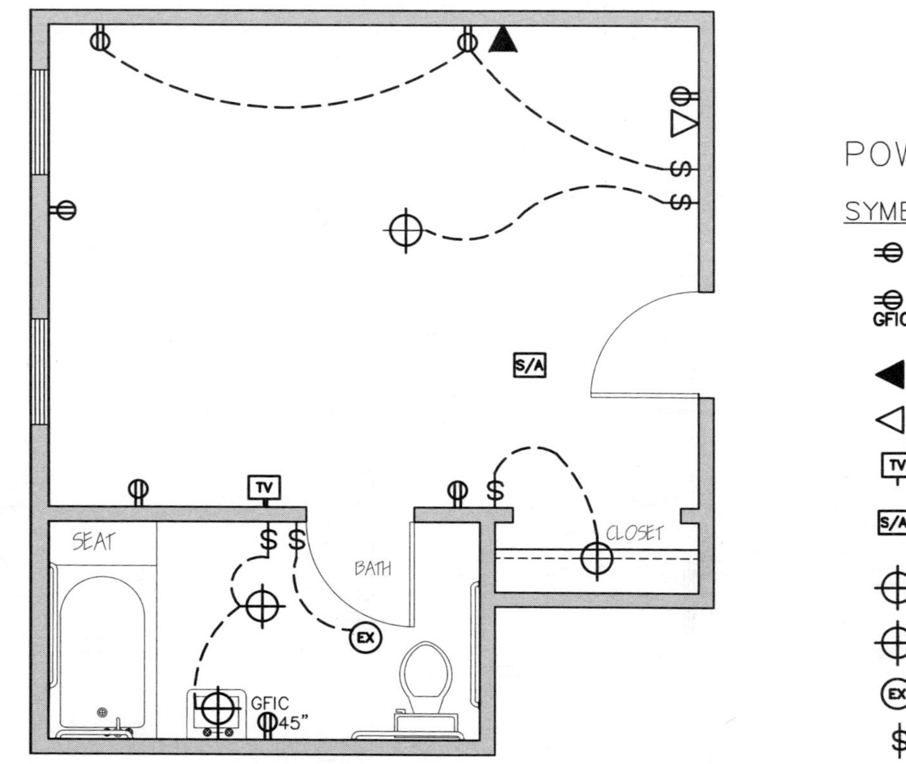

FIGURE 11–6
Exercise 11–1: Hotel Room Power/Communication/Lighting Plan (Scale: 3/16" = 1'0")

FIGURE 11–7
Exercise 11–2: Wheelchair Accessible Commercial Restroom Lighting Legend (Scale: 1/4" = 1'-0")

LIGHTING LEGEND

SYMBOL	DESCRIPTION
(R)	RECESSED LIGHT FIXTURE
$	SWITCH
	EMERGENCY LIGHT WALL MOUNTED

Exercise 11–2: Wheelchair Accessible Commercial Restroom Lighting Legend and Plan

1. Draw the wheelchair accessible commercial restroom lighting symbols as shown in Figure 11–7. Do not redraw any symbols you have already drawn and Wblocked to a folder. Use an architectural scale to measure the symbols and draw them full scale.
2. Wblock each symbol to the appropriate folder.
3. Complete the wheelchair accessible commercial restroom lighting plan as shown in Figure 11–8.
4. Plot or print the drawing to scale.

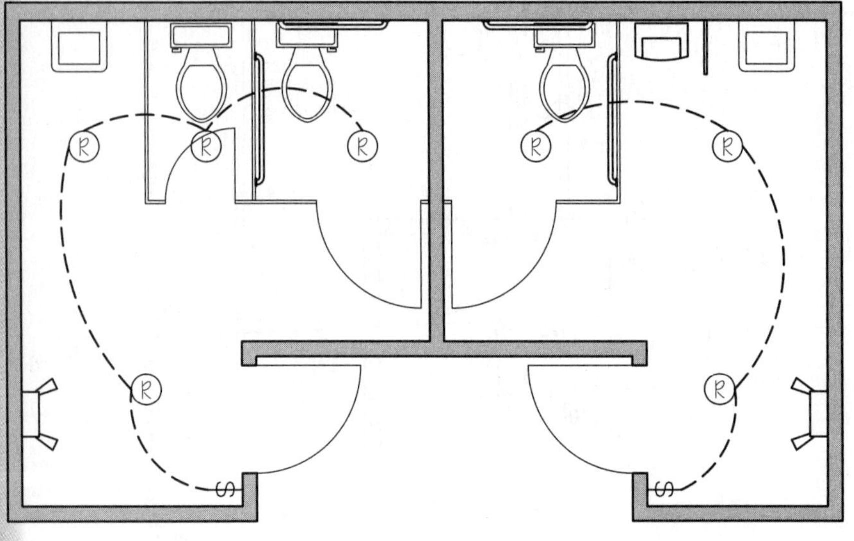

LIGHTING LEGEND

SYMBOL	DESCRIPTION
(R)	RECESSED LIGHT FIXTURE
$	SWITCH
	EMERGENCY LIGHT WALL MOUNTED

LIGHTING PLAN
SCALE: 3/16"=1'-0"

FIGURE 11–8
Exercise 11–2: Wheelchair Accessible Commercial Restroom Lighting Plan (Scale: 3/16" = 1'-0")

Exercise 11–3: Wheelchair Accessible Residential Bathroom Power/Communication/Lighting Legend and Plan

1. Draw the wheelchair accessible residential bathroom power/communication/lighting symbols as shown in Figure 11–9. Do not redraw any symbols you have already drawn and Wblocked to a folder. Use an architectural scale to measure the symbols and draw them full scale.
2. Wblock each symbol to the appropriate folder.
3. Complete the wheelchair accessible residential bathroom lighting plan as shown in Figure 11–10.
4. Plot or print the drawing to scale.

POWER/COMMUNICATION/LIGHTING LEGEND

SYMBOL	DESCRIPTION
⦵	DUPLEX RECEPTACLE
⦵ GFIC	DUPLEX RECEPTACLE WITH GROUND FAULT INTERUPTER CIRCUIT
◀	TELEPHONE OUTLET
Ⓡ	RECESSED LIGHT FIXTURE
⊕	WALL MOUNTED LIGHT FIXTURE
(EX)	EXHAUST FAN
$	SWITCH

FIGURE 11–9
Exercise 11–3: Wheelchair Accessible Residential Restroom Power/Communication/Lighting Legend (Scale: 1/4″ = 1′-0″)

POWER/COMMUNICATION/LIGHTING LEGEND

SYMBOL	DESCRIPTION
⊖	DUPLEX RECEPTACLE
⊖ GFIC	DUPLEX RECEPTACLE WITH GROUND FAULT INTERUPTER CIRCUIT
◀	TELEPHONE OUTLET
Ⓡ	RECESSED LIGHT FIXTURE
⊕	WALL MOUNTED LIGHT FIXTURE
(EX)	EXHAUST FAN
$	SWITCH

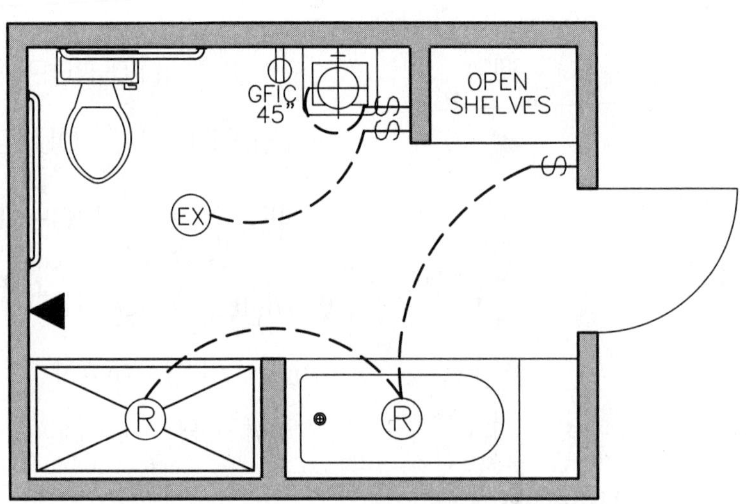

POWER/COMMUNICATION/LIGHTING PLAN
SCALE: 1/4"=1'–0"

FIGURE 11–10
Exercise 11–3: Wheelchair Accessible Residential Bathroom Power/Communication/Lighting Plan (Scale: 1/4" = 1'-0")

Exercise 11–4: Log Cabin Lighting Legend and Plan

1. Draw the log cabin lighting symbols as shown in Figure 11–11. Do not redraw any symbols you have already drawn and Wblocked to a folder. Use an architectural scale to measure the symbols and draw them full scale.
2. Wblock each symbol to the appropriate folder.
3. Complete the log cabin lighting plan as shown in Figure 11–12.
4. Plot or print the drawing to scale.

LIGHTING LEGEND

SYMBOL	DESCRIPTION
Ⓡ	RECESSED LIGHT FIXTURE
	CEILING MOUNTED LIGHT FIXTURE
	WALL MOUNTED LIGHT FIXTURE
	RECESSED WALL WASHER LIGHT FIXTURE
EX	EXHAUST FAN/LIGHT COMBINATION
	CEILING FAN WITH INTEGRAL LIGHT(S) PROVIDE SEPARATE SWITCHING FOR FAN AND LIGHT(S)
$	SWITCH
$3	3–WAY SWITCH

FIGURE 11–11
Exercise 11–4: Log Cabin Lighting Legend (Scale: 1/4″ = 1′-0″)

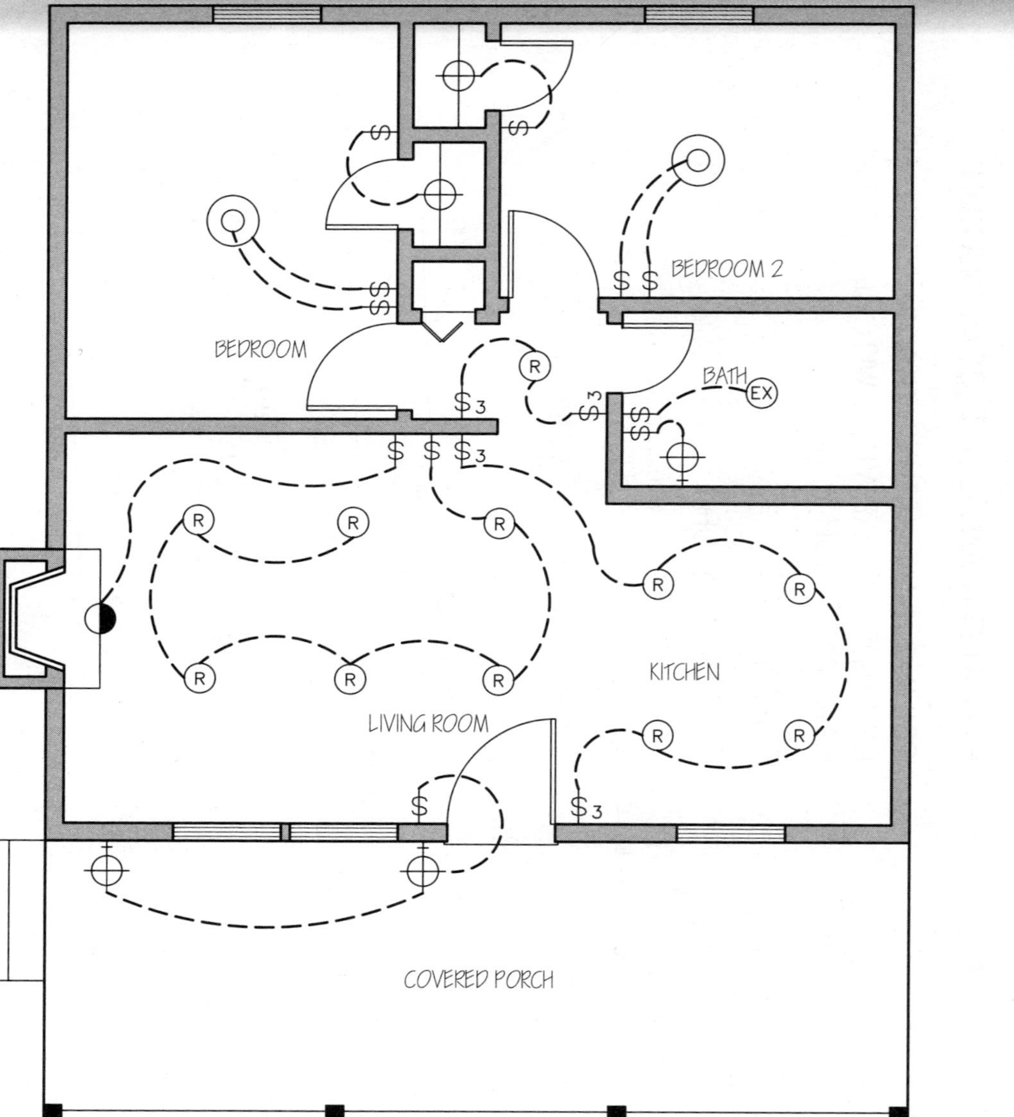

LIGHTING LEGEND

SYMBOL	DESCRIPTION
(R)	RECESSED LIGHT FIXTURE
⊕	CEILING MOUNTED LIGHT FIXTURE
⊕	WALL MOUNTED LIGHT FIXTURE
◒	RECESSED WALL WASHER LIGHT FIXTURE
(EX)	EXHAUST FAN/LIGHT COMBINATION
◎	CEILING FAN WITH INTEGRAL LIGHT(S) PROVIDE SEPARATE SWITCHING FOR FAN AND LIGHT(S)
$	SWITCH
$_3	3-WAY SWITCH

FIGURE 11–12
Exercise 11–4: Log Cabin Lighting Plan (Scale: 3/16″ = 1′0″)

Exercise 11–5: Log Cabin Power/Communication Legend and Plan

1. Draw the log cabin power and communication symbols as shown in Figure 11–13. Do not redraw any symbols you have already drawn and Wblocked to a folder. Use an architectural scale to measure the symbols and draw them full scale.
2. Wblock each symbol to the appropriate folder.
3. Complete the log cabin power/communication plan as shown in Figure 11–14. The 45″ notation on three of the receptacles shows the distance from the floor to the receptacle.
4. Plot or print the drawing to scale.

POWER/COMMUNICATION LEGEND

SYMBOL	DESCRIPTION
⊖	DUPLEX RECEPTACLE
⊖ GFIC	DUPLEX RECEPTACLE WITH GROUND FAULT INTERRUPTER CIRCUIT
R⊖	RANGE OUTLET
◀	TELEPHONE OUTLET
◁	DATA OUTLET
TV	CABLE TV OUTLET
S/A	SMOKE ALARM WIRE DIRECT W/BATTERY BACKUP
$	SWITCH

FIGURE 11–13
Exercise 11–5: Log Cabin Power/Communication Legend (Scale: 1/4″ = 1′-0″)

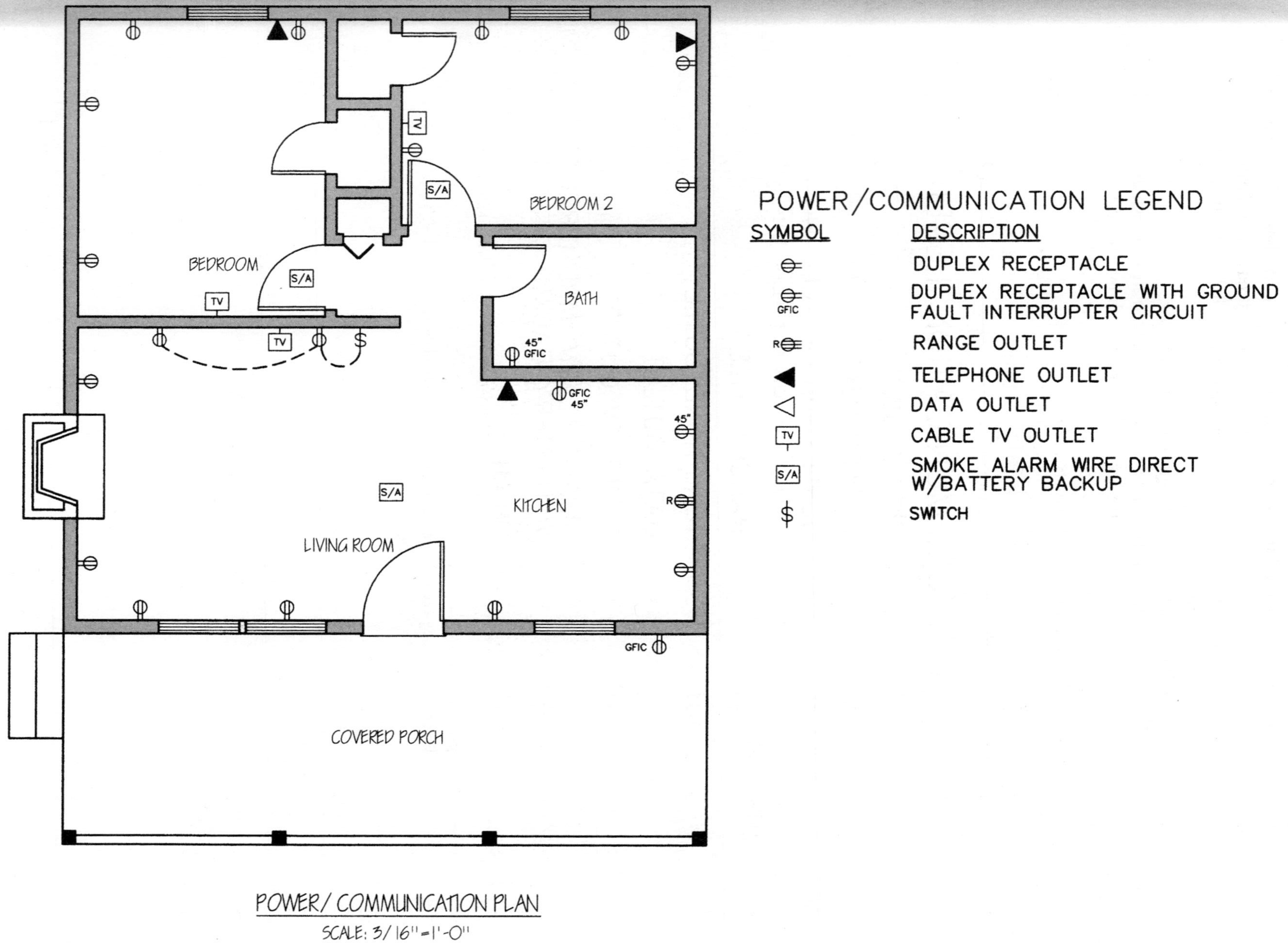

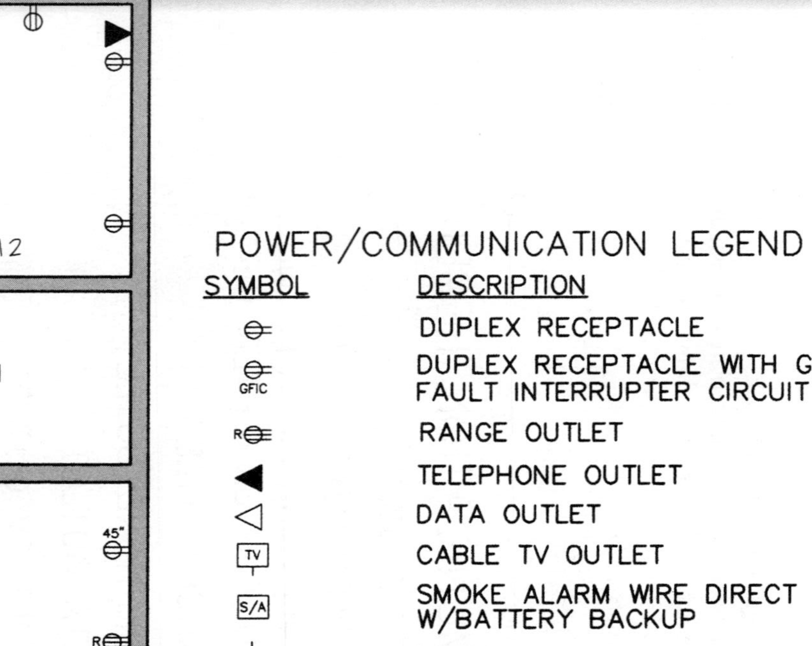

FIGURE 11–14
Exercise 11–5: Log Cabin Power/Communication Plan (Scale: 3/16″ = 1′-0″)

Exercise 11–6: House Power/Communication/Lighting Legend and Plan

1. Draw the house power/communication/lighting symbols as shown in Figure 11–15. Do not redraw any symbols you have already drawn and Wblocked to a folder. Use an architectural scale to measure the symbols and draw them full scale.
2. Wblock each symbol to the appropriate folder.
3. Complete the house power/communication/lighting plan—Lower Level and Upper Level as shown in Figure 11–16, Sheets 1 and 2.
4. Plot or print the drawing to scale.

FIGURE 11–15
Exercise 11–6: House Power/Communication/Lighting Legend (Scale: 1/8″ = 1′-0″)

POWER/COMMUNICATION/LIGHTING LEGEND

SYMBOL	DESCRIPTION
	DUPLEX RECEPTACLE
WP	DUPLEX RECEPTACLE WEATHERPROOF
	220 VOLT OUTLET
	FLOOR DUPLEX RECEPTACLE
◀	TELEPHONE
	SURFACE MOUNTED INCANDESCENT TRACK LIGHTING
⊙	CHANDELIER
Ⓡ	RECESSED INCANDESCENT FIXTURE
Ⓢ	SURFACE MOUNTED INCANDESCENT FIXTURE
Ⓡ WP	RECESSED FIXTURE WEATHERPROOF
	WALL FIXTURE
WP	WALL FIXTURE WEATHERPROOF
Ⓟ	PENDANT FIXTURE
	FLUORESCENT FIXTURE
$	SWITCH
$3	3–WAY SWITCH

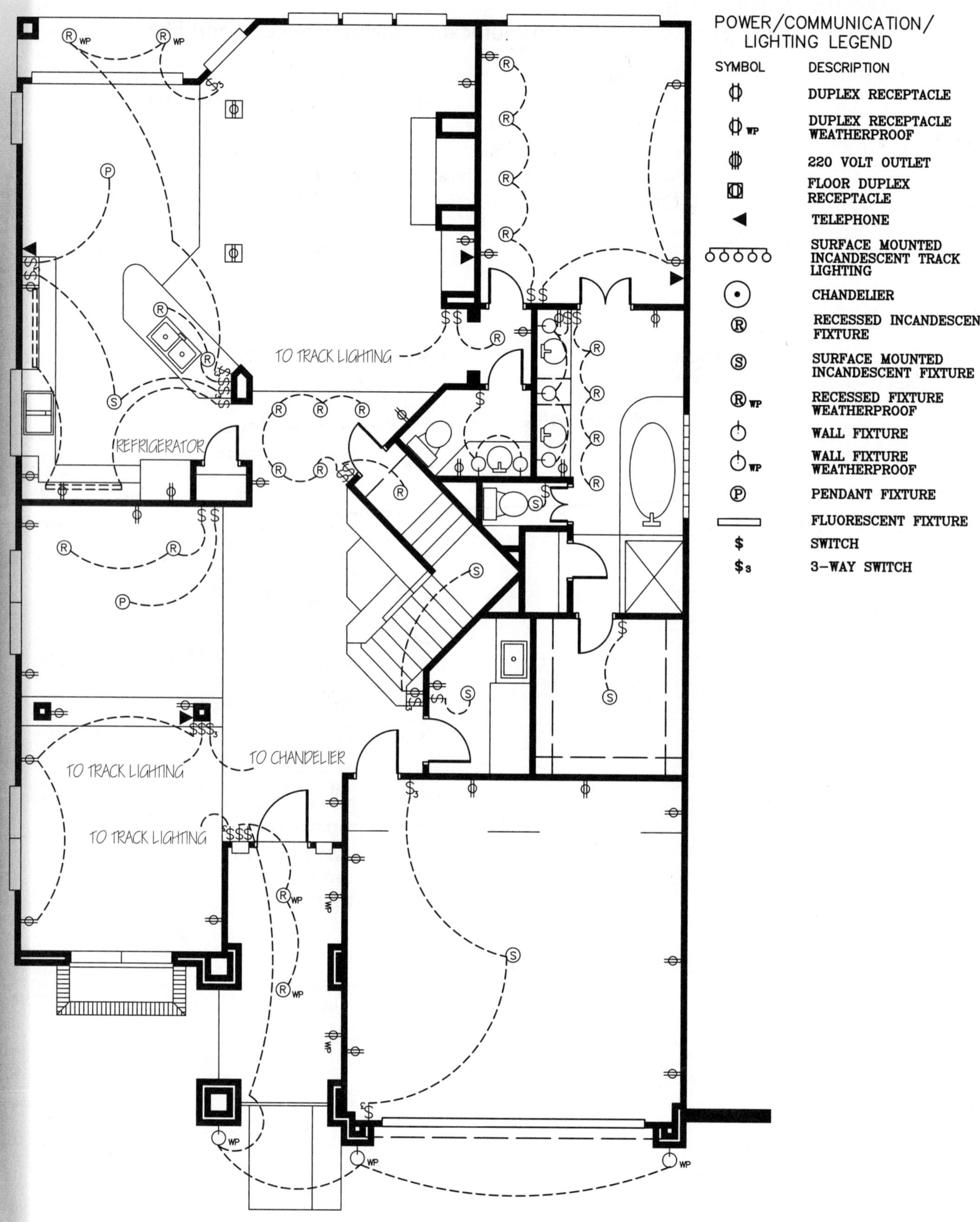

FIGURE 11–16
Sheet 1 of 2, Exercise 11–6: House Power/Communication/Lighting Plan (Scale: 1/8″ = 1′-0″) (Courtesy of John Brooks, AIA, Dallas, Texas)

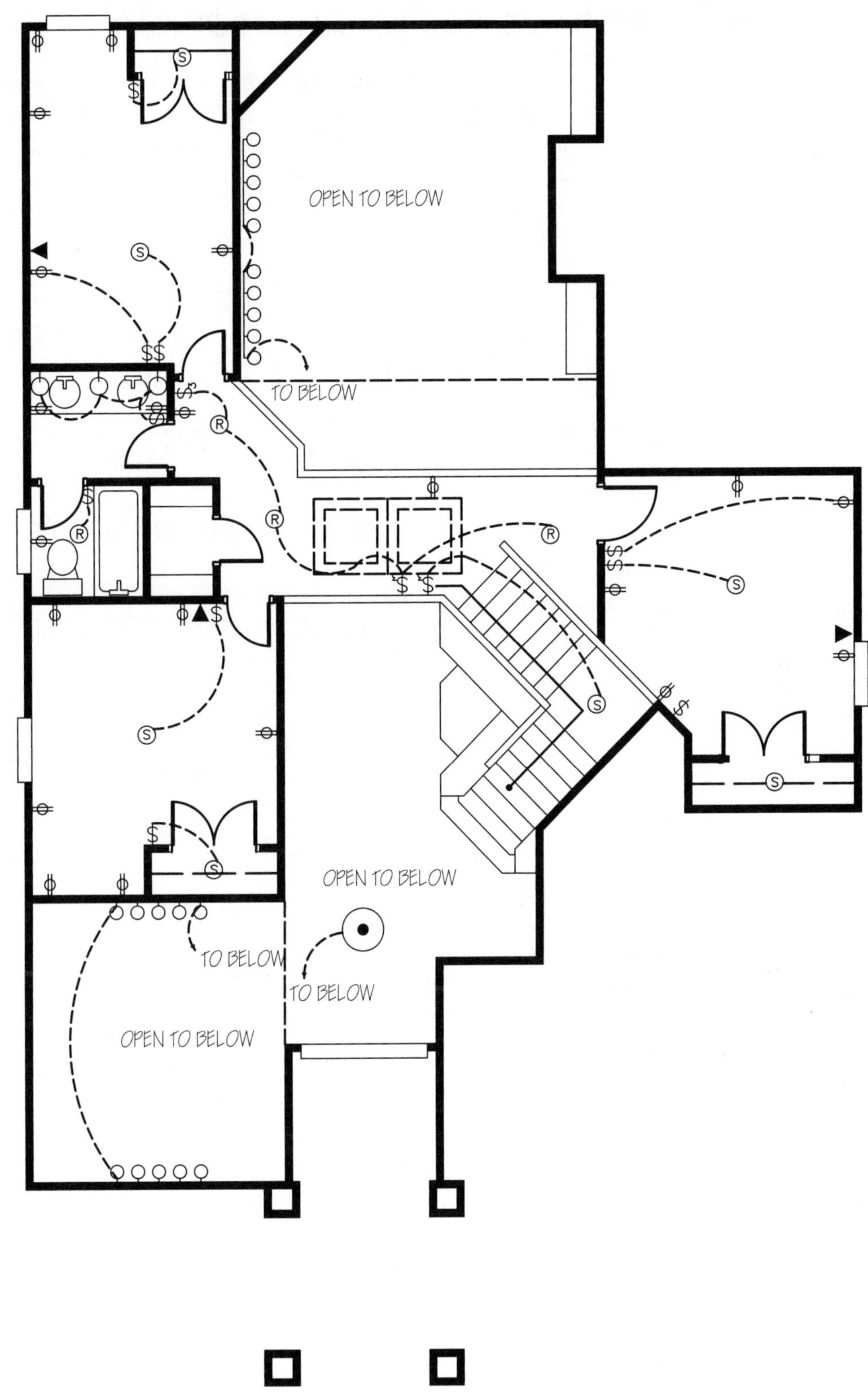

FIGURE 11–16
Sheet 2 of 2, Exercise 11–6: House Power/Communication/Lighting Plan (Scale: 1/8″ = 1′-0″) (Courtesy of John Brooks, AIA, Dallas, Texas)

Exercise 11–7: Bank Lighting Legend and Reflected Ceiling Plan

1. Draw the bank lighting symbols as shown in Figure 11–17. Do not redraw any symbols you have already drawn and Wblocked to a folder. Use an architectural scale to measure the symbols and draw them full scale.
2. Wblock each symbol to the appropriate folder.
3. Complete the bank reflected ceiling plan as shown in Figure 11–18.
4. Plot or print the drawing to scale.

LIGHTING LEGEND

SYMBOL	DESCRIPTION
▭	2 X 4 FLUORESCENT LIGHT
⌖	WALL MOUNTED LIGHT FIXTURE
(R)	RECESSED LIGHT FIXTURE
(EX)	EXHAUST FAN
$	SWITCH
$3	3–WAY SWITCH

FIGURE 11–17
Exercise 11–7: Bank Lighting Legend (Scale: 1/4″ = 1′-0″)

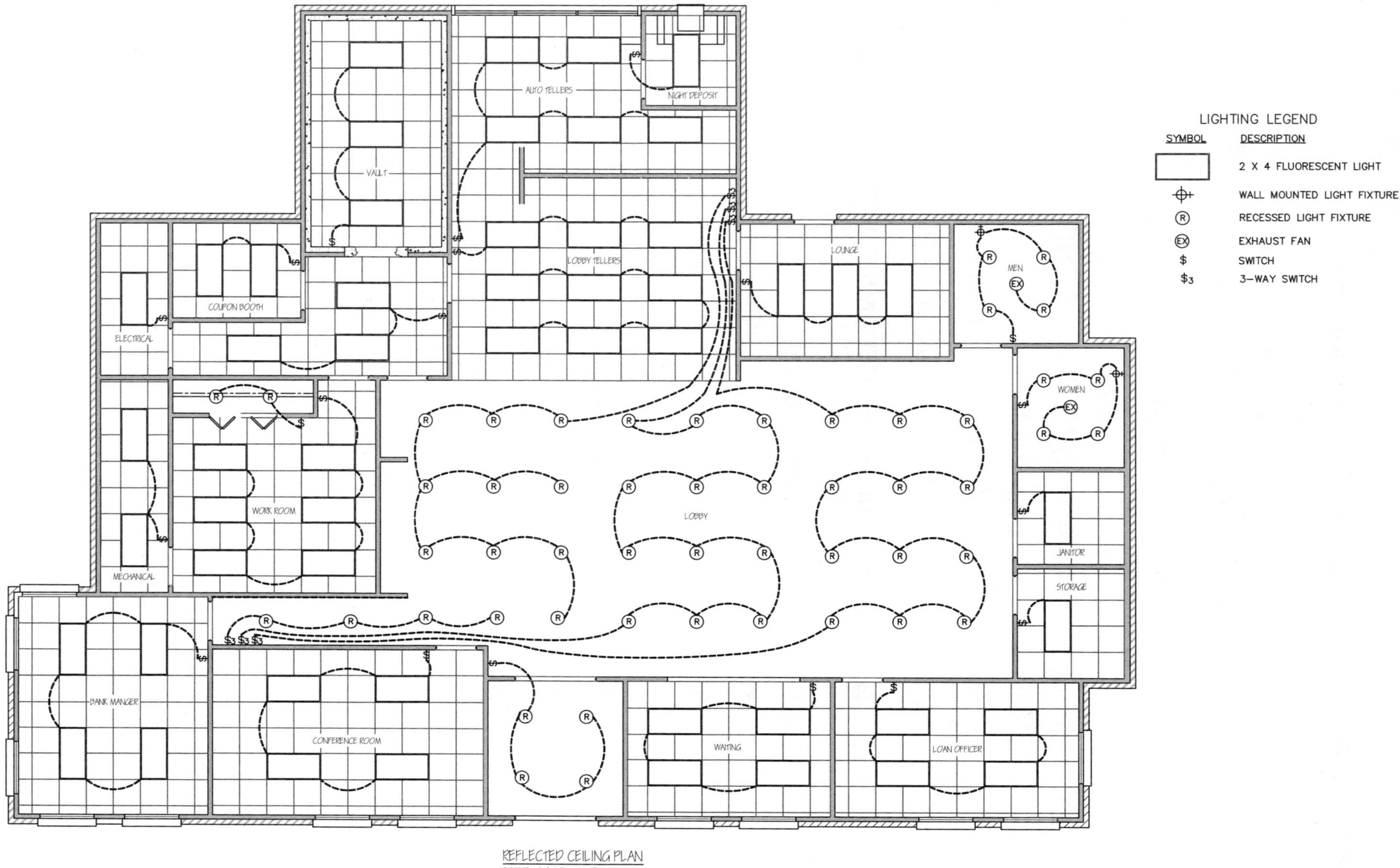

FIGURE 11–18
Exercise 11–7: Bank Reflected Ceiling Plan (Scale: 3/32″ = 1′-0″)

Exercise 11–8: Bank Voice/Data/Power Legend and Plan

1. Draw the bank voice/data/power symbols as shown in Figure 11–19. Do not redraw any symbols you have already drawn and Wblocked to a folder. Use an architectural scale to measure the symbols and draw them full scale.
2. Wblock each symbol to the appropriate folder.
3. Complete the bank voice/data/power plan as shown in Figure 11–20.
4. Plot or print the drawing to scale.

VOICE/DATA/POWER LEGEND

SYMBOL	DESCRIPTION
⊖=	DUPLEX RECEPTACLE
⊖	DUPLEX FLOOR RECEPTACLE
⊖= GFIC	DUPLEX RECEPTACLE WITH GROUND FAULT INTERRUPTER CIRCUIT
R ⊖≡	RANGE OUTLET
◀	TELEPHONE OUTLET
◀ (in circle)	FLOOR TELEPHONE OUTLET
◁	DATA OUTLET
◁ (in circle)	FLOOR DATA OUTLET
⊙	FLOOR JUNCTION BOX
Ⓙ+	WALL JUNCTION BOX

FIGURE 11–19
Exercise 11–8: Bank Voice/Data/Power Legend (Scale: 1/4″ = 1′-0″)

VOICE/DATA/POWER LEGEND

SYMBOL	DESCRIPTION
⊖	DUPLEX RECEPTACLE
⊕	DUPLEX FLOOR RECEPTACLE
GFIC	DUPLEX RECEPTACLE WITH GROUND FAULT INTERRUPTER CIRCUIT
R	RANGE OUTLET
◀	TELEPHONE OUTLET
	FLOOR TELEPHONE OUTLET
◁	DATA OUTLET
	FLOOR DATA OUTLET
⊙	FLOOR JUNCTION BOX
Ⓙ+	WALL JUNCTION BOX

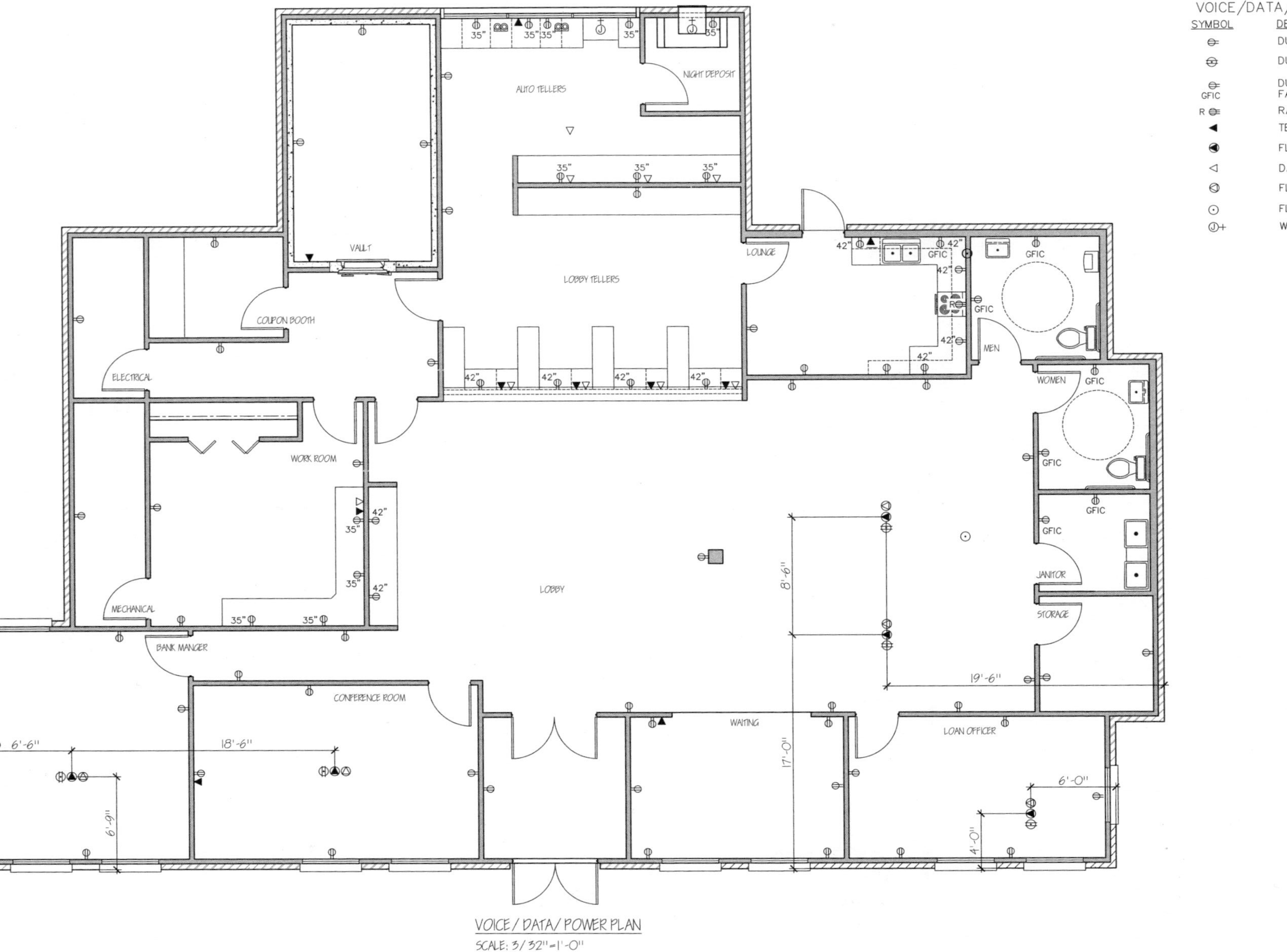

FIGURE 11–20
Exercise 11–8: Bank Voice/Data/Power Plan (Scale: 3/32″ = 1′-0″)

chapter 12

Creating Presentations with Layouts and Sheet Sets

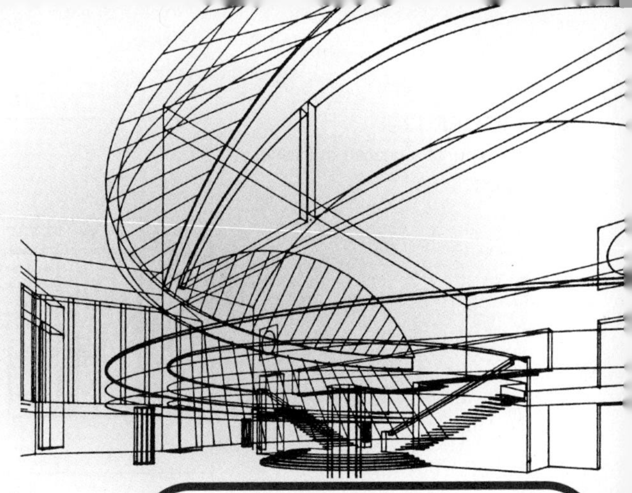

objectives

When you have completed this chapter, you will be able to:

Correctly use the following commands and settings:

Create Layout Wizard
eTransmit...
Layer Properties Manager
Model Space
MVIEW
MVSETUP
Paper Space
Quick View
Redraw
RedrawAll
Regen
RegenAll
Sheet Set
Tilemode
Viewports (VPORTS)

MODEL SPACE AND PAPER SPACE

Model space is the 2D environment in which you have been working to this point. While in model space, you can use the Viewports command to divide the display screen into multiple viewports, as shown in Figure 12–1. Model space is limited in that, although several viewports may be visible on the display screen, only one viewport can be active on the display screen at a time, and only one viewport can be plotted. Model space is where your 2D or 3D model (drawing) is created and modified. When you start a new drawing, you are in model space. When the Model tab is clicked, you are in model space.

Paper space shows a piece of paper on which you can arrange a single plan (viewport) or as many plans or views (viewports) as you need. The MVIEW command is used to create and control a viewport display. Each viewport can be copied, stretched, erased, moved, or scaled, as shown in Figure 12–2. You cannot edit the drawing within the viewport while it is in paper space; however, you can draw something over the viewport—for example, you can add labels to a drawing. You can even overlap a viewport over

FIGURE 12–1
Viewports Created in Model Space

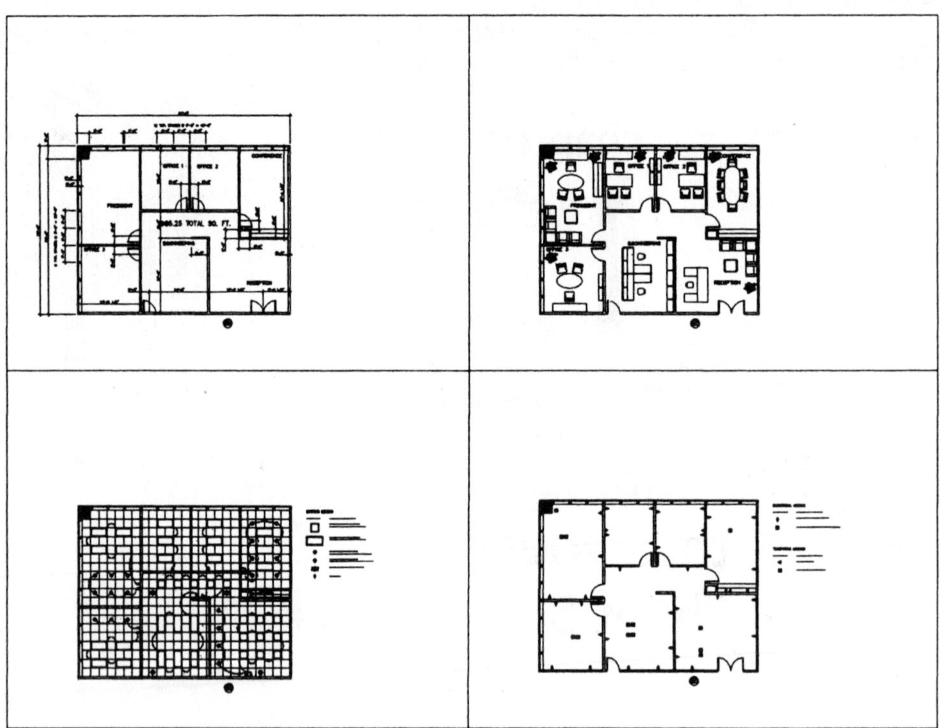

FIGURE 12–2
Viewports Moved and Overlapping in Paper Space

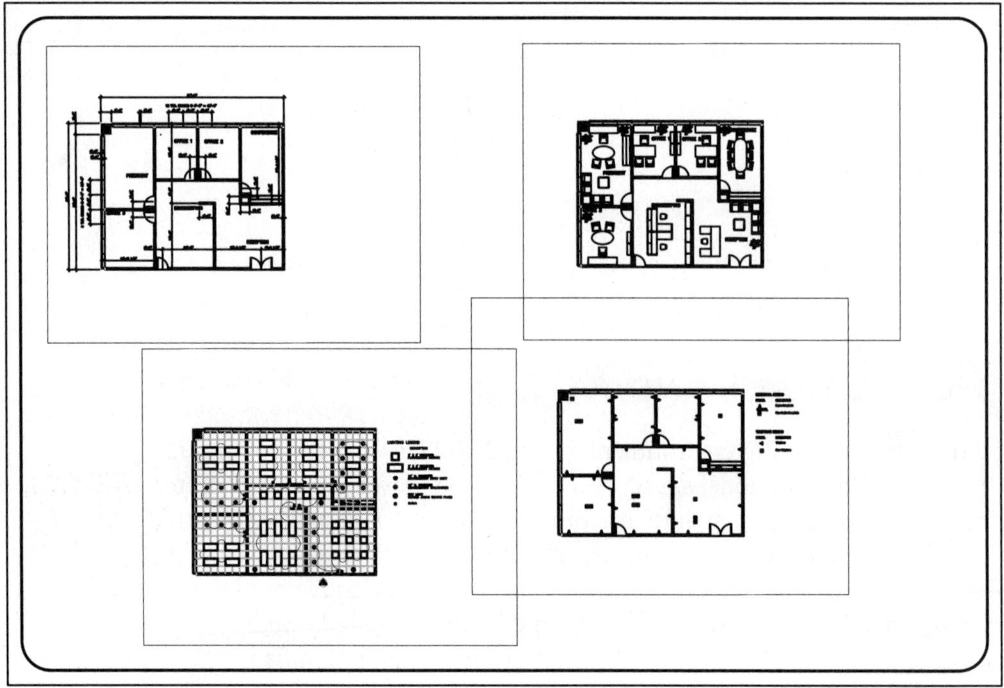

one or more of the other viewports. You can also place the viewports into a single architectural format sheet, and you can plot all the viewports at the same time. When you click any of the Layout tabs, your drawing is in paper space.

Tutorial 12–1: Creating a Printed Presentation of the Tenant Space Project by Combining Multiple Plans on One Sheet of Paper

When you have completed Tutorial 12–1, your drawing will look similar to Figure 12–3.

FIGURE 12–3
Tutorial 12–1: A Presentation of the Tenant Space Plans on One Sheet of Paper

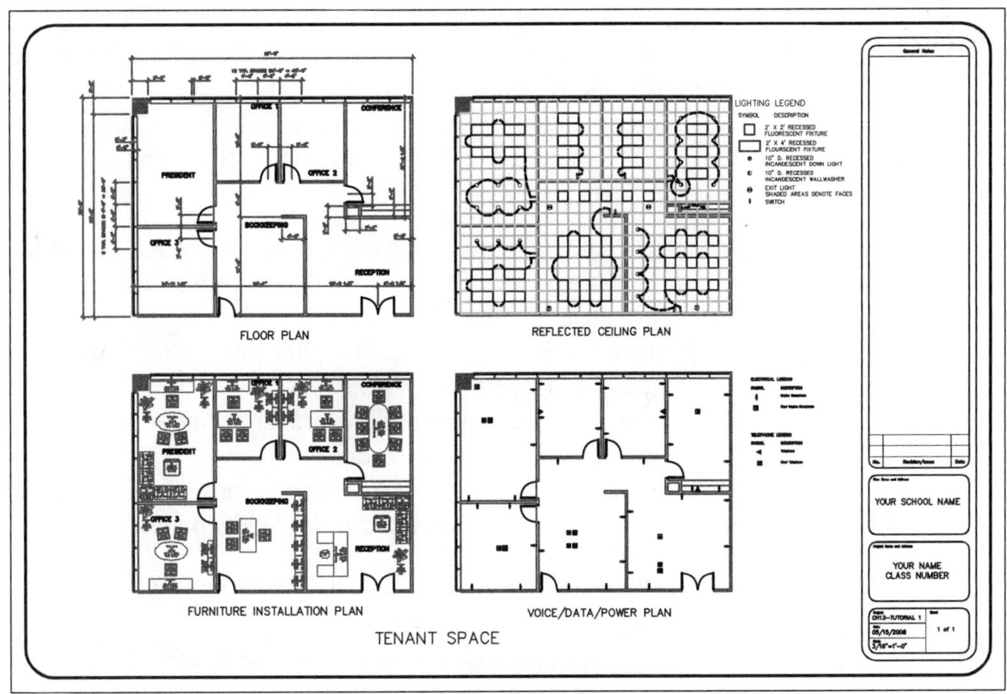

Step 1. **Open existing drawing CH11-TUTORIAL1-VOICE-DATA-POWER; erase the title text, the scale, your name, class, and date; and save it as CH12-TUTORIAL1.**

Step 2. **Use Zoom-All to view the limits of the drawing.**

VIEWPORTS (VPORTS)

Begin by dividing the screen into four viewports. Remember that while it is in model space the model (drawing) is the same in each viewport. If you edit the model in any one viewport, you are doing it in all viewports. You may, however, freeze different layers in each viewport, which you will do later in this tutorial; display a different UCS in each viewport; and zoom in or out in a viewport without affecting other viewport magnification.

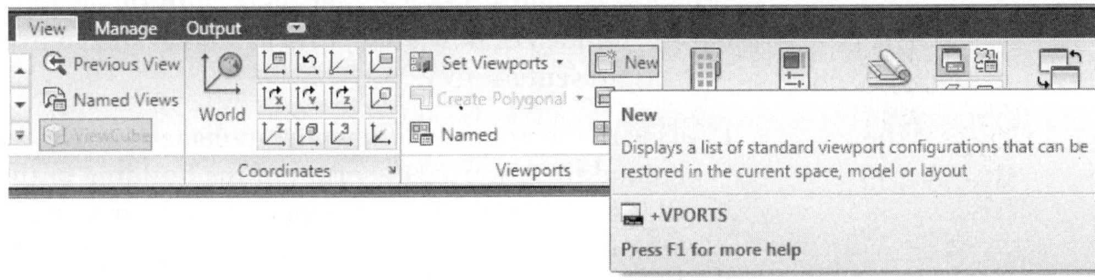

Step 3. **Divide the screen into four viewports, as described next:**

Prompt	Response
Command:	**New** (or TYPE: **VPORTS<enter>**)
The Viewports dialog box appears:	CLICK: **Four: Equal** (on the New Viewports tab) CLICK: **OK** (The screen is divided into four viewports.)

The screen is now divided into four viewports. The active viewport, outlined with a solid line, displays the lines of the cursor when the cursor is moved into it. Inactive viewports display an arrow when the cursor is moved into those areas. To make a different viewport active, position the arrow in the desired viewport and press CLICK:. When you TYPE: **-VPORTS<enter>**, the options of the viewports command are:

Save Allows you to name a set of viewports and save it for future use. Restore recalls the saved viewports. Any number of sets of viewports may be named, saved, and recalled.

Restore Restores a saved set of viewports. AutoCAD prompts you for the name of the saved viewport.

Delete Deletes a named viewport set. AutoCAD prompts you for the name of the saved viewport set to be deleted.

Join Joins two viewports into a larger one. The resulting view is the dominant viewport. AutoCAD prompts for the following when Join is picked:

Prompt	Response
Select dominant viewport <current viewport>:	**<enter>** (to accept the current active viewport, or click the one you want)
Select viewport to join:	CLICK: **the other viewport**

Single Returns the display to a Single viewport. The resulting view is the current active viewport before single was selected.

? Lists the identification numbers and the screen positions of the current arrangement of viewports and all previously saved viewports by name if you accept the default **<*>** when AutoCAD prompts you for the viewport configuration to list.

2,3,4 Divides the current viewport into two, three, or four viewports with the same view, snap, grid, and layer settings. Selections 2 and 3 also allow you to select a vertical or horizontal arrangement. Selection 3 allows for two smaller viewports to the left or right of one larger one. You can divide the screen into as many as 64 viewports depending on your display.

Step 4. See Figure 12–4. Experiment with the viewports so that you can get an idea of how viewports can be useful in drawing as well as in presentation:

1. CLICK: **the upper left viewport to make it active, and Zoom a window around the lower right corner of the building in the upper left viewport.**
2. CLICK: **the upper right viewport to make it active, and Zoom a window around the upper left corner of the building in the upper right viewport.**
3. **Draw a line from the lower right corner of the building to the upper left corner.** CLICK: **the upper left viewport to make it active, start the Line command in the upper left viewport, and then** CLICK: **the upper right viewport to make it active, ending the line in the upper right viewport.** (Be sure Ortho is OFF.)
4. **Erase the line and Zoom-All in each viewport to return all displays to their original magnification.**
5. **Use Redraw in the View menu on the Menu Bar to refresh the display in all viewports at the same time.**

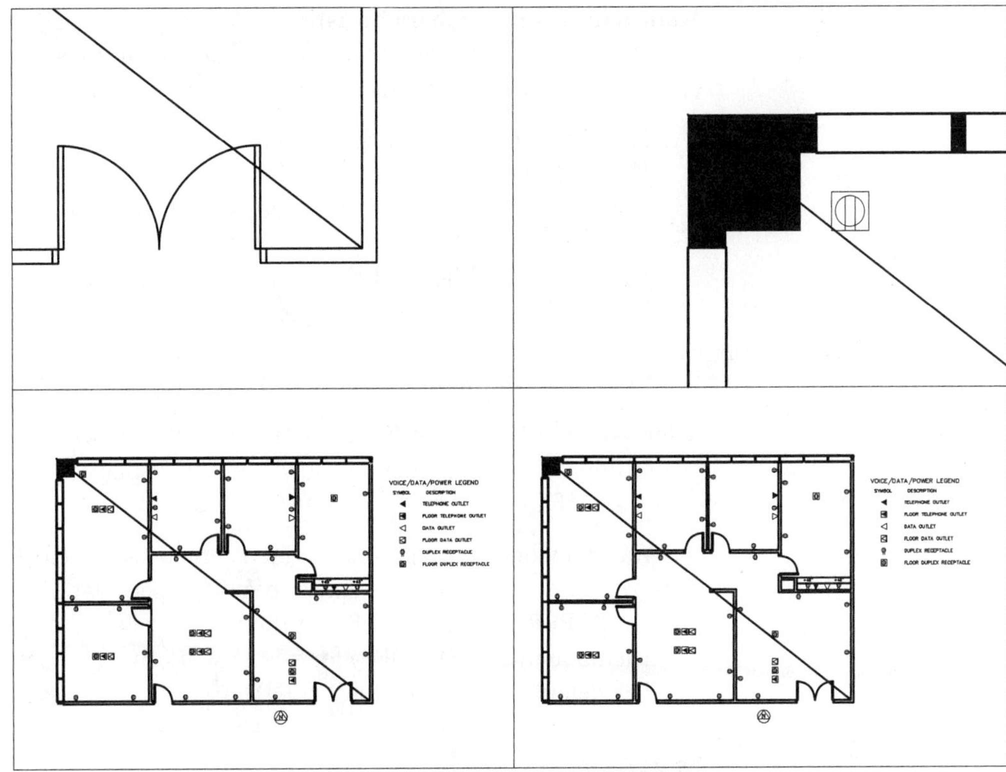

FIGURE 12–4
Start a Command in One Viewport and End It in Another

REDRAW, REDRAWALL, REGEN, AND REGENALL

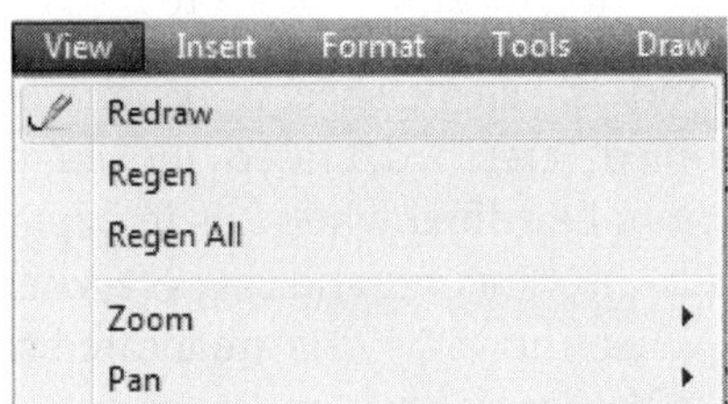

The Redraw and Regen commands redraw or regenerate the drawing in the current viewport only. The RedrawAll and RegenAll commands redraw or regenerate the drawing in all viewports at the same time. When you TYPE: **R<enter>**, you activate Redraw. When you CLICK: **Redraw** on the View menu, you activate RedrawAll.

TILEMODE

Two types of viewports, tiled and nontiled, are available to you in AutoCAD.

Tiled Viewport Characteristics (When you CLICK: **the Model tab**, Tilemode is ON.) Tiled viewports are those that exist in model space with Tilemode ON. They have the following characteristics:

They fill the graphics screen, lie side-by-side like ceramic tiles, and cannot be moved.
They are fixed and cannot overlap.
They can be deleted only by changing the viewport configuration.
Only one tiled viewport can be active at a time.
Only the active viewport can be plotted.
Nothing drawn in a tiled viewport can be edited in a nontiled viewport.

Nontiled Viewport Characteristics (When you CLICK: **a Layout tab**, Tilemode is OFF.) Nontiled viewports are those that exist in paper space or model space. They have the following characteristics:

They may or may not fill the graphics screen.
They can overlap.
They can be moved, copied, scaled, stretched, or erased while they are in paper space.
They can have different layers frozen in any viewport.
All nontiled viewports can be plotted at the same time when they are in paper space.
Nothing drawn in paper space can be edited in model space.

Tilemode Settings Settings for Tilemode are 1 (ON) and 0 (OFF). The Tilemode setting determines whether the viewports displayed are tiled (1—ON) or nontiled (0—OFF).

You can work in model space with Tilemode set to either 1 (ON) or 0 (OFF). You can move from paper space to model space with Tilemode OFF by clicking **PAPER** on the Status Bar at the bottom of your display or typing **MS<enter>**.
Tilemode must be 0 (OFF) for you to work in paper space.
The default for Tilemode is 1 (ON).

MVIEW

The MVIEW command operates only when Tilemode is set to 0 (OFF) and is used to create and control viewport display in model space and paper space. When you TYPE: **MV<enter>**, the Tilemode setting must first be set to 0 (OFF). The MVIEW options are:

OFF Think of each viewport as a single sheet of paper lying on a much larger sheet. The viewport can be copied, stretched, erased, moved, or scaled. The drawing within the viewport cannot be edited while it is in paper space. The OFF option turns off the views inside the viewport and saves regeneration time while you are editing the viewports. When the viewports are located so that you are pleased with the format, you can turn the views back on.
ON Turns ON the model space view (drawing inside the viewport).
Shadeplot Allows you to choose from four options: Wireframe, As displayed, Hidden, and Rendered. These options are discussed in the 3D chapters.
Lock Allows you to lock the scale of a viewport so it does not change when you zoom in or out.
Object Allows you to create a new viewport by selecting an existing object such as a circle.
Polygonal Allows you to draw an irregular-shaped viewport using polyline lines and arcs.
Fit Creates a single viewport to fill current paper space limits. Other viewports can be erased before or after the Fit option is used.
LAyer Allows you to remove viewport property overrides (such as VPLAYER settings described in the tutorials in this chapter).
2,3,4 Creates two, three, or four viewports in a specified area or to fit the current paper space limits.
Restore Restores saved model space viewports (saved with the Viewports [VPORTS] command) into paper space.
Specify Corner of Viewport Creates a new viewport defined by picking two corners or by typing the X and Y coordinates of the lower left and upper right corners.

CREATE LAYOUT WIZARD

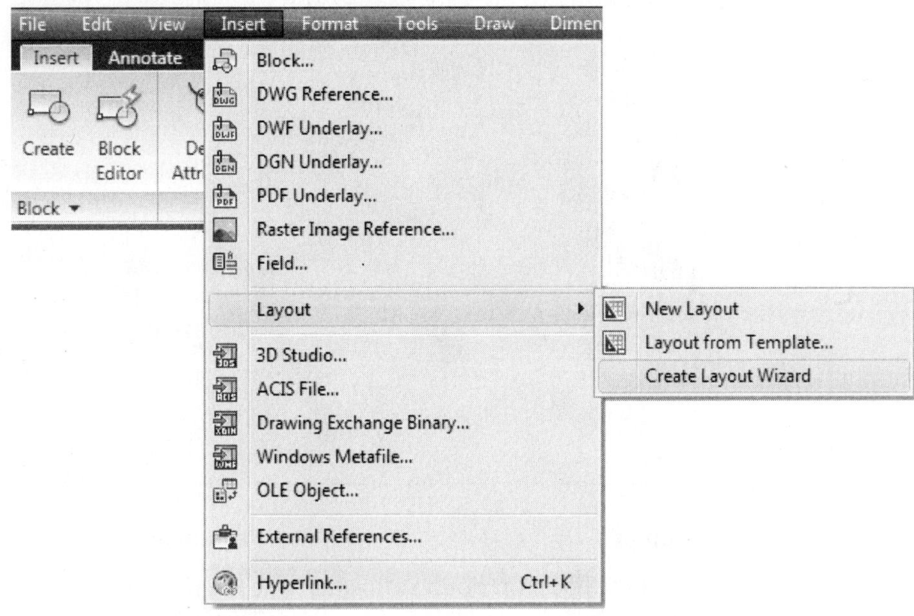

Step 5. Use the Layout Wizard to save the current viewport configuration in model space and restore it in paper space in an architectural format measuring 24″ × 36″ with all viewports at a scale of 3/16″ = 1′, as described next.

Prompt	Response
Command:	**Set the 0 Layer Current.**
Command:	CLICK: **Create Layout Wizard** (from the Insert-Layout menu)
The Create Layout Wizard appears with the name Layout3:	CLICK: **Next**
The Printer option appears:	CLICK: **DWF6 ePlot.pc3** (or a plotter that plots ARCH D size [24.00 × 36.00 inches])
	CLICK: **Next**
The Paper Size option appears:	LOCATE: **ARCH D (24.00 × 36.00 inches) in the paper size list and** CLICK: **on it**
	CLICK: **Next**
The Orientation option appears:	CLICK: **Landscape**
	CLICK: **Next**
The Title Block option appears:	CLICK: **Architectural Title Block.dwg**
	CLICK: **Next**
The Define Viewports option appears:	CLICK: **Array in the Viewport setup list** (Figure 12–5)
	CLICK: **3/16″ = 1′-0″ in the Viewport scale: input box**
	TYPE: **2 in the Rows: input box**
	TYPE: **2 in the Columns: input box**
	TYPE: **0 in the Spacing between rows: input box**
	TYPE: **0 in the Spacing between columns: input box**
	CLICK: **Next**

FIGURE 12–5
Defining Viewports in the Layout Wizard

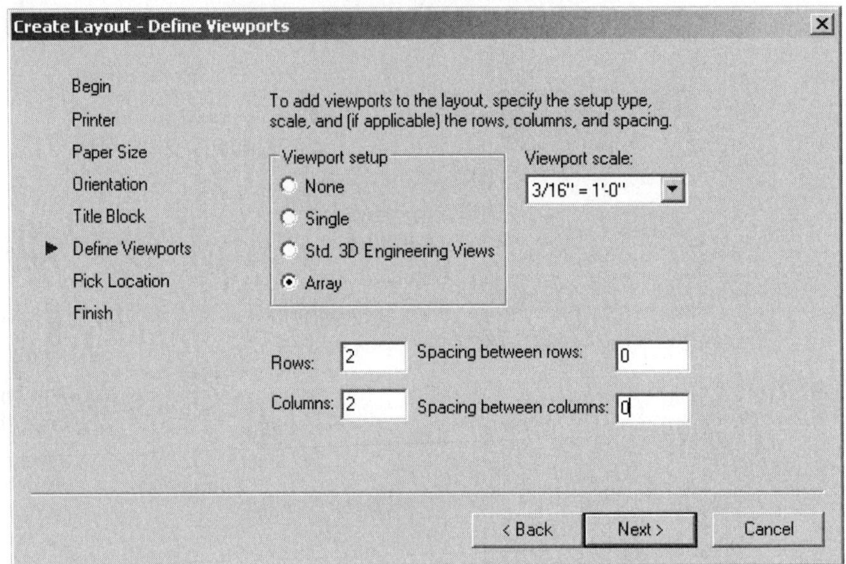

Prompt	Response
The Pick Location option appears:	CLICK: **Select location:**
Specify first corner:	TYPE: **2,2<enter>**
Specify opposite corner:	TYPE: **28,22<enter>**
The Finish option appears:	CLICK: **Finish**
Command:	TYPE: **PS<enter>** or CLICK: **MODEL** on the Status Bar if you are not already in paper space (if **MODEL** is not visible, RIGHT-CLICK: on a blank space in the Status Bar and CLICK: **Paper/Model**.)

NOTE: The UCS icon appears as a triangle in paper space.

Step 6. **Complete the title block as shown in Figure 12–6:**

Use the Single Line Text (TYPE: **DT<enter>**) **command for the following:**

YOUR NAME (3/16″ High, simplex font, center justification)
YOUR COURSE NUMBER (3/16″ High, simplex font, center justification)
YOUR SCHOOL NAME (3/16″ High, simplex font, center justification)

Assign a variable attribute (TYPE: **ATT<enter> center justification—1/8″ high) as follows:**

Tag	Prompt	Default Value
PLAN-NAME	Type the plan name	PRESENTATION

Assign variable attributes (left justification—1/8″ high) as follows:

Tag	Prompt	Default Value
TUTORIAL	Type the tutorial number.	CHX-TUTORIALX
DATE	Type today's date.	09/15/2009

FIGURE 12–6
Use Single Line Text for Your Name, Course Number, and School Name. Assign Variable Attributes for Plan-Name, Tutorial, Date, Scale, and Sheet

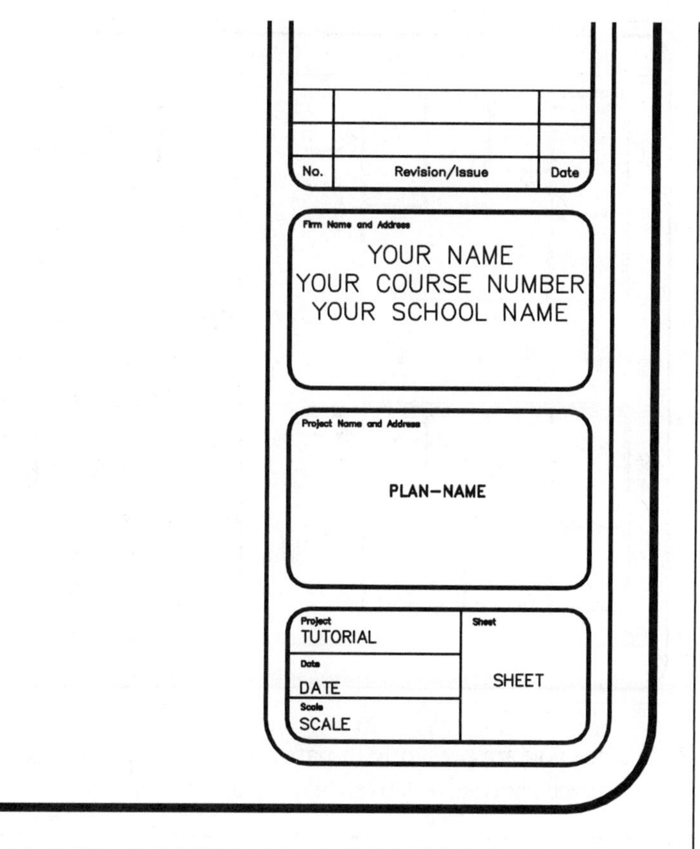

Tag	Prompt	Default Value
SCALE	Type the scale.	3/16″ = 1′-0″
SHEET	Type Sheet of Sheet.	1 of 1

Step 7. Wblock the border and title block (be sure you do not include the viewports in the wblock). CLICK: the lower left corner of the border as the Base point. Name the wblock, ARCH D FORMAT. Check the radio button in Delete from drawing so the format disappears.

Step 8. Insert the ARCH D FORMAT drawing (not the Architectural Title Block drawing) into the drawing around the paper space viewports (Figure 12–7). Change the attribute values as needed:

Tag	Prompt	New Value
PLAN-NAME	Type the plan name.	PRESENTATION
TUTORIAL	Type the tutorial number.	CH12-TUTORIAL1
DATE	Type today's date.	Today's date
SCALE	Type the scale.	3/16″ = 1′-0″
SHEET	Type Sheet of Sheet.	1 of 1

WORKING IN MODEL SPACE WITH PAPER SPACE VIEWPORTS VISIBLE

The MS (Model Space) command (with Tilemode OFF) switches you from paper space to model space with paper space viewports visible. You may work in model space with Tilemode either ON or OFF.

FIGURE 12–7
Insert the ARCH D Format Drawing Around the Paper Space Viewports

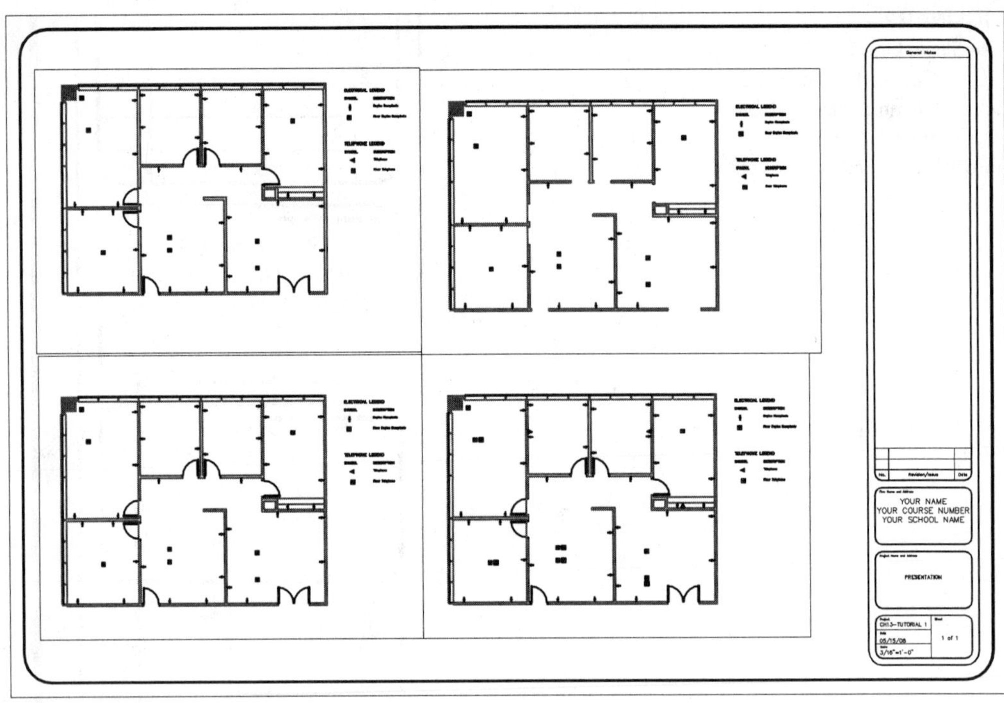

Since you are presently in paper space, you know that Tilemode is 0 (OFF) because paper space cannot be active unless Tilemode is 0.

Step 9. Return to model space with Tilemode set to 0, as described next:

Prompt	Response
Command:	TYPE: **MS<enter>** (or CLICK: **PAPER** on the Status Bar)

Step 10. CLICK: **each model space viewport and Zoom-All so that all viewports show the entire drawing.**

Step 11. Use the Layer Properties Manager to thaw all frozen layers and to turn all layers on. When all layers are thawed and turned on, they will all be visible in all viewports, and you will be able to create a unique drawing in each viewport by turning individual layers off.

Step 12. Use the Layer Properties Manager to freeze layers in the upper left viewport so only the dimensioned floor plan is visible (Figures 12–8 and 12–9), as described next:

Prompt	Response
Command:	CLICK: **The upper left viewport to make it active**
Command:	TYPE: **LA<enter>**
The Layer Properties Manager appears:	In the VP Freeze column, CLICK: **the Freeze/Thaw symbol to freeze all layers not used to view the dimensioned floor plan in the upper left viewport:** **a-anno-area** **a-clng-grid** **e-lite**

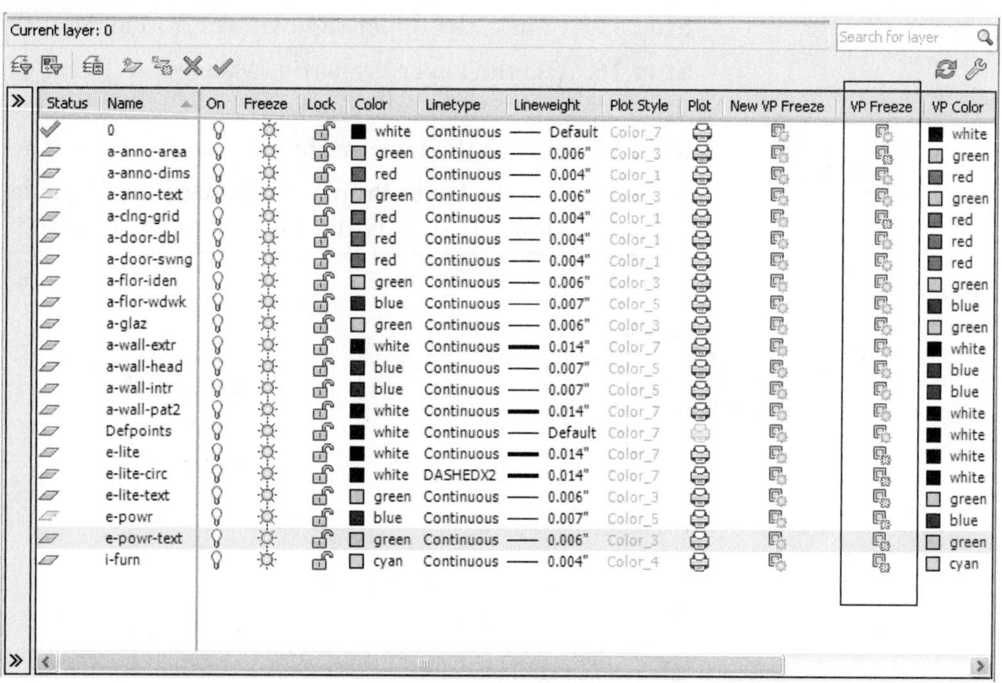

FIGURE 12–8
Frozen Layers in the Upper Left Viewport

Prompt	Response
	e-lite-circ
	e-lite-text
	e-powr
	e-powr-text
	i-furn

Step 13. CLICK: the lower left viewport to make it active.

Step 14. Use the Layer Properties Manager to freeze layers in the lower left viewport so only the furniture installation plan is visible (Figure 12–9).

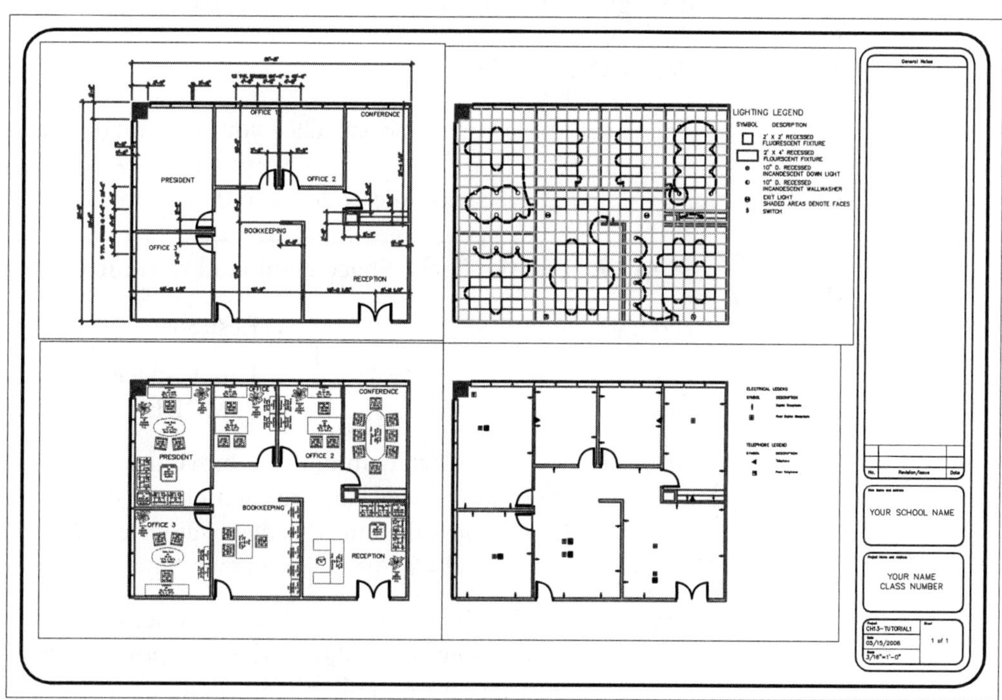

FIGURE 12–9
Position the Paper Space Viewports in the Format and Freeze Different Layers in Each Viewport

Step 15. CLICK: **the upper right viewport to make it active.**

Step 16. **Use the Layer Properties Manager to freeze layers in the upper right viewport so only the Reflected Ceiling Plan is visible (Figure 12–9).**

Step 17. CLICK: **the lower right viewport to make it active.**

Step 18. **Use the Layer Properties Manager to freeze layers in the lower right viewport so only the Voice-Data-Power Plan is visible (Figure 12–9).**

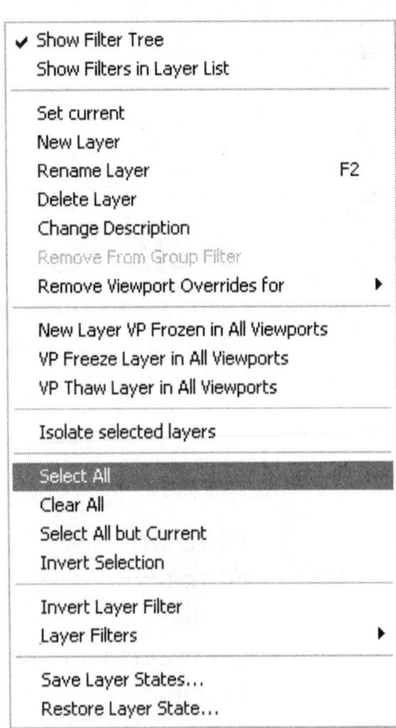

There will be occasions when you will want to select or deselect all layers at the same time. To do that, position the cursor in an open area in the dialog box and PRESS: **the right mouse button**, then CLICK: **Select All** or **Clear All**.

PAPER SPACE

The Paper Space command switches you from model space to paper space. Tilemode must be 0 (OFF) for Paper Space to work. Tilemode is still set to 0. You have been working in model space with Tilemode set to 0.

Step 19. **Use the Paper Space command to return to paper space:**

Prompt	Response
Command:	**Paper Space** (or TYPE: **PS<enter>**) (or CLICK: **MODEL** on the Status Bar—not the Model tab)

Step 20. **Use the Move command to move the viewports so that they are centered in the space approximately, as shown in Figure 12–9**. You will have to pick the outside edge of any viewport to move it, or select all four viewports by using a crossing window.

Step 21. While in paper space, you can also make the viewports larger or smaller. **Pick the outside edge of the viewport and use grips to make the viewport larger or smaller, if needed**.

FIGURE 12–10
Use Properties to Set a Scale of 3/16″ = 1′-0″ for All Viewports

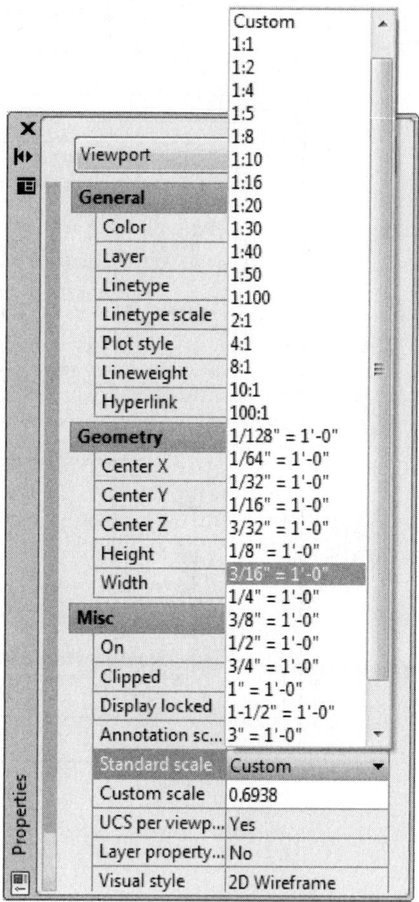

Step 22. CLICK: **the boundary line of all paper space viewports, then** CLICK: **Properties and set a standard scale of 3/16″ = 1′-0″ in all four viewports, as shown in Figure 12–10.**

MVSETUP

Because the viewports have been moved, it is possible that your model space views (of the plans) are not lined up vertically and horizontally. The MVSETUP command can be used to align the views (drawings) within each viewport.

Step 23. **Return to MODEL SPACE.**

Step 24. **Use Pan in model space to center images in each viewport. Do not zoom in or out, while in model space.** If you do zoom in or out while in model space, you will have to reset the scale of the drawing.

Step 25. **Use the MVSETUP command to align the plans in the viewports (Figure 12–11), as described next:**

Prompt	Response
Command:	TYPE: **MVSETUP<enter>**
Enter an option [Align/Create/Scale viewports/Options/Title block/Undo]:	TYPE: **A<enter>**

FIGURE 12–11
Use MVSETUP to Align the Views in Adjacent Viewports

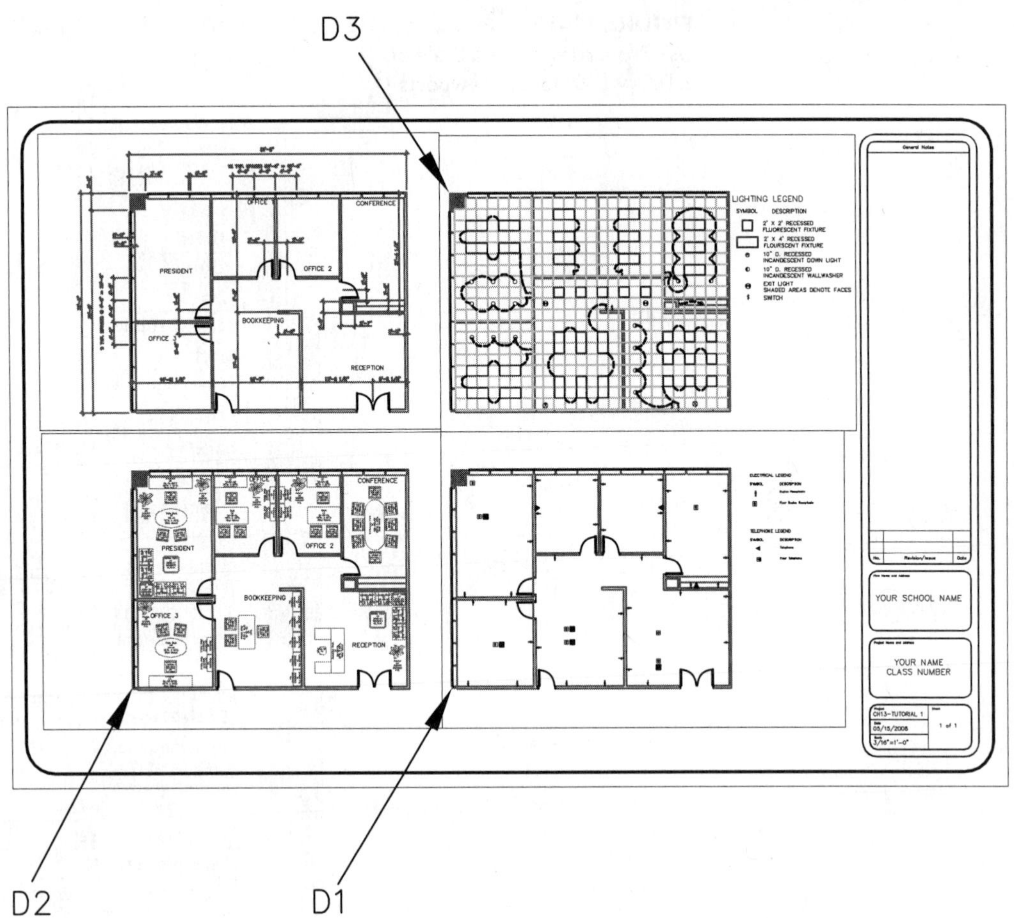

Prompt	Response
Enter an option [Angled/Horizontal/ Vertical alignment/Rotate view/ Undo]:	TYPE: **H<enter>**
Specify basepoint:	CLICK: **the lower right viewport to make it active** **OSNAP-Intersection**
of	**D1** (Figure 12–11)
Specify point in viewport to be panned:	CLICK: **the lower left viewport to make it active** **OSNAP-Intersection**
of	**D2**
Enter an option [Angled/Horizontal/ Vertical alignment/Rotate view/ Undo]:	TYPE: **V<enter>**
Specify basepoint:	**OSNAP-Intersection** CLICK: **the upper right viewport to make it active**
of	**D3**
Specify point in viewport to be panned:	CLICK: **the lower right viewport to make it active**

Prompt	Response
	OSNAP-Intersection
of	D1

Step 26. Align, horizontally and vertically, any remaining model space views that need to be aligned.

A brief description of the MVSETUP options follows:

Tilemode Set to 1 (ON)

When Tilemode is ON, MVSETUP allows you to set Units, Scale, and Paper Size using prompts for each setting.

Tilemode Set to 0 (OFF)

When Tilemode is OFF, MVSETUP has the following options:

Align This option lets you pan the view so that it aligns with a basepoint in another viewport. You may align viewports horizontally and vertically, you may align them at a specified distance and angle from a basepoint in another viewport, and you may rotate the view in a viewport about a basepoint. This option also has an undo feature.

Create This option allows you to delete existing viewports. It also allows you to create one or more standard-size viewports. If more than one is created, this option allows you to specify the distance between viewports. It also allows you to create an array of viewports. This option also has an undo feature.

Scale viewports This option allows you to set the scale of the drawing displayed in the viewports. The Properties command is now used for scaling viewports.

Options This option allows you to specify a layer for the title block, reset paper space limits, change different units, or attach an Xref as the title block.

Title block This option allows you to delete objects from paper space and to select the origin point for this sheet. It then prompts you to select one of 13 standard formats. This option also has an undo feature.

Undo This is an undo option for the major routine.

LABEL THE VIEWS WHILE IN PAPER SPACE

Step 27. Return to PAPER SPACE.

Step 28. Create a new layer named VP. While in paper space, change the outside edges of the four viewports to the VP Layer. Use the layer list to turn the VP Layer OFF. The outside edges of the viewports will no longer be visible and will not print.

Step 29. Label the views using Dtext (single line text) with the STYLE name Label, FONT—simplex, HEIGHT—1/4″, as shown in Figure 12–12. Use the Zoom-Window command to zoom in and out of the drawing as needed.

Step 30. Use the same font, 1/2″ high, to label the entire drawing TENANT SPACE.

Step 31. When you have completed Tutorial 12–1, save your work in at least two places.

Step 32. Plot or print Tutorial 12–1 at a plotting ratio of 1 = 1. You will be plotting on a 36″ × 24″ sheet.

FIGURE 12–12
Tutorial 12–1: Complete

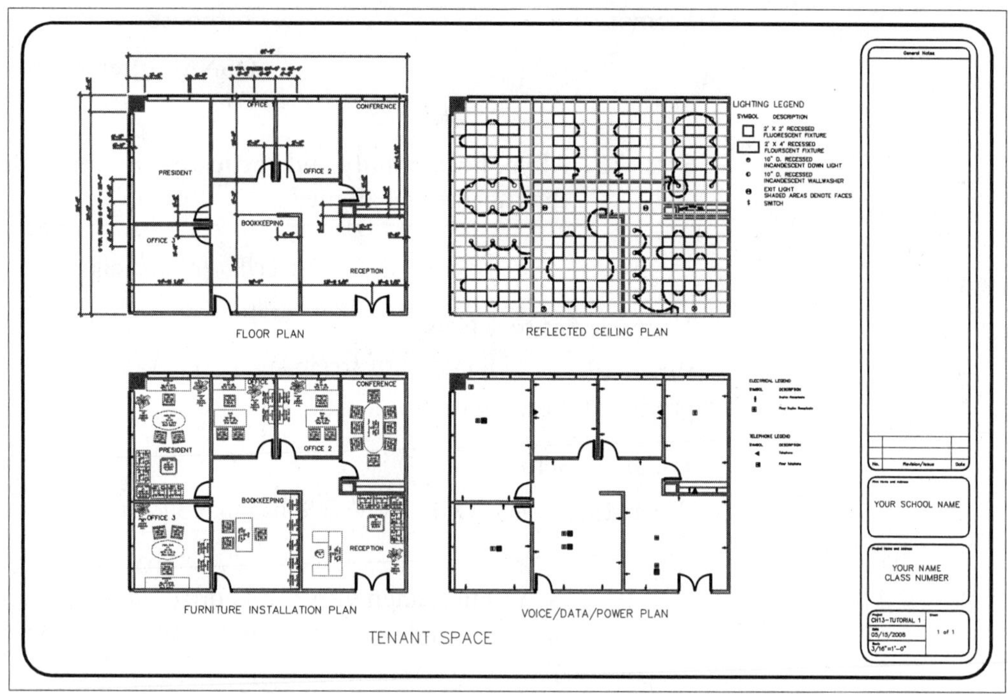

NOTE: You may notice in the preview of your plot that the ARCH D FORMAT border and title block do not fit within the 36″ × 24″ sheet size. You can use the Scale command to scale the border and title block .97 percent (or more if needed). Also, do not include both border lines in your plot. Eliminate the outside rectangular border line. When plotting, window the plot and make a tight window around the border with curved corners to eliminate the rectangular border line in your selection.

Tutorial 12–2: Creating a Four-Sheet Drawing with Different Layers Frozen on Each Sheet

When you have completed Tutorial 12–2, your drawing will contain four sheets and will look similar to Figure 12–13, sheets 1 through 4.

Step 1. Use your workspace to make the following settings:

1. Open drawing CH11-TUTORIAL1-VOICE-DATA-POWER; erase your name, class, date, the title text, and the scale; and save it with the name CH12-TUTORIAL2.
2. Thaw all frozen layers and turn all layers on.

Step 2. Delete any existing layout tabs. CLICK: **the layout tab name,** RIGHT-CLICK: **to get the right-click menu, and** CLICK: **Delete.**

NOTE: You may not be able to delete Layout1 at this time. If not, delete it after you create the layout named Sheet 1.

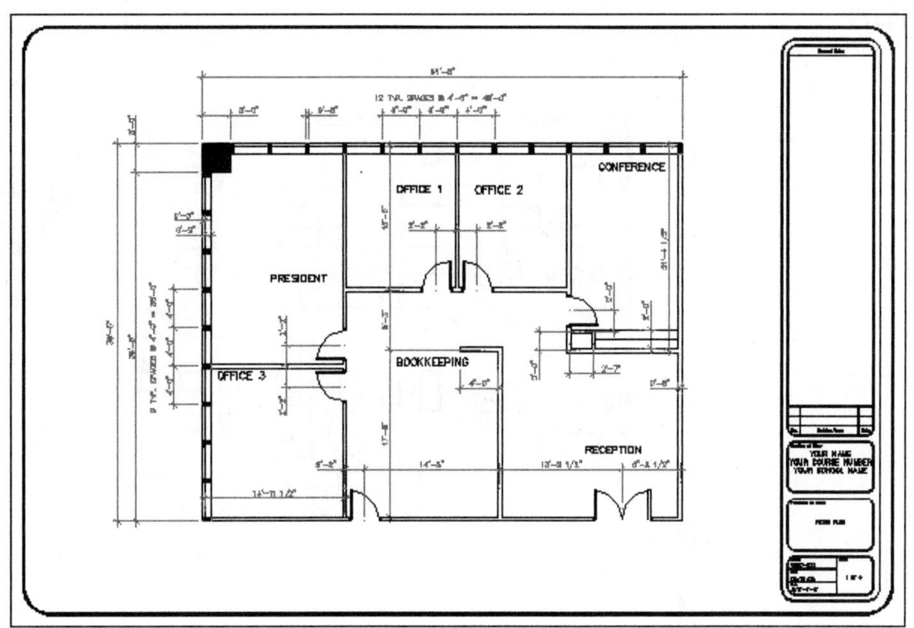

Model | Sheet 1 | Sheet 2 | Sheet 3 | Sheet 4

FIGURE 12–13
Tutorial 12–2 Sheet 1 of 4

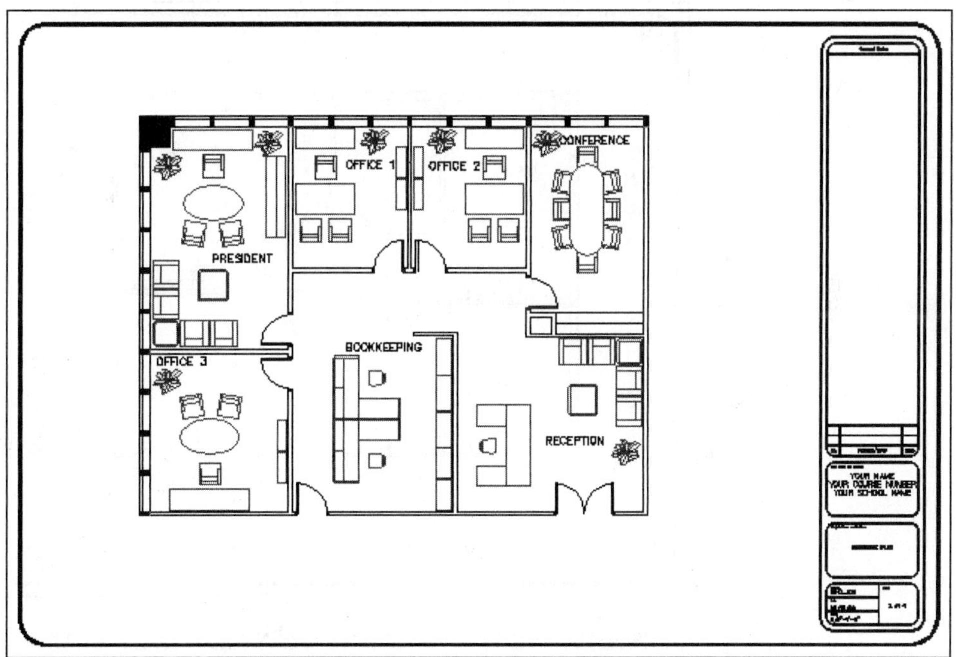

Model | Sheet 1 | Sheet 2 | Sheet 3 | Sheet 4

FIGURE 12–13
Tutorial 12–2 Sheet 2 of 4

Step 3. **Add a new layout named Sheet 1, as described next:**

Prompt	Response
Command:	CLICK: **Create Layout Wizard** (from the Insert-Layout menu)

FIGURE 12–13
Tutorial 12–2 Sheet 3 of 4

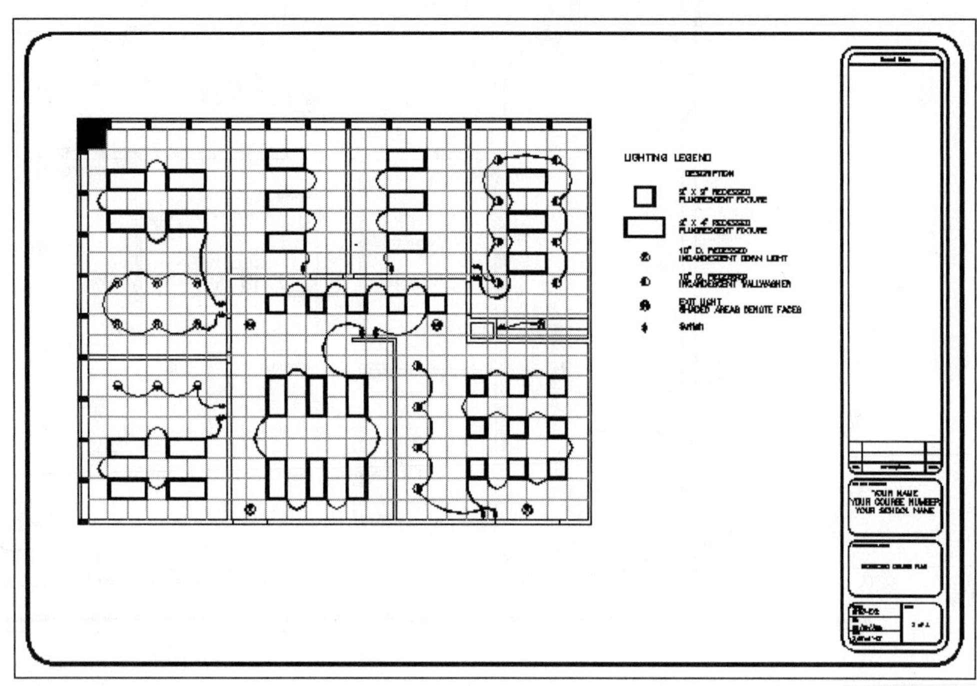

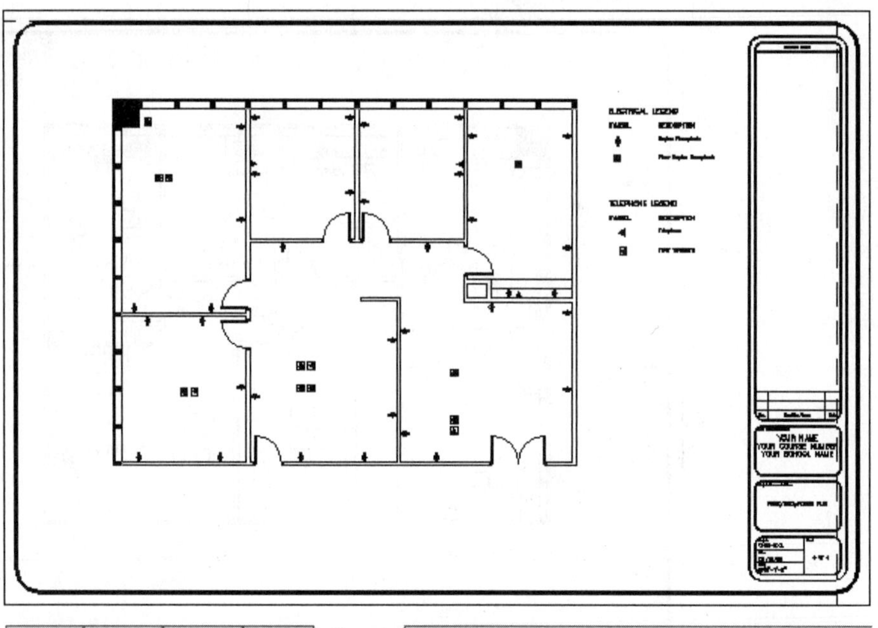

FIGURE 12–13
Tutorial 12–2 Sheet 4 of 4

Prompt	Response
The Create Layout Wizard appears with the name Layout1 (or Layout2 if Layout1 could not be deleted):	TYPE: **Sheet 1** (over the Layout2 text) CLICK: **Next**

Prompt	Response
The Printer option appears:	CLICK: **the appropriate printer configured for your computer** CLICK: **Next**

NOTE: If your printer does not print a 24″ × 36″ sheet, use the DWF6 ePlot.pc3 printer.

The Paper Size option appears:	LOCATE: **ARCH D (24 × 36 inches) in the paper size list and** CLICK: **on it** CLICK: **Next**
The Orientation option appears:	CLICK: **Landscape** CLICK: **Next**
The Title Block option appears:	CLICK: **None** CLICK: **Next**
The Define Viewports option appears:	CLICK: **Single** CLICK: **3/8″ = 1′-0″ in the Viewport scale: input box** CLICK: **Next**
The Pick Location option appears:	CLICK: **Select location<**
Specify first corner:	TYPE: **3,1<enter>**
Specify other corner:	TYPE: **28,22<enter>**
The Finish option appears:	CLICK: **Finish**

Step 4. CLICK: **PAPER to go to model space.**

Step 5. **Use the Layer Properties Manager to freeze the following layers in the VP Freeze column, so only the dimensioned floor plan is visible:**

a-anno-area
a-clng-grid
e-lite
e-lite-circ
e-lite-text
e-powr
e-powr-text
i-furn

Step 6. **Use Pan to center your drawing.**

Step 7. CLICK: **MODEL to return to paper space.**

Step 8. CLICK: **any point on the viewport boundary, select Properties, check to make sure 3/8″ = 1′-0″ scale is selected.**

Step 9. CLICK: **Display locked..., and select Yes to lock this viewport at that scale.**

Step 10. **Make a new layer named VP, place the viewport boundary on that layer, and turn the new layer off.**

Step 11. **Make a new layer named FORMAT, select the color white, and set it current. Insert the ARCH D FORMAT (made in CH12-TUTORIAL1)**

around the paper space viewport (dimensioned floor plan), Figure 12–13, Sheet 1 of 4. Change attributes as needed:

Tag	Prompt	New Value
PLAN-NAME	Type the plan name.	FLOOR PLAN
TUTORIAL	Type the tutorial number.	CH12-TUTORIAL2
DATE	Type today's date.	Today's date
SCALE	Type the scale.	3/8″ = 1′-0″
SHEET	Type Sheet of Sheet.	1 of 4

Step 12. Now is the time to delete Layout1 if you have not done so.

Step 13. Add a new layout named Sheet 2 using the Create Layout Wizard. Use the same settings as you did for Sheet 1.

Step 14. Use the Layer Properties Manager to freeze layers in the VP Freeze column, so only the Furniture Plan is visible.

Step 15. Select a scale of 3/8″ = 1′-0″ and lock the viewport at that scale.

Step 16. Move the viewport boundary line to the VP layer so it is not visible.

Step 17. Insert the ARCH D FORMAT around the FURNITURE PLAN and change the attributes as needed.

Step 18. Complete Steps 13 through 17 to create Sheet 3, REFLECTED CEILING PLAN.

Step 19. Complete Steps 13 through 17 to create Sheet 4, VOICE-DATA-POWER PLAN.

Step 20. Save your drawing in at least two places.

QUICK VIEW

You can use the Quick View tool to preview open drawings and layouts in a drawing.

When you click the Quick View Drawings icon, any drawings you have open are displayed as thumbnail images. When you move your cursor over a thumbnail drawing, all of the layouts and the model tab for that drawing are displayed in a row. You can also click an image to make that drawing become the current drawing.

When you click Quick View Layouts, the model space and and paper space layouts in the current drawing are displayed as thumbnail images (Figure 12–14). If you click an image of a layout, it becomes the current layout. You can also click the Publish or Plot icons on the image to plot or publish each individual layout.

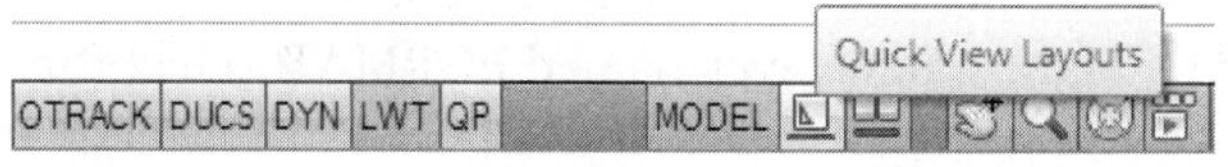

FIGURE 12–14
Quick View Layouts

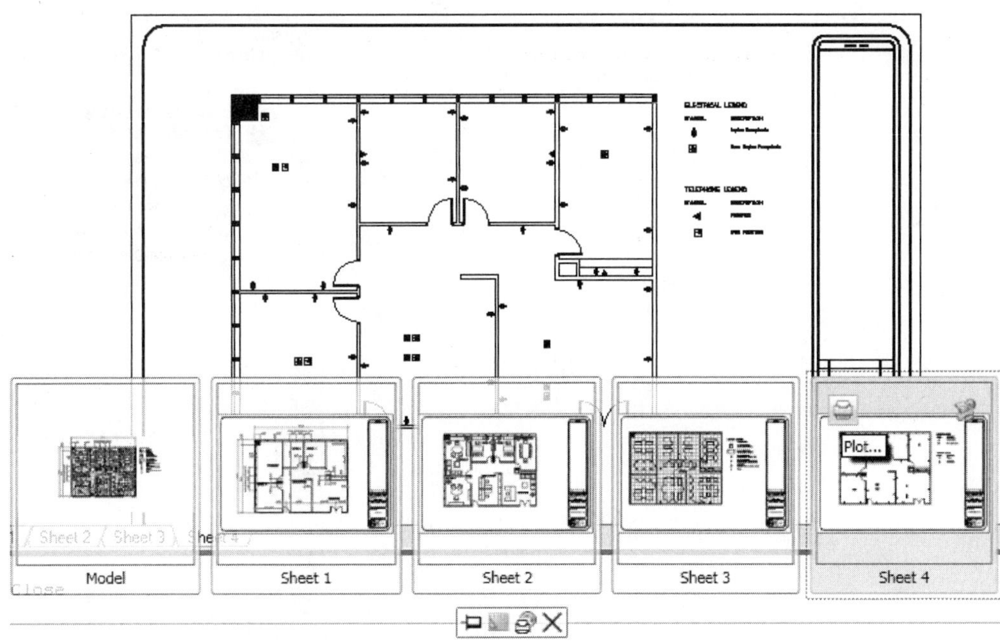

Step 21. CLICK: **Quick View Layout to display the model space layout and all four paper space layouts.**

Step 22. CLICK: **the Plot icon in each of the four Quick View paper space layouts and plot each layout on 24″ × 36″ sheets full scale or plot half-size on 12″ × 18″ sheets.**

Tutorial 12–3: Making a Sheet Set Containing Four Drawing Layouts and a Title Page

The New Sheet Set... command allows you to organize drawing layouts from several drawings into a single set that may easily be transmitted to a client. Any drawing to be used in a sheet set must contain one or more paper space layouts. The layouts are used to make up the sheet set.

In Tutorial 12–3, you will use the drawing made in CH12-TUTORIAL2. You will also make a blank drawing with a layout titled TITLE PAGE. The Sheet Set Manager will automatically create a table that will be inserted into the layout. For simplicity, these two drawings will be placed in a separate folder.

When you have completed Tutorial 12–3, your Sheet Set Manager will look similar to Figure 12–15.

Step 1. **Make a new folder labeled Tenant Space Sheet Set, on the drive where you want to work.**

Step 2. **Open drawing CH12-TUTORIAL2 and save it in the Tenant Space Sheet Set folder.** Be sure to save the drawing instead of copying the drawing so AutoCAD recognizes the completed layout tabs.

Step 3. **Start a new drawing and use your workspace to make the following settings:**

1. **Use Save As... to save the drawing in the folder Tenant Space Sheet Set with the name TITLE PAGE.**

FIGURE 12–15
Sheet Set Manager for Tutorial 12–3

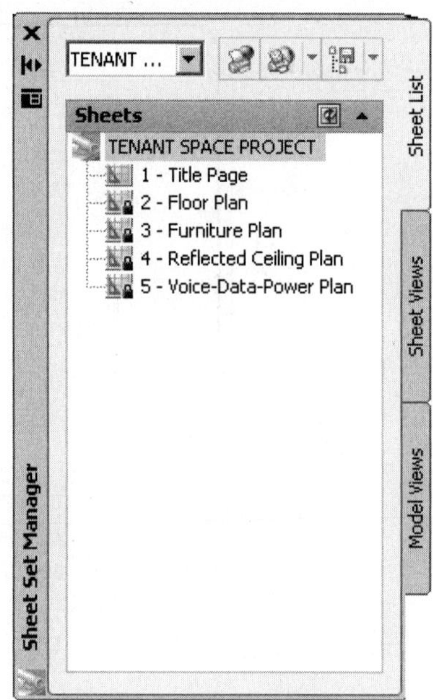

2. Set drawing Units: **Architectural**
3. Set Drawing Limits: **36, 24**
4. Set GRIDDISPLAY: **0**
5. Set Grid: **1**
6. Set Snap: **1/2**
7. Make the following layers:

LAYER NAME	COLOR	LINETYPE	LINEWEIGHT
Table	white	continuous	default

8. Set **Layer Table** current.

MAKE A TITLE PAGE

Step 4. Make the layout named Title Page and insert your ARCH D FORMAT drawing, as described next:

Prompt	Response
Command:	CLICK: **Create Layout Wizard** (from the Insert-Layout menu)
The Create Layout dialog box appears:	TYPE: **Title Page** in the name box
	CLICK: **Next**
The Printer tab appears:	CLICK: **DWF6 ePlot.pc3** (if your printer does not print a 24″ × 36″ sheet)
	CLICK: **Next**
The Paper Size tab appears:	CLICK: **ARCH D (36.00 × 24.00 inches)**
	CLICK: **Next**
The Orientation tab appears:	CLICK: **Landscape**
	CLICK: **Next**
The Title Block tab appears:	CLICK: **None**
	CLICK: **Next**

Prompt	Response
The Define Viewports tab appears:	CLICK: **Single** CLICK: **Next**
The Pick Location tab appears:	CLICK: **Next**
The Finish tab appears:	CLICK: **Finish**
The Title Page layout appears:	RIGHT-CLICK: **on Layout1 and Layout2 tabs** and CLICK: **Delete** so that no other paper space layouts exist

Step 5. **Insert the ARCH D FORMAT (made in CH12-TUTORIAL1) around the paper space viewport and change attributes as needed:**

Tag	Prompt	New Value
PLAN-NAME	**Type the plan name.**	**TITLE PAGE**
TUTORIAL	**Type the tutorial number.**	**CH12-TUTORIAL3**
DATE	**Type today's date.**	**Today's date**
SCALE	**Type the scale.**	**NONE**
SHEET	**Type Sheet of Sheet.**	**1 of 5**

Step 6. **Use the Text Style command to change the Arial font in the Standard style to the simplex font.**

Step 7. **Create a new layer named VP. While in paper space, change the outside edges of the viewport to the VP Layer. Turn the VP Layer OFF. The outside edges of the viewport are no longer visible.**

Step 8. Save the drawing.

SHEET SET...

Step 9. **Make a new sheet set with the name TENANT SPACE PROJECT, as described next:**

Prompt	Response
Command:	**New Sheet Set...** (or TYPE: **NEWSHEETSET <enter>**)

FIGURE 12–16
Create Sheet Set—Name of New Sheet Set

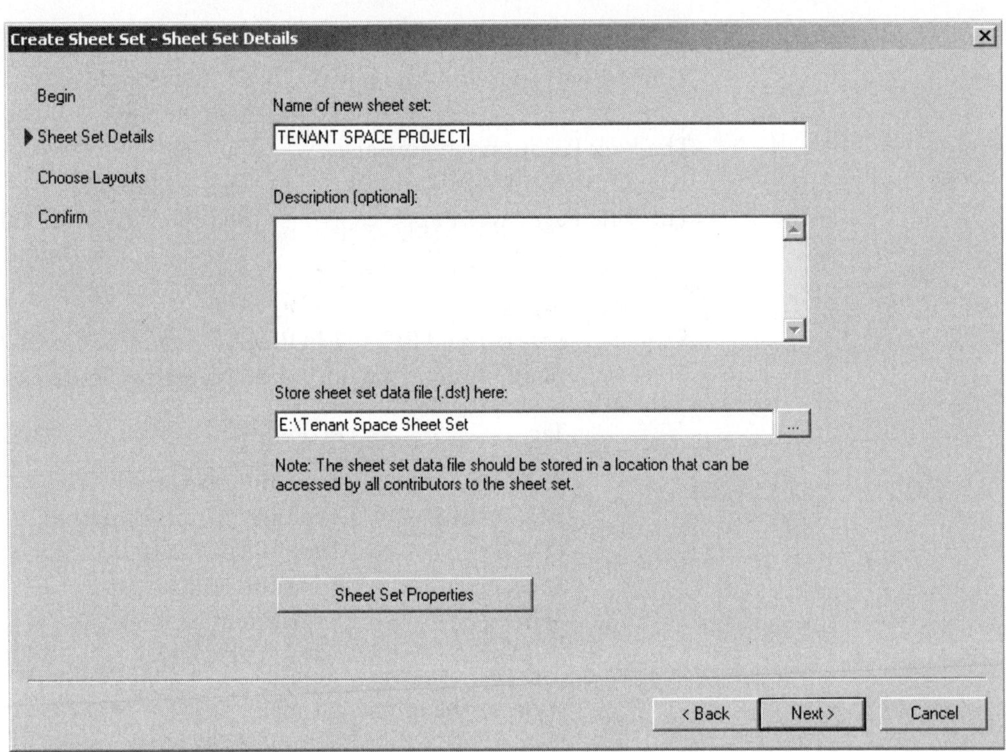

Prompt	Response
The Create Sheet Set - Begin tab appears:	CLICK: **Existing drawings** in the Create a sheet set using: area CLICK: **Next**
The Sheet Set Details tab appears:	TYPE: **TENANT SPACE PROJECT** in the Name of new sheet set: input box (Figure 12–16) CLICK: **the ellipsis (three dots) button** to the right of Store sheet set data file (.dst) here: CLICK: **the Tenant Space Sheet Set folder** CLICK: **Open** CLICK: **Next**
The Choose Layouts tab appears:	CLICK: **Browse**
The Browse for Folder dialog box appears:	CLICK: **the Tenant Space Sheet Set folder** CLICK: **OK**
The layouts in the drawings in that folder appear as shown in Figure 12–17.	CLICK: **Next**
The Confirm Sheet Set Preview (Figure 12–18) appears:	CLICK: **Finish** (if all the layouts shown in Figure 12–18 are there. If not, you may need to open and save one or more of the drawings so the layouts are in the list.)

Step 10. Rename and renumber all the layouts so you can identify each layout, as described next:

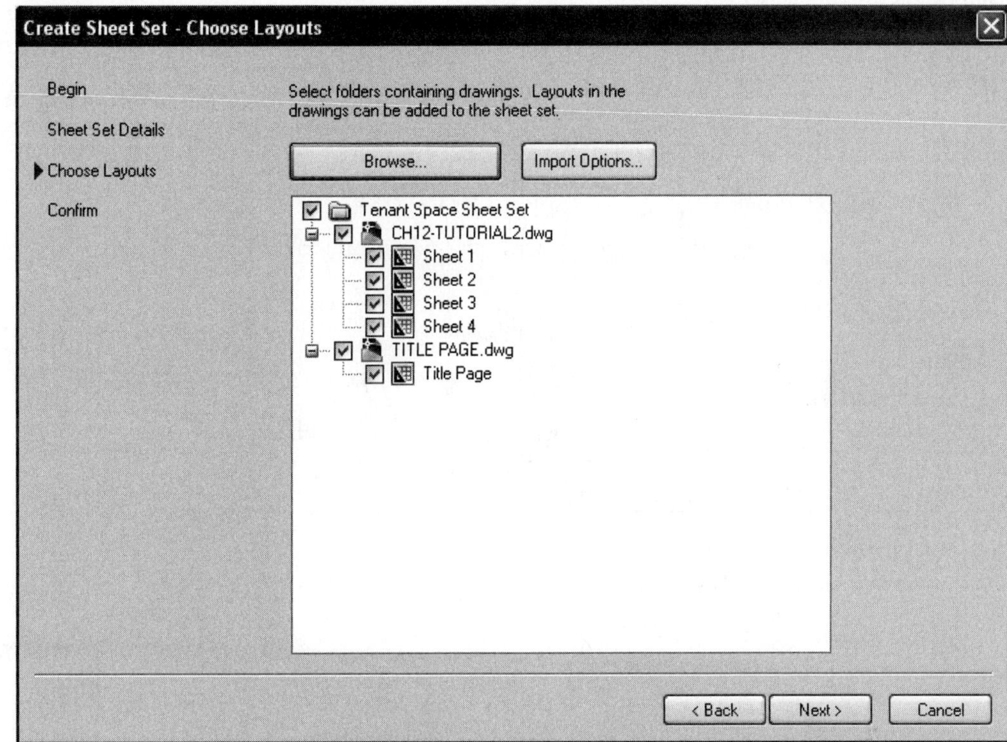

FIGURE 12–17
Choose Layouts

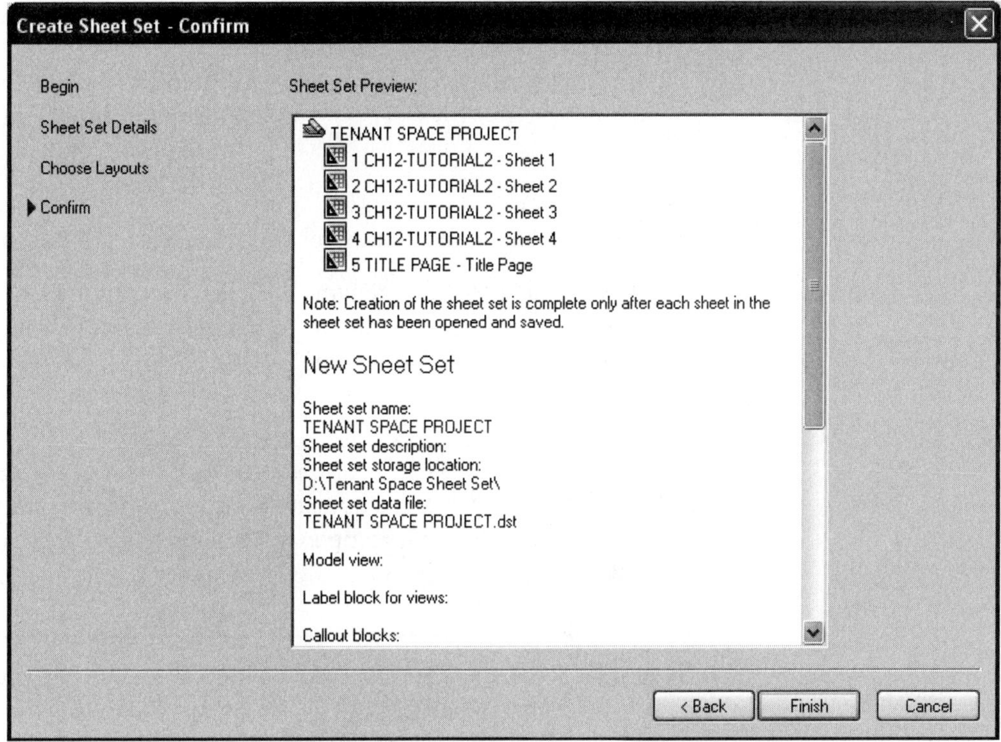

FIGURE 12–18
Confirm Sheet Set Preview

Prompt	Response
With the SHEET SET MANAGER open:	RIGHT-CLICK: **on CH12-TUTORIAL2-Sheet 1**.
The right-click menu appears:	CLICK: **Rename and Renumber...**
The Rename and Renumber Sheet dialog box (Figure 12–19) appears:	TYPE: **2** (in the Number: input box)

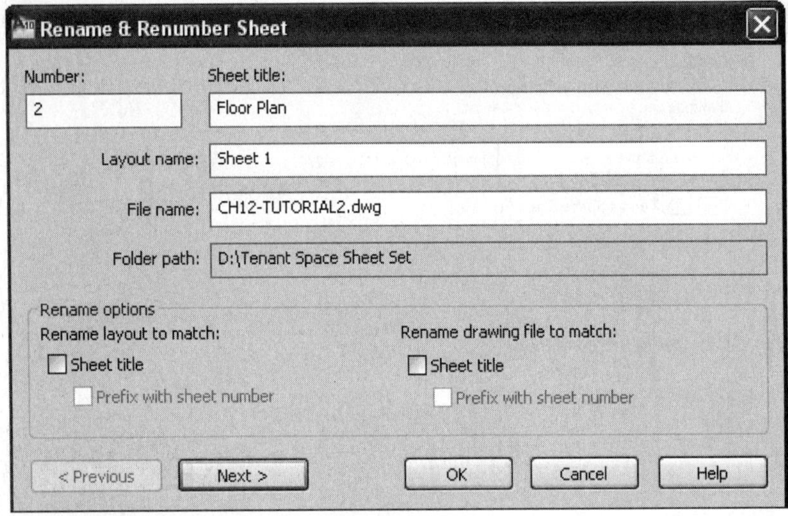

FIGURE 12–19
Rename and Renumber Sheet Dialog Box

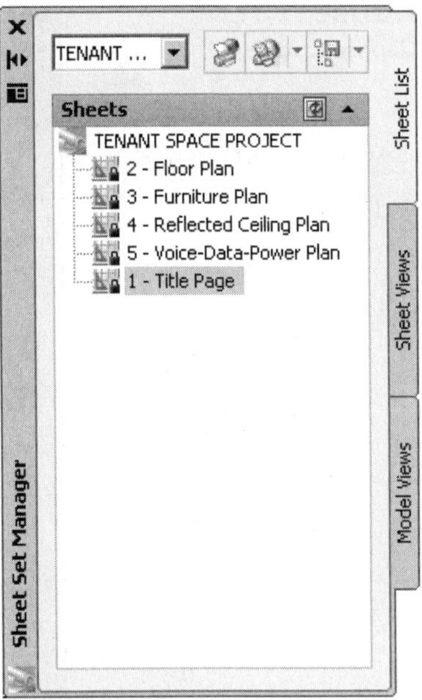

FIGURE 12–20
Sheets Renumbered and Renamed

Prompt	Response
	TYPE: **Floor Plan** (in the Sheet title: input box) CLICK: **Next** (in the lower left)
CH12-TUTORIAL2-Sheet 2 appears in the dialog box:	TYPE: **3** (in the Number: input box) TYPE: **Furniture Plan** (in the Sheet title: input box) CLICK: **Next**

Step 11. Rename and renumber the remaining layouts, as shown in Figure 12–20.

No. 3: Renumber to 4 and rename to Reflected Ceiling Plan
No. 4: Renumber to 5 and rename to Voice-Data-Power Plan
No. 5: Renumber to 1 and rename to Title Page

CLICK: **OK**

TIP: If you are not sure which drawing you are renumbering, DOUBLE-CLICK: on it to open it. Then close it so you have only the TITLE PAGE drawing open.

Step 12. Move the sheet labeled 1-Title Page to its correct location (Figure 12–21), as described next:

Prompt	Response
With the SHEET SET MANAGER open:	CLICK: **1-Title Page and hold down the** CLICK: **button as you move your mouse up so a black line appears at the top of the list, as shown in Figure 12–21** **Release the** CLICK: **button**

FIGURE 12–21
Move Title Page So It Is the First Sheet in the List

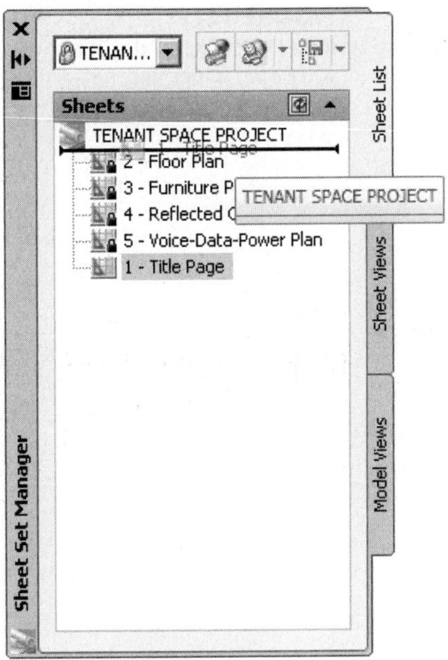

Prompt	Response
The Title Page sheet is now the first sheet in the list:	**Rearrange any remaining Sheets that are not in numerical order**

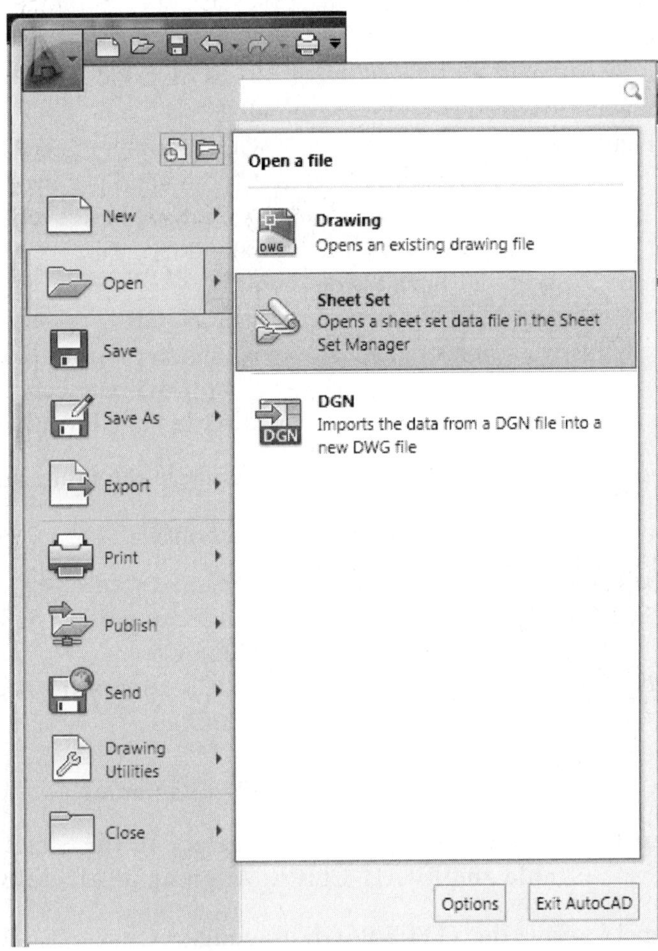

FIGURE 12–22
RIGHT-CLICK: on the TENANT SPACE PROJECT Title and CLICK: Insert Sheet List Table

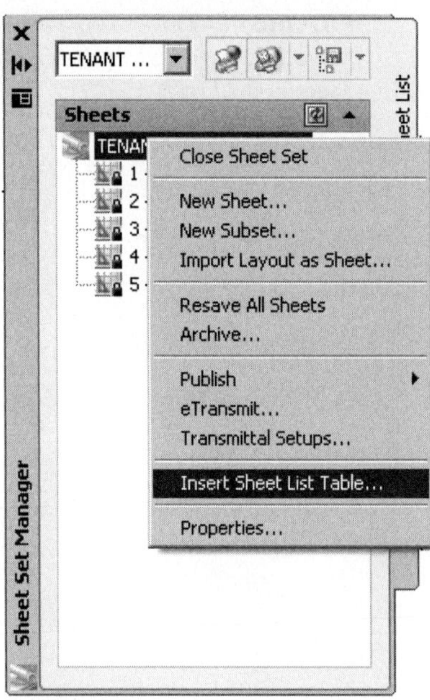

Step 13. Make a table showing the contents of the sheet set on the TITLE PAGE, as described next:

Prompt	Response
With the SHEET SET MANAGER open:	RIGHT-CLICK: **the Sheet Set Title, TENANT SPACE PROJECT**
The right-click menu (Figure 12–22) appears:	CLICK: **Insert Sheet List Table...** (If this command is grayed out, save the TITLE PAGE drawing to the Tenant Space Project folder and try again.)
The Insert Sheet List Table dialog box appears:	CLICK: **OK**
Specify Insertion Point:	CLICK: **a point to place the table in the approximate center of the space on the Title Page layout (Figure 12–23).**

Step 14. Use the Scale command to enlarge the table, as described next:

Prompt	Response
Command:	TYPE: **SC<enter>**
Select objects:	CLICK: **any point on the table**
Select objects:	**<enter>**
Specify base point:	CLICK: **any point near the center of the table**
Specify scale factor or [Copy/Reference] <0′-1″>:	TYPE: **3<enter>**

Step 15. Use a crossing window to select all the Sheet Titles in the Sheet List Table and RIGHT CLICK: **Alignment—Middle Left (Figure 12–23).**

Step 16. Save the TITLE PAGE drawing.

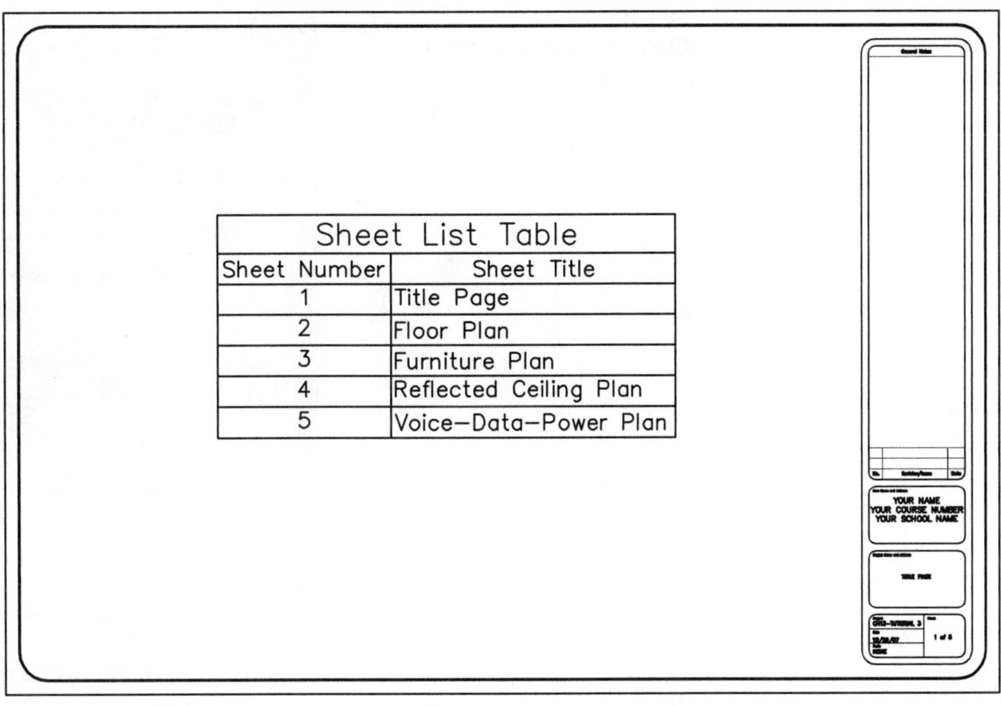

Sheet List Table	
Sheet Number	Sheet Title
1	Title Page
2	Floor Plan
3	Furniture Plan
4	Reflected Ceiling Plan
5	Voice–Data–Power Plan

FIGURE 12–23
Place the Sheet List Table in the Center of the Sheet, Use the Scale Command to Enlarge It, and Align Sheet Titles Middle Left

Step 17. With the Sheet Set Manager open, test your sheet set by double-clicking on each sheet in the drawing set.

Step 18. Make sure each sheet has the correct name and number. If not, rename and renumber as needed.

eTRANSMIT...

Step 19. Use eTransmit... to save all layouts to a .zip file (so they can be attached to an email and electronically transmitted), as described next:

Prompt	Response
With the SHEET SET MANAGER open:	RIGHT-CLICK: **the Sheet Set Title, TENANT SPACE PROJECT**

TIP: If you get a message telling you that some drawings need to be saved, CLICK: on the sheet that is contained within the drawing and save the drawing.

The right-click menu (Figure 12–24) appears:	CLICK: **eTransmit...**

FIGURE 12–24
CLICK: eTransmit... on the Right-Click Menu

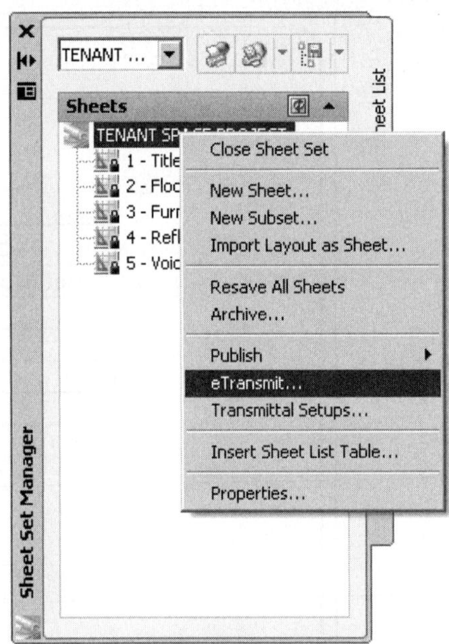

Prompt	Response
The Create Transmittal dialog box appears:	CLICK: **OK**
The Specify Zip file dialog box (Figure 12–25) appears:	CLICK: **on the Tenant Space Sheet Set folder** and CLICK: **Save**

The Sheet Set is now saved as a Zip file and can be attached to an email and sent to anyone you choose. The Sheet Set Manager can also be used to publish these sheet sets to a website by using one of the icons above the sheet set title.

FIGURE 12–25
Specify Zip File Dialog Box

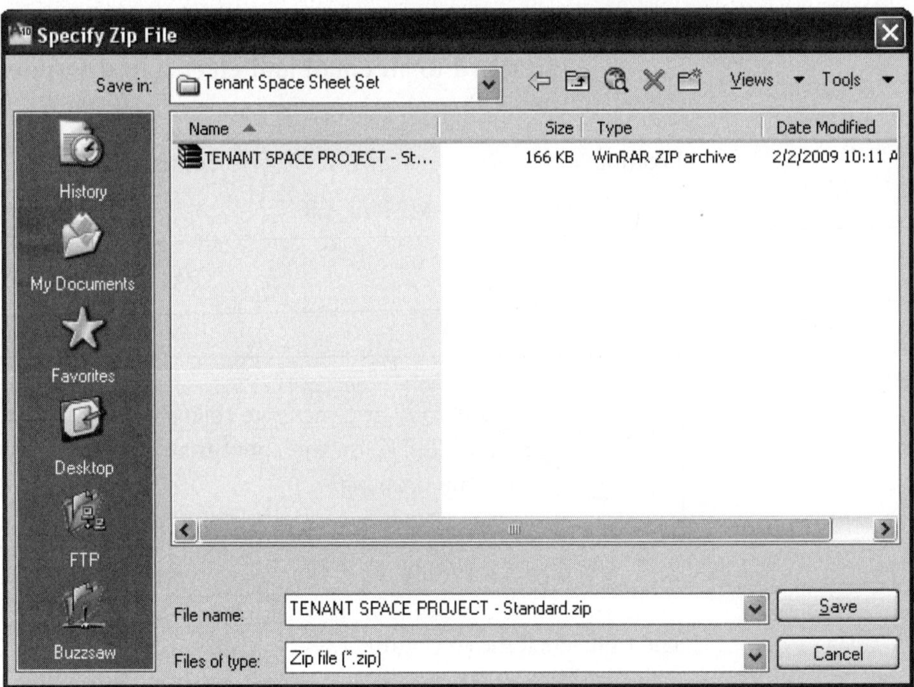

review questions

1. Which of the following is a characteristic of paper space?
   a. Viewports are tiled.
   b. Tilemode is set to 1.
   c. Viewports can overlap.
   d. Models are created.
   e. The -VPORTS command will work.
2. What is the maximum number of model space viewports that can be created on any one drawing?
   a. 2
   b. 4
   c. 16
   d. 64
   e. Unlimited
3. The Create Layout Wizard does *not* do which of the following?
   a. Turn viewport on and off
   b. Scale viewports
   c. Allow you to specify the corners of a viewport's location
   d. Allow you to name the layout
   e. Allow you to create an array of viewports
4. Which VPORTS command option returns the screen to a single viewport?
   a. Single
   b. One
   c. Delete
   d. MVIEW
   e. ?
5. A command can be started in one model space viewport and completed in a different model space viewport.
   a. True
   b. False
6. Which of the following is a characteristic of a nontiled viewport?
   a. Fills the graphics screen and touches all other viewports
   b. Is fixed and cannot overlap
   c. Can be erased or moved
   d. Only one of these viewports may be plotted at one time
   e. Only one viewport may be active at one time
7. Model space may be active with Tilemode set at either 0 or 1.
   a. True
   b. False
8. Which of the following MVIEW options creates several viewports at the same time?
   a. ON
   b. OFF
   c. Fit
   d. 2,3,4
   e. <First point>
9. Which command can be used to set a standard scale of 1/4″ = 1′ in paper space viewports?
   a. Paper Space
   b. Tilemode
   c. Properties
   d. Scale
   e. Model Space

10. Which of the following can be used to align objects in adjacent viewports accurately in model space?
   a. MVIEW
   b. VPORTS
   c. Move
   d. MVSETUP
   e. OSNAP

Complete.

11. List the command that regenerates all model space viewports at the same time.

   ____

12. List the command and its option that will restore a set of saved model space viewports into paper space.

   ____

13. List the title of the column in the Layer Properties Manager that is used to freeze layers in a single viewport or layout.

   ____

14. List the two letters that can be typed (and then press **<enter>**) to switch from model space to paper space when Tilemode is OFF.

   ____

15. List the setting in the Properties palette that is used to lock the scale of a viewport.

   ____

16. List the command that can be used to align objects in adjacent viewports.

   ____

17. Why is the viewport boundary often moved to a layer that is turned OFF?

   ____

18. When you RIGHT-CLICK: on a Sheet Set Title, which command do you CLICK: to create a table listing of all the sheets in the sheet set?

   ____

19. List the name of the dialog box used to renumber a sheet.

   ____

20. List the command used to make a .zip file of a sheet set with the Sheet Set Manager open.

   ____

chapter

13

Isometric Drawing and Gradient Hatch Rendering

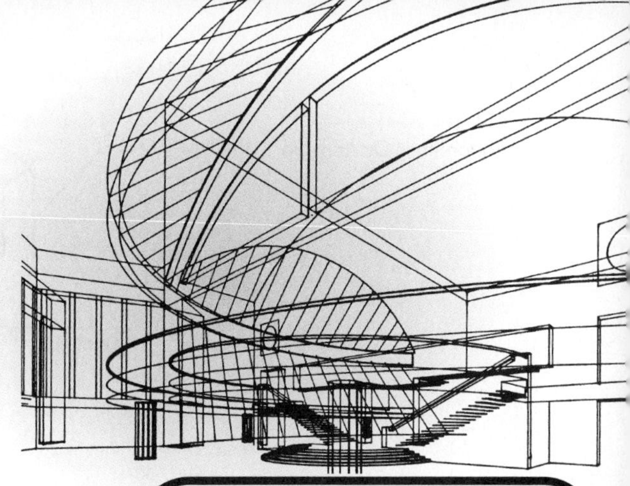

objectives

When you have completed this chapter, you will be able to:

Make isometric drawings to scale from two-dimensional drawings.

Correctly use the following commands and settings:

ELLIPSE-Isocircle
SNAP-Style Iso

Use the Ctrl-E or F5 keys to change from one isoplane to another.

Use gradient hatch patterns to render isometric drawings.

AXONOMETRIC DRAWING

The forms of axonometric drawing are isometric, dimetric, and trimetric, as shown in Figure 13–1. The trimetric form has the most pleasing appearance because each of the three axes uses a different scale. Dimetric uses the same scale on two axes, and isometric uses the same scale on all three axes. Isometric drawing is the axonometric drawing form covered in this book.

ISOMETRIC DRAWING

Isometric drawing is commonly used to show how objects appear in three dimensions. This drawing method is a two-dimensional one that is used to give the appearance of three dimensions. It is not a 3D modeling form such as those that are covered in later chapters. In 3D modeling you actually create three-dimensional objects that can be viewed from any angle and can be placed into a perspective mode.

FIGURE 13–1
Axonometric Drawing Forms

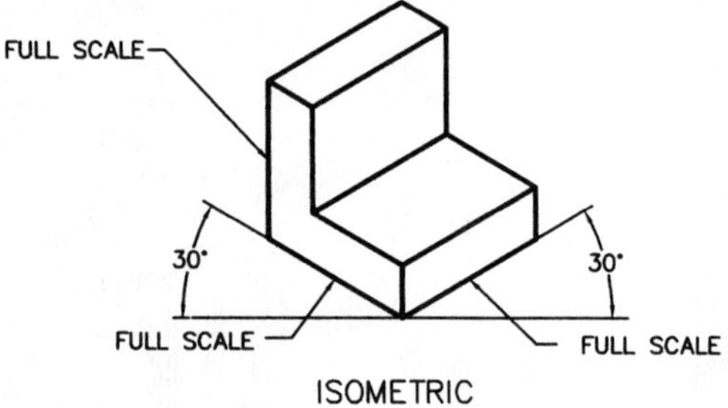

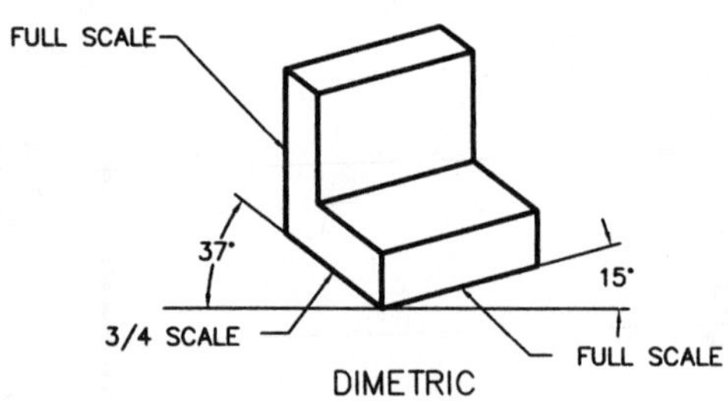

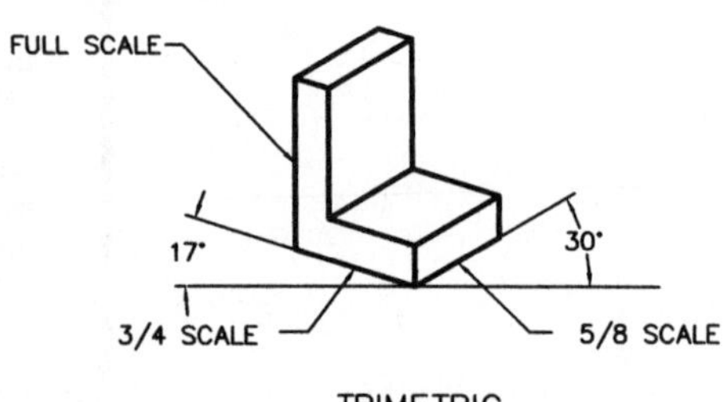

You can make isometric drawings quickly and easily using AutoCAD software. Once the proper Grid and Snap settings are made, the drawing itself proceeds with little difficulty. The three isometric axes are 30° right, 30° left, and vertical.

Tutorial 13–1: Fundamentals of Isometric Drawing

Seven isometric shapes are drawn in this exercise to acquaint you with the fundamentals of making isometric drawings using AutoCAD. We will begin with a simple isometric box so that you can become familiar with drawing lines on an isometric axis. All seven of these shapes are drawn on the same sheet and plotted on one 8-1/2″ × 11″ sheet. When you have completed Tutorial 13–1, your drawing will look similar to Figure 13–2.

Step 1. Use your workspace to make the following settings:

1. **Use SaveAs... to save the drawing with the name CH13-TUTORIAL1.**
2. Set drawing Units: **Architectural**
3. Set Drawing Limits: **11′, 8′6″** (be sure to use the foot symbol)
4. Set Snap for an isometric grid, as described next:

Prompt	Response
Command:	TYPE: **SN<enter>**
Specify snap spacing or [ON/OFF/Aspect/Style/Type] <0′-0 1/2″>:	TYPE: **S<enter>**

FIGURE 13–2
Tutorial 13–1 Complete

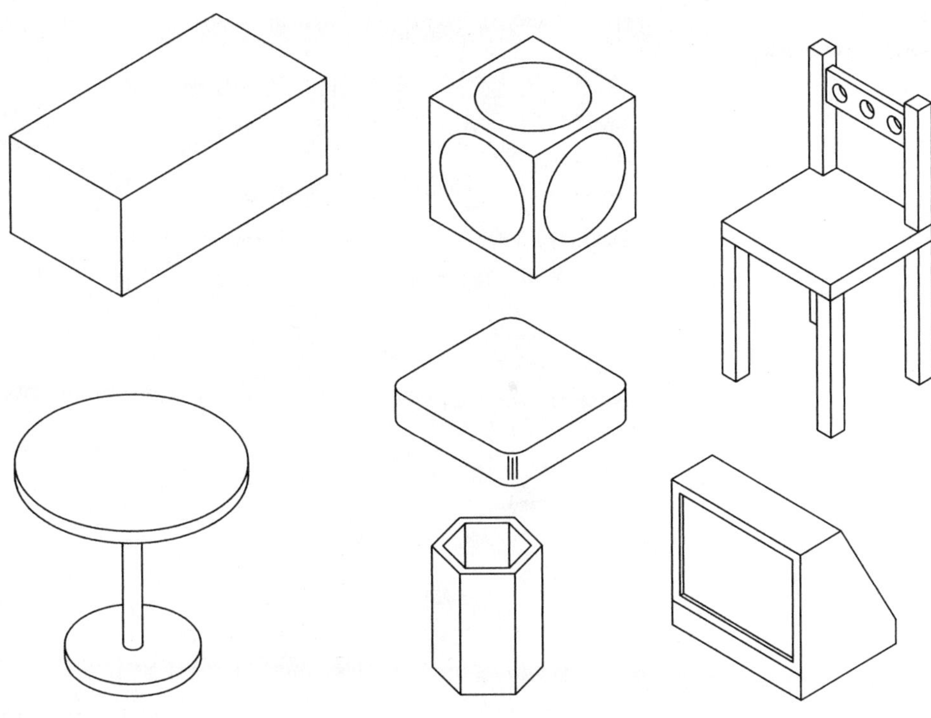

Prompt	Response
Enter snap grid style [Standard/ Isometric] <S>:	TYPE: **I<enter>** (I for isometric)
Specify vertical spacing <0′-6″>:	TYPE: **1<enter>** (if 1″ is not the default)

When you want to exit the isometric grid, TYPE: **SN<enter>** and then TYPE: **S<enter>**, then TYPE: **S<enter>** again to select the standard grid. Keep the isometric grid for this exercise.

5. Set GRIDDISPLAY: **0**
6. Set Grid: **3″**
7. Create the following Layers:

LAYER NAME	COLOR	LINETYPE	LINEWEIGHT
Layer1	blue	continuous	.007″ (.18mm)

8. Set **Layer1** current.
9. **Zoom-All.**

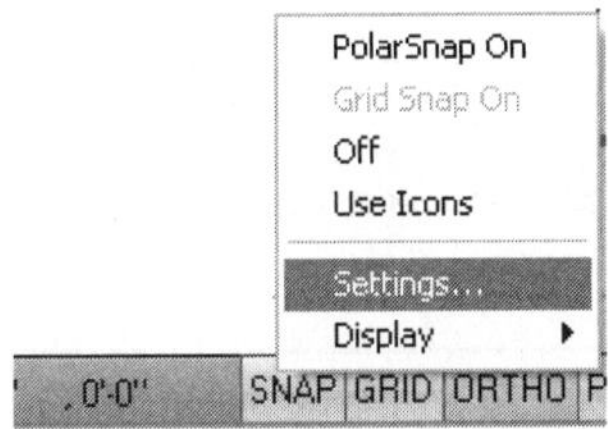

DRAFTING SETTINGS DIALOG BOX

When the isometric 1″ snap and 3″ grid are set, and GRIDDISPLAY is set to 0, the Drafting Settings dialog box will appear as shown in Figure 13–3. Grid and snap settings can also be made using the Drafting Settings dialog box.

FIGURE 13–3
Drafting Settings Dialog Box

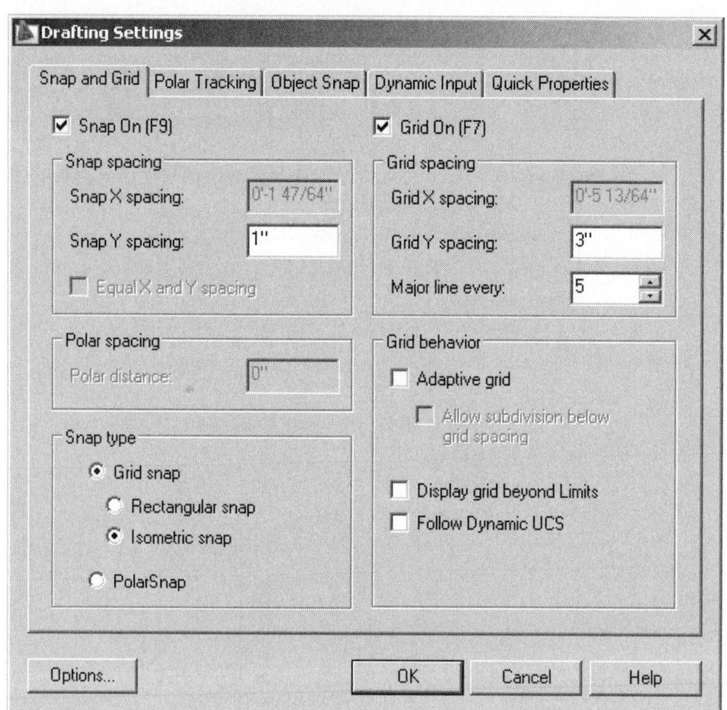

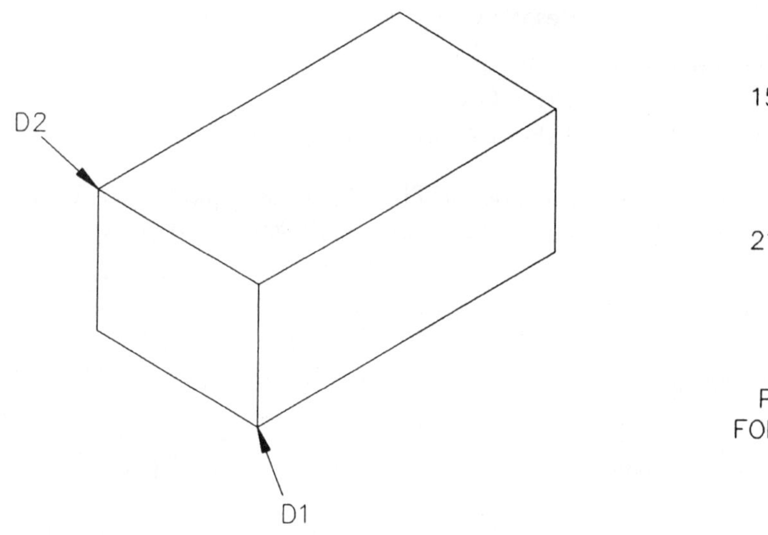

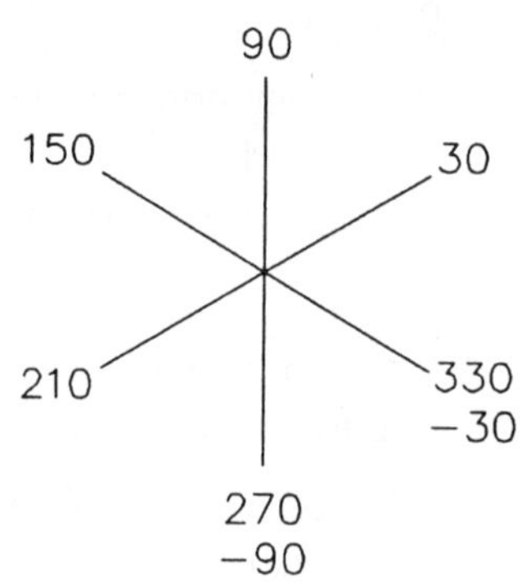

FIGURE 13–4
Shape 1: Drawing the Isometric Rectangle

SHAPE 1: DRAWING THE ISOMETRIC RECTANGLE

Drawing Shape 1 (Figure 13–4) helps you become familiar with drawing lines using isometric polar coordinates.

Step 2. Draw the right face of an isometric rectangular box measuring 12″ × 16″ × 30″ using isometric polar coordinates, as described next:

Prompt	Response
Command:	**Line** (or TYPE: **L<enter>**)
Specify first point:	**D1** (Figure 13–4) (absolute coordinates 1′7-1/16, 4′11″—this is an isometric snap point)

Prompt	Response
Specify next point or [Undo]:	TYPE: **@30<30<enter>**
Specify next point or [Undo]:	TYPE: **@12<90<enter>**
Specify next point or [Close/Undo]:	TYPE: **@30<210<enter>**
Specify next point or [Close/Undo]:	TYPE: **C<enter>**

Step 3. Draw the left face of the isometric rectangular box, as described next:

Prompt	Response
Command:	**<enter>** (Repeat LINE)
Specify first point:	**D1** (Figure 13–4) **(OSNAP-Endpoint)**
Specify next point or [Undo]:	TYPE: **@16<150<enter>**
Specify next point or [Undo]:	TYPE: **@12<90<enter>**
Specify next point or [Close/Undo]:	TYPE: **@16<330<enter>**
Specify next point or [Close/Undo]:	**<enter>**

Step 4. Draw the top of the isometric rectangular box, as described next:

Prompt	Response
Command:	**<enter>** (Repeat LINE)
Specify first point:	**D2**
Specify next point or [Undo]:	TYPE: **@30<30<enter>**
Specify next point or [Undo]:	TYPE: **@16<-30<enter>**
Specify next point or [Close/Undo]:	**<enter>**

SHAPE 2: DRAWING ISOMETRIC ELLIPSES

When using polar coordinates to draw lines in isometric, you can ignore Isoplanes. Isoplanes are isometric faces—Top, Right, and Left. Pressing two keys, Ctrl and E, at the same time toggles your drawing to the correct Isoplane—Top, Right, or Left. The function key F5 can also be used to toggle to the correct Isoplane.

Shape 2 (Figure 13–5) has a circle in each of the isometric planes of a cube. When drawn in isometric, circles appear as ellipses. You must use the isoplanes when drawing isometric circles using the Ellipse command. The following part of the tutorial starts by drawing a 15″ isometric cube.

FIGURE 13–5
Shape 2: Drawing an Isometric Cube with an Ellipse in Each Isoplane

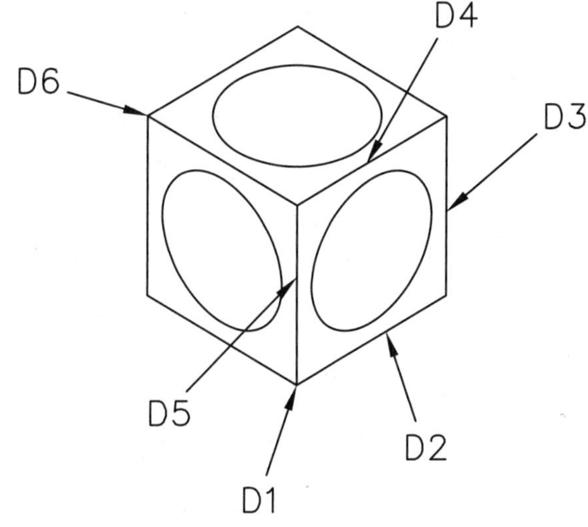

Step 5. Draw the right face of a 15″ isometric cube using direct distance entry, as described next:

Prompt	Response
Command:	**Toggle to the right isoplane** (PRESS: **F5** until <Isoplane Right> appears) **and** CLICK: **Line** (or TYPE: **L<enter>**)
Specify first point:	**D1** (absolute coordinates 6′3/4″, 5′3″)
Specify next point or [Undo]:	**With ORTHO ON, move your mouse upward 30° to the right, and** TYPE: **15<enter>**
Specify next point or [Undo]:	**Move the mouse straight up, and** TYPE: **15<enter>**
Specify next point or [Close/Undo]:	**Move the mouse downward 210° to the left, and** TYPE: **15<enter>**
Specify next point or [Close/Undo]:	TYPE: **C <enter>**

Step 6. Use the Mirror command to draw the left face of the isometric cube, as described next:

Prompt	Response
Command:	**Mirror** (or TYPE: **MI<enter>**)
Select objects:	**D2,D3,D4<enter>** (Figure 13–5)
Specify first point of mirror line:	**D1** (be sure Ortho is ON) **(OSNAP-Endpoint)**
Specify second point of mirror line:	**D5** (PRESS: **F5** to be sure you are in either the right or left isoplane)
Erase source objects? [Yes/No]<N>:	**<enter>**

Step 7. Complete the top face of the isometric cube, as described next:

Prompt	Response
Command:	**Toggle to the top isoplane and** CLICK: **Line** (or TYPE: **L<enter>**)
Specify first point:	**D6 (OSNAP-Endpoint)**
Specify next point or [Undo]:	**Move the mouse upward 30° to the right, and** TYPE: **15<enter>**
Specify next point or [Undo]:	**Move the mouse downward 330° to the right, and** TYPE: **15<enter>**
Specify next point or [Close/Undo]:	**<enter>**

NOTE: If you do not have the isometric snap style active, the Ellipse command will not prompt you with Isocircle as one of the options for the command.

NOTE: Select Ellipse-Axis, End if you select from the Ribbon. Ellipse-Center or Ellipse-Arc does not allow you to draw an isometric ellipse.

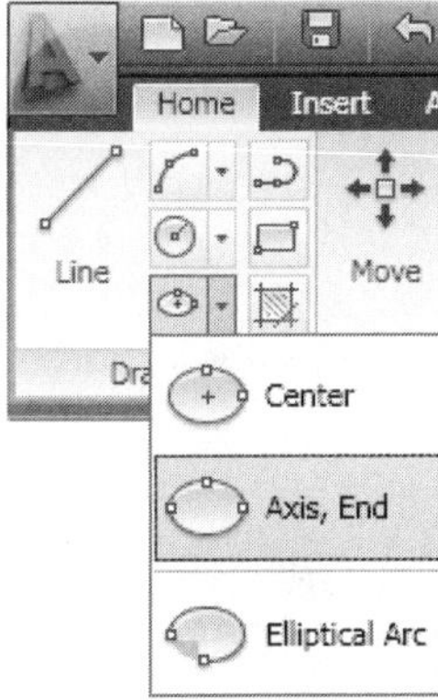

Step 8. **Draw an isometric ellipse (6″ radius) that represents a circle in the LEFT ISOPLANE, as described next:**

Prompt	Response
Command:	**Ellipse Axis, End** (or TYPE: **EL<enter>**)
Specify axis endpoint of ellipse or [Arc/Center/Isocircle]:	TYPE: **I<enter>**
Specify center of isocircle:	**OSNAP-Mid Between 2 Points**
First point of mid:	**D1**
Second point of mid:	**D6**
Specify radius of isocircle or [Diameter]:	PRESS: **the F5 function key until the command line reads <Isoplane Left>, then** TYPE: **6<enter>**

When you type and enter **D** in response to the prompt "Specify radius of Isocircle or Diameter:", you can enter the diameter of the circle. The default is radius.

Step 9. **Follow a similar procedure to draw ellipses in the right and top isoplanes. Be sure to specify Isocircle after you have selected the Ellipse command, and be sure you are in the correct isoplane before you draw the ellipse. Use F5 to toggle to the correct isoplane.**

When you have completed this part of the tutorial, you have the essentials of isometric drawing. Now you are going to apply these essentials to a more complex shape.

TIP: After you become familiar with isometric angles and toggling to isoplanes, use direct distance entry with Ortho ON to draw lines. Just move your mouse in the isometric direction and TYPE: the number that tells AutoCAD how far you want to go. You may choose to watch the dynamic display of distance and polar angles and simply pick the desired point.

SHAPE 3: DRAWING A CHAIR WITH ELLIPSES THAT SHOW THE THICKNESS OF A MATERIAL

Step 10. **Draw the right side of the front chair leg, as described next:**

Prompt	Response
Command:	**Toggle to the right isoplane and** CLICK: **Line** (or TYPE: **L<enter>**) (be sure Ortho is ON)
Specify first point:	**D1** (Figure 13–6) (pick a point in the approximate location **[9′-7/8″,4′11″]** shown in Figure 13–2)
Specify next point or [Undo]:	**With Ortho ON, move your mouse straight down 270° and** TYPE: **1′5<enter>**

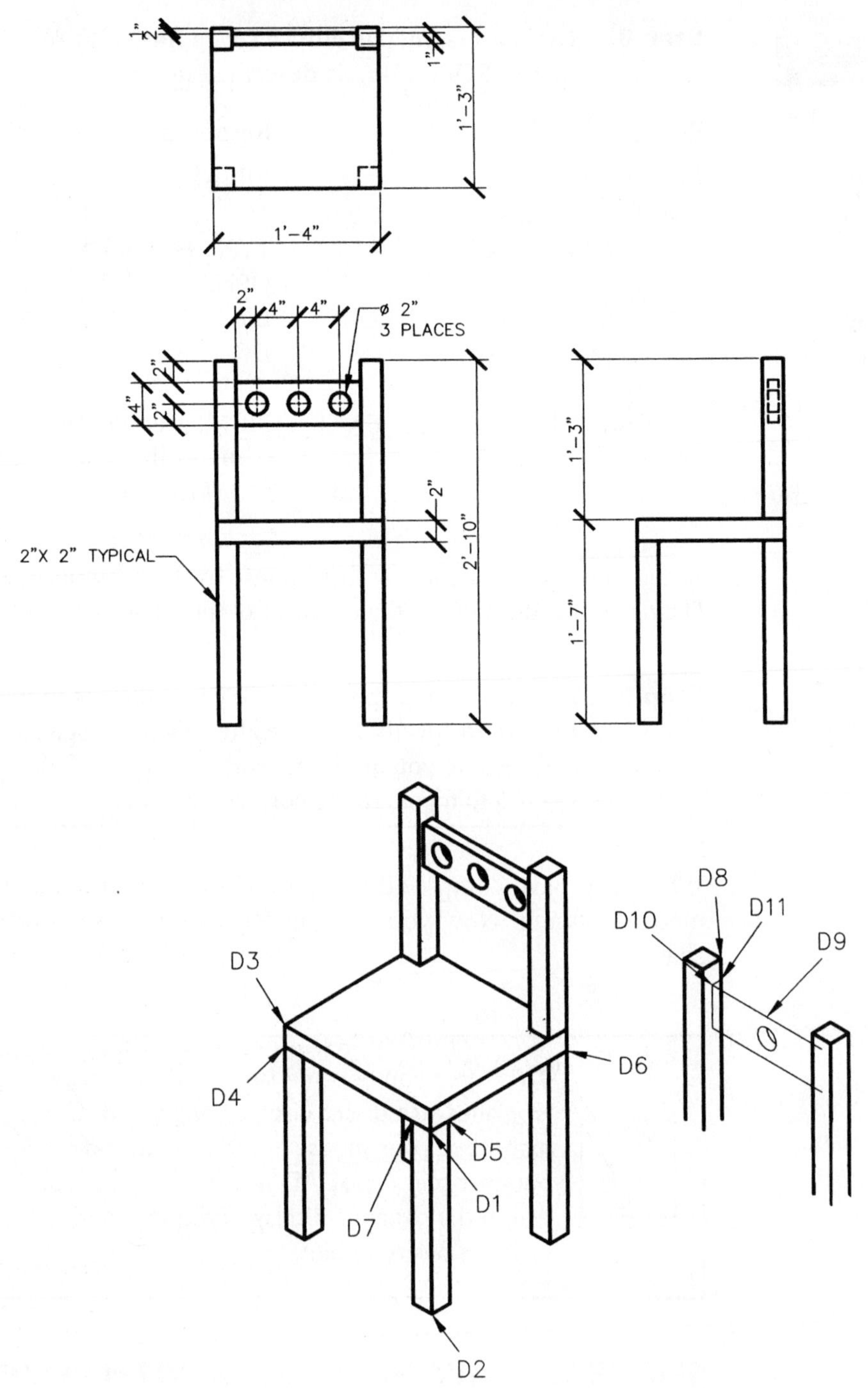

FIGURE 13–6
Shape 3: Drawing a Chair with Ellipses That Show the Thickness of a Material

Prompt	Response
Specify next point or [Undo]:	**Move your mouse upward 30° to the right and** TYPE: **2<enter>**
Specify next point or [Close/Undo]:	**Move your mouse straight up 90° and** TYPE: **1′5<enter>**
Specify next point or [Close/Undo]:	**<enter>**

Step 11. **Draw the left side of the front chair leg, as described next:**

Prompt	Response
Command:	**Toggle to the left isoplane and** CLICK: **Line** (or TYPE: **L<enter>**)
Specify first point:	**D2 (OSNAP-Endpoint)** (Figure 13–6)
Specify next point or [Undo]:	**Move your mouse upward 150° to the left, and** TYPE: **2<enter>**
Specify next point or [Undo]:	**Move your mouse straight up 90° and** TYPE: **1′5<enter>**
Specify next point or [Close/Undo]:	**<enter>**

Step 12. **Draw the chair seat, as described next:**

Prompt	Response
Command:	**Line** (or TYPE: **L<enter>**)
Specify first point:	**D1 (OSNAP-Endpoint)** (Figure 13–6)
Specify next point or [Undo]:	**Move your mouse 150° upward to the left** and TYPE: **1′4<enter>**
Specify next point or [Undo]:	**Move your mouse straight up and** TYPE: **2<enter>**
Specify next point or [Close/Undo]:	**Move your mouse 330° downward to the right and** TYPE: **1′4<enter>**
Specify next point or [Close/Undo]:	TYPE: **C<enter>**
Command:	**<enter>** (to begin the Line command)
Specify first point:	**D1 (OSNAP-Endpoint)**
Specify next point or [Undo]:	**Toggle to the right isoplane and with Ortho ON, move your mouse 30° upward to the right and** TYPE: **1′3<enter>**
Specify next point or [Undo]:	**Move your mouse straight up and** TYPE: **2<enter>**
Specify next point or [Close/Undo]:	**Move your mouse 210° downward to the left and** TYPE: **1′3<enter>**
Specify next point or [Close/Undo]:	**<enter>** (to end the Line command)
Command:	**<enter>** (to begin the Line command)
Specify first point:	**D3 (OSNAP-Intersection)**
Specify next point or [Undo]:	**Toggle to the top isoplane and with Ortho ON, move your mouse 30° upward to the right and** TYPE: **1′3<enter>**
Specify next point or [Close/Undo]:	**Move your mouse 330° downward to the right and** TYPE: **1′4<enter>**
Specify next point or [Close/Undo]:	**<enter>**

Step 13. **Copy the front leg to the other three positions.**

1. **Using the Copy command, select the lines of the front leg. Use D5 (Osnap-Endpoint) (Figure 13–6) as the base point and D6 (Osnap-Intersection) as the second point of displacement.**
2. **Using the Copy command, select both legs on the right side. Use D7 (Osnap-Endpoint) (Figure 13–6) as the base point and D4 (Osnap-Intersection) as the second point of displacement.**
3. **Use the Trim and Erase commands to delete any unnecessary lines.**

Step 14. Use the Line command to draw one of the upright posts, and use the Copy command to copy it to the other position. Follow the dimensions shown in Figure 13–6.

Step 15. Draw the 1″ × 4″ × 12″ piece containing the three holes, as described next:

Prompt	Response
Command:	**Line** (or TYPE: **L<enter>**)
Specify first point:	TYPE: **FRO<enter>**
Base point:	CLICK: **D8 (OSNAP-Intersection)** (Figure 13–6)
<Offset>:	TYPE: **@2<-90<enter>**
Specify next point or [Undo]:	TYPE: **@1<210<enter>**
Specify next point or [Undo]:	TYPE: **@12<-30<enter>**
Specify next point or [Close/Undo]:	**<enter>**
Command:	**Toggle to the left isoplane, and with Ortho OFF, Ellipse Axis, End** (or TYPE: **EL<enter>**)
Specify axis endpoint of ellipse or [Arc/Center/Isocircle]:	TYPE: **I<enter>**
Specify center of isocircle:	TYPE: **FRO<enter>**
Base point:	CLICK: **D9 (OSNAP-Midpoint)**
<Offset>:	TYPE: **@2<-90<enter>**
Specify radius of isocircle or [Diameter]:	TYPE: **1<enter>**
Command:	**COPY** (or TYPE: **CP<enter>**)
Select objects:	CLICK: **the ellipse just drawn**
Select objects:	**<enter>**
Specify base point or [Displacement] <Displacement>:	CLICK: **D10 (OSNAP-Endpoint)**
Specify second point or <use first point as displacement>:	CLICK: **D11 (OSNAP-Endpoint)**
Specify second point or [Exit/Undo] <Exit>:	**<enter>**

Step 16. Trim the copied ellipse so that only the part within the first ellipse remains.

Step 17. Copy the hole described by the ellipses 4″ 330° downward to the right, and 4″ 150° upward to the left.

Step 18. Draw a 4″ line straight down from D10 (Endpoint) and a 12″ line 330° downward to the right from the end of the 4″ line.

Step 19. Draw a 12″ line 330° downward to the right from D11 (Endpoint).

Step 20. Use the Move command to move the 1″ × 4″ × 12″ piece and three holes 210° downward to the left 1/2″.

Step 21. Trim to complete the drawing.

SHAPE 4: DRAWING A SHAPE THAT HAS A SERIES OF ISOMETRIC ELLIPSES LOCATED ON THE SAME CENTERLINE

Shape 4 (Figure 13–7), similar to a round table, will help you become familiar with drawing a shape that has a series of ellipses located on the same centerline. Five ellipses must be drawn. The centers of two of them, the extreme top and bottom ellipses, can be located by using endpoints of the centerline.

The following part of the tutorial begins by drawing a centerline through the entire height of the object.

Step 22. Begin to draw a shape containing several ellipses of different sizes located on the same centerline by drawing the centerline, as described next:

Prompt	Response
Command:	**Line** (or TYPE: **L<enter>**)
Specify first point:	**D1** (1′11-7/16,1′4-1/2)
Specify next point or [Undo]:	TYPE: **@24<90<enter>**
Specify next point or [Undo]:	**<enter>**

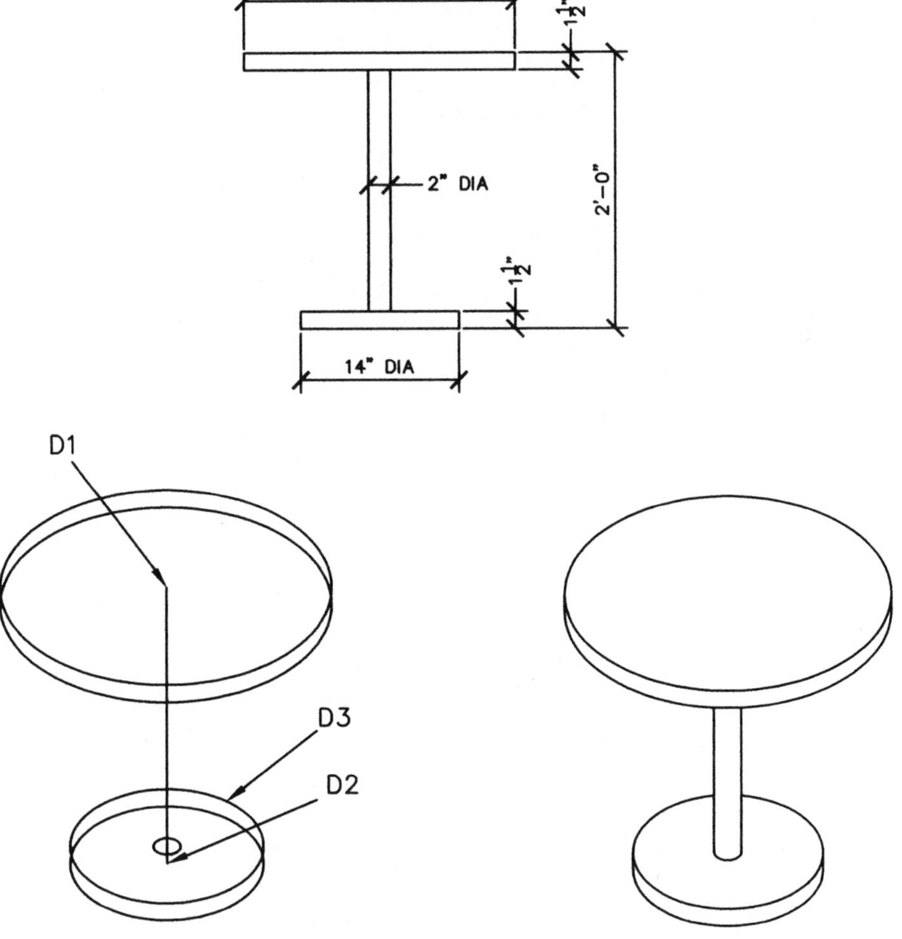

FIGURE 13–7
Shape 4: Drawing a Shape That Has a Series of Isometric Ellipses Located on the Same Centerline

Step 23. Draw five ellipses:

1. Toggle to the top isoplane and use Endpoint to locate the center of the uppermost isometric ellipse on the endpoint of the vertical line. Draw it with a diameter of 24″.
2. Draw a second 24″-diameter isometric ellipse by copying the 24″ ellipse 1-1/2″ straight down.
3. Draw the 14″-diameter ellipse using the bottom Endpoint of the vertical line as its center. Copy the 14″-diameter ellipse 1-1/2″ straight up.
4. Draw the 2″-diameter ellipse at the center of the copied 14″-diameter ellipse using Osnap-Center to locate its center.

NOTE: Although Osnap-Nearest can be used to end an isometric line on another line, the position is not exact. A more exact method is to draw the line beyond where it should end and trim it to the correct length.

Step 24. To draw the 2″ column, toggle to the right or left isoplane (the top isoplane does not allow you to draw vertical lines using a mouse if Ortho is ON). Turn Ortho (F8) ON. Draw a vertical line from the quadrant of one side of the 2″-diameter ellipse to just above the first 24″-diameter ellipse. Draw a similar line to form the other side of the column.

Step 25. With Ortho (F8) ON and toggled to the right or left isoplane, draw vertical lines from the quadrants of the ellipse segments to connect each side of the top and bottom ellipses, as shown in Figure 13–8.

Step 26. Use Trim and Erase to remove unneeded lines. The drawing is complete as shown in the lower right corner of Figure 13–7.

SHAPE 5: ISOMETRIC DETAIL WITH ROUNDED CORNERS

The fifth drawing (Figure 13–9) in this tutorial is a shape that has rounded corners. Rounded corners are common in many items. In two-dimensional drawing, the Fillet

FIGURE 13–8
Shape 4: Drawing Tangents to the Ellipses

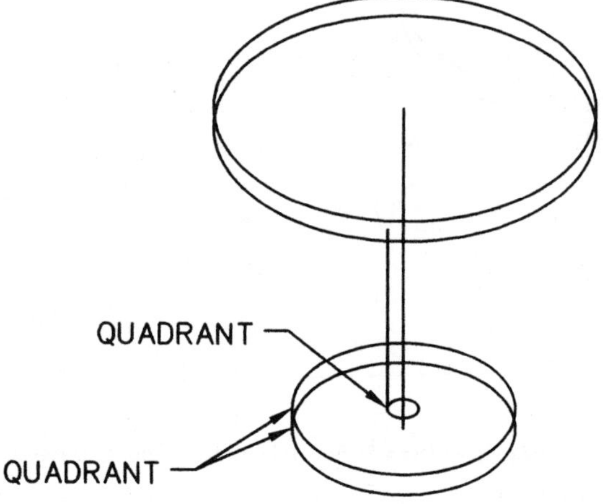

FIGURE 13–9
Shape 5: Isometric Detail with Rounded Corners

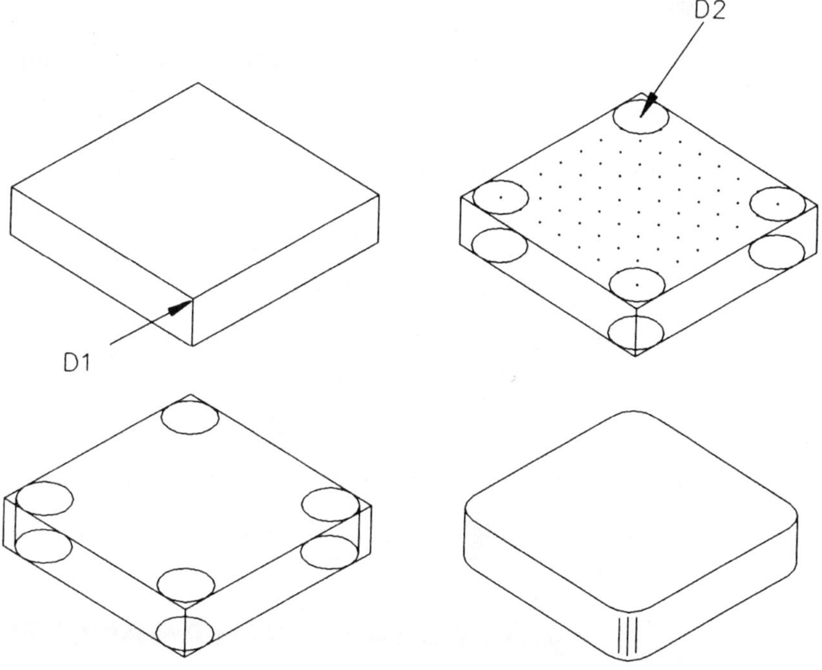

command allows you to obtain the rounded corners quickly and easily. This is not so in isometric. Drawing Shape 5 will help you become familiar with how rounded corners must be constructed with isometric ellipses.

Step 27. Turn Ortho and Snap ON, and toggle to the top isoplane. Draw an 18″ × 18″ square shape in the top isoplane (Figure 13–9), as described next:

Prompt	Response
Command:	**Line** (or TYPE: **L<enter>**)
Specify first point:	**D1** (on a grid mark) **(5′11, 3′3)**
Specify next point or [Undo]:	TYPE: **@18<30<enter>**
Specify next point or [Undo]:	TYPE: **@18<150<enter>**
Specify next point or [Close/Undo]:	TYPE: **@18<210<enter>**
Specify next point or [Close/Undo]:	TYPE: **C<enter>**

Step 28. Copy the 18″ × 18″ square 4″ down:

1. **Copy the front two edges of the square to form the bottom of the shape. Copy using @4<270 (4″ is the depth) as the polar coordinates for the second point of displacement.**
2. **Draw lines connecting the top and bottom edges.** (These lines are for reference only. You may skip this step if you choose.)

Step 29. Draw a 2″ radius ellipse in the top isoplane, as described next:

Prompt	Response
Command:	**Ellipse** (or TYPE: **EL<enter>**) (toggle to the top isoplane)
Specify axis endpoint of ellipse or [Arc/Center/Isocircle]:	TYPE: **I<enter>**

Prompt	Response
Specify center of isocircle:	**D2** (Count 2″ in both the 330 and 210 directions from the corner to locate the center of the ellipse. Make sure Snap is ON.)
Specify radius of isocircle or [Diameter]:	TYPE: **2<enter>**

Step 30. **Copy the ellipse just drawn to the other four top corners, locating them in a similar manner.**

Step 31. **Copy the front three ellipses 4″ in the 270 direction to form corners in the bottom plane. Make sure Snap is ON.**

Step 32. **Draw lines connecting the two outside ellipses using Osnap-Quadrant.**

Step 33. **Use the Trim and Erase commands to remove the extra lines.**

Step 34. **Add highlights on the front corner to complete the drawing.**

SHAPE 6: A TV SHAPE WITH AN ANGLED BACK

While drawing in isometric, you will often need to draw angles. To do that you will need to locate both ends of the angle and connect them. You will not be able to draw any angle otherwise, such as the 62° angle in Figure 13–10.

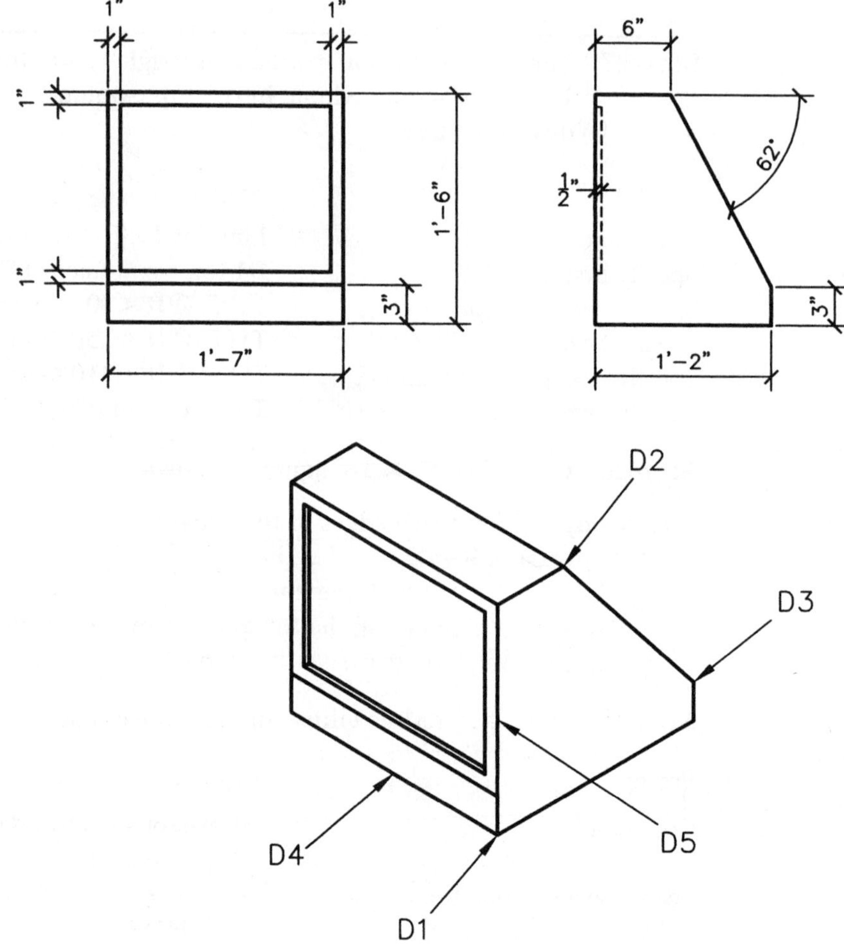

FIGURE 13–10
Shape 6: A TV Shape with an Angled Block

Step 35. Draw the right side of Figure 13–10, as described next:

Prompt	Response
Command:	**Line** (or TYPE: **L<enter>**)
Specify first point:	**D1** (8′9-5/8″,9″)
Specify next point or [Undo]:	**Toggle to the right isoplane and with Ortho ON, move your mouse 30° upward to the right and** TYPE: **1′2<enter>**
Specify next point or [Undo]:	**Move your mouse straight up and** TYPE: **3<enter>**
Specify next point or [Close/Undo]:	**<enter>**
Command:	**<enter>** (to get the Line command back)
Specify first point:	**D1** (again) **(Endpoint)**
Specify next point or [Undo]:	**Move your mouse straight up and** TYPE: **1′6<enter>**
Specify next point or [Close/Undo]:	**Move your mouse 30° upward to the right and** TYPE: **6<enter>**
Specify next point or [Undo]:	**D3 (Endpoint)**
Specify next point or [Close/Undo]:	**<enter>**

Step 36. Draw the left side and top of Figure 13–10, as described next:

Prompt	Response
Command:	**Line** (or TYPE: **L<enter>**)
Specify first point:	CLICK: **D1** (Figure 13–10)
Specify next point or [Undo]:	**Toggle to the left isoplane and with Ortho ON, move your mouse 150° upward to the left and** TYPE: **1′7<enter>**
Specify next point or [Undo]:	**Move your mouse straight up and** TYPE: **1′6<enter>**
Specify next point or [Close/Undo]:	**Toggle to the top isoplane and move your mouse 30° upward to the right and** TYPE: **6<enter>**
Specify next point or [Close/Undo]:	CLICK: **D2**
Specify next point or [Close/Undo]:	**<enter>**
Command:	**COPY** (or TYPE: **CP<enter>**)
Select objects:	CLICK: **D4**
Select objects:	**<enter>**
Specify base point or [Displacement/mOde] <Displacement>:	CLICK: **any point**
Specify second point or <use first point as displacement>:	**Toggle to the left isoplane and move your mouse straight up and** TYPE: **3<enter>**
Specify second point or [Exit/Undo] <Exit>:	**Move your mouse straight up and** TYPE: **4<enter>**

Prompt	Response
Specify second point or [Exit/Undo] <Exit>:	**Move your mouse straight up and** TYPE: **1′5<enter>**
Specify second point or [Exit/Undo] <Exit>:	**Move your mouse straight up and** TYPE: **1′6<enter>**
Specify second point or [Exit/Undo] <Exit>:	**<enter>**
Command:	**<enter>**(to repeat the COPY command)
Select objects:	CLICK: **D5**
Select objects:	**<enter>**
Specify base point or [Displacement/mOde] <Displacement>:	CLICK: **any point**
Specify second point or <use first point as displacement>:	**Move your mouse 150° upward to the left and** TYPE: **1<enter>**
Specify second point or [Exit/Undo] <Exit>:	**Move your mouse 150° upward to the left and** TYPE: **1′6<enter>**
Specify second point or [Exit/Undo] <Exit>:	**<enter>**

Step 37. **Use the Trim command to trim unnecessary lines.**

Step 38. **Use the Copy command to draw the two lines forming the inside edge of the TV screen. Copy them 1/2″, 30° upward to the right.**

Step 39. **Draw a line at the intersection of those copied lines.**

Step 40. **Use the Trim command to trim unnecessary lines. The drawing is complete.**

SHAPE 7: ISOMETRIC DETAIL—A HEXAGONAL-SHAPED VASE

The final shape in this tutorial combines several features (Figure 13–11).

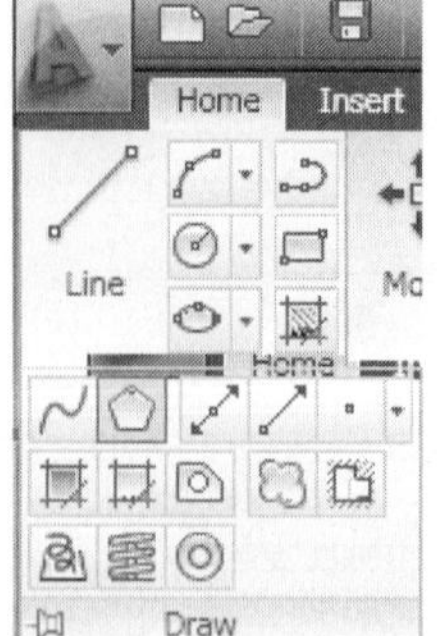

Step 41. **Draw the hexagonal shape of the vase (Figure 13–11A), as described next:**

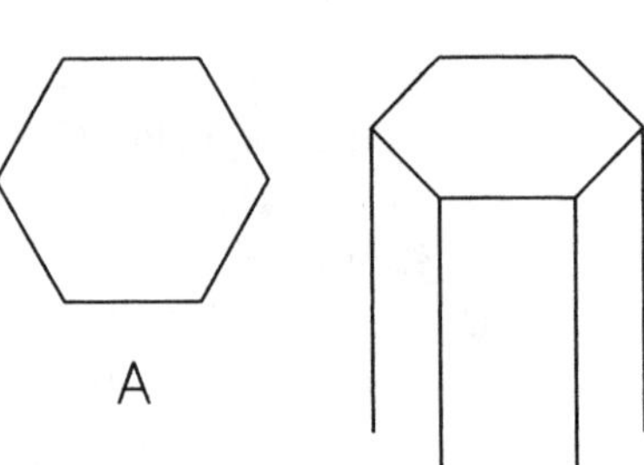

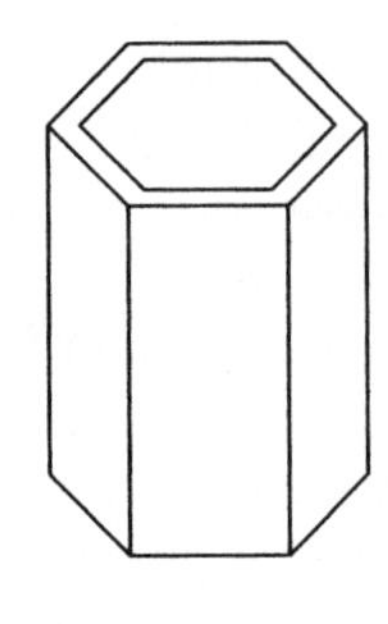

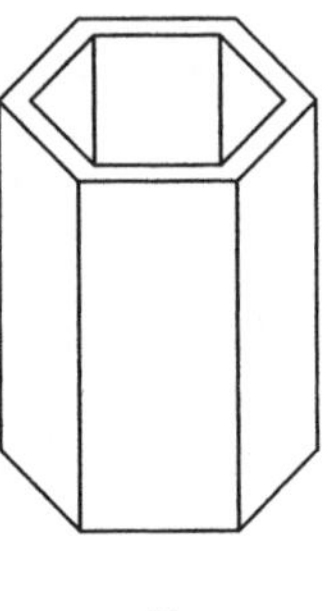

B C D

FIGURE 13–11
Shape 7: Isometric Detail—A Hexagonal-Shaped Vase

Prompt	Response
Command:	**Polygon** (or TYPE: **POL<enter>**)
Enter number of sides <4>:	TYPE: **6<enter>**
Specify center of polygon or [Edge]:	CLICK: **a point on a grid mark, in the approximate location shown in Figure 13–2 (with SNAP ON)**
Enter an option [Inscribed in circle/ Circumscribed about circle] <1>:	TYPE: **C<enter>**
Specify radius of circle:	TYPE: **6<enter>**

Now you have a hexagon that cannot be used in isometric drawing. To use it, you must block the hexagon and then insert it with different X and Y values. **Be sure to toggle to the top isoplane when you insert the hexagonal block.**

Step 42. Block and insert the hexagon (Figure 13–11B), as described next:

Prompt	Response
Command:	**Block** (or TYPE: **B<enter>**)
The Block Definition dialog box appears:	TYPE: **HEX in the Name: input box. Make sure Delete is selected.**
	CLICK: **Pick point**
Specify insertion base point:	CLICK: **the center of the hexagon**
The Block Definition dialog box appears:	CLICK: **Select objects**
Select objects:	CLICK: **any point on the hexagon**
Select objects:	**<enter>**
The Block Definition dialog box appears:	CLICK: **OK**
The hexagon disappears:	
Command:	**Insert-Block...** (or TYPE: **I<enter>**)
The Insert dialog box appears:	CLICK: **the down arrow in the Name: input box**
	CLICK: **HEX** (if it is not already in the Name: input box)
	CLICK: **the checks in Uniform Scale and Rotation - Specify on screen to remove them**
	CHANGE: **Y: in the Scale area to .58** (This is a very close approximation to the isometric scale factor.)
	CLICK: **OK**
Specify insertion point or [Basepoint/ Scale/X/Y/X/Rotate]:	PICK: **the location of the isometric hexagon as shown in Figure 13–2 (SNAP ON)** (5′7-9/16″, 2′-4″)

Step 43. Draw 1′-3″ vertical lines from each of the visible corners of the hexagon in the 270 direction (Figure 13–11B). (You can draw one line, then copy it three times.)

Step 44. Using Osnap-Endpoint, draw lines to form the bottom of the hexagon (Figure 13–11C).

Step 45. Copy the HEX block and pick the same point for the base point and second point of displacement so that the copied HEX lies directly on top of the first HEX.

Step 46. Use the Scale command to scale the copied HEX to a .8 scale factor. Be sure to CLICK: the center of the HEX block as the base point.

Step 47. Draw vertical lines on the inside of the vase, as shown in Figure 13–11D.

Step 48. When you have completed Tutorial 13–1, save your work in at least two places.

Step 49. Plot or print the drawing on an 8-1/2″ × 11″ sheet of paper; use Fit to paper.

Tutorial 13–2: Tenant Space Reception Desk in Isometric

The tenant space reception desk is drawn in isometric in Tutorial 13–2. When you have completed Tutorial 13–2, your drawing will look similar to Figure 13–12.

Step 1. Use your workspace to make the following settings:

1. **Use SaveAs... to save the drawing on the hard drive with the name CH13-TUTORIAL2.**
2. Set drawing Units: **Architectural**
3. Set Drawing Limits: **15′,15′**
4. Set Snap: **Style-Isometric-1″**
5. Set GRIDDISPLAY: **0**
6. Set Grid: **4″**

FIGURE 13–12
Tutorial 13–2: Tenant Space Reception Desk in Isometric

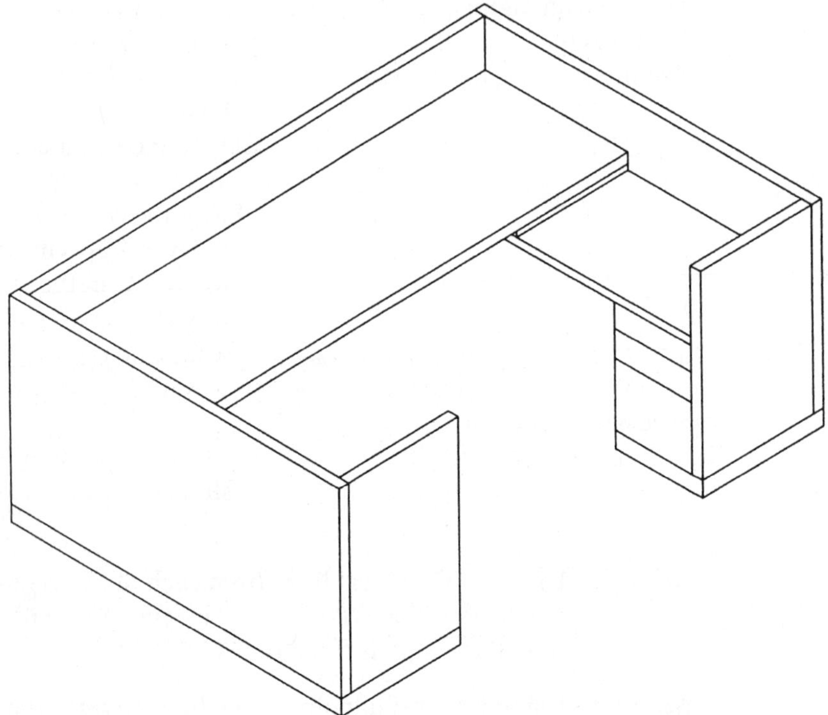

FIGURE 13–13
Drawing the Top Edge of the Panels

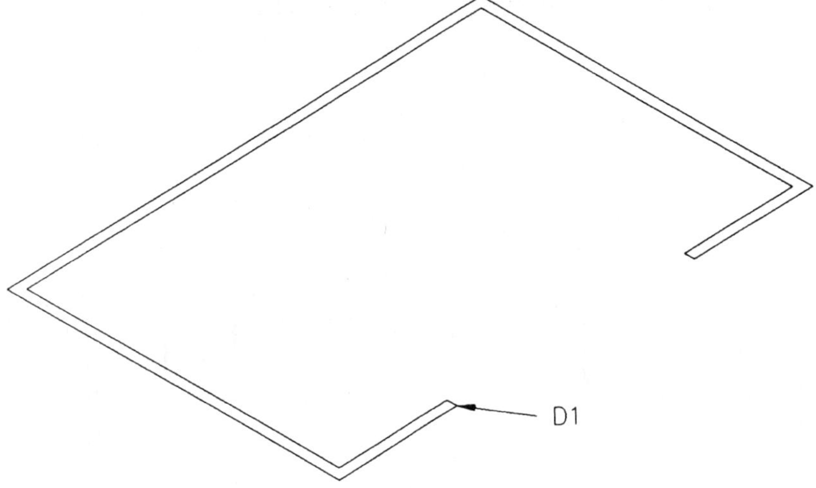

7. Create the following layer:

LAYER NAME	COLOR	LINETYPE	LINEWEIGHT
Layer1	green	continuous	Default

8. Set **Layer1** current.
9. **Zoom-All.**

This tutorial is a series of straight lines, all of which are on the isometric axes. Follow the step-by-step procedure described next so that you get some ideas about what you can and cannot do when using the isometric drawing method. To draw an isometric view of the reception desk (Figure 13–12), use the dimensions shown in Figure 13–14.

Step 2. Set Snap and Ortho ON. Toggle to the top isometric plane. Draw the top edge of the panels (Figure 13–13), as described next:

Prompt	Response
Command:	**Line** (or TYPE: **L<enter>**)
Specify first point:	**D1** (Figure 13–13) (absolute coordinates 8′1,7′4)
Specify next point or [Undo]:	TYPE: **@24<210<enter>** (or **move the mouse downward 30° to the left and** TYPE: **24<enter>**)
Specify next point or [Undo]:	TYPE: **@66<150<enter>**
Specify next point or [Close/Undo]:	TYPE: **@96<30<enter>**
Specify next point or [Close/Undo]:	TYPE: **@66<-30<enter>**
Specify next point or [Close/Undo]:	TYPE: **@24<210<enter>**
Specify next point or [Close/Undo]:	TYPE: **@2<150<enter>**
Specify next point or [Close/Undo]:	TYPE: **@22<30<enter>**
Specify next point or [Close/Undo]:	TYPE: **@62<150<enter>**
Specify next point or [Close/Undo]:	TYPE: **@92<210<enter>**
Specify next point or [Close/Undo]:	TYPE: **@62<330<enter>**
Specify next point or [Close/Undo]:	TYPE: **@22<30<enter>**
Specify next point or [Close/Undo]:	TYPE: **C<enter>**

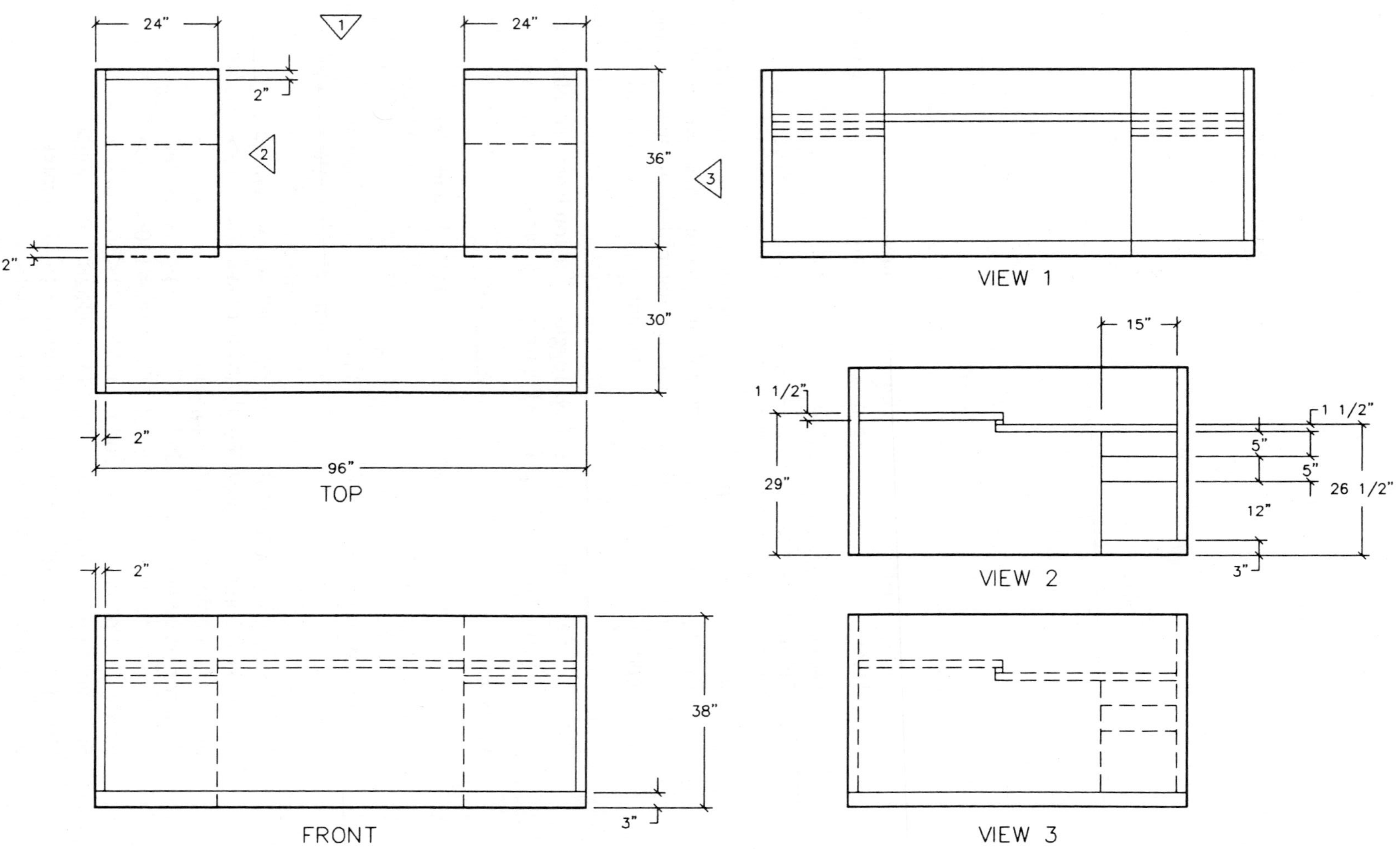

FIGURE 13–14
Dimensions of the Tenant Space Reception Desk (Scale: 3/8″ = 1′-0″)

FIGURE 13–15
Extend Lines to Form the Separate Panels

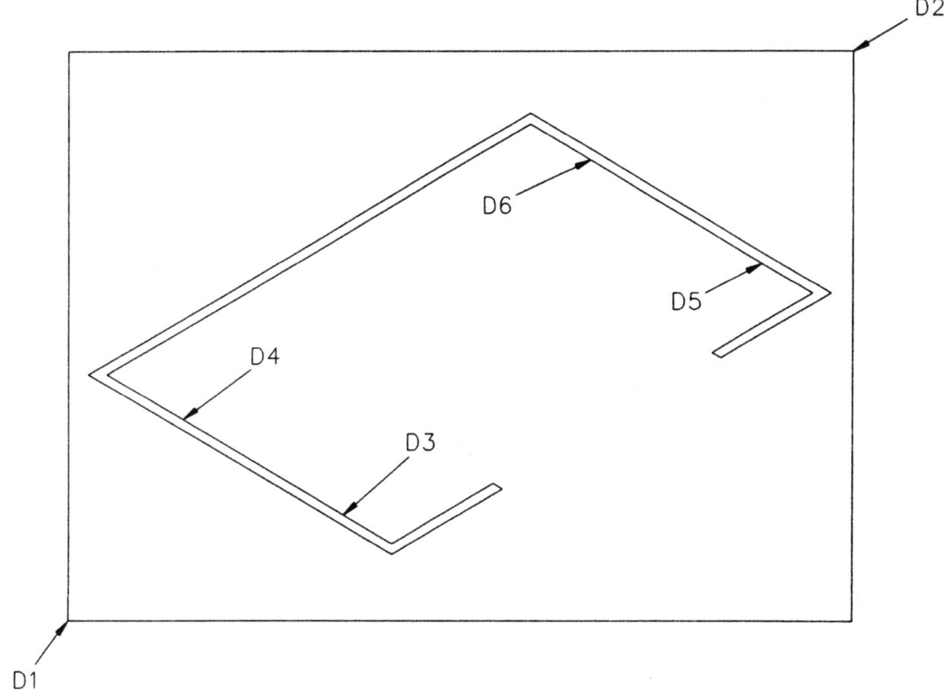

Step 3. **Use the Extend command to extend the inside lines of the panels to form the separate panels (Figure 13–15), as described next:**

Prompt	Response
Command:	**Extend** (or TYPE: **EX<enter>**)
Select objects or <select all>:	**<enter>** (enter Select all objects as boundary edges)
Select object to extend or shift-select to trim or [Fence/ Crossing/Project/Edge/Undo]:	**D3,D4,D5,D6<enter>**

Step 4. **Copy the top edges of the panels to form the lower kickplate surfaces (Figure 13–16), as described next:**

TIP: You can also use direct distance entry to specify distances when you copy if you toggle to the correct isoplane.

Prompt	Response
Command:	**Copy** (or TYPE: **CP<enter>**)
Select objects:	**D1,D2,D3,D4**
Select objects:	**<enter>**
Specify base point or [Displacement/ mOde] <Displacement>:	**D1** (any point is OK)
Specify second point or <use first point as displacement>:	TYPE: **@35<270<enter>**

FIGURE 13–16
Copy the Top Edges to Form the Lower Kickplate Surfaces and the Edge of the Main Work Surface

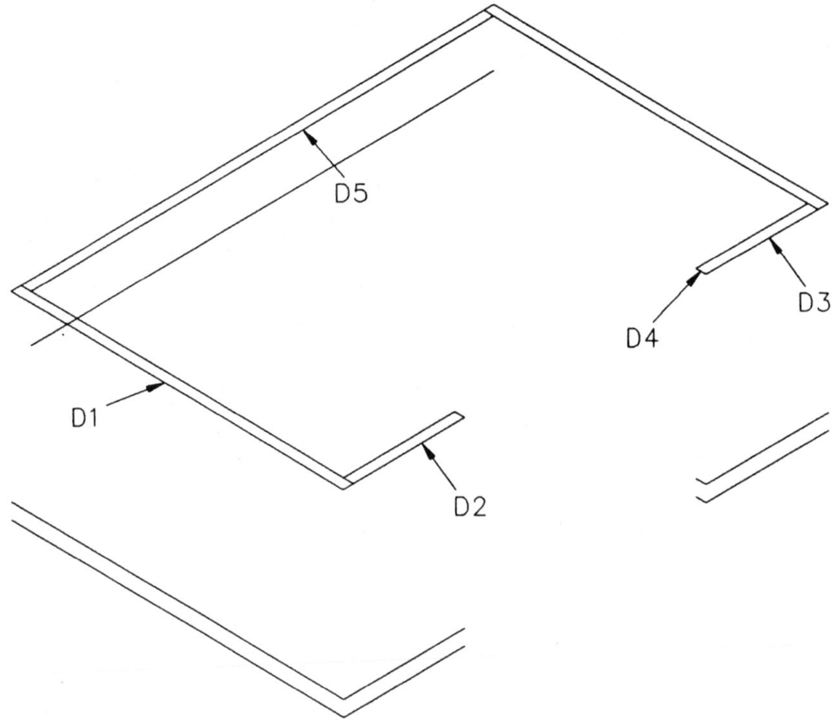

Prompt	Response
Specify second point or [Exit/Undo] <Exit>:	TYPE: **@38<270<enter>**
Specify second point or [Exit/Undo] <Exit>:	**<enter>**

Step 5. **Repeat the Copy command to draw the edge of the main work surface against the inside of the panel (Figure 13–16), as described next:**

Prompt	Response
Command:	**<enter>**
Select objects:	**D5**
Select objects:	**<enter>**
Specify base point or [Displacement/mOde] <Displacement>:	**D5** (any point is OK)
Specify second point or <use first point as displacement>:	TYPE: **@9<270<enter>**

Step 6. **Set a running Osnap mode of Endpoint and draw vertical lines connecting top and bottom outside lines and the inside corner above the work surface (Figure 13–17).**

Step 7. **Draw the work surfaces (Figure 13–17), as described next:**

Prompt	Response
Command:	**Line** (or TYPE: **L<enter>**)
Specify first point:	**OSNAP-Endpoint, D1**
Specify next point or [Undo]:	TYPE: **@28<330<enter>**
Specify next point or [Undo]:	**D2** (With Ortho ON and the top isoplane active, move your mouse downward 30° to the left and pick any point beyond the inside of the left partition; you can Trim these later.)

FIGURE 13–17
Draw the Vertical Lines Connecting Top and Bottom Edges; Draw the Work Surfaces

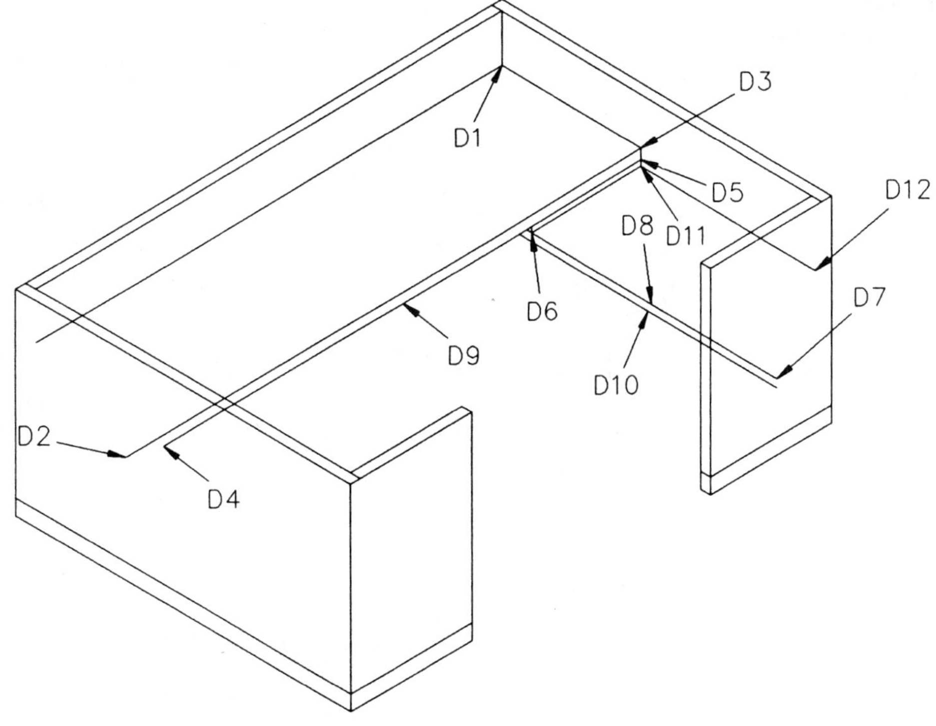

Prompt	Response
Specify next point or [Close/Undo]:	**<enter>**
Command:	**<enter>** (repeat LINE)
Specify first point:	**OSNAP-Endpoint, D3**
Specify next point or [Undo]:	TYPE: **@1-1/2<270<enter>**
Specify next point or [Undo]:	**D4** (pick another point outside the left partition)
Specify next point or [Close/Undo]:	**<enter>**
Command:	**<enter>** (repeat LINE)
Specify first point:	**OSNAP-Endpoint, D5**
Specify next point or [Undo]:	TYPE: **@1<270<enter>**
Specify next point or [Undo]:	TYPE: **@22<210<enter>**
Specify next point or [Close/Undo]:	TYPE: **@1<90<enter>**
Specify next point or [Close/Undo]:	**<enter>**
Command:	**<enter>** (repeat LINE)
Specify first point:	**OSNAP-Endpoint, D6 (Figure 13–17)**
Specify next point or [Undo]:	**D7** (move the mouse downward 30° to the right and pick a point outside the right rear panel)
Specify next point or [Undo]:	**<enter>**
Command:	**<enter>** (Repeat LINE)
Specify first point:	**OSNAP-Endpoint, D11**
Specify next point or [Undo]:	**D12** (pick a point outside the right rear panel) **<enter>**
Command:	**Copy** (or TYPE: **CP<enter>**)
Select objects:	**D8**
Select objects:	**<enter>**
Specify base point or [Displacement/ mOde] <Displacement>:	**D8 (any point)**
Specify second point or <use first point as displacement>:	TYPE: **@1-1/2<270<enter>**
Command:	Extend (or TYPE: **EX<enter>**)

FIGURE 13–18
Trim Lines and Draw the Drawer Pedestal

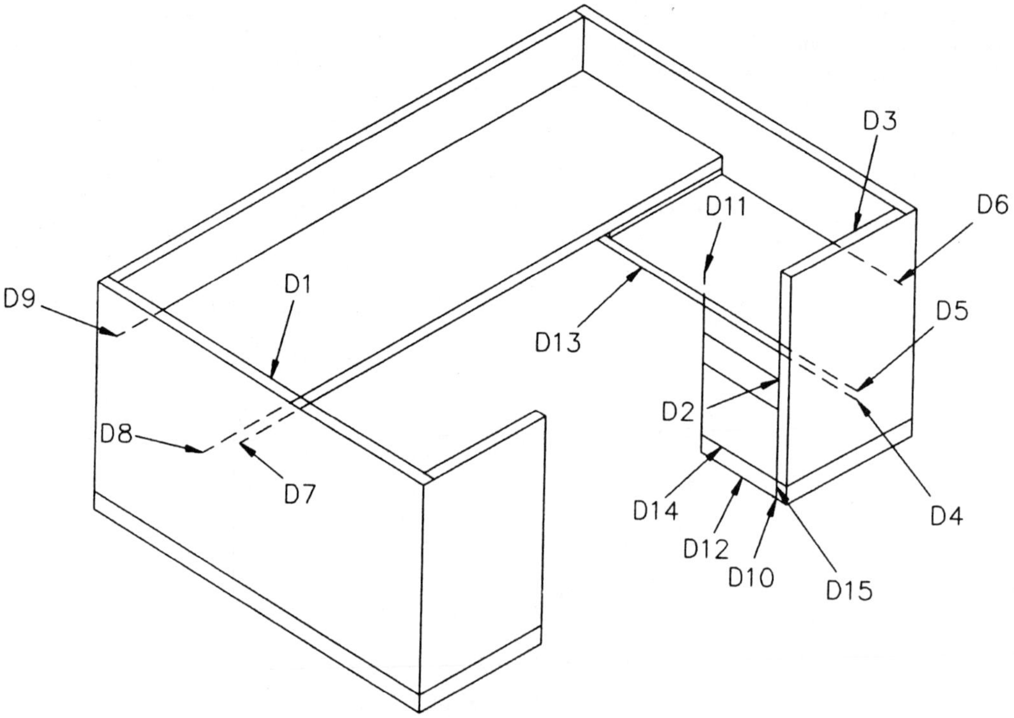

Prompt	Response
Select objects or <select all>:	**D9<enter>**
Select object to extend or [Fence/Crossing/Project/ Edge/Undo]:	**D8,D10<enter>**

Step 8. Trim lines that extend outside the panels (Figure 13–18), as described next:

Prompt	Response
Command:	**Trim** (or TYPE: **TR<enter>**)
Select objects or <select all>:	**D1,D2,D3<enter>**
Select object to trim or shift-select to extend or [Fence/Crossing/ Project/Edge/eRase/Undo]:	**D4,D5,D6,D7,D8,D9<enter>**

Step 9. Draw the drawer pedestal (Figure 13–18), as described next:

Prompt	Response
Command:	**Line** (or TYPE: **L<enter>**)
Specify first point:	**OSNAP-Endpoint, D10**
Specify next point or [Undo]:	**Toggle to the left isoplane and** TYPE: **@15<150<enter>**
Specify next point or [Undo]:	**D11** (with Ortho ON, pick a point above the bottom edge of the desktop)
Specify next point or [Close/Undo]:	**<enter>**
Command:	**Copy** (or TYPE: **CP<enter>**)
Select objects:	**D12** (Figure 13–18)
Select objects:	**<enter>**
Specify base point or [Displacement/ mOde] <Displacement>:	**D12 (any point)**

Prompt	Response
Specify second point or <use first point as displacement>:	TYPE: **@3<90<enter>**
Specify second point or [Exit/Undo] <Exit>:	TYPE: **@15<90<enter>**
Specify second point or [Exit/Undo] <Exit>:	TYPE: **@20<90<enter>**
Specify second point or [Exit/Undo] <Exit>:	**<enter>**

Step 10. Trim the extra lines, as described next:

Prompt	Response
Command:	**Trim** (or TYPE: **TR<enter>**)
Select objects or <select all>:	**D13,D14<enter>**
Select object to trim or shift-select to extend or [Fence/Crossing/Project/Edge/eRase/Undo]:	**D15,D11<enter>**

Step 11. When you have completed Tutorial 13–2, save your work in at least two places.

Step 12. CLICK: **Layout1**, CLICK: **the viewport boundary**, RIGHT-CLICK, **and use the Properties menu to set a standard scale of 1/2″ = 1′. Plot or print the drawing on an 8-1/2″ × 11″ sheet of paper.**

DIMENSIONING IN ISOMETRIC

You can resolve the problem of placing dimensions on an isometric drawing by buying a third-party software dimensioning package designed specifically for isometric. Other methods, such as using the aligned option in dimensioning and using an inclined font with the style setting, solve only part of the problem. Arrowheads must be constructed and individually inserted for each isoplane. If you spend a little time blocking the arrowheads and customizing your menu, you can speed up the process significantly.

GRADIENT HATCH

Gradient (the tab on the Hatch and Gradient dialog box) can be used to render two-dimensional drawings such as the isometric drawings in this chapter (Figure 13–19). The appearance of these renderings is very similar to air brush renderings. The three means you can use to change the pattern appearance are

1. Select one of the nine pattern buttons.
2. Check: Centered (or Uncheck: centered).
3. Change the angle of the pattern.

In addition, you can select a color and vary its shade.

In general, follow these guidelines:

1. When selecting a gradient pattern, you should place those on left and right isoplanes at a 60° angle to a horizontal line. Top isoplanes can vary from a horizontal pattern (90° of rotation) to 30°.

FIGURE 13–19
Tutorial 13–3 Complete

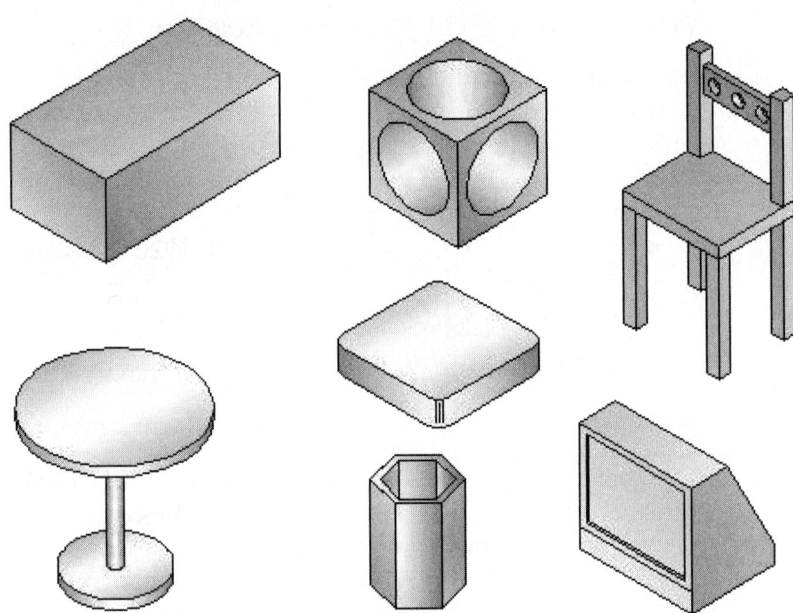

2. Use the center pattern on the top row to shade holes. This pattern should be at a 0° angle in the top isoplane, 120° in the left isoplane, and 60° in the right isoplane. The Centered button should be unchecked so that the pattern shows a darker area on one side of the hole than on the other side.
3. Do not be too concerned about where the light is coming from. Consider that there are varying sources of light. Just try to keep light areas next to dark ones and do not be afraid to experiment with any of the nine patterns. Some figures will be challenging and will require several tries before the rendering looks right.
4. Use the Draw order: command to "Send to back" all your gradient patterns so that the lines of the drawing show in front of the gradient patterns.

Tutorial 13–3: Using Gradient Patterns to Render the Shapes of Tutorial 13–1

Step 1. **Open drawing CH13-TUTORIAL1.**

Step 2. **Save the drawing as CH13-TUTORIAL3.**

Step 3. **Open the Hatch and Gradient dialog box and select a color, as described next:**

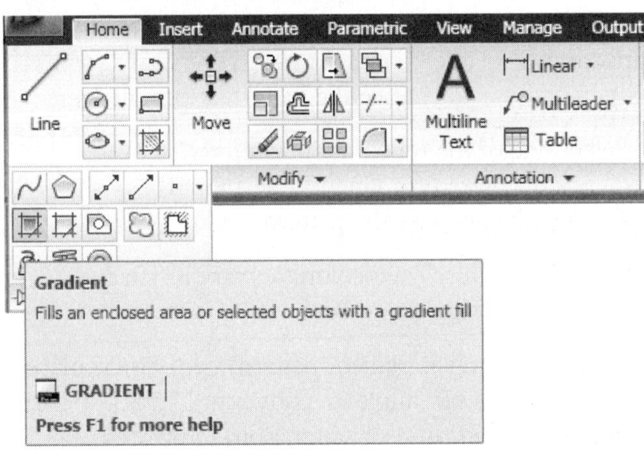

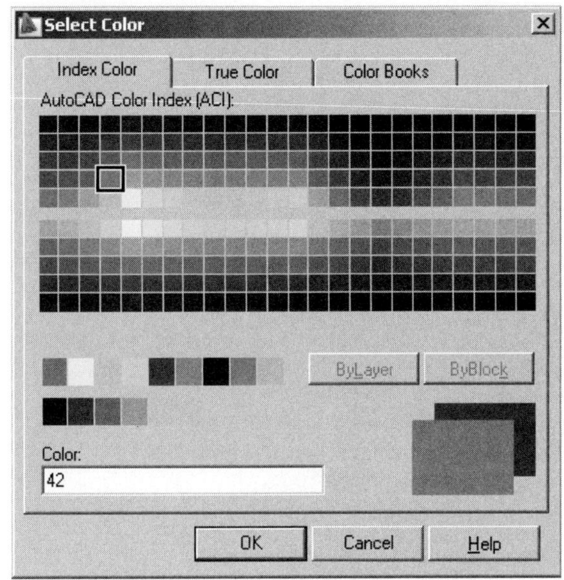

FIGURE 13–20
Select a Color for Gradient Hatch

Prompt	Response
Command:	**Hatch...** (or TYPE: **H<enter>**)
The Hatch and Gradient dialog box appears:	**With the Gradient tab selected:** CLICK: **the ellipsis (the three dots) to the right of the one color swatch**
The Select Color dialog box (Figure 13–20) appears:	CLICK: **the Index Color tab** CLICK: **a color (for now, number 42)** CLICK: **OK**

Step 4. Hatch the top plane of Shape 1, Figure 13–21, as described next:

Prompt	Response
The Hatch and Gradient dialog box appears:	CLICK: **the first pattern from the left on the top row to select it** **Uncheck the Centered box** **Change the Angle to 300** CLICK: **Send to back** (in the Draw order: list) so the lines are visible CLICK: **Add: Pick points**
Pick internal point or [Select objects/remove Boundaries]:	CLICK: **any point inside the top plane of Shape 1**
Pick internal point or [Select objects/remove Boundaries]:	**<enter>**
The Hatch and Gradient dialog box appears:	CLICK: **Preview**
Pick or press Esc to return to dialog or <Right-click to accept hatch>:	**RIGHT-CLICK** (if the pattern looks right) or PRESS: **Esc and fix the dialog box**
Command:	**<enter>** (Repeat Hatch)

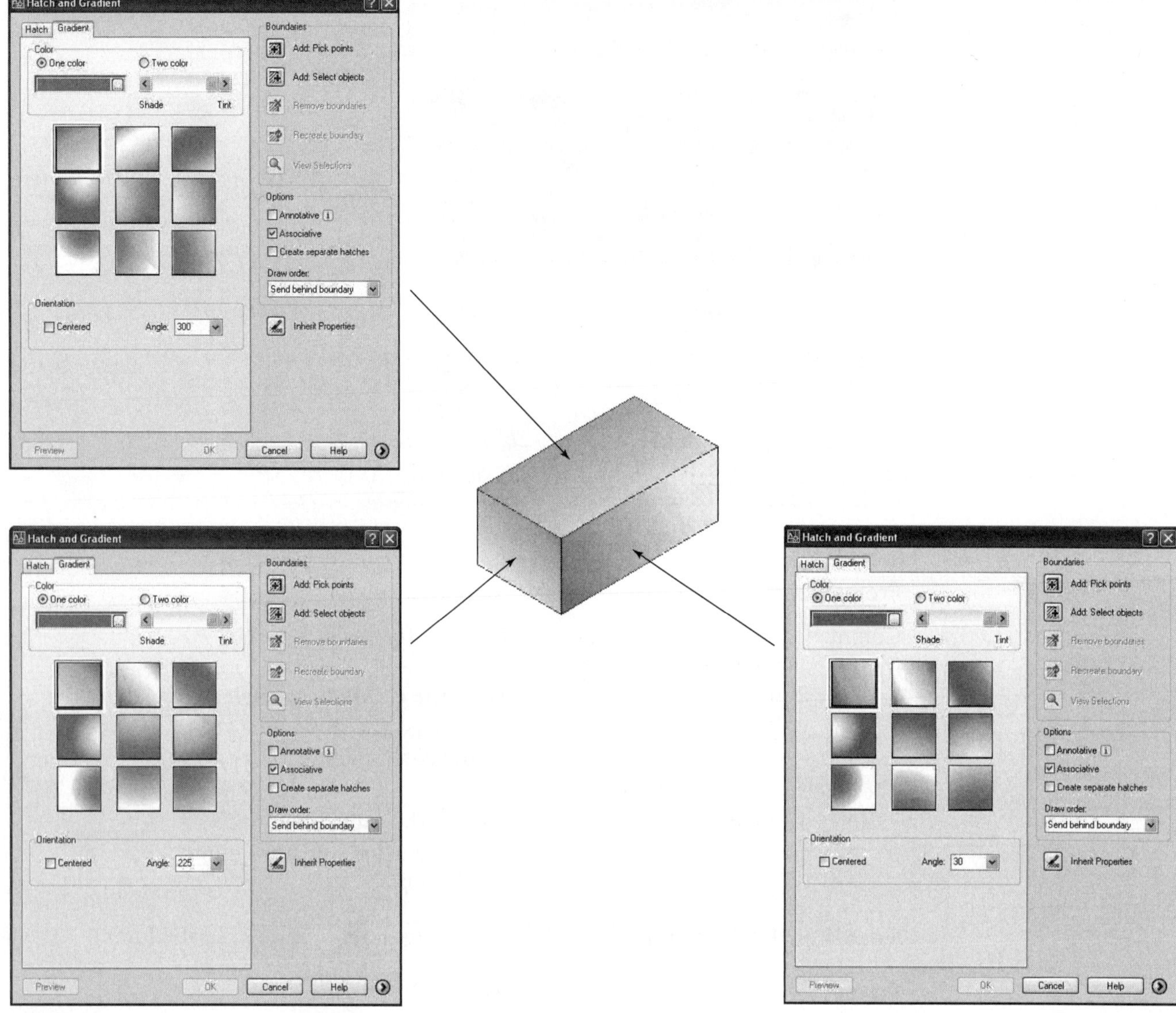

FIGURE 13–21
Apply Gradient Hatch Patterns to Shape 1

Step 5. **Hatch the left plane of Shape 1, Figure 13–21, as described next:**

Prompt	Response
The Hatch and Gradient dialog box appears:	CLICK: **the first pattern from the left on the top row to select it.** **Uncheck the Centered box** **Change the Angle to 225** CLICK: **Send to back** CLICK: **Add: Pick points**
Pick internal point or [Select objects/remove Boundaries]:	CLICK: **any point inside the left plane of Shape 1**
Pick internal point or [Select objects/remove Boundaries]:	**<enter>**

Prompt	Response
The Hatch and Gradient dialog box appears:	CLICK: **Preview**
Pick or press Esc to return to dialog or <Right-click to accept hatch>:	**RIGHT-CLICK** (if the pattern looks right) or PRESS: **Esc and fix the dialog box**
Command:	**<enter>**(Repeat Hatch)

Step 6. Hatch the right plane of Shape 1, Figure 13–21, as described next:

Prompt	Response
The Hatch and Gradient dialog box appears:	CLICK: **the first pattern from the left on the top row to select it** **Uncheck the Centered box** **Change the Angle to 30** CLICK: **Send to back** CLICK: **Add: Pick points**
Pick internal point or [Select objects/remove Boundaries]:	CLICK: **any point inside the right plane of Shape 1**
Pick internal point or [Select objects/remove Boundaries]:	**<enter>**
The Hatch and Gradient dialog box appears:	CLICK: **Preview**
Pick or press Esc to return to dialog or <Right-click to accept hatch>:	**RIGHT-CLICK** (if the pattern looks right) or PRESS: **Esc and fix the dialog box**

Step 7. Hatch the top planes of Shape 4, Figure 13–22, as described next:

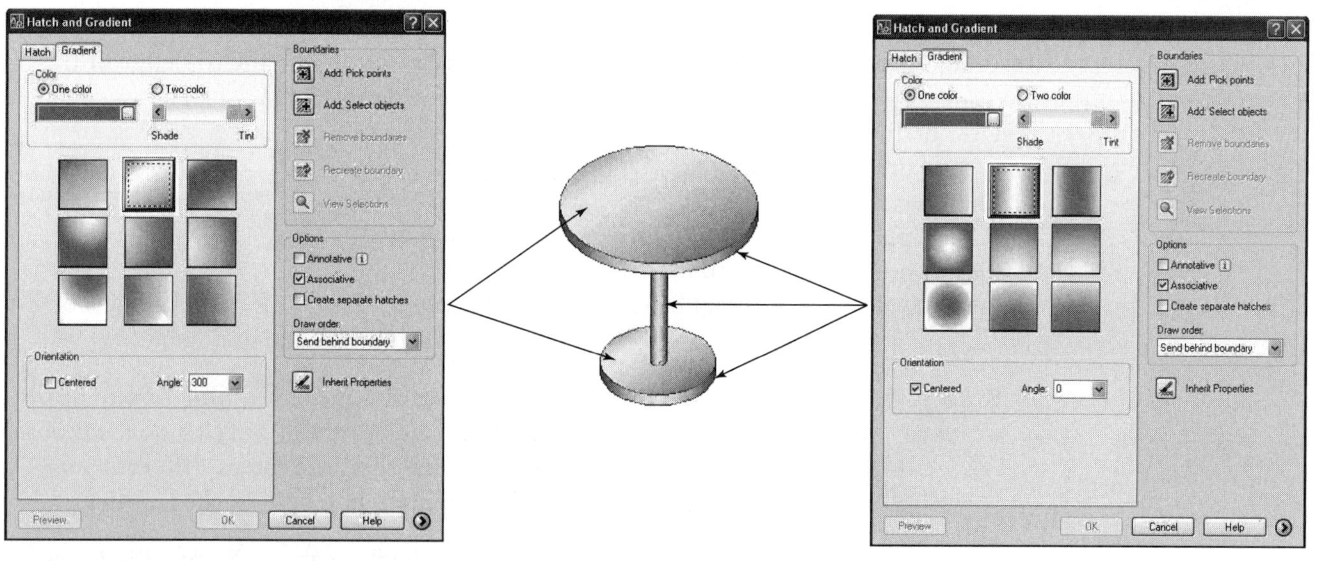

FIGURE 13–22
Gradient Hatch Patterns for Shape 4

Prompt	Response
Command:	TYPE: **H<enter>**
The Hatch and Gradient dialog box appears:	CLICK: **the second pattern from the left on the top row to select it** **Uncheck the Centered box** **Change the Angle to 300** CLICK: **Send to back** CLICK: **Add: Pick points**
Pick internal point or [Select objects/remove Boundaries]:	CLICK: **any point inside the top plane of Shape 4, then** CLICK: **any point inside the top plane of the base, as shown in Figure 13–22.**
Pick internal point or [Select objects/remove Boundaries]:	**<enter>**
The Hatch and Gradient dialog box appears:	CLICK: **Preview**
Pick or press Esc to return to dialog or <Right-click to accept hatch>:	**RIGHT-CLICK** (if the pattern looks right) or PRESS: **Esc and fix the dialog box**

Step 8. **Hatch the cylindrical planes of Shape 4, Figure 13–22, as described next:**

Prompt	Response
Command:	TYPE: **H<enter>**
The Hatch and Gradient dialog box appears:	CLICK: **the second pattern from the left on the top row to select it** **Check the Centered box** **Change the Angle to 0** CLICK: **Send to back** CLICK: **Add: Pick points**
Pick internal point or [Select objects/remove Boundaries]:	CLICK: **any point inside the top edge of the tabletop, Figure 13–22.**
Pick internal point or [Select objects/remove Boundaries]:	**<enter>**
The Hatch and Gradient dialog box appears:	CLICK: **Preview**
Pick or press Esc to return to dialog or <Right-click to accept hatch>:	**RIGHT-CLICK** (if the pattern looks right) or PRESS: **Esc and fix the dialog box**

Step 9. **Use the same settings in the Hatch and Gradient dialog box to apply patterns to the post and the base edge. You will have to do each one separately because the areas to be hatched are much different in size. (You can also check "Create separate hatches" in the Gradient tab.)**

Step 10. **Use the Inherit Properties option to Hatch Shape 5, Figure 13–23, as described next:**

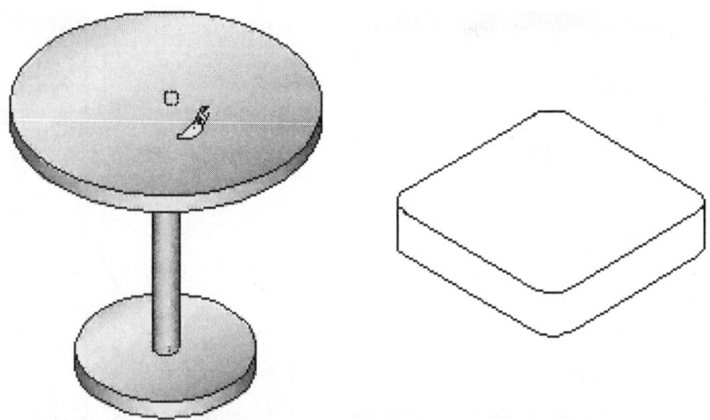

FIGURE 13–23 Use Inherit Properties to Hatch Shape 5—Select Associative Hatch Object

Prompt	Response
Command:	TYPE: **H<enter>**
The Hatch and Gradient dialog box appears:	CLICK: **Inherit Properties**
Select hatch object:	CLICK: **the top surface of Shape 4, Figure 13–23.**
Pick internal point or [Select objects/remove Boundaries]:	CLICK: **the top surface of Shape 5, Figure 13–24**
Pick internal point or [Select objects/remove Boundaries]:	**<enter>** CLICK: **Send to back** CLICK: **OK**
Command:	**<enter>**(Repeat Hatch)
The Hatch and Gradient dialog box appears:	CLICK: **Inherit Properties**
Select hatch object:	CLICK: **the post pattern of Shape 4**
Pick internal point or [Select objects/remove Boundaries]:	CLICK: **the unshaded surface of Shape 5**
Pick internal point or [Select object/remove Boundaries]:	**<enter>** CLICK: **OK**

Step 11. **Use the gradient hatch patterns shown in Figure 13–25 to hatch five of the areas of Shape 3. Use Inherit Properties to select hatch patterns from Shapes 1 and 5 to complete Shape 3.**

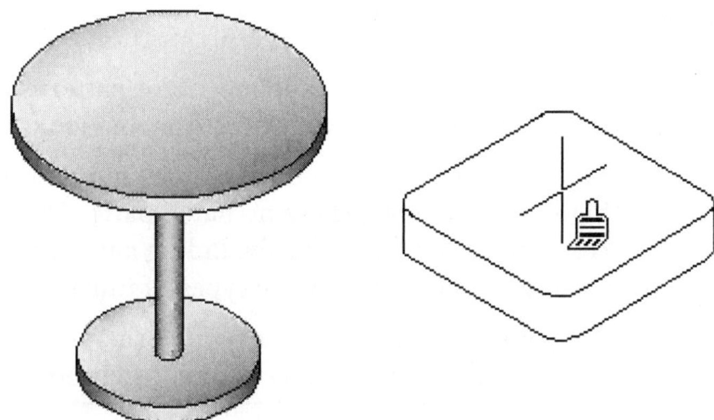

FIGURE 13–24 Select Internal Point

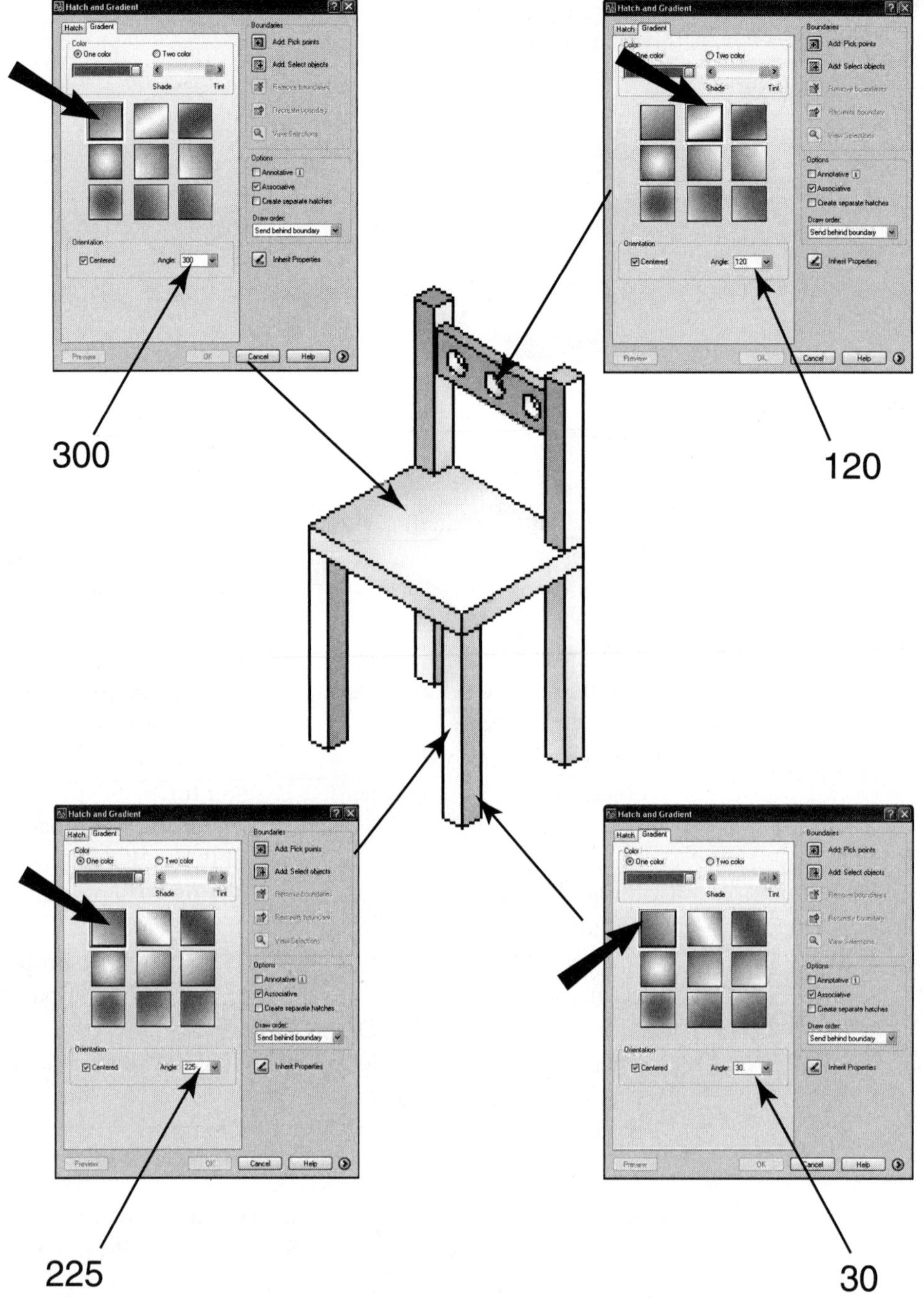

FIGURE 13–25
Gradient Hatch Patterns for Shape 3

Step 12. Use Inherit Properties and any other patterns you need to shade the remaining shapes so your final drawing looks similar to Figure 13–19.

Step 13. Experiment with the Wipeout command on the Draw menu to create highlights in areas where no hatch pattern should appear. Wipeout completely covers any image hiding any part or all of it. You will find uses for Wipeout in several types of illustrating.

Step 14. Put your name in the lower right corner and plot the drawing at a scale of 1″ = 1′. Be sure the Shade plot: input box shows: As Displayed.

review questions

1. From which of the following dialog boxes are the isometric snap and grid obtained?
   a. Layer Control...
   b. Drafting Settings...
   c. Set SysVars
   d. Grid On/Off
   e. UCS Control...
2. From which of the Snap options is the isometric snap obtained?
   a. ON
   b. OFF
   c. Aspect
   d. Rotate
   e. Style
3. Which isoplane is used to draw the ellipse shown at left?
   a. Top
   b. Left
   c. Right
4. From which of the Ellipse prompts is the isometric ellipse obtained?
   a. <Axis endpoint 1>
   b. Center
   c. Isocircle
   d. Axis endpoint 2
   e. Rotation
5. Which of the following is *not* one of the normal isometric axes?
   a. 30
   b. 60
   c. 90
   d. 210
   e. 330
6. Which isoplane is used to draw the ellipse shown at left?
   a. Top
   b. Left
   c. Right
7. Which tab on the Hatch and Gradient dialog box allows you to apply patterns shown in Figure 13–19?
   a. Gradient
   b. Advanced
   c. Hatch
8. Which key(s) toggle from one isoplane to another?
   a. Ctrl-C
   b. F9
   c. F7
   d. F5
   e. Alt-F1
9. Which of the following is the same as –30°?
   a. 60°
   b. 150°
   c. 180°
   d. 210°
   e. 330°
10. Which isoplane is used to draw the ellipse shown at left?
    a. Top
    b. Left
    c. Right

Complete.

11. Which function key is used to turn the isometric grid ON and OFF?

    ____

12. Write the correct syntax (letters and numbers) to draw a line 5.25″ at a 30° angle upward to the right.

    ____

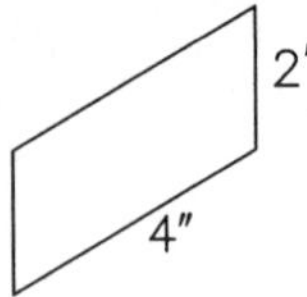

13. Write the correct sequence of keystrokes, using polar coordinates, to draw the right side of the isometric rectangle shown at left, after the first point (lower left corner) has been picked. Draw to the right and up.
    a. ______________________________
    b. ______________________________
    c. ______________________________
    d. ______________________________
14. In Tutorial 13–2, why were lines drawn beyond where they should stop and then trimmed to the correct length?

    ____

    ____
15. Which of the isoplanes will not allow vertical lines to be drawn with a mouse when ORTHO is ON?

    ____
16. List the six angles used for polar coordinates in drawing on isometric axes.

    ____
17. Describe how to draw an angled line that is *not* on one of the isometric axes.

    ____

    ____
18. Describe how to use the Draw order: option in the Hatch and Gradient dialog box to make lines appear more prominent than a gradient hatch pattern.

    ____

    ____
19. Describe two problems that must be solved to place dimensions on an isometric drawing.

    ____

    ____
20. Describe the difference between isometric drawing and 3D modeling.

    ____

    ____

exercises

Exercise 13–1: Using Gradient Patterns to Render the Reception Desk of Tutorial 13–2

Open CH13-TUTORIAL2 and use gradient hatch patterns to shade this drawing so it looks similar to Figure 13–26. When you have completed the hatching, put your name in the lower right corner and plot this drawing at a scale of 1/2″ = 1′-0″. Be sure the Shade plot: input box shows: As Displayed.

FIGURE 13–26
Exercise 13–1, Completed

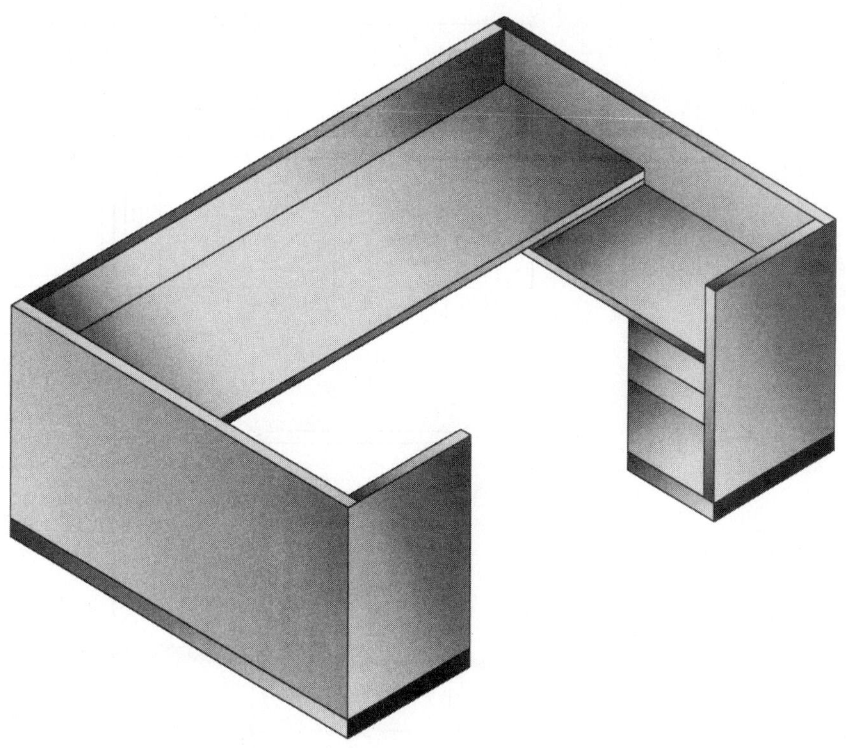

Exercise 13–2: Tenant Space Reception Seating Area in Isometric

1. Make an isometric drawing, full size, of the chairs, coffee table, and corner table to show the entire reception room seating area. Use the dimensions shown in Figure 13–27.
2. CLICK: **Layout1**, CLICK: **the viewport boundary**, and use Properties from the Modify menu to set a standard scale of 1/2″ = 1′. Plot or print the drawing on an 8-1/2″ × 11″ sheet of paper.

Exercise 13–3: Tenant Space Conference Chair in Isometric

1. Make an isometric drawing, full size, of the conference room chair. Use the dimensions shown in Figure 13–28.
2. CLICK: **Layout1**, CLICK: **the viewport boundary**, and use Properties from the Modify menu to set a standard scale of 1/2″ = 1′. Plot or print the drawing on an 8-1/2″ × 11″ sheet of paper.

Exercise 13–4: Conference Room Walls and Table in Isometric

1. Make an isometric drawing, full size, of the conference room shown in Figure 13–29. Draw a view from the direction shown by the arrow in Figure 13–29(A). The following figures provide the information needed to complete Exercise 13–4:

   Figure 13–29(A): Plan view of the north part of the conference room
   Figure 13–29(B): Elevation of the north wall of the conference room

FIGURE 13–27
Exercise 13–2: Tenant Space Reception Seating Dimensions (Scale: 3/8″ = 1′-0″)

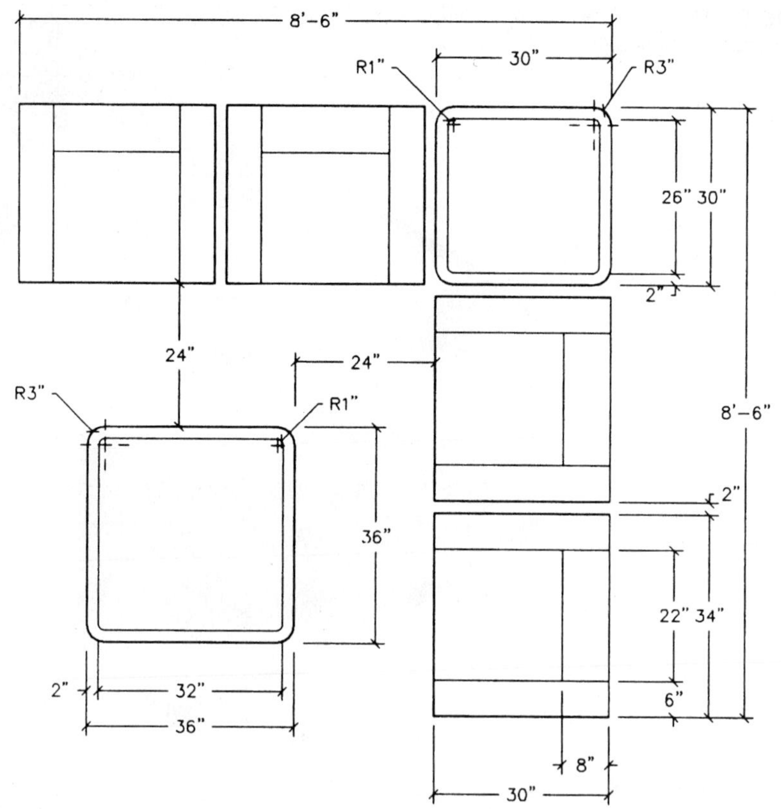

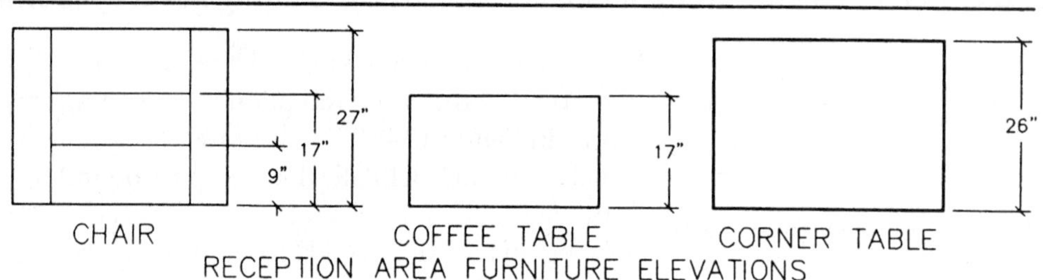

FIGURE 13–28
Exercise 13–3: Tenant Space Conference Chair Dimensions (Scale: 3/8″ = 1′-0″)

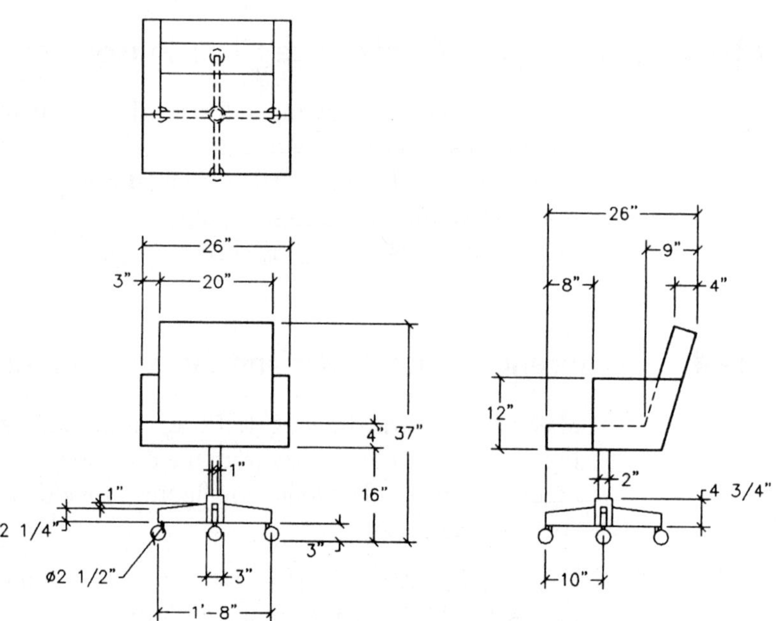

FIGURE 13–29(A)
Exercise 13–4: Plan View of the North Part of the Conference Room (Scale: 3/8″ = 1′-0″)

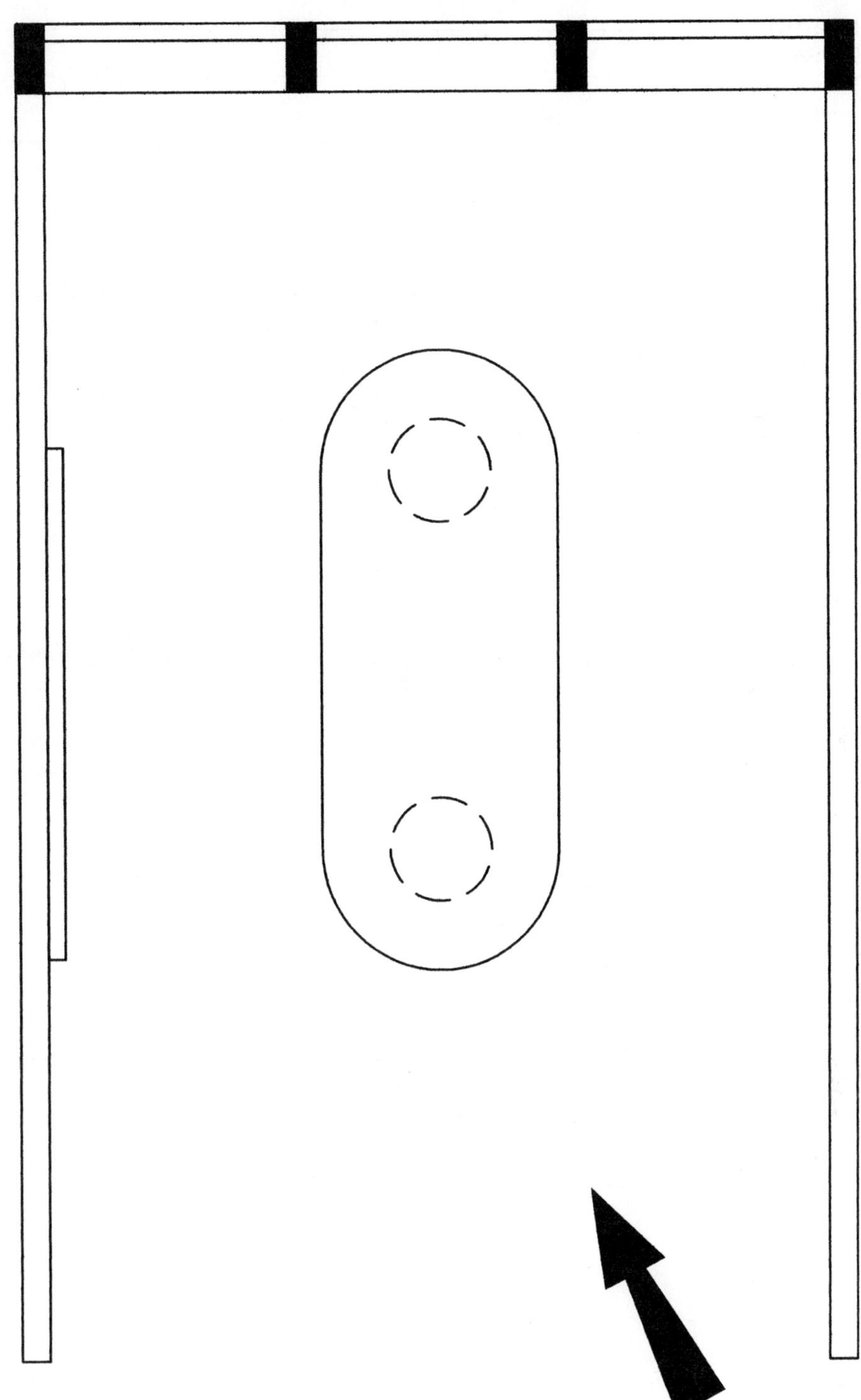

Figure 13–29(C): Elevation of the east wall of the conference room
Figure 13–29(D): Plan and elevation views of the conference table

Your final drawing should look similar to Figure 13–29(E).

2. CLICK: **Layout1**, CLICK: **the viewport boundary**, and use Properties from the Modify menu to set a standard scale of 1/4″ = 1′. Plot or print the drawing on an 8-1/2″ × 11″ sheet of paper.

FIGURE 13–29(B)
Exercise 13–4: Elevation of the North Wall of the Conference Room (Scale: 3/8″ = 1′-0″)

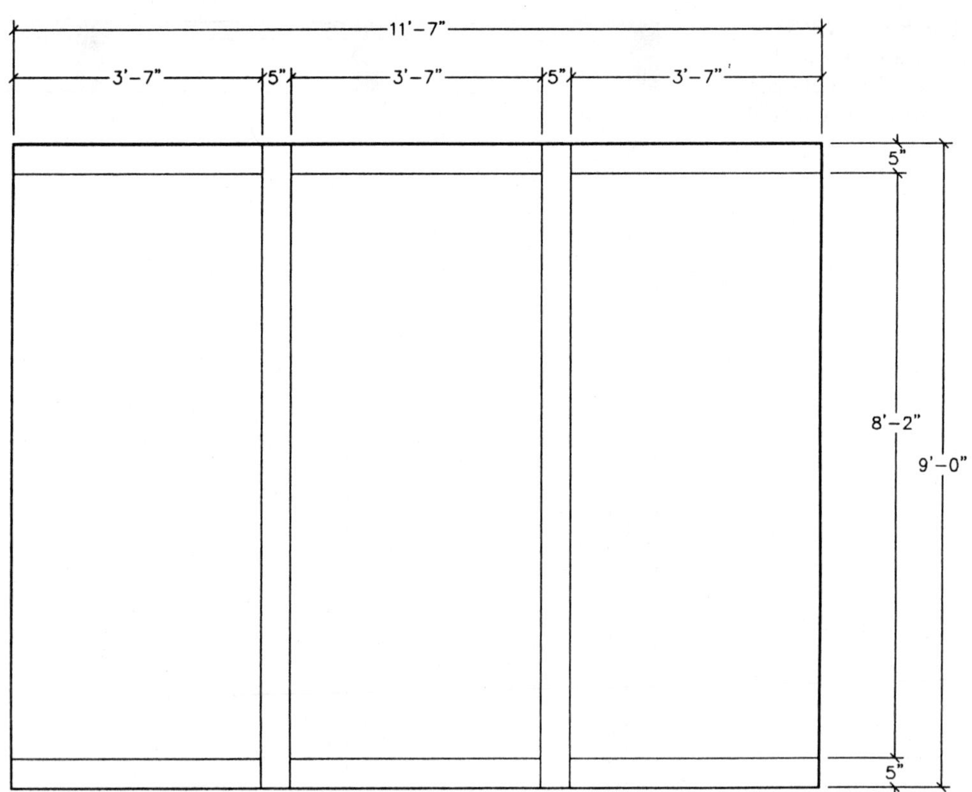

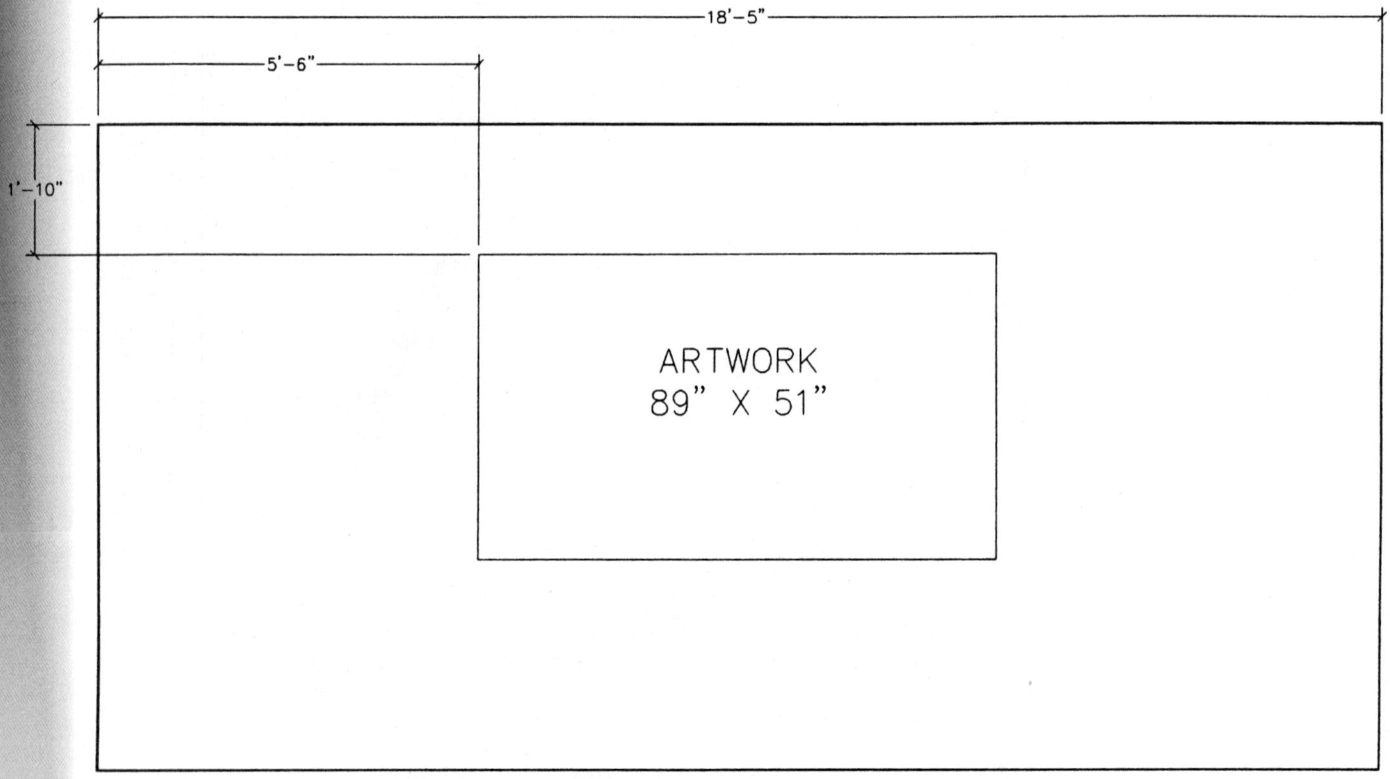

FIGURE 13–29(C)
Exercise 13–4: Elevation of the East Wall of the Conference Room (Scale: 3/8″ = 1′-0″)

FIGURE 13–29(D)
Exercise 13–4: Plan and Elevation Views of the Conference Table (Scale: 3/8″ = 1′-0″)

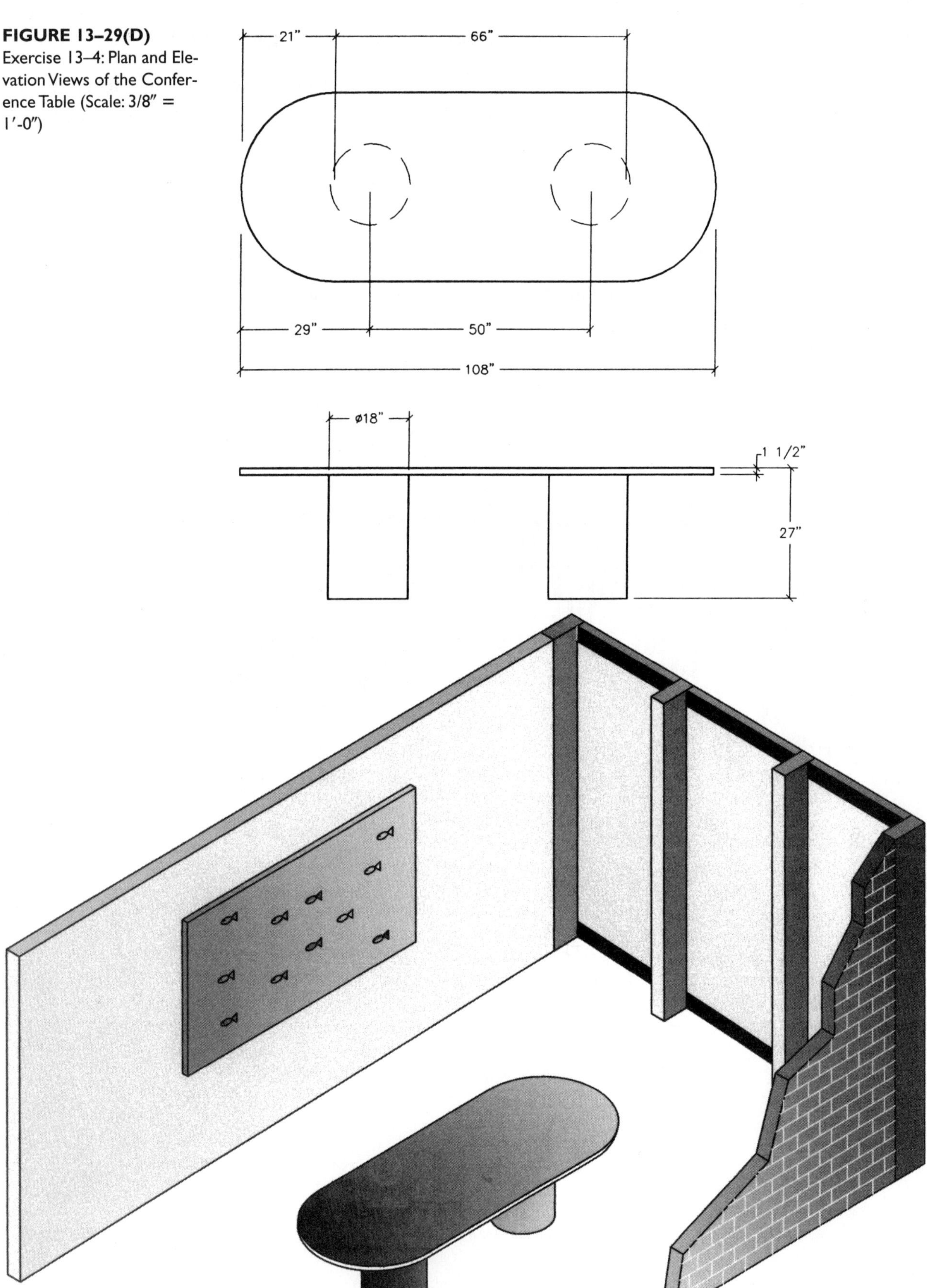

FIGURE 13–29(E)
Exercise 13–4: Gradient Hatch Isometric View of the North Part of the Conference Room (Scale: 1/4″ = 1′-0″)

Exercise 13–5: Log Cabin Kitchen Isometric Cutaway Drawing

Exercise 13–5 is an isometric cutaway drawing of the log cabin kitchen, Figure 13–30. When you have completed Exercise 13–5, your drawing will look similar to Figure 13–30, but your drawing will be in color.

Use the dimensions from Figures 13–32 and 13–33 and, if necessary, measure some of the features in the isometric drawings (Figures 13–30 and 13–31) using the scales indicated.

1. Use your workspace to make the following settings:

    1. **Use SaveAs... to save the drawing with the name CH13-EX5.**

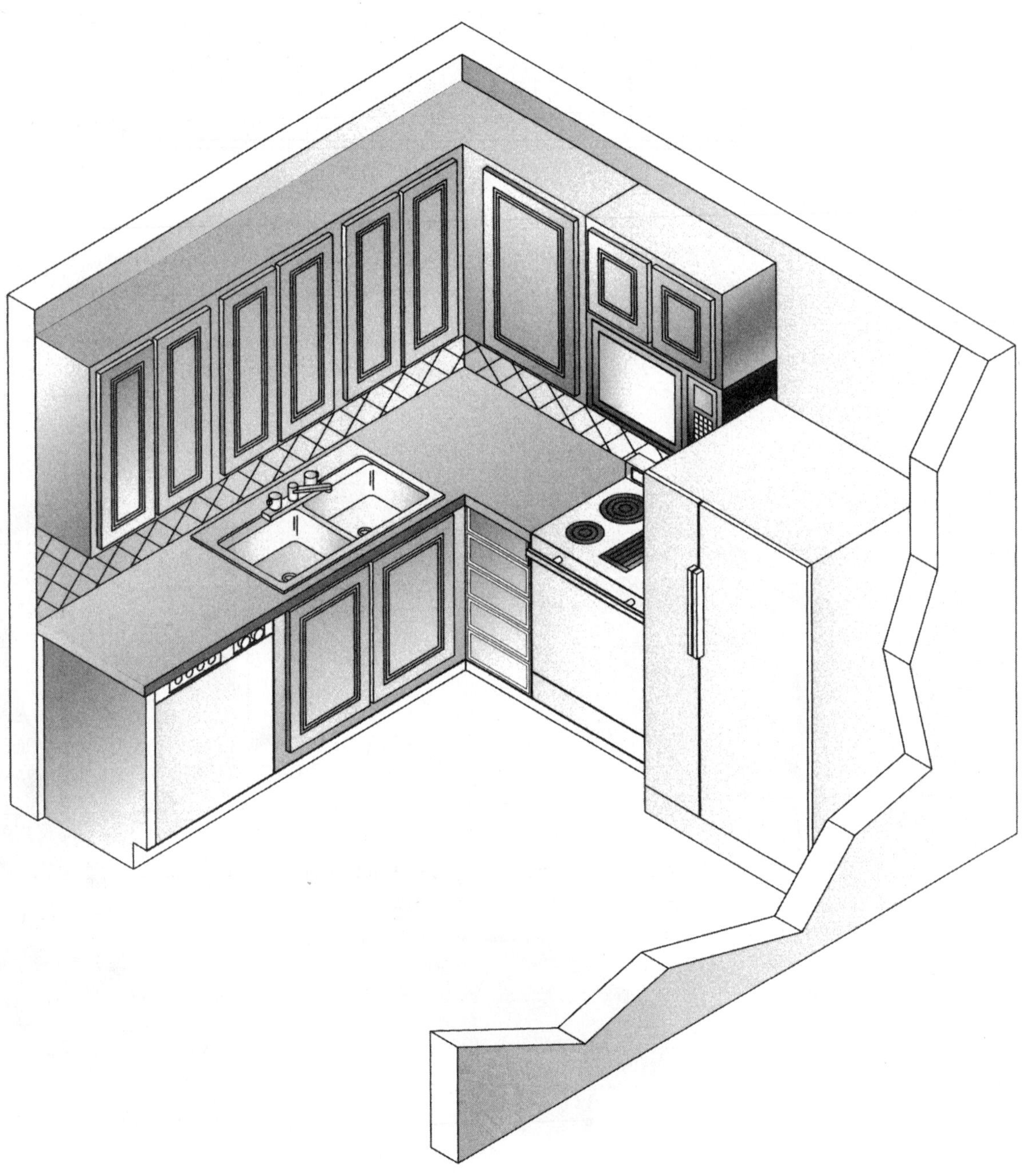

FIGURE 13–30
Exercise 13–5: Log Cabin Kitchen Cutaway (Scale: 3/8″ = 1′-0″)

FIGURE 13–31
Log Cabin Kitchen Sink (Scale: 1″ = 1′-0″)

2. Set drawing Units: **Architectural**
3. Set Drawing Limits: **30′,40′**
4. Set GRIDDISPLAY: **0**
5. Set Grid: **12″**
6. Set Isometric Snap: **3″**
7. Create the following layers:

LAYER NAME	COLOR	LINETYPE	LINEWEIGHT
Kitchen	white	continuous	0.15 mm
Kitchen Thin	magenta	continuous	0.05 mm
Text	white	continuous	Default
Hatch	varies	continuous	Default
Walls	white	continuous	0.30 mm

2. You will be able to draw one of the doors as a polyline, offset it to the inside 2″ once, 1/2″ twice, and then copy it and stretch it to make all the other doors. It may be helpful to block the doors and insert them as you are drawing.
3. Use different colors in the gradient hatch box (CLICK: **the ellipsis... in the Color area**) to apply gradient hatch patterns to each of the areas such as wood, appliances, and sink.
4. The backsplash is a combination of two hatch patterns, a gradient pattern (send to back) and a double, user-defined 60° angle with 4″ spacing on the left side and a double, user-defined 120° angle with 4″ spacing on the right side.
5. You can also insert the appliances from the DesignCenter to get measurements of many of the details.
6. Plot the drawing at a scale of 3/8″ = 1′-0″ centered vertically on an 8-1/2″ × 11″ sheet.

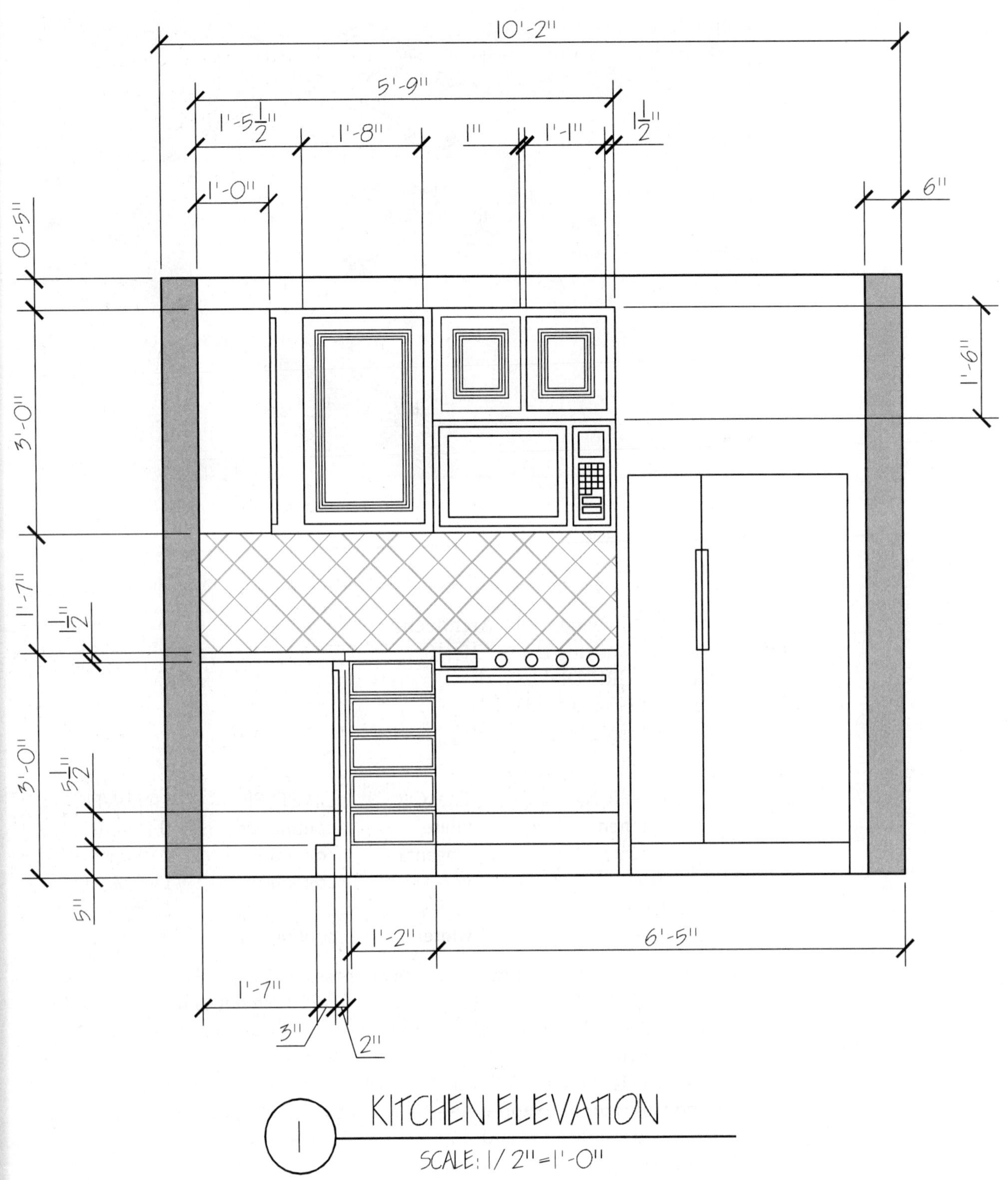

FIGURE 13–32
Exercise 13–5: Kitchen Elevation 1 (Scale: 1/2″ = 1′-0″)

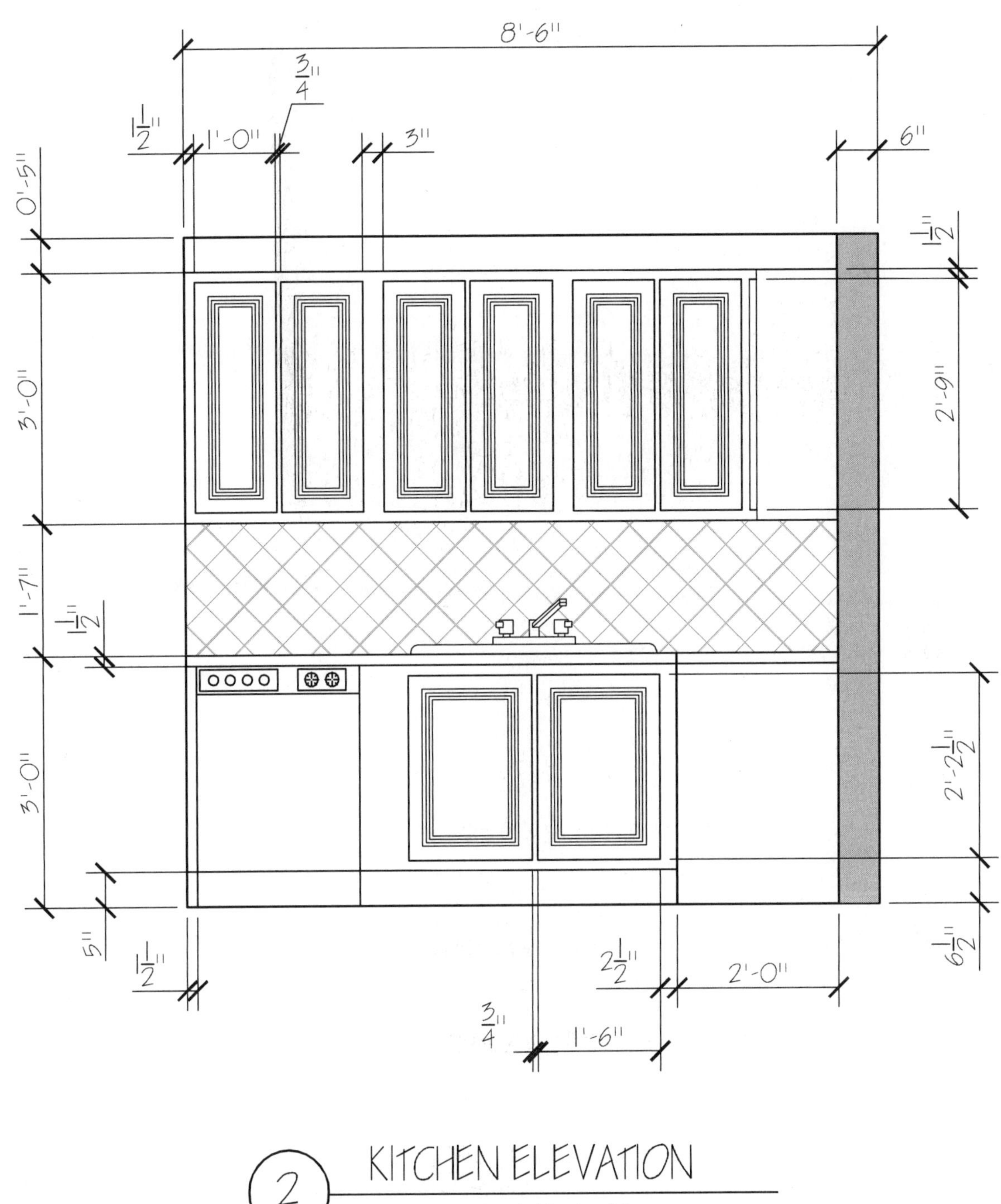

FIGURE 13–33
Exercise 13–5: Kitchen Elevation 2 (Scale: 1/2" = 1'-0")

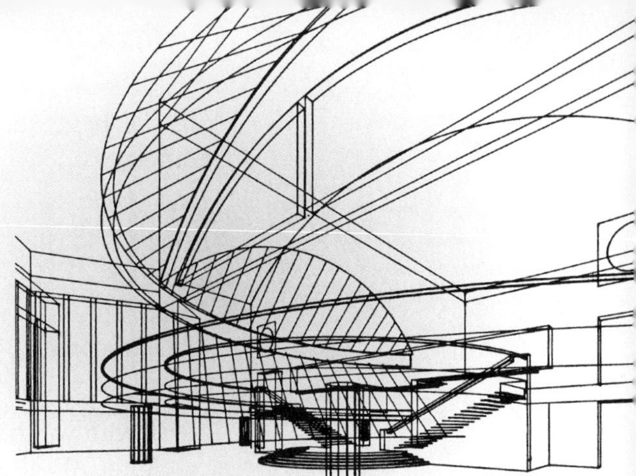

chapter 14

Solid Modeling

objectives

When you have completed this chapter, you will be able to:

- Use the 3D workspace to create solids.
- Draw the following primitive solids: box, sphere, wedge, cone, cylinder, torus, pyramid, helix, polysolid, and planar surface.
- Make settings to display solids smoothly.
- Use Steering Wheels and ViewCube to change views of a model.
- Draw extruded solids.
- Draw revolved solids.
- Use grips to modify solid shapes.
- Rotate solids about the X, Y, or Z axis.
- Form chamfers and fillets on solid edges.
- Join two or more solids.
- Subtract one or more solids from another solid.
- Use the Solidedit command to change existing solids.
- Form a solid model from the common volume of two intersecting solids.
- Use Mesh modeling to create and modify freeform solid models.
- Obtain perspective views of complex solid models.
- Use Orbit and Render to render solids and print the rendered model.

INTRODUCTION

AutoCAD provides four means of creating 3D models: basic 3D using elevation and thickness, surface modeling, solid modeling and organic modeling. Basic 3D has very limited uses. Surface modeling uses commands similar to those used in solid modeling but requires a wire frame on which surfaces are placed to give the illusion of a solid model. Models cannot be subtracted from other models when surface modeling is used, nor can they be joined to form a composite model. Neither basic 3D nor surface modeling is covered in this book. Solid modeling creates solids that are much more useful and easier to modify than basic 3D or surface models. A solid may be a single object called a *primitive,* or it may be a combination of objects called a *composite.* Mesh modeling is used to create solids that have flowing freeform shapes.

SOLIDS COMMANDS USED TO CREATE BASIC SHAPES

A primitive solid is a single solid shape that has had nothing added to or subtracted from it. There are ten solid primitives (box, sphere, wedge, helix, planar surface, polysolid, cone, cylinder, torus, and pyramid) that are the basic shapes often used in solid modeling. They are drawn by using ten commands:

Box
Cone
Cylinder
Helix
Planar Surface
Polysolid
Pyramid
Sphere
Torus
Wedge

The Polysolid command may also be used to convert lines, arcs, and polylines into a wall with width and height.

AutoCAD also allows you to form solids by extruding (adding height), sweeping (extruding along a path), lofting (selecting cross-sectional areas), and revolving (rotating about an axis) two-dimensional drawing entities such as polylines, circles, ellipses, rectangles, polygons, and donuts. The commands that extrude, sweep, loft, and revolve drawing entities to form solids are:

Extrude
Revolve
Sweep
Loft

SOLIDS COMMANDS USED TO CREATE COMPOSITE SOLIDS

Composite solids are formed by joining primitive solids, other solids, or a combination of the two. These combinations may also be added to or subtracted from other solids to form the composite model needed. The following commands used to create composite solids are described in this chapter:

Union Allows you to join several solids to form a single solid.

Intersect Allows you to create composite solids from the intersection of two or more solids. Intersect creates a new solid by calculating the common volume of two or more existing solids.

Subtract Allows you to subtract solids from other solids.

Interfere Does the same thing as Intersect except it retains the original objects.

SOLIDS COMMANDS USED TO EDIT SOLIDS

Slice Used to create a new solid by cutting the existing solid into two pieces and removing or retaining either or both pieces.

Section Used to create the cross-sectional area of a solid. That area may then be hatched using the Hatch command with any pattern you choose. Be sure the section is parallel with the current UCS when you hatch the area.

Thicken Used to make a surface thicker.

MESH MODELING

The basic shapes in mesh modeling are made using commands similar to the ones used in solid modeling. Those commands are:

Meshbox
Meshcone
Meshcylinder
Meshpyramid
Meshsphere
Meshtorus
Meshwedge

Meshsmooth This command is used to convert solids to meshes.

Meshsmoothless This command makes a selected mesh less smooth by one level. You can repeat this command until the object looks just as you want it to look.

Meshsmoothmore This command makes a selected mesh more smooth by one level. You can repeat this command until the object looks just as you want it to look.

These commands will be used in exercises that allow you to create objects that are quite different from those commonly seen in solid modeling assignments.

SOLIDEDIT

With SOLIDEDIT, you can change solid objects by extruding, moving, rotating, offsetting, tapering, copying, coloring, separating, shelling, cleaning, checking, or deleting features such as holes, surfaces, and edges.

CONTROLLING UCS IN THREE DIMENSIONS

Understanding and controlling the UCS is extremely important in creating three-dimensional models. The UCS is the *location and orientation* of the origin of the X, Y, and Z axes. If you are going to draw parts of a 3D model on a slanted surface, you can create a slanted UCS. If you are going to draw a 3D object, such as the handles on the drawer pedestal, you can locate your UCS so that it is flush with the front plane of the pedestal. An extrusion is then made from that construction plane, and the handles are easily created in the correct location.

The UCS command options Origin, OBject, Previous, Restore, Save, Delete, World, and ? were described in Chapter 8. The options described in this chapter are Move, Origin, 3point, OBject, View, and X/Y/Z.

Dynamic UCS

You can draw on any face of a 3D solid without changing the UCS orientation with one of the UCS options by activating DUCS on the status bar. The UCS then changes automatically when your cursor is over a face of an object, and dynamic UCS is on.

COMMANDS TO VIEW SOLIDS

3D Views Menu Options

Viewpoint Presets The Viewpoint Presets dialog box, Figure 14–1, appears when **vp<enter>** is typed.

From X Axis: Chart Specifies the viewing angle from the X axis. The button allows you to type the angle; the chart above it allows you to specify a new angle by clicking the inner region on the circle. The chart, consisting of a square with a circle in it, may be thought of as a viewpoint looking down on the top of an object:

270 Places your view directly in front of the object.
315 Places your view to the right and in front of the object.
0 Places your view on the right side of the object.
45 Places your view to the right and behind the object.
90 Places your view directly behind the object.
135 Places your view to the left and behind the object.
180 Places your view on the left side of the object.
225 Places your view to the left and in front of the object.

From XY Plane: Chart Specifies the viewing angle from the XY plane. The button allows you to type the angle, and the chart above it allows you to specify a new angle by clicking the inner region on the half circle. Consisting of two semicircles,

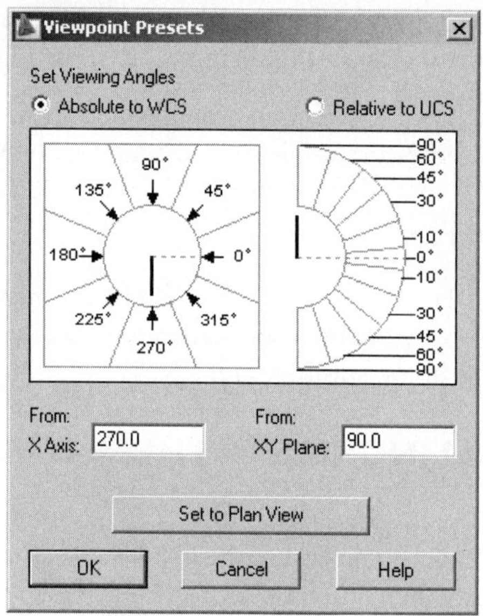

Viewpoint Presets

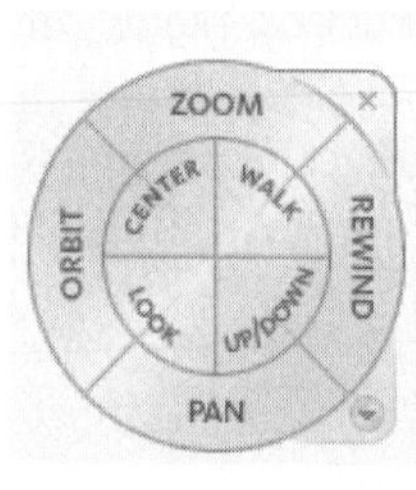

Steering Wheel

View Cube

FIGURE 14–1
Navigation Tools

the chart allows you to specify whether the viewpoint is to be above or below the object:

0 Places your view directly perpendicular to the chosen angle. For example, a view of 270 on the left chart and 0 on the right chart places the viewpoint directly in front of the object.

10 to 60 Places your view above the object.

90 Places your view perpendicular to the top view of the chosen angle.

−10 to −60 Places your view below the object.

−90 Places your view perpendicular to the bottom view of the chosen angle.

Set to Plan View Sets the viewing angles to plan view (270,90) relative to the selected UCS.

Now, let's look at other 3D Views options:

Plan View Allows you to select the plan view of the current UCS, the World UCS, or a saved and named UCS.

SW Isometric Gives you an isometric view from the front, to the left, above.

SE Isometric Gives you an isometric view from the front, to the right, above.

NE Isometric Gives you an isometric view from the back, to the right, above.

NW Isometric Gives you an isometric view from the back, to the left, above.

3DFLY Changes your view of a 3D model so that it is as if you were flying through the model.

ORBIT Allows you to control the viewing of a 3D model using an orbit.

3DWALK Changes your view of a 3D model so that it is as if you were walking through the model.

STEERINGWHEELS

SteeringWheels, Figure 14–1, are icons that are divided into sections. Each section on the steering wheel is a tool that allows you to pan, zoom, or show the motion of the current view of a model.

SteeringWheels can save you time because they combine several of the common navigation tools so they all appear on the wheel. There are several different wheels that can be used. You can change the size, transparency, and other settings for each of the wheels.

VIEWCUBE

The ViewCube, Figure 14–1, is a another 3D viewing tool that can be used to switch from one view of the model to another.

When the ViewCube is displayed, it appears in one of the corners of the drawing area over the model and displays the current viewpoint of the model. When you hold your mouse over the ViewCube, you can switch to one of the preset views, CLICK: on the cube, and move your mouse to rotate the model or return to the Home view of the model.

OTHER COMMANDS THAT CAN BE USED TO EDIT SOLIDS

3D Move Moves solids easily.

3D Array Used to create three-dimensional arrays of objects.

3D Rotate Used to rotate solids about the X, Y, or Z axis.

3D Mirror Used to create mirror images of solids about a plane specified by three points.

Fillet Used to create fillets and rounds. Specify the radius for the fillet and then click the edge or edges to be filleted.

Chamfer Used to create chamfers. Specify the distances for the chamfer and then click the edge or edges to be chamfered.

Align Used to move a solid so that a selected plane on the first solid is aligned with a selected plane on a second solid.

Explode Used to explode a solid into regions or planes. (Example: An exploded solid box becomes six regions: four sides, a top, and a bottom.) Use care with Explode. When you explode a solid, you destroy it as a solid shape.

Interference Checking Alerts you if your camera is about to bump into something.

SETTINGS THAT CONTROL HOW THE SOLID IS DISPLAYED

FACETRES Used to make shaded solids and those with hidden lines removed appear smoother. Values range from 0.01 to 10.0. The default value is 0.5. Higher values take longer to regenerate but look better. Four is a good compromise. If you change this value, you can update the solid to the new value by using the Shade or Hide command again.

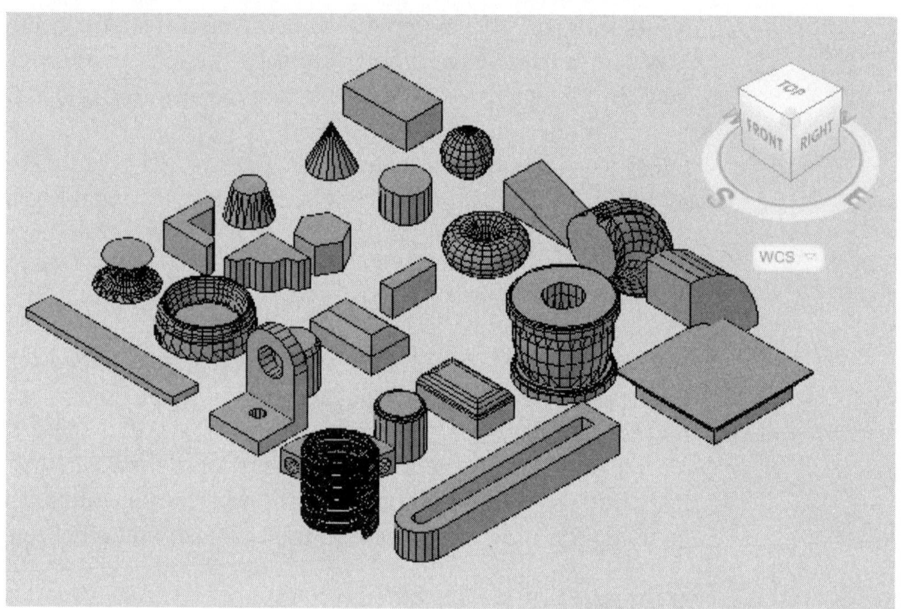

FIGURE 14–2
Tutorial 14–1 Complete

ISOLINES Sets the number of lines on rounded surfaces of solids. Values range from 0 to 2047. The default value is 4. Twenty is a good middle ground. If you change this value, you can update the solid to the new value by regenerating the drawing.

Tutorial 14–1: Part 1, Drawing Primitive Solids

Tutorial 14–1, Parts 1 through 6, provides step-by-step instructions for using the solid commands just described. These basic commands will also be used to create complex solid models in Tutorial 14–2. Upon completion of this chapter, and mastery of the commands included in the chapter, you will have a sound foundation for learning solid modeling.

When you have completed Tutorial 14–1, Parts 1 through 6, your drawing will look similar to Figure 14–2.

Step 1. Make a new workspace for all of your 3D drawings as described next:

1. CLICK: **3D Modeling** on the workspace switching tab (in the lower right of the screen). **Close the palettes on the right to give yourself more room.**

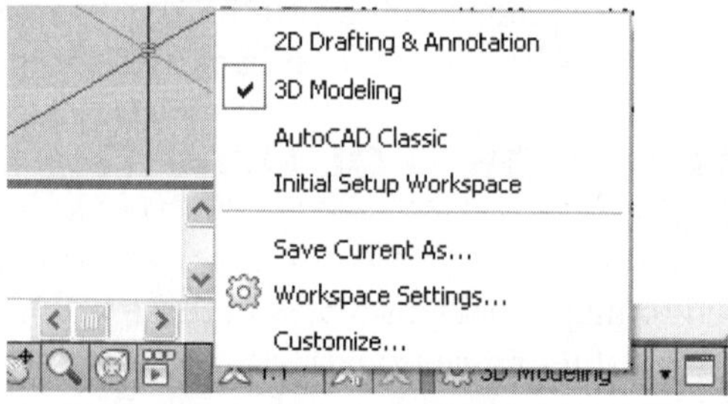

2. RIGHT-CLICK: **the SNAP icon** and CLICK: **Use Icons** so icons are not used (words are used instead of icons).

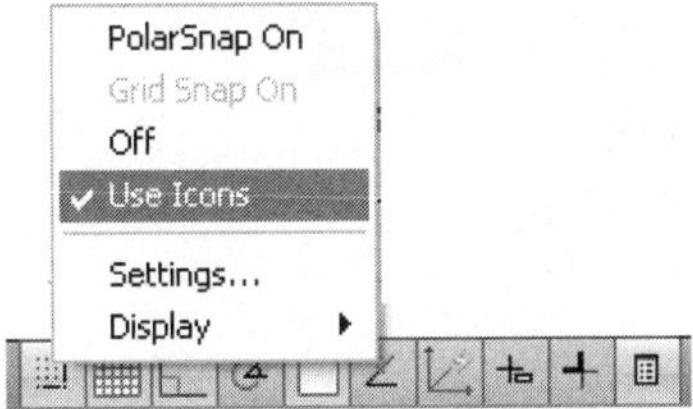

3. RIGHT-CLICK: **the MODEL icon** and CLICK: **Display Layout and Model Tabs.**

4. CLICK: **3D Modeling-Save Current as...** and TYPE: **YOUR NAME-3D** (in the Name: box), then CLICK: **Save.**

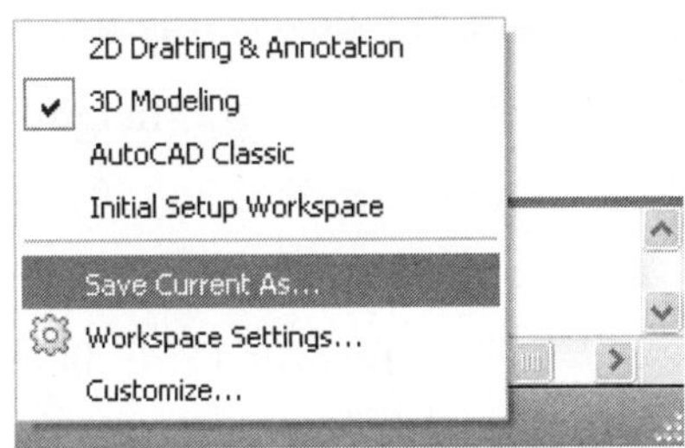

Step 2. **Use your new 3D workspace to make the following settings:**

1. **Use SaveAs... to save the drawing on the hard drive with the name CH14-TUTORIAL1.**
2. Set drawing Units: **Architectural**
3. Set Drawing Limits: **11, 8-1/2**
4. Set GRIDDISPLAY: **0**
5. Set Grid: **1/2**
6. Set Snap: **1/16**
7. Create the following layers:

LAYER NAME	COLOR	LINETYPE	LINEWEIGHT
3d-m	magenta	continuous	default
3d-r	red	continuous	default
3d-g	green	continuous	default

8. **Set Layer 3d-m current.**
9. **Use the Vports command to make two vertical viewports. Zoom-All in both viewports to start, then Zoom in closer so your view is similar to the figures shown.** Either viewport may be active as you draw. You will need to Zoom-All occasionally in both viewports to see the entire drawing.
10. CLICK: **SE Isometric from 3D Views on the View menu to set a viewpoint for the right viewport.**
11. Set **FACETRES** to 4 (TYPE: **FACETRES<enter>**)
12. Set **ISOLINES** to 20 (TYPE: **ISOLINES<enter>**)

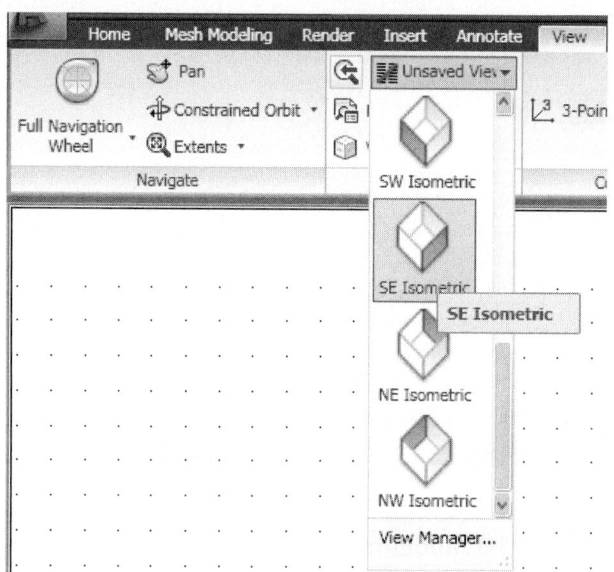

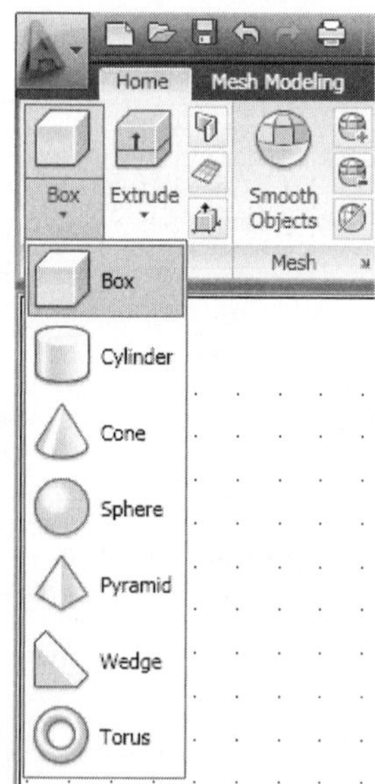

BOX

Step 3. Draw a solid box, 1 1/4″ × 3/4″ × 1/2″ height (Figure 14–3), as described next:

Prompt	Response
Command:	**Box** (or TYPE: **BOX<enter>**)
Specify first corner or [Center] <0,0,0>:	TYPE: **1/2,7-1/2<enter>**
Specify other corner or [Cube/Length]:	TYPE: **@1-1/4,3/4<enter>**
Specify height or [2Point]:	TYPE: **1/2<enter>**

Center Allows you to draw a box by first locating its center.
Cube Allows you to draw a cube by specifying the length of one side.
Length Allows you to draw a box by specifying its length (X), width (Y), and height (Z).

SPHERE

Step 4. Draw a solid sphere, 3/8 radius (Figure 14–4), as described next:

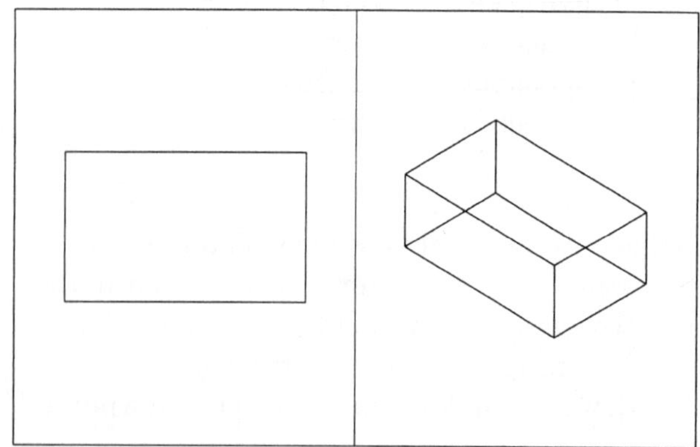

FIGURE 14–3
Draw a Solid Box

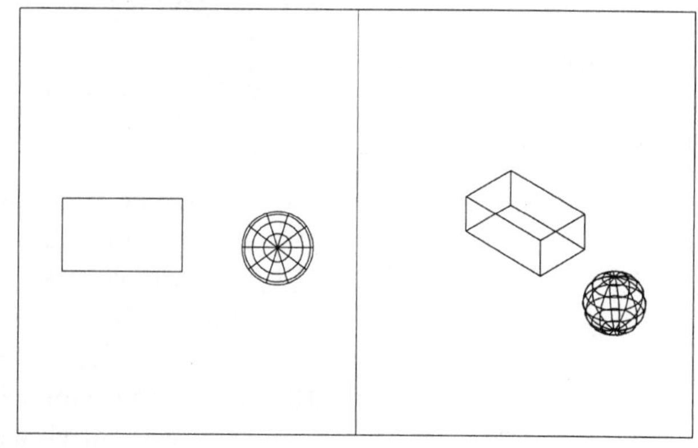

FIGURE 14–4
Draw a Solid Sphere

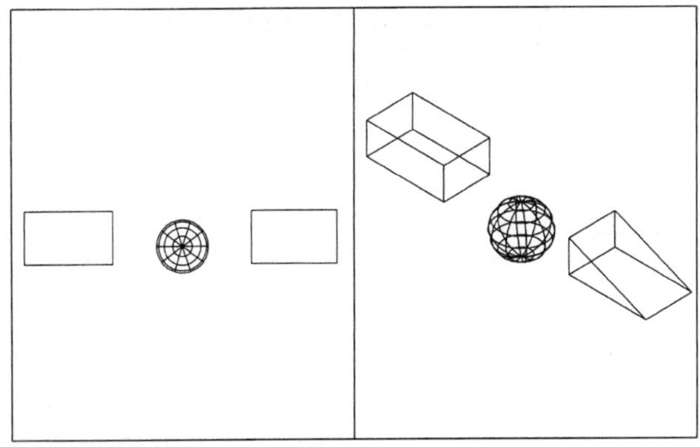

FIGURE 14–5
Draw a Solid Wedge

Prompt	Response
Command:	**Sphere** (or TYPE: **SPHERE<enter>**)
Specify center point or [3P/2P/Ttr]:	TYPE: **2-3/4,7-3/4<enter>**
Specify radius or [Diameter]:	TYPE: **3/8<enter>**

WEDGE

Step 5. Draw a solid wedge, 3/4 × 1-1/4 × 1/2 height (Figure 14–5), as described next:

Prompt	Response
Command:	**Wedge** (or TYPE: **WE<enter>**)
Specify first corner or [Center]:	TYPE: **3-3/4,7-1/2<enter>**
Specify other corner or [Cube/Length]:	TYPE: **@1-1/4, 3/4<enter>**
Specify height or [2Point]<1/2″>:	TYPE: **1/2<enter>**

CONE

Step 6. Draw a solid cone, 3/8 radius, 3/4 height (Figure 14–6), as described next:

Prompt	Response
Command:	**Cone** (or TYPE: **CONE<enter>**)
Specify center point of base or [3P/2P/Ttr/Elliptical]:	TYPE: **1-1/4,6-1/2<enter>**

FIGURE 14–6
Draw a Solid Cone

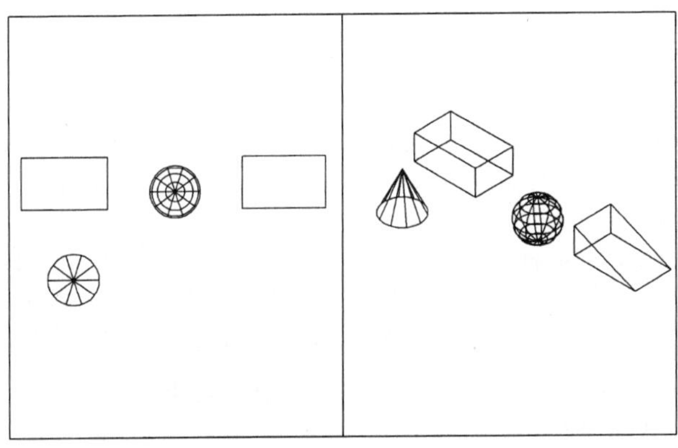

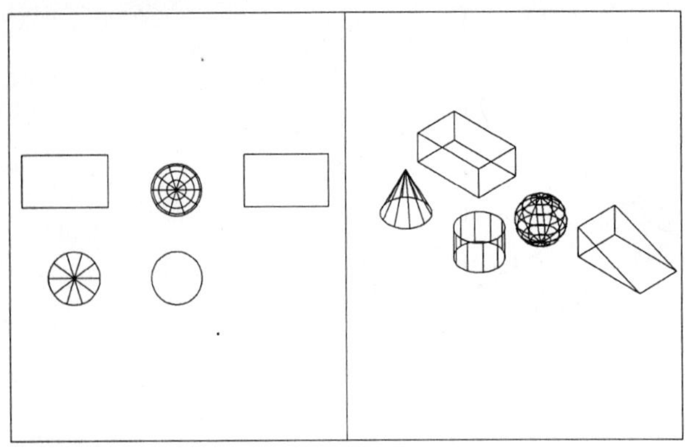

FIGURE 14–7
Draw a Solid Cylinder

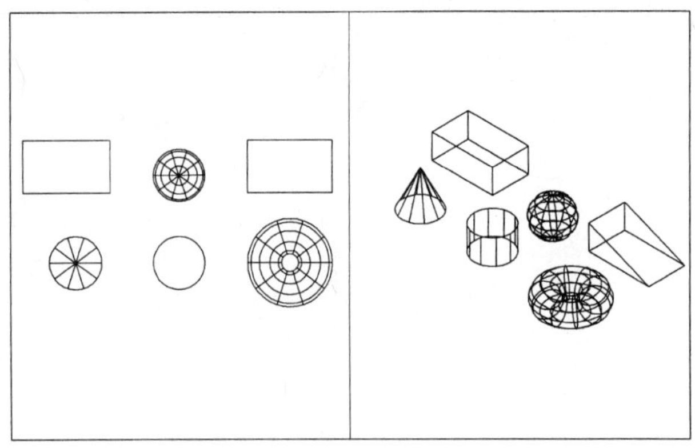

FIGURE 14–8
Draw a Solid Torus

Prompt	Response
Specify base radius or [Diameter]<0′-3/8″>:	TYPE: **3/8<enter>**
Specify height or [2Point/Axis endpoint/Top radius]<0′-0 1/2″>:	TYPE: **3/4<enter>**

CYLINDER

Step 7. Draw a solid cylinder, 3/8 radius, 1/2 height (Figure 14–7), as described next:

Prompt	Response
Command:	**Cylinder** (or TYPE: **CYL<enter>**)
Specify center point of base or [3P/2P/Ttr/Elliptical]:	TYPE: **2-3/4,6-1/2<enter>**
Specify base radius or [Diameter]<default>:	TYPE: **3/8<enter>**
Specify height or [2Point/Axis endpoint]<default>:	TYPE: **1/2<enter>**

TORUS

Step 8. Draw a solid torus (a 3D donut), 3/8 torus radius, 1/4 tube radius (Figure 14–8), as described next:

Prompt	Response
Command:	**Torus** (or TYPE: **TOR<enter>**)
Specify center point or [3P/2P/Ttr]:	TYPE: **4-3/8,6-1/2<enter>**
Specify radius or [Diameter]:	TYPE: **3/8<enter>**
Specify tube radius or [2Point/Diameter]:	TYPE: **1/4<enter>**

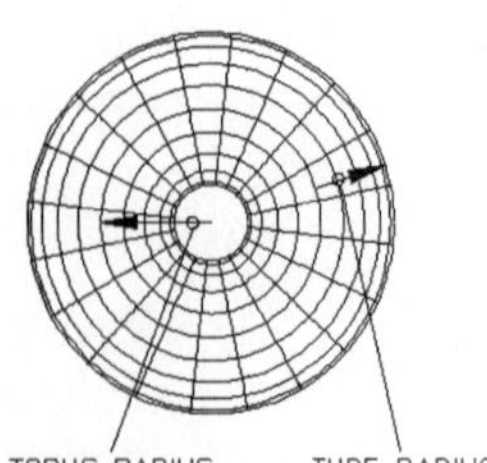

FIGURE 14–9
Radius of the Tube and Radius of the Torus

The radius of the torus is the distance from the center of the 3D donut to the center of the tube that forms the donut. The radius of the tube is the radius of the tube forming the donut (Figure 14–9).

FIGURE 14–10
Extruding and Tapering a Circle

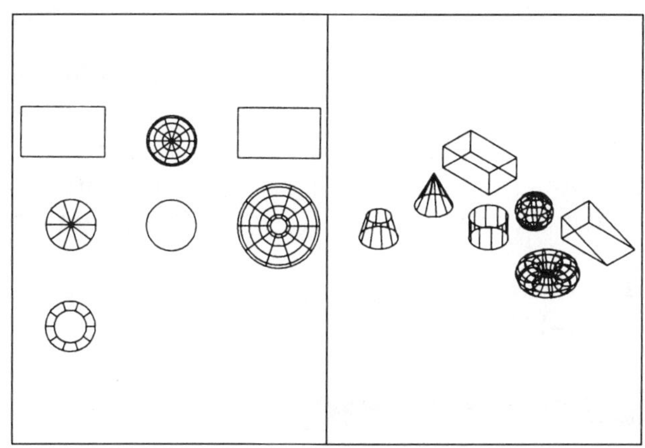

Tutorial 14–1: Part 2, Using Extrude to Draw Extruded Solids

DRAW AN EXTRUDED CIRCLE

Step 9. **Draw a circle (Figure 14–10), as described next:**

Prompt	Response
Command:	TYPE: **C<enter>**
Specify center point of circle or [3P/2P/Ttr (tan tan radius)]:	TYPE: **1-1/4,5<enter>**
Specify radius of circle or [Diameter]:	TYPE: **3/8<enter>**

Step 10. **Extrude the circle, 1/2 height, 15° extrusion taper angle (Figure 14–10), as described next:**

Prompt	Response
Command:	**Extrude** (or TYPE: **EXT<enter>**)
Select objects to extrude:	CLICK: **the circle**
Select objects to extrude:	**<enter>**
Specify height of extrusion or [Direction/Path/Taper angle] <0′-0 1/2″>:	TYPE: **T<enter>**
Specify angle of taper for extrusion <0:>	TYPE: **15<enter>**
Specify height of extrusion or [Direction/Path/Taper angle] <′-0 1/2″:>	TYPE: **1/2<enter>**

DRAW AN EXTRUDED POLYGON

Step 11. **Draw a polygon (Figure 14–11), as described next:**

Prompt	Response
Command:	**Polygon** (or TYPE: **POL<enter>**)
Enter number of sides <4>:	TYPE: **6<enter>**

Prompt	Response
Specify center of polygon or [Edge]:	TYPE: **2-3/4,5<enter>**
Enter an option [Inscribed in circle/ Circumscribed about circle] <I>:	TYPE: **C<enter>**
Specify radius of circle:	TYPE: **3/8<enter>**

Step 12. Extrude the polygon, 1/2 height, using the Press/Pull command (Figure 14–11), as described next:

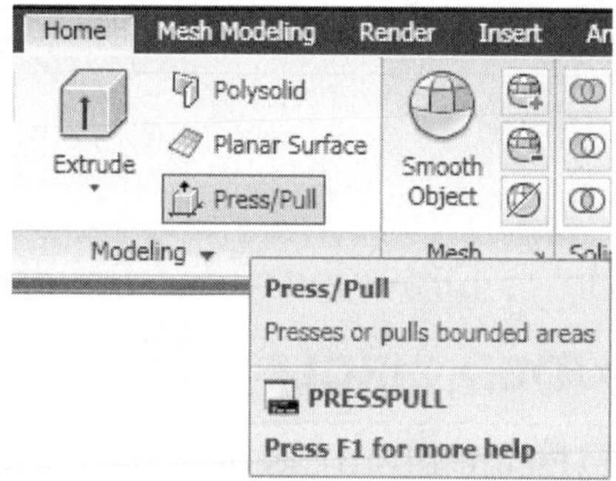

Prompt	Response
Command:	**Press/Pull** (or TYPE: **PRESSPULL <enter>**)
Click inside bounded areas to press or pull.	CLICK: **any point inside the polygon (in the SE Isometric viewport)**
	Move your mouse up and TYPE: **1/2 <enter>**

DRAW AN EXTRUDED RECTANGLE

Step 13. Draw a rectangle (Figure 14–12), as described next:

Prompt	Response
Command:	**Rectangle** (or TYPE: **REC<enter>**)

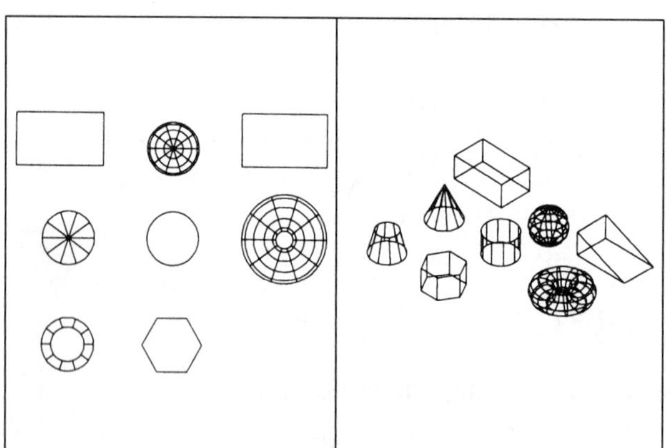

FIGURE 14–11
Extruding a Polygon

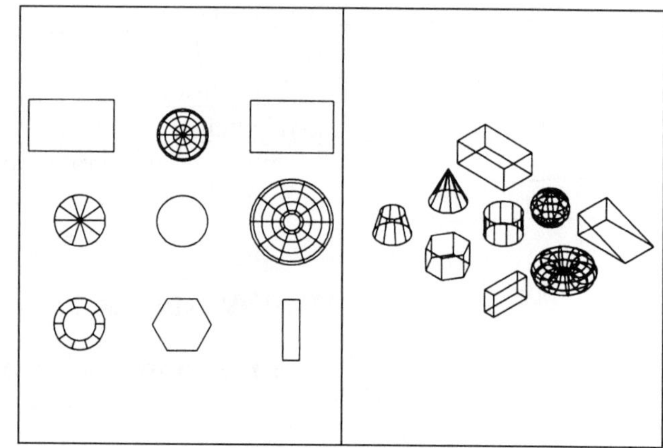

FIGURE 14–12
Extruding a Rectangle

Prompt	Response
Specify first corner point or [Chamfer/Elevation/Fillet/ Thickness/Width]:	TYPE: **4-1/4,4-1/2<enter>**
Specify other corner point or [Area/Dimensions/Rotation]:	TYPE: **@1/4,7/8<enter>**

Step 14. Extrude the rectangle, 1/2 height, 0° extrusion taper angle (Figure 14–12), as described next:

Prompt	Response
Command:	**Extrude** (or TYPE: **EXT<enter>** or use **PRESSPULL**)
Select objects to extrude:	CLICK: **the rectangle**
Select objects to extrude:	**<enter>**
Specify height of extrusion or [Direction/Path/Taper angle] <0′-0 1/2″>:	TYPE: **1/2<enter>**

DRAW AN EXTRUDED STRUCTURAL ANGLE

Step 15. Draw the outline of the cross section of a structural angle (Figure 14–13), as described next:

Prompt	Response
Command:	TYPE: **L<enter>**
Specify first point:	TYPE: **1,3<enter>**
Specify next point or [Undo]:	TYPE: **@7/8,0<enter>** (or turn ORTHO ON and use direct distance entry)
Specify next point or [Undo]:	TYPE: **@0,1/4<enter>**
Specify next point or [Close/Undo]:	TYPE: **@-5/8,0<enter>**
Specify next point or [Close/Undo]:	TYPE: **@0,5/8<enter>**
Specify next point or [Close/Undo]:	TYPE: **@-1/4,0<enter>**
Specify next point or [Close/Undo]:	TYPE: **C<enter>**

Step 16. Add a 1/8 radius fillet to the outline (Figure 14–13), as described next:

Prompt	Response
Command:	**Fillet** (or TYPE: **F<enter>**)

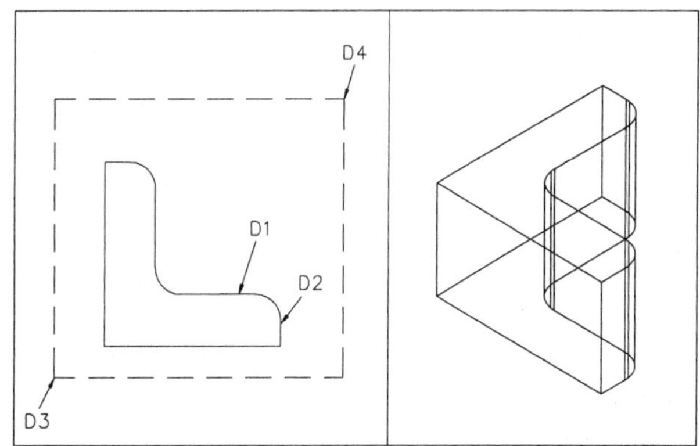

FIGURE 14–13
Extruding a Structural Steel Angle

TIP: TYPE: **M<enter>** before you select the first object for the fillet so you can fillet all corners without repeating the command.

Prompt	Response
Select first object or [Undo/Polyline/ Radius/Trim/Multiple]:	TYPE: **R<enter>**
Specify fillet radius <0′-0 1/2″>:	TYPE: **1/8<enter>**
Select first object or [Undo/Polyline/ Radius/Trim/Multiple]:	**D1** (Use the Zoom-Window command if needed to allow you to pick the necessary lines.)
Select second object or shift-select to apply corner:	**D2**

Step 17. Draw 1/8 radius fillets (Figure 14–13) at the other two intersections shown.

Step 18. Use Edit Polyline (Pedit) to combine all the lines and fillets into a single entity (Figure 14–13), as described next:

Prompt	Response
Command:	**Edit Polyline** (or TYPE: **PE<enter>**)
Select polyline or [Multiple]:	CLICK: **one of the lines forming the structural angle**
Object selected is not a polyline	
Do you want to turn it into one? <Y>	**<enter>**
Enter an option [Close/Join/Width/ Edit vertex/Fit/Spline/Decurve/ Ltype gen/Undo]:	TYPE: **J<enter>** (to select the Join option)
Select objects:	TYPE: **ALL<enter>**
Select objects:	**<enter>**
8 segments added to polyline	
Enter an option [Open/Join/Width/ Edit vertex/Fit/Spline/Decurve/ Ltype gen/Undo]:	**<enter>** (to exit from the Pedit command)

Step 19. Extrude the cross section of the structural angle, 1/2 height, 0° extrusion taper angle (Figure 14–13), as described next:

Prompt	Response
Command:	**Extrude** (or TYPE: **EXT<enter>**)
Select objects to extrude:	CLICK: **the polyline**
Select objects to extrude:	**<enter>**
Specify height of extrusion or [Direction/Path/Taper angle] <0′-0 1/2″>:	TYPE: **1/2<enter>**

FIGURE 14–14
Extruding a Molding Shape

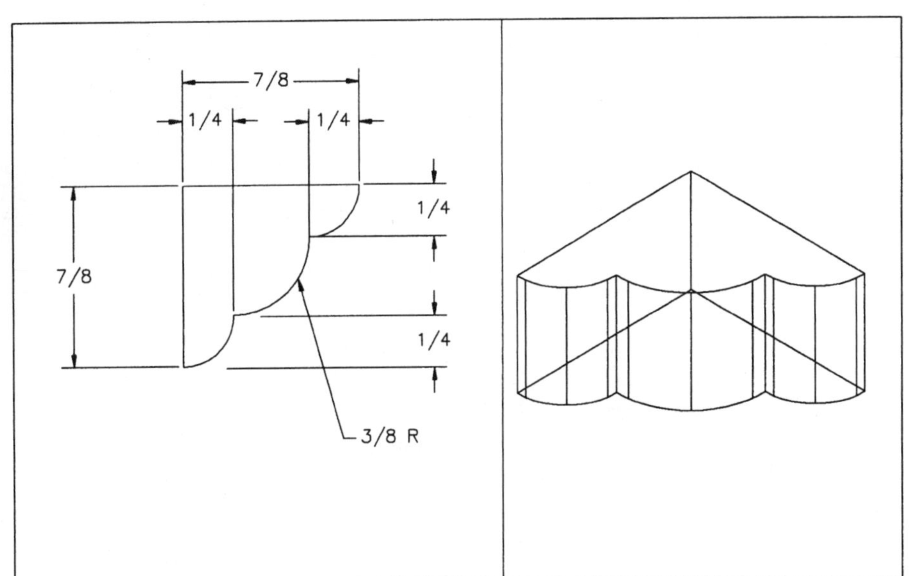

TIP: Presspull works well for Extrude in cases where the extrusion is just up or down. In addition, you do not have to have a single polyline.

DRAW AN EXTRUDED SHAPE

Step 20. Draw the shape shown as Figure 14–14 in the approximate location shown in Figure 14–2. When you draw the shape, be sure that you draw only what is needed. If you draw extra lines, the Edit Polyline command cannot join the lines into a single polyline.

Step 21. Use the Edit Polyline command to join all lines and arcs into a single polyline or use Presspull without joining all lines.

Step 22. Extrude the figure to a height of 1/2.

Tutorial 14–1: Part 3, Using Revolve to Draw Revolved Solids; Using 3D Rotate to Rotate Solids About the X, Y, and Z Axes

DRAW REVOLVED SHAPE 1

Step 23. Draw two circles (Figure 14–15), as described next:

Prompt	Response
Command:	TYPE: **C<enter>**
Specify center point for circle or [3P/2P/Ttr (tan tan radius)]:	TYPE: **6-1/4,7-3/4<enter>**
Specify radius of circle or [Diameter]:	TYPE: **1/2<enter>**
Command:	**<enter>**

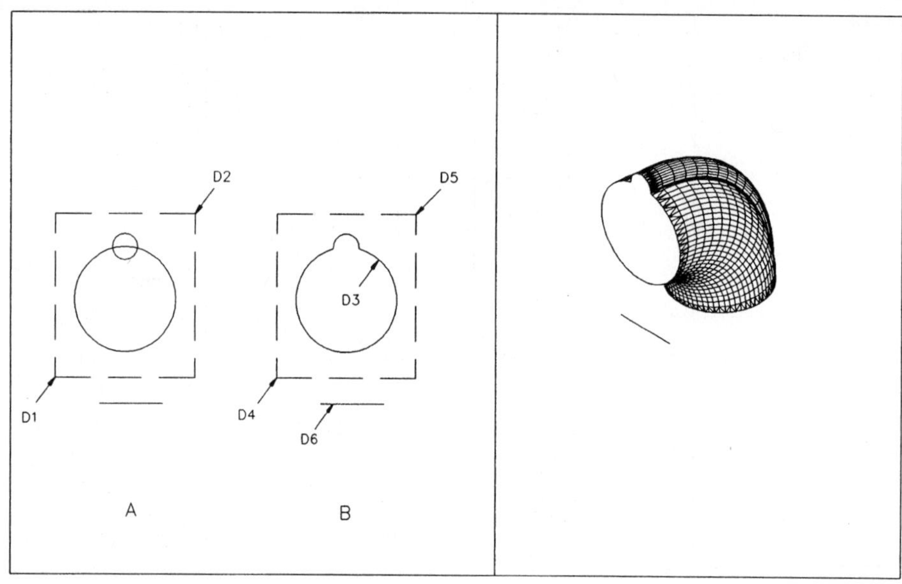

FIGURE 14–15
Revolving a Shape 90°

Prompt	Response
Specify center point for circle or [3P/2P/Ttr (tan tan radius)]:	TYPE: **6-1/4,8-1/4<enter>**
Specify radius of circle or [Diameter] <0′-1/2″>:	TYPE: **1/8<enter>**

Step 24. Use the Trim command to trim parts of both circles (Figures 14–15A and 14–15B), as described next:

Prompt	Response
Command:	**Trim** (or TYPE: **TR<enter>**)
Select cutting edges...	
Select objects or <select all>:	**<enter>**
Select object to trim or shift-select to extend or [Fence/Crossing/Project Edge/eRase/Undo]:	**Trim the circles as shown in Figure 14–15B** (Zoom-Window to get in closer if needed.) **<enter>**

Step 25. Join all segments of the circles into one polyline (Figure 14–15B), as described next:

Prompt	Response
Command:	**Edit Polyline** (or TYPE: **PE<enter>**)
Select polyline:	**D3<enter>**
Object selected is not a polyline	
Do you want to turn it into one? <Y>	**<enter>**
Enter an option [Close/Join/Width/ Edit vertex/Fit/Spline/Decurve/ Ltype gen/Undo]:	TYPE: **J<enter>**

Prompt	Response
Select objects:	TYPE: **ALL<enter>**
Select objects:	**<enter>**
1 segment added to polyline	
Enter an option [Open/Join/Width/ Edit vertex/Fit/Spline/Decurve/ Ltype gen/Undo]:	**<enter>** (to exit from the Edit Polyline command)

Step 26. **Draw the axis of revolution (Figure 14–15), as described next:**

Prompt	Response
Command:	**Line** (or TYPE: **L<enter>**)
Specify first point:	TYPE: **6,6-3/4<enter>**
Specify next point or [Undo]:	**With ORTHO ON, move your mouse to the right and** TYPE: **5/8<enter>**
Specify next point or [Undo]:	**<enter>**

Step 27. **Use Revolve to form a revolved solid created by revolving a single polyline 90° counterclockwise about an axis (Figure 14–15B), as described next:**

Prompt	Response
Command:	**Revolve** (or TYPE: **REV<enter>**)
Select objects to revolve:	**D3**
Select objects to revolve:	**<enter>**
Specify axis start point or define axis by [Object/X/Y/Z] <Object>:	**<enter>**
Select an object:	**D6** (Be sure to click the left end of the line for counterclockwise rotation.)
Specify angle of revolution or [STart angle]<360>:	TYPE: **90<enter>**

DRAW A REVOLVED RECTANGLE

Step 28. **Draw a rectangle (Figure 14–16), as described next:**

Prompt	Response
Command:	**Rectangle** (or TYPE: **REC<enter>**)
Specify first corner point or [Chamfer/Elevation/Fillet/ Thickness/Width]:	TYPE: **7-3/8,7-3/8<enter>**
Specify other corner point or [Area/ Dimensions/Rotation]:	TYPE: **@7/8,7/8<enter>**

Step 29. **Draw the axis of revolution (Figure 14–16), as described next:**

Prompt	Response
Command:	TYPE: **L<enter>**
Specify first point:	TYPE: **7-3/8,6-3/4<enter>**

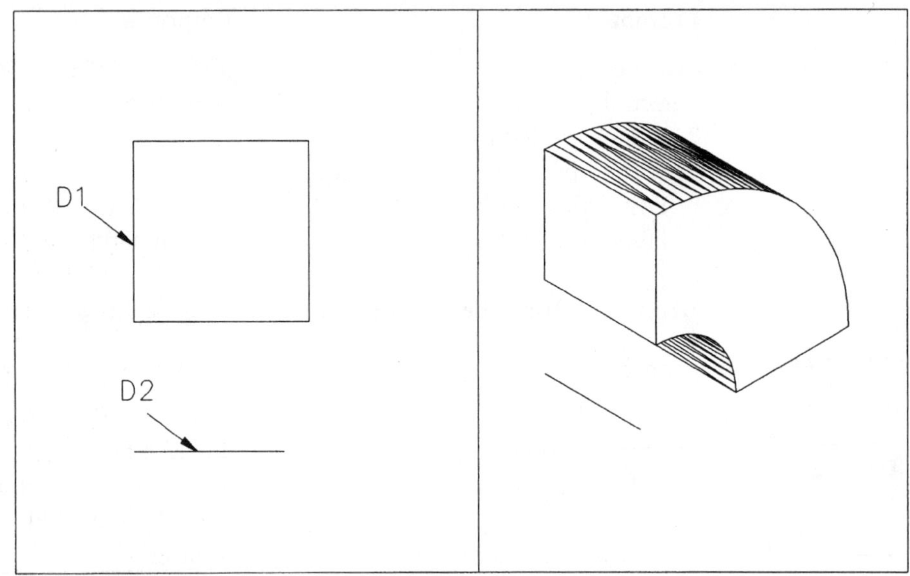

FIGURE 14–16
Revolving a Rectangle

Prompt	Response
Specify next point or [Undo]:	**Move your mouse to the right and** TYPE: **3/4<enter>** (Be sure ORTHO is ON.)
Specify next point or [Undo]:	**<enter>**

Step 30. **Use the Revolve command to form a revolved solid created by revolving the rectangle 90 counterclockwise about an axis (Figure 14–16), as described next:**

Prompt	Response
Command:	**Revolve**
Select objects to revolve:	**D1<enter>**
Select objects to revolve:	**<enter>**
Specify axis start point or define axis by [Object/X/Y/Z] <Object>:	**<enter>**
Select an object:	**D2** (CLICK: **the left end of the line**)
Specify angle of revolution or [STart angle] <360>:	TYPE: **90<enter>**

DRAW A REVOLVED PAPER CLIP HOLDER

Step 31. **Draw the cross-sectional shape of the object shown in Figure 14–17 using the Line and Arc commands in the left viewport in the approximate locations shown in Figure 14–2.**

Step 32. **Use the Edit Polyline command to join all entities of the shape into a single closed polyline.**

Step 33. **Locate the axis of revolution for the shape in the position shown.**

Step 34. **Use Revolve to revolve the shape full circle about the axis.**

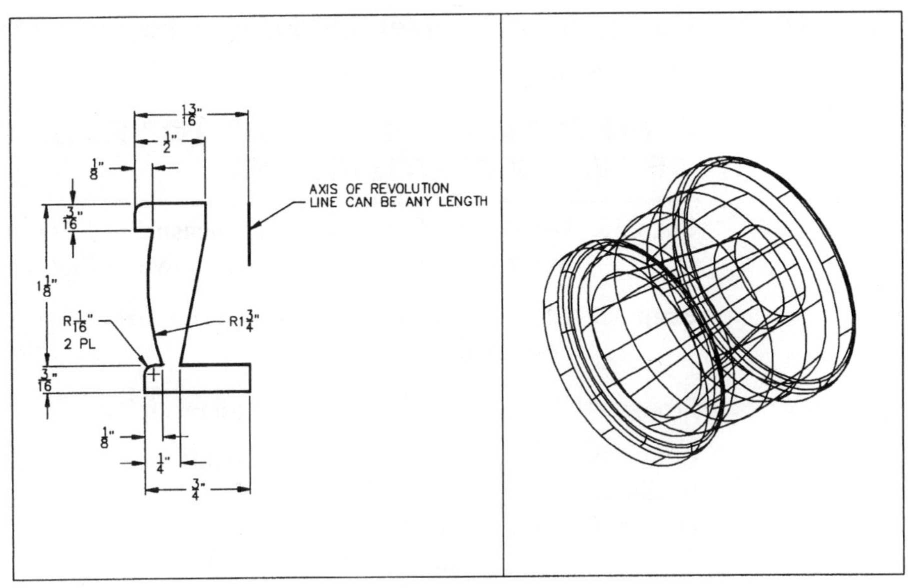

FIGURE 14–17
Revolving a Paper Clip Holder

ROTATE 3D

Step 35. Use Rotate 3D to rotate the paper clip holder 90° about the X axis so that it assumes the position shown in Figure 14–18, as described next:

Prompt	Response
Command:	TYPE: **ROTATE3D<enter>**
Select objects:	CLICK: **the paper clip holder**
Select objects:	**<enter>**
Specify first point on axis or define axis by [Object/Last/View/Xaxis/Yaxis/Zaxis/2points]:	TYPE: **X<enter>**
Specify a point on the X axis <0,0,0>:	**OSNAP-Center**
of	**D1**
Specify rotation angle or [Reference]:	TYPE: **90<enter>**

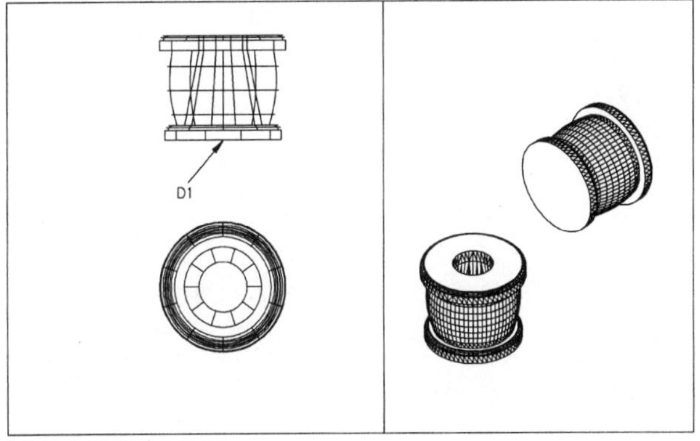

FIGURE 14–18
Rotating an Object About the X Axis

Tutorial 14–1: Part 4, Using Chamfer and Fillet to Form Chamfers and Fillets on Solid Edges

CHAMFER AND FILLET THE TOP FOUR EDGES OF TWO SEPARATE BOXES

Step 36. Use Box to draw two boxes measuring 1-1/4″ × 3/4″ × 1/2″ H each, in the approximate locations shown in Figure 14–2.

Step 37. Chamfer the top four edges of the first box (Figure 14–19), as described next:

Prompt	Response
Command:	**Chamfer** (or TYPE: **CHA<enter>**)
(TRIM mode) Current chamfer Dist1 = 0′-0 1/2″, Dist2 = 0′-0 1/2″	
Select first line or [Undo/Polyline/Distance/Angle/Trim/mEthod/Multiple]:	TYPE: **D<enter>**
Specify first chamfer distance <0′-0 1/2″>:	TYPE: **3/16<enter>**
Specify second chamfer distance <0′-0 3/16″>:	**<enter>**
Select first line or [Undo/Polyline/Distance/Angle/Trim/mEthod/Multiple]:	**D1** (Figure 14–19)
Base surface selection...	
Enter surface selection option [Next/OK (current)] <OK>:	

If the top surface of the box turns dotted, showing it as the selected surface, continue. If one of the side surfaces is selected, TYPE: **N<enter>** until the top surface is selected.

Prompt	Response
Enter surface selection option [Next/OK (current)] <OK>:	**<enter>**
Specify base surface chamfer distance <0′-0 3/16″>:	**<enter>**

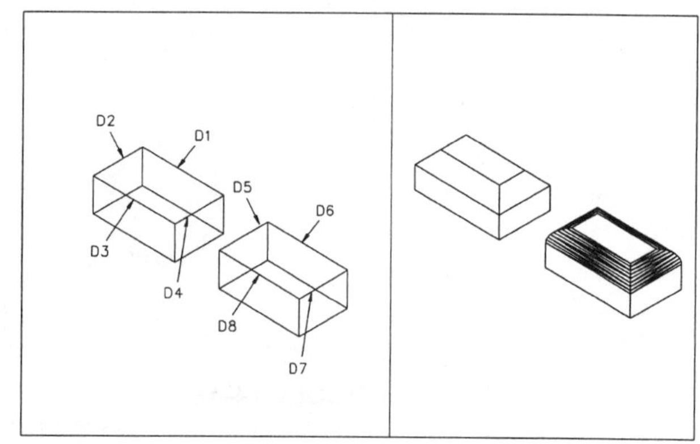

FIGURE 14–19
Chamfering and Filleting Solid Edges

Prompt	Response
Specify other surface chamfer distance <0′-0 3/16″>:	**<enter>**
Select an edge or [Loop]:	**D1, D2, D3, D4**
Select an edge or [Loop]:	**<enter>**

Step 38. Fillet the top four edges of the second box (Figure 14–19), as described next:

Prompt	Response
Command:	**Fillet** (or TYPE: **F<enter>**)
Current settings: Mode = TRIM, Radius = 0′-0 1/8″	
Select first object or [Undo/Polyline/Radius/Trim/Multiple]:	**D5** (Figure 14–19)
Enter fillet radius <0′-0 1/8″>:	TYPE: **3/16<enter>**
Select an edge or [Chain/Radius]:	**D6,D7,D8**
Select an edge or [Chain/Radius]:	**<enter>**

CHAMFER AND FILLET ON THE TOP EDGE OF TWO SEPARATE CYLINDERS

Step 39. Draw two cylinders using Cylinder with a radius of 3/8 and a height of 3/4 in the approximate location shown in Figure 14–20 (in front of the two boxes).

Step 40. Chamfer the top edge of the first cylinder (Figure 14–20) using chamfer distances of 1/16. CLICK: **D1 when you select edges to be chamfered.**

Step 41. Fillet the top edge of the second cylinder (Figure 14–20) using a fillet radius of 1/16. CLICK: **D2 when you select edges to be filleted.**

The edges of the cylinders should appear as shown in Figure 14–20.

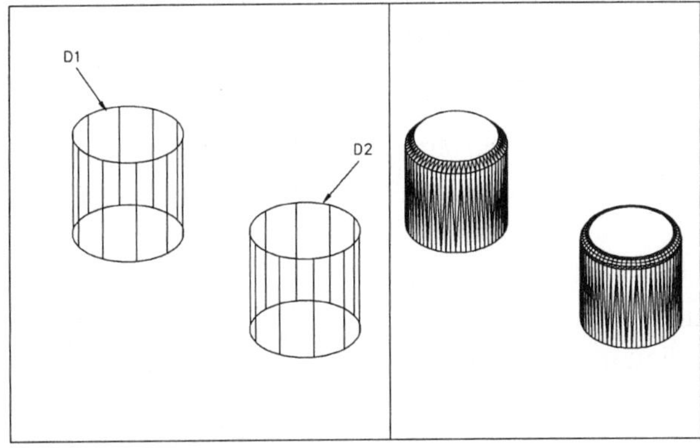

FIGURE 14–20
Chamfering and Filleting Cylinders

Tutorial 14–1: Part 5, Using Union to Join Two Solids; Using Subtract to Subtract Solids from Other Solids

DRAW SOLID SHAPE 1

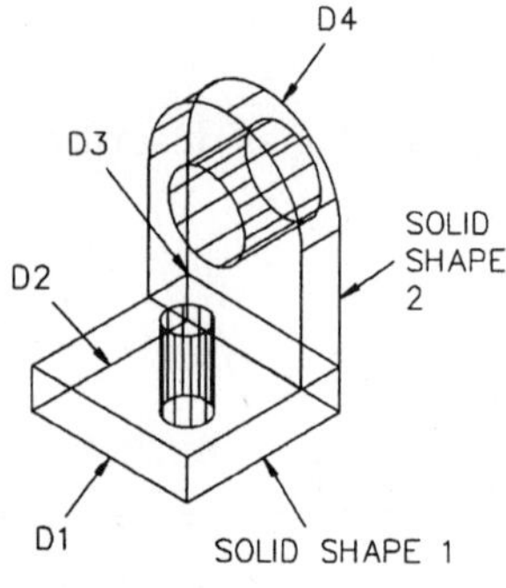

FIGURE 14–21
Drawing a Composite Solid

Step 42. Draw Solid Shape 1 (the base of the shape) and a cylinder that will be the hole in the base (Figure 14–21) with UCS set to World, as described next:

Prompt	Response
Command:	TYPE: **UCS<enter>**
Specify origin of UCS or [Face/NAmed/OBject/Previous/View/World/X/Y/Z/ZAxis] <World>:	**<enter>**
Command:	**Box**
Specify corner of box or [Center] <0,0,0>:	TYPE: **4-1/2,3/4<enter>**
Specify corner or [Cube/Length]:	TYPE: **@1,1<enter>**
Specify height:	TYPE: **1/4<enter>**
Command:	**Cylinder**
Specify center point of base or [3P/2P/Ttr/Elliptical]:	TYPE: **.X<enter>**
of	**OSNAP-Midpoint**
of	**D1**
(need YZ):	**OSNAP-Midpoint**
of	**D2**
Specify base radius or [Diameter]:	TYPE: **1/8<enter>**
Specify height or [2Point/Axis endpoint]:	TYPE: **1/2<enter>** (Make the height of the hole tall enough so you can be sure it goes through the model.)

DRAW SOLID SHAPE 2

Step 43. Set the UCS Icon command to ORigin so you will be able to see the UCS icon move when the origin is relocated (TYPE: **UCSICON <enter>, then OR<enter>**).

Step 44. Rotate the UCS 90° about the X axis, and move the origin of the UCS to the upper left rear corner of the box (Figure 14–21), as described next:

Prompt	Response
Command:	CLICK: **the right viewport** (so the UCS changes there and not in the left viewport)
Command:	TYPE: **UCS<enter>**
Specify origin of UCS or [Face/NAmed/OBject/Previous/View/World/X/Y/Z/ZAxis] <World>:	TYPE: **X<enter>**
Specify rotation angle about X axis <90>:	**<enter>**

Prompt	Response
Command:	TYPE: **UCS<enter>**
Specify origin of UCS or [Face/ NAmed/OBject/Previous/View/ World/X/Y/Z/ZAxis] <World>:	TYPE: **O<enter>**
Specify new origin point <0,0,0>:	**OSNAP-Endpoint** **D3**

Step 45. Draw Solid Shape 2 (the vertical solid) and a cylinder that will be the hole in the vertical solid (Figure 14–21), as described next:

Prompt	Response
Command:	**Polyline** (or TYPE: **PL<enter>**)
Specify start point:	TYPE: **0,0<enter>**
Specify next point or [Arc/Close/ Halfwidth/Length/Undo/Width]:	**With ORTHO ON, move your mouse right** and TYPE: **1<enter>**
Specify next point or [Arc/Close/ Halfwidth/Length/Undo/Width]:	**Move your mouse up** and TYPE: **3/4 <enter>**
Specify next point or [Arc/ Close/Halfwidth/Length/ Undo/Width]:	TYPE: **A<enter>**
Specify endpoint of arc or [Angle/ CEnter/CLose/Direction/ Halfwidth/Line/Radius/ Second pt/Undo/Width]:	**Move your mouse left** and TYPE: **1<enter>**
Specify endpoint of arc or [Angle/ CEnter/CLose/Direction/ Halfwidth/Line/Radius/ Second pt/Undo/Width]:	TYPE: **CL<enter>**
Command:	**Extrude** (or TYPE: **EXT<enter>**)
Select objects to extrude:	CLICK: **the polyline just drawn**
Select objects to extrude:	**<enter>**
Specify height of extrusion or [Direction/Path/Taper angle]:	TYPE: **1/4<enter>** **<enter>**
Command:	**Cylinder**
Specify center point of base or [3P/2P/Ttr/Elliptical]:	**OSNAP-Center**
of	**D4**
Specify base radius or [Diameter]:	TYPE: **1/4<enter>**
Specify height or [2point/ Axis endpoint]:	TYPE: **1/2<enter>**

The cylinder is longer than the thickness of the upright piece so you can be sure that the hole goes all the way through it.

Make sure the base of the cylinder is located on the back surface of the upright piece. If the cylinder is located on the front surface of the upright piece, move the cylinder 3/8 in the negative Z direction.

UNION

Step 46. **Join the base and the vertical shape together to form one model, as described next:**

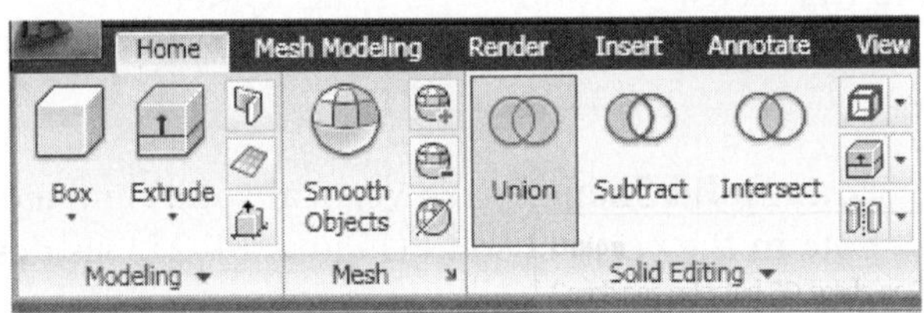

Prompt	Response
Command:	**Union** (from Modify-Solid Editing) (or TYPE: **UNION<enter>**)
Select objects:	CLICK: **the base (Shape 1) and the vertical solid (Shape 2).**
Select objects:	**<enter>**

SUBTRACT

Step 47. **Subtract the holes from the model, as described next:**

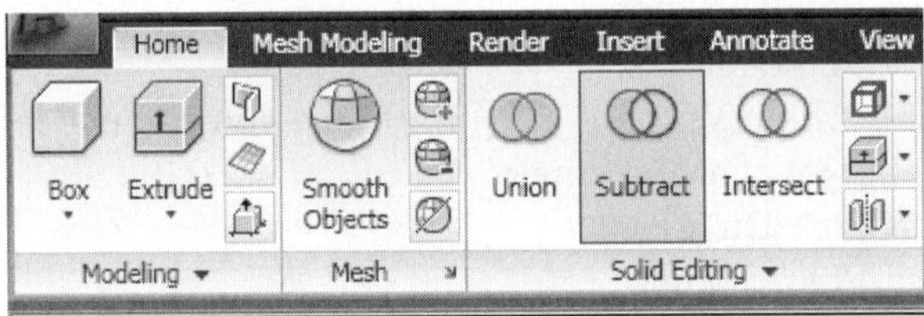

Prompt	Response
Command:	**Subtract** (from Modify-Solid Editing) (or TYPE: **SU<enter>**)
Select solids and regions to subtract from...	
Select objects:	CLICK: **any point on the model**
Select objects:	**<enter>**
Select solids and regions to subtract...	
Select objects:	CLICK: **the two cylinders**
Select objects:	**<enter>**

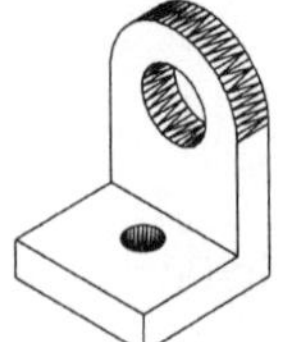

FIGURE 14–22
The Completed Model After a Hide

HIDE

Step 48. **Perform a Hide to be sure the model is correct (Figure 14–22), as described next:**

Prompt	Response
Command:	**Hide** (or TYPE: **HI<enter>**)

The model should appear as shown in Figure 14–22.

Step 49. Return to the World UCS.

Tutorial 14–1: Part 6, Using Sweep, Helix, Subtract, Loft, Planar Surface, Thicken, and Polysolid to Draw Solid Shapes

The commands in this part of Tutorial 14–1 are extremely powerful. Sweep and Subtract are used in the first shape. Helix, Sweep, and Subtract are used in the second shape.

SWEEP

The Sweep command gives you the ability to create a new solid by sweeping an object along a path. You have the options of selecting a base point, scaling the object as it is swept along the path, and twisting the object as it is swept.

Step 50. Draw an arc in the approximate location shown in Figure 14–23. It should be about 1-1/2″ long and approximately the shape shown.

Step 51. Draw a 1/8″ radius circle in the approximate location shown in Figure 14–23.

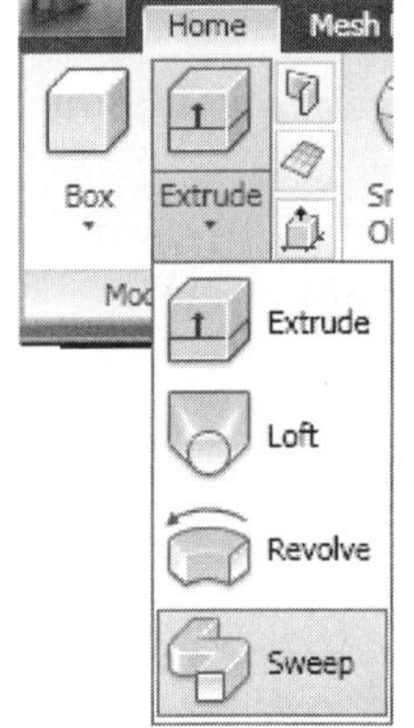

Step 52. Draw a 3/8″ square using the Rectangle command in the approximate location shown.

Step 53. Use the Sweep command to create the shape shown in Figure 14–24, as described next:

Prompt	Response
Command:	**Sweep** (or TYPE: **SWEEP<enter>**)
Select objects to sweep:	CLICK: **any point on the circle**
Select objects to sweep:	**<enter>**
Select sweep path or Alignment/ Base point/Scale/Twist]:	CLICK: **any point on the arc**

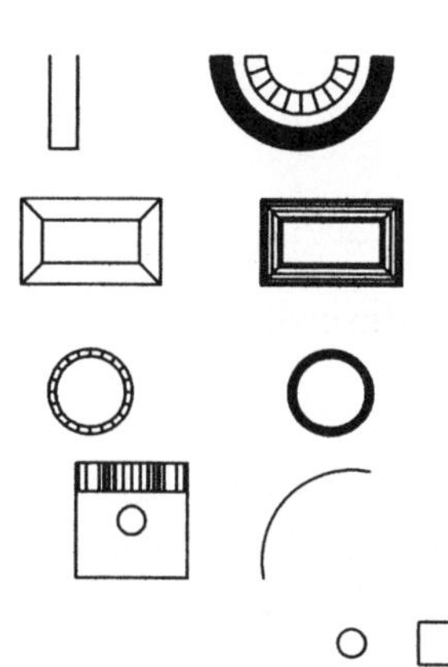

FIGURE 14–23
Draw an Arc, a Circle, and a Square

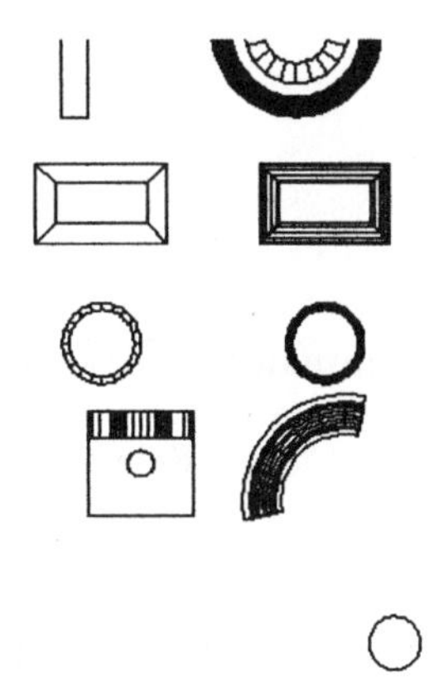

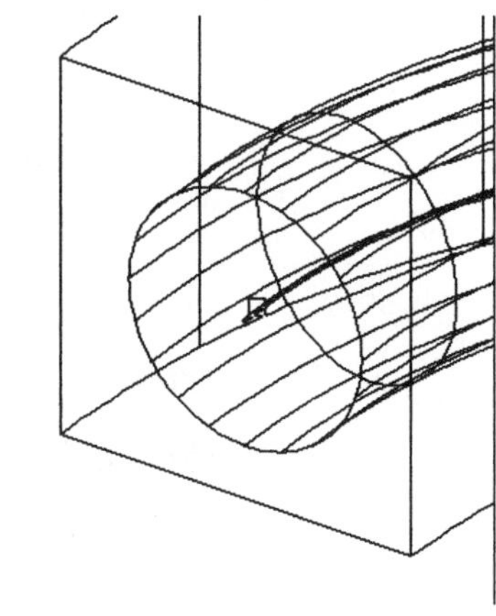

FIGURE 14–24
Zoom in Close to CLICK: the Arc in the Center of the Swept Circle

FIGURE 14–25
Use Subtract to Create a Hole in the Swept Square

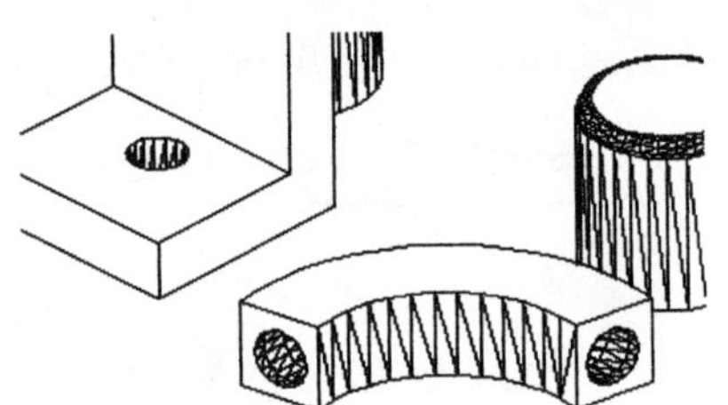

Prompt	Response
Command:	**<enter>** (repeat the Sweep command)
Select objects to sweep:	CLICK: **any point on the square**
Select objects to sweep:	**<enter>**
Select sweep path or Alignment/ Base point/Scale/Twist]:	CLICK: **any point on the arc**

You will have to CLICK: **in the 3D view, then zoom in close to** CLICK: **the arc as shown in Figure 14–24.**

Step 54. Use the Subtract command to create a hole throughout the swept square and use the Hide command to check the shape (Figure 14–25), as described next:

Prompt	Response
Command:	**Subtract** (or TYPE: **SU<enter>**)
Select solids and regions to subtract from:	
Select objects:	CLICK: **any point on the swept square**
Select solids and regions to subtract:	
Select objects:	CLICK: **any point on the swept circle**
Command:	**Hide** (or TYPE: **HI<enter>**)

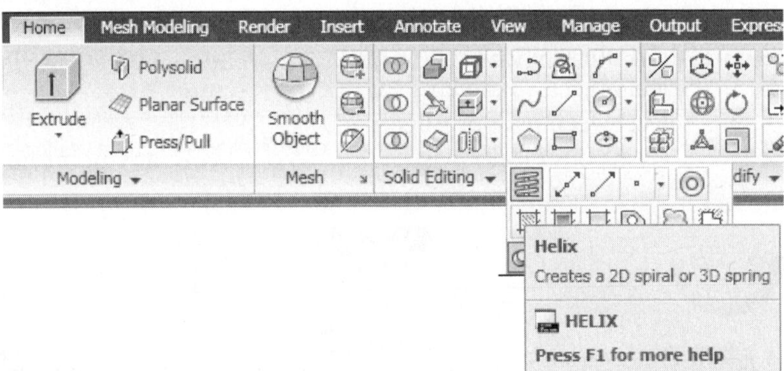

Step 55. Use the Helix command to make a helix as described next:

Prompt	Response
Command:	**Helix** (or TYPE: **HELIX<enter>**)
Specify center point of base:	CLICK: **a point in the approximate location shown in Figure 14–26.**
Specify base radius or [Diameter] <0′-0″>:	TYPE: **1/2<enter>**
Specify top radius or [Diameter] <0′-0 1/2″>:	**<enter>**

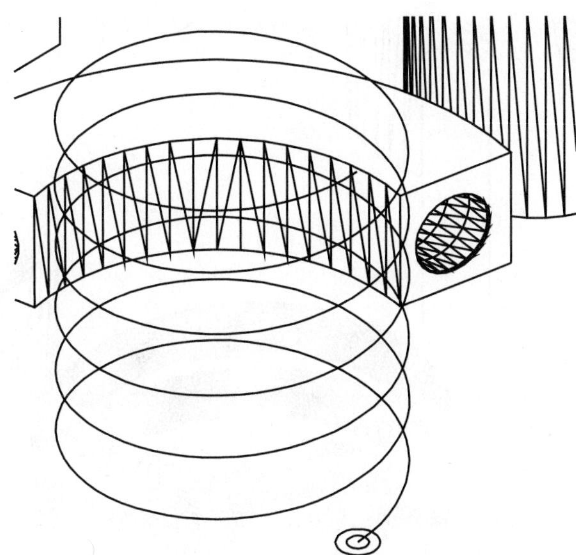

FIGURE 14–26
Draw the Helix and 1/16″ Radius and 1/32″ Radius Circles on the Helix Endpoint

Prompt	Response
Specify helix height or [Axis endpoint/Turns/turn Height/ tWist] <0′-1/2″>:	TYPE: **T<enter>**
Enter number of turns <3.0000>:	TYPE: **6<enter>**
Specify helix height or [Axis endpoint/Turns/turn Height/ tWist] <0′-1″>:	TYPE: **1-1/4<enter>**

Step 56. **Draw a 1/16″ radius circle and a 1/32″ radius circle on the endpoint of the base of the helix (Figure 14–26).**

Step 57. **Use the Sweep command to sweep the circles around the helix as described next:**

Prompt	Response
Command:	**SWEEP** (or TYPE: **SWEEP<enter>**)
Select objects to sweep:	CLICK: **both the 1/16″ and the 1/32″ radius circles**
Select objects to sweep:	**<enter>**
Select sweep path or [Alignment/ Base point/Scale/Twist]:	CLICK: **any point on the helix**

Step 58. **Use the Subtract command to subtract the inner swept circle from the outer swept circle (Figure 14–27), as described next:**

Prompt	Response
Command:	**SUBTRACT** (or TYPE: **SU<enter>**)
Select solids and regions to subtract from...	CLICK: **the 1/16″ radius swept circle**
Select objects:	**<enter>**
Select objects: Select solids and regions to subtract...	CLICK: **the 1/32″ radius swept circle**
Select objects:	**<enter>**

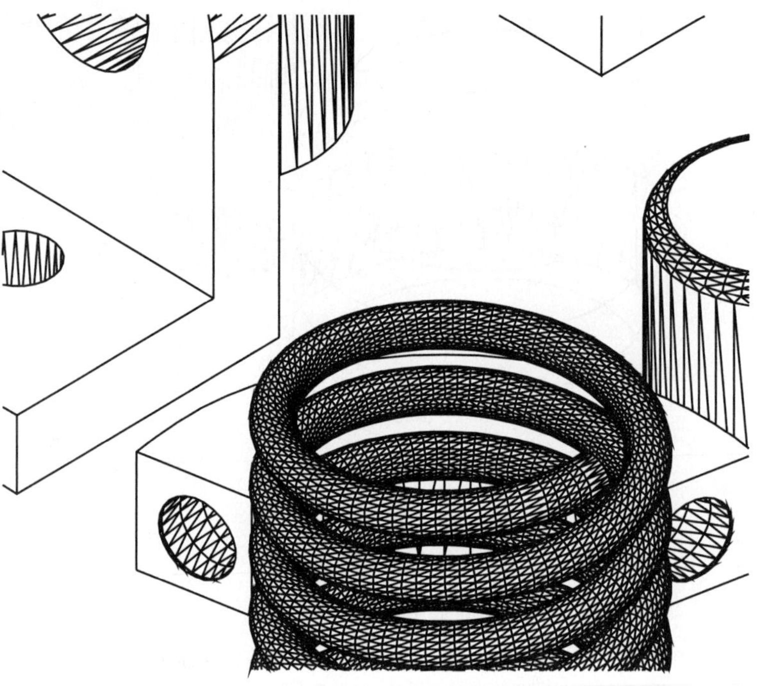

FIGURE 14–27
Inner Swept Circle Subtracted from Outer Swept Circle

LOFT

The Loft command gives you the ability to create a 3D solid or surface selecting a set of two or more cross-sectional areas.

If you select two or more closed cross-sectional areas, a solid is created.

If you select two or more open cross-sectional areas, a surface is created.

You cannot use both open and closed cross-sectional areas in a set. You have to choose one or the other.

When you make a lofted shape, you can use the Loft Settings dialog box to control the shape of the surface or solid.

Step 59. **Draw three circles (1/2″ radius, 3/8″ radius, and 1/4″ radius) in the approximate location shown in Figure 14–28.**

Step 60. **Move the 1/4″ radius circle up 1/4″ in the Z direction. You may use the Move command and** TYPE: **@0,0,1/4 <enter> for the second point of displacement OR in the 3D view (with ORTHO ON)** CLICK: **on the circle,** CLICK: **the center grip, move your mouse up, and** TYPE: **1/4 <enter>.**

Step 61. **Move the 3/8″ radius circle up 1/2″ in the Z direction.**

Step 62. **Use the Loft command to create a lofted solid and use the Hide command to check it (Figure 14–29), as described next:**

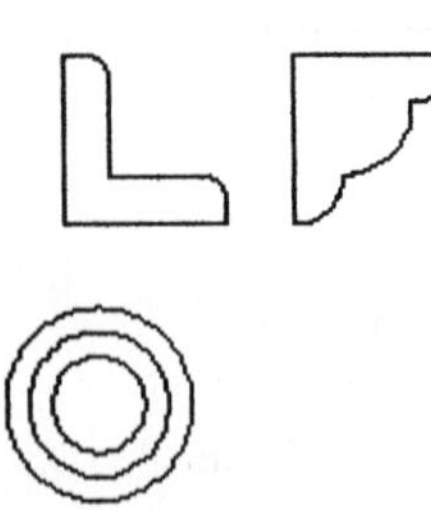

FIGURE 14–28
Draw 1/4″, 3/8″, and 1/2″ Radius Circles

Prompt	Response
Command:	**Loft** (or TYPE: **LOFT<enter>**)
Select cross-sections in lofting order:	CLICK: **the 1/2″ radius circle** (the one on the bottom)

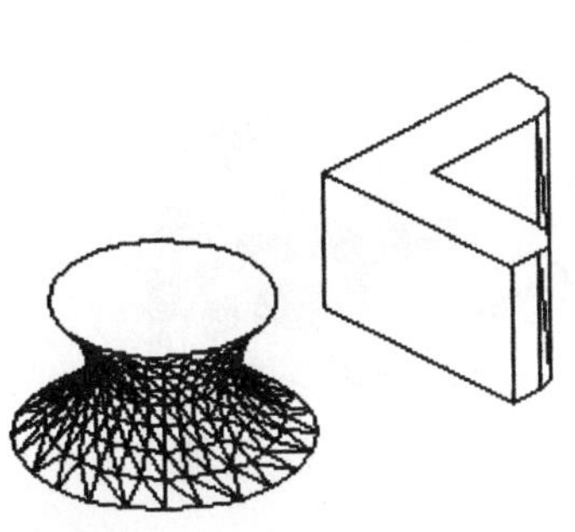

FIGURE 14–29
Lofted Shape Complete

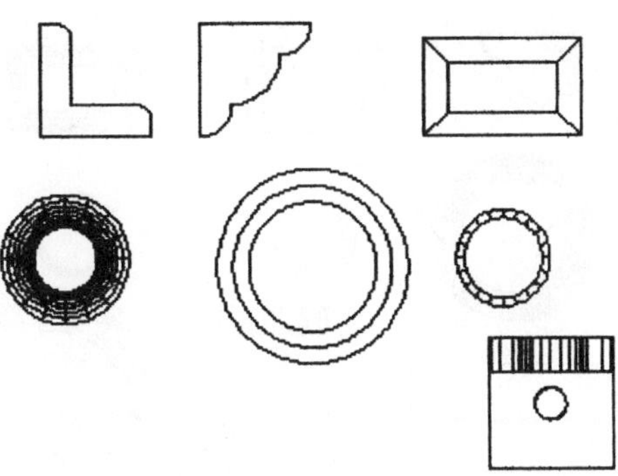

FIGURE 14–30
Draw 1/2", 5/8", and 3/4" Radius Circles

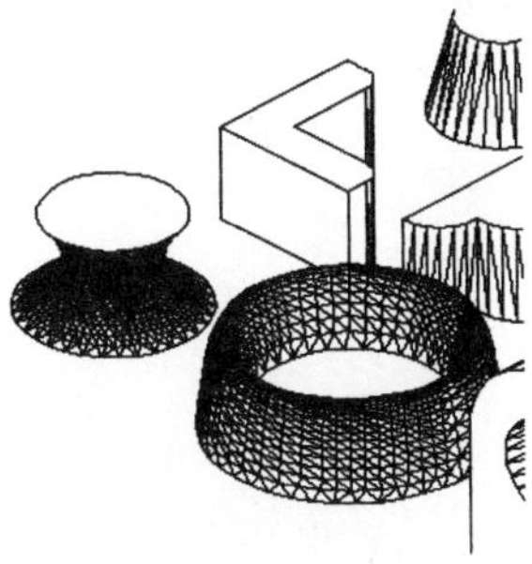

FIGURE 14–31
Lofted Bowl Shape Complete

Prompt	Response
Select cross-sections in lofting order:	CLICK: **the 1/4" radius circle** (the next one up)
Select cross-sections in lofting order:	CLICK: **the 3/8" radius circle** (the one on top)
Select cross-sections in lofting order:	**<enter>**
Enter an option [Guides/Path/ Cross-sections only] <Cross-sections only>:	**<enter>**
The Loft Settings dialog box appears;	CLICK: **OK**
Command:	**Hide** (or TYPE: **HI<enter>**)

Create a Bowl-Shaped Object

The Loft command also enables you to create a bowl-shaped object as described next.

Step 63. **Draw three circles (3/4" radius, 5/8" radius, and 1/2" radius) in the approximate location shown in Figure 14–30.**

Step 64. **Move the 1/2" radius circle up 1/8" in the Z direction.**

Step 65. **Move the 5/8" radius circle up 1/2" in the Z direction.**

Step 66. **Use the Loft command to create the bowl but pick the circles in a different order:** CLICK: **the one on the bottom first, the one on the top next, and the one in between the two others last.**

Step 67. **Use the Hide command to check its shape, Figure 14–31.**

PLANAR SURFACE

You can use the Planar Surface (PLANESURF) command to make a surface using one of the following:

Select one or more objects that form an enclosed area.
Draw a rectangle so that the surface is created parallel to the rectangle.

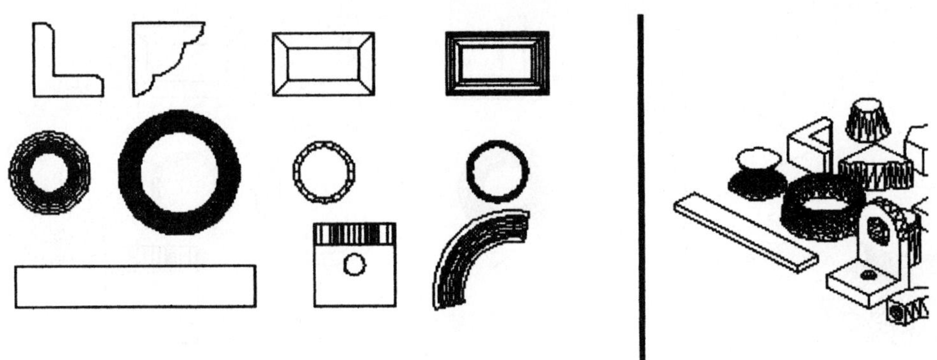

FIGURE 14–32
Draw the Planar Surface and Thicken It

Step 68. Draw a planar surface and thicken it (Figure 14–32), as described next:

Prompt	Response
Command:	**Planar Surface** (or TYPE: **PLANESURF<enter>**)
Specify first corner or [Object] <Object>:	CLICK: **the lower left corner in the approximate location shown in Figure 14–32**
Specify other corner:	TYPE: **@3,1/2<enter>**
Command:	**Thicken** (or TYPE: **THICKEN<enter>**)

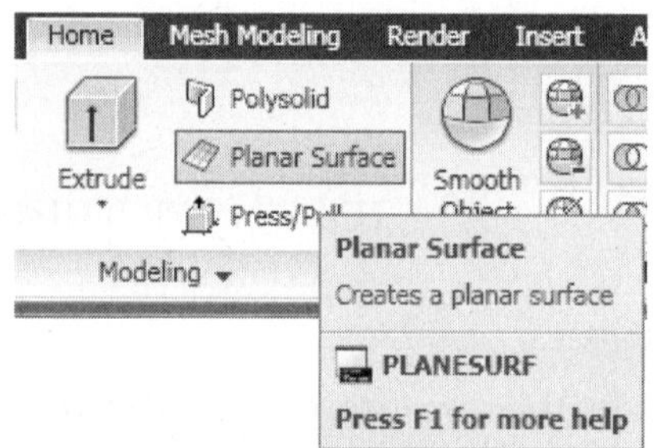

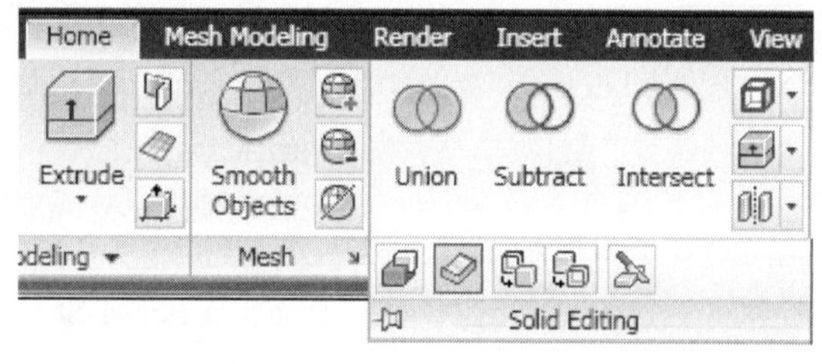

Prompt	Response
Select surfaces to thicken:	CLICK: **the planar surface**
Select surfaces to thicken:	**<enter>**
Specify thickness <0′-0″>:	TYPE: **1/8<enter>**

POLYSOLID

You can use the Polysolid command to draw walls by specifying the wall width and its height. You can also create a polysolid from an existing line, polyline, arc, or circle. If the width and height have been set, clicking on the object from the polysolid prompt such as a line or an arc will change it to a polysolid that is the height and width of the polysolid setting.

Step 69. Draw a polysolid that has a height of 1/2″ and a width of 1/4″ (Figure 14–33), as described next. (Be sure you are in the World UCS.)

Prompt	Response
Command:	**Polysolid** (or TYPE: **POLYSOLID<enter>**)
Specify start point or [Object/Height/Width/Justify] <Object>:	TYPE: **H<enter>**
Specify height <0′-0″>:	TYPE: **1/2<enter>**

FIGURE 14–33
Draw a Polysolid with a Height of 1/2″ and a Width of 1/4″

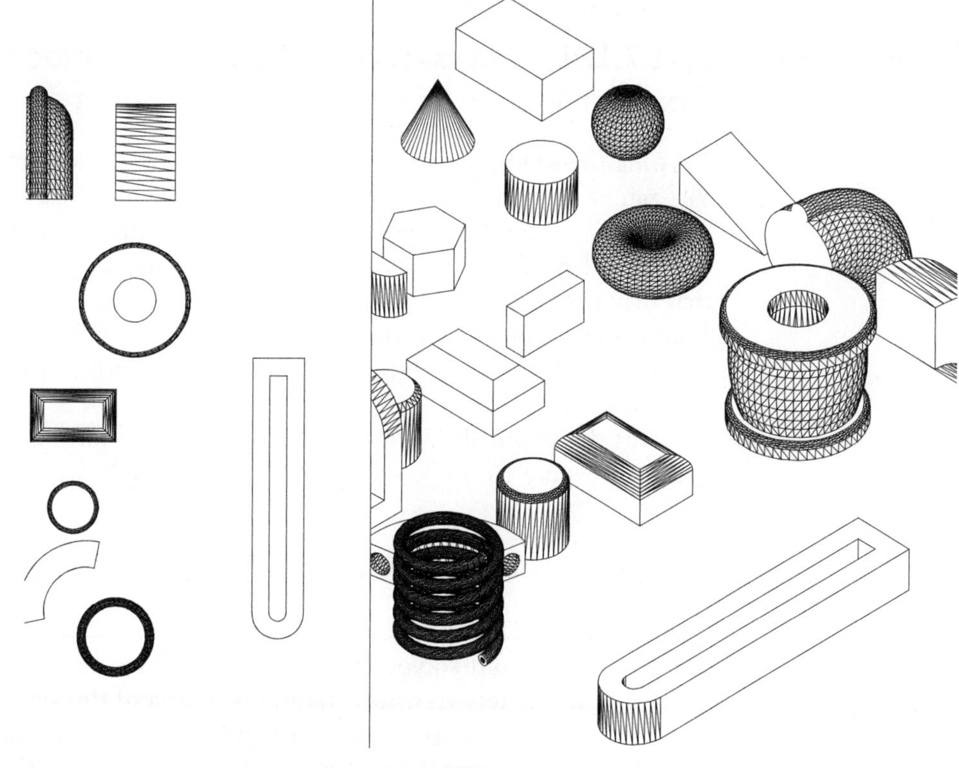

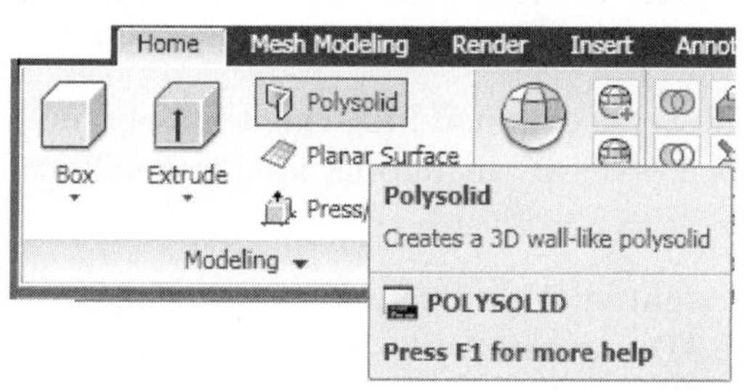

Prompt	Response
Specify start point or [Object/ Height/Width/Justify] <Width>:	TYPE: **W<enter>**
Specify width <0′-0 ″>:	TYPE: **1/4<enter>**
Specify start point or [Object/ Height/Width/Justify] <Width>:	TYPE: **8-1/2,4<enter>**
Specify next point or [Arc/Undo]: <Ortho on>	**Move your mouse down 3″ and** CLICK:
Specify next point or [Arc/Undo]:	TYPE: **A<enter>**
Specify endpoint of arc or [Close/ Direction/Line/Second point/Undo]:	**Move your mouse to the left 1/2″ and** CLICK:
Specify next point or [Arc/Close/ Undo]:	
Specify endpoint of arc or [Close/ Direction/Line/Second point/Undo]:	TYPE: **L<enter>**
Specify next point or [Arc/Close/ Undo]:	**Move your mouse up 3″ and** CLICK:
Specify next point or [Arc/Close/ Undo]:	TYPE: **C<enter>**
Command:	**Hide** (or TYPE: **HI<enter>**)

Tutorial 14–1: Part 7, Using Intersection to Form a Solid Model from the Common Volume of Two Intersecting Solids

Drawing the solid model in Tutorial 14–1, Part 7, demonstrates another powerful tool that can be used to form complex models.

In this tutorial two separate solid shapes are drawn (in this case the same shape is copied and rotated so the two shapes are at right angles to each other) and moved so that they intersect. Intersection is used to combine the shapes to form one solid model from the common volume of the two intersecting solids. Figure 14–34 shows the two separate solid shapes, and the solid model that is formed from the common volume of the two solid shapes.

This shape will also be used in Tutorial 15–2 to form the cornices at the top of the columns (Figure 15–7).

DRAW TWO EXTRUDED SHAPES AT RIGHT ANGLES TO EACH OTHER

Step 70. Zoom out so you can draw the full size shape shown in Figure 14–35 in the left viewport. In an open area of the screen, draw Figure 14–35 using Polyline and Fillet commands. Use Polyline to draw the shape with square corners shown in the top half of the figure, then use 1″ radius fillets to form the rounded corners.

Step 71. Use the Scale command to scale the polyline to 1/12 its size. (This is a scale of 1″ = 1′-0″. In Tutorial 15–2 you will scale this model to its original size.)

Step 72. In the right viewport, set UCS to World, copy the shape once, and use Rotate 3D to rotate both shapes 90° about the X axis.

Step 73. Use Rotate 3D to rotate the shape on the right 90° about the Z axis (Figure 14–36).

Step 74. Extrude both shapes 2″ (Figure 14–37) (or use **Press/Pull** to extrude both shapes 2″).

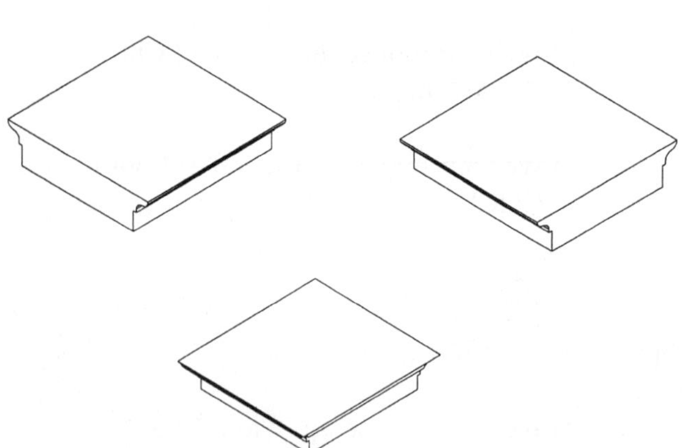

FIGURE 14–34
Two Shapes and the Shape Formed from the Intersected Volume of the Two Shapes

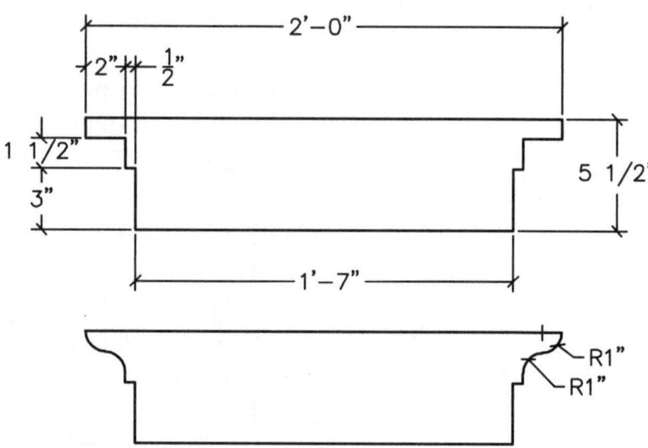

FIGURE 14–35
Dimensions for the Extruded Shapes

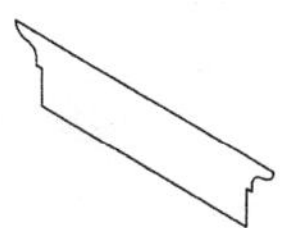

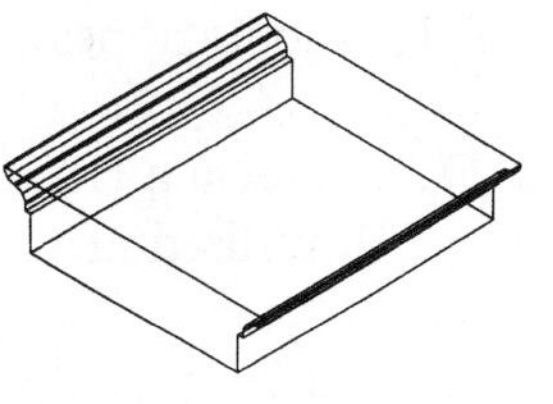

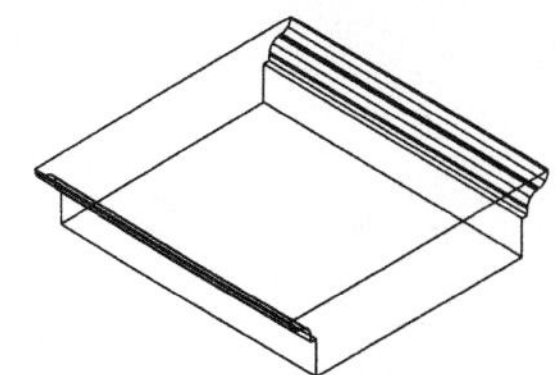

FIGURE 14–36
Two Shapes Rotated 90° to Each Other

FIGURE 14–37
Both Shapes Extruded

Step 75. **Use the Move command to move the solid on the left to intersect with the other solid (Figure 14–38), as described next:**

Prompt	Response
Command:	**Move**
Select objects:	CLICK: **the shape on the left**
Select objects:	**<enter>**
Specify base point or [Displacement] <Displacement>:	**OSNAP-Endpoint**
of	**D1**
Specify second point or <use first point as displacement>:	**OSNAP-Endpoint**
of	**D2**

INTERSECT

Step 76. **Use Intersect to form a solid model from the common volume of the two intersecting solids (Figure 14–39), as described next:**

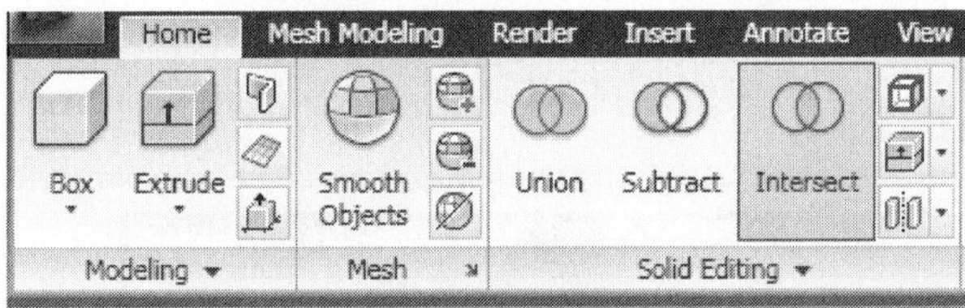

Prompt	Response
Command:	**Intersect** (from Modify-Solid Editing) (or TYPE: **IN<enter>**)
Select objects:	CLICK: **both shapes**
2 solids intersected	

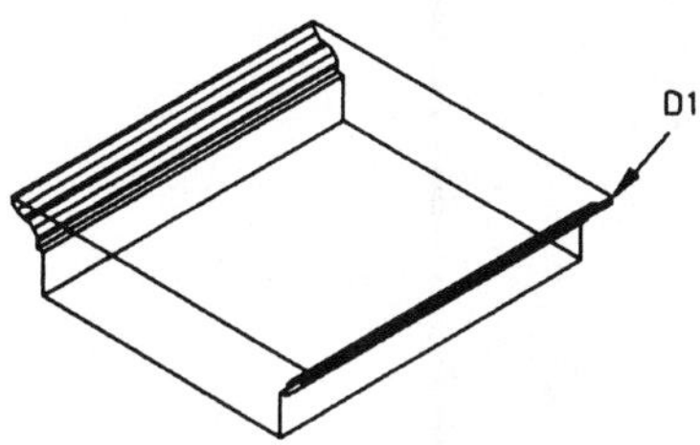

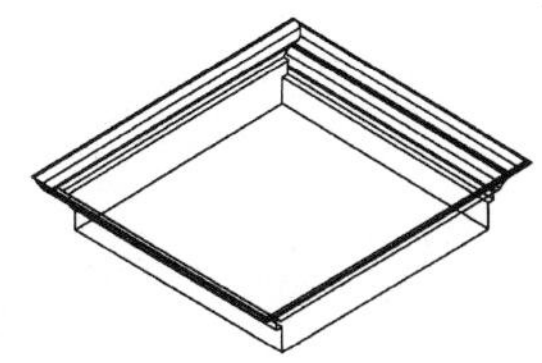

FIGURE 14–38
Moving One Shape to Intersect with the Other

FIGURE 14–39
The Shape Formed from the Intersected Shapes

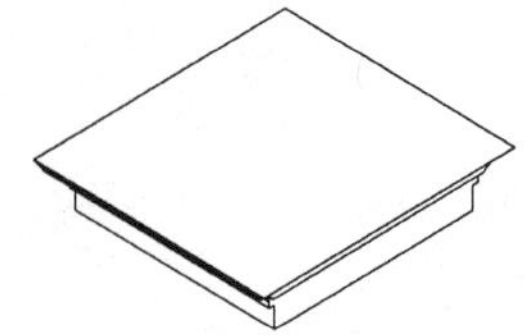

FIGURE 14–40
The Intersected Solid After a Hide

The display should appear as shown in Figure 14–39.

Step 77. Perform a Hide to be sure the solid model is correct (Figure 14–40), as described next:

Prompt	Response
Command:	**Hide** (or TYPE: **HI<enter>**)

The display should appear as shown in Figure 14–40.

Step 78. Return the UCS to World so you will not be surprised at the position the model will assume when it is inserted.

WBLOCK THE INTERSECTED MODEL

You should now Wblock the intersected model so you can use it in Tutorial 15–2 to form the cornices at the tops of the columns (see Figure 15–7).

Step 79. Use Wblock to save the model to a disk (Figure 14–41), as described next:

Prompt	Response
Command:	TYPE: **W<enter>**
The Write Block dialog box appears:	CLICK: **the three dots to the far right of the File name and path: input box** **Locate the disk and folder where you store drawings and** DOUBLE-CLICK: **the folder**
The Browse for Drawing File dialog box appears:	TYPE: **14-3** in the File name: input box, then CLICK: **Save** CLICK: **Pick point**

FIGURE 14–41
Wblocking the Intersected Shape

Prompt	Response
Specify insertion base point:	TYPE: **END<enter>**
of	CLICK: **the bottom corner of the intersected shape using OSNAP-Endpoint. It will be the lowest point on the display.**
The Write Block dialog box appears:	CLICK: **Select Objects**
Select objects:	CLICK: **the intersected shape**
Select objects:	**<enter>**
The Write Block dialog box appears:	**If Retain is not on,** CLICK: **that option button**
	CLICK: **OK**

The shape now exists on your disk as 14–3.dwg, and it is also on the current drawing.

COMPLETE TUTORIAL 14–1

Step 80. **Use the Move command to move the intersected shape to the approximate location shown in Figure 14–2.**

Step 81. **Use the VPORTS command to return to a single viewport of the 3D viewport (Figure 14–2).**

Step 82. CLICK: **Visual Styles Manager and** DOUBLE-CLICK: **Conceptual to shade the drawing, as shown in Figure 14–42.**

Step 83. **Save the drawing in two places.**

Step 84. **Plot the 3D viewport from the Model tab on a standard size sheet of paper. Be sure to click Conceptual from the Shade plot: list in the Plot dialog box so the final plot appears as shown in Figure 14–42.**

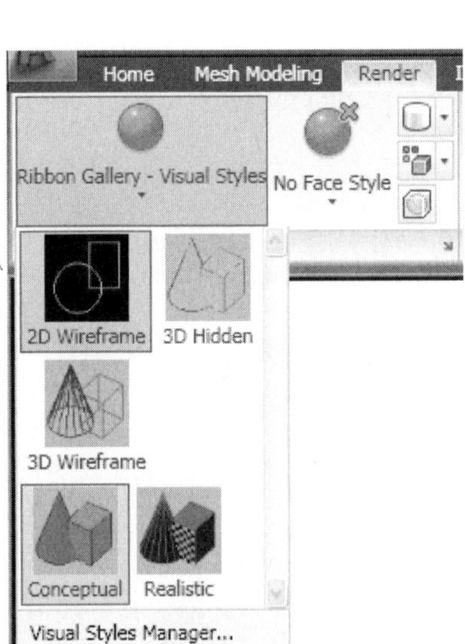

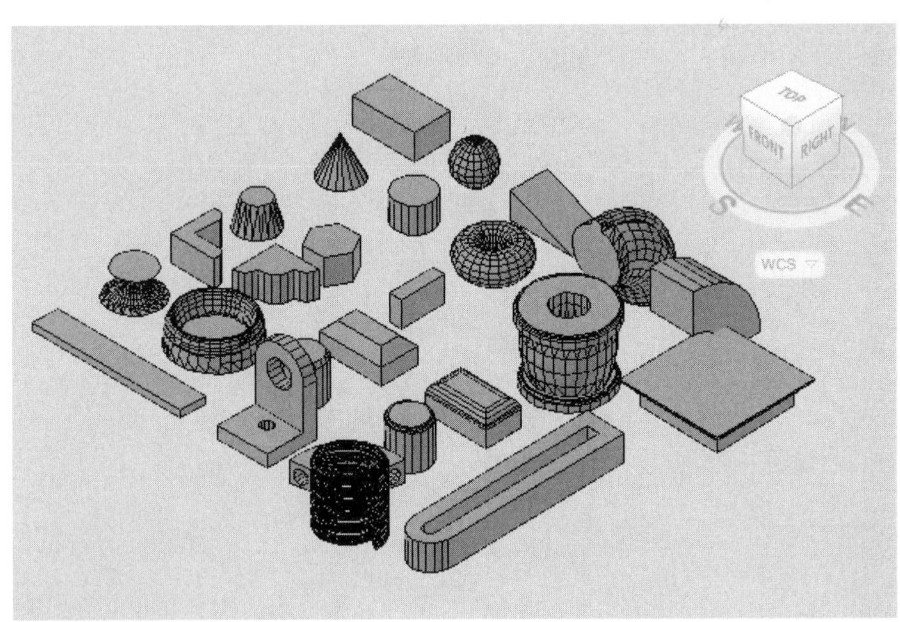

FIGURE 14–42
Rendered Image of Tutorial 14–1

Tutorial 14–2: Using Grips to Modify Solid Shapes

Grips for solids make changing the size and shape of solids much easier. In this tutorial you will draw some solid shapes and use grips to change them.

Step 1. Use your **3D** workspace to make the following settings:

1. **Use SaveAs... to save the drawing on the hard drive with the name CH14-TUTORIAL2.**
2. Set drawing Units: **Architectural**
3. Set Drawing Limits: **8-1/2,11**
4. Set GRIDDISPLAY: **0**
5. Set Grid: **1/4**
6. Set Snap: **1/8**
7. **Create the following Layers:**

LAYER NAME	COLOR	LINETYPE	LINEWEIGHT
3d-r	red	continuous	default
3d-m	magenta	continuous	default
3d-g	green	continuous	default

8. **Set Layer 3d-m current.**
9. **Use the Viewports command to make two vertical viewports. Zoom-All in both viewports to start, then Zoom in closer as needed.**
10. CLICK: **SE Isometric from 3D Views for the right viewport.**
11. **Set FACETRES to 4, ISOLINES to 20.**

Step 2. Draw the following solids in the approximate locations shown in Figure 14–43:

1. **Use the Box command to draw a box 2″ long × 1-1/2″ deep × 2″ high.**
2. **Use the Cylinder command to draw a cylinder with a radius of 3/4″ × 2″ high.**

FIGURE 14–43
Draw Solids in This Approximate Location

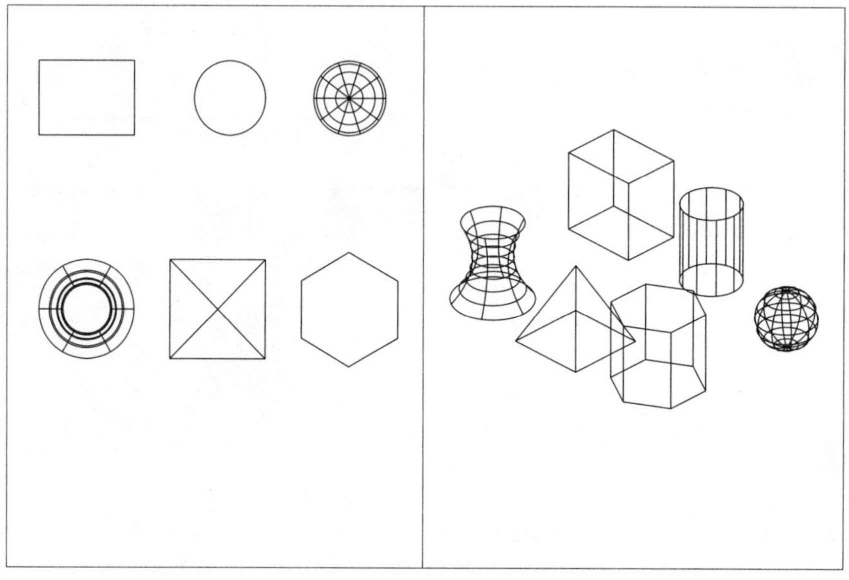

3. Use the Sphere command to draw a 3/4″ radius sphere.
4. Use the Circle command to draw three circles; 1″ radius, 3/4″ radius, 1/2″ radius. Move the 1/2″ radius circle up 1″ in the Z direction and the 3/4″ radius circle up 2″ in the Z direction. Use the Loft command to create the shape shown.
5. Use the Pyramid command to draw a pyramid with a 1″ radius base, 2″ high.
6. Use the Polygon command to draw a 6-sided polygon with a 1″ radius circumscribed.
7. Use the Extrude or Press/Pull command to extrude the polygon 2″.

Step 3. Use grips to change the box to make it 2″ taller and 1″ deeper:

1. With no command active, CLICK: **any point on the box.**
2. CLICK: **the up grip to make it active (it changes color) and move your mouse up (in the Z direction) until the dynamic input reads 2″, as shown in Figure 14–44, then** CLICK: **to choose 2″** (or TYPE: **2<enter>**). Then PRESS: **Esc.**
3. With no command active, CLICK: **any point on the box.**
4. CLICK: **the grip in front to make it active and move your mouse forward (in the Y direction) until the dynamic input reads 1″, as shown in Figure 14–45, then** CLICK: **to choose 1″ (or TYPE: 1<enter>).**
5. Then PRESS: **Esc.**

Step 4. Use grips to make the cylinder 4″ taller with a radius of 1/2″:

1. With no command active, CLICK: **any point on the cylinder.**
2. CLICK: **the up grip to make it active, and move your mouse up (in the Z direction) until the dynamic input reads 4″, as shown in Figure 14–46, then** CLICK: **to choose 4″** (or TYPE: **4<enter>**). Then PRESS: **Esc.**
3. With no command active, CLICK: **any point on the cylinder.**
4. CLICK: **one of the grips on the quadrants to make it active and move your mouse in until the dynamic input reads 1/4″, as shown in Figure 14–47, then** CLICK: **to choose 1/4″** (or TYPE: **1/4<enter>**).
5. Then PRESS: **Esc.**

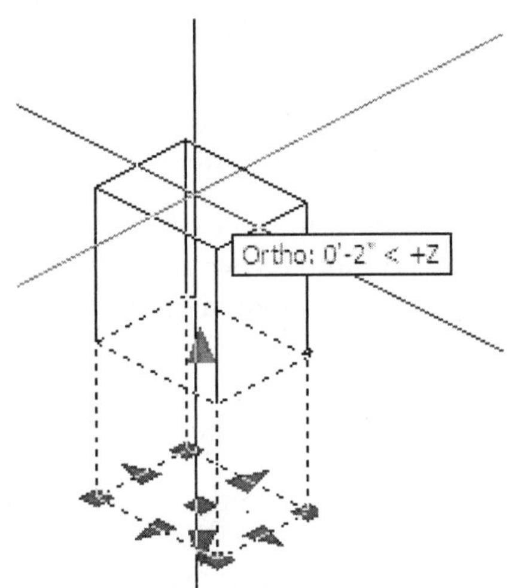

FIGURE 14–44
Use Grips to Make the Box 2″ Taller

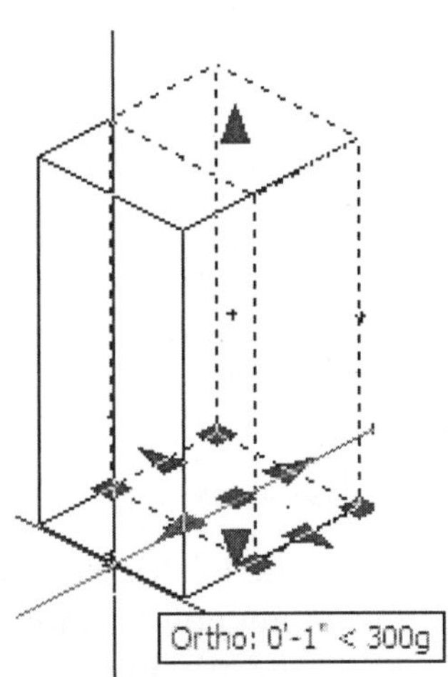

FIGURE 14–45
Use Grips to Make the Box 1″ Deeper

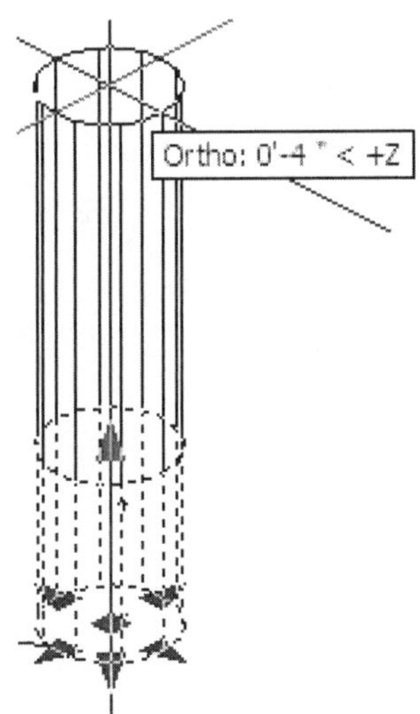

FIGURE 14–46
Use Grips to Make the Cylinder 4″ Taller

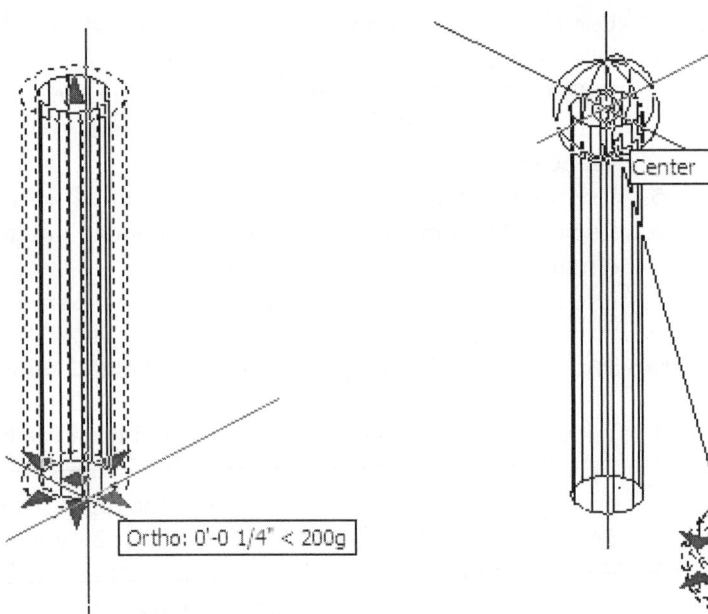

FIGURE 14–47
Use Grips to Make the Cylinder Radius 1/4″ Smaller

FIGURE 14–48
Use Grips to Move the Sphere to the Top of the Cylinder

Step 5. **Use grips to move the sphere to the top of the cylinder:**

1. With no command active, CLICK: **any point on the sphere.**
2. CLICK: **the grip in the center to make it active, turn ORTHO OFF, activate Osnap-Center, and** CLICK: **the top of the cylinder, as shown in Figure 14–48.** Then, PRESS: **Esc.**

Step 6. **Use grips to move the extruded polygon back 4″:**

1. With no command active, CLICK: **any point on the extruded polygon.**
2. CLICK: **one of the grips to make it active, turn ORTHO ON,** PRESS: **the space bar or toggle to the MOVE grip mode, and move your mouse back in the Y direction until the dynamic input reads 4″, as shown in Figure 14–49.**

Step 7. **Use grips to make the extruded polygon 4″ taller:**

1. With no command active, CLICK: **any point on the extruded polygon.**
2. CLICK: **the up grip to make it active and move your mouse up (in the Z direction) until the dynamic input reads 4″, as shown in Figure 14–50, then** CLICK: **to choose 4″** (or TYPE: **4<enter>**). Then, PRESS: **Esc.**

Step 8. **Use grips to move the pyramid 2-3/4″ to the right:**

1. CLICK: **the left viewport to make it active, and with no command active** CLICK: **any point on the pyramid.**
2. CLICK: **the grip in the center to make it active, turn ORTHO ON, and move your mouse to the right until the dynamic input reads 2-3/4″, as shown in Figure 14–51.** CLICK: **to choose 2-3/4″** (or TYPE: **2-3/4<enter>**). Then, PRESS: **Esc.**

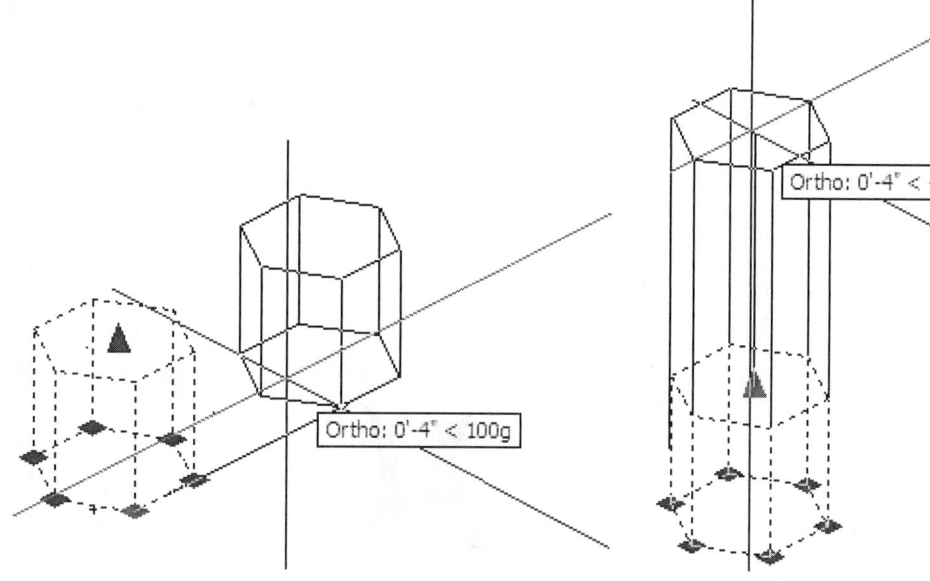

FIGURE 14–49
Use Grips to Move the Extruded Polygon Back 4″ in the Y Direction

FIGURE 14–50
Use Grips to Make the Extruded Polygon 4″ Taller

FIGURE 14–51
Use Grips to Move the Pyramid 2-3/4″ to the Right

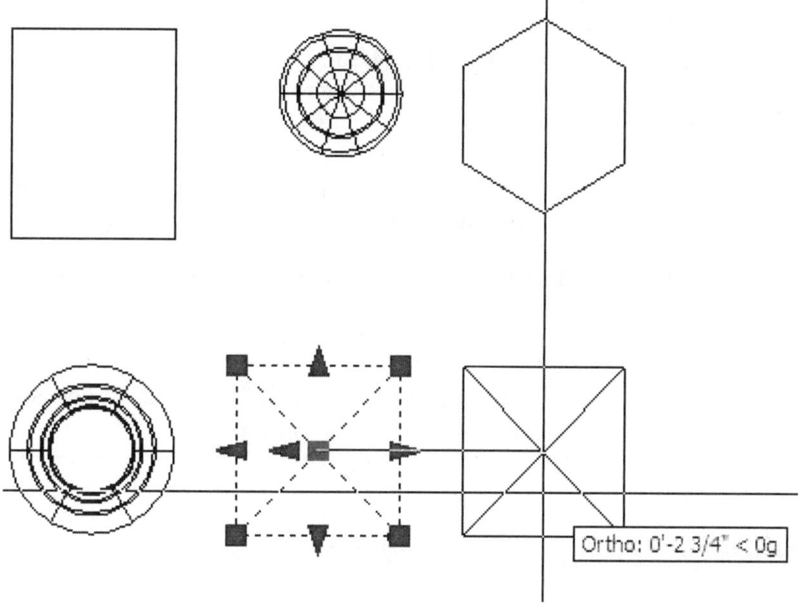

Step 9. **Use grips to make the pyramid 4″ taller:**

1. With no command active, CLICK: **any point on the pyramid.**
2. CLICK: **the up grip to make it active, move your mouse up (in the Z direction) until the dynamic input reads 4″, as shown in Figure 14–52, then** CLICK: **to choose 4″** (or TYPE: **4<enter>**). Then, PRESS: **Esc.**

Step 10. **Use grips to scale the lofted solid 1-1/4 larger than it is:**

1. With no command active, CLICK: **any point on the lofted solid.**
2. CLICK: **the grip in the center to make it active,** PRESS: **the space bar several times to toggle to the SCALE grip mode, and** TYPE: **1-1/4<enter>.** Then, PRESS: **Esc.**

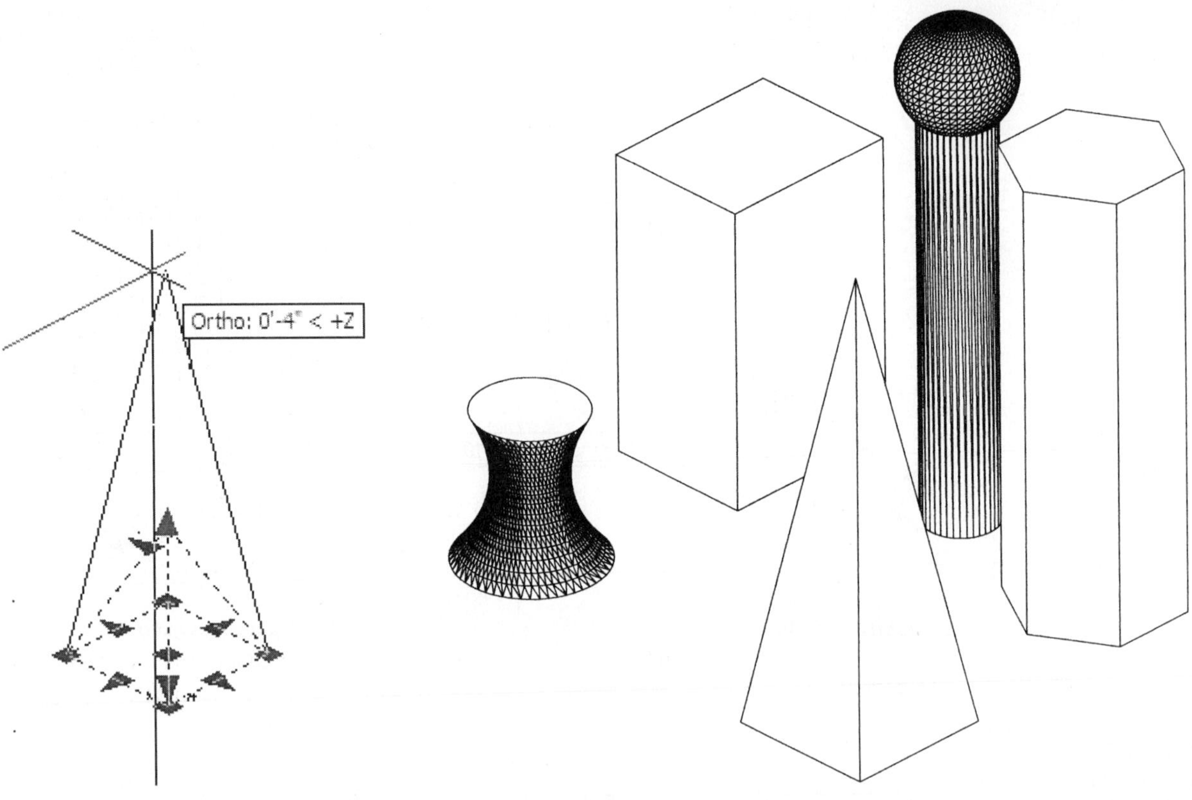

FIGURE 14–52
Use Grips to Make the Pyramid 4″ Taller

FIGURE 14–53
Tutorial 14–2 Complete

Step 11. CLICK: **the 3D viewport to make it active, and change the display to a single viewport.**

Step 12. **Use the Hide command to remove hidden lines, as shown in Figure 14–53.**

Step 13. **Save your drawing in two places.**

Step 14. **Plot the drawing on an 11″ × 8-1/2″ sheet, scale: 1:2;** CLICK: **3D Hidden in the Shade plot area.**

Tutorial 14–3: Creating a Solid Model of Chair 1

In this tutorial you will create a solid model of chair 1 (Figure 14–54) using many of the commands you used in Tutorial 14–1 and many of the options of the SOLIDEDIT command.

Step 1. **Use your 3D workspace to make the following settings:**

1. **Use SaveAs... to save the drawing on the hard drive with the name CH14-TUTORIAL3.**
2. Set drawing Units: **Architectural**
3. Set Drawing Limits: **50,50**
4. Set GRIDDISPLAY: **0**
5. Set Grid: **1**
6. Set Snap: **1/2**

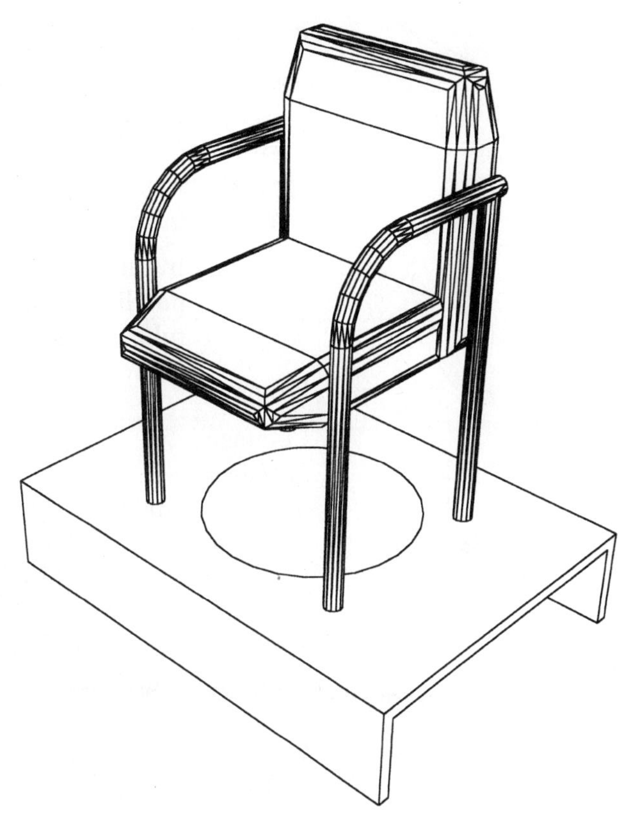

FIGURE 14–54
Tutorial 14–3 Complete

7. Create the following Layers:

LAYER NAME	COLOR	LINETYPE	LINEWEIGHT
3d-r	red	continuous	default
3d-m	magenta	continuous	default
3d-g	green	continuous	default

8. **Set Layer 3d-r current.**
9. **Use the Viewports command to make two vertical viewports. Zoom-All in both viewports to start, then Zoom in closer as needed.** You will need both viewports as aids in creating this model.
10. CLICK: **SE Isometric from 3D Views for the right viewport.**
11. **Set FACETRES to 4, ISOLINES to 20.**

DRAW ONE SIDE OF THE CHAIR LEGS AND ARMS

Step 2. Define a UCS that is parallel to the side of the chair legs and arms in the right viewport, as described next:

Prompt	Response
Command:	CLICK: **The right viewport**
Command:	TYPE: **UCS<enter>**
Specify origin of UCS or [Face/NAmed/OBject/Previous/View/World/X/Y/Z/ZAxis] <World>:	TYPE: **X<enter>**
Specify rotation angle about X axis <90>:	**<enter>**
Command:	**<enter>**

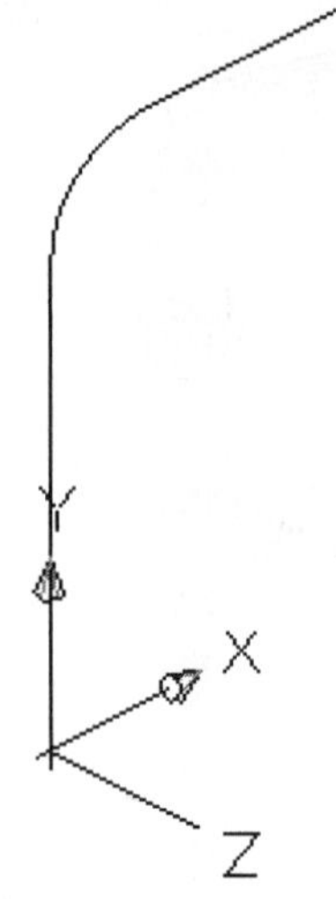

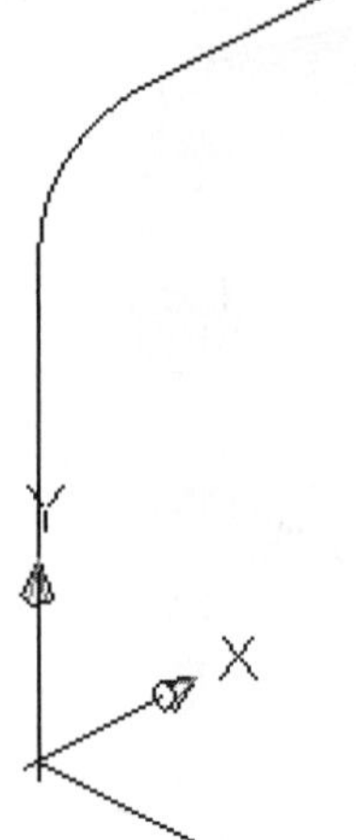

FIGURE 14–55
Draw a Path to Sweep a Circle

Prompt	Response
Specify origin of UCS or [Face/ NAmed/OBject/Previous/View/ World/X/Y/Z/ZAxis] <World>:	TYPE: **Y<enter>**
Specify rotation angle about Y axis <90>:	**<enter>**

Step 3. **In the right viewport draw a path for the chair arm and front leg (two polylines and a fillet) (Figure 14–55). Draw a circle to form the metal tube, and sweep it along the path, as described next:**

Prompt	Response
Command:	TYPE: **PL<enter>**
Specify start point:	TYPE: **8,12<enter>**
Specify next point or [Arc/Halfwidth/ Length/Undo/Width]:	TYPE: **@0,27<enter>**
Specify next point or [Arc/Halfwidth/ Length/Undo/Width]:	TYPE: **@16.5,0<enter>**
Specify next point or [Arc/Halfwidth/ Length/Undo/Width]:	**<enter>**
Command:	TYPE: **F<enter>**
Select first object or [Undo/Polyline/ Radius/Trim/Multiple]:	TYPE: **R<enter>**
Specify fillet radius <0′-0″>:	TYPE: **5<enter>**
Select first object or [Undo/Polyline/ Radius/Trim/Multiple] to apply corner:	CLICK: **one of the lines**
Select second object or shift-select:	CLICK: **the other line**
Command:	TYPE: **C<enter>**
Specify center point for circle or [3P/2P/Ttr (tan tan radius)]:	TYPE: **END<enter>**
of	CLICK: **the lower end of the vertical line**
Specify radius of circle or [Diameter]:	TYPE: **1<enter>**
Command:	**Sweep** (or TYPE: **SWEEP<enter>**)
Select objects to sweep:	CLICK: **the circle**
Select objects to sweep:	**<enter>**
Select sweep path or [Alignment/ Base point/Scale/Twist]:	CLICK: **the polyline**

The right viewport should appear as shown in Figure 14–56.

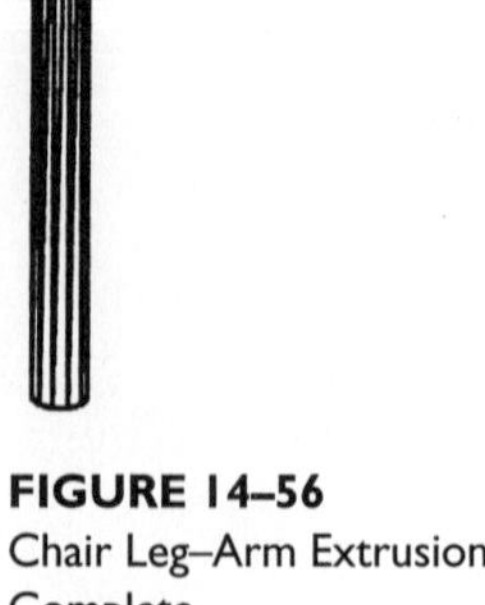

FIGURE 14–56
Chair Leg–Arm Extrusion Complete

DRAW THE CUSHION OF THE CHAIR

Step 4. **Set a new UCS that is parallel to the World UCS (the cushion of the chair) that has an origin at the bottom of the chair leg, as described next:**

Prompt	Response
Command:	TYPE: **UCS<enter>**
Specify origin of UCS or [Face/ NAmed/OBject/Previous/View/ World/X/Y/Z/ZAxis] <World>:	**<enter>**
Command:	**<enter>**

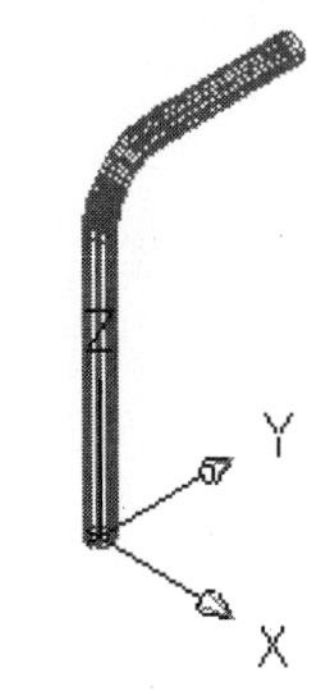

FIGURE 14–57
Move the UCS

Prompt	Response
Specify origin of UCS or [Face/ NAmed/OBject/Previous/View/ World/X/Y/Z/ZAxis] <World>:	**OSNAP-Center**
of	CLICK: **the bottom of the chair leg** (Figure 14–57)
Specify point on X-axis or <Accept>:	**<enter>**

Step 5. **Set Layer 3d-m current.**

Step 6. **Draw a box for the chair cushion and extrude and taper the front of it, as described next:**

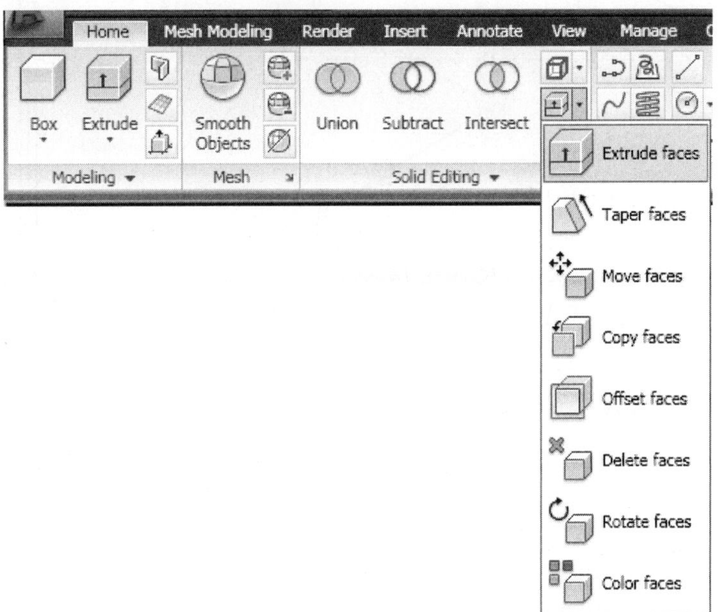

Prompt	Response
Command:	**Box** (or TYPE: **BOX<enter>**)
Specify corner of box or [Center]:	TYPE: **.75,13,14<enter>**
Specify corner or [Cube/Length]:	TYPE: **@18,-13** (Be sure to include the minus.)
Specify height or [2Point]:	TYPE: **5<enter>**
	CLICK: **Extrude faces**
Select faces or [Undo/Remove]:	CLICK: **D1** (Figure 14–58)
Select faces or [Undo/Remove/ALL]:	TYPE: **R<enter>** (to remove any surfaces that you do not want to extrude. You will probably have one that needs to be removed.)
Remove faces or [Undo/Add/ALL]:	CLICK: **any extra faces so the model appears as shown in Figure 14–59**
Remove faces or [Undo/Add/ALL]:	**<enter>**
Specify height of extrusion or [Path]:	TYPE: **5<enter>**
Specify angle of taper for extrusion <0>:	TYPE: **15<enter>**
Enter a face editing option [Extrude/ Move/Rotate/Offset/Taper/Delete/ Copy/coLor/Undo/eXit] <eXit>:	**<enter>**
Enter a solids editing option [Face/ Edge/Body/Undo/eXit] <eXit>:	**<enter>**

The model appears as shown in Figure 14–60.

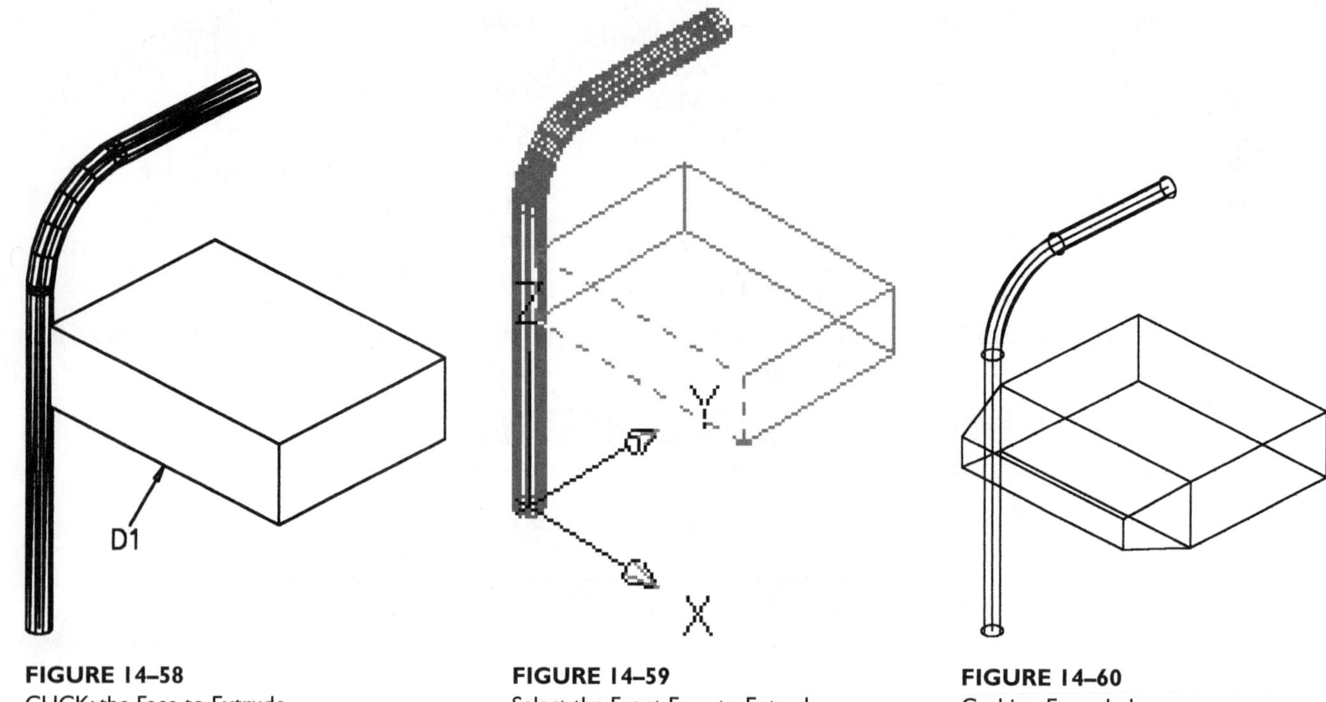

FIGURE 14–58
CLICK: the Face to Extrude

FIGURE 14–59
Select the Front Face to Extrude

FIGURE 14–60
Cushion Extruded

DRAW THE BACK OF THE CHAIR

Step 7. Draw a box for the back of the chair, as described next:

Prompt	Response
Command:	**Box** (or TYPE: **BOX<enter>**)
Specify first corner or [Center]	**OSNAP-Endpoint**
of	CLICK: **D1** (Figure 14–61)
Specify corner or [Cube/Length]:	TYPE: **@20,5<enter>**
Specify height or [2Point]:	TYPE: **16<enter>**

Oops, the back is too long. Correct it by moving the right surface of the box 2″ to the left using Grips.

Step 8. Use the Extrude Faces option of the Solid Editing (SOLIDEDIT) command to extrude the top of the chair back 5″ with a 15° taper (Figure 14–62). You can skip several prompts by using either the Solid Editing toolbar or Solid Editing-Extrude Faces from the Modify menu on the menu bar.

Step 9. Use the Fillet command to round all sharp edges of the chair cushion and back. TYPE: F <enter> for fillet, then TYPE: R <enter> for radius, then TYPE: 1 <enter> to set the radius, then select edges when you get the prompt: "Select an edge or [Chain/Radius]:". Pick the edges of the right side of the cushion, for example, then PRESS: <enter>. If you try to select all edges at the same time, you will get an error message.

COMPLETE THE LEG AND ARM ASSEMBLY

Step 10. Draw a circle for one of the back legs, extrude it, and combine front and back legs into a single object using the Union command (Figure 14–63), as described below:

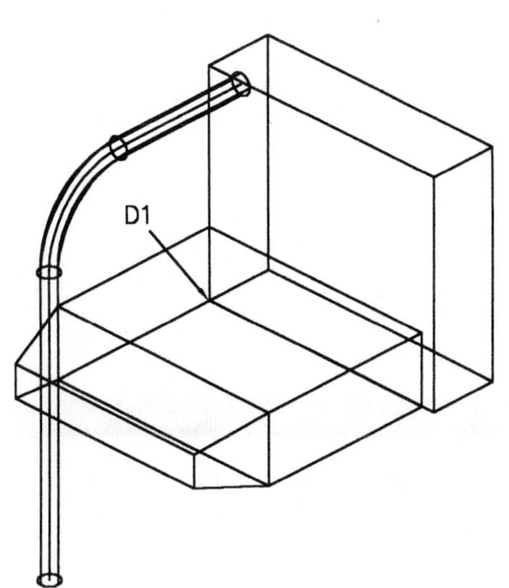

FIGURE 14–61
Draw the Box for the Back of the Chair

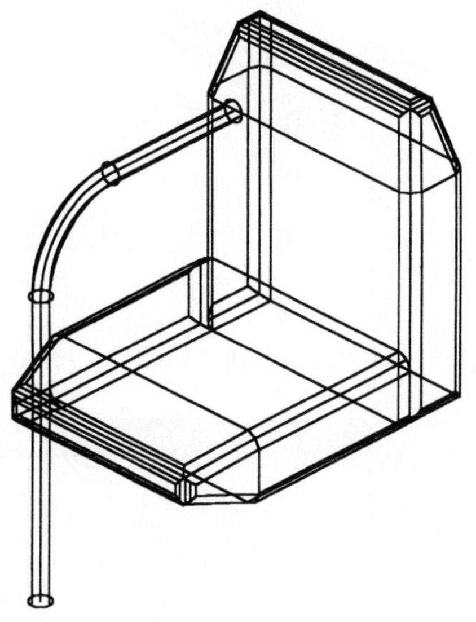

FIGURE 14–62
Correct the Back, Extrude Its Top Surface, and Fillet All Sharp Edges 1″

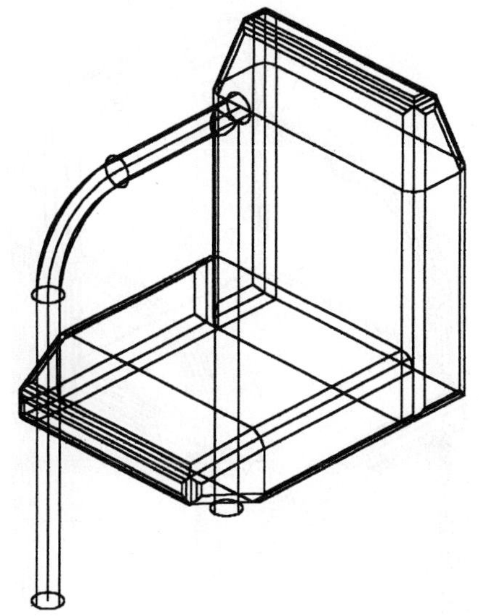

FIGURE 14–63
Draw a Circle for the Back Leg, Extrude It, and Union It with the Front Leg and Arm

Set Layer 3d-g current:

Prompt	Response
Command:	TYPE: **C<enter>**
Specify center point for circle or [3P/2P/Ttr (tan tan radius)]:	TYPE: **0,15–1/2<enter>** (This makes the center point of the circle 15 1/2″ in the Y direction from the UCS origin.)
Specify radius of circle or [Diameter]:	TYPE: **1<enter>**
Command:	TYPE: **EXT<enter>**
Select objects to extrude:	CLICK: **the circle you just drew**
Select objects to extrude:	**<enter>**
Specify height of extrusion or [Direction/Path/Taper angle]:	TYPE: **27<enter>** (The back leg is 27″ high.)
Command	**Union** (or TYPE: **UNION<enter>**)
Select objects:	CLICK: **the chair front leg and the back leg** (This makes the two pieces into a single piece.)
Select objects:	**<enter>**

Step 11. Copy the leg assembly to the right side of the chair (Figure 14–64), as described next:

Prompt	Response
Command:	TYPE: **CP<enter>**
Select objects:	CLICK: **the chair leg assembly**
Select objects:	**<enter>**
Specify base point or [Displacement] <Displacement>:	CLICK: **any point**
Specify second point or <use first point as displacement>:	TYPE: **@20<0<enter>**
Specify second point or [Exit/Undo] <Exit>:	**<enter>**

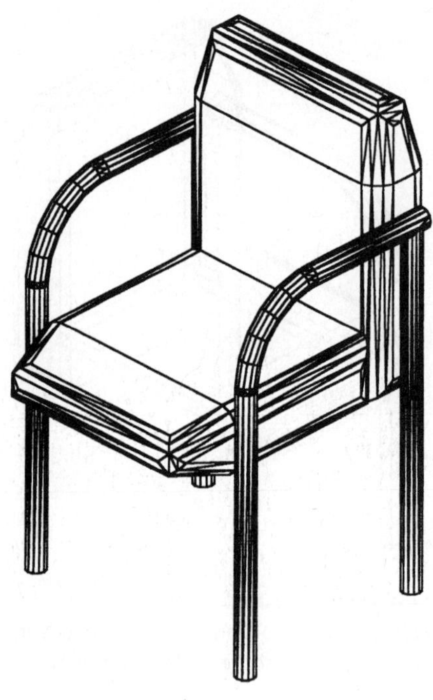

FIGURE 14–64
Copy the Leg Assembly to the Right Side of the Chair

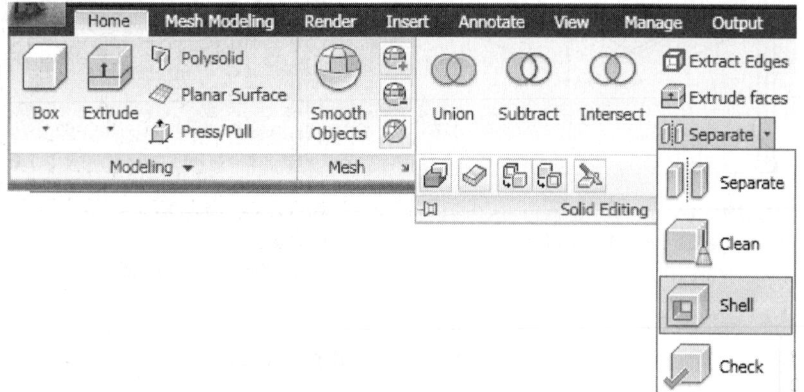

DRAW THE CHAIR PLATFORM

Step 12. **Draw a box and make a shell out of it, as described next:**

Prompt	Response
Command:	TYPE: **BOX<enter>**
Specify corner of box or [Center]:	TYPE: **-10,-8,-6<enter>** (Notice that these are absolute coordinates based on the UCS located on the bottom of the front left leg.)
Specify corner or [Cube/Length]:	TYPE: **30,23.5,0<enter>** (absolute coordinates again)
Command:	**Solid Editing-Shell**
Select a 3D solid:	CLICK: **the box you just drew**
Remove faces or [Undo/Add/ALL]:	CLICK: **D1 and D2** (Figure 14–65)
Remove faces or [Undo/Add/ALL]:	**<enter>**
Enter the shell offset distance:	TYPE: **1<enter>**
[Imprint/seParate solids/Shell/cLean/Check/Undo/eXit]<eXit>:	**<enter><enter>**

Step 13. **Draw a circle and imprint it on the shell (Figure 14–66), as described next:**

Prompt	Response
Command:	TYPE: **C<enter>**
Specify center point for circle or [3P/2P/Ttr (tan tan radius)]:	TYPE: **10,7-3/4<enter>**
Specify radius of circle or [Diameter]<0′-1″>:	TYPE: **8<enter>**
Command:	**Solid Editing-Imprint Edges**

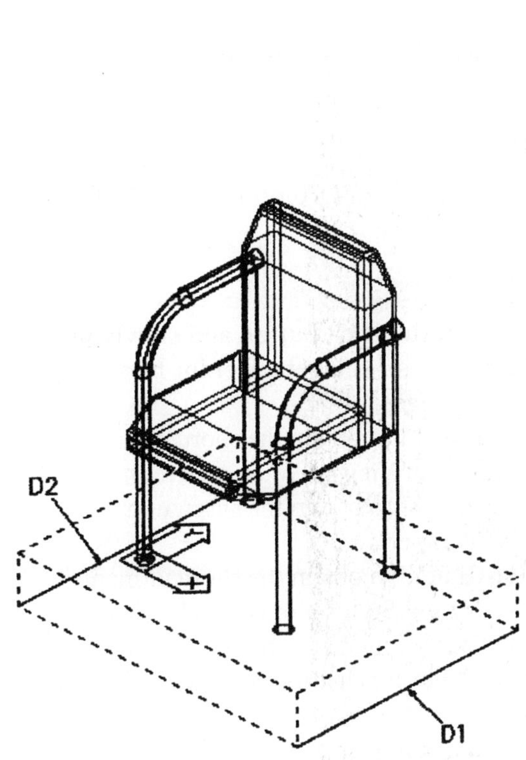

FIGURE 14–65
Draw a Box and Make a Shell of It

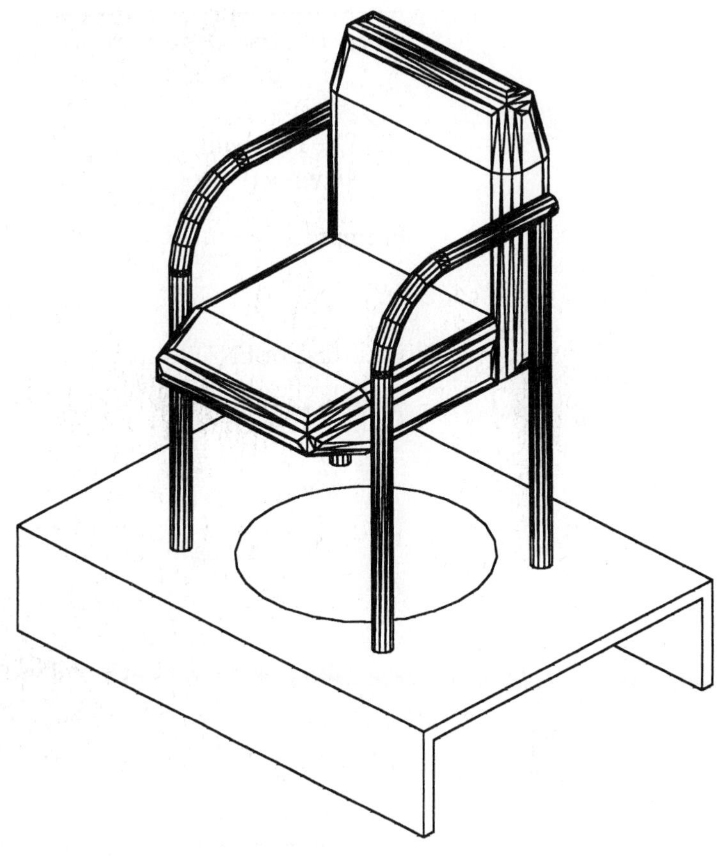

FIGURE 14–66
Draw a Circle and Imprint It on the Shell

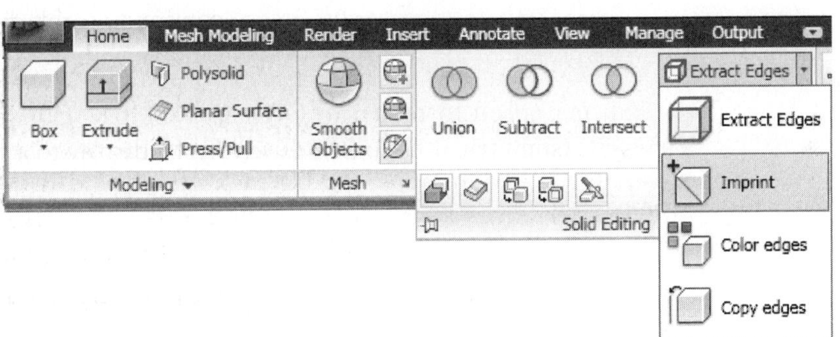

Prompt	Response
Select a 3D solid:	CLICK: **the shell under the chair**
Select an object to imprint:	CLICK: **the circle you just drew**
Delete the source object <N>:	TYPE: **Y<enter>**
Select an object to imprint:	**<enter>**

ORBIT

Orbit allows you to obtain a 3D view in the active viewport. When Orbit is active, you can right-click in the drawing area to activate the shortcut menu. This menu allows you to render the object and select parallel or perspective views while the object is being orbited. You can also access these options from the Orbit toolbar.

Step 14. Use Orbit to render and animate the model you have just completed, as described next:

CLICK: **The right viewport to make it active and turn the display to a single viewport.**

Prompt	Response
Command:	**Orbit-Constrained Orbit** (or TYPE: **3DO <enter>**)
Press ESC or ENTER to exit, or right-click to display shortcut-menu.	**Hold down the click button and slowly move the mouse so you get a feel for how the view changes.** RIGHT-CLICK: to obtain the shortcut menu CLICK: **Preset Views-SW Isometric** RIGHT-CLICK: to obtain the shortcut menu CLICK: **Perspective** RIGHT-CLICK: to obtain the shortcut menu CLICK: **Visual Styles-Conceptual** RIGHT-CLICK: to obtain the shortcut menu CLICK: **Other Navigation modes-Continuous Orbit** CLICK: **a point at the upper left edge of the display, hold down the click button, and describe a very small circle so the model rotates continuously.** Experiment with the continuous orbit display until you feel comfortable with it.

You may need to return to Orbit and CLICK: **Constrained Orbit and Preset Views-SE Isometric** occasionally to return the display to a manageable view.

Prompt	Response
	CLICK: **Orbit and Preset Views-SE Isometric with perspective projection and Conceptual Visual Style to obtain a view similar to Figure 14–67.**

Step 15. CLICK: **your workspace to exit from the 3D Modeling workspace, and** CLICK: **Layout 1.**

Step 16. Use Dtext to place your name in the lower right corner in the simplex font.

Step 17. Put the viewport boundary on a new layer and turn that layer OFF.

Step 18. Plot the drawing from the Plot dialog box. Be sure to CLICK: **Conceptual from the Shade plot: list. Plot to fit on an 11″ × 8-1/2″ sheet.** If the Shade plot option is grayed out, CLICK: **the viewport boundary** and CLICK: **Properties.** Then, CLICK: **Conceptual** from the Shade plot options.

FIGURE 14–67
Tutorial 14–3 Complete

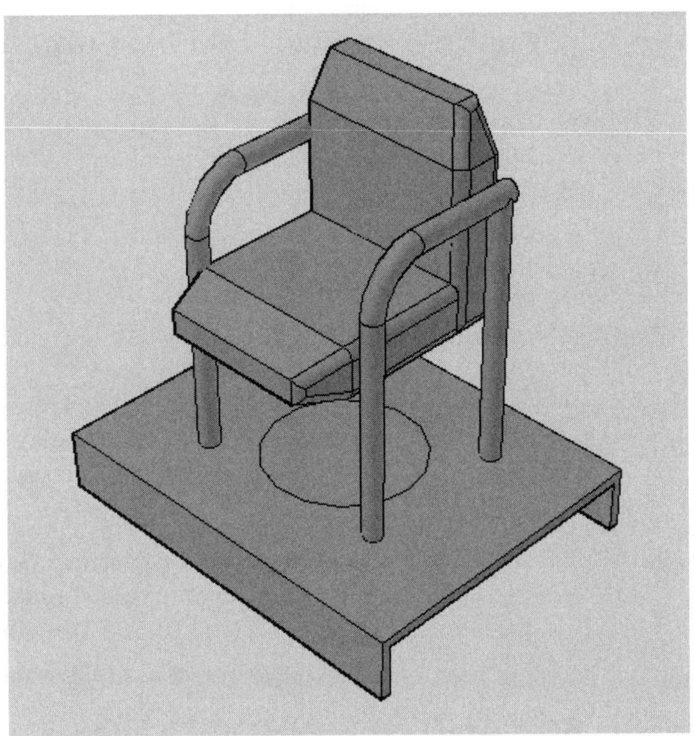

Tutorial 14–4: Creating Mesh Models

Mesh models can be made using mesh modeling primitives, or solid models can be converted into mesh models quite easily. This tutorial provides practice in both methods. The tutorial begins with mesh model primitives. In the next part of the tutorial, solid models are made and converted to mesh models using the MESHSMOOTH command. When you have completed Tutorial 14–4, your drawing will look similar to Figure 14–68.

FIGURE 14–68
Tutorial 14–4 Complete

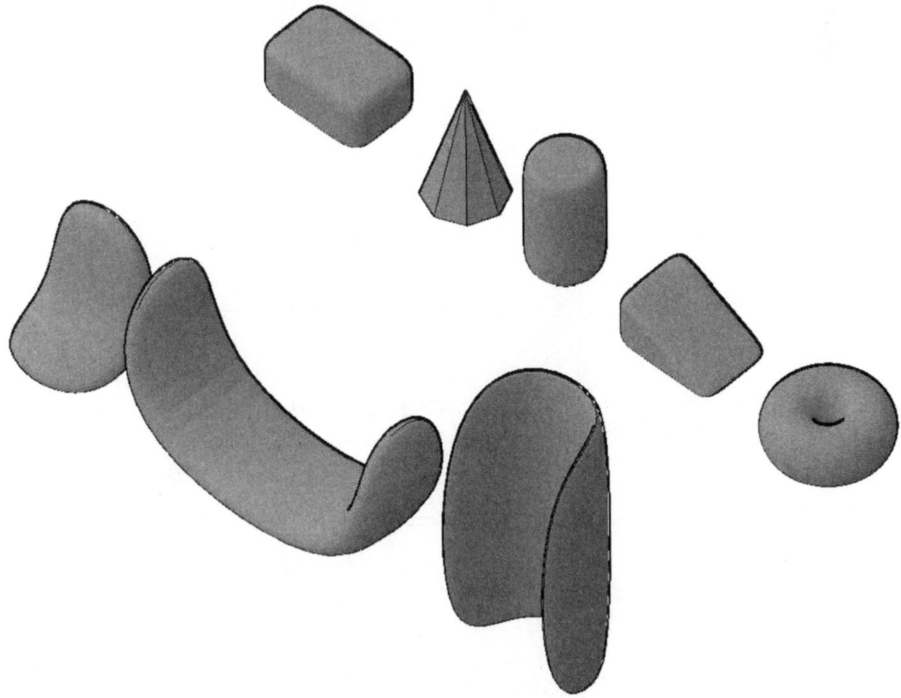

Step 1. Use your 3D Workspace to make the following settings:

1. **Use SaveAs... to save the drawing on the hard drive with the name CH14-TUTORIAL4.**
2. Set Drawing Units: **Architectural**
3. Set Drawing Limits: **8-1/2,11**
4 Set Grid: 1/2″
5. Set Snap: 1/8″
6. Set GRIDDISPLAY: **0**
7. **Create the following layers:**

LAYER NAME	COLOR	LINETYPE	LINEWEIGHT
3d-m	**magenta**	**continuous**	**default**
3d-w	**white**	**continuous**	**default**

8. **Set Layer 3d-m current.**
9. **Use the VPORTS command to make two vertical viewports. Zoom-All in both viewports, then Zoom in closer so your view is similar to the figures shown.**
10. CLICK: **SE Isometric from 3D Views on the View menu to set a viewpoint for the right viewport.**

MESH BOX AND MESHSMOOTHMORE

Step 2. Draw a mesh box, 1-1/2″ × 1″ × 3/4″ height (Figure 14–69) and change its level of smoothness as described next:

Prompt	Response
Command:	**MESH BOX** (or TYPE: **MESH<enter>** then **B<enter>**)
Select primitive [Box/Cone/ CYlinder/Pyramid/Sphere/ Wedge/Torus]<Box>:_BOX Specify first corner or [Center]:	TYPE: **1,6-1/2<enter>**
Specify other corner or [Cube/ Length]:	TYPE: **@1-1/2,1<enter>**

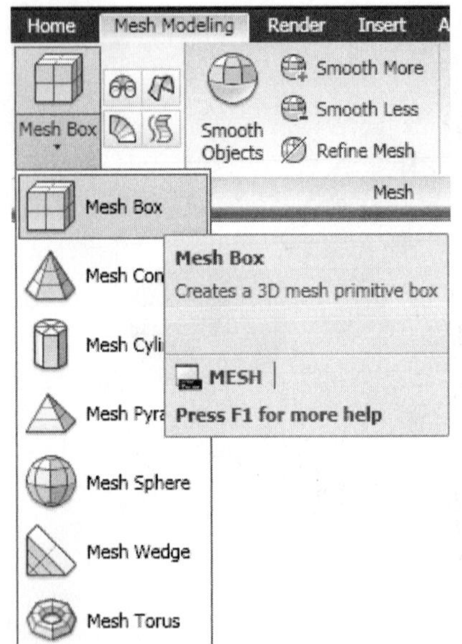

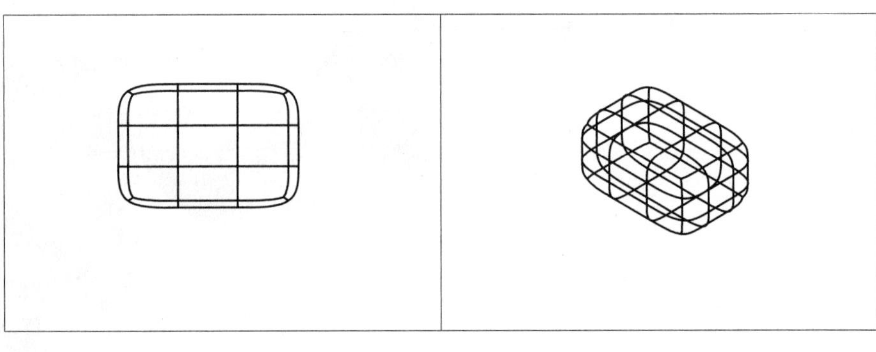

FIGURE 14–69
Draw a Mesh Box

Prompt	Response
Specify height or [2Point] <0′-0″>:	TYPE: **3/4<enter>**
Specify level of smoothness <1>:	**<enter>**

Step 3. Make the mesh box one level smoother as described next:

Prompt	Response
Command:	**Smooth More** (or TYPE: **MESHSMOOTHMORE<enter>**
Select mesh objects to increase the smoothness level:	CLICK: **The mesh box you just drew**
Select mesh objects to increase the smoothness level:	**<enter>**

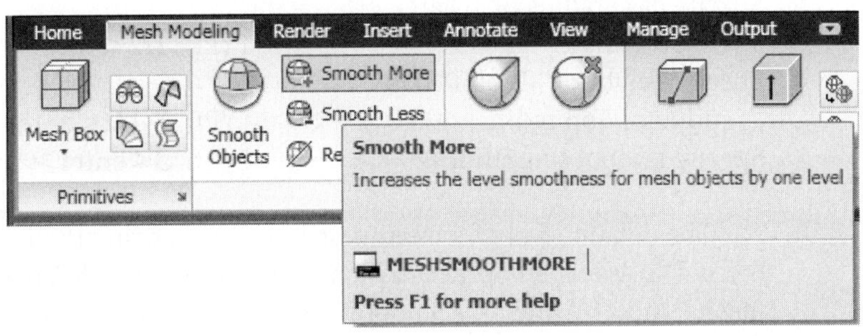

Step 4. Use the Hide command to see how MESHSMOOTHMORE changes the model.

MESH CONE

Step 5. Draw a mesh cone, 1/2″ base radius × 1-1/2″ height (Figure 14-70) as described next:

Prompt	Response
Command:	**MESH CONE**(or TYPE: **MESH<enter>then, C<enter>**)
Select primitive [Box/Cone/CYlinder/Pyramid/Sphere/Wedge/Torus] <Cone>:_CONE Specify center point of base or [3P/2P/Ttr/Elliptical]:	TYPE: **3-3/4,7<enter>**

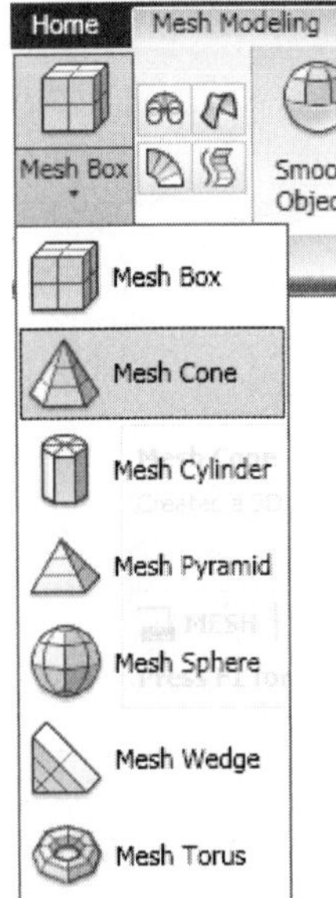

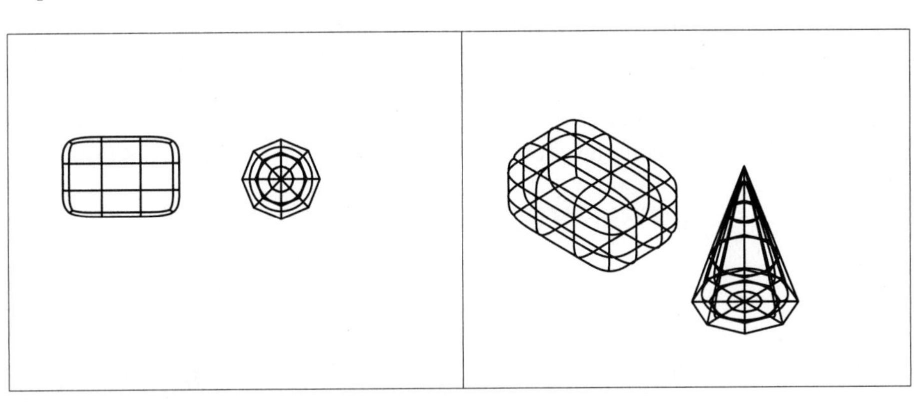

FIGURE 14–70
Draw a Mesh Cone

FIGURE 14–71
Draw a Mesh Cylinder

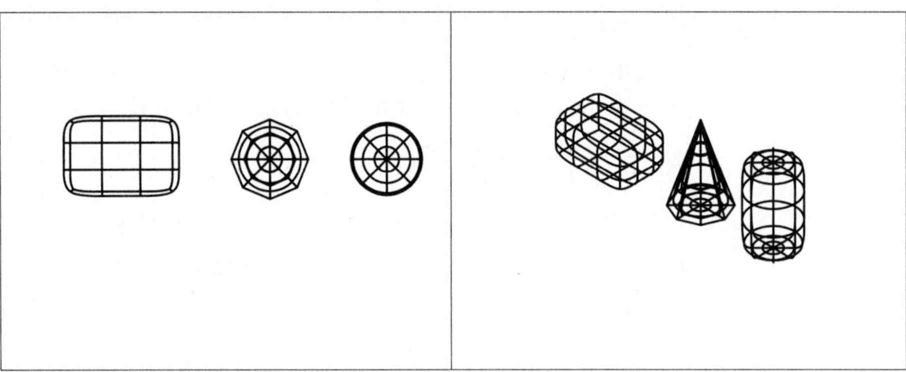

Prompt	Response
Specify base radius or [Diameter] <0′-0 1/2″>:	TYPE: **1/2<enter>**
Specify height or [2Point/Axis endpoint/Top radius]<0′-0 3/4″>:	TYPE: **1-1/2<enter>**
Specify level of smoothness<1>:	TYPE: **3<enter>**

The default level of smoothness is 1. By changing the level to 3, you have made the mesh two levels smoother, which makes quite a difference in the appearance of the mesh. Smooth More and Smooth Less can be used to change appearances until you get the exact mesh you want. The suggested range is between 0 and 7 for AutoCAD to perform well. Numbers above 7 can slow the program considerably.

MESH CYLINDER

Step 6. **Draw a mesh cylinder, 1/2″ base radius × 1-1/2″ height (Figure 14–71) as described next:**

Prompt	Response
Command:	**MESH CYLINDER** (or TYPE: **MESH<enter>** then, **CY<enter>**
Select primitive [Box/Cone/CYlinder/Pyramid/Sphere/Wedge/Torus] <Cone>: CYLINDER Specify center point of base or [3P/2P/Ttr/Elliptical]:	TYPE: **5-1/4,7<enter>**
Specify base radius or [Diameter] <0′-0 1/2″>:	TYPE: **1/2<enter>**
Specify height or [2Point/Axis endpoint]<0′-1 1/2″>:	TYPE: **1-1/2<enter>**
Specify level of smoothness <1>:	TYPE: **3<enter>**

MESH WEDGE

Step 7. **Draw a mesh wedge, 1-1/2″ × 1″ × 3/4″ height (Figure 14–72) as described next:**

Prompt	Response
Command:	**MESH WEDGE** (or TYPE: **MESH<enter>** then, **W<enter>**)

FIGURE 14–72
Draw a Mesh Wedge

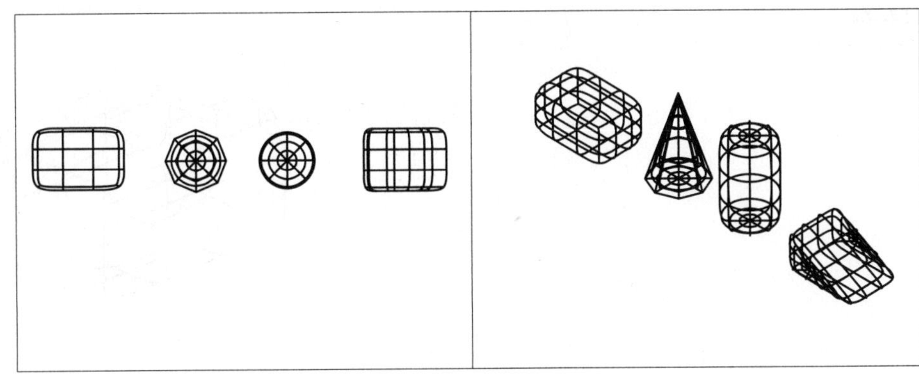

Prompt	Response
Select primitive [Box/Cone/CYlinder/ Pyramid/Sphere/Wedge/Torus] <Torus>:_WEDGE Specify first corner or [Center]:	Type: **6-1/2,6-1/2<enter>**
Specify other corner or [Cube/Length]:	TYPE: **@1-1/2,1<enter>**
Specify height or [2Point]<0′-0 3/4″>:	TYPE: **3/4<enter>**
Specify level of smoothness <1>:	TYPE: **3<enter>**

MESH TORUS

Step 8. Draw a mesh torus, 1/2″ radius × 1-1/2″ height (Figure 14–73) as described next:

Prompt	Response
Command:	**MESH TORUS** (or TYPE: **MESH<enter>** then, **T<enter>**)
Select Primitive [Box/Cone/CYlinder/ Pyramid/Sphere/Wedge/Torus] <Wedge>:_TORUS Specify center point or [3P/2PTtr]:	TYPE: **9-1/4,7<enter>**
Specify radius or [Diameter] <0′-0 1/2″>:	TYPE: **1/2<enter>**
Specify tube radius or [2Point/ Diameter]:	TYPE: **3/8<enter>**
Specify level of smoothness<1>:	TYPE: **3<enter>**

In the remaining part of this tutorial, solid models will be drawn and converted to mesh models.

FIGURE 14–73
Draw a Mesh Torus

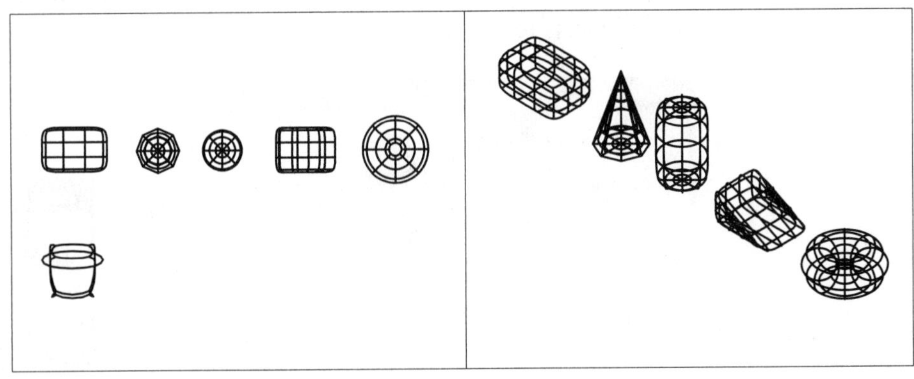

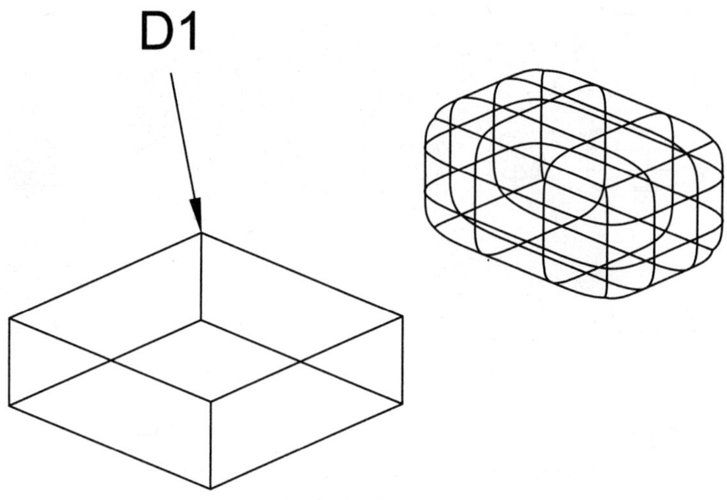

FIGURE 14–74
Draw the Second Box

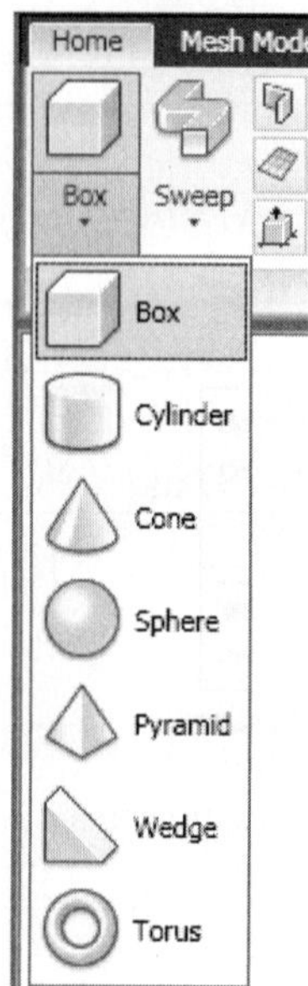

MAKE SOLID MODELS

Step 9. **Draw two solid boxes and use the Union command to make a single solid of the two boxes as described next:**

Prompt	Response
Command:	**BOX** (or TYPE: **BOX<enter>**)
Specify first corner or [Center]:	TYPE: **1,1-1/2<enter>**
Specify other corner or [Cube/ Length]:	TYPE: **@1-1/2,1-1/2<enter>**
Specify height or [2Point]<0′-5″>:	TYPE: **1/2<enter>**
Command:	**BOX**
Specify first corner or [Center]:	CLICK: **D1** (Figure 14–74)
Specify other corner or [Cube/ Length]:	TYPE: **@1-1/2,-1/2<enter>**
Specify height or [2Point] <0′-0 1/2″>:	TYPE: **1-1/2<enter>**
Command:	**UNION** (or TYPE: **UNION<enter>**)
Select objects:	CLICK: **The two boxes just drawn**
Select objects:	**<enter>**

Step 10. **Convert the solid model to a mesh model and smooth it as described next:**

Prompt	Response
Command:	**SMOOTH OBJECTS**
Select objects to convert:	CLICK: **The boxes that were just combined using the UNION command**
Select objects to convert:	**<enter>**

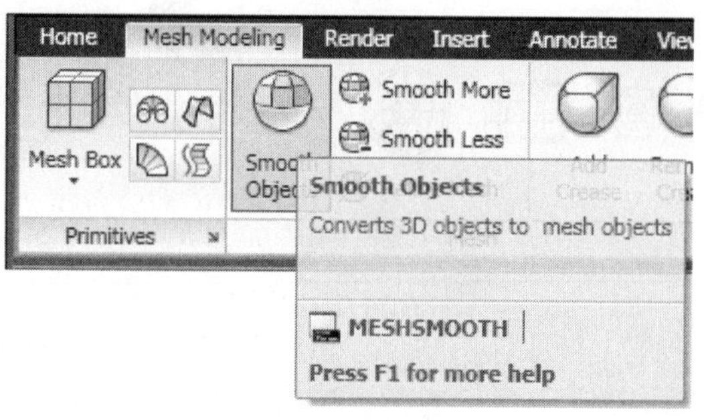

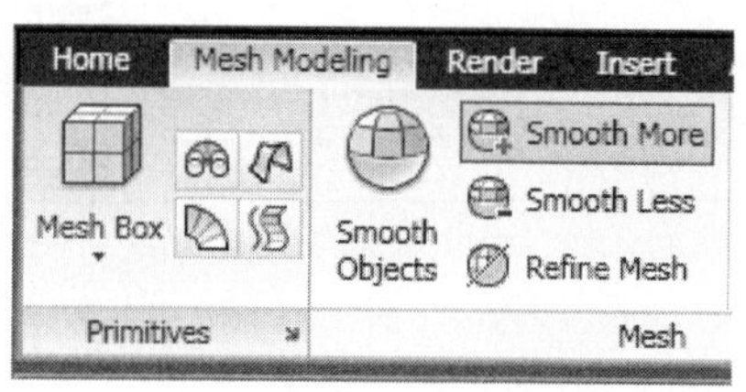

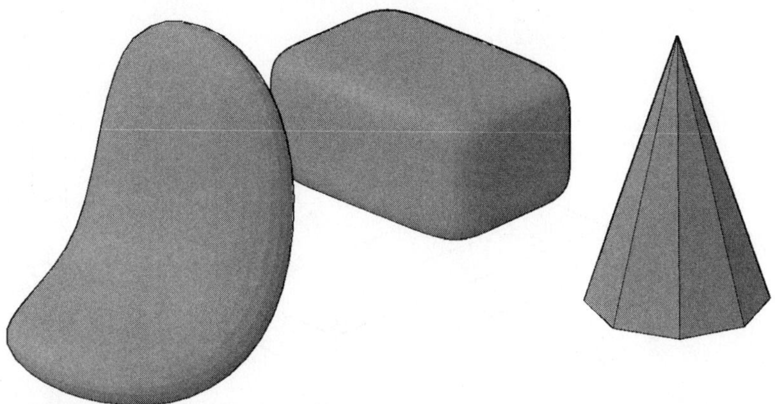

FIGURE 14–75
Using MESHSMOOTH to Convert a Solid Model to a Mesh Model

Prompt	Response
The warning box appears:	CLICK: **Create mesh**
Command:	**MESHSMOOTHMORE**
Select mesh objects to increase the smoothness level:	CLICK: **The new mesh**
Select mesh objects to increase the smoothness level:	**<enter>**
Command:	**MESHSMOOTHMORE**
Select mesh objects to increase the smoothness level:	CLICK: **The same mesh again**
Select mesh objects to increase the smoothness level:	**<enter>**
Command:	TYPE: **HI<enter> or use Conceptual Visual Style** to get an idea of what the new mesh looks like (Figure 14–75).

Step 11. Draw three solid boxes and use the Union command to make a single solid of the three boxes as described next:

Prompt	Response
Command:	**Box**
Specify first corner or [Center]:	TYPE: **3-1/2,1-1/2<enter>**
Specify other corner or [Cube/ Length]:	TYPE: **@4,1-1/2<enter>**
Specify height or [2Point]:	TYPE: **1/2<enter>**
Command:	**BOX**
Specify first corner or [Center]:	CLICK: **D1** (Figure 14–76)
Specify other corner or [Cube/ Length]:	TYPE: **@1/2,1-1/2<enter>**
Specify height or [2Point] <0′-0 1/2″>:	TYPE: **2<enter>**
Command:	**COPY the box just drawn to the other end as shown in Figure 14–77)**
Command:	**UNION**
Select Objects:	CLICK: **the three boxes just drawn**
Select objects:	**<enter>**

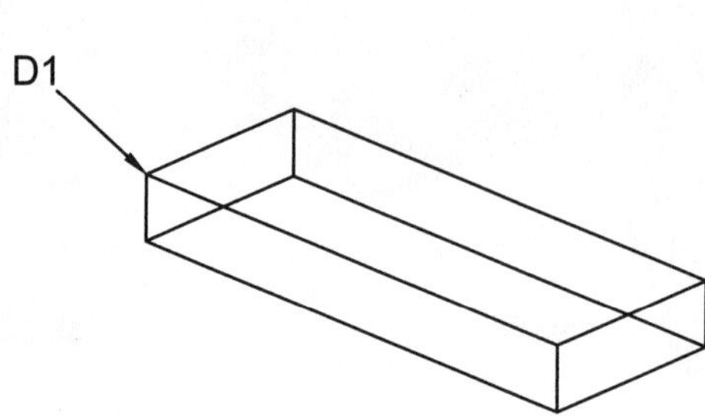

FIGURE 14–76
CLICK: the Corner for Another Box

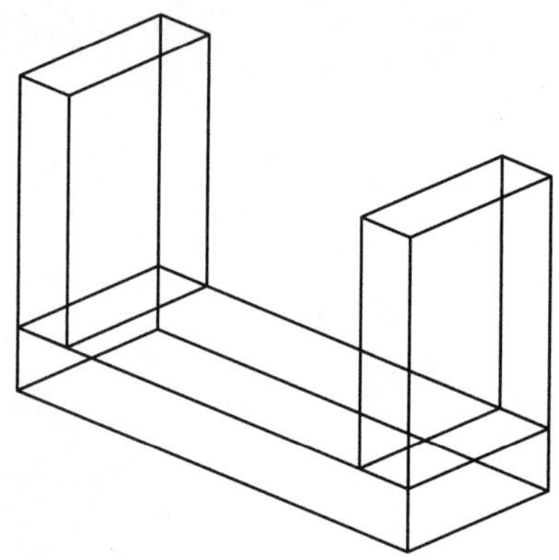

FIGURE 14–77
Copy the Box

Step 12. Convert the solid model to a mesh model and smooth it as described next:

Prompt	Response
Command:	**SMOOTH OBJECTS**
Select objects to convert:	CLICK: **The boxes that were just combined using the UNION command**
Select objects to convert:	**<enter>**
The warning box appears:	CLICK: **Create mesh**
Command:	**MESHSMOOTHMORE**
Select mesh objects to increase the smoothness level:	CLICK: **The new mesh**
Select mesh objects to increase the smoothness level:	**<enter>**
Command:	**MESHSMOOTHMORE**
Select mesh objects to increase the smoothness level:	CLICK: **The same mesh again**
Select mesh objects to increase the smoothness level:	**<enter>**
Command:	TYPE: **HI<enter> or use Conceptual Visual Style** to get an idea of what the new mesh looks like (Figure 14–78).

Step 13. Draw a polysolid as described next:

Prompt	Response
Command:	**POLYSOLID**
Specify start point or [Object/Height/Width/Justify]<Object>:	TYPE: **H<enter>**

FIGURE 14–78
Convert a Solid Model to a Mesh Model and Smooth It

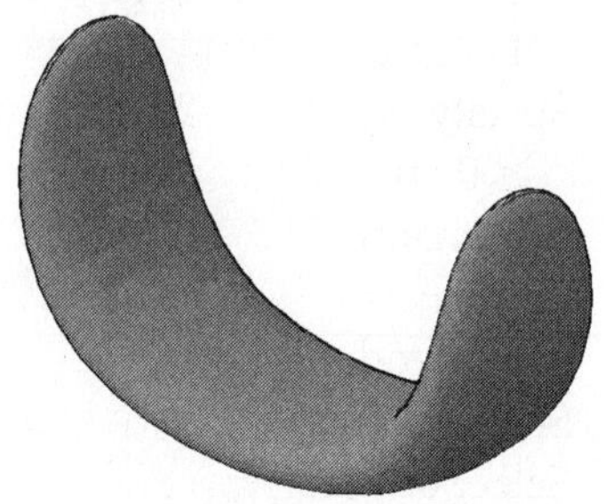

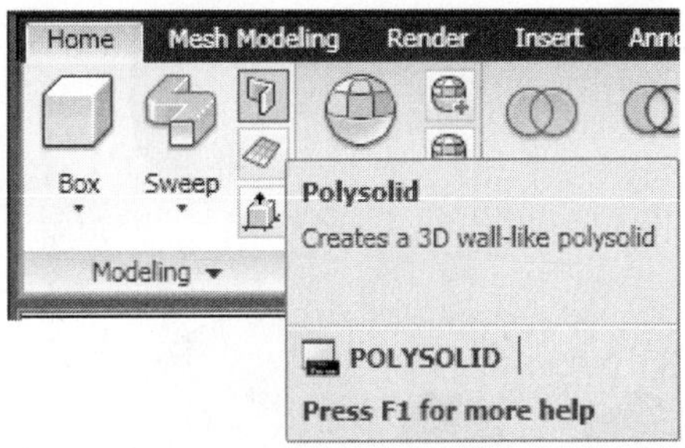

Prompt	Response
Specify height<0′-2″>:	TYPE: **4<enter>**
Specify start point or [Object /Height/Width/Justify] <Object>:	TYPE: **W<enter>**
Specify width<1/8″>	TYPE: **1/4<enter>**
Specify start point or [Object/ Height/Width/Justify] <Object>:	TYPE: **8-1/2,1-1/2<enter>**
Specify next point or [Arc/Undo]:	**With ORTHO ON, move the mouse up 1-1/2″ and** CLICK:
Specify next point or [Arc/Undo]:	**Move the mouse to the right 1-1/2″ and** CLICK:
Specify next point or [Arc/Close/ Undo]:	**Move the mouse down 1-1/2″ and** CLICK:
Specify next point or [Arc/Close/ Undo]:	**<enter>**

Step 14. Convert the polysolid to a mesh model and smooth it as described next:

Prompt	Response
Command:	SMOOTH OBJECTS
Select objects to convert:	CLICK: **The polysolid just drawn**

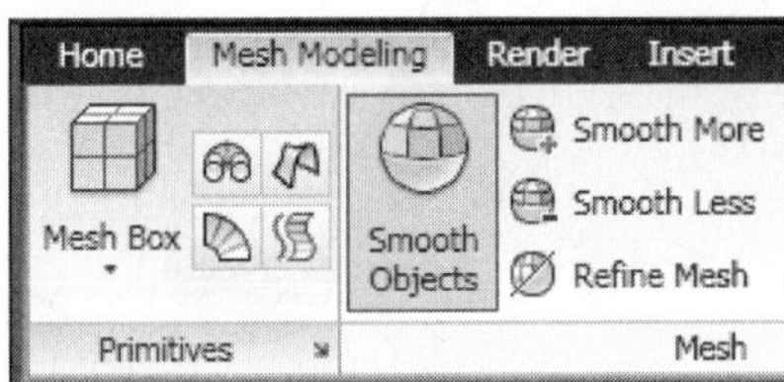

Prompt	Response
Select objects too convert:	**<enter>**
The warning box appears:	CLICK: **Create mesh**
Command:	**MESHSMOOTHMORE**
Select mesh objects to increase the smoothness level:	CLICK: **The new mesh**
Select mesh objects to increase the smoothness level:	**<enter>**
Command:	**MESHSMOOTHMORE**
Select mesh objects to increase the smoothness level:	CLICK: **The same mesh again**
Select mesh objects to increase the smoothness level:	**<enter>**

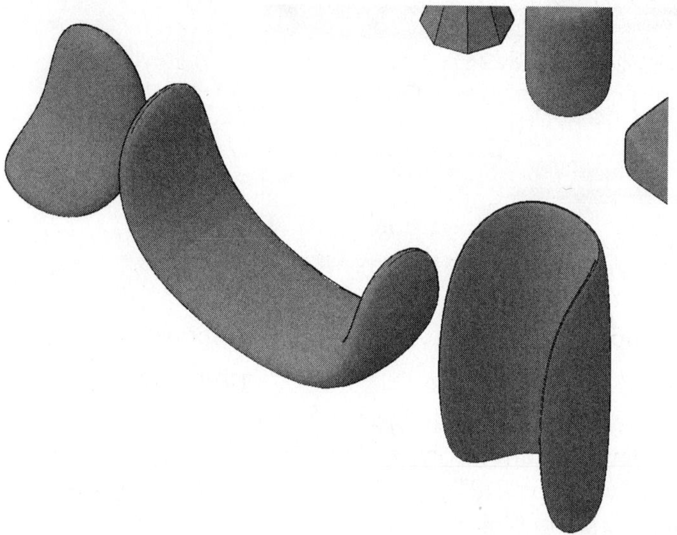

FIGURE 14–79
Convert the Polysolid to a Mesh Model and Smooth It

Prompt	Response
Command:	TYPE: **HI<enter> or use Conceptual Visual Style** to get an idea of what the new mesh looks like (Figure 14–79).

Step 15. Plot the 3D viewport from the Model tab on a standard size sheet of paper. Be sure to click Conceptual from the Shade plot: list in the Plot dialog box so the final plot appears as shown in Figure 14–80.

FIGURE 14–80
Tutorial 14–4 Complete

review questions

1. Which of the following is *not* a SOLID command used to draw solid primitives?
   a. Box
   b. Cylinder
   c. Rectangle
   d. Wedge
   e. Sphere
2. Which of the following is used to make rounded corners on a solid box?
   a. Chamfer
   b. Extrude
   c. Intersection
   d. Round
   e. Fillet
3. Which is the last dimension called for when the Box command is activated?
   a. Height
   b. Width
   c. Length
   d. First corner of box
   e. Other corner
4. Which is the first dimension called for when the Sphere command is activated?
   a. Segments in Y direction
   b. Segments in X direction
   c. Radius
   d. Center of sphere
   e. Diameter
5. Which of the following *cannot* be extruded with the Extrude command?
   a. Polylines
   b. Circles
   c. Rectangles
   d. Polygons
   e. Solids
6. Which of the following commands is used to join several lines into a single polyline?
   a. Edit Polyline
   b. Offset
   c. Union
   d. Intersection
   e. Extrude
7. Which of the following is used to make a solid by revolving a polyline about an axis?
   a. Revolve
   b. Extrude
   c. Intersection
   d. Round
   e. Fillet
8. Which of the following adjusts the smoothness of objects rendered with the Hide command?
   a. SURFTAB1
   b. MESH
   c. SEGS
   d. WIRE
   e. FACETRES
9. Which of the following allows you to rotate an object around an X, Y, or Z axis?
   a. Rotate
   b. 3D Rotate
   c. Extrude
   d. Solrot
   e. Offset
10. Which of the following sets the number of lines on rounded surfaces of solids?
    a. FACETRES
    b. ISOLINES
    c. Union
    d. Fillet
    e. Interfere

Complete.

11. List eight Solid commands used to make specific solid objects.

_______________ _______________ _______________

_______________ _______________ _______________

_______________ _______________

12. List the Solid command used to extrude a polyline into a solid.

____

13. List the Solid command used to create a new solid by cutting the existing solid into two pieces and removing or retaining either or both pieces.

____

14. List the Solid command that allows you to join several solids into a single object.

____

15. List the Solid command used to subtract solids from other solids.

____

16. List the command and its option that is used to move the UCS icon so that it is displayed at the origin of the current coordinate system.

_______________ _______________

command option

17. List the Solid command used to create a cross-sectional area of a solid.

____

18. List the command that can convert a line, arc, or polyline to a wall with width and height.

____

19. List the Solid command used to create a solid from the common volume of two intersecting solids.

____

20. List three sections on a SteeringWheel.

_______________ _______________ _______________

21. The mesh box command can be activated by typing **MESH<enter>**, then:
    a. **MB<enter>**
    b. **B<enter>**
    c. **MEB<enter>**
    d. **L<enter>**
    e. **ML<enter>**
22. Boxes made with the BOX command and combined with the UNION command cannot be made into mesh objects.
    a. True
    b. False
23. Which of the following is NOT a mesh object?
    a. MESH BOX
    b. MESH CYLINDER
    c. MESH TORUS
    d. MESH SOLID
    e. MESH WEDGE
24. Which of the following is not a mesh command?
    a. SMOOTH OBJECTS
    b. MESHSMOOTHMORE
    c. MESHSMOOTHLESS
    d. UNSMOOTH OBJECTS
    e. MESH CONE
25. A polysolid can be made into a mesh object.
    a. True
    b. False

Exercise 14–1: Drawing Solid Models of Eight Objects

1. Draw solid models of the eight objects shown in Figure 14–81. Use the dimensions shown in the top and front views of A through H:
   Draw the top view, join it to form a continuous polyline, and extrude it to the height shown in the front view.
   Rotate the UCS 90° about the X axis, draw a rectangle at the angle shown in the front view, extrude it, move it in the Z direction so it covers the area of the extruded top view that must be removed, and subtract it from the extruded top view.
2. Arrange the objects so that they are well spaced on the page and take up most of a 9″ × 7″ area on an 11″ × 8-1/2″ sheet. Use the Hide command to remove hidden lines.

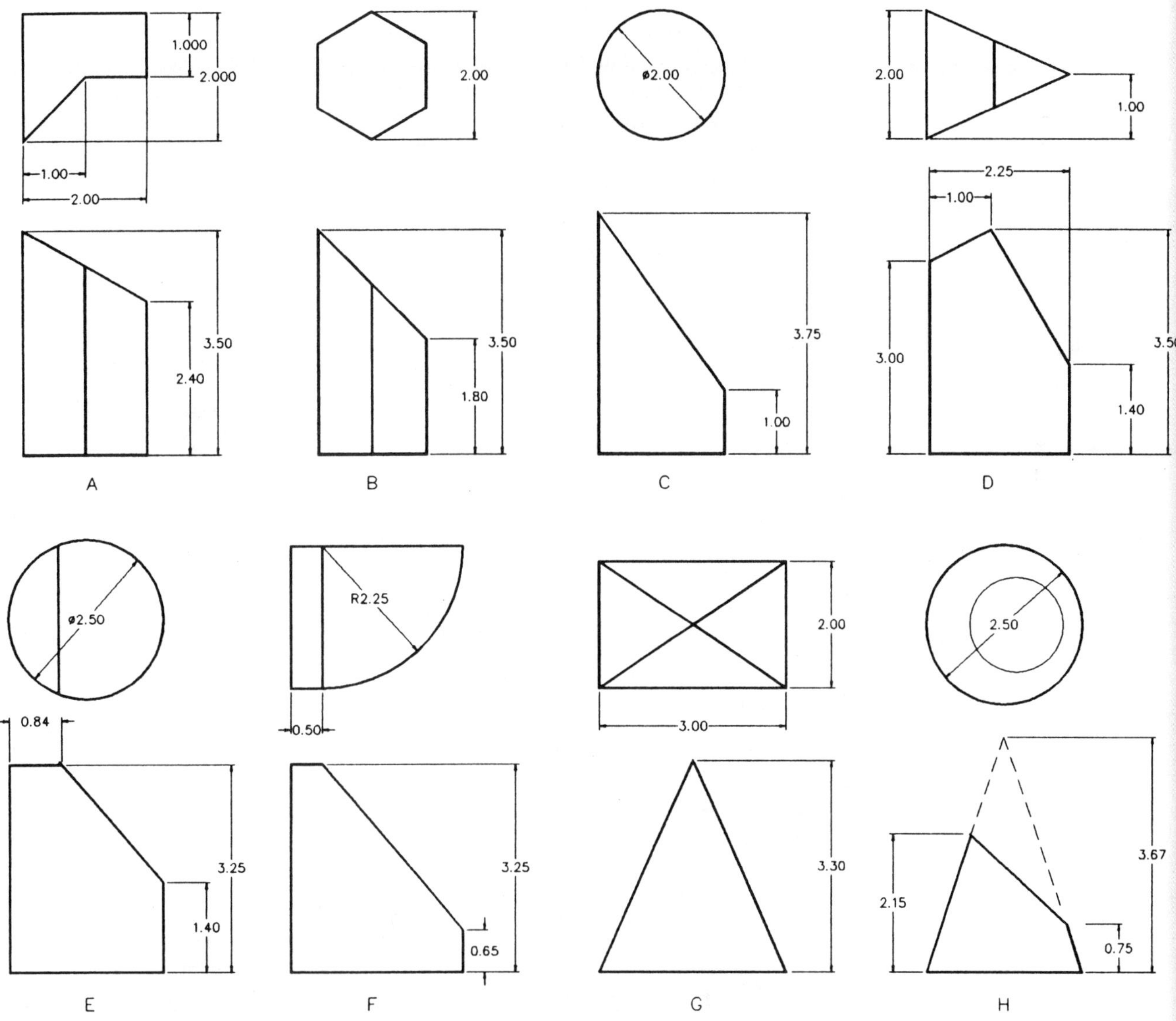

FIGURE 14–81
Exercise 14–1: Draw Solid Models of Eight Objects

3. Your final drawing should show eight solid objects in a viewpoint similar to Figure 14–42 (Tutorial 14–1).
4. CLICK: **Layout1**, place your name in the lower right corner in 1/8″ letters, use Shade plot - As displayed, and plot or print the drawing on an 11″ × 8-1/2″ sheet at a scale of 1 = 1.
5. Save your drawing in two places with the name CH14-EX1.

Exercise 14–2: Drawing a Solid Model of a Lamp Table

1. Draw a solid model of the lamp table shown in Figure 14–82. Scale the top and front views using a scale of 1″ = 1′-0″ to obtain the correct measurements for the model.
2. Use Revolve for the table pedestal. Use Polyline and Extrude for one table leg, and duplicate it with Polar Array. The tabletop can be an extruded circle or a solid cylinder.
3. Use Orbit to obtain a perspective view of your final model and CLICK: **Layout1** before you plot.
4. Place your name in the lower right corner in 1/8″ letters using simplex or an architectural font.
5. Plot the drawing at a scale of 1 = 1 on an 11″ × 8-1/2″ sheet.
6. Return to the Model tab (World UCS current) and Wblock the lamp table to a disk with the name TABLE.
7. Save your drawing with the name CH14-EX2.

FIGURE 14–82
Exercise 14–2: Create a Solid Model of a Table (Scale: 1″=1′-0″)

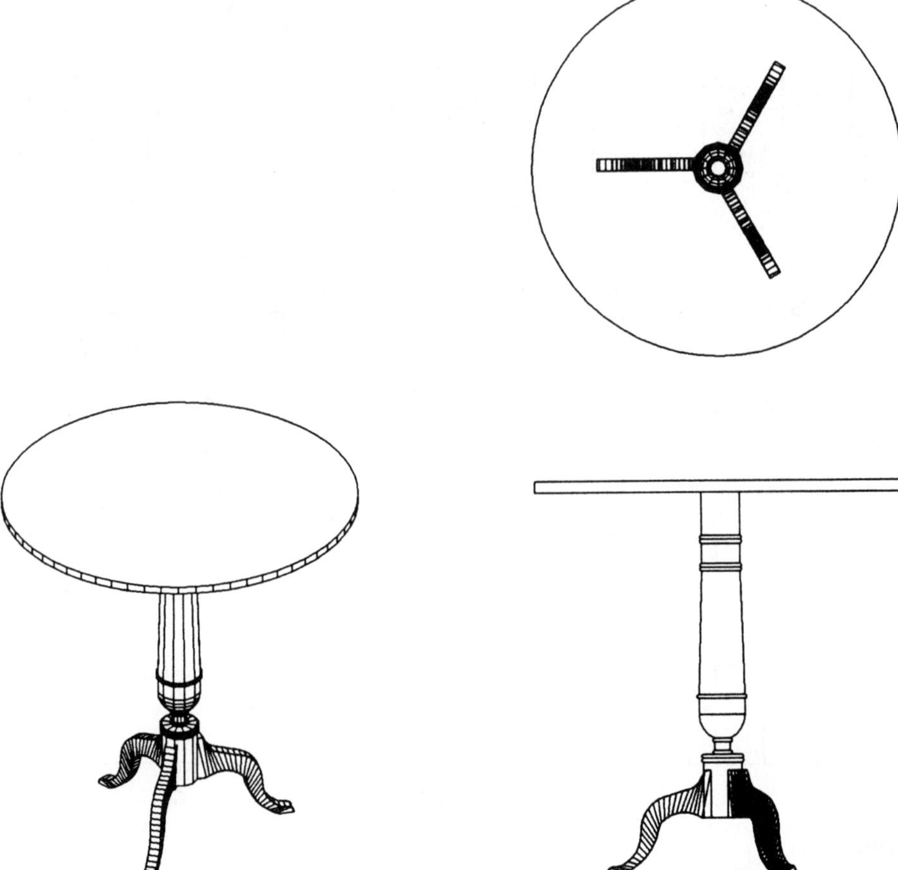

Exercise 14–3: Drawing a Solid Model of a Sofa

1. Use the dimensions from Figure 14–83 to draw the sofa. Draw a mesh box measuring 27″ × 27″ × 6″ high with a smoothness level of 5 to form a bottom cushion.
2. Draw a back cushion in a similar manner.
3. Draw the arms, back, and base of the sofa using the Rectangle and Polyline commands, and extrude them to the dimensions shown.
4. Copy the cushions and move them to their correct locations using the Move and Rotate 3D commands.
5. Use Orbit to obtain a perspective view of your final model and CLICK: **Layout1** before you plot.
6. Place your name in the lower right corner in 1/8″ letters using simplex or an architectural font.
7. Plot the drawing at a scale of 1 = 1 on an 11″ × 8-1/2″ sheet.
8. Return to the Model tab (World UCS current) and Wblock the sofa to a disk with the name SOFA. CHECK: **Retain** so the drawing stays on the screen.
9. Save your drawing in two places with the name CH14-EX3.

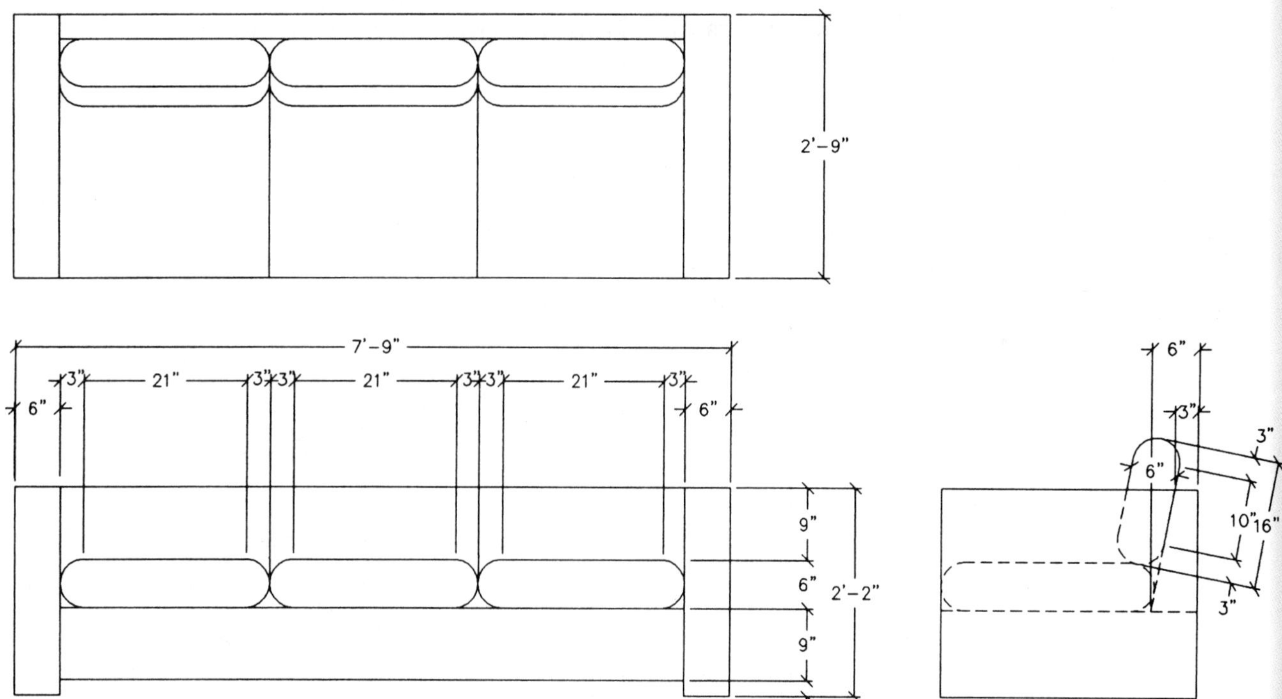

FIGURE 14–83
Exercise 14–3: Sofa Dimensions (Scale: 1/2″=1′-0″)

Exercise 14–4: Drawing a Solid Model of a Lamp and Inserting It and the Lamp Table into the Sofa Drawing

1. Draw the lamp and the shade from the dimensions shown in Figure 14–84. Use your 1/8″ architect's scale for any dimensions not shown. Make sure the lamp is a closed polyline and the shade is a closed polyline. You will have to give the shade some thickness by offsetting its shape and closing the ends with a line. Then join all parts of the shade to form a closed polyline.
2. Revolve the two polylines to form the lamp.
3. Rotate the lamp 90° about the X axis so it is in an upright position.
4. With the World UCS current, Wblock the lamp to a disk with the name LAMP. Use the center of the bottom of the lamp as the insertion point.
5. Open the drawing SOFA that you have Wblocked to the disk.
6. Insert the TABLE and LAMP models from the disk into the SOFA drawing. Place the table to the right of the sofa, and center the base of the lamp on the tabletop as shown in Figure 14–85.
7. Use Orbit to obtain a perspective view of your final model and CLICK: **Layout1** before you plot.
8. Place your name in the lower right corner in 1/8″ letters using simplex or an architectural font.
9. Plot the drawing at a scale of 1 = 1 on an 11″ × 8-1/2″ sheet.
10. Save your drawing in two places with the name CH14-EX4.

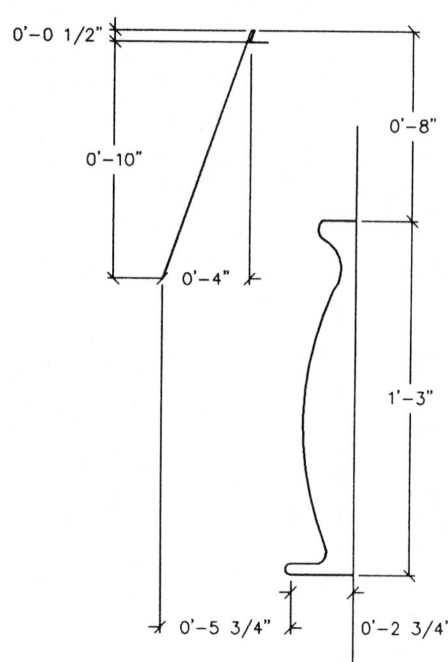

FIGURE 14–84
Exercise 14–4: Overall Dimensions of the Lamp (Scale: 1/8″=1″)

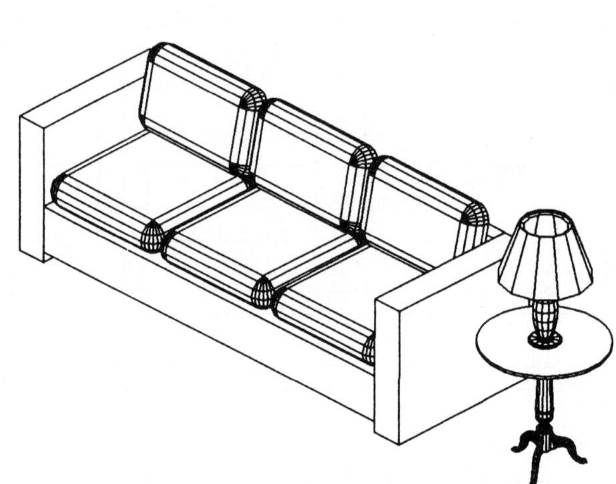

FIGURE 14–85
Exercise 14–4: Combine Solid Models

Exercise 14–5: Drawing a Solid Model of the Tenant Space Reception Seating

1. Draw the chair coffee table and corner table with a series of boxes (Figure 14–86).
2. Fillet the vertical edges of the coffee table and corner table.
3. Use the Rectangle command with 1″ fillets to draw the coffee table and corner table inlays. Extrude the rectangles 1″ and place them so they are flush with the top of the tables. Subtract the extruded rectangles from the tables and replace them with other extruded rectangles that are slightly smaller to form the inlays.
4. Use Orbit to obtain a perspective view of your final model and CLICK: **Layout1** before you plot.
5. Place your name in the lower right corner in 1/8″ letters using simplex or an architectural font.
6. Plot the drawing at a scale of 1 = 1 on an 11″ × 8-1/2″ sheet.
7. Save your drawing in two places with the name CH14-EX5.

FIGURE 14–86
Exercise 14–5: Tenant Space Reception Seating Dimensions (Scale: 3/8″=1′-0″)

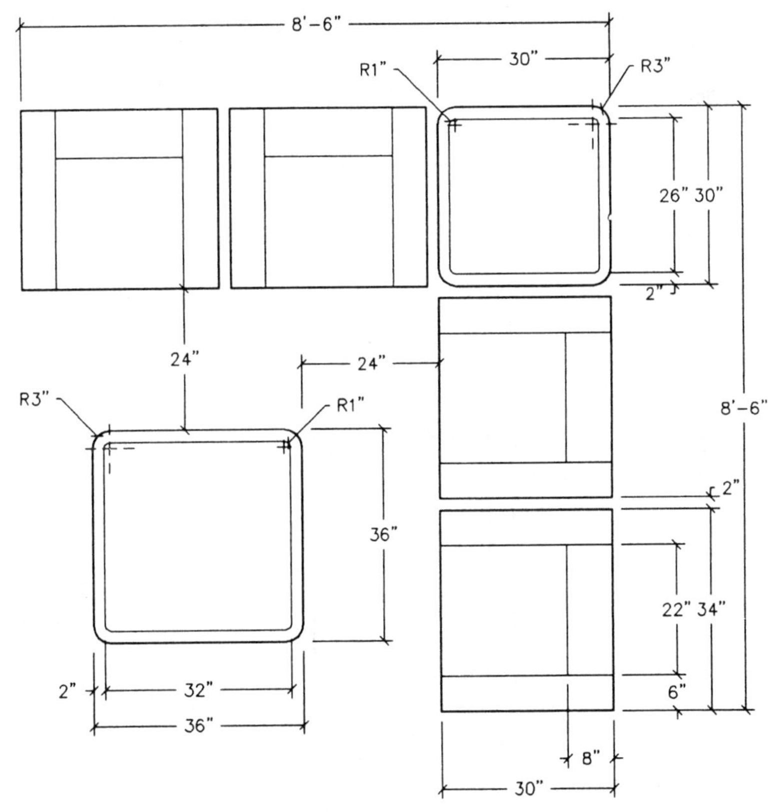

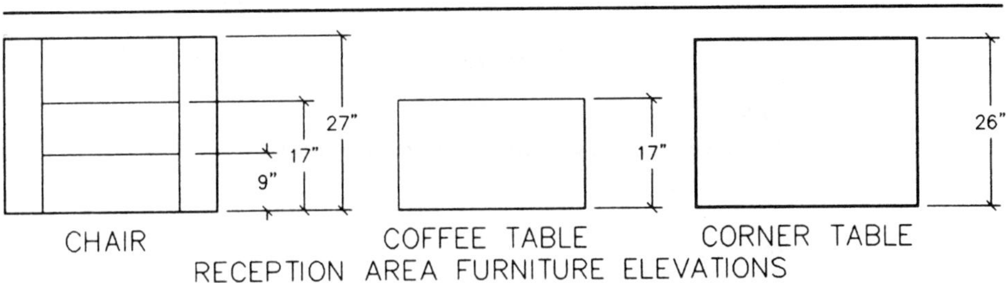

Exercise 14–6: Drawing a Solid Model of a Conference Chair

1. Use the dimensions from Figure 14–87 to draw the chair. Draw one caster with the solid Sphere command and use the Polar Array command to copy it three times.
2. The chair base can be formed with two cylinders and an extruded polyline copied three times using Polar Array.
3. Draw the bottom and back cushion with a single extruded polyline.
4. Draw the arms with a single extruded polyline.
5. Use Orbit to obtain a perspective view of your final model and CLICK: **Layout1** before you plot.
6. Place your name in the lower right corner in 1/8″ letters using simplex or an architectural font.
7. Plot the drawing at a scale of 1 = 1 on an 11″ × 8-1/2″ sheet.
8. Return to model space with Tilemode ON and Wblock the conference chair to a disk with the name C-CHAIR. Use the bottom of one of the casters as the insertion point. Make sure the option button Retain is on before you select objects.
9. Save your drawing with the name CH14-EX6.

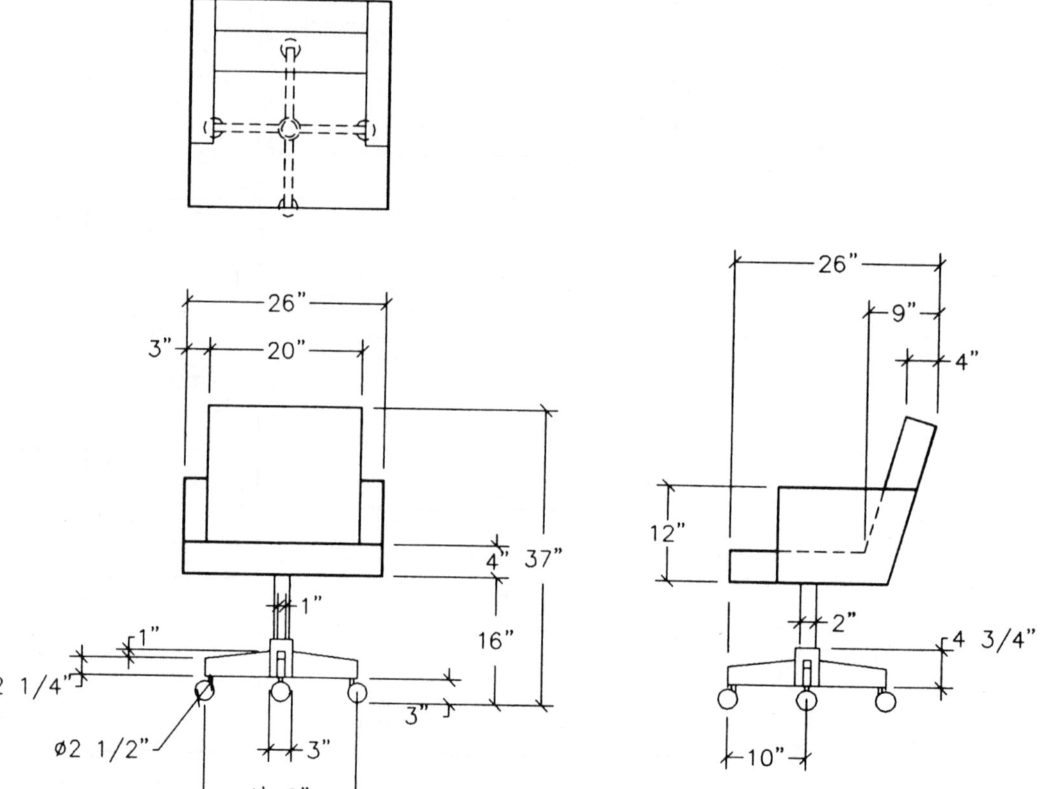

FIGURE 14–87
Exercise 14–6: Tenant Space Conference Chair Dimensions

Exercise 14–7: Drawing a Solid Model of a Conference Table and Inserting Chairs Around It

1. Use the dimensions from Figure 14–88 to draw the conference table. Draw the table bases with the Cylinder command.
2. Draw the table top with the Rectangle command using a 21″ fillet radius. The rectangle will measure 108″ × 42″.
3. Insert the C-CHAIR drawing into the conference table drawing.
4. Copy the chair seven times, and position the chairs as shown in Figure 14–89.
5. Use Orbit to obtain a perspective view of your final model and CLICK: **Layout1** before you plot.
6. Place your name in the lower right corner in 1/8″ letters using simplex or an architectural font.
7. Plot the drawing at a scale of 1 = 1 on an 11″ × 8-1/2″ sheet.
8. Save your drawing in two places with the name CH14-EX7.

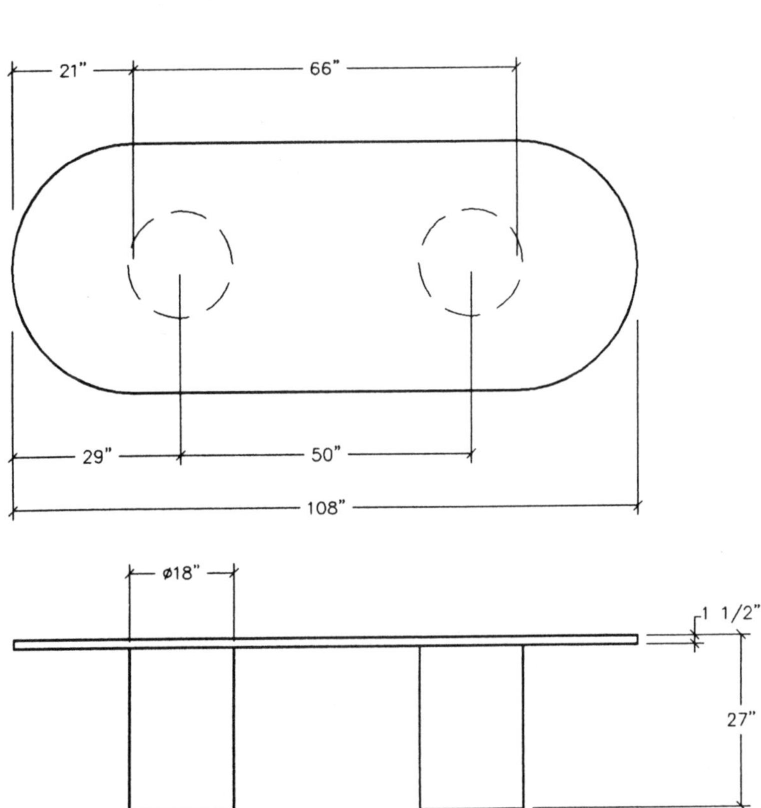

FIGURE 14–88
Exercise 14–7: Plan and Elevation Views of the Conference Table (Scale: 3/8″ = 1′-0″)

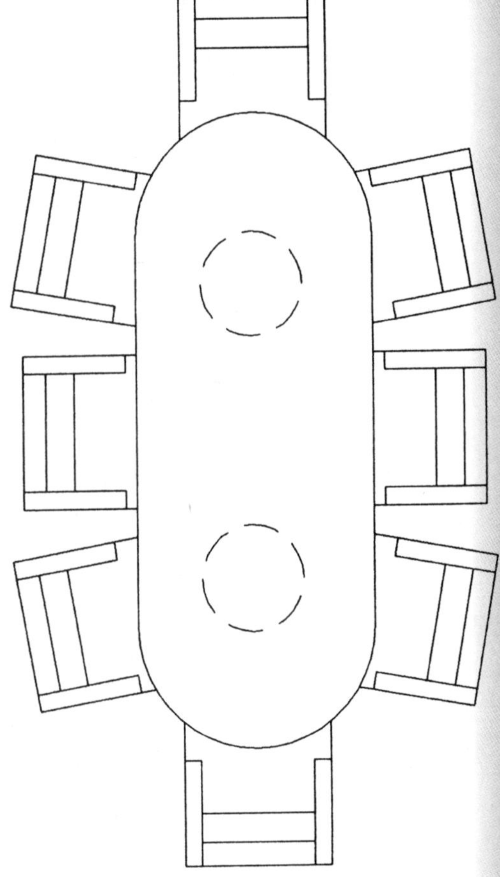

FIGURE 14–89
Exercise 14–7: Conference Table and Chair Locations

chapter

15

Complex Solid Models with Materials, Lighting, Rendering, and Animation

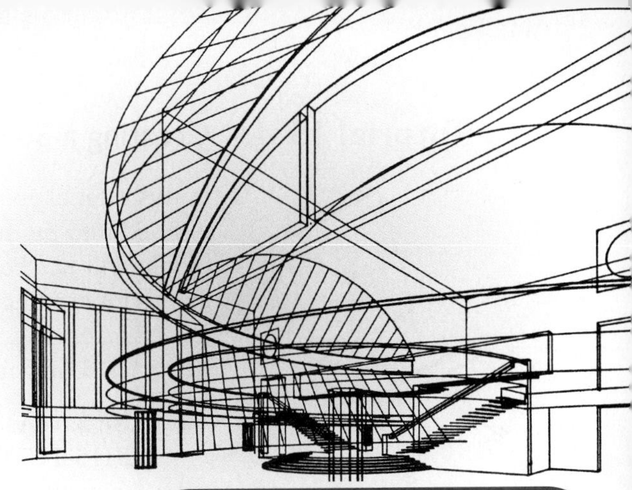

objectives

When you have completed this chapter, you will be able to:

Correctly use the following commands and settings:

- Animation
- Background
- Landscape
- Light
- Materials
- Materials Library
- Orbit
- Printing of 3D Models
- Render

INTRODUCTION

This chapter presents more complex models using the Solids commands from Chapter 14.

This chapter also covers the Render and Animation commands, which allow you to use lights, to attach materials, and to apply backgrounds so that a photo-realistic rendering of a 3D scene can be created and an animated file produced. Although there are many means of locating lights in a 3D scene, you will use the endpoints of lines and other objects in this tutorial to place lights. You will also use the existing materials in the materials library and existing backgrounds to begin using the render commands.

The first two tutorials, creating a chair and a patio, will give you the complex models needed to assign materials, place lights, render, and create an animated file.

Tutorial 15–1: Creating a Solid Model of Chair 2

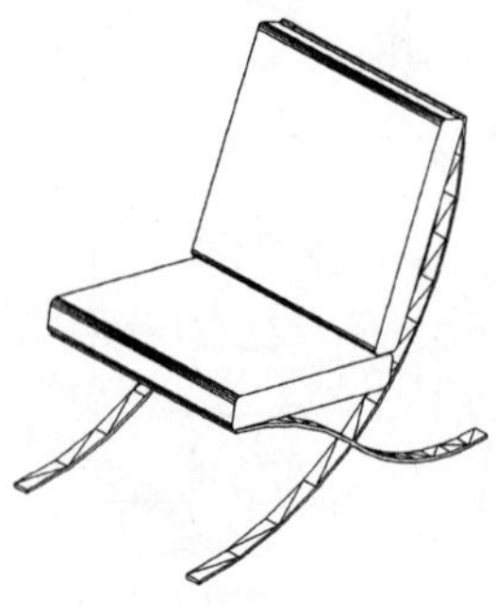

FIGURE 15–1
Tutorial 15–1: Complete

In this tutorial you will create a solid model of a chair (Figure 15–1). This chair will be inserted into the structure that you will create in Tutorial 15–2. The Prompt/Response format will not be used in this tutorial. The steps will be listed with suggested commands for creating this model.

Step 1. Use your 3D workspace to make the following settings:

1. **Use SaveAs... to save the drawing on the hard drive with the name CH15-TUTORIAL1.**
2. Set drawing Units: **Architectural**
3. Set Drawing Limits: **5′,5′**
4. Set GRIDDISPLAY: **0**
5. Set Grid: **1**
6. Set Snap: **1/4**
7. Create the following layers:

LAYER NAME	COLOR	LINETYPE
Fabric	magenta	continuous
Metal	green	continuous

8. **Set Layer Fabric current.**
9. **Use the Vports command to make two vertical viewports. Zoom-All in both viewports to start, then Zoom in closer as needed.** You will find it easier to draw in the left viewport and use the right viewport to determine whether the model is proceeding as it should.
10. **Use SW Isometric to select a view for the right viewport.**
11. **Set FACETRES to 4; set ISOLINES to 20.**

Step 2. Draw two 32″ × 5″ cushions using the dimensions from Figure 15–2:

1. **Draw two temporary construction lines near the bottom of your drawing in the left viewport. With Ortho ON, draw the first line 50″ to the right; draw the second line 51″ up (Figure 15–2).**
2. **Use Rectangle to draw the bottom cushion in a horizontal position 16″ above the temporary horizontal construction line and 12″ to the left of the vertical**

FIGURE 15–2
Two Construction Lines, One Horizontal 50″ and One Vertical 51″; Two 32″ × 5″ Rectangles, One Horizontal Rotated −10° and One Vertical Rotated 20°

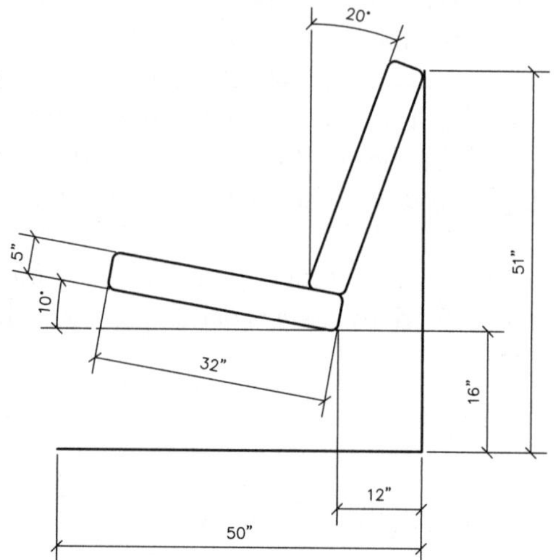

construction line. (Use the From option @-12,16 from the intersection of the construction lines. Draw the rectangle to the left and up @-32,5.) Use the Fillet option of the Rectangle command to create the 1″ fillet on all four corners at the same time.

3. Use Rectangle to draw the back cushion in a vertical position, and fillet all four corners.
4. Use Rotate to rotate the bottom cushion minus 10° and the back cushion minus 20°.
5. Move the back cushion so it sits on the right endpoint of the bottom, and use Stretch to form the bottom of the back cushion so it fits flush against the bottom cushion.

Step 3. Draw chair legs and back support (Figure 15–3):

1. Set Layer Metal current.
2. Draw temporary construction lines to locate the beginning and ending points of the three arcs; from the left end of the 50″ construction line, draw a 21″ line straight up. Then offset it 7″ to the right. Offset that line 24″ to the right.
3. Use Arc, Start-End-Radius to draw the three arcs. First arc: start point D1, endpoint D2, radius 47″. Second arc: start point D3, endpoint D4, radius 48″. Third arc: start point D3, endpoint D5, radius 34″.
4. Use Edit Polyline to join the arcs with the 34″ and 48″ radii.
5. Use Offset to offset the joined arcs 1/2″ up.
6. Use Offset to offset the arc with the 47″ radius 1/2″ to the left.
7. Use the Line command to draw lines at the ends of all arcs so that the two metal legs have a thickness.
8. Use Polyline Edit to join all parts of each leg so they can be extruded.

Step 4. Draw chair supports:

1. Draw the three supports in Figure 15–4 in the locations shown.
2. Use the Rectangle command to draw the 2″ × 1/2″ supports in either a vertical or horizontal position, as needed.

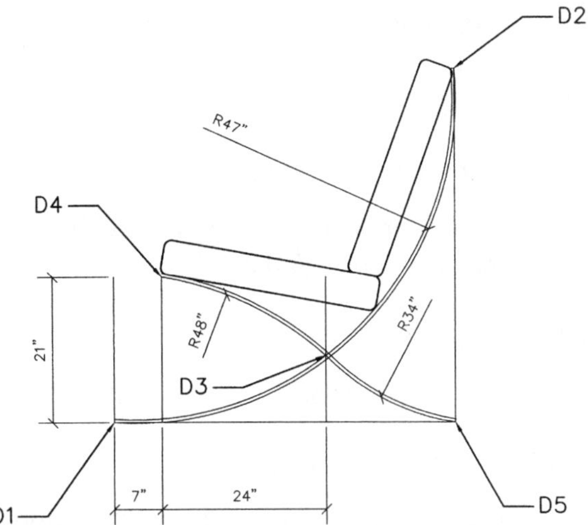

FIGURE 15–3
Draw Three Arcs, Use Polyline Edit to Join the Two Smaller Arcs

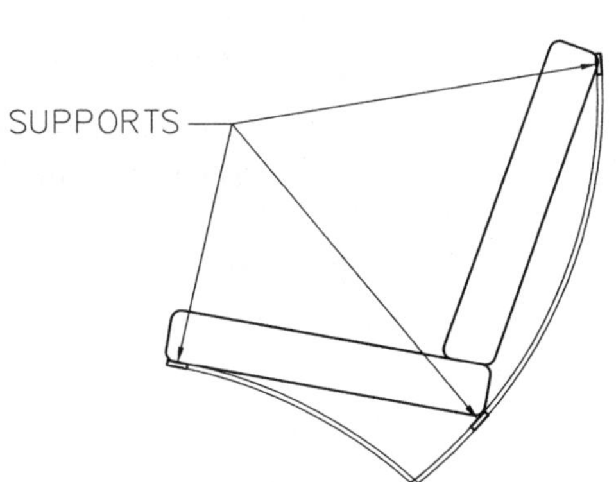

FIGURE 15–4
Draw Three 2″ × 1/2″ Rectangles, Move and Rotate into Position

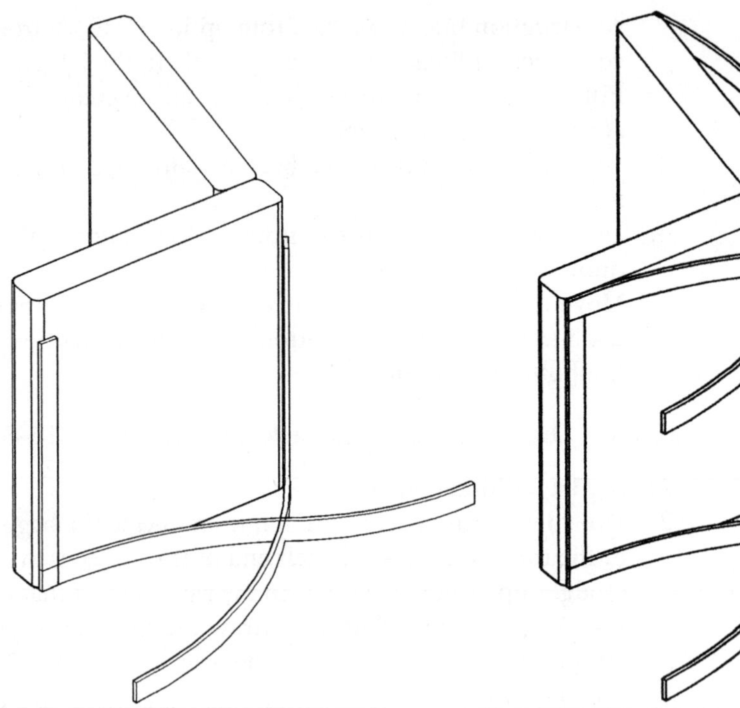

FIGURE 15–5
Extrude Cushions 36″, Legs 2-1/2″, and Supports 31″

FIGURE 15–6
Supports Moved, Legs Copied, and All Metal Parts Joined with the Union Command

3. Use the Rotate and Move commands to locate the supports in the positions shown.

Step 5. Extrude cushions, legs, and supports:

1. Set Layer Fabric current so the extruded cushions will be on that layer.
2. Use the Extrude command to extrude the two cushions 36″.
3. Set Layer Metal current.
4. Use the Extrude command to extrude the polylines forming the legs 2-1/2″.
5. Use the Extrude command to extrude the supports 31″.
6. Use the Hide command so the drawing appears as shown in Figure 15–5.

Step 6. Move supports so they sit on top of the legs (Figure 15–6):

1. Use the Move command to move the three supports 2-1/2″ in the positive Z direction (second point of displacement will be @0,0,2-1/2).

Step 7. Join extruded legs to form a single piece:

1. Use the Union command to join the two extruded legs to form a single piece.

Step 8. Add the other set of legs and join legs and supports:

1. Use the Copy command to copy the legs 33-1/2″ in the positive Z direction (second point of displacement will be @0,0,33-1/2).
2. Use the Union command to join both sets of legs and the three supports into a single object.

Step 9. Rotate chair to the upright and forward position:

1. Use the 3D Rotate command to rotate the chair 90° about the X axis. CLICK: one of the lowest points of the end of one of the chair legs as the Point on the X axis.
2. Use the 3D Rotate command to rotate the chair 90° about the Z axis. CLICK: one of the lowest points of the end of one of the chair legs as the Point on the Z axis.

Step 10. Remove hidden lines:

1. Use the Hide command to remove hidden lines so the chair appears as shown in Figure 15–1.

Step 11. Save the drawing as a Wblock:

1. Use the Wblock command to save the drawing on a disk with the name CH15-TUTORIAL1. Use the bottom of the front of the left leg as the insertion point. CLICK: Retain to keep the drawing on the screen.
2. Make a Layout in paper space. Use Properties to set a scale of 1/2″=1′-0″.
3. Place your name in the upper right corner of the viewport 3/16″ high, simplex font.
4. Save the drawing as CH15-TUTORIAL1.

Step 12. Plot:

1. Plot or print the drawing at a scale of 1 = 1 from paper space (the Layout1 tab) in the center of an 8-1/2″ × 11″ sheet. CLICK: 3D Hidden in the Shade plot: list. (If the 3D Hidden option is gray, close the Plot dialog box, CLICK: the viewport boundary, and use the Properties command to change Shade plot to 3D Hidden. Then plot.)

Tutorial 15–2: Creating a Solid Model of a Patio

In this tutorial you will create a solid model of a patio area and insert your chair into it (Figure 15–7). The Prompt/Response format will not be used in this tutorial. The steps will be listed with suggested commands for creating this model.

Step 1. Use your 3D workspace to make the following settings:

1. Use SaveAs... to save the drawing on the hard drive with the name CH15-TUTORIAL2.
2. Set drawing Units: **Architectural**
3. Set Drawing Limits: **50′,40′**
4. Set GRIDDISPLAY: **0**
5. Set Grid: **2′**
6. Set Snap: **6″**
7. Create the following layers:

LAYER NAME	COLOR	LINETYPE
Border	red	continuous
Column	white	continuous
Cornice	white	continuous
Roof	white	continuous
Pad	red	continuous

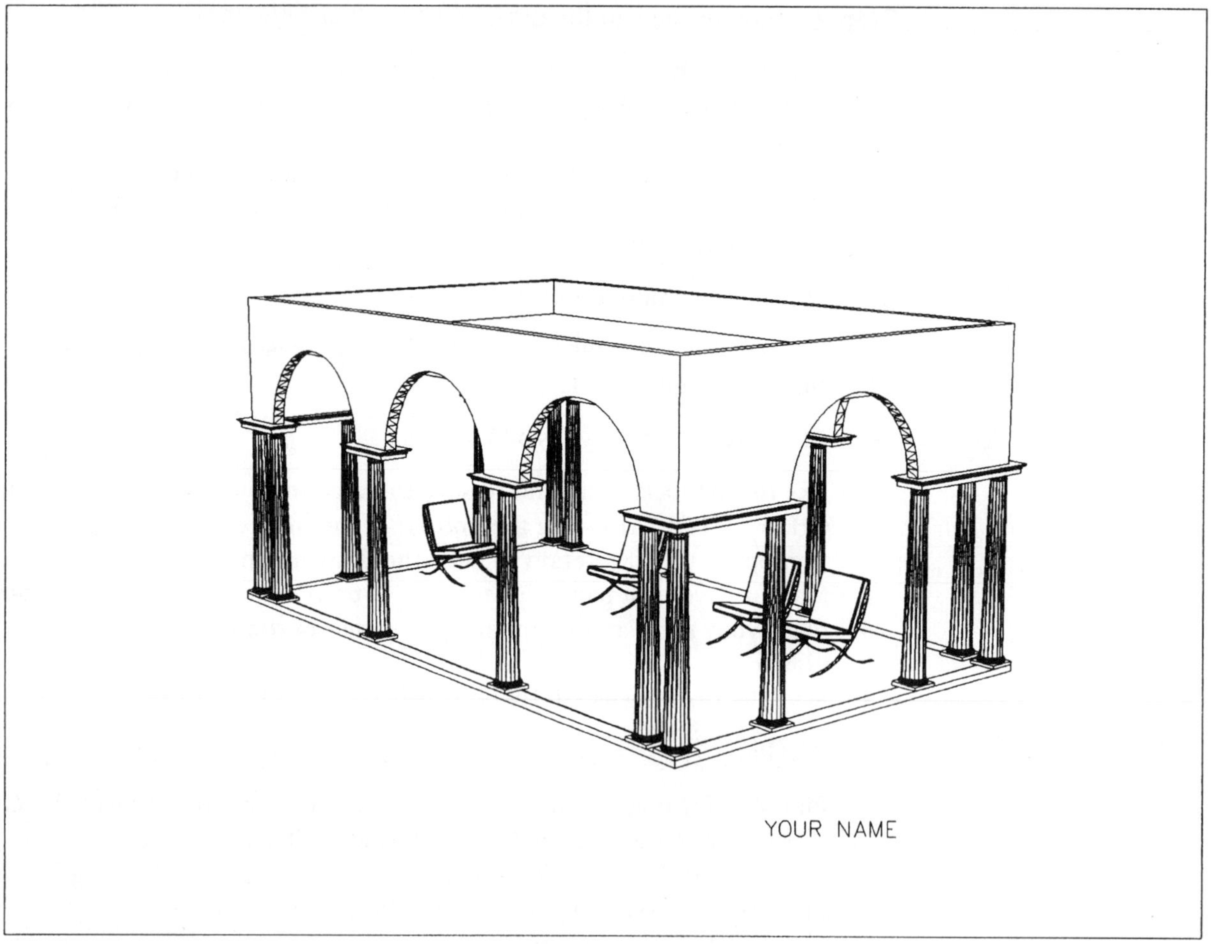

YOUR NAME

FIGURE 15–7
Tutorial 15–2: Complete

8. **Set Layer Pad current.**
9. **Use the Vports command to make two vertical viewports. Zoom-All in both viewports to start, then Zoom in closer as needed.** You will find it easier to draw in the left viewport and use the right viewport to determine whether the model is proceeding as it should.
10. **Use SE Isometric to set a viewpoint for the right viewport.**
11. **Set FACETRES to 4; set ISOLINES to 20.**

Let's begin at the bottom and work up.

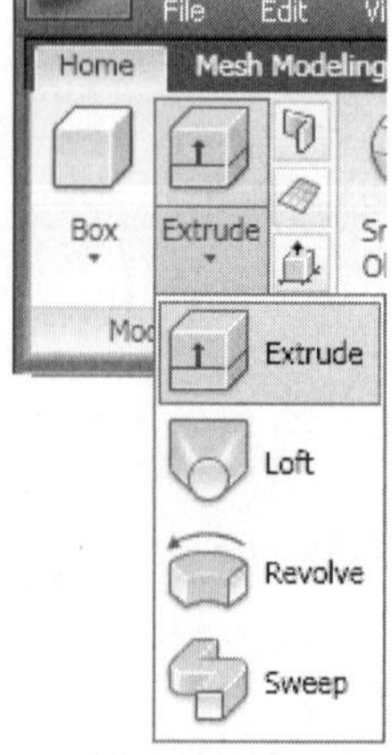

Step 2. Draw the concrete pad with a border around it:

The concrete pad and the border have to be two separate objects extruded to a height of 4″. Draw the outside edge of the border and extrude it, then draw the inside edge, extrude it, and subtract it from the outside edge. Finally, draw the pad and extrude it (Figure 15–8):

1. **Use the Rectangle command to draw a rectangle measuring 39′ × 24′. Start the first corner at absolute coordinates 6′,8′.**
2. **Offset the first rectangle 1′ to the inside.**
3. **Use the Offset command to offset the 37′ × 22′ rectangle 1/2″ to the inside to form the concrete pad with a 1/2″ space between it and the border.**

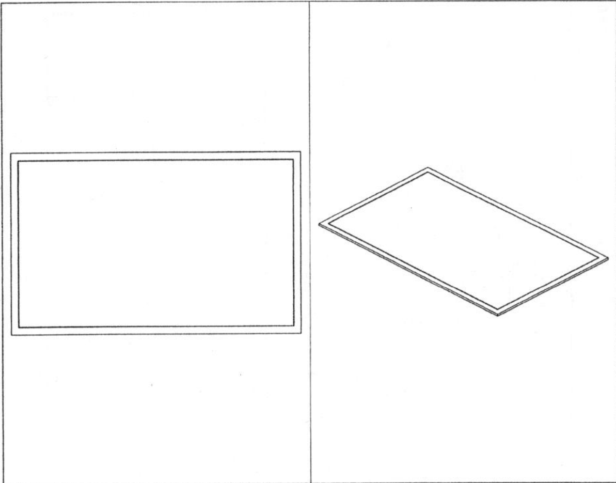

FIGURE 15–8
The Concrete Pad with a 1′ Border

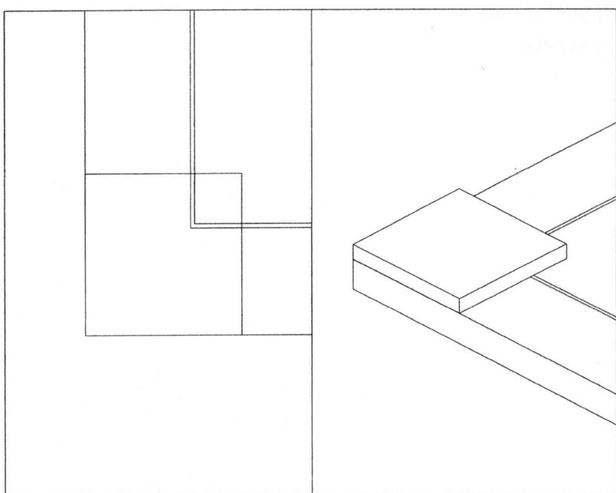

FIGURE 15–9
Draw the Base of the Column

4. Use the Extrude command to extrude all three rectangles 4″.
5. Use the Subtract command to subtract the inside of the border (the 1′ offset extruded rectangle) from the outside of the border. You will have to Zoom a window so you can get close enough to pick the correct rectangle to subtract.
6. Put the border on the Border layer.

Step 3. Draw the base of the columns:

Draw the base of the columns on the lower left corner of the drawing. They will be copied after the columns are placed on them (Figure 15–9):

1. Set Layer Column current.
2. Zoom in on the lower left corner of the drawing, as shown in Figure 15–9 in both viewports.
3. Use Box to draw the column base. The box measures 18″ × 18″ × 2″ height. Locate the "Corner of box" on the lower left corner of the border as shown. Use Osnap-Endpoint to click the first corner, then @18,18 to specify the other corner.

Step 4. Draw the columns:

Draw the column and rotate it so it sits on top of the base (Figures 15–10, 15–11, 15–12, 15–13, and 15–14):

1. Use the dimensions in Figure 15–10 to draw the column in an open area of your drawing. Use the Line and Circle commands to draw this figure. After you have drawn the circles and lines at the bottom and top of the column, draw a line from the quadrant of the lower circle on the top to the quadrant of the upper circle on the column bottom. Then trim the circles to form the arcs.

WARNING: Be sure to trim all parts of the circles so there are no double lines.

FIGURE 15–10
Dimensions for Drawing the Column

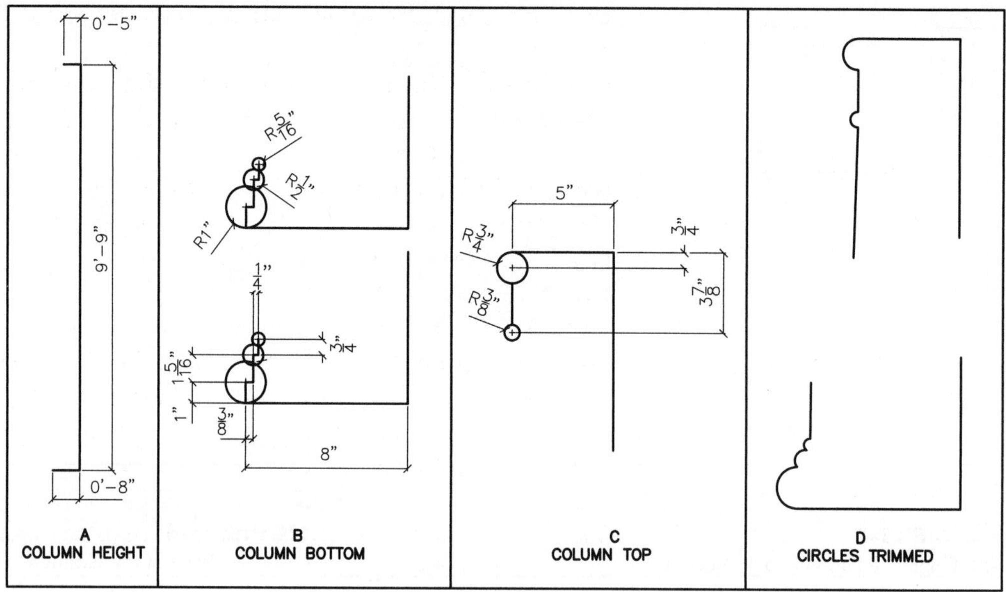

FIGURE 15–11
The Column Revolved

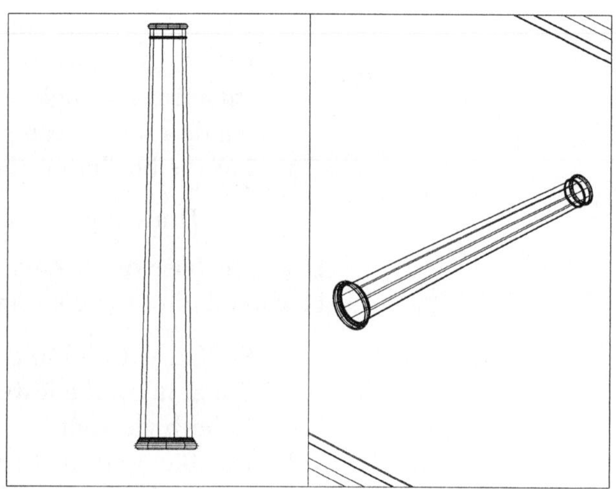

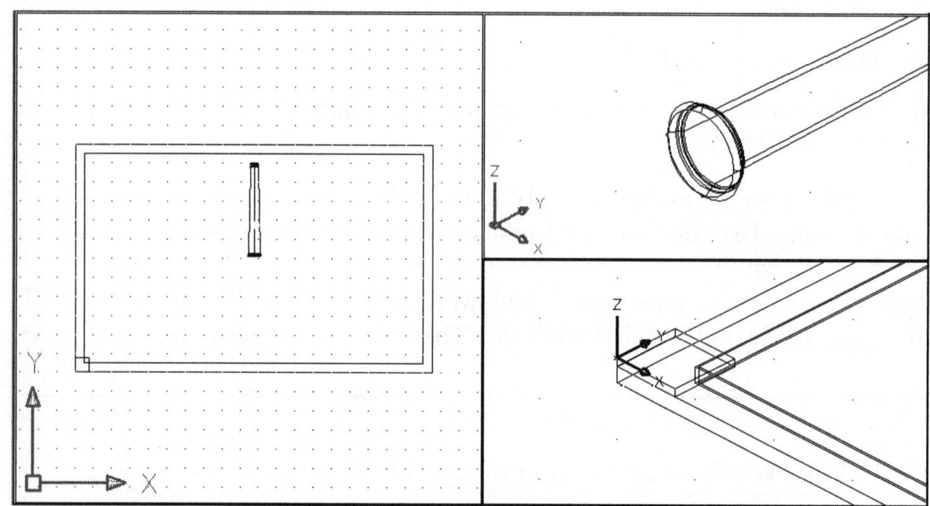

FIGURE 15–12
Move the UCS to the Top Lower Left Corner of the Base

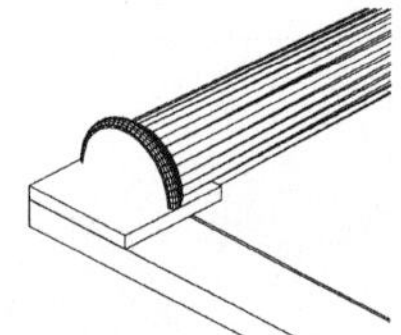

FIGURE 15–13
Move the Column to the Center of the Base

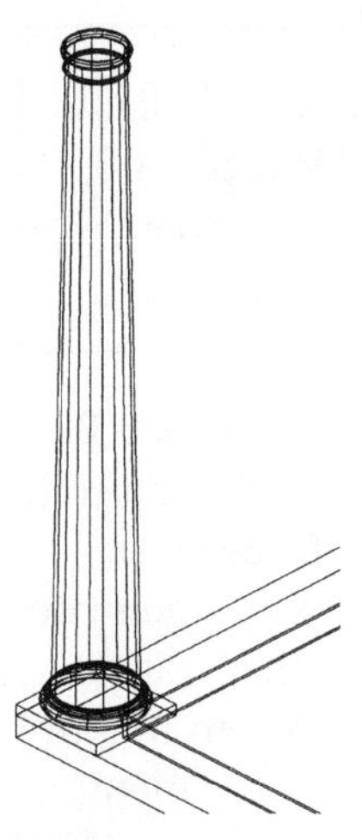

FIGURE 15–14
Rotate the Column to Its Upright Position

2. Use Polyline Edit to join all the parts of Figure 15–10 into a single polyline.
3. Use the Revolve command to create the solid column as shown in Figure 15–11. Select both ends of the vertical line using Osnap-Endpoint as the Axis of revolution.
4. Use the VPORTS command to split the right viewport into two horizontal viewports (three:left) and Zoom in on the bottom of the column and the box you drew as the column base, as shown in Figure 15–12 in both horizontal viewports. (You may need to adjust your view in the left viewport—TYPE: **PLAN <enter>.**)
5. Use the UCS command to move your UCS to the lower left corner of the top plane of the base, as shown in Figure 15–12 in both right viewports.
6. Use the Move command to move the column to the center of the base, as shown in Figure 15–13. Use Osnap-Center as the Base point, and CLICK: the extreme bottom circular center of the column in the upper right viewport. TYPE: **9,9** as the second point of displacement to move the column to the center of the base.
7. Use the 3D Rotate command to rotate the column 90° about the X axis, as shown in Figure 15–14.
8. Use the VPORTS command to return the display to two vertical viewports.

Step 5. Add the cornice at the top of the column:

Insert drawing 14–3 (from Tutorial 14–1, Figures 14–35 through 14–40) to form the cornice at the top of the column (Figures 15–15 and 15–16):

1. Set Layer Cornice current.
2. Use the Move option of the UCS command to move the UCS to the extreme top of the column as shown in Figure 15–15. Use Osnap-Center to locate the UCS at that point.
3. Use the Insert command to insert drawing 14–3 onto the top of the column (Figure 15–16). Use the following:

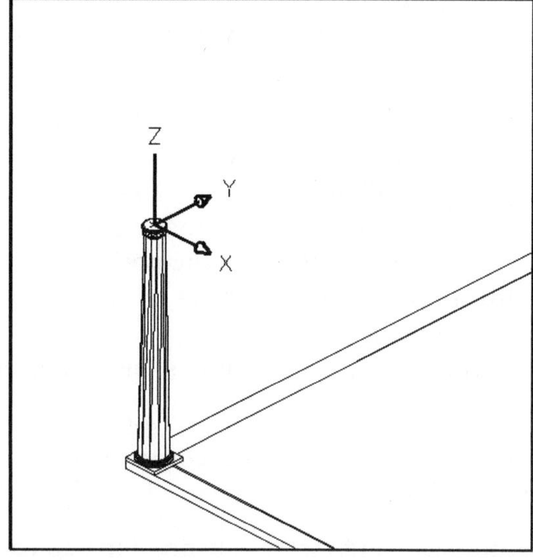

FIGURE 15–15
Move the UCS to the Center of the Top of the Column

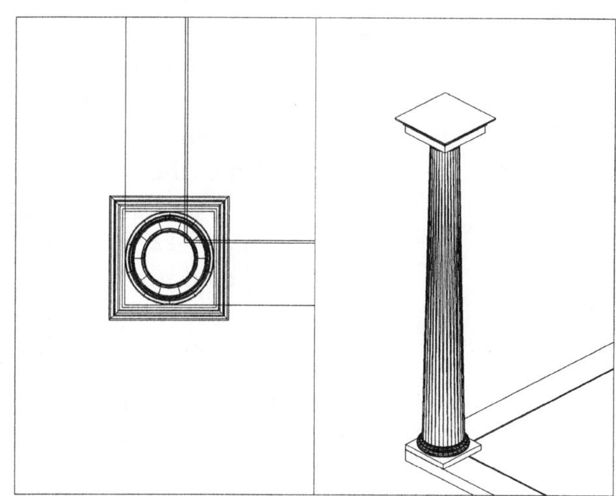

FIGURE 15–16
Inserting the Cornice

TIP: Be sure the insertion point is positive 9-1/2, negative −9-1/2. If you did not pick the correct insertion point when you Wblocked 14-3, draw a line from a bottom corner to the diagonally opposite corner. Use the midpoint of that line to move 14-3 to coordinates 0,0.

Insertion point: TYPE: **9-1/2 in the X: box and −9-1/2 in the Y: box. (Be sure to include the minus in the Y: direction.) Leave Z: at 0.** (The bottom of the cornice drawing measures 19″, as shown in Figure 14–35. Because you picked the endpoint of the lower corner as the insertion point when you Wblocked the shape, 9-1/2,−9-1/2 will place the center of the shape at the center of the column top. The shape must measure 24″ × 24″ when it is inserted. The arithmetic requires you to subtract 5″ from both measurements and divide by 2.)

After you have typed the insertion point in the X: and Y: boxes of Insertion point, TYPE: **12 in the X: Scale box and** CHECK: **Uniform Scale.**

(The shape measures 2″ square, so an X scale factor of 12 will make the shape 24″ long.)

(The shape must also be 24″ in the Y direction so Uniform Scale must be checked.)

(The height of the original shape was reduced to 1/12 of the 5-1/2″ dimension shown in Figure 14–35, so a scale factor of 12 will make it 5-1/2″ in this drawing.)

Leave Rotation angle: 0. CLICK: **OK**

4. **Use the Explode command to explode the inserted cornice so it can be joined to form longer cornices. EXPLODE IT ONLY ONCE. If you explode it more than once, you destroy it as a solid. If you are not sure if you have exploded it, use the List command to find out. List should tell you it is a 3D solid, not a block.**
5. **Go to 3D Views-Front** (on the View menu) or use **ViewCube-Front** occasionally to be sure all parts are in the correct location, then return to the previous view.

Step 6. Draw the columns and cornices at the center and one corner of the structure:

Copy the column and cornice to create supports at the center of the structure (Figures 15–17 and 15–18):

1. **With Ortho ON, use the Copy command and direct distance entry to copy the column, its base, and cornice three times: 2′ and 12′9″ in the positive X direction, and once 6′2″ in the positive Y direction (Figure 15–17).**
2. **With Ortho ON, use the Copy command and direct distance entry to copy the cornice on the column that is to the far right 12″ in the positive X direction and 12″ in the negative X direction so that the cornice on this column will measure 48″ when the three are joined.**
3. **Use Union to join the cornice and the two copies to form a single cornice that is 48″ long (Figure 15–18).**

Copy the cornice and join all the cornice shapes on the three corner columns to create the L-shaped cornice at the corner of the structure (Figure 15–19):

1. **With Ortho ON, use the Copy command and direct distance entry to copy the cornice on the corner column six times: 12″ and 24″ in the positive X direction and 12″, 24″, 36″, 48″, 60″, and 72″ in the positive Y direction so**

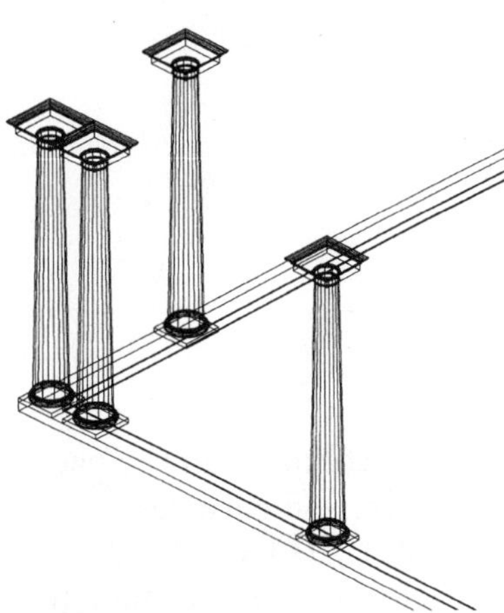

FIGURE 15–17
Copy the Base, Column, and Cornice Twice in the X Direction and Once in the Y Direction

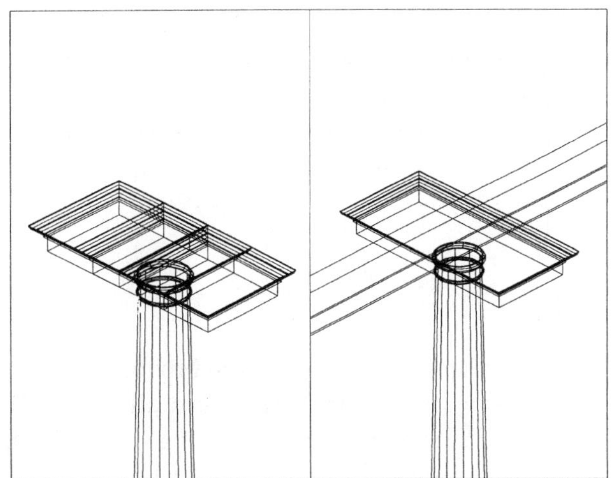

FIGURE 15–18
Copy the Cornice in the Positive X Direction and the Negative X Direction and Union the Three Cornice Shapes

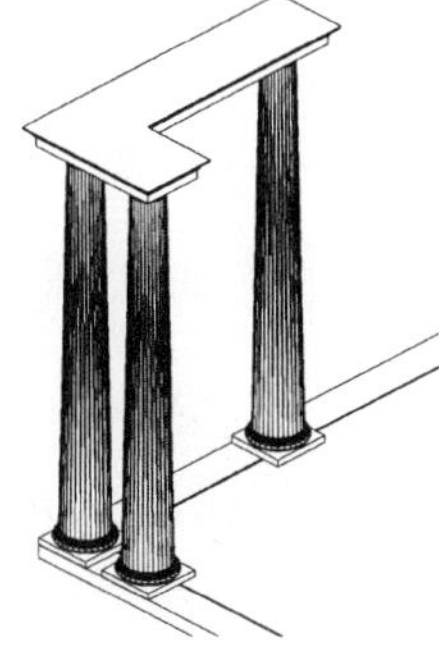

FIGURE 15–19
The L-Shaped Cornice After Using the Union and Hide Commands

that the cornice on the three corner columns will measure 48″ in the X direction and 96″ in the Y direction when all these shapes are joined.

2. Use Union to join all the cornice shapes on the three corner columns to form a single L-shaped cornice (Figure 15–19).

Step 7. Draw all the remaining columns:

Mirror the existing columns twice to form the remaining columns (Figure 15–20):

1. Use the UCS command to return to the World UCS.
2. With Ortho ON, use the Mirror command to form the columns on the right side of the structure. Select all existing columns, bases, and cornices. PRESS: <enter>, then using Osnap-Midpoint, CLICK: D1 (Figure 15–20) as the first point of the mirror line, then CLICK: any point directly above or below D1. Do not erase source objects.

FIGURE 15–20
Copying the Columns Using the Mirror Command

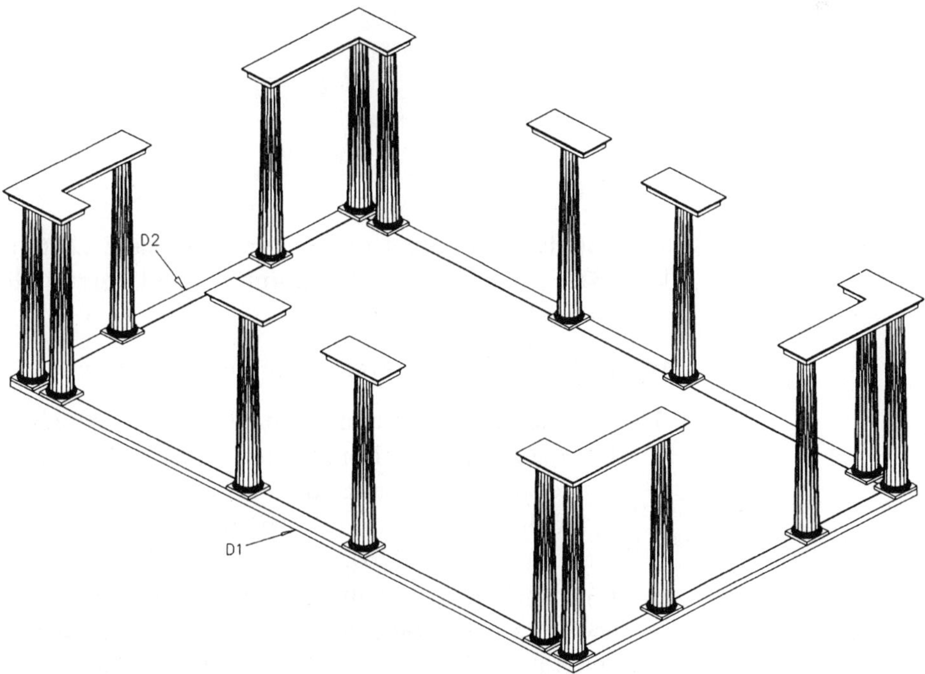

FIGURE 15–21
Dimensions for the Front and Rear Elevations of the Upper Structure

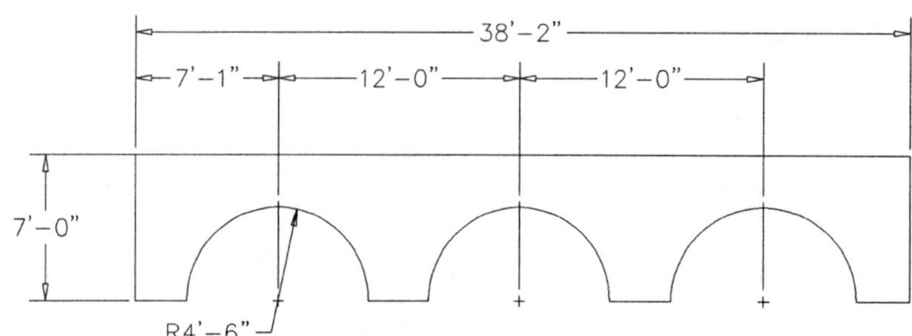

3. With Ortho ON, use the Mirror command to form the columns on the back side of the structure. Select all existing columns, bases, and cornices. PRESS: <enter>, then using Osnap-Midpoint, CLICK: D2 (Figure 15–20) as the first point of the mirror line, then CLICK: any point directly to the left or right of D2. Do not erase source objects.

Step 8. Draw the upper part of the structure:

Draw the front and rear elevations of the upper structure (Figure 15–21):

1. Set Layer Roof current.
2. Use the UCS command to rotate the UCS 90° about the X axis.
3. Draw the upper part of the structure in an open area. You will move it to its correct location after it is completed.
4. Use the dimensions from Figure 15–21 to draw that shape with the Rectangle, Circle, and Trim commands.
5. Use the Press/Pull command to extrude the polyline 8″. With Press/Pull it is not necessary to have a closed Polyline. Just CLICK: inside the boundary and move your extrusion in the direction you want, and TYPE: the distance (8).

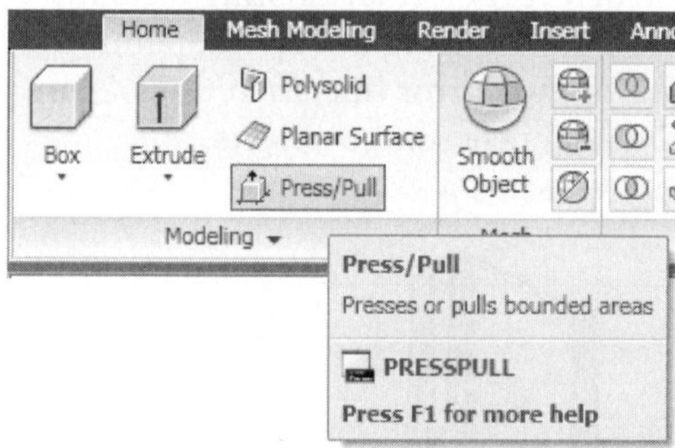

6. Use the Copy command to copy this shape 22′-6″ in the negative Z direction (Base point—CLICK: any point; Second point of displacement—TYPE: @0,0,-22′6 <enter>).

Draw the left and right elevations of the upper structure (Figures 15–22 and 15–23):

1. Use the UCS command to rotate the UCS 90° about the Y axis.
2. Use the dimensions from Figure 15–22 to draw that shape with the Rectangle, Circle, and Trim commands across the ends of the front and rear elevations.
3. Draw the right side of the structure on the right ends of the front and rear planes (Figure 15–23).
4. Use the Press/Pull command to extrude the polyline 8″.
5. Use the Copy command to copy this shape 37′-6″ in the negative Z direction (Base point—CLICK: any point; Second point of displacement—TYPE:

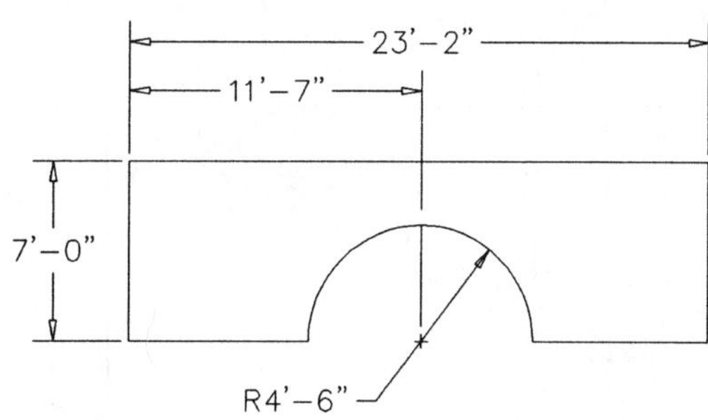

FIGURE 15–22
Dimensions for the Left and Right Elevations of the Upper Structure

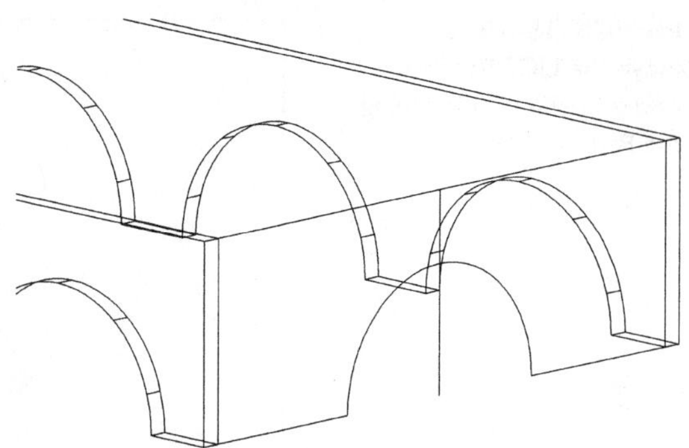

FIGURE 15–23
Draw the Right Elevation on the Right Ends of the Front and Rear Planes

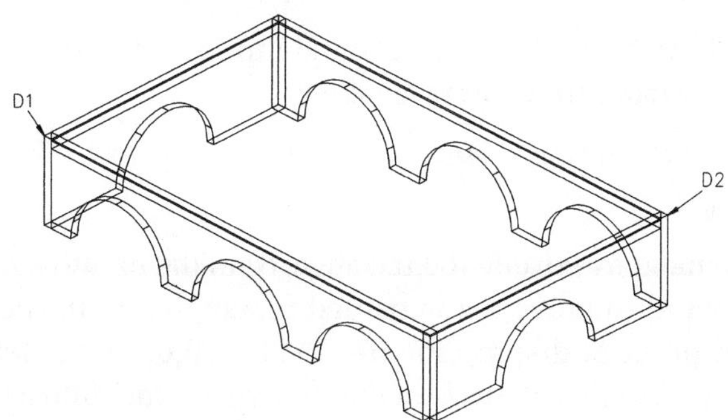

FIGURE 15–24
Draw a Rectangle to Form the Roof

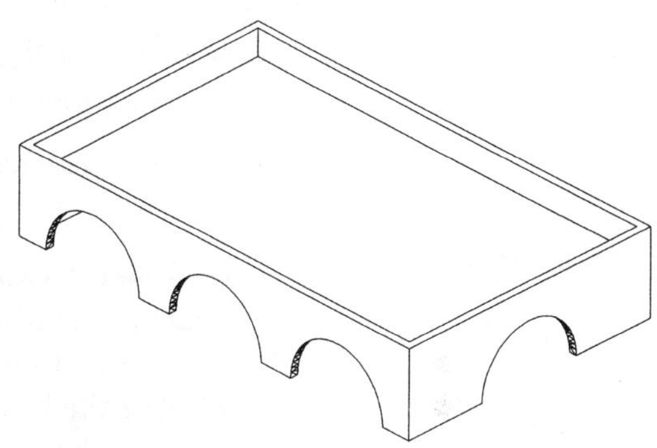

FIGURE 15–25
The Completed Upper Structure

@0,0,-37′6<enter> or move your mouse in the negative Z direction with ORTHO ON and TYPE: **37′6<enter>).**

Draw the roof and complete the upper part of the structure (Figures 15–24, 15–25, 15–26, and 15–27):

1. **Make the Roof Layer current.**
2. **Use the UCS command to return to the World UCS.**

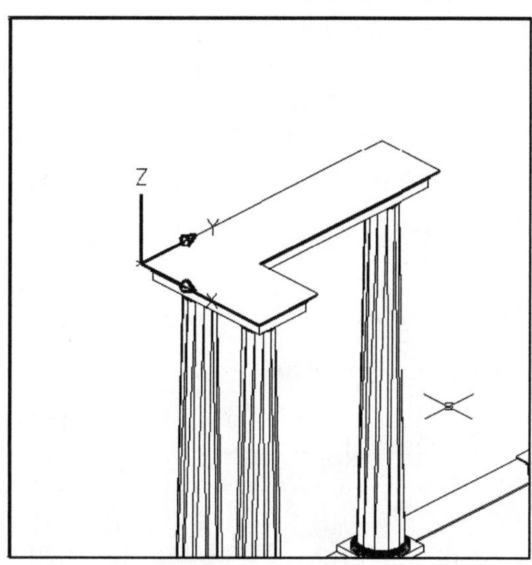

FIGURE 15–26
Move the UCS to the Top of the Cornice Corner

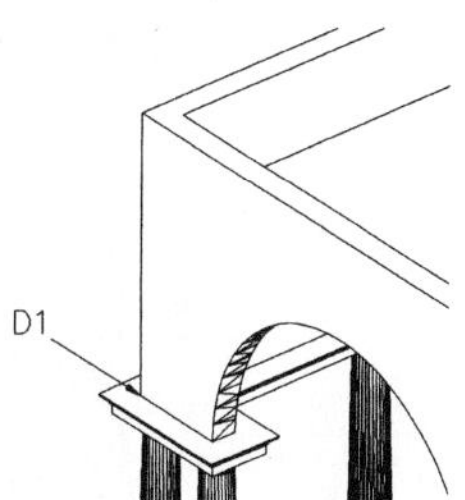

FIGURE 15–27
Move the Upper Structure into Position

FIGURE 15–28
Move the UCS to the Top of the Border Surrounding the Pad

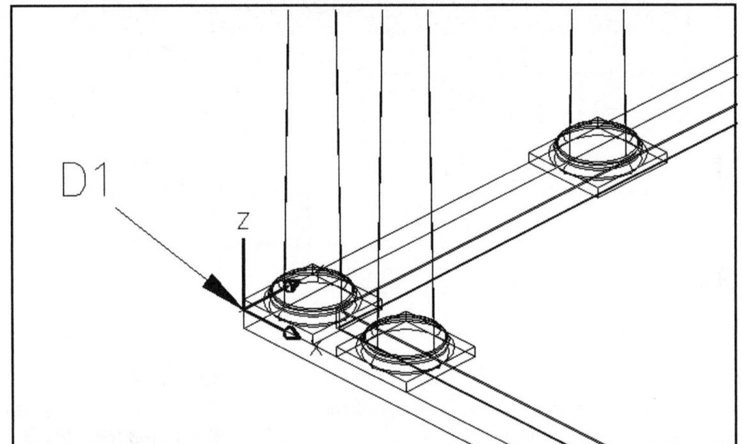

3. Use the Rectangle command to draw a rectangle to form the flat roof inside the upper part of the structure (Figure 15–24):

   First corner—D1
   Other corner—D2

4. Use the Extrude command to extrude the rectangle 8″ in the negative Z direction.
5. Use the Move command to move the extruded rectangle 18″ in the negative Z direction (Second point of displacement—TYPE: @0,0,-18<enter>).
6. Use the Union command to join all parts of the upper structure into a single unit.
7. Use the Hide command to make sure your model is OK (Figure 15–25).
8. Use the UCS command to move the origin of the UCS to the endpoint of the lower left cornice (Figure 15–26).
9. Use the Move command to move the endpoint, D1 (Figure 15–27), of the lower right corner of the upper part of the structure to absolute coordinates 8,8,0. Be sure you do not put the @ symbol in front of the coordinates.

Step 9. Insert chairs to complete the model:

Insert a chair at the correct elevation, copy it, rotate it, and complete Tutorial 15–2 (Figures 15–28 and 15–29):

1. Use the UCS command to move the origin of the UCS to the top of the border surrounding the concrete pad, D1 (Figure 15–28).
2. Use the Insert command to insert the chair drawing, CH15-TUTORIAL1, at absolute coordinates 18′,14′,0.
3. Explode the inserted chair ONCE, If you explode it more than once, you will have destroyed it as a solid.

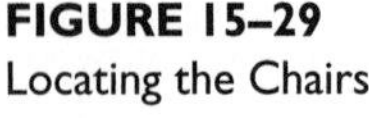

FIGURE 15–29
Locating the Chairs

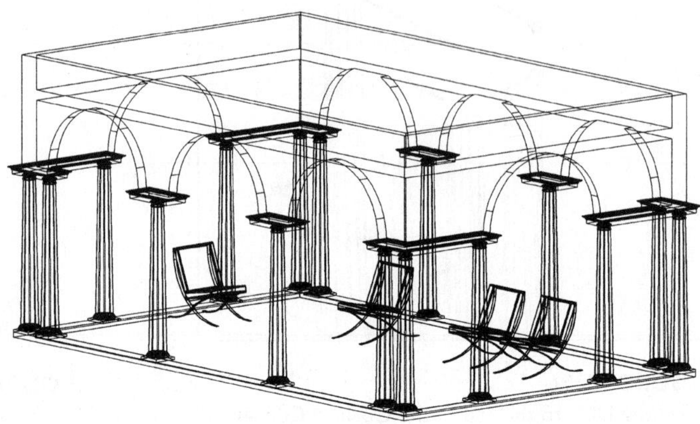

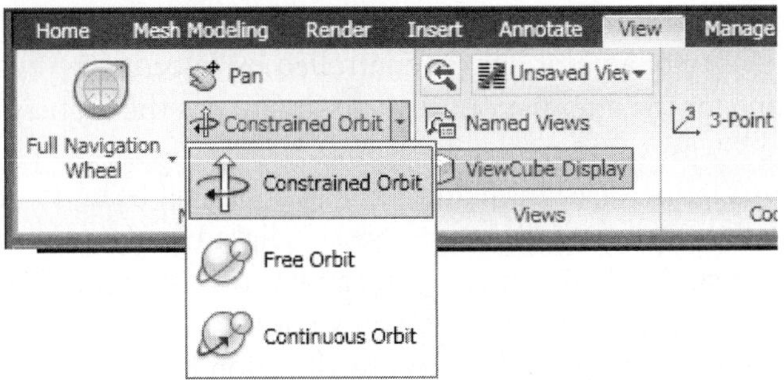

4. **With Ortho ON, use the Copy command to copy the chair three times to the approximate locations shown in Figure 15–29.**
5. **Use the Rotate command to rotate the chair on the far left 90°.**
6. **Use the Viewpoint Presets dialog box to select a viewpoint of 315,10.**
7. **Use Orbit-Free Orbit** (RIGHT-CLICK) **with Perspective projection and Visual Styles - 3D Hidden to obtain a view similar to Figure 15–7.**
8. **With the right viewport active, use the SIngle option of the VPORTS command to return the display to a single viewport.**
9. CLICK: **Layout1 and place the viewport boundary on a new layer that is turned off.**
10. **Use the Single Line Text command** (TYPE: **DT<enter>**) **to place your name in the lower right corner 1/8″ high in the simplex font. Your final drawing should appear as shown in Figure 15–7.**
11. **Use the Shade plot-As Displayed option in the Plot dialog box to remove hidden lines when you plot.**

Step 10. Use the SaveAs command to save your drawing in two places.

Step 11. Plot or print the drawing at a scale of 1 = 1.

RENDER

The Render program uses objects, lighting, and materials to obtain a realistic view of a model.

Render Quality

There are five preset rendering quality options: draft, low, medium, high, and presentation. Draft produces very low-quality rendering but results in the fastest rendering speed. Presentation is used for high-quality, photo-realistic rendered images and requires the greatest amount of time to render.

Destinations

Render Window Choosing Render Window as your render destination means the image will be displayed in the render window when processing is complete.

Save rendering to a file Allows you to save the rendering to a disk with the file name you choose.

Viewport Anything currently displayed in the viewport gets rendered.

LIGHTS

Render has five types of light that are used to light any scene. They are:

Sun This light is present in all scenes and is used to lighten or darken all the images in the scene by the same amount. You can turn off the sunlight to simulate darkness and use only the other types of light to render the scene.

Point Lights Point lights shine in all directions much like a common lightbulb. The intensity of a point light is controlled by selecting inverse linear, inverse square, or none for the attenuation. Inverse square has the highest intensity value; none has the lowest value.

Distant Lights Distant lights shine as a parallel beam in one direction illuminating all objects that the light strikes. This light can be used to simulate the sun or another similar light source. You can use one or more distant lights and vary their intensity to achieve the result you want.

Spotlights Spotlights shine in one direction in a cone shape. One of the settings for this light is the hotspot, at which the light has the greatest intensity. The other setting is the falloff, at which the light begins to decrease in intensity. Spotlights can be used in a manner similar to spotlights in a theater or to light a display.

Photometric Lights These lights are similar to those bought in a store: fluorescent, low-pressure sodium, incandescent, and high-intensity discharge.

AutoCAD has three lighting options: standard (generic), International (SI), and American. The default lighting for AutoCAD 2010 is a photometric based on American lighting units. This option is physically correct lighting. American differs from International in that illuminance values are measured in foot-candles rather than lux.

You can change the lighting option by typing: **LIGHTINGUNITS <enter>**, then change the number to 0, 1, or 2:

0 is standard (generic) lighting
1 is photometric lighting in International SI units
2 is photometric lighting in American units

Photometric properties can be added to both artificial lights and natural lights. Natural lights are the sun and the sky.

You can create lights with various distribution and color characteristics or import specific photometric files available from lighting manufacturers. Photometric lights always attenuate using an inverse-square falloff and rely on your scene using realistic units.

Which of these options you use will depend on how your scene is constructed and what your preferences are.

Often with photometric lights and the sun you will need to perform tone mapping. The RENDEREXPOSURE command allows you to adjust the tone mapping. TYPE: **RENDEREXPOSURE<enter>** to display The Adjust Rendered Exposure dialog box which provides a preview and controls to adjust the tone mapping.

MATERIALS

AutoCAD has several palettes containing materials that can be attached to the surfaces of 3D objects in your drawing. You can also create new materials from scratch and modify existing materials and save them with a new name. In this tutorial, only existing materials will be used. If you attach a material to an object and decide you do not like its appearance, the Material Editor allows you to detach the material from that object.

OTHER COMMANDS AVAILABLE TO RENDER, ANIMATE, AND SHADE 3D MODELS

Orbit As discussed in previous chapters, the Orbit command has several features that can be used to give a 3D model a photo-realistic appearance.

New View This command allows you to add a solid, a gradient, or an image background to your model.

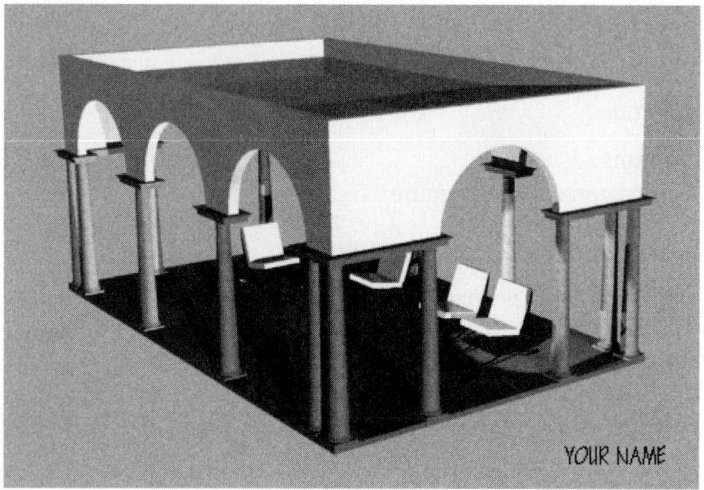

FIGURE 15–30
Tutorial 15–3: Complete

Render Environment This command allows you to simulate an atmosphere that enhances the illusion of depth. The color of the fog can be changed to create different visual effects.

Motion Path Animations... This command moves a camera along a path you choose.

3D Walk This command allows you to walk through your model controlling height and speed.

3D Fly This command allows you to fly through or around the model.

Tutorial 15–3: Use Render Commands to Make a Photo-Realistic Rendering of the Solid Model in Tutorial 15–2

In this tutorial you will use the Material Editor and the Materials palettes to select materials to attach to your model. You will then place lights in a manner that will illuminate your model. You will then give the model perspective projection, and finally, the model will be rendered using the Render command and the Visual Styles Manager (Figure 15–30).

Step 1. Use your 3D workspace to make the following settings:

1. **Open drawing CH15-TUTORIAL2 and save it as CH15-TUTORIAL3.**
2. CLICK: **the MODEL tab to return to model space**
3. CLICK: **in the right viewport to make it active and change the display to a single viewport if it is not already a single viewport.**

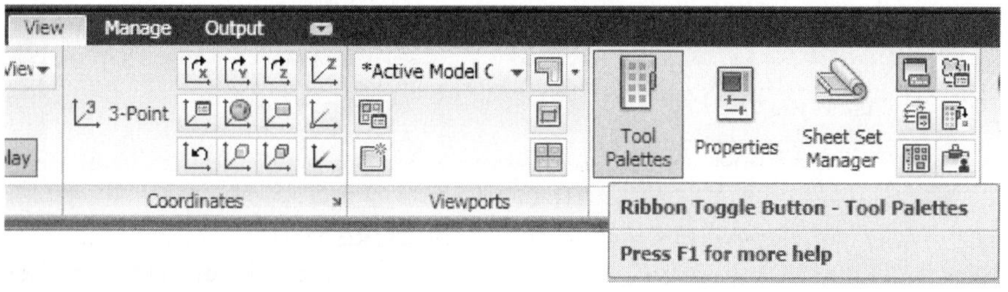

Step 2. **Select materials from the palettes and place them in your drawing on the Material Editor:**

Prompt	Response
Command:	**Materials...** **(from the View-3D Palettes Panel)**
The Material Editor (Figure 15–31) appears:	CLICK: **Tool Palettes from the Tools-Palettes menu**
The tool palettes appear:	CLICK: **The tabs that are not fully visible in a lower corner of the palettes,** so that a list of all palettes is available, as shown in Figure 15–32
	CLICK: **Fabric - Materials Sample; hold your mouse over the Furnishings, Fabrics, Canvas, White icon; and drag and drop it into the Material Editor. Use this material for the chair cushions.**

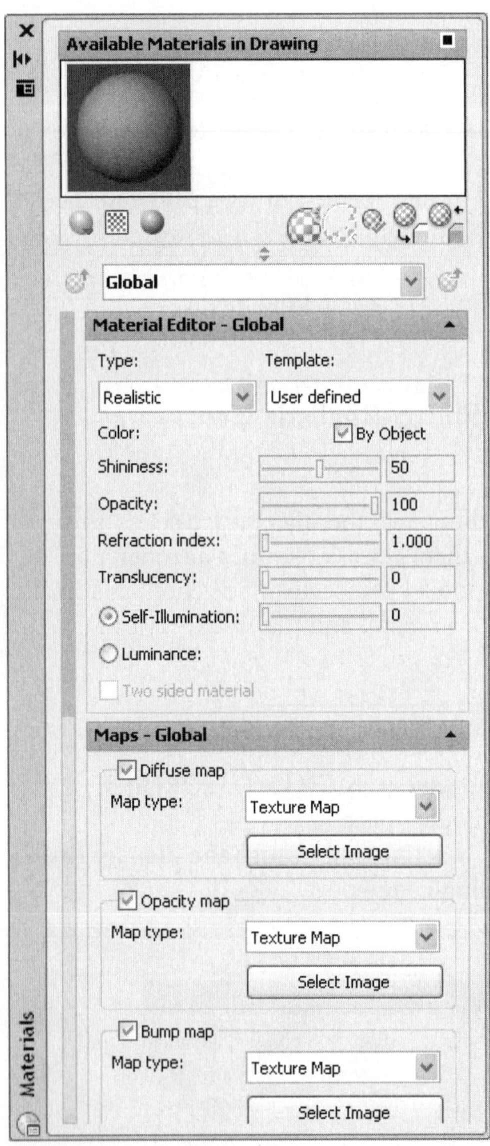

FIGURE 15–31
The Material Editor

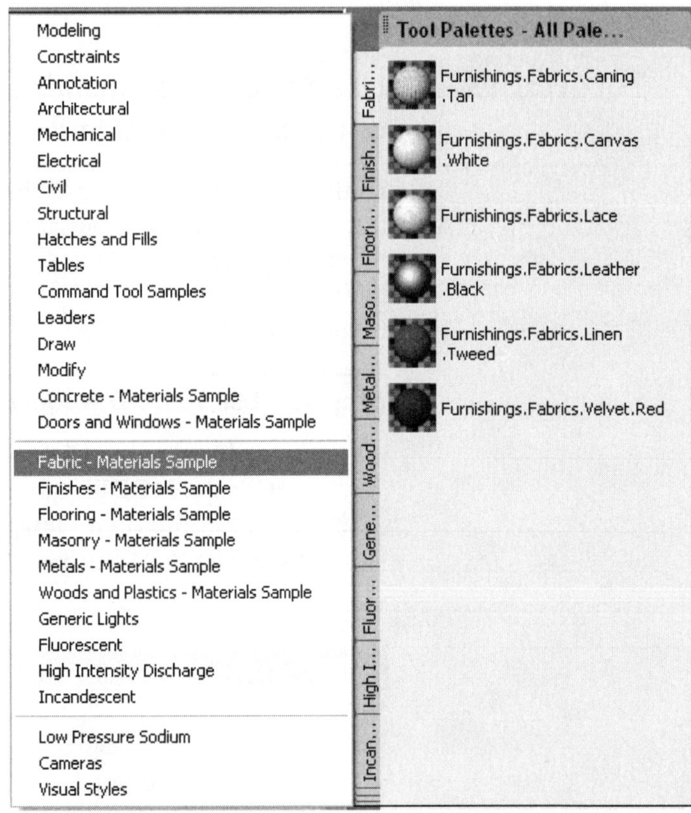

FIGURE 15–32
Display List of Palettes and CLICK: Fabric - Materials Sample

FIGURE 15–33
Drag and Drop Materials from the Masonry - Materials Sample Palette onto the Materials Editor

You have the choice now of placing the materials in the Material Editor, checking them over, and then attaching them to the solid model shapes or placing them directly onto the shapes. In this tutorial the materials are placed into the Material Editor and then dropped onto the solid shapes.

Prompt	Response
	CLICK: **the Metals - Materials Sample name in the list so the Metals - Materials Sample tab is active, and drag and drop the Structural Metal Framing, Steel material onto the Material Editor for the chair legs and supports**
	CLICK: **the Masonry - Materials Sample tab (Figure 15–33), scroll down through the many materials, and drag and drop the following materials onto the Material Editor:**
	Masonry, Unit Masonry, Brick, Modular, Herringbone, 1 for the patio floor pad
	Masonry, Unit Masonry, Brick, Modular, Common for the border around the patio floor pad
	Masonry, Unit Masonry, CMU, Sandblasted, Grey for the columns and bases
	Masonry, Unit Masonry, CMU, Sandblasted, Tan for the roof
	Masonry, Unit Masonry, CMU, Split Face, Running for the cornices
	CLICK: **the Masonry, Unit Masonry, Brick, Modular, Herringbone, 1 material** to make it active, and CLICK: **the Swatch Geometry flyout in the lower left of the Available Materials in Drawing icons**, and CLICK: **the cube icon (Figure 15–34)**

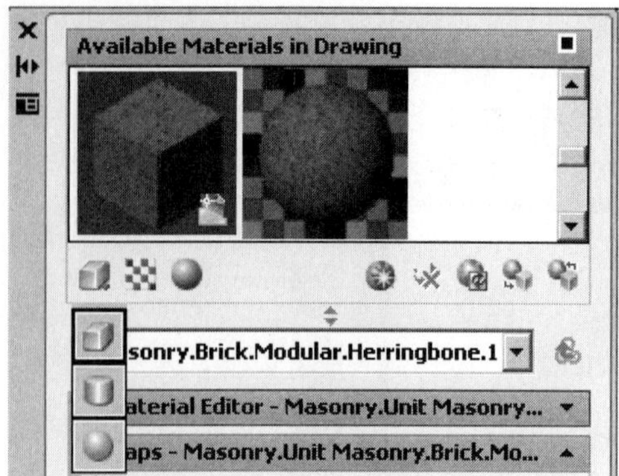

FIGURE 15–34
Available Materials with Square Geometry Selected for a Material

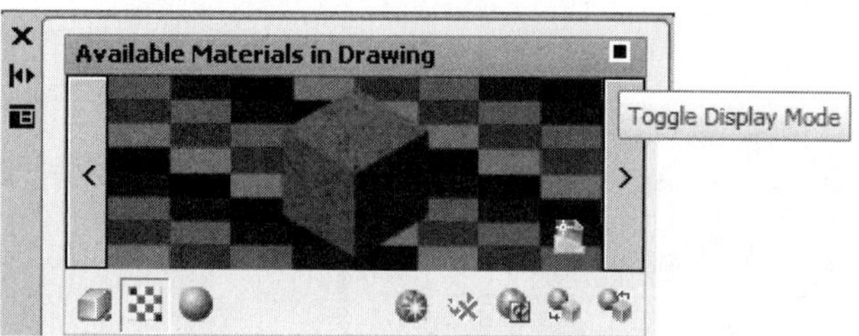

FIGURE 15–35
Toggle the Display Mode to View the Material Closely

Prompt	Response
	Then CLICK: **the Checkered Underlay icon to the right to turn it off so you can see the material a little more clearly**
	Finally, CLICK: **the Toggle Display mode in the extreme upper right of the Material Editor to enlarge the display of that material (Figure 15–35)**

Several features of any material in the Material Editor can be changed before or after materials are attached to the solids. In this tutorial you may use the materials without editing. The five icons in the lower right of the materials display activate the following commands. From left to right they are:

Create New Material
Purge from Drawing (if the material is attached to a solid, it cannot be purged until it is removed from the solid)
Indicate Materials in Use
Apply Material to Objects
Remove Material from Selected Objects

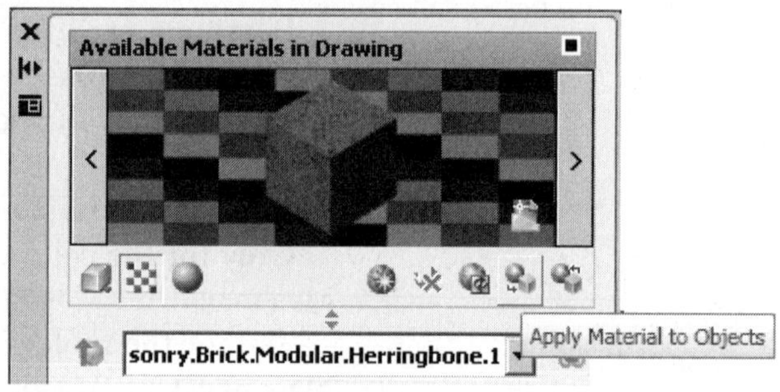

Step 3. **Attach materials to the solid shapes in your drawing:**

Prompt	Response
	Close the Tool Palettes
	CLICK: **the Masonry, Unit Masonry, Brick, Modular, Herringbone, 1 material** to make it active in the Material Editor

Prompt	Response
	CLICK: **Apply Material to Objects (or just DOUBLE-CLICK: the material)**
Select objects:	With the Paintbrush, CLICK: **the patio pad** (the solid forming the floor)
Select objects or [Undo]:	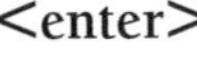 **<enter>**

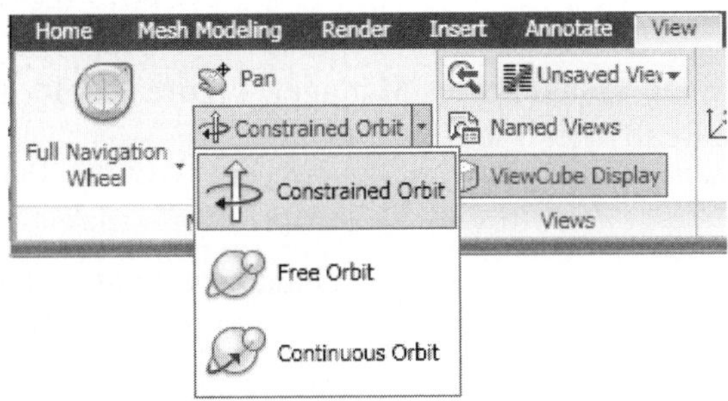

1. **Use the Constrained Orbit command to rotate the model to a view similar to Figure 15–36.**
2. **Attach the following materials to the remaining solids:**

Material	Attach to
Furnishings, Fabrics, Canvas, White,	**chair cushions**
Structural metal, Framing, Steel	**chair legs and supports**
Masonry, Unit Masonry, Brick, Modular, Common	**border around the patio floor pad**
Masonry, Unit Masonry, CMU, Sandblasted, Grey	**columns and bases**
Masonry, Unit Masonry, CMU, Sandblasted, Tan	**roof**
Masonry, Unit Masonry, CMU, Split Face, Running	**cornices**

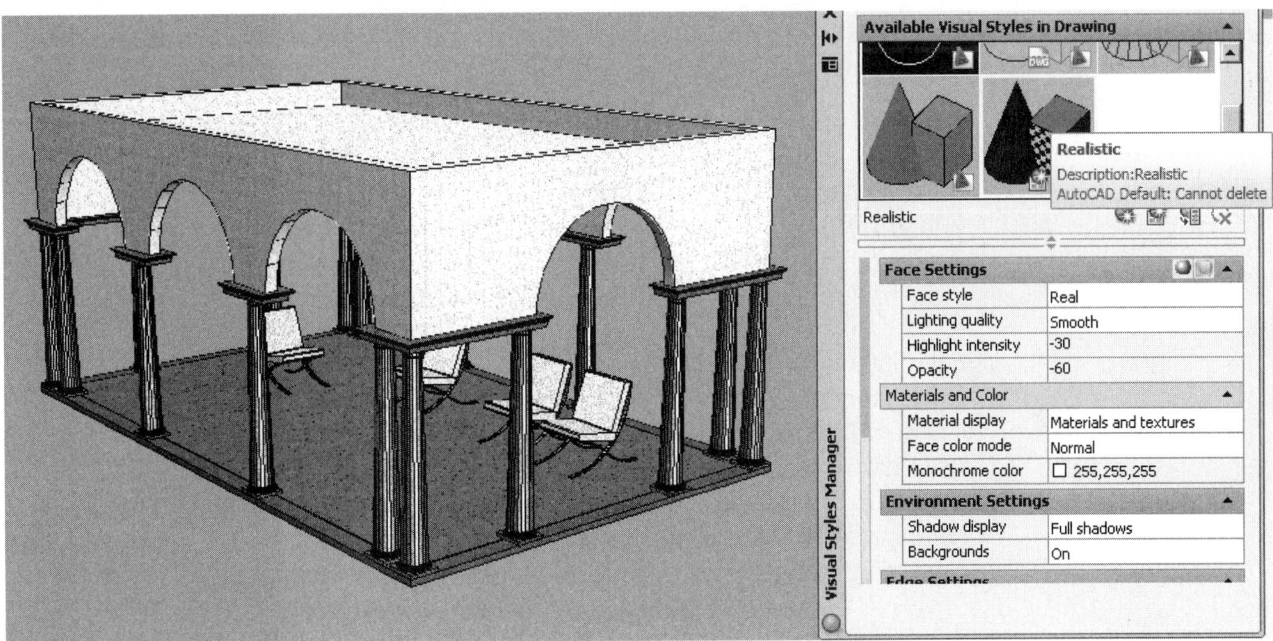

FIGURE 15–36
Realistic Visual Style

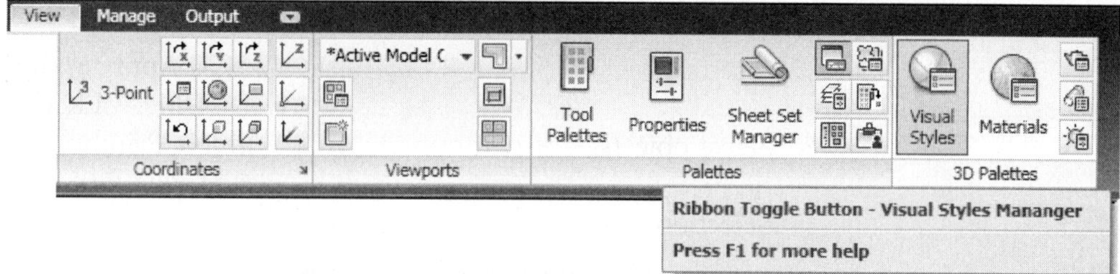

Step 4. Use the Visual Styles Manager, Figure 15–36, to render the model with the Realistic style.

Prompt	Response
Command:	**Visual Styles Manager** DOUBLE-CLICK: **the Realistic style icon**

The model is rendered as shown in Figure 15–36.

Now, lighting will be added, shadows turned on, the background selected, and the model rendered with the Render command to produce a realistic image.

Step 5. Add distant lights using lines to locate the lights and targets:

1. With ORTHO ON, use the Line command to draw 30′ lines from the midpoints of the arches on the front and right side of the patio, as shown in Figure 15–37.
2. Draw a line from the midpoint of one side of the roof to the opposite side of the roof, then draw a 30′ line straight up with ORTHO ON.

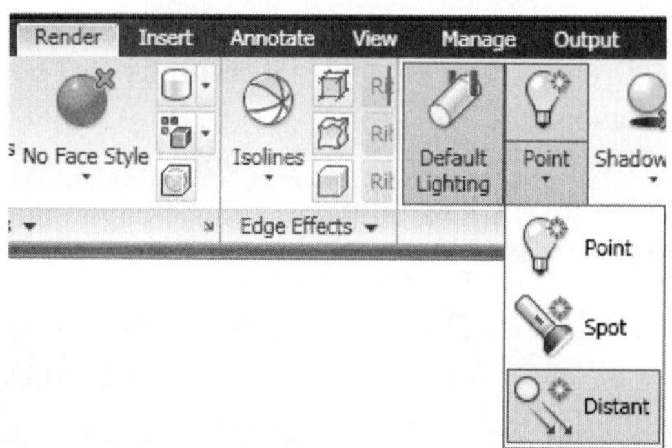

Prompt	Response
Command:	TYPE: **LIGHT<enter>** (you can also CLICK: **Distant Light on the Ribbon and skip the next prompt**) (A warning regarding default lighting may appear. If it does, CLICK: **Yes.**)
Enter light type [Point/Spot/Web/Targetpoint/Freespot/freeweB/Distant] <Freespot>:	TYPE: **D<enter>**
The Viewport Lighting Mode warning appears:	CLICK: **Turn off the default lighting**
Photometric Distant Lights warning appears:	CLICK: **Disable Distant Lights when the lighting unit is photometric**
Specify light direction FROM <0,0,0> or [Vector]:	**OSNAP-Endpoint** CLICK: **the end farthest from the model of one of the 30′ lines**

FIGURE 15–37
Add Lines for Distant Lights

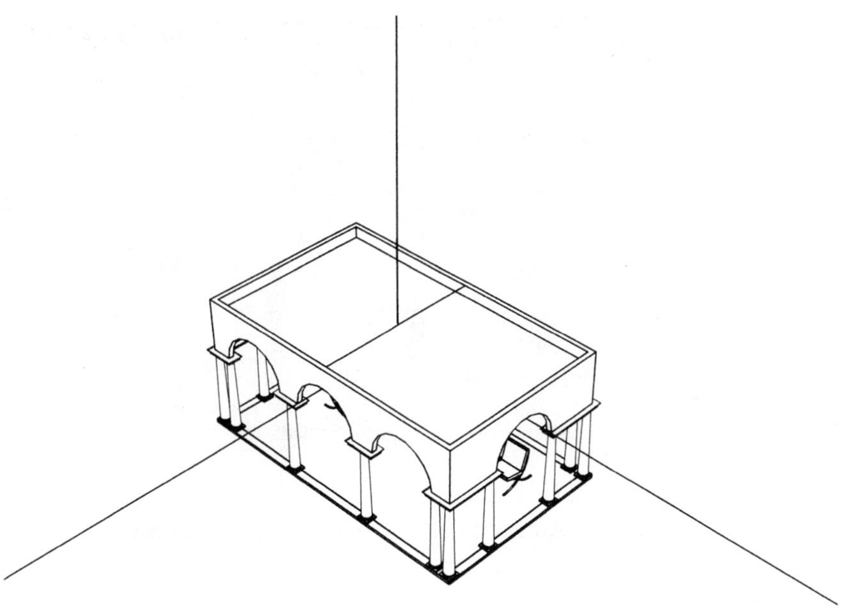

Prompt	Response
Specify light direction TO <1,1,1>:	**OSNAP-Endpoint** CLICK: **the other end of the same line**
Enter an option to change [Name/Intensity/Status/shadoW/Color/eXit] <eXit>:	TYPE: **N<enter>**
Enter light name <Distantlight1>:	**<enter>** (to accept the name Distantlight1)
Enter an option to change [Name/Intensity/Status/shadoW/Color/eXit] <eXit>:	**<enter>**

1. **Add two more distant lights at the ends of the other two 30′ lines pointed toward the model.**
2. **Erase the construction lines locating the distant lights.**

Distant lights shine uniform parallel light rays in one direction only. The intensity of a distant light does not diminish over distance; it shines as brightly on each surface it strikes no matter how far away the surface is from the light. Distant lights are used to light the model uniformly. You can change the intensity of a distant light if you want all surfaces on that side to be lighter or darker.

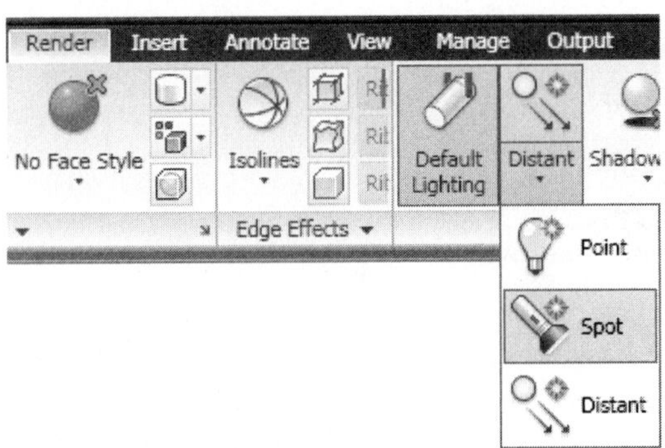

FIGURE 15–38
Locate Spotlights and Point Lights

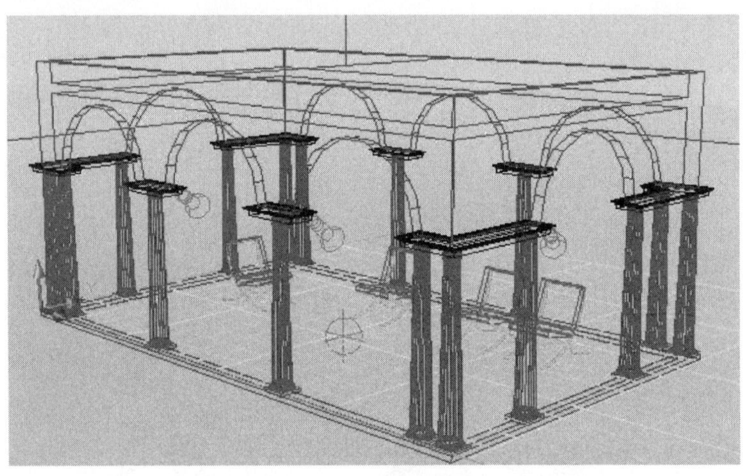

Step 6. Add spotlights to shine on the chairs:

Prompt	Response
Command:	**Spot** (or TYPE: **SPOTLIGHT<enter>**)
The Viewport Lighting Mode warning appears:	CLICK: **Turn off the default lighting.**
Specify source location <0,0,0>:	CLICK: **an Endpoint on the L-shaped cornice on the right side of the model, as shown in Figure 15–38**
Specify target location <0,0,-10>:	Using **OSNAP-Endpoint**, CLICK: **a point on the two chairs closest together.**
Enter an option to change [Name/Intensity/Status/Hotspot /Falloff/shadoW/ Attenuation/ Color/eXit] <eXit>:	TYPE: **N<enter>**
Enter light name <Spotlight1>:	**<enter>**
Enter an option to change [Name/Intensity/Status/Hotspot /Falloff/shadoW/ Attenuation/ Color/eXit] <eXit>:	**<enter>**

1. **Add two more spotlights on the cornices of the two single columns on the front pointing to points on the other two chairs, as shown in Figure 15–38. Name the lights Spotlight2 and Spotlight3.**

A spotlight shines light in the shape of a cone. You can control the direction of the spotlight and the size of the cone. The intensity of a spotlight decreases the farther it is from the object. Spotlights are used to light specific areas of the model.

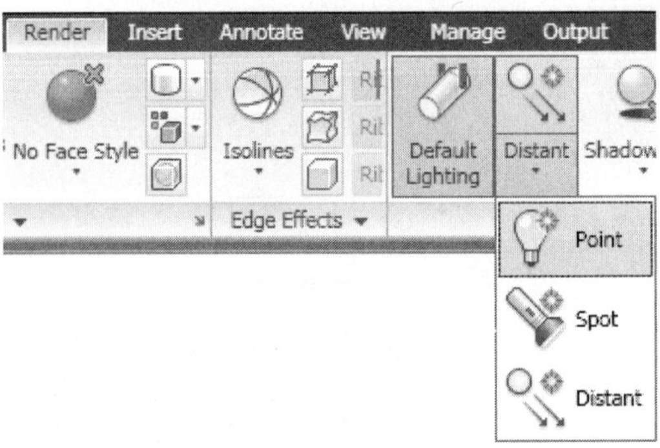

Step 7. Add a point light near the center of the patio:

Prompt	Response
Command:	**Point** (or TYPE: **POINTLIGHT<enter>**)
The Viewport Lighting Mode warning appears:	CLICK: **Turn off the default lighting.**
Specify source location <0,0,0>:	**OSNAP-Endpoint**, CLICK: **a point near the center of the floor of the patio**
Enter an option to change [Name/Intensity/Status/shadoW/Attenuation/Color/eXit] <eXit>:	TYPE: **N<enter>**
Enter light name <Pointlight1>:	**<enter>**
Enter an option to change [Name/Intensity/Status/shadoW/Attenuation/Color/eXit] <eXit>:	**<enter>**

A point light shines light in all directions. The intensity of a point light fades the farther the object is from it unless attenuation is set to None. Point lights are used for general lighting.

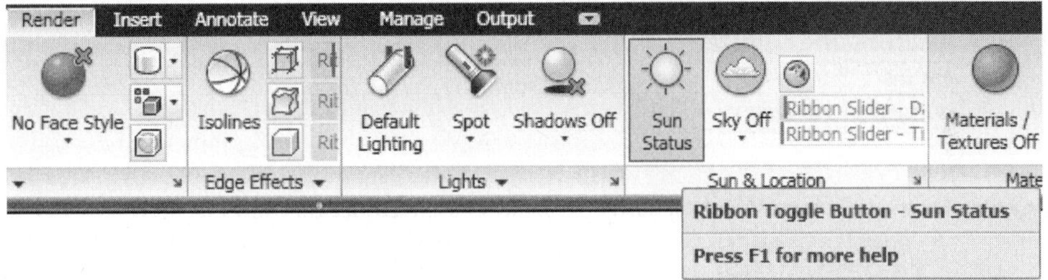

Step 8. **Turn on the Sun light and adjust it to a summer month at midday.** CLICK: **Sun Status: OFF to turn it ON.**

Step 9. CLICK: **Constrained Orbit**, then RIGHT-CLICK: and CLICK: **Perspective to change the view to a perspective view.**

TIP: Be aware that you will not be able to CLICK: points to view a window or complete many commands that require you to CLICK: a point when Perspective Projection is active.

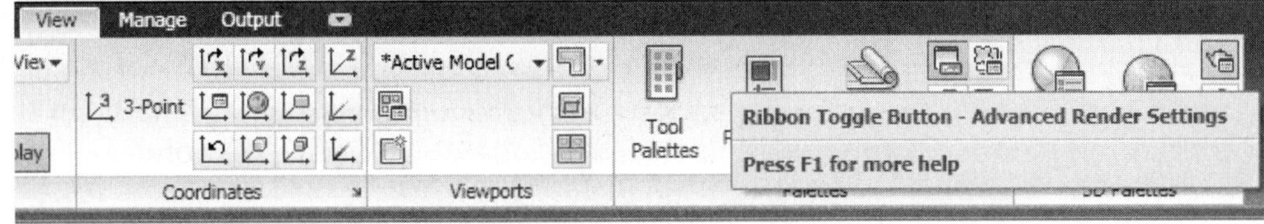

Step 10. Make Advanced Render Settings:

Prompt	Response
Command:	**Advanced Render Settings...** (or TYPE: **RPREF<enter>**) **Set Render Quality to High** (Figure 15–39)

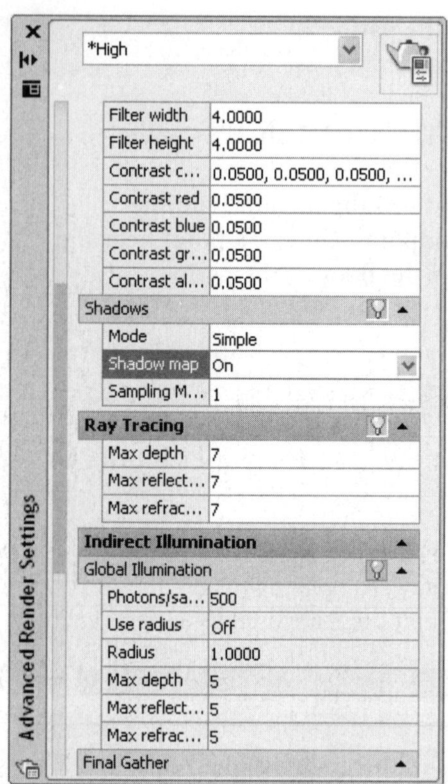

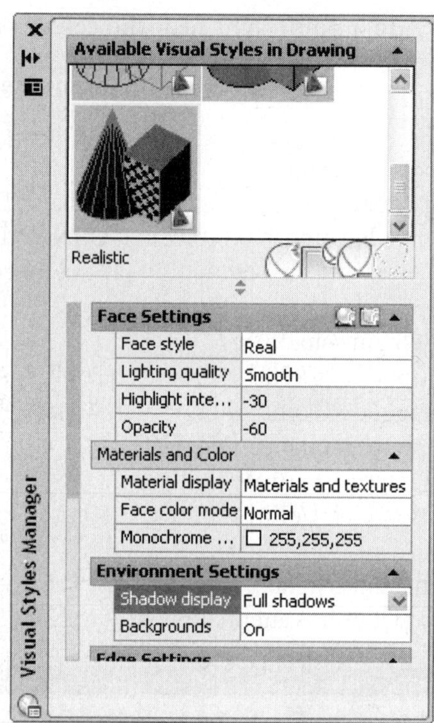

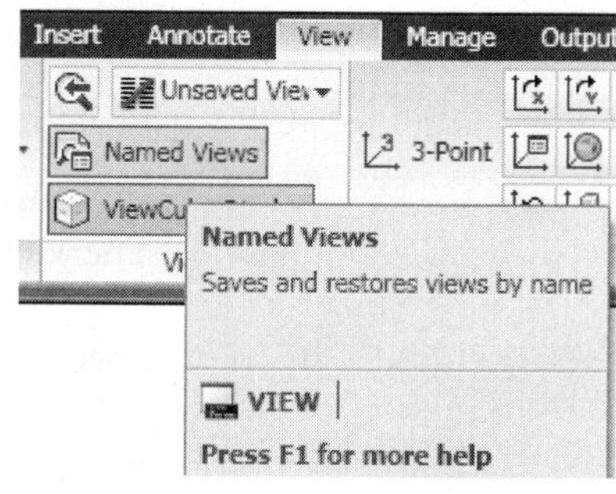

FIGURE 15–39
Render Quality High, Render to a Window, Turn Full Shadows on, Activate the View Manager

Prompt	Response
The Advanced Render Settings palette appears:	**Set Destination to Window** **Set Shadow Map ON** (in the middle of the first screen in this figure) **Close this palette** CLICK: **Full shadows** on the Visual Styles Manager to turn shadows on

Step 11. Change the background to a color before rendering:

Prompt	Response
Command:	**Named Views...** (or TYPE: **VIEW<enter>**)
The View Manager appears:	CLICK: **New...**
The New View dialog box appears:	TYPE: **VIEW 1** in the View name: input box CLICK: **Default (in the Background area), then** CLICK: **Solid**
The Background dialog box appears:	CLICK: **Color:** (the area beneath the word Color:)
The Select Color dialog box, Figure 15–40, appears:	CLICK: **the Index Color tab** and CLICK: color **33.** CLICK: **OK**
The Background dialog box appears:	CLICK: the Type: list (Figure 15–41)

This list allows you to have a single color background or a two- or three-color gradient background or to select an image file for the background of your rendering.

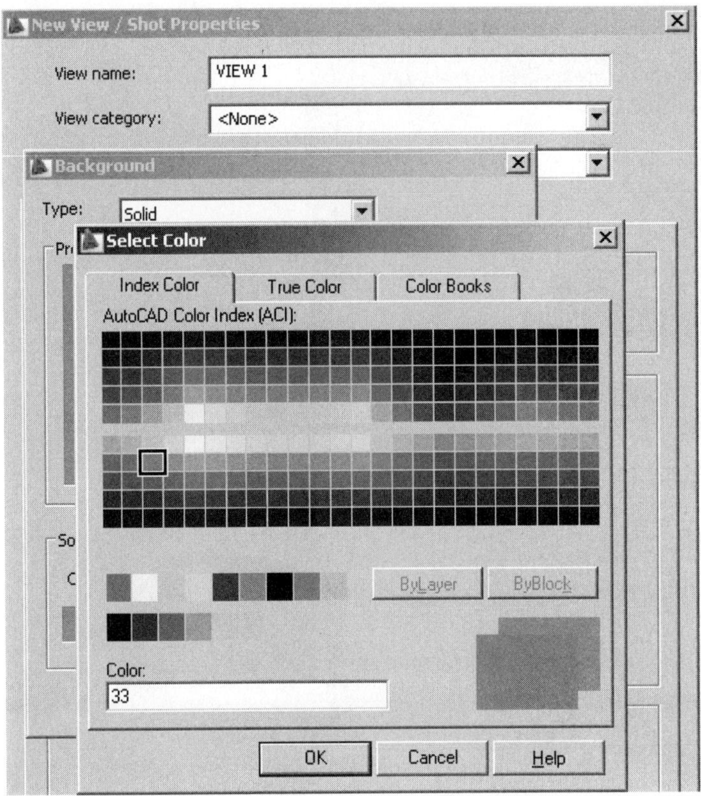

FIGURE 15–40
Set Background Color for Rendering

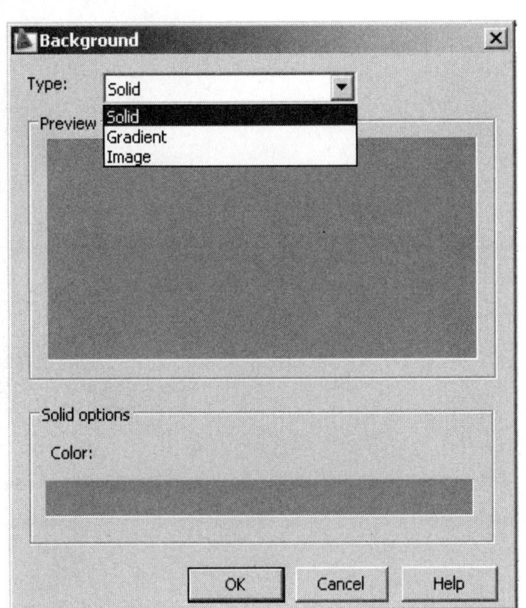

FIGURE 15–41
Background Types

Prompt	Response
	Close the list with Solid selected and CLICK: **OK**
The New View dialog box appears:	CLICK: **OK**
The View Manager appears:	CLICK: **VIEW 1** in the list to the left CLICK: **Set Current** CLICK: **OK**

Step 12. Render the drawing and insert it into a paper space viewport:

Prompt	Response
Command:	**Render** (or TYPE: **RENDER<enter>**)
The rendered model appears similar to Figure 15–42.	CLICK: **File-Save...** (if you like what you see—if not, add, erase, or change the intensity of lights, replace materials, and so forth)
The Render Output File dialog box appears:	TYPE: **CH15-TUTORIAL3** (in the File Name: input box) SELECT: **TIF** in the Files of type: input box **Save the file on a disk and make note of the disk and folder.**
The **TIFF** Image Options dialog box appears:	CLICK: **OK**

FIGURE 15–42
Tutorial 15–3: Complete

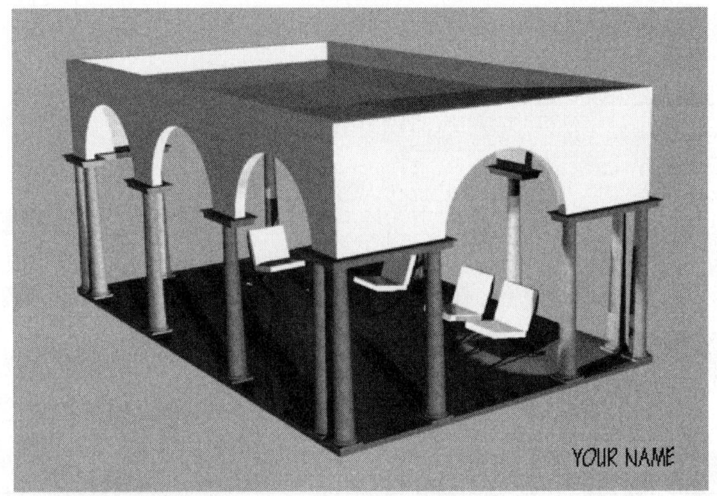

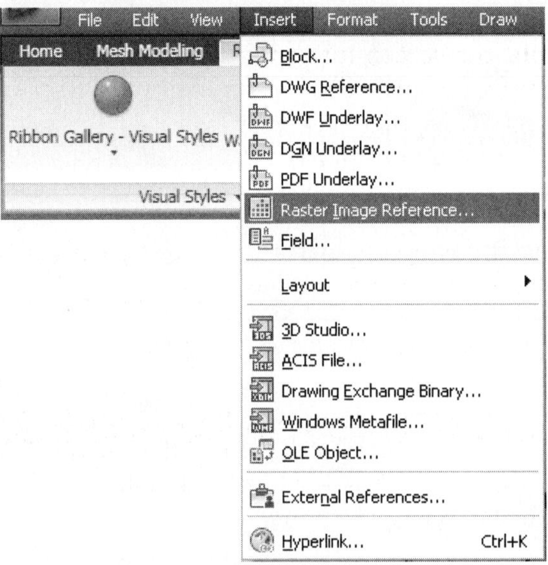

Prompt	Response
	Close the Render Window
The drawing returns:	CLICK: **Layout1**
The active model space viewport appears:	CLICK: **any point on the viewport border and erase the viewport**
Command:	**Insert - Raster Image Reference...**
The Select Image File dialog box appears:	CLICK: the file **CH15-TUTORIAL3** (on the disk where you saved it). You may need to make Files of type: read **All Image files**)
	CLICK: **Open**
The Image dialog box appears:	With a **check in Specify on Screen for Scale**
	CLICK: **OK**
Specify scale factor <1>:	**Drag the upper right corner of the image to fill the viewport, then** CLICK:

The rendered image fills the viewport.

Step 13. TYPE: **your name 3/16″ high in the CityBlueprint font in the lower right corner of the drawing.**

Step 14. **Save the drawing in two places.**

Step 15. **Plot the drawing to fit on an 8-1/2″ × 11″ sheet, landscape.**

Tutorial 15–4: Create a Walk-Through AVI File for the Rendered 3D Patio

Step 1. **Begin CH15-TUTORIAL4 on the hard drive or network drive by opening existing drawing CH15-TUTORIAL3 and saving it as CH15-TUTORIAL4.**

Step 2. **Make a new layer, name it Path, color White, and make the Path Layer current.**

Step 3. **Split the screen into two vertical viewports, and make the left viewport a plan view of the World UCS.** (TYPE: **UCS<enter>**, then PRESS: **<enter>** again to accept World as the UCS, then TYPE: **PLAN<enter>**, then PRESS: **<enter>** again to get the plan view of the World UCS.)

Step 4. **Use the Polyline command to draw a path similar to Figure 15–43.** The exact size and angle are not important.

Step 5. **Make the settings for the camera:**

Prompt	Response
Command:	**Create Camera** (or TYPE: **CAM<enter>**)
Specify camera location:	CLICK: **OSNAP-Endpoint**, CLICK: **D1, Figure 15–43**
Specify target location:	CLICK: **OSNAP-Endpoint** CLICK: **D2, Figure 15–43**
Enter an option [?/Name/LOcation/ Height/Target/ LEns/Clipping/ View/eXit]<eXit>:	TYPE: **N<enter>**
Enter name for new camera <Camera1>:	**<enter>**
Enter an option [?/Name/LOcation/ Height/Target/LEns/Clipping/ View/eXit]<eXit>:	TYPE: **H<enter>**

FIGURE 15–43
Draw a Path and Locate the Camera and Target

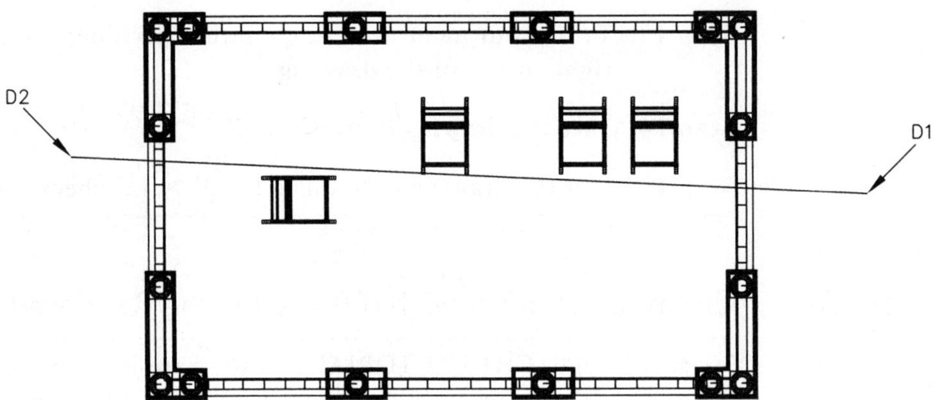

Prompt	Response
Specify camera height <0″>:	TYPE: **6′<enter>**
Enter an option [?/Name/LOcation/Height/Target/LEns/Clipping/View/eXit]<eXit>:	TYPE: **V<enter>**
Switch to camera view? [Yes/No] <No>:	TYPE: **Y<enter>**

The camera view should be similar to Figure 15–44.

Step 6. Make Walk and Fly settings as shown in Figure 15–45.

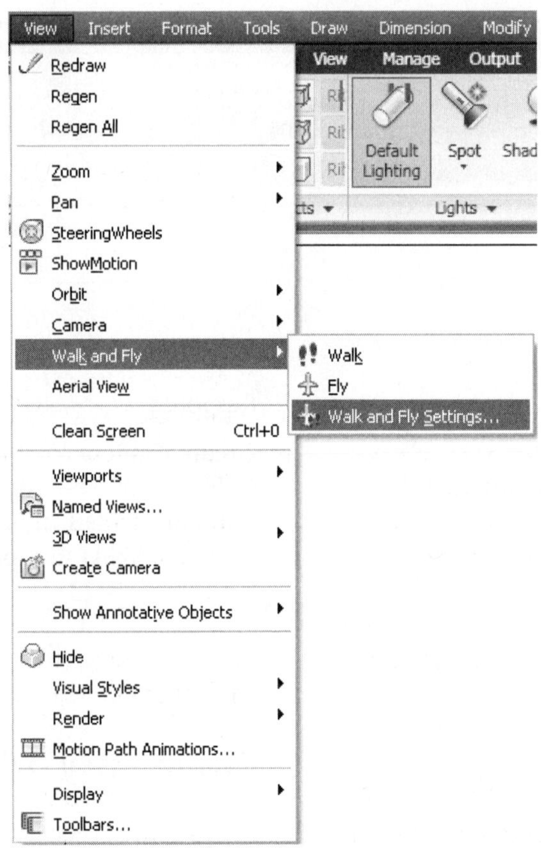

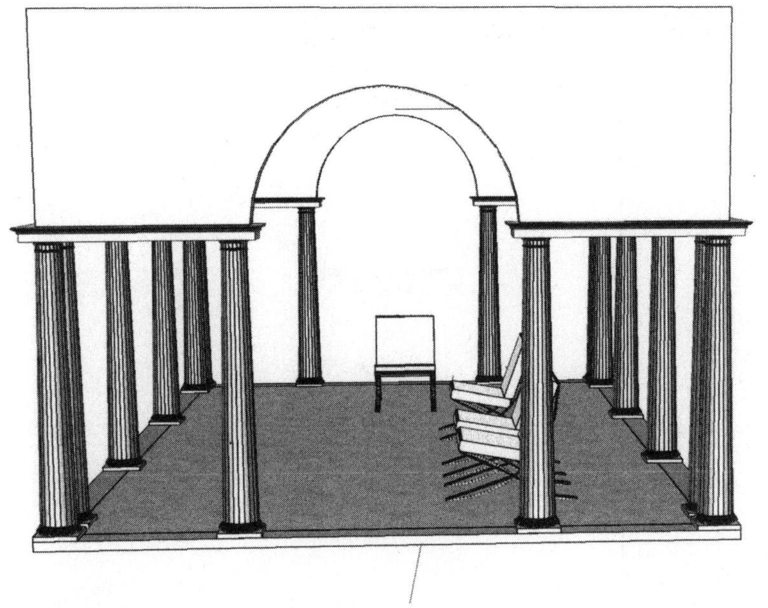

FIGURE 15–44
Camera View

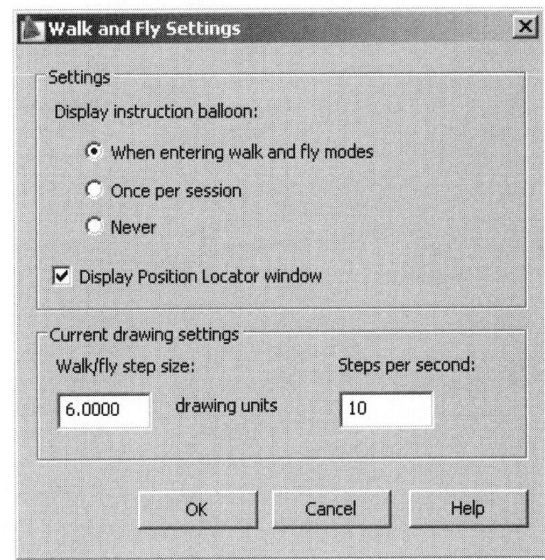

FIGURE 15–45
Walk and Fly Settings Dialog Box

Step 7. Activate the 3dwalk command and make an animation file:

Prompt	Response
Command:	**Walk** (or TYPE: **3DWALK<enter>**)

To move forward, you can press and hold the up arrow or the W key. Similarly, use the left arrow or the A key to move left, down arrow or S to move back, and right arrow or D to move right. You can also hold down the CLICK: button on your mouse and move the display in the Position Locator palette, as shown in Figure 15–46.

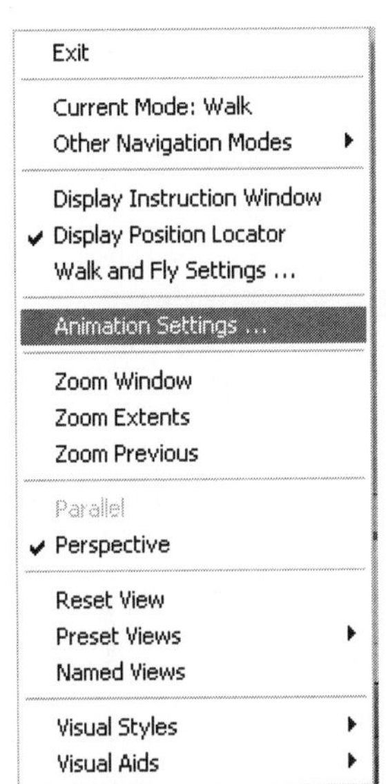

Prompt	Response
Press Esc or Enter to exit: or right-click to display shortcut menu:	**Hold your mouse over the drawing and** RIGHT-CLICK:
The right-click menu appears:	CLICK: **Animation Settings...**
The Animation Settings dialog box appears:	**Make the setting as shown in Figure 15–47** CLICK: **OK**
	Hold your mouse over the drawing and RIGHT-CLICK:
The right-click menu appears:	**Make any other necessary changes to your settings**—you probably will not have to make any
	CLICK: **any point in the drawing to get rid of the right-click menu**
	CLICK: **Start Recording Animation** on the Ribbon

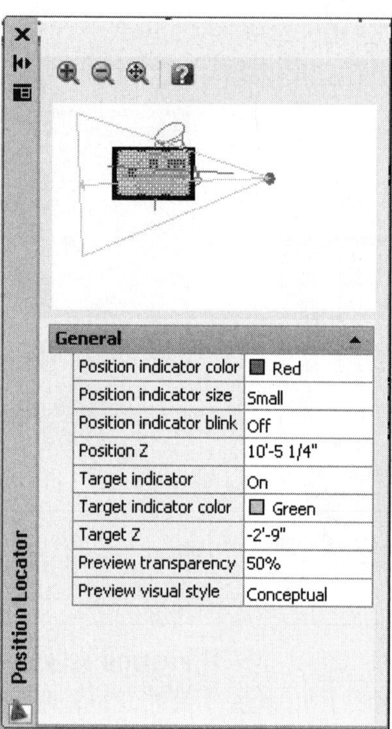

FIGURE 15–46
Use the Mouse to Move the Camera Through the Walk

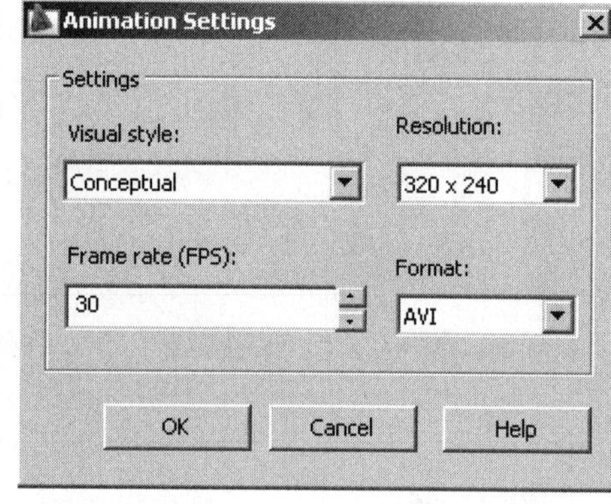

FIGURE 15–47
Animation Settings Dialog Box

Prompt	Response
	Use the up, down, left, and right arrows to move the camera along the path moving forward, back, left, and right
	When you have moved through the patio, CLICK: **Save Animation**

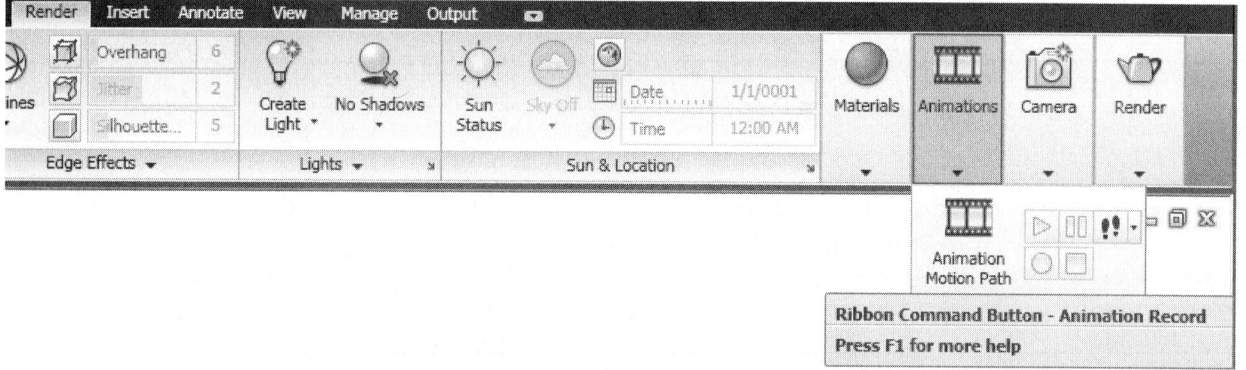

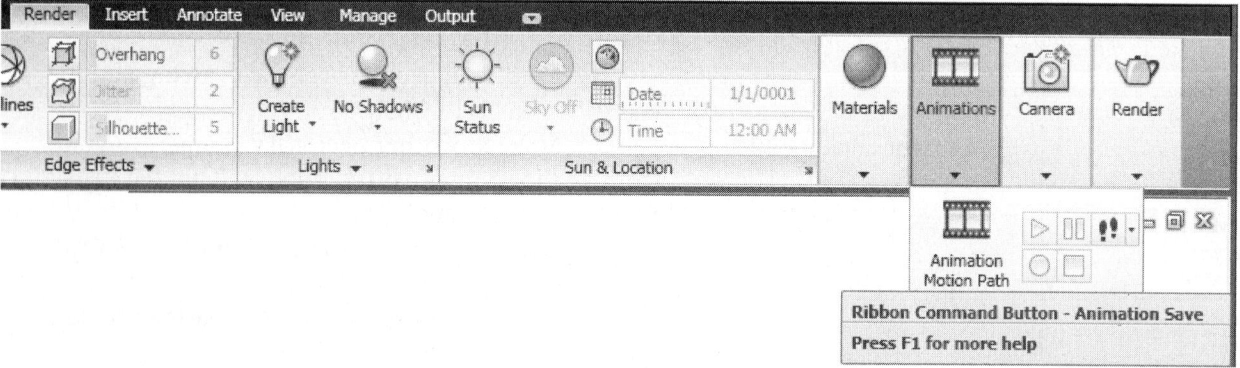

FIGURE 15–48
Save Animation File as an .avi File

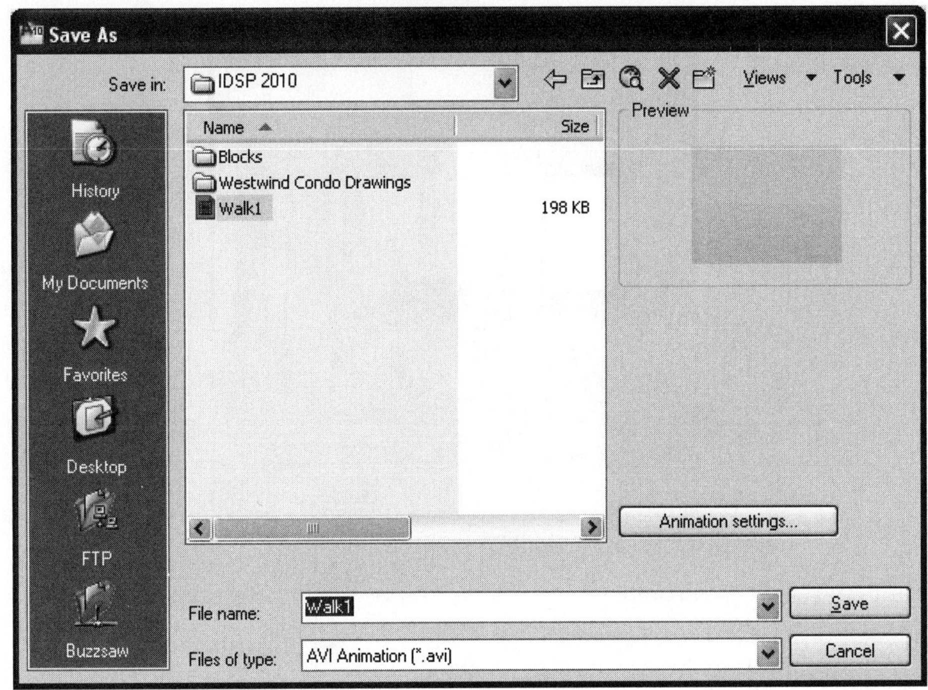

Prompt	Response
The Save As dialog box, Figure 15–48, appears:	TYPE: **Walk1** in the File name: box Select: **AVI Animation** (*.avi) in the Files of type: box **Be sure to save the file on a disk and in a folder where you can find it.**

Step 8. Preview the animation file, then exit from the 3Dwalk command. Make changes if needed:

Prompt	Response
Press Esc or Enter to exit, or right-click to display shortcut menu:	CLICK: **Play Animation**
The Animation Preview program appears:	CLICK: **the Play button and view your Animation, Figure 15–49**

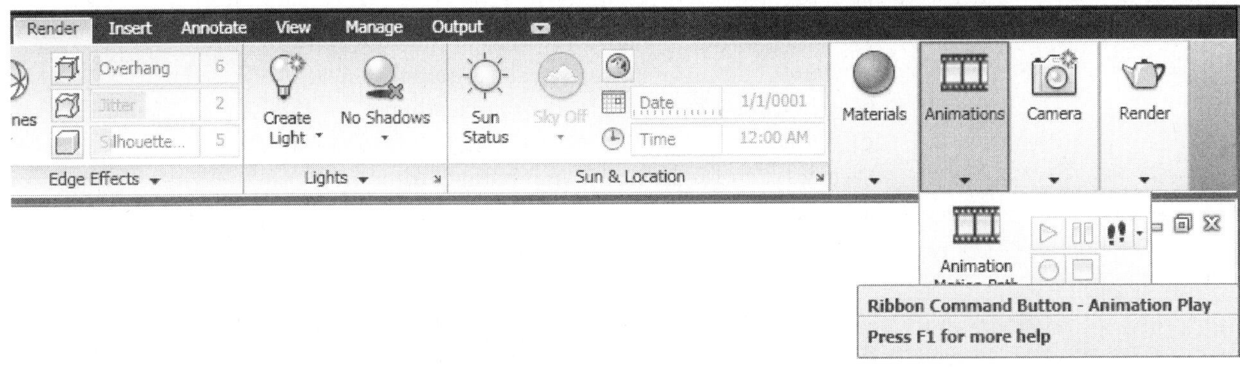

FIGURE 15–49
Play Animation Preview

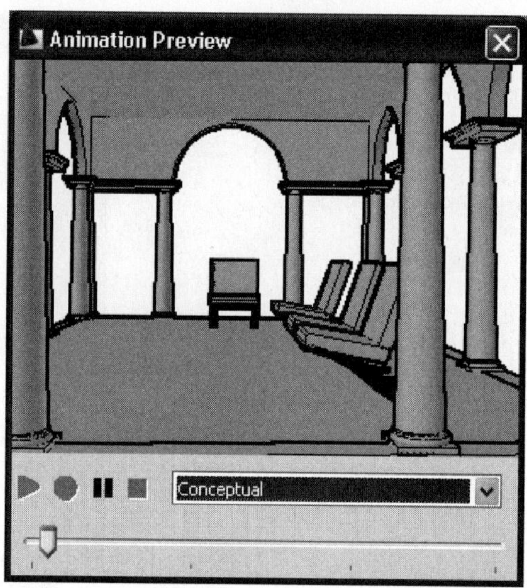

Prompt	Response
	Close the Animation Preview box
	PRESS: **Esc or <enter> to exit the 3Dwalk command**

If you like your animation, keep it. You can view it outside of AutoCAD by simply clicking on the .avi file using Windows Explorer. If you want to make lighting or material changes, you can do that easily and then do another 3Dwalk and save it with the same name to overwrite the original file.

review questions

1. Which type of light is used to lighten or darken all the images in the scene by the same amount?
   a. Sun
   b. Point
   c. Distant
   d. Spotlight
   e. Headlight
2. Which type of light shines in one direction in a cone shape?
   a. Sun
   b. Point
   c. Distant
   d. Spotlight
   e. Headlight
3. Which type of light can be used as an incandescent lightbulb?
   a. Sun
   b. Photometric
   c. Distant
   d. Spotlight
   e. Headlight
4. Which type of light shines in a parallel direction?
   a. Sun
   b. Point
   c. Distant
   d. Spotlight
   e. Headlight
5. Materials cannot be detached after they are attached to a model.
   a. True
   b. False

6. Which icon do you have to click to copy a material from the Material Editor onto a solid?
   a. Attach
   b. Detach
   c. Apply Material to Objects
   d. Preview
   e. Scene
7. The material preview uses either a cube or a sphere so you can see what the material looks like.
   a. True
   b. False
8. Which of the following lights is not on the Render Ribbon?
   a. Point
   b. Blue Point
   c. Spotlight
   d. Distant
   e. Sun
9. When you select a new distant light, which of the following is the first prompt AutoCAD gives you?
   a. Locate distant light
   b. Click: First Point
   c. Specify light direction TO<1,1,1>:
   d. Specify light direction FROM<0,0,0> or [Vector]:
   e. Specify light location<0,0,0>:
10. Which command is used to obtain a Perspective projection of a solid model?
    a. Shade
    b. Constrained Orbit
    c. SW Isometric
    d. Viewpoint
    e. Viewport

Complete.

11. List five types of lights that can be used with the Render command.

    __________ __________ __________ __________ __________

12. List the type of light that illuminates all parts of the scene by the same amount.

    ____

13. List the type of light that should be used for a lightbulb.

    ____

14. List the type of light that should be used to light a display.

    ____

15. List three types of backgrounds that can be used in a rendering.

    __________ __________ __________

16. List the dialog box used to change the background in Tutorial 15–3.

    ____

17. List the two types of Projection available to you.

    __________ __________

18. List three panels on the Render Ribbon.

    __________ __________ __________

19. Which Ribbon on the 3D Modeling Workspace contains the Create Camera command?

    ____

20. Which panel on the Render Ribbon contains the Ground shadows, Full shadows, and Shadows off settings?

    ____

chapter

16

Advanced Modeling

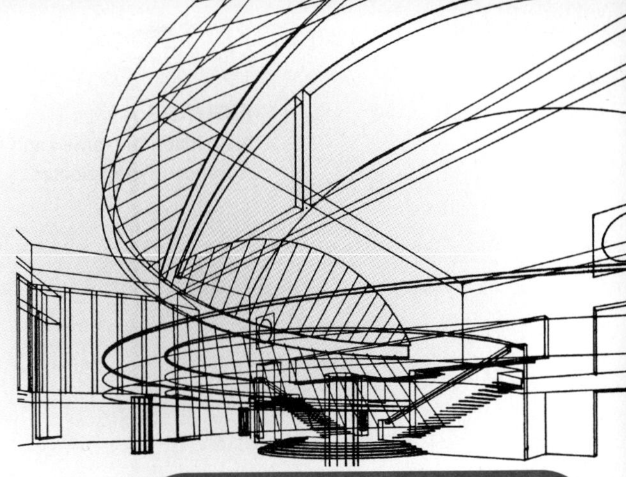

objectives

When you have completed this chapter, you will be able to:

- Make new materials.
- Use images of manufacturer's products to make new materials.
- Make advanced render settings.
- Continue using solid modeling commands to build solid models of rooms with furniture.
- Build solid models on your own from sketches.

INTRODUCTION

In this chapter you will continue using solid commands to make a room with furniture and attach existing materials as before. You will also make new materials, obtain an image of a material commonly used by designers from a manufacturer's website to make a new material, and attach these materials to solids. Finally, you will make advanced render settings to change the appearance of a final rendering.

Tutorial 16–1: Make a New Material Using the Advanced Material Type, Attach It to a Model, and Render the Model

In this tutorial, you will name a new material, specify colors, make settings for the material, and use a texture map to add texture to your material.

After you have selected a map, you can use any texture map, or you can use one of the procedural maps. If you want a brick wall, you can select a brick texture map. You will use a brick texture map in this tutorial.

FIGURE 16–1
New Material Named and the Advanced Type Selected

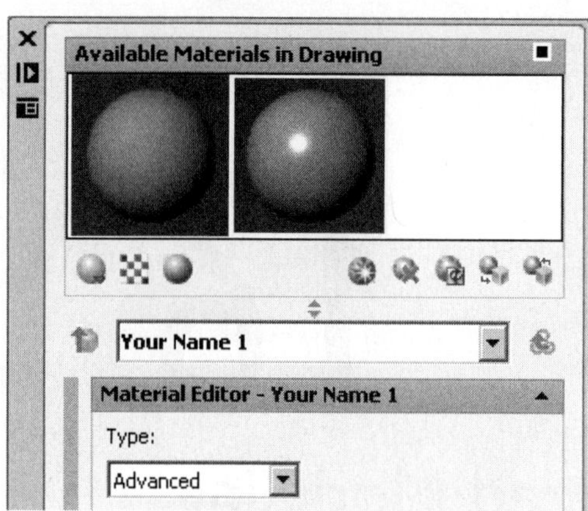

Procedural maps are also available. The procedural maps have properties that can be adjusted, such as the tiling size and mortar spacing for bricks or grains in wood materials.

Maps can be scaled, or they can be fit to the object. The patterns can be tiled or rotated. You can use more than one map for the same material.

Step 1. Use your 3D workspace to make the following settings:

1. **Use SaveAs . . . to save the drawing with the name CH16-TUTORIAL1.**
2. Set drawing Units: **Architectural**
3. Set Drawing Limits: **15′,10′**
4. Set GRIDDISPLAY: **0**
5. Set Grid: **12**
6. Set Snap: **3**
7. Set a viewpoint of **SW Isometric**

Step 2. Draw a 10′ × 4′ rectangle and extrude it 4″.

Step 3. Open the Masonry - Materials Sample palette.

Step 4. Open the Material Editor.

Step 5. Name the new material and select the material type:

1. CLICK: **Create New Material:** TYPE: **Your Name 1 in the Create New Material dialog box.**
2. CLICK: **OK.**
3. Select: **Advanced** in the Type: list box (Figure 16–1).

Step 6. Specify the material color options (you can select one or more colors):

1. CLICK: **the box to the right of the word Ambient. Then, select the color that you want to appear on the object faces that have only ambient lighting.** (CLICK: **By Object to use the color of the object to which the material is attached.**)

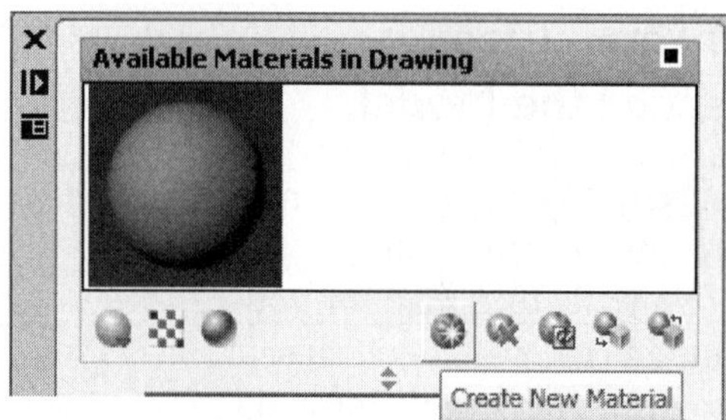

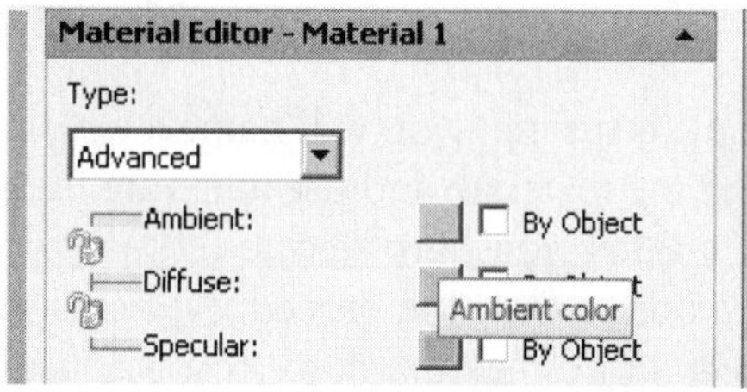

2. CLICK: **the box to the right of the word Diffuse. Then, select the color you want to assign to the material.**
3. CLICK: **The first lock to make the ambient color the same as the diffuse color.** When a color is locked to another color, changing one changes both.
4. CLICK: **the box to the right of the word Specular. Then, select the color that you want to appear as a highlight on a shiny material.** You can now lock the specular color to the other two or leave the highlight color a different one.
5. **Use the sliders to set the properties for the shininess, opacity, reflection, refraction index, translucency, and self-illumination.** Watch the material geometry to see how your new material will appear. The material preview at the bottom of the material editor also tells you how your settings change the material.

   Applying lights in the model will change the appearance even more later.

Step 7. Specify the Texture map to add texture to the material:

1. CLICK: **Select Image** in the Diffuse Map area.
2. CLICK: **Masonry, Unit Masonry, Brick Modular, Common** in the Select Image File dialog box. You may have to look for this image here: C:\Documents and Settings\All\Users. WINDOWS\Application Data\Autodesk\AutoCAD 2010\R17.2\enu\Texture.

   At this point you can select any image file for your material. You can select an image of a landscape, a pattern, a person, ... anything.

3. CLICK: the **Click for Texture Map settings icon**

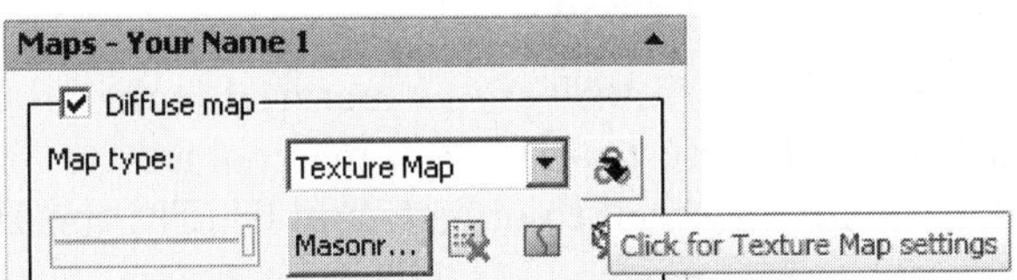

4. Change Scale units: to **Inches,** Width: to **140.0000** and Height: to **50.0000** (Figure 16–2). (If Inches is not available as a scale unit, go to Material Scaling and Tiling on the Parent Map and select it there.)

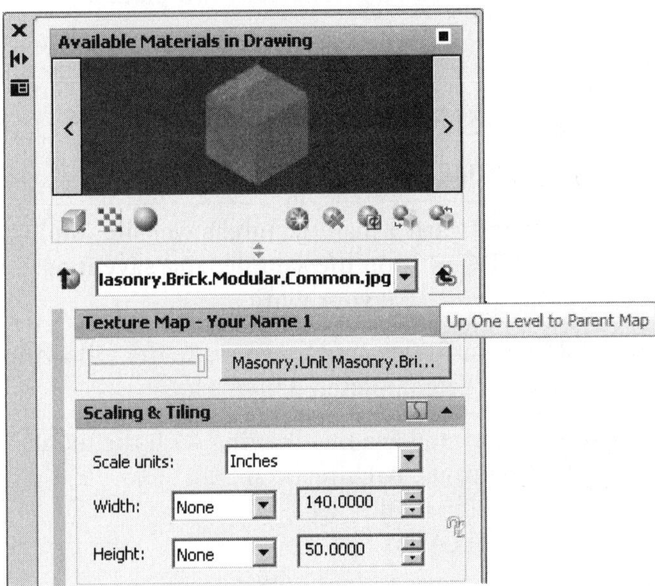

FIGURE 16–2
Change Scaling

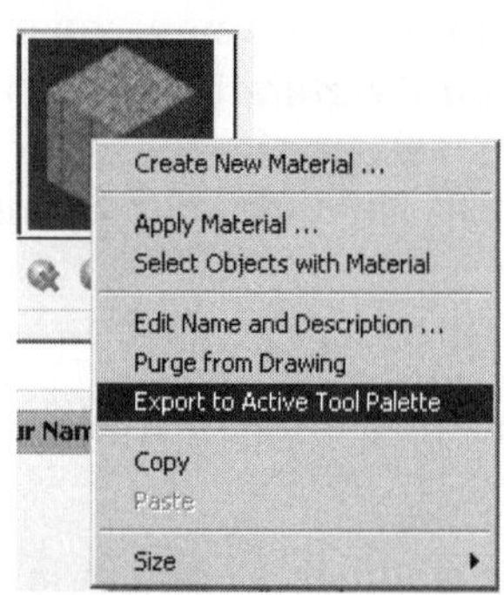

FIGURE 16–3
Add Your New Material to an Existing Palette

FIGURE 16–4
Rendered Model with Your Name 1 Material Attached

5. CLICK: the **Up One Level to Parent Map** icon (Figure 16–2).

Step 8. **Save your new material to the Masonry - Materials Sample palette and attach it to the model:**

1. RIGHT-CLICK: the **Your Name 1 material icon** and CLICK: **Export to Active Tool Palette (Figure 16–3).** (Your material is now on the Masonry palette.)
2. CLICK: **Apply material to objects** and CLICK: **the 10′ × 4′ extruded rectangle.**

Step 9. **Render the model (Figure 16–4) and save the rendering as a .jpg file in the folder where you save your work.** (CLICK: **Files of type in the Save dialog box to get the .jpg extension.)**

Step 10. **Save the drawing in at least two places.**

Tutorial 16–2: Save a Carpet Sample Image from a Manufacturer's Website and Use the Image to Make a New Material

Step 1. **Locate a carpet manufacturer's website, find the carpet sample displays,** RIGHT-CLICK **on the sample, and save it as CARPET1 in the folder where you save your work.**

Step 2. **Use your 3D workspace to make the following settings (Figure 16–10 shows the completed drawing):**

1. **Use SaveAs... to save the drawing with the name CH16-TUTORIAL2.**
2. Set drawing Units: **Architectural**
3. Set Drawing Limits: **15′,10′**
4. Set GRIDDISPLAY: **0**
5. Set Grid: **12**

6. Set Snap: **3**
7. Set a viewpoint of **SW Isometric**

Step 3. **Draw a 10′ × 4′ rectangle and extrude it 4″.**

Step 4. **Open the Flooring - Materials Sample palette.**

Step 5. **Open the Material Editor.**

Step 6. **Name the new material and select the material type:**

1. CLICK: **Create New Material:**, TYPE: **Your Name 2 in the Create New Material dialog box.**
2. CLICK: **OK.**
3. Select: **Realistic** in the Type: list box.

Step 7. **Specify the Texture map to display the carpet sample material:**

1. CLICK: **Select Image** in the Diffuse Map area. CLICK: **Carpet1.jpg** (in the folder where you saved it) **in the Select Image File dialog box.** CLICK: **Open.**
2. **Scroll to the Material Scaling and Tiling area.**
3. Change Scale units: to **Inches,** Width: to **1.0000** and **Height: to 1.0000** (Figure 16–5).

Step 8. **Save your new material to the Flooring - Materials Sample palette and attach it to the model:**

1. RIGHT-CLICK: the **Your Name 2 material icon** and CLICK: **Export to Active Tool Palette** (Figure 16–6). (Your material is now on the Flooring palette.)
2. CLICK: **Apply material to objects** and CLICK: **the 10′ × 4′ extruded rectangle.**

Step 9. **Render the model (Figure 16–7) and save the rendering as a .jpg file in the folder where you save your work. (CLICK: Files of Type in the Save dialog box to get the .jpg extension.)**

Step 10. **Save the drawing in at least two places.**

You will now have two new materials—one on the Masonry - Materials Sample palette and one on the Flooring - Materials Sample palette (Figure 16–8).

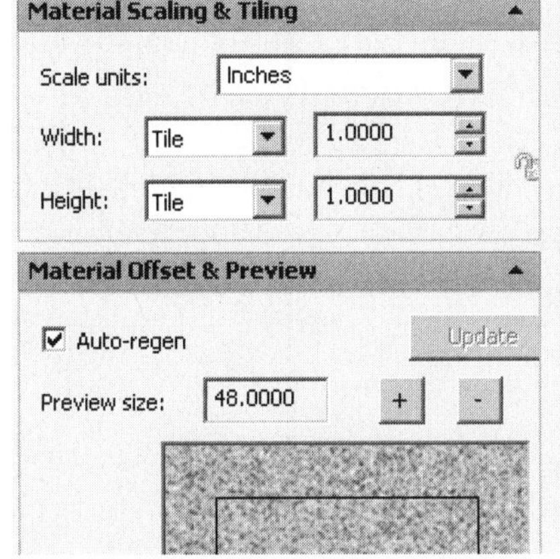

FIGURE 16–5
Select Scale Units and Set Width and Height

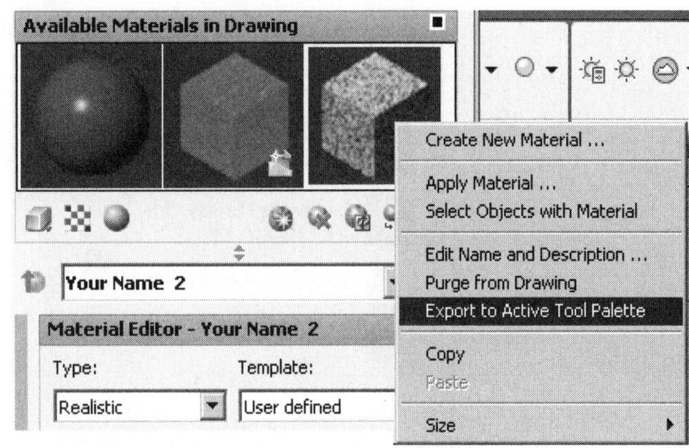

FIGURE 16–6
Save Your Name 2 Material to the Flooring Palette

FIGURE 16–7
Rendered Model with Your Name 2 Material Attached

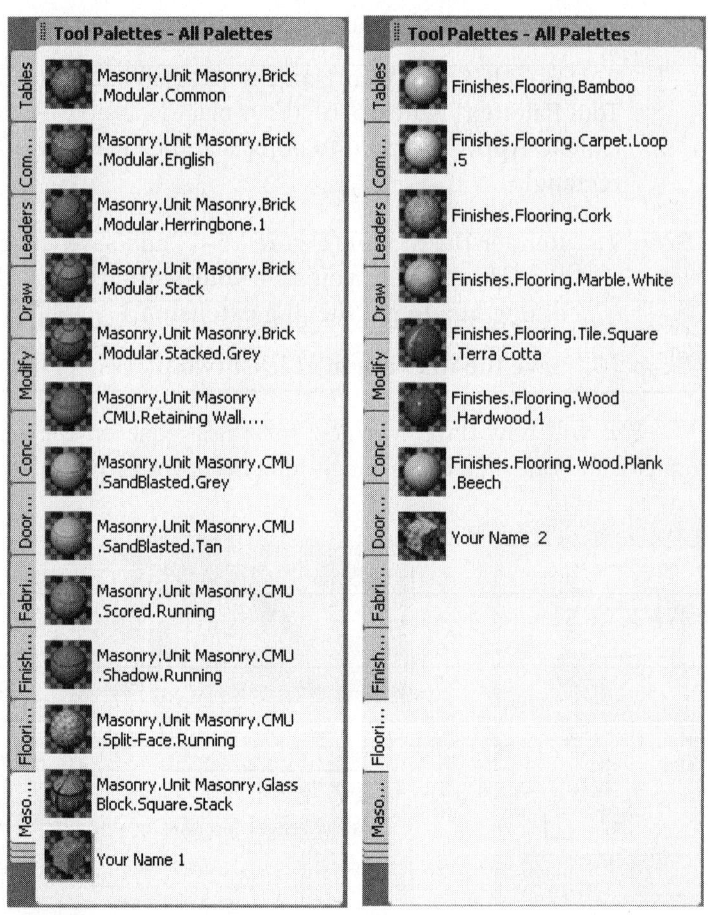

FIGURE 16–8
Your Name 1 Material on the Masonry Palette and Your Name 2 Material on the Flooring Palette

FIGURE 16–9
Advanced Render Settings Palette

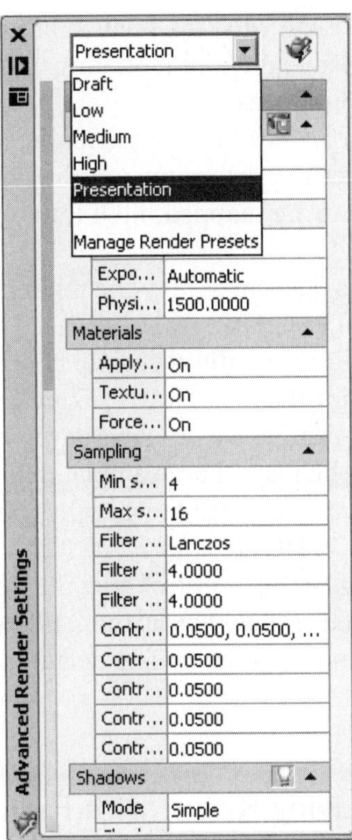

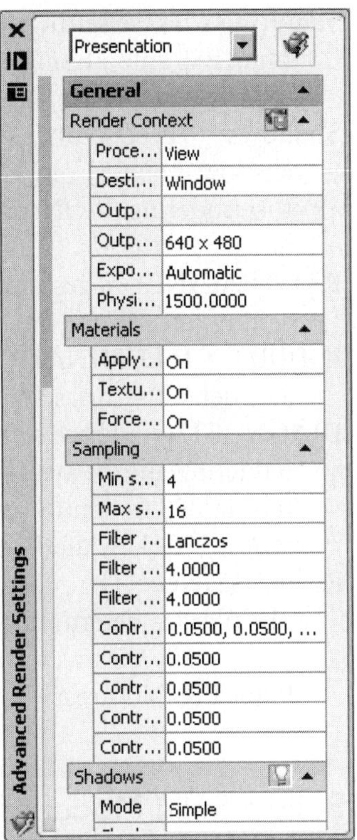

Before you begin Tutorial 16–3, examine further the details contained in the Advanced Render Settings palette. This palette controls how your solid models are rendered.

ADVANCED RENDER SETTINGS

The RPREF command opens the Advanced Render Settings palette (Figure 16–9). The palette contains five standard render presets that you can simply select and ignore the remaining categories. These are Draft, Low, Medium, High, and Presentation. Draft takes the least time to render and is the lowest quality; Presentation takes the most time and is the highest quality.

The palette is divided into five sections with settings in each section:

General

The general section is divided into four sections:

Render Context This area allows you to specify what part of the drawing you want to render: the whole view, a selected area of the view, or selected objects. This is helpful when you want to test your rendering and don't want to take the time to render an entire scene. It also can be used to specify where the rendering will be displayed: in the viewport or in the render window.

Materials The Apply material setting in this area allows you to specify whether you want to render the drawings using the materials you have attached. If you specify OFF, solid objects in the scene are rendered in the color in which they were made. If you have spent the time to attach materials, you will probably want this setting to say ON.

When the Texture filtering property is ON, there are fewer edges that will appear slightly distorted on textured materials.

When the Force 2-sided property is ON, both sides of all faces are rendered. In most cases, both of these should be ON.

Sampling These settings determine what the final color will be. Increasing the sampling will smooth out rounded edges and rendering will take longer. The default settings are OK for the sampling area.

Shadows These settings control how shadows are rendered in a scene. Turning the shadow map ON or OFF does not determine whether shadows are generated in the rendering. If ON, shadows are mapped; if OFF, they are raytraced. The default is OK.

RAY TRACING These settings determine how the rendering is shaded. The default settings are OK for the RAY TRACING area.

INDIRECT ILLUMINATION These settings control how bounced light is displayed. The default settings are OK for the RAY TRACING area.

DIAGNOSTIC These settings can be used to determine where problems exist in the rendering and how they can be fixed. For example, if your rendering is too slow, setting BPS to depth may give you a clue to what the problem is. The default settings are OK for the DIAGNOSTIC area.

PROCESSING The processing settings control how the final rendering is processed. The tile size determines into how many areas the rendered image is divided. Larger tiles usually mean shorter rendering times. The default settings are OK for the PROCESSING area.

Tutorial 16–3: Build a Solid Model of a Living Room with Furniture, Attach Materials, Add Lights, and Render It

Step 1. Use your 3D workspace to make the following settings (Figure 16–10 shows the completed drawing):

1. **Use SaveAs... to save the drawing with the name CH16-TUTORIAL3.**
2. Set drawing Units: **Architectural**
3. Set Drawing Limits: **45′,45′**

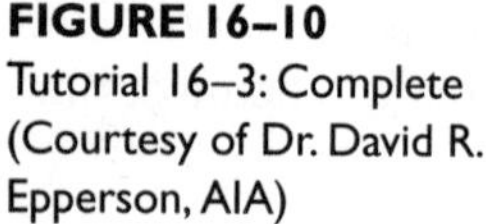
FIGURE 16–10
Tutorial 16–3: Complete (Courtesy of Dr. David R. Epperson, AIA)

4. Set GRIDDISPLAY: **0**
5. Set Grid: **12**
6. Set Snap: **3**
7. Create the following layers:

LAYER NAME	COLOR	LINETYPE
Ceiling	white	continuous
Chair	green	continuous
Coffee Table	white	continuous
Couch	green	continuous
Couch cushions-back	yellow	continuous
Door	cyan	continuous
End Table	white	continuous
Floor	white	continuous
Glass	white	continuous
Picture	cyan	continuous
Rug	magenta	continuous
Supports	green	continuous
Standing Lamp	cyan	continuous
SL Shade	magenta	continuous
Table Lamp	red	continuous
T Shade	yellow	continuous
Walls	white	continuous
Woodwork	yellow	continuous

8. Set **Layer Floor** current.

Step 2. Split the screen into two vertical viewports, and make the left viewport a plan view of the world UCS. (TYPE: **UCS <enter>**, then PRESS: **<enter>** again to accept World as the UCS, then TYPE: **PLAN<enter>**, then PRESS: **<enter>** again to get the plan view of the world UCS.) **Set the right viewport to SE Isometric.**

Step 3. Use the Rectangle and Extrude commands to draw the floor:

1. **The rectangle should measure 19′ × 21′**.
2. **Extrude the rectangle −4″** (be sure to include the minus).

Step 4. Use Rectangle, Extrude, 3D Rotate, Copy, and Union commands to draw the end table (Figure 16–11, Sheet 1):

1. **Set Layer End Table current.**
2. **Draw three 1″ × 1″ rectangles.**
3. **Extrude one 24″, another 18″, and the last one 28″.**
4. **Use 3D Rotate to rotate the extruded rectangles into position** (Figure 16–12).
5. **Copy the extruded rectangles from endpoint to endpoint to form the end table.**
6. **Use the Union command to make all extruded rectangles a single object.**
7. **Set Layer Glass current. Use the Rectangle command to draw the glass insert in the top of the end table and extrude it a negative 1/4″.**

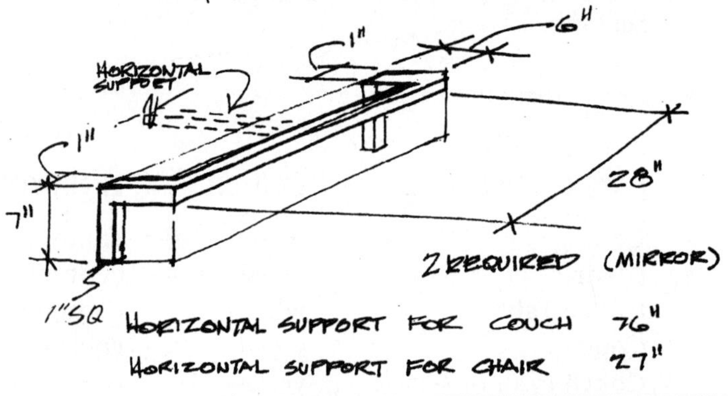

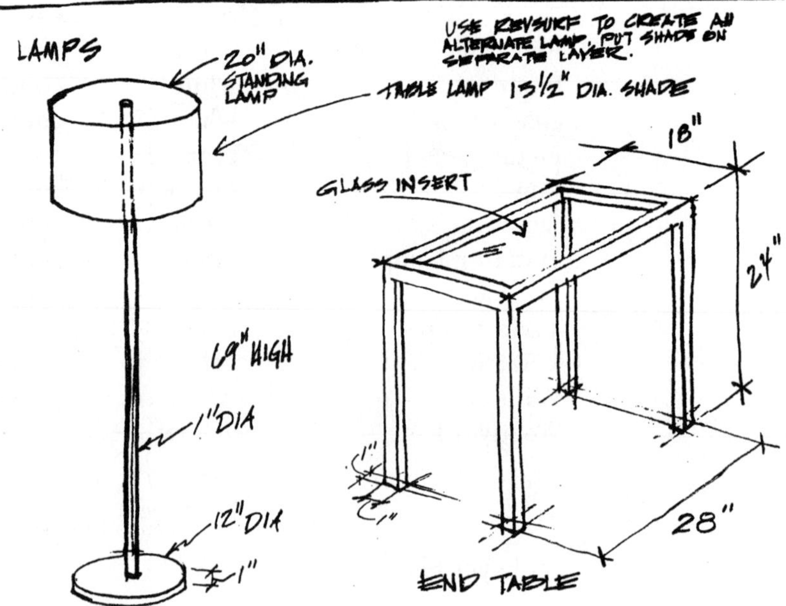

FIGURE 16–11
Sheet 1 of 2, Furniture Dimensions (Courtesy of Dr. David R. Epperson, AIA)

Step 5. Use Rectangle, Extrude, 3D Rotate, Copy, and Union commands to draw the supports for the couch and chair (Figure 16–11, Sheet 2):

1. Set Layer Supports current.
2. Draw three 1″ × 1″ rectangles.
3. Extrude one 7″, another 6″, and the last one 28″.
4. Use 3D Rotate to rotate the extruded rectangles into position (Figure 16–13).
5. Copy the extruded rectangles from endpoint to endpoint to form the support.
6. Draw two more 1″ × 1″ rectangles and extrude one 76″, the other 27″.
7. Use 3D Rotate to rotate the extruded rectangles into position, and use Move to move those rectangles from midpoint to midpoint (Figure 16–14).
8. Use Mirror to copy the supports to the other end of the 76″ and 27″ extruded rectangles (Figure 16–14).
9. Use the Union command to make all extruded rectangles for the couch a single object, and all the extruded rectangles for the chair another single object.

FIGURE 16–11
Sheet 2 of 2, Furniture Dimensions (Courtesy of Dr. David R. Epperson, AIA)

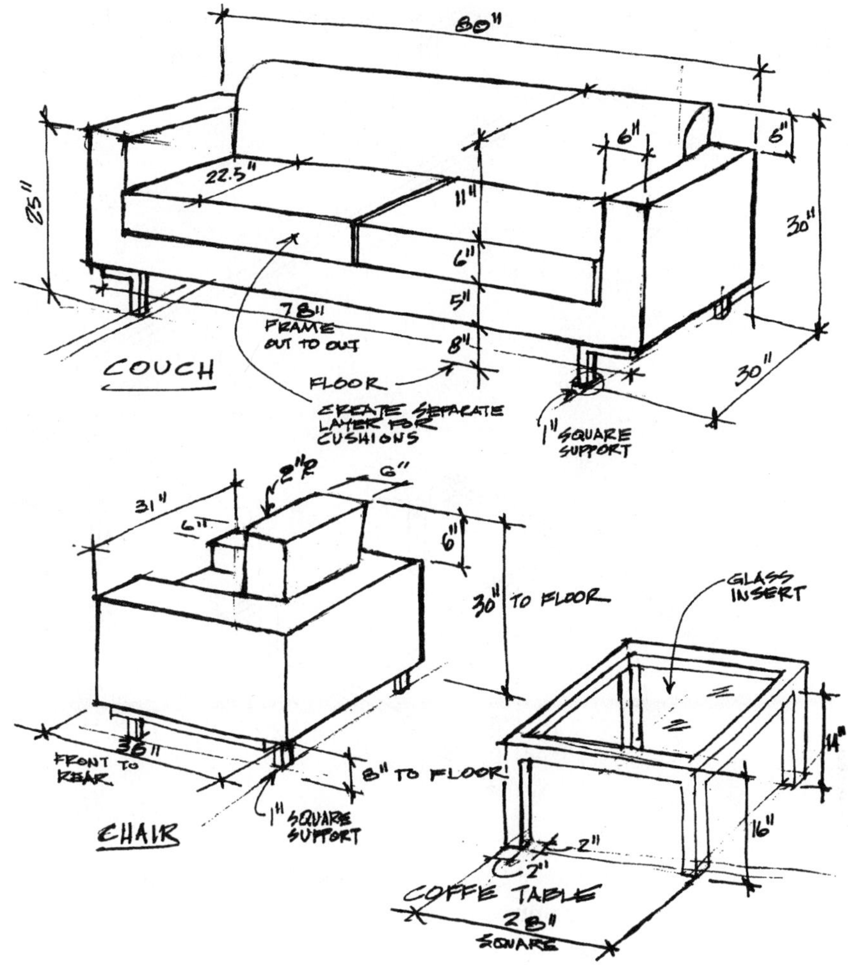

Step 6. Use the dimensions from the sketch, Figure 16–11, Sheet 2, to make the solid model of the couch and place it on the couch support:

1. Set Layer Couch current, rotate the UCS 90° about the X axis, and draw the U shape of the couch base and arms.
2. Extrude the U shape 30″.

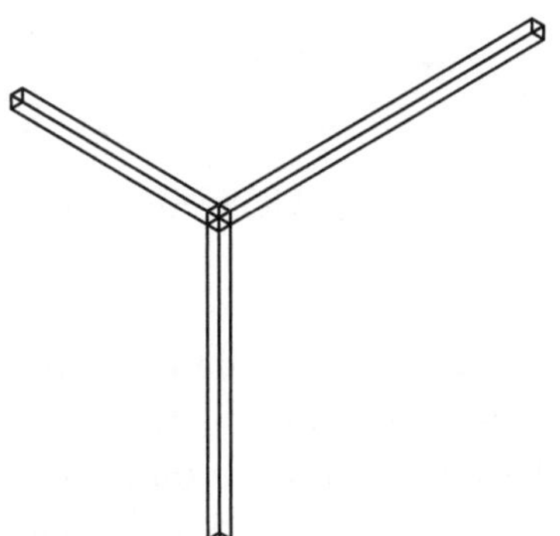

FIGURE 16–12
Use 3D Rotate to Rotate Extruded Rectangles to Form the End Table

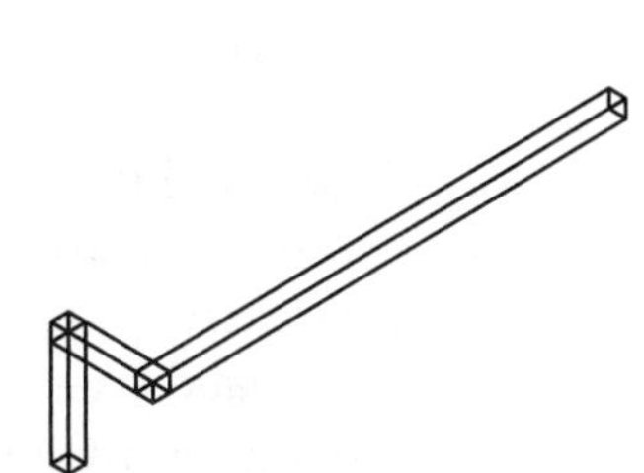

FIGURE 16–13
Use 3D Rotate to Rotate Extruded Rectangles to Form the Support

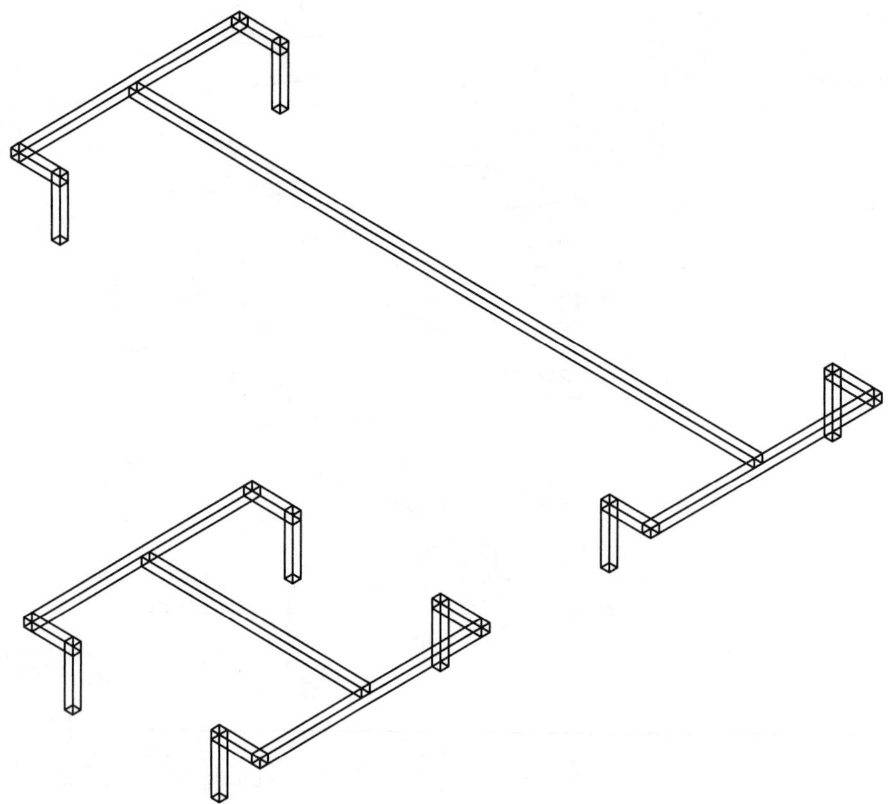

FIGURE 16–14
Rotate Horizontal Supports and Mirror Supports to the Other End

3. Set Layer Couch cushions - back current and draw the cushions using the Box command, or draw a rectangle and extrude it.
4. Rotate the UCS 90° about the Y axis, draw the back, and extrude it 68″. Return to the World UCS.
5. Move all parts of the couch (Figure 16–15), so they fit together to form a couch as shown in the sketch. Use Osnap-Endpoint to select base points and second points of displacement.
6. Use ViewCube to change the 3D view to Front, then Right (Figure 16–16), and determine whether the couch must be moved to the right or left to center it on the supports. Be sure ORTHO is ON when you move the couch, and do not use Osnap so you can be sure the couch is moved correctly.
7. Return the model to a SE Isometric view and use the Hide command to be sure the view is as it should be.

Step 7. Use the dimensions from the sketch, Figure 16–11, Sheet 2, to make the solid model of the chair and place it on the chair support:

1. Set Layer Chair current, rotate the UCS 90° about the X axis, and draw the U shape of the chair base and arms.
2. Extrude the U shape 36″.
3. Draw the cushion and the back using the Box command, or draw rectangles and extrude them. Use the Union command to make one object of the back, arms, and base. Do not include the cushion in the union.
4. Rotate the UCS 90° about the Y axis, draw the back cushion, and extrude it 19″. Return to the World UCS.
5. Move all parts of the chair (Figure 16–17), so they fit together to form a chair as shown in the sketch. Use Osnap-Endpoint to select base points and second points of displacement.

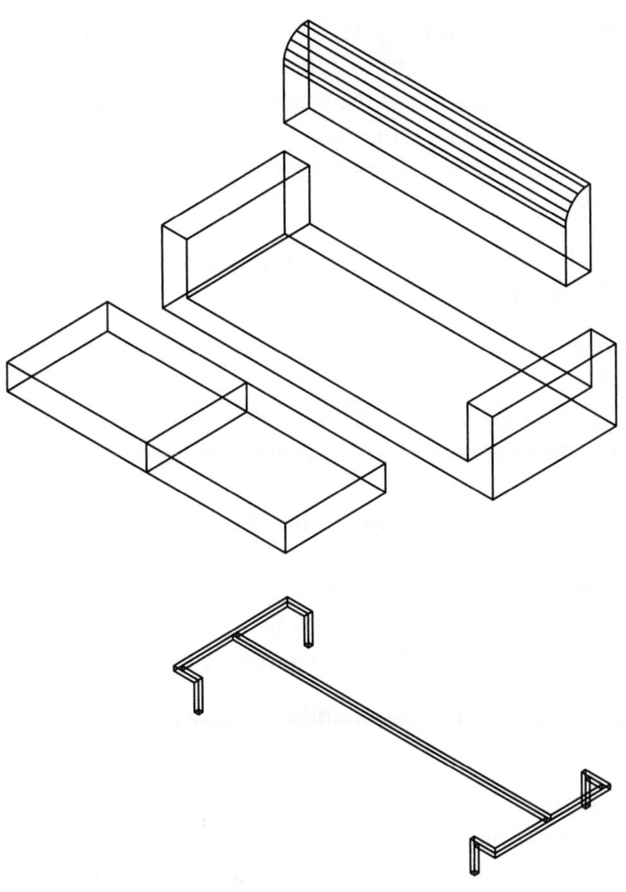

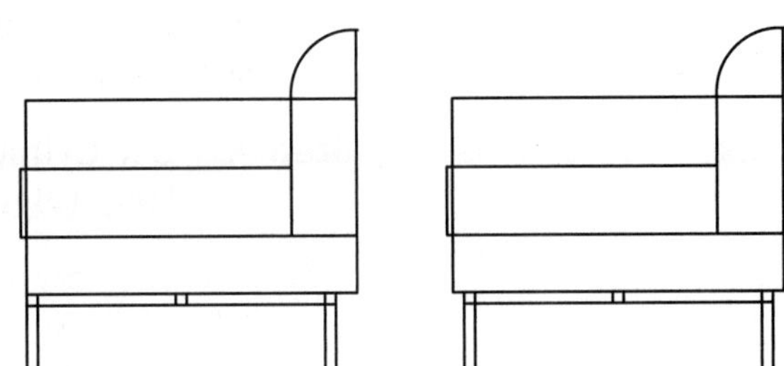

FIGURE 16–15
Pieces of the Couch

FIGURE 16–16
Move Couch So It Is Centered on the Supports

FIGURE 16–17
Pieces of the Chair

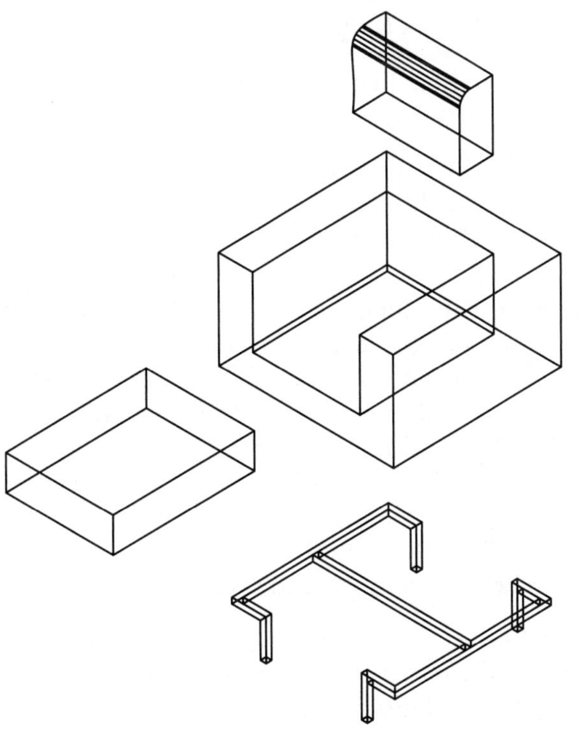

6. Change the 3D view to Front, then Right (Figure 16–16), and determine whether the chair must be moved to the right or left to center it on the supports. Be sure ORTHO is ON when you move the chair, and do not use Osnap so you can be sure the chair is moved correctly.
7. Return the model to a SE Isometric view and use the Hide command to be sure the view is as it should be.

Step 8. Use Rectangle, Extrude, 3D Rotate, Copy, and Union commands to draw the coffee table (Figure 16–11, Sheet 2):

1. Set Layer Coffee Table current.
2. Draw three 2″ × 2″ rectangles.
3. Extrude one 16″, another 28″, and the last one 28″.
4. Use 3D Rotate to rotate the extruded rectangles into position as you did for the end table.
5. Copy the extruded rectangles from endpoint to endpoint to form the coffee table.
6. Use the Union command to make all extruded rectangles a single object.
7. Set Layer Glass current. Use the Rectangle command to draw the glass insert in the top of the coffee table and extrude it a negative 1/4″.

Step 9. Use Cylinder, Rectangle, and Revolve commands to draw the floor lamp (Figure 16–11, Sheet 1):

1. Set Layer Standing Lamp current.
2. With UCS set to World, draw a cylinder, 6″ radius and 1″ high.
3. In the same center, draw another cylinder, 1/2″ radius and 69″ high.
4. Use the Union command to make the two cylinders a single object.
5. Set UCS to World, then rotate the UCS 90° about the X axis.
6. Set Layer SL Shade current.
7. Draw a line from D1 to D2 (Figure 16–18), 9-3/4″ long.
8. From D2, draw a 1/4″ × 12″ rectangle and rotate it −15°.
9. Use the Revolve command to revolve the rectangle 360° around the 1/2″ cylinder to form a lamp shade.

Step 10. Use Polyline, Rectangle, and Revolve commands to draw the table lamp (Figure 16–19):

1. Set Layer Table Lamp current.
2. Set UCS to World, then rotate the UCS 90° about the X axis in the left viewport and TYPE: PLAN<enter><enter> to see the plan view of the current UCS.
3. Use the Polyline command to draw the lamp without the shade. Draw the straight lines first and end the command, then draw short polylines to draw the curved line and end the command. Use Polyline Edit to smooth the curve and join all polylines into a single polyline.
4. Draw a 1/4″ × 12″ rectangle that is 4″ up and 4-1/2″ to the left of the lamp, as shown in Figure 16–19. Then, rotate the rectangle −15°.
5. Use the Revolve command to revolve the polyline 360° to form the lamp.
6. Set Layer T Shade current.
7. Use the Revolve command to revolve the rectangle 360° to form the lamp shade.

Step 11. Copy the chairs and end tables, and place furniture in the room, as shown in Figure 16–20.

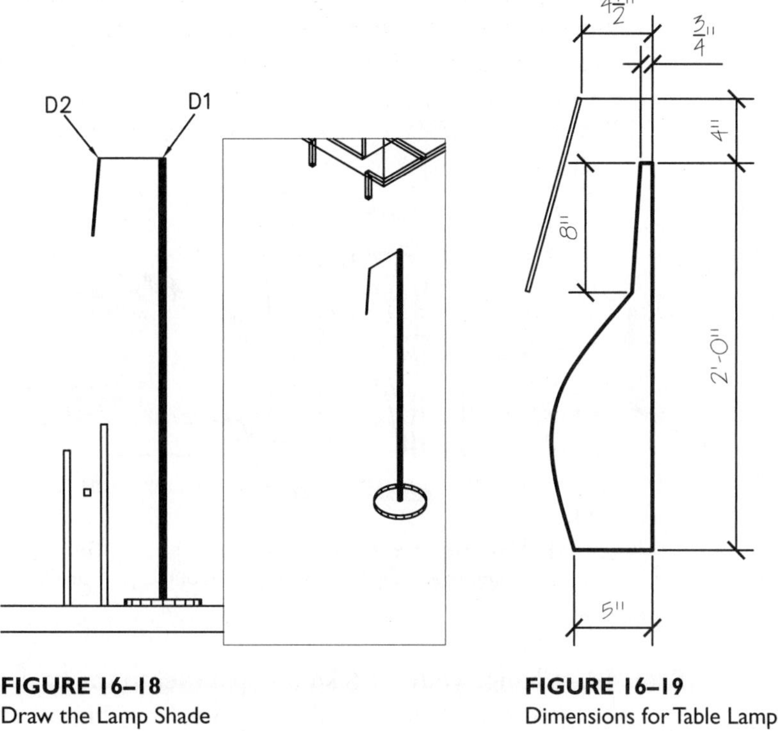

FIGURE 16–18
Draw the Lamp Shade

FIGURE 16–19
Dimensions for Table Lamps

Step 12. Set Layer Rug current. Use the Rectangle command to draw an 8′-0″ × 11′-0″ rug centered on the floor beneath the couch and chairs, and extrude it 1″.

Step 13. Use the Polysolid command (6″ width, 8′4″ height) to draw the back wall by selecting the endpoints of the back of the floor, then move the wall down 4″.

FIGURE 16–20
Copy and Place Furniture

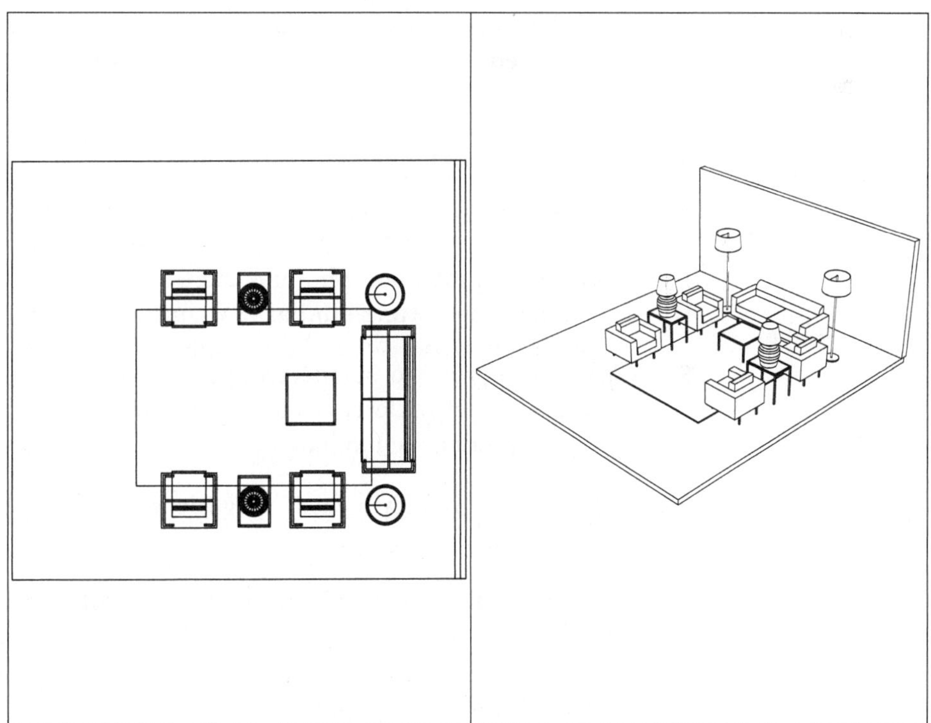

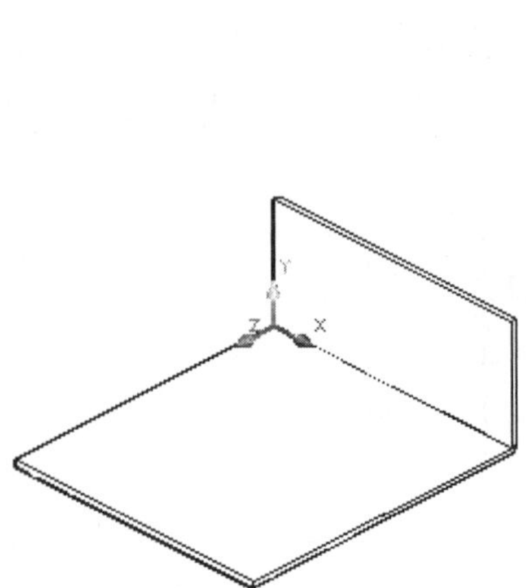

FIGURE 16–21
UCS Parallel to Back Wall

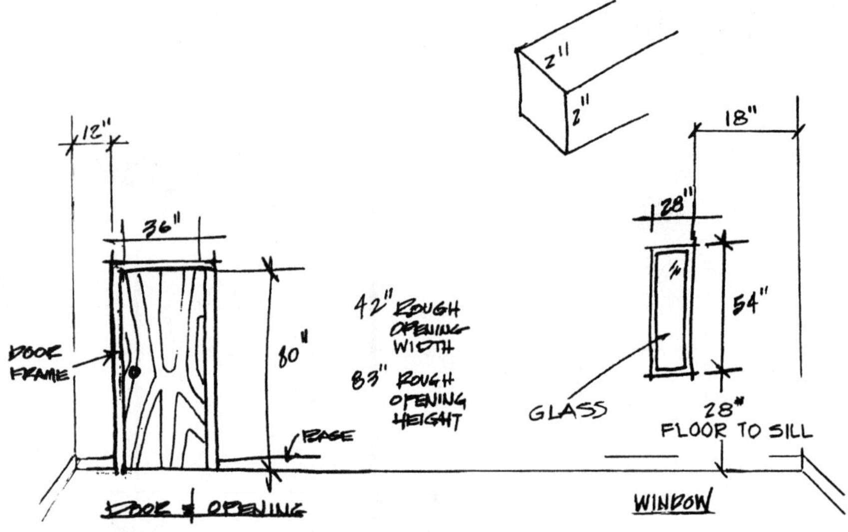

FIGURE 16–22
Window and Door Dimensions (Courtesy of Dr. David R. Epperson, AIA)

Step 14. Change your UCS so it is parallel to the back wall as shown in Figure 16–21, and use the dimensions from Figure 16–22 to make openings in the back wall for the window and the door.

Step 15. Turn off all furniture layers if necessary so you can draw more easily.

Step 16. Use the Polysolid command (6″ width, 8′4″ height) to draw the side walls, move them down 4″, then move them to the outside of the floor (3″ to the right or left so they lie on the edge of the floor).

Step 17. Draw windows (2″ × 2″ sill and a rectangle for glass on the inside of the sill extruded 1/2″), doors (3″ jamb and header extruded 7″ and moved so they extend 1/2″ from the wall), and baseboards (make the baseboards 4″ × 1″).

Step 18. Draw the ceiling and extrude it 4″.

Step 19. Attach appropriate materials to all objects.

Step 20. Place point, spot, photometric, and distant lights in locations to obtain a lighting pattern similar to Figure 16–10.

Step 21. Set the view to Perspective projection with a view similar to Figure 16–23, set preferences using the Advanced Render Settings dialog box, and render the model.

Step 22. Save the rendering as a .jpeg file and insert it into paper space (Layout1).

Step 23. Put your name on the drawing and plot it to fit on a 11″ × 8-1/2″ sheet.

Step 24. Save the drawing in two places.

FIGURE 16–23
Perspective View

review questions

1. Which command in the Materials Editor do you select to begin making a new material?
   a. Start New Material
   b. Create New Material
   c. Apply Material to Objects
   d. Indicate Material in Use
   e. Name the New Material
2. The diffuse color for a new material is assigned to which of the following?
   a. Faces lit by ambient light only
   b. Highlights on shiny materials
   c. The material
   d. All maps
   e. Realistic types only
3. The ambient color for a new material is assigned to which of the following?
   a. Faces lit by ambient light only
   b. Highlights on shiny material
   c. The material
   d. All maps
   e. Realistic types only
4. The specular color for a new material is assigned to which of the following?
   a. Faces lit by ambient light only
   b. Highlights on shiny materials
   c. The material
   d. All maps
   e. Realistic types only
5. Some maps can be scaled or fit to the object.
   a. True
   b. False

6. Which of the following is used to save a new material to an open palette?
   a. Save to open palette
   b. Open Active Palette
   c. Export to Active Tool Palette
   d. Save New Material
   e. Export Material
7. When a new material is started and the Realistic type is specified, which of the following must be selected in the diffuse map area to find a saved image?
   a. Select Image
   b. Select Map
   c. Specify Image
   d. Search for Image
   e. Search Image
8. Which of the following opens the Advanced Render Settings palette?
   a. ARS
   b. Render
   c. Render Pref
   d. RPREF
   e. Pref
9. In which section of the Advanced Render Settings palette is the Apply material setting located?
   a. General
   b. Ray Tracing
   c. Indirect Illumination
   d. Diagnostic
   e. Processing
10. In which section of the Advanced Render Settings palette is the Tile size setting located?
    a. General
    b. Ray Tracing
    c. Indirect Illumination
    d. Diagnostic
    e. Processing

Complete.

11. List the five standard render presets shown in the Advanced Render Settings palette.

    ________ ________ ________ ________ ________

12. List the five sections in the Advanced Render Settings palette.

    ________________ ________________ ________________

    ________________ ________________

13. Describe what the Sampling settings are used for in the Advanced Render Settings palette.

    ____

14. Describe what the Diagnostic settings are used for in the Advanced Render Settings palette.

    ____

15. Describe what the Indirect Illumination settings are used for in the Advanced Render Settings palette.

    ____

exercises

Exercise 16–1: Make a Solid Model of the Chair Shown in the Sketch. Use Render Commands to Make a Photo-Realistic Rendering of the Solid Model

1. Draw a solid model of the chair shown in Figure 16–24.
2. Attach appropriate materials to the legs, back, and seat. Use one material for the legs and another for the back and seat.
3. Position distant, point, or spotlights to illuminate the chair. Adjust the sunlight so the chair shows well.
4. Change the view to Perspective projection.
5. Use the Render command to render the scene in a single viewport.
6. Print the rendered drawing centered on an 11″ × 8-1/2″ sheet.

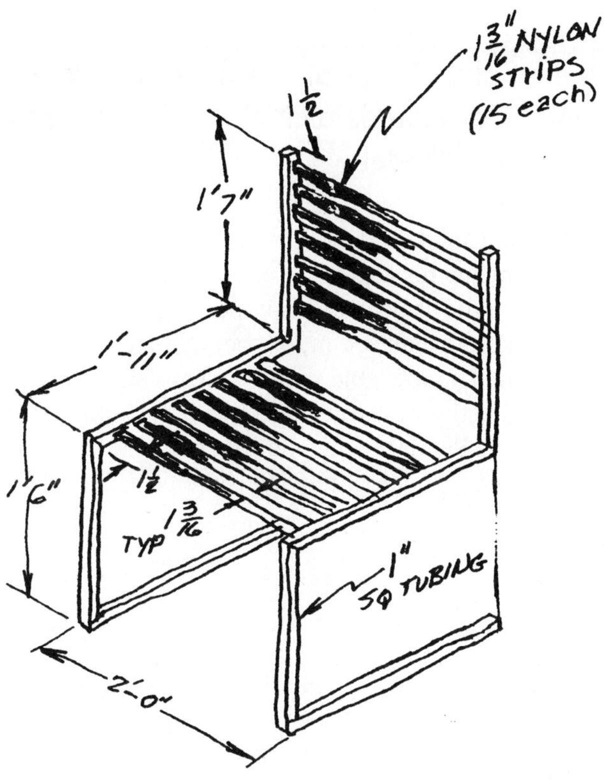

FIGURE 16–24
Exercise 16–1: Chair

Exercise 16–2: Make a Solid Model of the Picnic Table Shown in the Sketch. Use Render Commands to Make a Photo-Realistic Rendering of the Solid Model

1. Draw a solid model of the picnic table shown in Figure 16–25.
2. Attach the same wooden-appearing material to the entire drawing.
3. Position distant, point, or spotlights to illuminate the picnic table. Adjust the sunlight so the picnic table shows well.

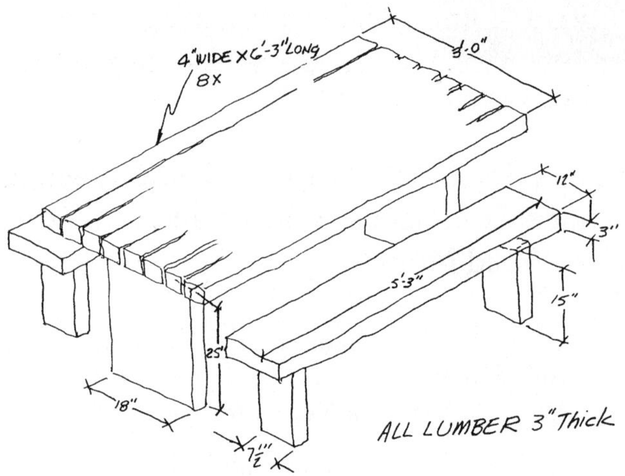

FIGURE 16–25
Exercise 16–2: Picnic Table

4. Change the view to Perspective projection.
5. Use the Render command to render the scene in a single viewport.
6. Print the rendered drawing centered on an 11″ × 8-1/2″ sheet.

Exercise 16–3: Make a Solid Model of the Table Shown in the Sketch. Use Render Commands to Make a Photo-Realistic Rendering of the Solid Model

1. Draw a solid model of the table shown in Figure 16–26. Estimate any measurements not shown.
2. Attach the same wooden-appearing material to the entire drawing.
3. Position distant, point, or spotlights to illuminate the table. Adjust the sunlight so the table shows well.
4. Change the view to Perspective projection.
5. Use the Render command to render the scene in a single viewport.
6. Print the rendered drawing centered on an 11″ × 8-1/2″ sheet.

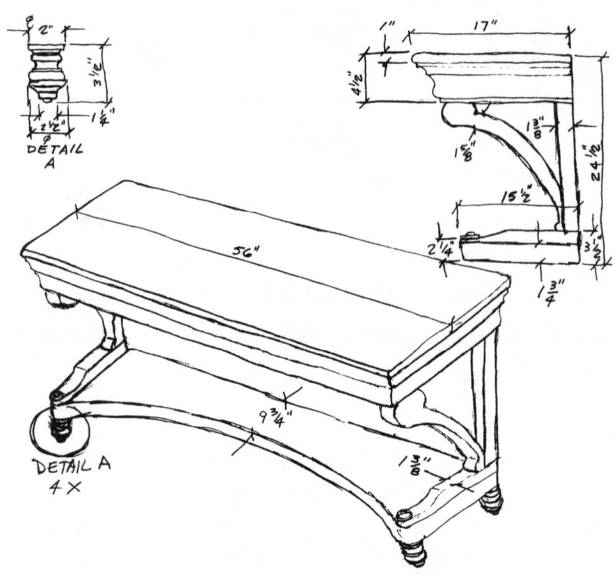

FIGURE 16–26
Exercise 16–3: Table

Exercise 16–4: Make a Solid Model of the Lounge Shown in the Sketch. Use Render Commands to Make a Photo-Realistic Rendering of the Solid Model

1. Draw a solid model of the lounge shown in Figure 16–27. Estimate any measurements not shown.
2. Attach appropriate materials to the tubing and pad. Use one material for the legs and another for the pad.
3. Position distant, point, or spotlights to illuminate the lounge. Adjust the sunlight so the lounge shows well.
4. Change the view to Perspective projection.
5. Use the Render command to render the scene in a single viewport.
6. Print the rendered drawing centered on an 11″ × 8-1/2″ sheet.

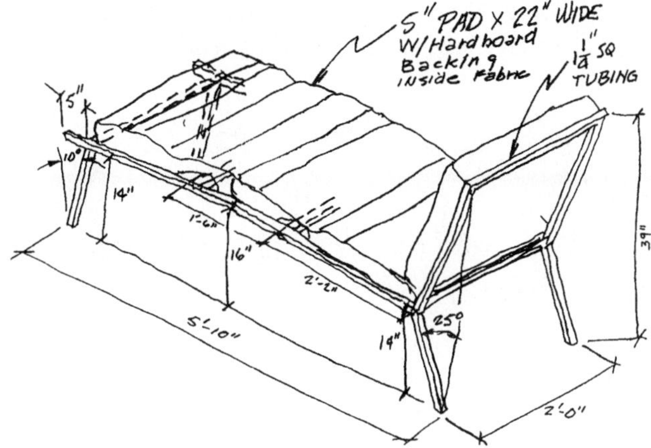

FIGURE 16–27
Exercise 16–4: Lounge

appendix

Keyboard Shortcuts

This appendix contains the AutoCAD command aliases (also called keyboard macros) that you can type to activate a command. Aliases and commands with a minus sign before the letters do not display a dialog box but instead show prompts at the command line.

Alias	Command
3A	3DARRAY
3DMIRROR	MIRROR3D
3DNavigate	3DWALK
3DO	3DORBIT
3DP	3DPRINT
3DPLOT	3DPRINT
3DW	3DWALK
3F	3DFACE
3M	3DMOVE
3P	3DPOLY
3R	3DROTATE
3S	3DSCALE
A	ARC
AC	BACTION
ADC	ADCENTER
AECTOACAD	-ExportToAutoCAD
AA	AREA
AL	ALIGN
3AL	3DALIGN
AP	APPLOAD
APLAY	ALLPLAY
AR	ARRAY
-AR	-ARRAY
ARR	ACTRECORD
ARM	ACTUSERMESSAGE
-ARM	-ACTUSERMESSAGE
ARU	ACTUSERINPUT
ARS	ACTSTOP
-ARS	-ACTSTOP
ATI	ATTIPEDIT
ATT	ATTDEF
-ATT	-ATTDEF
ATE	ATTEDIT
-ATE	-ATTEDIT
ATTE	-ATTEDIT
B	BLOCK
-B	-BLOCK
BC	BCLOSE
BE	BEDIT
BH	HATCH
BO	BOUNDARY
-BO	-BOUNDARY
BR	BREAK
BS	BSAVE
BVS	BVSTATE
C	CIRCLE
CAM	CAMERA
CBAR	CONSTRAINTBAR
CH	PROPERTIES
-CH	CHANGE

Alias	Command
CHA	CHAMFER
CHK	CHECKSTANDARDS
CLI	COMMANDLINE
COL	COLOR
COLOUR	COLOR
CO, or CP	COPY
CPARAM	BCPARAMETER
CREASE	MESHCREASE
CSETTINGS	CONSTRAINTSETTINGS
CT	CTABLESTYLE
CUBE	NAVVCUBE
CYL	CYLINDER
D	DIMSTYLE
DAL	DIMALIGNED
DAN	DIMANGULAR
DAR	DIMARC
JOG	DIMJOGGED
DBA	DIMBASELINE
DBC	DBCONNECT
DC	ADCENTER
DCE	DIMCENTER
DCENTER	ADCENTER
DCO	DIMCONTINUE
DCON	DIMCONSTRAINT
DDA	DIMDISASSOCIATE
DDI	DIMDIAMETER
DED	DIMEDIT
DELCON	DELCONSTRAINT
DI	DIST
DIV	DIVIDE
DJL	DIMJOGLINE
DJO	DIMJOGGED
DL	DATALINK
DLI	DIMLINEAR
DLU	DATALINKUPDATE
DO	DONUT
DOR	DIMORDINATE
DOV	DIMOVERRIDE
DR	DRAWORDER
DRA	DIMRADIUS
DRE	DIMREASSOCIATE
DRM	DRAWINGRECOVERY
DS	DSETTINGS
DST	DIMSTYLE
DT	TEXT
DV	DVIEW
DX	DATAEXTRACTION
E	ERASE
ED	DDEDIT
EL	ELLIPSE

Alias	Command	Alias	Command
ER	EXTERNALREFERENCES	-LT	-LINETYPE
ESHOT	EDITSHOT	LTYPE	LINETYPE
EX	EXTEND	-LTYPE	-LINETYPE
EXIT	QUIT	LTS	LTSCALE
EXP	EXPORT	LW	LWEIGHT
EXT	EXTRUDE	M	MOVE
F	FILLET	MA	MATCHPROP
FI	FILTER	MAT	MATERIALS
FREEPOINT	POINTLIGHT	ME	MEASURE
FSHOT	FLATSHOT	MEA	MEASUREGEOM
G	GROUP	MI	MIRROR
-G	-GROUP	ML	MLINE
GCON	GEOMCONSTRAINT	MLA	MLEADERALIGN
GD	GRADIENT	MLC	MLEADERCOLLECT
GEO	GEOGRAPHICLOCATION	MLD	MLEADER
GR	DDGRIPS	MLE	MLEADEREDIT
H	HATCH	MLS	MLEADERSTYLE
-H	-HATCH	MO	PROPERTIES
HE	HATCHEDIT	MORE	MESHSMOOTHMORE
HI	HIDE	MOTION	NAVSMOTION
I	INSERT	MOTIONCLS	NAVSMOTIONCLOSE
-I	-INSERT	MS	MSPACE
IAD	IMAGEADJUST	MSM	MARKUP
IAT	IMAGEATTACH	MT	MTEXT
ICL	IMAGECLIP	MV	MVIEW
IM	IMAGE	NORTH	GEOGRAPHICLOCATION
-IM	-IMAGE	NORTHDIR	GEOGRAPHICLOCATION
IMP	IMPORT	NSHOT	NEWSHOT
IN	INTERSECT	NVIEW	NEWVIEW
INF	INTERFERE	O	OFFSET
IO	INSERTOBJ	OP	OPTIONS
QVD	QVDRAWING	ORBIT	3DORBIT
QVDC	QVDRAWINGCLOSE	OS	OSNAP
QVL	QVLAYOUT	-OS	-OSNAP
QVLC	QVLAYOUTCLOSE	P	PAN
J	JOIN	-P	-PAN
JOGSECTION	SECTIONPLANEJOG	PA	PASTESPEC
L	LINE	RAPIDPROTOTYPE	3DPRINT
LA	LAYER	PAR	PARAMETERS
-LA	-LAYER	-PAR	-PARAMETERS
LAS	LAYERSTATE	PARAM	BPARAMETER
LE	QLEADER	PARTIALOPEN	-PARTIALOPEN
LEN	LENGTHEN	PE	PEDIT
LESS	MESHSMOOTHLESS	PL	PLINE
LI	LIST	PO	POINT
LINEWEIGHT	LWEIGHT	POFF	HIDEPALETTES
LMAN	LAYERSTATE	POL	POLYGON
LO	-LAYOUT	PON	SHOWPALETTES
LS	LIST	PR	PROPERTIES
LT	LINETYPE	PRCLOSE	PROPERTIESCLOSE

Alias	Command
PROPS	PROPERTIES
PRE	PREVIEW
PRINT	PLOT
PS	PSPACE
PSOLID	POLYSOLID
PTW	PUBLISHTOWEB
PU	PURGE
-PU	-PURGE
PYR	PYRAMID
QC	QUICKCALC
QCUI	QUICKCUI
R	REDRAW
RA	REDRAWALL
RC	RENDERCROP
RE	REGEN
REA	REGENALL
REC	RECTANG
REFINE	MESHREFINE
REG	REGION
REN	RENAME
-REN	-RENAME
REV	REVOLVE
RO	ROTATE
RP	RENDERPRESETS
RPR	RPREF
RR	RENDER
RW	RENDERWIN
S	STRETCH
SC	SCALE
SCR	SCRIPT
SE	DSETTINGS
SEC	SECTION
SET	SETVAR
SHA	SHADEMODE
SL	SLICE
SMOOTH	MESHSMOOTH
SN	SNAP
SO	SOLID
SP	SPELL
SPL	SPLINE
SPLANE	SECTIONPLANE
SPLAY	SEQUENCEPLAY
SPLIT	MESHSPLIT
SPE	SPLINEDIT

Alias	Command
SSM	SHEETSET
ST	STYLE
STA	STANDARDS
SU	SUBTRACT
T	MTEXT
-T	-MTEXT
TA	TABLET
TB	TABLE
TEDIT	TEXTEDIT
TH	THICKNESS
TI	TILEMODE
TO	TOOLBAR
TOL	TOLERANCE
TOR	TORUS
TP	TOOLPALETTES
TR	TRIM
TS	TABLESTYLE
UC	UCSMAN
UN	UNITS
-UN	-UNITS
UNCREASE	MESHUNCREASE
UNI	UNION
V	VIEW
VGO	VIEWGO
VPLAY	VIEWPLAY
-V	-VIEW
VP	DDVPOINT
-VP	VPOINT
VS	VSCURRENT
VSM	VISUALSTYLES
-VSM	-VISUALSTYLES
W	WBLOCK
-W	-WBLOCK
WE	WEDGE
WHEEL	NAVSWHEEL
X	EXPLODE
XA	XATTACH
XB	XBIND
-XB	-XBIND
XC	XCLIP
XL	XLINE
XR	XREF
-XR	-XREF
Z	ZOOM

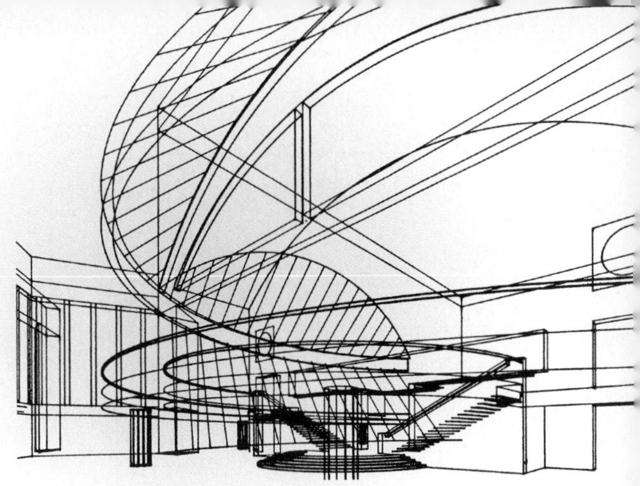

appendix

B

Shortcut and Temporary Override Keys

This appendix contains a listing of the combination of keys that can be used to perform the described actions. For example, a shortcut key shown as Ctrl+1 requires you to hold down the Ctrl key and press the 1 key while you continue to hold down the Ctrl key. This combination will display the Properties palette if it is not displayed or turn off the Properties palette if it is displayed.

F1 through F12 keys are not used in combination with other keys to perform the stated functions. Just press the key.

CTRL+A	Select All
CTRL+C	Copy to the Windows Clipboard
CTRL+D	Turns On and Off Dynamic UCS (DUCS)
CTRL+E	Cycles through isoplanes in isometric drawing
CTRL+F	Turns OSNAP On and Off
CTRL+G	Turns the GRID On and Off
CTRL+H	Toggles PICKSTYLE
CTRL+I	Turns Coordinates On and Off
CTRL+J	Repeats the last command
CTRL+K	Inserts a hyperlink
CTRL+L	Turns ORTHO On and Off
CTRL+N	Starts a new drawing
CTRL+O	Opens existing drawings
CTRL+P	Plots or Prints the current drawing
CTRL+Q	Exit the AutoCAD program
CTRL+R	Cycles through the viewports on the current layout
CTRL+S	Saves the current drawing
CTRL+T	Turns the TABLET On and Off
CTRL+V	Paste from the Windows Clipboard
CTRL+X	Cut to the Windows Clipboard
CTRL+Y	Redo
CTRL+Z	Undo
CTRL+SHIFT+C	Copy with Base Point
CTRL+SHIFT+S	Save As...
CTRL+SHIFT+V	Paste as Block
CTRL+SHIFT+P	Turns On and Off Quick Properties
CTRL+0	Toggles Clean Screen
CTRL+1	Displays and closes the Properties Palette
CTRL+2	Displays and closes the DesignCenter
CTRL+3	Displays and closes the Tool Palettes
CTRL+4	Displays and closes the Sheet Set Manager
CTRL+6	Displays and closes the dbConnect Manager
CTRL+7	Displays and closes the Markup Set Manager
CTRL+8	Displays and closes the QuickCalculator
CTRL+9	Displays and closes the Command Line
F1	Displays and closes Help
F2	Displays and closes the Text window
F3	Turns OSNAP On and Off
F4	Turns the TABLET On and Off
F5	Cycles through isoplanes in isometric drawing
F6	Turns Dynamic UCS On and Off (DUCS)
F7	Turns the GRID On and Off
F8	Turns ORTHO On and Off
F9	Turns SNAP On and Off
F10	Turns POLAR On and Off
F11	Turns OTRACK On and Off
F 12	Suppresses Dynamic Input(DYN)

appendix C

Floor Plans and Interior Elevations of a 15-Unit Condominium Building

The floor plans and interior elevations can be found as Figures C-1 through C-10, which are placed at the end of the book following the index.

All figures in Appendix C are courtesy of:

Kelly McCarthy
McCarthy Architecture
620 Main Street, Suite 100
Garland, Texas 75040

Figures C–1 and C–2

Figure C–1 is a floor plan of the first floor of the entire building. Notice that individual condos are labeled as Unit Types A through E. Unit E has a lower floor and an upper floor with an interior circular stairway. All other units are on either the lower floor or the upper floor. Notice that there are several Type A and Type B units on both floors. There are four stairways shown. These stairways lead to the second floor and are shown on both the first and second floor.

Figure C–2 is a floor plan of the second floor of the entire building. Here again the individual units are numbered as Type A through E units. Unit E shows the circular stairway leading to the lower floor. The second floor is almost identical to the first floor, with the exception of Unit E and the areas lying outside the dashed lines.

Figures C–3 Through C–8

Figures C3 through C–8 are floor plans of the individual condos. Units on the first floor have a patio next to the storage area. Units on the second floor have a balcony next to the storage area.

Figures C7 and C8 are the lower and upper floors of the Type E unit.

These figures can be assigned as a project, with individual units drawn and attached as external references to the floor plans of the upper and lower floors of the entire building.

Figures C–9 and C–10

These figures show typical interior elevations of all the units. Many of the items are blocks that can be obtained from Autodesk Seek in the DesignCenter. The circular stairway shown as Item 31 in Figure C–10 is such a block.

Index

A

Absolute coordinates, 39, 40
Add Color-Dependent Plot Style Table, 176–78
Add selection, 52
Advanced render settings, 621–25, 639, 640
Align columns, 392
Align command, 533
All Selection, 52
Animation, play, 629
Animation settings dialog box, 627, 628
Annotation Scale, 34
Annotative Attributes, 374
Annotative Dimensioning, 263, 264
Annotative Hatch, 337
Annotative Multileader, 321, 322
Annotative Text, 228, 229
Aperture size, 103, 104
Apparent intersection Osnap mode, 102
Application menu button, 3, 4
Arc, polyline, 117, 118
Arc command, 55–57
Area command, 281–84
Array command:
  Polar, 120
  Rectangular, 111, 112, 202–04
Attribute, 371–88
  Annotative, 374
  ATTDEF (attribute definition), 371–78
  ATTDIA (system variable), 380
  ATTDISP (attribute display), 385
  ATTEDIT (edit attribute), 383, 384
  Attribute, Global (edit), 383
  Attribute, Single (edit), 382, 383
  ATTSYNC (synchronize attributes), 386
  BATTMAN (block attribute manager), 386
  Data Extraction, 388–92
  EATTEDIT (enhanced attribute edit), 382, 383
  Edit Text (DDEDIT) command, 379
AutoCAD:
  Beginning a drawing, 18, 19
  close, 13
  screen, 2–11
Autodesk Seek, 236, 238, 411
AutoStack Properties dialog box, 148
AVI file, 625–30
Axonometric drawing, 485, 486

B

Background, 622, 623
Backup files, 21, 22
.bak, 21, 22
Blipmode command, 48
Blips, removing, 48
Block, dynamic, 410–21
Block Attribute Manager (BATTMAN), 386
Block Definition dialog box, 221
Block Editor, 411–21
Block-make command, 219–22
Block parameters, 411–22
Blocks. *See also* Block-make command
  advantages of, 230, 231
  inserting, 225–28
  redefining, 231

Box command, 536
Break command, 106, 107, 332, 333
  at point, 333

C

CAD Layer Guidelines, 173
Calculator, 284, 285
Camera, 625, 626
Cartesian Coordinate System, 24
Center Osnap mode, 102
Chamfer command, 89–92, 548, 549
  zero for making square corners, 92
Check spelling, 152
Circle command, 42–45
Color command, 216, 217
Color dependent plot style (STB), 176–78
Command Line window, 7
Cone command, 537, 538
Constrained orbit, 576, 621
Convert plot styles command, 178
Coordinates:
  absolute, 39, 40
  polar, 40, 41
  relative, 40
Copy command, 94, 95, 98, 99
Create Camera command, 625, 626
Create Layout Wizard, 164, 165, 459–72
Create New Material command, 634–36
Crosshair size, 7
Crossing window, 52
Cursor, 7
Customization button, 5
Cylinder command, 538

D

Data Extraction, 388–92
DDEDIT (edit text), 149–52
Defpoints layer, 278
Design Center, AutoCAD, 235, 236, 402–10
DIMASSOC system variable, 274
Dimension Edit command, 276, 277
  Align text, 276
Dimensioning, 251–77
  adjust space, 273
  aligned, 269
  annotative, 263, 264
  associative, 274–77
  baseline, 270
  break, 272–73
  continue, 266–69
  defpoints layer, 278
  editing, 276, 277
  grips, 278, 279
  isometric, 509
  leader, 319–29
  linear, 254, 255, 265–69
  oblique, 276
  override, 277
  QDIM, 286–88
  six basic types, 251, 252
  status, 252, 253
  update, 277
  variables, 252, 253, 255–64
Dimension Style Manager dialog box, 256–62
  fit tab, 261, 262
  lines tab, 259
  primary units tab, 258
  symbols and arrows tab, 258
  text tab, 260
DIMSCALE, 262, 263
Direct distance entry, 41
DIST (Distance command), 113
Divide command, 97, 98
Donut command, 59, 60
Drafting Settings dialog box, 26, 27, 487
Drawing extents, 47, 66
Drawing limits, 24
Drawing names, 21, 22
Drawing precision, 23
Drawing scale, 23
Drawing window, 7
Draw order command, (send to back), 512–15
Dtext command. *See* Single Line Text command
DUCS, 531
.dwg files, 21, 22
.dwt files, 19, 81, 82
DYN, 42
Dynamic blocks, 410–21
  Linear parameter, 411, 412
  Lookup parameter, 413, 414
  Visibility parameter, 419–21
Dynamic input, 42
Dynamic UCS, 531

E

Edit Attributes dialog box, 381
Edit multiline, 211–13
Edit Text (DDEDIT), 379
Ellipse command, 57–59
Endpoint osnap mode, 102
Enhanced attribute edit (EATTEDIT), 382, 383

Erase command, 38
Esc key, 22, 53
Etransmit, 481, 482
Explode command, 85, 606
Extend command, 213, 214
Extension, filename, 21, 22
Extension, osnap mode, 102
External Reference command, 421–27
Extracting attributes, 388–92
Extrude command, 539–43

F

FACETRES, 533
Fence selection option, 52
File Names, 21, 22
Fill, 118
Fillet command, 92–94, 549
  3D objects, 549
  zero radius for making square corners, 125, 312
Flyouts, 5
Font, text, 137, 138
Freezing layers, 33
From, 106, 124
Function keys, 660

G

Gradient hatch, 509–16
Graphics cursor, 7
Grid, 25
Griddisplay, 25
Grips, 53, 54, 278, 279, 564–67
  to modify solids, 564–67

H

Hatch and Gradient dialog box, 335–44
Hatch command, 108–10, 202, 233, 234, 331–45
  Annotative, 337
  associative hatching, 337
  gap tolerance, 334
  gradient hatch, 335–44
  inherit properties, 337
  origin, 336
  pattern palette, 336, 341, 342
Hatchedit command, 343
Hatch styles, 337, 355, 356
Helix command, 554, 555
Hide command, 552, 553
Highlight, 49

I

ID Point command, 86, 87
Imageattach command, 166, 167
Image clip command, 166, 167
Image frame command, 168
Imprint, solidedit, 574, 575
Inherit properties, 337
Insert command, 225–28, 380, 381
Insertion Osnap mode, 102
Interference checking, 533
Intersect command, 561, 562
Intersection Osnap mode, 102
Isolines, 534
Isometric drawing, 485–509
  angles in, 498–500
  dimensioning, 509
  ellipses, 489–91
  fundamentals, 486–91
  F5 function key, 489–90
  hatching, 509–16
  isoplanes, 489–94
  snap/grid mode, 486, 487
  Y-scale factor, 501

J

Joining:
  Polylines, 108
  Viewports, 456

K

Keyboard shortcuts, 655–58

L

Last selection, 52, 53
Layer Properties Manager dialog box, 28–32
Layers:
  assigning colors to, 28, 29
  assigning linetypes to, 29, 30
  creating, 27–34
  defpoints, 278
  freezing/thawing, 33
  lineweight, 30–32
  locking and unlocking, 33
  making a layer current, 32
  naming, 27
  plot style, 33
  plottable or nonplottable, 34
  turning on/off, 33
  used in this book, 175

Layout Wizard, 164, 165
Lights, 611, 612
  Distant, 612, 618, 619
  photometric, 612
  point, 612, 621
  spotlight, 612, 620
  sun, 611
Limits command, 24
Line command, 36–42
Linetype command, 217
Linetypes, 30
Linetype scale, 45
Lineweight command, 217
List command, 215, 216
Loading linetypes, 29, 30
Loft command, 556, 557
LTSCALE command, 45

M

Magnet, osnap, 103
Make Object's Layer Current command, 218
Marker size, 103
Match Properties command, 218, 278
Materials, 612, 614–18
Materials editor, 614–18
Measure command, 98
Menu bar, 12, 13
Mesh box, 578, 579
Mesh cone, 579, 580
Mesh cylinder, 580
MESHSMOOTH, 582–85
MESHSMOOTHLESS, 580
MESHSMOOTHMORE, 579, 580
Mesh torus, 581
Mesh wedge, 580, 581
Mid Between 2 Points Osnap mode, 101
Midpoint Osnap mode, 94, 95, 98, 99, 102
Mirror command, 304–06
Mirroring text. *See* MIRRTEXT system variable
MIRRTEXT system variable, 305
Model and layout tabs, 12, 62, 179, 180
Model space, 179, 180, 453–72
Mouse, 35
Move command, 49–52
Multileader command, 319–29
  Add, 328, 329
  Align, 323, 324
  Collect, 327, 328
Multileader Style command, 320–22, 324, 325
  Annotative, 321, 322
Multileader Style dialog box, 320–22
Multiline, edit, 211–13
Multiline command, 206–13
Multiline style command, 204–06
Multiline text command, 147, 148
  AutoStack Properties dialog box, 148
Multiline text ribbon, 148
Mview command, 458
Mvsetup command, 465–67

N

Named plot style (STB), 174
Navigation tools, 10
Nearest Osnap mode, 102
New View, 622, 623
Node Osnap mode, 98, 99, 102
Nontiled viewports, 458

O

Offset command, 84, 85
Options dialog box, 7, 8, 103, 104
Orbit, 575, 576, 611, 621
  Constrained, 576, 621
ORTHO mode, 36
Osnap modes, 94, 95, 98, 99, 101–04
  display osnap tooltip, 103
OTRACK, 348–53
Override keys, temporary, 659, 660

P

Palettes, 613–16
Pan command:
  realtime, 48
  wheel mouse, 48
Paper space, 179, 180, 453–72
Paragraph text. *See* Multiline text command
Parallel osnap mode, 103
Parallel projection, 575, 576
Parameters, dynamic block, 411–14, 419–21
Pdmode, 96
PDF file, 193–95
pdsize, 96
Perpendicular Osnap mode, 102
Perspective projection, 611
Pickbox, 100
Planar surface, 557, 558
plan view, 605
Play animation, 629

Plot command (Plot dialog box), 62–69, 179–93
  annotative property, 67
  annotation scale, 67
  area, 66
    display, 66
    extents, 66
    limits, 66
    window, 66
  center the plot, 67
  create layout wizard, 183–87
  custom properties, 63
  drawing orientation, 68
  landscape, 68
  layout tabs, 179, 180
  model tab, 62, 179, 180
  multiple viewports, 183–93
  name, 63
  offset, 67
  page setup, 63
  Page setup manager, 180–82, 187–93
  paper size, 65
  PDF file, 193–95
  plot to file, 64
  portrait, 68
  preview, 68, 69
  printer/plotter, 63
  properties, 63
  scale, 66
  shade plot options, 67
  styles, 174–83
  Style table, 64, 65
Plot styles, 174–83
Plot style table list, 176
Point command, 96, 97
Point filters, 348–51
Point style, 96, 97
Point Style dialog box, 96
Polar angles, 41
Polar coordinates, 40, 41
Polar tracking, 122–24
Polygon command, 118, 119
Polyline command, 82–84, 105–07
  arc, 116, 117
  chamfering, 91, 92
  close, 116
  exploding, 85
  joining, 108
  length, 116
  offsetting, 84, 85
  undo, 84
  width, 116
Polyline edit, 107, 108, 125, 126
Polysolid command, 558, 559
Precision, 23
Presspull command, 540, 543
Previous selection, 52, 53
Printing. *See* Plot command
Prompt and Response, 1, 17
Properties command, 149, 152, 214, 278

Q

QDIM, 286–88
Quadrant osnap mode, 102
Quick access toolbar, 5, 6
QuickCalc, 285
Quick dimension command, 286–88
Quick view drawings, 10, 472
Quick view layouts, 10, 472, 473

R

Raster image command, 166–69, 624
Realtime Pan command, 48
Realtime Zoom command, 47
Rectangle command, 127, 201, 202
Redo command, 54
Redrawall command, 457
Redraw command, 48, 457
Regenall command, 457
Regen command, 49, 457
Relative coordinates, 40
Remove, selection, 52
Rename and renumber sheet dialog box, 478
Render command, 611–25
  destinations, 422
  environment, 613
  motion path animations, 613
  3D fly, 613
  3D walk, 613, 627–30
Revolve command, 543–46
Ribbon, 4–7
Right click customization, 35, 36
Rotate command, 95, 96
Rotate 3D command, 547
RPREF command, 639, 640
Running osnap modes, 103

S

SaveAs command, 19
Save as type, 21
Save command, 19, 34
Save Drawing As dialog box, 21
Saving:
  drawing, 19–21, 34
  template, 19, 81, 82
Scale command, 60, 61
Section command, 530

Select all, 52
Selecting objects, 49–53
Selection set, 49, 50
Sheet set command, 475–82
- eTransmit, 481, 482
- title page, 478–81
- zip file, 482

Sheet Set Manager, 477–82
Shell, solids edit, 574, 575
Shortcuts, keyboard, 655–58
Single Line Text command, 61, 62, 140–46
- align, 142
- alignment, 143
- center, 142
- editing, 148–52
- fit, 142
- justification, 142
- middle, 142
- right, 143
- standard codes, 144, 145
- style, 136–40
- vertical, 143

Slice command, 530
Snap, 25, 26
- isometric, 486, 487

Solid modeling, 529–86
Solids commands, 529–86
- box, 536
- cone, 537, 538
- cylinder, 538
- extrude, 539–43
- helix, 554, 555
- intersect (intersection), 561, 562
- loft, 556, 557
- mesh box, 578, 579
- mesh cone, 579, 580
- mesh cylinder, 580
- MESHSMOOTH, 582–85
- MESHSMOOTHLESS, 580
- MESHSMOOTHMORE, 579, 580
- mesh torus, 581
- mesh wedge, 580, 581
- planar surface, 557, 558
- polysolid, 558, 559
- presspull, 540, 543
- revolve, 543–46
- sphere, 536, 537
- subtract, 552
- sweep, 553–55
- thicken, 558
- torus, 538
- union, 552
- wedge, 537

Solids Editing command (solidedit), 572–75
Spelling command, 152
Sphere command, 536, 537
Start recording animation, 627, 628
Status bar, 9
Steering wheels, 533
Stretch command, 306–09
Subtract command, 552
Sun, 611
Sweep command, 553–55
Synchronize attributes (ATTSYNC), 386

T

Table command, 153–62
Tangent Osnap mode, 102
Templates, 19, 81, 82
Text:
- Annotative, 228, 229
- Multiline, 147, 148
- single line, 140–46

Text fonts, 137, 138
Text Formatting editor, 148
Text Style command, 136–40
Text Style dialog box, 137–40
Texture map, 635, 636
Thicken command, 558
3D fly, 613
3D rotate command, 547
3D views, 531, 532
3D walk command, 613, 627–30
3D workspace, 534, 535
Tick marks, 252, 259
Tiled viewports, 457
Tilemode command, 457, 458
Title page, 478–81
Tooltips, 5
Torus command, 538
Tracking, 127, 128
Transparent commands, 48
Trim command, 88

U

UCS command, 301–03, 605, 608
UCS Icon, 8, 302, 303
UCS Icon dialog box, 303
Undo command, 38, 54
Undo selection, 53
Union command, 552
Units command, 22, 23
User Coordinate Systems. *See* UCS command

V

View, 622, 623
View cube, 533

Viewpoint command, 531
  presets dialog box, 531, 532
Viewports command, 455–71
  delete, 456
  hiding boundaries of, 475
  join, 456
  nontiled, 458
  restore in paper space, 456
  save, 456
  scale, 467, 471
  single, 456
  tilemode command, 457, 458
  tiled, 457
Visual styles manager, 618
VPORTS command. *See* Viewports command

W

Walk and Fly settings, 626, 627
Walk through, 625–30
Wblock command, 222–24, 379
Wedge command, 537
Wheel mouse, 48
Wide polylines, 116
Window, 52
Window, crossing, 52
Windows:
  Explorer, 21, 22
  Folder options, 21
Workspace, 2D, 11, 12
Workspace, 3D, 534, 535
World Coordinate System, 8, 301, 531
Write Block dialog box, 223, 379

X

XATTACH command, 421–26
XBIND command, 422
XREF command, 421–27

Z

Zip file, 481, 482
Zoom command:
  all, 26, 46, 47
  extents, 47
  object, 47
  previous, 47
  realtime, 47
  wheel mouse, 48
  window, 45

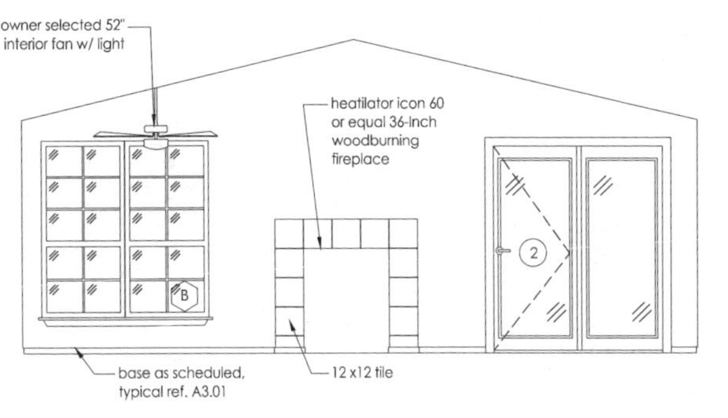

41 **Unit Type 'E' Typical**
1/8=1'-0" elevation

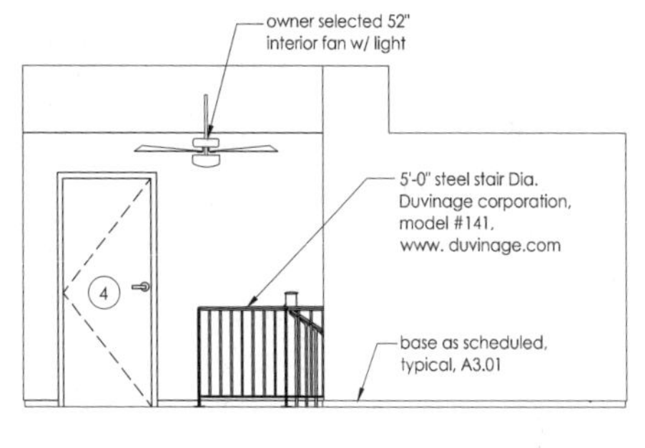

40 **Unit Type 'E' Typical**
1/8=1'-0" elevation

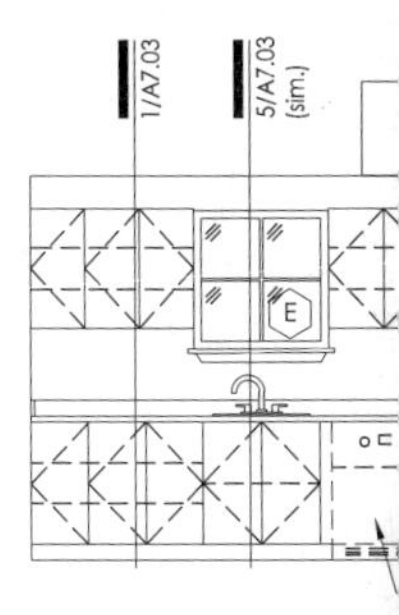

39
1/8=1'-0"

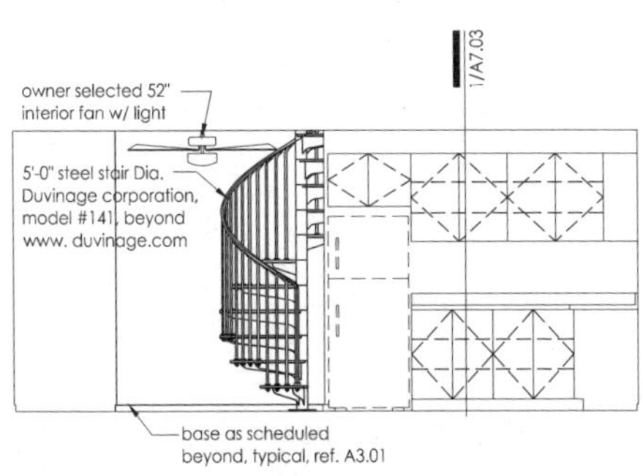

35 **Unit Type 'E' 1st Floor Typ**
1/8=1'-0" elevation

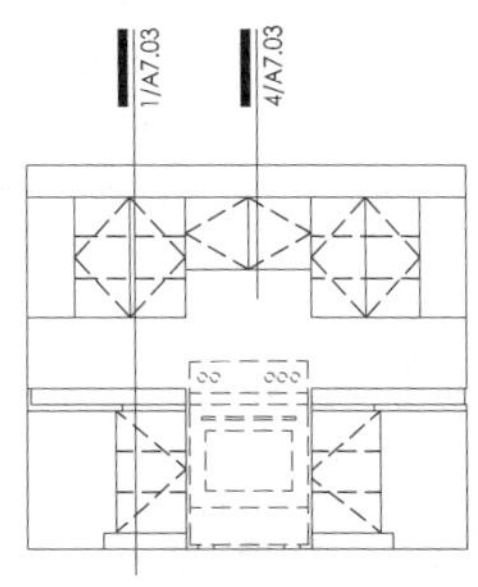

34 **Unit Type 'E' 1st Floor Typ**
1/8=1'-0" elevation

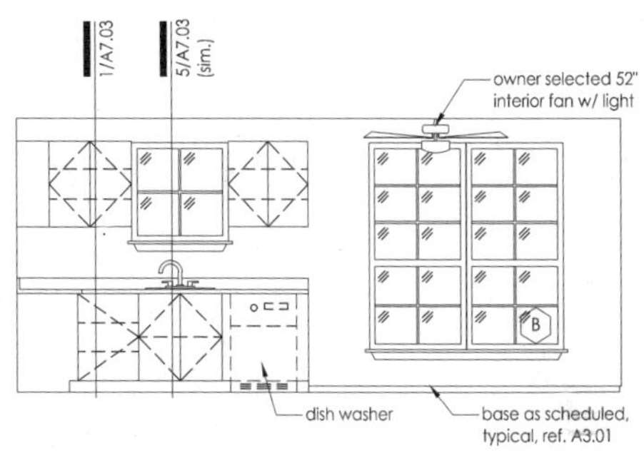

33 **Unit Type 'E' 1st Floor Typ**
1/8=1'-0" elevation

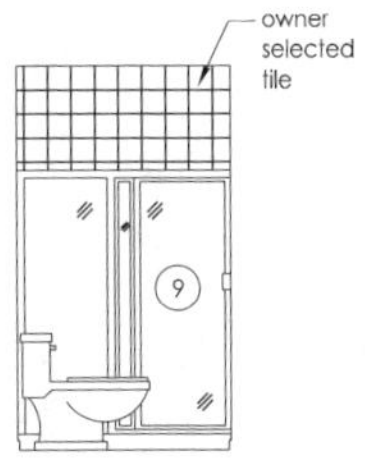

29 **Unit Type 'E' 1st Floor Typ**
1/8=1'-0" elevation

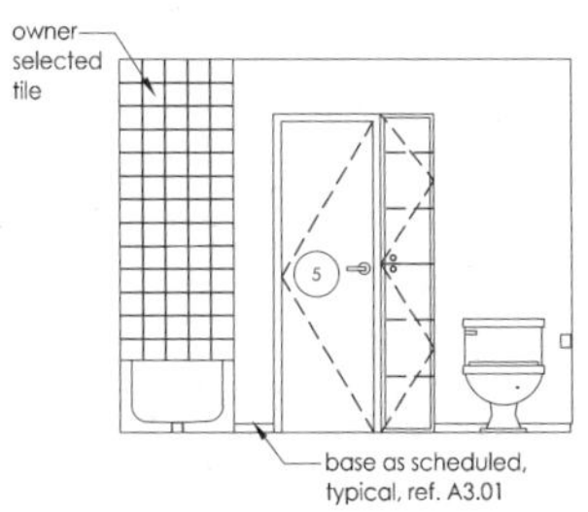

28 **Unit Type 'D' Typical**
1/8=1'-0" elevation

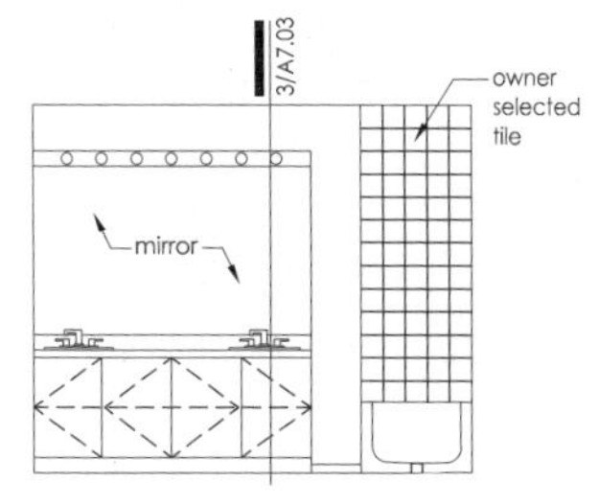

27 **Unit Type 'D' Typical**
1/8=1'-0" elevation

26
1/8=

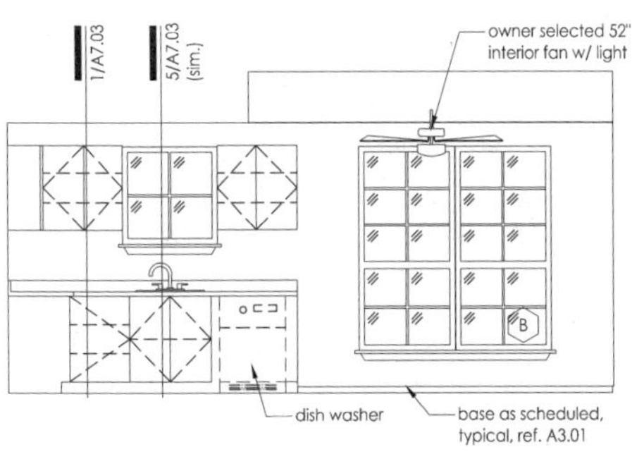

23 **Unit Type 'D' Typical**
1/8=1'-0" elevation

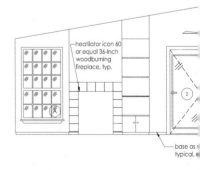

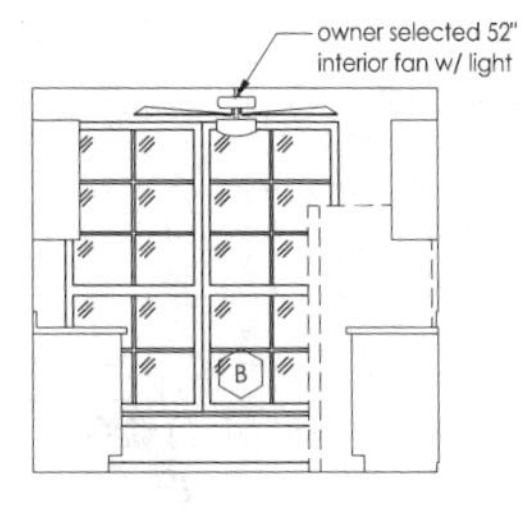

22 **Unit Type 'D' Typical**
1/8=1'-0" elevation

heatilator icon 60 or equal 36-inch woodburning fireplace, typ.

base as s
typical,

21 **Unit Type '**
1/8=1'-0"

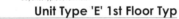

FIGURE C–10
Elevations (Scale: 1/8" = 1'-0")
Courtesy of Kelly McCarthy, McCarthy Architecture

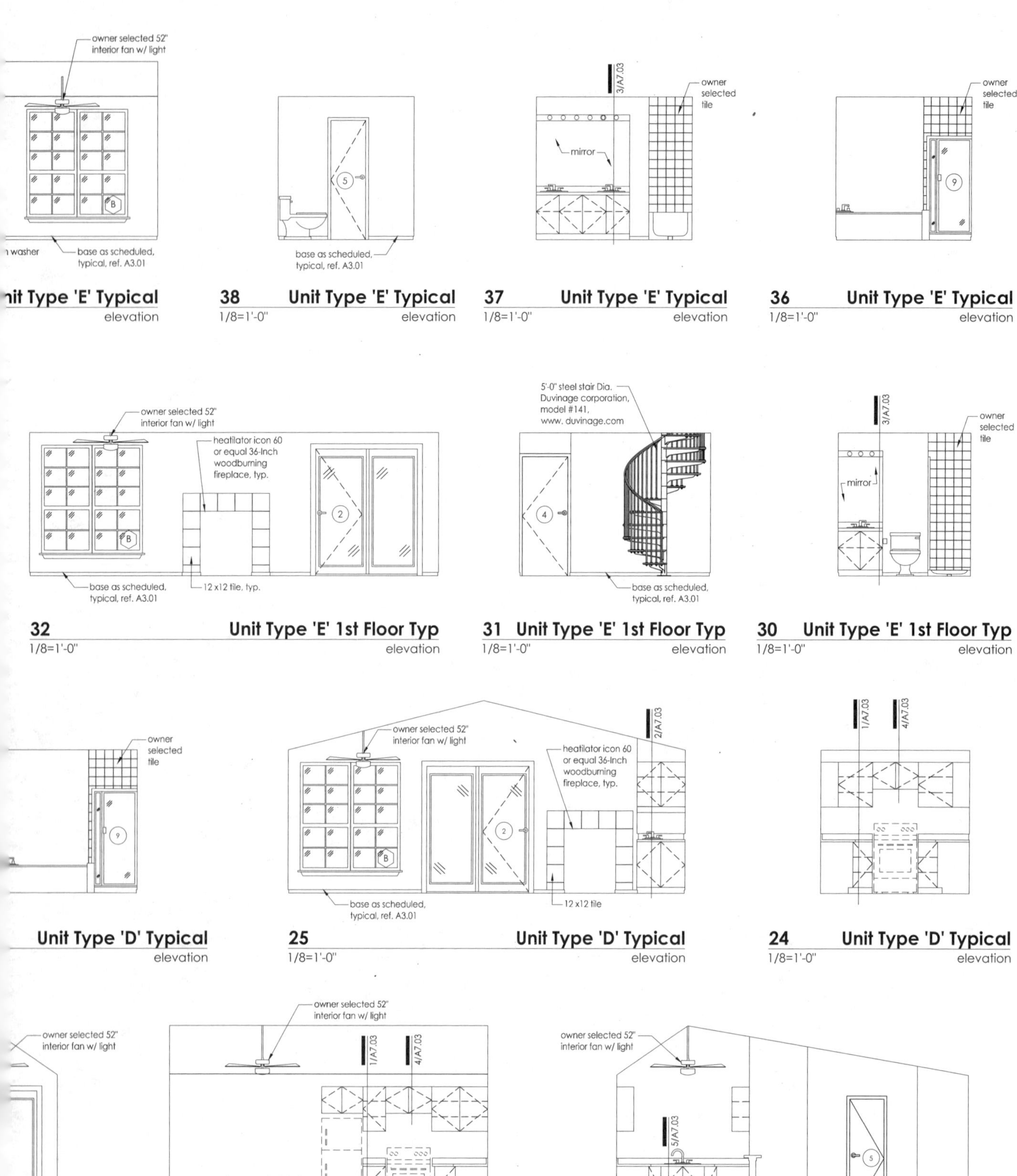

'pical
levation

20 Unit Type 'C' Typical
1/4=1'-0" elevation

19 Unit Type 'C' Typical
1/8=1'-0" elevation

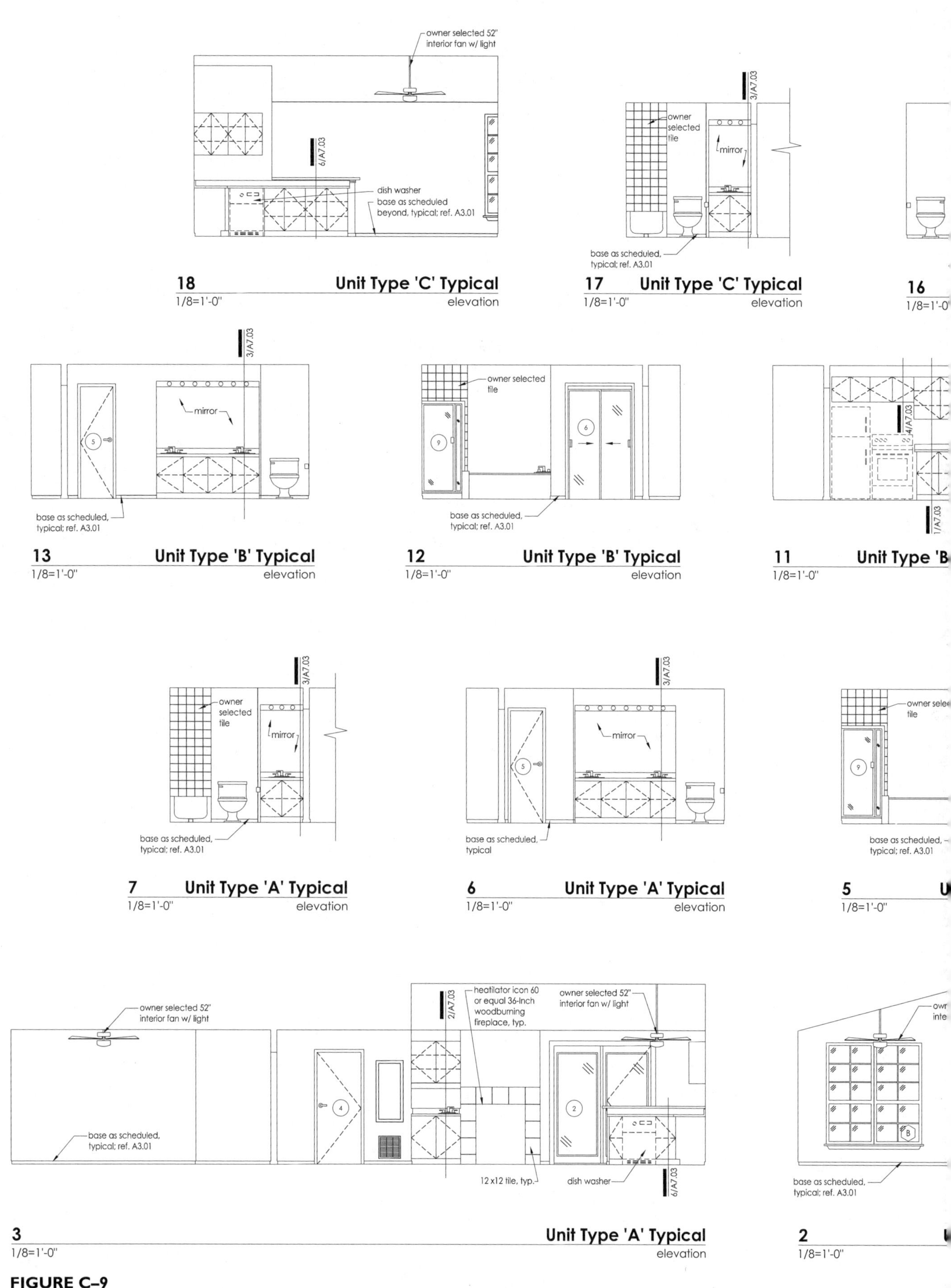

FIGURE C–9
Elevations (Scale: 1/8″ = 1′-0″)
Courtesy of Kelly McCarthy, McCarthy Architecture

3/A7.03
mirror
base as scheduled, typical; ref. A3.01
Unit Type 'C' Typical
elevation
owner selected tile
base as scheduled, typical
base as scheduled, typical; ref. A3.01
15
Unit Type 'C' Typical
1/8=1'-0"
elevation
2/A7.03
heatilator icon 60 or equal 36-Inch woodburning fireplace, typ.
base as scheduled, typical; ref. A3.01
12 x12 tile, typ.
14
Unit Type 'B' Typical
1/8=1'-0"
elevation
ypical
elevation
2/A7.03 (sim.)
5/A7.03
10
Unit Type 'B' Typical
1/8=1'-0"
elevation
dish washer
6/A7.03
base as scheduled, typical; ref. A3.01
9
Unit Type 'B' Typical
1/8=1'-0"
elevation
3/A7.03
mirror
base as scheduled, typical; ref. A3.01
8
Unit Type 'B' Typical
1/8=1'-0"
elevation
owner selected 52" interior fan w/ light
base as scheduled, typical
2/A7.03
heatilator icon 60 or equal 36-Inch woodburning fireplace, typ.
owner selected 52" interior fan w/ light
12 x12 tile, typ.
t Type 'A' Typical
elevation
4
Unit Type 'A' Typical
1/8=1'-0"
elevation
1/A7.03
2/A7.03 (sim.)
5/A7.03
4/A7.03
base as scheduled, typical; ref. A3.01
it Type 'A' Typical
elevation
1
Unit Type 'A' Typical
1/8=1'-0"
elevation

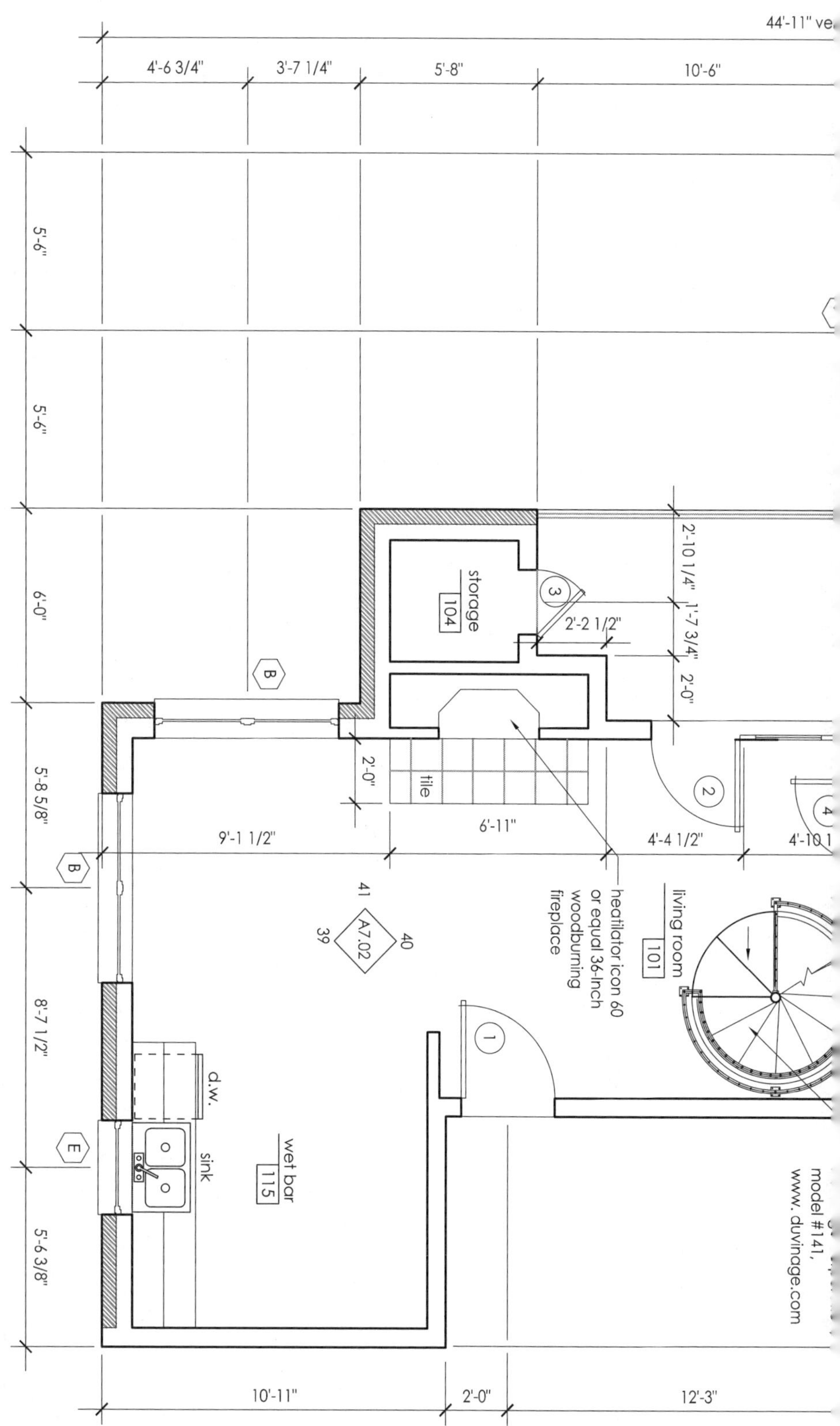

FIGURE C–8
Unit Type E Floor Plan—Upper Floor (Scale: 3/16″ = 1′-0″)
Courtesy of Kelly McCarthy, McCarthy Architecture

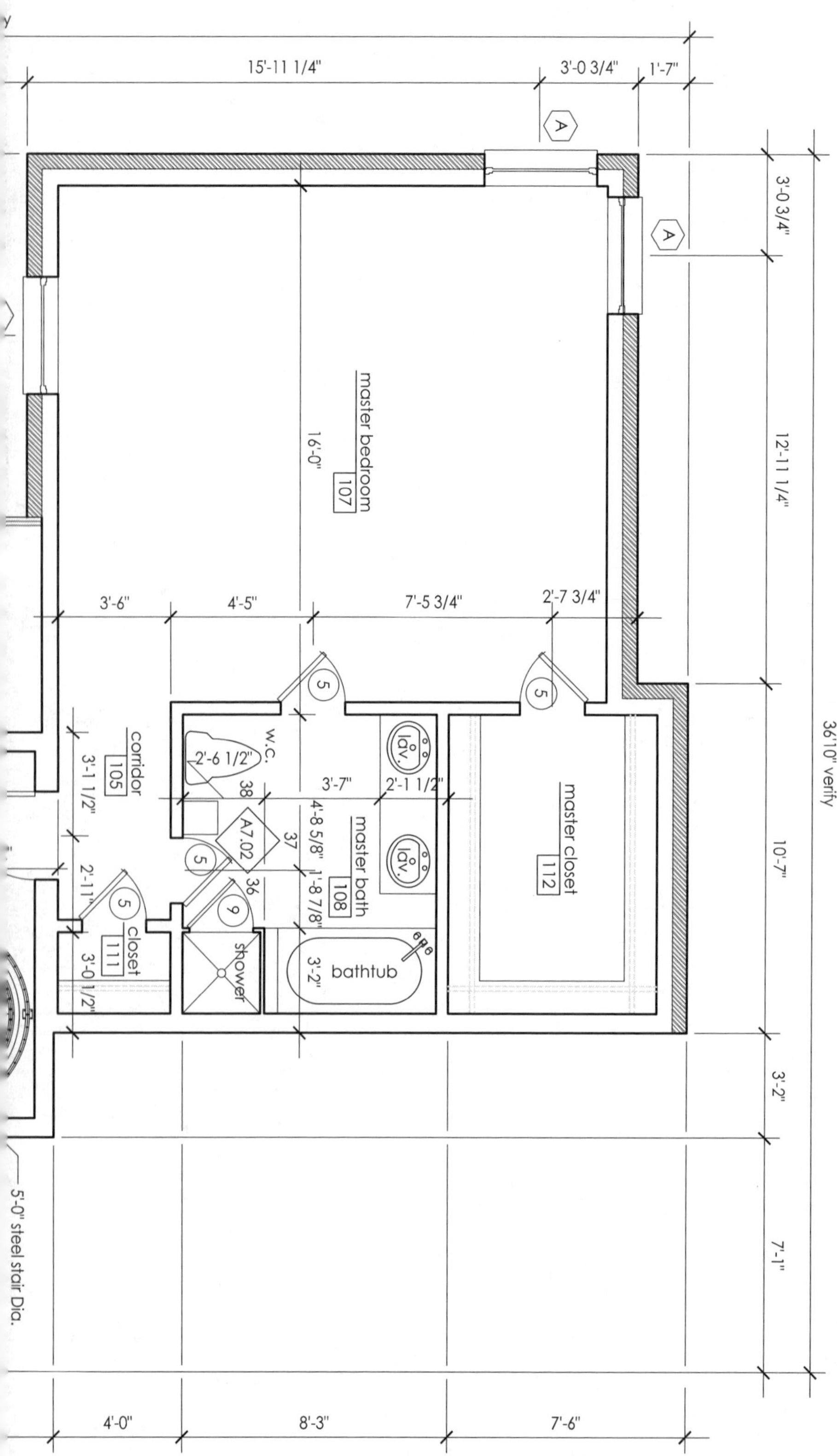
15'-11 1/4"
3'-0 3/4"
1'-7"
A
A
3'-0 3/4"
master bedroom
107
16'-0"
12'-11 1/4"
3'-6"
4'-5"
7'-5 3/4"
2'-7 3/4"
5
5
36'10" verify
w.c.
2'-6 1/2"
38
3'-7"
2'-1 1/2"
lav.
lav.
corridor
105
3'-1 1/2"
A7.02
37
4'-8 5/8"
master bath
108
1'-8 7/8"
36
master closet
112
10'-7"
2'-11"
5
5
9
closet
111
3'-0 1/2"
shower
bathtub
3'-2"
3'-2"
7'-1"
5'-0" steel stair Dia.
4'-0"
8'-3"
7'-6"

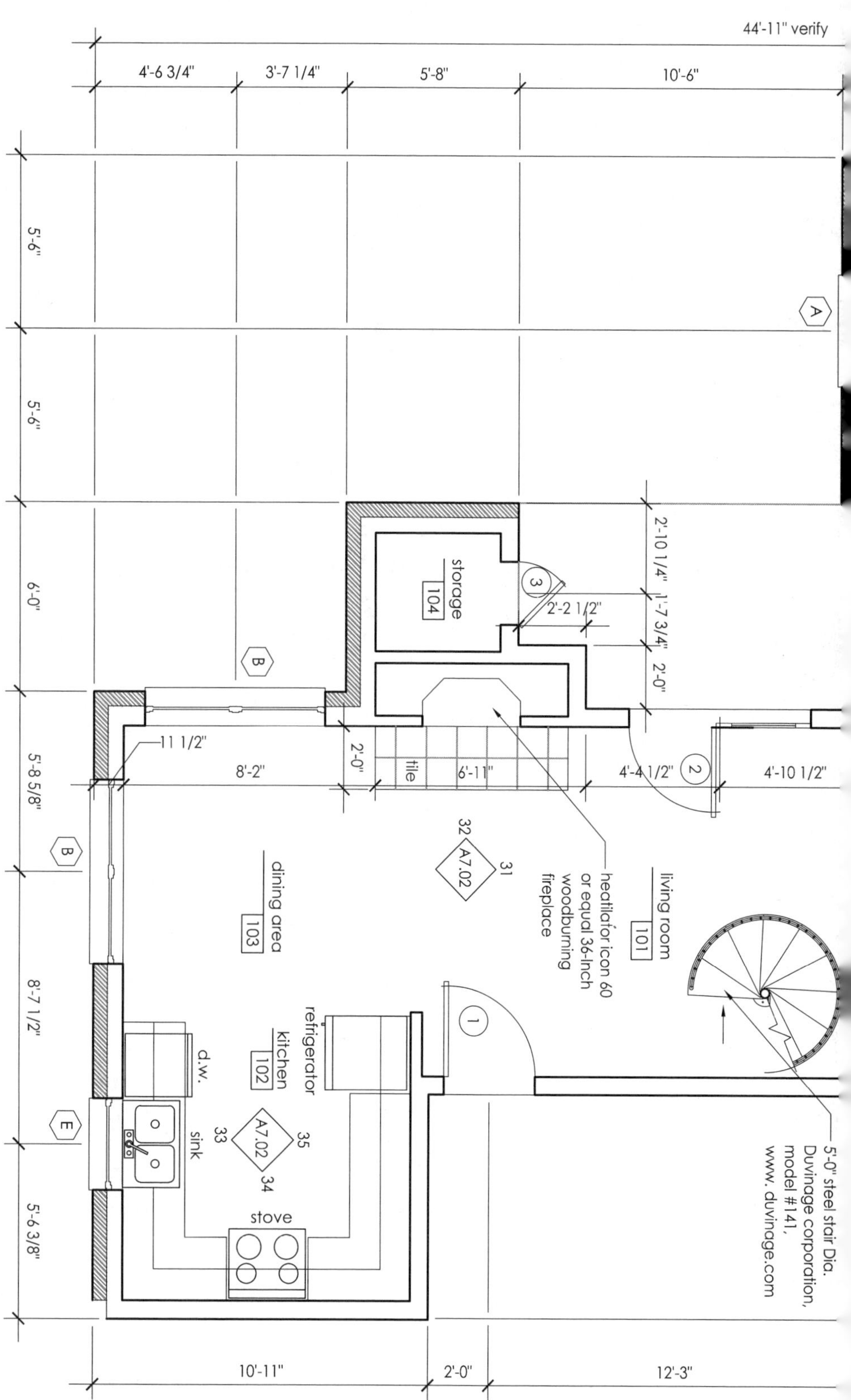

FIGURE C–7
Unit Type E Floor Plan—Lower Floor (Scale: 3/16″ = 1′-0″)
Courtesy of Kelly McCarthy, McCarthy Architecture

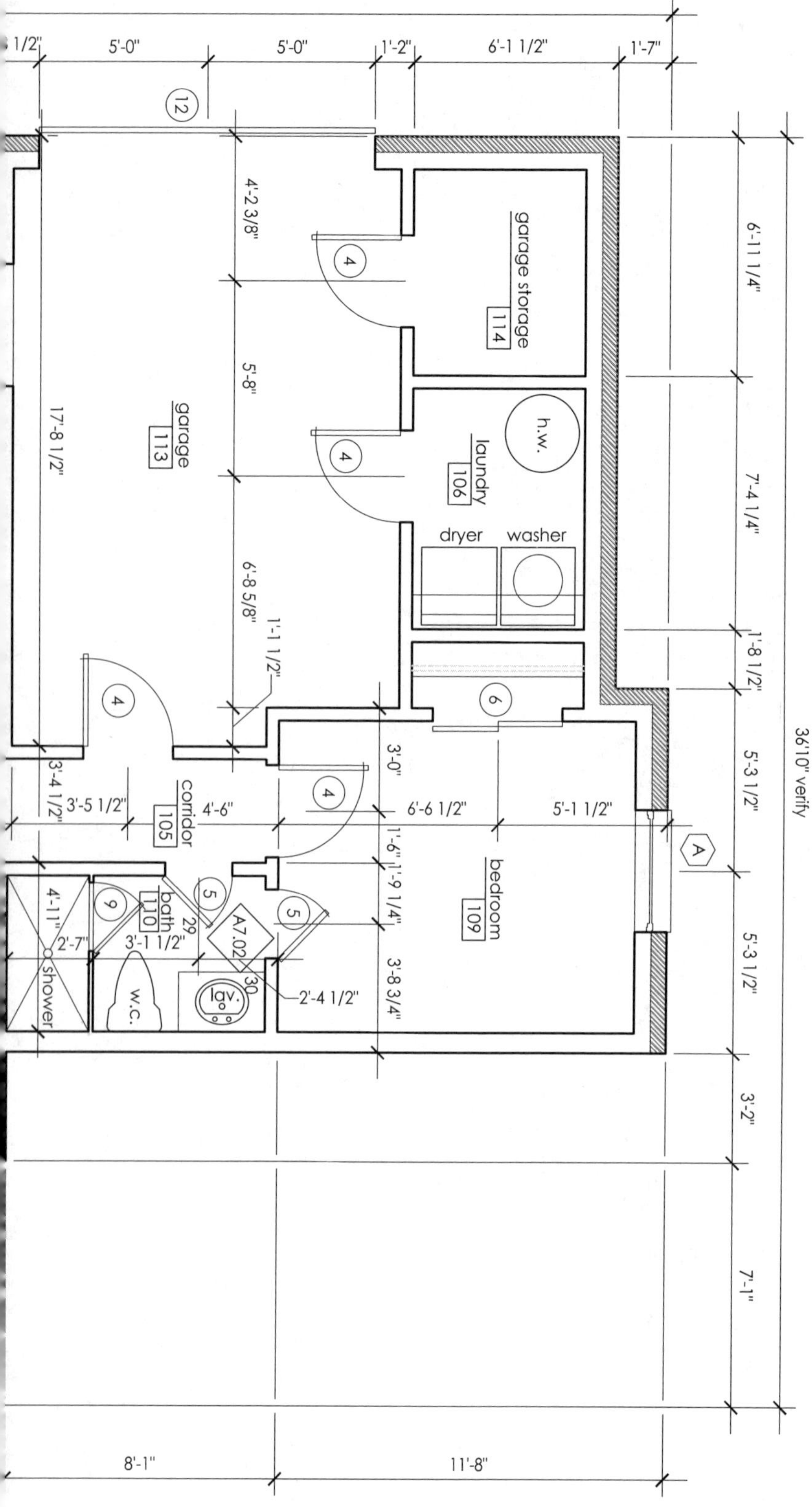
garage
113
garage storage
114
laundry
106
h.w.
dryer
washer
bedroom
109
corridor
105
bath
110
shower
w.c.
lav.
36'10" verify

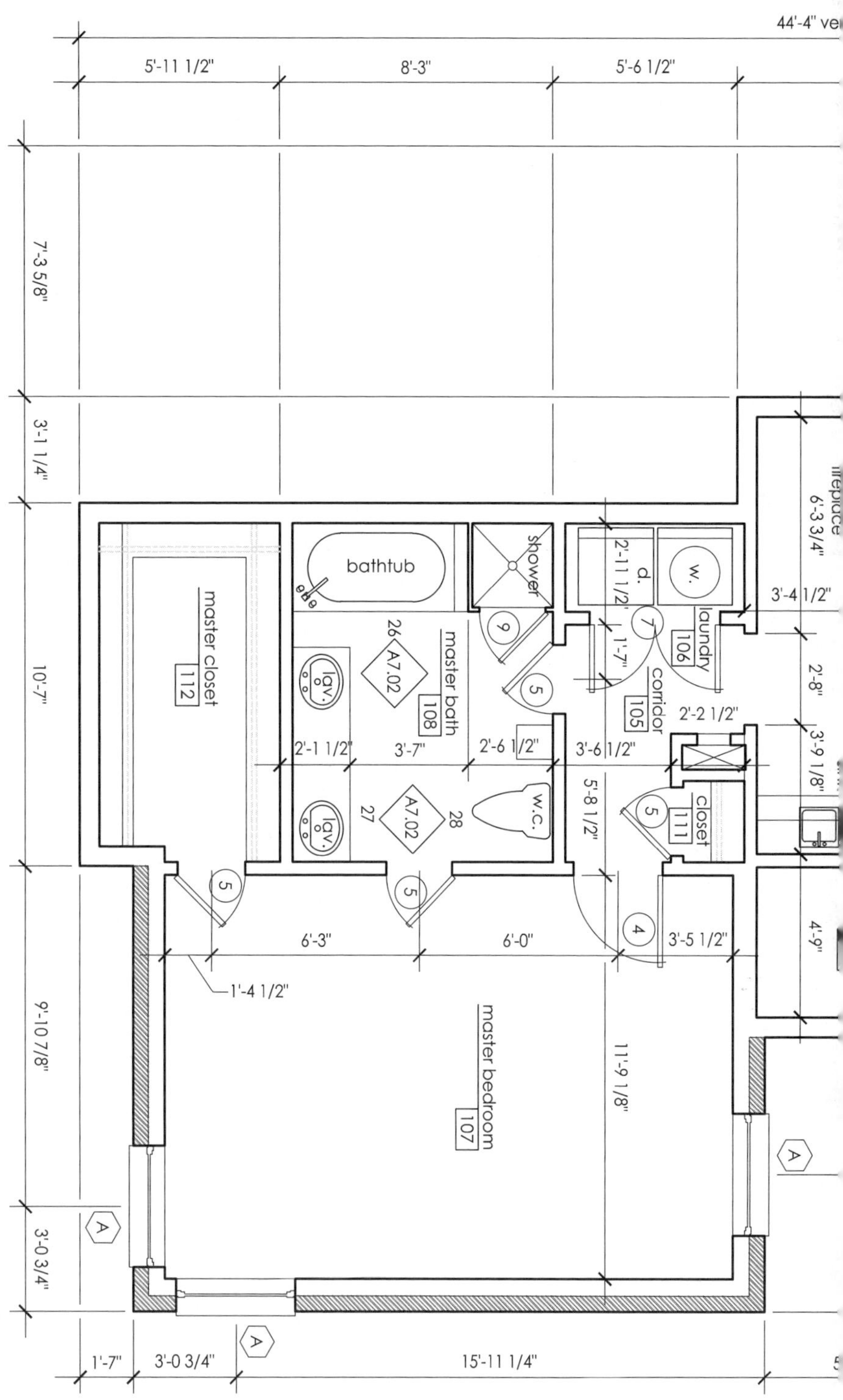

FIGURE C–6

Unit Type D Floor Plan (Scale: 1/4″ = 1′-0″)

Courtesy of Kelly McCarthy, McCarthy Architecture

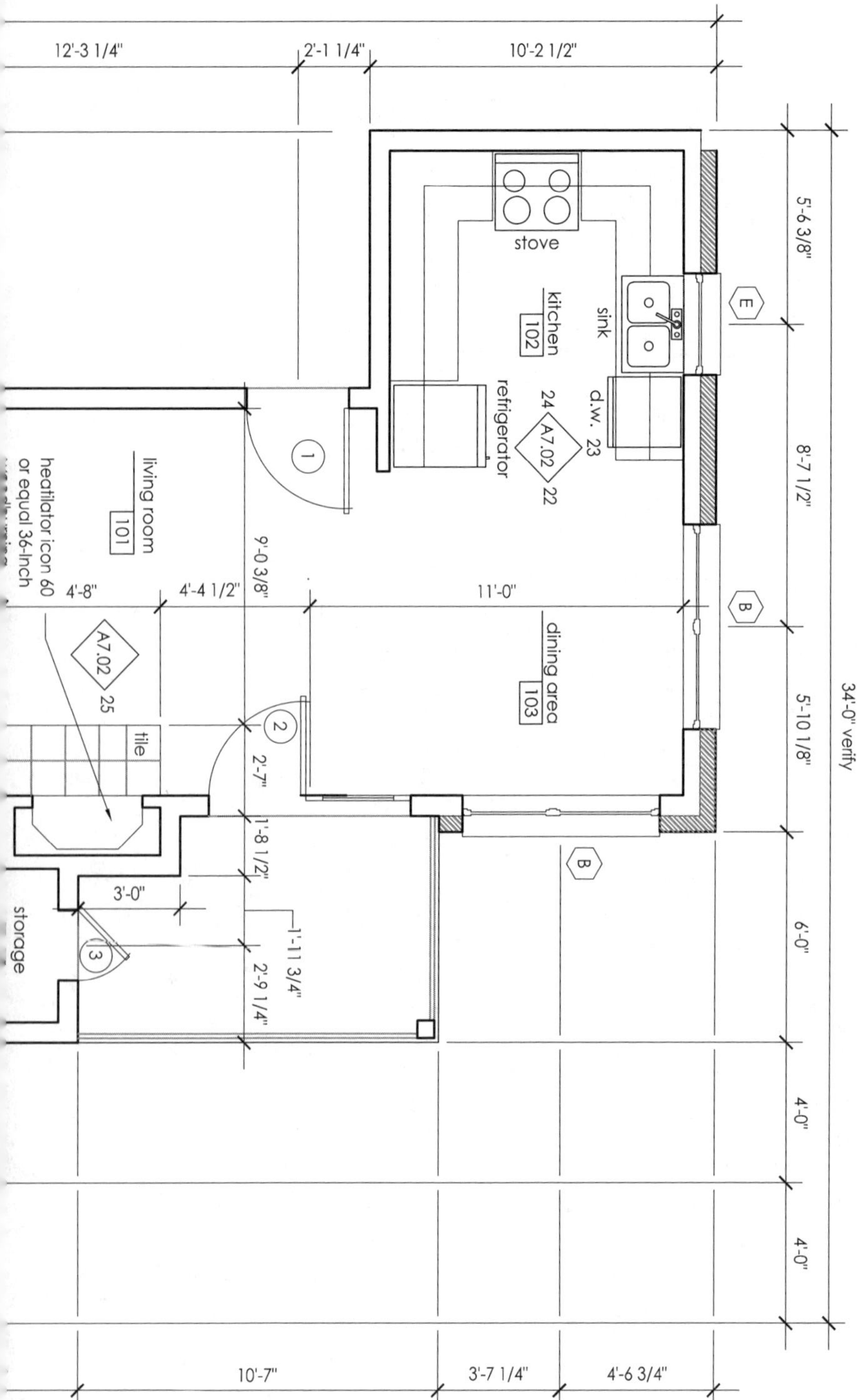
12'-3 1/4"
2'-1 1/4"
10'-2 1/2"
stove
kitchen
102
sink
refrigerator
d.w.
A7.02
23
24
22
living room
101
heatilator icon 60
or equal 36-inch
9'-0 3/8"
4'-8"
4'-4 1/2"
11'-0"
dining area
103
A7.02
25
tile
2'-7"
1'-8 1/2"
3'-0"
1'-11 3/4"
2'-9 1/4"
storage
5'-6 3/8"
8'-7 1/2"
5'-10 1/8"
6'-0"
4'-0"
4'-0"
34'-0" verify
10'-7"
3'-7 1/4"
4'-6 3/4"

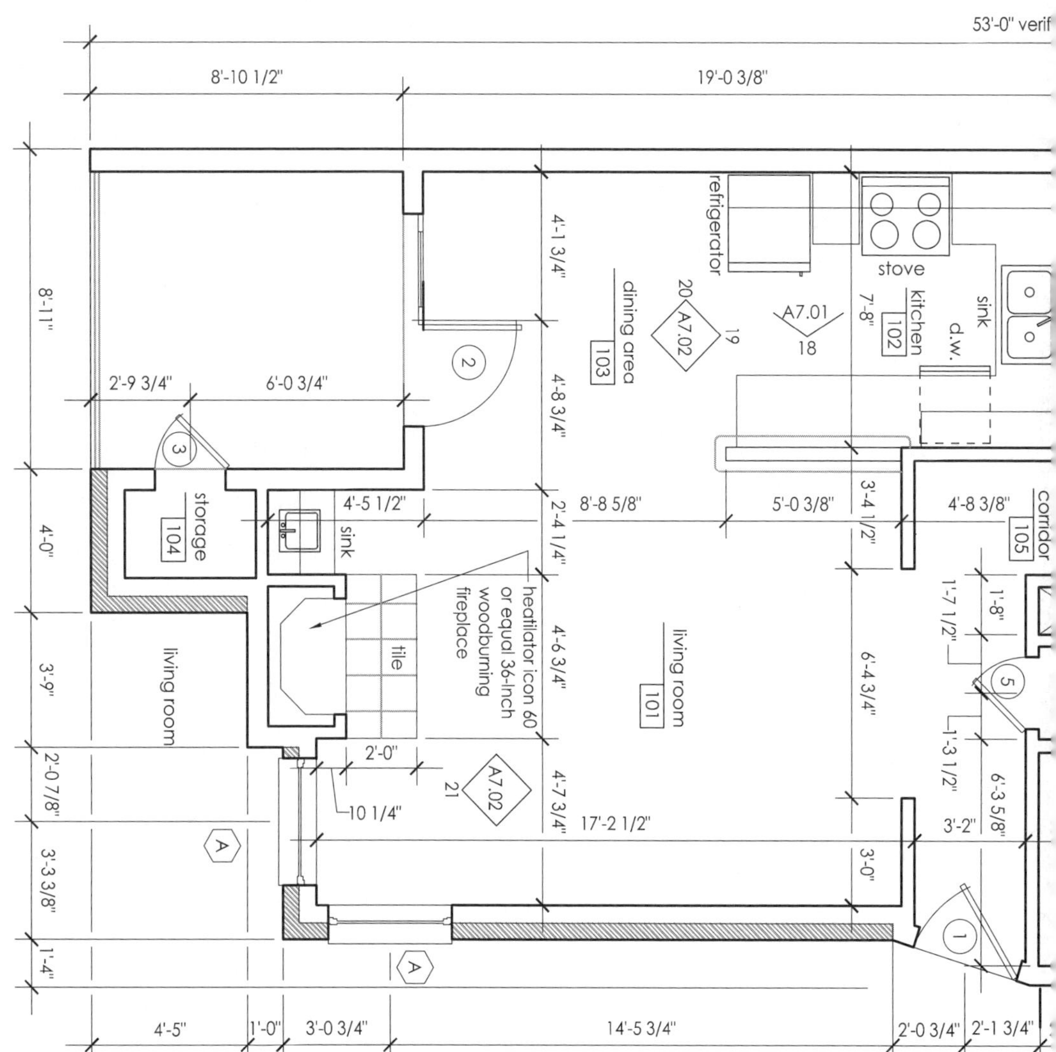

FIGURE C–5
Unit Type C Floor Plan (Scale: 1/4″ = 1′-0″)
Courtesy of Kelly McCarthy, McCarthy Architecture

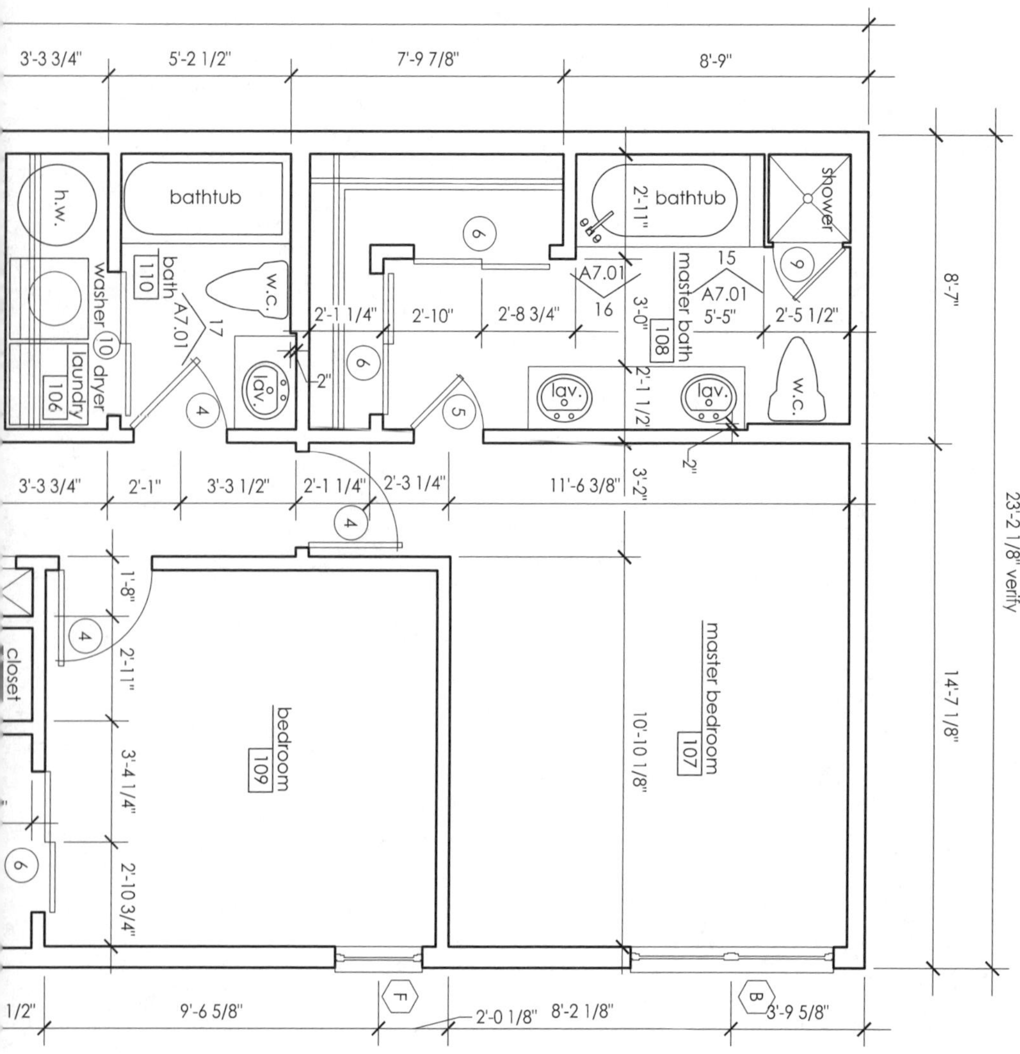
bathtub
bath
110
w.c.
lav.
h.w.
washer
dryer
laundry
106
bathtub
shower
master bath
108
lav.
lav.
w.c.
bedroom
109
master bedroom
107
closet
23'-2 1/8" verify

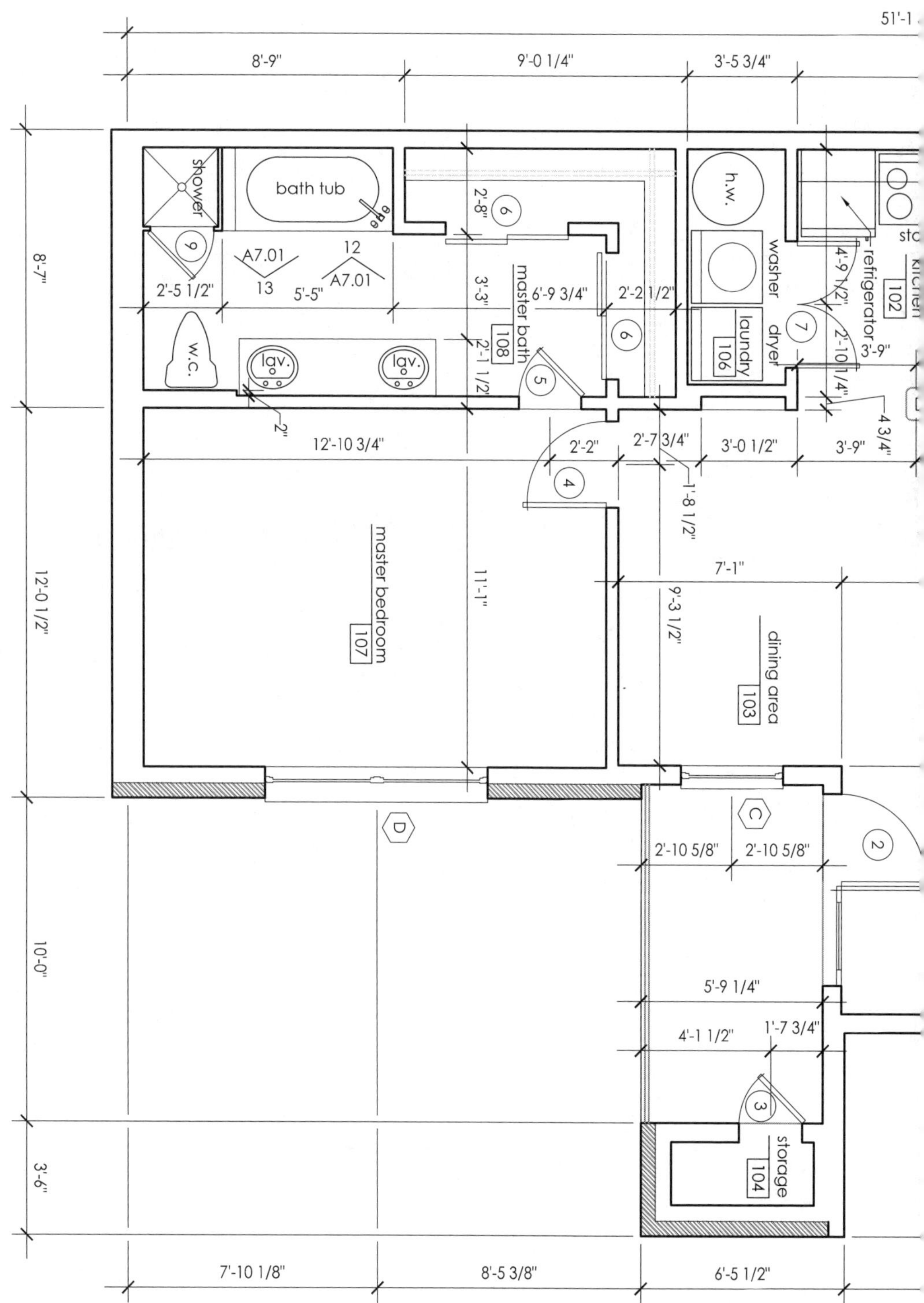

FIGURE C–4
Unit Type B Floor Plan (Scale: 1/4" = 1'-0")
Courtesy of Kelly McCarthy, McCarthy Architecture

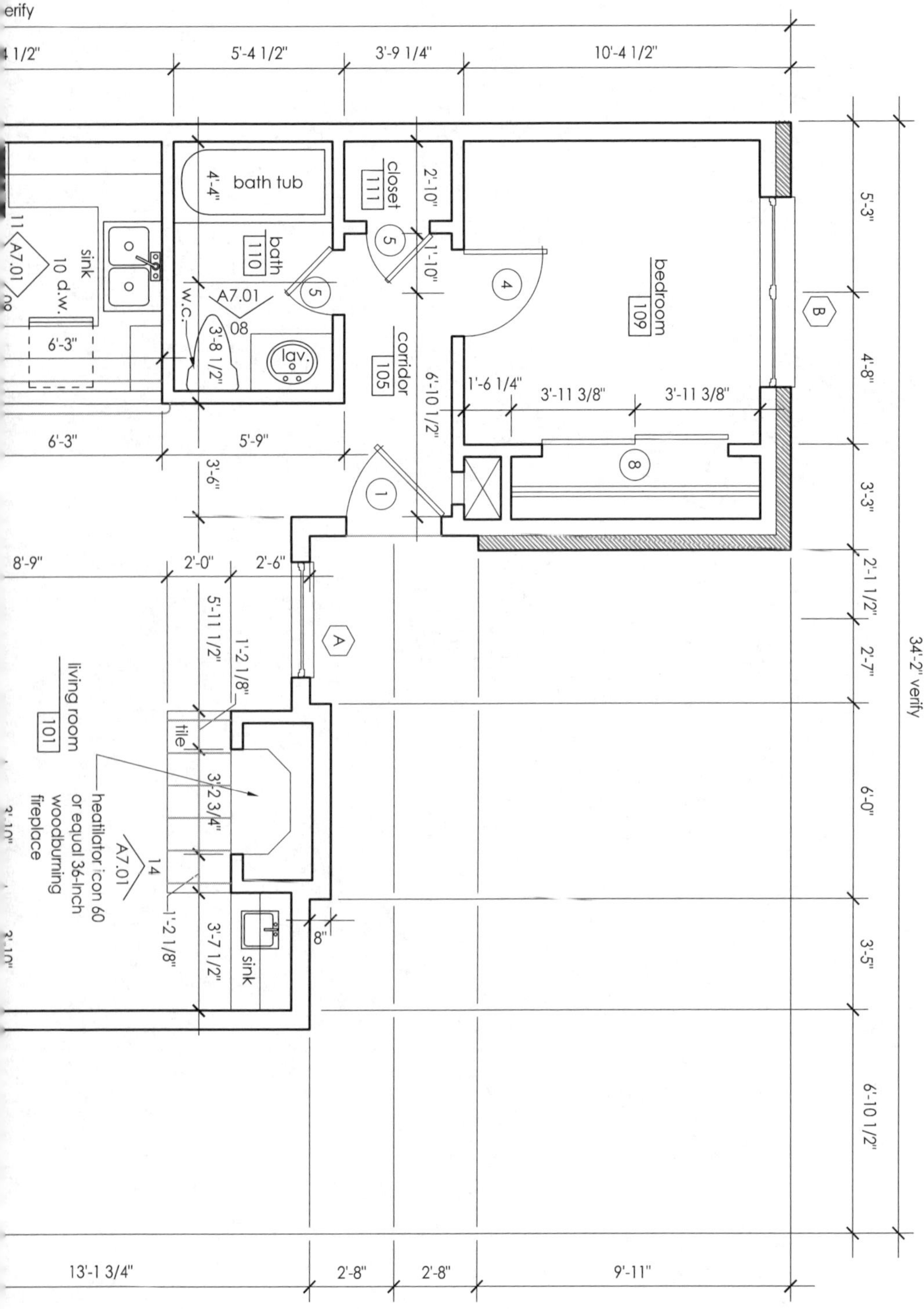
bath tub
closet
111
bath
110
corridor
105
bedroom
109
living room
101
sink
10 d.w.
w.c.
lav.
tile
heatilator icon 60 or equal 36-inch woodburning fireplace
34'-2" verify

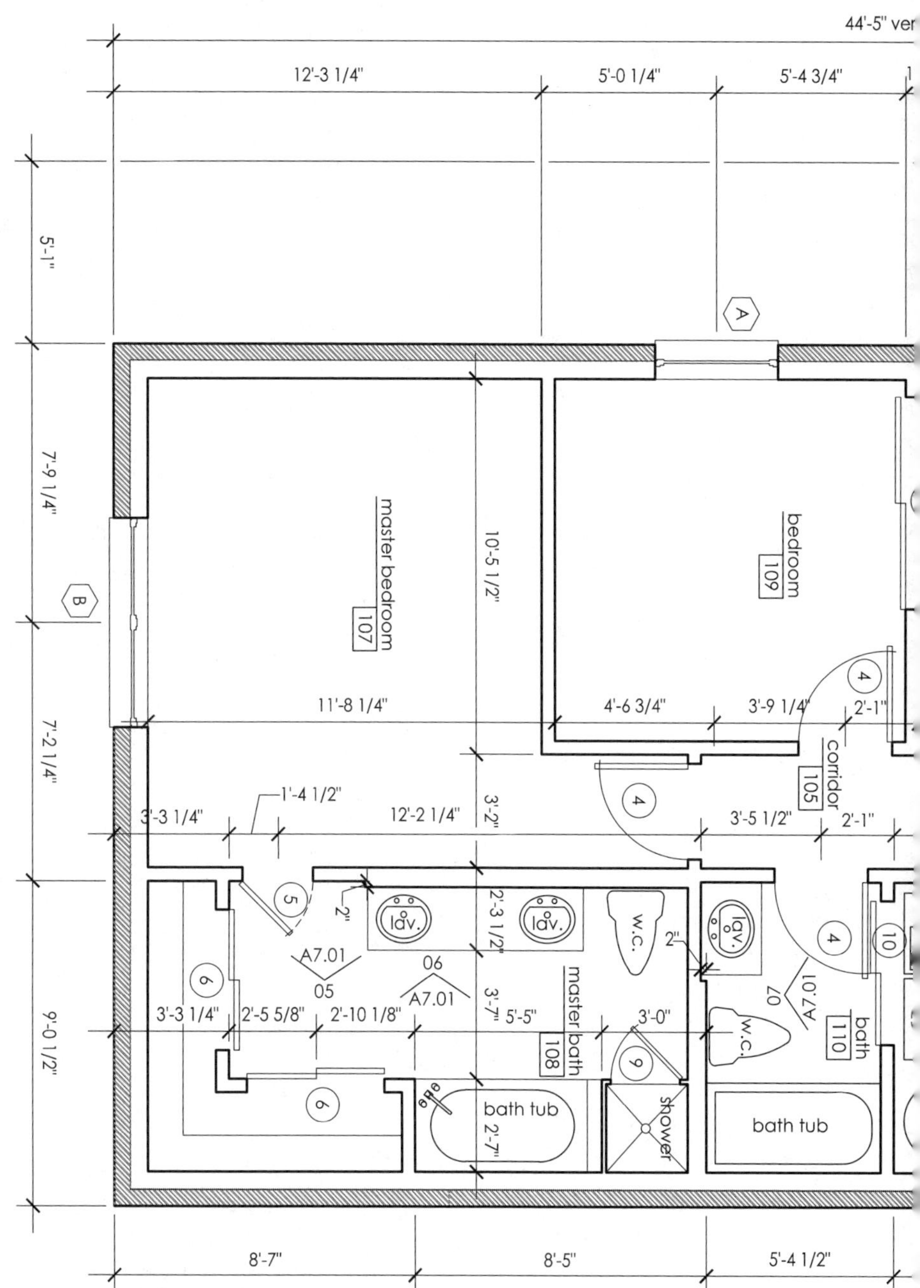

FIGURE C–3

Unit Type A Floor Plan (Scale: 1/4″ = 1′-0″)

Courtesy of Kelly McCarthy, McCarthy Architecture

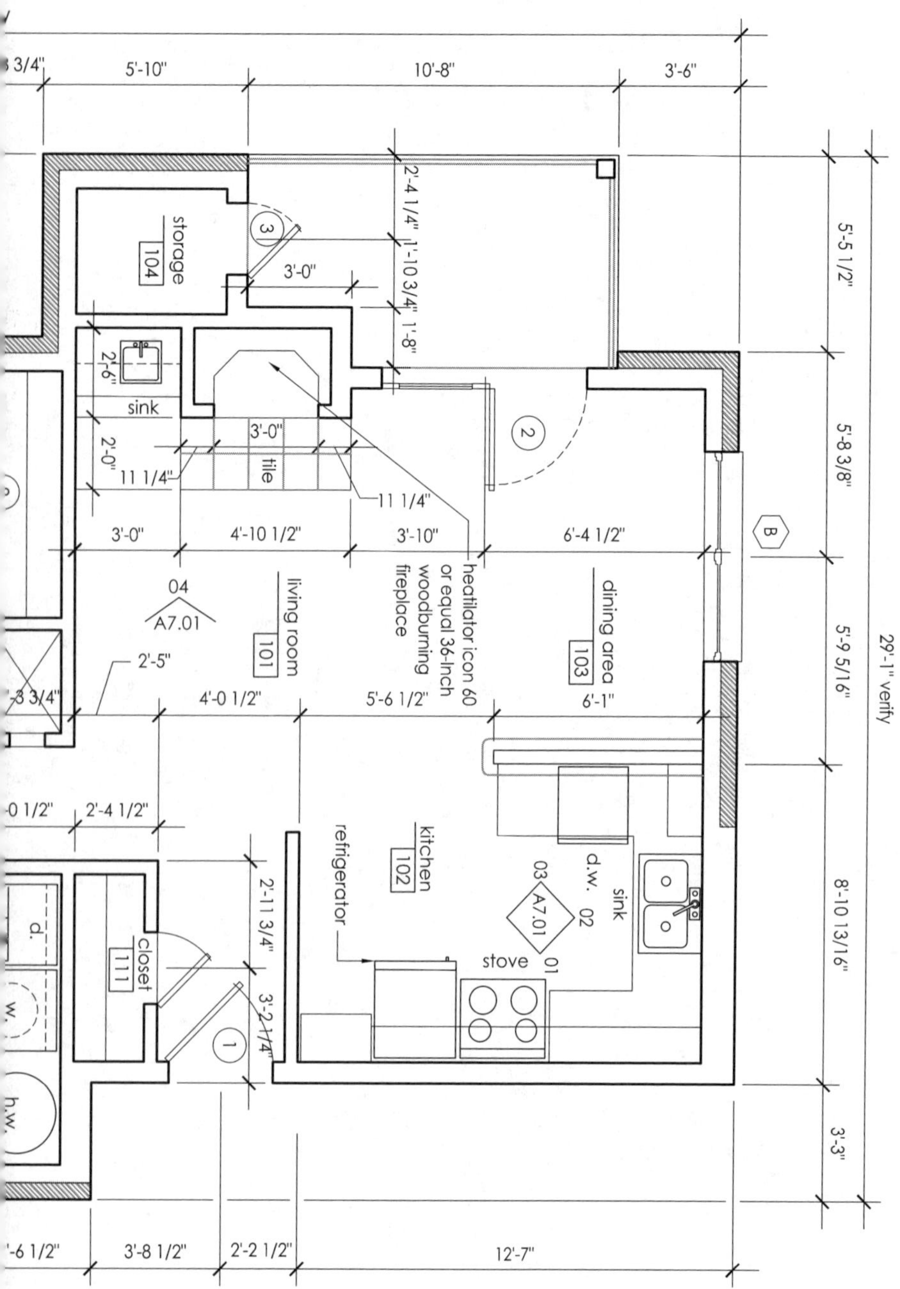

5'-10"
10'-8"
3'-6"
storage
104
3'-0"
2'-4 1/4"
1'-10 3/4"
1'-8"
2'-6"
sink
2'-0"
3'-0"
tile
11 1/4"
11 1/4"
3'-0"
4'-10 1/2"
3'-10"
6'-4 1/2"
04
A7.01
living room
101
heatilator icon 60 or equal 36-Inch woodburning fireplace
dining area
103
2'-5"
4'-0 1/2"
5'-6 1/2"
6'-1"
2'-4 1/2"
kitchen
102
refrigerator
sink
d.w.
03
A7.01
02
01
stove
closet
111
2'-11 3/4"
3'-2 1/4"
d.
w.
h.w.
3'-8 1/2"
2'-2 1/2"
12'-7"
5'-5 1/2"
5'-8 3/8"
5'-9 5/16"
8'-10 13/16"
3'-3"
29'-1" verify
B

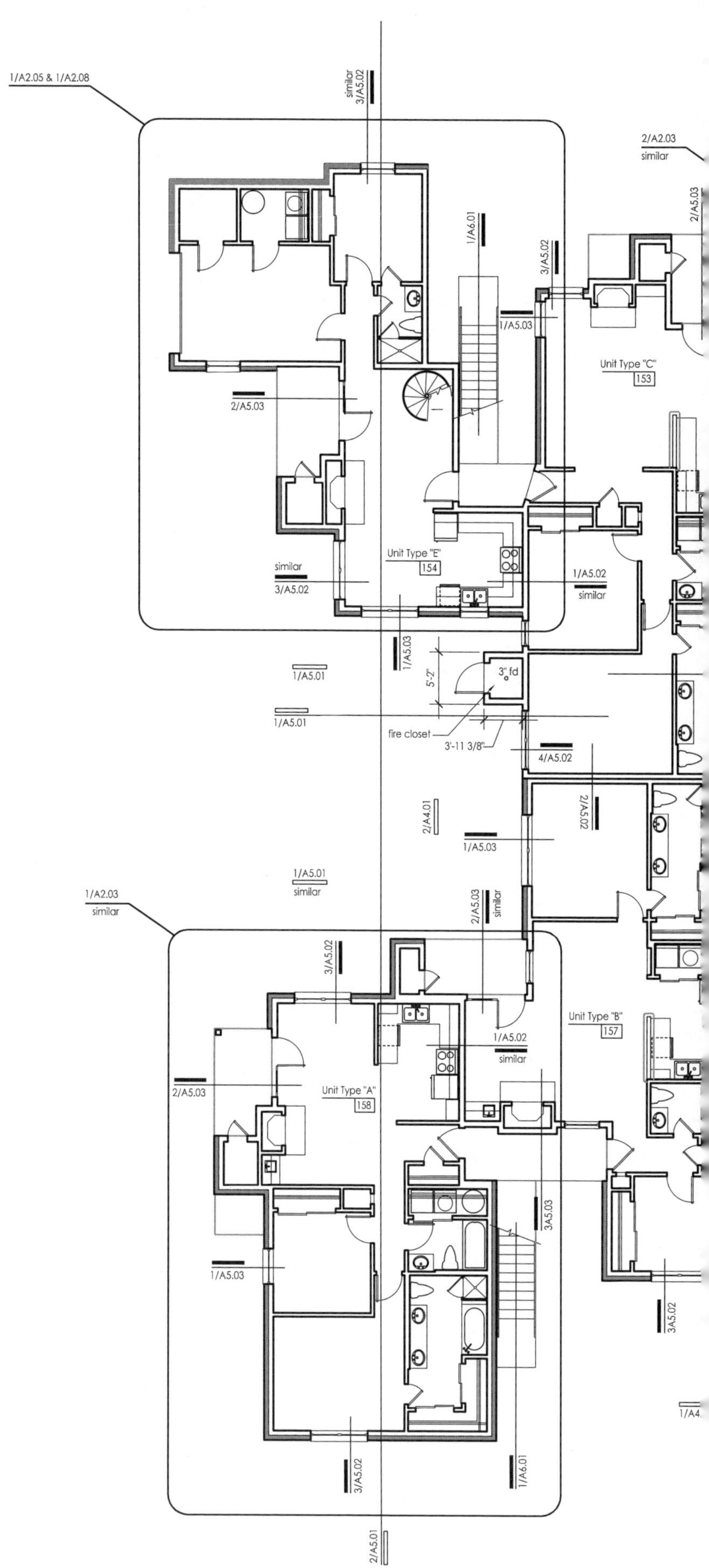

FIGURE C–2

Second Floor Condominium Project (Scale: 1/16″ = 1′-0″)

Courtesy of Kelly McCarthy, McCarthy Architecture

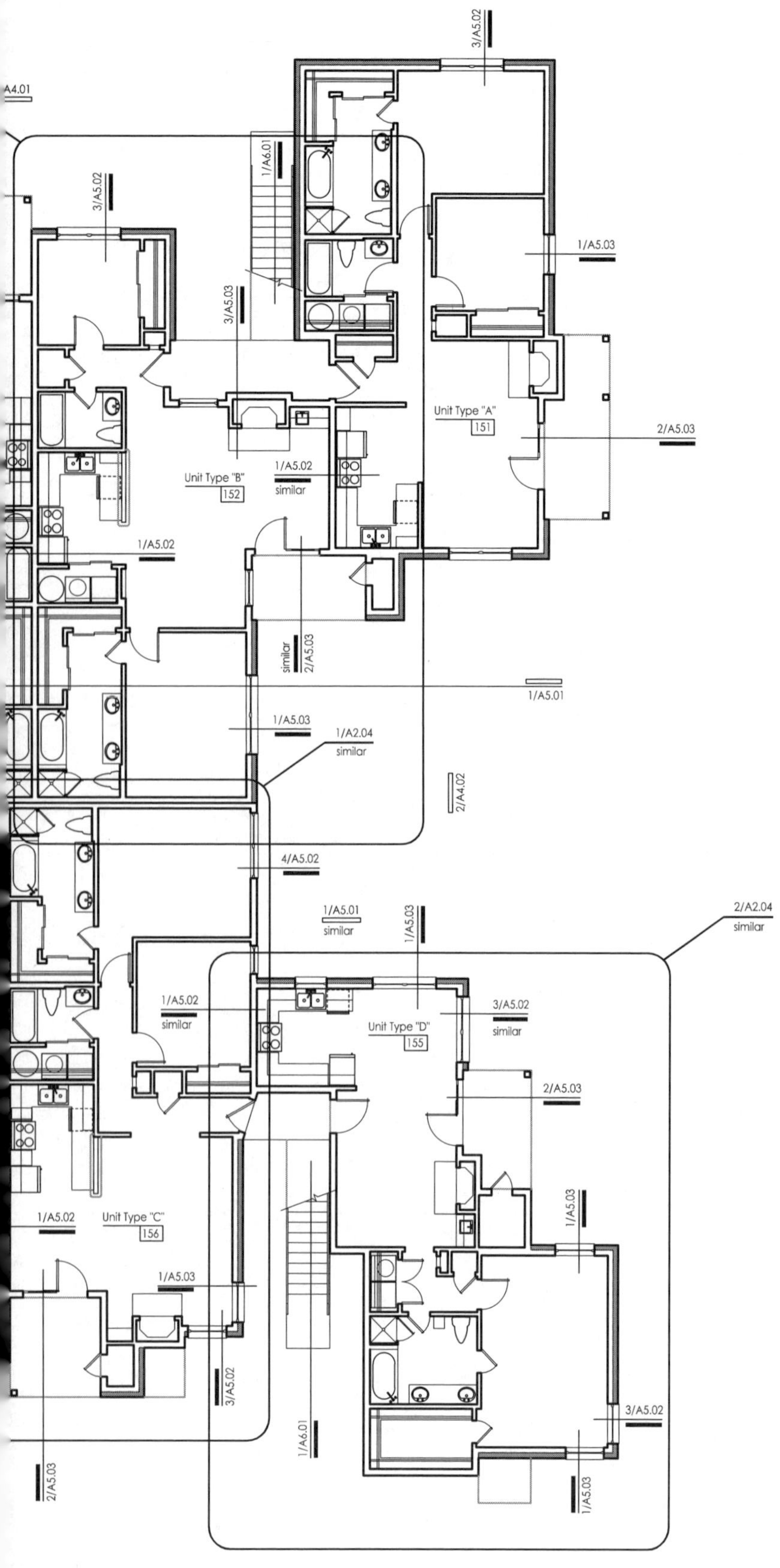

A4.01
3/A5.02
1/A6.01
3/A5.03
1/A5.03
Unit Type "A"
151
2/A5.03
Unit Type "B"
152
1/A5.02
similar
1/A5.02
similar
2/A5.03
1/A5.01
1/A5.03
1/A2.04
similar
2/A4.02
4/A5.02
1/A5.01
similar
1/A5.03
2/A2.04
similar
1/A5.02
similar
Unit Type "D"
155
3/A5.02
similar
2/A5.03
1/A5.02
Unit Type "C"
156
1/A5.03
1/A5.03
3/A5.02
3/A5.02
1/A6.01
2/A5.03
1/A5.03

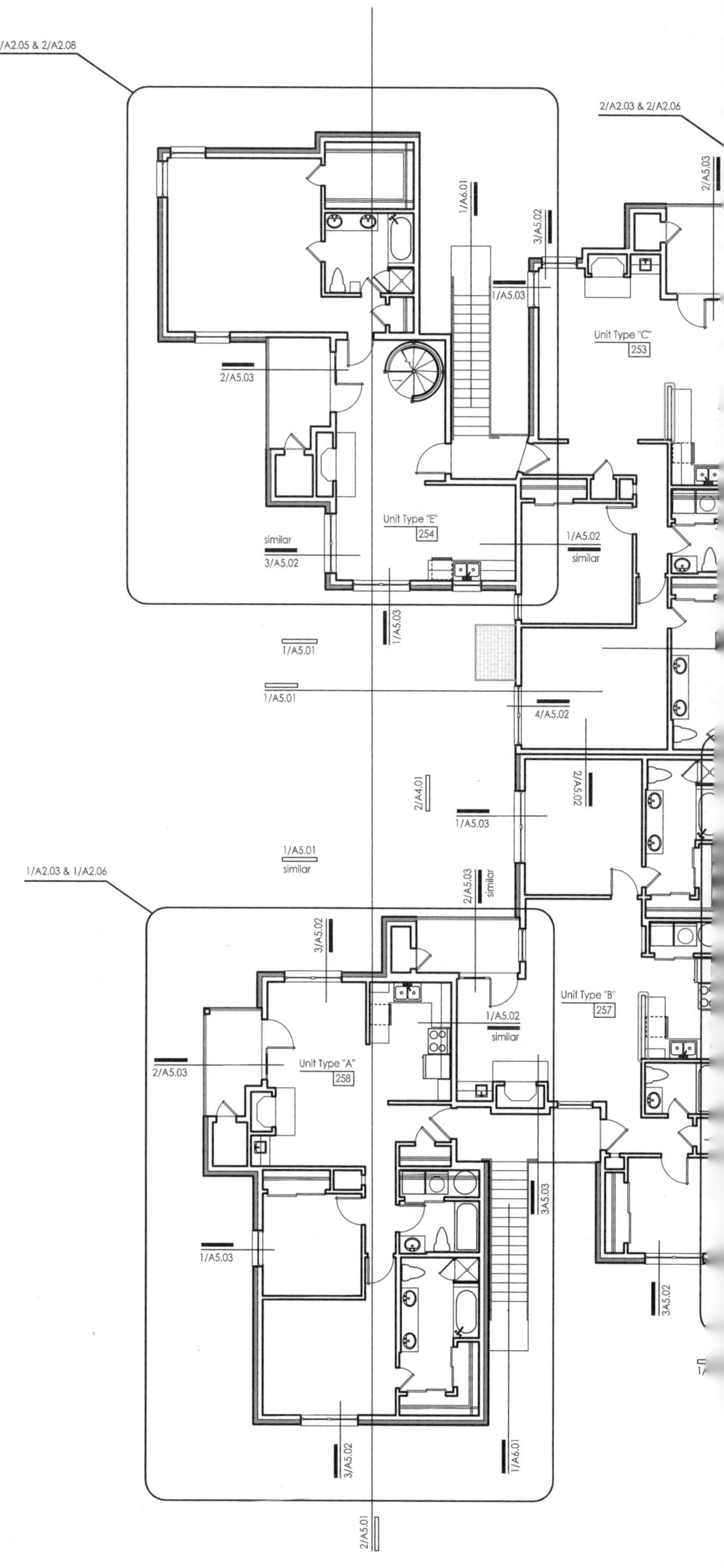

FIGURE C–1
First Floor Condominium Project (Scale: 1/16″ = 1′-0″)
Courtesy of Kelly McCarthy, McCarthy Architecture

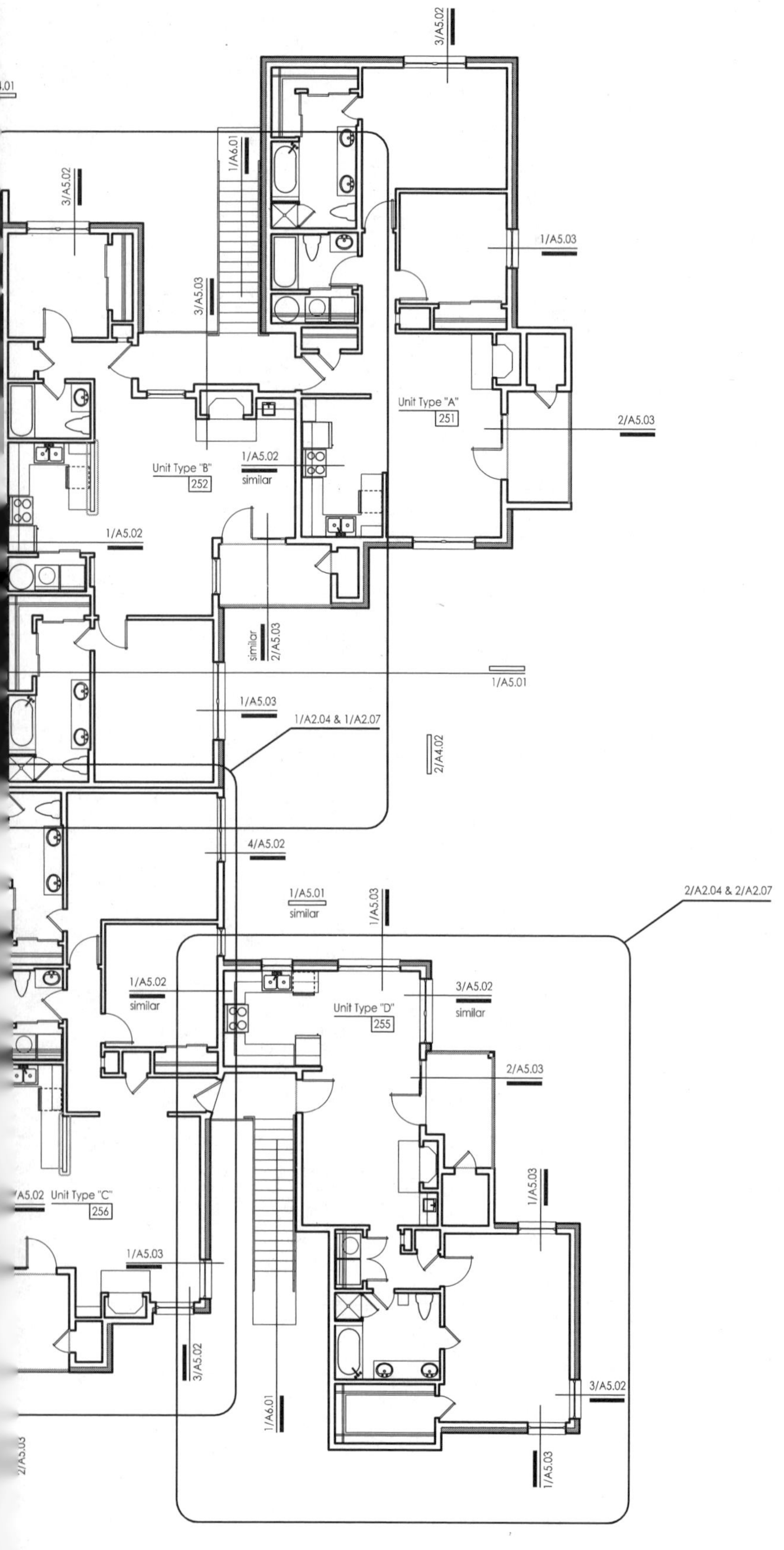

Unit Type "A"
251
Unit Type "B"
252
Unit Type "C"
256
Unit Type "D"
255
1/A2.04 & 1/A2.07
2/A2.04 & 2/A2.07
similar